W9-AMC-857

Holt Online Learning

HOLT MATH

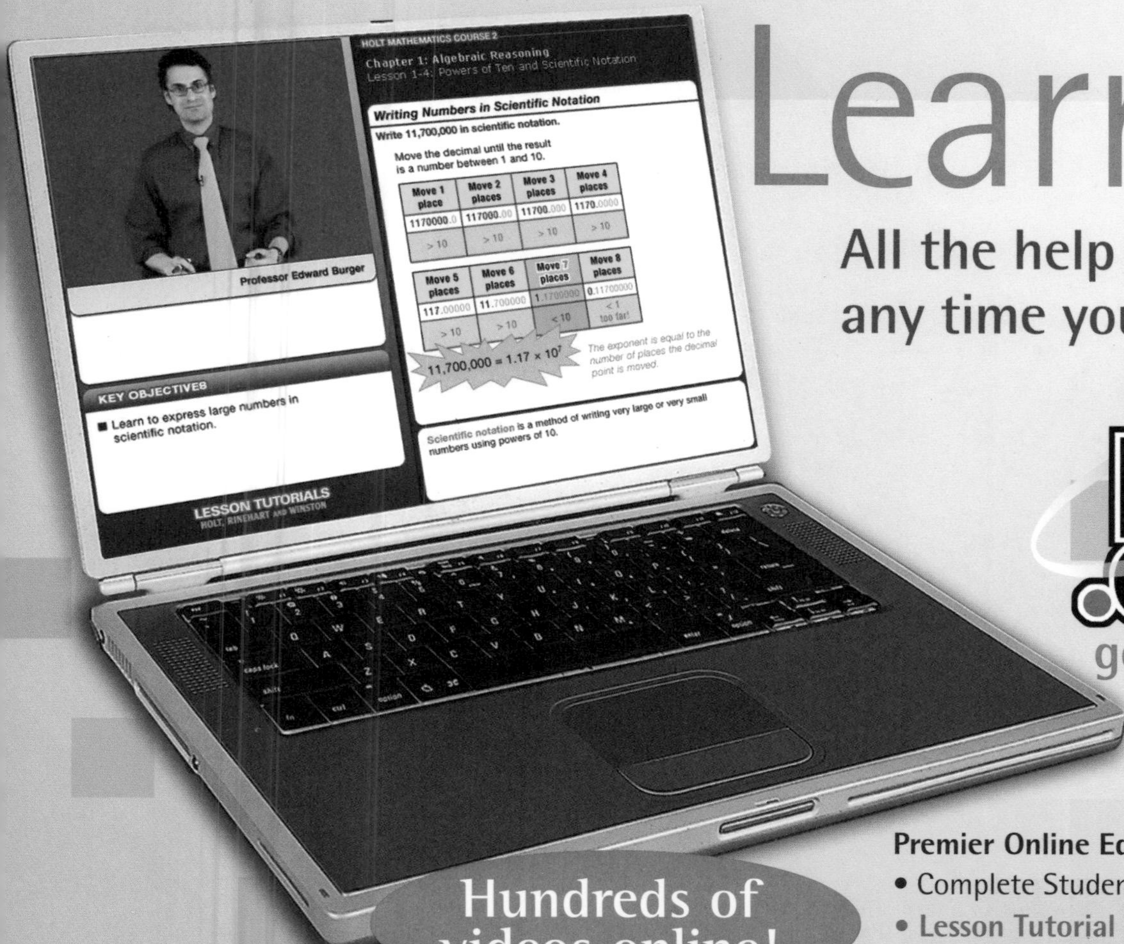

All the help you need, any time you need it.

go.hrw.com

Hundreds of videos online!

Lesson Tutorial Videos feature entertaining and enlightening videos that illustrate every example in your textbook!

Premier Online Edition
- Complete Student Edition
- **Lesson Tutorial Videos** for every example
  - > **Course 1**: 279 videos
  - > **Course 2**: 294 videos
  - > **Course 3**: 333 videos
- Interactive practice with feedback

Extra Practice
- Homework Help Online
- Intervention and enrichment exercises
- State test practice

Online Tools
- Graphing calculator
- TechKeys "How-to" tutorials on graphing calculators
- Virtual Manipulatives
- Multilingual glossary

For Parents
- Parent Resources Online

Log on to **www.go.hrw.com** to access Holt's online resources.

HOLT

Mathematics

Course 3

Jennie M. Bennett

Edward B. Burger

David J. Chard

Audrey L. Jackson

Paul A. Kennedy

Freddie L. Renfro

Janet K. Scheer

Bert K. Waits

HOLT, RINEHART AND WINSTON

A Harcourt Education Company

Orlando • Austin • New York • San Diego • London

Course 3 Contents in Brief

CHAPTER 1 Principles of Algebra 2
CHAPTER 2 Rational Numbers 60
CHAPTER 3 Graphs, Functions, and Sequences 114
CHAPTER 4 Exponents and Roots 158
CHAPTER 5 Ratios, Proportions, and Similarity 212
CHAPTER 6 Percents 270
CHAPTER 7 Foundations of Geometry 320
CHAPTER 8 Perimeter, Area, and Volume 384
CHAPTER 9 Data and Statistics 458
CHAPTER 10 Probability 518
CHAPTER 11 Multi-Step Equations and Inequalities 580
CHAPTER 12 Graphing Lines 624
CHAPTER 13 Sequences and Functions 678
CHAPTER 14 Polynomials 730

Student Handbook

Extra Practice 782
Problem Solving Handbook 810
Skills Bank 820
Selected Answers 847
Glossary 859
Index 898
Formulas and Symbols . . . . . Inside Back Cover

Copyright © 2007 by Holt, Rinehart and Winston

All rights reserved. No part of this publication may be reproduced or transmitted in any form or by any means, electronic or mechanical, including photocopy, recording, or any information storage and retrieval system, without permission in writing from the publisher.

Requests for permission to make copies of any part of the work should be mailed to the following address: Permissions Department, Holt, Rinehart and Winston, 10801 N. MoPac Expressway, Building 3, Austin, Texas 78759.

HOLT and the **"Owl Design"** are trademarks licensed to Holt, Rinehart and Winston, registered in the United States of America and/or other jurisdictions.

Printed in the United States of America

ISBN 0-03-038542-3

1 2 3 4 5 073 09 08 07 06

Cover photo: Getty Center, Los Angeles, CA. © Richard Cummins/ SuperStock

Authors

Jennie M. Bennett, Ph.D. is a mathematics teacher at Hartman Middle School in Houston, Texas. Jennie is past president of the Benjamin Banneker Association, the Second Vice-President of NCSM, and a former board member of NCTM.

Paul A. Kennedy, Ph.D. is a professor in the Department of Mathematics at Colorado State University. Dr. Kennedy is a leader in mathematics education. His research focuses on developing algebraic thinking by using multiple representations and technology. He is the author of numerous publications.

Edward B. Burger, Ph.D. is Professor of Mathematics and Chair at Williams College and is the author of numerous articles, books, and videos. He has won several of the most prestigious writing and teaching awards offered by the Mathematical Association of America. Dr. Burger has appeared on NBC TV, National Public Radio, and has given innumerable mathematical performances around the world.

Freddie L. Renfro, BA, MA, has 35 years of experience in Texas education as a classroom teacher and director/coordinator of Mathematics PreK-12 for school districts in the Houston area. She has served as TEA TAAS/TAKS reviewer, team trainer for Texas Math Institutes, TEKS Algebra Institute writer, and presenter at math workshops.

David J. Chard, Ph.D., is an Associate Dean of Curriculum and Academic Programs at the University of Oregon. He is the President of the Division for Research at the Council for Exceptional Children, is a member of the International Academy for Research on Learning Disabilities, and is the Principal Investigator on two major research projects for the U.S. Department of Education.

Janet K. Scheer, Ph.D., Executive Director of Create A VisionTM, is a motivational speaker and provides customized K-12 math staff development. She has taught internationally and domestically at all grade levels.

Audrey L. Jackson is on the Board of Directors for NCTM. She is the Program Coordinator for Leadership Development with the St. Louis, public schools and is a former school administrator for the Parkway School District.

Bert K. Waits, Ph.D., is a Professor Emeritus of Mathematics at The Ohio State University and co-founder of T3 (Teachers Teaching with Technology), a national professional development program.

Contributing Authors

Linda Antinone
Fort Worth, TX

Ms. Antinone teaches mathematics at R. L. Paschal High School in Fort Worth, Texas. She has received the Presidential Award for Excellence in Teaching Mathematics and the National Radio Shack Teacher award. She has coauthored several books for Texas Instruments on the use of technology in mathematics.

Carmen Whitman
Pflugerville, TX

Ms. Whitman travels nationally helping districts improve mathematics education. She has been a program coordinator on the mathematics team at the Charles A. Dana Center, and has served as a secondary math specialist for the Austin Independent School District.

Reviewers

Thomas J. Altonjy
Assistant Principal
Robert R. Lazar Middle School
Montville, NY

Jane Bash, M.A.
Math Education
Eisenhower Middle School
San Antonio, TX

Charlie Bialowas
District Math Coordinator
Anaheim Union High School District
Anaheim, CA

Lynn Bodet
Math Teacher
Eisenhower Middle School
San Antonio, TX

Sharon Butler
Adjunct Faculty
Montgomery College of The Woodlands
Spring, TX

Judy Cass
Mathematics Department Chair
Corpus Christi ISD
Corpus Christi, TX

Louis D'Angelo, Jr.
Math Teacher
Archmere Academy
Claymont, DE

Troy Deckebach
Math Teacher
Tredyffrin-Easttown Middle School
Berwyn, PA

Mary Gorman
Math Teacher
Sarasota, FL

Brian Griffith
Supervisor of Mathematics, K-12
Mechanicsburg Area School District
Mechanicsburg, PA

Ruth Harbin-Miles
District Math Coordinator
Instructional Resource Center
Olathe, KS

Kim Hayden
Math Teacher
Milford Jr. High School
Milford, OH

Susan Howe
Math Teacher
Lime Kiln Middle School
Fulton, MD

Sharron Ingram
Mathematics Teacher
Eanes ISD
Austin, TX

Paula Jenniges
Austin, TX

Lendy Jones
Mathematics Teacher
Killeen ISD
Killeen, TX

Ronald J. Labrocca
District Mathematics Coordinator
Manhasset Public Schools
Plainview, NY

Victor R. Lopez
Math Teacher
Washington School
Union City, NJ

George Maguschak
Math Teacher/Building Chairperson
Wilkes-Barre Area
Wilkes-Barre, PA

Mende Mays
Mathematics Teacher
Ector County ISD
Odessa, TX

Dianne McIntire
Math Teacher
Garfield School
Kearny, NJ

Kenneth McIntire
Math Teacher
Lincoln School
Kearny, NJ

Francisco Pacheco
Math Teacher
IS 125
Bronx, NY

Vivian Perry
Edwards, IL

Vicki Perryman Petty
Math Teacher
Central Middle School
Murfreesbro, TN

Jennifer Sawyer
Math Teacher
Shawboro, NC

Russell Sayler
Math Teacher
Longfellow Middle School
Wauwatosa, WI

Raymond Scacalossi
Math Chairperson
Hauppauge Schools
Hauppauge, NY

Richard Seavey
Math Teacher, retired
Metcalf Jr. High
Eagan, MN

Sherry Shaffer
Math Teacher
Honeoye Central School
Honeoye Falls, NY

Gail M. Sigmund
Math Teacher
Charles A. Mooney Preparatory School
Cleveland, OH

Jonathan Simmons
Math Teacher
Manor Middle School
Killeen, TX

Jeffrey L. Slagel
Math Department Chair
South Eastern Middle School
Fawn Grove, PA

Cassandra Slayton
Mathematics Teacher
Lubbock ISD
Lubbock, TX

Karen Smith, Ph.D.
Math Teacher
East Middle School
Braintree, MA

Cecilia Thomas
Mathematics Teacher, retired
Dallas ISD
Dallas, TX

Bonnie Thompson
Math Teacher
Tower Heights Middle School
Dayton, OH

Mary Thoreen
Mathematics Subject Area Leader
Wilson Middle School
Tampa, FL

Paul Turney
Math Teacher
Ladue School District
St. Louis, MO

Preparing for Standardized Tests

Holt Mathematics Course 3 provides many opportunities for you to prepare for standardized tests.

Test Prep Exercises

Use the Test Prep Exercises for daily practice of standardized test questions in various formats.

Multiple Choice—choose your answer.

Gridded Response—write your answer in a grid and fill in the corresponding bubbles.

Short Response—write open-ended responses that are scored with a 2-point rubric.

Extended Response—write open-ended responses that are scored with a 4-point rubric.

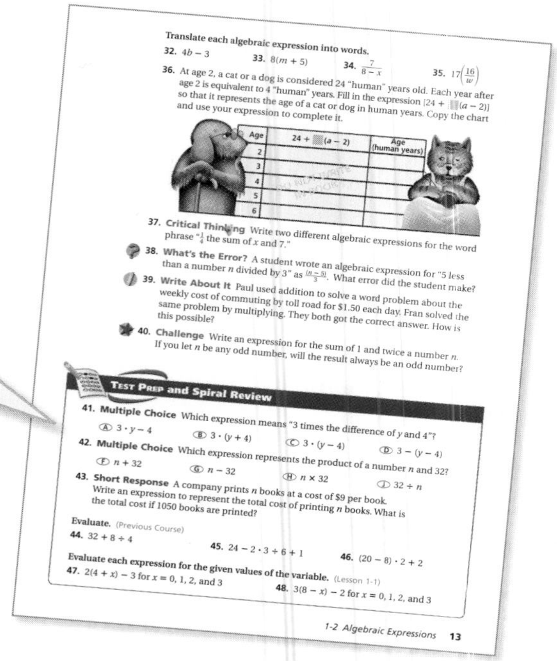
Translate each algebraic expression into words.

32. $4b - 3$ 33. $8(m + 5)$ 34. $\frac{7}{8-x}$ 35. $17\left(\frac{16}{w}\right)$

36. At age 2, a cat or a dog is considered 24 "human" years old. Each year after age 2 is equivalent to 4 "human" years. Fill in the expression [24 + ▒(a − 2)] so that it represents the age of a cat or dog in human years. Copy the chart and use your expression to complete it.

Age	24 + ▒(a − 2)	Age (human years)
2		
3		
4		
5		
6		

37. **Critical Thinking** Write two different algebraic expressions for the word phrase "$\frac{1}{4}$ the sum of x and 7."

38. **What's the Error?** A student wrote an algebraic expression for "5 less than a number n divided by 3" as $\frac{n-5}{3}$. What error did the student make?

39. **Write About It** Paul used addition to solve a word problem about the weekly cost of commuting by toll road for \$1.50 each day. Fran solved the same problem by multiplying. They both got the correct answer. How is this possible?

40. **Challenge** Write an expression for the sum of 1 and twice a number n. If you let n be any odd number, will the result always be an odd number?

Test Prep and Spiral Review

41. **Multiple Choice** Which expression means "3 times the difference of y and 4"?
Ⓐ $3 \cdot y - 4$ Ⓑ $3 \cdot (y + 4)$ Ⓒ $3 \cdot (y - 4)$ Ⓓ $3 - (y - 4)$

42. **Multiple Choice** Which expression represents the product of a number n and 32?
Ⓕ $n + 32$ Ⓖ $n - 32$ Ⓗ $n \times 32$ Ⓙ $32 \div n$

43. **Short Response** A company prints n books at a cost of \$9 per book. Write an expression to represent the total cost of printing n books. What is the total cost if 1050 books are printed?

Evaluate. (Previous Course)

44. $32 + 8 \div 4$ 45. $24 - 2 \cdot 3 + 6 + 1$ 46. $(20 - 8) \cdot 2 + 2$

Evaluate each expression for the given values of the variable. (Lesson 1-1)

47. $2(4 + x) - 3$ for $x = 0, 1, 2,$ and 3 48. $3(8 - x) - 2$ for $x = 0, 1, 2,$ and 3

1-2 Algebraic Expressions 13

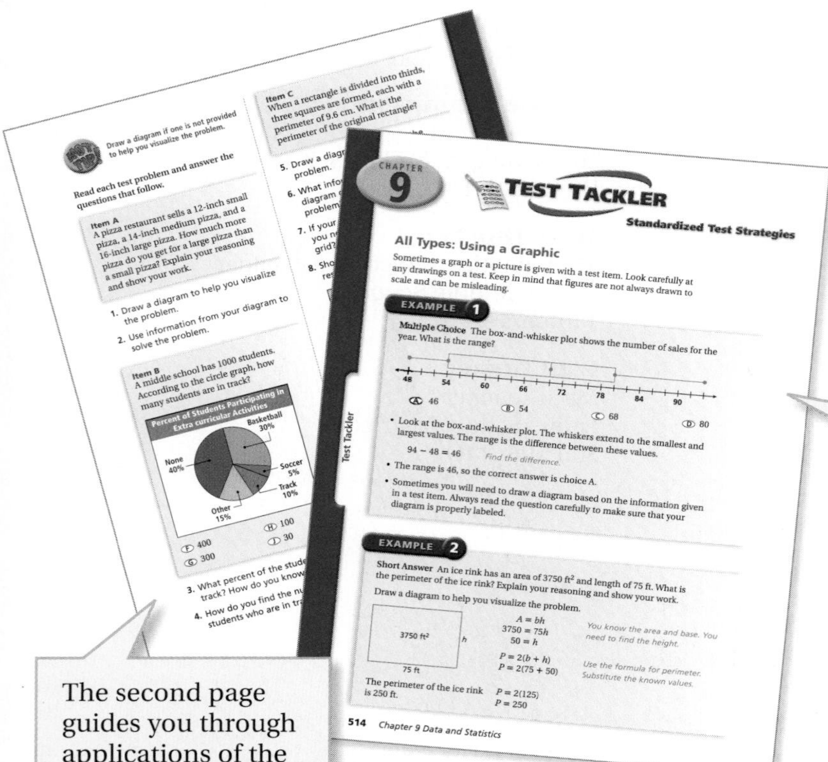
Draw a diagram if one is not provided to help you visualize the problem.

Read each test problem and answer the questions that follow.

Item A
A pizza restaurant sells a 12-inch small pizza, a 14-inch medium pizza, and a 16-inch large pizza. How much more pizza do you get for a large pizza than a small pizza? Explain your reasoning and show your work.

1. Draw a diagram to help you visualize the problem.
2. Use information from your diagram to solve the problem.

Item B
A middle school has 1000 students. According to the circle graph, how many students are in track?

Percent of Students Participating in Extra curricular Activities

Basketball 30%, None 40%, Soccer 5%, Track 10%, Other 15%

Ⓕ 400 Ⓗ 100
Ⓖ 300 Ⓙ 30

3. What percent of the stude… track? How do you know…
4. How do you find the nu… students who are in tr…

Item C
When a rectangle is divided into thirds, three squares are formed, each with a perimeter of 9.6 cm. What is the perimeter of the original rectangle?

5. Draw a diag… problem.
6. What info… diagram… problem…
7. If your… you n… grid?
8. Sho… re…

CHAPTER 9 TEST TACKLER

Standardized Test Strategies

All Types: Using a Graphic

Sometimes a graph or a picture is given with a test item. Look carefully at any drawings on a test. Keep in mind that figures are not always drawn to scale and can be misleading.

EXAMPLE 1

Multiple Choice The box-and-whisker plot shows the number of sales for the year. What is the range?

Ⓐ 46 Ⓑ 54 Ⓒ 68 Ⓓ 80

- Look at the box-and-whisker plot. The whiskers extend to the smallest and largest values. The range is the difference between these values.

$94 - 48 = 46$ *Find the difference.*

- The range is 46, so the correct answer is choice A.
- Sometimes you will need to draw a diagram based on the information given in a test item. Always read the question carefully to make sure that your diagram is properly labeled.

EXAMPLE 2

Short Answer An ice rink has an area of 3750 ft² and length of 75 ft. What is the perimeter of the ice rink? Explain your reasoning and show your work.

Draw a diagram to help you visualize the problem.

$A = bh$
$3750 = 75h$
$50 = h$
You know the area and base. You need to find the height.

$P = 2(b + h)$
$P = 2(75 + 50)$
Use the formula for perimeter. Substitute the known values.

$P = 2(125)$
$P = 250$

The perimeter of the ice rink is 250 ft.

514 Chapter 9 Data and Statistics

The second page guides you through applications of the test-taking strategy.

Test Tackler

Use the Test Tackler to become familiar with and practice test-taking strategies.

The first page of this feature explains and shows an example of a test-taking strategy.

Standardized Test Prep

Use the Standardized Test Prep to apply test-taking strategies.

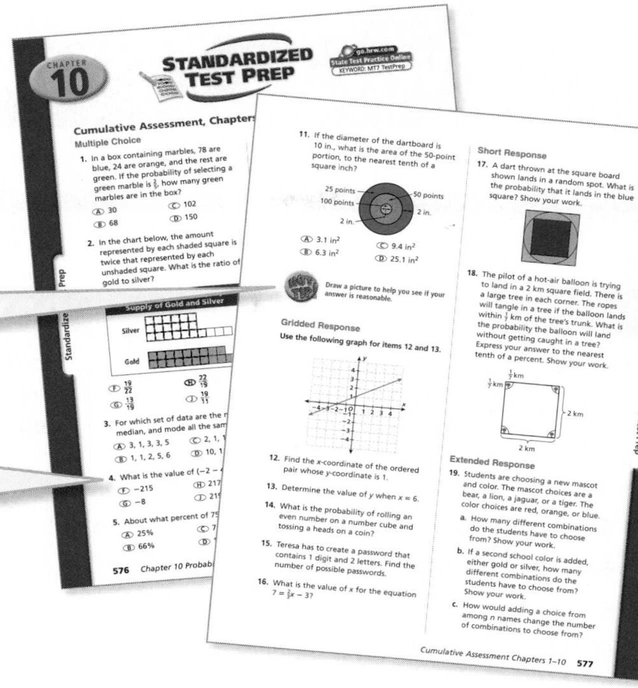

The Hot Tip provides test-taking tips to help you suceed on your tests.

These pages include practice with multiple choice, gridded response, short response, and extended response test items.

Countdown to Testing

Use the Countdown to Testing to practice for your state test every day.

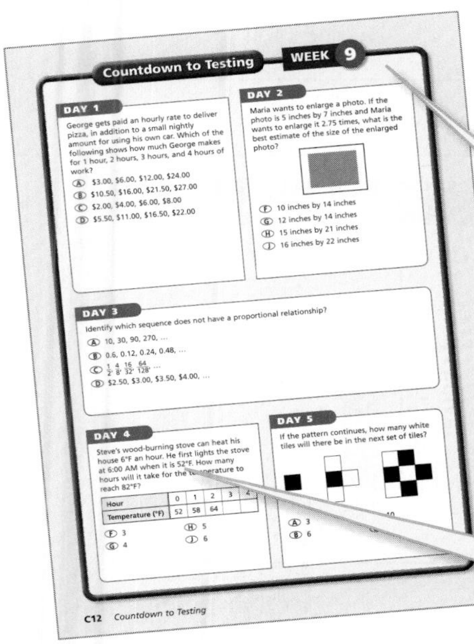

There are 24 pages of practice for your state test. Each page is designed to be used in a week so that all practice will be completed before your state test is given.

Each week's page has five practice test items, one for each day of the week.

Test-Taking Tips

- Get plenty of sleep the night before the test. A rested mind thinks more clearly and you won't feel like falling asleep while taking the test.
- Draw a figure when one is not provided with the problem. If a figure is given, write any details from the problem on the figure.
- Read each problem carefully. As you finish each problem, read it again to make sure your answer is reasonable.
- Review the formula sheet that will be supplied with the test. Make sure you know when to use each formula.
- First answer problems that you know how to solve. If you do not know how to solve a problem, skip it and come back to it when you have finished the others.
- Use other test-taking strategies that can be found throughout this book, such as working backward and eliminating answer choices.

Countdown to Testing

Week 1

Day 1

Six friends went to the movies. Admission cost $7.50. Two of them bought a bag of popcorn for $3.50. Which expression can be used to find the total amount they spent?

Ⓐ 6(7.50 + 3.50)

Ⓑ 6(7.50) + 2(3.50)

Ⓒ 6 · (7.50 + 3.50)

Ⓓ 6(7.50) + 2 + (3.50)

Day 2

How many feet of wood molding would Jeremy need to trim all the walls of his bedroom?

Ⓕ 4 feet

Ⓖ 32 feet

Ⓗ 72 feet

Ⓙ 320 feet

Day 3

In which month were the savings greatest?

Ⓐ June

Ⓑ July

Ⓒ August

Ⓓ September

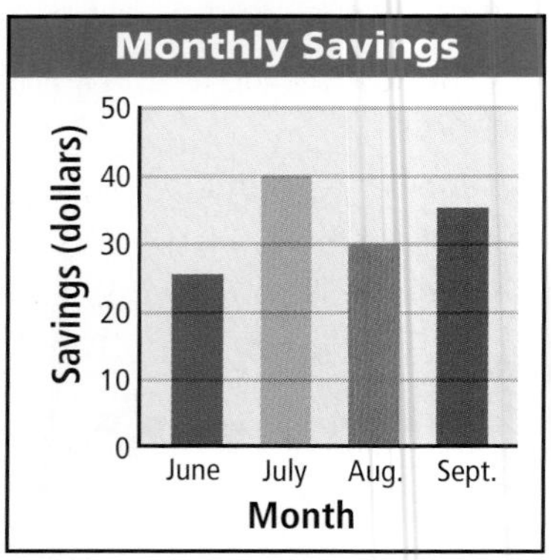

Day 4

Ravi is studying fruit flies. What is the length of the smallest fly?

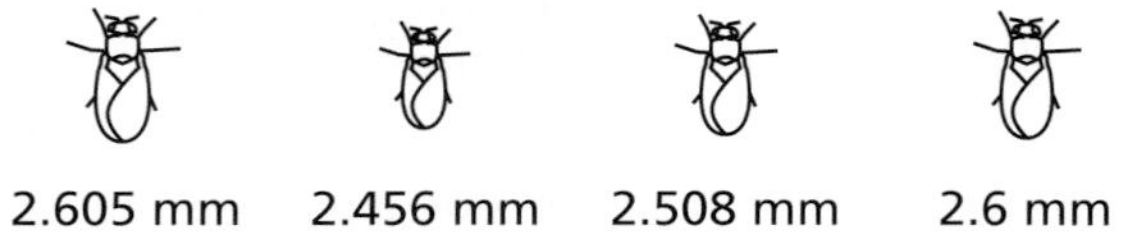

Ⓕ 2.605 mm

Ⓖ 2.501 mm

Ⓗ 2.6 mm

Ⓙ 2.456 mm

Day 5

The science club is raising money for a trip. It needs to raise $240.50 so that the entire club can go. So far it has raised $169.75. How much more money does it need to raise?

Ⓐ $70.50

Ⓑ $70.75

Ⓒ $70.85

Ⓓ $71.75

Countdown to Testing WEEK 2

DAY 1

Craig has 0.38 milliliters of a solution to pour into four equal parts. He determines that each part will contain 0.095 milliliters of the solution. Which of the following shows that Craig's solution is reasonable?

Ⓐ $4 \cdot 0.01 = 0.04$

Ⓑ $0.4 \cdot 4 = 1.6$

Ⓒ $0.1 \cdot 4 = 0.4$

Ⓓ $0.4 \cdot 0.01 = 0.004$

DAY 2

Missy's car can travel 30 miles per gallon. If Missy fills up her tank with 16 gallons of gas, which equation can be used to show how many gallons of gas are left in Missy's tank after she travels 90 miles?

Ⓕ $16(90 \div 30)$

Ⓖ $16 - \frac{90}{30}$

Ⓗ $30 + 30 + 30 - 16$

Ⓙ $90 \cdot 16 - 30$

DAY 3

What information does the circle graph not tell you about Chris?

Ⓐ Chris spends more time at soccer practice than at the library.

Ⓑ Chris spends the most amount of time doing his chores.

Ⓒ Chris spends less time at guitar practice than at soccer practice.

Ⓓ Chris spends more time doing chores than at the library.

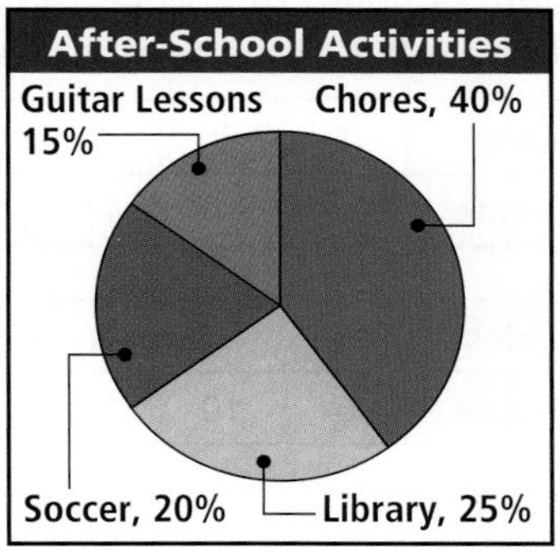

DAY 4

Ivy's Fresh Eggs transports its eggs in crates. How many crates will 8 trucks carry?

Trucks	2	3	4	5
Crates	80	120	160	200

Ⓕ 220

Ⓖ 280

Ⓗ 320

Ⓙ 360

DAY 5

When Kit woke up, it was –15°C outside. By that afternoon, the temperature had risen 20 degrees. What was the afternoon temperature?

Ⓐ –5°C

Ⓑ 5°C

Ⓒ 20°C

Ⓓ 35°C

Countdown to Testing WEEK 3

DAY 1

Annie makes gift baskets of mini muffins. If Annie needs 20 baskets with 25 muffins in each basket, which equation shows how many dozens of muffins she must make?

Ⓐ 12(20) – 25

Ⓑ 25(20) + 12

Ⓒ 20(25) ÷ 12

Ⓓ 12(25 + 20)

DAY 2

Beth saved $2,200. A laptop costs $2199.99, extra memory is $149.50, and an extra battery is $59.95. Beth also has a coupon for $300 off one purchase at the store. Which of the following shows that Beth has saved enough for all of these items?

Ⓕ 2200 – 300 + 150 – 60 = 1,890

Ⓖ 2200 – 150 – 60 – 300 = 1,690

Ⓗ 2200 + 150 + 60 = 2,410

Ⓙ 2200 + 150 + 60 – 300 = 2,110

DAY 3

At a restaurant, a rectangular table can seat 1 person on each end and 2 on each side. When 2 tables are pushed together end to end, 10 people can sit. Which table shows the number of people who can sit at 4 tables pushed together?

Ⓐ

Tables	1	2	3	4
People	6	10	14	18

Ⓑ

Tables	1	2	3	4
People	6	10	18	24

Ⓒ

Tables	1	2	3	4
People	6	10	12	16

Ⓓ

Tables	1	2	3	4
People	6	10	24	48

DAY 4

Rita is playing a board game. If she had 13 points before landing on the shown spot, how many points does she have now?

Ⓕ –33

Ⓖ –7

Ⓗ 7

Ⓙ 33

DAY 5

Jorge recorded the following information while studying the effects of sunlight on plant growth. Which plant grew the most?

Plant	1	2	3	4
Change in Height (in.)	$\frac{1}{2}$	$-\frac{3}{8}$	$-\frac{1}{4}$	$\frac{7}{16}$

Ⓐ 1

Ⓑ 2

Ⓒ 3

Ⓓ 4

Countdown to Testing WEEK 4

DAY 1

Juan deposits $200 at his bank. The first quarter, Juan withdraws $150. He deposits another $100 in each of the next two quarters. How much money does Juan have now?

Ⓐ $50
Ⓑ $250
Ⓒ $350
Ⓓ $450

DAY 2

Sandra uses 3.6 meters of ribbon to weave a small rug and 4.2 meters to weave a large rug. Which expression can be used to find the total length of ribbon used for 12 small rugs and 18 large rugs?

Ⓕ 12(3.6) + 18(4.2)
Ⓖ 18(3.6) + 12(4.2)
Ⓗ 12 + 18(3.6 • 4.2)
Ⓙ 12 + 18 + 3.6 + 4.2

DAY 3

To do his homework, Ethan estimates that he will need about 185 minutes, or 4 hours. What mistake did Ethan make?

Ⓐ He rounded 185 minutes to 200.
Ⓑ He multiplied 4 by 60.
Ⓒ He underestimated the time needed.
Ⓓ He divided 185 by 60 incorrectly.

DAY 4

Andre recorded the high temperature for each day this week. What was the temperature on the warmest day?

Day	M	T	W	Th	F
(°C)	5	−15	−10	−10	−20

Ⓕ −20
Ⓖ −15
Ⓗ −10
Ⓙ 5

DAY 5

At the factory, boxes of paper clips are packed into shipping cases. How many boxes come in 5 cases?

Cases	2	3	4	5
Boxes	192	288	384	?

Ⓐ 384
Ⓑ 480
Ⓒ 500
Ⓓ 672

Countdown to Testing WEEK 5

DAY 1

Ari had 15.3 centimeters of metal pipe. He needed to make 3 equal-size pieces for a project. Should he add, subtract, multiply, or divide to find the length of each piece?

Ⓐ Add 15.3 and 3

Ⓑ Subtract 3 from 15.3

Ⓒ Multiply 15.3 by 3

Ⓓ Divide 15.3 by 3

DAY 2

Sue needed $3\frac{2}{7}$ yards of fringe to trim each drape. If she had 8 drapes to trim, how much fringe did she need?

Ⓕ $4\frac{6}{7}$ yards

Ⓖ $11\frac{2}{7}$ yards

Ⓗ $24\frac{3}{7}$ yards

Ⓙ $26\frac{2}{7}$ yards

DAY 3

Cara used the following table to predict the number of sit-ups she would do on Sunday. She predicted 40. Is her prediction reasonable?

Day	M	T	W	Th	F	S	Su
Number of Sit-ups	2	3	5	8	12		

Ⓐ Yes, it is about right.

Ⓑ No, it is too low.

Ⓒ No, it is too high.

Ⓓ No, there is no pattern in the table.

DAY 4

The table shows how much different numbers of tickets to a hockey game cost. How many dollars would 10 tickets cost?

Tickets	2	3	5	8
Cost ($)	4.80	7.20	12.00	19.20

Ⓕ $21.60

Ⓖ $24.00

Ⓗ $29.20

Ⓙ $32.00

DAY 5

Which is the greatest number in the list?

3.3, $3\frac{1}{4}$, 3.1, 3.13, 3.11, 3.31

Ⓐ 3.13

Ⓑ $3\frac{1}{4}$

Ⓒ 3.3

Ⓓ 3.31

Countdown to Testing WEEK 6

DAY 1

Which point is located at (2, –3)?

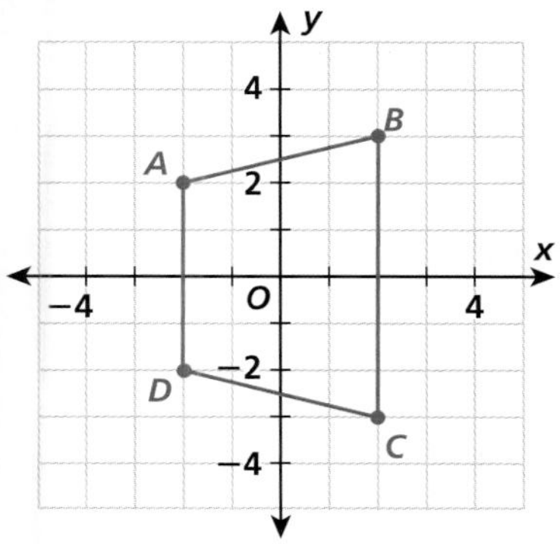

Ⓐ *A*

Ⓑ *B*

Ⓒ *C*

Ⓓ *D*

DAY 2

What are the coordinates of *F*?

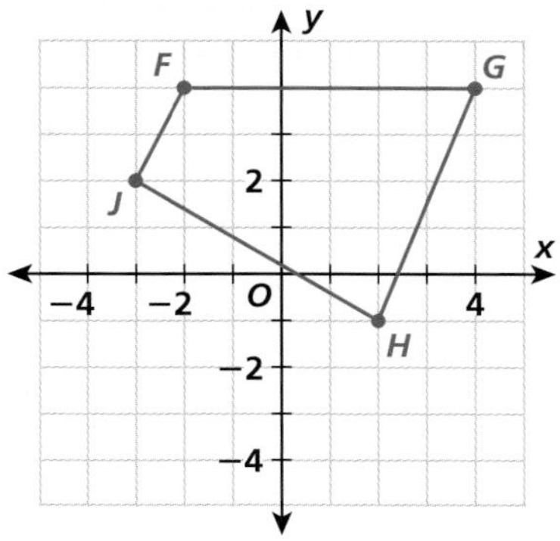

Ⓕ (–3, 2)

Ⓖ (–2, 4)

Ⓗ (4, 4)

Ⓙ (2, –1)

DAY 3

Carla is making a table based on the information in the graph. Complete the table for Monday.

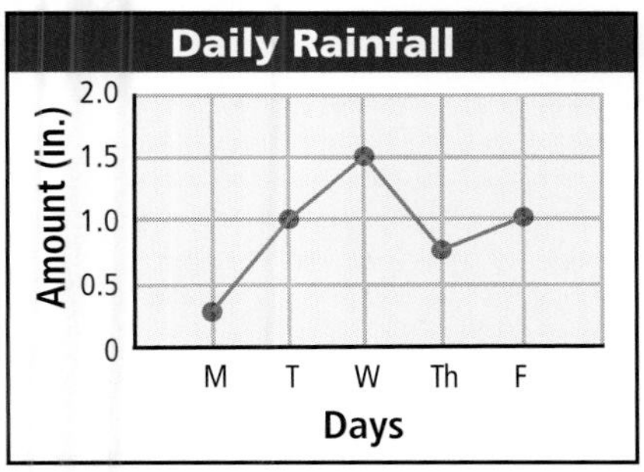

Day	M	T	W	Th	F
Inches		1	$1\frac{1}{2}$		1

Ⓐ $\frac{1}{4}$

Ⓑ $\frac{1}{2}$

Ⓒ $\frac{3}{4}$

Ⓓ 1

DAY 4

Blake works in a cheese store. The table shows how many cheese tidbits he has made at the end of each hour. If he continues at the same pace, how many tidbits will Blake have made in 6 hours?

Hours	2	3	4	5	6
Cheese Tidbits	234	351	468		

Ⓕ 585

Ⓖ 702

Ⓗ 819

Ⓙ 1404

DAY 5

Six samples of water (A, B, C, D, E, F) were collected from the lake.

A = 591.25 mL, B = 591.85 mL,
C = 591.5 mL, D = 591.75 mL,
E = 591.8 mL

If sample F measured between the greatest and least amounts, which of the following could be the amount of sample F?

Ⓐ 591.15 mL

Ⓑ 591.2 mL

Ⓒ 591.45 mL

Ⓓ 591.90 mL

Countdown to Testing WEEK 7

DAY 1

Chandra gets paid 1.5 times her hourly wage of $12.50 per hour when she works overtime. This month she worked 20 hours of overtime.

Which of the following expressions shows how much extra money Chandra will earn this month?

Ⓐ $1.5(12.50) + 20$

Ⓑ $12.50 \div 1.5 \cdot 20$

Ⓒ $1.5(12.50) \cdot 20$

Ⓓ $20 \div 12.50 \cdot 1.5$

DAY 2

Which of the following describes the distance of the E ring from the surface of Saturn?

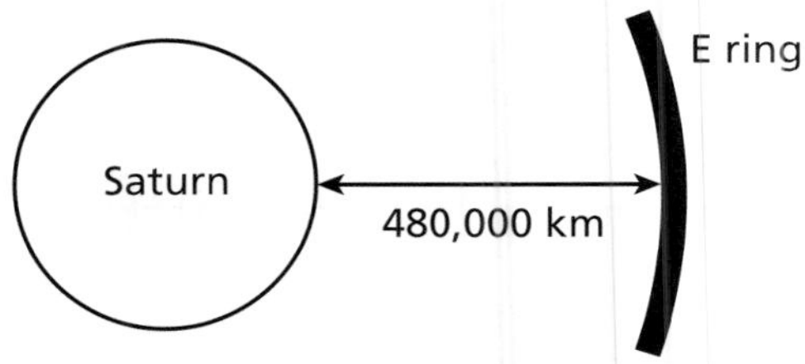

Ⓕ $4.8 \cdot 10^5$

Ⓖ $4.8 \cdot 10^6$

Ⓗ $0.48 \cdot 10^4$

Ⓙ $48 \cdot 10^5$

DAY 3

Which expression describes the following sequence?

10, 17, 31, 59, …

Ⓐ $x + 7$

Ⓑ $2x - 3$

Ⓒ $2(x - 2)$

Ⓓ $3x - 13$

DAY 4

How many dots could be in the next figure in this sequence?

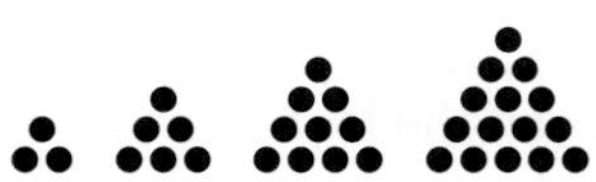

Ⓕ 20

Ⓖ 21

Ⓗ 22

Ⓙ 23

DAY 5

Every 2 hours, a hive of honeybees can produce 150 grams of honey. How many grams of honey does the hive produce in 5 hours?

Ⓐ 300

Ⓑ 375

Ⓒ 450

Ⓓ 750

Countdown to Testing WEEK 8

DAY 1

Ronnie ties his dog to an 8-foot length of rope attached to a pole. What is the distance around the circle the dog can run? Use 3.14 for π.

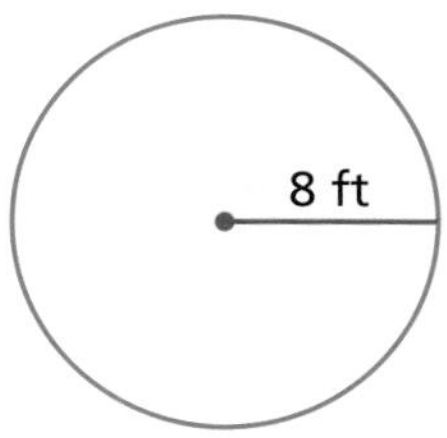

Ⓐ 25.12 feet
Ⓑ 50.24 feet
Ⓒ 100.48 feet
Ⓓ 200.96 feet

DAY 2

Shawn uses a ramp to get in and out of his house. What is the height of the ramp? Round your answer to the nearest tenth.

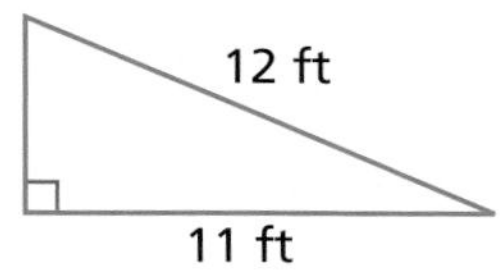

Ⓕ 1.09 feet
Ⓖ 2.5 feet
Ⓗ 3.6 feet
Ⓙ 4.8 feet

DAY 3

Carla receives a special offer from an online bookseller. For every \$50 she spends, she'll receive \$5 off her purchases. Carla spends \$142.50 and estimates she'll pay about \$133. Which of the following shows that Carla's estimate is reasonable?

Ⓐ $142.50 - 50 = 92.50$
Ⓑ $142.50 + 50 - 50 = 197.50$
Ⓒ $142.50 - 2(5) = 132.50$
Ⓓ $142.50 - 3(5) = 127.50$

DAY 4

Jerry is building two triangular tables from a piece of rectangular wood. If the wood measures 24 inches by 36 inches, how many inches will the third side of each table be? Round to the nearest tenth.

Ⓕ 24.7 inches
Ⓖ 36.3 inches
Ⓗ 43.3 inches
Ⓙ 60 inches

DAY 5

Carolyn is building a triangular headboard for her bed. What is its height? Round your answer to the nearest tenth.

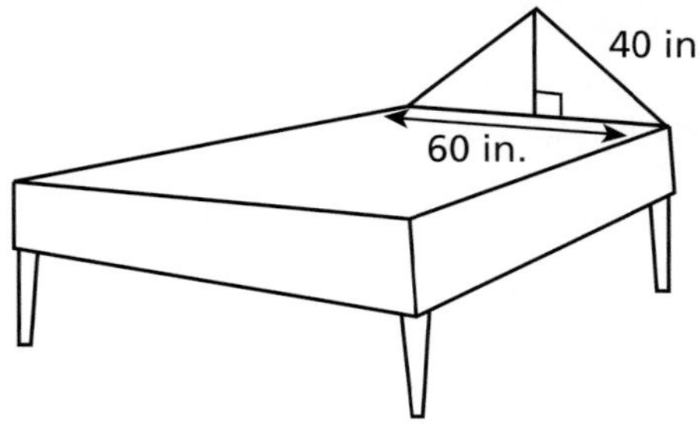

Ⓐ 8.3 inches
Ⓑ 10 inches
Ⓒ 26.5 inches
Ⓓ 100 inches

Countdown to Testing WEEK 9

DAY 1

George gets paid an hourly rate to deliver pizza, in addition to a small nightly amount for using his own car. Which of the following shows how much George makes for 1 hour, 2 hours, 3 hours, and 4 hours of work?

Ⓐ $3.00, $6.00, $12.00, $24.00

Ⓑ $10.50, $16.00, $21.50, $27.00

Ⓒ $2.00, $4.00, $6.00, $8.00

Ⓓ $5.50, $11.00, $16.50, $22.00

DAY 2

Maria wants to enlarge a photo. If the photo is 5 inches by 7 inches and Maria wants to enlarge it 2.75 times, what is the best estimate of the size of the enlarged photo?

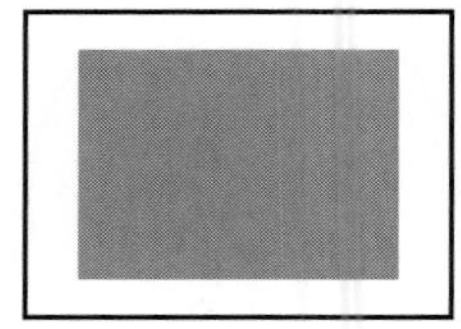

Ⓕ 10 inches by 14 inches

Ⓖ 12 inches by 14 inches

Ⓗ 15 inches by 21 inches

Ⓙ 16 inches by 22 inches

DAY 3

Identify which sequence does not have a proportional relationship?

Ⓐ 10, 30, 90, 270, …

Ⓑ 0.6, 0.12, 0.24, 0.48, …

Ⓒ $\frac{1}{2}, \frac{4}{8}, \frac{16}{32}, \frac{64}{128}, \ldots$

Ⓓ $2.50, $3.00, $3.50, $4.00, …

DAY 4

Steve's wood-burning stove can heat his house 6°F an hour. He first lights the stove at 6:00 AM when it is 52°F. How many hours will it take for the temperature to reach 82°F?

Hour	0	1	2	3	4
Temperature (°F)	52	58	64		

Ⓕ 3

Ⓖ 4

Ⓗ 5

Ⓙ 6

DAY 5

If the pattern continues, how many white tiles will there be in the next set of tiles?

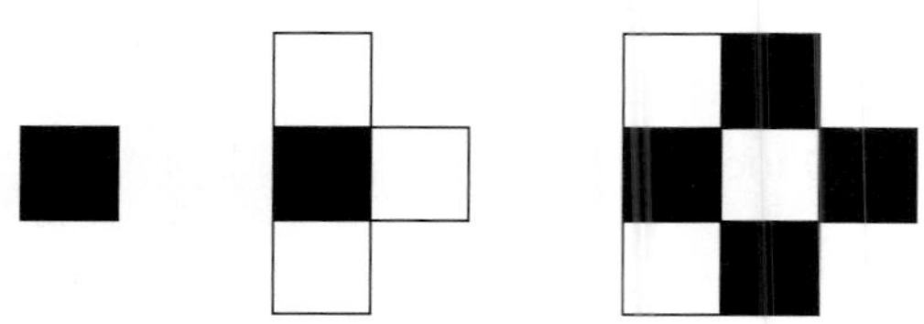

Ⓐ 3

Ⓑ 6

Ⓒ 10

Ⓓ 12

Countdown to Testing WEEK 10

DAY 1

The table shows the typing rates of four applicants for a job. Based on typing rates, which applicant is the best choice to hire?

Applicant	Words	Minute
Ann	112	6
Theo	206	8
June	195	7
Andy	120	5

Ⓐ June
Ⓑ Ann
Ⓒ Andy
Ⓓ Theo

DAY 2

If figure *ABCD* is dilated by a scale factor of 3, which ordered pair describes the new location of *C*?

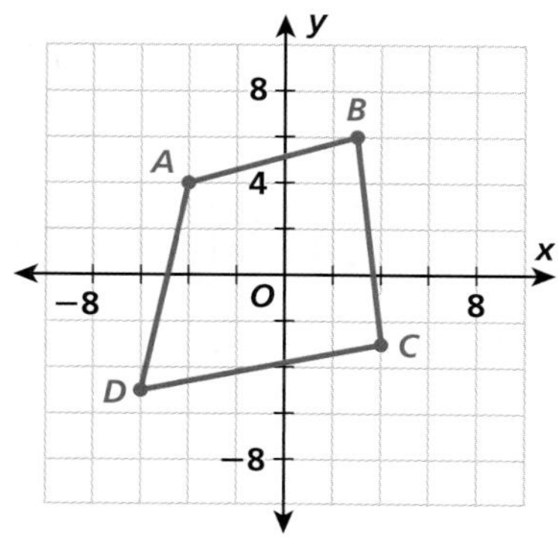

Ⓕ (–12, 9)
Ⓖ (9, 18)
Ⓗ (4, –3)
Ⓙ (12, –9)

DAY 3

Dylan is making a circular garden. Its diameter is 3.2 ft. What is its circumference? Use 3.14 for π. Round to the nearest tenth.

Ⓐ 6.4 ft
Ⓑ 10 ft
Ⓒ 20.1 ft
Ⓓ 32.2 ft

DAY 4

A chandelier uses three different sizes of bulbs. Each bulb is twice as large as the previous one. What is the diameter of the largest bulb?

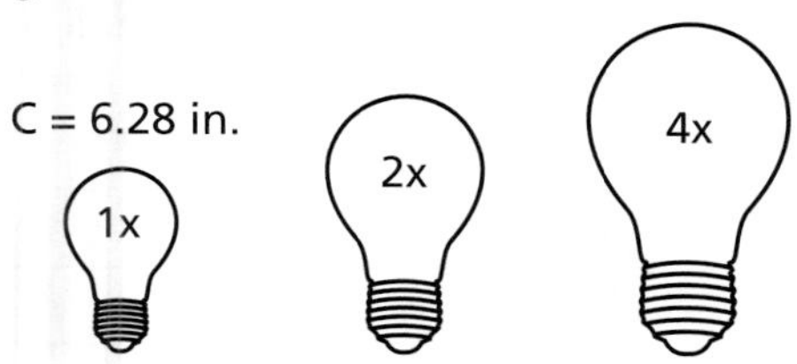

Ⓕ 2 inches
Ⓖ 3.14 inches
Ⓗ 8 inches
Ⓙ 12.56 inches

DAY 5

Mr. Bryce bought a hybrid car that can travel 240 miles on 8 gallons of gas. How far can Mr. Bryce travel on 10 gallons of gas?

Ⓐ 280 miles
Ⓑ 300 miles
Ⓒ 480 miles
Ⓓ 2400 miles

DAY 1

Simon is shopping for a new mountain bike. He finds one that costs $179.95, but he has a coupon. By which number should Simon multiply the price of the bike to calculate how much money he'll save?

Ⓐ 0.01
Ⓑ 0.1
Ⓒ 1.0
Ⓓ 10.0

DAY 2

Christina wants to paint a circle with a radius of 4 feet on her bedroom wall. If 1 can of paint covers 26 square feet, how many cans of paint will Christina need to buy?

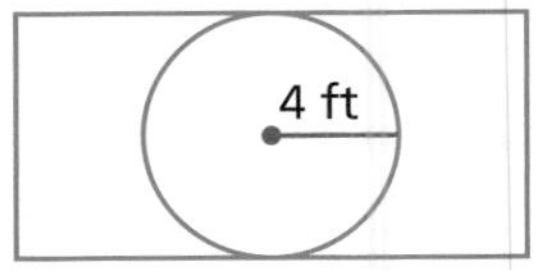

Ⓕ 1
Ⓖ 2
Ⓗ 3
Ⓙ 4

DAY 3

Jake is a reporter for a local newspaper. He has rewritten 68% of an interview that lasted 87 minutes. Which is the best estimate of the number of minutes Jake has transcribed?

Ⓐ 18 minutes
Ⓑ 48 minutes
Ⓒ 54 minutes
Ⓓ 63 minutes

DAY 4

Four people are playing a trivia game. Their scores are shown in the table. Which player has the lowest score?

Player	1	2	3	4
Score	−30	10	−25	50

Ⓕ 1
Ⓖ 2
Ⓗ 3
Ⓙ 4

DAY 5

For every 3 scarves that Kendall knits, Rhonda can knit 4 hats. When Kendall has knit 15 scarves, how many hats will Rhonda have knit?

Kendall	3	6	9	12
Rhonda	4	8		

Ⓐ 20
Ⓑ 24
Ⓒ 30
Ⓓ 60

Countdown to Testing WEEK 12

DAY 1

A manufacturer of doll clothes produces more white dresses than blue dresses by a factor of 3.5. Given *b*, the number of blue dresses produced, which equation shows *w*, the number of white dresses produced?

Ⓐ $w = b \div 3.5$

Ⓑ $w = \frac{3.5}{b}$

Ⓒ $w = 3.5b$

Ⓓ $w = 3.5 + b$

DAY 2

At dinner, Mr. and Mrs. Brandt decide to leave a 20% tip for their server. Which is the best estimate of their tip if their meals total $63.20?

Ⓕ $1.20

Ⓖ $12.00

Ⓗ $14.00

Ⓙ $120.00

DAY 3

Tom is working with his lab group on a chemistry project. Each group member recorded the weight of a sample after a chemical reaction. Which number, rounded to the nearest hundredth, should be used for the weight of solution B?

Solution	A	B	C	D
Weight (g)	42.28	$47\frac{12}{17}$	50.16	44.09

Ⓐ 47.17 grams

Ⓑ 47.7 grams

Ⓒ 47.71 grams

Ⓓ 48.42 grams

DAY 4

Ronald followed this recipe for fruit punch. How many cups did he make? Write your answer in simpest terms.

Fantastic Fruit Punch

$1\frac{3}{4}$ cups orange juice
$\frac{2}{3}$ cup cranberry juice
$1\frac{1}{3}$ cups white grape juice
$\frac{1}{4}$ cup lime juice

Combine ingredients. Chill until ready to serve.

Ⓕ 3 cups

Ⓖ $3\frac{1}{2}$ cups

Ⓗ 4 cups

Ⓙ $4\frac{2}{3}$ cups

DAY 5

Mark is researching the effects of diet on mice. The table below shows the percent change in weight of each mouse studied. If the mice weighed the same at the start of the experiment, which mouse lost the most weight?

Mouse	% Change in Weight
1	−9.2
2	3.25
3	−9.05
4	−9.095

Ⓐ 1

Ⓑ 2

Ⓒ 3

Ⓓ 4

DAY 1

Which of the following correctly shows the length of the Earth's equator?

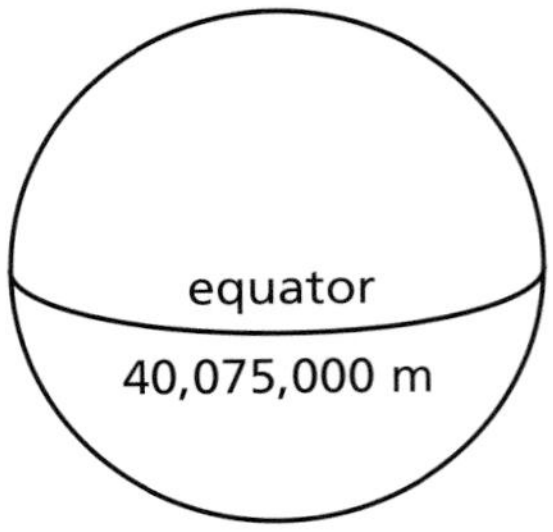

Ⓐ 0.40075×10^7 meters
Ⓑ 4.0075×10^7 meters
Ⓒ 40.075×10^7 meters
Ⓓ $4{,}007.5 \times 10^7$ meters

DAY 2

Figure *ABCD* is dilated by a scale factor of $\frac{3}{2}$. What are the coordinates of *C* after the dilation?

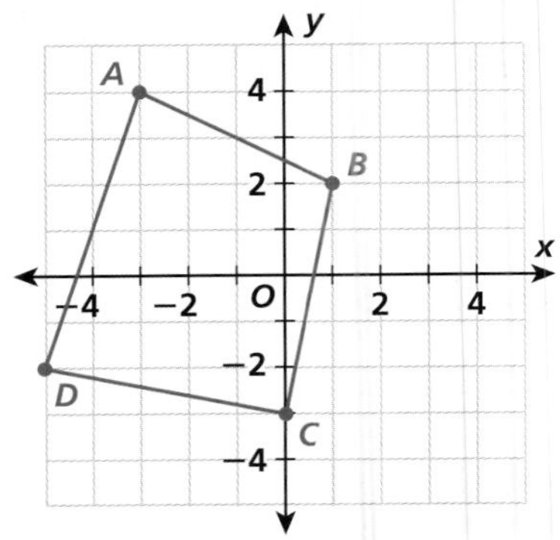

Ⓕ (2, –4)
Ⓖ $(0, -4\frac{1}{2})$
Ⓗ $(0, -1\frac{1}{2})$
Ⓙ (0, –2)

DAY 3

The Gordon family is driving to the Grand Canyon from Lubbock, Texas. If they drive an average of 55 miles per hour for *h* hours, which equation shows *d,* the distance they traveled?

Ⓐ $d = 55h$
Ⓑ $d = 55 \div h$
Ⓒ $d = \frac{h}{55}$
Ⓓ $d = 55 + h$

DAY 4

This rectangle is enlarged by a scale factor of 3. What is the new length in centimeters?

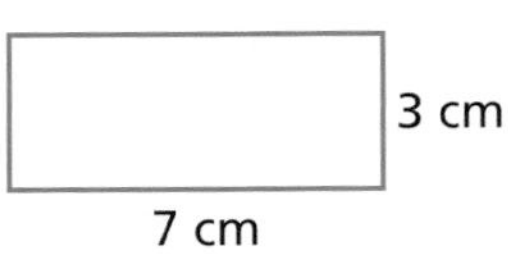

Ⓕ 9 centimeters
Ⓖ 10 centimeters
Ⓗ 20 centimeters
Ⓙ 21 centimeters

DAY 5

If these two figures are similar, what is the missing length of figure B?

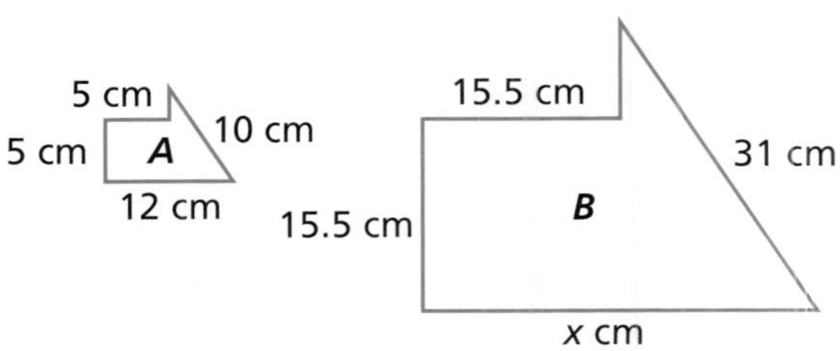

Ⓐ 3.1 centimeters
Ⓑ 22.5 centimeters
Ⓒ 25.2 centimeters
Ⓓ 37.2 centimeters

Countdown to Testing WEEK 14

DAY 1

Television screen size is measured on the diagonal. What is the height of this screen? Round your answer to the nearest tenth.

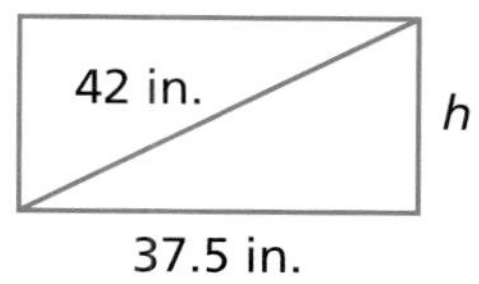

Ⓐ 4.5 inches
Ⓑ 9.0 inches
Ⓒ 18.9 inches
Ⓓ 20.3 inches

DAY 2

Which point is at $(-5, -1\frac{1}{2})$?

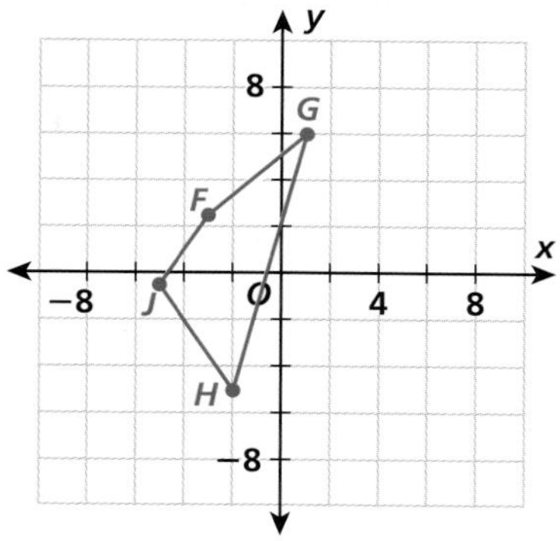

Ⓕ F
Ⓖ G
Ⓗ H
Ⓙ J

DAY 3

Martin can repair 7 watches in 1 hour when he begins work in the morning. The next hour, Martin repairs one less watch. If this pattern continues, which of the following shows how many watches Martin repairs in the third, fourth, fifth, and sixth hours?

Ⓐ 5, 4, 3, 2
Ⓑ 6, 4, 2, 1
Ⓒ 14, 21, 28, 35
Ⓓ 8, 9, 10, 11

DAY 4

If these two figures are similar, what is the missing measure in figure B?

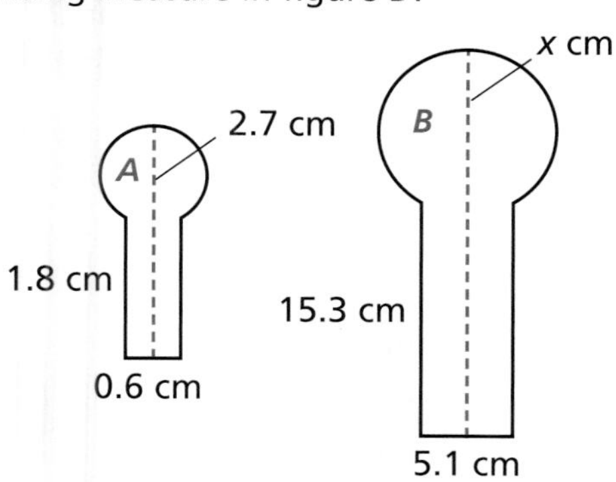

Ⓕ 18 centimeters
Ⓖ 20.4 centimeters
Ⓗ 22.95 centimeters
Ⓙ 30.6 centimeters

DAY 5

Gina is drawing a scale model of a park. If the scale factor is 1 inch = 4 feet, what is the perimeter of the actual park?

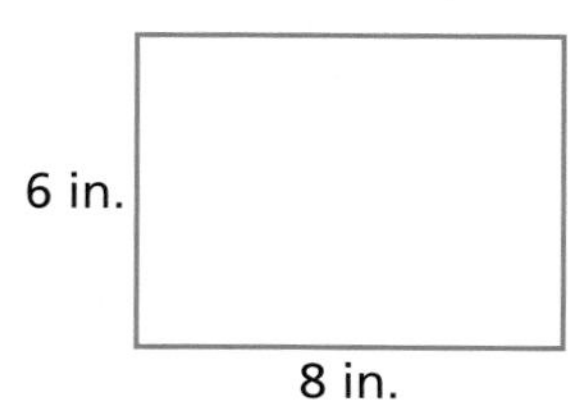

Ⓐ 28 feet
Ⓑ 56 feet
Ⓒ 112 feet
Ⓓ 768 feet

Countdown to Testing — WEEK 15

DAY 1

If figure *LMNO* is reflected across the *x*-axis, which point(s) will **not** change locations?

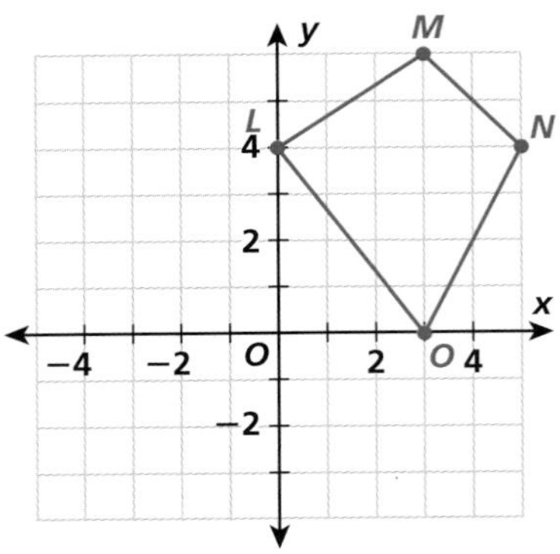

Ⓐ *L* and *O*
Ⓑ *L*
Ⓒ *O*
Ⓓ *L* and *N*

DAY 2

If figure *PQRS* is dilated by a scale factor of $\frac{1}{2}$, which point will be located at $(2, -1\frac{1}{2})$?

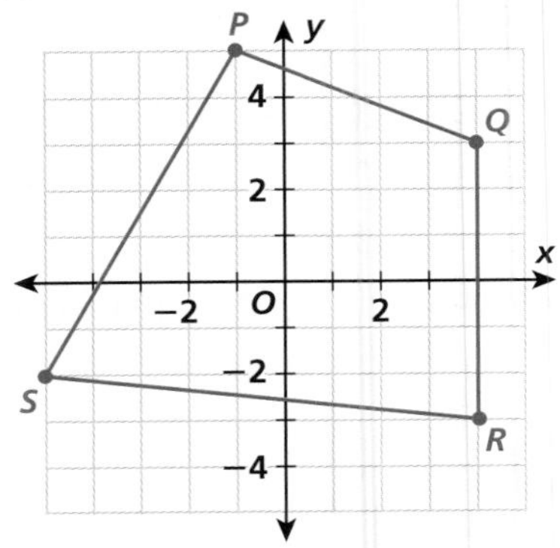

Ⓕ *P*
Ⓖ *Q*
Ⓗ *R*
Ⓙ *S*

DAY 3

The number 48 is 6% of which number?

Ⓐ 28.8
Ⓑ 80
Ⓒ 288
Ⓓ 800

DAY 4

Which figure does **not** form a tessellation?

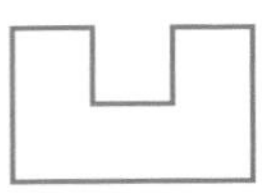

Figure 1

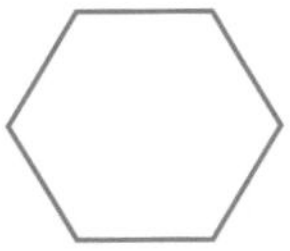

Figure 2

Figure 3

Figure 4

Ⓕ Figure 1
Ⓖ Figure 2
Ⓗ Figure 3
Ⓙ Figure 4

DAY 5

What is the side length of this square? Round your answer to the nearest tenth.

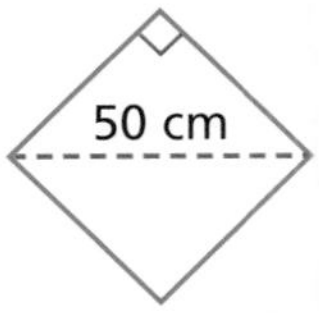

Ⓐ 5.0 centimeters
Ⓑ 11.2 centimeters
Ⓒ 25.0 centimeters
Ⓓ 35.4 centimeters

Countdown to Testing — WEEK 16

DAY 1

A computer's hard drive spins at 5400 revolutions per minute. If the hard drive has been running for *m* minutes, which expression shows *r*, the number of revolutions?

Ⓐ $r = m \div 5400$

Ⓑ $r = 5400 \cdot m$

Ⓒ $r = 5400 + m$

Ⓓ $r = \frac{5400}{m}$

DAY 2

Which expression describes this sequence?

…, 23, 25, 27, 29, …

Ⓕ $3x - 3$

Ⓖ $3 + 2x$

Ⓗ $2x - 2$

Ⓙ $x^2 + 1$

DAY 3

Figures A and B are similar. If the area of Figure A is 218.75 square centimeters, which expression could you use to determine the area of Figure B?

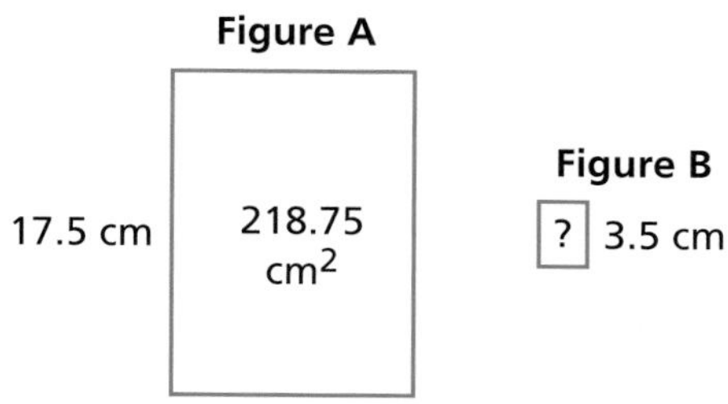

Ⓐ $17.5 \div 3.5$

Ⓑ $218.75 \div 25$

Ⓒ $5 \cdot 218.75$

Ⓓ $3.5 \cdot 17.5$

DAY 4

Katie wants to frame this stained-glass window with wood. What length of wood does she need to buy? Round your answer to the nearest tenth.

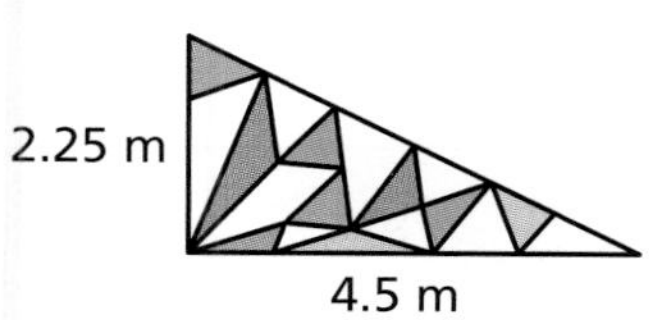

Ⓕ 5 meters

Ⓖ 6.8 meters

Ⓗ 11.8 meters

Ⓙ 13.5 meters

DAY 5

What is the length of side *c*?

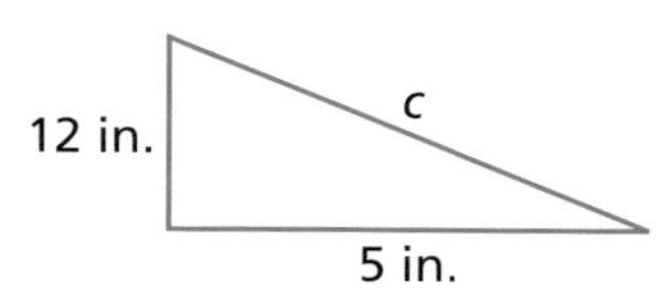

Ⓐ 12 inches

Ⓑ 13 inches

Ⓒ 25 inches

Ⓓ 169 inches

Countdown to Testing — WEEK 17

DAY 1

The Great Pyramid in Giza, Egypt, is a rectangular pyramid. Which formula could you use to determine the volume of the pyramid?

Ⓐ $V = \frac{1}{2}Bh$

Ⓑ $V = \frac{1}{3}Bh$

Ⓒ $V = Bh$

Ⓓ $V = \frac{4}{3}\pi r^3$

DAY 2

For which of the following shapes could you **not** use the formula $V = Bh$ to find the volume?

Ⓕ hexagonal prism

Ⓖ cylinder

Ⓗ rectangular prism

Ⓙ triangular pyramid

DAY 3

Nick buys a new fish tank for his living room. Which is the best estimate of the volume of water Nick needs to fill the tank?

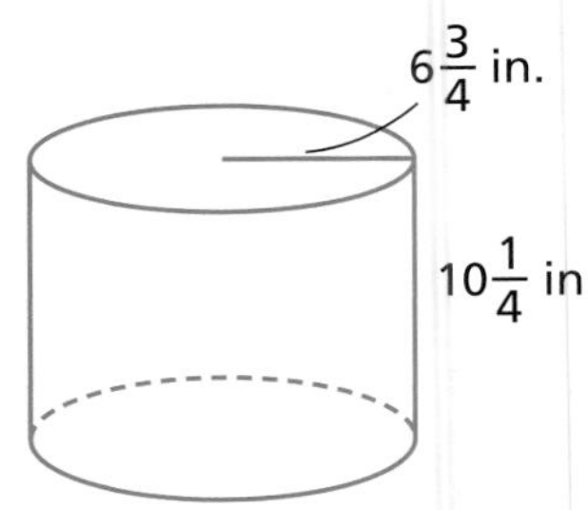

Ⓐ 70 cubic inches

Ⓑ 147 cubic inches

Ⓒ 1080 cubic inches

Ⓓ 1470 cubic inches

DAY 4

If $\triangle ACE$ is similar to $\triangle BCD$, what is the length of AC?

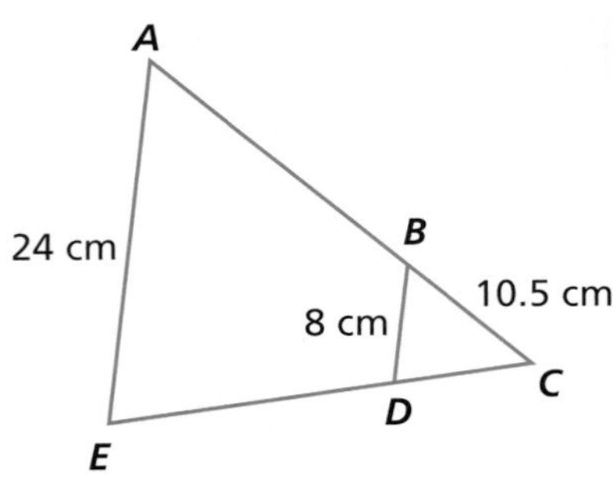

Ⓕ 5.5 centimeters

Ⓖ 13.5 centimeters

Ⓗ 21.5 centimeters

Ⓙ 31.5 centimeters

DAY 5

Candace is building a bookcase with shelves that are right triangles. What is the measure across the front of the bookcase? Round your answer to the nearest whole unit.

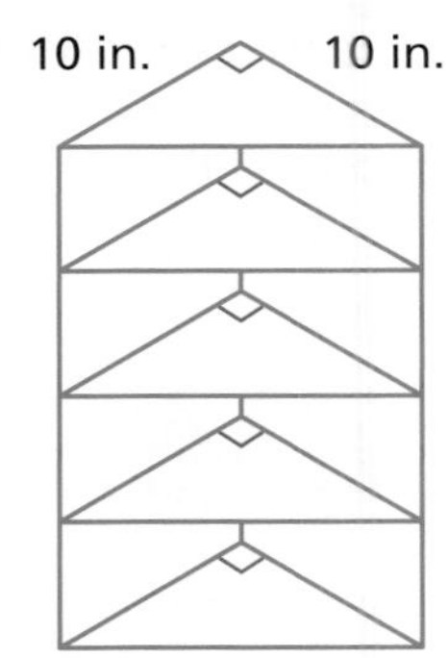

Ⓐ 4 inches

Ⓑ 14 inches

Ⓒ 50 inches

Ⓓ 72 inches

Countdown to Testing WEEK 18

DAY 1

What is the surface area of this square pyramid?

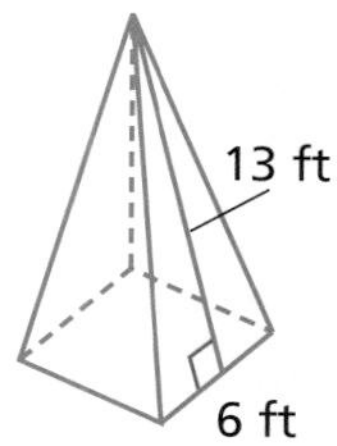

Ⓐ 75 square feet

Ⓑ 156 square feet

Ⓒ 192 square feet

Ⓓ 348 square feet

DAY 2

Sherman wants to paint the lateral surface area of the base for a sculpture he made. Which is the best estimate of the area Sherman wants to paint?

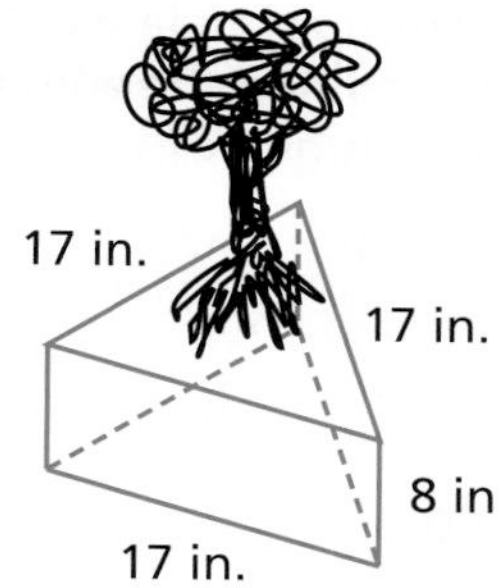

Ⓕ 51 square inches

Ⓖ 136 square inches

Ⓗ 408 square inches

Ⓙ 533 square inches

DAY 3

At a garage sale, Curtis buys a planter for his backyard. With base area B and height h, which formula should Curtis use to find the volume of soil he will need to fill the planter?

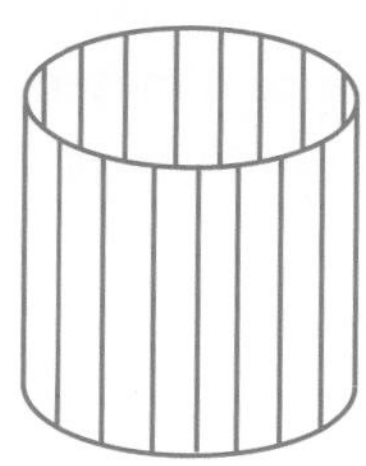

Ⓐ $V = Bh$

Ⓑ $V = \frac{1}{2}Bh$

Ⓒ $V = \frac{4}{3}\pi r^3$

Ⓓ $V = \frac{1}{3}Bh$

DAY 4

Nina is designing a pattern that is made up of equilateral triangles. If all the triangles are similar, what is the combined area of three shaded triangles?

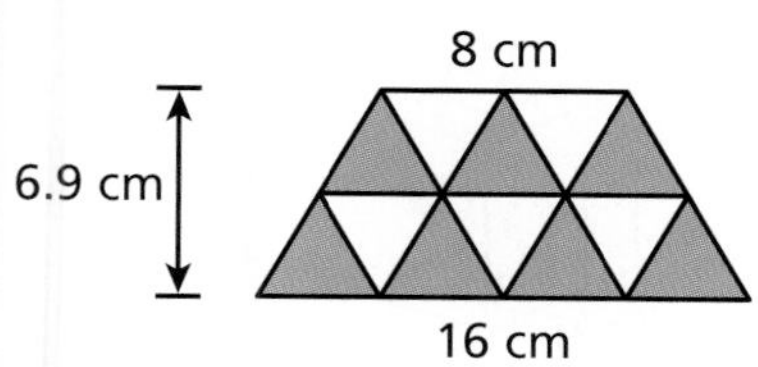

Ⓕ 6.9 square centimeters

Ⓖ 20.7 square centimeters

Ⓗ 27.6 square centimeters

Ⓙ 82.8 square centimeters

DAY 5

What percent of the larger rectangle's area is the smaller rectangle's area?

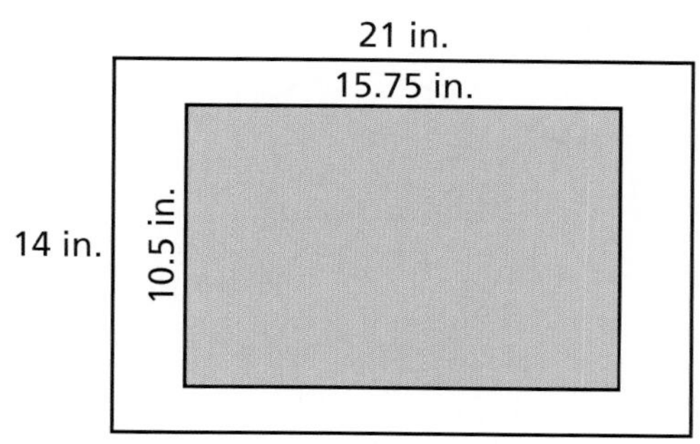

Ⓐ 0.75%

Ⓑ 5.25%

Ⓒ 56.25%

Ⓓ 103%

Countdown to Testing WEEK 19

DAY 1

Which formula would you use to find the volume of this globe?

Ⓐ $V = \frac{4}{3}\pi r^2$

Ⓑ $V = Bh$

Ⓒ $V = \frac{1}{3}Bh$

Ⓓ $V = \frac{1}{2}Bh$

DAY 2

What is the best estimate of the lateral surface area of this vase if the radius is 6 inches and the slant height is 13 inches?

Ⓕ 117 square inches

Ⓖ 234 square inches

Ⓗ 468 square inches

Ⓙ 1404 square inches

DAY 3

Mia made this net of a triangular prism. What is the surface area of the prism?

Ⓐ 615 square centimeters

Ⓑ 840 square centimeters

Ⓒ 877.5 square centimeters

Ⓓ 915 square centimeters

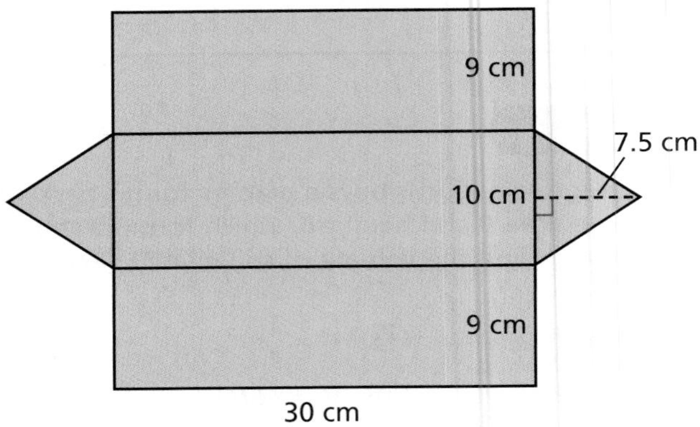

DAY 4

Paola drew a circle with four congruent circles inside it. If the area of the large circle is 167.2 square meters, what is the area of one small circle?

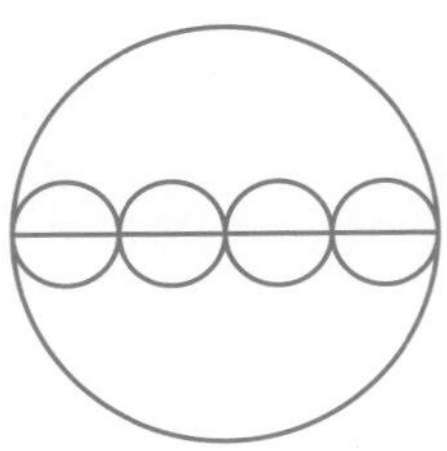

Ⓕ 5.65 square meters

Ⓖ 10.45 square meters

Ⓗ 18.54 square meters

Ⓙ 41.83 square meters

DAY 5

The roof of the greenhouse, which forms half a cylinder, is covered in glass. What is the surface area of the glass roof?

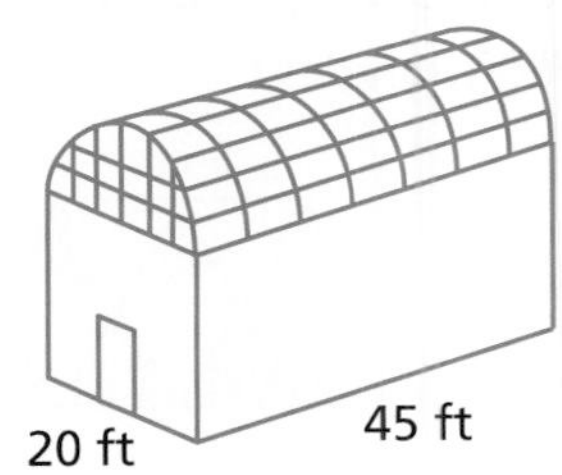

Ⓐ 1,727 square feet

Ⓑ 2,041 square feet

Ⓒ 3,140 square feet

Ⓓ 3,454 square feet

DAY 1

What is the best measure of the central tendency of these test scores?

92, 85, 89, 93, 74, 94

Ⓐ mean
Ⓑ median
Ⓒ mode
Ⓓ range

DAY 2

What is the lateral surface area of this pentagonal prism? Every side on the base has the same measurement.

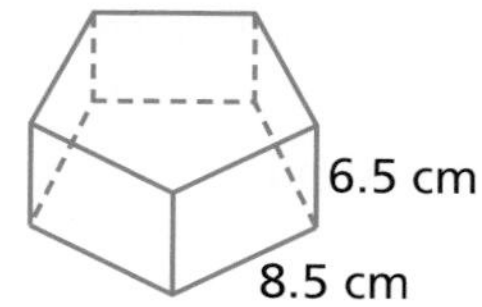

Ⓕ 120 square centimeters
Ⓖ 211.25 square centimeters
Ⓗ 212.5 square centimeters
Ⓙ 276.25 square centimeters

DAY 3

Philip created this table for the data in the graph. What mistake did he make?

Plant	A	B	C	D
Height (in.)	$1\frac{1}{2}$	3	1	$2\frac{1}{4}$

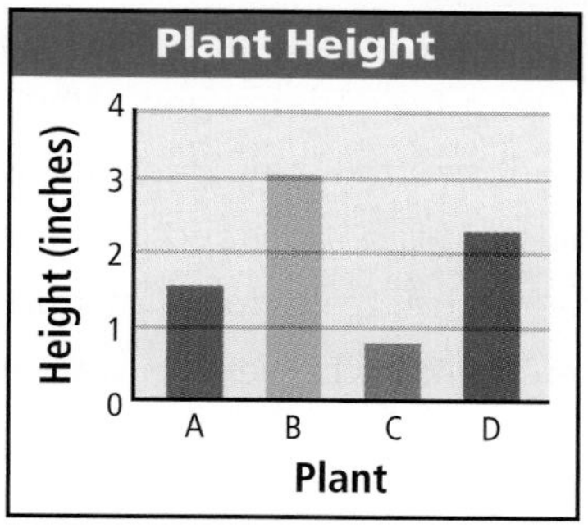

Ⓐ He confused the data for plants A and C.
Ⓑ He misread the data for plant C.
Ⓒ He rounded the data to the nearest $\frac{1}{4}$ inch.
Ⓓ He misread the data for plant D.

DAY 4

In this figure, each rectangle has $\frac{1}{4}$ less area than the rectangle directly enclosing it. What is the area of the smallest rectangle in this figure?

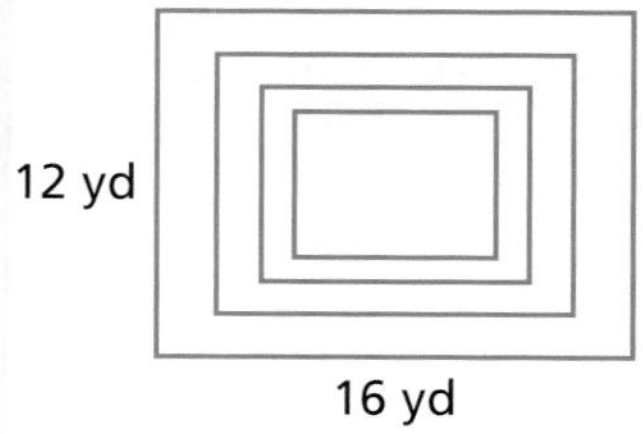

Ⓕ 81 square yards
Ⓖ 108 square yards
Ⓗ 144 square yards
Ⓙ 192 square yards

DAY 5

What is the possible next term in this pattern?

1, 8, 64, 512, ▢

Ⓐ 576
Ⓑ 582
Ⓒ 2,048
Ⓓ 4,096

DAY 1

Liu is researching the speeds of some of the fastest animals on Earth. Which of the following is the most appropriate method for her to display the data she finds on animals and their top speeds?

Ⓐ stem-and-leaf plot
Ⓑ scatter plot
Ⓒ line graph
Ⓓ bar graph

DAY 2

Bruno surveys his classmates about their favorite pet. What is the best measure of central tendency of this data?

Ⓕ mode
Ⓖ range
Ⓗ mean
Ⓙ median

DAY 3

This graph shows a company's monthly profits, but it gives a false impression. Why?

Ⓐ The horizontal scale does not start with 0.
Ⓑ The scale is not divided into equal increments.
Ⓒ The vertical scale does not start at 0.
Ⓓ The break in the vertical scale exaggerates the data.

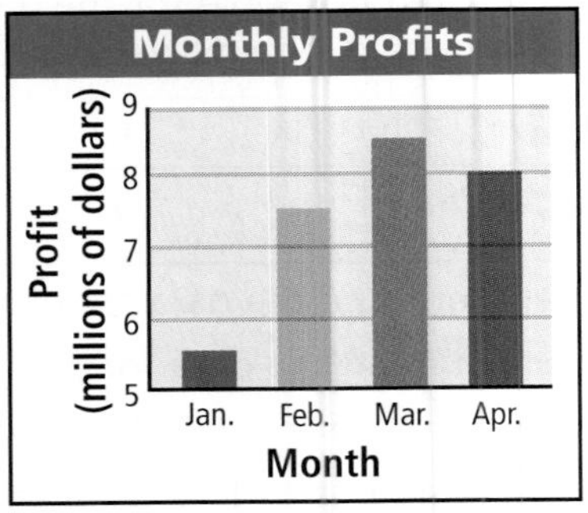

DAY 4

Keenan creates a sequence using blocks. The pattern of the sequence is shown in the table. How many blocks will he use for the fourteenth figure in the sequence?

Figure	1	2	3	4
Blocks	1	3	6	9

Ⓕ 36
Ⓖ 39
Ⓗ 42
Ⓙ 45

DAY 5

Jimmy buys 44 feet of wood to build a square frame for a sandbox. He decides to make the sandbox smaller and reduces its perimeter by 20%. How much wood will be left over?

Ⓐ 8.8 feet
Ⓑ 17.6 feet
Ⓒ 26.4 feet
Ⓓ 35.2 feet

Countdown to Testing WEEK 22

DAY 1

Which conclusion can you draw about worker productivity based on the scatter plot?

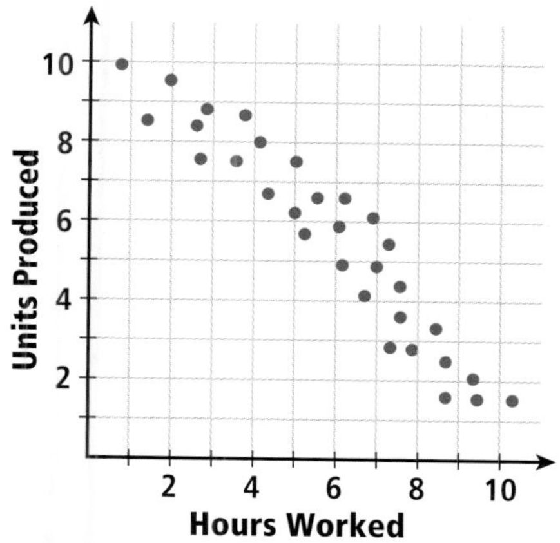

Ⓐ Productivity increases during the work day.

Ⓑ There is no trend for productivity in the scatter plot.

Ⓒ As the work day progresses, productivity declines.

Ⓓ Productivity remains constant during the work day.

DAY 2

Why is this bar graph misleading?

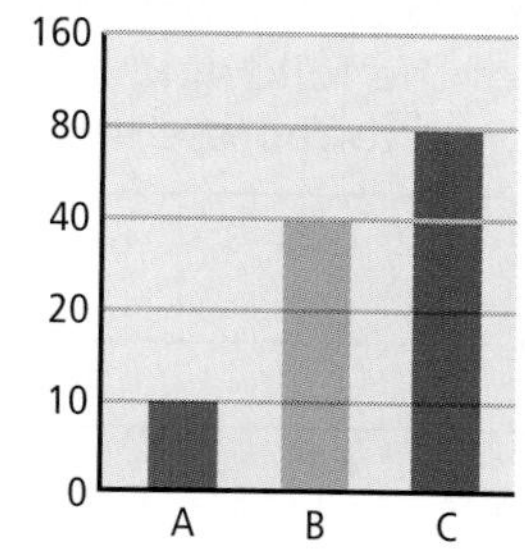

Ⓕ The scale is not divided into equal intervals, so the differences among the data seems less than than really are.

Ⓖ The horizontal scale does not start at 0, which skews the data.

Ⓗ The scale is not divided into equal intervals, so the differences among the data seems greater than they really are.

Ⓙ The bar graph is not misleading.

DAY 3

Kyle is studying the speed of cars as they drive by his house. Which of the following is the most appropriate way for Kyle to display his data?

Ⓐ circle graph
Ⓑ bar graph
Ⓒ stem-and-leaf plot
Ⓓ line graph

DAY 4

Ben is building a wall. What length of wood does Ben need to buy to create two cross beams for the frame? Round your answer to the nearest tenth.

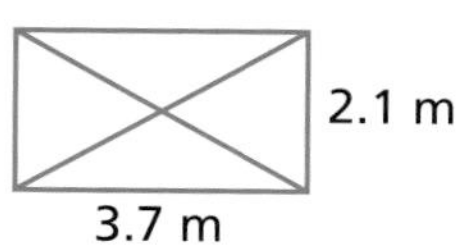

Ⓕ 4.3 meters
Ⓖ 5.8 meters
Ⓗ 8.5 meters
Ⓙ 11.6 meters

DAY 5

If this pattern continues, how many circles will be in the eighth group in this sequence?

Ⓐ 2
Ⓑ 3
Ⓒ 4
Ⓓ 5

Countdown to Testing — WEEK 23

DAY 1

The frequency table shows the number of days of rain in each month for one year. Which of the following is the most appropriate way to represent this data?

Days of Rain	0–2	3–5	6–8	9–11
Frequency	4	6	2	0

Ⓐ histogram
Ⓑ bar graph
Ⓒ circle graph
Ⓓ line plot

DAY 2

Which conclusion can you draw based on the data in this scatter plot?

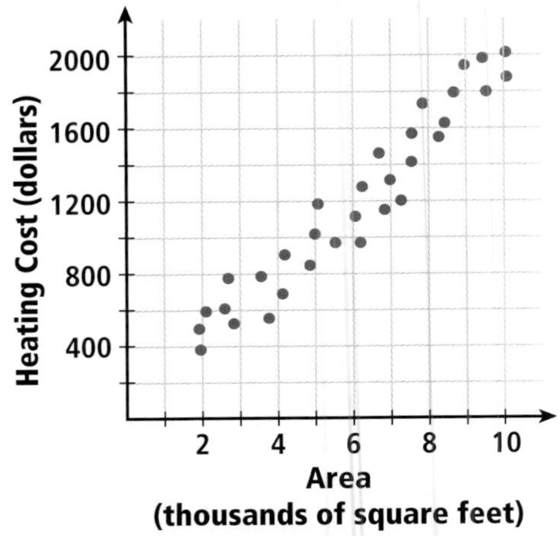

Ⓕ The smaller the area, the more expensive the heating costs.
Ⓖ Heating costs remain constant.
Ⓗ The scatter plot does not show a trend.
Ⓙ The larger the area, the greater the heating costs.

DAY 3

Tamara records the high temperature for each day this month. Which would be the most appropriate way for Tamara to display the data if she wants to see the change in temperature over time?

Ⓐ circle graph
Ⓑ line plot
Ⓒ line graph
Ⓓ scatter plot

DAY 4

If the two rectangles are similar, what is the length of the smaller rectangle?

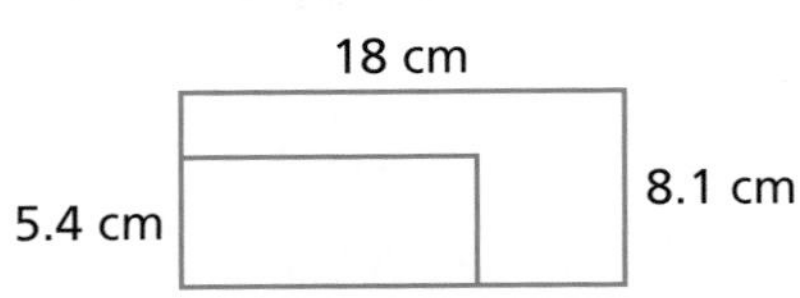

Ⓕ 6.7 centimeters
Ⓖ 12 centimeters
Ⓗ 14.1 centimeters
Ⓙ 15 centimeters

DAY 5

If the side of this triangle is increased by a factor of 1.3, what is the perimeter of the new triangle?

Ⓐ 7.3 meters
Ⓑ 7.8 meters
Ⓒ 21.9 meters
Ⓓ 23.4 meters

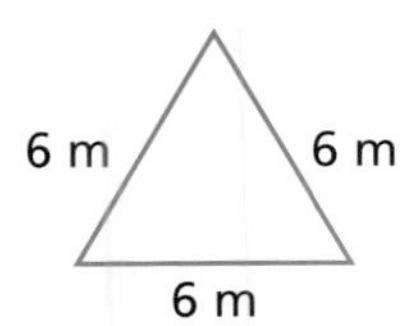

Countdown to Testing WEEK 24

DAY 1

What kind of correlation would you expect to find in a scatter plot comparing people's ages and favorite colors?

Ⓐ negative

Ⓑ no correlation

Ⓒ positive

Ⓓ There is not enough information to answer the question.

DAY 2

Megan recorded the weight of each tomato in her garden this week. Which is the best measure of the central tendency for this data set?

220 grams, 225 grams,
213 grams, 140 grams,
210 grams, 209 grams

Ⓕ mean

Ⓖ range

Ⓗ mode

Ⓙ median

DAY 3

This graph shows a local politician's approval ratings for the last four months. What effect does the unequal scale interval have on the visual impression of the data?

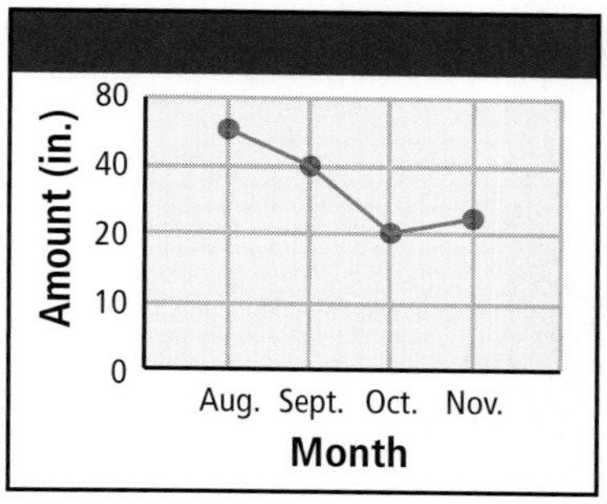

Ⓐ It makes the drop in his approval ratings look more dramatic.

Ⓑ It makes the drop in his approval ratings look less dramatic.

Ⓒ It makes the politician appear less popular than he is.

Ⓓ It does not have any effect.

DAY 4

Mrs. Weyland is making 7 cups of juice for her children's friends. If she wants to serve each guest $\frac{3}{4}$ cup of juice, how many children will the juice serve?

Ⓕ 8

Ⓖ 9

Ⓗ 10

Ⓙ 11

DAY 5

Which number is missing from this sequence?

254, ▒, 22.86, 6.858, ...

Ⓐ 76.2

Ⓑ 99.06

Ⓒ 115.57

Ⓓ 138.43

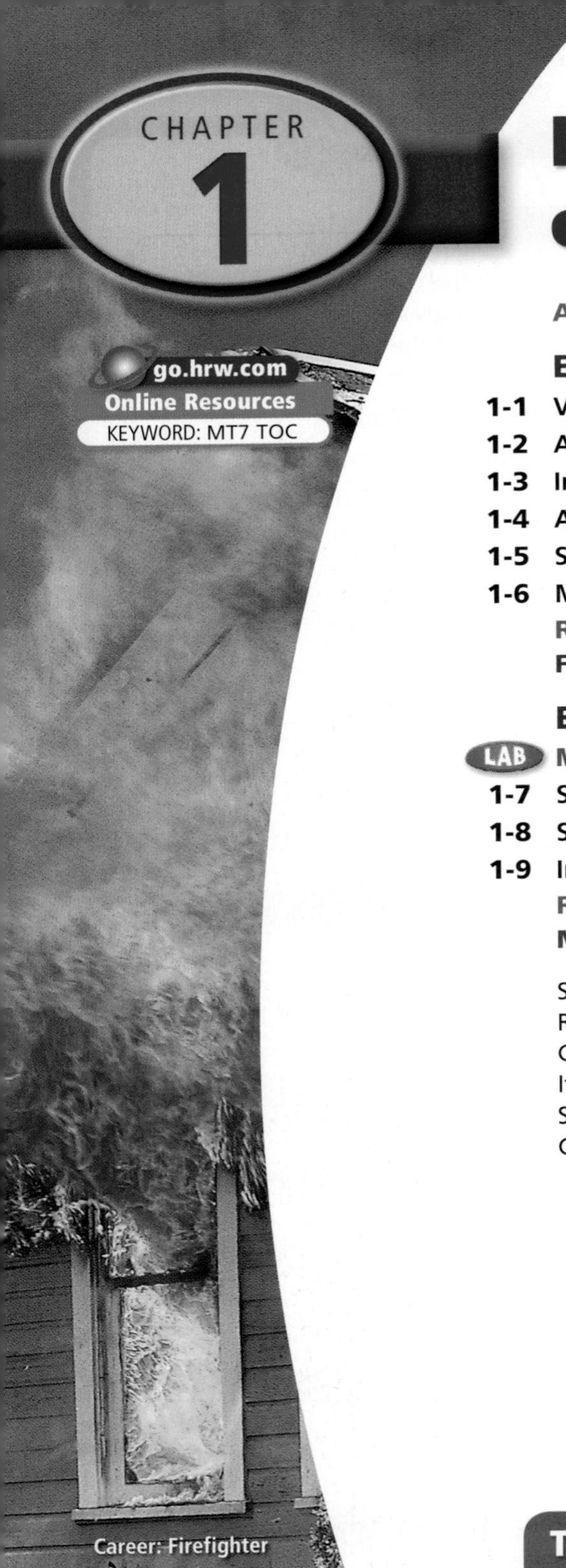

Career: Firefighter

CHAPTER 1

Principles of Algebra

go.hrw.com
Online Resources
KEYWORD: MT7 TOC

ARE YOU READY? 3

Expressions and Integers

1-1 Variables and Expressions 6
1-2 Algebraic Expressions 10
1-3 Integers and Absolute Value 14
1-4 Adding Integers 18
1-5 Subtracting Integers 22
1-6 Multiplying and Dividing Integers 26
READY TO GO ON? QUIZ 30
Focus on Problem Solving: Solve 31

Equations and Inequalities

LAB Model Solving Equations 32
1-7 Solving Equations by Adding or Subtracting 34
1-8 Solving Equations by Multiplying or Dividing 39
1-9 Introduction to Inequalities 44
READY TO GO ON? QUIZ 48
MULTI-STEP TEST PREP 49

Study Guide: Preview 4
Reading and Writing Math 5
Game Time: Math Magic 50
It's in the Bag!: Note-Taking Taking Shape 51
Study Guide: Review 52
Chapter Test 55

Tools for Success

Reading and Writing Math

Reading Math 5
Writing Math 9, 13, 17, 21, 25, 29, 38, 43, 47
Vocabulary 6, 14, 34, 44

Study Skills

Know-It Notebook Chapter 1
Homework Help Online 8, 12, 16, 20, 24, 28, 37, 41, 46
Study Skills 6, 14, 44, 45

TEST PREP

Test Prep and Spiral Review 9, 13, 17, 21, 25, 29, 38, 43, 47
Multi-Step Test Prep 49
Test Tackler 56
Standardized Test Prep 58

Rational Numbers

CHAPTER 2

ARE YOU READY? 61

Rational Number Operations

2-1 Rational Numbers 64
2-2 Comparing and Ordering Rational Numbers 68
2-3 Adding and Subtracting Rational Numbers 72
2-4 Multiplying Rational Numbers 76
2-5 Dividing Rational Numbers 80
2-6 Adding and Subtracting with Unlike Denominators 85
LAB Add and Subtract Fractions 89
READY TO GO ON? QUIZ 90
Focus on Problem Solving: Look Back 91

Equations with Rational Numbers

2-7 Solving Equations with Rational Numbers 92
LAB Model Two-Step Equations 96
2-8 Solving Two-Step Equations 98
READY TO GO ON? QUIZ 102
MULTI-STEP TEST PREP 103
Problem Solving on Location: New Jersey 112

Study Guide: Preview 62
Reading and Writing Math 63
Game Time: Egyptian Fractions 104
It's in the Bag!: Canister Carry-All 105
Study Guide: Review 106
Chapter Test 109

go.hrw.com
Online Resources
KEYWORD: MT7 TOC

Career: Nutritionist

Tools for Success

Reading and Writing Math

Writing Math 63, 65, 67, 71, 75, 79, 84, 88, 95, 101
Vocabulary 64, 68, 80

Study Skills

Know-It Notebook Chapter 2
Homework Help Online 66, 70, 74, 78, 83, 87, 94, 100
Student Help 64, 68, 73, 77, 92

TEST PREP

Test Prep and Spiral Review 67, 71, 75, 79, 84, 88, 95, 101
Multi-Step Test Prep 103
Standardized Test Prep 110

CHAPTER 3

Graphs, Functions, and Sequences

go.hrw.com
Online Resources
KEYWORD: MT7 TOC

Career: Pharmacist

ARE YOU READY? 115

Tables and Graphs

3-1 Ordered Pairs 118
3-2 Graphing on a Coordinate Plane 122
LAB Graph Points 126
3-3 Interpreting Graphs and Tables 127
READY TO GO ON? QUIZ 132
Focus on Problem Solving: Make a Plan 133

Functions and Sequences

3-4 Functions 134
3-5 Equations, Tables, and Graphs 138
3-6 Arithmetic Sequences 142
READY TO GO ON? QUIZ 146
MULTI-STEP TEST PREP 147

Study Guide: Preview 116
Reading and Writing Math 117
Game Time: Find the Phony! 148
It's in the Bag!: Clipboard Solutions for Graphs, Functions, and Sequences 149
Study Guide: Review 150
Chapter Test 153

Tools for Success

Reading and Writing Math

Reading Math 117
Writing Math 121, 125, 131, 137, 141, 145
Vocabulary 118, 122, 134, 142

Study Skills

Know-It Notebook Chapter 3
Homework Help Online 120, 124, 129, 136, 140, 144

TEST PREP

Test Prep and Spiral Review 121, 125, 131, 137, 141, 145
Multi-Step Test Prep 147
Test Tackler 154
Standardized Test Prep 156

Exponents and Roots

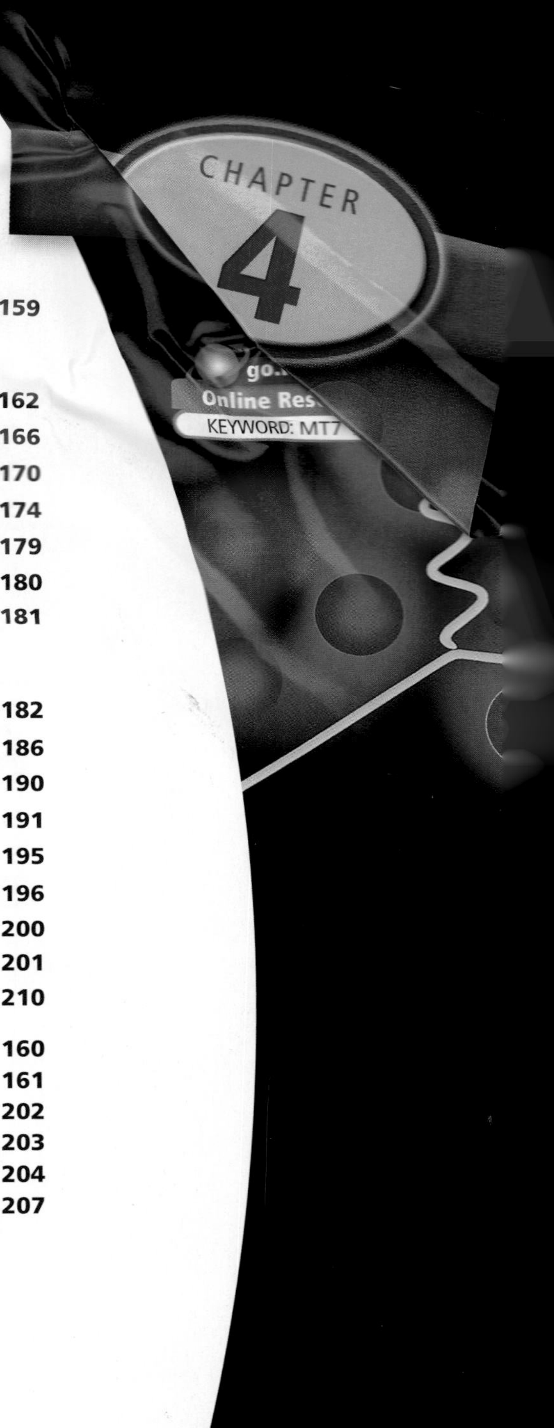

ARE YOU READY? 159

Exponents

4-1 Exponents 162
4-2 Look for a Pattern in Integer Exponents 166
4-3 Properties of Exponents 170
4-4 Scientific Notation 174
LAB Multiply and Divide Numbers in Scientific Notation 179
READY TO GO ON? QUIZ 180
Focus on Problem Solving: Solve 181

Roots

4-5 Squares and Square Roots 182
4-6 Estimating Square Roots 186
LAB Evaluate Powers and Roots 190
4-7 The Real Numbers 191
LAB Explore Right Triangles 195
4-8 The Pythagorean Theorem 196
READY TO GO ON? QUIZ 200
MULTI-STEP TEST PREP 201
Problem Solving on Location: Ohio 210

Study Guide: Preview 160
Reading and Writing Math 161
Game Time: Magic Squares 202
It's in the Bag!: It's a Wrap 203
Study Guide: Review 204
Chapter Test 207

Career:
Nuclear Physicist

Tools for Success

Reading and Writing Math

Reading Math 162, 171

Writing Math 165, 169, 173, 178, 185, 189, 194, 199

Vocabulary 162, 174, 182, 191, 196

Study Skills

Know-It Notebook Chapter 4

Study Strategy 161

Homework Help Online 164, 168, 172, 176, 184, 188, 193, 198

Student Help 163, 167, 182, 183, 191

TEST PREP

Test Prep and Spiral Review 165, 169, 173, 178, 185, 189, 194, 199

Multi-Step Test Prep 201

Standardized Test Prep 208

Ratios, Proportions, and Similarity

Are You Ready? 213

Ratios, Rates, and Proportions

5-1 Ratios and Proportions 216
5-2 Ratios, Rates, and Unit Rates 220
5-3 Dimensional Analysis 224
5-4 Solving Proportions 229
Ready to Go On? Quiz 234
Focus on Problem Solving: Solve 235

Similarity and Scale

LAB Explore Similarity 236
5-5 Similar Figures 238
LAB Explore Dilations 242
5-6 Dilations 244
5-7 Indirect Measurement 248
5-8 Scale Drawings and Scale Models 252
LAB Make a Scale Model 256
Ready to Go On? Quiz 258
Multi-Step Test Prep 259

Study Guide: Preview 214
Reading and Writing Math 215
Game Time: Copy-Cat 260
It's in the Bag!: A Worthwhile Wallet 261
Study Guide: Review 262
Chapter Test 265

Tools for Success

Reading and Writing Math

Reading Math 216, 238, 252
Writing Math 215, 219, 223, 228, 233, 241, 247, 251, 255
Vocabulary 216, 220, 224, 229, 238, 244, 248, 252

Study Skills

Know-It Notebook Chapter 5
Homework Help Online 218, 222, 226, 231, 240, 246, 250, 254
Student Help 224

Test Prep

Test Prep and Spiral Review 219, 223, 228, 233, 241, 247, 251, 255
Multi-Step Test Prep 259
Test Tackler 266
Standardized Test Prep 268

Percents

go.hrw.com
Online Resources
KEYWORD: MT7 TOC

CHAPTER 6

ARE YOU READY? 271

Proportions and Percents

6-1 Relating Decimals, Fractions, and Percents 274
6-2 Estimate with Percents 278
6-3 Finding Percents 283
6-4 Finding a Number When the Percent is Known 288
READY TO GO ON? QUIZ 292
Focus on Problem Solving: Make a Plan 293

Applying Percents

6-5 Percent Increase and Decrease 294
6-6 Applications of Percents 298
6-7 Simple Interest 302
LAB Compute Compound Interest 306
READY TO GO ON? QUIZ 308
MULTI-STEP TEST PREP 309
Problem Solving on Location: Pennsylvania 318

Study Guide: Preview 272
Reading and Writing Math 273
Game Time: Percent Puzzlers 310
It's in the Bag!: Origami Percents 311
Study Guide: Review 312
Chapter Test 315

Career: Sports Statistician

Tools for Success

Reading and Writing Math

Reading Math 273, 274
Writing Math 277, 282, 287, 291, 297, 301, 305
Vocabulary 274, 278, 294, 298, 302

Study Skills

Know-It Notebook Chapter 6
Homework Help Online 276, 280, 285, 290, 296, 300, 304
Student Help 275

TEST PREP

Test Prep and Spiral Review 277, 282, 287, 291, 297, 301, 305
Multi-Step Test Prep 309
Standardized Test Prep 316

CHAPTER 7

Foundations of Geometry

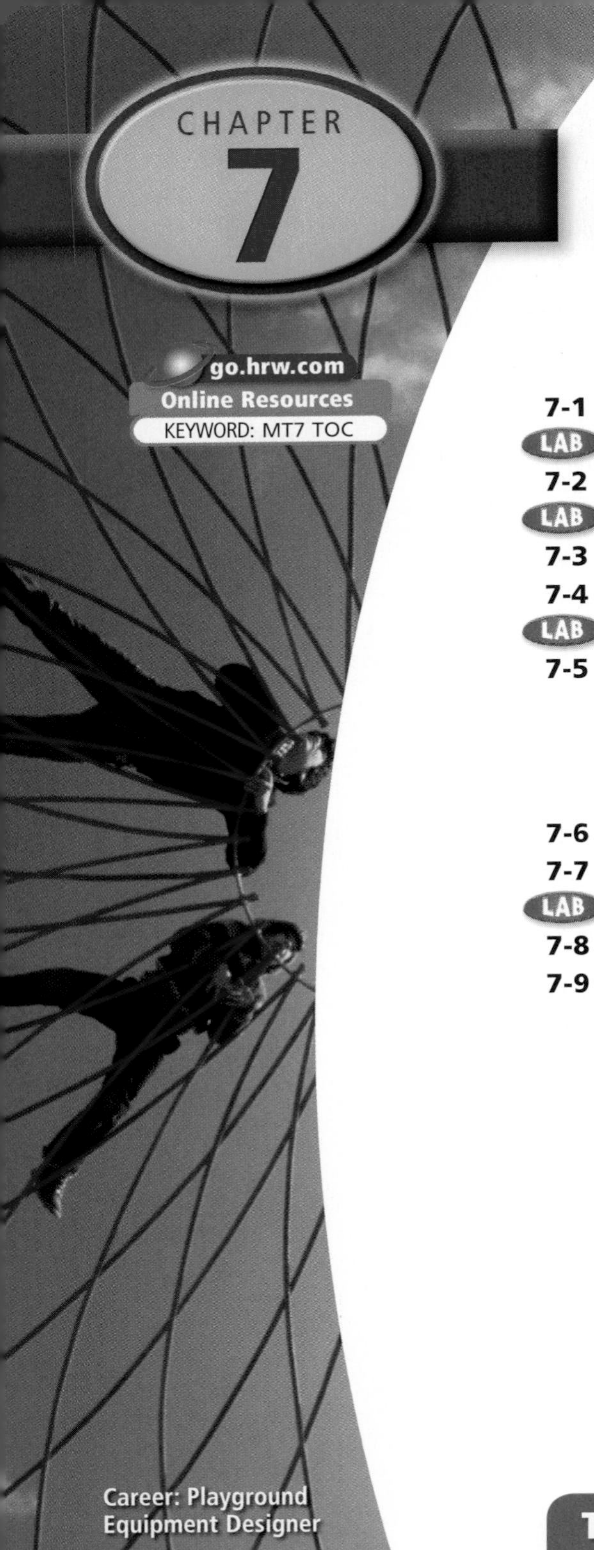

go.hrw.com
Online Resources
KEYWORD: MT7 TOC

Career: Playground Equipment Designer

ARE YOU READY? 321

Two-Dimensional Geometry

7-1 Points, Lines, Planes, and Angles 324
LAB Bisect Figures 329
7-2 Parallel and Perpendicular Lines 330
LAB Constructions 334
7-3 Angles in Triangles 336
7-4 Classifying Polygons 341
LAB Exterior Angles of a Polygon 346
7-5 Coordinate Geometry 347
READY TO GO ON? QUIZ 352
Focus on Problem Solving: Understand the Problem 353

Patterns in Geometry

7-6 Congruence 354
7-7 Transformations 358
LAB Combine Transformations 362
7-8 Symmetry 364
7-9 Tessellations 368
READY TO GO ON? QUIZ 372
MULTI-STEP TEST PREP 373

Study Guide: Preview 322
Reading and Writing Math 323
Game Time: Coloring Tessellations 374
It's in the Bag!: Project CD Geometry 375
Study Guide: Review 376
Chapter Test 379

Tools for Success

Reading and Writing Math

Reading Math 325, 358, 364
Writing Math 323, 328, 331, 333, 340, 345, 351, 357, 361, 367, 371
Vocabulary 324, 330, 336, 341, 354, 358, 368

Study Skills

Know-It Notebook Chapter 7
Homework Help Online 326, 332, 338, 343, 349, 356, 360, 366, 369
Student Help 330, 347, 349

TEST PREP

Test Prep and Spiral Review 328, 333, 340, 345, 351, 357, 361, 367, 371
Multi-Step Test Prep 373
Test Tackler 380
Standardized Test Prep 382

Perimeter, Area, and Volume

CHAPTER 8

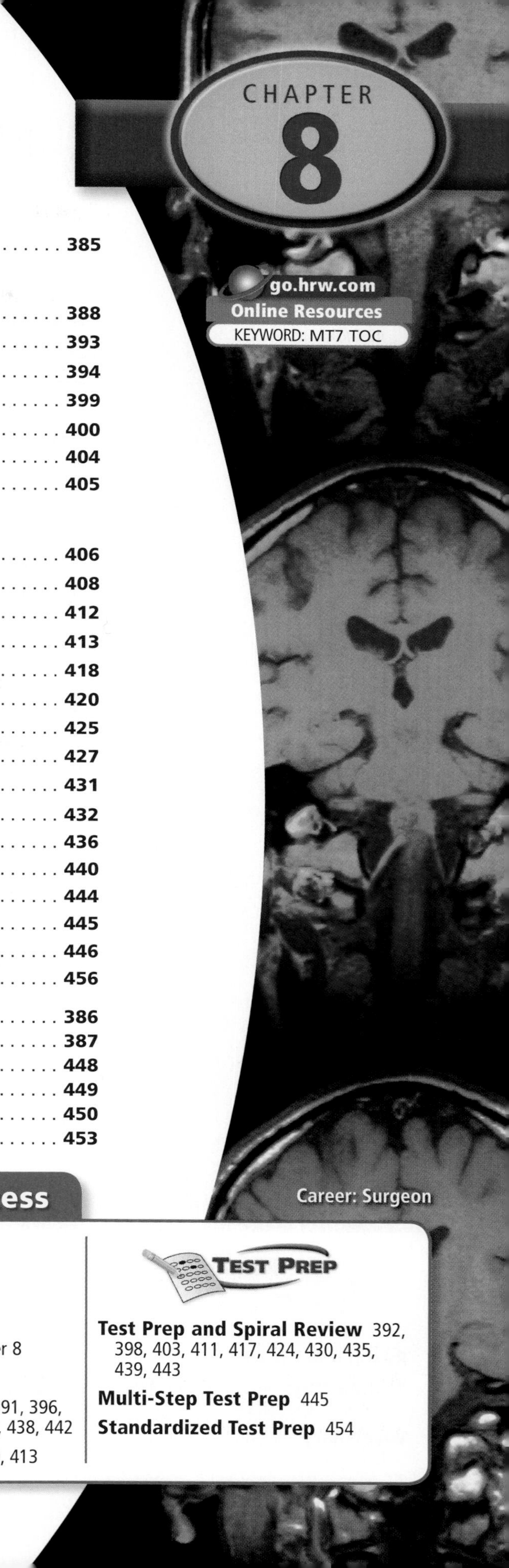

ARE YOU READY? 385

Perimeter and Area

8-1 Perimeter and Area of Rectangles & Parallelograms 388
LAB Explore the Effects of Changing Dimensions 393
8-2 Perimeter and Area of Triangles and Trapezoids 394
LAB Approximate *Pi* by Measuring 399
8-3 Circles 400
READY TO GO ON? QUIZ 404
Focus on Problem Solving: Look Back 405

Three-Dimensional Geometry

LAB Construct Nets 406
8-4 Drawing Three-Dimensional Figures 408
LAB Find Volume of Prisms and Cylinders 412
8-5 Volume of Prisms and Cylinders 413
LAB Find Volume of Pyramids and Cones 418
8-6 Volume of Pyramids and Cones 420
LAB Find Surface Area of Prisms and Cylinders 425
8-7 Surface Area of Prisms and Cylinders 427
LAB Find the Surface Area of Pyramids 431
8-8 Surface Area of Pyramids and Cones 432
8-9 Spheres 436
8-10 Scaling Three-Dimensional Figures 440
READY TO GO ON? QUIZ 444
MULTI-STEP TEST PREP 445
EXT Symmetry in Three Dimensions 446
Problem Solving on Location: Nevada 456

Study Guide: Preview 386
Reading and Writing Math 387
Game Time: Planes in Space 448
It's in the Bag!: The Tube Journal 449
Study Guide: Review 450
Chapter Test 453

Tools for Success

Reading and Writing Math

Reading Math 395
Writing Math 392, 398, 403, 411, 417, 424, 430, 435, 439, 443
Vocabulary 388, 400, 408, 413, 420, 427, 432, 436, 440, 446

Study Skills

Know-It Notebook Chapter 8
Study Strategy 387
Homework Help Online 391, 396, 402, 410, 416, 422, 429, 434, 438, 442
Student Help 388, 390, 400, 413

TEST PREP

Test Prep and Spiral Review 392, 398, 403, 411, 417, 424, 430, 435, 439, 443
Multi-Step Test Prep 445
Standardized Test Prep 454

Career: Quality Assurance Specialist

CHAPTER 9

Data and Statistics

ARE YOU READY? 458

Collecting and Describing Data

9-1 Samples and Surveys 462
LAB Explore Samples 466
9-2 Organizing Data 467
9-3 Measures of Central Tendency 472
9-4 Variability 476
LAB Create Box-and-Whisker Plots 481
READY TO GO ON? QUIZ 482
Focus on Problem Solving: Make a Plan 483

Displaying Data

LAB Make a Circle Graph 484
9-5 Displaying Data 485
LAB Create Histograms 489
9-6 Misleading Graphs and Statistics 490
9-7 Scatter Plots 494
LAB Create a Scatter Plot 498
9-8 Choosing the Best Representation of Data 500
LAB Use a Spreadsheet to Create Graphs 504
READY TO GO ON? QUIZ 506
MULTI-STEP TEST PREP 507

Study Guide: Preview 460
Reading and Writing Math 461
Game Time: Distribution of Primes 508
It's in the Bag!: Data Pop-Ups 509
Study Guide: Review 510
Chapter Test 513

Tools for Success

Reading and Writing Math

Reading Math 461
Writing Math 465, 471, 475, 480, 488, 493, 497, 503
Vocabulary 462, 467, 472, 476, 485, 494

Study Skills

Know-It Notebook Chapter 9
Homework Help Online 464, 469, 474, 478, 487, 492, 496, 502

TEST PREP

Test Prep and Spiral Review 465, 471, 475, 480, 488, 493, 497, 503
Multi-Step Test Prep 507
Test Tackler 514
Standardized Test Prep 516

Probability

CHAPTER 10

ARE YOU READY? 519

Experimental Probability

10-1 Probability 522
10-2 Experimental Probability 527
LAB Generate Random Numbers 531
10-3 Use a Simulation 532
LAB Use Different Models for Simulations 536
READY TO GO ON? QUIZ 538
Focus on Problem Solving: Understand the Problem 539

Theoretical Probability and Counting

10-4 Theoretical Probability 540
10-5 Independent and Dependent Events 545
10-6 Making Decisions and Predictions 550
10-7 Odds 554
10-8 Counting Principles 558
10-9 Permutations and Combinations 563
READY TO GO ON? QUIZ 568
MULTI-STEP TEST PREP 569
Problem Solving on Location: South Carolina 578

Study Guide: Preview 520
Reading and Writing Math 521
Game Time: The Paper Chase 570
It's in the Bag!: Probability Post-Up 571
Study Guide: Review 572
Chapter Test 575

go.hrw.com
Online Resources
KEYWORD: MT7 TOC

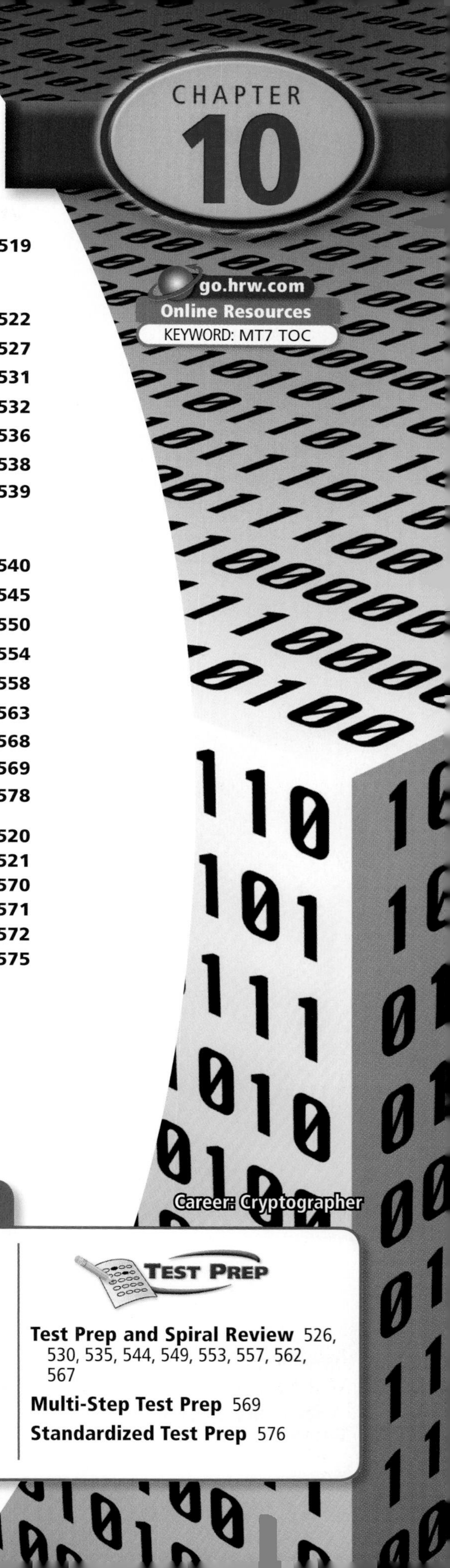

Tools for Success

Reading and Writing Math

Reading Math 521, 563
Writing Math 526, 530, 535, 544, 549, 553, 557, 562, 567
Vocabulary 522, 527, 532, 540, 545, 554, 558, 563

Study Skills

Know-It Notebook Chapter 10
Homework Help Online 525, 529, 534, 543, 548, 552, 556, 560, 566

TEST PREP

Test Prep and Spiral Review 526, 530, 535, 544, 549, 553, 557, 562, 567
Multi-Step Test Prep 569
Standardized Test Prep 576

CHAPTER 11

Multi-Step Equations and Inequalities

Career: Hydrologist

ARE YOU READY? 581

Solving Linear Equations

11-1 Simplifying Algebraic Expressions 584
11-2 Solving Multi-Step Equations 588
LAB Model Equations with Variables on Both Sides 592
11-3 Solving Equations with Variables on Both Sides 593
READY TO GO ON? QUIZ 598
Focus on Problem Solving: Make a Plan 599

Solving Equations and Inequalities

11-4 Solving Inequalities by Multiplying or Dividing 600
11-5 Solving Two-Step Inequalities 604
11-6 Systems of Equations 608
READY TO GO ON? QUIZ 612
MULTI-STEP TEST PREP 613

Study Guide: Preview 582
Reading and Writing Math 583
Game Time: Trans-Plants 614
It's in the Bag!: Picture Envelopes 615
Study Guide: Review 616
Chapter Test 619

Tools for Success

Reading and Writing Math

Writing Math 583, 587, 591, 597, 603, 607, 611
Vocabulary 584, 608

Study Skills

Know-It Notebook Chapter 11
Homework Help Online 586, 590, 596, 602, 606, 610
Student Help 585, 589, 600

TEST PREP

Test Prep and Spiral Review 587, 591, 597, 603, 607, 611
Multi-Step Test Prep 613
Test Tackler 620
Standardized Test Prep 622

CHAPTER 12

Graphing Lines

ARE YOU READY? 625

Linear Equations

12-1 Graphing Linear Equations 628
12-2 Slope of a Line 633
12-3 Using Slopes and Intercepts 638
LAB Graph Equations in Slope-Intercept Form 643
12-4 Point-Slope Form 644
READY TO GO ON? QUIZ 648
Focus on Problem Solving: Understand the Problem 649

Linear Relationships

12-5 Direct Variation 650
12-6 Graphing Inequalities in Two Variables 655
12-7 Lines of Best Fit 660
READY TO GO ON? QUIZ 664
MULTI-STEP TEST PREP 665
EXT Solving Systems of Equations by Graphing 666
Problem Solving on Location: Maryland 676

Study Guide: Preview 626
Reading and Writing Math 627
Game Time: Graphing in Space 668
It's in the Bag!: Graphing Tri-Fold 669
Study Guide: Review 670
Chapter Test 673

go.hrw.com
Online Resources
KEYWORD: MT7 TOC

Career: Wildlife Ecologist

Tools for Success

Reading and Writing Math

Reading Math 628
Writing Math 627, 632, 637, 642, 647, 654, 659, 663
Vocabulary 628, 638, 644, 650, 655

Study Skills

Know-It Notebook Chapter 12
Homework Help Online 631, 635, 641, 646, 653, 658, 662
Student Help 633, 660

TEST PREP

Test Prep and Spiral Review 632, 637, 642, 647, 654, 659, 663
Multi-Step Test Prep 665
Standardized Test Prep 674

CHAPTER 13

Sequences and Functions

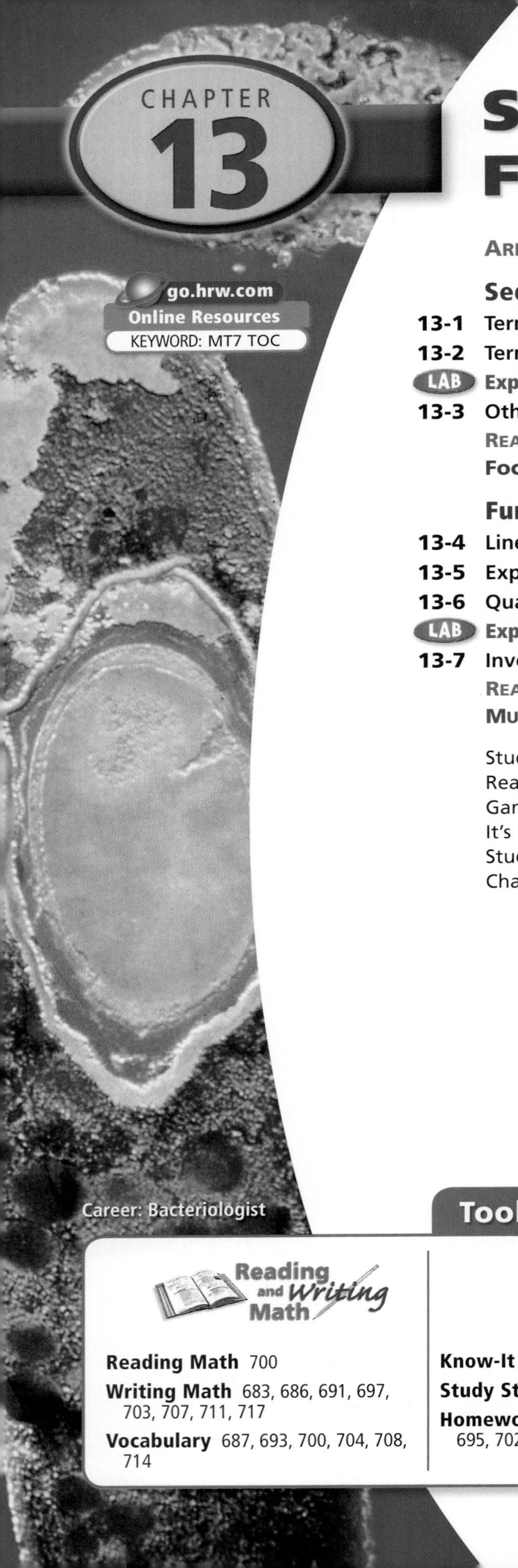

Career: Bacteriologist

go.hrw.com
Online Resources
KEYWORD: MT7 TOC

ARE YOU READY? 679

Sequences

13-1 Terms of Arithmetic Sequences 682
13-2 Terms of Geometric Sequences 687
LAB Explore the Fibonacci Sequence 692
13-3 Other Sequences 693
READY TO GO ON? QUIZ 698
Focus on Problem Solving: Solve 699

Functions

13-4 Linear Functions 700
13-5 Exponential Functions 704
13-6 Quadratic Functions 708
LAB Explore Cubic Functions 712
13-7 Inverse Variation 714
READY TO GO ON? QUIZ 718
MULTI-STEP TEST PREP 719

Study Guide: Preview 680
Reading and Writing Math 681
Game Time: Squared Away 720
It's in the Bag!: Springboard to Sequences 721
Study Guide: Review 722
Chapter Test 725

Tools for Success

Reading and Writing Math

Reading Math 700
Writing Math 683, 686, 691, 697, 703, 707, 711, 717
Vocabulary 687, 693, 700, 704, 708, 714

Study Skills

Know-It Notebook Chapter 13
Study Strategy 681
Homework Help Online 685, 689, 695, 702, 706, 710, 716

TEST PREP

Test Prep and Spiral Review 686, 691, 697, 703, 707, 711, 717
Multi-Step Test Prep 719
Test Tackler 726
Standardized Test Prep 728

CHAPTER 14

Polynomials

Are You Ready? 730

Introduction to Polynomials

14-1 Polynomials 734
LAB Model Polynomials 738
14-2 Simplifying Polynomials 740
Ready to Go On? Quiz 744
Focus on Problem Solving: Look Back 745

Polynomial Operations

LAB Model Polynomial Addition 746
14-3 Adding Polynomials 747
LAB Model Polynomial Subtraction 751
14-4 Subtracting Polynomials 752
14-5 Multiplying Polynomials and Monomials 756
LAB Multiply Binomials 760
14-6 Multiplying Binomials 762
Ready to Go On? Quiz 766
Multi-Step Test Prep 767
EXT Dividing Polynomials by Monomials 768
Problem Solving on Location: Mississippi 778

Study Guide: Preview 732
Reading and Writing Math 733
Game Time: Short Cuts 770
It's in the Bag!: Polynomial Petals 771
Study Guide: Review 772
Chapter Test 775

go.hrw.com
Online Resources
KEYWORD: MT7 TOC

Career: Financial Analyst

Tools for Success

Reading and Writing Math

Writing Math 737, 743, 750, 755, 759, 765
Vocabulary 734, 762

Study Skills

Know-It Notebook Chapter 14
Study Strategy 733
Homework Help Online 736, 742, 749, 754, 758, 764
Student Help 768

Test Prep

Test Prep and Spiral Review 737, 743, 750, 755, 759, 765
Multi-Step Test Prep 767
Standardized Test Prep 776

Interdisciplinary Connections

Many fields of study require knowledge of the mathematical skills and concepts taught in ***Holt Mathematics Course 3.*** Examples and exercises throughout the book highlight the math you will need to understand in order to study other subjects, such as art or finance, or to pursue a career in fields such as medicine or architecture.

13. Earth Science When the Moon is between the Sun and Earth, it casts a conical shadow called the *umbra.* If the shadow is 2140 mi in diameter and 260,955 mi along the edge, what is the lateral surface area of the umbra?

14. Social Studies The Pyramid Arena in Memphis, Tennessee, is 321 feet tall and has a square base with side length 200 yards. What is the lateral surface area of the pyramid in feet?

15. The table shows the dimensions of three square pyramids.

a. Complete the table.

Dimensions of Giza Pyramids (ft)			
Pyramid	Height	Slant Height	Side of Base

Science

Anatomy 176
Animals 79
Astronomy 37, 172, 475, 709
Chemistry 17, 220
Computer 183
Earth Science 17, 23, 28, 29, 94, 297, 345, 435, 480, 557, 647, 659
Environment 217
Life Science 71, 165, 177, 227, 228, 252, 253, 284, 288, 290, 294-295, 417, 433, 535, 567, 647, 654, 691, 742
Meteorology 71
Physical Science 7, 38, 177, 226, 231, 232, 241, 275, 281, 288, 333, 401, 591, 597, 630, 631, 635, 652, 691, 701, 706, 711, 717
Physics 735
Technology 562

Language Arts

Language Arts 184, 287
Literature 297

Fine and Performing Arts

Art 241, 411, 428, 442, 567, 748
Crafts 610
Design 74
Entertainment 9, 218, 223, 403, 535, 606, 611, 632
Graphic Design 9
Music 125, 415, 715
Photography 247

Social Studies

Architecture 254, 424, 637
Geography 248, 254, 277, 285, 480
History 121
Social Studies 37, 69, 84, 178, 282, 286, 340, 367, 392, 417, 421, 435, 602, 657
Transportation 227, 228, 632, 737
Travel 140, 143, 589

Economics

Business 46, 136, 172, 218, 230, 281, 441, 465, 473, 557, 587, 595, 703, 711, 741, 750, 753, 755
Consumer Math 100, 119
Economics 21, 607, 691, 703
Finance 8, 281, 717
Home Economics 137
Money 40, 175, 305, 689

Health and Fitness

Cooking 567
Fitness 503, 686
Food 227, 403, 658
Games 185, 549
Health 19, 79, 759
Hobbies 185, 219, 586, 710
Medical 645
Nutrition 94
Recreation 42, 77, 86, 284, 443, 465, 686, 703
Safety 528, 637
Sports 14, 27, 47, 66, 70, 72, 74, 137, 145, 184, 227, 281, 403, 430, 503, 567, 587, 591, 607, 661, 690, 710

WHY LEARN MATHEMATICS?

Throughout the text, links to interesting application topics, such as entertainment, photography, and technology, will help you see how math is used in the real world. Some of these links have additional information and activities at go.hrw.com. For a complete list of all real-world problems in *Holt Mathematics Course 3,* see page 898 in the Index.

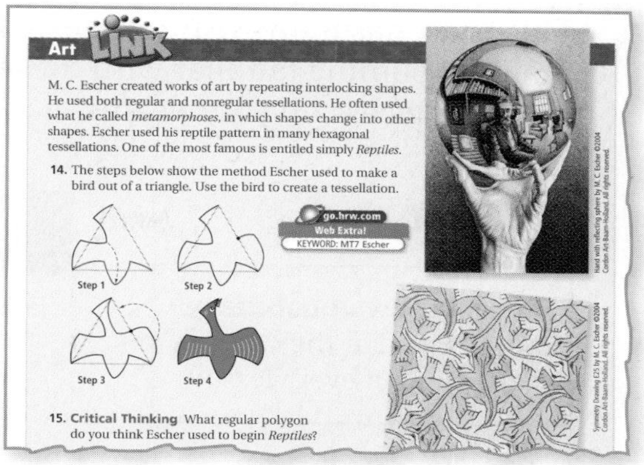

Art LINK

M. C. Escher created works of art by repeating interlocking shapes. He used both regular and nonregular tessellations. He often used what he called *metamorphoses,* in which shapes change into other shapes. Escher used his reptile pattern in many hexagonal tessellations. One of the most famous is entitled simply *Reptiles.*

14. The steps below show the method Escher used to make a bird out of a triangle. Use the bird to create a tessellation.

Step 1 Step 2 Step 3 Step 4

go.hrw.com Web Extra! KEYWORD: MT7 Escher

15. **Critical Thinking** What regular polygon do you think Escher used to begin *Reptiles*?

Hand with reflecting sphere by M. C. Escher ©2004 Cordon Art-Baarn-Holland. All rights reserved.

Symmetry Drawing E25 by M. C. Escher ©2004 Cordon Art-Baarn-Holland. All rights reserved.

Real-World LINKS

Animals 79
Architecture 255
Art 241, 371, 567, 743
Business 465, 750
Career 424
Earth Science 17, 29, 88, 131, 345, 530, 647, 659
Economics 21, 301, 663
Entertainment 403, 611
Games 185, 549

Games LINK

In 1997, Deep Blue became the first computer to win a match against a chess grand master when it defeated world champion Garry Kasparov.

Health 233, 707
History 121
Home Economics 137
Language Arts 471
Life Science 101, 165, 177, 289, 417, 433, 439, 497, 535, 544, 642, 654, 765
Literature 297
Meteorology 71
Money 305

Money LINK

Many bank ATMs in Bangkok, Thailand, are located in sculptures to attract customers.

Music 125 , 697
Photography 247
Physical Science 328, 333, 398, 597, 691, 705
Recreation 86, 703

Recreation LINK

The volume of a typical hot air balloon is between 65,000 and 105,000 cubic feet. Most hot air balloons fly at altitudes of 1000 to 1500 feet.

Science 169, 189
Social Studies 25, 291, 367, 735
Sports 47, 430, 503, 591
Technology 562
Transportation 632

USING YOUR BOOK FOR SUCCESS

This book has many features designed to help you learn and study math. Becoming familiar with these features will prepare you for greater success on your exams.

Learn

Preview new **vocabulary** terms listed at the beginning of every lesson.

Look for the **Student Help** for hints and reminders.

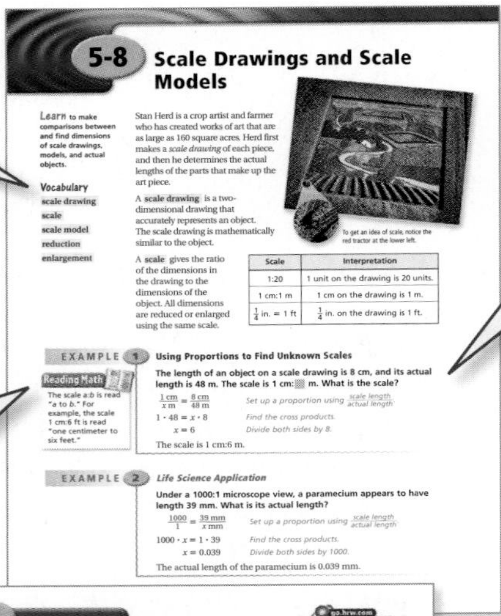
5-8 Scale Drawings and Scale Models

Learn to make comparisons between and find dimensions of scale drawings, models, and actual objects.

Vocabulary: scale drawing, scale, scale model, reduction, enlargement

Stan Herd is a crop artist and farmer who has created works of art that are as large as 160 square acres. Herd first makes a *scale drawing* of each piece, and then he determines the actual lengths of the parts that make up the art piece.

A **scale drawing** is a two-dimensional drawing that accurately represents an object. The scale drawing is mathematically similar to the object.

A **scale** gives the ratio of the dimensions in the drawing to the dimensions of the object. All dimensions are reduced or enlarged using the same scale.

To get an idea of scale, notice the red tractor at the lower left.

Scale	Interpretation
1:20	1 unit on the drawing is 20 units.
1 cm:1 m	1 cm on the drawing is 1 m.
$\frac{1}{4}$ in. = 1 ft	$\frac{1}{4}$ in. on the drawing is 1 ft.

EXAMPLE 1 Using Proportions to Find Unknown Scales

The length of an object on a scale drawing is 8 cm, and its actual length is 48 m. The scale is 1 cm: ■ m. What is the scale?

$\frac{1 \text{ cm}}{x \text{ m}} = \frac{8 \text{ cm}}{48 \text{ m}}$ Set up a proportion using $\frac{\text{scale length}}{\text{actual length}}$.

$1 \cdot 48 = x \cdot 8$ Find the cross products.

$x = 6$ Divide both sides by 8.

The scale is 1 cm:6 m.

Reading Math: The scale a:b is read "a to b." For example, the scale 1 cm:6 ft is read "one centimeter to six feet."

EXAMPLE 2 Life Science Application

Under a 1000:1 microscope view, a paramecium appears to have length 39 mm. What is its actual length?

$\frac{1000}{1} = \frac{39 \text{ mm}}{x \text{ mm}}$ Set up a proportion using $\frac{\text{scale length}}{\text{actual length}}$.

$1000 \cdot x = 1 \cdot 39$ Find the cross products.

$x = 0.039$ Divide both sides by 1000.

The actual length of the paramecium is 0.039 mm.

Study the **examples** to learn new math ideas and skills. The examples include step-by-step solutions.

Practice

Look back at examples from the lesson to solve the **Guided Practice** exercises.

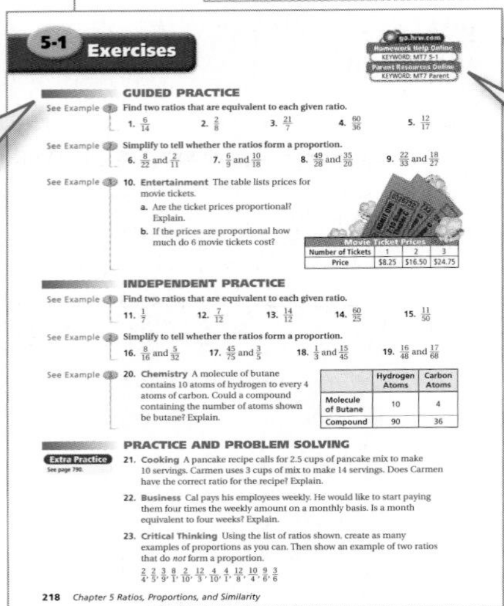
5-1 Exercises

go.hrw.com Homework Help Online KEYWORD: MT7 5-1 Parent Resources Online KEYWORD: MT7 Parent

GUIDED PRACTICE

See Example 1 Find two ratios that are equivalent to each given ratio.

1. $\frac{6}{14}$ 2. $\frac{2}{8}$ 3. $\frac{21}{7}$ 4. $\frac{60}{36}$ 5. $\frac{12}{17}$

See Example 2 Simplify to tell whether the ratios form a proportion.

6. $\frac{8}{22}$ and $\frac{2}{11}$ 7. $\frac{6}{9}$ and $\frac{10}{18}$ 8. $\frac{49}{28}$ and $\frac{35}{20}$ 9. $\frac{22}{33}$ and $\frac{18}{27}$

See Example 3 10. **Entertainment** The table lists prices for movie tickets.

a. Are the ticket prices proportional? Explain.

b. If the prices are proportional how much do 6 movie tickets cost?

Movie Ticket Prices			
Number of Tickets	1	2	3
Price	$8.25	$16.50	$24.75

INDEPENDENT PRACTICE

See Example 1 Find two ratios that are equivalent to each given ratio.

11. $\frac{1}{7}$ 12. $\frac{7}{12}$ 13. $\frac{14}{12}$ 14. $\frac{60}{25}$ 15. $\frac{11}{30}$

See Example 2 Simplify to tell whether the ratios form a proportion.

16. $\frac{8}{16}$ and $\frac{5}{32}$ 17. $\frac{45}{75}$ and $\frac{3}{5}$ 18. $\frac{1}{3}$ and $\frac{15}{45}$ 19. $\frac{16}{48}$ and $\frac{17}{68}$

See Example 3 20. **Chemistry** A molecule of butane contains 10 atoms of hydrogen to every 4 atoms of carbon. Could a compound containing the number of atoms shown be butane? Explain.

	Hydrogen Atoms	Carbon Atoms
Molecule of Butane	10	4
Compound	90	36

PRACTICE AND PROBLEM SOLVING

Extra Practice See page 790.

21. **Cooking** A pancake recipe calls for 2.5 cups of pancake mix to make 10 servings. Carmen uses 3 cups of mix to make 14 servings. Does Carmen have the correct ratio for the recipe? Explain.

22. **Business** Cal pays his employees weekly. He would like to start paying them four times the weekly amount on a monthly basis. Is a month equivalent to four weeks? Explain.

23. **Critical Thinking** Using the list of ratios shown, create as many examples of proportions as you can. Then show an example of two ratios that do *not* form a proportion.

218 Chapter 5 Ratios, Proportions, and Similarity

If you get stuck, use the internet for **Homework Help Online**.

Review

Study and review **vocabulary** from the entire chapter.

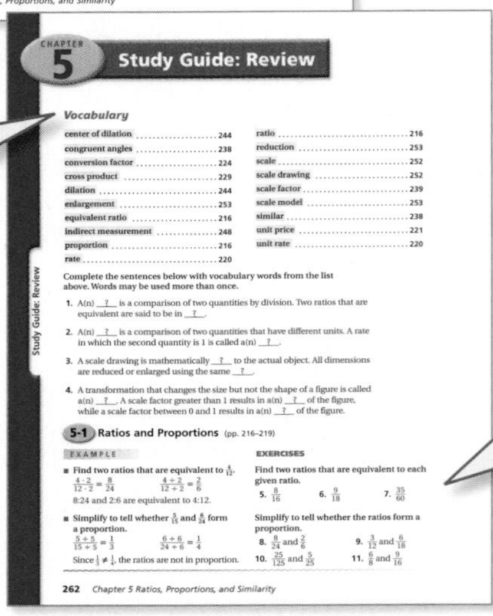
Chapter 5 Study Guide: Review

Vocabulary

center of dilation 244, congruent angles 238, conversion factor 224, cross product 229, dilation 244, enlargement 253, equivalent ratio 216, indirect measurement 248, proportion 216, rate 220, ratio 216, reduction 253, scale 252, scale drawing 252, scale factor 239, scale model 253, similar 238, unit price 221, unit rate 220

Complete the sentences below with vocabulary words from the list above. Words may be used more than once.

1. A(n) _?_ is a comparison of two quantities by division. Two ratios that are equivalent are said to be in _?_.

2. A(n) _?_ is a comparison of two quantities that have different units. A rate in which the second quantity is 1 is called a(n) _?_.

3. A scale drawing is mathematically _?_ to the actual object. All dimensions are reduced or enlarged using the same _?_.

4. A transformation that changes the size but not the shape of a figure is called a(n) _?_. A scale factor greater than 1 results in a(n) _?_ of the figure, while a scale factor between 0 and 1 results in a(n) _?_ of the figure.

5-1 Ratios and Proportions (pp. 216–219)

262 Chapter 5 Ratios, Proportions, and Similarity

Test yourself with **practice problems** from every lesson in the chapter.

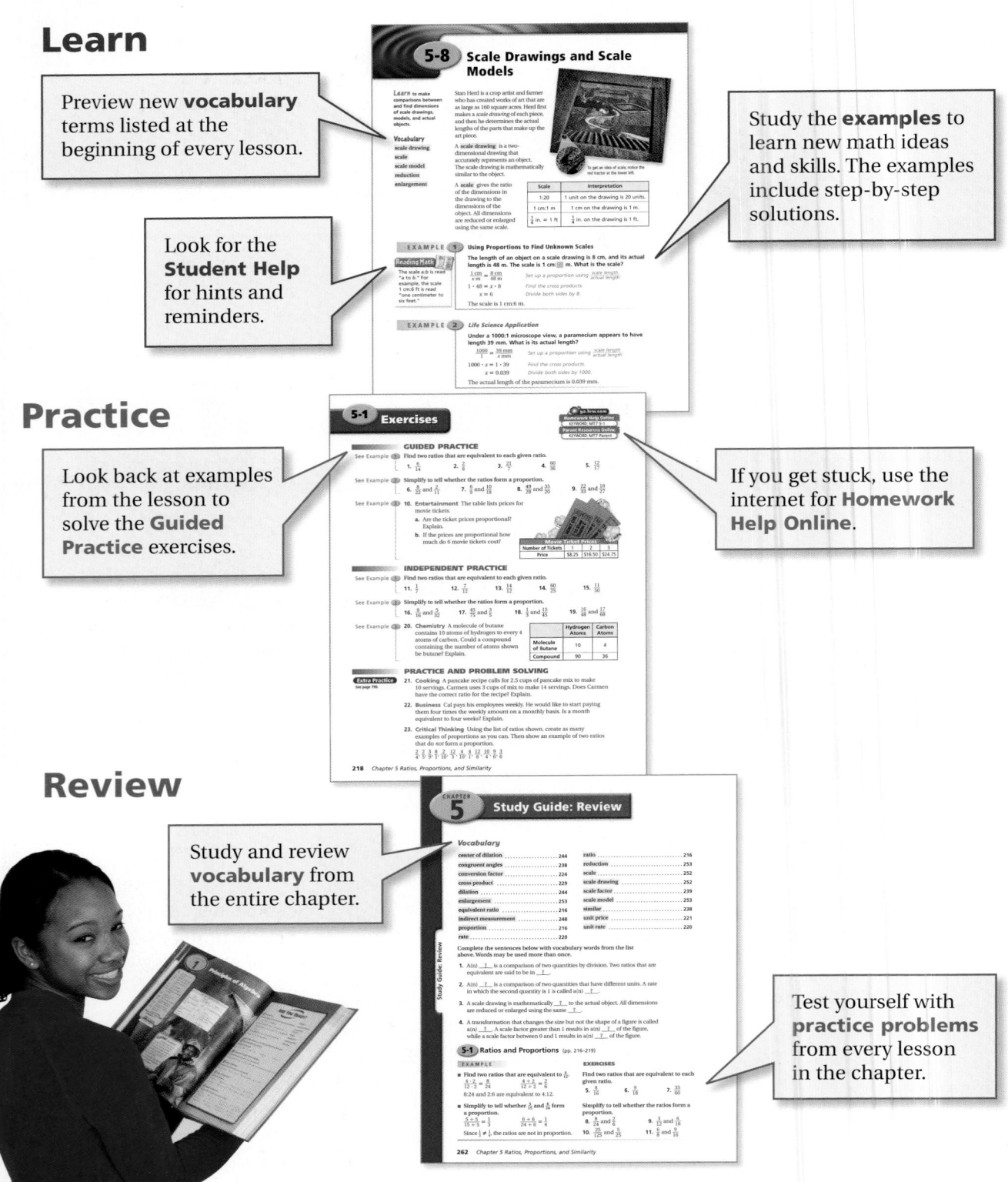

Focus on Problem Solving

PROBLEM SOLVING

The Problem Solving Plan

In order to be a good problem solver, you need to use a good problem-solving plan. The plan used in this book is detailed below. If you have another plan that you like to use, you can use it as well.

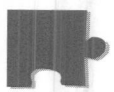

UNDERSTAND the Problem

- **What are you asked to find?** Restate the question in your own words.
- **What information is given?** Identify the important facts in the problem.
- **What information do you need?** Determine which facts are needed to answer the question.
- **Is all the information given?** Determine whether all the facts are given.
- **Is there any information given you will not use?** Determine which facts, if any, are unnecessary to solve the problem.

Make a PLAN

- **Have you ever solved a similar problem?** Think about other problems like this that you successfully solved.
- **What strategy or strategies can you use?** Determine a strategy that you can use and how you will use it.

SOLVE

- **Follow your plan.** Show the steps in your solution. Write your answer as a complete sentence.

LOOK BACK

- **Have you answered the question?** Be sure that you answered the question that is being asked.
- **Is your answer reasonable?** Your answer should make sense in the context of the problem.
- **Is there another strategy you could use?** Solving the problem using another strategy is a good way to check your work.
- **Did you learn anything that could help you solve similar problems in the future?** Try to remember the problems you have solved and the strategies you used to solve them.

CHAPTER 1

Principles of Algebra

1A Expressions and Integers

1-1 Variables and Expressions

1-2 Algebraic Expressions

1-3 Integers and Absolute Value

1-4 Adding Integers

1-5 Subtracting Integers

1-6 Multiplying and Dividing Integers

1B Equations and Inequalities

LAB Model Solving Equations

1-7 Solving Equations by Adding or Subtracting

1-8 Solving Equations by Multiplying or Dividing

1-9 Introduction to Inequalities

MULTI-STEP TEST PREP

go.hrw.com
Chapter Project Online
KEYWORD: MT7 Ch1

Toxic Gases Released by Fires

Gas	Danger Level (ppm)	Source
Carbon monoxide (CO)	1200	Incomplete burning
Hydrogen chloride (HCl)	50	Plastics
Hydrogen cyanide (HCN)	50	Wool, nylon, polyurethane foam, rubber, paper
Phosgene ($COCl_2$)	2	Refrigerants

Career *Firefighter*

A firefighter approaching a fire should be aware of ventilation, space, what is burning, and what could be ignited. Oxygen, fuel, heat, and chemical reactions are at the core of a fire, but the amounts and materials differ.

The table above lists some of the toxic gases that firefighters frequently encounter.

ARE YOU READY?

Vocabulary

Choose the best term from the list to complete each sentence.

addition
Associative Property
Commutative Property
division
multiplication
opposite operation
subtraction

1. __?__ is the __?__ of addition.
2. The expressions $3 \cdot 4$ and $4 \cdot 3$ are equal by the __?__.
3. The expressions $1 + (2 + 3)$ and $(1 + 2) + 3$ are equal by the __?__.
4. Multiplication and __?__ are opposite operations.
5. __?__ and __?__ are commutative.

Complete these exercises to review skills you will need for this chapter.

Whole Number Operations

Simplify each expression.

6. $8 + 116 + 43$
7. $2431 - 187$
8. $204 \cdot 38$
9. $6447 \div 21$

Compare and Order Whole Numbers

Order each sequence of numbers from least to greatest.

10. 1050; 11,500; 105; 150
11. 503; 53; 5300; 5030
12. 44,400; 40,040; 40,400; 44,040

Inverse Operations

Rewrite each expression using the inverse operation.

13. $72 + 18 = 90$
14. $12 \cdot 9 = 108$
15. $100 - 34 = 66$
16. $56 \div 8 = 7$

Order of Operations

Simplify each expression.

17. $2 + 3 \cdot 4$
18. $50 - 2 \cdot 5$
19. $6 \cdot 3 \cdot 3 - 3$
20. $(5 + 2)(5 - 2)$
21. $5 - 6 \div 2$
22. $16 \div 4 + 2 \cdot 3$
23. $(8 - 3)(8 + 3)$
24. $12 \div 3 \div 2 + 5$

Evaluate Expressions

Determine whether the given expressions are equal.

25. $(4 \cdot 7) \cdot 2$ and $4 \cdot (7 \cdot 2)$
26. $(2 \cdot 4) \div 2$ and $2 \cdot (4 \div 2)$
27. $2 \cdot (3 - 3)$ and $(2 \cdot 3) - 3$
28. $5 \cdot (50 - 44)$ and $5 \cdot 50 - 44$
29. $9 - (4 \cdot 2)$ and $(9 - 4) \cdot 2$
30. $2 \cdot 3 + 2 \cdot 4$ and $2 \cdot (3 + 4)$
31. $(16 \div 4) + 4$ and $16 \div (4 + 4)$
32. $5 + (2 \cdot 3)$ and $(5 + 2) \cdot 3$

CHAPTER 1

Study Guide: Preview

Where You've Been

Previously, you

- simplified numerical expressions involving order of operations.
- compared and ordered integers and positive rational numbers.
- used concrete models to solve equations.

In This Chapter

You will study

- using an algebraic expression to find any term in a sequence.
- comparing and ordering rational numbers in various forms, including integers.
- estimating and finding solutions to application problems using algebraic equations.
- finding the absolute value of a number.

Where You're Going

You can use the skills learned in this chapter

- to find differences between extreme temperatures.
- to balance a checkbook.
- to solve a formula for a variable.
- to solve complex equations in later math courses.

Key Vocabulary/Vocabulario

absolute value	valor absoluto
constant	constante
equation	ecuación
inequality	desigualdad
integer	entero
inverse operation	operacione inversa
opposite	opuesto
variable	variable

Vocabulary Connections

To become familiar with some of the vocabulary terms in the chapter, consider the following. You may refer to the chapter, the glossary, or a dictionary if you like.

1. The word *constant* means "unchanging." What do you think a **constant** is in math?
2. The word **equation** looks like the word *equal,* which means "having the same value." How do you think this meaning applies to an equation?
3. The word **inequality** begins with the prefix *in-,* which means "not," and has the same root as the word *equation.* Together, what do you think the prefix and root mean?
4. The word *vary,* which is the root of **variable**, means "to change." How do you think this applies to math?

Study Guide: Preview

Reading and Writing Math

Reading Strategy: Use Your Book for Success

Understanding how your textbook is organized will help you locate and use helpful information.

As you read through an example problem, pay attention to the **margin notes**, such as Helpful Hints, Reading Math notes, and Caution notes. These notes will help you understand concepts and avoid common mistakes.

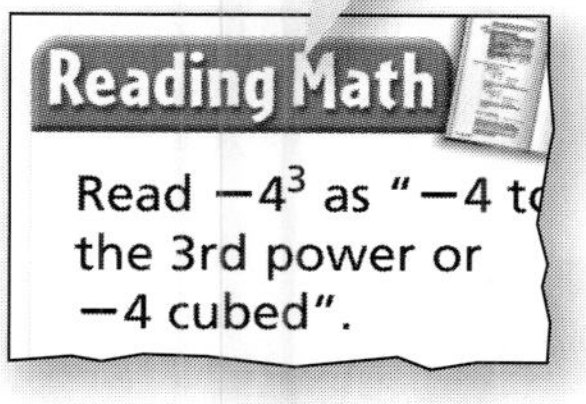

Reading Math
Read -4^3 as "−4 to
the 3rd power or
−4 cubed".

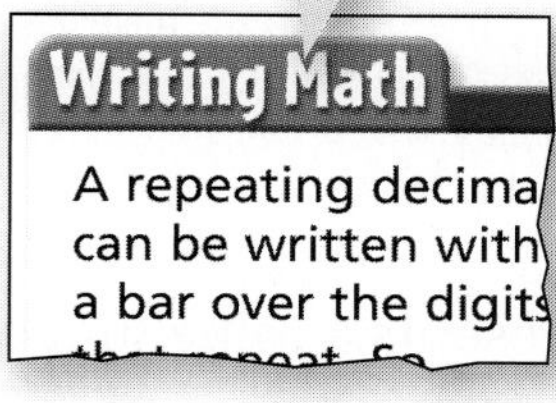

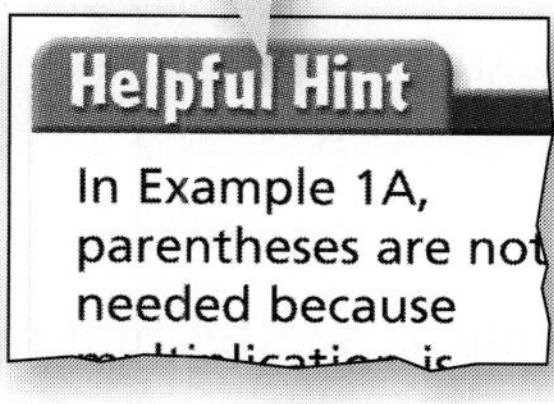

Helpful Hint
In Example 1A,
parentheses are not
needed because

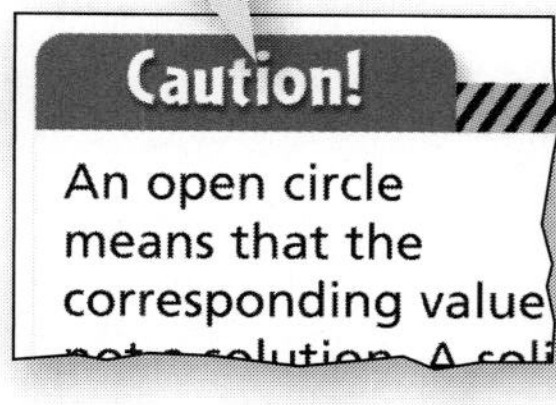

The **glossary** is found in the back of your textbook. Use it to find definitions and examples of unfamiliar words or properties.

The **index** is located at the end of your textbook. Use it to find the page where a particular concept is taught.

The **Skills Bank** is found in the back of your textbook. These pages review concepts from previous math courses.

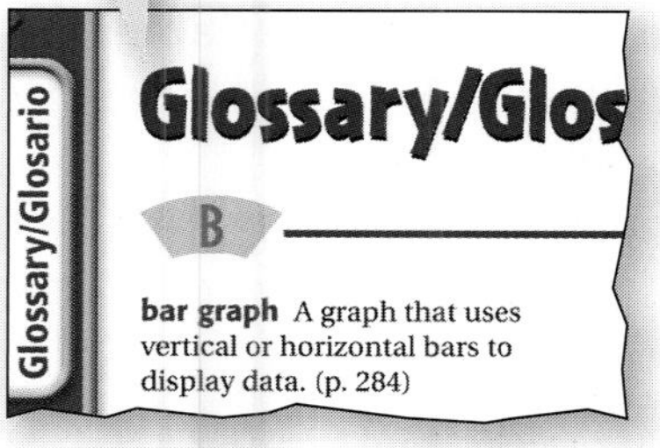

Try This

Use your textbook for the following problems.

1. Use the glossary to find the definition of *supplementary angles.*
2. Where can you review factors and multiples?
3. Use the Problem Solving Handbook to list three different strategies for solving problems.
4. Use the index to find the page numbers where *algebraic expressions, mean,* and *volume of prisms* are explained.

1-1 Variables and Expressions

Learn to evaluate algebraic expressions.

Vocabulary

variable
coefficient
algebraic expression
constant
evaluate
substitute

Adult giant pandas in the wild spend almost 12 hours each day feeding. On average, an adult panda eats about 30 pounds of food each day.

There are about 1500 giant pandas that live in the wild.

Let n be the number of adult pandas in the wild. You can approximate the total number of pounds of food they eat in one day using this expression:

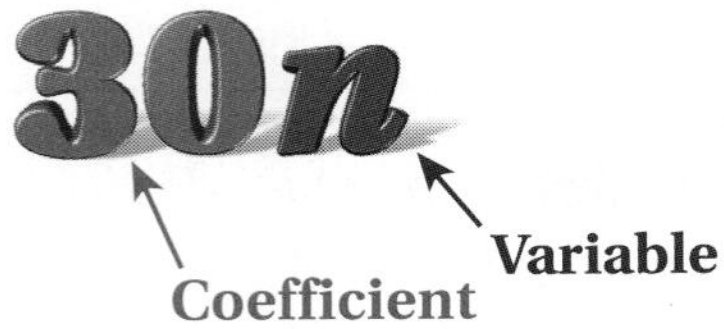

A **variable** is a letter that represents a value that can change or vary. The **coefficient** is the number multiplied by the variable. An **algebraic expression** has one or more variables.

In the algebraic expression $x + 6$, the number 6 is a **constant** because it does not change. To **evaluate** an algebraic expression, **substitute** a given number for the variable, and find the value of the resulting numerical expression.

EXAMPLE 1 Evaluating Algebraic Expressions with One Variable

Evaluate each expression for the given value of the variable.

A $x + 5$ **for** $x = 11$

$11 + 5$ *Substitute 11 for x.*

16 *Add.*

B $2a + 3$ **for** $a = 4$

$2(4) + 3$ *Substitute 4 for a.*

$8 + 3$ *Multiply.*

11 *Add.*

C $4(3 + n) - 2$ **for** $n = 0, 1, 2$

n	Substitute	Parentheses	Multiply	Subtract
0	$4(3 + 0) - 2$	$4(3) - 2$	$12 - 2$	10
1	$4(3 + 1) - 2$	$4(4) - 2$	$16 - 2$	14
2	$4(3 + 2) - 2$	$4(5) - 2$	$20 - 2$	18

Remember!

Order of Operations
PEMDAS:
1. Parentheses
2. Exponents
3. Multiply and Divide from left to right.
4. Add and Subtract from left to right.

EXAMPLE 2 Evaluating Algebraic Expressions with Two Variables

Evaluate each expression for the given values of the variables.

A $5x + 2y$ for $x = 13$ and $y = 11$

$5(13) + 2(11)$	*Substitute 13 for x and 11 for y.*
$65 + 22$	*Multiply.*
87	*Add.*

B $2.5p - 4q$ for $p = 12$ and $q = 6.5$

$2.5(12) - 4(6.5)$	*Substitute 12 for p and 6.5 for q.*
$30 - 26$	*Multiply.*
4	*Subtract.*

EXAMPLE 3 *Physical Science Application*

If *c* is a temperature in degrees Celsius, then 1.8*c* + 32 can be used to find the temperature in degrees Fahrenheit. Convert each temperature from degrees Celsius to degrees Fahrenheit.

A **freezing point of water: 0°C**

$1.8c + 32$	
$1.8(0) + 32$	*Substitute 0 for c.*
$0 + 32$	*Multiply.*
32	*Add.*

0°C = 32°F

Water freezes at 32°F.

B **highest recorded temperature in the United States: 57°C**

$1.8c + 32$	
$1.8(57) + 32$	*Substitute 57 for c.*
$102.6 + 32$	*Multiply.*
134.6	*Add.*

57°C = 134.6°F

The highest recorded temperature in the United States is 134.6°F.

Think and Discuss

1. **Give an example** of an expression that is algebraic and of an expression that is not algebraic.
2. **Tell** how to evaluate an algebraic expression for a given value.
3. **Explain** why you cannot find a numerical value for the expression $4x - 5y$ for $x = 3$.

1-1 Exercises

go.hrw.com
Homework Help Online
KEYWORD: MT7 1-1
Parent Resources Online
KEYWORD: MT7 Parent

GUIDED PRACTICE

See Example 1

Evaluate each expression for the given value of the variable.

1. $x + 4$ for $x = 11$ **2.** $2a + 7$ for $a = 7$ **3.** $2(4 + n) - 5$ for $n = 0$

See Example 2

Evaluate each expression for the given values of the variables.

4. $3x + 2y$ for $x = 8$ and $y = 10$ **5.** $1.6p - 3q$ for $p = 4.5$ and $q = 1.4$

See Example 3

You can make papier-mâché paste by mixing $\frac{1}{4}$ as many cups of flour as water. How much flour do you need for each number of cups of water?

6. 12 cups **7.** 8 cups **8.** 7 cups **9.** 10 cups

INDEPENDENT PRACTICE

See Example 1

Evaluate each expression for the given value of the variable.

10. $x + 7$ for $x = 23$ **11.** $7t + 2$ for $t = 5$ **12.** $4(3 + k) - 7$ for $k = 0$

See Example 2

Evaluate each expression for the given values of the variables.

13. $4x + 7y$ for $x = 9$ and $y = 3$ **14.** $4m - 2n$ for $m = 25$ and $n = 2.5$

See Example 3

If c is the number of cups, then $\frac{1}{2}c$ can be used to find the number of pints. Find the number of pints for each of the following.

15. 26 cups **16.** 12 cups **17.** 20 cups **18.** 34 cups

PRACTICE AND PROBLEM SOLVING

Extra Practice
See page 782.

Evaluate each expression for the given value of the variable.

19. $13d$ for $d = 1$ **20.** $x + 4.3$ for $x = 6$ **21.** $30 - n$ for $n = 8$

22. $5t + 5$ for $t = 1$ **23.** $3a - 4$ for $a = 8$ **24.** $2 + 4b$ for $b = 2.2$

25. $11 - 6m$ for $m = 0$ **26.** $4g + 5$ for $g = 12$ **27.** $x + 6.6$ for $x = 3.4$

28. $18 - 3y$ for $y = 6$ **29.** $4y + 2$ for $y = 3.5$ **30.** $3(z + 9)$ for $z = 6$

Evaluate each expression for $t = 0$, $x = 1.5$, $y = 6$, and $z = 23$.

31. $3z - 3y$ **32.** yz **33.** $4.2y - 3x$ **34.** $1.4z - y$

35. $4(y - x)$ **36.** $4(3 + y)$ **37.** $4(2 + z) + 5$ **38.** $3(y - 6) + 8$

39. $5(4 + t) - 6$ **40.** $y(3 + t) - 7$ **41.** $x + y + z$ **42.** $10x + z - y$

43. $2y + 6(x + t)$ **44.** $4(z - 5t) + 3$ **45.** $8txz$ **46.** $2z - 3xy$

47. **Finance** A bank charges interest on money it loans. Interest is sometimes a fixed amount of the loan. The expression $a(1 + i)$ gives the total amount due for a loan of a dollars with interest rate i. Find the amount due for a loan of \$100 with an interest rate of 0.1.

48. **Graphic Design** Rectangular shapes with a length-to-width ratio of approximately 5 to 3 are pleasing to the eye. This ratio is known as the golden ratio. A designer can use the expression $\frac{1}{3}(5w)$ to find the length of such a rectangle with a given width w. Find the length of such a rectangle with width 6 inches.

49. **Entertainment** There are 24 frames, or still shots, in one second of movie footage.

   a. Write an expression to determine the number of frames in a movie.

   b. Using the running time of *E.T. the Extra-Terrestrial*, determine how many frames are in the movie.

E.T. the Extra-Terrestrial (1982) has a running time of 115 minutes, or 6900 seconds.

50. **Choose a Strategy** A basketball league has 288 players and 24 teams, with an equal number of players per team. If the number of teams is reduced by 6 but the total number of players stays the same, there will be ___?___ players per team.

   Ⓐ 6 more　　Ⓑ 4 more　　Ⓒ 4 fewer　　Ⓓ 6 fewer

51. **Write About It** A student says that the algebraic expression $5 + x \cdot 7$ can also be written as $5 + 7x$. Is the student correct? Explain.

52. **Challenge** Can the expressions $2x$ and $x + 2$ ever have the same value? If so, what must the value of x be?

TEST PREP and Spiral Review

53. **Multiple Choice** What is the value of the expression $3x + 4$ for $x = 2$?

   Ⓐ 4　　Ⓑ 6　　Ⓒ 9　　Ⓓ 10

54. **Multiple Choice** A bakery charges \$7 for a dozen muffins and \$2 for a loaf of bread. If a customer bought 2 dozen muffins and 4 loaves of bread, how much did she pay?

   Ⓕ \$22　　Ⓖ \$38　　Ⓗ \$80　　Ⓙ \$98

55. **Gridded Response** What is the value of $7x + 9$ when $x = 2$?

Identify the odd number(s) in each list of numbers. (Previous course)

56. 15, 18, 22, 34, 21, 61, 71, 100

57. 101, 114, 122, 411, 117, 121

58. 4, 6, 8, 16, 18, 20, 49, 81, 32

59. 9, 15, 31, 47, 65, 93, 1, 3, 43

Find each sum, difference, product, or quotient. (Previous course)

60. $200 + 2$

61. $200 \div 2$

62. $200 \cdot 2$

63. $200 - 2$

64. $200 + 0.2$

65. $200 \div 0.2$

66. $200 \cdot 0.2$

67. $200 - 0.2$

1-2 Algebraic Expressions

Learn to translate between algebraic expressions and word phrases.

Each 30-second block of commercial time during Super Bowl XXXIX cost an average of $2.4 million.

This information can be used to write an algebraic expression to determine how much a given number of 30-second blocks would have cost.

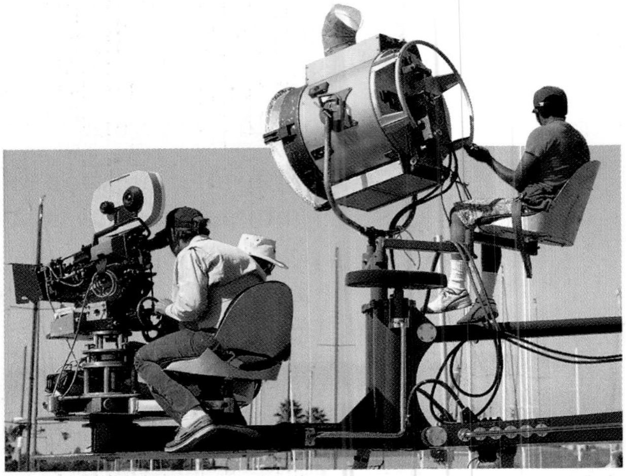

Sixty-eight different commercials aired during the 2005 Super Bowl.

	Word Phrases	Expression
+	• add 5 to a number • sum of a number and 5 • 5 more than a number	$n + 5$
−	• subtract 11 from a number • difference of a number and 11 • 11 less than a number	$x - 11$
×	• 3 multiplied by a number • product of 3 and a number	$3m$
÷	• 7 divided into a number • quotient of a number and 7	$\frac{a}{7}$ or $a \div 7$

EXAMPLE 1 Translating Word Phrases into Math Expressions

Write an algebraic expression for each word phrase.

Helpful Hint

In Example 1A, parentheses are not needed because multiplication is performed first by the order of operations.

A **1 more than the product of 12 and *p***

1 **more than** the **product of** 12 and p

$1 \quad + \quad (12 \quad \cdot \quad p)$

$1 + 12p$

B **4 less than a number *n* divided by 2**

4 **less than** n **divided by** 2

$(n \quad \div \quad 2) \quad - \quad 4$ *4 is being subtracted from $n \div 2$*

$\frac{n}{2} - 4$

EXAMPLE 2 **Translating Math Expressions into Word Phrases**

Write a word phrase for the algebraic expression $4 - 7b$.

$4 - 7b$

4	−	7	·
			b

4 **minus** the **product of** 7 and b

4 minus the product of 7 and b

To solve a word problem, first interpret the action you need to perform and then choose the correct operation for that action.

EXAMPLE 3 **Writing and Evaluating Expressions in Word Problems**

Helpful Hint

When a word problem involves groups of equal size, use multiplication or division. Otherwise, use addition or subtraction.

A company aired its 30-second commercial n times during Super Bowl XXXIX at a cost of \$2.4 million each time. Write an algebraic expression to evaluate what the cost would be if the commercial had aired 2, 3, and 4 times.

\$2.4 million · n *Combine n equal amounts of \$2.4 million.*

$2.4n$ *In millions of dollars*

n	$2.4n$	Cost
2	2.4(2)	\$4.8 million
3	2.4(3)	\$7.2 million
4	2.4(4)	\$9.6 million

Evaluate for n = 2, 3, and 4.

EXAMPLE 4 **Writing a Word Problem from a Math Expression**

Write a word problem that can be evaluated by the algebraic expression $14{,}917 + m$, and evaluate the expression for $m = 633$.

At the beginning of the month, Benny's car had 14,917 miles on the odometer. If Benny drove m miles during the month, how many miles were on the odometer at the end of the month?

$14{,}917 + m$

$14{,}917 + 633 = 15{,}550$ *Substitute 633 for m.*

The car had 15,550 miles on the odometer at the end of the month.

Think and Discuss

1. **Give** two words or phrases that can be used to express each operation: addition, subtraction, multiplication, and division.
2. **Express** $5 + 7n$ in words in at least two different ways.

1-2 Exercises

go.hrw.com
Homework Help Online
KEYWORD: MT7 1-2
Parent Resources Online
KEYWORD: MT7 Parent

GUIDED PRACTICE

See Example 1
Write an algebraic expression for each word phrase.

1. 5 less than the product of 3 and p

2. 77 more than the product of 2 and u

3. 16 more than the quotient of d and 7

4. 6 minus the quotient of u and 2.

See Example 2
Write a word phrase for each algebraic expression.

5. $18 + 43s$

6. $\frac{22}{r} - 37$

7. $10 + \frac{y}{31}$

8. $29b - 93$

See Example 3
9. Mark is going to work for his father's pool cleaning business during the summer. Mark's father will pay him \$5 for each pool he helps clean. Write an algebraic expression to evaluate how much Mark will earn if he cleans 15, 25, 35, or 45 pools.

See Example 4
10. Write a word problem that can be evaluated by the algebraic expression $x - 450$, and then evaluate the expression for $x = 1325$.

INDEPENDENT PRACTICE

See Example 1
Write an algebraic expression for each word phrase.

11. 1 more than the quotient of 5 and n

12. 2 minus the product of 3 and p.

13. 45 less than the product of 78 and j

14. 4 plus the quotient of r and 5.

15. 14 more than the product of 59 and q

See Example 2
Write a word phrase for each algebraic expression.

16. $142 - 19t$

17. $16g + 12$

18. $14 + \frac{5}{d}$

19. $\frac{w}{182} - 51$

See Example 3
20. A community center is trying to raise \$1680 to purchase exercise equipment. The center is hoping to receive equal contributions from members of the community. Write an algebraic expression to evaluate how much will be needed from each person if 10, 12, 14, or 16 people contribute.

See Example 4
21. Write a word problem that can be evaluated by the algebraic expression $372 + r$, and evaluate it for $r = 137$.

PRACTICE AND PROBLEM SOLVING

Extra Practice
See page 782.

Write an algebraic expression for each word phrase.

22. 6 times the sum of 4 and y

23. half the sum of m and 5

24. $\frac{1}{3}$ of the sum of 4 and p

25. 1 divided by the sum of 3 and g

26. 9 more than the product of 6 and y

27. 6 less than the product of 13 and y

28. 2 less than m divided by 8

29. twice the quotient of m and 35

30. $\frac{3}{4}$ of the difference of p and 7

31. 8 times the sum of $\frac{2}{3}$ and x

Translate each algebraic expression into words.

32. $4b - 3$ **33.** $8(m + 5)$ **34.** $\frac{7}{8 - x}$ **35.** $17\left(\frac{16}{w}\right)$

36. At age 2, a cat or a dog is considered 24 "human" years old. Each year after age 2 is equivalent to 4 "human" years. Fill in the expression $[24 + \blacksquare(a - 2)]$ so that it represents the age of a cat or dog in human years. Copy the chart and use your expression to complete it.

Age	$24 + \blacksquare(a - 2)$	Age (human years)
2		
3		
4		
5		
6		

DO NOT WRITE IN BOOK

37. Critical Thinking Write two different algebraic expressions for the word phrase "$\frac{1}{4}$ the sum of x and 7."

38. What's the Error? A student wrote an algebraic expression for "5 less than a number n divided by 3" as $\frac{(n - 5)}{3}$. What error did the student make?

39. Write About It Paul used addition to solve a word problem about the weekly cost of commuting by toll road for $1.50 each day. Fran solved the same problem by multiplying. They both got the correct answer. How is this possible?

40. Challenge Write an expression for the sum of 1 and twice a number n. If you let n be any odd number, will the result always be an odd number?

Test Prep and Spiral Review

41. Multiple Choice Which expression means "3 times the difference of y and 4"?

Ⓐ $3 \cdot y - 4$ Ⓑ $3 \cdot (y + 4)$ Ⓒ $3 \cdot (y - 4)$ Ⓓ $3 - (y - 4)$

42. Multiple Choice Which expression represents the product of a number n and 32?

Ⓕ $n + 32$ Ⓖ $n - 32$ Ⓗ $n \times 32$ Ⓙ $32 \div n$

43. Short Response A company prints n books at a cost of $9 per book. Write an expression to represent the total cost of printing n books. What is the total cost if 1050 books are printed?

Evaluate. (Previous Course)

44. $32 + 8 \div 4$ **45.** $24 - 2 \cdot 3 \div 6 + 1$ **46.** $(20 - 8) \cdot 2 + 2$

Evaluate each expression for the given values of the variable. (Lesson 1-1)

47. $2(4 + x) - 3$ for $x = 0, 1, 2,$ and 3 **48.** $3(8 - x) - 2$ for $x = 0, 1, 2,$ and 3

1-3 Integers and Absolute Value

Learn to compare and order integers and to evaluate expressions containing absolute values.

Vocabulary

integer

opposite

additive inverse

absolute value

In disc golf, a player tries to throw a disc to a target, or "hole," in as few throws as possible. The standard number of throws expected to complete a course is called "par." A player's score tells you how many throws he or she is above or below par.

Fred completes the course in 5 fewer throws than par. His score is 5 under par. Trevor completes the course in 3 more throws than par. His score is 3 over par. Monique is 4 over par, and Julie is 2 under par.

These scores can be written as *integers*. **Integers** are the set of whole numbers and their *opposites*. **Opposites**, or **additive inverses**, are numbers that are the same distance from 0, but on opposite sides of 0 on a number line.

Expressed as integers, the scores relative to par are Fred −5, Trevor 3, Monique 4, and Julie −2.

EXAMPLE 1 *Sports Application*

Remember!

Numbers on a number line increase in value as you move from left to right.

A **Use <, >, or = to compare Trevor's and Julie's scores.**

Trevor's score is 3, and Julie's score is −2.

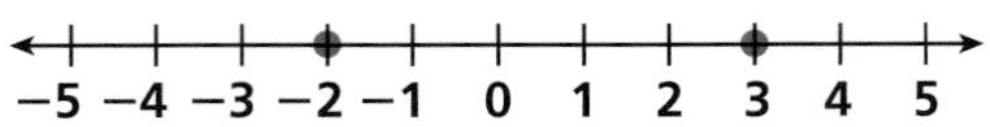

Place the scores on a number line.

$-2 < 3$ *−2 is to the left of 3.*

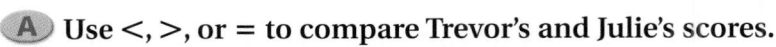

Julie's score is less then Trevor's.

B **List the golfers in order from the lowest score to the highest.**

The scores are −5, 3, 4, and −2.

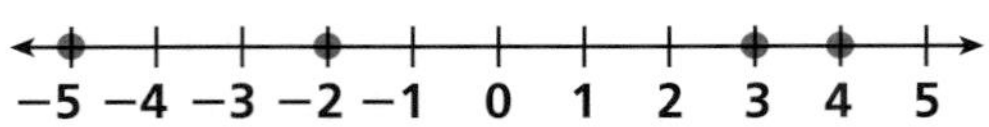

Place the scores on a number line and read them from left to right.

In order from the lowest score to the highest, the golfers are Fred, Julie, Trevor, and Monique.

EXAMPLE 2 Ordering Integers

Write the integers 7, −4, and 3 in order from least to greatest.

$7 > -4$, $7 > 3$, and $-4 < 3$ — *Compare each pair of integers.*

$-4, 3, 7$ — *−4 is less than both 3 and 7.*

EXAMPLE 3 Finding Additive Inverses

Find the additive inverse of each integer.

A 8

-8 — *−8 is the same distance from 0 as 8 is on the number line.*

B -15

15 — *15 is the same distance from 0 as −15 is on the number line.*

C 0

0 — *Zero is its own additive inverse.*

A number's **absolute value** is its distance from 0 on a number line. Absolute value is always positive because distance is always positive. "The absolute value of -4" is written as $|-4|$. Additive inverses have the same absolute value.

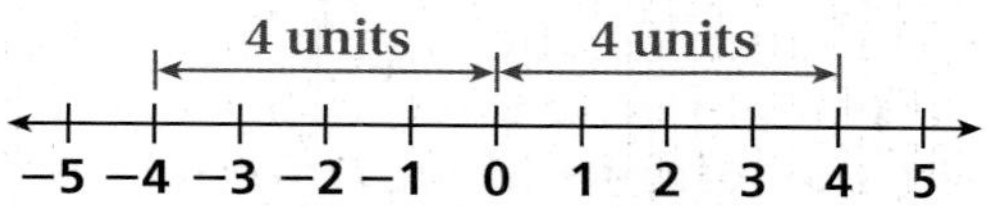

$|-4| = |4| = 4$ — *Both 4 and −4 are 4 units from 0.*

EXAMPLE 4 Evaluating Absolute-Value Expressions

Evaluate each expression.

A $|-9| + |7|$

$|-9| = 9$ — *−9 is 9 units from 0.*

$|7| = 7$ — *7 is 7 units from 0.*

$9 + 7 = 16$

B $|20 - 20|$

$|0|$ — *20 − 20 = 0*

0 — *0 is 0 units from 0.*

Think and Discuss

1. **Explain** how integers are used in real life to manage a bank account.
2. **Explain** whether -1, -4, and 5 are additive inverses.

1-3 Exercises

go.hrw.com
Homework Help Online
KEYWORD: MT7 1-3
Parent Resources Online
KEYWORD: MT7 Parent

GUIDED PRACTICE

See Example 1

1. After the first round of the 2005 Masters golf tournament, scores relative to par were Tiger Woods 2, Vijay Singh −4, Phil Mickelson −2, and Justin Leonard 5. Use <, >, or = to compare Vijay Singh's and Phil Mickelson's scores, and then list the golfers in order from the lowest score to the highest.

See Example 2

Write the integers in order from least to greatest.

2. −5, 2, −3 **3.** −17, 6, −8 **4.** −9, −21, −14 **5.** 3, −7, 0

See Example 3

Find the additive inverse of each integer.

6. −7 **7.** 13 **8.** −1 **9.** 25 **10.** −13

See Example 4

Evaluate each expression.

11. $|-3| + |11|$ **12.** $|-12| + |-9|$ **13.** $|22 - 7|$ **14.** $|8 - 8|$

INDEPENDENT PRACTICE

See Example 1

15. During a very cold week, the temperature in Philadelphia was −7°F on Monday, 4°F on Tuesday, 2°F on Wednesday, and −3°F on Thursday. Use <, >, or = to compare the temperatures on Wednesday and Thursday, and then list the days in order from the coldest to the warmest.

See Example 2

Write the integers in order from least to greatest.

16. −6, 5, −2 **17.** 8, −11, −5 **18.** −25, −30, −27 **19.** 4, −2, −1

See Example 3

Find the additive inverse of each integer.

20. 9 **21.** −15 **22.** 0 **23.** −31 **24.** 8

See Example 4

Evaluate each expression.

25. $|7| + |-14|$ **26.** $|-19| + |-13|$ **27.** $|28 - 18|$ **28.** $|6 + 3|$

PRACTICE AND PROBLEM SOLVING

Extra Practice
See page 782.

Compare. Write <, >, or =.

29. −9 ▒ 15 **30.** 13 ▒ −17 **31.** −23 ▒ −23 **32.** −14 ▒ 0

33. $|-7|$ ▒ $|6|$ **34.** $|-3|$ ▒ $|3|$ **35.** $|-13|$ ▒ $|2|$ **36.** $|20|$ ▒ $|-21|$

Write the integers in order from least to greatest.

37. 24, −16, −12 **38.** −46, −31, −52 **39.** −45, 35, −25

Evaluate each expression.

40. $|17| + |-24|$ **41.** $|-22| + |-28|$ **42.** $|53 - 37|$ **43.** $|21 - 20|$

44. $|7| \cdot |-9|$ **45.** $|-6| \cdot |-12|$ **46.** $|72| \div |8|$ **47.** $|3| + |-3|$

LINK Earth Science

The Ice Hotel in Jukkasjärvi, Sweden, is rebuilt every winter from 30,000 tons of snow and 4000 tons of ice.

Find the additive inverse of each integer and then perform the operation.

48. $-48, -7$; addition

49. $-8, -6$; multiplication

50. $-60, -5$; division

51. $-27, -25$; subtraction

52. Chemistry The boiling point of nitrogen is -196°C. The boiling point of oxygen is -183°C. Which element has the greater boiling point? Explain your answer.

53. Earth Science The table shows the lowest recorded temperatures for each continent. Write the continents in order from the lowest recorded temperature to the highest recorded temperature.

Lowest Recorded Temperatures

Continent	Temperature
Africa	−11°F
Antarctica	−129°F
Asia	−90°F
Australia	−9°F
Europe	−67°F
North America	−81°F
South America	−27°F

54. Critical Thinking Write rules for using absolute value to compare two integers. Be sure to take all of the possible combinations into account.

55. Write About It Explain why there is no number that can replace n to make the equation $|n| = -1$ true.

56. Challenge List the integers that can replace n to make the statement $-|8| < n \leq -|-5|$ true.

TEST PREP and Spiral Review

57. Multiple Choice Which set of integers is in order from greatest to least?

Ⓐ $-10, 8, -5$ Ⓑ $8, -5, -10$ Ⓒ $-5, 8, -10$ Ⓓ $-10, -5, 8$

58. Multiple Choice Which integer is between -4 and 2?

Ⓕ 0 Ⓖ 3 Ⓗ 4 Ⓙ -5

59. Short Answer After the final round of a golf tournament, the scores of the top 5 finishers were McKenna -3, Bernie -5, Shonda 0, Matt -1, and Kelly 1. Who won the tournament, and who came in fifth?

Evaluate each expression for $a = 3$, $b = 2.5$, and $c = 24$. (Lesson 1-1)

60. $c - 15$

61. $9a + 8$

62. $8(a + 2b)$

63. $bc - a$

Write an algebraic expression for each word phrase. (Lesson 1-2)

64. 8 more than the product of 7 and a number t

65. A pizzeria delivered p pizzas on Thursday. On Friday, it delivered 3 more than twice the number of pizzas delivered on Thursday. Write an expression to show the number of pizzas delivered on Friday.

1-4 Adding Integers

Learn to add integers.

Melanie keeps a health journal. She knows that when she eats she adds calories, and when she exercises she burns calories. Melanie can add positive and negative integers to find the total number of calories she takes in.

You can model integer addition on a number line. Starting at zero, move to the first number in the addition expression. Then move the number of units represented by the second number.

EXAMPLE 1 Using a Number Line to Add Integers

Helpful Hint

To add a **positive** number, move to the **right.** To add a **negative** number, move to the **left.**

Use a number line to find each sum.

A $3 + (-7)$

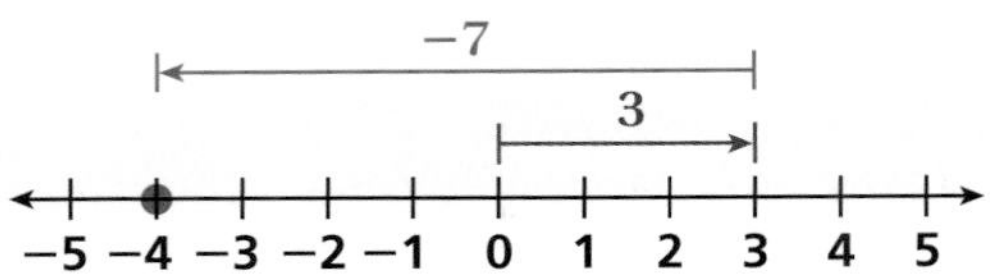

Move right 3 units.

From 3, move left 7 units.

You finish at -4, so $3 + (-7) = -4$.

B $-2 + (-5)$

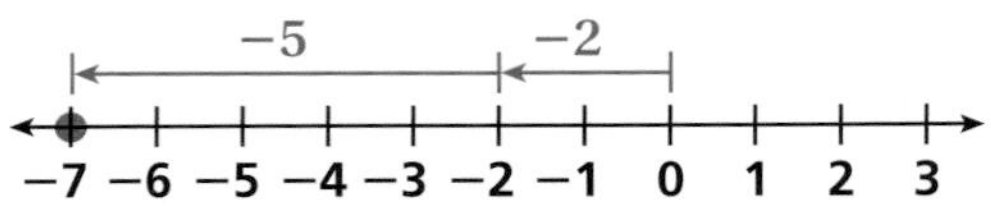

Move left 2 units.

From −2, move left 5 units.

You finish at -7, so $-2 + (-5) = -7$.

Another way to add integers is to use absolute value.

ADDING INTEGERS

If the signs are the same. . .	If the signs are different. . .
find the sum of the absolute values. Use the same sign as the integers.	find the difference of the absolute values. Use the sign of the integer with the greater absolute value.

EXAMPLE 2 Using Absolute Value to Add Integers

Add.

A $-4 + (-6)$

$-4 + (-6)$ — *Think: Find the sum of $|-4|$ and $|-6|$.*

-10 — *Same sign; use the sign of the integers.*

B $8 + (-9)$

$8 + (-9)$ — *Think: Find the difference of $|8|$ and $|-9|$.*

-1 — *$9 > 8$; use the sign of 9.*

C $-5 + 11$

$-5 + 11$ — *Think: Find the difference of $|-5|$ and $|11|$.*

6 — *$11 > 5$; use the sign of 11.*

EXAMPLE 3 Evaluating Expressions with Integers

Evaluate $b + 11$ for $b = -6$.

$b + 11$

$-6 + 11$ — *Replace b with −6.*

Think: Find the difference of $|11|$ and $|-6|$.

$-6 + 11 = 5$ — *$11 > 6$; use the sign of 11.*

EXAMPLE 4 *Health Application*

Monday Morning
Calories
Oatmeal 145
Toast w/jam 62
8 fl oz juice 111
Calories burned
Walked six laps 110
Swam six laps 40

Melanie wants to check her calorie count after breakfast and exercise. Use information from the journal entry to find her total.

$145 + 62 + 111 + (-110) + (-40)$ — *Use a positive sign for calories and a negative sign for calories burned.*

$(145 + 62 + 111) + (-110 + -40)$ — *Group integers with same signs.*

$318 + (-150)$ — *Add integers within each group.*

168 — *$318 > 150$; use the sign of 318.*

Melanie's calorie count after breakfast and exercise is 168 calories.

Think and Discuss

1. **Compare** the sums $10 + (-22)$ and $-10 + 22$.
2. **Explain** whether an absolute value is ever negative.
3. **Describe** how to add the following addition expressions on a number line: $9 + (-13)$ and $-13 + 9$. Then compare the sums.

1-4 Exercises

go.hrw.com
Homework Help Online
KEYWORD: MT7 1-4
Parent Resources Online
KEYWORD: MT7 Parent

GUIDED PRACTICE

See Example 1 **Use a number line to find each sum.**

1. $5 + 1$ **2.** $6 + (-4)$ **3.** $-7 + 9$ **4.** $-4 + (-2)$

See Example 2 **Add.**

5. $-12 + 5$ **6.** $7 + (-3)$ **7.** $-11 + 17$ **8.** $-6 + (-8)$

See Example 3 **Evaluate each expression for the given value of the variable.**

9. $t + 16$ for $t = -5$ **10.** $m + 7$ for $m = -5$ **11.** $p + (-5)$ for $p = -5$

See Example 4 **12.** Lee opens a checking account. In the first month, he makes two deposits and writes three checks, as shown at right. Find what his balance is at the end of the month. (*Hint:* Checks count as negative amounts.)

Checks	Deposits
$134	$600
$56	$225
$302	

INDEPENDENT PRACTICE

See Example 1 **Use a number line to find each sum.**

13. $5 + (-7)$ **14.** $-7 + 7$ **15.** $4 + (-9)$ **16.** $-4 + 7$

See Example 2 **Add.**

17. $8 + 14$ **18.** $-6 + (-7)$ **19.** $-8 + (-8)$ **20.** $19 + (-5)$

21. $22 + (-15)$ **22.** $17 + 9$ **23.** $-20 + (-12)$ **24.** $-18 + 7$

See Example 3 **Evaluate each expression for the given value of the variable.**

25. $q + 13$ for $q = 10$ **26.** $x + 21$ for $x = -7$ **27.** $z + (-7)$ for $z = 16$

See Example 4 **28.** On Monday morning, a mechanic has no cars in her shop. The table at right shows the number of cars dropped off and picked up each day. Find the total number of cars left in her shop on Friday.

	Cars Dropped Off	Cars Picked Up
Monday	8	4
Tuesday	11	6
Wednesday	9	12
Thursday	14	9
Friday	7	6

PRACTICE AND PROBLEM SOLVING

Extra Practice
See page 782.

Write an addition equation for each number line diagram.

29.

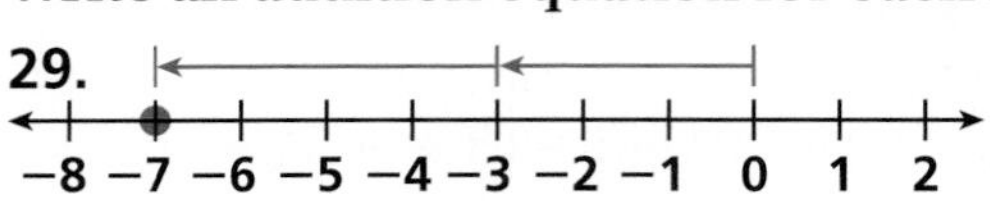

30.

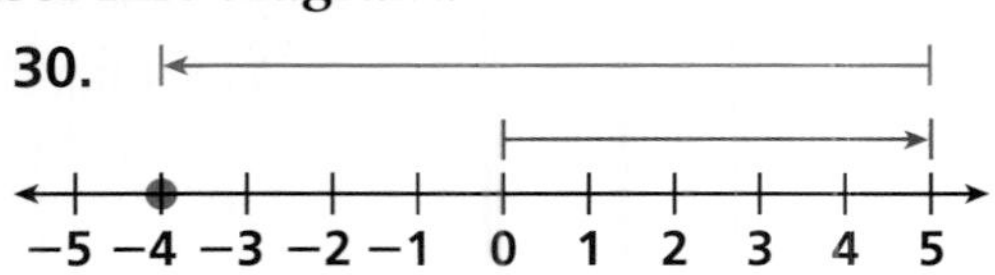

LINK

Economics

The number one category of imported goods in the United States is industrial supplies, including petroleum and petroleum products. In 2004, this category accounted for over $412 million of imports.

Use a number line to find each sum.

31. $-9 + (-3)$ **32.** $16 + (-22)$ **33.** $-34 + 17$ **34.** $44 + 39$

35. $45 + (-67)$ **36.** $-14 + 85$ **37.** $52 + (-9)$ **38.** $-31 + (-31)$

Evaluate each expression for the given value of the variable.

39. $c + 17$ for $c = -9$ **40.** $k + (-12)$ for $k = 4$ **41.** $b + (-6)$ for $b = -24$

42. $13 + r$ for $r = -19$ **43.** $-9 + w$ for $w = -6$ **44.** $3 + n + (-8)$ for $n = 5$

45. **Economics** Refer to the data at right about U.S. international trade for the year 2004. Consider values of exports as positive quantities and values of imports as negative quantities.

	Exports	Imports
Goods	$807,584,000,000	$1,473,768,000,000
Services	$338,553,000,000	$290,095,000,000

Source: U.S. Census Bureau

a. What was the total of U.S. exports in 2004?

b. What was the total of U.S. imports in 2004?

c. The sum of exports and imports is called the *balance of trade.* Approximate the 2004 U.S. balance of trade to the nearest billion dollars.

46. **What's the Error?** A student evaluated $-4 + d$ for $d = -6$ and gave an answer of 2. What might the student have done wrong?

47. **Write About It** Explain the different ways it is possible to add two integers and get a negative answer.

48. **Challenge** What is the sum of $3 + (-3) + 3 + (-3) + \ldots$ when there are 10 terms? 19 terms? 24 terms? 25 terms? Explain any patterns that you find.

TEST PREP and Spiral Review

49. **Multiple Choice** Which of the following is the value of $-7 + 3h$ when $h = 5$?

Ⓐ -22 Ⓑ -8 Ⓒ 8 Ⓓ 22

50. **Gridded Response** Evaluate the expression $12 - y$ for $y = -8$.

Evaluate each expression for the given values of the variables. (Lesson 1-1)

51. $2x - 3y$ for $x = 8$ and $y = 4$ **52.** $6s - t$ for $s = 7$ and $t = 12$

Evaluate each expression. (Lesson 1-3)

53. $|-3| + |-9|$ **54.** $|-4 + (-7)|$ **55.** $|18| - |-5|$ **56.** $|-27| - |-5|$

1-5 Subtracting Integers

Learn to subtract integers.

Carlsbad Caverns in New Mexico is one of the world's largest underground caves. A tour of the chambers in the cavern takes explorers on many descents and climbs.

Distances above or below the entrance level of a cave can be represented by integers. Negative integers represent distances below, and positive integers represent distances above.

Subtracting a lesser number from a greater number is the same as finding how far apart the two numbers are on a number line. Subtracting an integer is the same as adding its opposite.

SUBTRACTING INTEGERS

Words	Numbers	Algebra
To subtract an integer, add its opposite.	$3 - 7 = 3 + (-7)$	$a - b = a + (-b)$
	$5 - (-8) = 5 + 8$	$a - (-b) = a + b$

EXAMPLE 1 Subtracting Integers

Subtract.

A $-7 - 7$

$-7 - 7 = -7 + (-7)$ *Add the opposite of 7.*

$= -14$ *Same sign; use the sign of the integers.*

B $2 - (-4)$

$2 - (-4) = 2 + 4$ *Add the opposite of −4.*

$= 6$ *Same sign; use the sign of the integers.*

C $-13 - (-5)$

$-13 - (-5) = -13 + 5$ *Add the opposite of −5.*

$= -8$ *13 > 5; use the sign of 13.*

EXAMPLE 2 Evaluating Expressions with Integers

Evaluate each expression for the given value of the variable.

A $6 - t$ for $t = -4$

$6 - t$	
$6 - (-4)$	*Substitute −4 for t.*
$6 + 4$	*Add the opposite of −4.*
10	*Same sign; use the sign of the integers.*

B $-4 - s$ for $s = -9$

$-4 - s$	
$-4 - (-9)$	*Substitute −9 for s.*
$-4 + 9$	*Add the opposite of −9*
5	*9 > 4; use the sign of 9.*

C $-3 - x$ for $x = 5$

$-3 - x$	
$-3 - 5$	*Substitute 5 for x.*
$-3 + (-5)$	*Add the opposite of 5.*
-8	*Same sign; use the sign of the integers.*

EXAMPLE 3 *Earth Science Application*

James enters a cave and climbs to a height 30 feet above the entrance level. Then he descends 210 feet. How far below the entrance level did James go?

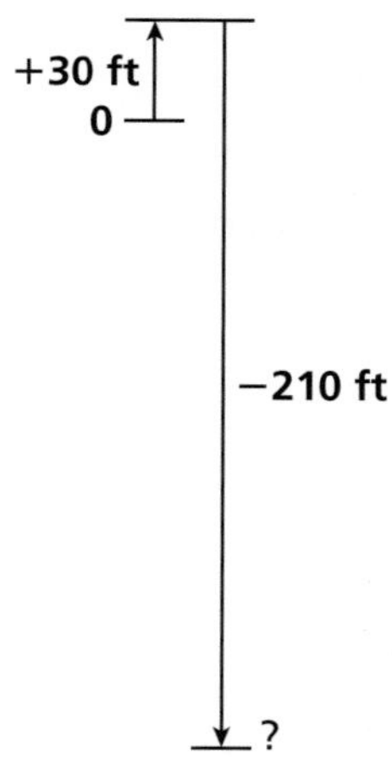

$30 - 210$	*Subtract the descent from the climb.*
$= 30 + (-210)$	*Add the opposite of 210.*
$= -180$	*210 > 30; use the sign of 210.*

James went 180 feet below the entrance level.

Think and Discuss

1. **Explain** why $10 - (-10)$ does not equal $-10 - 10$.
2. **Describe** the answer that you get when you subtract a greater number from a lesser number.

1-5 Exercises

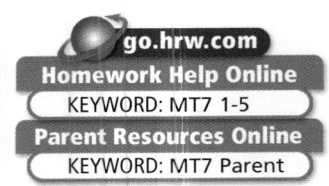

go.hrw.com
Homework Help Online
KEYWORD: MT7 1-5
Parent Resources Online
KEYWORD: MT7 Parent

GUIDED PRACTICE

See Example 1
Subtract.

1. $-5 - 9$
2. $-8 - (-6)$
3. $8 - (-4)$
4. $-11 - (-6)$

See Example 2
Evaluate each expression for the given value of the variable.

5. $9 - h$ for $h = -8$
6. $-7 - m$ for $m = -5$
7. $-3 - k$ for $k = 12$

See Example 3
8. The temperature rose from −4°F to 45°F in Spearfish, South Dakota, on January 22, 1943, in only 2 minutes! By how many degrees did the temperature change?

INDEPENDENT PRACTICE

See Example 1
Subtract.

9. $-3 - 7$
10. $14 - (-9)$
11. $11 - (-6)$
12. $-8 - (-2)$

See Example 2
Evaluate each expression for the given value of the variable.

13. $14 - b$ for $b = -3$
14. $-7 - q$ for $q = -15$
15. $-5 - f$ for $f = 12$

See Example 3
16. A submarine cruising at 27 m below sea level, or −27 m, descends 14 m. What is its new depth?

PRACTICE AND PROBLEM SOLVING

Extra Practice
See page 783.

Write a subtraction equation for each number line diagram.

17.
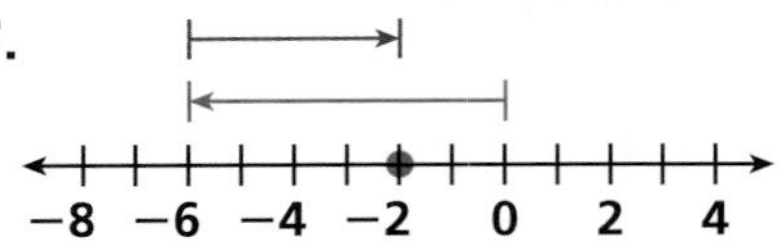

18.
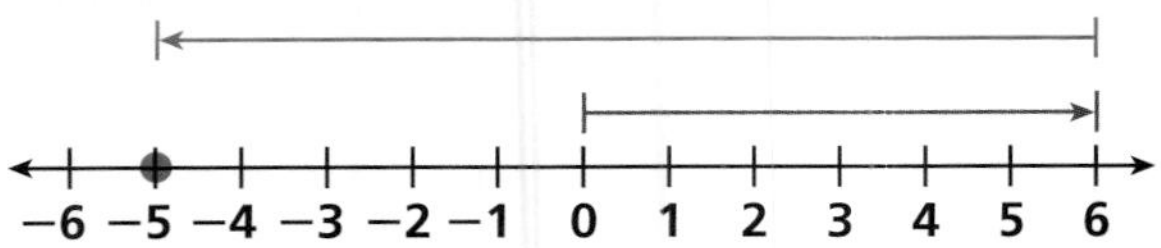

Perform the given operations.

19. $-8 - (-11)$
20. $24 - (-27)$
21. $-43 - 13$
22. $-26 - 26$
23. $-13 - 7 + (-6)$
24. $-11 - (-4) + (-9)$

Evaluate each expression for the given value of the variable.

25. $x - 16$ for $x = -4$
26. $8 - t$ for $t = -5$
27. $-16 - y$ for $y = 8$
28. $s - (-22)$ for $s = -18$

29. **Estimation** A roller coaster starts with a 160-foot climb and then plunges 228 feet down a canyon wall. It then climbs a gradual 72 feet before a steep climb of 189 feet. Approximately how far is the coaster above or below its starting point?

Social Studies LINK

Use the timeline to answer the questions. Use negative numbers for years B.C.E. Assume that there was a year 0 (there wasn't) and that there have been no major changes to the calendar (there have been).

30. How long was the Greco-Roman era, when Greece and Rome ruled Egypt?

31. Which was a longer period of time: from the Great Pyramid to Cleopatra, or from Cleopatra to the present? By how many years?

32. Queen Neferteri ruled Egypt about 2900 years before the Turks ruled. In what year did she rule?

33. There are 1846 years between which two events on this timeline?

34. **Write About It** What is it about years B.C.E. that make negative numbers a good choice for representing them?

35. **Challenge** How would your calculations differ if you took into account the fact that there was no year 0?

go.hrw.com
Web Extra!
KEYWORD: MT7 Egypt

TEST PREP and Spiral Review

36. Multiple Choice Which of the following is equivalent to $|7 - (-3)|$?

Ⓐ $|7| - |-3|$ Ⓑ $|7| + |-3|$ Ⓒ -10 Ⓓ 4

37. Gridded Response Subtract: $-4 - (-12)$.

Write an algebraic expression to evaluate each word problem. (Lesson 1-2)

38. Tate bought a compact disc for \$17.99. The sales tax on the disc was t dollars. What was the total cost including sales tax?

Evaluate each expression for $m = -3$. (Lesson 1-4)

39. $m + 6$ **40.** $m + -5$ **41.** $-9 + m$ **42.** $m + 3$

1-6 Multiplying and Dividing Integers

Learn to multiply and divide integers.

When a football team has possession of the football, its goal is to move the ball toward its opponent's goal line. Each play run can result in a gain of yards, a loss of yards, or no change. If a team loses 10 yards in each of 3 successive plays, the net change in yards can be represented by $3(-10)$.

A positive number multiplied by an integer can be written as repeated addition.

$$3(-10) = -10 + (-10) + (-10) = -30$$

From what you know about adding integers, you can see that a positive integer times a negative integer is negative.

You know that multiplying two positive integers together gives you a positive answer. The pattern in the integer multiplication at right can help you understand the rules for multiplying two negative integers.

$3(-10) = -30$
  + 10
$2(-10) = -20$
  + 10
$1(-10) = -10$
  + 10
$0(-10) = 0$
$-1(-10) = 10$
$-2(-10) = 20$
$-3(-10) = 30$

The product of two negative integers is a positive integer.

MULTIPLYING AND DIVIDING TWO INTEGERS

If the signs are the same, the sign of the answer is **positive.**

If the signs are different, the sign of the answer is **negative.**

EXAMPLE 1 Multiplying and Dividing Integers

Multiply or divide.

A $5(-8)$ — *Signs are different.*

-40 — *Answer is* ***negative.***

B $\frac{-45}{9}$ — *Signs are different.*

-5 — *Answer is* ***negative.***

C $-12(-3)$ — *Signs are the same.*

36 — *Answer is* ***positive.***

D $\frac{32}{-8}$ — *Signs are different.*

-4 — *Answer is* ***negative.***

EXAMPLE 2 Using the Order of Operations with Integers

Simplify.

A $-3(2 - 8)$

$-3(2 - 8)$	*Subtract inside the parentheses.*
$= -3(-6)$	*Think: The signs are the same.*
$= 18$	*The answer is positive.*

B $4(-7 - 2)$

$4(-7 - 2)$	*Subtract inside the parentheses.*
$= 4(-9)$	*Think: The signs are different.*
$= -36$	*The answer is negative.*

C $-2(14 - 6)$

$-2(14 - 6)$	*Subtract inside the parentheses.*
$= -2(8)$	*Think: The signs are different.*
$= -16$	*The answer is negative.*

EXAMPLE 3 *Sports Application*

A football team runs 10 plays. On 6 plays, it has a gain of 4 yards each. On 4 plays, it has a loss of 5 yards each. Each gain in yards can be represented by a positive integer, and each loss can be represented by a negative integer. Find the total net change in yards.

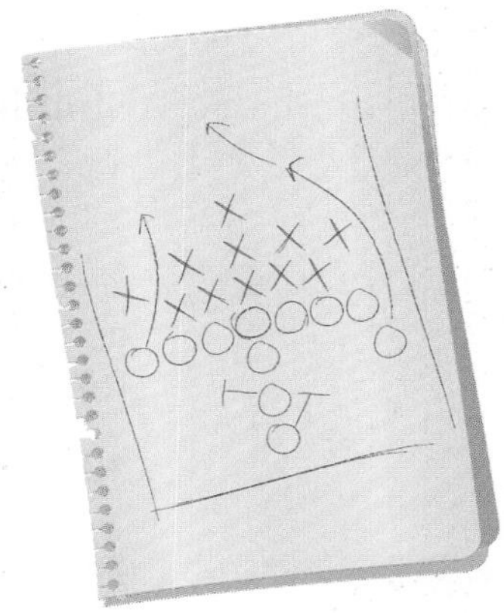

$6(4) + 4(-5)$	*Add the losses to the gains.*
$= 24 + (-20)$	*Multiply.*
$= 4$	*Add.*

The team gained 4 yards.

Think and Discuss

1. **List** all possible multiplication and division statements for the integers with absolute values of 5, 6, and 30. For example, $5 \cdot 6 = 30$.
2. **Compare** the sign of the product of two negative integers with the sign of the sum of two negative integers.
3. **Suppose** the product of two integers is positive. What do you know about the signs of the integers?

1-6 Exercises

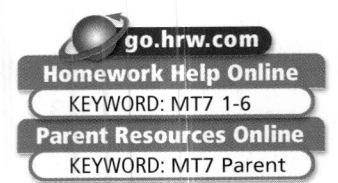

go.hrw.com
Homework Help Online
KEYWORD: MT7 1-6
Parent Resources Online
KEYWORD: MT7 Parent

GUIDED PRACTICE

See Example 1

Multiply or divide.

1. $8(-4)$
2. $\frac{-54}{9}$
3. $-7(-4)$
4. $\frac{32}{-8}$

See Example 2

Simplify.

5. $-7(5 - 12)$
6. $4(-3 - 9)$
7. $-6(-5 + 9)$
8. $11(-7 + 3)$

See Example 3

An investor buys shares of stock A and stock B. Stock A loses $8 per share, and stock B gains $5 per share. Given the number of shares, how much does the investor lose or gain?

9. stock A: 20 shares, stock B: 35 shares
10. stock A: 30 shares, stock B: 20 shares

INDEPENDENT PRACTICE

See Example 1

Multiply or divide.

11. $-3(-7)$
12. $\frac{72}{-6}$
13. $12(-7)$
14. $\frac{-42}{6}$

See Example 2

Simplify.

15. $12(9 - 14)$
16. $-13(-2 - 8)$
17. $13(8 - 11)$
18. $10 + 4(5 - 8)$

See Example 3

A student puts $50 in the bank each time he makes a deposit. He takes $20 each time he makes a withdrawal. Given the number of transactions, what is the net change in the student's account?

19. deposits: 4, withdrawals: 5
20. deposits: 3, withdrawals: 8

PRACTICE AND PROBLEM SOLVING

Extra Practice
See page 783.

21. **Earth Science** Ocean tides are the result of the gravitational force between the sun, the moon, and the earth. When ocean tides occur, the earth's crust also moves. This is called an earth tide. The formula for the height of an earth tide is $y = \frac{x}{3}$, where x is the height of the ocean tide. Fill in the table.

Ocean Tide Height (x)	$\frac{x}{3}$	Earth Tide Height (y)
15		
−6		
9		
−15		

Perform the given operations.

22. $-7(6)$
23. $\frac{-144}{12}$
24. $-7(-7)$
25. $\frac{160}{-40}$
26. $2(-3)(-5)$
27. $\frac{-96}{-12}$
28. $12(3)(-2)$
29. $\frac{-18(6)}{-3}$

LINK

Earth Science

Anoplogaster cornuta, often called a fangtooth or ogrefish, is a predatory fish that reaches a maximum length of 15 cm. It can be found in tropical and temperate waters at −16,000 ft.

Evaluate the expressions for the given value of the variable.

30. $-4t - 5$ for $t = 3$

31. $-x + 2$ for $x = -9$

32. $6(s + 9)$ for $s = -1$

33. $\frac{-r}{8}$ for $r = 64$

34. $\frac{-42}{t}$ for $t = -6$

35. $\frac{y - 11}{-4}$ for $y = 35$

36. Earth Science The ocean floor is extremely uneven. It includes underwater mountains, ridges, and extremely deep areas called *trenches.* To the nearest foot, find the average depth of the trenches shown.

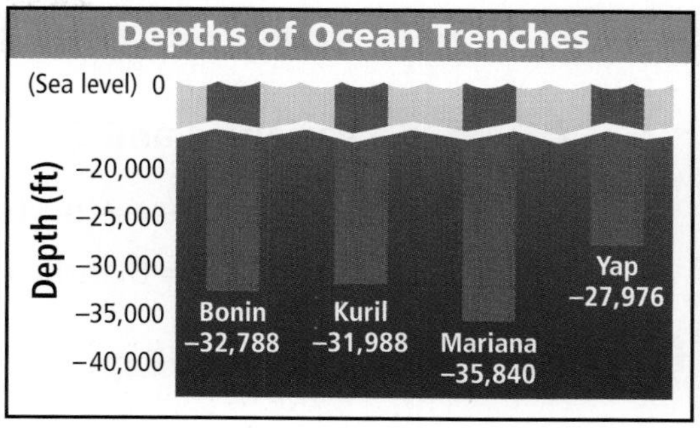

37. Critical Thinking A football team runs 11 plays. There are 3 plays that result in a loss of 2 yards each and 8 plays that result in a gain of 4 yards each. To find the total yards gained, Art evaluates the expression $3(-2) + 8(4)$. Bella first finds the total yards lost, 6, and the total yards gained, 32. Then she subtracts 6 from 32. Compare these two methods.

38. Choose a Strategy P is the set of positive factors of 30, and Q is the set of negative factors of 18. If x is a member of set P and y is a member of set Q, what is the greatest possible value of $x \cdot y$?

Ⓐ 540 Ⓑ 180 Ⓒ 90 Ⓓ −1

39. Write About It If you know that the product of two integers is negative, what can you say about the two integers? Give examples.

40. Challenge How many yards must be gained after a loss of 3 yards to have a total gain of 10 yards?

TEST PREP and Spiral Review

41. Multiple Choice What is the product of −7 and −10?

Ⓐ −70 Ⓑ −17 Ⓒ −3 Ⓓ 70

42. Short Response Brenda donates part of her salary to the local children's hospital each month by having $15 deducted from her monthly paycheck. Write an integer to represent the deduction recorded on each paycheck. Find an integer to represent the change in the amount of money in Brenda's paychecks after 1.5 years.

Write an algebraic expression for each word phrase. (Lesson 1-2)

43. j decreased by 18

44. twice b less 12

45. 22 less than y

Find each sum or difference. (Lessons 1-4 and 1-5)

46. $-7 + 3$

47. $5 - (-4)$

48. $-3 + (-6)$

49. $-513 - (-259)$

CHAPTER 1

READY TO GO ON?

SECTION 2B

Quiz for Lessons 1-1 Through 1-6

1-1 Variables and Expressions

Evaluate each expression for the given values of the variables.

1. $5x + 6y$ for $x = 8$ and $y = 4$
2. $6(r - 7t)$ for $r = 80$ and $t = 8$

1-2 Algebraic Expressions

Write an algebraic expression for each word phrase.

3. one-sixth the sum of r and 7
4. 10 plus the product of 16 and m

Write a word phrase for each algebraic expression.

5. $7y - 46$
6. $2(18 + t)$
7. $\frac{x - 10}{3}$
8. $15 + \frac{p}{32}$

1-3 Integers and Absolute Value

Write the integers in order from least to greatest.

9. $-17, 25, 18, -2$
10. $0, -8, 9, 1$

Evaluate each expression.

11. $|14 - 7|$
12. $|-15| - |-12|$
13. $|26| + |-14|$

1-4 Adding Integers

Evaluate each expression for the given value of the variable.

14. $p + 14$ for $p = -8$
15. $w + (-9)$ for $w = -4$
16. In Loma, Montana, on January 15, 1972, the temperature increased 103 degrees in a 24-hour period. If the lowest temperature on that day was −54°F, what was the highest temperature?

1-5 Subtracting Integers

Subtract.

17. $12 - (-8)$
18. $-7 - (-5)$
19. $-5 - (-16)$
20. $-22 - 5$
21. The point of highest elevation in the United States is on Mount McKinley, Alaska, at 20,320 feet. The point of lowest elevation is in Death Valley, California, at −282 feet. What is the difference in the elevations?

1-6 Multiplying and Dividing Integers

Multiply or divide.

22. $(-8)(-6)$
23. $\frac{-28}{7}$
24. $\frac{39}{-3}$
25. $(-2)(-5)(-6)$

Ready to Go On?

Focus on Problem Solving

Solve

- **Choose an operation: Addition or Subtraction**

To decide whether to add or subtract, you need to determine what action is taking place in the problem. If you are combining numbers or putting numbers together, you need to add. If you are taking away or finding out how far apart two numbers are, you need to subtract.

Action	Operation	Illustration
Combining or putting together	Add	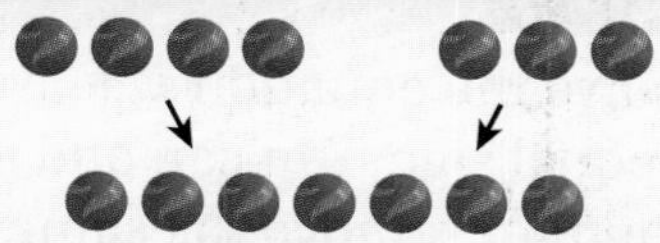
Removing or taking away	Subtract	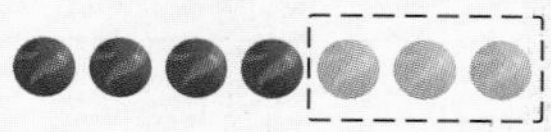
Finding the difference	Subtract	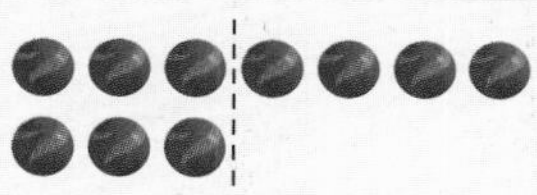

Jan has 10 red marbles. Joe gives her 3 more. How many marbles does Jan have now? The action is combining marbles. Add 10 and 3.

Determine the action in each problem. Use the actions to restate the problem. Then give the operation that must be used to solve the problem.

1. Lake Superior is the largest of the Great Lakes and contains approximately 3000 mi^3 of water. Lake Michigan is the second largest Great Lake by volume and contains approximately 1180 mi^3 of water. Estimate the difference in volumes of water.

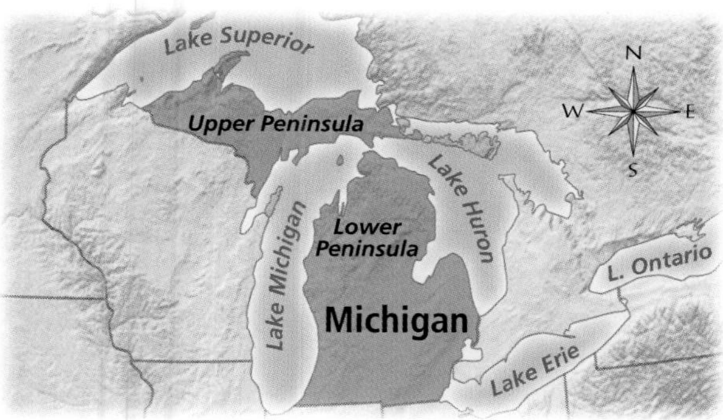

2. The average temperature in Homer, Alaska, is approximately 53°F in July and approximately 24°F in December. Find the difference between the average temperature in Homer in July and in December.

3. Einar has $18 to spend on his friend's birthday presents. He buys one present that costs $12. How much does he have left to spend?

4. Dinah got 87 points on her first test and 93 points on her second test. What is her combined point total for the first two tests?

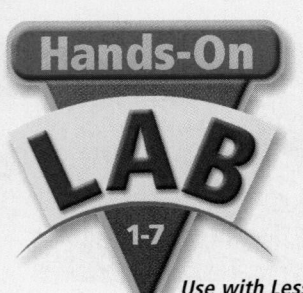

Hands-On LAB 1-7

Model Solving Equations

Use with Lesson 1-7

go.hrw.com
Lab Resources Online
KEYWORD: MT7 Lab1

KEY

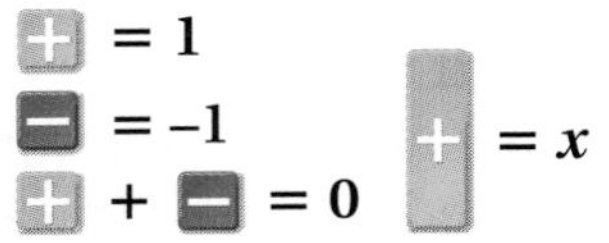

REMEMBER

It will not change the value of an expression if you add or remove zero.

You can use algebra tiles to help you solve equations.

Activity

To solve the equation $x + 3 = 5$, you need to get x alone on one side of the equal sign. You can add or remove tiles as long as you add the same amount or remove the same amount on both sides.

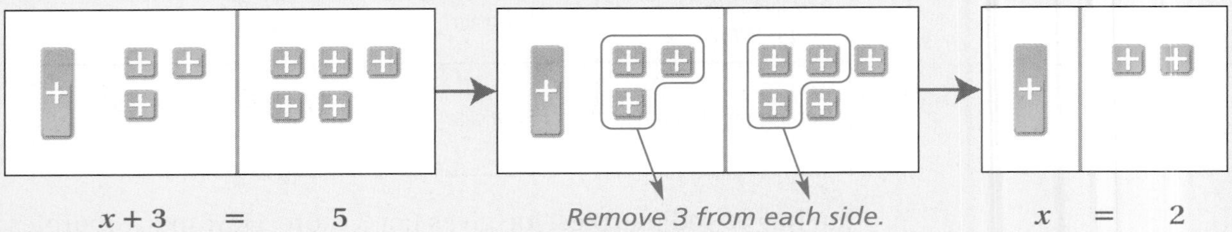

1 Use algebra tiles to model and solve each equation.

a. $x + 2 = 6$ **b.** $x + 2 = 7$ **c.** $x + (-4) = -7$ **d.** $x + 7 = 7$

The equation $x + 4 = 2$ is more difficult to solve because there are not enough yellow tiles on the right side. You can use the fact that the sum of two opposites is equal to zero to help you solve the equation.

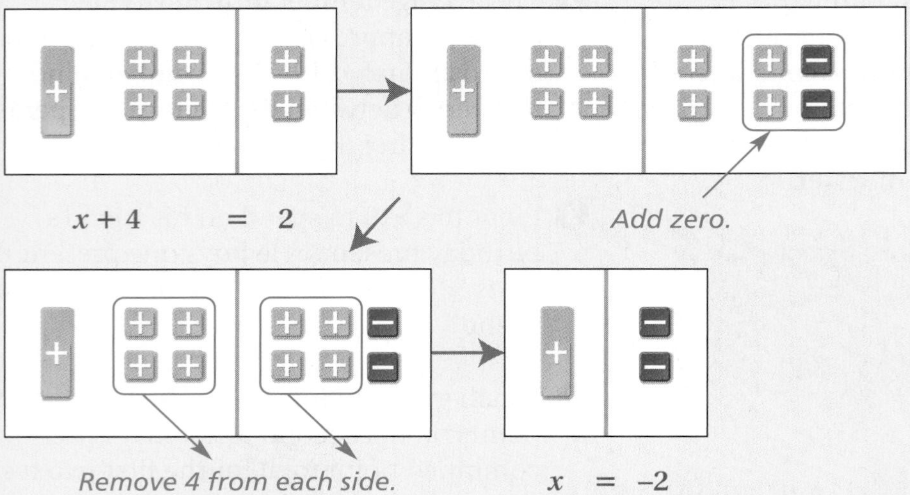

2 Use algebra tiles to model and solve each equation.

a. $x + 5 = 8$ **b.** $x + 8 = 3$ **c.** $x + (-5) = -2$ **d.** $x + (-11) = -4$

Modeling $x - 4 = 2$ is similar to modeling $x + 4 = 2$. Remember that you can add the same amount to both sides of an equation and the equation's value does not change.

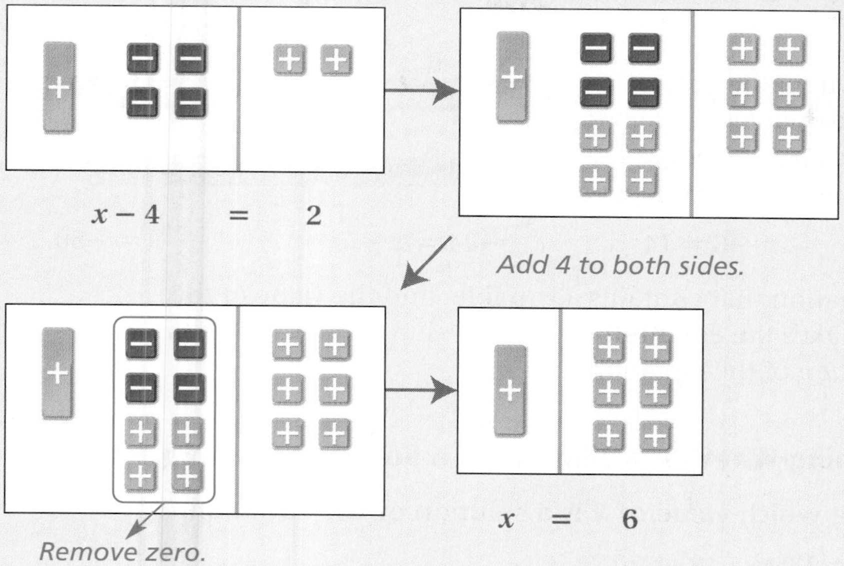

3 Use algebra tiles to model and solve each equation.

a. $x - 1 = 2$ **b.** $x - 3 = 7$ **c.** $x - 6 = -4$ **d.** $x - 8 = 3$

Think and Discuss

1. When you add zero to an equation, how do you know the numbers of yellow square tiles and red square tiles that you need to represent the addition?
2. When you remove tiles, what operation are you representing? When you add tiles, what operation are you representing?
3. How can you use the original model to check your solution?
4. Give an example of an equation with a negative solution that would require your adding 2 red square tiles and 2 yellow square tiles to model and solve it.
5. Give an example of an equation with a positive solution that would require your adding 2 red square tiles and 2 yellow square tiles to model and solve it.

Try This

Use algebra tiles to model and solve each equation.

1. $x - 8 = 12$ 2. $x + 3 = -9$ 3. $x + (-2) = -8$ 4. $x - 9 = -6$
5. Kensho used a gift card to buy a \$6 book. After the purchase, he had \$14 left on his card. Model and solve an equation to find the original value of the gift card.
6. Sari ran a total of 15 miles on two days. On the first day, she ran 6 miles. Model and solve an equation to find how far she ran on the second day.

1-7 Solving Equations by Adding or Subtracting

Learn to solve equations using addition and subtraction.

Vocabulary

equation

inverse operation

An **equation** is a mathematical sentence that uses an equal sign to show that two expressions have the same value. All of these are equations.

$3 + 8 = 11$ $\qquad r + 6 = 14$ $\qquad -24 = x - 7$ $\qquad \frac{-100}{2} = -50$

To *solve* an equation that contains a variable, find the value of the variable that makes the equation true. This value of the variable is called the *solution* of the equation.

EXAMPLE 1 Determining Whether a Number Is a Solution of an Equation

Determine which value of *x* is a solution of the equation.

$x - 7 = 13$; $x = 12$ or 20

Substitute each value for *x* in the equation.

$x - 7 = 13$

$12 - 7 \stackrel{?}{=} 13$ *Substitute 12 for x.*

$5 \stackrel{?}{=} 13$ ✗

So 12 **is not** a solution.

$x - 7 = 13$

$20 - 7 \stackrel{?}{=} 13$ *Substitute 20 for x.*

$13 \stackrel{?}{=} 13$ ✓

So 20 **is** a solution.

Helpful Hint

The phrase "subtraction 'undoes' addition" can be understood with this example:
If you start with 3 and add 4, you can get back to 3 by subtracting 4.

$$\begin{array}{r} 3 + 4 \\ -\ 4 \\ \hline 3 \end{array}$$

Addition and subtraction are **inverse operations**, which means they "undo" each other. To solve an equation, use inverse operations to isolate the variable. In other words, get the variable alone on one side of the equal sign.

To solve a subtraction equation, like $y - 15 = 7$, you would use the *Addition Property of Equality.*

ADDITION PROPERTY OF EQUALITY

Words	Numbers	Algebra
You can add the same number to both sides of an equation, and the statement will still be true.	$\begin{array}{rr} 2 + 3 = & 5 \\ +\ 4 & +\ 4 \\ \hline 2 + 7 = & 9 \end{array}$	$x = y$ $x + z = y + z$

There is a similar property for solving addition equations, like $x + 9 = 11$. It is called the *Subtraction Property of Equality*.

SUBTRACTION PROPERTY OF EQUALITY		
Words	**Numbers**	**Algebra**
You can subtract the same number from both sides of an equation, and the statement will still be true.	$\begin{array}{rr} 4 + 7 = & 11 \\ \underline{\;\; - 3} & \underline{-3} \\ 4 + 4 = & 8 \end{array}$	$x = y$ $x - z = y - z$

EXAMPLE 2 **Solving Equations Using Addition and Subtraction Properties**

Solve.

A $6 + t = 28$

$$\begin{array}{rrl} 6 + t = & 28 & \\ \underline{-6 \quad\;\;} & \underline{-6} & \textit{Subtract 6 from both sides.} \\ 0 + t = & 22 & \\ t = & 22 & \textit{Identity Property of Zero: } 0 + t = t \end{array}$$

Check

$$\begin{array}{rl} 6 + t = 28 & \\ 6 + 22 \stackrel{?}{=} 28 & \textit{Substitute 22 for t.} \\ 28 \stackrel{?}{=} 28 \checkmark & \end{array}$$

B $m - 8 = -14$

$$\begin{array}{rrl} m - 8 = & -14 & \\ \underline{+8} & \underline{+8} & \textit{Add 8 to both sides.} \\ m + 0 = & -6 & \\ m = & -6 & \end{array}$$

Check

$$\begin{array}{rl} m - 8 = -14 & \\ -6 - 8 \stackrel{?}{=} -14 & \textit{Substitute } -6 \textit{ for m.} \\ -14 \stackrel{?}{=} -14 \checkmark & \end{array}$$

C $15 = w + (-14)$

$$\begin{array}{rl} 15 = w + (-14) & \\ 15 - (-14) = w + (-14) - (-14) & \textit{Subtract } -14 \textit{ from both sides.} \\ 29 = w + 0 & \\ 29 = w & \\ w = 29 & \textit{Definition of Equality} \end{array}$$

EXAMPLE 3 PROBLEM SOLVING APPLICATION

PROBLEM SOLVING

Net force is the sum of all forces acting on an object. Expressed in newtons (N), it tells you in which direction and how quickly the object will move. If two dogs are playing tug-of-war, and the dog on the right pulls with a force of 12 N, what force is the dog on the left exerting on the rope if the net force is 2 N?

1 Understand the Problem

The **answer** is the force that the left dog exerts on the rope.

List the **important information:**

- The dog on the right pulls with a force of 12 N.
- The net force is 2 N.

Show the **relationship** of the information:

net force = **left dog's force** + **right dog's force**

2 Make a Plan

Write an equation and solve it. Let f represent the left dog's force on the rope, and use the equation model.

$$2 = f + 12$$

3 Solve

$$\begin{aligned} 2 &= f + 12 \\ \underline{-12} & \quad \underline{\;\;\; -12} \\ -10 &= f \end{aligned}$$

Subtract 12 from both sides.

The left dog is exerting a force of −10 newtons on the rope.

4 Look Back

The problem states that the net force is 2 N, which means that the dog on the right must be pulling with more force. The absolute value of the left dog's force is less than the absolute value of the right dog's force, $|-10| < |12|$, so the answer is reasonable.

Helpful Hint

Force is measured in newtons (N). The number of newtons tells the size of the force and the sign tells its direction. Positive is to the right, and negative is to the left.

Think and Discuss

1. **Explain** what the result would be in the tug-of-war match in Example 3 if the dog on the left pulled with a force of −7 N and the dog on the right pulled with a force of 6 N.
2. **Describe** the steps to solve $y - 5 = 16$.

1-7 Exercises

go.hrw.com
Homework Help Online
KEYWORD: MT7 1-7
Parent Resources Online
KEYWORD: MT7 Parent

GUIDED PRACTICE

See Example 1

Determine which value of x is a solution of each equation.

1. $x + 6 = 18$; $x = 10, 12,$ or 25
2. $x - 7 = 14$; $x = 2, 7,$ or 21

See Example 2

Solve.

3. $m - 9 = -23$
4. $8 + t = 13$
5. $p - (-13) = -10$
6. $q + (-25) = 81$
7. $26 = t - 13$
8. $52 = p + (-41)$

See Example 3

9. A team of mountain climbers descended 3600 feet to a camp that was at an altitude of 12,035 feet. At what altitude did they start?

INDEPENDENT PRACTICE

See Example 1

Determine which value of x is a solution for each equation.

10. $x - 14 = 8$; $x = 6, 22,$ or 32
11. $x + 23 = 55$; $x = 15, 28,$ or 32

See Example 2

Solve.

12. $9 = w + (-8)$
13. $m - 11 = 33$
14. $4 + t = 16$
15. $z + (-22) = -96$
16. $102 = p - (-130)$
17. $27 = h + (-8)$

See Example 3

18. Olivia owns 43 CDs. This is 15 more CDs than Angela owns. How many CDs does Angela own?

PRACTICE AND PROBLEM SOLVING

Extra Practice
See page 783.

Solve. Check your answer.

19. $7 + t = 12$
20. $h - 21 = -52$
21. $15 = m + (-9)$
22. $m - 5 = -10$
23. $h + 8 = 11$
24. $-6 + t = -14$
25. $1785 = t - (-836)$
26. $m + 35 = -172$
27. $x - 29 = 81$
28. $p + 8 = 23$
29. $n + (-14) = -31$
30. $20 = -8 + w$
31. $8 + t = -130$
32. $57 = c - 28$
33. $-987 = w + 797$

34. **Social Studies** In 1990, the population of Cheyenne, Wyoming, was 73,142. By 2000, the population had increased to 81,607. Write and solve an equation to find n, the increase in Cheyenne's population from 1990 to 2000.

35. **Astronomy** Mercury's surface temperature has a range of 600°C. This range is the broadest of any planet in the solar system. Given that the lowest temperature on Mercury's surface is −173°C, write and solve an equation to find the highest temperature.

Determine which value of the variable is a solution of the equation.

36. $d + 4 = 24$; $d = 6, 20,$ or 28

37. $k + (-13) = 27$; $k = 40, 45,$ or 50

38. $d - 17 = -36$; $d = 19, 17,$ or -19

39. $k + 3 = 4$; $k = 1, 7,$ or 17

40. $12 = -14 + s$; $s = 20, 26,$ or 32

41. $-32 = 27 + g$; $g = 58, -25, -59$

42. Physical Science An ion is a charged particle. Each proton in an ion has a charge of +1 and each electron has a charge of −1. The ion charge is the electron charge plus the proton charge. Write and solve an equation to find the electron charge for each ion.

Hydrogen sulfate ion (HSO_4^-)

Name of Ion	Proton Charge	Electron Charge	Ion Charge
Aluminum ion (Al^{3+})	+13		+3
Hydroxide ion (OH^-)	+9		−1
Oxide ion (O^{2-})	+8		−2
Sodium ion (Na^+)	+11		+1

43. What's the Error? A student evaluated the expression $-7 - (-3)$ and came up with the answer −10. What did the student do wrong?

44. Write About It Explain what a gain of negative yardage means in football.

45. Challenge Explain how you could solve for h in the equation $14 - h = 8$ using algebra. Then find the value of h.

TEST PREP and Spiral Review

46. Multiple Choice Which value of x is the solution of the equation $x - 5 = 8$?

Ⓐ 3 Ⓑ 11 Ⓒ 13 Ⓓ 15

47. Multiple Choice Len bought a pair of $12 flip-flops and a shirt. He paid $30 in all. Which equation can you use to find the price p he paid for the shirt?

Ⓕ $12 - p = 30$ Ⓖ $12 + p = 30$ Ⓗ $30 + p = 12$ Ⓙ $p - 12 = 30$

48. Gridded Response What value of x is the solution of the equation $-4x - 3 = -19$?

Add. (Lesson 1-4)

49. $-5 + (-9)$ **50.** $16 + (-22)$ **51.** $-64 + 51$ **52.** $82 + (-75)$

Multiply or divide. (Lesson 1-6)

53. $7(-8)$ **54.** $-63 \div (-7)$ **55.** $\frac{38}{-19}$ **56.** $-8(-13)$

1-8 Solving Equations by Multiplying or Dividing

Learn to solve equations using multiplication and division.

Helene plays baritone in her school's marching band. The band has been invited to compete in a national band festival, but they need to raise money in order to make the trip. So far, the band's fundraisers have brought in \$720, but that's only one-third of what is needed.

You can write and solve a multiplication equation to figure out how much the band needs to raise in all.

You can solve a multiplication equation using the *Division Property of Equality.*

DIVISION PROPERTY OF EQUALITY

Words	Numbers	Algebra
You can divide both sides of an equation by the same nonzero number, and the statement will still be true.	$4 \cdot 3 = 12$ $\frac{4 \cdot 3}{2} = \frac{12}{2}$ $\frac{12}{2} = 6$	$x = y$ $\frac{x}{z} = \frac{y}{z}$, $z \neq 0$

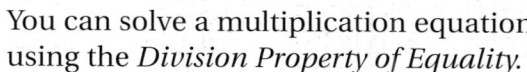

EXAMPLE 1 Solving Equations Using Division

Solve and check.

A $8x = 32$

$8x = 32$

$\frac{8x}{8} = \frac{32}{8}$ *Divide both sides by 8.*

$1x = 4$ *$1 \cdot x = x$*

$x = 4$

Check

$8x = 32$

$8(4) \stackrel{?}{=} 32$ *Substitute 4 for x.*

$32 \stackrel{?}{=} 32$ ✔

B $-7y = -91$

$-7y = -91$

$\frac{-7y}{-7} = \frac{-91}{-7}$ *Divide both sides by −7.*

$1y = 13$ *$1 \cdot y = y$*

$y = 13$

Check

$-7y = -91$

$-7(13) \stackrel{?}{=} -91$ *Substitute 13 for y.*

$-91 \stackrel{?}{=} -91$ ✔

You can solve division equations using the *Multiplication Property of Equality.*

MULTIPLICATION PROPERTY OF EQUALITY

Words	Numbers	Algebra
Multiply both sides of an equation by the same number, and the statement will still be true.	$2 \cdot 3 = 6$ $4 \cdot 2 \cdot 3 = 4 \cdot 6$ $8 \cdot 3 = 24$	$x = y$ $zx = zy$

EXAMPLE 2 Solving Equations Using Multiplication

Solve $\frac{h}{-3} = 6$.

$\frac{h}{-3} = 6$

$-3 \cdot \frac{h}{-3} = -3 \cdot 6$ *Multiply both sides by −3.*

$h = -18$

Check

$\frac{h}{-3} = 6$

$\frac{-18}{-3} \stackrel{?}{=} 6$ *Substitute −18 for h.*

$6 \stackrel{?}{=} 6$ ✓

EXAMPLE 3 *Money Application*

Helene's band needs money to go to a national competition. So far, band members have raised $720, which is only one-third of what they need. What is the total amount needed?

fraction of total amount raised so far	·	total amount needed	=	amount raised so far
$\frac{1}{3}$	·	x	=	$720

$\frac{1}{3}x = 720$ *Write the equation.*

$3 \cdot \frac{1}{3}x = 3 \cdot 720$ *Multiply both sides by 3.*

$x = 2160$

The band needs to raise a total of $2160.

Sometimes it is necessary to solve equations by using two inverse operations. For instance, the equation $6x - 2 = 10$ has multiplication and subtraction.

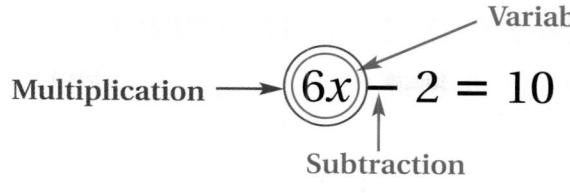

Variable term

Multiplication → $6x - 2 = 10$

Subtraction

To solve this equation, add to isolate the term with the variable in it. Then divide to solve.

EXAMPLE 4 Solving a Simple Two-Step Equation

Solve $2x + 1 = -7$.

Step 1:

$$\begin{aligned} 2x + 1 &= -7 \\ -1 &= -1 \\ 2x \quad &= -8 \end{aligned}$$

Subtract 1 from both sides to isolate the term with x in it.

Step 2:

$$\frac{2x}{2} = \frac{-8}{2}$$

Divide both sides by 2.

$$x = -4$$

Think and Discuss

1. Explain what property you would use to solve $\frac{k}{2.5} = 6$.

2. Give the equation you would solve to figure out how much money the band would need to raise if their trip cost twice as much.

1-8 Exercises

go.hrw.com
Homework Help Online
KEYWORD: MT7 1-8
Parent Resources Online
KEYWORD: MT7 Parent

GUIDED PRACTICE

See Example 1 **Solve and check.**

1. $-4x = 28$ **2.** $7t = -49$ **3.** $3y = 42$ **4.** $2w = 26$

5. $-12q = -24$ **6.** $25m = -125$ **7.** $13p = 39$ **8.** $22y = -88$

See Example 2

9. $\frac{l}{-15} = 4$ **10.** $\frac{k}{8} = 9$ **11.** $\frac{h}{19} = -3$ **12.** $\frac{m}{-6} = 1$

13. $\frac{t}{23} = -9$ **14.** $\frac{t}{13} = 52$ **15.** $\frac{w}{-12} = 7$ **16.** $\frac{f}{45} = -3$

See Example 3

17. Gary needs to buy a suit to go to a formal dance. Using a coupon, he can save \$60, which is $\frac{1}{4}$ of the cost of the suit. Write and solve an equation to determine the cost c of the suit.

See Example 4 **Solve and check.**

18. $3x + 2 = 23$ **19.** $\frac{k}{-5} - 1 = 7$ **20.** $-3y - 8 = 1$ **21.** $\frac{m}{6} + 4 = 10$

INDEPENDENT PRACTICE

See Example 1 **Solve and check.**

22. $3d = 57$ **23.** $-7x = 105$ **24.** $-4g = -40$ **25.** $16y = 112$

26. $-8p = 88$ **27.** $17n = 34$ **28.** $-212b = -424$ **29.** $41u = -164$

See Example 2

30. $\frac{n}{9} = -63$ **31.** $\frac{h}{-27} = -2$ **32.** $\frac{a}{6} = 102$ **33.** $\frac{j}{8} = 12$

34. $\frac{y}{-9} = 11$ **35.** $\frac{d}{7} = -23$ **36.** $\frac{t}{5} = 60$ **37.** $\frac{p}{-84} = 3$

See Example 3

38. Fred gathered 150 eggs on his family's farm today. This is $\frac{1}{3}$ the number he usually gathers. Write and solve an equation to determine the number of eggs n that Fred usually gathers.

See Example 4 **Solve.**

39. $6x - 5 = 7$ **40.** $\frac{n}{-3} - 4 = 1$ **41.** $2y + 5 = -9$ **42.** $\frac{h}{7} + 2 = 2$

PRACTICE AND PROBLEM SOLVING

Extra Practice
See page 783.

Solve.

43. $-2x = 14$ **44.** $4y = -80$ **45.** $6y = 12$ **46.** $-9m = -9$

47. $\frac{k}{8} = 7$ **48.** $\frac{1}{5}x = 121$ **49.** $\frac{b}{6} = -12$ **50.** $\frac{n}{15} = 1$

51. $3x = 51$ **52.** $15g = 75$ **53.** $16y - 18 = -66$ **54.** $3z - 14 = 58$

55. $\frac{b}{-4} = 12$ **56.** $\frac{m}{24} = -24$ **57.** $\frac{n}{5} - 3 = 4$ **58.** $\frac{a}{-2} + 8 = 14$

59. **Critical Thinking** Will the solution of $\frac{x}{-5} = 11$ be greater than 11 or less than 11? Explain how you know.

60. **Multi-Step** Joy earns \$8 per hour at an after-school job. Each month she earns \$128. How many hours does she work each month? After six months, she gets a \$2 per hour raise. How much money does she earn per month now?

61. Elvira estimates that meetings take up about $\frac{1}{4}$ of the time she spends at work. If Elvira spent 12 hours in meetings last week, how many hours did she work?

62. **Recreation** While on vacation, Milo drove his car a total of 370 miles. This was 5 times as many miles as he drives in a normal week. How many miles does Milo drive in a normal week?

63. **Multi-Step** Forty-two students and 6 faculty members at Byrd Middle School chose to retake their school pictures. These numbers represent $\frac{1}{12}$ of the students and $\frac{1}{6}$ of the faculty. What is the combined number of students and faculty members at Byrd Middle School?

Social Studies LINK

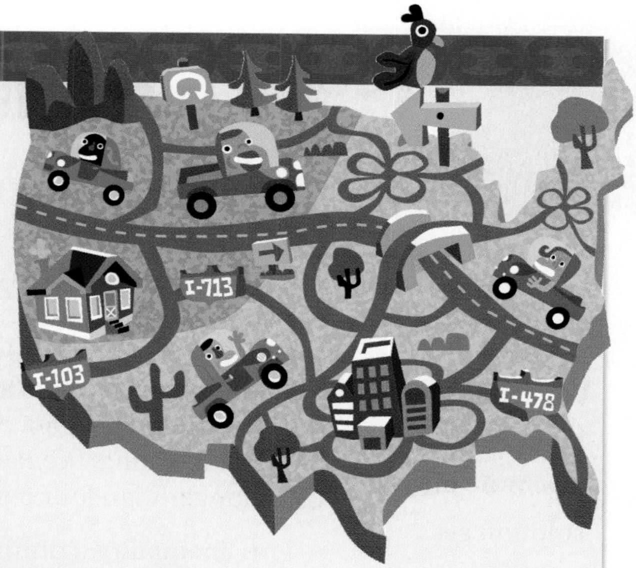

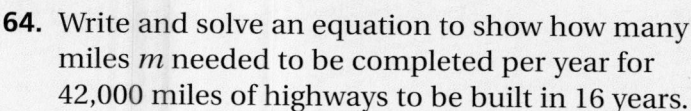

In 1956, during President Eisenhower's term, construction began on the United States interstate highway system. The original plan was for 42,000 miles of highways to be completed within 16 years. It actually took 37 years to complete. The last part, Interstate 105 in Los Angeles, was completed in 1993.

64. Write and solve an equation to show how many miles m needed to be completed per year for 42,000 miles of highways to be built in 16 years.

65. Interstate 35 runs north and south from Laredo, Texas, to Duluth, Minnesota, covering 1568 miles. There are 505 miles of I-35 in Texas and 262 miles in Minnesota. Write and solve an equation to find m, the number of miles of I-35 that are not in either state.

66. A portion of I-476 in Pennsylvania, known as the Blue Route, is about 22 miles long. The length of the Blue Route is about one-sixth the total length of I-476. Write and solve an equation to calculate the length of I-476 in miles m.

67. **Challenge** Interstate 80 extends from California to New Jersey. At right are the number of miles of Interstate 80 in each state the highway passes through.

a. __?__ has 134 more miles than __?__.

b. __?__ has 174 fewer miles than __?__.

Number of I-80 Miles

State	Miles
California	195
Nevada	410
Utah	197
Wyoming	401
Nebraska	455
Iowa	301
Illinois	163
Indiana	167
Ohio	236
Pennsylvania	314
New Jersey	68

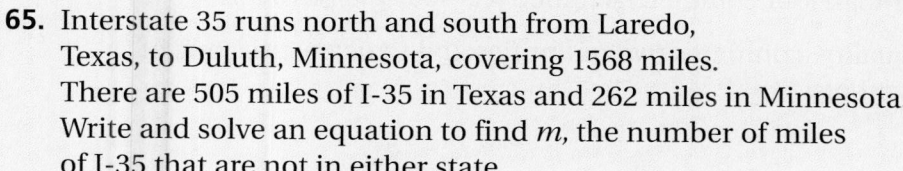

TEST PREP and Spiral Review

68. **Multiple Choice** Solve the equation $7x = -42$.

Ⓐ $x = -49$ Ⓑ $x = -35$ Ⓒ $x = -6$ Ⓓ $x = 6$

69. **Gridded Response** On a game show, Paul missed q questions, each worth -100 points. Paul received a total of -900 points. How many questions did he miss?

Subtract. (Lesson 1-5)

70. $-8 - 8$ **71.** $-3 - (-7)$ **72.** $-10 - 2$ **73.** $11 - (-9)$

Solve each equation. (Lesson 1-7)

74. $4 + x = 13$ **75.** $x - 4 = -9$ **76.** $-17 = x + 9$ **77.** $19 = x + 11$

1-9 Introduction to Inequalities

Learn to solve and graph inequalities.

Vocabulary

inequality

algebraic inequality

solution set

The aircraft carrier USS *Ronald Reagan* was commissioned on July 12, 2003, over five years after construction began. At 1092 feet long, the *Reagan* is longer than four commercial jumbo jets sitting nose to tail.

An **inequality** compares two quantities and typically uses one of these symbols:

$<$	$>$	$\le$	$\ge$
is less than	*is greater than*	*is less than or equal to*	*is greater than or equal to*

EXAMPLE 1 Completing an Inequality

Compare. Write $<$ or $>$.

A $13 - 9 \; \blacksquare \; 6$

$4 \; \blacksquare \; 6$

$4 < 6$

B $2(8) \; \blacksquare \; 10$

$16 \; \blacksquare \; 10$

$16 > 10$

Remember!

The inequality symbol opens to the side with the greater number.
$2 < 10$

An inequality that contains one or more variables is an **algebraic inequality**. A number that makes an inequality true is a *solution of the inequality.*

The set of all solutions is called the **solution set**. The solution set can be shown by graphing it on a number line.

Word Phrase	Inequality	Sample Solutions		Solution Set
x is less than 5	$x < 5$	$x = 4$ $x = 2.1$	$4 < 5$ $2.1 < 5$	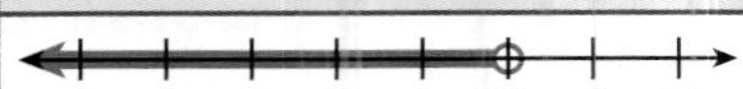
a is greater than 0 a is more than 0	$a > 0$	$a = 7$ $a = 25$	$7 > 0$ $25 > 0$	
y is less than or equal to 2 y is at most 2	$y \le 2$	$y = 0$ $y = 1.5$	$0 \le 2$ $1.5 \le 2$	
m is greater than or equal to 3 m is at least 3	$m \ge 3$	$m = 17$ $m = 3$	$17 \ge 3$ $3 \ge 3$	

Most inequalities can be solved the same way equations are solved. Use inverse operations on both sides of the inequality to isolate the variable.

EXAMPLE 2 Solving and Graphing Inequalities

Solve and graph each inequality.

A $\mathbf{x + 7 < -10}$

$x + 7 < -10$

$\underline{\ \ -7 \quad\ \ -7}$ *Subtract 7 from both sides.*

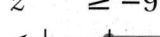

$x \qquad < -17$

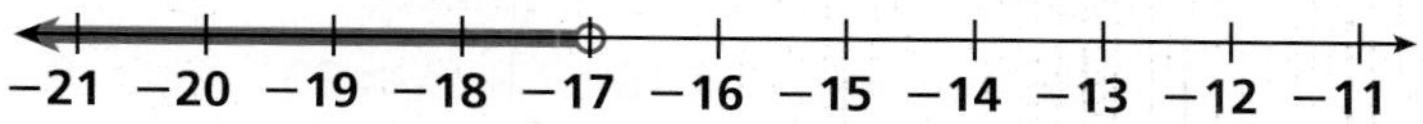

Caution!

An open circle means that the corresponding value is not a solution. A solid circle means that the value is part of the solution set.

Check

According to the graph, -20 should be a solution, since $-20 < -17$, and 3 should not be a solution because $3 > -17$.

$x + 7 < -10$

$-20 + 7 \overset{?}{<} -10$ *Substitute −20 for x.*

$-13 \overset{?}{<} -10$ ✔

So -20 is a solution.

$x + 7 < -10$

$3 + 7 \overset{?}{<} -10$ *Substitute 3 for x.*

$10 \overset{?}{<} -10$ ✘

And 3 is not a solution.

B $\mathbf{t - 11 \leq -22}$

$t - 11 \leq -22$

$\underline{\ \ +11 \quad\ \ +11}$ *Add 11 to both sides.*

$t \qquad \leq -11$

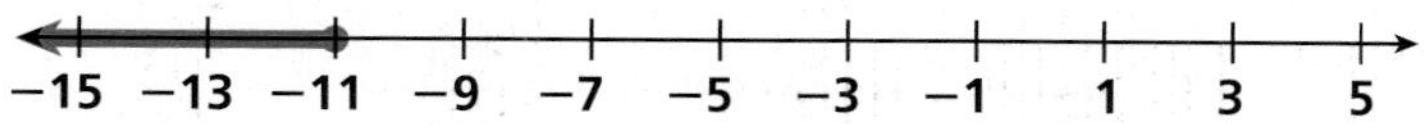

C $\mathbf{z + 6 \geq -3}$

$z + 6 \geq -3$

$\underline{\ \ -6 \quad\ \ -6}$ *Subtract 6 from both sides.*

$z \qquad \geq -9$

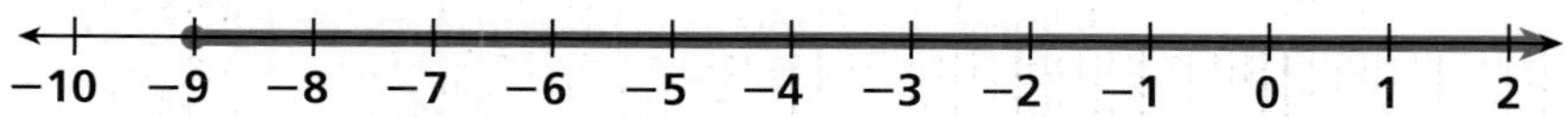

Think and Discuss

1. **Give** all the symbols that make 5 + 8 ▒ 13 true. Explain.
2. **Compare** and contrast expressions, equations, and inequalities.

1-9 Exercises

go.hrw.com
Homework Help Online
KEYWORD: MT7 1-9
Parent Resources Online
KEYWORD: MT7 Parent

GUIDED PRACTICE

See Example 1

Compare. Write $<$ or $>$.

1. $5 + 9$ ■ 13 **2.** $4(-2)$ ■ 7 **3.** $27 - 13$ ■ 11

4. $5(9)$ ■ 42 **5.** $9 + (-2)$ ■ 10 **6.** $3(8)$ ■ -27

See Example 2

Solve and graph each inequality.

7. $x + 3 < -4$ **8.** $4 + b \geq 20$ **9.** $m - 4 \leq 28$ **10.** $x + (-3) < 5$

11. $y + 8 \geq 25$ **12.** $-6 + f < -30$ **13.** $z - 8 > 13$ **14.** $x + 2 \geq -7$

INDEPENDENT PRACTICE

See Example 1

Compare. Write $<$ or $>$.

15. $4 + 7$ ■ 12 **16.** $6(8)$ ■ 25 **17.** $15 - 9$ ■ 4

18. $7(-6)$ ■ -40 **19.** $13 + 5$ ■ 17 **20.** $5 + (-23)$ ■ -12

See Example 2

Solve and graph each inequality.

21. $b + 4 < 8$ **22.** $-7 + x \geq 49$ **23.** $h - 2 \geq 3$ **24.** $1 < t - 4$

25. $6 + a > 9$ **26.** $-3 + x \geq 12$ **27.** $f - 9 \leq 2$ **28.** $2 < a + (-5)$

PRACTICE AND PROBLEM SOLVING

Extra Practice
See page 783.

Write the inequality shown by each graph.

29.
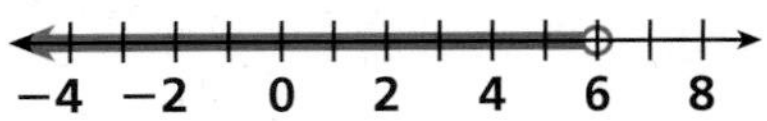

30.
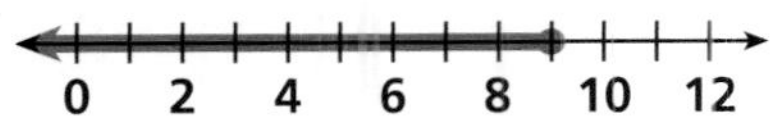

31.
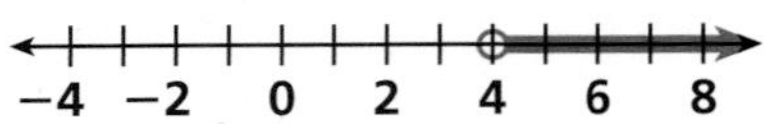

32.
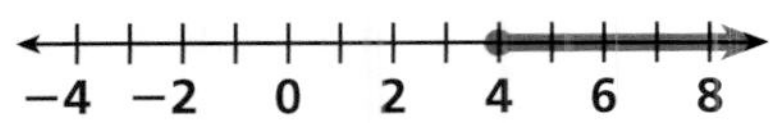

33.
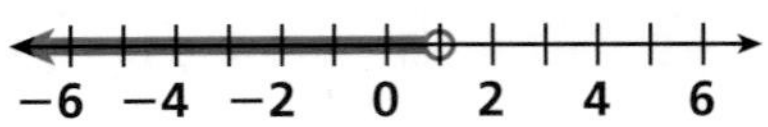

34.

35. **Business** The financial officers of Toshi Business Solutions are looking at the budget for the current fiscal year. They estimate that the company will have operating costs of at least \$201,522 for the entire year. So far, the company has had sales of \$98,200. At least how much money must Toshi earn in sales for the remainder of the year in order to show a profit?

36. Suly earned an 87 on her first test. She needs a total of 140 points on her first two tests to pass the class. What score must Suly make on her second test to ensure that she passes the class?

37. Reginald's cement truck can travel up to 300 miles on a single tank of gas. Reginald has driven 246 miles so far today, and now he has to make a delivery to a construction site that is 30 miles away. Write and solve an inequality to determine whether Reginald will be able to get to the construction site and back without having to fill his gas tank.

LINK **Sports**

The Global Challenge 2004–2005 began on October 31, 2004, and ended July 2005.

Compare. Write < or >.

38. 52 − 37 ■ 14 **39.** 8(7) ■ 54 **40.** 2 − 7 ■ −10

41. −5(7) ■ −30 **42.** 15 + (−7) ■ −9 **43.** −23 + (−15) ■ −39

44. Sports After each leg of the Global Challenge 2004–2005 yacht race, the yachts are given points for that leg. Through the first four legs, the *BP Explorer* led the *Team Save the Children* by as many as 9 points in a leg. If the *Team Save the Children's* lowest score for a leg of the race was 4 points, at least how many points did the *BP Explorer* score in its best of the first 4 legs?

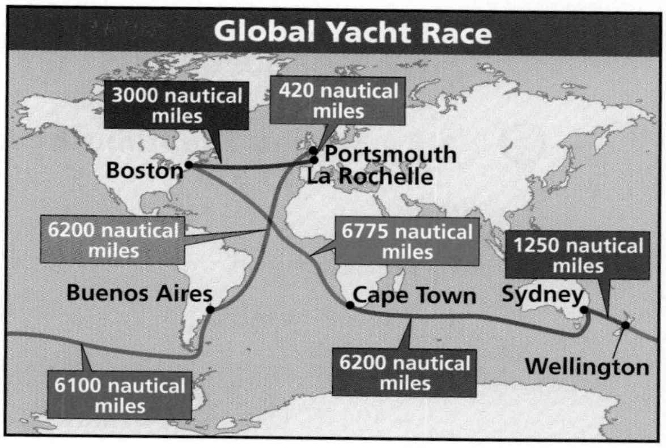

Solve and graph each inequality.

45. $-21 + b \geq 13$ **46.** $p - 54 < -21$ **47.** $q + 13 \geq -22$ **48.** $25 + y > -13$

49. $p - 1 \leq -17$ **50.** $10 + k > -22$ **51.** $y - 2 \geq -6$ **52.** $z + 4 < -5$

53. Write a Problem The weight limit for an elevator is 2500 pounds. Passengers and cargo weighing a total of 2342 pounds are already on the elevator. Write and solve a problem to find the maximum additional weight the elevator can carry.

54. Write About It In mathematics, the conventional way to write an inequality is with the variable on the left, such as $x > 5$. Explain how to rewrite the inequality $4 \leq x$ in the conventional way.

55. Challenge The inequality $3 \leq x < 5$ means both $3 \leq x$ and $x < 5$ are true at the same time. Solve and graph $6 < x \leq 12$.

Test Prep and Spiral Review

56. Short Answer Solve $x + 7 < 15$.

57. Multiple Choice Which number is NOT a solution of $n - 7 < 1$?

Ⓐ 2 Ⓑ 4 Ⓒ 6 Ⓓ 8

Write each set of integers in order from least to greatest. (Lesson 1-3)

58. −22, −18, −35 **59.** 1, −2, 0, 3 **60.** −17, −22, −29 **61.** −15, 0, −23

Solve each equation. (Lesson 1-8)

62. $7x = -45.5$ **63.** $\frac{x}{6} = 11.2$ **64.** $-1{,}032 = -129x$ **65.** $14y = -42$

CHAPTER 1

READY TO GO ON?

SECTION 1B

Quiz for Lessons 1-7 Through 1-9

1-7 Solving Equations by Adding or Subtracting

Solve.

1. $p - 12 = -5$
2. $w + (-9) = 14$
3. $t + (-14) = 8$
4. $23 + k = -5$
5. $-52 + p = 17$
6. $y - (-6) = -74$
7. The approximate surface temperature of Pluto, the coldest planet, is -391°F. This is approximately 1255 degrees cooler than the approximate surface temperature of Venus, the hottest planet. What is the approximate surface temperature of Venus?

1-8 Solving Equations by Multiplying or Dividing

Solve.

8. $\frac{x}{6} = -48$
9. $3x = 21$
10. $14y = -84$
11. $\frac{y}{12} = -72$
12. $-5p = 75$
13. $\frac{r}{-7} = 3$
14. $\frac{d}{12} = -10$
15. $8y = -96$
16. Ahmed's baseball card collection consists of 228 cards. This is 4 times as many cards as Ming has. How many baseball cards are in Ming's collection?
17. The College of Liberal Arts at Middletown University has 342 students. This is $\frac{1}{8}$ the size of the entire student body. How many students attend Middletown University?

1-9 Introduction to Inequalities

Solve and graph each inequality.

18. $t - 12 < -4$
19. $x + 3 \geq 9$
20. $x - 7 > -91$
21. $u + 88 \geq -107$
22. $p - 17 < 74$
23. $76 + v \leq -18$
24. Barbara is saving money so that she can buy a new CD player and a couple of CDs. She knows that she needs at least \$60, and she has saved \$22 so far. At least how much more money does Barbara need to save?
25. Montel is playing in a four-round golf tournament. He estimates that he needs to have a score of at most -3 after the second round in order to make the cut and play the third and fourth rounds. If Montel scored $+4$ in the first round of the tournament, how high can he score at most in the second round and still make the cut?

MULTI-STEP TEST PREP

Have a Ball A physical education class is playing a variation of basketball. When a team makes a basket from inside the three-point line, the team scores a "Climb" (C), or 2 points. When a team makes a basket from outside the three-point line, the other team scores a "Slide" (S), or -1 point.

Game Results	
Team 1	**Team 2**
C	C
S	C
S	C
S	S
S	S
C	S
C	S
C	S

1. During the first 20 minutes of the game, a team scores the following: C, C, S, S, C, S, C, C, and S. Evaluate the expression $2 + 2 + (-1) + (-1) + 2 + (-1) + 2 + 2 + (-1)$ to determine the team's score.
2. The points scored by two teams during a game are shown in the table. Which team won the game? What was the difference in the teams' scores?
3. Diego's team scores 3 Climbs and 2 Slides, but not necessarily in that order. Find his team's score by substituting $S = -1$ and $C = 2$ in the expression $3C + 2S$.
4. After four consecutive baskets are made, Leann's team's score is -8. After the next basket is made, the team's score is -6. Write and solve an equation for the last made basket.
5. Daryl's team finishes the game with a score of 12. If his team scored 9 times, how many Climbs did the team score?
6. Is it possible to finish with a score of 2 after five baskets are made? Explain your reasoning.

Game Time

Math Magic

You can guess what your friends are thinking by learning to "operate" your way into their minds! For example, try this math magic trick.

Think of a number. Multiply the number by 8, divide by 2, add 5, and then subtract 4 times the original number.

No matter what number you choose, the answer will always be 5. Try another number and see. You can use what you know about variables to prove it. Here's how:

	What you say:	What the person thinks:	What the math is:
Step 1:	Pick any number.	6 (for example)	n
Step 2:	Multiply by **8**.	$8(6) = 48$	$8n$
Step 3:	Divide by **2**.	$48 \div 2 = 24$	$8n \div 2 = 4n$
Step 4:	Add **5**.	$24 + 5 = 29$	$4n + 5$
Step 5:	Subtract **4** times the original number.	$29 - 4(6) = 29 - 24 = 5$	$4n + 5 - 4n = 5$

Invent your own math magic trick that has at least five steps. Show an example using numbers and variables. Try it on a friend!

Crazy Cubes

This game, called The Great Tantalizer around 1900, was reintroduced in the 1960s as "Instant Insanity™." Make four cubes with paper and tape, numbering each side as shown.

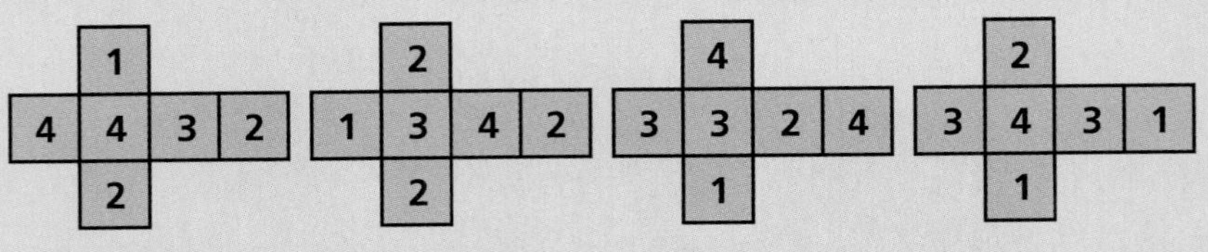

The goal is to line up the cubes so that 1, 2, 3, and 4 can be seen along the top, bottom, front, and back of the row of cubes. They can be in any order, and the numbers do not have to be right-side up.

A complete copy of the rules is available online.

go.hrw.com
Game Time Extra
KEYWORD: MT7 Games

FOLDNOTES

It's in the Bag!

Materials
- **sheet of decorative paper ($8\frac{1}{2}$ by 11 in.)**
- **ruler**
- **pencil**
- **scissors**
- **glue**
- **markers**

PROJECT Note-Taking Taking Shape

Make this notebook to help you organize examples of algebraic expressions.

Directions

1. Hold the sheet of paper horizontally. Make two vertical lines $3\frac{5}{8}$ in. from each end of the sheet.

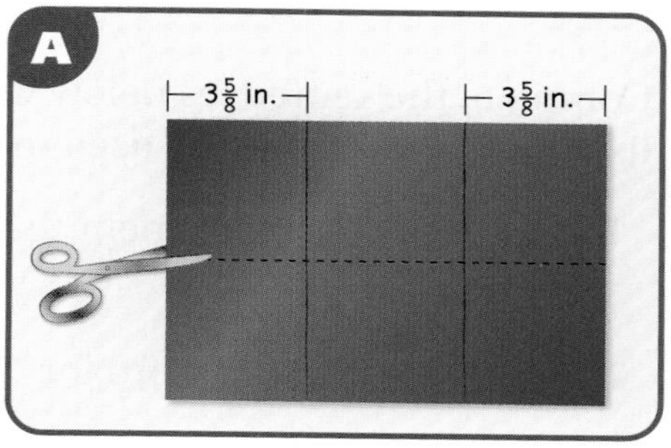

2. Fold the sheet in half lengthwise. Then cut it in half by cutting along the fold. **Figure A**

3. On one half of the sheet, cut out rectangles A and B. On the other half, cut out rectangles C and D. **Figure B**

   Rectangle A: $\frac{3}{4}$ in. by $3\frac{5}{8}$ in.
   Rectangle B: $1\frac{1}{2}$ in. by $3\frac{5}{8}$ in.
   Rectangle C: $2\frac{1}{4}$ in. by $3\frac{5}{8}$ in.
   Rectangle D: 3 in. by $3\frac{5}{8}$ in.

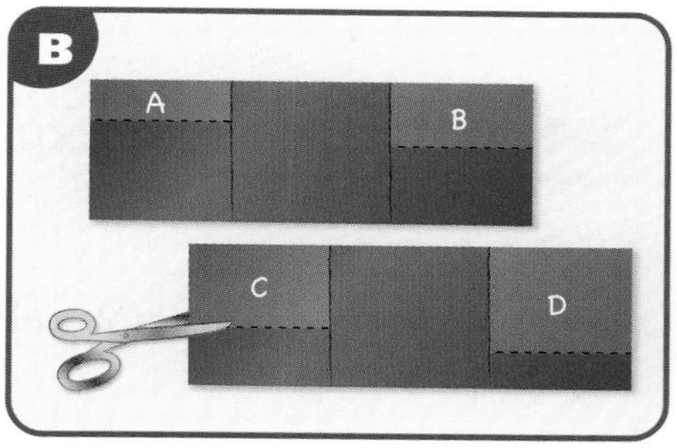

4. Place the piece with the taller rectangular panels on top of the piece with the shorter rectangular panels. Glue the middle sections of the two pieces together. **Figure C**

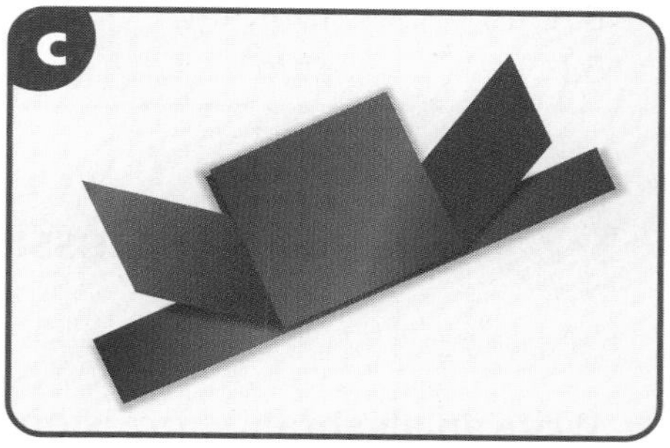

5. Fold the four panels into the center, starting with the tallest panel and working your way down to the shortest.

Taking Note of the Math

Write "Addition," "Subtraction," "Multiplication," and "Division" on the tabs at the top of each panel. Use the space below the name of each operation to list examples of verbal, numerical, and algebraic expressions.

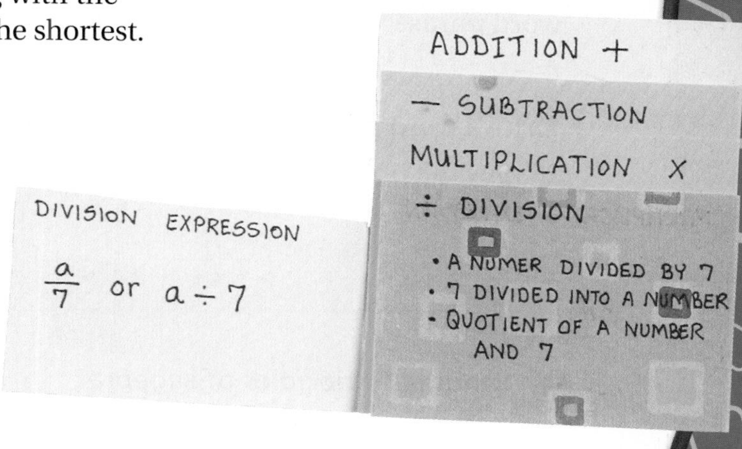

ADDITION +
− SUBTRACTION
MULTIPLICATION X
÷ DIVISION
DIVISION EXPRESSION
a/7 or a ÷ 7
• A NUMER DIVIDED BY 7
• 7 DIVIDED INTO A NUMBER
• QUOTIENT OF A NUMBER AND 7

CHAPTER 1

Study Guide: Review

Vocabulary

absolute value 15
additive inverse 14
algebraic expression 6
algebraic inequality 44
coefficient 6
constant 6
equation 34
evaluate 6
inequality 44
integer 14
inverse operation 34
opposite 14
solution set 44
substitute 6
variable 6

Complete the sentences below with vocabulary words from the list above. Words may be used more than once.

1. An ___?___ is a statement that two expressions have the same value.
2. ___?___ is another word for "additive inverse."
3. The ___?___ of 3 is 3.

1-1 Variables and Expressions (pp. 6–9)

EXAMPLE

■ **Evaluate $4x + 9y$ for $x = 2$ and $y = 5$.**

$4x + 9y$
$4(2) + 9(5)$ *Substitute 2 for x and 5 for y.*
$8 + 45$ *Multiply.*
53 *Add.*

EXERCISES

Evaluate each expression.

4. $9a + 7b$ for $a = 7$ and $b = 12$
5. $17m - 3n$ for $m = 10$ and $n = 6$
6. $1.5r + 19s$ for $r = 8$ and $s = 14$

1-2 Algebraic Expressions (pp. 10–13)

EXAMPLE

■ **Write an algebraic expression for the word phrase "2 less than a number n."**

$n - 2$ *Write as subtraction.*

■ **Write a word phrase for $25 + 13t$.**

25 plus the product of 13 and t

EXERCISES

Write an algebraic expression for each phrase.

7. twice the sum of k and 4
8. 5 more than the product of 4 and t

Write a word phrase for each algebraic expression.

9. $5b - 10$
10. $32 + 23s$
11. $\frac{10}{r} - 12$
12. $16 + \frac{y}{8}$

1-3 Integers and Absolute Value (pp. 14–17)

EXAMPLE

■ **Evaluate the expression.** $|-9| - |3|$

$\|-9\| - \|3\|$	
$9 - 3$	*$\|9\| = 9$ and $\|3\| = 3$*
6	*Subtract.*

EXERCISES

Evaluate each expression.

13. $|7 - 6|$
14. $|-8| + |-7|$
15. $|15| + |19|$
16. $|14 + 7|$
17. $|16 - 20|$
18. $|-7| - |-8|$

1-4 Adding Integers (pp. 18–21)

EXAMPLE

■ **Add.**

$-8 + 2$	*Find the difference of $\|-8\|$ and $\|2\|$.*
-6	*$8 > 2$; use the sign of the 8.*

■ **Evaluate.**

$-4 + a$ for $a = -7$

$-4 + (-7)$	*Substitute.*
-11	*Same sign*

EXERCISES

Add.

19. $-6 + 4$
20. $-3 + (-9)$
21. $4 + (-7)$
22. $4 + (-3)$
23. $-11 + (-5) + (-8)$

Evaluate.

24. $k + 11$ for $k = -3$
25. $-6 + m$ for $m = -2$

1-5 Subtracting Integers (pp. 22–25)

EXAMPLE

■ **Subtract.**

$-3 - (-5)$	
$-3 + 5$	*Add the opposite of −5.*
2	*$5 > 3$; use the sign of the 5.*

■ **Evaluate.**

$-9 - d$ for $d = 2$

$-9 - 2$	*Substitute.*
$-9 + (-2)$	*Add the opposite of 2.*
-11	*Same sign*

EXERCISES

Subtract.

26. $-7 - 9$
27. $8 - (-9)$
28. $-2 - (-5)$
29. $13 - (-2)$
30. $-5 - 17$
31. $16 - 20$

Evaluate.

32. $9 - h$ for $h = -7$
33. $12 - z$ for $z = 17$

1-6 Multiplying and Dividing Integers (pp. 26–29)

EXAMPLE

Multiply or divide.

■ $4(-9)$	*The signs are **different.***
-36	*The answer is **negative.***
■ $\frac{-33}{-11}$	*The signs are the **same.***
3	*The answer is **positive.***

EXERCISES

Multiply or divide.

34. $7(-5)$
35. $\frac{72}{-4}$
36. $-4(-13)$
37. $\frac{-100}{-4}$
38. $8(-3)(-5)$
39. $\frac{10(-5)}{-25}$

1-7 Solving Equations by Adding or Subtracting (pp. 34–38)

EXAMPLE

Solve.

■ $x + 7 = 12$
$\quad -7 \quad -7$ *Subtract 7 from both sides.*
$x + 0 = 5$
$x = 5$ *Identity Property of Zero*

■ $y - 3 = 1.5$
$\quad +3 \quad +3$ *Add 3 to both sides.*
$y + 0 = 4.5$
$y = 4.5$ *Identity Property of Zero*

EXERCISES

Solve and check.

40. $z - 9 = 14$
41. $t + 3 = 11$
42. $6 + k = 21$
43. $x + 2 = -13$

Write an equation and solve.

44. A polar bear weighs 715 lb, which is 585 lb less than a sea cow. How much does the sea cow weigh?

45. The Mojave Desert, at 15,000 mi^2, is 11,700 mi^2 larger than Death Valley. What is the area of Death Valley?

1-8 Solving Equations by Multiplying or Dividing (pp. 39–43)

EXAMPLE

Solve.

■ $4h = 24$
$\frac{4h}{4} = \frac{24}{4}$ *Divide both sides by 4.*
$1h = 6$ *$4 \div 4 = 1$*
$h = 6$ *$1 \cdot h = h$*

■ $\frac{t}{4} = 16$
$4 \cdot \frac{t}{4} = 4 \cdot 16$ *Multiply both sides by 4.*
$1t = 64$ *$4 \div 4 = 1$*
$t = 64$ *$1 \cdot t = t$*

EXERCISES

Solve and check.

46. $-7g = 56$
47. $108 = 12k$
48. $0.1p = -8$
49. $-\frac{w}{4} = 12$
50. $-20 = \frac{y}{2}$
51. $\frac{z}{24} = 8$

52. The Lewis family drove 235 mi toward their destination. This was $\frac{1}{3}$ of the total distance. What was the total distance?

53. Luz will pay a total of \$9360 on her car loan. Her monthly payment is \$390. For how many months is the loan?

1-9 Introduction to Inequalities (pp. 44–47)

EXAMPLE

Solve and graph.

■ $x + 5 \leq 8$
$\quad -5 \quad -5$
$x \leq 3$

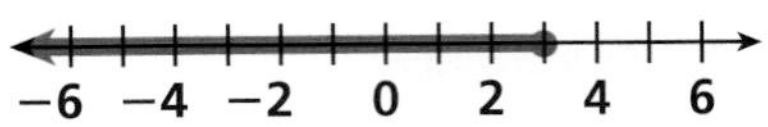

■ $w - 3 \geq 18$
$\quad +3 \quad +3$
$w \geq 21$

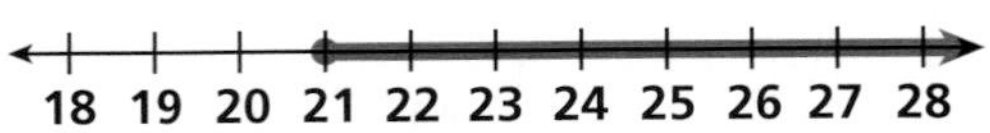

EXERCISES

Solve and graph.

54. $h - 3 < 7$
55. $y - 2 > 5$
56. $2 + x \geq 8$
57. $w + 2 \geq 4$
58. $x - 3 \leq 1$
59. $3 + q \leq 0$
60. $4 + p < 2$
61. $m - 2 \leq 46$
62. $y + 4 > 4$
63. $4 < x + 1$
64. $2 < y - 4$
65. $8 \geq 4 + x$

CHAPTER TEST

CHAPTER 1

Evaluate each expression for the given value of the variable.

1. $16 - p$ for $p = -12$
2. $t - 7$ for $t = -14$
3. $13 - x + (-2)$ for $x = 4$
4. $-8y + 27$ for $y = -9$

Write an algebraic expression for each word phrase.

5. 15 more than the product of 33 and y
6. 18 less than the quotient of x and 7
7. 4 times the sum of -7 and h
8. 18 divided by the difference of t and 9

Write each set of integers in order from least to greatest.

9. $-7, 7, 2, -3, 0, 1$
10. $-12, -45, 13, 100, 20$
11. $120, -7, 54, 41, 7$
12. $-41, -78, 5, 0, 2$
13. $-25, -8, -70, -2, -13$
14. $-100, 12, 9, 0, -23$

Perform the given operations.

15. $-9 + (-12)$
16. $11 - 17$
17. $6(-22)$
18. $(-20) \div (-4)$
19. $42 - (-5)$
20. $-18 \div 3$
21. $-9 - (-13)$
22. $12 - (-6) + (-5)$
23. $-2(-21 - 17)$
24. $(-15 + 3) \div (-4)$
25. $(54 \div 6) - (-1)$
26. $-(16 + 4) - 20$
27. The temperature on a winter day increased 37°F. If the beginning temperature was −9°F, what was the temperature after the increase?

Solve.

28. $y + 19 = 9$
29. $4z = -32$
30. $52 = p - 3$
31. $\frac{w}{3} = 9$
32. $\frac{t}{7} = 12$
33. $-9p = -27$
34. $\frac{q}{-5} = 18$
35. $\frac{g}{4} = -11$
36. The O'Malley family is driving cross-country to see their cousins. So far, they have traveled 275 miles. This is $\frac{1}{5}$ of the way to their cousins' house. How far do the O'Malleys live from their cousins?

Solve and graph each inequality.

37. $x + 7 > -4$
38. $n - 14 \le -3$
39. $74 + p \ge -26$
40. $-4 + t < 7$
41. $z - 52 \le -18$
42. $p + 22 > 8$
43. $-4 + u \le -20$
44. $8 + z > -6$
45. The choir is selling tickets to the school's fall musical. The auditorium can hold at most 435 people. So far, 237 tickets have been sold. At most, how many more tickets can be sold?
46. Anthony is working on a term paper for his literature class. The teacher wants the papers to be at least 1000 words long. So far, Anthony's paper is 698 words long. At least how many more words must Anthony's paper have?

TEST TACKLER

Standardized Test Strategies

Multiple Choice: Eliminate Answer Choices

With some multiple-choice test items, you can use logical reasoning or estimation to eliminate some of the answer choices. Test writers often create the incorrect choices, called distracters, using common student errors.

EXAMPLE 1

Which choice represents "4 times the sum of x and 8"?

Ⓐ $4 \cdot (x + 8)$	Ⓒ $4 \cdot x + 8$
Ⓑ $4 \cdot (x - 8)$	Ⓓ $4 \div (x + 8)$

Read the question. Then try to eliminate some of the answer choices.

Use logical reasoning.

Times means "to multiply," and *sum* means "to add." You can eliminate any option without a multiplication symbol and an addition symbol. You can eliminate B and D.

The sum of x and 8 is being multiplied by 4, so you need to add before you multiply. Because multiplication comes before addition in the order of operations, $x + 8$ should be in parentheses. The correct answer is A.

EXAMPLE 2

Which value for k is a solution to the equation $k - 3.5 = 12$?

Ⓕ $k = 8.5$	Ⓗ $k = 42$
Ⓖ $k = 15.5$	Ⓙ $k = 47$

Read the question. Then try to eliminate some of the answer choices.

Use estimation.

You can eliminate H and J immediately because they are too large. Estimate by rounding 3.5 to 4. If $x = 47$, then $47 - 4 = 43$. This is not even close to 12. Similarly, if $x = 42$, then $42 - 4 = 38$, which is also too large to be correct.

Choice F is called a *distracter* because it was created using a common student error, subtracting 3.5 from 12 instead of adding 3.5 to 12. Therefore, F is also incorrect. The correct answer is G.

HOT TIP! Even if the answer you calculated is an answer choice, it may not be the correct answer. It could be a distracter. Always check your answers!

Read each test problem and answer the questions that follow.

Item A
The table shows average high temperatures for Nome, Alaska. Which answer choice lists the months in order from coolest to warmest?

Month	Temperature (°C)
Jan.	−11
Feb	−10
Mar	−8
Apr	−3
May	6
Jun	12
Jul	15
Aug	13
Sep	9
Oct	1
Nov	−5
Dec	−9

(A) Jul, Aug, Jun, Sep, May, Oct, Apr, Nov, Mar, Dec, Feb, Jan

(B) Jul, Jun, Aug, Jan, Feb, Sep, Dec, Mar, May, Nov, Apr, Oct

(C) Jan, Apr, Jun, Jul, Sep, Nov, Feb, Mar, May, Jul, Sep, Nov

(D) Jan, Feb, Dec, Mar, Nov, Apr, Oct, May, Sep, Jun, Aug, Jul

1. Which two choices can you eliminate by using logic? Explain your reasoning.
2. What common error does choice A represent?

Item B
Which value for p is a solution to the equation $p + 5.2 = 15$?

(F) $p = -30.2$ (H) $p = 20.2$

(G) $p = 9.8$ (J) $p = 78$

3. Which choices can you eliminate by using estimation? Explain your reasoning.
4. What common error does choice H represent?

Item C
Which inequality corresponds to the graph below?

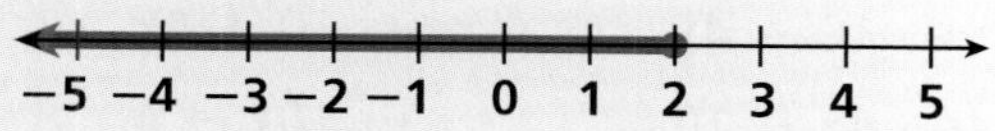

(A) $x < 2$ (C) $x > 2$

(B) $x \leq 2$ (D) $x \geq 2$

5. Is $x = 2$ a solution to the inequality? How do you know?
6. Which two choices can you eliminate by using the answer in Problem 5?

Item D
Which word phrase can be translated into the algebraic expression $2x - 6$?

(F) six more than twice a number

(G) the sum of twice a number and six

(H) twice the difference of a number and six

(J) six less than twice a number

7. Can you eliminate any of the choices immediately by using logic? Explain your reasoning.
8. Describe how you can determine the correct answer from the remaining choices.

CHAPTER 1

STANDARDIZED TEST PREP

go.hrw.com
State Test Practice Online
KEYWORD: MT7 TestPrep

Cumulative Assessment, Chapter 1

Multiple Choice

1. Which expression has a value of 12 when $x = 2$, $y = 3$, and $z = 1$?

(A) $3xyz$ (C) $3xz + 2y$

(B) $2x + 3y + z$ (D) $4xyz + 2$

2. The word phrase "10 less than 4 times a number" can be represented by which expression?

(F) $10 - 4x$ (H) $10 + 4x$

(G) $4x - 10$ (J) $10x - 4$

3. A copy center prints c copies at a cost of \$0.10 per copy. What is the total cost of the copies?

(A) $0.10c$ (C) $\frac{0.10}{c}$

(B) $0.10 + c$ (D) $\frac{c}{0.10}$

4. Which value of x makes the equation $x - 15 = 20$ true?

(F) $x = 5$ (H) $x = 35$

(G) $x = 30$ (J) $x = 300$

5. What is the solution of $s + 12 = 16$?

(A) $s = 4$ (C) $s = 28$

(B) $s = 8$ (D) $s = 192$

6. Carlos owes his mother money. His paycheck is \$105. If he pays his mother the money he owes her, he will have \$63 left. Which equation represents this situation?

(F) $-x + 63 = 105$

(G) $x - 63 = 105$

(H) $105 - x = 63$

(J) $x - 105 = 63$

7. To ride a roller coaster at the local amusement park, a person must be at least 48 inches tall. Which inequality represents this requirement?

(A) $h < 48$ (C) $h \leq 48$

(B) $h > 48$ (D) $h \geq 48$

8. Which addition equation represents the number line diagram below?

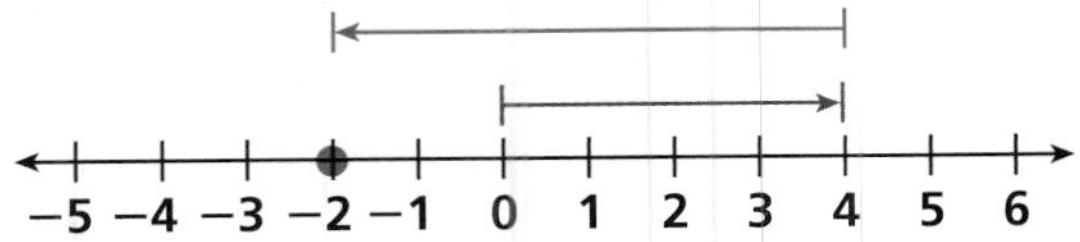

(F) $4 + (-2) = 2$

(G) $4 + (-6) = -2$

(H) $4 + 6 = 10$

(J) $-4 + (-6) = -10$

9. Which equation has the solution $x = 16$?

(A) $x - 16 = 4$ (C) $2x = 32$

(B) $\frac{x}{2} = 32$ (D) $x + 2 = 16$

10. Which inequality is represented by this graph?

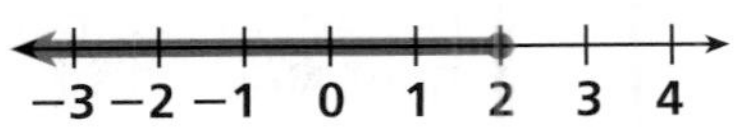

(F) $x < 2$ (H) $x \leq 2$

(G) $x > 2$ (J) $x \geq 2$

11. A scuba diver swimming at a depth of 35 ft below sea level, or −35 ft, dives another 15 ft deeper to get a closer look at a fish. What is the diver's new depth?

(A) −50 ft (C) 20 ft

(B) −20 ft (D) 50 ft

Standardized Test Prep

HOT TIP! The incorrect answer choices in a multiple-choice test item are called distracters. They are the results of common mistakes. Be sure to check your work!

12. Which set of numbers is in order from least to greatest?

    (F) $-15, 13, -10$
    (G) $13, -10, -15$
    (H) $-10, -15, 13$
    (J) $-15, -10, 13$

13. Which expression is equivalent to $|9 - (-5)|$?

    (A) $|9| + |-5|$
    (B) $|9| - |-5|$
    (C) -14
    (D) 4

Gridded Response

14. What is the value of the expression $2xy - y$ when $x = 3$ and $y = 5$?

15. What is the solution to the equation $x - 27 = -16$?

16. Evaluate the expression $m + 11 + (-3)$ for $m = -5$.

17. Nora collects 15 magazines every week for 6 weeks. She plans to use the magazines for an art project. After 6 weeks, however, she still does not have enough magazines to complete the project. If Nora needs 20 more magazines to complete the project, how many total magazines does she need?

18. Patricia works twice as many days as Laura works each month. Laura works 3 more days than Jaime. If Jaime works 10 days each month, how many days does Patricia work?

19. On a trip, the Parker family stopped to rest after covering $\frac{3}{5}$ of the distance. They still had 750 miles to travel to complete their trip. How far did they travel?

Short Response

20. The Hun family plans to visit the Sea Center. Tickets cost $7 each.
    a. Write an expression to represent the cost of admission for any number of tickets t.
    b. How much will it cost the Hun family if they buy 6 tickets? Explain your answer.
    c. Mrs. Hun pays with three $20 bills. How much change will she get back? Explain your answer.

21. It costs $0.15 per word to place an advertisement in the school newspaper. Let w represent the number of words in an advertisement and C represent the cost of the advertisement.
    a. Write an equation that relates the number of words to the cost of the advertisement.
    b. If Bernard has $12.00, how many words can he use in his advertisement? Explain your answer.

Extended Response

22. **Statement 1:** Currently there are 8 more students in the student council than there are officers. There are 18 students total in the student council.

    Statement 2: In addition, there have to be at least 4 officers in the council.

    a. Write an equation to represent Statement 1 and an inequality to represent Statement 2.
    b. Solve the equation, and plot the solution to the equation on a number line.
    c. Graph the solution set to the inequality.
    d. Explain what the solution sets have in common, and then explain how they are different.

CHAPTER 2

Rational Numbers

2A Rational Number Operations

- **2-1** Rational Numbers
- **2-2** Comparing and Ordering Rational Numbers
- **2-3** Adding and Subtracting Rational Numbers
- **2-4** Multiplying Rational Numbers
- **2-5** Dividing Rational Numbers
- **2-6** Adding and Subtracting with Unlike Denominators
- **LAB** Add and Subtract Fractions

2B Equations with Rational Numbers

- **2-7** Solving Equations with Rational Numbers
- **LAB** Model Two-Step Equations
- **2-8** Solving Two-Step Equations

MULTI-STEP TEST PREP

go.hrw.com
Chapter Project Online
KEYWORD: MT7 Ch2

Nutrient Requirements

Nutrient	Girls and Boys 9–13 Years	Girls 14–18 Years	Boys 14–18 Years
Protein (g)	46	55	66
Iron (mg)	8	15	11
Calcium (mg)	1300	1300	1300
Calories	2200–2500	2200	3000

The table lists recommended nutrient requirements for boys and girls age 9–18.

Career *Nutritionist*

Nutritionists use their knowledge of the nutrient content of food to help promote healthful eating. Together with food scientists they develop guidelines for people who must follow medically necessary diets as well as for people who just want to improve their eating habits.

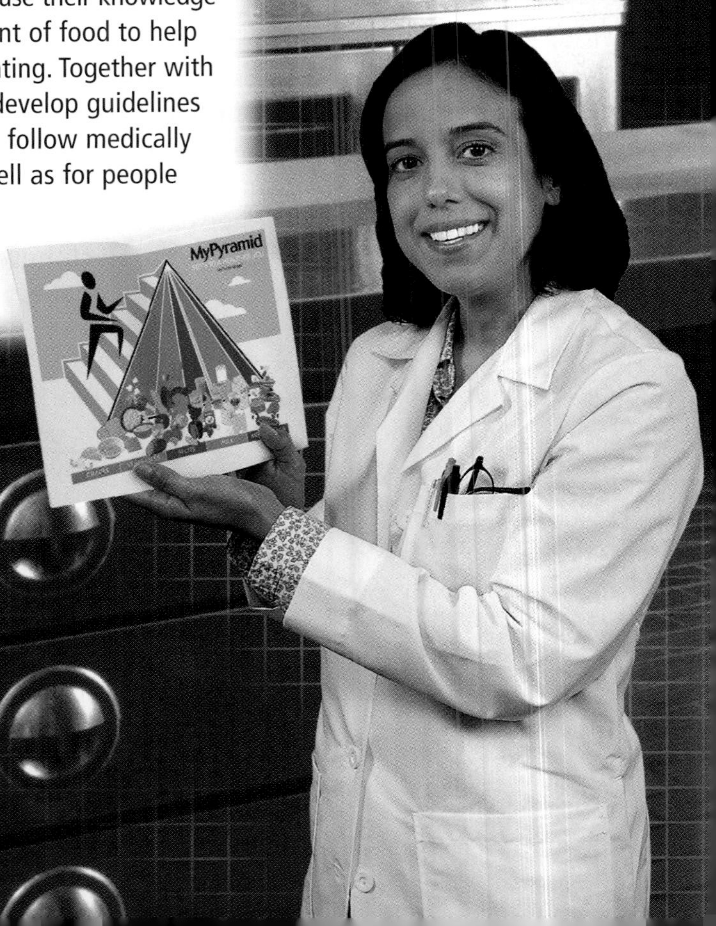

ARE YOU READY?

Vocabulary

Choose the best term from the list to complete each sentence.

equivalent fraction
fraction
improper fraction
mixed number
proper fraction

1. A number that consists of a whole number and a fraction is called a(n) __?__.
2. A(n) __?__ is a number that represents a part of a whole.
3. A fraction whose absolute value is greater than 1 is called a(n) __?__, and a fraction whose absolute value is between 0 and 1 is called a(n) __?__.
4. A(n) __?__ names the same value.

Complete these exercises to review skills you will need for this chapter.

Model Fractions

Write a fraction to represent the shaded portion of each diagram.

5. 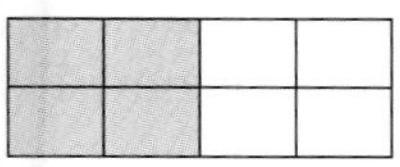

6. 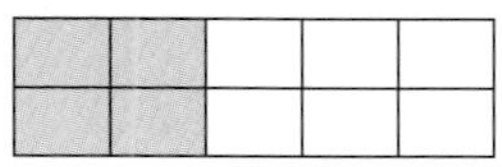

7. 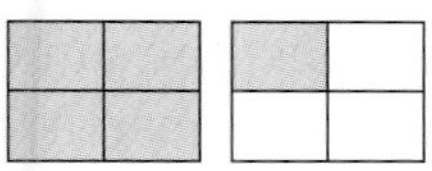

8. 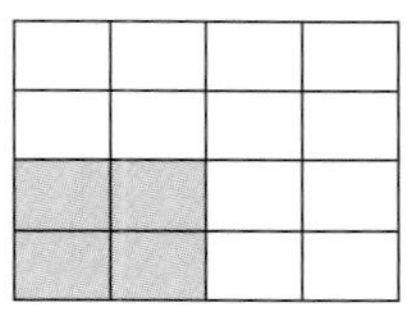

Write a Fraction as a Mixed Number

Write each improper fraction as a mixed number.

9. $\frac{22}{7}$ **10.** $\frac{18}{5}$ **11.** $\frac{104}{25}$ **12.** $\frac{65}{9}$ **13.** $\frac{37}{3}$

Write a Mixed Number as a Fraction

Write each mixed number as an improper fraction.

14. $7\frac{1}{4}$ **15.** $10\frac{3}{7}$ **16.** $5\frac{3}{8}$ **17.** $11\frac{1}{11}$ **18.** $3\frac{5}{6}$

Write Equivalent Fractions

Supply the missing information.

19. $\frac{3}{8} = \frac{\blacksquare}{24}$ **20.** $\frac{5}{13} = \frac{\blacksquare}{52}$ **21.** $\frac{7}{12} = \frac{\blacksquare}{36}$ **22.** $\frac{8}{15} = \frac{\blacksquare}{45}$ **23.** $\frac{3}{5} = \frac{\blacksquare}{75}$

CHAPTER 2

Study Guide: Preview

Where You've Been

Previously, you

- compared and ordered positive rational numbers.
- added, subtracted, multiplied, and divided integers.
- used models to solve equations.

In This Chapter

You will study

- comparing and ordering positive and negative fractions and decimals.
- using appropriate operations to solve problems involving fractions and decimals.
- finding solutions to application problems using equations.
- solving two-step equations.

Where You're Going

You can use the skills learned in this chapter

- to compare and manipulate measurements.
- to find the size of a fraction of a group or an item.
- to solve more-complicated equations in future math courses.

Key Vocabulary/Vocabulario

least common denominator (LCD)	mínimo común denominador (mcd)
rational number	número racional
reciprocal	recíproco
relatively prime	primos relativos

Vocabulary Connections

To become familiar with some of the vocabulary terms in the chapter, consider the following. You may refer to the chapter, the glossary, or a dictionary if you like.

1. The word *rational* has as its root the word *ratio* and sounds somewhat like the word *fraction*. What do you think a **rational number** is in math?
2. The word *least* means "smallest," and the word *common* means "the same." What do you think these words mean in combination in **least common denominator**?
3. The word *relative* means "in relation to each other." What do you think **relatively prime** numbers are?

Study Guide: Preview

Writing Strategy: Translate Between Words and Math

When reading a real-world math problem, look for key words to help you translate between the words and the math.

There are several different ways to indicate a mathematical operation in words.

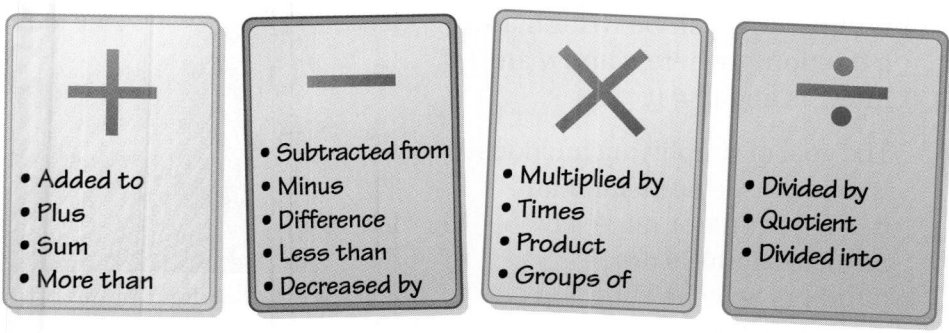

+
- Added to
- Plus
- Sum
- More than

−
- Subtracted from
- Minus
- Difference
- Less than
- Decreased by

×
- Multiplied by
- Times
- Product
- Groups of

÷
- Divided by
- Quotient
- Divided into

In the problem below, use the highlighted terms to translate the words into math.

The Montez family went to the state fair over the weekend. They spent \$52.50 on rides, food, and drinks, in addition to the \$5.50-per-person price of admission. How much did the Montez family spend at the fair?

They spent \$52.50 **in addition to** \$5.50 **per** **person**.

Let p represent the number of people.

$$\$52.50 \quad + \quad \$5.50 \quad \times \quad p \quad = 52.5 + 5.5p$$

Try This

Identify the mathematical operation described by the key terms in each statement. Explain your choice.

1. The male calf weighs 0.55 pounds less than the female calf.
2. Bob has 9 more books than Kerri.
3. The number of treats is divided by the number of students.
4. The rate is \$15 plus two times the cost of the paint.

2-1 Rational Numbers

Learn to write rational numbers in equivalent forms.

Vocabulary

rational number

relatively prime

In 2005, there were 325 NCAA Division I women's basketball teams. At the end of the season, 64 teams were selected for the women's NCAA basketball tournament. Only $\frac{64}{325}$ of the teams qualified for the tournament.

The Baylor women's basketball team won its first national championship in 2005.

A **rational number** is any number that can be written as a fraction $\frac{n}{d}$, where n and d are integers and $d \neq 0$.

The goal of simplifying fractions is to make the numerator and the denominator *relatively prime.* **Relatively prime** numbers have no common factors other than 1.

You can often simplify fractions by dividing both the numerator and denominator by the same nonzero integer. You can simplify the fraction $\frac{12}{15}$ to $\frac{4}{5}$ by dividing both the numerator and denominator by 3.

12 of the 15 boxes are shaded.

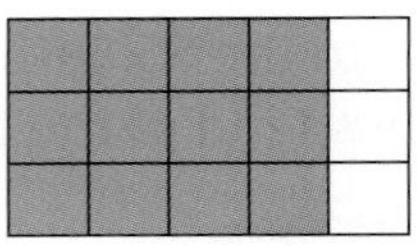

$$\frac{12 \div 3}{15 \div 3} = \frac{4}{5}$$

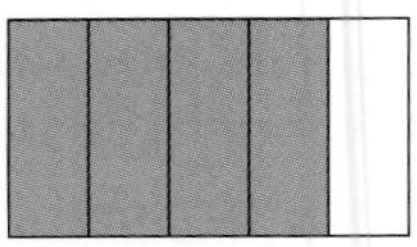

4 of the 5 boxes are shaded.

The same total area is shaded.

EXAMPLE 1 Simplifying Fractions

Remember!

$\frac{0}{a} = 0$ for $a \neq 0$

$\frac{a}{a} = 1$ for $a \neq 0$

$\frac{-7}{8} = \frac{7}{-8} = -\frac{7}{8}$

Simplify.

A $\frac{9}{55}$

$9 = 3 \cdot 3$, $55 = 5 \cdot 11$; there are no common factors.

$\frac{9}{55} = \frac{9}{55}$ *9 and 55 are relatively prime.*

B $\frac{-24}{32}$

$\frac{-24}{32} = \frac{-24 \div 8}{32 \div 8}$ *$24 = (2 \cdot 2 \cdot 2) \cdot 3$, $32 = (2 \cdot 2 \cdot 2) \cdot 2 \cdot 2$ 8 is a common factor.*

$= \frac{-3}{4}$, or $-\frac{3}{4}$ *Divide the numerator and denominator by 8.*

Writing Math

A repeating decimal can be written with a bar over the digits that repeat. So $0.13333\ldots = 0.1\overline{3}$.

Decimals that terminate or repeat are rational numbers.

Rational Number	Description	Written as a Fraction
-3.2	Terminating decimal	$-\frac{32}{10}$
$0.1\overline{3}$	Repeating decimal	$\frac{2}{15}$

To write a terminating decimal as a fraction, identify the place value of the digit farthest to the right. Then write all of the digits after the decimal point as the numerator with the place value as the denominator.

EXAMPLE 2 Writing Decimals as Fractions

Write each decimal as a fraction in simplest form.

A -5.59

$-5.59 = -5\frac{59}{100}$ *9 is in the hundredths place.*

B 0.5714

$0.5714 = \frac{5714}{10{,}000}$ *4 is in the ten-thousandths place.*

$= \frac{2857}{5000}$ *Simplify by dividing by the common factor 2.*

To write a fraction as a decimal, divide the numerator by the denominator.

EXAMPLE 3 Writing Fractions as Decimals

Write each fraction as a decimal.

A $\frac{5}{4}$

$$\begin{array}{r} 1.25 \\ 4\overline{)5.00} \\ -4 \\ \hline 1\,0 \\ -8 \\ \hline 20 \\ -20 \\ \hline 0 \end{array}$$

The remainder is 0. This is a terminating decimal.

The fraction $\frac{5}{4}$ is equivalent to the decimal 1.25.

B $-\frac{1}{6}$

$$\begin{array}{r} 0.1\overline{6} \\ 6\overline{)1.000} \\ -6 \\ \hline 40 \\ -36 \\ \hline 40 \end{array}$$

Leave the negative sign off while dividing. The pattern repeats.

The fraction $-\frac{1}{6}$ is equivalent to the decimal $-0.1\overline{6}$.

Think and Discuss

1. **Explain** how you can be sure that a fraction is simplified.
2. **Give** the sign of a fraction in which the numerator is negative and the denominator is negative.

2-1 Exercises

go.hrw.com
Homework Help Online
KEYWORD: MT7 2-1
Parent Resources Online
KEYWORD: MT7 Parent

GUIDED PRACTICE

See Example 1

Simplify.

1. $\frac{11}{22}$ **2.** $\frac{6}{10}$ **3.** $-\frac{16}{24}$ **4.** $\frac{14}{25}$ **5.** $\frac{17}{51}$

6. $\frac{57}{69}$ **7.** $-\frac{6}{8}$ **8.** $\frac{9}{28}$ **9.** $\frac{49}{112}$ **10.** $\frac{22}{44}$

See Example 2

Write each decimal as a fraction in simplest form.

11. 0.75 **12.** 1.125 **13.** 0.4 **14.** 0.35

15. −2.2 **16.** 0.625 **17.** 3.21 **18.** −0.3878

See Example 3

Write each fraction as a decimal.

19. $\frac{5}{8}$ **20.** $-\frac{3}{5}$ **21.** $\frac{5}{12}$ **22.** $\frac{1}{4}$ **23.** $\frac{1}{9}$

24. $-\frac{18}{9}$ **25.** $\frac{3}{8}$ **26.** $-\frac{14}{5}$ **27.** $\frac{5}{4}$ **28.** $\frac{2}{3}$

INDEPENDENT PRACTICE

See Example 1

Simplify.

29. $\frac{21}{28}$ **30.** $\frac{25}{65}$ **31.** $-\frac{17}{34}$ **32.** $-\frac{17}{21}$ **33.** $\frac{25}{30}$

34. $\frac{13}{17}$ **35.** $\frac{22}{35}$ **36.** $\frac{64}{76}$ **37.** $-\frac{78}{126}$ **38.** $\frac{14}{22}$

See Example 2

Write each decimal as a fraction in simplest form.

39. 0.6 **40.** 3.5 **41.** 0.72 **42.** −0.183

43. 1.377 **44.** 1.450 **45.** −1.4 **46.** −2.9

See Example 3

Write each fraction as a decimal.

47. $-\frac{3}{8}$ **48.** $\frac{7}{12}$ **49.** $-\frac{9}{5}$ **50.** $\frac{13}{20}$ **51.** $\frac{8}{5}$

52. $\frac{18}{40}$ **53.** $-\frac{23}{5}$ **54.** $\frac{28}{25}$ **55.** $\frac{4}{3}$ **56.** $-\frac{7}{4}$

PRACTICE AND PROBLEM SOLVING

Extra Practice
See page 784.

57. Make up a fraction that cannot be simplified and has 36 as its denominator.

58. Make up a fraction that cannot be simplified and has 24 as its denominator.

59. **Sports** The thickness of a surfboard is often matched to the weight of the rider. For example, a person weighing 170 pounds might need a surfboard that is 3.375 inches thick. Write 3.375 as a fraction in simplest form.

60. Bondi weighed his mobile phone and found it to be approximately $\frac{7}{25}$ pound. What is the weight of Bondi's phone written as a decimal?

61. a. Simplify each fraction.

$\frac{8}{18}$ $\frac{8}{48}$ $\frac{5}{20}$ $\frac{21}{45}$ $\frac{18}{32}$ $\frac{24}{50}$ $\frac{45}{72}$ $\frac{36}{96}$

b. Write the denominator of each simplified fraction as the product of prime factors.

c. Write each simplified fraction as a decimal. Label each as a terminating or repeating decimal.

62. The ruler is marked at every $\frac{1}{16}$ in. Do the labeled measurements convert to terminating or repeating decimals?

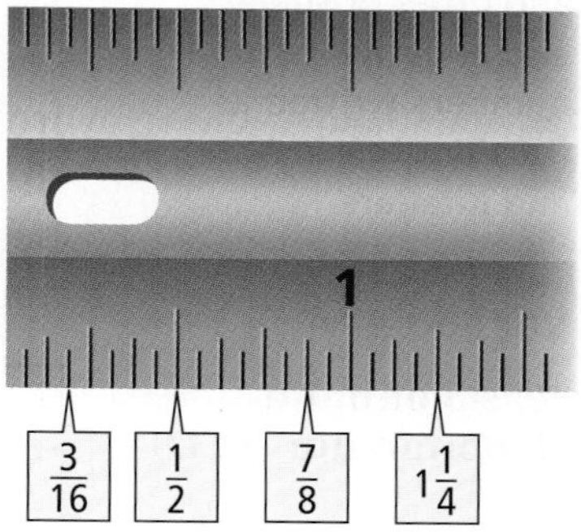

63. Critical Thinking The greatest common factor, GCF, is the largest common factor of two or more given numbers. Find and remove the GCF of 42 and 68 from the fraction $\frac{42}{68}$. Can the resulting fraction be further simplified? Explain.

64. What's the Error? A student simplified a fraction in this manner: $\frac{-25}{-30} = -\frac{5}{6}$. What error did the student make?

65. Write About It Using your answers to Exercise 61, examine the prime factors in the denominators of the simplified fractions that are equivalent to terminating decimals. Then examine the prime factors in the denominators of the simplified fractions that are equivalent to repeating decimals. What pattern do you see?

66. Challenge A student simplified a fraction to $-\frac{2}{9}$ by removing the common factors, which were 2 and 9. What was the original fraction?

Test Prep and Spiral Review

67. Multiple Choice If $y = -\frac{3}{9}$, which is NOT equal to y?

Ⓐ $\frac{-1}{3}$ Ⓑ $-\frac{1}{3}$ Ⓒ $-\left(\frac{-1}{3}\right)$ Ⓓ $-\left(\frac{-1}{-3}\right)$

68. Multiple Choice Which shows the decimal 0.68 as a fraction in simplest form?

Ⓕ $\frac{17}{25}$ Ⓖ $\frac{34}{50}$ Ⓗ $\frac{3}{4}$ Ⓙ $\frac{6}{8}$

69. Gridded Response What is the decimal equivalent of the fraction $\frac{119}{8}$?

Evaluate each expression for the given values of the variable. (Lesson 1-1)

70. $3x + 5$ for $x = 2$ and $x = 3$

71. $4(x + 1)$ for $x = 6$ and $x = 11$

Simplify. (Lesson 1-6)

72. $-3(6 - 8)$

73. $4(-3 - 2)$

74. $-5(3 + 2)$

75. $-3(1 - 8)$

76. $-12(-4 - 9)$

77. $15(11 - (-1))$

78. $6(-5 - (-4))$

79. $-7(1 - (-17))$

2-2 Comparing and Ordering Rational Numbers

Learn to compare and order positive and negative rational numbers written as fractions, decimals, and integers.

Vocabulary

least common denominator (LCD)

The population within the United States is constantly changing. The table shows the percent change in populations from 2000 to 2003 for three states and the District of Columbia. A negative percent indicates that the population declined.

Population Change from 2000–2003			
Location	**Change (%)**	**Location**	**Change (%)**
Maine	$\frac{12}{5}$	Washington	4.0
North Dakota	−1.3	Washington, D.C.	$-1\frac{1}{2}$

To compare or order rational numbers, first write them in the same form. To compare fractions, find a common denominator. This could be the **least common denominator** (LCD), which is the least common multiple of the denominators.

EXAMPLE 1 Comparing Fractions by Finding a Common Denominator

Compare. Write <, >, or =.

A $\frac{5}{8} \;\square\; \frac{7}{12}$

Method 1: Multiply to find a common denominator.

$8 \cdot 12 = 96$ — *Multiply 8 and 12 to find a common denominator.*

$\frac{5}{8} \cdot \frac{12}{12} = \frac{5 \cdot 12}{8 \cdot 12} = \frac{60}{96}$

$\frac{7}{12} \cdot \frac{8}{8} = \frac{7 \cdot 8}{12 \cdot 8} = \frac{56}{96}$ — *Write the fractions with a common denominator.*

$\frac{60}{96} > \frac{56}{96}$, so $\frac{5}{8} > \frac{7}{12}$ — *Compare the fractions.*

B $\frac{3}{4} \;\square\; \frac{5}{6}$

Method 2: Find the least common denominator.

4: 4, 8, 12. . . 6: 6, 12. . . — *List multiples of 4 and 6. The LCM is 12.*

$\frac{3}{4} \cdot \frac{3}{3} = \frac{3 \cdot 3}{4 \cdot 3} = \frac{9}{12}$

$\frac{5}{6} \cdot \frac{2}{2} = \frac{5 \cdot 2}{6 \cdot 2} = \frac{10}{12}$ — *Write the fractions with a common denominator.*

$\frac{9}{12} < \frac{10}{12}$, so $\frac{3}{4} < \frac{5}{6}$ — *Compare the fractions.*

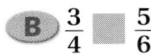

Remember!

The least common multiple (LCM) of two numbers is the smallest number, other than 0, that is a multiple of both numbers.

EXAMPLE 2 Comparing by Using Decimals

Compare. Write <, >, or =.

A $3\frac{3}{8} \;\square\; 3\frac{3}{5}$

$3\frac{3}{8} = 3.375$ and $3\frac{3}{5} = 3.6$ — *Write the fractions as decimals.*

$3.375 < 3.6$, so $3\frac{3}{8} < 3\frac{3}{5}$ — *Compare the decimals.*

B $-0.53 \;\square\; -\frac{6}{10}$

$-\frac{6}{10} = -0.6$ — *Write $-\frac{6}{10}$ as a decimal.*

$-0.53 > -0.6$, so $-0.53 > -\frac{6}{10}$ — *Compare the decimals.*

C $\frac{9}{11} \;\square\; 0.8$

$\frac{9}{11} = 0.\overline{81}$ — *Write $\frac{9}{11}$ as a decimal.*

$0.\overline{81} > 0.8$, so $\frac{9}{11} > 0.8$ — *Compare the decimals.*

To order fractions and decimals, you can either write them all in the same form and then compare them, or place them on a number line.

EXAMPLE 3 *Social Studies Application*

From 2000 to 2003, the percent changes in populations for three states and the District of Columbia were as follows: $\frac{12}{5}$ for Maine, -1.3 for North Dakota, 4.0 for Washington, and $-1\frac{1}{2}$ for Washington, D.C. List these numbers in order from least to greatest.

Place the numbers on a number line and read them from left to right.

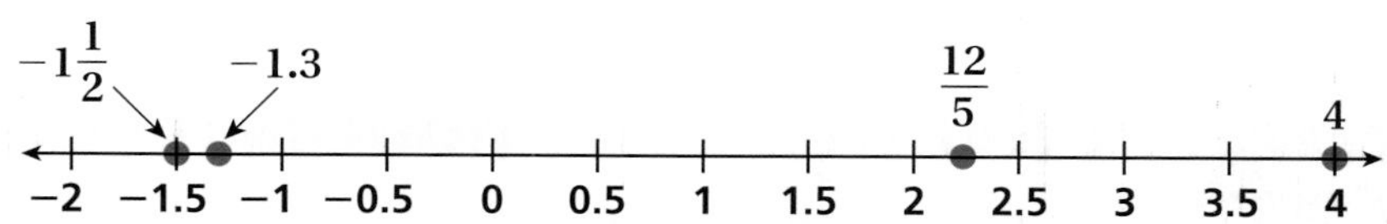

The percent changes in population from least to greatest are $-1\frac{1}{2}$, -1.3, $\frac{12}{5}$, and 4.0.

Think and Discuss

1. **Explain** whether you need to find a common denominator to compare $\frac{2}{3}$ and $-\frac{1}{2}$.
2. **Describe** the steps you would use to compare 0.235 and 0.239.

2-2 Exercises

go.hrw.com
Homework Help Online
KEYWORD: MT7 2-2
Parent Resources Online
KEYWORD: MT7 Parent

GUIDED PRACTICE

See Example 1

Compare. Write <, >, or =.

1. $\frac{3}{8}$ $\square$ $\frac{3}{7}$ **2.** $\frac{9}{11}$ $\square$ $\frac{9}{10}$ **3.** $\frac{6}{15}$ $\square$ $\frac{2}{5}$ **4.** $-\frac{7}{10}$ $\square$ $-\frac{5}{8}$

See Example 2

5. $\frac{7}{8}$ $\square$ $\frac{9}{11}$ **6.** 4.2 $\square$ $4\frac{1}{5}$ **7.** $-\frac{3}{7}$ $\square$ -0.375 **8.** $-1\frac{1}{2}$ $\square$ $-1\frac{7}{9}$

See Example 3

9. In Mr. Corsetti's shop class, students were instructed to measure and cut boards to a length of 8 inches. In checking four students' work, Mr. Corsetti found that one board was 8.25 inches, the second was $8\frac{1}{8}$ inches, the third was 7.5 inches, and the fourth was $7\frac{5}{16}$ inches. List these measurements in order from least to greatest.

INDEPENDENT PRACTICE

See Example 1

Compare. Write <, >, or =.

10. $\frac{5}{8}$ $\square$ $\frac{16}{21}$ **11.** $\frac{13}{11}$ $\square$ $\frac{8}{7}$ **12.** $-\frac{1}{3}$ $\square$ $-\frac{1}{4}$ **13.** $-\frac{3}{4}$ $\square$ $-\frac{9}{12}$

14. $-\frac{2}{3}$ $\square$ $-\frac{5}{7}$ **15.** $-\frac{16}{9}$ $\square$ $-\frac{8}{3}$ **16.** $\frac{17}{20}$ $\square$ $\frac{5}{6}$ **17.** $-\frac{2}{9}$ $\square$ $-\frac{1}{8}$

See Example 2

18. $5\frac{8}{9}$ $\square$ $5\frac{7}{8}$ **19.** $-\frac{1}{6}$ $\square$ $-\frac{1}{5}$ **20.** $-\frac{4}{7}$ $\square$ $-\frac{2}{5}$ **21.** $\frac{6}{7}$ $\square$ 0.87

22. $-\frac{9}{7}$ $\square$ $-\frac{10}{8}$ **23.** $1\frac{2}{3}$ $\square$ $1\frac{8}{12}$ **24.** $\frac{15}{22}$ $\square$ $0.6\overline{81}$ **25.** $\frac{13}{20}$ $\square$ 0.65

See Example 3

26. Sports During the qualifying for the first NASCAR event at Texas Motor Speedway in 2005, the fastest speed was 192.582 mi/h. The next four fastest speeds, relative to the fastest speed, were approximately $-\frac{17}{25}$ mi/h, -0.15 mi/h, -1.15 mi/h, and $-1\frac{1}{40}$ mi/h. List these relative speeds in order from least to greatest.

PRACTICE AND PROBLEM SOLVING

Extra Practice
See page 784.

Compare. Write <, >, or =.

27. $-\frac{5}{7}$ $\square$ $-\frac{6}{10}$ **28.** -5.00 $\square$ $-\frac{20}{5}$ **29.** 7.2 $\square$ $7\frac{2}{9}$ **30.** 14.7 $\square$ 14.6885

Write a fraction or decimal that has a value between the given numbers.

31. $\frac{1}{4}$ and $\frac{1}{3}$ **32.** 0.89 and 0.9 **33.** $-\frac{2}{3}$ and 0.5 **34.** 0.27 and $\frac{4}{5}$

35. Critical Thinking On Tuesday, stock A's price fell -0.56 and stock B's price fell -0.50. Stock C's price did not fall as much as stock A's, but it fell more than stock B's. What is a reasonable answer for how much stock C's price fell? Explain.

36. Multi-Step Alejandro, Becky, Marcus, and Kathy ate lunch at a restaurant. The total amount of the bill, including tax and tip, was \$34.20. Alejandro paid \$10.00, Becky paid $\frac{1}{4}$ of the bill, Marcus paid 0.2 of the bill, and Kathy paid the rest. Who paid the greatest part of the bill?

37. **Life Science** The lengths of some butterflies' wingspans are shown in the table.

Butterfly	Wingspan (in.)
Great white	3.75
Large orange sulphur	$3\frac{3}{8}$
Apricot sulphur	2.625
White-angled sulphur	3.5

a. List the butterflies in order from smallest to largest wingspan.

b. The pink-spotted swallowtail's wingspan can measure $3\frac{5}{16}$ inches. Between which two butterflies should the pink-spotted swallowtail be in your list from part **a**?

LINK Meteorology

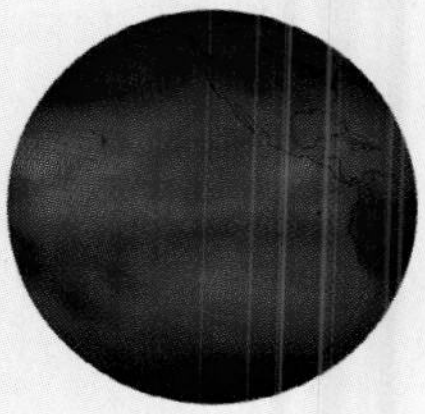

NASA uses satellite imagery to gather information about temperatures on Earth, such as the amount of heat radiated into space from Earth's surface and atmosphere.

38. **Meteorology** One measure of average global temperature shows how each year varies from a base measure. The table shows results for several years.

Year	1958	1964	1965	1978	2002
Difference from Base	0.10°C	−0.17°C	−0.10°C	$\frac{1}{50}$°C	0.54°C

a. Order the five years from coldest to warmest.

b. In 1946, the average temperature varied by −0.03°C from the base measure. Between which two years should 1946 fall when the years are ordered from coldest to warmest?

39. **What's the Error?** A student compared $-\frac{1}{4}$ and −0.3. He changed $-\frac{1}{4}$ to the decimal −0.25 and wrote, "Since 0.3 is greater than 0.25, −0.3 is greater than −0.25." What was the student's error?

40. **Write About It** Describe two methods to compare $\frac{13}{17}$ and 0.82. Which do you think is easier? Why?

41. **Challenge** Write $\left|-\frac{2}{3}\right|$, $|-0.75|$, $|0.62|$, and $\left|\frac{5}{6}\right|$ in order from least to greatest.

Test Prep and Spiral Review

42. **Multiple Choice** Which pair of numbers does $\frac{3}{7}$ NOT come between?

(A) 0.3 and 0.45 (B) $\frac{9}{25}$ and $\frac{1}{2}$ (C) 0.2 and $\frac{1}{3}$ (D) $\frac{2}{5}$ and 0.65

43. **Multiple Choice** Which list of numbers is in order from least to greatest?

(F) 0.3, $\frac{4}{5}$, $\frac{1}{4}$, 0 (G) $\frac{4}{5}$, 0.3, 0, $\frac{1}{4}$ (H) $\frac{1}{4}$, $\frac{4}{5}$, 0, 0.3 (J) 0, $\frac{1}{4}$, 0.3, $\frac{4}{5}$

Simplify. (Lesson 1-5)

44. −5 − (−4) 45. 8 − (−2) 46. −19 − 13 47. 72 − 119 48. 24 − 37

Write each fraction as a decimal. (Lesson 2-1)

49. $\frac{3}{4}$ 50. $\frac{1}{8}$ 51. $\frac{10}{4}$ 52. $\frac{9}{15}$ 53. $\frac{19}{20}$

2-3 Adding and Subtracting Rational Numbers

Learn to add and subtract decimals and rational numbers with like denominators.

Olympic swimming events are measured in hundredths of a second. In the Athens 2004 Summer Olympic Games, the difference in times between the gold and silver medal winners in the men's 100-meter backstroke was 0.29 second.

EXAMPLE 1 *Sports Application*

In the Athens 2004 Olympic Games, Aaron Piersol of the United States won the gold medal in the 100-meter backstroke with a time of 54.06 seconds. The eighth place finisher, Marco di Carli, completed the race in 55.27 seconds. What was the difference in times between the first- and eighth-place finishers?

$$\begin{array}{r} 55.27 \\ -54.06 \\ \hline 1.21 \end{array}$$

Write the numbers so that the decimals line up.

The difference between the first- and eighth-place finishers was 1.21 seconds.

EXAMPLE 2 Using a Number Line to Add Rational Numbers

Use a number line to find each sum.

A $-0.4 + 1.3$

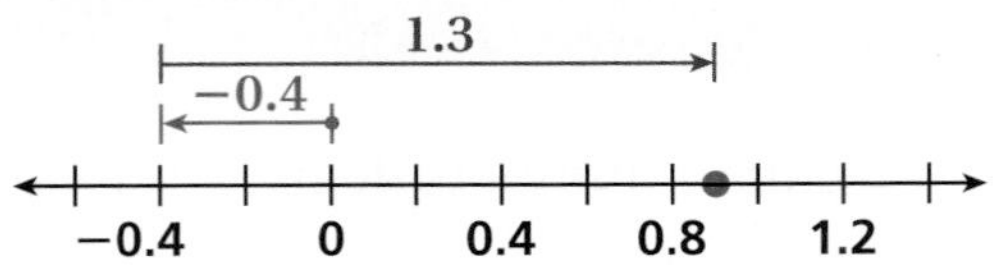

Move left 0.4 units. From −0.4, move right 1.3 units.

You finish at 0.9, so $-0.4 + 1.3 = 0.9$.

B $-\frac{7}{8} + \left(-\frac{3}{8}\right)$

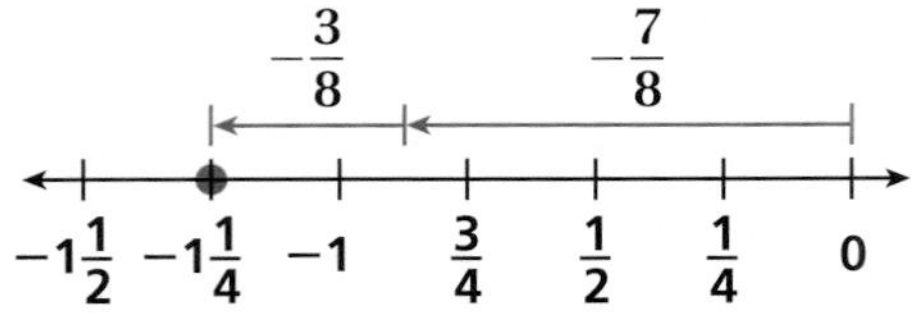

Move left $\frac{7}{8}$ units. From $-\frac{7}{8}$, move left $\frac{3}{8}$ units.

You finish at $-1\frac{1}{4}$, so $-\frac{7}{8} + \left(-\frac{3}{8}\right) = -1\frac{1}{4}$.

ADDING AND SUBTRACTING WITH LIKE DENOMINATORS

Words	Numbers	Algebra
To add or subtract rational numbers with the same denominator, add or subtract the numerators and keep the denominator.	$\frac{1}{5} + \left(-\frac{4}{5}\right) = \frac{1 + (-4)}{5}$ $= \frac{-3}{5}$, or $-\frac{3}{5}$	$\frac{a}{d} + \frac{b}{d} = \frac{a + b}{d}$

EXAMPLE 3 Adding and Subtracting Fractions with Like Denominators

Remember!

Subtracting a number is the same as adding its opposite.

Add or subtract. Write each answer in simplest form.

A $\frac{7}{13} + \frac{11}{13}$

$\frac{7}{13} + \frac{11}{13} = \frac{7 + 11}{13}$ *Add numerators. Keep the denominator.*

$= \frac{18}{13}$, or $1\frac{5}{13}$

B $-\frac{3}{8} - \frac{5}{8}$

$-\frac{3}{8} - \frac{5}{8} = \frac{-3}{8} + \frac{-5}{8}$ *$-\frac{5}{8}$ can be written as $\frac{-5}{8}$.*

$= \frac{-3 + (-5)}{8} = \frac{-8}{8} = -1$

EXAMPLE 4 Evaluating Expressions with Rational Numbers

Evaluate each expression for the given value of the variable.

A $33.5 + x$ for $x = -48.2$

$33.5 + (-48.2)$ *Substitute −48.2 for x.*

-14.7 *Think: 48.2 > 33.5. Use sign of 48.2.*

B $-\frac{3}{8} + c$ for $c = 1\frac{7}{8}$

$-\frac{3}{8} + 1\frac{7}{8}$ *Substitute $1\frac{7}{8}$ for c.*

$\frac{-3}{8} + \frac{15}{8}$ *$1\frac{7}{8} = \frac{1(8) + 7}{8} = \frac{15}{8}$*

$\frac{-3 + 15}{8} = \frac{12}{8}$ *Add numerators. Keep the denominator.*

$\frac{3}{2}$, or $1\frac{1}{2}$ *Simplify.*

Think and Discuss

1. **Give an example** of an addition problem that involves simplifying an improper fraction in the final step.
2. **Explain** why $\frac{7}{9} + \frac{7}{9}$ does not equal $\frac{14}{18}$.

2-3 Exercises

go.hrw.com
Homework Help Online
KEYWORD: MT7 2-3
Parent Resources Online
KEYWORD: MT7 Parent

GUIDED PRACTICE

See Example 1

1. **Sports** In the Athens 2004 Olympic Games, Jodie Henry of Australia won the gold medal in the 100-meter freestyle swim with a time of 53.84 seconds. The bronze medal winner, Natalie Coughlin of the United States, completed the race in 54.4 seconds. What was the difference between the two times?

See Example 2

Use a number line to find each sum.

2. $-0.9 + 3.2$ 3. $-\frac{7}{3} + \left(-\frac{2}{3}\right)$ 4. $-2.7 + 0.5$ 5. $-\frac{1}{2} + \left(-\frac{4}{2}\right)$

See Example 3

Add or subtract. Write each answer in simplest form.

6. $\frac{1}{6} - \frac{5}{6}$ 7. $-\frac{3}{10} - \frac{9}{10}$ 8. $\frac{3}{12} + \frac{7}{12}$ 9. $\frac{9}{25} + \left(-\frac{4}{25}\right)$

See Example 4

Evaluate each expression for the given value of the variable.

10. $3.7 + x$ for $x = -9.3$ 11. $-\frac{4}{9} + x$ for $x = \frac{8}{9}$ 12. $-\frac{14}{15} + x$ for $x = 1$

INDEPENDENT PRACTICE

See Example 1

13. **Sports** Reaction time measures how quickly a runner reacts to the starter pistol. In the 100-meter dash at the 2004 Olympic Games, Lauryn Williams had a reaction time of 0.214 second. Her total race time, including reaction time, was 11.03 seconds. How long did it take her to run the actual distance?

See Example 2

Use a number line to find each sum.

14. $-3.2 + 1.6$ 15. $-\frac{7}{8} + \left(-\frac{7}{8}\right)$ 16. $-0.5 + 9.1$ 17. $-\frac{5}{18} + \left(-\frac{1}{18}\right)$

See Example 3

Add or subtract. Write each answer in simplest form.

18. $\frac{7}{13} - \frac{5}{13}$ 19. $-\frac{1}{17} - \frac{13}{17}$ 20. $\frac{9}{17} + \frac{16}{17}$ 21. $\frac{11}{33} + \left(-\frac{19}{33}\right)$

See Example 4

Evaluate each expression for the given value of the variable.

22. $47.3 + x$ for $x = -18.6$ 23. $\frac{11}{12} + x$ for $x = -\frac{7}{12}$ 24. $-\frac{23}{25} + x$ for $x = \frac{7}{25}$

PRACTICE AND PROBLEM SOLVING

Extra Practice
See page 784.

Evaluate each expression for the given value of the variable.

25. $8.25 - x$ for $x = \frac{5}{16}$ 26. $x + \left(-\frac{3}{7}\right)$ for $x = \frac{2}{3}$ 27. $x + \left(-\frac{3}{8}\right)$ for $x = 4.72$

28. **Design** The distance from the floor of one level of a building to the floor of the level above it is 9 feet $\frac{3}{8}$ inches. If the distance from the floor to the ceiling is 8 feet $2\frac{1}{2}$ inches, how thick is the space between the ceiling of one floor and the floor of the level above it?

29. **Sports** The circumference of a women's NCAA college softball must be between $11\frac{7}{8}$ inches and $12\frac{1}{8}$ inches. What is the greatest possible difference in circumference between two softballs that meet the standards?

Add or subtract. Write each answer in simplest form.

30. $\frac{4}{9} - \frac{1}{9}$ **31.** $-\frac{7}{11} + \frac{3}{11} - \frac{2}{11}$ **32.** $\frac{13}{5} + \frac{8}{5}$ **33.** $-\frac{17}{18} - \frac{29}{18}$

34. $-1.7 + 3\frac{3}{5}$ **35.** $-\frac{13}{21} + \left(-\frac{8}{21}\right)$ **36.** $-8 + 6\frac{4}{5}$ **37.** $-\frac{15}{16} + \left(-\frac{9}{16}\right)$

Energy The circle graph shows the sources of renewable energy and their use in the United States in British thermal units (Btu).

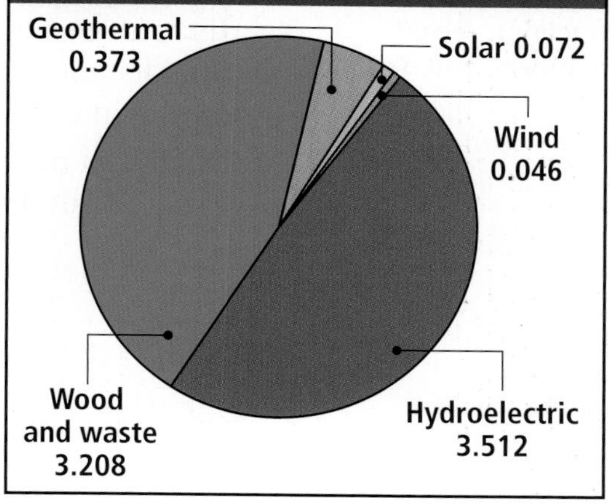

38. How many quadrillion Btu's from geothermal, wood and waste, and hydroelectric sources combined were used?

39. How many more Btu's from hydroelectric sources were used than those from wind, solar, and wood and waste sources combined?

40. Write a Problem Write a problem that requires a decimal to be converted to a fraction and that also involves addition or subtraction of fractions.

41. Write About It Explain how to subtract fractions.

42. Challenge The gutter of a bowling lane measures $9\frac{5}{16}$ inches wide. This is $\frac{3}{16}$ inch less than the widest gutter permitted and $\frac{5}{16}$ inch greater than the narrowest gutter permitted. What is the greatest possible difference in the width of two gutters?

Test Prep and Spiral Review

43. Multiple Choice Evaluate the expression $25.18 - x$ for $x = -18.7$.

Ⓐ 6.48 Ⓑ 23.31 Ⓒ 27.05 Ⓓ 43.88

44. Multiple Choice Gregory filled a fish tank with $4\frac{5}{12}$ gallons of water. Linda added $3\frac{11}{12}$ more gallons of water. How many gallons of water were in the tank?

Ⓕ $7\frac{1}{2}$ gal Ⓖ $8\frac{1}{3}$ gal Ⓗ $8\frac{5}{12}$ gal Ⓙ $8\frac{2}{3}$ gal

45. Gridded Response Evaluate $\frac{7}{15} - x$ for $x = -\frac{4}{15}$.

Solve. (Lesson 1-7)

46. $x + 13 = 22$ **47.** $b + 5 = -2$ **48.** $2y + 9 = 19$ **49.** $4a + 2 = -18$

Compare. Write <, >, or =. (Lesson 2-2)

50. $0.25 \;\square\; \frac{1}{3}$ **51.** $-0.5\overline{3} \;\square\; -0.5$ **52.** $\frac{4}{7} \;\square\; 0.57$ **53.** $-\frac{9}{11} \;\square\; -0.\overline{81}$

2-4 Multiplying Rational Numbers

Learn to multiply fractions, mixed numbers, and decimals.

Andrew walks his dog each day. His route is $\frac{1}{8}$ mile. What is the total distance that Andrew walks his dog in a 5-day week?

Recall that multiplication is repeated addition.

$$3\left(\frac{1}{4}\right) = \frac{1}{4} + \frac{1}{4} + \frac{1}{4}$$
$$= \frac{1+1+1}{4}$$
$$= \frac{3}{4}$$

Notice that multiplying a fraction by a whole number is the same as multiplying the whole number by just the numerator of the fraction and keeping the same denominator.

RULES FOR MULTIPLYING TWO RATIONAL NUMBERS

If the signs of the factors are the same, the product is positive.

$(+) \cdot (+) = (+)$ **or** $(-) \cdot (-) = (+)$

If the signs of the factors are different, the product is negative.

$(+) \cdot (-) = (-)$ **or** $(-) \cdot (+) = (-)$

EXAMPLE 1 Multiplying a Fraction and an Integer

Multiply. Write each answer in simplest form.

A $6\left(\frac{2}{3}\right)$

$6\left(\frac{2}{3}\right)$

$\frac{6 \cdot 2}{3}$

$\frac{12}{3}$ *Multiply*

4 *Simplify.*

B $-2\left(3\frac{1}{5}\right)$

$-2\left(3\frac{1}{5}\right)$

$-2\left(\frac{16}{5}\right)$ $\quad 3\frac{1}{5} = \frac{3(5)+1}{5} = \frac{16}{5}$

$-\frac{32}{5}$ *Multiply $(-) \cdot (+) = (-)$.*

$-6\frac{2}{5}$ *Simplify.*

Helpful Hint

To write $-\frac{32}{5}$ as a mixed number, divide:

$-\frac{32}{5} = -6$ **R2**

$= -6\frac{2}{5}$

EXAMPLE 2 Multiplying Fractions

Caution!

A fraction is in lowest terms, or simplest form, when the numerator and denominator have no common factors.

Multiply. Write each answer in simplest form.

A $-\frac{3}{5}\left(-\frac{1}{4}\right)$

$-\frac{3}{5}\left(-\frac{1}{4}\right) = \frac{-3}{5}\left(\frac{-1}{4}\right)$

$= \frac{(-3)(-1)}{5(4)}$ *Multiply numerators. Multiply denominators.*

$= \frac{3}{20}$ *Simplify.*

B $\frac{5}{12}\left(-\frac{12}{5}\right)$

$\frac{5}{12}\left(-\frac{12}{5}\right) = \frac{5}{12}\left(\frac{-12}{5}\right)$

$= \frac{\overset{1}{\cancel{5}}(-\overset{-1}{\cancel{12}})}{\underset{1}{\cancel{12}}(\underset{1}{\cancel{5}})}$ *Look for common factors: 12, 5.*

$= \frac{-1}{1} = -1$ *Simplify.*

EXAMPLE 3 Multiplying Decimals

Multiply.

A $-5.2(-5)$

$-5.2 \cdot (-5) = 26.0$ *Product is positive with 1 decimal place.*

$= 26$

You can drop the zero after the decimal point.

B $-0.07(4.6)$

$-0.07 \cdot 4.6 = -0.322$

Product is negative with 3 decimal places.

EXAMPLE 4 *Recreation Application*

Andrew walks his dog $\frac{1}{8}$ mile each day. What is the total distance that Andrew walks his dog in a 5-day week?

$\frac{1}{8}(5) = \frac{1 \cdot 5}{8}$

$= \frac{5}{8}$ *Multiply.*

Andrew walks his dog $\frac{5}{8}$ mile in a 5-day week.

Think and Discuss

1. **Name** the number of decimal places in the product of 5.625 and 2.75.
2. **Give an example** of two fractions whose product is an integer due to common factors.

2-4 Exercises

go.hrw.com
Homework Help Online
KEYWORD: MT7 2-4
Parent Resources Online
KEYWORD: MT7 Parent

GUIDED PRACTICE

See Example 1

Multiply. Write each answer in simplest form.

1. $5\left(\frac{1}{2}\right)$
2. $-7\left(1\frac{3}{4}\right)$
3. $3\left(\frac{5}{8}\right)$
4. $-4\left(5\frac{2}{3}\right)$

See Example 2

5. $-\frac{1}{4}\left(-\frac{5}{8}\right)$
6. $\frac{3}{8}\left(-\frac{7}{10}\right)$
7. $6\frac{3}{7}\left(\frac{7}{8}\right)$
8. $-\frac{3}{5}\left(-\frac{5}{9}\right)$

See Example 3

Multiply.

9. $-2.1(-7)$
10. $0.03(5.4)$
11. $-4.8(-2)$
12. $-0.15(2.8)$

See Example 4

13. Tran jogs $\frac{3}{4}$ mile each day. What is the total distance Tran jogs in 6 days?

INDEPENDENT PRACTICE

See Example 1

Multiply. Write each answer in simplest form.

14. $5\left(\frac{1}{7}\right)$
15. $-3\left(1\frac{5}{6}\right)$
16. $9\left(\frac{4}{21}\right)$
17. $-7\left(1\frac{2}{3}\right)$
18. $9\left(\frac{14}{15}\right)$
19. $-3\left(6\frac{7}{9}\right)$
20. $8\left(\frac{3}{4}\right)$
21. $-7\left(3\frac{1}{5}\right)$

See Example 2

22. $-\frac{2}{3}\left(-\frac{5}{6}\right)$
23. $\frac{2}{9}\left(-\frac{7}{8}\right)$
24. $5\frac{7}{8}\left(\frac{5}{11}\right)$
25. $-\frac{1}{3}\left(-\frac{7}{8}\right)$
26. $\frac{3}{7}\left(-\frac{5}{6}\right)$
27. $2\frac{1}{7}\left(\frac{7}{10}\right)$
28. $-\frac{2}{3}\left(-\frac{1}{9}\right)$
29. $\frac{7}{8}\left(\frac{3}{5}\right)$

See Example 3

Multiply.

30. $-1.7(-4)$
31. $-0.05(4.7)$
32. $-6.2(-7)$
33. $-0.75(5.5)$
34. $-6.2(-9)$
35. $-0.08(6.2)$
36. $-2.4(-9)$
37. $-0.04(9.2)$

See Example 4

38. There was $\frac{3}{4}$ of a pizza left over from a family gathering. The next day, Tina ate $\frac{1}{2}$ of what was left. How much of the whole pizza did Tina eat?

PRACTICE AND PROBLEM SOLVING

Extra Practice
See page 784.

39. **Consumer Economics** At a bookstore, the ticketed price of a book is $\frac{1}{4}$ off the original price. Kayla has a discount coupon for $\frac{1}{2}$ off the ticketed price. What fraction of the original price is the additional discount?

Multiply.

40. $6\left(\frac{3}{7}\right)$
41. $-5\left(1\frac{8}{11}\right)$
42. $7\left(\frac{4}{5}\right)$
43. $5\left(3\frac{1}{9}\right)$
44. $-5.9(-7)$
45. $0.7(2.6)$
46. $-3.6(-4)$
47. $-0.06(9.3)$
48. $\frac{4}{11}\left(-\frac{4}{7}\right)$
49. $3\frac{5}{6}\left(\frac{7}{9}\right)$
50. $-\frac{8}{9}\left(-\frac{3}{5}\right)$
51. $\frac{5}{12}\left(-\frac{11}{16}\right)$

52. **Health** The directions for a pain reliever recommend that children 96 pounds and over take 4 tablets every 4 hours as needed, and children who weigh between 60 and 71 pounds take only $2\frac{1}{2}$ tablets every 4 hours as needed. Each tablet is $\frac{4}{25}$ gram.

a. If a 105-pound child takes 4 tablets, how many grams of pain reliever is he or she receiving?

b. How many grams of pain reliever is the recommended dose for a child weighing 65 pounds?

LINK

Animals

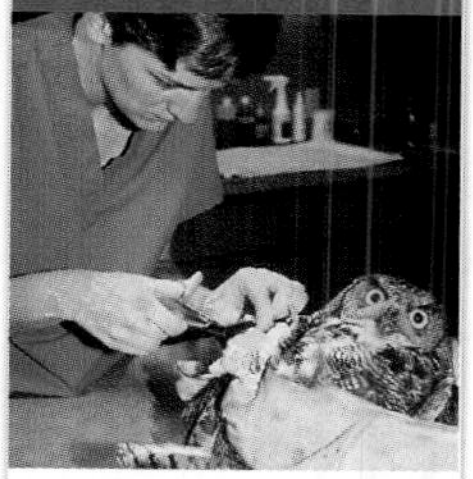

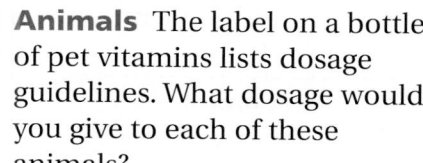

There are fewer than 30 veterinary colleges in the United States.

53. **Animals** The label on a bottle of pet vitamins lists dosage guidelines. What dosage would you give to each of these animals?

a. a 50 lb adult dog

b. a 12 lb cat

c. a 40 lb pregnant dog

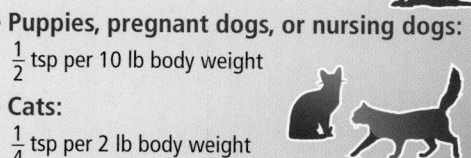

Do-Good Pet Vitamins

- **Adult dogs:** $\frac{1}{2}$ tsp per 20 lb body weight
- **Puppies, pregnant dogs, or nursing dogs:** $\frac{1}{2}$ tsp per 10 lb body weight
- **Cats:** $\frac{1}{4}$ tsp per 2 lb body weight

54. **What's the Error?** A student multiplied two mixed numbers in the following fashion: $2\frac{4}{7} \cdot 3\frac{1}{4} = 6\frac{1}{7}$. What's the error?

55. **Write About It** In the pattern $\frac{1}{3} + \frac{1}{4} + \frac{1}{5} + \ldots$, which fraction makes the sum greater than 1? Explain.

56. **Challenge** Of the 42 presidents who preceded George W. Bush, $\frac{1}{3}$ were elected to a second term. Of those elected to a second term, $\frac{1}{7}$ were former vice presidents of the United States. What fraction of the first 42 presidents were elected to a second term and were former vice presidents?

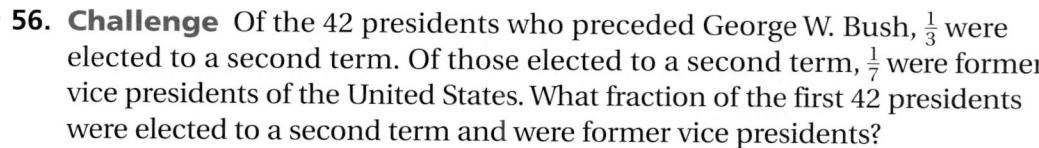

TEST PREP and Spiral Review

57. **Multiple Choice** Lindsay walked $\frac{3}{4}$ mile on Monday. She walked $1\frac{5}{8}$ that distance on Tuesday. How far did she walk on Tuesday?

Ⓐ $1\frac{7}{32}$ miles Ⓑ $1\frac{15}{32}$ miles Ⓒ $2\frac{3}{8}$ miles Ⓓ $2\frac{15}{32}$ miles

58. **Multiple Choice** What is the product of $-5\frac{1}{3}$ and $3\frac{3}{4}$?

Ⓕ -20 Ⓖ $-15\frac{1}{4}$ Ⓗ $15\frac{1}{4}$ Ⓙ 20

59. **Multiple Choice** Multiply: -0.98×-8.4.

Ⓐ -82.83 Ⓑ -8.232 Ⓒ 8.232 Ⓓ 82.83

Compare. Write <, >, or =. (Lesson 1-3)

60. $|-9|$ ▢ -9 61. -13 ▢ -22 62. $|5|$ ▢ $|-5|$ 63. $|-17|$ ▢ $|-13|$

Find each sum. (Lesson 2-3)

64. $-1.7 + 2.3$ 65. $-\frac{2}{3} + \left(-\frac{1}{6}\right)$ 66. $23.75 + (-25.15)$ 67. $-\frac{4}{9} + \frac{2}{9}$

2-5 Dividing Rational Numbers

Learn to divide fractions and decimals.

Vocabulary

reciprocal

A number and its **reciprocal** have a product of 1. To find the reciprocal of a fraction, exchange the numerator and the denominator. Remember that an integer can be written as a fraction with a denominator of 1.

Number	Reciprocal	Product
$\frac{3}{4}$	$\frac{4}{3}$	$\frac{3}{4}\left(\frac{4}{3}\right) = 1$
$-\frac{5}{12}$	$-\frac{12}{5}$	$-\frac{5}{12}\left(-\frac{12}{5}\right) = 1$
6	$\frac{1}{6}$	$6\left(\frac{1}{6}\right) = 1$

Multiplication and division are inverse operations. They undo each other.

$$\frac{1}{3}\left(\frac{2}{5}\right) = \frac{2}{15} \longrightarrow \frac{2}{15} \div \frac{2}{5} = \frac{1}{3}$$

Notice that multiplying by the reciprocal gives the same result as dividing.

$$\left(\frac{2}{15}\right)\left(\frac{5}{2}\right) = \frac{2 \cdot 5}{15 \cdot 2} = \frac{10}{30} = \frac{1}{3}$$

DIVIDING RATIONAL NUMBERS IN FRACTION FORM

Words	Numbers	Algebra
To divide by a fraction, multiply by the reciprocal.	$\frac{1}{7} \div \frac{4}{5} = \frac{1}{7} \cdot \frac{5}{4} = \frac{5}{28}$	$\frac{a}{b} \div \frac{c}{d} = \frac{a}{b} \cdot \frac{d}{c} = \frac{ad}{bc}$

EXAMPLE 1 Dividing Fractions

Divide. Write each answer in simplest form.

A $\frac{7}{15} \div \frac{4}{5}$

$\frac{7}{15} \div \frac{4}{5} = \frac{7}{15} \cdot \frac{5}{4}$ *Multiply by the reciprocal.*

$= \frac{7 \cdot \cancel{5}^{1}}{_{3}\cancel{15} \cdot 4}$ *Remove common factors.*

$= \frac{7}{12}$ *Simplest form*

Divide. Write each answer in simplest form.

B $5\frac{1}{3} \div (-7)$

$5\frac{1}{3} \div (-7) = \frac{16}{3} \div \left(-\frac{7}{1}\right)$ *Write as improper fractions.*

$= \frac{16}{3}\left(-\frac{1}{7}\right)$ *Multiply by the reciprocal.*

$= \frac{16 \cdot (-1)}{3 \cdot 7}$ *No common factors*

$= -\frac{16}{21}$ *Simplest form*

When dividing a decimal by a decimal, multiply both numbers by a power of 10 so you can divide by a whole number. To decide which power of 10 to multiply by, look at the denominator. The number of decimal places is the number of zeros to write after the 1.

$$\frac{1.32}{0.4} = \frac{1.32}{0.4}\left(\frac{10}{10}\right) = \frac{13.2}{4}$$

1 decimal place *1 zero*

EXAMPLE 2 Dividing Decimals

Find 7.48 ÷ 0.4.

$7.48 \div 0.4 = \frac{7.48}{0.4}\left(\frac{10}{10}\right) = \frac{74.8}{4}$ *0.4 has 1 decimal place, so use $\frac{10}{10}$.*

$= 18.7$ *Divide.*

EXAMPLE 3 Evaluating Expressions with Fractions and Decimals

Evaluate each expression for the given value of the variable.

A $\frac{7.2}{n}$ **for** $n = -0.24$

$-\frac{7.2}{0.24} = -\frac{7.2}{0.24}\left(\frac{100}{100}\right)$ *0.24 has 2 decimal places, so use $\frac{100}{100}$.*

$= -\frac{720}{24}$ *Divide.*

$= -30$

When $n = -0.24$, $\frac{7.2}{n} = -30$.

B $m \div \frac{5}{24}$ **for** $m = 3\frac{3}{4}$

$3\frac{3}{4} \div \frac{5}{24} = \frac{15}{4} \cdot \frac{24}{5}$ *Rewrite $3\frac{3}{4}$ as an improper fraction and multiply by the reciprocal.*

$= \frac{\overset{3}{\cancel{15}} \cdot \overset{6}{\cancel{24}}}{\underset{1}{\cancel{4}} \cdot \underset{1}{\cancel{5}}}$ *Remove common factors.*

$= \frac{18}{1} = 18$

When $m = 3\frac{3}{4}$, $m \div \frac{5}{24} = 18$.

EXAMPLE 4 PROBLEM SOLVING APPLICATION

PROBLEM SOLVING

Ella ate $\frac{2}{3}$ cup of lowfat yogurt. The serving size listed on the container is 6 ounces, or $\frac{3}{4}$ cup. How many servings did Ella eat? How many calories did Ella eat?

1 Understand the Problem

The number of calories Ella ate is the number of calories in the fraction of a serving.

List the **important information:**

- Ella ate $\frac{2}{3}$ cup.
- A full serving is $\frac{3}{4}$ cup.
- There are 100 calories in one serving.

2 Make a Plan

Set up an equation to find the number of servings Ella ate.

amount Ella ate ÷ serving size = number of servings

Using the number of servings, find the number of calories Ella ate.

number of servings · calories per serving = total calories

3 Solve

Let n = number of servings. Let c = total calories.

Servings: $\frac{2}{3} \div \frac{3}{4} = n$

$$\frac{2}{3} \cdot \frac{4}{3} = n$$

$$\frac{8}{9} = n$$

Calories: $\frac{8}{9} \cdot 100 = c$

$$\frac{8 \cdot 100}{9} = c$$

$$\frac{800}{9} \approx 88.9$$

Ella ate $\frac{8}{9}$ of a serving, which is about 88.9 calories.

4 Look Back

Ella did not eat a full serving, so $\frac{8}{9}$ of a serving is a reasonable answer. Since $\frac{8}{9}$ is less than 1 and 88.9 calories is less than 100, the calories in a full serving, 88.9 calories is a reasonable answer.

Think and Discuss

1. **Tell** what happens when you divide a fraction by itself. Show that you are correct using multiplication by the reciprocal.
2. **Model** the product of $\frac{2}{3}$ and $\frac{1}{4}$.

2-5 Exercises

go.hrw.com
Homework Help Online
KEYWORD: MT7 2-5
Parent Resources Online
KEYWORD: MT7 Parent

GUIDED PRACTICE

See Example 1
Divide. Write each answer in simplest form.

1. $\frac{1}{2} \div \frac{3}{4}$
2. $4\frac{1}{5} \div 5\frac{2}{3}$
3. $-\frac{6}{7} \div 3$
4. $\frac{5}{6} \div \frac{3}{8}$
5. $5\frac{1}{18} \div 4\frac{4}{9}$
6. $-\frac{5}{8} \div 12$
7. $\frac{14}{15} \div \frac{2}{3}$
8. $4\frac{3}{10} \div \frac{3}{5}$

See Example 2
Find each quotient.

9. $3.72 \div 0.3$
10. $2.1 \div 0.07$
11. $10.71 \div 0.7$
12. $1.72 \div 0.2$
13. $2.54 \div 0.6$
14. $11.04 \div 0.4$
15. $2.45 \div 0.005$
16. $4.41 \div 0.7$

See Example 3
Evaluate each expression for the given value of the variable.

17. $\frac{9.7}{x}$ for $x = -0.5$
18. $\frac{6.2}{x}$ for $x = 0.2$
19. $\frac{40.5}{x}$ for $x = 0.9$
20. $\frac{9.2}{x}$ for $x = 2.3$
21. $\frac{32.4}{x}$ for $x = -1.8$
22. $\frac{14.7}{x}$ for $x = 0.07$

See Example 4
23. You eat $\frac{1}{4}$ ounce of cheddar cheese. One serving of cheddar cheese is $1\frac{1}{2}$ ounces. How much of a serving did you eat?

INDEPENDENT PRACTICE

See Example 1
Divide. Write each answer in simplest form.

24. $\frac{1}{6} \div \frac{3}{4}$
25. $4\frac{2}{5} \div 3\frac{1}{2}$
26. $-\frac{5}{12} \div \frac{2}{3}$
27. $\frac{4}{5} \div \frac{1}{2}$
28. $1\frac{2}{3} \div 2\frac{1}{6}$
29. $-\frac{2}{9} \div \frac{7}{12}$
30. $\frac{2}{3} \div \frac{3}{10}$
31. $2\frac{3}{8} \div 1\frac{1}{6}$

See Example 2
Find each quotient.

32. $12.11 \div 0.7$
33. $2.49 \div 0.03$
34. $6.64 \div 0.4$
35. $4.85 \div 0.5$
36. $5.49 \div 0.003$
37. $32.44 \div 0.8$
38. $9.36 \div 0.03$
39. $12.24 \div 0.9$

See Example 3
Evaluate each expression for the given value of the variable.

40. $\frac{7.2}{x}$ for $x = -0.4$
41. $\frac{9.6}{x}$ for $x = 0.8$
42. $\frac{15}{x}$ for $x = -0.05$
43. $\frac{15.4}{x}$ for $x = -1.4$
44. $\frac{4.24}{x}$ for $x = 0.8$
45. $\frac{22.2}{x}$ for $x = 0.06$

See Example 4
46. The platform on the school stage is $8\frac{3}{4}$ feet wide. Each chair is $1\frac{5}{12}$ feet wide. How many chairs will fit across the platform?

PRACTICE AND PROBLEM SOLVING

Extra Practice
See page 785.

47. Maya is drinking her favorite juice. There are $2\frac{3}{4}$ servings remaining in the bottle. Maya pours only $\frac{1}{4}$ of a serving into her glass at a time. How many glasses can Maya have before the bottle is empty?

48. The width of a DVD case is about $\frac{1}{3}$ inch. How many DVD cases are in a box set if the set is about $1\frac{2}{3}$ inches thick?

49. Social Studies Nesting dolls called *matrushkas* are a well-known type of Russian folk art. Use the information in the picture to find the height of the largest doll.

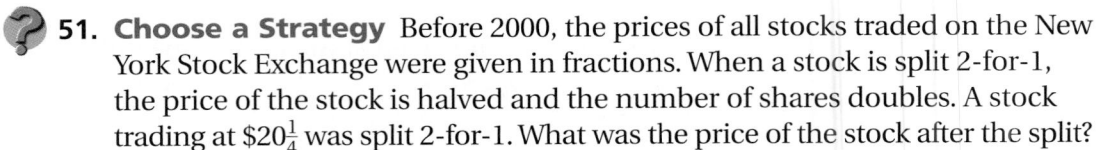

50. Estimation Leo's bowl contains 16 ounces of cereal. His spoon can hold $1\frac{1}{8}$ ounces. Approximately how many spoonfuls are in the bowl?

51. Choose a Strategy Before 2000, the prices of all stocks traded on the New York Stock Exchange were given in fractions. When a stock is split 2-for-1, the price of the stock is halved and the number of shares doubles. A stock trading at $\$20\frac{1}{4}$ was split 2-for-1. What was the price of the stock after the split?

52. Write About It A proper fraction with denominator 10 is divided by a proper fraction with denominator 5. Will the denominator of the quotient be odd or even? Explain.

53. Challenge In 2003, the U.S. Census Bureau estimated that about $\frac{1}{25}$ of the U.S. population resided in Los Angeles County. At that time, about $\frac{3}{25}$ of the U.S. population resided in California. Approximately what fraction of the California population resided in Los Angeles County?

Test Prep and Spiral Review

54. Multiple Choice Evaluate the expression $\frac{7.92}{x}$ for $x = 3.3$.

Ⓐ 2.4 Ⓑ 4.62 Ⓒ 11.22 Ⓓ 26.136

55. Multiple Choice A recipe calls for $2\frac{1}{2}$ cups of sugar to make a batch of cookies. To make one-third of a batch, Betty needs to divide the amount of each ingredient in the recipe by 3. How many cups of sugar will she use?

Ⓕ $\frac{3}{4}$ cup Ⓖ $\frac{5}{6}$ cup Ⓗ $1\frac{1}{5}$ cups Ⓙ $7\frac{1}{2}$ cups

56. Gridded Response Frank bought 12.6 gallons of gasoline for $26.96. How much, to the nearest cent, was the cost per gallon of gasoline?

Evaluate each expression for the given values of the variables. (Lesson 1-1)

57. $7x - 4y$ for $x = 5$ and $y = 6$

58. $6.5p - 9.1q$ for $p = 2.5$ and $q = 0$

Write each decimal as a fraction or mixed number in simplest form. (Lesson 2-1)

59. 0.65 **60.** -1.25 **61.** 0.723 **62.** 11.17 **63.** -0.8

2-6 Adding and Subtracting with Unlike Denominators

Learn to add and subtract fractions with unlike denominators.

North Dome trail in Yosemite National Park is $5\frac{3}{4}$ miles to the summit. Two hikers walk $2\frac{1}{8}$ miles before taking a break. They then hike another $1\frac{1}{2}$ miles before taking a second break. How many more miles do they have to hike before reaching the summit?

To solve this problem, add and subtract rational numbers with unlike denominators. First find a common denominator using one of these methods:

Method 1 Find a common denominator by multiplying one denominator by the other denominator.

Method 2 Find the least common denominator (LCD).

EXAMPLE 1 Adding and Subtracting Fractions with Unlike Denominators

Add or subtract.

A $\frac{4}{5} + \frac{1}{6}$

Method 1: $\frac{4}{5} + \frac{1}{6}$ — *Find a common denominator: 5(6) = 30.*

$= \frac{4}{5}\left(\frac{6}{6}\right) + \frac{1}{6}\left(\frac{5}{5}\right)$ — *Multiply by fractions equal to 1.*

$= \frac{24}{30} + \frac{5}{30}$ — *Rewrite with a common denominator.*

$= \frac{29}{30}$ — *Simplify.*

B $2\frac{1}{6} - 2\frac{2}{9}$

Method 2: $2\frac{1}{6} - 2\frac{2}{9}$

$= \frac{13}{6} - \frac{20}{9}$ — *Write as improper fractions.*

Multiples of 6: 6, 12, (18), . . .
Multiples of 9: 9, (18), 27, . . . — *List the multiples of each denominator and find the LCD.*

$= \frac{13}{6}\left(\frac{3}{3}\right) - \frac{20}{9}\left(\frac{2}{2}\right)$ — *Multiply by fractions equal to 1.*

$= \frac{39}{18} - \frac{40}{18}$ — *Rewrite with the LCD.*

$= -\frac{1}{18}$ — *Simplify.*

EXAMPLE 2 Evaluating Expressions with Rational Numbers

Evaluate $n - \frac{11}{16}$ for $n = -\frac{1}{3}$.

$n - \frac{11}{16} = \left(-\frac{1}{3}\right) - \frac{11}{16}$ *Substitute $-\frac{1}{3}$ for n.*

$= \left(-\frac{1}{3}\right)\left(\frac{16}{16}\right) - \frac{11}{16}\left(\frac{3}{3}\right)$ *Multiply by fractions equal to 1.*

$= -\frac{16}{48} - \frac{33}{48}$ *Rewrite with a common denominator: 3(16) = 48.*

$= -\frac{49}{48}$, or $-1\frac{1}{48}$ *Simplify.*

EXAMPLE 3 *Recreation Application*

Recreation LINK

Abraham Lincoln established Yosemite National Park as a natural preserve in 1864.

Two hikers begin hiking the North Dome trail in Yosemite National Park, which is $5\frac{3}{4}$ miles to the summit. The hikers cover $2\frac{1}{8}$ miles before taking a break. They then hike another $1\frac{1}{2}$ miles before taking a second break. How many more miles do the hikers have to go before reaching the summit?

$2\frac{1}{8} + 1\frac{1}{2}$ *Add to find the distance hiked.*

$= \frac{17}{8} + \frac{3}{2}$ *Write as improper fractions.*

$= \frac{17}{8} + \frac{12}{8}$ *The LCD is 8.*

$= \frac{29}{8}$, or $3\frac{5}{8}$

The hikers have hiked $3\frac{5}{8}$ miles. Now find the number of miles remaining.

$5\frac{3}{4} - 3\frac{5}{8}$ *Subtract the distance hiked from the total distance.*

$= \frac{23}{4} - \frac{29}{8}$ *Write as improper fractions.*

$= \frac{46}{8} - \frac{29}{8}$ *The LCD is 8.*

$= \frac{17}{8}$, or $2\frac{1}{8}$ *Simplify.*

The hikers have $2\frac{1}{8}$ miles to go before reaching the summit.

Think and Discuss

1. **Give an example** of two denominators with no common factors.
2. **Tell** if $-2\frac{1}{5} - \left(-2\frac{3}{16}\right)$ is positive or negative. Explain.
3. **Explain** how to add $2\frac{2}{5} + 9\frac{1}{3}$ without first writing them as improper fractions.

2-6 Exercises

go.hrw.com
Homework Help Online
KEYWORD: MT7 2-6
Parent Resources Online
KEYWORD: MT7 Parent

GUIDED PRACTICE

See Example 1 **Add or subtract.**

1. $\frac{4}{7} + \frac{1}{3}$
2. $\frac{1}{2} - \frac{7}{8}$
3. $3\frac{1}{2} + \left(-7\frac{4}{5}\right)$
4. $3\frac{7}{12} + \left(-2\frac{4}{5}\right)$

See Example 2 **Evaluate each expression for the given value of the variable.**

5. $4\frac{3}{8} + x$ for $x = -3\frac{2}{9}$
6. $n - \frac{3}{8}$ for $n = -\frac{4}{5}$
7. $\frac{3}{7} + y$ for $y = \frac{1}{2}$

See Example 3

8. Gavin needs $2\frac{5}{8}$ yards of fabric each to make two shirts. This amount is cut from a bolt containing $9\frac{1}{4}$ yards of fabric. How much fabric remains on the bolt?

INDEPENDENT PRACTICE

See Example 1 **Add or subtract.**

9. $\frac{7}{13} + \frac{2}{7}$
10. $\frac{1}{3} + \frac{4}{7}$
11. $\frac{11}{12} - \frac{4}{5}$
12. $\frac{2}{5} + \frac{14}{15}$
13. $5\frac{4}{5} + \left(-3\frac{2}{7}\right)$
14. $\frac{5}{9} - \frac{11}{14}$
15. $2\frac{1}{4} - 4\frac{3}{7}$
16. $\frac{1}{5} + \frac{8}{9}$

See Example 2 **Evaluate each expression for the given value of the variable.**

17. $2\frac{3}{4} + x$ for $x = -3\frac{2}{3}$
18. $n - \frac{2}{3}$ for $n = \frac{3}{4}$
19. $r - \frac{4}{5}$ for $r = \frac{3}{4}$
20. $3\frac{1}{6} + x$ for $x = -2\frac{5}{7}$
21. $n - \frac{11}{13}$ for $n = \frac{2}{3}$
22. $\frac{12}{17} - n$ for $n = \frac{1}{2}$

See Example 3

23. An oxygen tank contained $212\frac{2}{3}$ liters of oxygen before $27\frac{1}{3}$ liters were used. If the tank can hold $240\frac{3}{8}$ liters, how much space in the tank is unused?

PRACTICE AND PROBLEM SOLVING

Extra Practice
See page 785.

24. **Multi-Step** The heights of the starting players for the Davis High School boy's basketball team are $78\frac{1}{8}$ in., 74 in., $71\frac{5}{8}$ in., $70\frac{3}{4}$ in., and $69\frac{1}{2}$ in. Find the average height of the starting players.

25. **Measurement** A water pipe has an outside diameter of $1\frac{1}{4}$ inches and a wall thickness of $\frac{5}{16}$ inch. What is the inside diameter of the pipe?

26. **Estimation** Georgia is making a rectangular gift box. She plans to glue ribbon along the bottom edge. The length of the box is $7\frac{3}{8}$ inches, and the width is $5\frac{1}{16}$ inches. She has 2 feet of ribbon. Does she have enough for the bottom edge? Explain your reasoning.

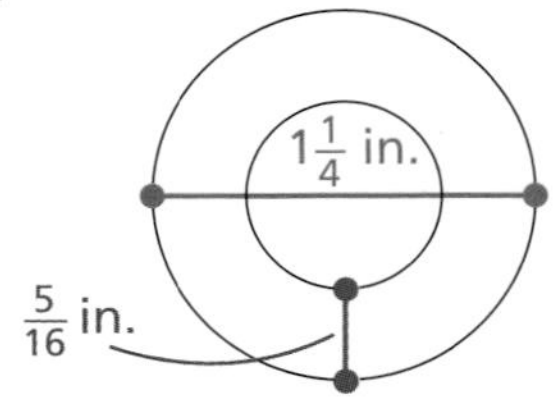

27. **Multi-Step** Karl rode his bike $16\frac{3}{8}$ miles. Neeka rode her bike m fewer miles.
    a. Write an expression to represent how many miles Neeka rode.
    b. How far did Neeka ride if she rode $5\frac{1}{4}$ fewer miles?
    c. Elda rode as far as Karl and Neeka combined. How far did Elda ride?

Earth Science LINK

Niagara Falls, on the border of Canada and the United States, has two major falls, Horseshoe Falls on the Canadian side and American Falls on the U.S. side. Surveys of the erosion of the falls began in 1842. From 1842 to 1905, Horseshoe Falls eroded $239\frac{2}{5}$ feet.

28. In 1986, Thomas Martin noted that American Falls eroded $7\frac{1}{2}$ inches and Horseshoe Falls eroded $2\frac{4}{25}$ feet. What is the difference between the two measurements?

29. From 1842 to 1875, the yearly erosion of Horseshoe Falls varied from a minimum of $\frac{61}{100}$ meter to a maximum of $1\frac{17}{50}$ meters. By how much did these rates of erosion differ?

30. In the 48 years between 1842 and 1890, the average rate of erosion at Horseshoe Falls was $\frac{33}{50}$ meter per year. In the 22 years between 1905 and 1927, the rate of erosion was $\frac{7}{10}$ meter per year. Approximately how much total erosion occurred during these two time periods?

31. **Challenge** Rates of erosion of American Falls have been recorded as $\frac{23}{100}$ meter per year for 33 years, $\frac{9}{40}$ meter per year for 48 years, and $\frac{1}{5}$ meter per year for 4 years. What is the total amount of erosion during these three time spans?

Test Prep and Spiral Review

32. Multiple Choice A $4\frac{5}{8}$ ft section of wood was cut from a $7\frac{1}{2}$ ft board. How much of the original board remained?

Ⓐ $3\frac{5}{8}$ ft Ⓑ $3\frac{9}{16}$ ft Ⓒ $2\frac{7}{8}$ ft Ⓓ $2\frac{3}{8}$ ft

33. Extended Response A rectangular swimming pool measured $75\frac{1}{2}$ feet by $25\frac{1}{4}$ feet. Schmidt Pool Supply computed the perimeter of the pool to be $200\frac{1}{3}$ feet. Explain what the company did incorrectly when computing the perimeter. What is the correct perimeter?

Evaluate each expression for the given value of the variable. (Lesson 1-4)

34. $c + 4$ for $c = -8$ **35.** $m - 2$ for $m = 13$ **36.** $5 + d$ for $d = -10$

Divide. Write each answer in simplest form. (Lesson 2-5)

37. $-\frac{4}{11} \div \frac{2}{7}$ **38.** $\frac{4}{9} \div 8$ **39.** $-\frac{7}{15} \div \frac{14}{25}$ **40.** $3\frac{1}{3} \div \frac{7}{9}$

Technology LAB 2-6

Add and Subtract Fractions

Use with Lesson 2-6

go.hrw.com
Lab Resources Online
KEYWORD: MT7 Lab2

You can add and subtract fractions using your graphing calculator. To display decimals as fractions, use the MATH key.

Activity

1 Use a graphing calculator to add $\frac{7}{12} + \frac{3}{8}$. Write the sum as a fraction.

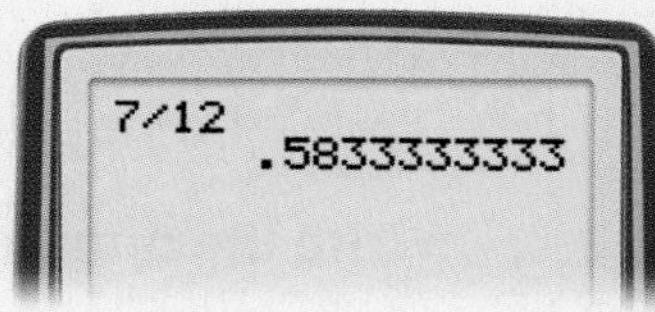

Type 7 ÷ 12 and press ENTER. You can see that the decimal equivalent is a repeating decimal, $0.58\overline{3}$.

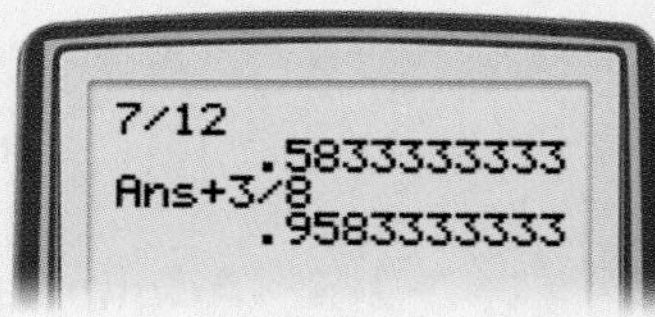

Type + 3 ÷ 8 ENTER. The decimal form of the sum is displayed.

Press MATH ENTER ENTER.

The fraction form of the sum, $\frac{23}{24}$, is displayed as 23/24.

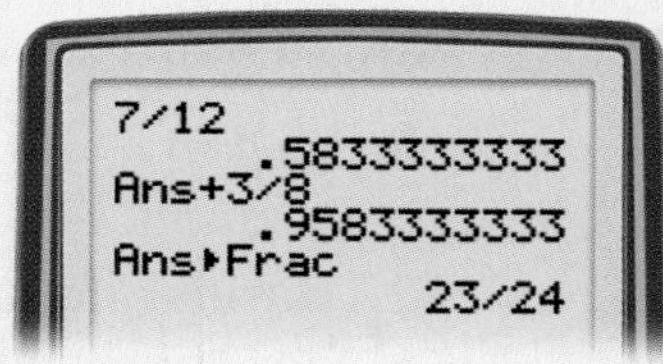

2 Use a graphing calculator to subtract $\frac{3}{5} - \frac{2}{3}$. Write the difference as a fraction.

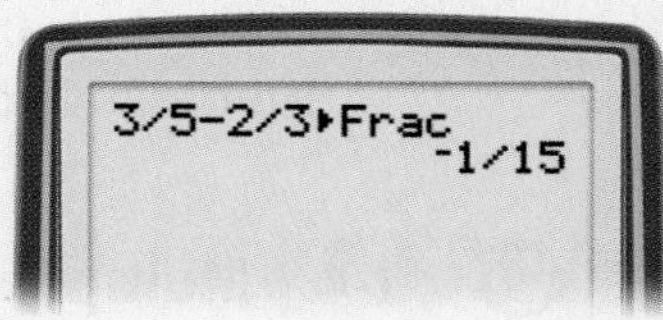

Type 3 ÷ 5 − 2 ÷ 3 MATH ENTER ENTER.

The answer is $-\frac{1}{15}$.

Think and Discuss

1. Why is the difference in **2** negative?

2. Type 0.33333 . . . (pressing 3 at least twelve times). Press MATH ENTER ENTER to write $0.\overline{3}$ as a fraction. Now do the same for $0.\overline{9}$. What happens to $0.\overline{9}$? How does the fraction for $0.\overline{3}$ help to explain this result?

Try This

Use a calculator to add or subtract. Write each result as a fraction.

1. $\frac{1}{4} + \frac{2}{7}$ **2.** $\frac{7}{8} - \frac{2}{3}$ **3.** $\frac{7}{15} + \frac{3}{10}$ **4.** $\frac{1}{3} - \frac{5}{7}$

5. $\frac{5}{32} + \frac{2}{11}$ **6.** $\frac{31}{101} - \frac{3}{5}$ **7.** $\frac{4}{15} + \frac{7}{16}$ **8.** $\frac{3}{35} - \frac{3}{37}$

READY TO GO ON?

SECTION 2A

Quiz for Lessons 2-1 Through 2-6

2-1 Rational Numbers

Simplify.

1. $\frac{12}{36}$
2. $\frac{15}{48}$
3. $\frac{33}{88}$
4. $\frac{55}{122}$

2-2 Comparing and Ordering Rational Numbers

Write the numbers in order from least to greatest.

5. $-1.2, \frac{2}{3}, 0.5, -\frac{3}{4}$
6. $3\frac{5}{7}, 0.1, \frac{7}{8}, 0.275$
7. $2.3, -\frac{3}{2}, -3, -3\frac{8}{9}$
8. $2\frac{10}{13}, 1.3, \frac{33}{8}, 2.99$

2-3 Adding and Subtracting Rational Numbers

Add or subtract. Write each answer in simplest form.

9. $65.8 - 24.24$
10. $-\frac{3}{7} + 2\frac{4}{7}$
11. $\frac{5}{6} + \left(-2\frac{1}{6}\right)$

12. Darius and Jamal ride their bicycles home from school every day. Each day this week, they have timed themselves to see how long the ride takes. On Monday, they made it home in about 0.25 hour. Today, it took them $\frac{3}{10}$ hour. How much longer did it take today?

2-4 Multiplying Rational Numbers

Multiply. Write each answer in simplest form.

13. $2\left(4\frac{2}{3}\right)$
14. $2\frac{2}{5}\left(\frac{7}{36}\right)$
15. $3.8(4)$
16. $\frac{-1}{7}\left(\frac{-3}{4}\right)$

17. Robert has a piece of twine that is $\frac{3}{4}$ yard long. He needs a piece of twine that is $\frac{2}{3}$ of this length. How long of a piece of twine does Robert need?

2-5 Dividing Rational Numbers

Divide. Write each answer in simplest form.

18. $\frac{3}{5} \div \frac{4}{15}$
19. $2.7 \div 3$
20. $-\frac{2}{3} \div 1$
21. $-4\frac{6}{7} \div 2\frac{5}{6}$

2-6 Adding and Subtracting with Unlike Denominators

Add or subtract. Write each answer in simplest form.

22. $\frac{2}{7} + \frac{1}{4}$
23. $1\frac{2}{3} + 3\frac{5}{9}$
24. $6\frac{4}{7} - 3\frac{1}{5}$
25. $3\frac{1}{6} - 1\frac{3}{4}$

Focus on Problem Solving

Look Back

- **Is your answer reasonable?**

After you solve a word problem, ask yourself if your answer makes sense. You can round the numbers in the problem and estimate to find a reasonable answer. It may also help to write your answer in sentence form.

Read the problems below and tell which answer is most reasonable.

1. Tonia calculates that she needs $47\frac{2}{3}$ pounds of compost to spread on her garden. There are 38.9 pounds of compost in her compost pile. How much compost does Tonia need to purchase?

   (A) about 9 pounds
   (B) about 87 pounds
   (C) about 6 pounds
   (D) about 15 pounds

2. The Qin Dynasty in China began about 2170 years before the People's Republic of China was formed in 1949. When did the Qin Dynasty begin?

   (F) before 200 B.C.E.
   (G) between 200 B.C.E. and 200 C.E.
   (H) between 200 C.E. and 1949 C.E.
   (J) after 1949 C.E.

3. On Mercury, the coldest temperature is about 600°C below the hottest temperature of 430°C. What is the coldest temperature on the planet?

   (A) about 1030°C
   (B) about −1030°C
   (C) about −170°C
   (D) about 170°C

4. Julie is balancing her checkbook. Her beginning balance is $325.46, her deposits add up to $285.38, and her withdrawals add up to $683.27. What is her ending balance?

   (F) about −$70
   (G) about −$600
   (H) about $700
   (J) about $1300

2-7 Solving Equations with Rational Numbers

Learn to solve equations with rational numbers.

Painting a house can be a difficult task. In order to have a good surface for the new paint, the old paint must be cleaned, and sometimes even scraped off completely.

Sully runs his own house-painting business. When he plans a job, he estimates that he can paint $\frac{2}{5}$ of a house in one work day. You can write and solve an equation to find how long it would take Sully to paint 3 houses.

EXAMPLE 1 Solving Equations with Decimals

Solve.

A $\mathbf{y - 17.5 = 11}$

$$y - 17.5 = 11$$
$$\underline{+17.5} \quad \underline{+17.5} \qquad \textit{Add 17.5 to both sides.}$$
$$y = 28.5$$

Remember!

Once you have solved an equation, it is a good idea to check your answer. To check your answer, substitute your answer for the variable in the original equation.

B $\mathbf{-4.2p = 12.6}$

$$-4.2p = 12.6$$
$$\frac{-4.2p}{-4.2} = \frac{12.6}{-4.2} \qquad \textit{Divide both sides by } -4.2.$$
$$p = -3$$

C $\mathbf{\frac{t}{7.5} = 4}$

$$\frac{t}{7.5} = 4$$
$$7.5 \cdot \frac{t}{7.5} = 7.5 \cdot 4 \qquad \textit{Multiply both sides by 7.5.}$$
$$t = 30$$

EXAMPLE 2 Solving Equations with Fractions

Solve.

A $\mathbf{x + \frac{1}{9} = -\frac{4}{9}}$

$$x + \frac{1}{9} = -\frac{4}{9}$$
$$x + \frac{1}{9} - \frac{1}{9} = -\frac{4}{9} - \frac{1}{9} \qquad \textit{Subtract } \frac{1}{9} \textit{ from both sides.}$$
$$x = -\frac{5}{9}$$

Solve.

B $x - \frac{1}{8} = \frac{9}{16}$

$$x - \frac{1}{8} = \frac{9}{16}$$

$$x - \frac{1}{8} + \frac{1}{8} = \frac{9}{16} + \frac{1}{8}$$ *Add $\frac{1}{8}$ to both sides.*

$$x = \frac{9}{16} + \frac{2}{16}$$ *Find a common denominator, 16.*

$$x = \frac{11}{16}$$

C $\frac{3}{5}w = \frac{3}{16}$

$$\frac{3}{5}w = \frac{3}{16}$$

$$\frac{3}{5}w \div \frac{3}{5} = \frac{3}{16} \div \frac{3}{5}$$ *Divide both sides by $\frac{3}{5}$.*

$$\frac{\cancel{3}}{\cancel{5}}w \cdot \frac{\cancel{5}}{\cancel{3}} = \frac{\cancel{3}}{16} \cdot \frac{5}{\cancel{3}}$$ *Multiply by the reciprocal. Simplify.*

$$w = \frac{5}{16}$$

EXAMPLE 3 Solving Word Problems Using Equations

Sully has agreed to paint 3 houses. If he knows that he can paint $\frac{2}{5}$ of a house in one day, how many days will it take him to paint all 3 houses?

Write an equation:

number of days	×	*houses per day*	=	*number of houses*
d	×	$\frac{2}{5}$	=	3

$$d \cdot \frac{2}{5} = 3$$

$$d \cdot \frac{2}{5} \div \frac{2}{5} = 3 \div \frac{2}{5}$$ *Divide both sides by $\frac{2}{5}$.*

$$d \cdot \frac{2}{5} \cdot \frac{5}{2} = 3 \cdot \frac{5}{2}$$ *Multiply by the reciprocal.*

$$d = \frac{15}{2}, \text{ or } 7\frac{1}{2}$$ *Simplify.*

Sully can paint 3 houses in $7\frac{1}{2}$ days.

Think and Discuss

1. **Explain** the first step in solving an addition equation with fractions having *like* denominators.
2. **Explain** the first step in solving an addition equation with fractions having *unlike* denominators.

2-7 Exercises

go.hrw.com
Homework Help Online
KEYWORD: MT7 2-7
Parent Resources Online
KEYWORD: MT7 Parent

GUIDED PRACTICE

See Example 1

Solve.

1. $y + 17.3 = -65$

2. $-5.2f = 36.4$

3. $\frac{m}{3.2} = -6$

4. $r - 15.8 = 24.6$

5. $\frac{s}{15.42} = 6.3$

6. $0.06g = 0.474$

See Example 2

7. $x + \frac{1}{9} = -\frac{4}{9}$

8. $-\frac{3}{8} + k = -\frac{7}{8}$

9. $\frac{5}{6}w = -\frac{7}{18}$

10. $m - \frac{4}{3} = -\frac{4}{3}$

11. $\frac{7}{17}y = -\frac{56}{17}$

12. $t + \frac{4}{13} = \frac{12}{39}$

See Example 3

13. Alonso runs a company called Speedy House Painters. His workers can paint $\frac{3}{4}$ of a house in one day. How many days would it take them to paint 6 houses?

INDEPENDENT PRACTICE

See Example 1

Solve.

14. $y + 16.7 = -49$

15. $4.7m = -32.9$

16. $-\frac{h}{7.8} = 2$

17. $k - 3.2 = -6.8$

18. $\frac{z}{11.4} = 6$

19. $c + 5.98 = 9.1$

See Example 2

20. $j + \frac{1}{3} = \frac{3}{4}$

21. $\frac{5}{6}d = \frac{3}{15}$

22. $7h = \frac{14}{33}$

23. $\frac{2}{3} + x = \frac{5}{8}$

24. $x - \frac{1}{16} = \frac{7}{16}$

25. $r + \frac{4}{7} = -\frac{1}{7}$

26. $\frac{5}{6}c = \frac{7}{24}$

27. $\frac{7}{8}d = \frac{11}{12}$

See Example 3

28. A professional lawn care service can mow $2\frac{3}{4}$ acres of lawn in one hour. How many hours would it take them to mow a lawn that is $6\frac{7}{8}$ acres?

PRACTICE AND PROBLEM SOLVING

Extra Practice
See page 785.

Earth Science The largest of all known diamonds, the Cullinan diamond, weighed 3106 carats before it was cut into 105 gems. The largest cut, Cullinan I, or the Great Star of Africa, weighs $530\frac{1}{3}$ carats. Another cut, Cullinan II, weighs $317\frac{2}{5}$ carats. Cullinan III weighs $94\frac{2}{5}$ carats, and Cullinan IV weighs $63\frac{3}{5}$ carats.

29. How many carats of the original Cullinan diamond were left after the Great Star of Africa and Cullinan II were cut?

30. How much more does Cullinan II weigh than Cullinan IV?

31. Which diamond weighs 223 carats less than Cullinan II?

32. **Nutrition** An entire can of chicken noodle soup has 6.25 grams of total fat. There are 2.5 servings per can. How many grams of total fat are in a single serving of chicken noodle soup?

Solve.

33. $z - \frac{2}{9} = \frac{1}{9}$ **34.** $-5f = -1.5$ **35.** $\frac{j}{7.2} = -3$ **36.** $\frac{2}{5} + x = 0.25$

37. $t - \frac{3}{4} = 6\frac{1}{4}$ **38.** $\frac{x}{0.5} = \frac{7}{8}$ **39.** $\frac{6}{7}d = -\frac{3}{7}$ **40.** $-4.7g = -28.2$

41. $\frac{v}{5.5} = -5.5$ **42.** $r + \frac{5}{6} = -3\frac{1}{6}$ **43.** $y + 2.8 = -1.4$

44. $-\frac{1}{15} + r = \frac{3}{5}$ **45.** $-3c = \frac{3}{20}$ **46.** $m - 2.34 = 8.2$

47. $y - 57 = -2.8$ **48.** $-18 = -9.6 + f$ **49.** $\frac{4m}{0.8} = -7$

50. **Multi-Step** Jack is tiling along the walls of the rectangular kitchen with the tile shown. The kitchen has a length of $243\frac{3}{4}$ inches and a width of $146\frac{1}{4}$ inches.

a. How many tiles will fit along the length of the room?

b. How many tiles will fit along its width?

c. If Jack needs 48 tiles to tile around all four walls of the kitchen, how many boxes of ten tiles must he buy? (*Hint:* He must buy whole boxes of tile.)

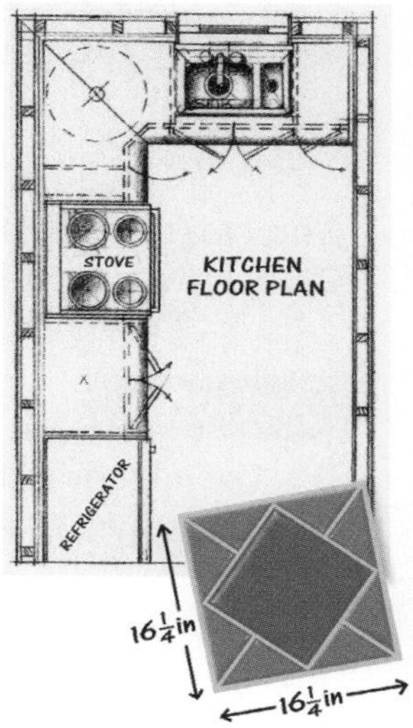

51. **What's the Error?** Janice is thinking about buying a CD writer that burns 1.8 megabytes of data per second. A computer salesperson told her that if she had 60 megabytes of data to burn, she could burn it in about 2 minutes with this writer. What was his error?

52. **Write About It** If a is $\frac{1}{3}$ of b, is it correct to say $\frac{1}{3}a = b$? Explain.

53. **Challenge** A 200-carat diamond was cut into two equal pieces to form two diamonds. One of the diamonds was cut again, reducing it by $\frac{1}{5}$ its weight. In a final cut, it was reduced by $\frac{1}{4}$ its new weight. How many carats remained?

Test Prep and Spiral Review

54. **Multiple Choice** If $\frac{12}{36} = 2w$, what is the value of w?

Ⓐ $\frac{24}{36}$ Ⓑ $\frac{24}{72}$ Ⓒ $\frac{1}{3}$ Ⓓ $\frac{1}{6}$

55. **Short Response** The performance of a musical arrangement lasted $6\frac{1}{4}$ minutes. The song consisted of 3 verses that each lasted the same number of minutes. Write and solve an equation to find the length of each verse.

Write an algebraic expression for each word phrase. (Lesson 1-2)

56. 15 less than a number p **57.** half of the sum of m and 19

Add or subtract. Write each answer in simplest form. (Lesson 2-6)

58. $\frac{7}{8} + \frac{1}{6}$ **59.** $4\frac{2}{3} + 5\frac{3}{4}$ **60.** $6\frac{5}{8} - 2\frac{1}{20}$ **61.** $2\frac{8}{9} - \frac{4}{5}$

Hands-On LAB 2-8

Model Two-Step Equations

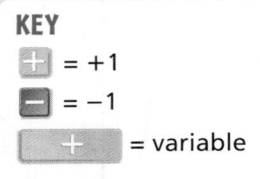

Use with Lesson 2-8

go.hrw.com
Lab Resources Online
KEYWORD: MT7 Lab2

KEY

= +1

= −1

= variable

REMEMBER

+ = 0

- **You can perform the same operation with the same numbers on both sides of an equation without changing the value of the equation.**

You can use algebra tiles to model and solve two-step equations. To solve a two-step equation, you use two different operations.

Activity

1. Use algebra tiles to model and solve $3s + 4 = 10$.

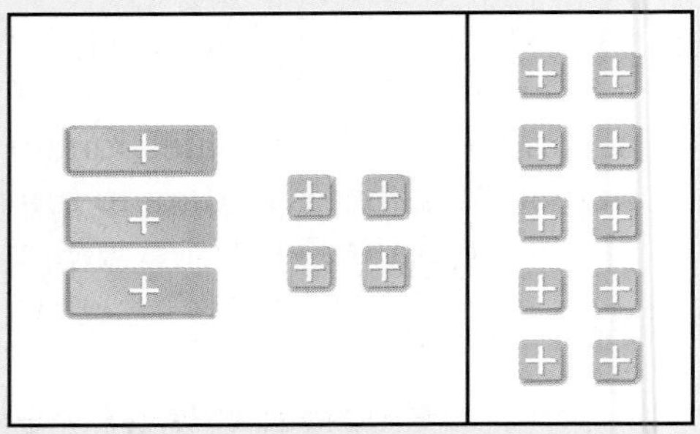

$3s + 4 = 10$

Two steps are needed to solve this equation.

Step 1: Remove 4 yellow tiles from each side.

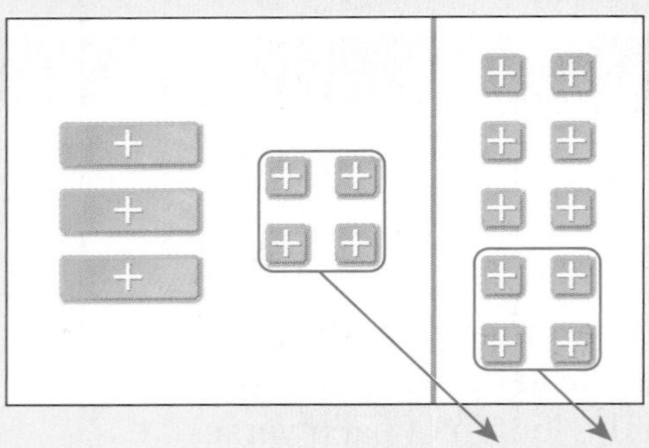

$3s = 6$

Step 2: Divide each side into 3 equal groups.

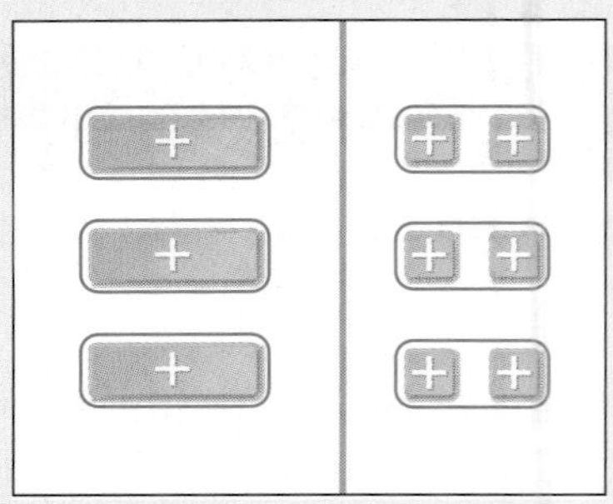

$s = 2$

Substitute to check:

$$3s + 4 = 10$$
$$3(2) + 4 \stackrel{?}{=} 10$$
$$6 + 4 \stackrel{?}{=} 10$$
$$10 \stackrel{?}{=} 10 \checkmark$$

2 Use algebra tiles to model and solve $2r + 4 = -6$.

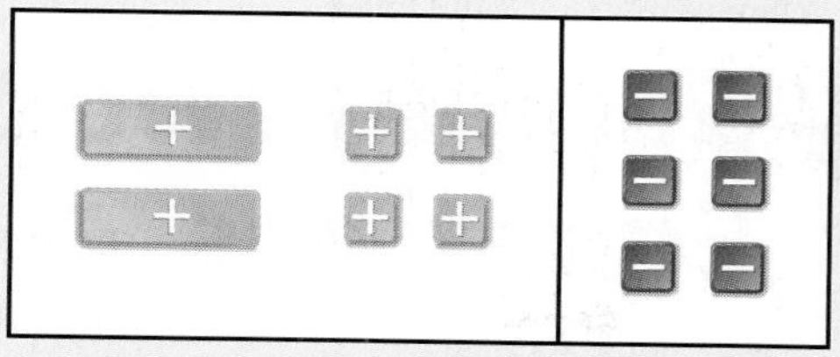

$2r + 4 = -6$

Step 1: Since 4 is being added to $2r$, add 4 red tiles to both sides and remove the zero pairs on the left side.

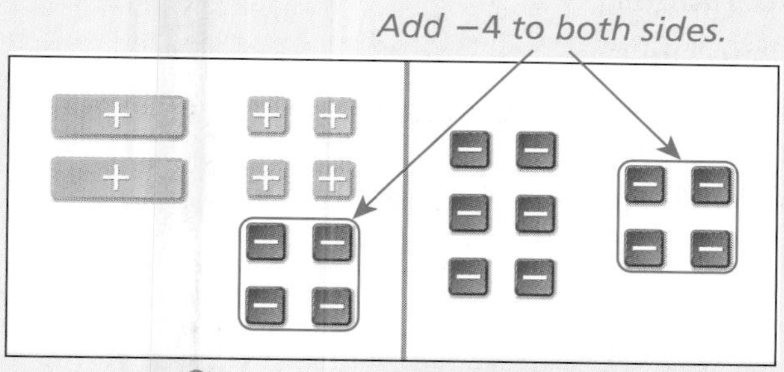

$2r = -10$

Step 2: Divide each side into 2 equal groups.

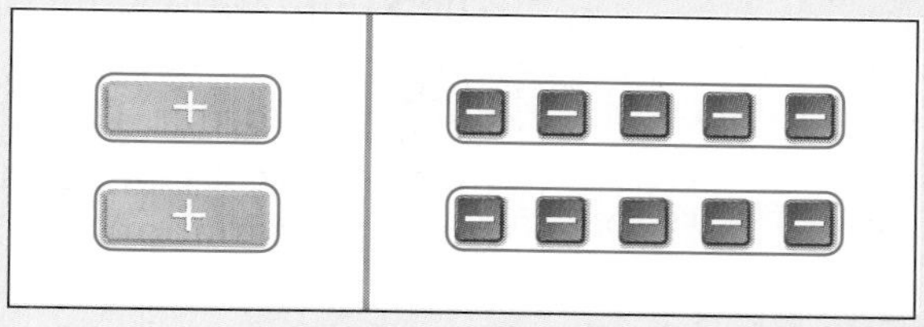

$r = -5$

Substitute to check:

$$\begin{aligned} 2r + 4 &\stackrel{?}{=} -6 \\ 2(-5) + 4 &\stackrel{?}{=} -6 \\ -10 + 4 &\stackrel{?}{=} -6 \\ -6 &\stackrel{?}{=} -6 \checkmark \end{aligned}$$

Think and Discuss

1. Why can you add zero pairs to one side of an equation without having to add them to the other side as well?
2. Show how you could have modeled to check your solution for each equation.

Try This

Use algebra tiles to model and solve each of the following equations.

1. $2x + 3 = 5$
2. $4p - 3 = 9$
3. $5r - 6 = -11$
4. $3n + 5 = -4$
5. $6b + 8 = 2$
6. $2a + 2 = 6$
7. $4m + 4 = 4$
8. $7h - 8 = 41$

9. Gerry walked dogs five times a week and got paid the same amount each day. One week his boss added on a $15 bonus. That week Gerry earned $90. What was his daily salary?

2-8 Solving Two-Step Equations

Learn to solve two-step equations.

Sometimes more than one inverse operation is needed to solve an equation. Before solving, ask yourself, "What is being done to the variable and in what order?" One method to solve the equation is to then work backward to undo the operations.

The Kuhr family bought tickets to see a circus. The ticket service charged a service fee for the order. The number of tickets the Kuhrs bought can be found by solving a two-step equation.

EXAMPLE 1 PROBLEM SOLVING APPLICATION

The Kuhr family spent \$52.00 for circus tickets. This cost included a \$3.25 service fee for the order, and the circus tickets cost \$9.75 each. How many tickets did the Kuhrs buy? Justify your answer.

1 Understand the Problem

The **answer** is the number of tickets that the Kuhrs bought. List the **important information:** The service fee is \$3.25 per order, the tickets cost \$9.75 each, and the total cost is \$52.

Let t represent the number of tickets bought.

Total cost	=	Tickets	+	Service Fee
52.00	=	$9.75t$	+	3.25

2 Make a Plan

Think: First the variable is multiplied by 9.75, and then 3.25 is added to the result. Work backward to solve the equation. Undo the operations in reverse order: First subtract 3.25 from both sides of the equation, and then divide both sides of the new equation by 9.75.

3 Solve

$$52.00 = 9.75t + 3.25$$

$$\underline{-3.25} \qquad \underline{-3.25} \qquad \textit{Subtract 3.25 from both sides.}$$

$$48.75 = 9.75t$$

$$\frac{48.75}{9.75} = \frac{9.75t}{9.75} \qquad \textit{Divide both sides by 9.75.}$$

$$5 = t$$

The Kuhrs bought 5 tickets.

4 Look Back

You can use a table to decide whether your answer is reasonable.

Tickets	Cost of Tickets	Service Charge	Total Cost
1	\$9.75	\$3.25	\$13.00
2	\$19.50	\$3.25	\$22.75
3	\$29.25	\$3.25	\$32.50
4	\$39.00	\$3.25	\$42.25
5	\$48.75	\$3.25	\$52.00

Five tickets is a reasonable answer.

Sometimes, a two-step equation contains a term or an expression with a denominator. In these cases, it is often easier to first multiply both sides of the equation by the denominator in order to remove it, and then work to isolate the variable.

EXAMPLE 2 Solving Two-Step Equations

Solve $\frac{r+7}{4} = 5$.

A Method 1: Work backward to isolate the variable.

$\frac{r+7}{4} = 5$

$\frac{r}{4} + \frac{7}{4} = 5$ *Rewrite the expression as the sum of two fractions.*

Think: First the variable is **divided by 4**, and then $\frac{7}{4}$ **is added.** To isolate the variable, **subtract** $\frac{7}{4}$, and then **multiply by 4.**

$\frac{r}{4} + \frac{7}{4} - \frac{7}{4} = 5 - \frac{7}{4}$ *Subtract $\frac{7}{4}$ from both sides.*

$(4)\frac{r}{4} = \frac{13}{4}(4)$ *Multiply both sides by 4.*

$r = 13$

B Method 2: Multiply both sides of the equation by the denominator.

$\frac{r+7}{4} = 5$

$(4)\frac{r+7}{4} = 5(4)$ *Multiply both sides by 4.*

$r + 7 = 20$

$\underline{-7} \quad \underline{-7}$ *Subtract 7 from both sides.*

$r = 13$

Think and Discuss

1. **Describe** how you would solve $4(x - 2) = 16$.
2. **Explain** how to check your solution to an equation.

2-8 Exercises

go.hrw.com
Homework Help Online
KEYWORD: MT7 2-8
Parent Resources Online
KEYWORD: MT7 Parent

GUIDED PRACTICE

See Example 1

1. Adele is paid a weekly salary of \$685. She is paid an additional \$23.50 for every hour of overtime he works. This week his total pay, including regular salary and overtime, was \$849.50. How many hours of overtime did Adele work this week?

See Example 2

Solve.

2. $\frac{t-3}{2} = 75$ **3.** $\frac{t+10}{6} = 11$ **4.** $\frac{r-12}{7} = 6$ **5.** $\frac{x+7}{11} = 11$

6. $\frac{b+24}{2} = 13$ **7.** $\frac{q-11}{5} = 23$ **8.** $\frac{a-3}{28} = 3$ **9.** $\frac{y-13}{8} = 14$

INDEPENDENT PRACTICE

See Example 1

10. The cost of a family membership at a health club is \$58 per month plus a one-time \$129 start-up fee. If a family spent \$651, how many months is their membership?

See Example 2

Solve.

11. $\frac{m+6}{-3} = 4$ **12.** $\frac{c-1}{2} = 12$ **13.** $\frac{g-2}{2} = -46$ **14.** $\frac{h+20}{9} = 11$

15. $\frac{h+19}{19} = 2$ **16.** $\frac{y-3}{4} = -27$ **17.** $\frac{z-4}{10} = 9$ **18.** $\frac{n-31}{10} = 22$

PRACTICE AND PROBLEM SOLVING

Extra Practice
See page 785.

Solve.

19. $5w + 2.7 = 12.8$ **20.** $15 - 3x = -6$ **21.** $\frac{m}{5} + 6 = 9$

22. $\frac{z+9}{4} = 2.1$ **23.** $2x + \frac{2}{3} = \frac{4}{5}$ **24.** $9 = -5g - 23$

25. $6z - 3 = 0$ **26.** $\frac{5}{2}d - \frac{3}{2} = -\frac{1}{2}$ **27.** $58k + 35 = 615$

28. $8 = 6 + \frac{p}{2}$ **29.** $40 - 3n = -23$ **30.** $\frac{17+s}{15} = -4$

31. $9y - 7.2 = 4.5$ **32.** $\frac{2}{3} - 6h = -\frac{13}{6}$ **33.** $-1 = \frac{5}{8}b + \frac{3}{8}$

Translate each sentence into an equation. Then solve the equation.

34. The quotient of a number and 2, minus 9, is 14.

35. A number decreased by 7 and then divided by 5 is 13.

36. The sum of 15 and 7 times a number is 99.

37. Show two ways to solve the equation $\frac{m-3}{2} = 37$. Check your answer.

38. **Consumer Math** A long distance phone company charges \$19.95 per month plus \$0.05 per minute for calls. If a family's monthly long distance bill is \$23.74, how many minutes of long distance did they use?

Life Science LINK

About 20% of the more than 2500 species of snakes are venomous. The United States has 20 domestic venomous snake species.

Venom is collected from snakes and injected into horses, which develop antibodies. The horses' blood is sterilized to make antivenom.

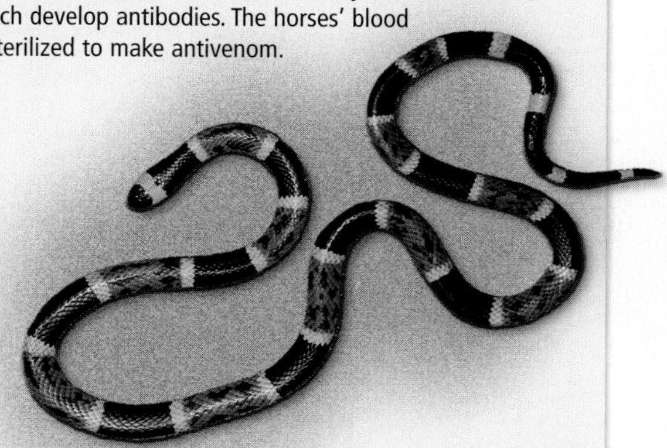

39. The inland taipan of central Australia is the world's most toxic venomous snake. Just 1 mg of its venom can kill 1000 mice. One bite contains up to 110 mg of venom. About how many mice could be killed with just one inland taipan bite?

40. A rattlesnake grows a new rattle segment each time it sheds its skin. Rattlesnakes shed their skin an average of three times per year. However, segments often break off. If a rattlesnake had 44 rattle segments break off in its lifetime and it had 10 rattles when it died, approximately how many years did the rattlesnake live?

41. All snakes shed their skin. The shed skin of a snake is an average of 10% longer than the actual snake. If the shed skin of a coral snake is 27.5 inches long, estimate the length of the coral snake.

42. **Challenge** Black mambas feed mainly on small rodents and birds. Suppose a black mamba is 100 feet away from an animal that is running at 8 mi/h. About how long will it take for the mamba to catch the animal? (*Hint*: 1 mile = 5280 feet)

go.hrw.com
Web Extra!
KEYWORD: MT7 Snakes

Records of World's Most Venomous Snakes

Category	Record	Type of Snake
Fastest	12 mi/h	Black mamba
Longest	18 ft 9 in.	King cobra
Heaviest	34 lb	Eastern diamondback rattlesnake
Longest fangs	2 in.	Gaboon viper

Test Prep and Spiral Review

43. Multiple Choice A plumber charges \$75 for a house call plus \$45 per hour. How many hours did the plumber work if he charged \$210?

Ⓐ 2 Ⓑ 3 Ⓒ 4 Ⓓ 6

44. Gridded Response What value of y makes the equation $4.4y + 1.75 = 43.99$ true?

Solve and graph each inequality. (Lesson 1-9)

45. $3x < 15$ **46.** $x + 2 \geq 4$ **47.** $x + 1 \leq 3$ **48.** $x - 4 < 4$

Solve. (Lesson 2-7)

49. $y - 27.6 = -32$ **50.** $-5.3f = 74.2$ **51.** $\frac{m}{3.2} = -8$ **52.** $x + \frac{1}{8} = -\frac{5}{8}$

CHAPTER 2

READY TO GO ON?

SECTION 2B

Quiz for Lessons 2-7 Through 2-8

2-7 Solving Equations with Rational Numbers

Solve.

1. $p - 1.2 = -5$

2. $-9w = 13.5$

3. $\frac{m}{3.7} = -8$

4. $x + \frac{1}{9} = -\frac{4}{7}$

5. $m - \frac{3}{4} = -\frac{4}{3}$

6. $\frac{7}{33}y = -\frac{56}{3}$

7. $\frac{y}{-2.6} = 3.2$

8. $s + 0.45 = 10.07$

9. $p + 2.7 = 4.5$

10. $\frac{h}{2.5} = 3.8$

11. $y - \frac{7}{8} = -\frac{25}{12}$

12. $\frac{8}{11}k = \frac{29}{44}$

13. The Montegro Flooring Company can replace 200 square feet of carpet with tile in one day. They accept a job replacing carpet with tile in an apartment that measures 977.5 square feet. How many days will it take the Montegro Flooring Company to complete this job?

14. From start to finish, Ellen took $15\frac{2}{3}$ days to write a research paper for her literature class. This was $\frac{9}{10}$ the time it took Rebecca to write her paper. How long did it take Rebecca to write her research paper?

2-8 Solving Two-Step Equations

Solve.

15. $\frac{x + 7}{6} = -48$

16. $3x + 4.2 = 21$

17. $\frac{1}{4}y - \frac{2}{3} = \frac{5}{6}$

18. $\frac{y}{12} + 6 = -72$

19. $-5p + 10 = 75$

20. $\frac{r - 2}{-7} = 3$

21. $2w + 7.1 = 2.85$

22. $-8.9y - 10.11 = 74.44$

23. $\frac{p + 17}{25} = 4$

24. Marvin sold newspaper subscriptions during summer break. He earned \$125.00 per week plus \$5.75 for each subscription that he sold. During the last week of the summer, Marvin earned \$228.50. How many subscriptions did he sell that week?

25. A cell phone company charges \$13.50 per month plus $3\frac{1}{2}$ cents for each minute used. If Angelina's cell phone bill was \$17.70 last month, how many minutes did she use?

MULTI-STEP TEST PREP

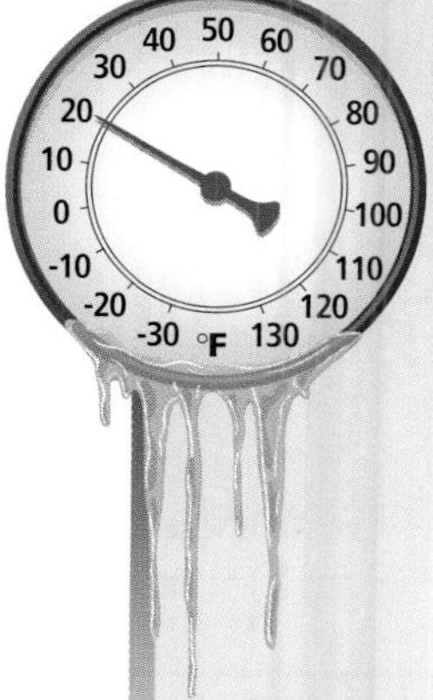

Some Like It Cold Scientists usually use the Celsius scale to measure temperatures. You can use the formula $C = \frac{5}{9}(F - 32)$ to convert a temperature in degrees Fahrenheit, °F, to a temperature in degrees Celsius, °C.

1. Water freezes at 32 degrees Fahrenheit (32°F) and boils at 212 degrees Fahrenheit (212°F). Use the formula to convert 32°F and 212°F to degrees Celsius. Why do you think scientists prefer the Celsius scale?
2. When temperatures are converted from Fahrenheit to Celsius, an interesting thing happens as the Fahrenheit temperature decreases. Convert −4°F, −22°F, and −40°F to degrees Celsius. What do you notice?
3. Use the above formula to write an equation to find the temperature in degrees Fahrenheit that corresponds to 40°C. Then solve the equation.
4. The formula $F = \frac{9}{5}C + 32$ converts a temperature in degrees Celsius to a temperature in degrees Fahrenheit. Use this formula to convert $-\frac{5}{18}$°C to degrees Fahrenheit.
5. The table shows the temperature in Nome, Alaska, recorded at several different times during a day in April. At which time was the lowest temperature recorded? Explain.

Temperature in Nome, Alaska

Time	Temperature
1:00 P.M.	25.7°F
3:00 P.M.	$25\frac{2}{5}$°F
5:00 P.M.	−3.5°C
7:00 P.M.	$-3\frac{4}{5}$°C

Wisconsin high school students participate in the annual Polar Plunge for Special Olympics.

Game Time

Egyptian Fractions

If you were to divide 9 loaves of bread among 10 people, you would give each person $\frac{9}{10}$ of a loaf. The answer was different on the ancient Egyptian Ahmes papyrus, because ancient Egyptians used only *unit fractions,* which have a numerator of 1. All other fractions were written as sums of different unit fractions. So $\frac{5}{6}$ could be written as $\frac{1}{2} + \frac{1}{3}$, but not as $\frac{1}{6} + \frac{1}{6} + \frac{1}{6} + \frac{1}{6} + \frac{1}{6}$.

Method	Example	
Suppose you want to write a fraction as a sum of different unit fractions.	$\frac{9}{10}$	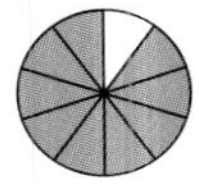
Step 1. Choose the largest fraction of the form $\frac{1}{n}$ that is less than the fraction you want.	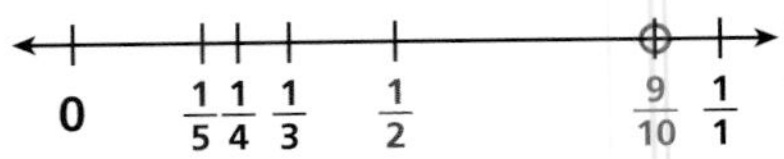	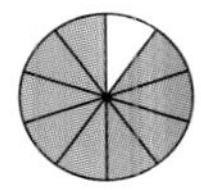
Step 2. Subtract $\frac{1}{n}$ from the fraction you want.	$\frac{9}{10} - \frac{1}{2} = \frac{2}{5}$ remaining	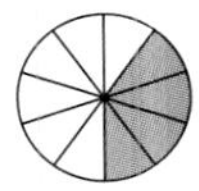
Step 3. Repeat steps 1 and 2 using the difference of the fractions until the result is a unit fraction.	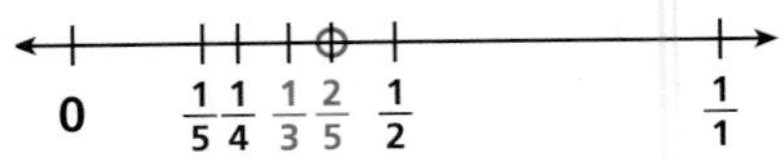 $\frac{2}{5} - \frac{1}{3} = \frac{1}{15}$ remaining	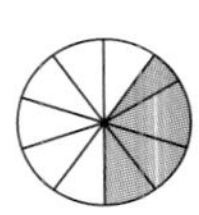
Step 4. Write the fraction you want as the sum of the unit fractions.	$\frac{9}{10} = \frac{1}{2} + \frac{1}{3} + \frac{1}{15}$	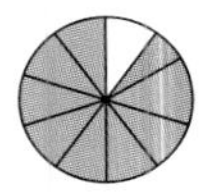

Write each fraction as a sum of different unit fractions.

1. $\frac{3}{4}$ **2.** $\frac{5}{8}$ **3.** $\frac{11}{12}$ **4.** $\frac{3}{7}$ **5.** $\frac{7}{5}$

Egg Fractions

This game is played with an empty egg carton. Each compartment represents a fraction with a denominator of 12. The goal is to place tokens in compartments with a given sum.

A complete copy of the rules is available online.

go.hrw.com
Game Time Extra
KEYWORD: MT7 Games

It's in the Bag!

FOLDNOTES

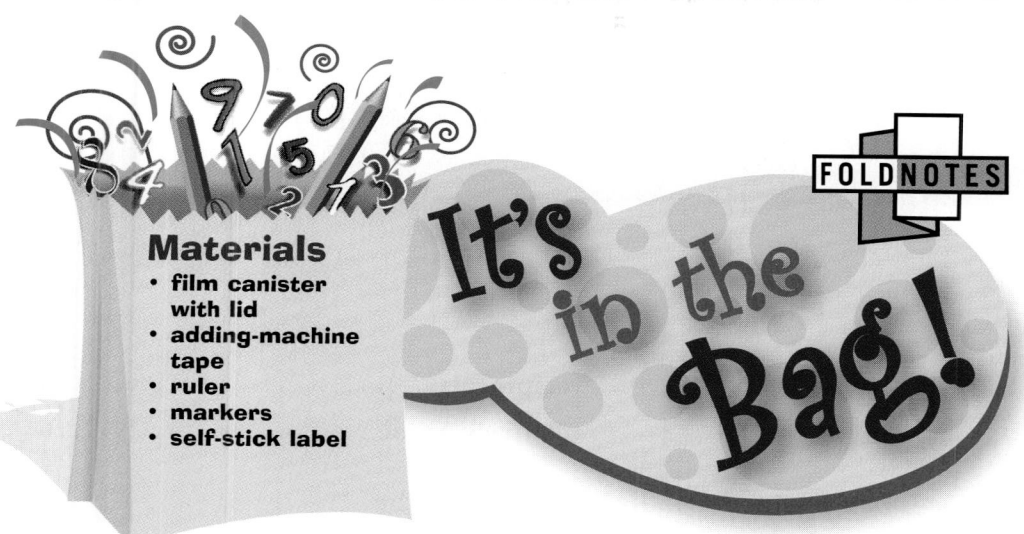

Materials
- film canister with lid
- adding-machine tape
- ruler
- markers
- self-stick label

PROJECT Canister Carry-All

Turn a film canister into a handy carrying case for a number line and notes about rational numbers.

Directions

1. If necessary, cut off a strip along the bottom edge of the adding-machine tape so that the tape will fit into the film canister when it is rolled up. When you're done, the tape should be about $1\frac{3}{4}$ in. wide. **Figure A**

2. Use a ruler to make a long number line on one side of the adding-machine tape. **Figure B**

3. Write the number and title of the chapter on a self-stick label. Then peel the backing off the label and place the label on the outside of the canister.

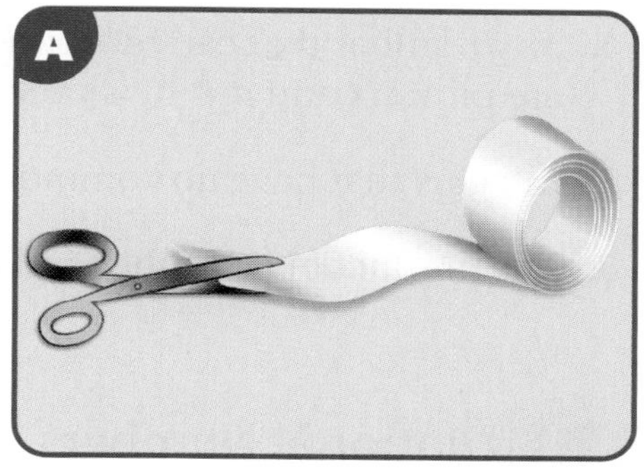

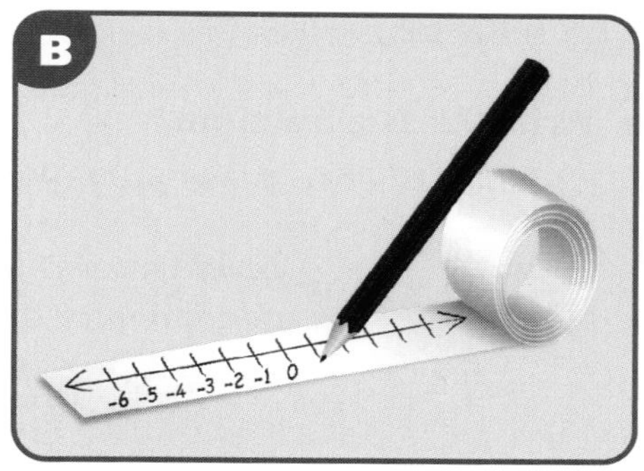

Taking Note of the Math

Place examples of rational numbers on the number line. Choose examples that will help you remember how to compare and order rational numbers. Then turn the adding-machine tape over, and use the other side to write notes and sample problems from the chapter.

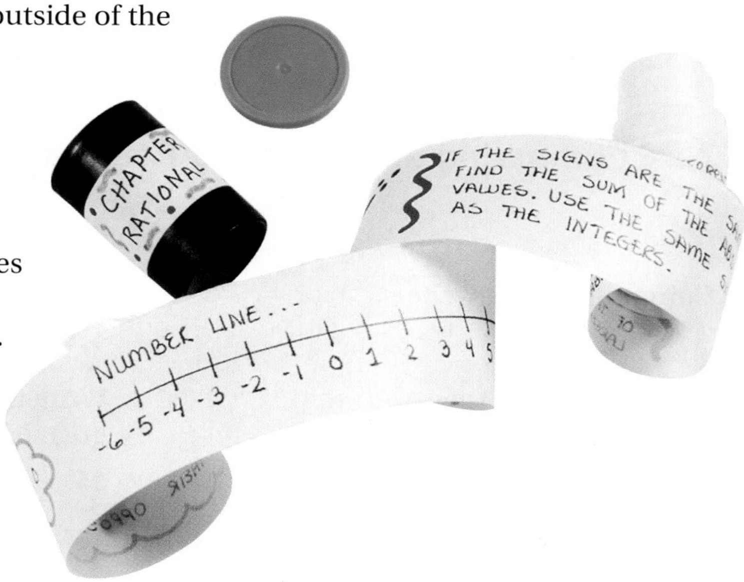

CHAPTER 2 Study Guide: Review

Vocabulary

least common denominator (LCD) 68

rational number 64

reciprocal 80

relatively prime 64

Complete the sentences below with vocabulary words from the list above.

1. Any number that can be written as a fraction $\frac{n}{d}$ (where n and d are integers and $d \neq 0$) is called a __?__.
2. Integers that have no common factors other than 1 are __?__.
3. The product of a number and its __?__ is 1.

2-1 Rational Numbers (pp. 64–67)

EXAMPLE

- **Write 0.8 as a fraction.**

$0.8 = \frac{8}{10}$ *8 is in the tenths place.*

$= \frac{8 \div 2}{10 \div 2}$ *Divide numerator and denominator by 2.*

$= \frac{4}{5}$

EXERCISES

Write each decimal as a fraction.

4. 0.6
5. 0.25
6. 0.525

Write each fraction as a decimal.

7. $\frac{7}{4}$
8. $\frac{4}{15}$
9. $\frac{7}{9}$

Simplify.

10. $\frac{14}{21}$
11. $\frac{22}{33}$
12. $\frac{75}{100}$

2-2 Comparing and Ordering Rational Numbers (pp. 68–71)

EXAMPLE

- **Compare $\frac{2}{3}$ ■ $\frac{5}{8}$. Write <, >, or =.**

$\frac{2}{3}$ ■ $\frac{5}{8}$

$\frac{2 \cdot 8}{3 \cdot 8} = \frac{16}{24}$ *24 is the LCD.*

$\frac{5 \cdot 3}{8 \cdot 3} = \frac{15}{24}$

$\frac{16}{24} > \frac{15}{24}$, so $\frac{2}{3} > \frac{5}{8}$

EXERCISES

Compare. Write <, >, or =.

13. $\frac{5}{7}$ ■ $\frac{9}{10}$
14. $\frac{7}{8}$ ■ $\frac{28}{32}$

Write the numbers in order from least to greatest.

15. $-\frac{2}{3}$, 0.25, $\frac{1}{2}$, −0.9
16. 0.67, $\frac{9}{10}$, 0, −0.11

2-3 Adding and Subtracting Rational Numbers (pp. 72–75)

EXAMPLE

Add or subtract.

■ $\frac{3}{7} + \frac{4}{7}$

$= \frac{3+4}{7} = \frac{7}{7} = 1$

■ $\frac{8}{11} - \left(-\frac{2}{11}\right)$

$= \frac{8-(-2)}{11} = \frac{8+2}{11} = \frac{10}{11}$

EXERCISES

Add or subtract.

17. $\frac{-8}{13} + \frac{2}{13}$

18. $\frac{3}{5} - \left(\frac{-4}{5}\right)$

19. $\frac{-2}{9} + \frac{7}{9}$

20. $\frac{-5}{12} - \left(\frac{-7}{12}\right)$

21. $\frac{-9}{11} + \frac{10}{11}$

22. $\frac{5}{13} - \frac{(-7)}{13}$

2-4 Multiplying Rational Numbers (pp. 76–79)

EXAMPLE

■ Multiply. Write the answer in simplest form.

$5\left(3\frac{1}{4}\right) = \left(\frac{5}{1}\right)\left(\frac{3(4)+1}{4}\right)$

$= \left(\frac{5}{1}\right)\left(\frac{13}{4}\right)$ *Write as improper fractions.*

$= \frac{65}{4} = 16\frac{1}{4}$ *Multiply and simplify.*

EXERCISES

Multiply. Write each answer in simplest form.

23. $3\left(-\frac{2}{5}\right)$

24. $2\left(3\frac{4}{5}\right)$

25. $\frac{-2}{3}\left(\frac{-4}{5}\right)$

26. $\frac{8}{11}\left(\frac{-22}{4}\right)$

27. $5\frac{1}{4}\left(\frac{3}{7}\right)$

28. $2\frac{1}{2}\left(1\frac{3}{10}\right)$

29. $4\frac{7}{8}\left(2\frac{2}{3}\right)$

30. $-\frac{8}{9}\left(\frac{7}{16}\right)$

2-5 Dividing Rational Numbers (pp. 80–84)

EXAMPLE

■ Divide. Write the answer in simplest form.

$\frac{7}{8} \div \frac{3}{4} = \frac{7}{8} \cdot \frac{4}{3}$ *Multiply by the reciprocal.*

$= \frac{7 \cdot 4}{8 \cdot 3}$ *Write as one fraction.*

$\frac{7 \cdot \cancel{4}^{1}}{{}_{2}\cancel{8} \cdot 3} = \frac{7 \cdot 1}{2 \cdot 3}$ *Remove common factors.*

$\frac{7}{6} = 1\frac{1}{6}$

EXERCISES

Divide. Write each answer in simplest form.

31. $\frac{3}{4} \div \frac{1}{8}$

32. $\frac{3}{10} \div \frac{4}{5}$

33. $\frac{2}{3} \div 3$

34. $4 \div \frac{-1}{4}$

35. $3\frac{3}{4} \div 3$

36. $1\frac{1}{3} \div \frac{2}{3}$

2-6 Adding and Subtracting with Unlike Denominators (pp. 85–88)

EXAMPLE

■ Add.

$\frac{3}{4} + \frac{2}{5}$ *Multiply denominators, 4 • 5 = 20.*

$\frac{3 \cdot 5}{4 \cdot 5} = \frac{15}{20} \quad \frac{2 \cdot 4}{5 \cdot 4} = \frac{8}{20}$

$\frac{15}{20} + \frac{8}{20} = \frac{15+8}{20} = \frac{23}{20} = 1\frac{3}{20}$ *Add and simplify.*

EXERCISES

Add or subtract.

37. $\frac{5}{6} + \frac{1}{3}$

38. $\frac{5}{6} - \frac{5}{9}$

39. $3\frac{1}{2} + 7\frac{4}{5}$

40. $7\frac{1}{10} - 2\frac{3}{4}$

41. $\frac{19}{20} + \frac{7}{3}$

42. $-1\frac{5}{9} - 7\frac{3}{4}$

2-7 Solving Equations with Rational Numbers (pp. 92–95)

EXAMPLE

Solve.

■ $x - 13.7 = -22$

$\underline{+13.7} = \underline{+13.7}$ *Add 13.7 to each side.*

$x = -8.3$

■ $\frac{7}{9}x = \frac{2}{5}$

$\frac{9}{7} \cdot \frac{7}{9}x = \frac{9}{7} \cdot \frac{2}{5}$ *Multiply both sides by $\frac{9}{7}$.*

$x = \frac{18}{35}$

EXERCISES

Solve.

43. $y + 7.8 = -14$

44. $2.9z = -52.2$

45. $w + \frac{3}{4} = \frac{1}{8}$

46. $\frac{3}{8}p = \frac{3}{4}$

47. $x - \frac{7}{9} = \frac{2}{11}$

48. $7.2x = -14.4$

49. $y - 18.7 = 25.9$

50. $\frac{19}{21}t = -\frac{38}{7}$

51. Freda paid \$126 for groceries for her family. This was $1\frac{1}{6}$ as much as she paid the previous time she shopped. How much did Freda pay on her previous shopping trip?

2-8 Solving Two-Step Equations (pp. 98–101)

EXAMPLE

Solve.

■ $7x + 12 = 33$

Think: First the variable is **multiplied by 7,** and then **12 is added.** To isolate the variable, **subtract 12,** and then **divide by 7.**

$7x + 12 = 33$

$\underline{\quad - 12} \quad \underline{- 12}$ *Subtract 12 from both sides.*

$7x = 21$

$\frac{7x}{7} = \frac{21}{7}$ *Divide both sides by 7.*

$x = 3$

■ $\frac{z}{3} - 8 = 5$

Think: First the variable is **divided by 3,** and then **8 is subtracted.** To isolate the variable, **add 8,** and then **multiply by 3.**

$\frac{z}{3} - 8 = 5$

$\underline{\quad + 8} \quad \underline{+8}$ *Add 8 to both sides.*

$\frac{z}{3} = 13$

$3 \cdot \frac{z}{3} = 3 \cdot 13$ *Multiply both sides by 3.*

$z = 39$

EXERCISES

Solve.

52. $3m + 5 = 35$

53. $55 = 7 - 6y$

54. $2c + 1 = -31$

55. $5r + 15 = 0$

56. $\frac{t}{2} + 7 = 15$

57. $\frac{w}{4} - 5 = 11$

58. $-25 = \frac{r}{3} - 11$

59. $\frac{h}{5} - 9 = -19$

60. $\frac{x + 2}{3} = 18$

61. $\frac{d - 3}{4} = -9$

62. $21 = \frac{a - 4}{3}$

63. $14 = \frac{c + 8}{7}$

64. A music club charges an annual membership fee of \$20.50 plus \$12.99 for each CD purchased. If Naomi's total bill for the year was \$163.39, how many CDs did she purchase?

Study Guide: Review

CHAPTER TEST

CHAPTER 2

Simplify.

1. $\frac{36}{72}$
2. $\frac{21}{35}$
3. $-\frac{16}{88}$
4. $\frac{18}{25}$

Write each decimal as a fraction in simplest form.

5. 0.225
6. 0.04
7. −0.101
8. 0.875

Write each fraction as a decimal.

9. $\frac{7}{8}$
10. $-\frac{13}{25}$
11. $\frac{5}{12}$
12. $\frac{4}{33}$

Write the numbers in order from least to greatest.

13. $\frac{2}{3}, -0.36, 0.2, -\frac{1}{4}$
14. $0.55, -\frac{7}{8}, -0.8, \frac{5}{6}$
15. $\frac{9}{10}, 0.7, 1.6, \frac{7}{5}$

Add or subtract. Write each answer in simplest form.

16. $\frac{-3}{11} - \left(\frac{-4}{11}\right)$
17. $7.25 - 2.75$
18. $\frac{5}{6} + \frac{7}{18}$
19. $\frac{5}{6} - \frac{8}{9}$
20. $4.5 + 5.875$
21. $8\frac{1}{5} - 1\frac{2}{3}$
22. Kory is making Thai food for several friends. She needs to triple her recipe. The recipe calls for $\frac{3}{4}$ teaspoon of curry. How much curry does she need?

Multiply or divide. Write each answer in simplest form.

23. $9(0.63)$
24. $\frac{7}{8} \div \frac{5}{24}$
25. $\frac{2}{3}\left(\frac{-9}{20}\right)$
26. $3\frac{3}{7}\left(1\frac{5}{16}\right)$
27. $34 \div 3.4$
28. $-4\frac{2}{3} \div 1\frac{1}{6}$
29. Lucie drank $\frac{3}{4}$ pint of bottled water. One serving of the water is $\frac{7}{8}$ pint. How much of a serving did Lucie drink?

Solve.

30. $x - \frac{1}{4} = -\frac{3}{8}$
31. $-3.14y = 53.38$
32. $\frac{x + 7}{12} = 11$
33. $-2k = \frac{1}{4}$
34. $2h - 3.24 = -1.1$
35. $4m = -29$
36. $\frac{4}{7}y + 7 = 31$
37. $\frac{x - 18}{32} = -3$
38. $s - \frac{2}{3} = \frac{7}{8}$
39. Rachel walked to a friend's house, then to the store, and then back home. The distance from Rachel's house to her friend's house is $1\frac{5}{6}$ miles. This is twice the distance from Rachel's house to the store. How far does Rachel live from the store?
40. Tickets to an orchestra concert cost $25.50 apiece plus a $2.50 handling fee for each order. If Jamal spent $79, how many tickets did he purchase?

Cumulative Assessment, Chapters 1–2

Multiple Choice

1. What is the value of the expression $12 - k$ if $k = -3$?

Ⓐ -15 Ⓒ 9

Ⓑ -9 Ⓓ 15

2. Which expression is equivalent to $2x - 5$ if $x = -4$?

Ⓕ -13 Ⓗ 3

Ⓖ -3 Ⓙ 13

3. Which of the following is equivalent to $|10 - (-5)|$?

Ⓐ -15 Ⓒ 5

Ⓑ -5 Ⓓ 15

4. Which value of x is the solution of the equation $\frac{x}{3} = -12$?

Ⓕ $x = -36$ Ⓗ $x = -4$

Ⓖ $x = -15$ Ⓙ $x = 9$

5. If a pitcher contains $\frac{3}{4}$ gallon of juice and each glass will hold $\frac{1}{8}$ gallon of juice, how many glasses can be filled?

Ⓐ $\frac{3}{32}$ glass Ⓒ 6 glasses

Ⓑ $\frac{3}{4}$ glass Ⓓ 8 glasses

6. Skip drove 55.6 miles. Then he drove another $42\frac{1}{5}$ miles. How many miles did he drive in all?

Ⓕ 97.7 miles Ⓗ 97.8 miles

Ⓖ 98.5 miles Ⓙ 13.4 miles

7. Which number is greater than $\frac{3}{4}$?

Ⓐ $\frac{4}{5}$ Ⓒ $\frac{5}{8}$

Ⓑ 0.75 Ⓓ $0.\overline{6}$

8. Which model correctly represents the number $\frac{1}{4}$?

Ⓕ 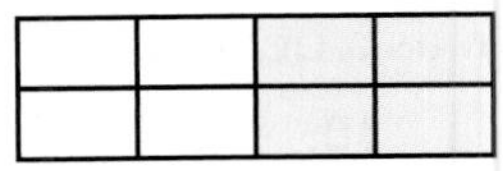

Ⓖ 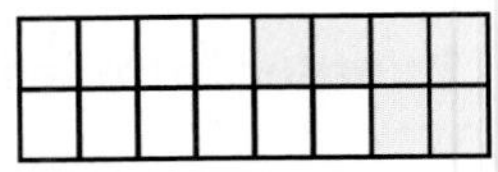

Ⓗ 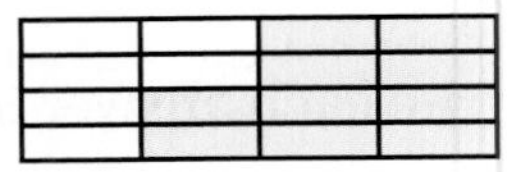

Ⓙ 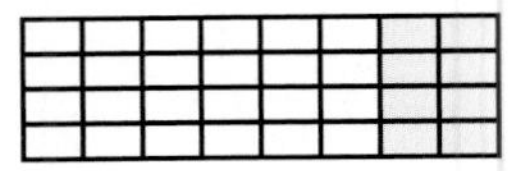

9. According to the graph, what fraction of games resulted in something other than a tie?

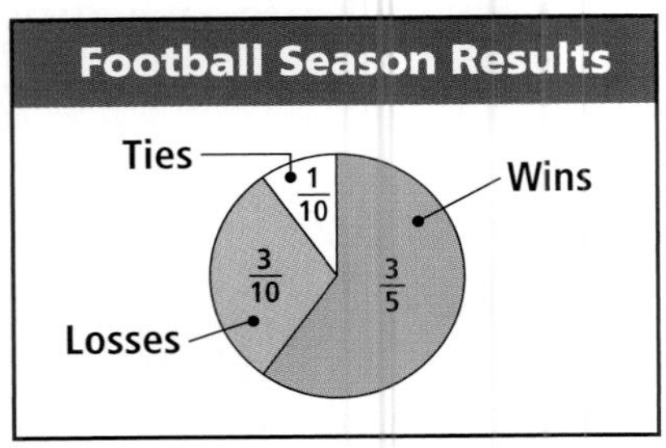

Ⓐ $\frac{9}{10}$ Ⓒ $\frac{6}{15}$

Ⓑ $\frac{3}{10}$ Ⓓ $\frac{9}{50}$

10. Which value of x makes the equation $\frac{2}{3}x = -\frac{5}{6}$ true?

Ⓕ $x = -\frac{5}{9}$ Ⓗ $x = -1\frac{1}{4}$

Ⓖ $x = \frac{1}{6}$ Ⓙ $x = 1\frac{1}{4}$

11. If $\frac{3}{5} = 9s$, what is the value of s?

Ⓐ 15 Ⓒ $\frac{5}{3}$

Ⓑ $\frac{27}{5}$ Ⓓ $\frac{1}{15}$

12. Jeremy has started drinking $\frac{1}{4}$ cup of grape juice every Wednesday at lunch. If he has had a total of 5 cups of juice so far, how many Wednesdays has Jeremy had grape juice?

(F) 4 (H) 20

(G) 5 (J) 80

HOT TIP! **Make sure you look at all the answer choices before making your decision. Try substituting each answer choice into the problem if you are unsure of the answer.**

13. Oscar bought a bag of almonds. He ate $\frac{3}{8}$ of the bag on Sunday. On Monday, he ate $\frac{2}{3}$ of the almonds left. What fraction of the entire bag did he eat on Monday?

(A) $\frac{9}{16}$ (C) $\frac{1}{4}$

(B) $\frac{5}{11}$ (D) $\frac{1}{12}$

Gridded Response

14. The diameter of a standard CD is $4\frac{3}{4}$ in. The diameter of the circular hole in the middle is $\frac{1}{2}$ in. Find the distance from the edge of the hole to the outer edge of the CD.

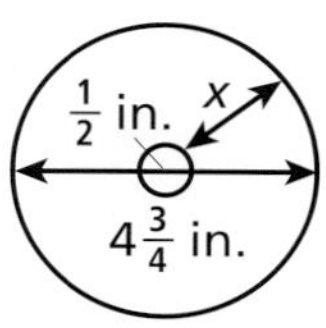

15. Evaluate the expression $|-3 - 8|$.

16. Alana has three times as many pairs of shoes as Marie. If Alana has 18 pairs of shoes, how many pairs of shoes does Marie have?

17. Fifteen students earned the National Merit Scholarship out of 600 students in the school. Write this value as a simplified fraction.

Short Response

18. A health club charges a one-time fee of \$99 and then \$39 per month for membership. Let m represent the number of months, and let C represent the total amount of money spent on the health club membership.

    a. Write an equation that relates m and C.

    b. If Jillian has spent \$801 on her membership, how many months has she been a member of the club?

19. The sum of 7 and the absolute value of a number is the same as 12.

    a. Write an equation that can be used to solve for the number.

    b. Describe the first step of solving the equation.

    c. Determine how many numbers make the equation true. Explain your reasoning.

20. Brigid has a $21\frac{1}{4}$ in. long ribbon. For a project she is cutting it into $\frac{3}{4}$ in. pieces. Into how many $\frac{3}{4}$ in. pieces can she cut the ribbon? Show or explain how you found your answer.

Extended Response

21. Use a diagram to model the expression $\frac{4}{5} \div \frac{4}{3}$.

    a. Draw a diagram to model the fraction $\frac{4}{5}$.

    b. What fraction do you multiply by that is equivalent to dividing by $\frac{4}{3}$?

    c. Use your answer from part b and shade that fraction of the $\frac{4}{5}$ that is already shaded. What does this shaded area represent?

    d. Use your diagram to write the quotient in simplest form.

Problem Solving on Location

NEW JERSEY

Ice House

Ice House, located in Hackensack, New Jersey, is one of the nation's premier ice-skating facilities. With its four regulation-size rinks, Ice House is used as a training facility by National Hockey League teams and by Olympic figure skaters. For those just starting out, Ice House offers skating lessons and four-day skate camps.

Choose one or more strategies to solve each problem.

1. Ice House has year-round public skating. Admission costs \$8.50 for adults and \$6.50 for children. Skate rentals are available for \$3.50 per person. A group of 4 visitors pays a total of \$42, with everyone in the group renting skates. How many adults and how many children are in the group?

For 2 and 3, use the table.

Ice Rink Surface Temperatures	
Time	**Temperature (°C)**
9:00 A.M.	10
9:30 A.M.	9
10:00 A.M.	8
10:30 A.M.	7

2. For figure skating, water is added to a rink and then frozen until it reaches a temperature of −2°C. Suppose water is added to a rink and cooled at the rate shown in the table. At what time will the water reach the proper temperature for figure skating?

3. Ice hockey requires colder, harder ice. To reach the appropriate temperature, water is added to a rink at 9:00 A.M. and cooled at the rate shown in the table for 7.5 hours. What is the temperature of the ice for ice hockey?

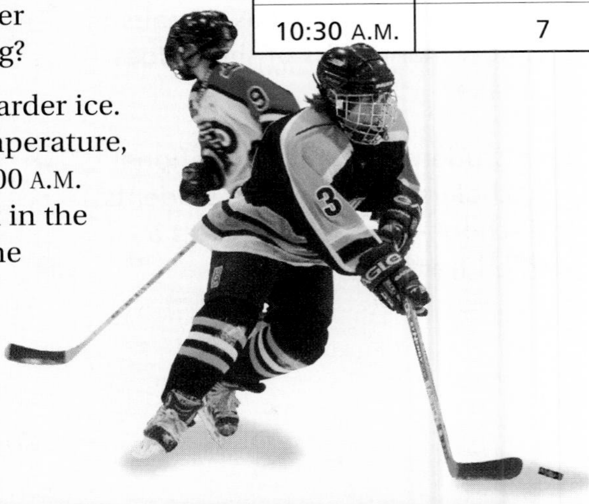

Problem Solving Strategies

- Draw a Diagram
- Make a Model
- Guess and Test
- Work Backward
- Find a Pattern
- Make a Table
- Solve a Simpler Problem
- Use Logical Reasoning
- Act It Out
- Make an Organized List

The Atlantic City Boardwalk

The first section of the famous Atlantic City boardwalk opened in 1870. Today the boardwalk stretches for 4 miles along the beachfront, offering a dazzling mix of restaurants, arcades, art galleries, and thrill rides.

Choose one or more strategies to solve each problem.

1. The city's tourist bureau proposes placing an information booth at each end of the boardwalk. It also recommends placing a booth every 0.8 mi along the boardwalk. How many booths would be needed?

2. Boardwalk Hall, located just off the boardwalk, hosts concerts and sporting events. Its total seating capacity is about 6.2 times the number of seats located on the arena floor. The number of seats on the arena floor is about 5.1 times the number of club seats. There are 432 club seats. What is the approximate seating capacity of Boardwalk Hall?

For 3, use the table.

3. The boardwalk has several piers with games and thrill rides. Steel Pier has three different plans for purchasing ride tickets. With one of the plans, a 5-ticket ride costs about $3.12. Which plan is it?

Steel Pier Tickets

Plan	Number of Tickets	Price
A	35	$25
B	80	$50
C	200	$100

CHAPTER

3

Graphs, Functions, and Sequences

3A Tables and Graphs

3-1 Ordered Pairs

3-2 Graphing on a Coordinate Plane

LAB Graph Points

3-3 Interpreting Graphs and Tables

3B Functions and Sequences

3-4 Functions

3-5 Equations, Tables, and Graphs

3-6 Arithmetic Sequences

MULTI-STEP TEST PREP

go.hrw.com
Chapter Project Online
KEYWORD: MT7 Ch3

Recommended Doses for Children

Weight of Child (lb)	Dose of Paracetamol (mg)	Dose of Ibuprofen (mg)
25	135	55
30	162	66
35	189	77

Career *Pharmacist*

In addition to dispensing medicine that has been prescribed by doctors, pharmacists advise patients about the uses and possible side effects of medications. Pharmacists may also make recommendations to help patients manage conditions such as diabetes and high blood pressure.

Although many pharmacists work in drugstores, others work closely with doctors and nurses in hospitals. Pharmacists in hospitals use tables like the one shown to help doctors provide correct doses of medicine to children.

ARE YOU READY?

Vocabulary

Choose the best term from the list to complete each sentence.

algebraic expression
equation
integer
rational number
variable

1. An __?__ states that two expressions have the same value.
2. Any number that can be written as a fraction is a __?__.
3. A __?__ serves as a placeholder for a number.
4. An __?__ can be a whole number or its opposite.

Complete these exercises to review skills you will need for this chapter.

Whole Number Operations

Evaluate each expression.

5. $5 + 12$ **6.** $18 - 9$ **7.** $25 \cdot 11$ **8.** $56 \div 4$

9. $8 \cdot 40$ **10.** $102 \div 3$ **11.** $250 - 173$ **12.** $107 + 298$

Decimal Operations

Evaluate each expression.

13. $1.25 + 3.7$ **14.** $52.7 - 12.9$ **15.** $3.2 \cdot 1.2$ **16.** $5.7 \div 0.3$

17. $2.84 \div 1.3$ **18.** $17.5 \cdot 12.1$ **19.** $17.5 - 12.45$ **20.** $2.75 + 13.254$

Operations with Fractions

Evaluate each expression.

21. $\frac{2}{3} - \frac{1}{2}$ **22.** $\frac{13}{18} + \frac{19}{24}$ **23.** $\frac{7}{8}\left(\frac{6}{11}\right)$ **24.** $\frac{9}{10} \div \frac{9}{13}$

25. $\frac{5}{6}\left(\frac{8}{15}\right)$ **26.** $\frac{11}{12} \div \frac{121}{144}$ **27.** $\frac{1}{6} + \frac{5}{8}$ **28.** $\frac{19}{20} - \frac{4}{5}$

Integer Operations

Evaluate each expression.

29. $-15 + 7$ **30.** $25 - (-23)$ **31.** $20(-13)$ **32.** $\frac{-108}{9}$

33. $\frac{161}{-7}$ **34.** $-13 + (-28)$ **35.** $-72 - 18$ **36.** $-31(14)$

CHAPTER 3 Study Guide: Preview

Where You've Been

Previously, you

- located and named pairs of integers on a coordinate plane.
- graphed data to demonstrate familiar relationships.
- interpreted graphs, tables, and equations.

In This Chapter

You will study

- locating ordered pairs of rational numbers on a coordinate plane.
- generating different representations of data using tables, graphs, and equations.
- using an algebraic expression to determine any term in an arithmetic sequence.
- using function notation to describe relationships among data.

Where You're Going

You can use the skills learned in this chapter

- to use functions to analyze and describe relationships among data.
- to make predictions based on analysis of data.

Key Vocabulary/Vocabulario

coordinate plane	plano cartesiano
domain	dominio
function	functión
ordered pair	par ordenado
origin	origin
quadrant	cuadrante
range	recorrido o rango
sequence	succesión
x-axis	eje de las *x*
y-axis	eje de las *y*

Vocabulary Connections

To become familiar with some of the vocabulary terms in the chapter, consider the following. You may refer to the chapter, the glossary, or a dictionary if you like.

1. The word **origin** means "beginning." How do you think this might apply to graphing?
2. The root of the word **quadrant** is *quad*, which means "four." What do you think a quadrant of a graph might be?
3. The word *ordered* means "arranged according to a rule." Do you think it matters which number comes first in an **ordered pair**? Explain.

Study Guide: Preview

Reading and Writing Math

CHAPTER 3

Reading Strategy: Read a Lesson for Understanding

You need to be actively involved as you work through each lesson in your textbook. To begin with, find the lesson's objective, which can be found at the top of the first page. As you progress through the lesson, keep the objective in mind while you work through examples and answer questions.

Lesson Features	Reading Tips
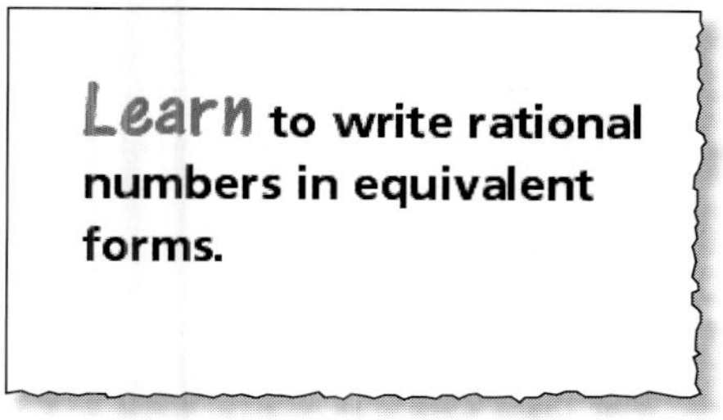 **Learn to write rational numbers in equivalent forms.**	Identify the objective of the lesson and look through the lesson to get a feel for how the objective is met.
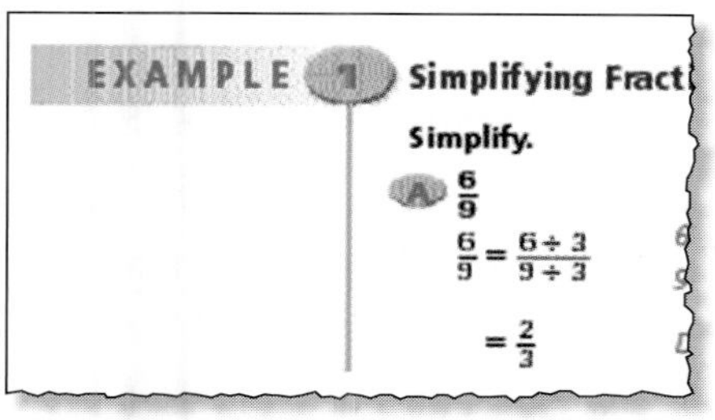 EXAMPLE 1 Simplifying Fract Simplify. A $\frac{6}{9}$ $\frac{6}{9} = \frac{6 \div 3}{9 \div 3}$ $= \frac{2}{3}$	Work through each example. The examples help to demonstrate the lesson objectives.
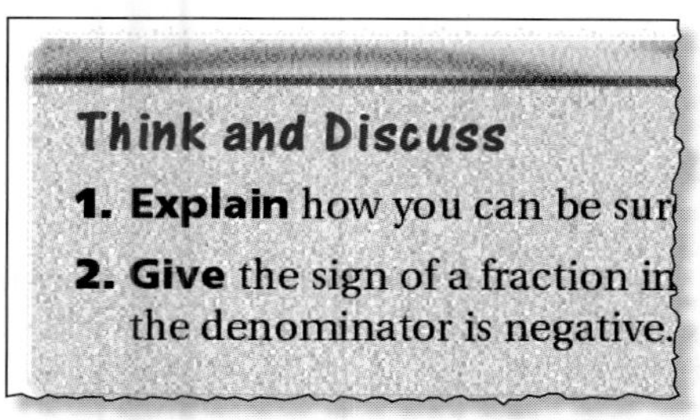 **Think and Discuss** **1. Explain** how you can be sur **2. Give** the sign of a fraction in the denominator is negative.	Check your understanding of the lesson by answering the *Think and Discuss* questions.

Try This

Use Lesson 3-1 in your textbook to answer each question.

1. What is the objective of the lesson?
2. What questions or problems did you have when you read the lesson?
3. Write your own example problem similar to Example 2.
4. What skill is being practiced in the first *Think and Discuss* question?

3-1 Ordered Pairs

Learn to write solutions of equations in two variables as ordered pairs.

Vocabulary

ordered pair

The company that makes team uniforms for a soccer league charges a \$20 fee for team artwork and \$10 for each jersey. Dominic's team has 14 players, and Alyssa's team has 12 players. Find the cost for a set of jerseys for each team.

Let y be the total cost of a set of jerseys and x be the number of jerseys needed.

total cost of jerseys = \$20 + \$10 · number of jerseys

$$y = \$20 + \$10 \cdot x$$

Dominic's team: $y = \$20 + (\$10 \cdot 14)$
$y = \$160$

Alyssa's team: $y = \$20 + (\$10 \cdot 12)$
$y = \$140$

An **ordered pair** (x, y) is a pair of numbers that can be used to locate a point on a coordinate plane. A solution of a two-variable equation can be written as an ordered pair.

The ordered pair (14, 160) is a solution because $160 = \$20 + (\$10 \cdot 14)$.
The ordered pair (12, 140) is a solution because $140 = \$20 + (\$10 \cdot 12)$.

EXAMPLE 1 Deciding Whether an Ordered Pair Is a Solution of an Equation

Determine whether each ordered pair is a solution of $y = 3x + 2$.

Helpful Hint

The order in which a solution is written is important. Always write x first, then y.

A (2, 5)

$y = 3x + 2$

$5 \stackrel{?}{=} 3(2) + 2$ *Substitute 2 for x and 5 for y.*

$5 \stackrel{?}{=} 8$ ✗ *Simplify.*

(2, 5) is *not* a solution.

B (3, 11)

$y = 3x + 2$

$11 \stackrel{?}{=} 3(3) + 2$ *Substitute 3 for x and 11 for y.*

$11 \stackrel{?}{=} 11$ ✔ *Simplify.*

(3, 11) is a solution.

EXAMPLE 2 Creating a Table of Ordered Pair Solutions

Helpful Hint

A table of solutions can be set up vertically or horizontally.

Use the given values to make a table of solutions.

A $y = 8x$ for $x = 1, 2, 3, 4$

x	8*x*	*y*	(*x*, *y*)
1	8(1)	8	(1, 8)
2	8(2)	16	(2, 16)
3	8(3)	24	(3, 24)
4	8(4)	32	(4, 32)

B $n = 4m - 3$ for $m = -4, -3, -2, -1$

m	−4	−3	−2	−1
4*m* − 3	4(−4) − 3	4(−3) − 3	4(−2) − 3	4(−1) − 3
n	−19	−15	−11	−7
(*m*, *n*)	(−4, −19)	(−3, −15)	(−2, −11)	(−1, −7)

EXAMPLE 3 *Consumer Math Application*

In most states, the price of each item is not the total cost. Sales tax must be added. If sales tax is 6%, the equation for total cost is $c = 1.06p$, where p is the price before tax.

A **How much will Dominic's $160 set of jerseys cost after sales tax?**

$c = 1.06(160)$ *The price of Dominic's set of jerseys before tax is $160.*

$c = 169.6$ *Multiply.*

After tax, Dominic's $160 set of jerseys will cost $169.60, so (160, 169.60) is a solution of the equation.

B **How much will Alyssa's $140 set of jerseys cost after sales tax?**

$c = 1.06(140)$ *The price of Alyssa's set of jerseys before tax is $140.*

$c = 148.4$ *Multiply.*

After tax, Alyssa's $140 set of jerseys will cost $148.40, so (140, 148.40) is a solution of the equation.

Think and Discuss

1. **Describe** how to find a solution of a two-variable equation.
2. **Explain** why an equation with two variables has an infinite number of solutions.
3. **Give** two equations using x and y that have (1, 2) as a solution.

3-1 Exercises

go.hrw.com
Homework Help Online
KEYWORD: MT7 3-1
Parent Resources Online
KEYWORD: MT7 Parent

GUIDED PRACTICE

See Example 1

Determine whether each ordered pair is a solution of $y = 2x - 4$.

1. (3, 2) **2.** (−4, 5) **3.** (6, 8) **4.** (2, 0)

See Example 2

Use the given values to make a table of solutions.

5. $y = 2x$ for $x = 1, 2, 3, 4$ **6.** $y = 4x - 1$ for $x = -4, -3, -2, -1$

See Example 3

7. The cost of a small frozen yogurt is \$2.50 plus \$0.15 per topping. The equation that gives the total cost c of a small frozen yogurt is $c = 0.15n + 2.50$, where n is the number of toppings. What is the cost of a small frozen yogurt with 3 toppings?

INDEPENDENT PRACTICE

See Example 1

Determine whether each ordered pair is a solution of $y = 4x + 3$.

8. (2, 9) **9.** (4, 20) **10.** (5, 23) **11.** (6, 28)

See Example 2

Use the given values to make a table of solutions.

12. $y = 2x - 1$ for $x = 1, 2, 3, 4$ **13.** $y = 3x + 9$ for $x = -4, -3, -2, -1$

14. $y = 4x - 5$ for $x = 2, 4, 6, 8$ **15.** $y = 3x - 4$ for $x = 2, 4, 6, 8$

See Example 3

16. The fine for speeding in one town is \$90 plus \$7 for every mile over the speed limit. The equation that gives the total cost c of a speeding ticket is $c = 90 + 7m$, where m is the number of miles over the posted speed limit. Rhonda was issued a ticket for going 63 mi/h in a 50 mi/h zone. What was the total cost of the ticket?

PRACTICE AND PROBLEM SOLVING

Extra Practice
See page 786.

Determine whether each ordered pair is a solution of $y = x + 3$.

17. (4, 7) **18.** (−3, 0) **19.** (5, 8) **20.** (2, 6)

Determine whether each ordered pair is a solution of $y = 3x - 5$.

21. (−2, 2) **22.** (4, 8) **23.** (3, 4) **24.** (6, 12)

25. **Multi-Step** A wireless phone company charges a monthly fee of \$39.99 plus \$0.49 per minute for usage that exceeds the included minutes. Write an equation for the monthly cost c in terms of the number of exceeded minutes m. Solve the equation to find the cost when the number of exceeded minutes is 29. Write your answer as an ordered pair.

26. **Geometry** The perimeter P of a square is four times the length of one side s, or $P = 4s$. Is (14, 55) a solution of this equation? If not, find a solution that uses one of the given values.

Use the given values to make a table of solutions.

27. $y = 2x - 2$ for $x = 1, 2, 3, 4$

28. $y = 3x - 1$ for $x = -4, -3, -2, -1$

29. $y = x + 7$ for $x = 1, 2, 3, 4, 5$

30. $y = 3x + 2$ for $x = 2, 4, 6, 8, 10$

LINK

History

In 1513, Ponce de León went in search of the legendary Fountain of Youth, which people believed would give them eternal youth. While searching, he discovered Florida, which he named Pascua de Florida.

31. **History** The life expectancy of Americans has been rising steadily since 1940. An ordered pair can be used to show the relationship between your birth year and life expectancy.

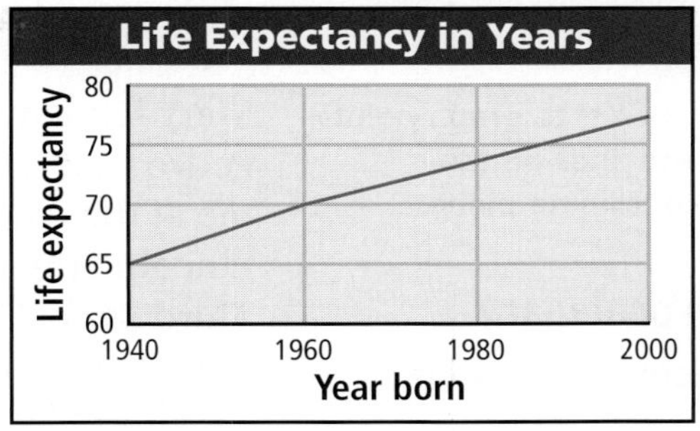

a. Write an ordered pair that shows the approximate life expectancy of an American born in 1980.

b. The data on the chart can be approximated by the equation $L = 0.2n - 323$, where L is the life expectancy and n is the year of birth. Use the equation to find an ordered pair that shows the approximate life expectancy for an American born in 2020.

32. **Critical Thinking** Two solutions of an equation are (6, 5) and (8, 5). What could the equation be? Explain.

33. **What's The Error?** A student thinks that (1, 2) is the solution to $y = 2x - 3$. While checking the solution, the student gets $1 = 2(2) - 3$. What is wrong with this calculation? Explain the error.

34. **Write About It** Write an equation that has (2, 6) as a solution. Explain how you found the equation.

35. **Challenge** In the NBA, a shot made from beyond the arc is worth 3 points. A shot made on or in front of the arc is worth 2 points. If x equals the number of 3-point baskets scored and y equals the number of 2-point baskets scored, find the possible solutions of the equation $36 = 3x + 2y$.

TEST PREP and Spiral Review

36. **Multiple Choice** Which ordered pair is a solution of $2y - 3x = 8$?

(A) (6, 13) (B) (19, 4) (C) (10, 4) (D) (4, 0)

37. **Multiple Choice** Which ordered pair is NOT a solution of $y = 3x - 2$?

(F) (0, −2) (G) (−2, −8) (H) (2, 4) (J) (2, 0)

Solve. (Lesson 2-7)

38. $y + 10.2 = -33$

39. $-\frac{x}{3.2} = -4$

40. $2.6m = -23.4$

Multiply or divide. Write each answer in simplest form. (Lessons 2-4 and 2-5)

41. $\frac{2}{3} \cdot \frac{9}{10}$

42. $\frac{4}{5} \cdot \frac{3}{8}$

43. $\frac{1}{3} \div \frac{2}{3}$

44. $\frac{11}{15} \div \frac{5}{22}$

3-2 Graphing on a Coordinate Plane

Learn **to graph points and lines on the coordinate plane.**

Vocabulary

coordinate plane

***x*-axis**

***y*-axis**

quadrant

***x*-coordinate**

***y*-coordinate**

origin

graph of an equation

Mary left a message for Pedro that read, "Meet me at the corner of East Lincoln Street and North Third Street." On the map, you can identify a location by the intersection of two streets. Finding points on a coordinate plane is like finding a location on a map.

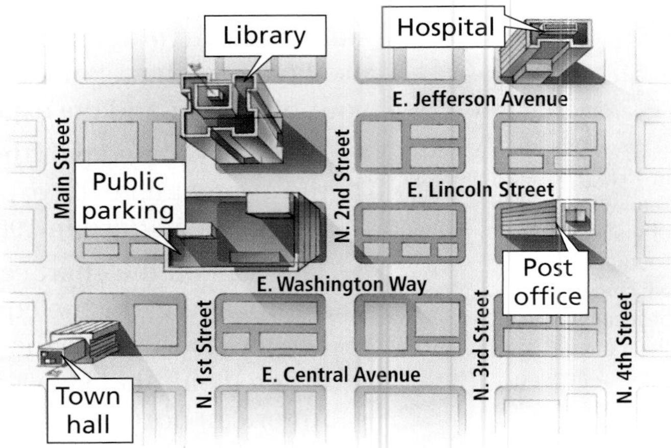

The **coordinate plane** is formed by two number lines, the ***x*-axis** and the ***y*-axis**. They intersect at right angles and divide the plane into four **quadrants**. The ***x*-coordinate** is the first number in an ordered pair. The ***y*-coordinate** is the second number of an ordered pair.

Helpful Hint

The sign of a number indicates which direction to move.
Positive: up or right
Negative: down or left

To plot an ordered pair, begin at the **origin**, the point (0, 0). It is the intersection of the x-axis and the y-axis. The x-coordinate tells how many units to move left or right; the y-coordinate tells how many units to move up or down.

move right 2 units **(2, 3)** *move up 3 units*

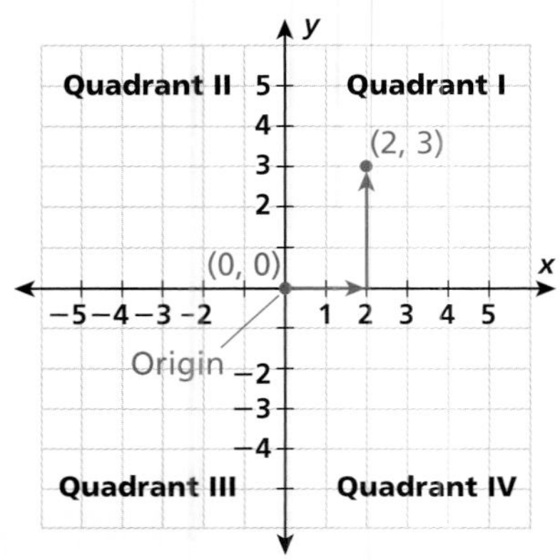

EXAMPLE 1 Finding the Coordinates and Quadrants of Points on a Plane

Give the coordinates and quadrant of each point.

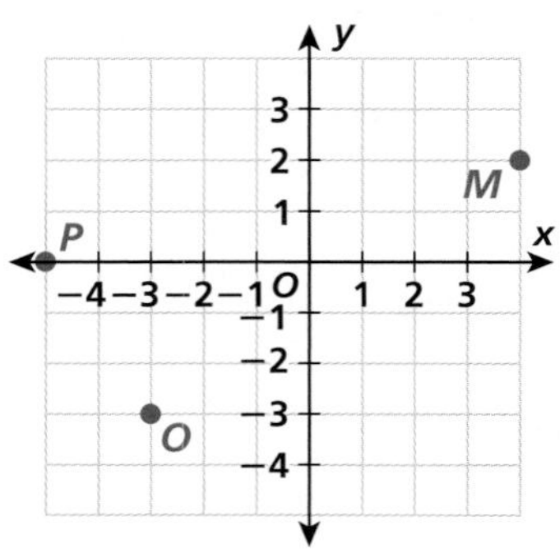

Point M is (4, 2); in Quadrant I.

4 units right, 2 units up

Point O is (−3, −3); in Quadrant III.

3 units left, 3 units down

Point P is (−5, 0); it has no quadrant because P is on the x-axis.

5 units left, 0 units up

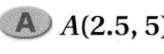

EXAMPLE 2 Graphing Points on a Coordinate Plane

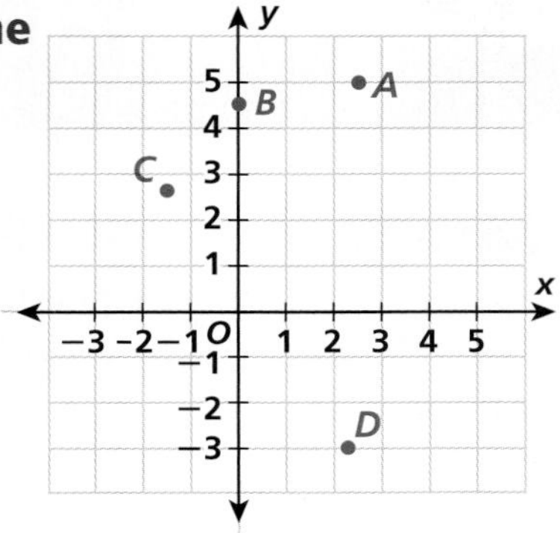

Graph each point on a coordinate plane.

A $A(2.5, 5)$

right 2.5, up 5

B $B\left(0, 4\frac{1}{2}\right)$

right 0, up $4\frac{1}{2}$

C $C\left(-1\frac{1}{5}, 2.7\right)$

left $1\frac{1}{5}$, up 2.7

D $D(2.3, -3)$

right 2.3, down 3

The **graph of an equation** is the set of all ordered pairs that are solutions of the equation.

EXAMPLE 3 Graphing an Equation of a Line

Complete each table of ordered pairs. Graph each ordered pair on a coordinate plane.

A $y = 2\frac{1}{2}x$

x	$2\frac{1}{2}x$	y	(x, y)
1	$2\frac{1}{2}(1)$	$2\frac{1}{2}$	$(1, 2\frac{1}{2})$
2	$2\frac{1}{2}(2)$	5	(2, 5)
3	$2\frac{1}{2}(3)$	$7\frac{1}{2}$	$(3, 7\frac{1}{2})$

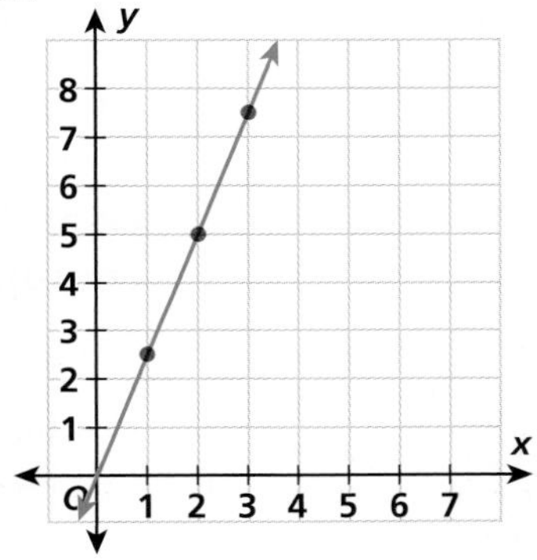

The points of each equation are on a straight line. Draw a line through the points to represent all possible solutions.

B $y = 3x - 2$

x	3x − 2	y	(x, y)
0	3(0) − 2	−2	(0, −2)
1	3(1) − 2	1	(1, 1)
2	3(2) − 2	4	(2, 4)

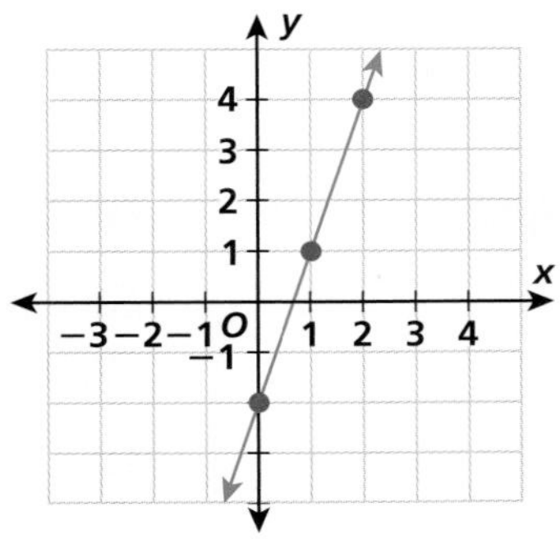

Think and Discuss

1. **Give** the coordinates of a point on the x-axis and a point on the y-axis.
2. **Give** the missing y-coordinates for the solutions to $y = 5x + 2$: $(1, y)$, $(3, y)$, $(10, y)$.

3-2 Exercises

go.hrw.com
Homework Help Online
KEYWORD: MT7 3-2
Parent Resources Online
KEYWORD: MT7 Parent

GUIDED PRACTICE

See Example 1 **Give the coordinates and quadrant of each point.**

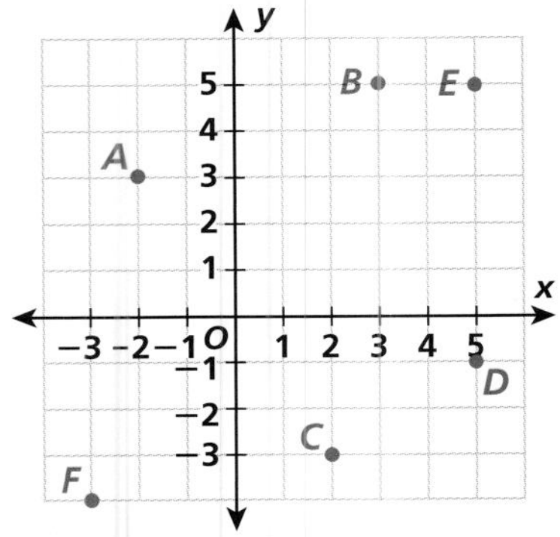

1. A **2.** B
3. C **4.** D
5. E **6.** F

See Example 2 **Graph each point on a coordinate plane.**

7. $A(3.5, 4)$ **8.** $B\left(6, 1\frac{1}{3}\right)$ **9.** $C(-1, 6)$ **10.** $D\left(2.7, -5\frac{1}{2}\right)$
11. $E(4.5, 7)$ **12.** $F(6, -2)$ **13.** $G\left(3, 7\frac{1}{2}\right)$ **14.** $H(1.5, -4)$

See Example 3 **Complete each table of ordered pairs. Graph each ordered pair on a coordinate plane.**

15. $y = x + 0.5$

x	$x + 0.5$	y	(x, y)
0			
1			
2			

16. $y = \frac{1}{2}x - 1$

x	$\frac{1}{2}x - 1$	y	(x, y)
0			
1			
2			

INDEPENDENT PRACTICE

See Example 1 **Give the coordinates and quadrant of each point.**

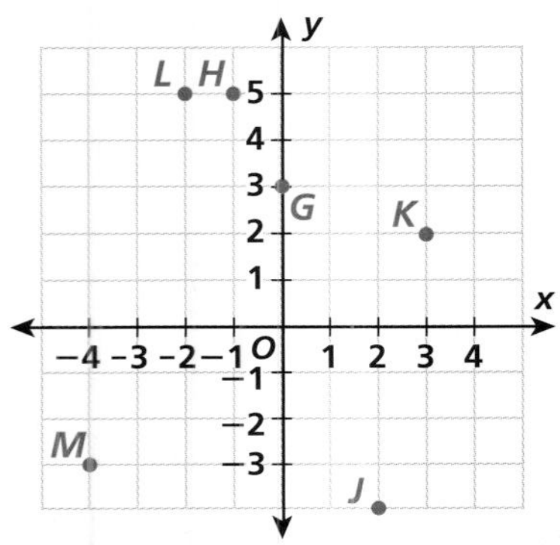

17. G **18.** H
19. J **20.** K
21. L **22.** M

See Example 2 **Graph each point on a coordinate plane.**

23. $A\left(2\frac{1}{3}, 6.5\right)$ **24.** $B(0.7, 4.2)$ **25.** $C(-1, -7)$ **26.** $D(-2.7, 0)$
27. $E\left(4\frac{1}{3}, 7\right)$ **28.** $F(-2, 5)$ **29.** $G(0, 3)$ **30.** $H(6.5, 3)$

See Example 3 **Complete each table of ordered pairs. Graph each ordered pair on a coordinate plane.**

31. $y = \frac{1}{3}x$

x	$\frac{1}{3}x$	y	(x, y)
0			
1			
2			

32. $y = 2x + 1.5$

x	$2x + 1.5$	y	(x, y)
0			
1			
2			

PRACTICE AND PROBLEM SOLVING

Extra Practice
See page 786.

33. Multi-Step A truck travels at 55 miles per hour. To find the distance traveled in x hours, use the equation $y = 55x$. Make a table of ordered pairs and graph the solution. How far will the truck travel in 7.5 hours?

34. Construction To build house walls, carpenters place a stud, or board, every 16 inches. Use the equation $y = \frac{x}{16} + 1$ to determine the number of studs in a wall of length x inches. Make a table of ordered pairs and graph the solution. How many studs should be placed in a wall 8 feet long?

35. Write a Problem Write an equation whose solution is in Quadrant IV.

36. Write About It The point (0, 0) on the coordinate plane is called the origin. Explain why this is.

37. Challenge Write a problem whose solution is a geometric shape on the coordinate plane.

TEST PREP and Spiral Review

38. Multiple Choice Which ordered pair lies on the line that is a graph of the equation $y = 2x + 1$?

Ⓐ (0, 0) Ⓒ (0, 1)

Ⓑ (2, 6) Ⓓ (5, 13)

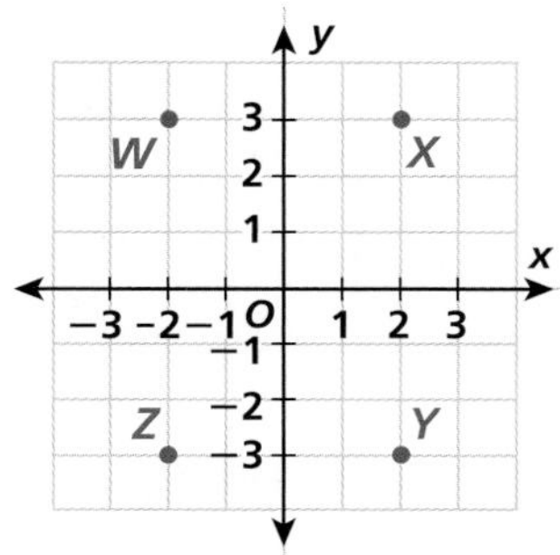

39. Multiple Choice Which ordered pair shows the coordinates for point W on the grid?

Ⓕ (2, 3) Ⓗ (2, −3)

Ⓖ (−2, 3) Ⓙ (−2, −3)

Solve and graph each inequality. (Lesson 1-9)

40. $y + 4 > 1$ **41.** $4p \leq 12$ **42.** $f - 3 \geq 2$ **43.** $4 < \frac{w}{3}$

Determine whether each ordered pair is a solution of $y = 4x - 3$. (Lesson 3-1)

44. (−3, −9) **45.** (0, −3) **46.** (−4, −19) **47.** (5, 23)

Technology LAB 3-2

Graph Points

Use with Lesson 3-2

go.hrw.com
Lab Resources Online
KEYWORD: MT7 Lab3

On a graphing calculator, the WINDOW menu settings determine which points you see and the spacing between those points. In the standard viewing window, the x- and y-values each go from -10 to 10, and the tick marks are one unit apart. The boundaries are set by **Xmin, Xmax, Ymin**, and **Ymax. Xscl** and **Yscl** give the distance between the tick marks.

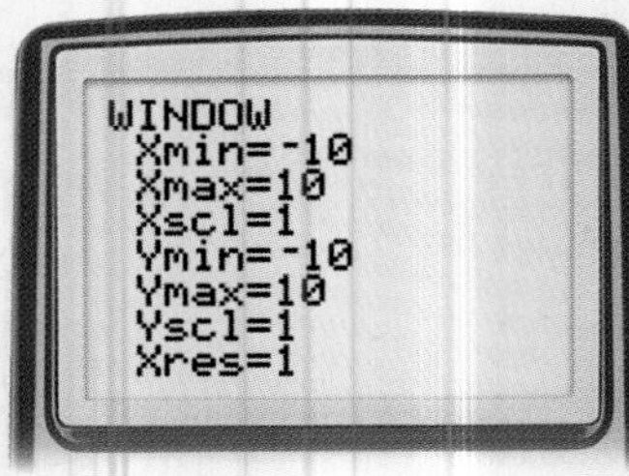

Activity

Plot the points (2, 5), (−2, 3), ($-\frac{3}{2}$, 4), and (1.75, −2) in the standard window. Then change the minimum and maximum x- and y-values of the window to −5 and 5.

Press WINDOW to check that you have the standard window settings.

To plot (2, 5), press 2nd DRAW PRGM **POINTS** ENTER .

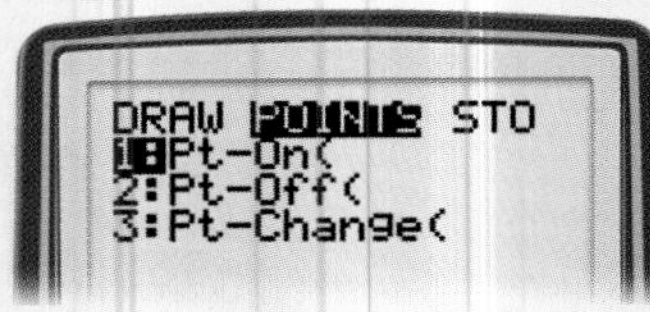

Then press 2 , 5 ENTER. After you see the grid with a point at (2, 5), press 2nd QUIT MODE to quit. Repeat the steps above to graph (−2, 3), ($-\frac{3}{2}$, 4), and (1.75, −2).

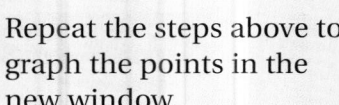

This is the graph in the standard window.

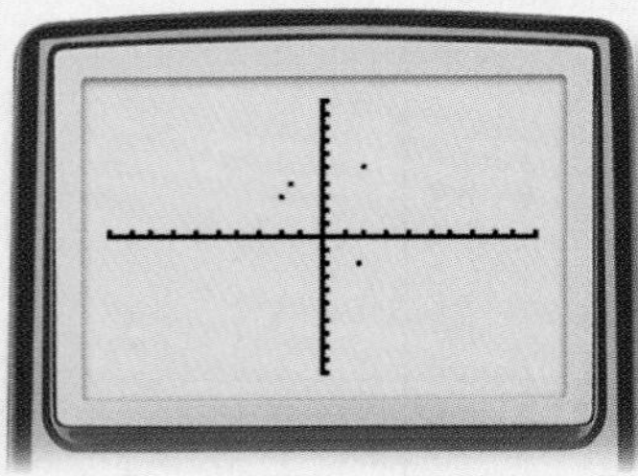

Press WINDOW. Change the **Xmin, Xmax, Ymin,** and **Ymax** values as shown.

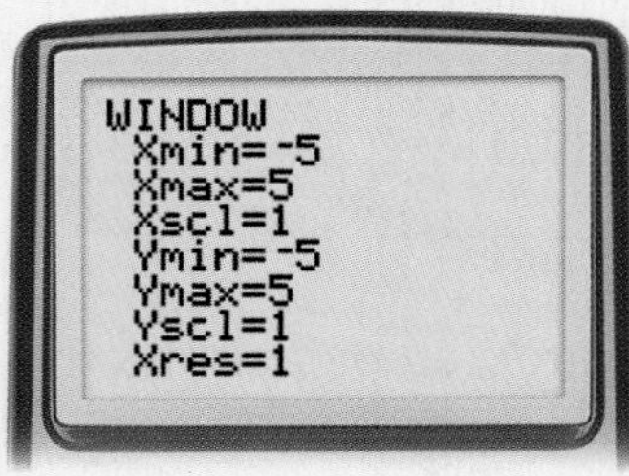

Repeat the steps above to graph the points in the new window.

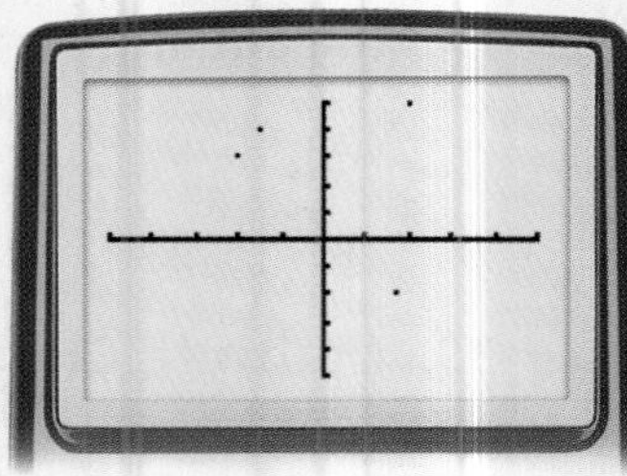

Think and Discuss

1. Compare the two graphs above. Describe and explain any differences you see.

Try This

Graph the points (−3, −8), (2, 3), (3.5, 6), (4, 9), and (−5.5, 11) in each window.

1. standard window
2. **Xmin** = −10; **Xmax** = 10; **Ymin** = −15; **Ymax** = 15; **Yscl** = 3

3-3 Interpreting Graphs and Tables

Learn to interpret information given in a graph or table and to make a graph to solve problems.

A commercial airliner climbs to an altitude of 30,000 feet to maintain cruising altitude. After a few hours it descends to the ground for a safe landing.

You can create a table of values to show the altitude of the airliner at different times during its flight. Plotting the values on a graph will give you a visual model of the airliner's flight.

EXAMPLE 1 Matching Situations to Tables

The table gives the speeds of three snowboarders in mi/h at given times during a race. Tell which snowboarder corresponds to each situation.

Time (s)	6.00	12.00	18.00	24.00	30.00
Snowboarder 1	15	18	22	19	24
Snowboarder 2	17	20	0	15	21
Snowboarder 3	16	19	22	25	26

A **Jordan gets off to a good start and continues through the course, picking up speed.**

Snowboarder 3—The racer's speed increases throughout the race.

B **Ethan gets off to a good start and picks up speed. Toward the end of the race, he nearly falls. He rights himself and finishes the race, reaching his greatest speed.**

Snowboarder 1—The racer's speed increases until the 24-second mark, when his speed decreases. The racer then picks up speed to finish the race.

C **Xavier gets off to a good start but falls around the middle of the race. He gets up and finishes the race, gaining speed through the finish line.**

Snowboarder 2—The racer's speed increases until the 18-second mark, when it is 0. After this, the racer's speed increases through the finish line.

EXAMPLE 2 Matching Situations to Graphs

Tell which graph corresponds to each situation described in Example 1.

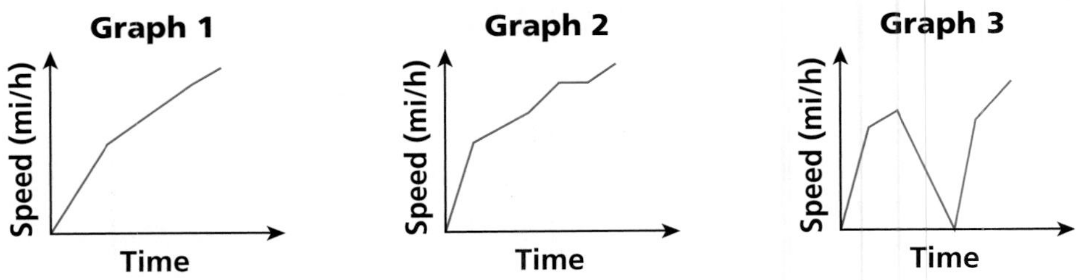

A Snowboarder 1

Graph 2—The racer's speed slows down near the end of the race and then increases.

B Snowboarder 2

Graph 3—The racer falls about halfway through the race.

C Snowboarder 3

Graph 1—The racer gains speed throughout the race.

EXAMPLE 3 Creating a Graph of a Situation

The flight of a commercial airliner can be modeled with a graph. Create a graph that models the flight of a commercial airliner.

Time (min)	Altitude (ft)
0	0
10	10,000
20	20,000
30	30,000
60	30,000
70	20,000
80	10,000
90	0

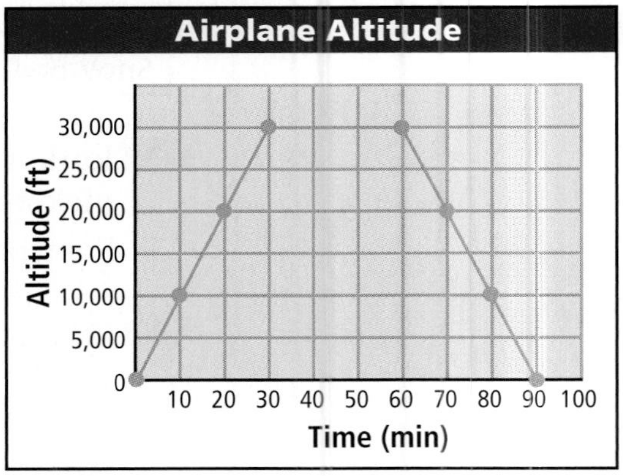

Think and Discuss

1. **Describe** what it means when a graph of speed starts at (0, 0).
2. **Give** a situation that, when graphed, would include a horizontal segment.

3-3 Exercises

go.hrw.com
Homework Help Online
KEYWORD: MT7 3-3
Parent Resources Online
KEYWORD: MT7 Parent

GUIDED PRACTICE

See Example 1

1. The table gives the speeds in mi/h of three people who are riding jet skis. Tell which rider corresponds to each situation.

Time	1:00	1:05	1:10	1:15	1:20
Rider 1	10	15	25	20	15
Rider 2	10	0	10	15	20
Rider 3	10	15	25	25	25

a. David begins his ride slowly but then stops to talk with some friends on jet skis. After a few minutes, he continues his ride, gradually increasing his speed.

b. Amber steadily increases her speed through most of her ride. After about 10 minutes, she slows down to turn around and returns to the boat dock.

c. Kai steadily increases his speed for the first part of his ride. He then keeps a constant speed as he continues his ride.

See Example 2

2. Tell which graph corresponds to each situation described in Exercise 1.

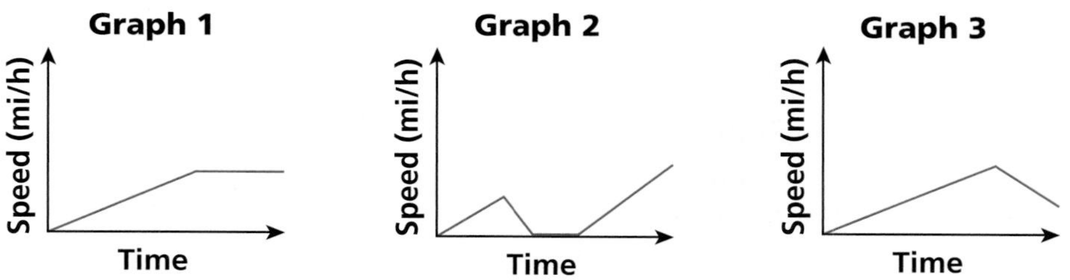

See Example 3

3. A ride at an amusement park can be modeled with a graph. Create a graph that illustrates the information in the table about the ride.

Time	3:20	3:21	3:22	3:23	3:24	3:25
Speed (mi/h)	0	14	41	62	8	0

4. You are watching a race at a local speedway. The lead car gets a flat tire 2 minutes into the race and has to stop. You collect the following data while watching the race. Construct a graph that models the information in the table.

Time (min)	0	0.5	1.0	1.5	2.0	2.5	3.0
Distance (mi)	0	1.0	1.75	3.0	4.25	4.25	4.25

INDEPENDENT PRACTICE

See Example 1

5. The table gives the speeds in mi/h of three dogs at given times during an obstacle course race. Tell which dog corresponds to each situation.

Time (s)	15.00	30.00	45.00	60.00
Dog 1	19	23	15	17
Dog 2	17	25	27	28
Dog 3	15	11	17	21

a. Brandy increases her speed throughout the race.

b. Bruno decreases his speed early in the race to run around cones on the course. After this, he steadily increases his speed.

c. Max gets off to a fast start and picks up speed for several seconds. He slows down to run through a tunnel but then increases his speed right afterward.

See Example 2

6. Tell which graph corresponds to each situation described in Exercise 4.

Graph 1

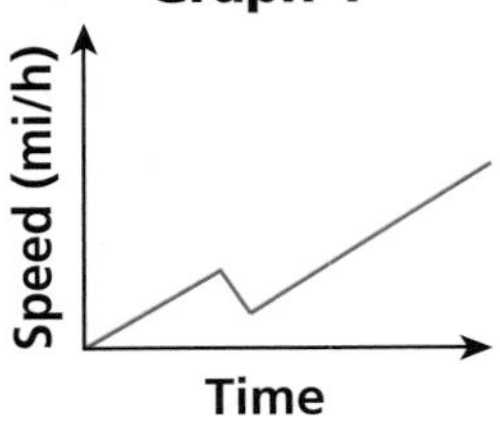

Graph 2

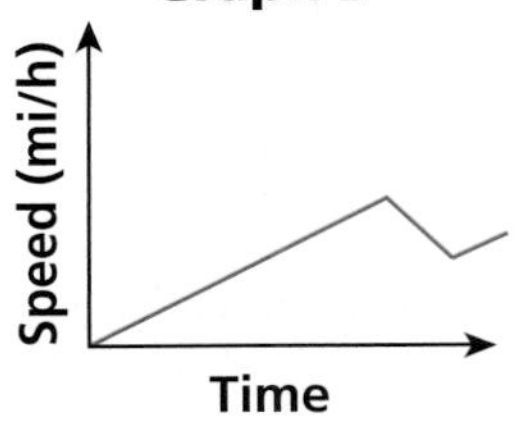

Graph 3

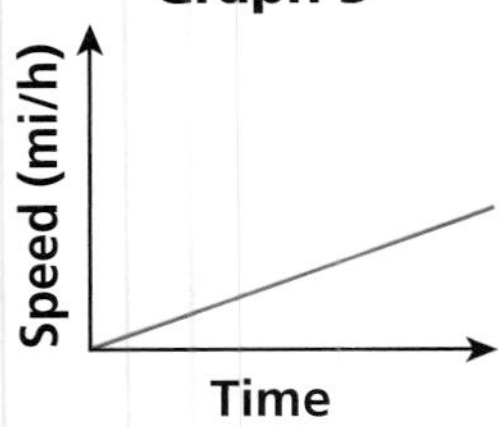

See Example 3

7. Create a graph that illustrates the information in the table about Mrs. Parr's commute from work to home.

Time	Speed (mi/h)	Time	Speed (mi/h)
6:04	5	6:07	34
6:05	27	6:08	14
6:06	6	6:09	0

PRACTICE AND PROBLEM SOLVING

Extra Practice
See page 786.

8. Create a graph that illustrates the information in the table about the movement of an electronic security gate.

Time (s)	0	10	20	30	40	50	60	70
Gate Opening (ft)	0	6	12	12	6	10	3	0

9. Physical Science Explain what the data tells about the flight of a model rocket. Make a graph.

Height of Model Rocket								
Time	1:00	1:01	1:02	1:03	1:04	1:05	1:06	1:07
Average Height (ft)	0	147	153	155	152	148	0	0

Earth Science LINK

10. Use the chart to choose the correct geyser name to label each graph.

Yellowstone National Park Geysers			
Geyser Name	Old Faithful	Grand	Riverside
Duration (min)	1.5 to 5	10	20

a.

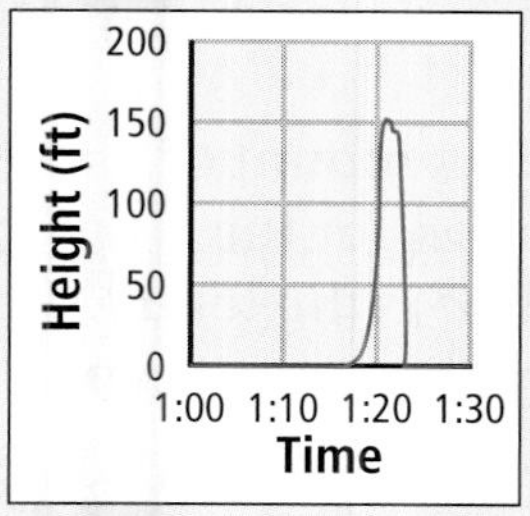

b.

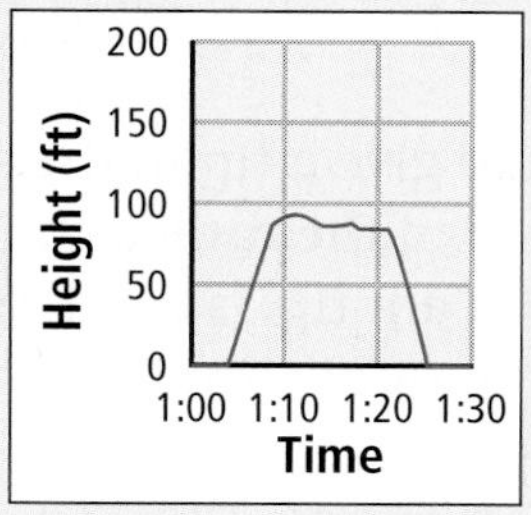

Old Faithful is the most famous geyser at Yellowstone National Park.

11. ★ **Challenge** Old Faithful erupts to heights between 105 ft and 184 ft. It erupted at 7:34 A.M. for 4.5 minutes. Later it erupted for 2.5 minutes. It then erupted a third time for 3 minutes. Use the table to determine how many minutes followed each of the three eruptions. Sketch a possible graph.

Old Faithful Eruption Information	
Duration	**Time Until Next Eruption**
2.5 min	70 min
3 min	72 min
3.5 min	74 min
4 min	82 min
4.5 min	93 min

go.hrw.com
Web Extra!
KEYWORD: MT7 Geyser

TEST PREP and Spiral Review

12. Multiple Choice Which graph most likely represents a car approaching a stop sign?

Ⓐ

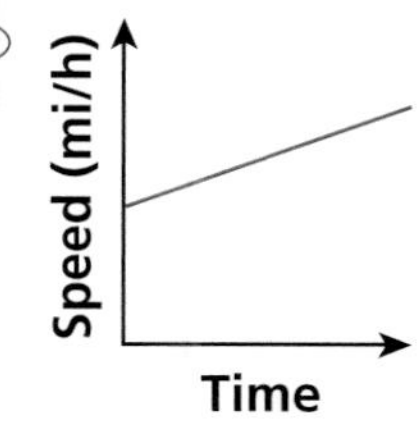

Ⓑ

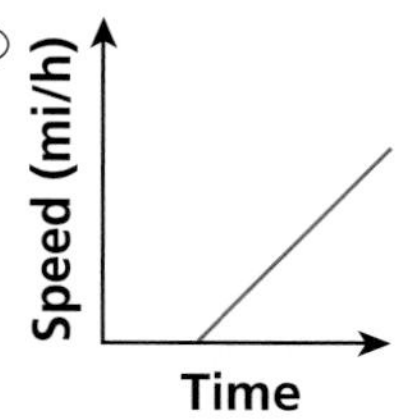

Ⓒ

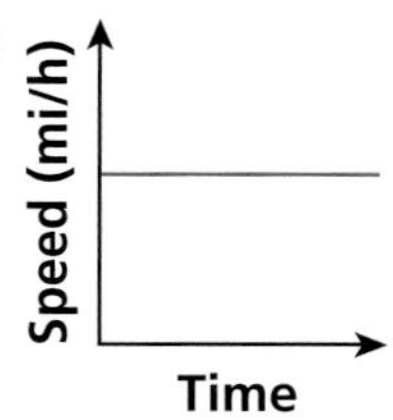

Ⓓ

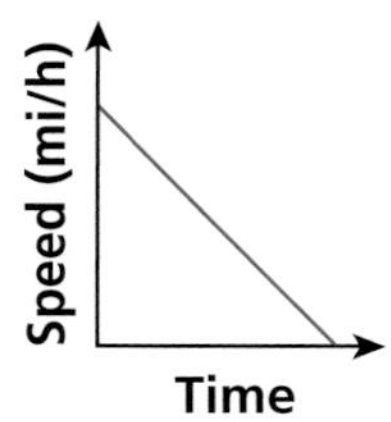

13. Short Response Lisa climbed up to the diving board, dove into the water, swam 10 meters, and returned to the surface of the water. Draw a graph to represent her distance from the surface of the water.

Add or subtract. (Lesson 2-6)

14. $\frac{5}{7} + \frac{2}{3}$ **15.** $\frac{4}{9} + \left(-1\frac{3}{4}\right)$ **16.** $\frac{3}{5} - \frac{7}{10}$ **17.** $2\frac{7}{9} - 1\frac{8}{11}$

Graph each point on a coordinate plane. (Lesson 3-2)

18. $(-3, 4)$ **19.** $(2, -7)$ **20.** $(-5, -1)$ **21.** $(0, 1)$

CHAPTER 3

READY TO GO ON?

SECTION 3A

Quiz for Lessons 3-1 Through 3-3

3-1 Ordered Pairs

Determine whether each ordered pair is a solution of $y = 2x - 7$.

1. (14, 21) **2.** (3, 13) **3.** (10, 13) **4.** (1.5, −4)

When dining out, it is customary to give a tip to the server. The amount of the tip is generally 15 to 20 percent of the total bill. The equation for the cost c of a meal, including a 15 percent tip, is $c = 1.15a$, where a is the total amount shown on the bill. Find the total cost of each meal to the nearest cent.

5. $a = \$35.20$ **6.** $a = \$40.00$ **7.** $a = \$22.35$ **8.** $a = \$15.50$

3-2 Graphing on a Coordinate Plane

Give the coordinates and quadrant of each point.

9. A **10.** B

11. C **12.** D

13. E **14.** F

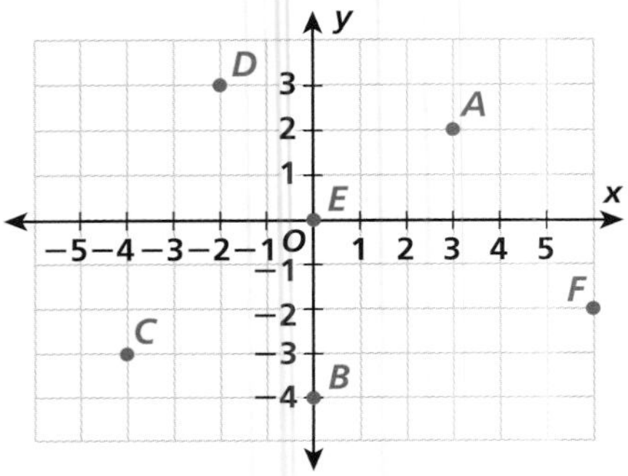

Make a table of ordered pairs for each equation and then graph the ordered pairs on a coordinate plane. Draw a line through the points.

15. $y = 7x + 3$ **16.** $y = -3x + 1$ **17.** $y = \frac{3}{4}x$ **18.** $y = 1.2x + 3$

3-3 Interpreting Graphs and Tables

Tell which graph corresponds to each situation below.

Graph 1

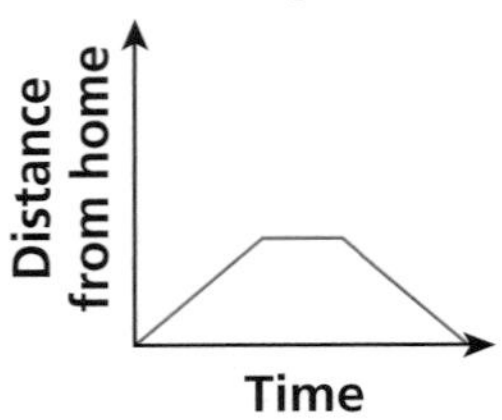

Graph 2

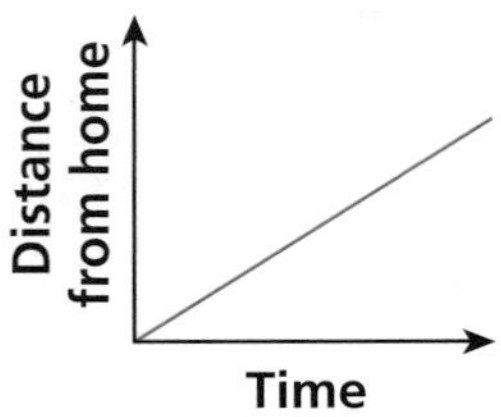

Graph 3

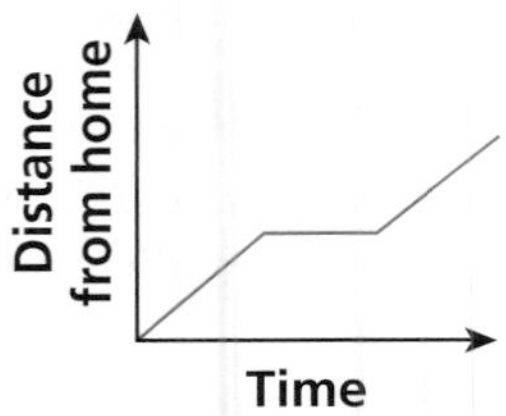

19. Gwendolyn started from home and walked to a friend's house. She stayed with her friend for a while and then walked to another friend's house farther from home.

20. Francisco started from home and walked to the store. After shopping, he walked back home.

Focus on Problem Solving

Make a Plan

- **Prioritize and sequence information**

Some problems contain a lot of information. Read the entire problem carefully to be sure you understand all of the facts. You may need to read it over several times—perhaps aloud so that you can hear yourself say the words.

Then decide which information is most important (prioritize). Is there any information that is absolutely necessary to solve the problem? This information is most important.

Finally, put the information in order (sequence). Use comparison words like *before, after, longer, shorter,* and so on to help you. Write down the sequence before you try to solve the problem.

Read each problem below, and then answer the questions that follow.

1 Five friends are standing in line for the opening of a movie. They are in line according to their arrival. Tiffany arrived 3 minutes after Cedric. Roy took his place in line at 8:01 P.M. He was 1 minute behind Celeste and 7 minutes ahead of Tiffany. The first person arrived at 8:00 P.M. Blanca showed up 6 minutes after the first person. List the time of each person's arrival.

a. Whose arrival information helped you determine each arrival time?

b. Can you determine the order without the time?

c. List the friends' order from the earliest to arrive to the last to arrive.

2 There are four children in the Putman family. Isabelle is half the age of Maxwell. Joe is 2 years older than Isabelle. Maxwell is 14. Hazel is twice Joe's age and 4 years older than Maxwell. What are the ages of the children?

a. Whose age must you figure out first before you can find Joe's age?

b. What are two ways to figure out Hazel's age?

c. List the Putman children from oldest to youngest.

3-4 Functions

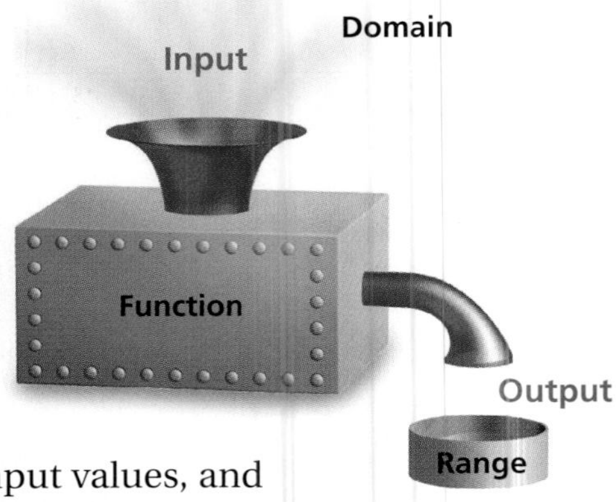

Learn to represent functions with tables, graphs, or equations.

Vocabulary
- function
- input
- output
- domain
- range
- vertical line test

A **function** is a rule that relates two quantities so that each **input** value corresponds to exactly one **output** value.

The **domain** is the set of all possible input values, and the **range** is the set of all possible output values.

Function

One input gives one output.

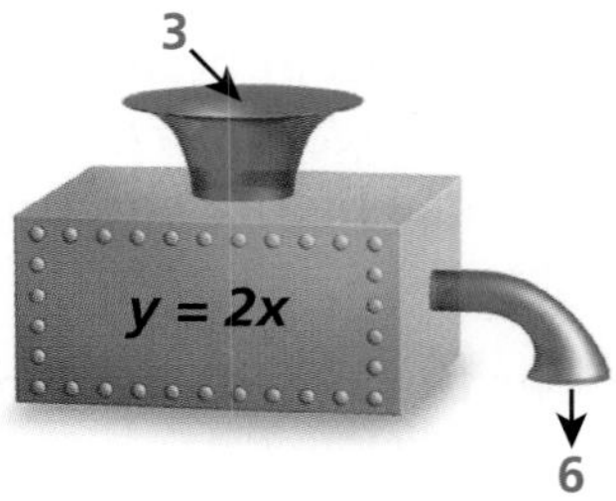

Example: The output is 2 times the input.

Not a Function

One input gives more than one output.

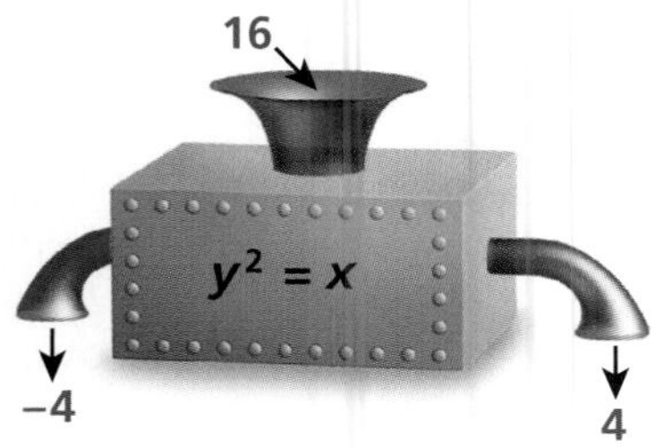

Example: The outputs are the square roots of the input.

Functions can be represented in many ways, including tables, graphs, and equations. If the domain of a function has infinitely many values, it is impossible to represent them all in a table, but a table can be used to show some of the values and to help in creating a graph.

EXAMPLE 1 Finding Different Representations of a Function

Make a table and a graph of $y = 2x + 1$.

Make a table of inputs and outputs. Use the table to make a graph.

x	$2x + 1$	y
-2	$2(-2) + 1$	-3
-1	$2(-1) + 1$	-1
0	$2(0) + 1$	1
1	$2(1) + 1$	3
2	$2(2) + 1$	5

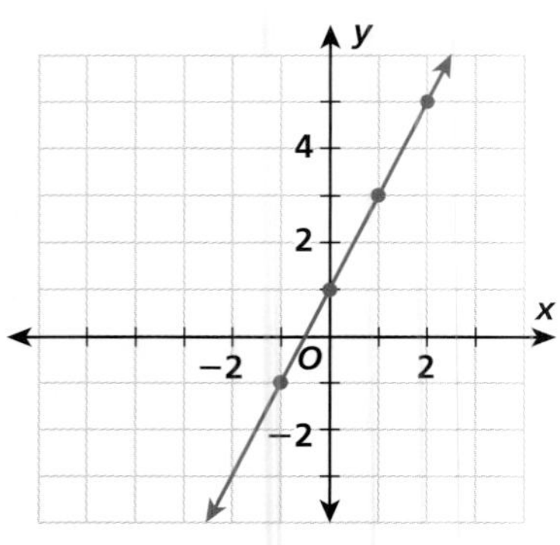

If a relationship is a function, each input has exactly one output. When the relationship is graphed, use the **vertical line test**. Place a vertical line on the graph. If the line intersects the graph at only one point, then the relationship is a function. If the line intersects the graph at more than one point, then the relationship is not a function.

EXAMPLE 2 Identifying Functions

Determine if each relationship represents a function.

A

x	y
0	5
1	4
2	3
3	2

Each input x has only one output y. The relationship is a function.

B

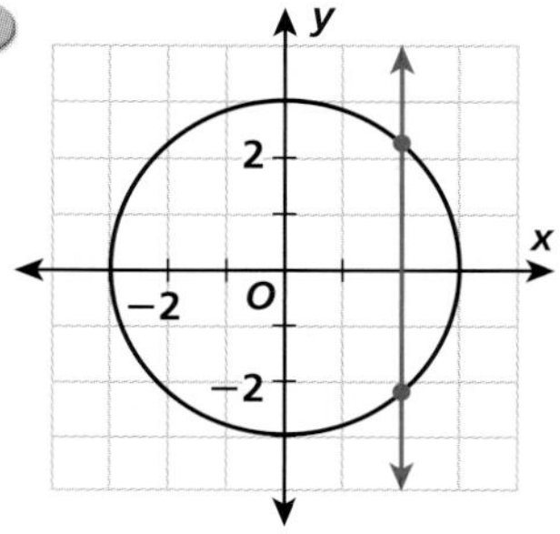

The vertical line intersects the graph at two points. The relationship is not a function.

C $y = x^2$

Make an input-output table and use it to graph $y = x^2$.

x	y
−2	$(-2)^2 = 4$
−1	$(-1)^2 = 1$
0	$(0)^2 = 0$
1	$(1)^2 = 1$
2	$(2)^2 = 4$

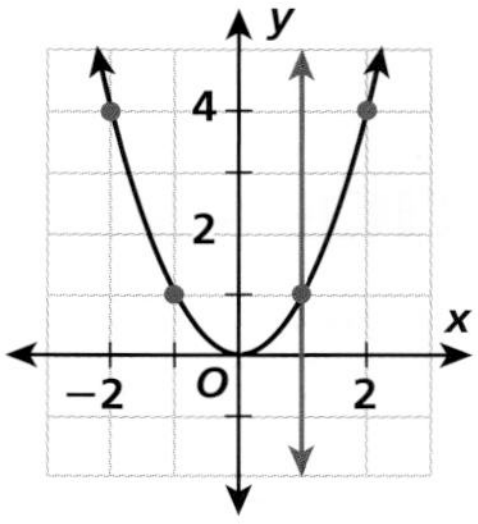

The vertical line intersects the graph at one point. The relationship is a function.

Think and Discuss

1. Describe the domain and range for $y = 2$.

2. Describe how to tell if a relationship is a function.

3. Identify the function, the domain, the range, an input, and the output.

x	y = 3x − 4	y
−1	3(−1) − 4	−7
0	3(0) − 4	−4
1	3(1) − 4	−1

3-4 Exercises

go.hrw.com
Homework Help Online
KEYWORD: MT7 3-4
Parent Resources Online
KEYWORD: MT7 Parent

GUIDED PRACTICE

See Example 1

Make a table and a graph of each function.

1. $y = 2x - 4$ **2.** $y = 3x + 4$ **3.** $y = 4x - 3$ **4.** $y = -x + 1$

See Example 2

Determine if each relationship represents a function.

5.

x	y
−1	−7
9	1
12	8
15	−7

6.

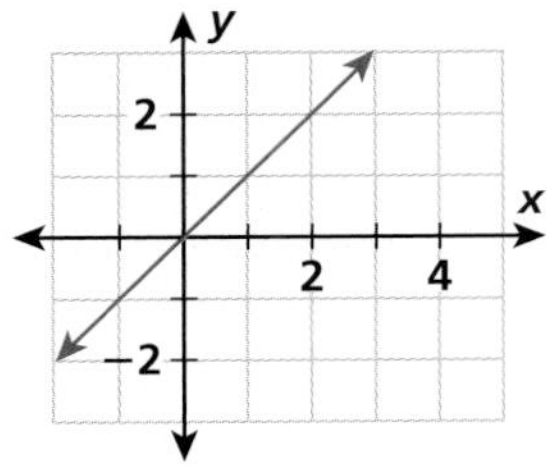

7. $y = 1.5x - 0.5$

INDEPENDENT PRACTICE

See Example 1

Make a table and a graph of each function.

8. $y = 2x + 5$ **9.** $y = 3(x + 1)$ **10.** $y = -(3 - x)$ **11.** $y = 2(1 - 2x)$

See Example 2

Determine if each relationship represents a function.

12.

x	y
2	4
5	5
8	6
2	7

13.

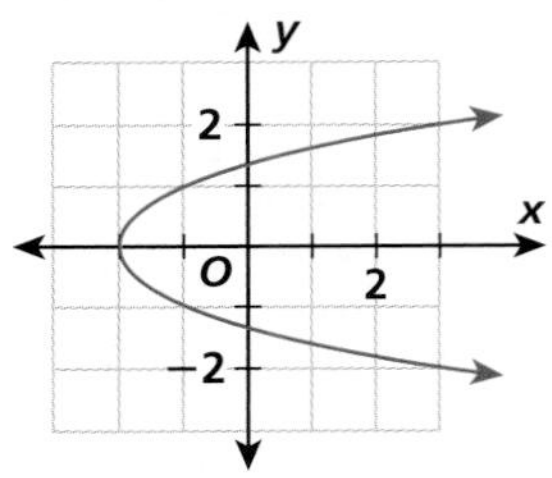

14. $y = -2x + 1$

PRACTICE AND PROBLEM SOLVING

Extra Practice
See page 787.

Give the domain and the range of each function.

15.

x	y
1	27
4	39
8	50
14	62

16.

x	y
100	5.4
120	3.5
150	2.7
170	0.2

17.

x	y
30	60
40	50
50	40
60	30

18.

x	y
20	12
25	15
35	21
40	24

19. **Sports** A distance runner trains by running 750 meters at a time. Her coach records the distance covered by the runner every 20 seconds. The results of one run are presented in the table.

Time *x* (s)	0	20	40	60	80	100
Distance *y* (m)	0	150	300	450	600	750

a. Does the relationship represent a function?

b. What is the domain of the function? What is the range?

c. Graph the data to verify your answer for part **a**.

20. **Business** The function $y = 50x - 750$ gives the daily profit of a company that manufactures x items. Make a table and a graph of the function to determine how many items the company must manufacture in order to break even. (*Hint:* When the company breaks even, $y = 0$.)

LINK Home Economics

In 1879, Thomas Edison used a carbonized piece of sewing thread to form a light bulb filament that lasted 13.5 hours before burning out.

21. **Home Economics** The cost of using a 60-watt light bulb is given by the function $y = 0.0036x$. The cost is in dollars, and x represents the number of hours the bulb is lit.

    a. How much does it cost to use a 60-watt light bulb 8 hours a day for a week?

    b. What is the domain of the function?

    c. If the cost of using a 60-watt bulb was \$1.98, for how many hours was it used?

22. **What's the Question?** The following set of points defines a function: $\{(3, 6), (-4, 1), (5, -5), (9, -6), (10, -2), (-2, 10)\}$. If the answer is 6, 1, -5, -6, -2, and 10, what is the question?

23. **Write About It** Can you tell if a relationship is a function by just looking at the range? Explain why or why not.

24. **Challenge** Create a table of values for $y = \frac{1}{x}$ using $x = -3, -2, -1, -0.5, -0.25, 0.5, 1, 2,$ and 3. Sketch the graph of the function. What happens when $x = 0$?

Test Prep and Spiral Review

25. **Multiple Choice** Which relationship does NOT represent a function?

Ⓐ (0, 8), (3, 8), (1, 6)

Ⓑ $y = 3x + 17$

Ⓒ

x	4	6	8
y	2	1	9

Ⓓ (0, 3), (2, 3), (2, 0)

26. **Gridded Response** For the function $y = 1.3x - 5.4$, find y when $x = 9$.

Evaluate each expression for the given value of the variable. (Lesson 1-5)

27. $7 - t$ for $t = -16$
28. $f - (-31)$ for $f = 76$
29. $-28 - g$ for $g = 32$
30. $65 + b$ for $b = -101$
31. $89 - d$ for $d = -15$
32. $62 - (-m)$ for $m = 71$

Solve. Check your answer. (Lesson 2-7)

33. $n + 10.7 = -23$
34. $-6.8x = 47.6$
35. $-\frac{2}{3}m = -\frac{1}{9}$

3-5 Equations, Tables, and Graphs

Learn to generate different representations of the same data.

Functions can be modeled as equations, tables, or graphs. Each representation shows the same data, but in a different way.

EXAMPLE 1 Using Equations to Generate Different Representations of Data

Helpful Hint

The number of minutes m is the input value. The depth d is the output value.

Make a table and sketch a graph of the path of a submarine diving at 50 ft per minute. The depth of the submarine is represented by the equation $d = -50m$, where d is the depth and m is the number of minutes.

Equation

$d = -50m$

An equation shows how the variables are related.

Table

m	$-50m$	d
0	$-50(0)$	0
1	$-50(1)$	-50
2	$-50(2)$	-100
3	$-50(3)$	-150
4	$-50(4)$	-200

A table identifies values that make the function true.

Graph

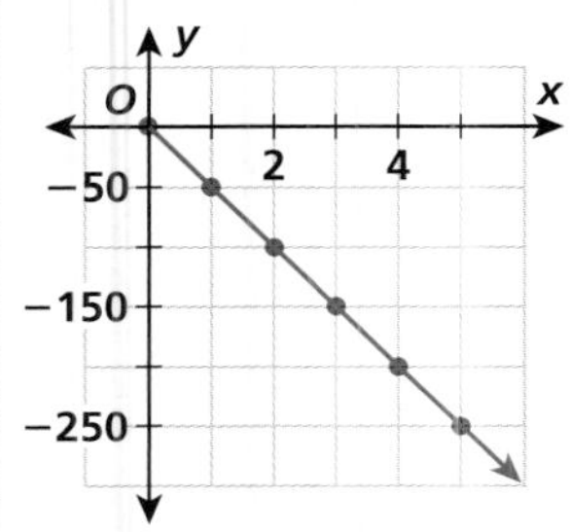

A graph is a visual image of the values in the table.

To write an equation from data in a table, you need to look for a pattern in the data. Look for the changes in the input values and the changes in the output values. Then see how the changes are related.

EXAMPLE 2 Using Tables to Generate Different Representations of Data

Use the table to make a graph and to write an equation.

x	0	1	2	3	4
y	0	6	12	18	24

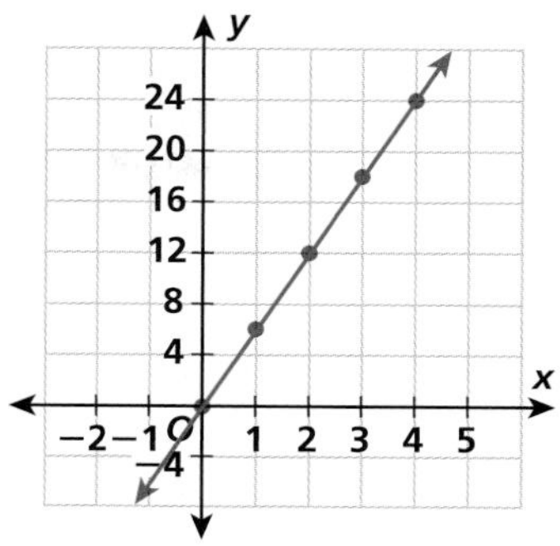

Look for a pattern in the values:

$6 = 6 \times 1$ *Each value of y is six times the value of x*

$12 = 6 \times 2$

$18 = 6 \times 3$

$y = 6 \times x$

To find an equation from a graph, it might be easier to first create a table of values from the graph. Then you can look for a pattern in the values as in Example 2.

EXAMPLE 3 Using Graphs to Generate Different Representations of Data

Use the graph to make a table and to write an equation.

Look for a pattern in the values:

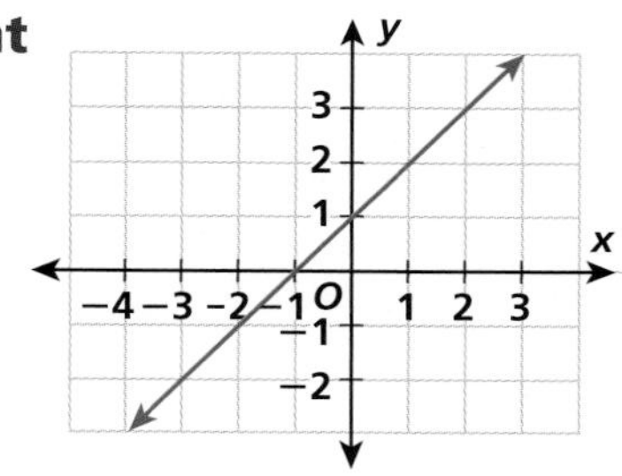

x	*y*
−3	−2
−2	−1
−1	0
0	1
2	3

$-2 = -3 + 1$

$-1 = -2 + 1$

$0 = -1 + 1$ *Each value of y is one more than the value of x.*

$1 = 0 + 1$

$3 = 2 + 1$

$y = x + 1$

Think and Discuss

1. **Which** representation of data do you think gives the most accurate information? Justify your answer.
2. **Which** representation of data do you think shows the relationship most quickly? Justify your answer.

3-5 Exercises

go.hrw.com
Homework Help Online
KEYWORD: MT7 3-5
Parent Resources Online
KEYWORD: MT7 Parent

GUIDED PRACTICE

See Example 1

1. The amount of water in a pool being filled is represented by the equation $g = 15m$, where g is the number of gallons of water in the pool and m is the number of minutes since filling began. Make a table and sketch a graph of the equation.

See Example 2

2. Use the table to make a graph and to write an equation.

x	0	2	5	9	12
y	3	5	8	12	15

See Example 3

3. Use the graph to make a table and to write an equation.

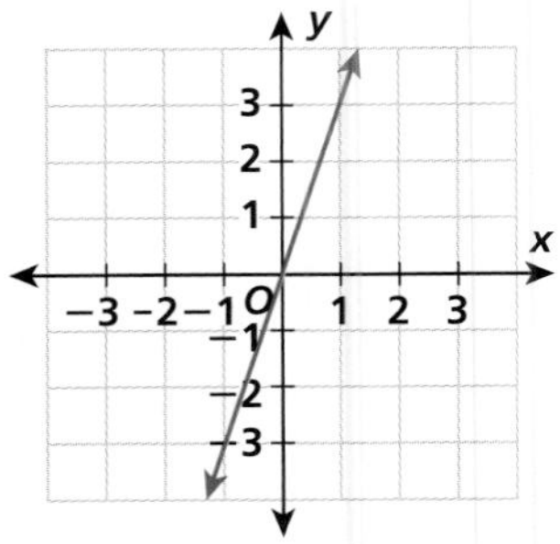

INDEPENDENT PRACTICE

See Example 1

4. The amount of sand in the top half of an hourglass is represented by the equation $h = -0.5s$, where h is the height of the sand in centimeters and s is the number of seconds since the top half began draining. Make a table and sketch a graph of the equation.

See Example 2

5. Use the table to make a graph and to write an equation.

x	0	2	4	6	8
y	12	10	8	6	4

See Example 3

6. Use the graph to make a table and to write an equation.

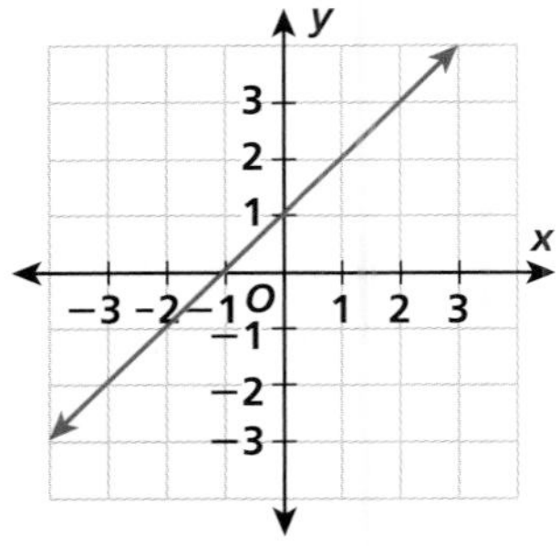

PRACTICE AND PROBLEM SOLVING

Extra Practice
See page 787.

7. Travel The distance Jackson can drive on a tank of gas is represented by the function $d = 20g$, where d is the distance in miles and g is the number of gallons of gas in the tank. Make a table and sketch a graph of the data.

8. Choose the representation that does not show the same relationship as the other two.

$y = 4x + 1$

x	0	3	6	9	12
y	1	13	25	37	49

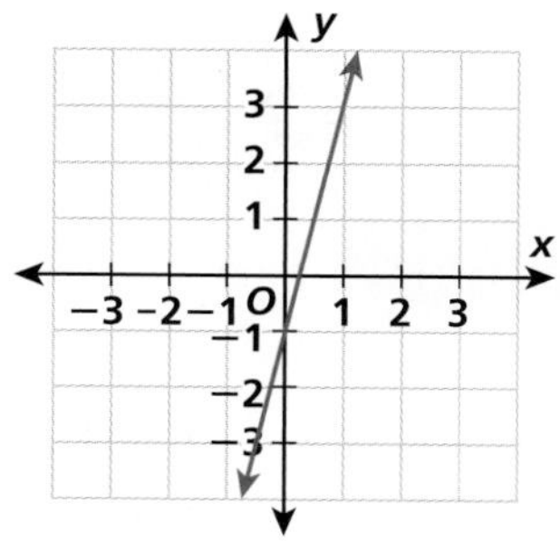

9. **Conservation** A faucet is leaking water at the rate of 2.5 gallons per hour. Let x be the number of hours the faucet leaks and y be the total number of gallons leaked. Write an equation and make a table.

10. **Write a Problem** Write a situation for each relationship.

a. $y = 2x + 3$

b.

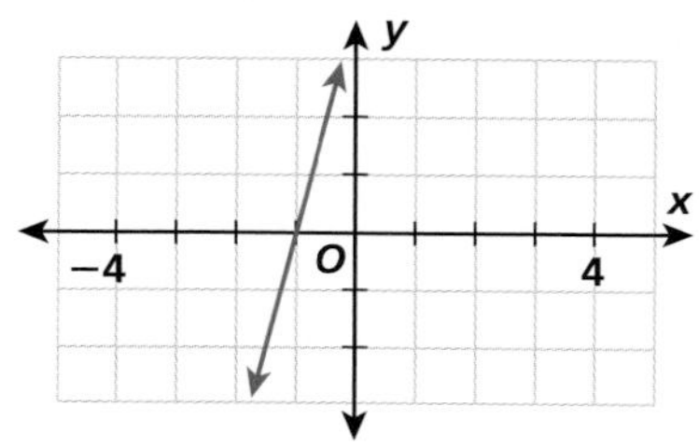

11. **Challenge** Graph the function $y = |x|$. Be sure to include negative values of x. How does the graph differ from the others in this lesson?

Test Prep and Spiral Review

12. **Multiple Choice** Jeff began the week with $30.00. He took a city bus to and from school, paying $0.75 for each trip. Let x be the number of trips he took and y be the amount of money he had left at the end of the week. Which equation represents the relationship in the situation?

Ⓐ $y = 0.75x + 30$

Ⓑ $y = 30 - 0.75x$

Ⓒ $x = 3 - 0.75y$

Ⓓ $y = 0.75x - 30$

13. **Extended Response** The equation $y = 2.5x - 2000$ represents the profit made by a manufacturer that sells a product for $2.50 each, where y is the profit and x is the number of units sold. Construct a table to find the number of units that must be sold for the manufacturer to break even. The break-even point is where profit is equal to 0. Explain the data in the table.

Simplify. (Lesson 1-6)

14. $-3(-9)$

15. $7(-3)$

16. $\frac{2(-6)}{4}$

17. $\frac{-8(-5)}{-10}$

Solve. Check your answer. (Lesson 2-8)

18. $5p - 2 = 0$

19. $\frac{s}{4} + 8 = 12$

20. $12 - 3x = -6$

3-6 Arithmetic Sequences

Learn to identify and evaluate arithmetic sequences.

Vocabulary

sequence

term

arithmetic sequence

common difference

A school choir is planning a trip to a water park. The choir must pay a \$100.00 transportation fee plus \$17.75 for each student to enter the park. Under the plan, one student would cost a total of \$117.75, two students \$135.50, three students \$153.25, and so on.

Number of Students	1	2	3	4
Total cost	\$117.25	\$135.50	\$153.25	\$171.00

\$17.75 \$17.75 \$17.75

A **sequence** is an ordered list of numbers or objects, called **terms**. In an **arithmetic sequence**, the difference between one term and the next is always the same. This difference is called the **common difference**. The common difference is added to each term to get the next term.

EXAMPLE 1 Finding the Common Difference in an Arithmetic Sequence

Find the common difference in each arithmetic sequence.

A **7, 10, 13, 16, . . .**

7, 10, 13, 16

+3 +3 +3 *The terms increase by 3.*

The common difference is 3

B **7.5, 6, 4.5, 3, . . .**

7.5, 6, 4.5, 3

−1.5 −1.5 −1.5 *The terms decrease by 1.5.*

The common difference is −1.5

EXAMPLE 2 Finding Missing Terms in an Arithmetic Sequence

Find the next three terms in the arithmetic sequence −12, −4, 4, 12, . . .

Each term is 8 more than the previous term.

$12 + 8 = 20$

$20 + 8 = 28$ *Use the common difference to find the next three terms.*

$28 + 8 = 36$

The next three terms are 20, 28, and 36.

You can use a function table to help identify the pattern in a sequence and to find missing terms. Each term's position in the sequence is the input, and the value of each term is the output.

EXAMPLE 3 Identifying Functions in Arithmetic Sequences

Find a function that describes each arithmetic sequence. Use y to identify each term in the sequence and n to identify each term's position.

A 2, 4, 6, 8, . . .

n	$n \cdot 2$	y
1	$1 \cdot 2$	2
2	$2 \cdot 2$	4
3	$3 \cdot 2$	6
4	$4 \cdot 2$	8
n	$n \cdot 2$	$2n$

Multiply n by 2.

$y = 2n$

B $-3, -6, -9, -12, \ldots$

n	$n \cdot (-3)$	y
1	$1 \cdot (-3)$	-3
2	$2 \cdot (-3)$	-6
3	$3 \cdot (-3)$	-9
4	$4 \cdot (-3)$	-12
n	$n \cdot (-3)$	$-3n$

Multiply n by −3.

$y = -3n$

EXAMPLE 4 *Travel Application*

A school choir is taking a trip to a water park. The choir must pay a transportation fee of \$100.00 plus \$17.75 for each student to enter the park. Find a function that describes the arithmetic sequence. Then find the total cost for a group of 23 students to enter the park.

n	$100 + 17.75n$	y
1	$100 + 17.75(1)$	117.75
2	$100 + 17.75(2)$	135.50
3	$100 + 17.75(3)$	153.25
4	$100 + 17.75(4)$	171.00
n	$100 + 17.75(n)$	$17.75n + 100$

Multiply n by \$17.75, and then add the \$100 transportation fee.

$17.75n + 100$ — *Write a function to find the 23rd term.*
$17.75(23) + 100$ — *Substitute 23 for n.*
$408.25 + 100$ — *Multiply.*
508.25 — *Add.*

It will cost a group of 23 students \$508.25 to go to the water park.

Think and Discuss

1. **How** are sequences useful in every day situations?
2. **Explain** how multiplication can be used to make a sequence with terms that decrease in value.

3-6 Exercises

go.hrw.com
Homework Help Online
KEYWORD: MT7 3-6
Parent Resources Online
KEYWORD: MT7 Parent

GUIDED PRACTICE

See Example 1 — Find the common difference in each arithmetic sequence.

1. 4, 8, 12, 16, . . .
2. 6, 13, 20, 27, . . .
3. 25, 19, 13, 7, . . .
4. 3.4, 4, 4.6, 5.2, . . .
5. 15, 12, 9, 6, 3, . . .
6. 10, 19, 28, 37, . . .

See Example 2 — Find the next three terms in each arithmetic sequence.

7. 5, 10, 15, 20, . . .
8. 1.5, 2, 2.5, 3, . . .
9. 40, 33, 26, 19, . . .
10. 6, 12, 18, 24, . . .
11. −2, −4, −6, −8, . . .
12. $\frac{1}{2}, 1, 1\frac{1}{2}, 2, \ldots$

See Example 3 — Find a function that describes each arithmetic sequence. Use *y* to identify each term in the sequence and *n* to identify each term's position.

13. 3, 6, 9, 12, . . .
14. 1, 4, 7, 10, . . .
15. 2, 6, 10, 14, . . .

See Example 4

16. A long distance phone plan costs $19.95 per month, plus $0.03 per minute used. Find a function that describes the arithmetic sequence. Then find the total charges for a month in which 3 hours of long distance were used.

INDEPENDENT PRACTICE

See Example 1 — Find the common difference in each arithmetic sequence.

17. 7, 14, 21, 28, . . .
18. −5, −1, 3, 7, . . .
19. 32, 26, 20, 14, . . .
20. 4.9, 6, 7.1, 8.2, . . .
21. 63, 56, 49, 42, . . .
22. 3, 15, 27, 39, . . .

See Example 2 — Find the next three terms in each arithmetic sequence.

23. 9, 18, 27, 36, . . .
24. 2.5, 5, 7.5, 10, . . .
25. 34, 25, 16, 7, . . .
26. 8, 16, 24, 32, . . .
27. −3, −6, −9, −12, . . .
28. $\frac{1}{3}, \frac{2}{3}, 1, 1\frac{1}{3}, \ldots$

See Example 3 — Find a function that describes each arithmetic sequence. Use *y* to identify each term in the sequence and *n* to identify each term's position.

29. 4, 8, 12, 16, . . .
30. 1, 6, 11, 16, . . .
31. 3, 10, 17, 24, . . .

See Example 4

32. A book club charges $10.50 to join. Members of the club pay $4.50 each for books sold by the club. Find a function that describes the arithmetic sequence. Then find the total charges for a member who buys 27 books.

PRACTICE AND PROBLEM SOLVING

Extra Practice
See page 787.

Find the missing term in each arithmetic sequence.

33. 13, 26, 39, 52, ▇, . . .
34. −8, −5, −2, ▇, 4, . . .
35. ▇, 24, 18, 12, 6, . . .
36. 2.7, 4.2, 5.7, ▇, 8.7, . . .
37. ▇, 37, 30, 23, 16, . . .
38. $\frac{7}{8}, \frac{13}{16}, \frac{3}{4}, \frac{11}{16}$, ▇, . . .

Find the given term in each arithmetic sequence. (*Hint:* To find a term *n* of an arithmetic sequence that has a common difference, add the 1st term of the sequence to the product of the common difference and (n − 1).

39. 11th term: 3, 9, 15, 21, . . .

40. 15th term: 4, 11, 18, 25, . . .

41. 18th term: 9, 13, 17, 21, . . .

42. 20th term: 2, 5, 8, 11, . . .

43. **Sports** Tyler ran 10 laps around the track on Monday. Each day after that, he ran 3 more laps than the day before. How many laps did Tyler run on the eighth day?

44. A restaurant has square tables. Each table can seat 4 people. If 2 square tables are pushed together, 6 people can be seated around the new table. If 12 square tables are pushed together to form one long table, how many people can be seated around the table?

45. **What's the Error?** A student said that the 10th term of the arithmetic sequence 2, 5, 8, 11, . . . is 32. What was the student's error?

46. **Critical Thinking** Matthew is making a sequence in which −3 is added to each successive term. The 6th term in his sequence is −1. What is the 1st term in his sequence?

47. **Challenge** Tell whether the given term belongs to the sequence defined by the given rule if n is a whole number.

a. 62; $4n$

b. 87; $3n$

c. 42; $-6n$

Test Prep and Spiral Review

48. **Multiple Choice** What is the next term in the sequence 25, 18, 11, 4, . . . ?

Ⓐ −11 Ⓑ −7 Ⓒ −3 Ⓓ 0

49. **Short Response** What is the 10th term in the sequence −10, −7, −4, −1, . . . ?

Find each sum, difference, product, or quotient. Write the answer in simplest form. (Lessons 2-4, 2-5, and 2-6)

50. $\frac{7}{12} - \frac{1}{4}$

51. $\frac{3}{8} \times \frac{4}{9}$

52. $\frac{3}{8} \div \frac{3}{4}$

Make a table and a graph of each function. (Lessons 3-4)

53. $y = 3x - 1$

54. $y = 2x + 2$

55. $y = -x$

Quiz for Lessons 3-4 Through 3-6

3-4 Functions

Make a table and a graph of each function.

1. $y = x + 7$ **2.** $y = 4x + 2$ **3.** $y = \frac{2}{3}x + \frac{1}{3}$ **4.** $y = 5.2x$

Determine if each relationship represents a function.

5.

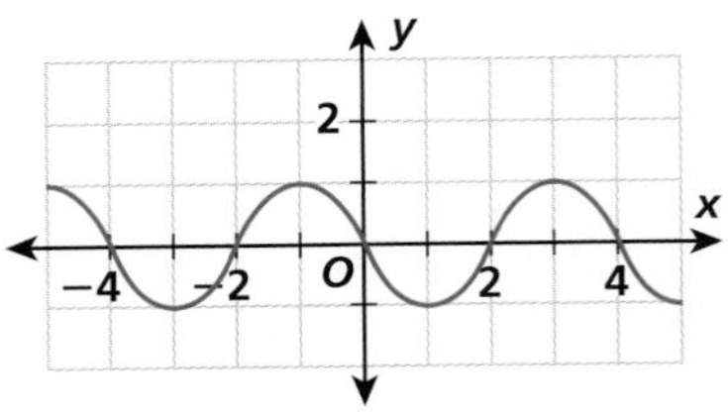

6.

x	y
0	9
1	8
2	7
3	8

7. $y = 4x - 8$ **8.** $y = x^2$

3-5 Equations, Tables, and Graphs

Use each table to make a graph and to write an equation.

9.

x	2	4	6	8
y	13	19	25	31

10.

x	3	6	9	12
y	3.5	5	6.5	8

Use each graph to make a table and to write an equation.

11.

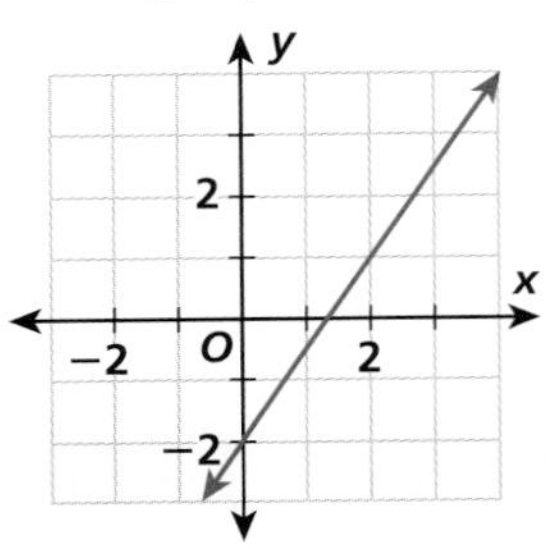

12.

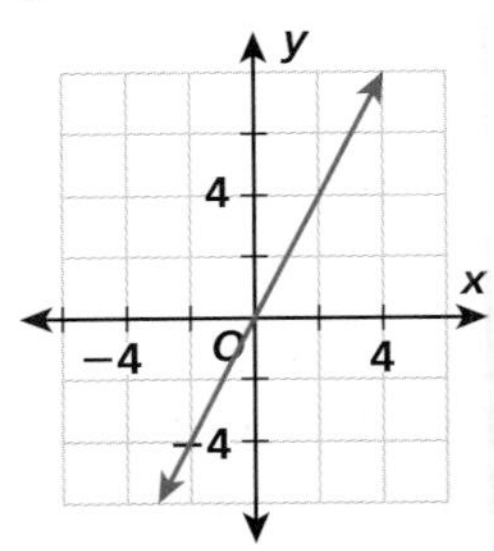

13. The number of tons of plankton that a blue whale eats during the summer is represented by the equation $p = 8d$, where d is the number of days. Make a table and sketch a graph of the equation.

3-6 Arithmetic Sequences

Find the missing term in each sequence.

14. 2, 5, 8, 11, ■, . . . **15.** ■, 8, 16, 24, 32, . . . **16.** 1.5, 3, ■, 6, 7.5, . . .

17. −5, ■, 5, 10, 15, . . . **18.** 1, 3, 5, 7, ■, . . . **19.** ■, 2.7, 4, 5.3, 6.6, . . .

20. Tickets to a dance cost \$5 each. Decorations, food, and music cost \$350. Find a function that describes the sequence. Then find the total profit if 93 tickets are sold.

MULTI-STEP TEST PREP

Start Your Engines Ms. Naranja's class is conducting an experiment with remote-controlled cars. The cars move in a straight line away from a wall. Students record each car's distance from the wall at one-second intervals.

1. The motion of car A is given by the equation, $y = 2.5x + 1.5$, where x is the time in seconds and y is the car's distance from the wall in feet. Complete the table of data for car A.

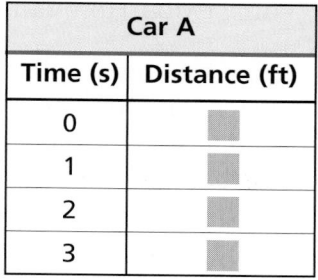

Car A	
Time (s)	Distance (ft)
0	
1	
2	
3	

2. Graph the data for car A on a coordinate plane.
3. How far is car A from the wall at the start of the experiment? How far is the car from the wall after 3 seconds?
4. Find the value of y when $x = 6$ for the function $y = 2.5x + 1.5$. What does this value represent?
5. The data for car B is shown in the graph. Make a table of data for car B. Include times from 0 to 6 seconds.
6. Describe the motion of car B in words. What do you think happened to the car after 3 seconds?

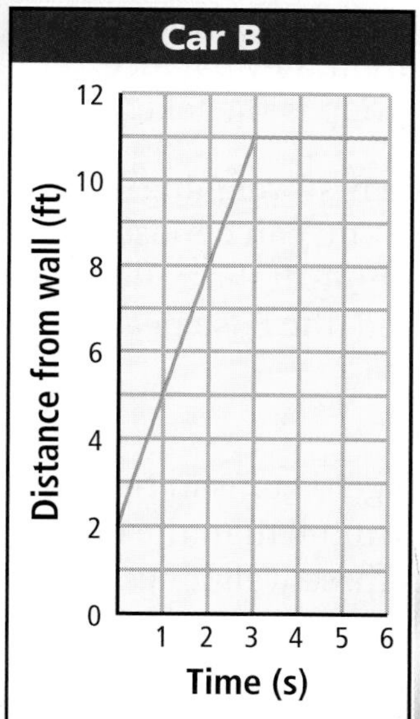

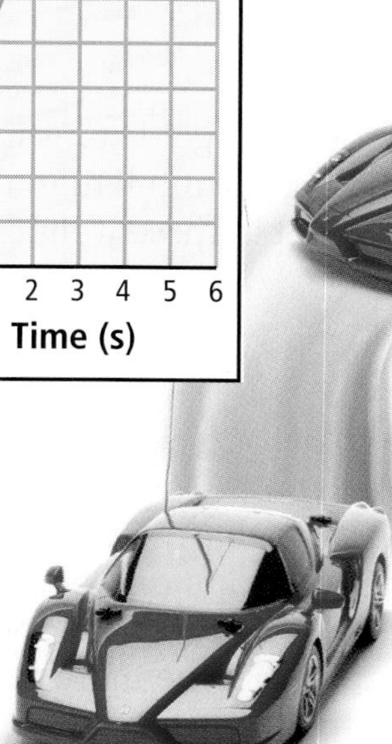

Game Time

Find the Phony!

Suppose you have nine identical-looking pearls. Eight are real, and one is fake. Using a balance scale that consists of two pans, you must find the bogus pearl. The real pearls weigh the same, and the fake weighs less. The scale can be used only twice. How can you find the phony?

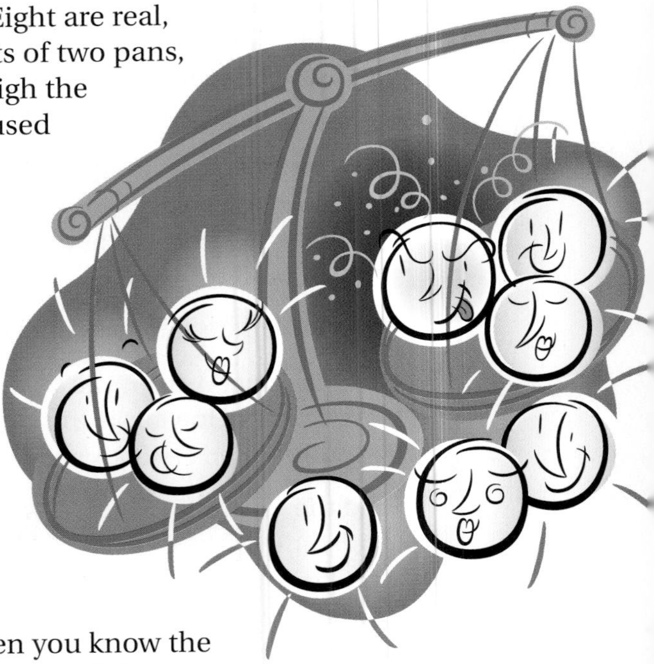

First you must split the pearls into equal groups. Place any three pearls on one side of the scale and any other three on the other side. If one side weighs less than the other, then the fake pearl is on that side. But you are not done yet! You still need to find the imitation, and you can use the scale only once more. Take any of the two pearls from the lighter pan, and weigh them against each other. If one pan is lighter, then that pan contains the fake pearl. If they balance, then the leftover pearl of the group is the fake.

If the scale balances during the first weighing, then you know the fake is in the third group. Then you can choose two pearls from that group for the second weighing. If the scale balances, the fake is the one left. If it is unbalanced, the false pearl is the lighter one.

You Play Detective

Suppose you have 12 identical gold coins in front of you. One is counterfeit and weighs slightly more than the others. How can you identify the counterfeit in three weighings?

Sprouts

You and a partner play against each other to try to make the last move in the game. You start with three dots. Player one draws a path to join two dots or a path that starts and ends at the same dot. A new dot is then placed somewhere on that path. No dot can have more than three paths drawn from it, and no path can cross another.

A complete copy of the rules is available online.

go.hrw.com
Game Time Extra
KEYWORD: MT7 Games

It's in the Bag!

FOLDNOTES

Materials
- paper lunch bag
- hole punch
- lined paper
- 2 brass fasteners
- string, ribbon, or yarn
- golf pencil
- card stock

PROJECT Clipboard Solutions for Graphs, Functions, and Sequences

Make your own clipboard for taking notes on graphs, functions, and sequences.

Directions

1. Fold the bag flat and hold it with the flap at the top. Punch two holes at the bottom of the flap, about 3 inches apart. The holes should go through only the flap, not the entire bag. **Figure A**

2. Slide about ten sheets of lined paper under the flap and mark where the holes should be punched. Then punch holes through the sheets.

3. Fasten the sheets under the flap using brass fasteners. **Figure B**

4. Punch holes in the upper left and upper right corners of the flap. Tie one end of the string to the left-hand hole. Thread the string through the right-hand hole and tie it there, leaving some slack at the top of the bag. Tie the golf pencil to the end of the string. **Figure C**

5. Slide a piece of card stock into the bag to make it more sturdy.

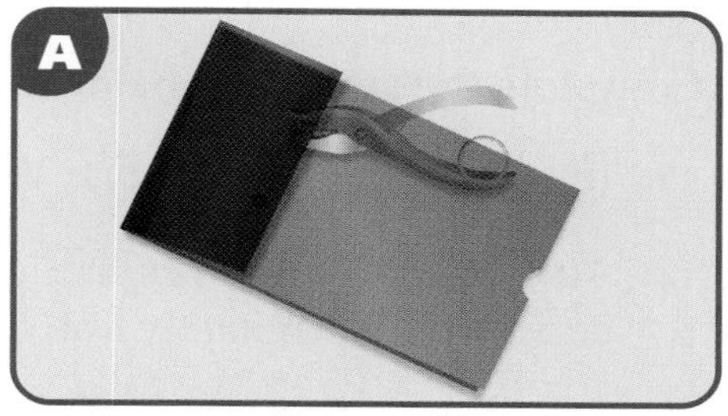
A

B

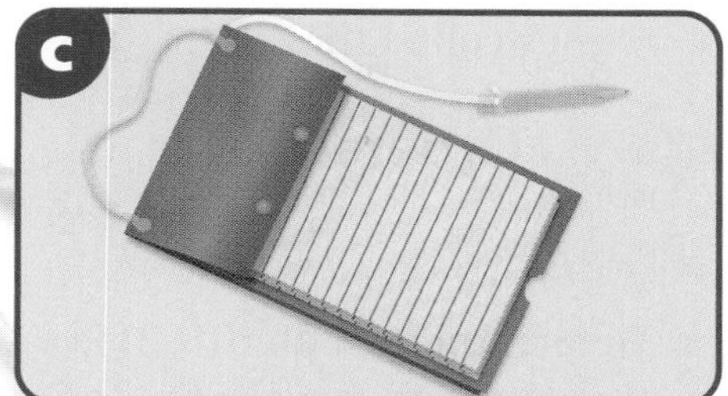
C

Taking Note of the Math

Summarize each lesson of the chapter on a separate page of the clipboard. Use any extra pages to write down sample problems.

CHAPTER 3

Study Guide: Review

Vocabulary

arithmetic sequence ... 142
common difference ... 142
coordinate plane ... 122
domain ... 134
function ... 134
graph of an equation ... 123
input ... 134
ordered pair ... 118
origin ... 122
output ... 134
quadrant ... 122
range ... 134
sequence ... 142
term ... 142
vertical line test ... 135
x-axis ... 122
x-coordinate ... 122
y-axis ... 122
y-coordinate ... 122

Complete the sentences below with vocabulary words from the list above.

1. In an arithmetic sequence, there is a(n) ___?___ between each term.
2. A(n) ___?___ is a mathematical relationship in which each input corresponds to exactly one output.
3. The ___?___ is the point (0, 0) on a coordinate plane.
4. A(n) ___?___ is an ordered list of numbers or objects, which are also called a(n) ___?___.
5. The ___?___ is a method for testing whether or not a graph represents a function.
6. The coordinate plane is formed by the intersection of two number lines called the ___?___ and the ___?___.

3-1 Ordered Pairs (pp. 118–121)

EXAMPLE

- **Determine whether (8, 3) is a solution of the equation $y = x - 6$.**

$y = x - 6$

$3 \stackrel{?}{=} 8 - 6$ Substitute 8 for *x* and 3 for *y*.

$3 \stackrel{?}{=} 2$ ✗

(8, 3) is not a solution.

- **Use the values to make a table of solutions. $y = 5x - 1$ for $x = 1, 2, 3$.**

x	5x − 1	y	(x, y)
1	5(1) − 1	4	(1, 4)
2	5(2) − 2	9	(2, 9)
3	5(3) − 1	14	(3, 14)

EXERCISES

Determine whether each ordered pair is a solution of the given equation.

7. (27, 0); $y = 81 - 3x$
8. (4, 5); $y = 5x$
9. (−3, 7); $y = 2x + 13$
10. (2, 4); $y = 3x$

Use the values to make a table of solutions.

11. $y = 3x + 2$ for $x = 0, 1, 2, 3, 4$
12. $y = \frac{7}{8}x + 5$ for $x = 0, 2, 4, 6$
13. $y = 2.2x - 1.7$ for $x = -4, -3, -2, -1$

3-2 Graphing on a Coordinate Plane (pp. 122–125)

EXAMPLE

- **Graph $A(3, -1)$, $B(0, 4)$, $C(-2, -3)$, and $D(1, 0)$ on a coordinate plane.**

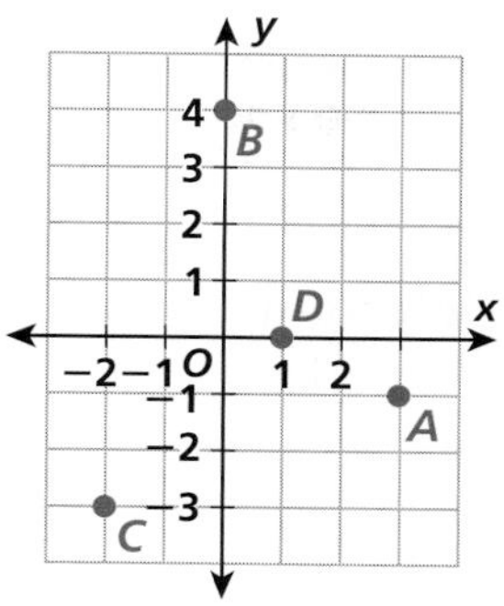

- **Give the missing coordinate for the solution of $y = -3x + 2$.**

$(11, y)$

$y = -3(11) + 2$ *Substitute 11 for x.*

$y = -33 + 2$ *Multiply.*

$y = -31$ *Add.*

$(11, -31)$

EXERCISES

Graph each point on a coordinate plane.

14. $A(3, 2)$ **15.** $B(-1, 0)$ **16.** $C(0, -5)$

17. $D(1, -3)$ **18.** $E(0, 4)$ **19.** $F(-3, -5)$

20. $G(5, 0)$ **21.** $H(-2, 3)$ **22.** $J(0, 0)$

Give the missing coordinate for the solutions of $y = 3x + 5$.

23. $(0, y)$ **24.** $(1, y)$ **25.** $(5, y)$

26. $(7, y)$ **27.** $(1.7, y)$ **28.** $\left(\frac{7}{9}, y\right)$

Complete the table of ordered pairs. Graph each ordered pair on a coordinate plane. Draw a line through the points.

29. $y = x - 2$

x	x − 2	y	(x, y)
0			
1			
2			

3-3 Interpreting Graphs and Tables (pp. 127–131)

EXAMPLE

- **Explain which car has the faster acceleration?**

Acceleration	Car A (s)	Car B (s)
0 to 30 mi/h	1.8	3.2
0 to 40 mi/h	2.8	4.7
0 to 50 mi/h	3.9	6.4
0 to 60 mi/h	5.1	8.8

Car A; Car A accelerates from 0 to each measured speed in fewer seconds than car B.

EXERCISES

30. Which oven had not been preheated? Explain.

Baking Time (min)	Oven D (°F)	Oven E (°F)
0	450°	70°
1	435°	220°
2	445°	440°
3	450°	440°

31. If there are 5 s between floors, which person rode an elevator? Explain.

Time (s)	Altitude of Person A (ft)	Altitude of Person B (ft)
0	0	0
5	5	10
10	10	20
15	15	30

3-4 Functions (pp. 134–137)

EXAMPLE

■ **Make a table and a graph of $y = x - 3$.**

x	$x - 3$	y
0	$0 - 3$	-3
1	$1 - 3$	-2
2	$2 - 3$	-1
3	$3 - 3$	0

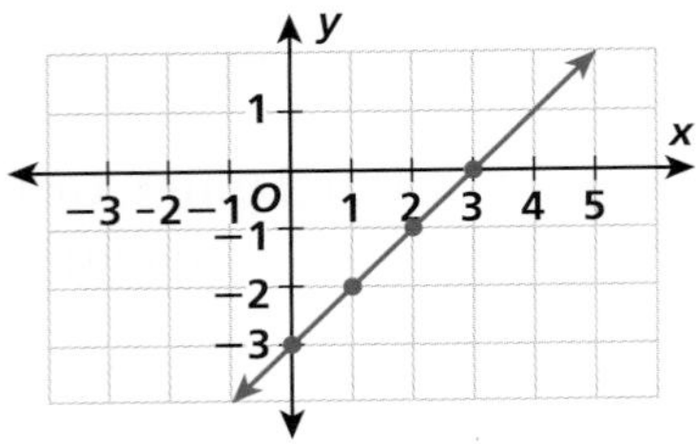

EXERCISES

Make a table and a graph of each function.

32. $y = 7x - 4$

33. $y = 6x + 1$

34. $y = -2x + 3$

35. $y = -3x + 4$

Determine if each relationship represents a function.

36.

x	1	2	3	4	5
y	17	19	21	23	25

37.

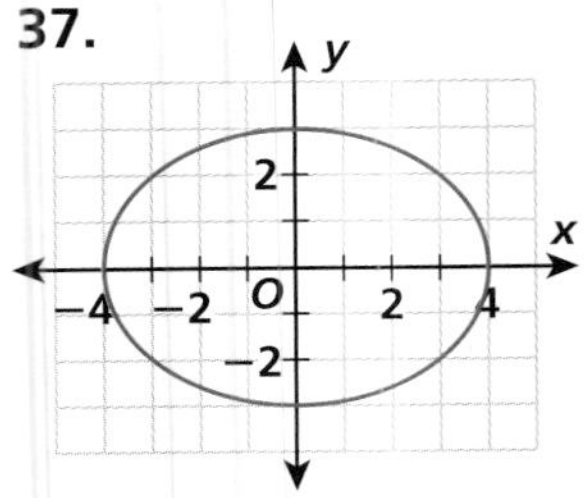

3-5 Equations, Tables, and Graphs (pp. 138–141)

EXAMPLE

■ **Use the table to make a graph and to write an equation.**

x	1	2	3	4	5
y	8	16	24	32	40

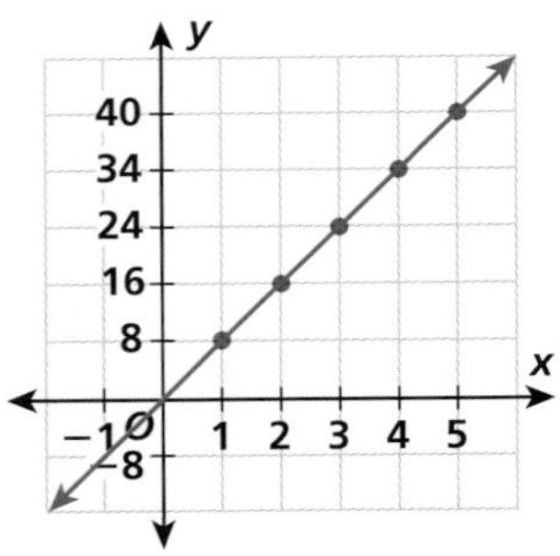

Each value of y is 8 times the corresponding value of x, so the equation is $y = 8x$.

EXERCISES

Use each table to make a graph and to write an equation.

38.

x	1	2	3	4	5
y	2.3	4.6	6.9	9.2	11.5

39.

x	1	2	3	4	5
y	$\frac{1}{2}$	1	$1\frac{1}{2}$	2	$2\frac{1}{2}$

40.

x	1	2	3	4	5
y	1	2	3	4	5

3-6 Arithmetic Sequences (pp. 142–145)

EXAMPLE

■ **Find the next three terms in the sequence $-7, -3, 1, 5, \ldots$**

Each term is 4 more than the previous term.

$5 + 4 = 9$

$9 + 4 = 13$

$13 + 4 = 17$

The next three terms are 9, 13, and 17.

EXERCISES

Find the next three terms in each sequence.

41. $1, 8, 15, 22, \ldots$

42. $1.5, 4, 6.5, 9, \ldots$

43. $\frac{2}{3}, 1\frac{1}{3}, 2, 2\frac{2}{3}, \ldots$

44. $5, 7, 9, 11, \ldots$

45. $-3, -6, -9, -12, \ldots$

CHAPTER TEST

Determine whether the ordered pair is a solution of the given equation.

1. (6, 5) for $y = 5x - 25$

2. (−3, 10) for $y = -3x - 1$

3. (2, 4) for $y = 5x - 6$

Give the coordinates for each point.

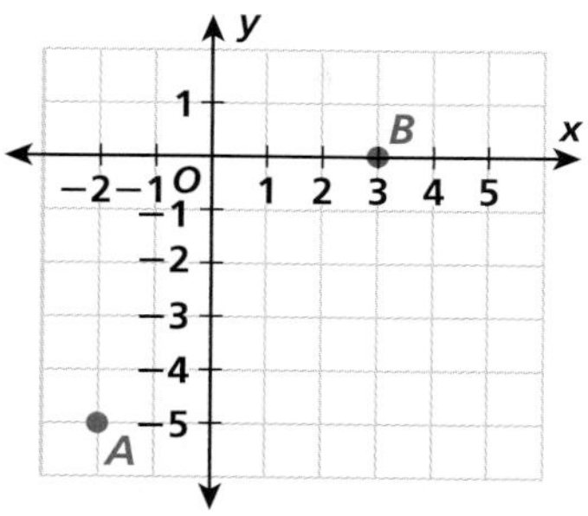

4. *A*

5. *B*

6. Suppose the cost of mailing a letter is \$0.23 per ounce plus \$0.14. The equation that gives the total cost c of mailing a letter is $c = 0.23w + 0.14$, where w is the weight in ounces. What is the cost of mailing a 6-ounce letter?

7. The cost of renting a sailboat at a lake is \$20 per hour plus \$12 for lifejackets. The total cost is represented by the equation $c = 20h + 12$, where h is the number of hours and c is the total cost. How much does it cost to rent a sailboat for 3.5 hours?

8. Use the table to graph the speed of the car over time.

Time (s)	0	5	10	15
Speed (mi/h)	0	20	30	35

Make a table and a graph of each function.

9. $y = 5x - 3$

10. $y = 9x + 2$

11. $y = -2x - 5$

12. $y = \frac{3}{5}x - \frac{2}{3}$

Use each table to make a graph and to write an equation.

13.

x	4	5	6	7
y	12	15	18	21

14.

x	$\frac{1}{2}$	1	$1\frac{1}{2}$	2
y	$3\frac{1}{2}$	7	$10\frac{1}{2}$	14

15. A pool contains 125 gallons of water. Every minute, an additional 55 gallons is added. Find a function to describe this sequence, and find the number of gallons of water in the pool after 1 hour.

16. An hourglass contains 10,235 beads in the top half. Every minute, 150 beads fall to the bottom half. Find a function to describe this sequence, and find the number of beads remaining in the top half of the hourglass after 35 minutes.

17. The amount of water being emptied from a pool is represented by the equation $g = -12m$, where g is the number of gallons of water emptied and m is the number of minutes since emptying began. Make a table and sketch a graph of the equation.

TEST TACKLER

Standardized Test Strategies

Gridded Response: Write Gridded Responses

When responding to a test item that requires you to place your answer in a grid, you must fill out the grid on your answer sheet correctly, or the item will be marked as incorrect.

EXAMPLE 1

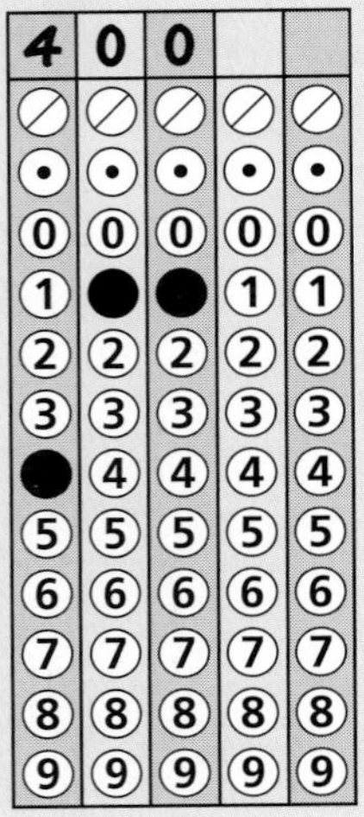

Gridded Response: Divide. 3000 ÷ 7.5

$3000 \div 7.5 = \frac{3000}{7.5}\left(\frac{10}{10}\right)$ *7.5 has 1 decimal place, so multiply by $\frac{10}{10}$.*

$= \frac{30{,}000}{75}$ *Divide.*

$= 400$ *Simplify.*

- Write your answer in the answer boxes at the top of the grid.
- Put only one digit in each box. Do not leave a blank box in the middle of an answer.
- Shade the bubble for each digit in the column beneath it.

EXAMPLE 2

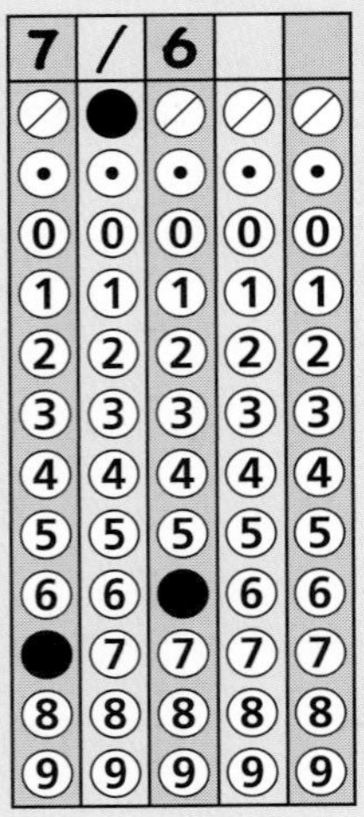

Gridded Response: Solve. $x - \frac{1}{2} = \frac{2}{3}$

$x - \frac{1}{2} + \frac{1}{2} = \frac{2}{3} + \frac{1}{2}$ *Add $\frac{1}{2}$ to both sides of the equation.*

$x = \frac{4}{6} + \frac{3}{6}$ *Find a common denominator.*

$x = \frac{7}{6}, 1\frac{1}{6}$; or $1.1\overline{6}$ *Add.*

- Mixed numbers and repeating decimals cannot be gridded, so you must grid the answer as $\frac{7}{6}$.
- Write your answer in the answer boxes at the top of the grid.
- Put only one digit or symbol in each box. On some grids, the fraction bar and the decimal point have a designated box. Do not leave a blank box in the middle of an answer.
- Shade the bubble for each digit or symbol in the column beneath it.

HOT TIP! You cannot grid a negative number in a gridded response item because the grid does not include the negative sign. If you get a negative answer to a test item, recalculate the problem because you probably made a math error.

Read each statement and then answer the questions that follow.

Item A

A student correctly evaluated an expression and got $\frac{9}{13}$ as a result. Then the student filled in the grid as shown.

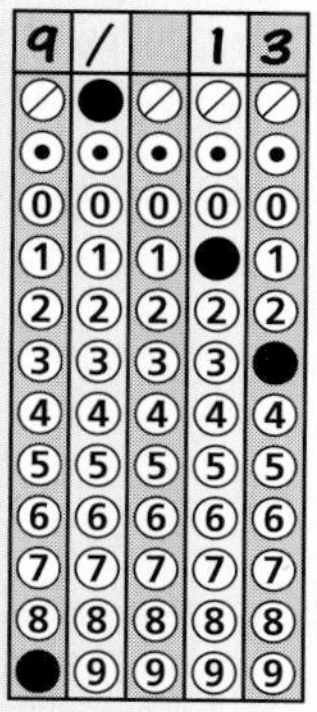

1. What error did the student make when filling in the grid?
2. Explain how to fill in the answer correctly.

Item B

A student added 0.21 and 0.49 and got an answer of 0.7. This answer is displayed in the grid.

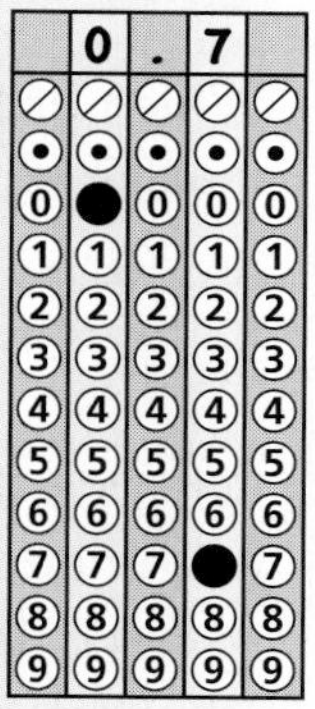

3. What errors did the student make when filling in the grid?
4. Explain how to fill in the answer correctly.

Item C

A student found -0.65 as the answer to $-5 \cdot (-0.13)$. Then the student filled in the grid as shown.

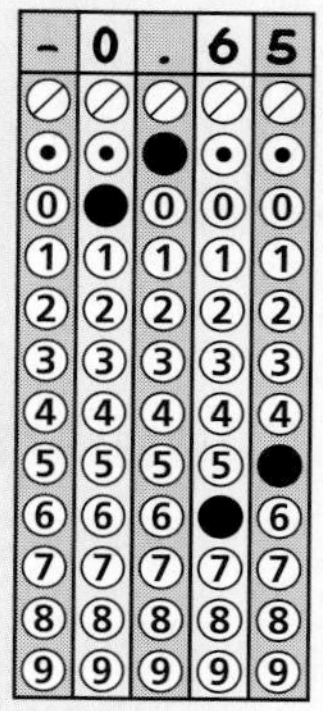

5. What error does the grid show?
6. Another student got an answer of -0.65. Explain why the student knew this answer was wrong.

Item D

A student found that $x = 5\frac{1}{2}$ was the solution to the equation $2x - 3 = 8$. Then the student filled in the grid as shown.

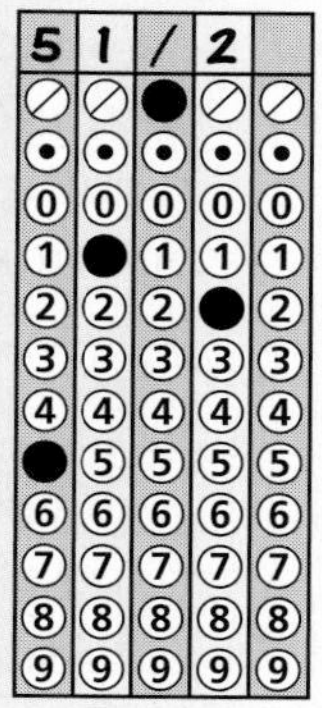

7. What answer does the grid show?
8. Explain why you cannot fill in a mixed number.
9. Write the answer $5\frac{1}{2}$ in two forms that could be entered in the grid correctly.

STANDARDIZED TEST PREP

go.hrw.com
State Test Practice Online
KEYWORD: MT7 TestPrep

Cumulative Assessment, Chapters 1–3

Multiple Choice

1. A cell phone company charges $0.21 per minute for phone calls. Which expression represents the cost of a phone call of m minutes?

Ⓐ $0.21m$ Ⓒ $0.21 - m$

Ⓑ $0.21 + m$ Ⓓ $0.21 \div m$

2. Laurie had $88 in her bank account on Sunday. The table below shows her account activity for the past 5 days. What is the balance in her account on Friday?

Day	Deposit	Withdraw
Monday	$25	
Tuesday		$58
Wednesday		$45
Thursday	$32	
Friday	$91	

Ⓕ $91 Ⓗ $133

Ⓖ $103 Ⓙ $236

3. Which equation has a solution of $x = -5$?

Ⓐ $2x + 8 = -2$ Ⓒ $\frac{1}{5}x - 6 = -10$

Ⓑ $\frac{1}{5}x + 10 = 5$ Ⓓ $-2x + 10 = -5$

4. You volunteer to bring in 7 gallons of juice for a class party. There are 28 students in the class. You plan to give each student an equal amount of juice. Which equation can you use to determine the amount of juice per student?

Ⓕ $7x = 28$ Ⓗ $28 + x = 7$

Ⓖ $\frac{x}{28} = 7$ Ⓙ $28x = 7$

5. In order to apply for a driver's permit in Ohio, you have to be at least 16 years old. Which graph correctly represents the possible ages of Ohioans who can apply for a driver's permit?

Ⓐ 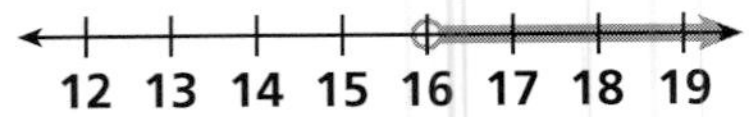

Ⓑ 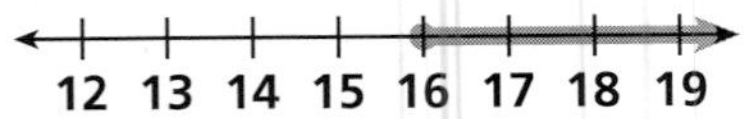

Ⓒ 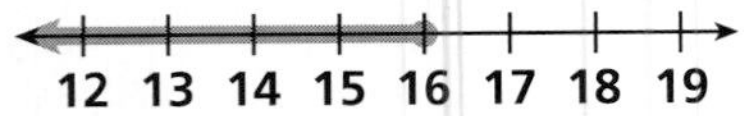

Ⓓ 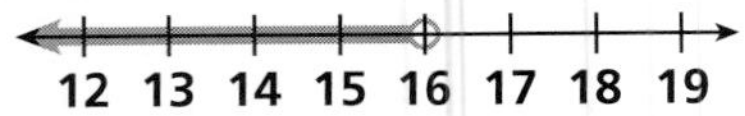

6. Which ordered pair is NOT a solution of $y = 2x - 6$?

Ⓕ (6, 6) Ⓗ (3, 0)

Ⓖ (0, −6) Ⓙ (−3, 0)

7. Which ordered pair is located on the x-axis?

Ⓐ (0, −3) Ⓒ (−3, 0)

Ⓑ (3, −3) Ⓓ (1, −3)

8. Which is the next term in this arithmetic sequence?
4, 8, 12, 16, . . .

Ⓕ 22 Ⓗ 18

Ⓖ 20 Ⓙ 17

9. A snack package has 4 ounces of mixed nuts, $1\frac{1}{2}$ ounces of wheat crackers, $5\frac{3}{4}$ ounces of pretzels, and $2\frac{1}{8}$ ounces of popcorn. What is the total weight of the snacks?

Ⓐ $13\frac{3}{8}$ ounces Ⓒ $12\frac{5}{8}$ ounces

Ⓑ $13\frac{1}{8}$ ounces Ⓓ $9\frac{3}{8}$ ounces

10. The graph of the line $y = 2x - 1$ is shown below.

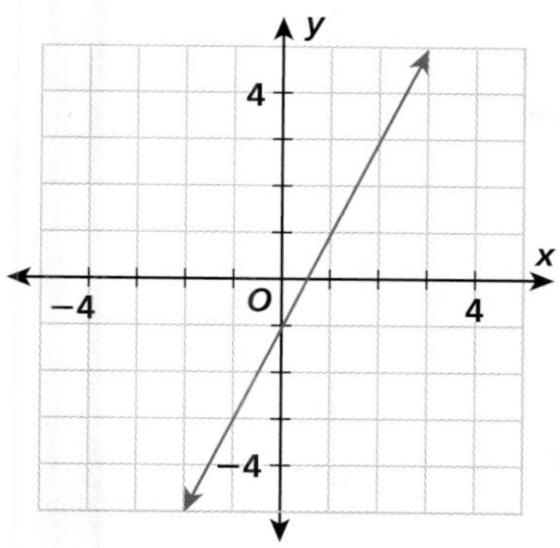

Which ordered pairs contains only points on this line?

(F) $(-1, -2), (0, 0), (1, 2), (2, 4)$

(G) $(-2, -3), (0, -1), (2, 1), (4, 3)$

(H) $(-4, 7), (-2, 3), (0, -1), (2, 3)$

(J) $(0, -1), (1, 1), (2, 3), (3, 5)$

HOT TIP! **Sometimes remembering the rules of integers can help you eliminate one or two of the answer choices.**

Gridded Response

11. In 2004, the minimum wage for workers was $5.85 per hour. To find the amount of money someone can make in x hours, use the equation $y = 5.85x$. How much money does a person who works 5 hours earn?

12. Solve the equation $\frac{4}{9}x = \frac{1}{3}$ for x.

13. The sum of two consecutive integers is 53. What is the smaller of the two numbers?

14. The function $d = -16t^2 + 35$ represents the distance a stone falls after t seconds when dropped from a bridge 35 feet over a river. How many feet does the stone fall after 1 second?

Short Response

15. Consider the set of coordinate points $\{(-1, 1), (0, 2), (1, 3), (2, 4), (3, 5), (4, 6), (5, 7), (x, x + 2)\}$.

a. Determine the domain and the range of the set.

b. Is the set a function? Explain why or why not.

c. Write an equation that will relate x and y.

16. Pablo leaves for school on his bike at 7:15 and arrives at 7:20. The table shows his rate of speed at one-minute intervals. Represent the information in the table with a line graph.

Time (min)	7:15	7:16	7:17	7:18	7:19	7:20
Speed (mi/h)	0	20	15	3	0	10

17. A craft club charges $12.95 to join. Members of the club pay $3.50 each month for a craft kit. Find a function that describes the arithmetic sequence, and then find the total charges for a member who buys a year's worth of craft kits. Show your work.

Extended Response

18. A train travels at a rate of 50 miles per hour from Baton Rouge, Louisiana, to Orlando, Florida. To find the distance y traveled in x hours, use the equation $y = 50x$.

a. Make a table of ordered pairs using the domain $x = 1, 2, 3, 4$, and 5.

b. Graph the solutions from the table of ordered pairs.

c. Maria leaves Baton Rouge at 5:30 A.M. on a train. She needs to be in Orlando by 6:30 P.M. If Baton Rouge is 602 miles from Orlando, will Maria make it on time? Explain.

CHAPTER 4

Exponents and Roots

4A Exponents
- **4-1** Exponents
- **4-2** Look for a Pattern in Integer Exponents
- **4-3** Properties of Exponents
- **4-4** Scientific Notation
- **LAB** Multiply and Divide Numbers in Scientific Notation

4B Roots
- **4-5** Squares and Square Roots
- **4-6** Estimating Square Roots
- **LAB** Evaluate Powers and Roots
- **4-7** The Real Numbers
- **LAB** Explore Right Triangles
- **4-8** The Pythagorean Theorem

MULTI-STEP TEST PREP

go.hrw.com
Chapter Project Online
KEYWORD: MT7 Ch4

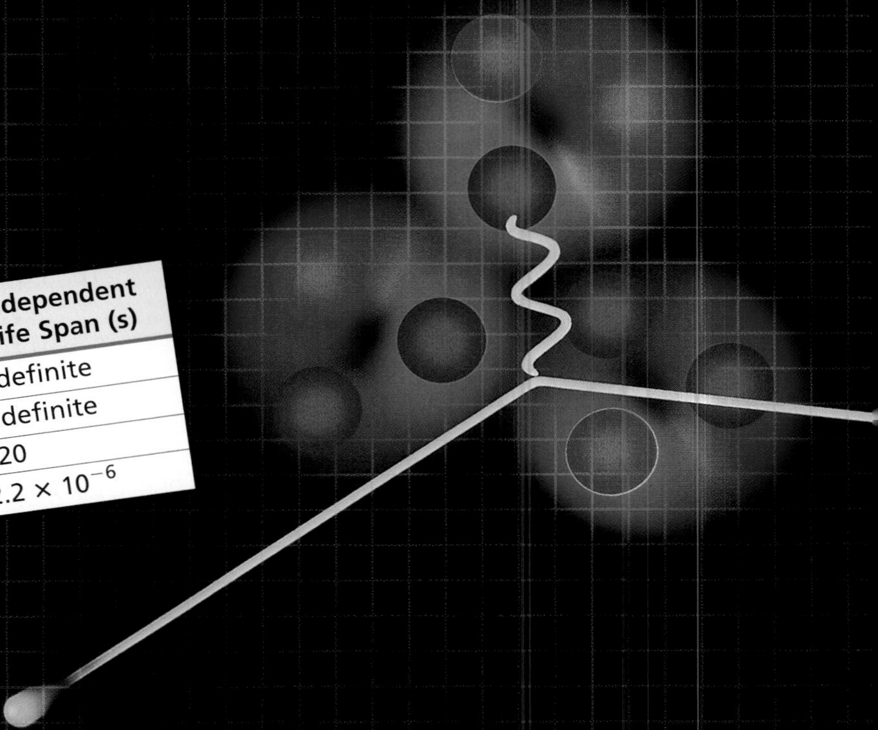

Atomic Particle	Independent Life Span (s)
Electron	Indefinite
Proton	Indefinite
Neutron	920
Muon	2.2×10^{-6}

Career *Nuclear Physicist*

The atom was defined by the ancient Greeks as the smallest particle of matter. We now know that atoms are made up of many smaller particles.

Nuclear physicists study these particles using large machines—such as linear accelerators, synchrotrons, and cyclotrons—that can smash atoms to uncover their component parts.

Nuclear physicists use mathematics along with the data they discover to create models of the atom and the structure of matter.

ARE YOU READY?

Vocabulary

Choose the best term from the list to complete each sentence.

1. According to the __?__, you must multiply or divide before you add or subtract when simplifying a numerical __?__.
2. An algebraic expression is a mathematical sentence that has at least one __?__.
3. In a(n) __?__, an equal sign is used to show that two quantities are the same.
4. You use a(n) __?__ to show that one quantity is greater than another quantity.

equation
expression
inequality
order of operations
variable

Complete these exercises to review skills you will need for this chapter.

Order of Operations

Simplify by using the order of operations.

5. $12 + 4(2)$
6. $12 + 8 \div 4$
7. $15(14 - 4)$
8. $(23 - 5) - 36 \div 2$
9. $12 \div 2 + 10 \div 5$
10. $40 \div 2 \cdot 4$

Equations

Solve.

11. $x + 9 = 21$
12. $3z = 42$
13. $\frac{w}{4} = 16$
14. $24 + t = 24$
15. $p - 7 = 23$
16. $12m = 0$

Use Repeated Multiplication

Find the product.

17. $7 \times 7 \times 7 \times 7 \times 7$
18. $12 \times 12 \times 12$
19. $3 \times 3 \times 3 \times 3$
20. $11 \times 11 \times 11 \times 11$
21. $8 \times 8 \times 8 \times 8 \times 8 \times 8$
22. $2 \times 2 \times 2$
23. $100 \times 100 \times 100 \times 100$
24. $9 \times 9 \times 9 \times 9 \times 9$
25. $1 \times 1 \times 1 \times 1$

Multiply and Divide by Powers of Ten

Multiply or divide.

26. $358(10)$
27. $358(1000)$
28. $358(100{,}000)$
29. $\frac{358}{10}$
30. $\frac{358}{1000}$
31. $\frac{358}{100{,}000}$

CHAPTER 4 Study Guide: Preview

Where You've Been

Previously, you

- simplified expressions involving order of operations and exponents.
- used models to represent squares and square roots.

In This Chapter

You will study

- expressing numbers in scientific notation, including negative exponents.
- approximating the values of irrational numbers.
- modeling the Pythagorean Theorem.
- using the Pythagorean Theorem to solve real-life problems.

Where You're Going

You can use the skills learned in this chapter

- to evaluate expressions containing exponents in future math courses.
- to express the magnitude of interstellar distances.
- to use right triangle geometry in future math courses.

Key Vocabulary/Vocabulario

exponent	exponente
hypotenuse	hipotenusa
irrational number	número irracional
perfect square	cuadrado perfecto
power	potencia
Pythagorean Theorem	teorema de Pitágoras
real number	número real
scientific notation	notación cientifica

Vocabulary Connections

To become familiar with some of the vocabulary terms in the chapter, consider the following. You may refer to the chapter, the glossary, or a dictionary if you like.

1. The word *irrational* contains the prefix *ir-*, which means "not." Knowing what you do about rational numbers, what do you think is true of **irrational numbers**?
2. The word *real* means "actual" or "genuine." How do you think this applies to math, and how do you think **real numbers** differ from numbers that are not real?

Reading and Writing Math

CHAPTER 4

Study Strategy: Take Effective Notes

Good note taking is an important study strategy. The Cornell system of note taking is an effective way to organize and review main ideas. This method involves dividing your notebook paper into three main sections. You take notes in the note-taking column during the lecture. You write questions and key phrases in the cue column as you review your notes. You write a brief summary of the lecture in the summary area.

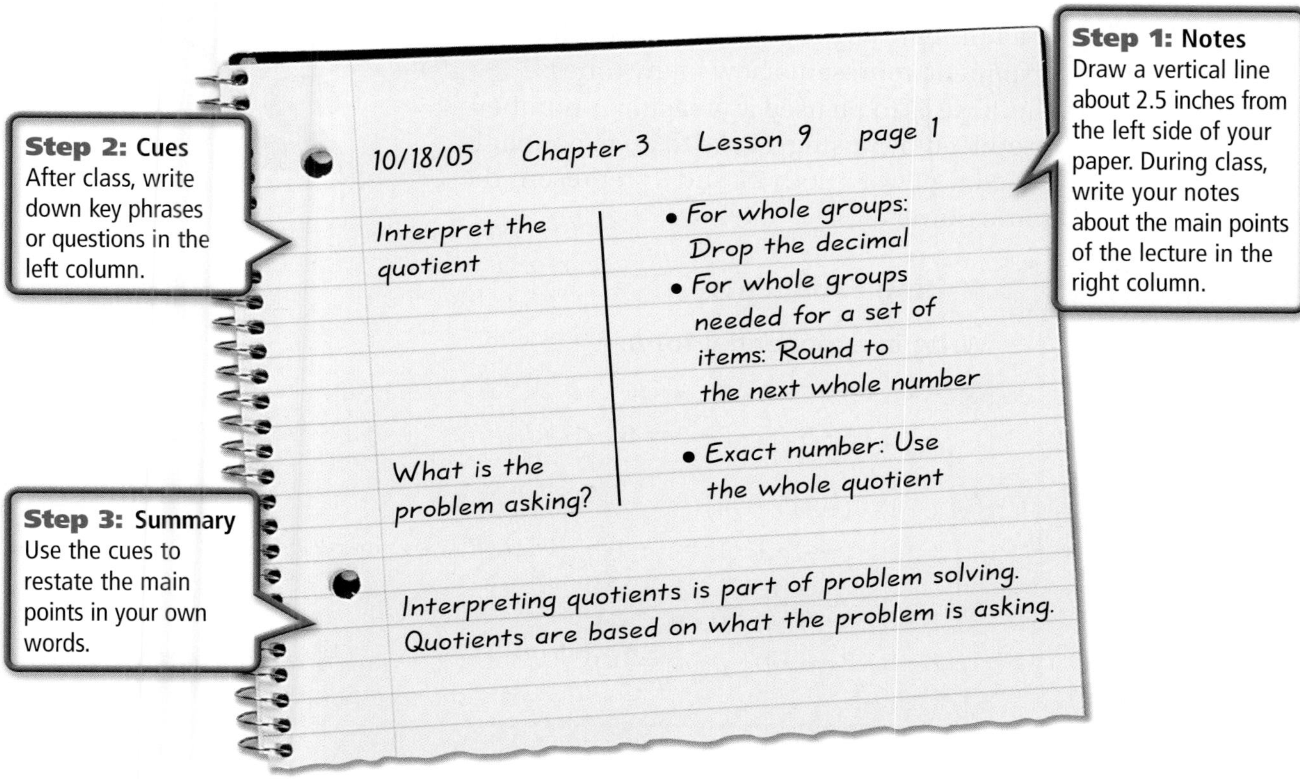

Step 1: Notes
Draw a vertical line about 2.5 inches from the left side of your paper. During class, write your notes about the main points of the lecture in the right column.
Step 2: Cues
After class, write down key phrases or questions in the left column.
Step 3: Summary
Use the cues to restate the main points in your own words.
10/18/05 Chapter 3 Lesson 9 page 1
Interpret the quotient
• For whole groups: Drop the decimal
• For whole groups needed for a set of items: Round to the next whole number
What is the problem asking?
• Exact number: Use the whole quotient
Interpreting quotients is part of problem solving.
Quotients are based on what the problem is asking.

Try This

1. Research and write a paragraph describing the Cornell system of note taking. Describe how you can benefit from using this type of system.
2. In your next class, use the Cornell system of note taking. Compare these notes to your notes from a previous lecture. Do you think your old notes or the notes using the Cornell system would better prepare you for tests and quizzes?

4-1 Exponents

Learn to evaluate expressions with exponents.

Vocabulary

exponential form

exponent

base

power

Fold a piece of $8\frac{1}{2}$-by-11-inch paper in half. If you fold it in half again, the paper is 4 sheets thick. After the third fold in half, the paper is 8 sheets thick. How many sheets thick is the paper after 7 folds?

With each fold the number of sheets doubles.

$2 \cdot 2 \cdot 2 \cdot 2 \cdot 2 \cdot 2 \cdot 2 = 128$ sheets thick after 7 folds

This multiplication problem can also be written in *exponential form.*

$2 \cdot 2 \cdot 2 \cdot 2 \cdot 2 \cdot 2 \cdot 2 = 2^7$ *The number 2 is a factor 7 times.*

If a number is in **exponential form**, the **exponent** represents how many times the **base** is to be used as a factor. A number produced by raising a base to an exponent is called a **power**. Both 27 and 3^3 represent the same power.

EXAMPLE 1 Writing Exponents

Write in exponential form.

A $5 \cdot 5 \cdot 5 \cdot 5 \cdot 5 \cdot 5 \cdot 5$

$5 \cdot 5 \cdot 5 \cdot 5 \cdot 5 \cdot 5 \cdot 5 = 5^7$ *Identify how many times 5 is a factor.*

B $(-4) \cdot (-4) \cdot (-4)$

$(-4) \cdot (-4) \cdot (-4) = (-4)^3$ *Identify how many times −4 is a factor.*

C $8 \cdot 8 \cdot 8 \cdot 8 \cdot p \cdot p \cdot p$

$8 \cdot 8 \cdot 8 \cdot 8 \cdot p \cdot p \cdot p = 8^4p^3$ *Identify how many times 8 and p are each used as a factor.*

Reading Math

Read (-4^3) as "−4 to the 3rd power or −4 cubed".

EXAMPLE 2 Evaluating Powers

Evaluate.

A 3^4

$3^4 = 3 \cdot 3 \cdot 3 \cdot 3$ *Find the product of four 3's.*

$= 81$

B 12^2

$12^2 = 12 \cdot 12$ *Find the product of two 12's.*

$= 144$

Caution!

Always use parentheses to raise a negative number to a power.

Evaluate.

C $(-8)^2$

$(-8)^2 = (-8) \cdot (-8)$ *Find the product of two −8's.*

$= 64$

D -2^3

$-2^3 = -(2 \cdot 2 \cdot 2)$ *Find the product of three 2's and then make the answer negative.*

$= -8$

EXAMPLE 3 Using the Order of Operations

Evaluate $x - y(z \cdot y^z)$ for $x = 20$, $y = 4$, and $z = 2$.

$x - y(z \cdot y^z)$

$20 - 4(2 \cdot 4^2)$ *Substitute 20 for x, 4 for y, and 2 for z.*

$= 20 - 4(2 \cdot 16)$ *Evaluate the exponent.*

$= 20 - 4(32)$ *Multiply inside the parentheses.*

$= 20 - 128$ *Multiply from left to right.*

$= -108$ *Subtract from left to right.*

EXAMPLE 4 *Geometry Application*

The number of diagonals of an n-sided figure is $\frac{1}{2}(n^2 - 3n)$. Use the formula to find the number of diagonals for a 6-sided figure.

$\frac{1}{2}(n^2 - 3n)$

$\frac{1}{2}(6^2 - 3 \cdot 6)$ *Substitute the number of sides for n.*

$\frac{1}{2}(36 - 18)$ *Simplify inside the parentheses.*

$\frac{1}{2}(18)$ *Subtract inside the parentheses.*

9 *Multiply.*

A 6-sided figure has 9 diagonals. You can verify your answer by sketching the diagonals.

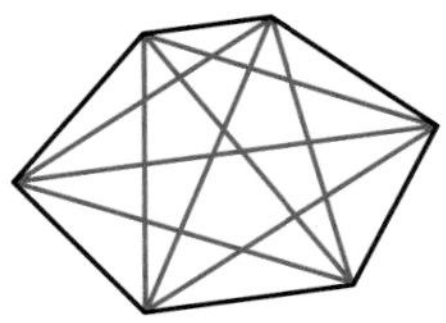

Think and Discuss

1. **Explain** the difference between $(-5)^2$ and -5^2.
2. **Compare** $3 \cdot 2$, 3^2, and 2^3.
3. **Show** that $(4 - 11)^2$ is not equal to $4^2 - 11^2$.

4-1 Exercises

go.hrw.com
Homework Help Online
KEYWORD: MT7 4-1
Parent Resources Online
KEYWORD: MT7 Parent

GUIDED PRACTICE

See Example 1

Write in exponential form.

1. 12 **2.** $18 \cdot 18$ **3.** $2b \cdot 2b \cdot 2b \cdot 2b$ **4.** $(-3) \cdot (-3)$

See Example 2

Evaluate.

5. 2^6 **6.** $(-7)^2$ **7.** $(-5)^3$ **8.** -7^4 **9.** 8^4

See Example 3

Evaluate each expression for the given values of the variables.

10. $a^5 + 4b$ for $a = 3$ and $b = 12$

11. $2x^9 - (y + z)$ for $x = -1$, $y = 7$, and $z = -4$

12. $s + (t^u - 1)$ for $s = 13$, $t = 5$, $u = 3$

13. $100 - n(p^{q-4})$ for $n = 10$, $p = 3$, and $q = 8$

See Example 4

14. The sum of the first n positive integers is $\frac{1}{2}(n^2 + n)$. Check the formula for the first 5 positive integers. Then use the formula to find the sum of the first 14 positive integers.

INDEPENDENT PRACTICE

See Example 1

Write in exponential form.

15. $5 \cdot 5 \cdot 5 \cdot 5 \cdot 5 \cdot 5$ **16.** $(-9) \cdot (-9) \cdot (-9)$ **17.** $3d \cdot 3d \cdot 3d$

18. -8 **19.** $(-4) \cdot (-4) \cdot c \cdot c \cdot c$ **20.** $x \cdot x \cdot y$

See Example 2

Evaluate.

21. 4^4 **22.** $(-3)^6$ **23.** 8^5 **24.** -2^9 **25.** $(-4)^2$

See Example 3

Evaluate each expression for the given values of the variables.

26. b^2 for $b = -7$

27. $2^c + 3d(g + 2)$ for $c = 7$, $d = 5$, and $g = 1$

28. $m + n^p$ for $m = 12$, $n = 11$, and $p = 2$

29. $x \div y^z$ for $x = 9$, $y = 3$, and $z = 2$

See Example 4

30. A circle can be divided by n lines into a maximum of $\frac{1}{2}(n^2 + n) + 1$ regions. Use the formula to find the maximum number of regions for 7 lines.

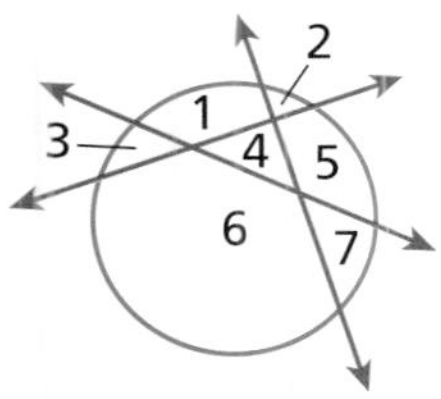

3 lines → 7 regions

PRACTICE AND PROBLEM SOLVING

Extra Practice
See page 788.

Write in exponential form.

31. $(-3) \cdot (-3) \cdot (-3) \cdot (-3)$ **32.** $5h \cdot 5h \cdot 5h$

33. $6 \cdot 6 \cdot 6 \cdot 6 \cdot 6 \cdot 6$ **34.** $(4)(4)(4)(4)(4)$

LINK Life Sciences

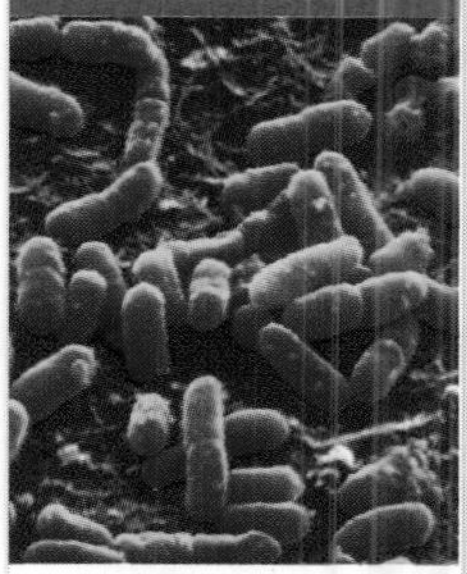

Most bacteria reproduce by a type of simple cell division known as binary fission. Each species reproduces best at a specific temperature and moisture level.

Evaluate.

35. 5^3 **36.** 8^2 **37.** $(-14)^3$ **38.** -4^5

Simplify.

39. $44 - (5 \cdot 4^2)$ **40.** $(4 + 4^4)$ **41.** $(6 - 7^1)$ **42.** $84 - [8 - (-2)^3]$

Evaluate each expression for the given value of the variable.

43. $m(p - n^q)$ for $m = 2$, $n = 6$, $p = 3$, and $q = 3$

44. $r + (t \cdot s^v)$ for $r = 42$, $s = 4$, $t = 3$, and $v = 2$

45. Life Science Bacteria can divide every 20 minutes, so 1 bacterium can multiply to 2 in 20 minutes, 4 in 40 minutes, and so on. How many bacteria will there be in 6 hours? Write your answer using exponents, and then evaluate.

46. Critical Thinking For any whole number n, $5^n - 1$ is divisible by 4. Verify this for $n = 4$ and $n = 6$.

47. Estimation A gift shaped like a cube has sides that measure 12.3 cm long. What is the approximate volume of the gift? (*Hint:* $V = s^3$)

48. Choose a Strategy Place the numbers 1, 2, 3, 4, and 5 in the boxes to make a true statement: $\square \cdot \square^3 = \square^2 - \square^{\square}$.

49. Write About It Compare 10^2 and 2^{10}. For any two numbers, make a conjecture about which usually gives the greater number, using the greater number as the base or as the exponent? Give at least one exception.

50. Challenge Write $(4^2)^3$ using a single exponent.

TEST PREP and Spiral Review

51. Multiple Choice Which expression has the greatest value?

Ⓐ 2^5 Ⓑ 3^4 Ⓒ 4^3 Ⓓ 5^2

52. Multiple Choice The volume of a cube is calculated by using the formula $V = s^3$, where s is the length of the sides of the cube. What is the volume of a cube that has sides 8 meters long?

Ⓕ 24 m^3 Ⓖ 512 m^3 Ⓗ 888 m^3 Ⓙ 6561 m^3

53. Gridded Response What is the value of 5^4?

Find each sum. (Lessons 1-4 and 1-5)

54. $-18 + -65$ **55.** $-123 + 95$ **56.** $87 - (-32)$ **57.** $-74 - (-27)$

Write each fraction as a decimal. (Lesson 2-1)

58. $\frac{7}{50}$ **59.** $\frac{4}{15}$ **60.** $\frac{3}{8}$ **61.** $\frac{5}{24}$

4-2 Look for a Pattern in Integer Exponents

Problem Solving Skill

Learn to evaluate expressions with negative exponents and to evaluate the zero exponent.

The nanoguitar is the smallest guitar in the world. It is no larger than a single cell, at about 10^{-5} meters long.

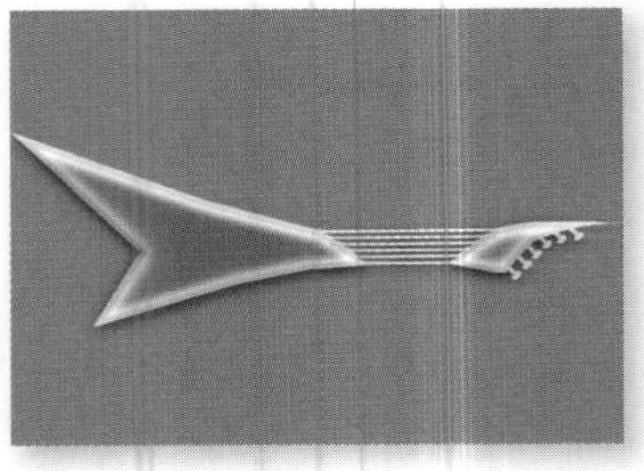

Look for a pattern in the table to extend what you know about exponents to include negative exponents.

10^2	10^1	10^0	10^{-1}	10^{-2}	10^{-3}
$10 \cdot 10$	10	1	$\frac{1}{10}$	$\frac{1}{10 \cdot 10}$	$\frac{1}{10 \cdot 10 \cdot 10}$
100	10	1	$\frac{1}{10} = 0.1$	$\frac{1}{100} = 0.01$	$\frac{1}{1000} = 0.001$

÷ 10   ÷ 10   ÷ 10   ÷ 10   ÷ 10

EXAMPLE 1 Using a Pattern to Evaluate Negative Exponents

Evaluate the powers of 10.

A 10^{-4}

$10^{-4} = \frac{1}{10 \cdot 10 \cdot 10 \cdot 10}$ *Extend the pattern from the table.*

$= \frac{1}{10{,}000}$ *Multiply.*

$= 0.0001$ *Write as a decimal.*

B 10^{-5}

$10^{-5} = \frac{1}{10 \cdot 10 \cdot 10 \cdot 10 \cdot 10}$ *Extend the pattern from Example 1A.*

$= \frac{1}{100{,}000}$ *Multiply.*

$= 0.00001$ *Write as a decimal.*

Remember!

The reciprocal of a number is 1 divided by that number.

NEGATIVE EXPONENTS

Words	Numbers	Algebra
Any number except 0 with a negative exponent equals its reciprocal with the opposite exponent.	$5^{-3} = \left(\frac{1}{5}\right)^3 = \frac{1}{125}$	$b^{-n} = \left(\frac{1}{b}\right)^n, b \neq 0$

EXAMPLE 2 Evaluating Negative Exponents

Evaluate.

A $(-2)^{-3}$

$(-2)^{-3}$

$= \left(\frac{1}{-2}\right)^3$ *Write the reciprocal; change the sign of the exponent.*

$= \frac{1}{-2} \cdot \frac{1}{-2} \cdot \frac{1}{-2}$ *Find the product of three $\left(\frac{1}{-2}\right)$'s.*

$= -\frac{1}{8}$ *Simplify.*

B 6^{-4}

6^{-4}

$= \left(\frac{1}{6}\right)^4$ *Write the reciprocal; change the sign of the exponent.*

$= \frac{1}{6} \cdot \frac{1}{6} \cdot \frac{1}{6} \cdot \frac{1}{6}$ *Find the product of four $\frac{1}{6}$'s.*

$= \frac{1}{1296}$ *Simplify.*

Notice from the table on the previous page that $10^0 = 1$. This is true for any number to the zero power.

THE ZERO POWER		
Words	**Numbers**	**Algebra**
The zero power of any number except 0 equals 1.	$100^0 = 1$ $(-7)^0 = 1$	$a^0 = 1$, if $a \neq 0$

EXAMPLE 3 Using the Order of Operations

Evaluate $2 + (-7)^0 - (4 + 2)^{-2}$.

$2 + (-7)^0 - (4 + 2)^{-2}$

$= 2 + (-7)^0 - 6^{-2}$ *Add inside the parentheses.*

$= 2 + 1 - \frac{1}{36}$ *Evaluate the exponents.*

$= 2\frac{35}{36}$ *Add and subtract from left to right.*

Think and Discuss

1. **Express** $\frac{1}{2}$ using a negative exponent.
2. **Tell** whether an integer raised to a negative exponent can ever be greater than 1. Justify your answer.

4-2 Exercises

go.hrw.com
Homework Help Online
KEYWORD: MT7 4-2
Parent Resources Online
KEYWORD: MT7 Parent

GUIDED PRACTICE

See Example 1

Evaluate the powers of 10.

1. 10^{-2} **2.** 10^{-7} **3.** 10^{-6} **4.** 10^{-10}

See Example 2

Evaluate.

5. $(2)^{-6}$ **6.** $(-3)^{-4}$ **7.** 3^{-3} **8.** $(-2)^{-5}$

See Example 3

9. $4 + 3(4 - 9^0) + 5^{-3}$ **10.** $7 - 8(2)^{-3} + 13$

11. $(2 + 2)^{-2} + (1 + 1)^{-4}$ **12.** $2 - (2^{-3})$

INDEPENDENT PRACTICE

See Example 1

Evaluate the powers of 10.

13. 10^{-1} **14.** 10^{-9} **15.** 10^{-8} **16.** 10^{-12}

See Example 2

Evaluate.

17. $(-4)^{-1}$ **18.** 5^{-2} **19.** $(-10)^{-4}$ **20.** $(-2)^{-6}$

See Example 3

21. $128(2 + 6)^{-3} + (4^0 - 3)$ **22.** $3 + (-3)^{-2} - (9 + 7)^0$

23. $12 - (-5)^0 + (3^{-3} + 9^{-2})$ **24.** $5^0 + 49(1 + 6)^{-2}$

PRACTICE AND PROBLEM SOLVING

Extra Practice
See page 788.

Evaluate.

25. $(18 - 16)^{-5}$ **26.** $25 + (6 \cdot 10^0)$ **27.** $(3 \cdot 3)^{-3}$ **28.** $(1 - 2^{-2})$

29. $3^{-2} \cdot 2^2 \cdot 4^0$ **30.** $10 + 4^3 \cdot 2^{-2}$

31. $6^2 - 3^2 + 1^{-1}$ **32.** $16 - [15 - (-2)^{-3}]$

Evaluate each expression for the given value of the variable.

33. $2(x^2 + x)$ for $x = 2.1$ **34.** $(4n)^{-2} + n$ for $n = 3$

35. $c^2 + c$ for $c = \frac{1}{2}$ **36.** $m^{-2} \cdot m^0 \cdot m^2$ for $m = 9$

Write each expression as repeated multiplication. Then evaluate the expression.

37. 11^{-4} **38.** 1^{-10} **39.** -6^{-3} **40.** $(-6)^{-3}$

41. Make a table with the column headings n, n^{-2}, and $-2n$. Complete the table for $n = -5, -4, -3, -2, -1, 0, 1, 2, 3, 4,$ and 5.

42. Pattern Describe the following pattern: $(-1)^1 =$ ▒; $(-1)^{-2} =$ ▒; $(-1)^{-3} =$ ▒; $(-1)^{-4} =$ ▒. Determine what $(-1)^{-100}$ would be. Justify your thinking.

43. Critical Thinking Evaluate $n^1 \cdot n^{-1}$ for $n = 1, 2,$ and 3. Then make a conjecture what $n^1 \cdot n^{-1}$ is for any value of n. Explain your reasoning.

Science LINK

44. The sperm whale is the deepest diving whale. It can dive to depths greater than 10^{12} nanometers. Evaluate 10^{12}.

45. Blubber makes up 27% of a blue whale's body weight. Davis found the average weight of blue whales and used it to calculate the average weight of their blubber. He wrote the amount as $2^2 \times 3^3 \times 5 \times 71$ pounds. Evaluate this amount.

46. Most baleen whales migrate an average of $2^5 \times 125$ km each way. The gray whale has the longest known migration of any mammal, a distance of $2^4 \times 3 \times 125$ km farther each way than the average baleen whale migration. How far does the gray whale migrate each way?

Krill are a food source for different species of baleen whales, such as the humpback whale, pictured above.

47. A blue whale may eat between 6 and 7 tons of krill each day. Krill are approximately $2^{-5} \times 3^{-1} \times 5^{-1}$ of the length of a blue whale. Evaluate this amount.

48. **Challenge** A cubic centimeter is the same as 1 mL. If a humpback whale has more than 1 kL of blood, how many cubic centimeters of blood does the humpback whale have?

Test Prep and Spiral Review

49. **Multiple Choice** Evaluate $(-5)^{-2}$.

Ⓐ -25 Ⓑ $-\frac{1}{25}$ Ⓒ $\frac{1}{25}$ Ⓓ 25

50. **Extended Response** Evaluate 8^3, 8^2, 8^1, 8^0, 8^{-1}, and 8^{-2}. Describe the pattern of the values. Use the pattern of the values to predict the value of 8^{-3}.

Give the coordinates and quadrant of each point. (Lesson 3-2)

51. A **52.** B **53.** C **54.** D

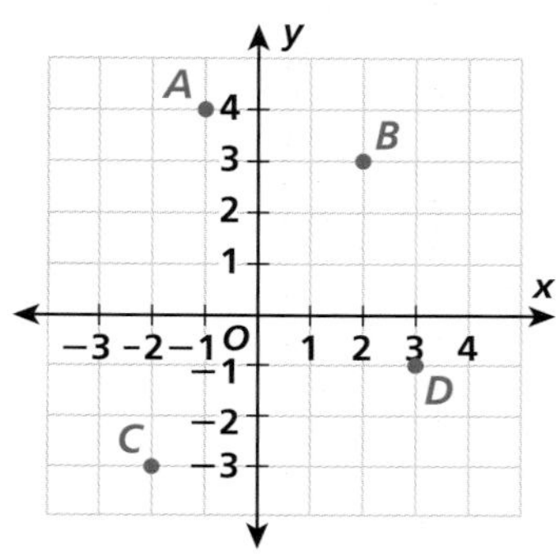

Evaluate. (Lesson 4-1)

55. $(-3)^4$ **56.** 5^2 **57.** $(10 - 15)^3$ **58.** $(-9)^3$

4-3 Properties of Exponents

Learn to apply the properties of exponents.

The factors of a power, such as 7^4, can be grouped in different ways. Notice the relationship of the exponents in each product.

$$7 \cdot 7 \cdot 7 \cdot 7 = 7^4$$
$$(7 \cdot 7 \cdot 7) \cdot 7 = 7^3 \cdot 7^1 = 7^4$$
$$(7 \cdot 7) \cdot (7 \cdot 7) = 7^2 \cdot 7^2 = 7^4$$

MULTIPLYING POWERS WITH THE SAME BASE

Words	Numbers	Algebra
To multiply powers with the same base, keep the base and add the exponents.	$3^5 \cdot 3^8 = 3^{5+8} = 3^{13}$	$b^m \cdot b^n = b^{m+n}$

EXAMPLE 1 Multiplying Powers with the Same Base

Multiply. Write the product as one power.

A $5^4 \cdot 5^3$

$5^4 \cdot 5^3$

5^{4+3} *Add exponents.*

5^7

B $a^{12} \cdot a^{12}$

$a^{12} \cdot a^{12}$

a^{12+12} *Add exponents.*

a^{24}

C $16 \cdot 16^{-7}$

$16 \cdot 16^{-7}$

$16^1 \cdot 16^{-7}$ *Think: $16 = 16^1$*

16^{1+-7} *Add exponents.*

16^{-6}

D $4^2 \cdot 2^2$

$4^2 \cdot 2^2$ *Cannot combine; the bases are not the same.*

Notice what occurs when you divide powers with the same base.

$$\frac{5^5}{5^3} = \frac{5 \cdot 5 \cdot 5 \cdot 5 \cdot 5}{5 \cdot 5 \cdot 5} = \frac{\not{5} \cdot \not{5} \cdot \not{5} \cdot 5 \cdot 5}{\not{5} \cdot \not{5} \cdot \not{5}} = 5 \cdot 5 = 5^2$$

DIVIDING POWERS WITH THE SAME BASE

Words	Numbers	Algebra
To divide powers with the same base, keep the base and subtract the exponents.	$\frac{6^9}{6^4} = 6^{9-4} = 6^5$	$\frac{b^m}{b^n} = b^{m-n}$

EXAMPLE 2 Dividing Powers with the Same Base

Divide. Write the quotient as one power.

A $\frac{10^8}{10^5}$

$\frac{10^8}{10^5}$

10^{8-5} *Subtract exponents.*

10^3

B $\frac{x^9}{y^4}$

$\frac{x^9}{y^4}$ *Cannot combine; the bases are not the same.*

To see what happens when you raise a power to a power, use the order of operations.

$(4^3)^2 = (4 \cdot 4 \cdot 4)^2$ *Evaluate the power inside the parentheses.*

$= (4 \cdot 4 \cdot 4) \cdot (4 \cdot 4 \cdot 4)$ *Evaluate the power outside the parentheses.*

$= 4^6$

Reading Math

$(9^4)^5$ is read as "nine to the fourth, to the fifth."

RAISING A POWER TO A POWER

Words	Numbers	Algebra
To raise a power to a power, keep the base and multiply the exponents.	$(9^4)^5 = 9^{4 \cdot 5} = 9^{20}$	$(b^m)^n = b^{m \cdot n}$

EXAMPLE 3 Raising a Power to a Power

Simplify.

A $(7^5)^3$

$(7^5)^3$ *Multiply exponents.*

$7^{5 \cdot 3}$

7^{15}

B $(8^9)^{11}$

$(8^9)^{11}$ *Multiply exponents.*

$8^{9 \cdot 11}$

8^{99}

C $(2^{-7})^{-2}$

$(2^{-7})^{-2}$

$2^{-7 \cdot (-2)}$ *Multiply exponents.*

2^{14}

D $(12^{10})^{-6}$

$(12^{10})^{-6}$ *Multiply exponents.*

$12^{10 \cdot (-6)}$

12^{-60}

Think and Discuss

1. **Explain** why the exponents cannot be added in the product $14^3 \cdot 18^3$.

2. **List** two ways to express 4^5 as a product of powers.

4-3 Exercises

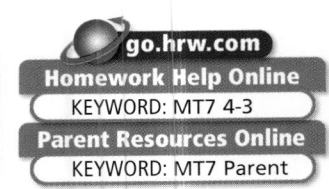

go.hrw.com
Homework Help Online
KEYWORD: MT7 4-3
Parent Resources Online
KEYWORD: MT7 Parent

GUIDED PRACTICE

See Example 1

Multiply. Write the product as one power.

1. $5^6 \cdot 5^9$
2. $12^3 \cdot 12^{-2}$
3. $m \cdot m^3$
4. $5^3 \cdot 7^3$

See Example 2

Divide. Write the quotient as one power.

5. $\frac{6^5}{6^3}$
6. $\frac{a^8}{a^{-1}}$
7. $\frac{12^5}{12^5}$
8. $\frac{5^{16}}{5^4}$

See Example 3

Simplify.

9. $(3^4)^5$
10. $(2^2)^0$
11. $(4^{-2})^3$
12. $(-y^2)^6$

INDEPENDENT PRACTICE

See Example 1

Multiply. Write the product as one power.

13. $10^{10} \cdot 10^7$
14. $3^4 \cdot 3^4$
15. $r^3 \cdot r^{-2}$
16. $18 \cdot 18^5$

See Example 2

Divide. Write the quotient as one power.

17. $\frac{5^{10}}{5^6}$
18. $\frac{m^{10}}{d^3}$
19. $\frac{t^9}{t^{-4}}$
20. $\frac{12^5}{12^5}$

See Example 3

Simplify.

21. $(5^0)^8$
22. $(6^4)^{-1}$
23. $(3^{-2})^2$
24. $(x^5)^2$

PRACTICE AND PROBLEM SOLVING

Extra Practice
See page 788.

Simplify. Write the product or quotient as one power.

25. $\frac{4^7}{4^3}$
26. $3^8 \cdot 3^{-1}$
27. $\frac{a^4}{a^{-3}}$
28. $\frac{10^{18}}{10^9}$
29. $x^3 \cdot x^7$
30. $a^6 \cdot b^9$
31. $(7^4)^3$
32. $2 \cdot 2^4$
33. $\frac{10^4}{5^2}$
34. $\frac{11^7}{11^6}$
35. $\frac{y^8}{y^8}$
36. $y^8 \cdot y^{-8}$

37. There are 26^3 ways to make a 3-letter "word" (from *aaa* to *zzz*) and 26^5 ways to make a 5-letter word. How many times more ways are there to make a 5-letter word than a 3-letter word?

38. **Astronomy** The mass of the sun is about 10^{27} metric tons, or 10^{30} kilograms. How many kilograms are in one metric ton?

39. **Business** Using the manufacturing terms below, tell how many dozen are in a great gross. How many gross are in a great gross?

1 dozen	$= 12^1$ items
1 gross	$= 12^2$ items
1 great gross	$= 12^3$ items

40. **Estimation** The distance from Earth to the moon is about 22^4 miles. The distance from Earth to Neptune is about 22^7 miles. Which distance is greater? About how much greater?

Find the missing exponent.

41. $b^{■} \cdot b^4 = b^8$ 42. $(v^2)^{■} = v^{-6}$ 43. $\frac{w^{■}}{w^3} = w^{-3}$ 44. $(a^4)^{■} = a^0$

45. A googol is the number 1 followed by 100 zeros.
    a. What is a googol written as a power?
    b. What is a googol times a googol written as a power?

Peanuts © Charles Schulz. Dist. by Universal Press Syndicate. Reprinted with Permission. All rights reserved.

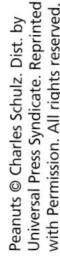

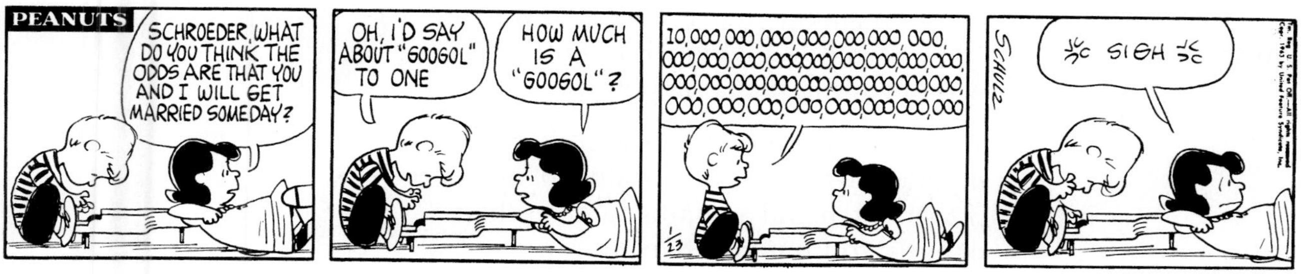

46. **What's the Error?** A student said that $\frac{3^5}{9^5}$ is the same as $\frac{1}{3}$. What mistake has the student made?

47. **Write About It** Why do you subtract exponents when dividing powers with the same base?

48. **Challenge** A number to the 11th power divided by the same number to the 8th power equals 64. What is the number?

Test Prep and Spiral Review

49. **Multiple Choice** In computer technology, a kilobyte is 2^{10} bytes in size. A gigabyte is 2^{30} bytes in size. The size of a terabyte is the product of the size of a kilobyte and the size of a gigabyte. What is the size of a terabyte?

Ⓐ 2^{20} bytes Ⓑ 2^{40} bytes Ⓒ 2^{300} bytes Ⓓ 4^{300} bytes

50. **Short Response** A student claims that $10^3 \cdot 10^{-5}$ is greater than 1. Explain whether the student is correct.

Evaluate each expression for the given value of the variable. (Lesson 2-3)

51. $19.4 - x$ for $x = -5.6$ 52. $11 - r$ for $r = 13.5$ 53. $p + 65.1$ for $p = -42.3$

54. $-\frac{3}{7} - t$ for $t = 1\frac{5}{7}$ 55. $3\frac{5}{11} + y$ for $y = -2\frac{4}{11}$ 56. $-\frac{1}{19} + g$ for $g = \frac{18}{19}$

Evaluate. (Lesson 4-2)

57. $(-3)^{-2}$ 58. $(-2)^{-3}$ 59. 1^{-3} 60. $-(2)^{-4}$

4-4 Scientific Notation

Learn to express large and small numbers in scientific notation and to compare two numbers written in scientific notation.

Vocabulary

scientific notation

An ordinary quarter contains about 97,700,000,000,000,000,000,000 atoms. The average size of an atom is about 0.00000003 centimeter across.

The length of these numbers in standard notation makes them awkward to work with. **Scientific notation** is a shorthand way of writing such numbers.

To express any number in scientific notation, write it as the product of a power of ten and a number greater than or equal to 1 but less than 10.

In scientific notation, the number of atoms in a quarter is 9.77×10^{22}, and the size of each atom is 3.0×10^{-8} centimeters across.

9.77×10^{22}

EXAMPLE 1 Translating Scientific Notation to Standard Notation

Write each number in standard notation.

Helpful Hint

A positive exponent means move the decimal to the right. A negative exponent means move the decimal to the left.

A $\mathbf{3.12 \times 10^9}$

3.12×10^9	
$3.12 \times 1{,}000{,}000{,}000$	*$10^9 = 1{,}000{,}000{,}000$*
$3{,}120{,}000{,}000$	*Think: Move the decimal right 9 places.*

B $\mathbf{1.35 \times 10^{-4}}$

1.35×10^{-4}	
$1.35 \times \frac{1}{10{,}000}$	*$10^{-4} = \frac{1}{10{,}000}$*
$1.35 \div 10{,}000$	*Divide by the reciprocal.*
0.000135	*Think: Move the decimal left 4 places.*

C $\mathbf{-4.7 \times 10^7}$

-4.7×10^7	
$-4.7 \times 10{,}000{,}000$	*$10^7 = 10{,}000{,}000$*
$-47{,}000{,}000$	*Think: Move the decimal right 7 places.*

EXAMPLE 2 Translating Standard Notation to Scientific Notation

Write 0.0000003 in scientific notation.

Helpful Hint

A number less than 1 will have a negative exponent when written in scientific notation.

0.0000003

3 — *Think: The decimal needs to move 7 places to get a number between 1 and 10.*

$3 \times 10^{\square}$ — *Set up scientific notation.*

Think: The decimal needs to move left to change 3 to 0.0000003, so the exponent will be negative.

So 0.0000003 written in scientific notation is 3×10^{-7}.

Check $3 \times 10^{-7} = 3 \times 0.0000001$
$= 0.0000003$

EXAMPLE 3 *Money Application*

Suppose you have a million dollars in pennies. A penny is 1.55 mm thick. How tall would a stack of all your pennies be? Write the answer in scientific notation.

$1.00 = 100 pennies

$1,000,000 = 100,000,000 pennies — *Multiply each side by 1,000,000.*

$1.55 \text{ mm} \times 100{,}000{,}000$ — *Find the total height.*

155,000,000 mm — *Multiply.*

$1.55 \times 10^{\square}$ — *Set up scientific notation.*

Think: The decimal needs to move 8 places.

Think: The decimal needs to move right to change 1.55 to 155,000,000, so the exponent will be positive.

In scientific notation the total height of one million dollars in stacked pennies is 1.55×10^{8} mm. This is about 96 miles tall.

To compare two numbers written in scientific notation, first compare the powers of ten. The number with the greater power of ten is greater. If the powers of ten are the same, compare the values between one and ten.

$2.7 \times 10^{13} > 2.7 \times 10^{9}$ — *$10^{13} > 10^{9}$*

$3.98 \times 10^{22} > 2.52 \times 10^{22}$ — *$3.98 > 2.52$*

EXAMPLE 4 *Life Science Application*

The major components of human blood are red blood cells, white blood cells, platelets, and plasma. A typical red blood cell has a diameter of approximately 7×10^{-6} meter. A typical platelet has a diameter of approximately 2.33×10^{-6} meter. Which has a greater diameter, a red blood cell or a platelet?

7×10^{-6} ▒ 2.33×10^{-6}

$10^{-6} = 10^{-6}$ *Compare powers of 10.*

$7 > 2.33$ *Compare the values between 1 and 10.*

$7 \times 10^{-6} > 2.33 \times 10^{-6}$

A typical red blood cell has a greater diameter than a typical platelet.

Think and Discuss

1. **Explain** the benefit of writing numbers in scientific notation.
2. **Describe** how to write 2.977×10^6 in standard notation.
3. **Determine** which measurement would be least likely to be written in scientific notation: size of bacteria, speed of a car, or number of stars in a galaxy.

4-4 Exercises

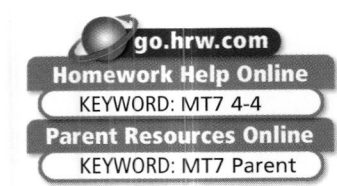

go.hrw.com
Homework Help Online
KEYWORD: MT7 4-4
Parent Resources Online
KEYWORD: MT7 Parent

GUIDED PRACTICE

See Example 1 **Write each number in standard notation.**

1. 4.17×10^3 2. 1.33×10^{-5} 3. 6.2×10^7 4. 3.9×10^{-4}

See Example 2 **Write each number in scientific notation.**

5. 0.000057 6. 0.0004 7. 6,980,000 8. 0.000000025

See Example 3

9. The distance from Earth to the Moon is about 384,000 km. Suppose an astronaut travels this distance a total of 250 times. How many kilometers does the astronaut travel? Write the answer in scientific notation.

See Example 4

10. The maximum length of a particle that can fit through a surgical mask is 1×10^{-4} millimeters. The average length of a dust mite is approximately 1.25×10^{-1} millimeters. Which is longer, the largest particle that can fit through a surgical mask or a dust mite of average length?

INDEPENDENT PRACTICE

See Example 1

Write each number in standard notation.

11. 9.2×10^6 **12.** 6.7×10^{-4} **13.** 3.6×10^{-2} **14.** 5.24×10^8

See Example 2

Write each number in scientific notation.

15. 0.00007 **16.** 6,500,000 **17.** 100,000,000 **18.** 0.00000003

See Example 3

19. Protons and neutrons are the most massive particles in the nucleus of an atom. If a nucleus were the size of an average grape, it would have a mass greater than 9 million metric tons. A metric ton is 1000 kg. What would the mass of a grape-size nucleus be in kilograms? Write your answer in scientific notation.

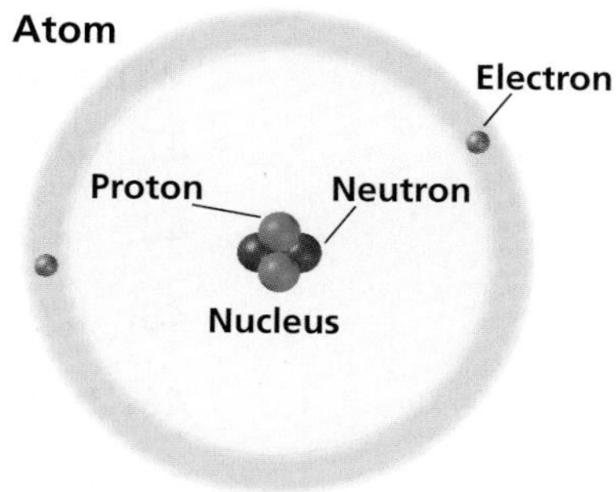

See Example 4

20. The orbits of Neptune and Pluto cross each other. Neptune's average distance from the Sun is approximately 4.5×10^9 kilometers. Pluto's average distance from the Sun is approximately 5.87×10^9 kilometers. Which planet has the greater average distance from the Sun?

PRACTICE AND PROBLEM SOLVING

Extra Practice
See page 788.

Write each number in standard notation.

21. 1.4×10^5 **22.** 3.24×10^{-2} **23.** 7.8×10^1 **24.** 2.1×10^{-6}

25. 5.3×10^{-8} **26.** 8.456×10^{-4} **27.** 5.59×10^5 **28.** 7.1×10^3

29. 7.113×10^6 **30.** 4.5×10^{-1} **31.** 2.9×10^{-4} **32.** 5.6×10^2

LINK

Life Science

This frog is covered with duckweed plants. Duckweed plants can grow both in sunlight and in shade and produce tiny white flowers.

33. Life Science Duckweed plants live on the surface of calm ponds and are the smallest flowering plants in the world. They weigh about 0.00015 g.

a. Write this number in scientific notation.

b. If left unchecked, one duckweed plant, which reproduces every 30–36 hours, could produce 1×10^{30} (a nonillion) plants in four months. How much would one nonillion duckweed plants weigh?

34. Life Science The diameter of a human red blood cell ranges from approximately 6×10^{-6} to 8×10^{-6} meters. Write this range in standard notation.

35. Physical Science The *atomic mass* of an element is the mass, in grams, of one *mole* (mol), or 6.02×10^{23} atoms.

a. How many atoms are there in 2.5 mol of helium?

b. If you know that 2.5 mol of helium weighs 10 grams, what is the atomic mass of helium?

c. Using your answer from part **b,** find the approximate mass of one atom of helium.

36. **Social Studies**

a. Express the population and area of Taiwan in scientific notation.

b. Divide the number of square miles by the population to find the number of square miles per person in Taiwan. Express your answer in scientific notation.

Taiwan	
Population:	22,113,250
Area:	14,032 mi^2
Capital:	Taipei
Number of televisions:	10,800,000
Languages:	Taiwanese (Min), Mandarin, Hakka dialects

Write each number in scientific notation.

37. 0.00858 **38.** 0.0000063 **39.** 5,900,000

40. 7,045,000,000 **41.** 0.0076 **42.** 400

43. 4200 **44.** 0.0000000082 **45.** 0.0000000003

46. 0.000005 **47.** 7,000,000 **48.** 0.0095678

49. Order the list of numbers below from least to greatest.
1.5×10^{-2}, 1.2×10^6, 5.85×10^{-3}, 2.3×10^{-2}, 5.5×10^6

50. Write a Problem An electron has a mass of about 9.11×10^{-31} kg. Use this information to write a problem.

51. Write About It Two numbers are written in scientific notation. How can you tell which number is greater?

52. Challenge Where on a number line does the value of a positive number in scientific notation with a negative exponent lie?

Test Prep and Spiral Review

53. Short Response Explain how you can determine the sign of the exponent when 29,600,000,000,000 is written in scientific notation?

54. Multiple Choice The distance light can travel in one year is 9.46×10^{12} kilometers. What is this distance in standard form?

(A) 94,600,000,000,000,000 km

(B) 946,000,000,000 km

(C) 9,460,000,000,000

(D) 0.000000000946

Use each table to make a graph and to write an equation. (Lesson 3-5)

55.

x	0	5	6	4
y	−4	11	14	20

56.

x	0	1	3	6
y	6	7	9	12

Simplify. Write each product or quotient as one power. (Lesson 4-3)

57. $\frac{7^4}{7^2}$ **58.** $5^3 \cdot 5^8$ **59.** $\frac{t^8}{t^5}$ **60.** $10^9 \cdot 10^{-3}$

Technology LAB 4-4

Multiply and Divide Numbers in Scientific Notation

Use with Lesson 4-4

go.hrw.com
Lab Resources Online
KEYWORD: MT7 Lab4

You can use a graphing calculator to perform operations with numbers written in scientific notation. Use the key combination 2nd EE , to enter numbers in scientific notation. On a graphing calculator, 9.5×10^{16} is displayed as 9.5E16.

Activity

Use a calculator to find $(4.8 \times 10^{12})(9.4 \times 10^{9})$.

Press 4.8 2nd EE , 12 × 9.4 2nd EE , 9 ENTER .

The calculator displays the answer 4.512 E22, which is the same as 4.512×10^{22}.

Think and Discuss

1. When you use the associative and communicative properties to multiply 4.8×10^{12} and 9.4×10^{9}, you get $(4.8 \cdot 9.4)(10^{12} \cdot 10^{9}) = 45.12 \times 10^{21}$. Explain why this answer is different from the answer you obtained in the activity.

Try This

Use a graphing calculator to evaluate each expression.

1. $(5.76 \times 10^{13})(6.23 \times 10^{-20})$
2. $\dfrac{9.7 \times 10^{10}}{2.9 \times 10^{7}}$
3. $(1.6 \times 10^{5})(9.65 \times 10^{9})$
4. $\dfrac{5.25 \times 10^{13}}{6.14 \times 10^{8}}$
5. $(1.1 \times 10^{9})(2.2 \times 10^{3})$
6. $\dfrac{8.56 \times 10^{97}}{2.34 \times 10^{80}}$
7. $(2.74 \times 10^{11})(3.2 \times 10^{-5})$
8. $\dfrac{5.82 \times 10^{-11}}{8.96 \times 10^{11}}$
9. $(4.5 \times 10^{12})(3.7 \times 10^{8})$
10. The star Betelgeuse, in the constellation of Orion, is approximately 3.36×10^{15} miles from Earth. This is approximately 1.24×10^{6} times as far as Pluto's minimum distance from Earth. What is Pluto's approximate minimum distance from Earth? Write your answer in scientific notation.
11. If 446 billion telephone calls were placed by 135 million United States telephone subscribers, what was the average number of calls placed per subscriber?

CHAPTER 4

READY TO GO ON?

SECTION 4A

Quiz for Lessons 4-1 Through 4-4

4-1 Exponents

Evaluate.

1. 10^1
2. 8^6
3. -3^4
4. $(-5)^3$
5. Write $5 \cdot 5 \cdot 5 \cdot 5$ in exponential form.
6. Evaluate $a^7 - 4b$ for $a = 3$ and $b = -1$.

4-2 Look for a Pattern in Integer Exponents

Evaluate.

7. 10^{-6}
8. $(-3)^{-4}$
9. -6^{-2}
10. 4^0
11. $8 + 10^0(-6)$
12. $5^{-1} + 3(5)^{-2}$
13. $-4^{-3} + 2^0$
14. $3^{-2} - (6^0 - 6^{-2})$

4-3 Properties of Exponents

Simplify. Write the product or quotient as one power.

15. $9^3 \cdot 9^5$
16. $\frac{5^{10}}{5^{10}}$
17. $q^9 \cdot q^6$
18. $3^3 \cdot 3^{-2}$

Simplify.

19. $(33)^{-2}$
20. $(4^2)^0$
21. $(-x^2)^4$
22. $(4^{-2})^5$
23. The mass of the known universe is about 10^{23} solar masses, which is 10^{50} metric tons. How many metric tons is one solar mass?

4-4 Scientific Notation

Write each number in scientific notation.

24. 0.00000015
25. 99,980,000
26. 0.434
27. 100

Write each number in standard notation.

28. 1.38×10^5
29. 4×10^6
30. 1.2×10^{-3}
31. 9.37×10^{-5}
32. The average distance from Earth to the Sun is approximately 149,600,000 kilometers. Pluto is about 39.5 times as far from the Sun as Earth is. What is the approximate average distance from Pluto to the Sun? Write your answer in scientific notation.
33. Picoplankton can be as small as 0.00002 centimeter. Microplankton are about 100 times as large as picoplankton. How large is a microplankton that is 100 times the size of the smallest picoplankton? Write your answer in scientific notation.

Ready to Go On?

Focus on Problem Solving

Solve

• Choose an operation

To decide whether to add, subtract, multiply, or divide to solve a problem, you need to determine the action taking place in the problem.

Action	Operation
Combining numbers or putting numbers together	Addition
Taking away or finding out how far apart two numbers are	Subtraction
Combining equal groups	Multiplication
Splitting things into equal groups or finding how many equal groups you can make	Division

Determine the action for each problem. Write the problem using the actions. Then show what operation you used to get the answer.

1. Mary is making a string of beads. If each bead is 7.0×10^{-1} cm wide, how many beads does she need to make a string that is 35 cm long?

2. The total area of the United States is 9.63×10^6 square kilometers. The total area of Canada is 9.98×10^6 square kilometers. What is the total area of both the United States and Canada?

3. Suppose $\frac{1}{3}$ of the fish in a lake are considered game fish. Of these, $\frac{2}{5}$ meet the legal minimum size requirement. What fraction of the fish in the lake are game fish that meet the legal minimum size requirement?

4. Part of a checkbook register is shown below. Find the amount in the account after the transactions shown.

RECORD ALL CHARGES OR CREDITS THAT AFFECT YOUR ACCOUNT

TRANSACTION	DATE	DESCRIPTION	AMOUNT	FEE	DEPOSITS	BALANCE $287.34
Withdrawal	11/16	autodebit for phone bill	$43.16			$43.16
Check 1256	11/18	groceries	$27.56			$27.56
Check 1257	11/23	new clothes	$74.23			$74.23
Withdrawal	11/27	ATM withdrawal	$40.00	$1.25		$41.25

4-5 Squares and Square Roots

Learn to find square roots.

Vocabulary

principal square root

perfect square

Think about the relationship between the area of a square and the length of one of its sides.

area = 36 square units
side length = $\sqrt{36} = 6$ units

Quilts are often pieced together from small squares to form a large design.

Taking the square root of a number is the inverse of squaring the number.

$6^2 = 36$ $\sqrt{36} = 6$

Every positive number has two square roots, one positive and one negative. One square root of 16 is 4, since $4 \cdot 4 = 16$. The other square root of 16 is -4, since $(-4)(-4)$ is also 16. You can write the square roots of 16 as ± 4, meaning "**plus or minus**" 4.

Caution!

$\sqrt{-49}$ is not the same as $-\sqrt{49}$. A negative number has no real square roots.

When you press the $\sqrt{}$ key on a calculator, only the nonnegative square root appears. This is called the **principal square root** of the number.

$+\sqrt{16} = 4$ $-\sqrt{16} = -4$

The numbers 16, 36, and 49 are examples of perfect squares. A **perfect square** is a number that has integers as its square roots. Other perfect squares include 1, 4, 9, 25, 64, and 81.

EXAMPLE 1 Finding the Positive and Negative Square Roots of a Number

Find the two square roots of each number.

A **81**

$\sqrt{81} = 9$ *9 is a square root, since $9 \cdot 9 = 81$.*

$-\sqrt{81} = -9$ *−9 is also a square root, since $-9 \cdot -9 = 81$.*

B **1**

$\sqrt{1} = 1$ *1 is a square root, since $1 \cdot 1 = 1$.*

$-\sqrt{1} = -1$ *−1 is also a square root, since $-1 \cdot -1 = 1$.*

C **144**

$\sqrt{144} = 12$ *12 is a square root, since $12 \cdot 12 = 144$.*

$-\sqrt{144} = -12$ *−12 is also a square root, since $-12 \cdot (-12) = 144$.*

EXAMPLE 2 Computer Application

Remember!

The area of a square is s^2, where s is the length of a side.

The square computer icon contains 676 pixels. How many pixels tall is the icon?

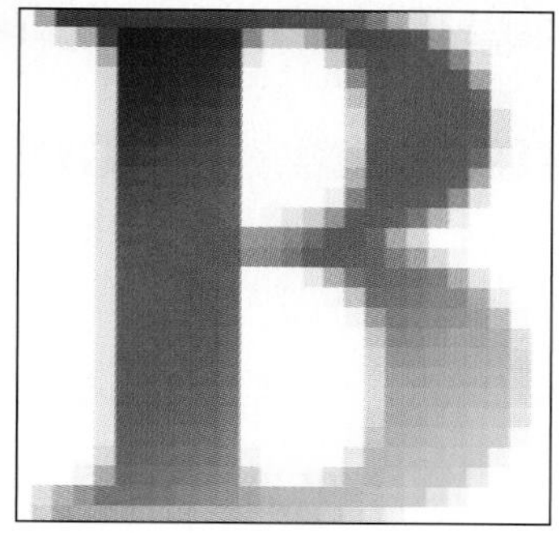

The square computer icon contains 676 colored dots that make up the picture. These dots are called *pixels.*

Find the square root of 676 to find the length of the side. Use the positive square root; a negative length has no meaning.

$26^2 = 676$

So $\sqrt{676} = 26$.

The icon is 26 pixels tall.

In the order of operations everything under the square root symbol is treated as if it were in parentheses. $\sqrt{5 - 3} = \sqrt{(5 - 3)}$

EXAMPLE 3 Evaluating Expressions Involving Square Roots

Evaluate each expression.

A $3\sqrt{25} + 4$

$3\sqrt{25} + 4 = 3(5) + 4$	*Evaluate the square root.*
$= 15 + 4$	*Multiply.*
$= 19$	*Add.*

B $\sqrt{\frac{16}{4}} + \frac{1}{2}$

$\sqrt{\frac{16}{4}} + \frac{1}{2} = \sqrt{4} + \frac{1}{2}$	$\frac{16}{4} = 4.$
$= 4 + \frac{1}{2}$	*Evaluate the square roots.*
$= 4\frac{1}{2}$	*Add.*

Think and Discuss

1. **Describe** what is meant by a perfect square. Give an example.
2. **Explain** how many square roots a positive number can have. How are these square roots different?
3. **Decide** how many square roots 0 has. Tell what you know about square roots of negative numbers.

4-5 Exercises

go.hrw.com
Homework Help Online
KEYWORD: MT7 4-5
Parent Resources Online
KEYWORD: MT7 Parent

GUIDED PRACTICE

See Example 1

Find the two square roots of each number.

1. 4 **2.** 16 **3.** 64 **4.** 121

5. 1 **6.** 441 **7.** 9 **8.** 484

See Example 2

9. A square court for playing the game four square has an area of 256 ft^2. How long is one side of the court?

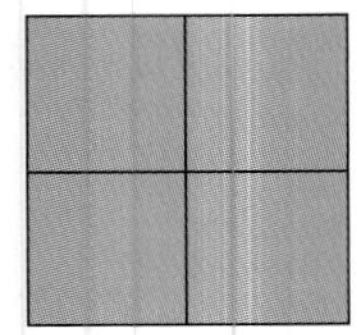

Area = 256 ft^2

See Example 3

Evaluate each expression.

10. $\sqrt{5 + 11}$ **11.** $\sqrt{\frac{81}{9}}$

12. $3\sqrt{400} - 125$ **13.** $-\left(\sqrt{169} - \sqrt{144}\right)$

INDEPENDENT PRACTICE

See Example 1

Find the two square roots of each number.

14. 25 **15.** 144 **16.** 81 **17.** 169

18. 196 **19.** 400 **20.** 361 **21.** 225

See Example 2

22. Elisa found a square digital image of a famous painting on a Web site. The image contained 360,000 pixels. How many pixels high is the image?

See Example 3

Evaluate each expression.

23. $\sqrt{25} - 6$ **24.** $\sqrt{\frac{64}{4}}$ **25.** $-\left(\sqrt{36}\sqrt{9}\right)$ **26.** $5(\sqrt{225} - 10)$

PRACTICE AND PROBLEM SOLVING

Extra Practice
See page 789.

Find the two square roots of each number.

27. 36 **28.** 100 **29.** 49 **30.** 900

31. 529 **32.** 289 **33.** 576 **34.** 324

35. Estimation Mr. Barada bought a square rug. The area of the rug was about 68.06 ft^2. He estimated that the length of a side was about 7 ft. Is Mr. Barada's estimate reasonable? Explain.

36. Language Arts *Crelle's Journal* is the oldest mathematics periodical in existence. Zacharias Dase's incredible calculating skills were made famous by *Crelle's Journal* in 1844. Dase produced a table of factors of all numbers between 7,000,000 and 10,000,000. He listed 7,022,500 as a perfect square. What is the square root of 7,022,500?

37. Sports A karate match is held on a square mat that has an area of 676 ft^2. What is the length of the mat?

LINK

Games

In 1997, Deep Blue became the first computer to win a match against a chess grand master when it defeated world champion Garry Kasparov.

go.hrw.com
Web Extra!
KEYWORD: MT7 Chess

Find the two square roots of each number.

38. $\frac{1}{9}$ **39.** $\frac{1}{121}$ **40.** $\frac{16}{9}$ **41.** $\frac{81}{16}$

42. $\frac{9}{4}$ **43.** $\frac{324}{81}$ **44.** $\frac{1000}{100,000}$ **45.** $\frac{169}{676}$

46. Multi-Step An office building has a square courtyard with an area of 289 ft^2. What is the distance around the edge of the courtyard?

47. Games A chessboard contains 32 black and 32 white squares. How many squares are along each side of the game board?

48. Hobbies A quilter wants to use as many of his 65 small fabric squares as possible to make one large square quilt.

a. How many small squares can the quilter use? How many small squares would he have left?

b. How many more small squares would the quilter need to make the next largest possible square quilt?

49. What's the Error? A student said that since the square roots of a certain number are 1.5 and −1.5, the number must be their product, −2.25. What error did the student make?

50. Write About It Explain the steps you would take to evaluate the expression $\sqrt{14 + 35} - 20$.

51. Challenge The square root of a number is four less than three times seven. What is the number?

Test Prep and Spiral Review

52. Multiple Choice Which number does NOT have a square root that is an integer?

Ⓐ 81 Ⓑ 196 Ⓒ 288 Ⓓ 400

53. Short Response Deanna knows that the floor in her kitchen is a square with an area of 169 square feet. The perimeter of her kitchen floor is found by adding the lengths of all its sides. What is the perimeter of her kitchen floor? Explain your answer.

Write each decimal as a fraction in simplest form. (Lesson 2-1)

54. 0.35 **55.** 2.6 **56.** −7.18 **57.** 0.125

Write each number in scientific notation. (Lesson 4-4)

58. 1,970,000,000 **59.** 2,500,000

60. 31,400,000,000 **61.** 5,680,000,000,000,000

4-6 Estimating Square Roots

Learn to estimate square roots to a given number of decimal places and solve problems using square roots.

A couple wants to install a square stained-glass window. The window has an area of 500 square inches with wood trim around it. You can calculate the length of the trim using your knowledge of squares and square roots.

EXAMPLE 1 Estimating Square Roots of Numbers

Each square root is between two integers. Name the integers. Explain your answer.

A $\sqrt{30}$ — *Think: What are perfect squares close to 30?*

$5^2 = 25$ — *$25 < 30$*

$6^2 = 36$ — *$36 > 30$*

$\sqrt{30}$ is between **5** and **6** because 30 is between 25 and 36.

B $-\sqrt{150}$ — *Think: What are perfect squares close to 150?*

$(-12)^2 = 144$ — *$144 < 150$*

$(-13)^2 = 169$ — *$169 > 150$*

$-\sqrt{150}$ is between **−12** and **−13** because 150 is between 144 and 169.

EXAMPLE 2 PROBLEM SOLVING APPLICATION

PROBLEM SOLVING

A couple wants to install a square stained-glass window that has an area of 500 square inches. Calculate the length of each side and the length of trim needed to the nearest tenth of an inch.

1 Understand the Problem

First find the length of a side. Then you can use the length of a side to find the *perimeter*, the length of the trim around the window.

2 Make a Plan

The length of a side, in inches, is the number that you multiply by itself to get 500. Find this number to the nearest tenth.

Use guess and check to find $\sqrt{500}$.

3 Solve

Because 500 is between 22^2 (484) and 23^2 (529), the square root of 500 is between 22 and 23.

Guess 22.5	Guess 22.2	Guess 22.4	Guess 22.3
$22.5^2 = 506.25$	$22.2^2 = 492.84$	$22.4^2 = 501.76$	$22.3^2 = 497.29$
Too high	Too low	Too high	Too low
Square root is between 22 and 22.5.	Square root is between 22.2 and 22.5.	Square root is between 22.2 and 22.4.	Square root is between 22.3 and 22.4.

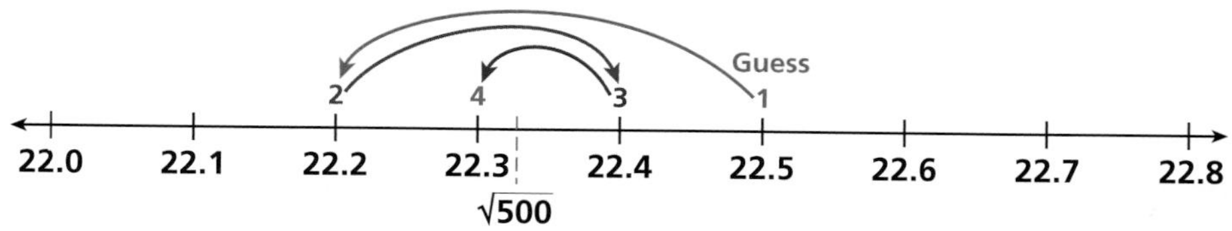

The square root is between 22.3 and 22.4. To round to the nearest tenth, consider 22.35.

$22.35^2 = 499.5225$ *Too low*

The square root must be *greater than* 22.35, so you can round *up*. To the nearest tenth, $\sqrt{500}$ is about 22.4.

Now estimate the length around the window. The length of a side of the window to the nearest tenth of an inch is 22.4 inches.

$4 \cdot 22.4 = 89.6$ *Perimeter = 4 · side*

The trim is about 89.6 inches long.

4 Look Back

The length 90 inches divided by 4 is 22.5 inches. A 22.5-inch square has an area of 506.25 square inches, which is close to 500, so the answers are reasonable.

EXAMPLE 3 Using a Calculator to Estimate the Value of a Square Root

Use a calculator to find $\sqrt{700}$. Round to the nearest tenth.

Using a calculator, $\sqrt{700} \approx 26.45751311\ldots$. Rounded, $\sqrt{700}$ is 26.5.

Think and Discuss

1. **Discuss** whether 9.5 is a good first guess for $\sqrt{75}$.
2. **Determine** which square root or roots would have 7.5 as a good first guess.

4-6 Exercises

go.hrw.com
Homework Help Online
KEYWORD: MT7 4-6
Parent Resources Online
KEYWORD: MT7 Parent

GUIDED PRACTICE

See Example 1
Each square root is between two integers. Name the integers. Explain your answer.

1. $\sqrt{40}$ **2.** $-\sqrt{90}$ **3.** $\sqrt{156}$ **4.** $-\sqrt{306}$ **5.** $\sqrt{250}$

See Example 2
6. A square photo is placed behind a piece of glass that has an area of 20 square inches. To the nearest hundredth, what length of frame is needed to go around all edges of the glass?

See Example 3
Use a calculator to find each value. Round to the nearest tenth.

7. $\sqrt{74}$ **8.** $\sqrt{34.1}$ **9.** $\sqrt{3600}$ **10.** $\sqrt{190}$ **11.** $\sqrt{5120}$

INDEPENDENT PRACTICE

See Example 1
Each square root is between two integers. Name the integers. Explain your answer.

12. $-\sqrt{52}$ **13.** $\sqrt{3}$ **14.** $\sqrt{600}$ **15.** $-\sqrt{2000}$ **16.** $\sqrt{410}$

See Example 2
17. Each square on Laura's chessboard is 13 square centimeters. A chessboard has 8 squares on each side. To the nearest hundredth, what is the width of Laura's chessboard?

See Example 3
Use a calculator to find each value. Round to the nearest tenth.

18. $\sqrt{58}$ **19.** $\sqrt{91.5}$ **20.** $\sqrt{550}$ **21.** $\sqrt{150}$ **22.** $\sqrt{330}$

PRACTICE AND PROBLEM SOLVING

Extra Practice
See page 789.

Write the letter that identifies the position of each square root.

23. $-\sqrt{3}$ **24.** $\sqrt{5}$ **25.** $\sqrt{7}$

26. $-\sqrt{8}$ **27.** $\sqrt{14}$ **28.** $\sqrt{0.75}$

Find each product to the nearest hundredth.

29. $\sqrt{51} \cdot \sqrt{25}$ **30.** $-\sqrt{70} \cdot \sqrt{16}$ **31.** $\sqrt{215} \cdot (-\sqrt{1})$

32. $-\sqrt{113} \cdot \sqrt{9}$ **33.** $\sqrt{22} \cdot (-\sqrt{49})$ **34.** $\sqrt{210} \cdot \sqrt{169}$

35. Multi-Step On a baseball field, the infield area created by the baselines is a square. In a youth baseball league for 9- to 12-year-olds, this area is 3600 ft^2. The distance between each base in a league for 4-year-olds is 20 ft less than it is for 9- to 12-year-olds. What is the distance between each base for 4-year-olds?

Science LINK

Tsunamis, sometimes called tidal waves, move across deep oceans at high speeds with barely a ripple on the water surface. It is only when tsunamis hit shallow water that their energy moves them upward into a mammoth destructive force.

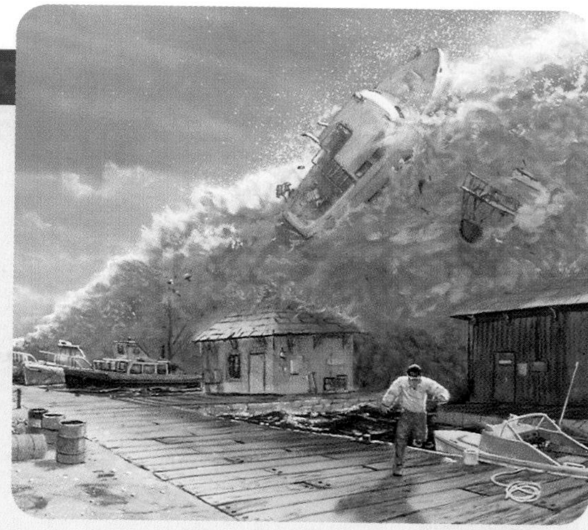

Tsunamis can be caused by earthquakes, volcanoes, landslides, or meteorites.

36. The rate of speed of a tsunami, in feet per second, can be found by the formula $r = \sqrt{32d}$, where d is the water depth in feet. Suppose the water depth is 20,000 ft. How fast is the tsunami moving?

37. The speed of a tsunami in miles per hour can be found using $r = \sqrt{14.88d}$, where d is the water depth in feet. Suppose the water depth is 25,000 ft.

a. How fast is the tsunami moving in miles per hour?

b. How long would it take a tsunami to travel 3000 miles if the water depth were a consistent 10,000 ft?

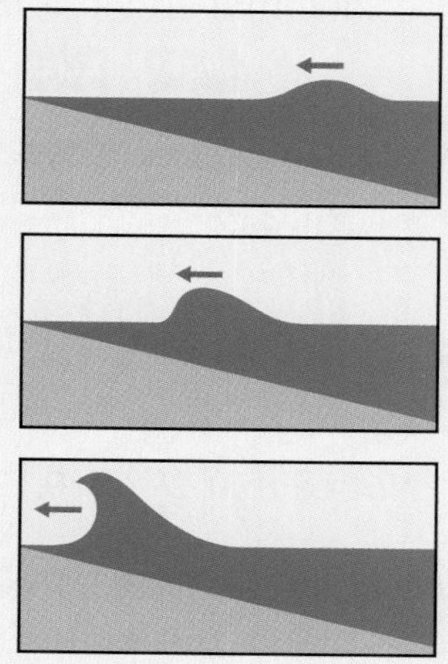

As the wave approaches the beach, it slows, builds in height, and crashes on shore.

38. **What's the Error?** Ashley found the speed of a tsunami, in feet per second, by taking the square root of 32 and multiplying by the depth, in feet. What was her error?

39. **Challenge** Find the depth of the water if a tsunami's speed is 400 miles per hour.

go.hrw.com
Lab Resources Online
KEYWORD: MT7 Wave

TEST PREP and Spiral Review

40. Multiple Choice Which expression has a value between 15 and 14?

Ⓐ $\sqrt{188}$ Ⓑ $\sqrt{200}$ Ⓒ $\sqrt{227}$ Ⓓ $\sqrt{324}$

41. Gridded Response Find the product $\sqrt{42} \cdot \sqrt{94}$ to the nearest hundredth.

Evaluate each expression for the given values of the variables. (Lesson 1-1)

42. $4x + 5y$ for $x = 3$ and $y = 9$

43. $7m - 2n$ for $m = 5$ and $n = 7$

44. $8h + 9j$ for $h = 11$ and $j = 2$

45. $6s - 2t$ for $s = 7$ and $t = 12$

Find the two square roots of each number. (Lesson 4-5)

46. 100 **47.** 64 **48.** 484 **49.** 1296

Technology LAB 4-6

Evaluate Powers and Roots

Use with Lesson 4-6

go.hrw.com
Lab Resources Online
KEYWORD: MT7 Lab4

A graphing calculator can be used to evaluate expressions that have negative exponents and square roots.

Activity

1 Use the STO▶ button to evaluate x^{-3} for $x = 2$. View the answer as a decimal and as a fraction.

2 STO▶ X,T,θ,n ENTER   X,T,θ,n ^ (–) 3 ENTER   MATH ENTER ENTER

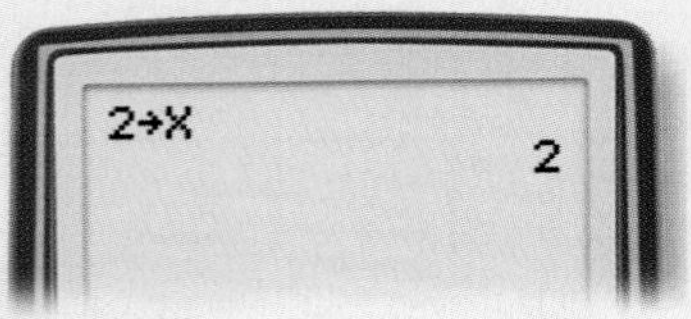

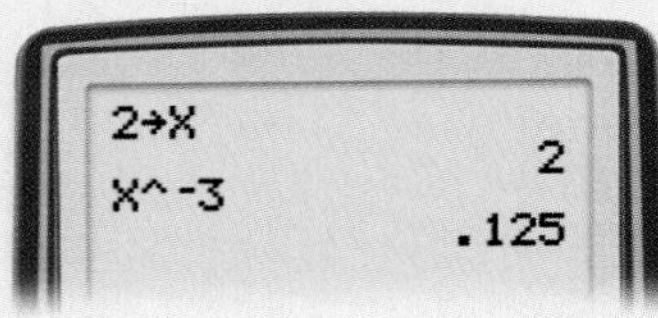

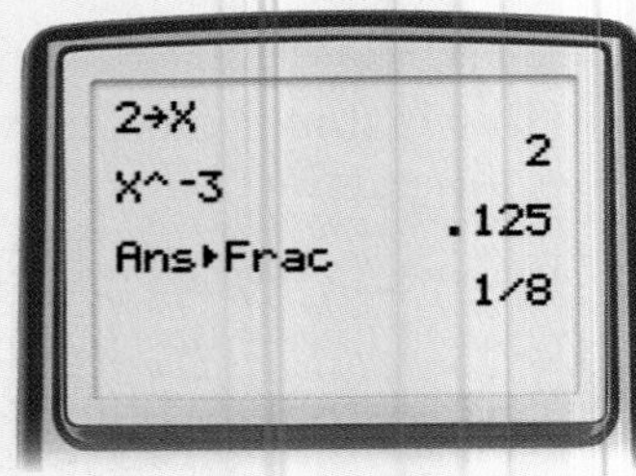

Notice that $2^{-3} = 0.125$, which is equivalent to $\frac{1}{2^3}$, or $\frac{1}{8}$.

2 Use the **TABLE** feature to evaluate $-\sqrt{x}$ for several x-values. Match the settings shown.

Y= (–) 2nd x^2 ($\sqrt{\ }$) X,T,θ,n ENTER   2nd WINDOW (TBLSET)   2nd GRAPH (TABLE)

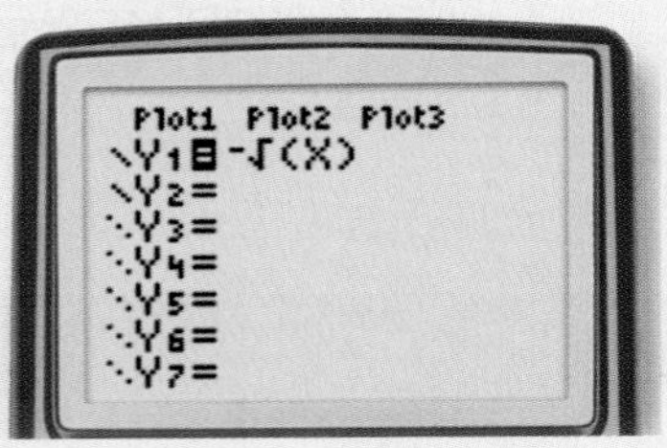

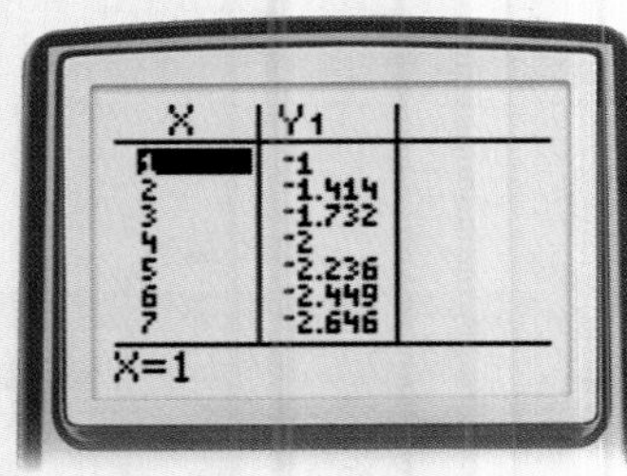

The **Y1** list shows the value of $-\sqrt{x}$ for several x-values.

Think and Discuss

1. When you evaluated 2^{-3} in Activity 1, the result was not a negative number. Is this surprising? Why or why not?

Try This

Evaluate each expression for the given x-value(s). Give your answers as fractions and as decimals rounded to the nearest hundredth.

1. 4^{-x}; $x = 2$ **2.** $\sqrt{x}$; $x = 1, 2, 3, 4$ **3.** x^{-2}; $x = 1, 2, 5$

4-7 The Real Numbers

Learn to determine if a number is rational or irrational.

Vocabulary

irrational number

real number

Density Property

Biologists classify animals based on shared characteristics. The horned lizard is an animal, a reptile, a lizard, and a gecko.

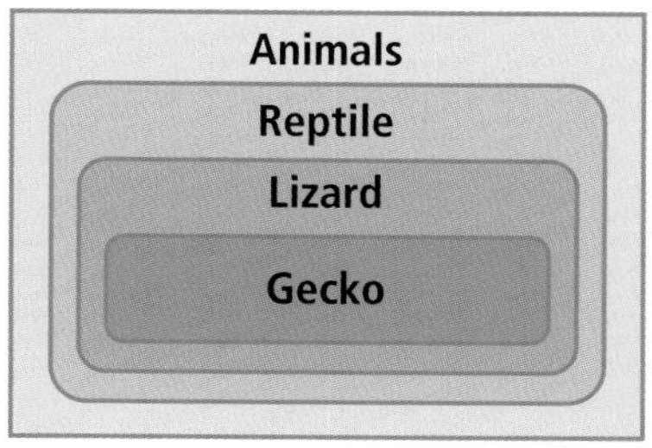

Horned lizards are commonly called "horny toads" because of their flattened, toad-like bodies.

You already know that some numbers can also be classified as whole numbers, integers, or rational numbers. The number 2 is a whole number, an integer, and a rational number. It is also a *real* number.

Rational numbers can be written as fractions and as decimals that either terminate or repeat.

$$3\frac{4}{5} = 3.8 \qquad \frac{2}{3} = 0.\overline{6} \qquad \sqrt{1.44} = 1.2$$

Caution!

A repeating decimal may not appear to repeat on a calculator because calculators show a finite number of digits.

Irrational numbers can only be written as decimals that do *not* terminate or repeat. If a whole number is not a perfect square, then its square root is an irrational number.

$\sqrt{2} \approx 1.4142135623730950488016\ldots$

The set of **real numbers** consists of the set of rational numbers and the set of irrational numbers.

Real Numbers

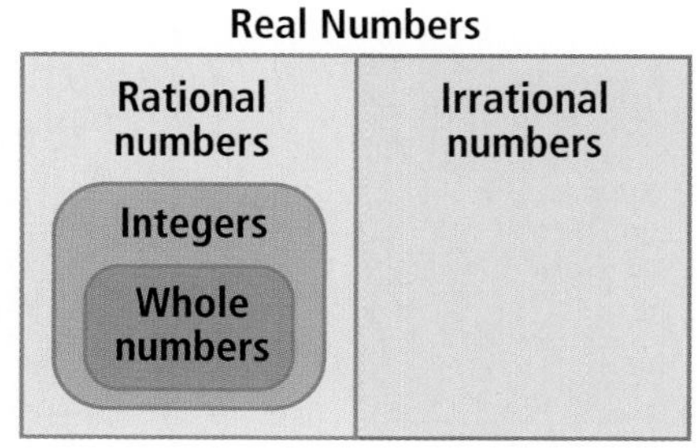

EXAMPLE 1 Classifying Real Numbers

Write all names that apply to each number.

A $\sqrt{3}$ — *3 is a whole number that is not a perfect square.*

irrational, real

B -52.28 — *−52.28 is a terminating decimal.*

rational, real

C $\frac{\sqrt{16}}{4}$ — $\frac{\sqrt{16}}{4} = \frac{4}{4} = 1$

whole, integer, rational, real

The square root of a negative number is not a real number. A fraction with a denominator of 0 is undefined because you cannot divide by zero. So it is not a number at all.

EXAMPLE 2 Determining the Classification of All Numbers

State if each number is rational, irrational, or not a real number.

A $\sqrt{15}$ *15 is a whole number that is not a perfect square.*

irrational

B $\frac{3}{0}$

undefined, so not a real number

C $\sqrt{\frac{1}{9}}$ $\left(\frac{1}{3}\right)\left(\frac{1}{3}\right) = \frac{1}{9}$

rational

D $\sqrt{-13}$

not a real number

The **Density Property** of real numbers states that between any two real numbers is another real number. This property is not true for whole numbers or integers. For instance, there is no integer between −2 and −3.

EXAMPLE 3 Applying the Density Property of Real Numbers

Find a real number between $1\frac{1}{3}$ and $1\frac{2}{3}$.

There are many solutions. One solution is halfway between the two numbers. To find it, add the numbers and divide by 2.

$\left(1\frac{1}{3} + 1\frac{2}{3}\right) \div 2$

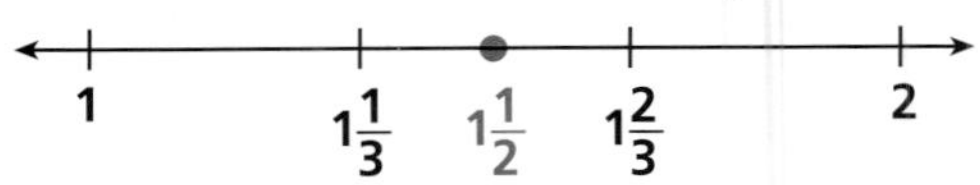

$= \left(2\frac{3}{3}\right) \div 2$

$= 3 \div 2 = 1\frac{1}{2}$

A real number between $1\frac{1}{3}$ and $1\frac{2}{3}$ is $1\frac{1}{2}$.

Think and Discuss

1. **Explain** how rational numbers are related to integers.
2. **Tell** if a number can be irrational and whole. Explain.
3. **Use** the Density Property to explain why there are infinitely many real numbers between 0 and 1.

4-7 Exercises

go.hrw.com
Homework Help Online
KEYWORD: MT7 4-7
Parent Resources Online
KEYWORD: MT7 Parent

GUIDED PRACTICE

See Example 1 — **Write all names that apply to each number.**

1. $\sqrt{10}$ **2.** $\sqrt{49}$ **3.** 0.25 **4.** $-\frac{\sqrt{16}}{3}$

See Example 2 — **State if each number is rational, irrational, or not a real number.**

5. $\sqrt{9}$ **6.** $\sqrt{\frac{9}{16}}$ **7.** $\sqrt{72}$ **8.** $-\sqrt{-3}$

9. $-\sqrt{25}$ **10.** $\sqrt{-9}$ **11.** $\sqrt{\frac{25}{-36}}$ **12.** $\frac{0}{0}$

See Example 3 — **Find a real number between each pair of numbers.**

13. $3\frac{1}{8}$ and $3\frac{2}{8}$ **14.** 4.14 and $\frac{29}{7}$ **15.** $\frac{1}{8}$ and $\frac{1}{4}$

INDEPENDENT PRACTICE

See Example 1 — **Write all names that apply to each number.**

16. $\sqrt{35}$ **17.** $\frac{5}{8}$ **18.** 3 **19.** $\frac{\sqrt{81}}{-3}$

See Example 2 — **State if each number is rational, irrational, or not a real number.**

20. $\frac{\sqrt{-16}}{-4}$ **21.** $-\sqrt{\frac{0}{4}}$ **22.** $\sqrt{-8(-2)}$ **23.** $-\sqrt{3}$

24. $\frac{\sqrt{25}}{8}$ **25.** $\sqrt{14}$ **26.** $\sqrt{-\frac{1}{4}}$ **27.** $-\sqrt{\frac{4}{0}}$

See Example 3 — **Find a real number between each pair of numbers.**

28. $3\frac{2}{5}$ and $3\frac{3}{5}$ **29.** $-\frac{1}{10}$ and 0 **30.** 4 and $\sqrt{9}$

PRACTICE AND PROBLEM SOLVING

Extra Practice
See page 789.

Write all names that apply to each number.

31. 6 **32.** $-\sqrt{36}$ **33.** $\sqrt{10}$ **34.** $\frac{1}{3}$

35. $\sqrt{2.56}$ **36.** $\sqrt{36} + 6$ **37.** $0.\overline{21}$ **38.** $\frac{\sqrt{100}}{20}$

39. -4.3134 **40.** $\sqrt{4.5}$ **41.** -312 **42.** $\frac{0}{7}$

43. Explain the difference between $-\sqrt{16}$ and $\sqrt{-16}$.

Give an example of each type of number.

44. an irrational number that is less than -3

45. a rational number that is less than 0.3

46. a real number between $\frac{5}{9}$ and $\frac{6}{9}$

47. a real number between $-3\frac{2}{7}$ and $-3\frac{3}{7}$

48. Find a rational number between $\sqrt{\frac{1}{9}}$ and $\sqrt{1}$.

49. Find a real number between $\sqrt{6}$ and $\sqrt{7}$.

50. Find a real number between $\sqrt{5}$ and $\sqrt{11}$.

51. Find a real number between $\sqrt{50}$ and $\sqrt{55}$.

52. Find a real number between $-\sqrt{20}$ and $-\sqrt{17}$.

53. a. Find a real number between 1 and $\sqrt{3}$.
b. Find a real number between 1 and your answer to part **a.**
c. Find a real number between 1 and your answer to part **b.**

For what values of x is the value of each expression a real number?

54. $\sqrt{2x}$
55. $3 - \sqrt{x}$
56. $\sqrt{x + 2}$
57. $\sqrt{3x - 6}$
58. $\sqrt{5x + 2}$
59. $\sqrt{1 - \frac{x}{5}}$

60. **What's the Error?** A student said that all integers are whole numbers. What mistake did the student make? Explain.

61. **Write About It** Can you ever use a calculator to determine if a number is rational or irrational? Explain.

62. **Challenge** The circumference of a circle divided by its diameter is an irrational number, represented by the Greek letter π (*pi*). Could a circle with a diameter of 2 have a circumference of 6? Why or why not?

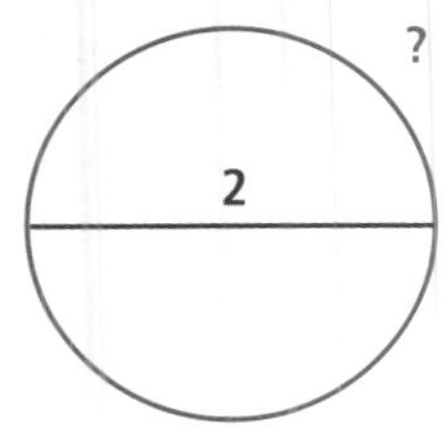

Test Prep and Spiral Review

63. **Multiple Choice** Which value is between -8 and -10?

Ⓐ -7.12 Ⓑ $-\sqrt{61}$ Ⓒ $-3 \cdot \pi$ Ⓓ $-\frac{123}{11}$

64. **Multiple Choice** Which value is NOT a rational number?

Ⓕ $0.\overline{7}$ Ⓖ $\frac{11}{13}$ Ⓗ $\sqrt{19}$ Ⓙ $\sqrt{225}$

65. **Multiple Choice** For which values of x is $\sqrt{x - 19}$ a real number?

Ⓐ $x \geq -19$ Ⓑ $x \leq -19$ Ⓒ $x \geq 19$ Ⓓ $x \leq 19$

Evaluate the function $y = -5x + 2$ for each value of x. (Lesson 3-4)

66. $x = 0$
67. $x = -3$
68. $x = 7$
69. $x = -1$

Evaluate. (Lesson 4-1)

70. 8^5
71. $(-3)^3$
72. $(-5)^4$
73. 9^2

Hands-On LAB 4-8

Explore Right Triangles

Use with Lesson 4-8

go.hrw.com
Lab Resources Online
KEYWORD: MT7 Lab4

REMEMBER

Right triangles have 1 right angle and 2 acute angles. The side opposite the right angle is called the *hypotenuse,* and the other two sides are called *legs.*

Activity

1 The Pythagorean Theorem states that if a and b are the lengths of the legs of a right triangle, then c is the length of the hypotenuse, where $a^2 + b^2 = c^2$. Prove the Pythagorean Theorem using the following steps.

a. Draw two squares side by side. Label one with side a and one with side b.

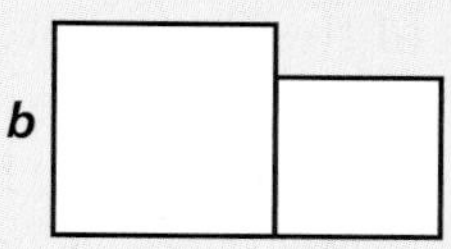

Notice that the area of this composite figure is $a^2 + b^2$.

b. Draw hypotenuses of length c, so that we have right triangles with sides a, b, and c. Use a protractor to make sure that the hypotenuses form a right angle.

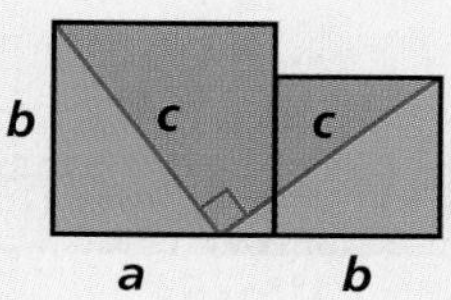

c. Cut out the triangles and the remaining piece.

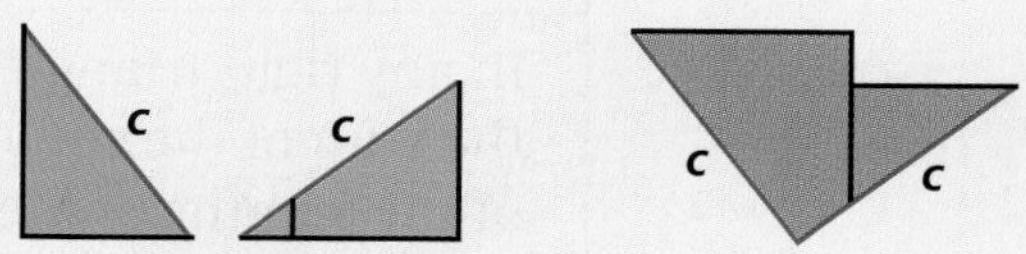

d. Fit the pieces together to make a square with sides c and area c^2. You have shown that the area $\boldsymbol{a^2 + b^2}$ can be cut up and rearranged to form the area $\boldsymbol{c^2}$, so $\boldsymbol{a^2 + b^2 = c^2}$.

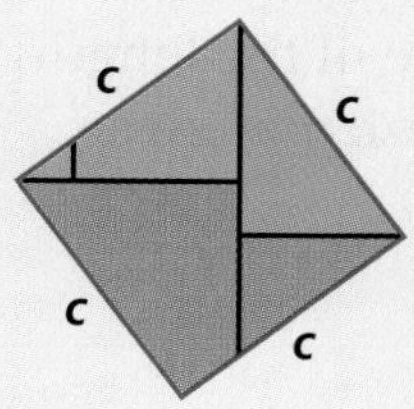

Think and Discuss

1. The diagram shows another way of understanding the Pythagorean Theorem. How are the areas of the squares shown in the diagram related.

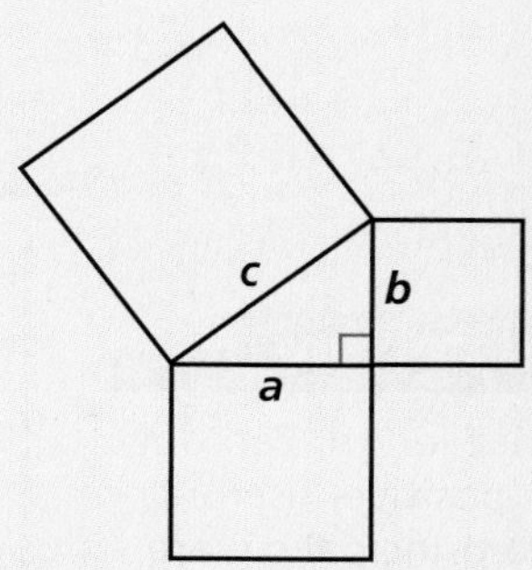

Try This

1. If you know that the lengths of two legs of a right triangle are 8 and 15, can you find the length of the hypotenuse? Show your work.

2. Take a piece of paper and fold the right corner down so that the top edge of the paper matches the side edge. Crease the paper. Without measuring, find the diagonal's length.

4-8 The Pythagorean Theorem

Learn to use the Pythagorean Theorem to solve problems.

Vocabulary

Pythagorean Theorem

leg

hypotenuse

Pythagoras was born on the Aegean island of Samos sometime between 580 B.C. and 569 B.C. He is best known for the *Pythagorean Theorem,* which relates the side lengths of a right triangle.

A Babylonian tablet known as Plimpton 322 provides evidence that the relationship between the side lengths of right triangles was known as early as 1900 B.C. Many people, including U.S. president James Garfield, have written proofs of the Pythagorean Theorem. In 1940, E. S. Loomis presented 370 proofs of the theorem in *The Pythagorean Proposition.*

This statue of Pythagoras is located in the Pythagorion Harbor on the island of Samos.

<table>
<tr><th colspan="3">THE PYTHAGOREAN THEOREM</th></tr>
<tr><th>Words</th><th>Numbers</th><th>Algebra</th></tr>
<tr><td>In any right triangle, the sum of the squares of the lengths of the two legs is equal to the square of the length of the hypotenuse.</td><td>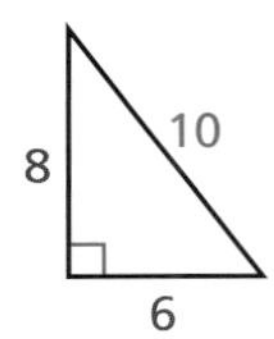

$6^2 + 8^2 = 10^2$
$36 + 64 = 100$</td><td>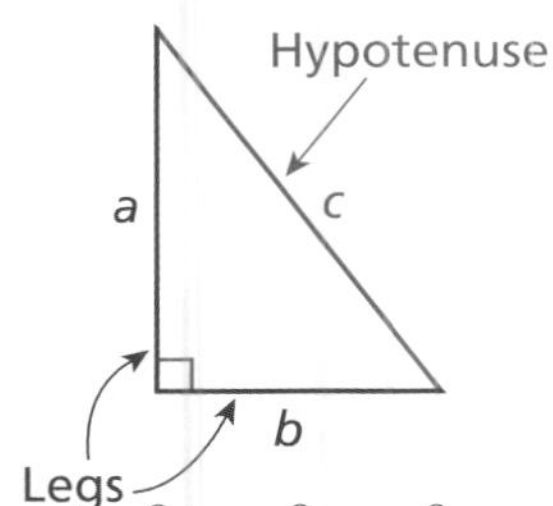

$a^2 + b^2 = c^2$</td></tr>
</table>

EXAMPLE 1 **Finding the Length of a Hypotenuse**

Find the length of each hypotenuse to the nearest hundredth.

Helpful Hint

Since length can only be positive, use only the principal square root.

A

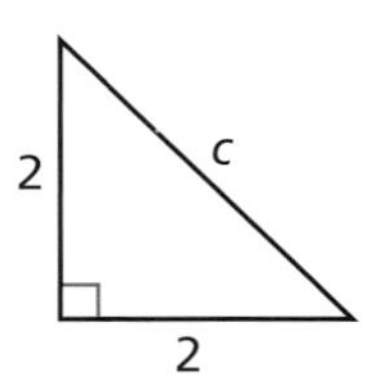

$a^2 + b^2 = c^2$	*Pythagorean Theorem*
$2^2 + 2^2 = c^2$	*Substitute 2 for a and 2 for b.*
$4 + 4 = c^2$	*Simplify powers.*
$8 = c^2$	*Add.*
$\sqrt{8} = \sqrt{c^2}$	*Find the square roots.*
$2.83 \approx c$	*Round to the nearest hundredth.*

Find the length of each hypotenuse to the nearest hundredth.

B **triangle with coordinates (3, 1), (0, 5), and (0, 1)**

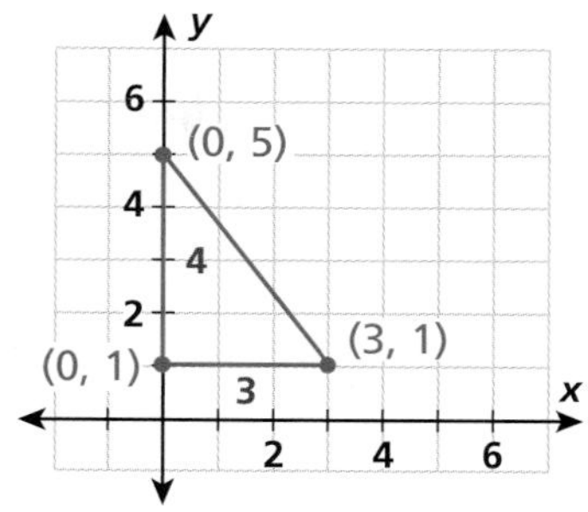

The points form a right triangle with $a = 4$ and $b = 3$.

$$\begin{aligned} a^2 + b^2 &= c^2 && \textit{Pythagorean Theorem} \\ 4^2 + 3^2 &= c^2 && \textit{Substitute for a and b.} \\ 16 + 9 &= c^2 && \textit{Simplify powers.} \\ 25 &= c^2 && \textit{Add.} \\ 5 &= c && \textit{Find the square roots.} \end{aligned}$$

EXAMPLE 2 Finding the Length of a Leg in a Right Triangle

Solve for the unknown side in the right triangle to the nearest tenth.

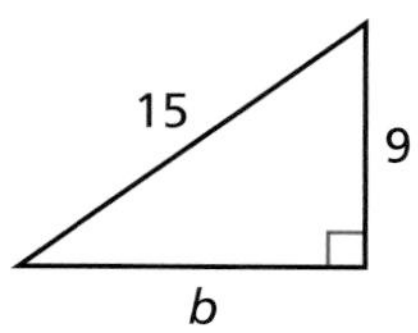

$$\begin{aligned} a^2 + b^2 &= c^2 && \textit{Pythagorean Theorem} \\ 9^2 + b^2 &= 15^2 && \textit{Substitute for a and b.} \\ 81 + b^2 &= 225 && \textit{Simplify powers.} \\ -81 \qquad &= -81 && \textit{Subtract 81 from each side.} \\ b^2 &= 144 && \\ b &= 12 && \textit{Find the square roots.} \end{aligned}$$

EXAMPLE 3 Using the Pythagorean Theorem for Measurement

Mark and Sarah start walking at the same point, but Mark walks 50 feet north while Sarah walks 75 feet east. How far apart are Mark and Sarah when they stop?

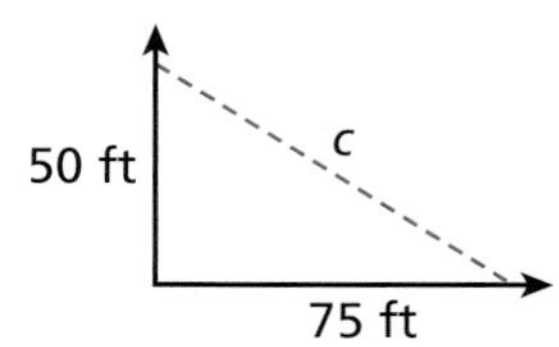

Mark and Sarah's distance from each other when they stop walking is equal to the hypotenuse of a right triangle.

$$\begin{aligned} a^2 + b^2 &= c^2 && \textit{Pythagorean Theorem} \\ 50^2 + 75^2 &= c^2 && \textit{Substitute for a and b.} \\ 2500 + 5625 &= c^2 && \textit{Simplify powers.} \\ 8125 &= c^2 && \textit{Add.} \\ 90.1 &\approx c && \textit{Find the square roots.} \end{aligned}$$

Mark and Sarah are approximately 90.1 feet apart.

Think and Discuss

1. **Tell** which side of a right triangle is always the longest side.
2. **Explain** if 2, 3, and 4 cm could be side lengths of a right triangle.

4-8 Exercises

go.hrw.com
Homework Help Online
KEYWORD: MT7 4-8
Parent Resources Online
KEYWORD: MT7 Parent

GUIDED PRACTICE

See Example 1

Find the length of each hypotenuse to the nearest hundredth.

1.
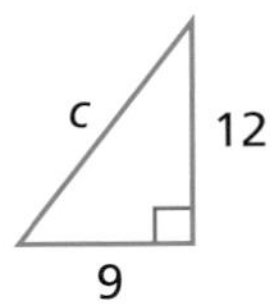

2.
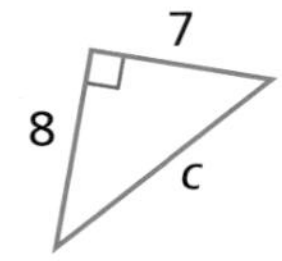

3.
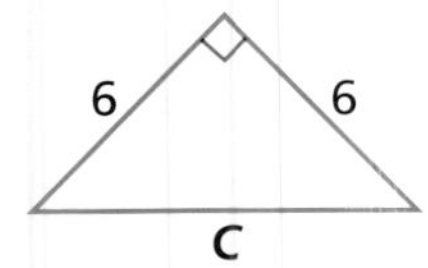

4. triangle with coordinates (−4, 0), (−4, 5), and (0, 5)

See Example 2

Solve for the unknown side in each right triangle to the nearest tenth.

5.
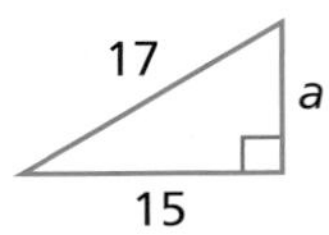

6.
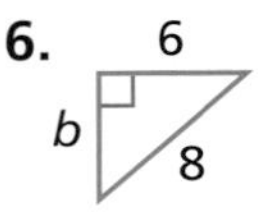

7.
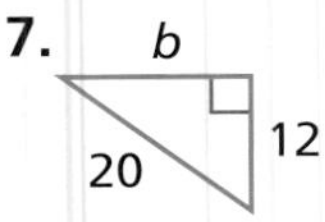

See Example 3

8. A traffic helicopter flies 10 miles due north and then 24 miles due east. Then the helicopter flies in a straight line back to its starting point. What was the distance of the helicopter's last leg back to its starting point?

INDEPENDENT PRACTICE

See Example 1

Find the length of each hypotenuse to the nearest hundredth.

9.
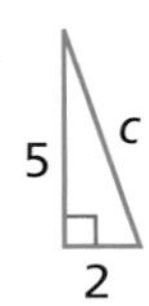

10.
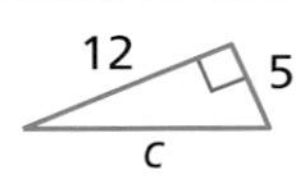

11.
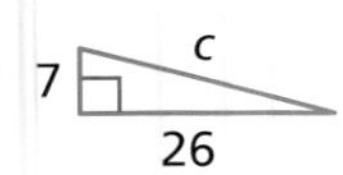

12. triangle with coordinates (−5, 3), (5, −3), and (−5, −3)

See Example 2

Solve for the unknown side in each right triangle to the nearest tenth.

13.
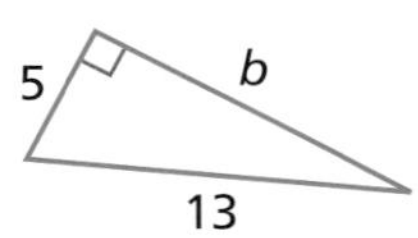

14.
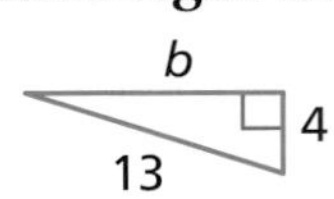

15.
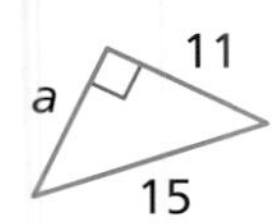

See Example 3

16. Mr. and Mrs. Flores commute to work each morning. Mr. Flores drives 8 miles east to his office. Mrs. Flores drives 15 miles south to her office. How many miles away do Mr. and Mrs. Flores work from each other?

PRACTICE AND PROBLEM SOLVING

Extra Practice
See page 789.

Find the missing length for each right triangle to the nearest tenth.

17. $a = 4$, $b = 7$, $c = \square$

18. $a = \square$, $b = 40$, $c = 41$

19. $a = 30$, $b = 72$, $c = \square$

20. $a = 16$, $b = \square$, $c = 38$

21. $a = \square$, $b = 47$, $c = 60$

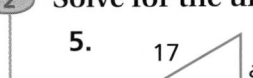

22. $a = 65$, $b = \square$, $c = 97$

The *converse* of the Pythagorean Theorem states that any three nonzero whole numbers that make the equation $a^2 + b^2 = c^2$ true are the side lengths of a right triangle. These numbers are called *Pythagorean triples.* Determine whether each set is a Pythagorean triple.

23. 3, 6, 9 **24.** 3, 4, 5 **25.** 5, 12, 13 **26.** 7, 24, 25

27. 10, 24, 26 **28.** 8, 14, 16 **29.** 10, 16, 19 **30.** 9, 40, 41

31. For safety reasons, the base of a 24-foot ladder must be placed at least 8 feet from the wall. To the nearest tenth of a foot, how high can a 24-foot ladder safely reach?

32. How far is the sailboat from the lighthouse, to the nearest kilometer?

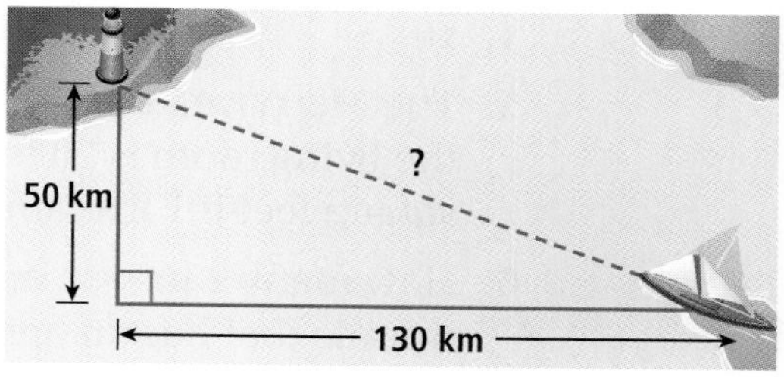

33. Critical Thinking A construction company is pouring a rectangular concrete foundation. The dimensions of the foundation are 24 ft by 48 ft. Describe a procedure to confirm that the sides of the foundation meet at a right angle.

34. Write a Problem Use a street map to write and solve a problem that requires the use of the Pythagorean Theorem.

35. Write About It Explain how to use the converse of the Pythagorean Theorem to show that a triangle is a right triangle. (See Exercises 23–30.)

36. Challenge A right triangle has legs of length $3x$ m and $4x$ m and hypotenuse of length 75 m. Find the lengths of the legs of the triangle.

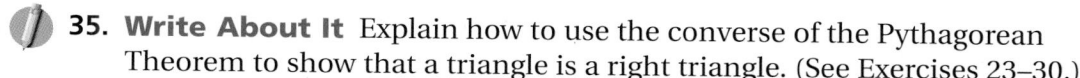

Test Prep and Spiral Review

37. Multiple Choice A flagpole is 40 feet tall. A rope is tied to the top of the flagpole and secured to the ground 9 feet from the base of the flagpole. What is the length of the rope to the nearest foot?

(A) 19 feet (B) 39 feet (C) 41 feet (D) 1519 feet

38. Gridded Response Brad leans his 15-foot ladder against his house. The base of the ladder is placed 4 feet from the base of the house. How far up the house does the ladder reach? Round your answer to the nearest hundredth.

Find the next term in each sequence. (Lesson 3-6)

39. −3, 0, 3, 6, . . . **40.** 0.55, 0.65, 0.75, 0.85, . . . **41.** 9, 16, 23, 30, 37, 44, . . .

42. 1, 1.5, 2, 2.5, . . . **43.** −1, 1, 3, 5, . . . **44.** 0, −2, −4, −6, . . .

Estimate each square root to two decimal places. (Lesson 4-6)

45. $\sqrt{30}$ **46.** $\sqrt{42}$ **47.** $\sqrt{55}$ **48.** $\sqrt{67}$

READY TO GO ON?

Quiz for Lessons 4-5 Through 4-8

4-5 Squares and Square Roots

Find the two square roots of each number.

1. 16
2. 9801
3. 10,000
4. 529
5. The Merryweathers want a new square rug for their living room. If the living room is 20 ft × 16 ft, will a square rug with an area of 289 square feet fit? Explain your answer.
6. How many 2 in. × 2 in. square tiles will fit along the edge of a square mosaic that has an area of 196 square inches?

4-6 Estimating Square Roots

Each square root is between two integers. Name the integers. Explain your answer.

7. $-\sqrt{72}$
8. $\sqrt{200}$
9. $-\sqrt{340}$
10. $\sqrt{610}$
11. A square table has a top with an area of 11 square feet. To the nearest hundredth, what length of edging is needed to go around all edges of the tabletop?
12. The area of a chess board is 110 square inches. Find the length of one side of the board to the nearest hundredth.

4-7 The Real Numbers

Write all names that apply to each number.

13. $\sqrt{12}$
14. 0.15
15. $\sqrt{1600}$
16. $-\sqrt{144}$
17. Give an example of an irrational number that is less than −5.
18. Find a real number between 5 and $\sqrt{36}$.

4-8 The Pythagorean Theorem

Find the missing length for each right triangle. Round your answer to the nearest tenth.

19. $a = 3, b = 6, c = \square$
20. $a = \square, b = 24, c = 25$
21. $a = 20, b = \square, c = 46$
22. $a = \square, b = 53, c = 70$
23. $a = 14, b = 15, c = \square$
24. $a = 8, b = \square, c = 17$
25. A construction company is pouring a concrete foundation. The measures of two sides that meet in a corner are 33 ft and 56 ft. For the corner to be a right angle, what would the length of the diagonal have to be?

MULTI-STEP TEST PREP

CHAPTER 4

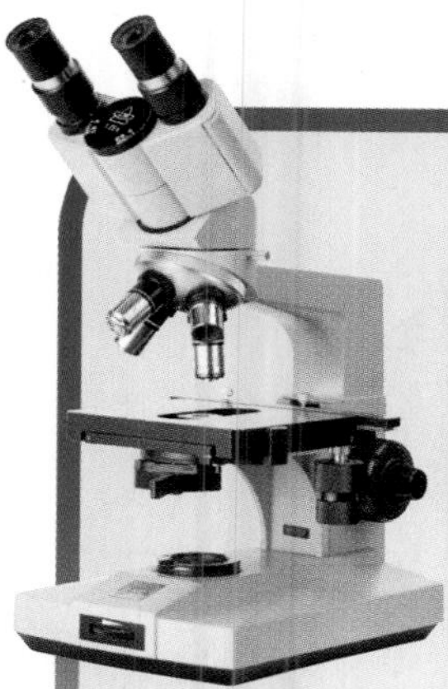

Divide and Conquer

A biologist is growing colonies of two bacteria. As shown in the table, the cells of bacterium A divide in two every hour. The cells of bacterium B divide in two every two hours.

Elapsed Time	Number of Cells	
	Bacterium A	Bacterium B
Start	1	1
1 hour	2^1	—
2 hours	2^2	2^1
3 hours	2^3	—
4 hours	2^4	2^2

1. After 8 hours, how many more cells are there of bacterium A than of bacterium B?
2. How many hours does it take until there are more than 1000 cells of bacterium A?
3. After 24 hours, how many times as many cells are there of bacterium A as bacterium B?
4. At the end of 24 hours, there are about 1.68×10^7 cells of bacterium A. The biologist divides this colony into 3 roughly equal portions. About how many cells are in each portion?
5. As a rule of thumb, if an experiment yields n colonies of bacteria, future experiments are likely to yield between $n - \sqrt{n}$ and $n + \sqrt{n}$ colonies. Suppose an experiment produces 170 colonies of bacterium A. Explain how you can estimate the range of the number of colonies that future experiments will produce.

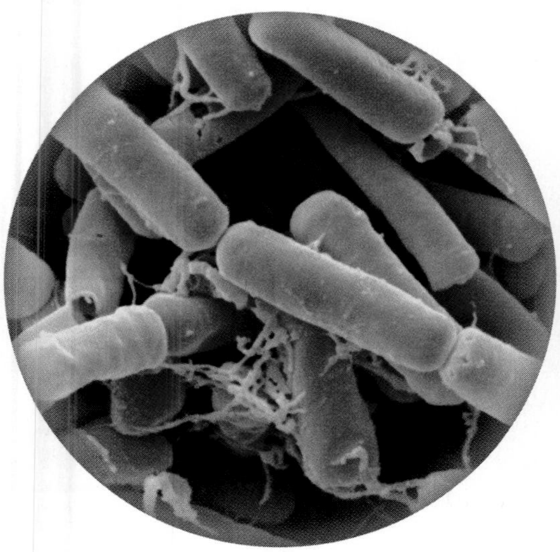

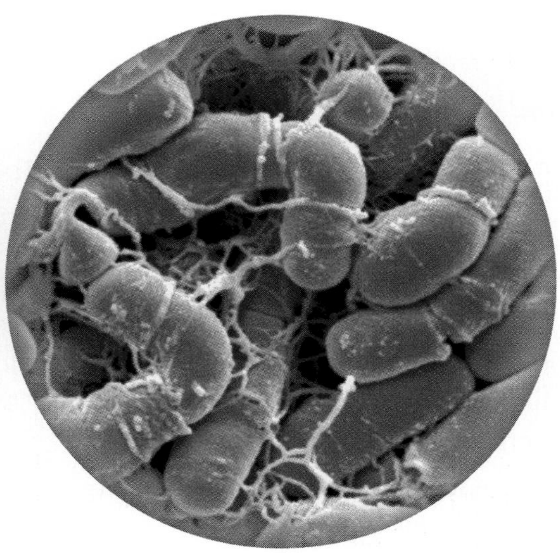

Game Time

Magic Squares

A *magic square* is a square with numbers arranged so that the sums of the numbers in each row, column, and diagonal are the same.

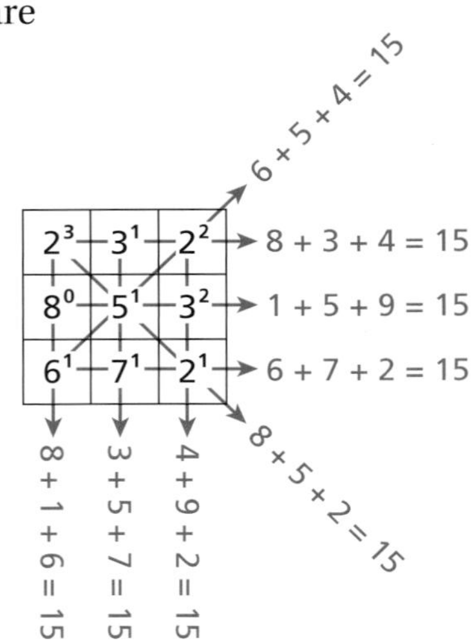

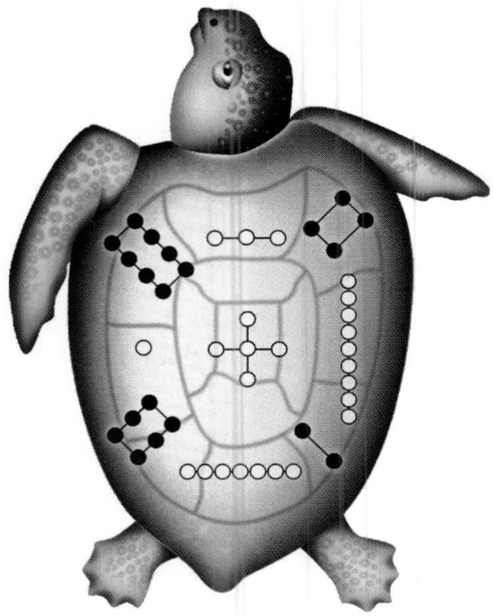

According to an ancient Chinese legend, a tortoise from the Lo river had the pattern of this magic square on its shell.

1 Complete each magic square below.

$\sqrt{36}$	■	2^2
8^0	$\sqrt{9}$	■
■	$3^2 - 2$	■

■	$-(\sqrt{4} + 4)$	$-(9^0)$
$-(\sqrt{16})$	■	0^3
$-(\sqrt{9})$	$2^0 + 1$	■

2 Use the numbers −4, −3, −2, −1, 0, 1, 2, 3, and 4 to make a magic square with row, column, and diagonal sums of 0.

Equation Bingo

Each bingo card has numbers on it. The caller has a collection of equations. The caller reads an equation, and then the players solve the equation for the variable. If players have the solution on their cards, they place a chip on it. The winner is the first player with a row of chips either down, across, or diagonally.

A complete copy of the rules and game boards are available online.

go.hrw.com
Game Time Extra
KEYWORD: MT7 Games

FOLDNOTES

It's in the Bag!

Materials

- strip of white paper (18 in. by 7 in.)
- piece of decorative paper (6 in. by 6 in.)
- tape
- scraps of decorative paper
- markers
- glue

PROJECT It's a Wrap

Design your own energy-bar wrapper to hold your notes on exponents and roots.

Directions

1. Make accordion folds on the strip of white paper so that there are six panels, each about 3 in. wide. **Figure A**
2. Fold up the accordion strip.
3. Wrap the decorative paper around the accordion strip. The accordion strip will stick out on either side. Tape the ends of the decorative paper together to make a wrapper. **Figure B**
4. Write the number and title of the chapter on scraps of decorative paper, and glue these to the wrapper.

A

B

Taking Note of the Math

Use the panels of the accordion strip to take notes on the key concepts in this chapter. Include examples that will help you remember facts about exponents, roots, and the Pythagorean Theorem. Fold up the strip and slide it back into the wrapper.

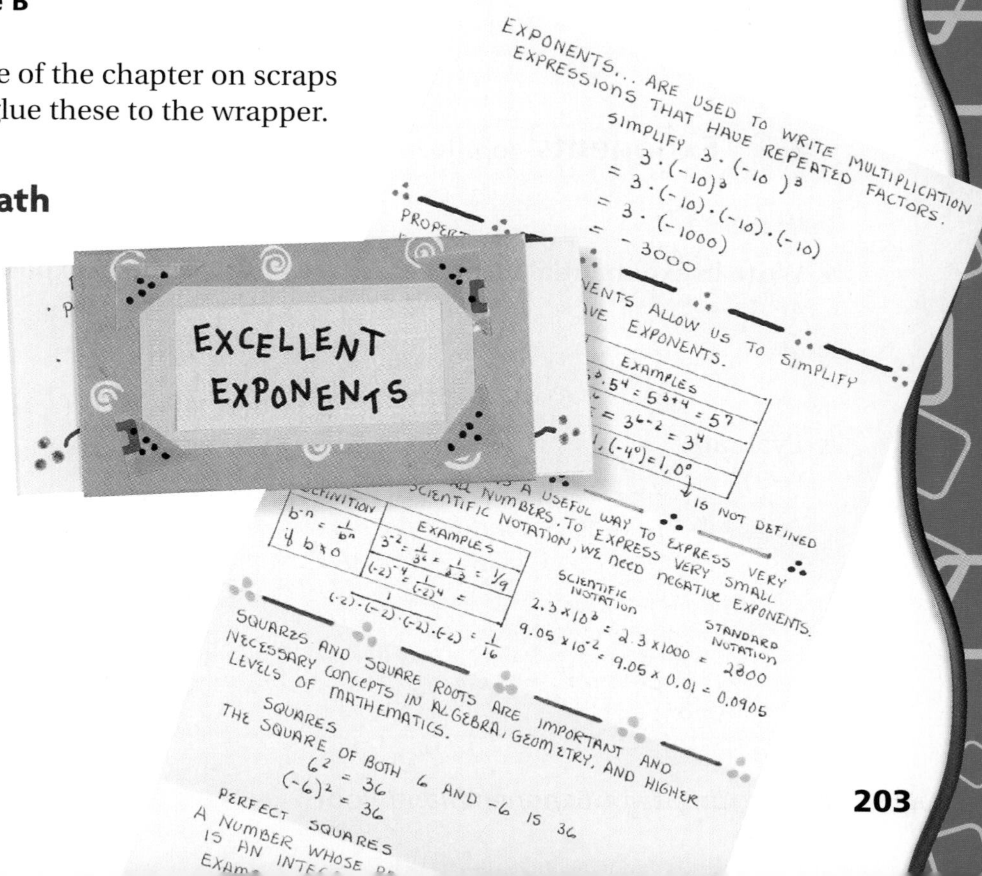

CHAPTER 4

Study Guide: Review

Vocabulary

base 162
Density Property 192
exponent 162
exponential form 162
hypotenuse 196
irrational number 191
leg 196
perfect square 182
power 162
principal square root 182
Pythagorean Theorem 196
real number 191
scientific notation 174

Complete the sentences below with vocabulary words from the list above.

1. A power consists of a(n) __?__ raised to a(n) __?__.
2. A(n) __?__ is a number that cannot be written as a fraction.
3. __?__ is a short-hand way of writing extremely large or extremely small numbers.
4. The __?__ states that the sum of the squares of the __?__ of a right triangle is equal to the square of the __?__.
5. The set of __?__ is the set of all rational and irrational numbers.

4-1 Exponents (pp. 162–165)

EXAMPLE

■ **Write in exponential form.**

$4 \cdot 4 \cdot 4$

4^3 *Identify how many times 4 is used as a factor.*

■ **Evaluate.**

$(-2)^3$

$(-2) \cdot (-2) \cdot (-2)$ *Find the product of three −2's.*

-8

EXERCISES

Write in exponential form.

6. $7 \cdot 7 \cdot 7$
7. $(-3) \cdot (-3)$
8. $k \cdot k \cdot k \cdot k$
9. -9
10. $(-2) \cdot (-2) \cdot d \cdot d$
11. $3n \cdot 3n \cdot 3n$
12. $6 \cdot x \cdot x$
13. 10,000

Evaluate.

14. 5^4
15. $(-2)^5$
16. $(-1)^9$
17. 2^8
18. $(-3)^1$
19. 4^3
20. $(-3)^3$
21. $(-5)^2$
22. 15^1
23. 6^4
24. 10^5
25. $(-2)^7$

4-2 Look for a Pattern in Integer Exponents (pp. 166–169)

EXAMPLE

Evaluate.

- $(-3)^{-2}$

  $\frac{1}{(-3)^2}$ *Write the reciprocal; change the sign of the exponent.*

  $\frac{1}{9}$

- 2^0

  1

EXERCISES

Evaluate.

26. 5^{-3} **27.** $(-4)^{-3}$ **28.** 11^{-1}

29. 10^{-4} **30.** 100^0 **31.** -6^{-2}

32. -3^{-4} **33.** $(-10)^{-2}$

34. $(9-7)^{-3}$ **35.** $(6-9)^{-3}$

36. $(8-5)^{-1}$ **37.** $(7-10)^0$

38. $4^{-1} + (5-7)^{-2}$ **39.** $3^{-2} \cdot 2^{-3} \cdot 9^0$

40. $10 - 9(3^{-2} + 6^0)$

4-3 Properties of Exponents (pp. 170–173)

EXAMPLE

Write the product or quotient as one power.

- $2^5 \cdot 2^3$

  2^{5+3} *Add exponents.*

  2^8

- $\frac{10^9}{10^2}$

  10^{9-2} *Subtract exponents.*

  10^7

EXERCISES

Write the product or quotient as one power.

41. $4^2 \cdot 4^5$ **42.** $9^2 \cdot 9^4$ **43.** $p \cdot p^3$

44. $15 \cdot 15^2$ **45.** $6^2 \cdot 3^2$ **46.** $x^4 \cdot x^6$

47. $\frac{8^5}{8^2}$ **48.** $\frac{9^3}{9}$ **49.** $\frac{m^7}{m^2}$

50. $\frac{3^5}{3^{-2}}$ **51.** $\frac{4^{-5}}{4^{-5}}$ **52.** $\frac{y^6}{y^{-3}}$

53. $5^0 \cdot 5^3$ **54.** $y^6 \div y$ **55.** $k^4 \div k^4$

4-4 Scientific Notation (pp. 174–178)

EXAMPLE

Write in standard notation.

- 3.58×10^4

  $3.58 \times 10{,}000$

  35,800

- 3.58×10^{-4}

  $3.58 \times \frac{1}{10{,}000}$

  $3.58 \div 10{,}000$

  0.000358

Write in scientific notation.

- $0.000007 = 7 \times 10^{-6}$
- $62{,}500 = 6.25 \times 10^4$

EXERCISES

Write in standard notation.

56. 1.62×10^3 **57.** 1.62×10^{-3}

58. 9.1×10^5 **59.** 9.1×10^{-5}

Write in scientific notation.

60. 0.000000008 **61.** 73,000,000

62. 0.0000096 **63.** 56,400,000,000

4-5 Squares and Square Roots (pp. 182–185)

EXAMPLE

- **Find the two square roots of 400.**

$20 \cdot 20 = 400$

$(-20) \cdot (-20) = 400$

The square roots are 20 and -20.

EXERCISES

Find the two square roots of each number.

64. 16 **65.** 900 **66.** 676

Evaluate each expression.

67. $\sqrt{4 + 21}$ **68.** $\frac{\sqrt{100}}{20}$ **69.** $\sqrt{3^4}$

4-6 Estimating Square Roots (pp. 186–189)

EXAMPLE

- **Find the side length of a square with area 359 ft^2 to one decimal place. Then find the distance around the square to the nearest tenth.**

Side $= \sqrt{359} \approx 18.9$

Distance around $\approx 4(18.9) \approx 75.6$ feet

EXERCISES

Find the distance around each square with the area given. Round to the nearest tenth.

70. Area of square *ABCD* is 500 in^2.

71. Area of square *MNOP* is 1750 cm^2.

72. Name the integers $\sqrt{82}$ is between.

4-7 The Real Numbers (pp. 191–194)

EXAMPLE

- **State if the number is rational, irrational, or not a real number.**

$-\sqrt{2}$ irrational — *The decimal equivalent does not repeat or end.*

$\sqrt{-4}$ not real — *Square roots of negative numbers are not real.*

EXERCISES

State if the number is rational, irrational, or not a real number.

73. $\sqrt{81}$ **74.** $\sqrt{122}$ **75.** $\sqrt{-16}$

76. $-\sqrt{5}$ **77.** $\frac{0}{-4}$ **78.** $\frac{7}{0}$

79. Find a real number between $\sqrt{9}$ and $\sqrt{16}$.

4-8 The Pythagorean Theorem (pp. 196–199)

EXAMPLE

- **Find the length of side *b* in the right triangle where $a = 8$ and $c = 17$.**

$a^2 + b^2 = c^2$

$8^2 + b^2 = 17^2$

$64 + b^2 = 289$

$b^2 = 225$

$b = \sqrt{225} = 15$

EXERCISES

Solve for the unknown side in each right triangle.

80. If $a = 6$ and $b = 8$, find c.

81. If $b = 24$ and $c = 26$, find a.

82. Find the length between opposite corners of a square with side lengths 10 inches to the nearest tenth.

CHAPTER TEST

Evaluate.

1. 10^9 **2.** 11^{-3} **3.** 2^7 **4.** 3^{-4}

Evaluate each expression. Write your answer as one power.

5. $\frac{3^3}{3^6}$ **6.** $7^9 \cdot 7^2$ **7.** $(5^{10})^6$ **8.** $\frac{11^{-7}}{11^7}$

9. $27^3 \cdot 27^{-18}$ **10.** $(52^{-7})^{-3}$ **11.** $13^0 \cdot 13^9$ **12.** $\frac{8^{12}}{8^7}$

Write each number in standard notation.

13. 2.7×10^{12} **14.** 3.53×10^{-2} **15.** 4.257×10^5 **16.** 9.87×10^{10}

17. -4.8×10^8 **18.** 6.09×10^{-3} **19.** -8.1×10^6 **20.** -3.5×10^{-4}

Write each number in scientific notation.

21. 19,000,000,000 **22.** 0.0000039 **23.** 1,980,000,000 **24.** 0.00045

25. A sack of cocoa beans weighs about 132 lb. How much would 1000 sacks of cocoa beans weigh? Write the answer in scientific notation.

Find the two square roots of each number.

26. 196 **27.** 1 **28.** 10,000 **29.** 625

30. The minimum area of a square, high school wrestling mat is 1444 square feet. What is the length of the mat?

Each square root is between two integers. Name the integers. Explain your answer.

31. $\sqrt{230}$ **32.** $\sqrt{125}$ **33.** $\sqrt{89}$ **34.** $-\sqrt{60}$

35. $-\sqrt{3}$ **36.** $\sqrt{175}$ **37.** $-\sqrt{410}$ **38.** $\sqrt{325}$

39. A square has an area of 13 ft^2. To the nearest tenth, what is its perimeter?

Write all names that apply to each number.

40. $-\sqrt{121}$ **41.** $-1.\overline{7}$ **42.** $\sqrt{-9}$ **43.** $\frac{\sqrt{225}}{}$

Find the missing length for each right triangle.

44. $a = 10, b = 24, c = \square$ **45.** $a = \square, b = 15, c = 175$ **46.** $a = 12, b = \square, c = 20$

47. Lupe wants to use a fence to divide her square garden in half diagonally. If each side of the garden is 16 ft long, how long will the fence have to be? Round your answer to the nearest hundredth of a foot.

48. A right triangle has a hypotenuse that is 123 in. long. If one of the legs is 75 in. long, how long is the other leg? Round your answer to the nearest tenth of an inch.

CHAPTER 4

STANDARDIZED TEST PREP

go.hrw.com
State Test Practice Online
KEYWORD: MT7 TestPrep

Standardized Test Prep

Cumulative Assessment, Chapters 1–4

Multiple Choice

1. Which expression is NOT equivalent to $3 \cdot 3 \cdot 3 \cdot 3 \cdot 3 \cdot 3$?

   (A) 3^6 (C) 18
   (B) 9^3 (D) 729

2. A number to the 8th power divided by the same number to the 4th power is 16. What is the number?

   (F) 2 (H) 6
   (G) 4 (J) 8

3. Which expression is equivalent to 81?

   (A) 2^9 (C) $\left(\frac{1}{3}\right)^{-4}$
   (B) 3^{-4} (D) $\left(\frac{1}{3}\right)^{4}$

4. The airports in the United States serve more than 635,000,000 people each year. Which of the following is the same number written in scientific notation?

   (F) 635×10^6 (H) 6.35×10^8
   (G) 6.35×10^{-8} (J) 6.35×10^9

5. For which equation is the ordered pair $(-3, 4)$ a solution?

   (A) $2x - y = -6$ (C) $\frac{1}{2}x - y = 6$
   (B) $x - 2y = 5$ (D) $x - \frac{1}{2}y = -5$

6. The population of India is close to 1.08×10^9. Which of the following represents this population written in standard notation?

   (F) 1,080,000,000 (H) 1,080,000
   (G) 180,000,000 (J) 108,000

7. Jenny finds that a baby lizard grows about 0.5 inch every week. Which equation best represents the number of weeks it will take for the lizard to grow to 1 foot long if it was 4 inches long when it hatched?

   (A) $0.5w + 4 = 1$ (C) $\frac{w + 4}{12} = 0.5$
   (B) $0.5w + 4 = 12$ (D) $\frac{w}{0.5 + 4} = 1$

8. A number k is decreased by 8, and the result is multiplied by 8. This product is then divided by 2. What is the final result?

   (F) $8k - 4$ (H) $4k - 32$
   (G) $4k - 8$ (J) $8k - 64$

9. Which ordered pair lies on the x-axis?

   (A) $(-1, 2)$ (C) $(0, 2)$
   (B) $(1, -2)$ (D) $(-1, 0)$

10. A quilt is made with 10 square pieces of fabric. If the area of each square piece is 169 square inches, what is the length of each square piece?

    (F) 12 inches (H) 14 inches
    (G) 13 inches (J) 15 inches

11. Which number is NOT between 1.5 and 1.75?

    (A) $1\frac{1}{4}$ (C) 1.62
    (B) 1.73 (D) $1\frac{13}{25}$

12. The $\sqrt{18}$ is between which pair of numbers?

    (F) 8 and 9 (H) 4 and 5
    (G) 7 and 8 (J) 3 and 4

13. Mrs. Graham ordered five pizzas for her top-performing class. The students ate $\frac{7}{8}$ of the pepperoni pizza, $\frac{3}{4}$ of the cheese pizza, $\frac{4}{5}$ of the veggie pizza, $\frac{2}{3}$ of the Hawaiian pizza, and $\frac{1}{2}$ of the barbecue chicken pizza. How much total pizza was left over?

(F) $3\frac{71}{120}$

(G) $2\frac{1}{8}$

(H) $1\frac{49}{120}$

(J) $1\frac{7}{15}$

HOT TIP! **Pay attention to the units given in a test question, especially if there are mixed units, such as inches and feet.**

Gridded Response

14. What exponent makes the statement $3^? = 27^2$ true?

15. Determine the value of x when $y = 3$ in the graph.

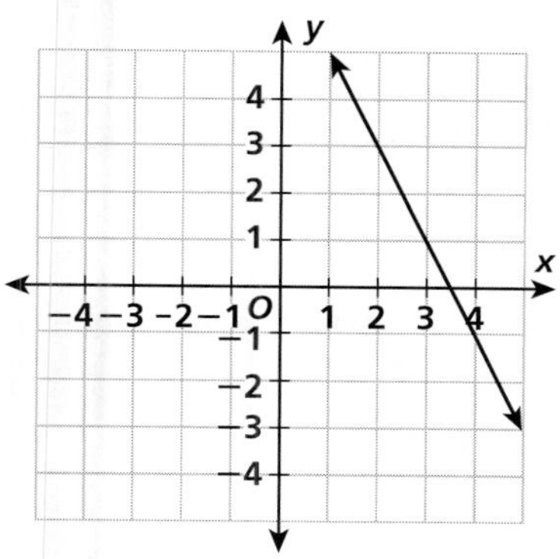

16. Chrissy is 25 years older than her dog. The sum of their ages is 37. How old is Chrissy's dog?

17. Evaluate the expression, $\frac{4}{5} - \left|\frac{1}{2} - x\right|$ for $x = \frac{1}{5}$.

18. The area of a square is 169 square feet. What is the length in feet of a side?

19. From her house, Lea rode her bike 8 miles north and then 15 miles west to a friend's house. How far in miles was she from her house along a straight path?

Short Response

20. A bag of pinto beans weighs 210 pounds.

    a. How much does 10,000 bags of pinto beans weigh? Write your answer in standard form.

    b. Write the numbers 210 and 10,000 in scientific notation.

    c. Explain how to use rules of exponents to write the weight of 10,000 bags of pinto beans in scientific notation.

21. Jack works part time with his dad installing carpet. They need to install carpet in a square room that has an area of about 876 square feet. Carpet can only be ordered in whole square yards.

    a. About how many feet long is the room?

    b. About how many square yards of carpet do Jack and his dad need in order to cover the floor of the room? Explain your reasoning.

Extended Response

22. Marissa's cat is stuck in a tree. The cat is on a branch 23 feet from the ground. Marissa is 5.5 feet tall, and she owns a 16-foot ladder.

    a. Create a table that shows how high up on the tree the top of the ladder will reach if Marissa places the base of the ladder 1 foot, 2 feet, 3 feet, 4 feet, and 5 feet from the tree.

    b. How high will Marissa be if she places the base of the ladder the distances from the tree in part **a** and stands on the rung 2.5-feet from the top of the ladder?

    c. Do you think Marissa can use this ladder to reach her cat? Explain your reasoning.

Problem Solving on Location

OHIO

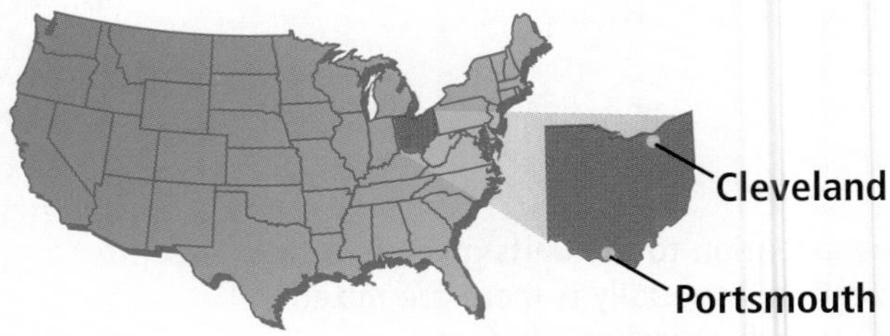

The Ohio and Erie Canal

In 1825, work began on the historic Ohio & Erie Canal, a waterway that connected the cities of Cleveland and Portsmouth. By 1832, traffic flowed along the entire 308-mile route. The Ohio & Erie is no longer a working canal, but its grassy towpath remains a popular destination for joggers and cyclists.

Choose one or more strategies to solve each problem. For Problems 1–3, use the graph.

1. A canal boat began at Frazee House, 14 miles south of Cleveland, and traveled south along the canal. The graph shows the boat's distance from Cleveland. At this rate, how many miles would the boat have been from Cleveland after 10 hours?

2. The boat traveled at the legal speed limit for the canal. What was the speed limit in miles per hour?

3. The canal used two types of locks to raise and lower the boats: lift locks and guard locks. There were 153 locks along the canal, and there were 139 more lift locks than guard locks. How many guard locks were there?

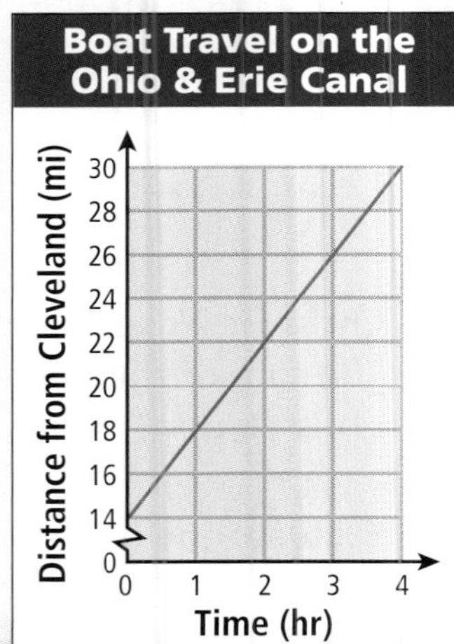

Problem Solving Strategies

- Draw a Diagram
- Make a Model
- Guess and Test
- Work Backward
- Find a Pattern
- Make a Table
- Solve a Simpler Problem
- Use Logical Reasoning
- Act It Out
- Make an Organized List

The Glenn Research Center

The Glenn Research Center, in northern Ohio, is one of NASA's key research facilities. The technologies developed at the Glenn Research Center have made it possible for humans to walk on the Moon, receive photographs from Mars, and explore the outer reaches of our solar system.

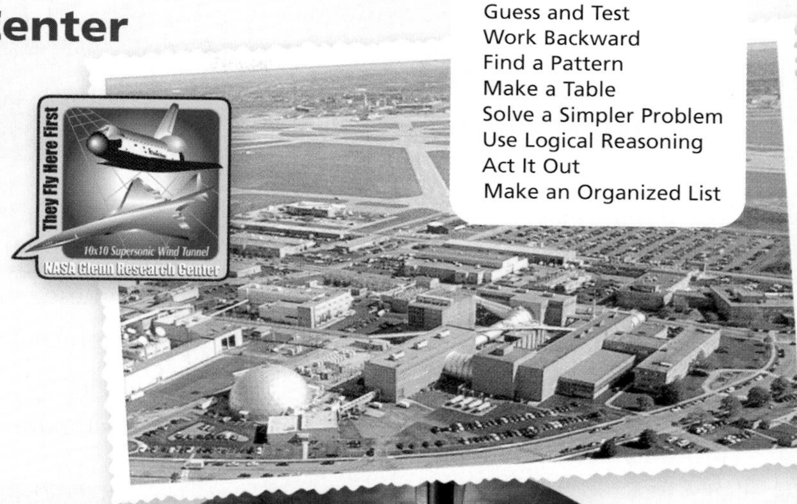

Choose one or more strategies to solve each problem.

1. The Flight Research Building is an enormous hangar that can hold several aircraft at the same time. The base of the hangar is a rectangle measuring 250 feet by 65 feet. To the nearest foot, what is the length of the longest pole that can be stored on the floor of the hangar?

2. The center's supersonic wind tunnel can produce wind speeds of up to 2280 mi/h. Here, scientists can test the effects of doubling wind speed. If scientists begin with a wind speed of 2^5 mi/h. How many times can they double the speed and still stay within the wind tunnel's capabilities?

For Problem 3, use the table.

3. The table shows some of the famous space missions that involved the Glenn Research Center. Use the following information to determine the destination of each mission.

- One mission went to Saturn, and one went to Mars.
- The shortest mission was a mission to the Moon.
- Saturn is farther from Earth than Mars.

What was the destination of the Pathfinder mission? the Apollo mission? the Cassini mission?

Glenn Research Center Missions

Name	Distance to Destination (mi)
Pathfinder	4×10^7
Apollo	2.4×10^5
Cassini	2×10^9

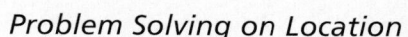

CHAPTER 5

Ratios, Proportions, and Similarity

5A Ratios, Rates, and Proportions
- **5-1** Ratios and Proportions
- **5-2** Ratios, Rates, and Unit Rates
- **5-3** Dimensional Analysis
- **5-4** Solving Proportions

5B Similarity and Scale
- **LAB** Explore Similarity
- **5-5** Similar Figures
- **LAB** Explore Dilations
- **5-6** Dilations
- **5-7** Indirect Measurement
- **5-8** Scale Drawings and Scale Models
- **LAB** Make a Scale Model

MULTI-STEP TEST PREP

go.hrw.com
Chapter Project Online
KEYWORD: MT7 Ch5

Tree	Natural Height (ft)	Bonsai Height (in.)
Chinese elm	60	10
Brush cherry	50	8
Juniper	10	6
Pitch pine	200	14
Eastern hemlock	80	18

Career *Horticulturist*

Chances are that a horticulturist helped create many of the varieties of plants at your local nursery. Horticulturists work in vegetable development, fruit growing, flower growing, and landscape design. Horticulturists who are also scientists work to develop new types of plants or ways to control plant diseases.

The art of *bonsai,* or making miniature plants, began in China and became popular in Japan. Now bonsai is practiced all over the world.

ARE YOU READY?

Vocabulary

Choose the best term from the list to complete each sentence.

common denominator
corresponding
inverse operations
least common denominator
multiplication equation

1. To solve an equation, you use __?__ to isolate the variable. So to solve the __?__ $3x = 18$, divide both sides by 3.
2. In the fractions $\frac{2}{3}$ and $\frac{1}{6}$, 18 is a(n) __?__, but 6 is the __?__.
3. If two polygons are congruent, all of their __?__ sides and angles are congruent.

Complete these exercises to review skills you will need for this chapter.

Simplify Fractions

Write each fraction in simplest form.

4. $\frac{8}{24}$ 5. $\frac{15}{50}$ 6. $\frac{18}{72}$ 7. $\frac{25}{125}$

Use a Least Common Denominator

Find the least common denominator for each set of fractions.

8. $\frac{2}{3}$ and $\frac{1}{5}$ 9. $\frac{3}{4}$ and $\frac{1}{8}$ 10. $\frac{5}{7}, \frac{3}{7}$, and $\frac{1}{14}$ 11. $\frac{1}{2}, \frac{2}{3}$, and $\frac{3}{5}$

Order Decimals

Write each set of decimals in order from least to greatest.

12. 4.2, 2.24, 2.4, 0.242 13. 1.1, 0.1, 0.01, 1.11 14. 1.4, 2.53, $1.\overline{3}$, $0.\overline{9}$

Solve Multiplication Equations

Solve.

15. $5x = 60$ 16. $0.2y = 14$ 17. $\frac{1}{2}t = 10$ 18. $\frac{2}{3}z = 9$

Customary Units

Change each to the given unit.

19. 18 yd = ▢ ft 20. 15 gal = ▢ qt 21. 30 lb = ▢ oz 22. 96 in. = ▢ ft
23. 46 c = ▢ pt 24. 160 oz = ▢ lb 25. 39 ft = ▢ yd 26. 108 qt = ▢ gal

CHAPTER 5

Study Guide: Preview

Where You've Been

Previously, you

- used division to find ratios and unit rates.
- used critical attributes to define similarity.
- found solutions to application problems involving related measurement units.

In This Chapter

You will study

- using unit rates to represent proportional relationships.
- estimating and finding solutions to application problems involving proportional relationships.
- generating similar figures using dilations.
- using proportional relationships in similar figures to find missing measurements.

Where You're Going

You can use the skills learned in this chapter

- to compare prices to find bargains
- to convert units in science courses
- to create scale drawings and scale models.

Key Vocabulary/Vocabulario

cross product	producto cruzado
dilation	dilatación
indirect measurement	medición indirecta
proportion	proporción
rate	tasa
ratio	razón
scale drawing	dibujo a escala
scale model	modelo a escala
similar	semejante
unit rate	tasa unitaria

Vocabulary Connections

To become familiar with some of the vocabulary terms in the chapter, consider the following. You may refer to the chapter, the glossary, or a dictionary if you like.

1. The word *cross* can mean "to intersect," forming an "X" shape. Since a *product* is the result of multiplying, what do you suppose you multiply to find the **cross products** of two fractions?
2. The word *indirect* means "not direct." What do you think it means to find the length of something using **indirect measurement**?
3. A **ratio** compares two quantities using a particular operation. Knowing what you do about *rational numbers*, which operation do you think you use in a ratio?

Reading and Writing Math

CHAPTER 5

Writing Strategy: Write a Convincing Argument

Your ability to write a convincing argument proves that you have a solid understanding of the concept. An effective argument should include the following four parts:

(1) A goal
(2) A response to the goal
(3) Evidence to support the response
(4) A summary statement

From Lesson 4-1

49. Write About It Compare 10^2 and 2^{10}. For any two numbers, which usually gives the greater number, using the greater number as the base or as the exponent? Give at least one exception.

Step 1 **Identify the goal.**

For any two numbers, explain whether using the greater number as the base or as the exponent will generally result in a greater number. Find one exception.

Step 2 **Provide a response to the goal.**

Using the greater number as the exponent usually gives the greater number.

Step 3 **Provide evidence to support your response.**

For the numbers 10 and 2, using the greater number, 10, as the exponent will result in a greater number.

$$10^2 = 100$$
$$2^{10} = 1024$$
$$100 < 1024$$
$$10^2 < 2^{10}$$

Exception: For the numbers 2 and 3, using the greater number, 3, as the exponent will not result in a greater number.

$$3^2 = 9$$
$$2^3 = 8$$
$$9 > 8$$
$$3^2 > 2^3$$

Step 4 **Summarize your argument.**

Generally, for any two numbers, using the greater number as the exponent instead of as the base will result in a greater number.

Try This

Write a convincing argument or explanation.

1. A student said a number raised to a negative power is always negative. What is the student's error?

5-1 Ratios and Proportions

Learn to find equivalent ratios to create proportions.

Vocabulary

ratio

equivalent ratio

proportion

On average, each person in the United States produces about 4.5 pounds of trash per day. About $\frac{27}{25}$, or 1.08 pounds, of this trash is recycled.

Comparisons of the number of people to total trash produced per day are shown in the table. These comparisons are *ratios* that are all equivalent.

The United States leads the world in both producing and recycling trash.

Comparisons of Number of People to Total Trash Produced per Day				
Number of People	1	2	3	4
Total Trash (lb)	4.5	9	13.5	18

Reading Math

Ratios can be written in several ways. 7 to 5, 7:5, and $\frac{7}{5}$ name the same ratio.

A **ratio** is a comparison of two quantities by division. Both rectangles have equivalent shaded areas. Ratios that make the same comparison are **equivalent ratios**.

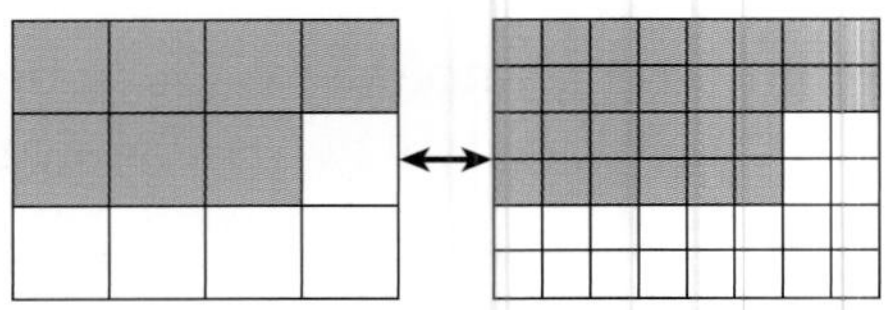

7 : 5 **28 : 20**

EXAMPLE 1 **Finding Equivalent Ratios**

Find two ratios that are equivalent to each given ratio.

A $\frac{6}{9}$

$\frac{6}{9} = \frac{6 \cdot 3}{9 \cdot 3} = \frac{18}{27}$

$\frac{6}{9} = \frac{6 \div 3}{9 \div 3} = \frac{2}{3}$

Multiply or divide the numerator and denominator by the same nonzero number.

Two ratios equivalent to $\frac{6}{9}$ are $\frac{18}{27}$ and $\frac{2}{3}$.

B $\frac{51}{36}$

$\frac{51}{36} = \frac{51 \cdot 2}{36 \cdot 2} = \frac{102}{72}$

$\frac{51}{36} = \frac{51 \div 3}{36 \div 3} = \frac{17}{12}$

Multiply or divide the numerator and denominator by the same nonzero number.

Two ratios equivalent to $\frac{51}{36}$ are $\frac{102}{72}$ and $\frac{17}{12}$.

Ratios that are equivalent are said to be *proportional*, or in **proportion**. Equivalent ratios are identical when they are written in simplest form.

EXAMPLE 2 Determining Whether Two Ratios Are in Proportion

Simplify to tell whether the ratios form a proportion.

A $\frac{9}{36}$ and $\frac{2}{8}$

$\frac{9}{36} = \frac{9 \div 9}{36 \div 9} = \frac{1}{4}$

$\frac{2}{8} = \frac{2 \div 2}{8 \div 2} = \frac{1}{4}$

Since $\frac{1}{4} = \frac{1}{4}$, the ratios are in proportion.

B $\frac{9}{12}$ and $\frac{16}{24}$

$\frac{9}{12} = \frac{9 \div 3}{12 \div 3} = \frac{3}{4}$

$\frac{16}{24} = \frac{16 \div 8}{24 \div 8} = \frac{2}{3}$

Since $\frac{3}{4} \neq \frac{2}{3}$, the ratios are *not* in proportion.

EXAMPLE 3 *Environment Application*

On average, each American recycles about 1.08 pounds of trash per day. To see how his family compared, Ahmed weighed the family's recycling on Earth Day and recorded the results in a table. Is Ahmed's family's recycling in proportion with the U.S. average? Explain.

Recycling		
	Number of People	Trash Recycled (lb)
Average in the U.S.	1	1.08
Ahmed's Family	4	5.1

$\frac{1}{1.08} \stackrel{?}{=} \frac{4}{5.1}$

$\frac{1}{1.08} \stackrel{?}{=} \frac{4 \div 4}{5.1 \div 4}$ *Divide.*

$\frac{1}{1.08} \neq \frac{1}{1.275}$ *Simplify.*

Since $\frac{1}{1.08}$ is not equal to $\frac{1}{1.275}$, the amount recycled by Ahmed's family is not in proportion with the average person in the United States. Ahmed's family recycles more than the average.

Think and Discuss

1. **Describe** how two ratios can form a proportion.
2. **Give** three ratios equivalent to 12:24.
3. **Explain** why the ratios 2:4 and 6:10 do not form a proportion.
4. **Give an example** of two ratios that are proportional and have numerators with different signs.

5-1 Exercises

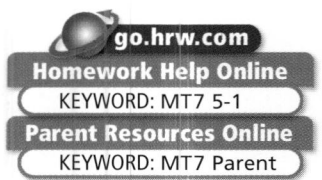

go.hrw.com
Homework Help Online
KEYWORD: MT7 5-1
Parent Resources Online
KEYWORD: MT7 Parent

GUIDED PRACTICE

See Example 1 **Find two ratios that are equivalent to each given ratio.**

1. $\frac{6}{14}$ **2.** $\frac{2}{8}$ **3.** $\frac{21}{7}$ **4.** $\frac{60}{36}$ **5.** $\frac{12}{17}$

See Example 2 **Simplify to tell whether the ratios form a proportion.**

6. $\frac{8}{22}$ and $\frac{2}{11}$ **7.** $\frac{6}{9}$ and $\frac{10}{18}$ **8.** $\frac{49}{28}$ and $\frac{35}{20}$ **9.** $\frac{22}{33}$ and $\frac{18}{27}$

See Example 3 **10. Entertainment** The table lists prices for movie tickets.

a. Are the ticket prices proportional? Explain.

b. If the prices are proportional how much do 6 movie tickets cost?

Movie Ticket Prices			
Number of Tickets	1	2	3
Price	$8.25	$16.50	$24.75

INDEPENDENT PRACTICE

See Example 1 **Find two ratios that are equivalent to each given ratio.**

11. $\frac{1}{7}$ **12.** $\frac{7}{12}$ **13.** $\frac{14}{12}$ **14.** $\frac{60}{25}$ **15.** $\frac{11}{50}$

See Example 2 **Simplify to tell whether the ratios form a proportion.**

16. $\frac{8}{16}$ and $\frac{5}{32}$ **17.** $\frac{45}{75}$ and $\frac{3}{5}$ **18.** $\frac{1}{3}$ and $\frac{15}{45}$ **19.** $\frac{16}{48}$ and $\frac{17}{68}$

See Example 3 **20. Chemistry** A molecule of butane contains 10 atoms of hydrogen to every 4 atoms of carbon. Could a compound containing the number of atoms shown be butane? Explain.

	Hydrogen Atoms	Carbon Atoms
Molecule of Butane	10	4
Compound	90	36

PRACTICE AND PROBLEM SOLVING

Extra Practice
See page 790.

21. Cooking A pancake recipe calls for 2.5 cups of pancake mix to make 10 servings. Carmen uses 3 cups of mix to make 14 servings. Does Carmen have the correct ratio for the recipe? Explain.

22. Business Cal pays his employees weekly. He would like to start paying them four times the weekly amount on a monthly basis. Is a month equivalent to four weeks? Explain.

23. Critical Thinking Using the list of ratios shown, create as many examples of proportions as you can. Then show an example of two ratios that do *not* form a proportion.

$\frac{2}{4}, \frac{2}{5}, \frac{3}{9}, \frac{8}{1}, \frac{2}{10}, \frac{12}{3}, \frac{4}{10}, \frac{4}{1}, \frac{12}{8}, \frac{10}{4}, \frac{9}{6}, \frac{3}{6}$

Tell whether the ratios form a proportion. If not, find a ratio that would form a proportion with the first ratio.

24. $\frac{4}{12}$ and $\frac{10}{15}$

25. $\frac{5}{7}$ and $\frac{100}{140}$

26. $\frac{4}{7}$ and $\frac{12}{49}$

27. $\frac{30}{36}$ and $\frac{15}{16}$

28. $\frac{15}{14}$ and $\frac{45}{42}$

29. $\frac{12}{25}$ and $\frac{24}{50}$

30. $\frac{18}{84}$ and $\frac{6}{56}$

31. $\frac{22}{12}$ and $\frac{42}{16}$

32. $\frac{22}{242}$ and $\frac{44}{484}$

33. Hobbies A bicycle chain moves along two sprockets when you shift gears. The number of teeth on the front sprocket and the number of teeth on the rear sprocket form a ratio. Equivalent ratios provide equal pedaling power. Find a ratio equivalent to the ratio $\frac{52}{24}$.

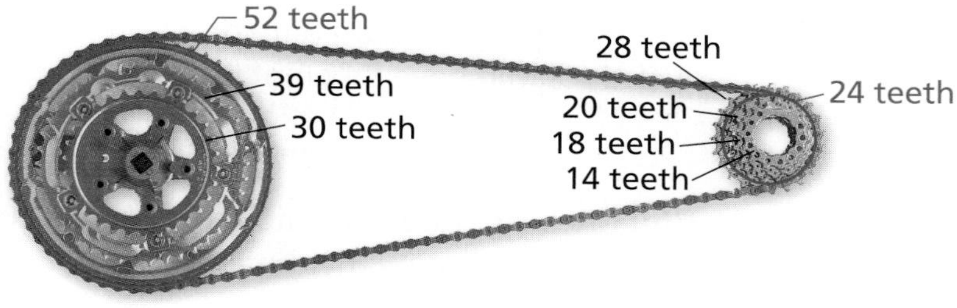

34. What's the Error? A student said that the ratios $\frac{3}{4}$ and $\frac{9}{16}$ were proportional. What error did the student make?

35. Write About It Describe at least two ways, given a ratio, to create a proportion.

36. Challenge Using each of the numbers 3, 9, 27, and 81 once, write all possible proportions.

Test Prep and Spiral Review

37. Multiple Choice Which of the following ratios is equivalent to the ratio 3:4?

Ⓐ 6:10 Ⓑ 8:6 Ⓒ 9:12 Ⓓ 10:40

38. Multiple Choice Which of the following does NOT form a proportion?

Ⓕ $\frac{5}{8} = \frac{10}{16}$ Ⓖ $\frac{15}{24} = \frac{10}{16}$ Ⓗ $\frac{5}{9} = \frac{10}{16}$ Ⓙ $\frac{25}{40} = \frac{10}{16}$

39. Short Response One ticket to the aquarium costs $10.50. Three tickets to the aquarium cost $31.50. Are ticket prices proportional? If so, how much would 4 tickets cost?

Compare. Write < or >. (Lesson 1-9)

40. 2 + 5 ■ 8 **41.** 27 − 11 ■ 15 **42.** 2(7) ■ 27 **43.** 17 + 18 ■ 27

Multiply. (Lesson 2-4)

44. −2.4(−7) **45.** 3.2(−1.7) **46.** −0.03(8.6) **47.** −1.07(−0.6)

5-2 Ratios, Rates, and Unit Rates

Learn to work with rates and ratios.

Vocabulary

rate

unit rate

unit price

Density is a ratio that compares mass and volume. Different substances have different densities. For example, gold has a density of $\frac{19{,}300 \text{ kg}}{1 \text{ m}^3}$, or 19,300 kilograms per cubic meter.

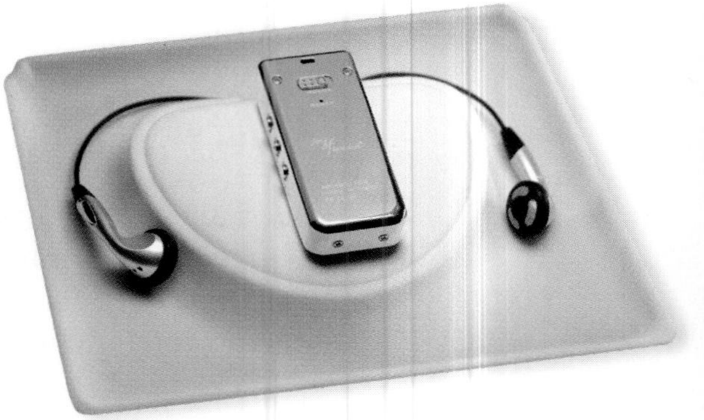

The Excentrique MP-400 MP3 player is made of 24-carat gold.

A **rate** is a comparison of two quantities that have different units.

ratio: $\frac{90}{3}$ rate: $\frac{90 \text{ miles}}{3 \text{ hours}}$ ← *Read as "90 miles per 3 hours."*

Unit rates are rates in which the second quantity is 1. The ratio $\frac{90}{3}$ can be simplified by dividing: $\frac{90}{3} = \frac{30}{1}$.

unit rate: $\frac{30 \text{ miles}}{1 \text{ hour}}$, or 30 mi/h

EXAMPLE 1 Finding Unit Rates

Miki can type 120 words in 3 minutes. How many words can she type per minute?

$\frac{120 \text{ words}}{3 \text{ minutes}}$ *Write the rate.*

$\frac{120 \text{ words} \div 3}{3 \text{ minutes} \div 3} = \frac{40 \text{ words}}{1 \text{ minute}}$ *Divide to find words per minute.*

Miki can type 40 words in one minute.

Since density is measured in units of mass per unit of volume, it is a unit rate.

EXAMPLE 2 *Chemistry Application*

A **Four cubic meters of silver has a mass of 41,960 kilograms. What is the density of silver?**

$\frac{41{,}960 \text{ kg}}{4 \text{ m}^3}$ *Write the rate.*

$\frac{41{,}960 \text{ kg} \div 4}{4 \text{ m}^3 \div 4}$ *Divide to find kilograms per 1 m^3.*

$\frac{10{,}490 \text{ kg}}{1 \text{ m}^3}$

Silver has a density of 10,490 kg/m^3

B **Aluminum weighing 1350 kilograms has a volume of 0.5 cubic meters. What is the density of aluminum?**

$\frac{1350 \text{ kg}}{0.5 \text{ m}^3}$ *Write the rate.*

$\frac{1350 \text{ kg} \cdot 2}{0.5 \text{ m}^3 \cdot 2}$ *Multiply to find kilograms per 1 m^3.*

$\frac{2700 \text{ kg}}{1 \text{ m}^3}$

Aluminum has a density of 2700 kg/m^3.

EXAMPLE 3 Estimating Unit Rates

Estimate each unit rate.

A 323 students to 11 teachers

$$\frac{323 \text{ students}}{11 \text{ teachers}} \approx \frac{319 \text{ students}}{11 \text{ teachers}}$$

Choose a number close to 323 that is divisible by 11.

$$\approx \frac{29 \text{ students}}{1 \text{ teacher}}$$

Divide to find students per teacher.

323 students to 11 teachers is approximately 29 students per teacher.

B 560 miles in 9 hours

$$\frac{560 \text{ miles}}{9 \text{ hours}} \approx \frac{560 \text{ miles}}{10 \text{ hours}}$$

Choose a number close to 9 that is a factor of 560.

$$\approx \frac{56 \text{ miles}}{1 \text{ hour}}$$

Divide to find miles per hour.

560 miles in 9 hours is approximately 56 miles per hour.

Unit price is a unit rate used to compare price per item.

EXAMPLE 4 Finding Unit Prices to Compare Costs

A Blank CD's can be purchased in packages of 3 for \$1.99 or 20 for \$10.99. Which is the better buy?

$$\frac{\text{price for package}}{\text{number of CD's}} = \frac{\$1.99}{3 \text{ CD's}} \approx \$0.66 \text{ per CD}$$

$$\frac{\text{price for package}}{\text{number of CD's}} = \frac{\$10.99}{20 \text{ CD's}} \approx \$0.55 \text{ per CD}$$

Divide the price by the number of CD's.

The better buy is the package of 20 for \$10.99.

B Arnie can buy a 16 oz box of cereal for \$5.49 or a 20 oz box for \$5.99. Which is the better buy?

$$\frac{\text{price for box}}{\text{number of ounces}} = \frac{\$5.49}{16 \text{ oz}} \approx \$0.34/\text{oz}$$

$$\frac{\text{price for box}}{\text{number of ounces}} = \frac{\$5.99}{20 \text{ oz}} \approx \$0.30/\text{oz}$$

Divide the price by the number of ounces.

The better buy is the 20 oz box for \$5.99.

Think and Discuss

1. **Choose** the quantity that has a lower unit price: 6 oz for \$1.29 or 15 oz for \$3.00. Explain your answer.
2. **Determine** two different units of measurement for speed.

5-2 Exercises

go.hrw.com
Homework Help Online
KEYWORD: MT7 5-2
Parent Resources Online
KEYWORD: MT7 Parent

GUIDED PRACTICE

See Example 1
1. Ana Maria walks 9 miles in 3 hours. How many miles does she walk per hour?

See Example 2
2. A nickel has a mass of 5 g and a volume of approximately 0.689 cm^3. What is the approximate density of a nickel?

See Example 3
Estimate each unit rate.

3. 121 students in 3 buses
4. $31.50 for 4 hours
5. 4008 Calories for 8 servings of pot pie
6. 10 laps in 22 minutes

See Example 4
7. A 16 oz box of crackers costs $3.99 and a 38 oz box of crackers costs $6.99. Which is the better buy?

INDEPENDENT PRACTICE

See Example 1
8. Kenji earns $32 in 4 hours. How much does he earn per hour?

See Example 2
9. The mass of a diamond is 1.76 g. The volume is 0.5 cm^3. What is the density of the diamond?

See Example 3
Estimate each unit rate.

10. 268 chairs in 9 rows
11. 9 cups of flour for 4 batches of muffins
12. $59.95 for 5 CDs
13. $2.19 for $\frac{1}{2}$ pound

See Example 4
14. One yard of ribbon costs $0.49 and 3 yards of ribbon costs $1.49. Which is the better buy?
15. A 16 oz package of brown rice costs $0.79 and a 32 oz package of brown rice costs $3.49. Which is the better buy?

PRACTICE AND PROBLEM SOLVING

Extra Practice
See page 790.

Find each unit rate.

16. travel 804 miles in 16 hours
17. score 84 points in 6 games
18. $7.05 for 3 tacos
19. 64 beats in 4 measures of music

Estimate each unit rate.

20. $107 for 22 magazines
21. 250 heartbeats in 6 minutes
22. 295 words in 6 minutes
23. 17 apples weigh 4 pounds

Find each unit price and tell which is the better buy.

24. $3.99 for 25 fl oz of detergent or $6.99 for 90 fl oz of detergent
25. $\frac{2}{3}$ pound of walnuts for $2.50 or $\frac{1}{2}$ pound of walnuts for $2.25

26. **Multi-Step** Before 1986, a gold bullion in the Federal Reserve Bank was rectangular and had a volume of approximately 727.7 cm^3. The density of gold is 19.3 g/cm^3. A pound is approximately 454 g. Find the weight of one gold bullion to the nearest tenth of a pound.

27. **Estimation** Maura received $790 for work she did for a catering company during one week. Find Maura's approximate daily rate.

28. **Entertainment** Tom, Cherise, and Tina work as film animators. The circle graph shows the number of frames each rendered in an 8-hour day.

    a. Find the hourly unit rendering rate for each employee.

    b. Who was the most efficient?

    c. How many more frames per hour did Cherise render than Tom?

    d. How many more frames per hour did Tom and Cherise together render than Tina?

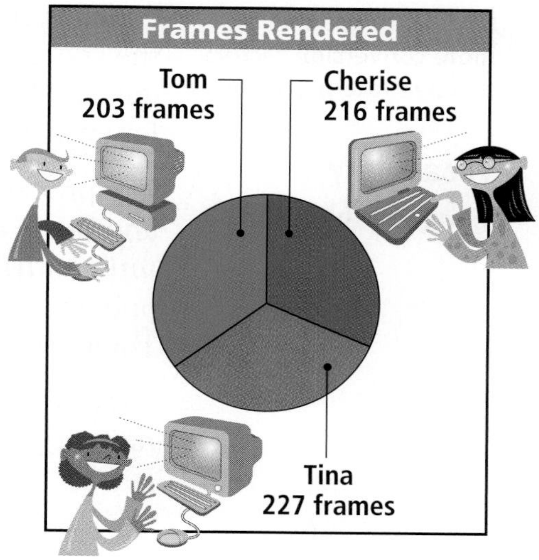

29. **What's the Error?** A clothing store charges $25 for 4 T-shirts. A student says that the unit price is $0.16 per T-shirt. What is the error? What is the correct unit price?

30. **Write About It** Explain how to find unit rates. Give an example, and explain how consumers can use unit rates to save money.

31. **Challenge** The size of a television (13 in., 25 in., 32 in., and so on) represents the length of the diagonal of the television screen. An aspect ratio describes a screen by comparing its width to its height. A 25 in. television has an aspect ratio of 4:3. What is the width and height of the screen?

Test Prep and Spiral Review

32. **Multiple Choice** A 24 lb bag of dog food sells for $10.56. What is the unit price per pound?

Ⓐ $0.44/lb Ⓑ $0.53/lb Ⓒ $13.44/lb Ⓓ $34.56/lb

33. **Extended Response** Flowers can be purchased in bunches of 4 for $2.48 or 6 for $3.96. Which is the better buy? Explain.

Solve. (Lesson 1-7)

34. $p - 8 = 12$ 35. $y + 9 = 15$ 36. $w - 7 = 8$ 37. $k + 4 = 11$

Find two ratios that are equivalent to each given ratio. (Lesson 5-1)

38. $\frac{3}{5}$ 39. $\frac{13}{26}$ 40. $\frac{4}{11}$ 41. $\frac{10}{9}$

5-3 Dimensional Analysis

Problem Solving Skill

Learn to use one or more conversion factors to solve rate problems.

Vocabulary

conversion factor

Officials at tennis tournaments can determine the speed of a serve by using radar. A radar gun sends out radio waves to determine how far away the ball is at given intervals of time.

The process of converting from one unit to another is called *dimensional analysis*, or *unit analysis*. To convert units, multiply by one or more ratios of equal quantities called **conversion factors**.

For example, to convert inches to feet use the ratio $\frac{1\text{ ft}}{12\text{ in.}}$ as a conversion factor.

$$\frac{1\text{ ft}}{12\text{ in.}} = \frac{12\text{ in.}}{12\text{ in.}} = \frac{1\text{ ft}}{1\text{ ft}}, = 1$$

Multiplying by a conversion factor is like multiplying by 1.

EXAMPLE 1 Finding Conversion Factors

Caution!

Be sure to put the units you are converting to in the numerator and the units you are converting from in the denominator.

Find the appropriate factor for each conversion.

A ounces to pounds

There are 16 ounces in 1 pound. To convert ounces to pounds, multiply the number of **ounces** by $\frac{1\text{ lb}}{16\text{ oz}}$.

B kilometers to meters

There are 1000 meters in 1 kilometer. To convert kilometers to meters, multiply the number of **kilometers** by $\frac{1000\text{ m}}{1\text{ km}}$.

EXAMPLE 2 Using Conversion Factors to Solve Problems

In the United States in 2003, the average person drank approximately 22 gallons of milk. Find the number of quarts of milk the average person drank.

Convert the ratio 22 *gallons* per year to *quarts* per year.

$\frac{22\text{ gal}}{1\text{ yr}} \cdot \frac{4\text{ qt}}{1\text{ gal}}$ *Multiply the ratio by the conversion factor.*

$= \frac{22 \cdot 4\text{ qt}}{1\text{ yr}}$ *Divide out like units.* $\frac{\cancel{gal}}{yr} \cdot \frac{qt}{\cancel{gal}} = \frac{qt}{yr}$

$= 88$ qt per year *Multiply 22 by 4 qt.*

The average person drank 88 quarts of milk in 2003.

EXAMPLE 3 PROBLEM SOLVING APPLICATION

PROBLEM SOLVING

A car traveled 330 feet down a road in 5 seconds. How many miles per hour was the car traveling?

1 Understand the Problem

The problem is stated in units of **feet** and **seconds**. The question asks for the **answer** in units of **miles** and **hours**. You will need to use several conversion factors.

List the important information:

- Feet to miles ⟶ $\frac{1 \text{ mi}}{5280 \text{ ft}}$
- Seconds to minutes ⟶ $\frac{60 \text{ s}}{1 \text{ min}}$
- Minutes to hours ⟶ $\frac{60 \text{ min}}{1 \text{ h}}$

2 Make a Plan

Multiply by each conversion factor separately, or **simplify the problem** and multiply by several conversion factors at once.

3 Solve

$\frac{330 \text{ ft}}{5 \text{ s}} = \frac{(330 \div 5) \text{ ft}}{(5 \div 5) \text{ s}} = \frac{66 \text{ ft}}{1 \text{ s}}$ *Convert 330 feet in 5 seconds into a unit rate.*

$\frac{60 \text{ s}}{1 \text{ min}} \cdot \frac{60 \text{ min}}{1 \text{ h}} = \frac{3600 \text{ s}}{1 \text{ h}}$ *Convert seconds directly to hours.*

$\frac{66 \text{ ft}}{1 \text{ s}} \cdot \frac{1 \text{ mi}}{5280 \text{ ft}} \cdot \frac{3600 \text{ s}}{1 \text{ h}}$ *Set up the conversion factors.*

$\frac{66 \cancel{\text{ft}}}{1 \cancel{\text{s}}} \cdot \frac{1 \text{ mi}}{5280 \cancel{\text{ft}}} \cdot \frac{3600 \cancel{\text{s}}}{1 \text{ h}}$ *Divide out like units.*

$= \frac{66 \cdot 1 \text{ mi} \cdot 3600}{1 \cdot 5280 \cdot 1 \text{ h}} = \frac{237{,}600 \text{ mi}}{5280 \text{ h}}$ *Multiply.*

$= \frac{45 \text{ mi}}{1 \text{ h}}$ *Divide.*

The car was traveling 45 miles per hour.

4 Look Back

A rate of 45 mi/h is less than 1 mi/min. 5 seconds is $\frac{1}{12}$ min. A car traveling 45 mi/h would go less than $\frac{1}{12}$ of 5280 ft in 5 seconds. It goes 330 ft, so 45 mi/h is a reasonable speed.

EXAMPLE 4 ***Physical Science Application***

On June 11, 2004, tennis player Andy Roddick delivered the fastest tennis serve ever recorded by radar. If the radar gun being used that day sent out signals every $\frac{1}{10}$s and recorded the ball moving 269.28 in. between flashes, how fast was Andy Roddick's serve in mi/h?

$$\frac{269.28 \text{ in.}}{\frac{1}{10} \text{ s}}$$ *Use rate = $\frac{\text{distance}}{\text{time}}$.*

$$\frac{269.28 \text{ in.}}{\frac{1}{10} \text{ s}} = \frac{10 \cdot 269.28 \text{ in.}}{10 \cdot \frac{1}{10} \text{ s}}$$ *Multiply top and bottom by 10 to eliminate the fraction in the denominator.*

$$= \frac{2692.8 \text{ in.}}{1 \text{ s}}$$

Now convert inches per second to miles per hour.

$$\frac{2692.8 \cancel{\text{in.}}}{1\cancel{\text{s}}} \cdot \frac{1 \text{ mi}}{63{,}360 \cancel{\text{in.}}} \cdot \frac{3600\cancel{\text{s}}}{1\text{h}}$$ *Divide out like units.*

$$= \frac{2692.8 \cdot 1 \text{ mi} \cdot 3600}{1 \cdot 63{,}360 \cdot 1 \text{ h}}$$ *Multiply.*

$= 153$ mi/h *Divide.*

The serve traveled 153 mi/h.

Think and Discuss

1. **Give** the conversion factor for converting $\frac{\text{lb}}{\text{yr}}$ to $\frac{\text{lb}}{\text{mo}}$.
2. **Explain** how to find whether 10 mi/h is faster than 15 ft/s.

5-3 Exercises

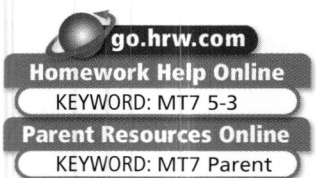

go.hrw.com
Homework Help Online
KEYWORD: MT7 5-3
Parent Resources Online
KEYWORD: MT7 Parent

GUIDED PRACTICE

See Example 1 **Find the appropriate factor for each conversion.**

1. minutes to seconds
2. quarts to gallons
3. grams to kilograms

See Example 2

4. Ali uses 12 gallons of gas for his car each week. Find the total number of quarts Ali uses in a year.

See Example 3

5. A model airplane flies 22 feet in 2 seconds. What is the airplane's speed in miles per hour?

See Example 4

6. If a bird flies 0.7 decimeter every tenth of a second, how fast in meters per second does it fly?

INDEPENDENT PRACTICE

See Example 1

Find the appropriate factor for each conversion.

7. meters to millimeters
8. feet to miles
9. minutes to hours

See Example 2

10. An Olympic athlete can run 110 yards in 10 seconds. How fast in miles per hour can the athlete run?

See Example 3

11. A yellow jacket can fly 4.5 meters in 9 seconds. How fast in kilometers per hour can a yellow jacket fly?

See Example 4

12. Anolin, Inc., produces cans at a rate of 0.03 per hundredth of a second. How many cans can be produced in a 7 hour day?

PRACTICE AND PROBLEM SOLVING

Extra Practice
See page 790.

Use conversion factors to find each of the following.

13. cereal boxes assembled in 4 minutes at a rate of 2 boxes per second
14. distance traveled in feet after 12 seconds at 87 miles per hour
15. fish caught in a day at a rate of 42 fish caught each week
16. concert tickets sold in an hour at a rate of 6 tickets sold per minute
17. miles jogged in 1 hour at an average rate of 8.5 feet per second
18. calls made in a 3 day telephone fund-raiser at a rate of 10 calls per hour
19. There are about 400 cocoa beans in a pound. There are 2.2 pounds in a kilogram. About how many grams does a cocoa bean weigh?
20. **Estimation** Assume that one dollar is equal to 1.14 euros. If 500 g of an item is selling for 25 euros, what is its approximate price in dollars per kilogram?
21. **Food** The largest block of cheese on record weighed 920,136 oz. How many tons is this?
22. **Sports** Use the graph to find each world-record speed in miles per hour. (*Hint:* 1 mi ≈ 1609 m.)
23. **Transportation** The rate of one knot equals one nautical mile per hour. One nautical mile is 1852 meters. What is the speed in meters per second of a ship traveling at 20 knots?

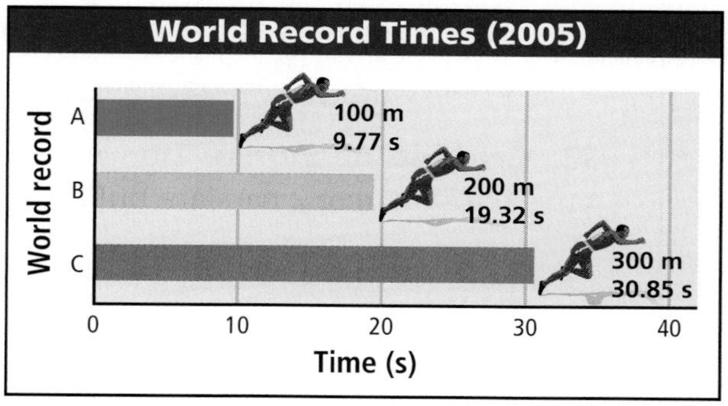

24. **Life Science** The Dolphin Bay exhibit at the Texas State Aquarium holds about 400,000 gallons of saltwater. How many days would it take to fill the exhibit at a rate of 1 gallon per second?

25. **Life Science** A vampire bat consumes approximately 2 tablespoons of animal blood each day. Approximately how many gallons of blood does a vampire bat consume in a year? (*Hint:* 1 tablespoon = 0.5 ounce)

26. **Transportation** The longest runway at Chicago's O'Hare International Airport is 13,001 ft long. The longest runway at New York's JFK International Airport is 2.76 miles long. Which runway is longer? Justify your answer.

27. **Choose a Strategy** Sondra's recipe for barbecue sauce calls for 3 tablespoons of brown sugar. Sondra does not have a tablespoon. Which spoon can Sondra use to measure the sugar? (*Hint:* 1 tablespoon = $\frac{1}{2}$ ounce)

    Ⓐ 2.5 oz spoon
    Ⓑ 2 oz spoon
    Ⓒ 1.5 oz spoon
    Ⓓ None of these

28. **What's the Error?** To convert 7 meters per second to kilometers per hour, a student wrote $\frac{7\text{ m}}{1\text{ s}} \cdot \frac{1\text{ km}}{1000\text{ m}} \cdot \frac{60\text{ s}}{1\text{ h}} = 0.42$ km/h. What error did the student make? What should the correct answer be?

29. **Write About It** Describe the important role that conversion factors play in solving rate problems. Give an example.

30. **Challenge** Convert each measure. (*Hint:* 1 oz = 28.35 g)

    a. 8 oz = ▒ g
    b. 198.45 g = ▒ oz
    c. 538.65 g = ▒ lb
    d. 1.5625 lb = ▒ g

Test Prep and Spiral Review

31. **Multiple Choice** A boat travels 110 feet in 5 seconds. What is the boat's speed in miles per hour?

    Ⓐ 11 mi/h Ⓑ 15 mi/h Ⓒ 20 mi/h Ⓓ 22.5 mi/h

32. **Multiple Choice** How long would it take to drain a 750-gallon hot tub at a rate of 112.5 gallons per minute?

    Ⓕ 45 minutes Ⓖ 55 minutes Ⓗ 60 minutes Ⓙ 80 minutes

33. **Gridded Response** How many cars are produced in 12 hours at a factory where 2 cars are built every 45 minutes?

Evaluate. (Lesson 4-3)

34. $\frac{3^9}{3^2}$
35. $2^5 \cdot 2^{-7}$
36. $\frac{w^5}{w^1}$
37. $\frac{10^2}{10^{-10}}$
38. $\frac{8^3}{8^2}$
39. $2^3 \cdot 2^4$
40. $\frac{4^7}{4^5}$
41. $m^5 \cdot m^8$

Find each unit price. (Lesson 5-2)

42. \$11.98 for 2 yd of fencing
43. 20 oz of cereal for \$3.49
44. 4 tickets for \$110
45. \$747 for 3 computer monitors

5-4 Solving Proportions

Learn to solve proportions.

Vocabulary

cross product

Unequal masses will not balance on a *fulcrum* if they are an equal distance from it; one side will go up and the other side will go down.

Alexander Calder's sculpture *Totem* stands in Paris. Calder is known as the father of the mobile.

Unequal masses will balance when the following proportion is true:

$$\frac{\text{mass 1}}{\text{length 2}} = \frac{\text{mass 2}}{\text{length 1}}$$

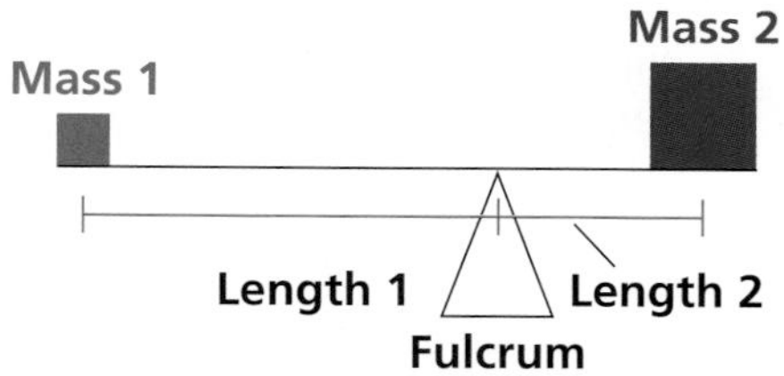

One way to find whether ratios are equal is to find a common denominator. Since $\frac{6}{8} = \frac{72}{96}$ and $\frac{9}{12} = \frac{72}{96}$, $\frac{6}{8}$ is equal to $\frac{9}{12}$.

Helpful Hint

The cross product represents the numerator of the fraction when a common denominator is found by multiplying the denominators.

CROSS PRODUCTS

Cross products in proportions are equal. If the ratios are *not* in proportion, the cross products are not equal.

Proportions		***Not* Proportions**	
$\frac{6}{8} = \frac{9}{12}$	$\frac{5}{2} = \frac{15}{6}$	$\frac{1}{6} \neq \frac{2}{7}$	$\frac{5}{12} \neq \frac{2}{5}$
$6 \cdot 12 = 8 \cdot 9$	$5 \cdot 6 = 2 \cdot 15$	$1 \cdot 7 \neq 6 \cdot 2$	$5 \cdot 5 \neq 12 \cdot 2$
$72 = 72$	$30 = 30$	$7 \neq 12$	$25 \neq 24$

EXAMPLE 1 Using Cross Products to Identify Proportions

A **Tell whether the ratios $\frac{5}{6}$ and $\frac{15}{21}$ are proportional.**

$\frac{5}{6} \stackrel{?}{=} \frac{15}{21}$

$\frac{5}{6} \times \frac{15}{21}$ → 90, 105 *Find the cross products.*

$105 \neq 90$

Since the cross products are not equal, the ratios are not proportional.

B A shade of paint is made by mixing 5 parts red paint with 7 parts blue paint. If you mix 21 quarts of blue paint with 15 quarts of red paint, will you get the correct shade? Explain.

$\frac{5 \text{ parts red}}{7 \text{ parts blue}} \stackrel{?}{=} \frac{15 \text{ quarts red}}{21 \text{ quarts blue}}$ *Set up equal ratios.*

$5 \cdot 21 = 105 \quad 7 \cdot 15 = 105$ *Find the cross products.*

$105 = 105$

The cross products are equal. You will get the correct shade of paint.

To solve problems involving proportional relationships, you can use unit rates, equivalent fractions, factors of change, or cross products.

EXAMPLE 2 Solving Proportions Using Unit Rates

Solve the proportion $\frac{\$d}{12 \text{ items}} = \frac{\$96}{4 \text{ items}}$.

$\frac{\$d}{12 \text{ items}} = \frac{\$96}{4 \text{ items}}$

$\frac{\$(d \div 12)}{1 \text{ item}} = \frac{\$24}{1 \text{ item}}$ *Find the unit rates.*

$d \div 12 = 24$ *The numerators are equal because the denominators are equal.*

$12(d \div 12) = 12(24)$ *Multiply both sides by 12.*

$d = \$288$ *Simplify.*

EXAMPLE 3 Solving Proportions Using Equivalent Fractions

Solve the proportion $\frac{x}{6} = \frac{4}{8}$.

$\frac{x}{6} = \frac{4}{8}$

$\frac{(x \cdot 4)}{(6 \cdot 4)} = \frac{(4 \cdot 3)}{(8 \cdot 3)}$ *Multiply to write the fractions with the LCD.*

$\frac{4x}{24} = \frac{12}{24}$

$4x = 12$ *The numerators are equal because the denominators are equal.*

$\frac{4x}{4} = \frac{12}{4}$ *Divide both sides by 4.*

$x = 3$ *Simplify.*

EXAMPLE 4 *Business Application*

On "2 fer Tuesday", 2 bagels with cream cheese cost \$2.50. Jimmy wants to buy 2 dozen. How much will this cost?

2 dozen bagels = 24 bagels

$\frac{2 \text{ bagels}}{\$2.50} = \frac{24 \text{ bagels}}{\$d}$ *Set up the proportion.*

$\frac{24 \text{ bagels}}{2 \text{ bagels}} = 12$ *Divide to find the factor of change.*

$\$2.50 \cdot 12 = \$30$ *Multiply by the factor of change to find cost.*

EXAMPLE 5 ***Physical Science Application***

Two children can be balanced on a seesaw when $\frac{\text{mass 1}}{\text{length 2}} = \frac{\text{mass 2}}{\text{length 1}}$. The child on the left and the child on the right are balanced. What is the mass of the child on the right?

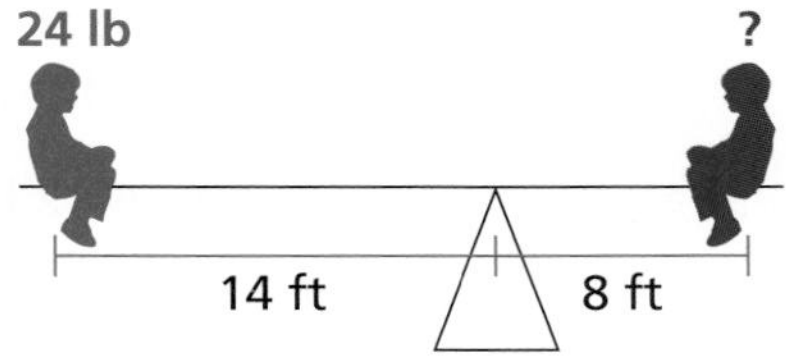

$\frac{24}{8} = \frac{m}{14}$ *Set up the proportion.*

$24 \cdot 14 = 8m$ *Find the cross products.*

$\frac{336}{8} = \frac{8m}{8}$ *Divide both sides by 8.*

$42 = m$ *Simplify.*

The mass of the child on the right is 42 lb.

Think and Discuss

1. **Explain** what the cross products of two ratios represent.
2. **Tell** what it means if the cross products are not equal.
3. **Describe** how to solve a proportion when one of the four numbers is a variable.

5-4 Exercises

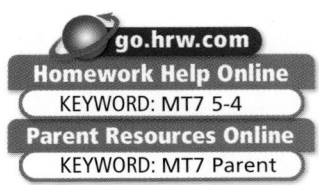

go.hrw.com
Homework Help Online
KEYWORD: MT7 5-4
Parent Resources Online
KEYWORD: MT7 Parent

GUIDED PRACTICE

See Example 1

Tell whether the ratios are proportional.

1. $\frac{6}{12} \stackrel{?}{=} \frac{12}{24}$
2. $\frac{2}{9} \stackrel{?}{=} \frac{6}{27}$
3. $\frac{5}{7} \stackrel{?}{=} \frac{10}{15}$
4. $\frac{10}{25} \stackrel{?}{=} \frac{6}{15}$
5. A bubble solution can be made with a ratio of 1 part detergent to 8 parts water. Would a mixture of 56 oz water and 8 oz detergent be proportional to this ratio? Explain.

See Example 2

Solve each proportion.

6. $\frac{\$d}{\text{12 hours}} = \frac{\$96}{\text{8 hours}}$
7. $\frac{m\text{ miles}}{\text{6 hours}} = \frac{\text{110 mile}}{\text{2 hours}}$
8. $\frac{s\text{ students}}{\text{6 teachers}} = \frac{\text{209 students}}{\text{11 teachers}}$
9. $\frac{\$d}{\text{4 enchiladas}} = \frac{\$13.50}{\text{6 enchiladas}}$
10. $\frac{c\text{ Calories}}{\text{3 servings}} = \frac{\text{290 Calories}}{\text{2 servings}}$
11. $\frac{p\text{ photos}}{\text{13 orders}} = \frac{\text{441 photos}}{\text{21 orders}}$

See Example 3 12. $\frac{x}{5} = \frac{3.78}{10}$ 13. $\frac{w}{20} = \frac{210}{8}$ 14. $\frac{s}{4} = \frac{15}{6}$ 15. $\frac{g}{6} = \frac{25}{15}$

See Example 4 16. Mitchell bought 3 postcards for $3.14. At this rate, how much would 12 postcards cost?

See Example 5 17. A 12 lb weight is positioned 8 in. from a fulcrum. At what distance from the fulcrum must an 18 lb weight be positioned to keep the scale balanced?

INDEPENDENT PRACTICE

See Example 1 **Tell whether the ratios are proportional.**

18. $\frac{22}{42} \stackrel{?}{=} \frac{3}{7}$ 19. $\frac{17}{51} \stackrel{?}{=} \frac{2}{6}$ 20. $\frac{40}{36} \stackrel{?}{=} \frac{20}{16}$ 21. $\frac{8}{9} \stackrel{?}{=} \frac{40}{45}$

22. An after-school club had 10 girls and 12 boys. Then 5 more girls and 6 more boys signed up. Did the ratio of girls to boys stay the same? Explain.

See Example 2 **Solve each proportion.**

23. $\frac{\$d}{8 \text{ CDs}} = \frac{\$38.97}{3 \text{ CDs}}$ 24. $\frac{c \text{ chairs}}{9 \text{ rows}} = \frac{27 \text{ chairs}}{3 \text{ rows}}$

25. $\frac{\$d}{4 \text{ tickets}} = \frac{\$72}{6 \text{ tickets}}$ 26. $\frac{m \text{ minutes}}{8 \text{ miles}} = \frac{24 \text{ minutes}}{3 \text{ miles}}$

27. $\frac{c}{\text{computers}} = \frac{20 \text{ computers}}{25 \text{ students}}$ 28. $\frac{t \text{ tissues}}{5 \text{ packages}} = \frac{1500 \text{ tissues}}{30 \text{ packages}}$

See Example 3 29. $\frac{b}{15} = \frac{6}{10}$ 30. $\frac{c}{9} = \frac{4}{6}$ 31. $\frac{h}{9} = \frac{16}{6}$ 32. $\frac{c}{9} = \frac{8}{6}$

33. $\frac{q}{7} = \frac{19}{133}$ 34. $\frac{j}{18} = \frac{10}{60}$ 35. $\frac{d}{24} = \frac{15}{40}$ 36. $\frac{s}{50} = \frac{3}{15}$

See Example 4 37. Zoe bought 4 book covers for $7.50. At this rate, how much would 12 book covers cost?

See Example 5 38. A 150 kg weight is positioned 3 m from a fulcrum. If a 200 kg weight is placed at the opposite end of the balance, how far from the fulcrum should it be positioned?

PRACTICE AND PROBLEM SOLVING

Extra Practice
See page 790.

For each set of ratios, find the two that are proportional.

39. $\frac{8}{4}, \frac{24}{12}, \frac{55}{27}$ 40. $\frac{1}{4}, \frac{4}{16}, \frac{110}{444}$ 41. $\frac{35}{26}, \frac{81}{39}, \frac{27}{13}$

42. $\frac{49}{182}, \frac{7}{26}, \frac{45}{160}$ 43. $\frac{0.5}{6}, \frac{0.25}{9}, \frac{1}{12}$ 44. $\frac{a}{c}, \frac{a}{b}, \frac{4a}{4b}$

45. $\frac{1.1}{11}, \frac{10}{110}, \frac{11}{121}$ 46. $\frac{13}{50}, \frac{91}{350}, \frac{26}{75}$ 47. $\frac{7}{15}, \frac{70}{165}, \frac{84}{180}$

48. **Physical Science** One molecule of nitrogen reacting with 3 molecules of hydrogen makes 2 molecules of ammonia. How many molecules of nitrogen must react with 42 molecules of hydrogen to make 28 molecules of ammonia?

49. **Multi-Step** Jacob is selling T-shirts at a music festival. Yesterday, he sold 51 shirts and earned $191.25. How many shirts must Jacob sell today and tomorrow to earn a total of $536.25 for all three days?

Health LINK

A doctor reports blood pressure in millimeters of mercury (mm Hg) as a ratio of *systolic* blood pressure to *diastolic* blood pressure (such as 140 over 80). Systolic pressure is measured when the heart beats, and diastolic pressure is measured when it rests. Refer to the table of blood pressure ranges for adults for Exercise 40.

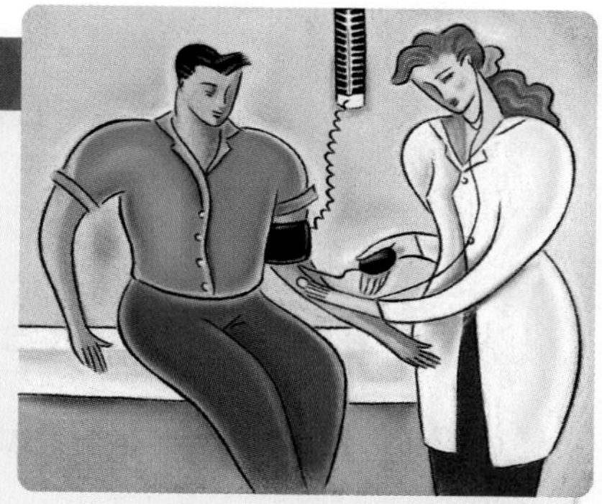

The disc-like shape of red blood cells allows them to pass through tiny capillaries.

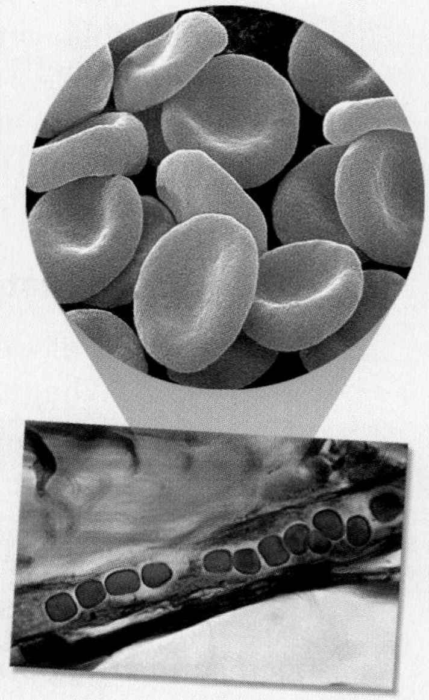

Blood Pressure Ranges

	Normal	Prehypertension	Hypertension (very high)
Systolic	under 120 mm Hg	120–139 mm Hg	140 mm Hg and above
Diastolic	under 80 mm Hg	80–89 mm Hg	90 mm Hg and above

50. **Estimation** Eduardo is a healthy 37-year-old man whose blood pressure is in the normal category.

a. Calculate an approximate ratio of systolic to diastolic blood pressure in the normal range.

b. If Eduardo's systolic blood pressure is 102 mm Hg, use the ratio from part **a** to predict his diastolic blood pressure.

51. **Write About It** A ratio related to heart health is LDL cholesterol to HDL cholesterol. The optimal ratio of LDL to HDL is below 3. A patient's total cholesterol is 168 and HDL is 44. Is the patient's ratio optimal? Explain.

52. **Challenge** The sum of Ken's LDL and HDL cholesterol is 210, and his LDL to HDL ratio is 2.75. What are his LDL and HDL?

go.hrw.com
Web Extra!
KEYWORD: MT7 Health

TEST PREP and Spiral Review

53. **Multiple Choice** A tree was 3.5 feet tall after 2 years and 8.75 feet tall after 5 years. If the tree grew at a constant rate, how tall was it after 3 years?

Ⓐ 5 feet Ⓑ 5.25 feet Ⓒ 5.75 feet Ⓓ 6.5 feet

54. **Gridded Response** What value of b makes the proportion $\frac{4}{5} = \frac{b}{20}$ true?

Divide. Write each answer in simplest form. (Lesson 2-5)

55. $\frac{3}{4} \div \frac{1}{2}$

56. $3\frac{1}{7} \div \left(-\frac{2}{21}\right)$

57. $-2\frac{1}{8} \div \left(-2\frac{1}{2}\right)$

58. A high speed train travels at 200 miles per hour. What is the train's speed in feet per second? (Lesson 5-3)

CHAPTER 5

READY TO GO ON?

SECTION 5A

Quiz for Lessons 5-1 Through 5-4

5-1 Ratios and Proportions

Simplify to tell whether the ratios form a proportion.

1. $\frac{6}{7}$ and $\frac{18}{21}$
2. $\frac{36}{48}$ and $\frac{12}{15}$
3. $\frac{12}{42}$ and $\frac{6}{21}$
4. $\frac{4}{5}$ and $\frac{16}{25}$

5. Cody is following a recipe that calls for 1.5 cups of flour to make 2 dozen mini corn muffins. He uses the amounts shown in the table to make 3 dozen mini corn muffins. Has he followed the recipe? Explain.

Flour (c)	Mini Corn Muffins (dozen)
1.5	2
2.5	3

5-2 Ratios, Rates, and Unit Rates

6. The mass of a piece of iron pyrite, or "fools gold," is 57.2 g. The volume is 11 cm^3. What is the density of the piece of iron pyrite?
7. Adela drinks 28 glasses of water per week. How many glasses does she drink per day?

Estimate each unit rate.

8. type 242 words in 6 minutes
9. $7.98 for 2 pounds

Determine the better buy.

10. a long distance phone charge of $1.40 for 10 min or $4.50 for 45 min
11. a dozen eggs for $2.78 or a half dozen for $1.49

5-3 Dimensional Analysis

Find the appropriate factor for each conversion.

12. pounds to ounces
13. feet to miles
14. minutes to days

Use conversion factors to find each unit to the nearest hundredth.

15. 10 quarts to gallons
16. 90 km per min to km per s
17. Driving at a constant rate, Shawna covered 325 miles 6.5 in hours. Express her driving rate in feet per minute.

5-4 Solving Proportions

Solve each proportion.

18. $\frac{\$180}{12 \text{ hours}} = \frac{\$d}{20 \text{ hours}}$
19. $\frac{360 \text{ miles}}{6 \text{ hours}} = \frac{m \text{ miles}}{4 \text{ hours}}$
20. Tim can input 110 data items in 2.5 minutes. Typing at the same rate, how many data items can he input in 7 minutes?

Ready to Go On?

Focus on Problem Solving

Solve

- **Choose an operation: multiplication or division**

When you are converting units, think about whether the number in the answer will be greater or less than the number given in the question. This will help you to decide whether to multiply or divide to convert the units.

For example, if you are converting feet to inches, you know that the number of inches will be greater than the number of feet because each foot is 12 inches. So you know that you should multiply by 12 to get a greater number.

In general, if you are converting to smaller units, the number of units will have to be greater to represent the same quantity.

For each problem, determine whether the number in the answer will be greater or less than the number given in the question. Use your answer to decide whether to multiply or divide by the conversion factor. Then solve the problem.

1. The speed a boat travels is usually measured in nautical miles per hour, or knots. The Staten Island Ferry in New York, which provides service between Manhattan and Staten Island, can travel at 15.5 knots. Find the speed in miles per hour. (*Hint:* 1 knot = 1.15 miles per hour)

2. When it is finished, the Crazy Horse Memorial in the Black Hills of South Dakota will be the world's largest sculpture. The sculpture's height will be 563 feet. Find the height in meters. (*Hint:* 1 meter = 3.28 feet)

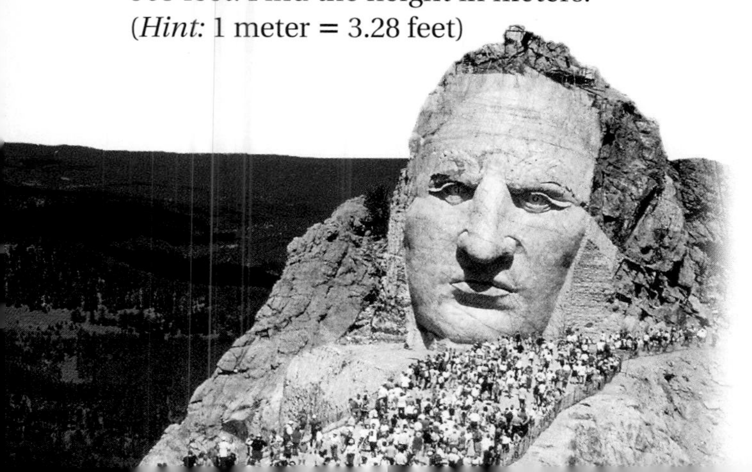

3. The grams of fat per serving of some common foods are given in the table below. Find the number of calories from fat for each serving. (*Hint:* 1 gram of fat = 9 calories)

Food	Fat per Serving (g)
Avocado (1 c, sliced)	22.3
Pretzels (1 oz)	1
Baked Potato (7 oz)	0.4
Plain Bagel (4 oz)	1.8

4. Nearly a quarter of the Texas Gulf Coast is national seashore or state park. At 372 miles long, it is undergoing a seaward advance at the rate of about 0.0095 miles per year. Find the length of the Texas shoreline in kilometers. (*Hint:* 1 mile = 1.61 kilometers)

Hands-On LAB 5-5

Explore Similarity

Use with Lesson 5-5

go.hrw.com
Lab Resources Online
KEYWORD: MT7 Lab5

WHAT YOU NEED:

- Two pieces of graph paper with different-sized boxes, such as 1 cm graph paper and $\frac{1}{4}$ in. graph paper
- Number cube
- Metric ruler
- Protractor

Triangles that have the same shape have some interesting relationships.

Activity

1 Follow the steps below to draw two triangles.

a. On a sheet of graph paper, plot a point below and to the left of the center of the paper. Label the point *A*. On the other sheet of paper, plot a point below and to the left of the center and label this point *D*.

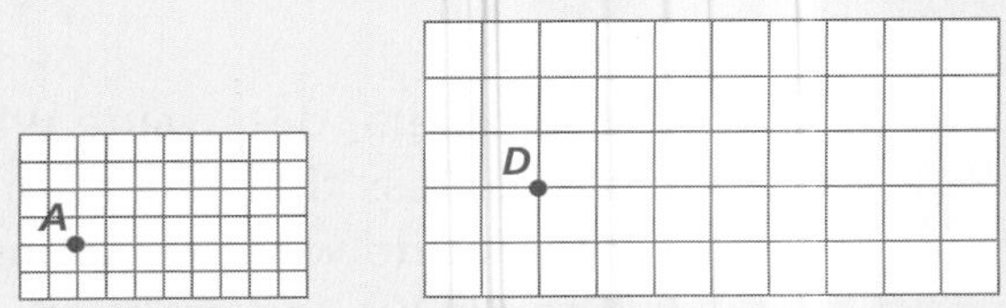

b. Roll a number cube twice. On each sheet of graph paper, move up the number on the first roll, move right the number on the second roll, and plot this location as point *B* on the first sheet and point *E* on the second sheet.

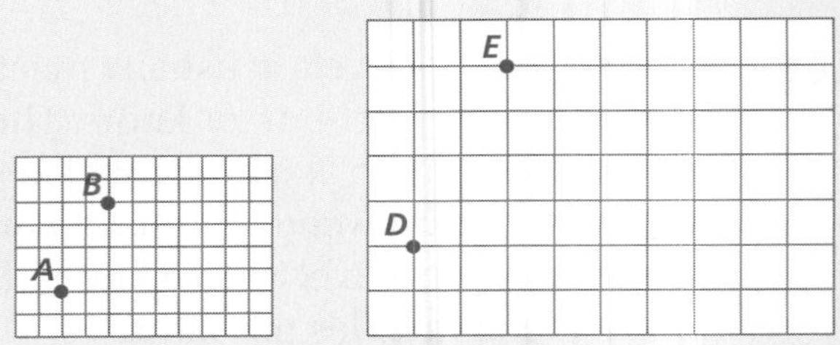

c. Roll the number cube twice again. On each sheet of graph paper, move down the number on the first roll, move right the number on the second roll, and plot point *C* on the first sheet and point *F* on the second sheet.

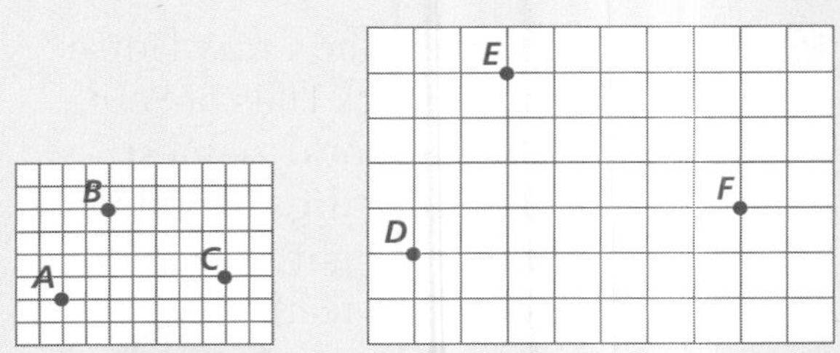

d. Connect the three points on each sheet of graph paper to form triangles *ABC* and *DEF*.

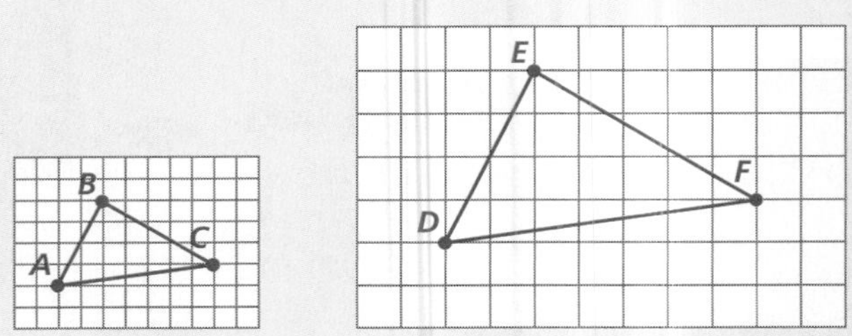

e. Measure the angles of each triangle. Measure the side lengths of each triangle to the nearest millimeter. Find the following:

$m\angle A$	$m\angle D$	$m\angle B$	$m\angle E$	$m\angle C$	$m\angle F$
AB	DE	$\frac{AB}{DE}$	BC	EF	$\frac{BC}{EF}$
AC	DF	$\frac{AC}{DF}$			

2 Follow the steps below to draw two triangles.

a. On one sheet of graph paper, plot a point below and to the left of the center of the paper. Label the point *A*.

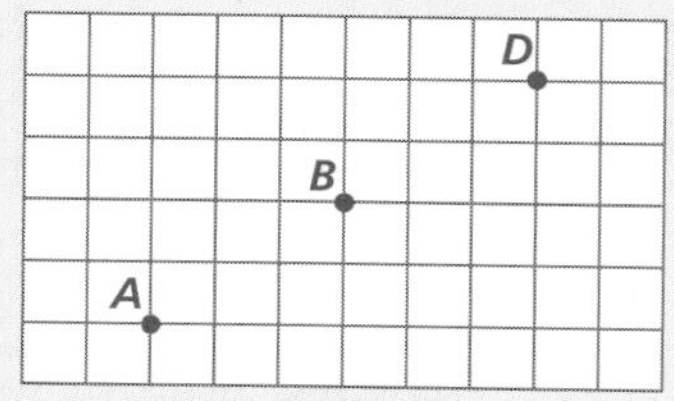

b. Roll a number cube twice. Move up the number on the first roll, move right the number on the second roll, and plot this location as point *B*. From *B*, move up the number on the first roll, move right the number on the second roll, and label this point *D*.

c. Roll a number cube twice. From *B*, move down the number on the first roll, move right the number on the second roll, and plot this location as point *C*.

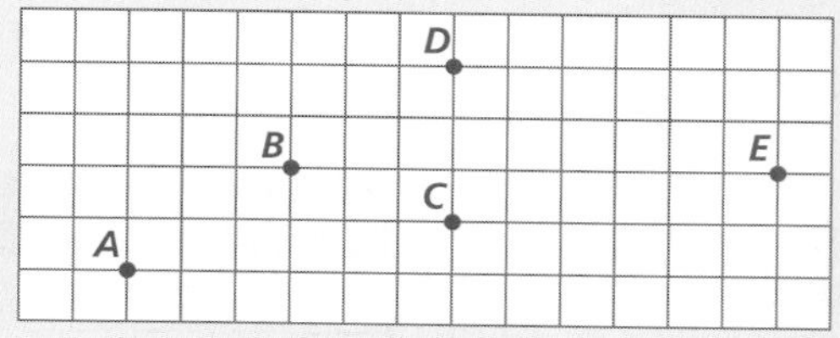

d. From *D*, move down twice the number on the first roll, move right twice the number on the second roll, and label this point *E*.

e. Connect points to form triangles *ABC* and *ADE*.

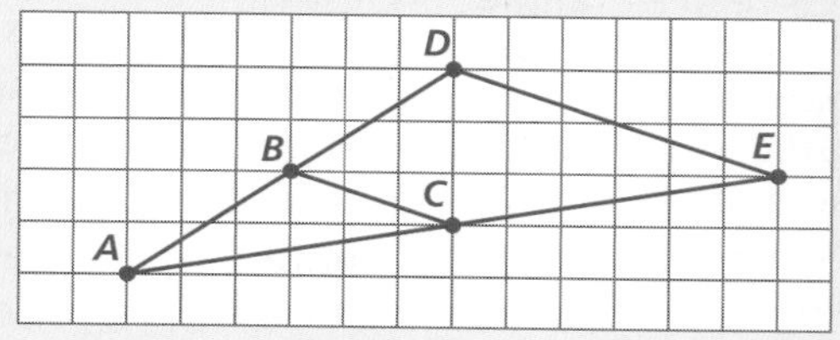

f. Measure the angles of each triangle. Measure the side lengths of each triangle to the nearest millimeter.

Think and Discuss

1. How do corresponding angles of triangles with the same shape compare?
2. How do corresponding side lengths of triangles with the same shape compare?
3. Suppose you enlarge a triangle on a copier machine. What measurements or values would be the same on the enlargement?

Try This

1. Make a small trapezoid on graph paper and triple the length of each side. Compare the angle measures and side lengths of the trapezoids.
2. Make a large polygon on graph paper. Use a copier to reduce the size of the polygon. Compare the angle measures and side lengths of the polygons.

5-5 Similar Figures

Learn to determine whether figures are similar, to use scale factors, and to find missing dimensions in similar figures.

Vocabulary

similar

congruent angles

scale factor

Photos that have been resized are examples of similar figures. Erin takes an 8 in. × 8 in. photo to a print shop. The printer reduces the image to a $3\frac{1}{2}$-inch × $3\frac{1}{2}$-inch photo and prints it onto a cube.

Similar figures have the same shape, but not necessarily the same size. Two triangles are similar if the lengths of corresponding sides are proportional and the corresponding angles are *congruent*. **Congruent angles** have equal measures.

Reading Math

$\angle A$ is read as "angle *A*." $\triangle ABC$ is read as "triangle *ABC*." "$\triangle ABC \sim \triangle EFG$" is read as "triangle *ABC* is similar to triangle *EFG*."

SIMILAR POLYGONS

Words	Diagram	Corresponding Parts
For two polygons to be similar, corresponding angles must be congruent, and corresponding sides must have lengths that form equivalent ratios.	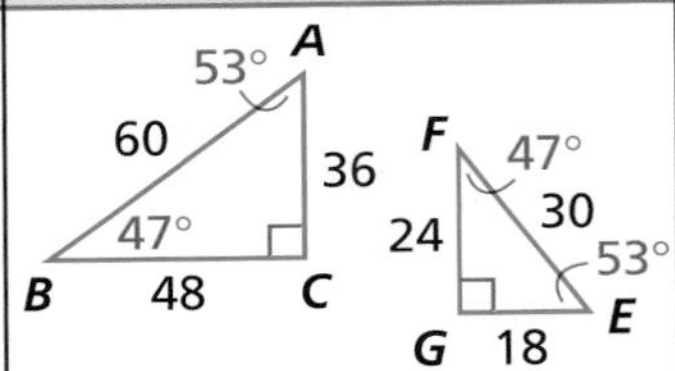 $\triangle ABC \sim \triangle EFG$	$\angle A$ and $\angle E$ $\angle B$ and $\angle F$ $\angle C$ and $\angle G$ $\frac{AB}{EF} = \frac{BC}{FG} = \frac{AC}{EG} = \frac{2}{1}$

EXAMPLE 1 Identifying Similar Figures

Which triangles are similar?

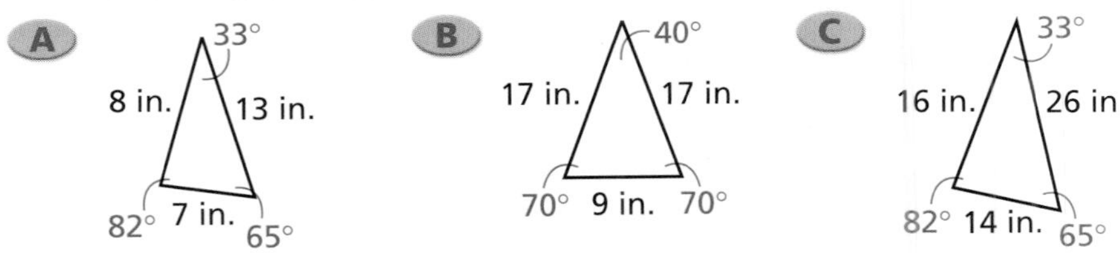

Both triangles *A* and *C* have angle measures of 82°, 33°, and 65°, while triangle *B* has angle measures of 70°, 40°, and 70°, so triangle *B* cannot be similar to triangles *A* or *C*.

Compare the ratios of corresponding sides in triangles *A* and *C* to see if they are equal.

$$\frac{13}{26} = \frac{7}{14} = \frac{8}{16} \text{ or } \frac{1}{2} = \frac{1}{2} = \frac{1}{2}$$

The ratios are equal. So triangle *A* is similar to triangle *C*.

The ratio formed by the corresponding sides is the **scale factor**.

EXAMPLE 2 Using Scale Factors to Find Missing Dimensions

A **A picture that is 8 in. tall and 10 in. wide is to be scaled to 3.5 in. tall to be displayed on a Web page. How wide should the picture be on the Web page for the two pictures to be similar?**

$\frac{3.5}{8} = 0.4375$ *Divide the height of the scaled picture by the corresponding height of the original picture.*

$0.4375 \cdot \mathbf{10}$ *Multiply the width of the original picture by the scale factor.*

4.375 *Simplify.*

The picture should be 4.375 in. wide.

B **In Jonathan Swift's *Gulliver's Travels,* the Lilliputians were only 6 inches tall. Suppose a Lilliputian's body is similar to a human's body. What is the length of a Lilliputian's femur, if a 5 ft tall person has a femur that is about 15 in. long?**

$\frac{6 \text{ in.}}{60 \text{ in.}} = 0.1$ *Divide the Lilliputian height by the human height, in inches, to find the scale factor.*

$0.1 \cdot \mathbf{15 \text{ in.}}$ *Multiply the length of the human femur by the scale factor.*

1.5 in. *Simplify.*

The Lilliputian's femur is approximately 1.5 in. long.

EXAMPLE 3 *Architecture Application*

Helpful Hint

Draw a diagram to help you visualize the problem.

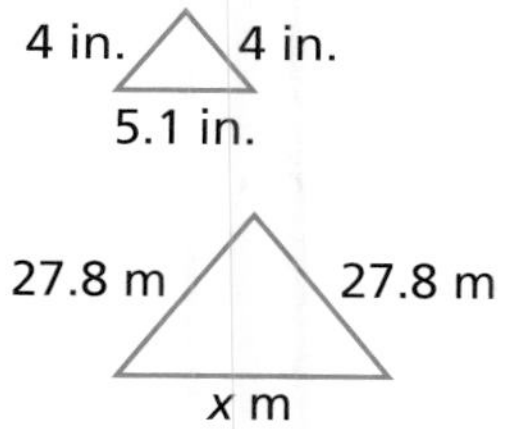

A souvenir model of the pyramid over the entrance of the Louvre in Paris has faces in the shape of a triangle. Two sides are each 4 in. long and the base is 5.1 in. long. On the actual pyramid, each triangular face has two sides that are each 27.8 m long. What is the length of the base of the actual pyramid?

$\frac{4 \text{ in.}}{27.8 \text{ m}} = \frac{5.1 \text{ in.}}{x \text{ m}}$ *Set up a proportion.*

$4 \text{ in.} \cdot x \text{ m} = 27.8 \text{ m} \cdot 5.1 \text{ in.}$ *Find the cross products.*

$4x = 27.8 \cdot 5.1$ *Divide out the units.*

$4x = 141.78$ *Multiply.*

$x = \frac{141.78}{4} = 35.445$ *Solve for x.*

The base of the actual pyramid is 35.445 m long.

Think and Discuss

1. **Compare** an image formed by a scale factor greater than 1 to an image formed by a scale factor less than 1.

5-5 Exercises

go.hrw.com
Homework Help Online
KEYWORD: MT7 5-5
Parent Resources Online
KEYWORD: MT7 Parent

GUIDED PRACTICE

See Example 1

1. Which triangles are similar?

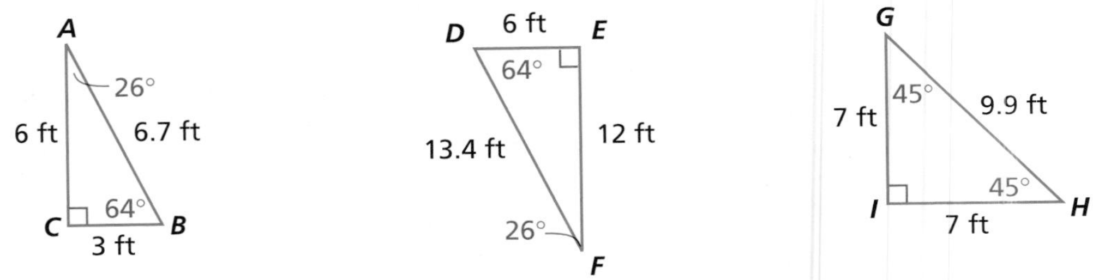

See Example 2

2. Gwen scans a photo that is 4 in. wide by 6 in. tall into her computer. If she scales the length down to 5 in., how wide should the similar photo be?

See Example 3

3. A triangle has a base of 11 cm and legs measuring 16 cm. How wide is the base of a similar triangle with legs measuring 24 cm?

INDEPENDENT PRACTICE

See Example 1

4. Which triangles are similar?

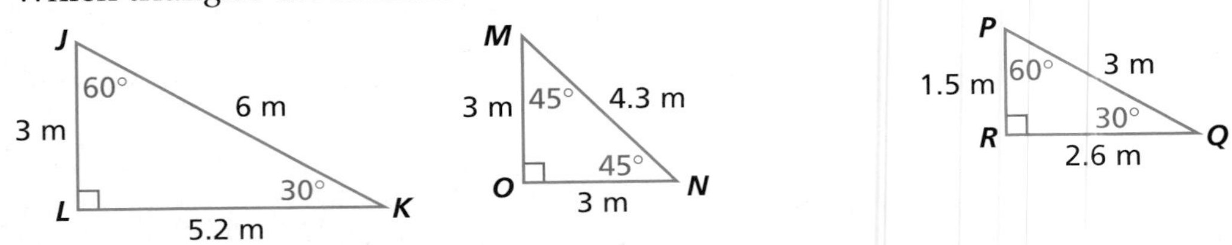

See Example 2

5. A rectangular park measures 6.5 mi wide and 9.1 mi long. On a map, the width of the park is 2.13 in. How long is the park on the map?

See Example 3

6. Vernon drew an 8 in. by 5 in. picture that will be turned into a 48 ft wide billboard. How tall will the billboard be?

PRACTICE AND PROBLEM SOLVING

Extra Practice
See page 791.

Tell whether the figures are similar. If they are not similar, explain.

7.

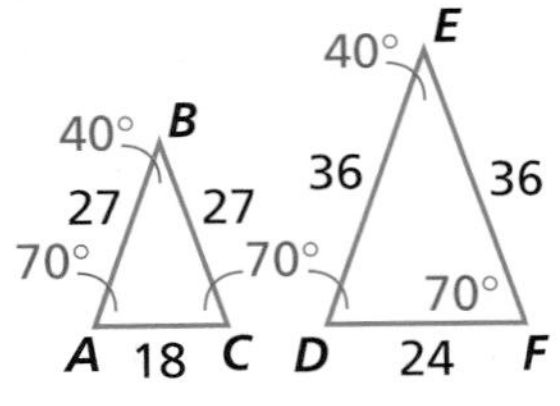

8.

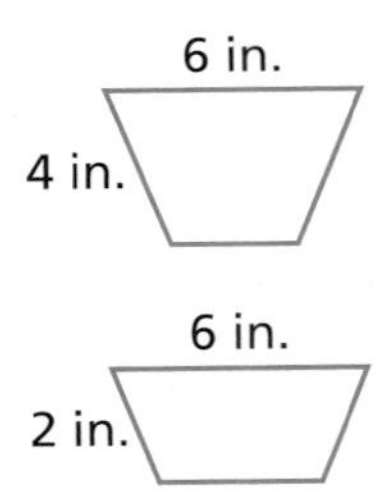

9.

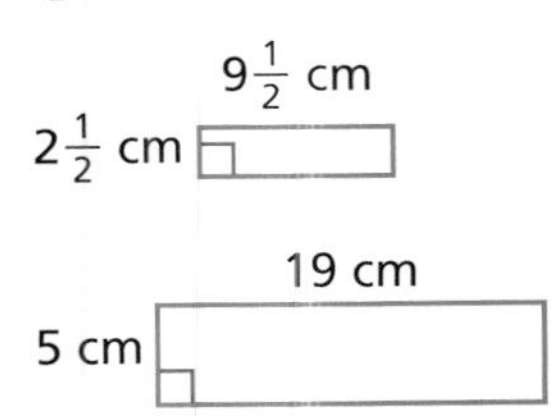

10. Draw a right triangle with vertices (0, 0), (6, 0), and (6, 4) on a coordinate plane. Draw another triangle with vertices (9, 6), (0, 0) and (9, 0). Are the triangles similar? Explain.

11. Sari's garden is 12 ft by 16 ft 6 in. Her sketch of the garden is 8 in. by 11 in. Is Sari's sketch a scale drawing? If so, what scale factor did she use?

LINK

Art

Many reproductions of artwork have been enlarged to fit unusual surfaces.

The figures in each pair are similar. Use the scale factor to solve for *x*.

12.

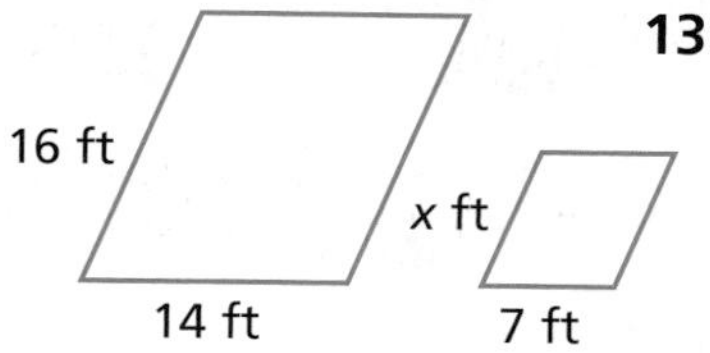

13.

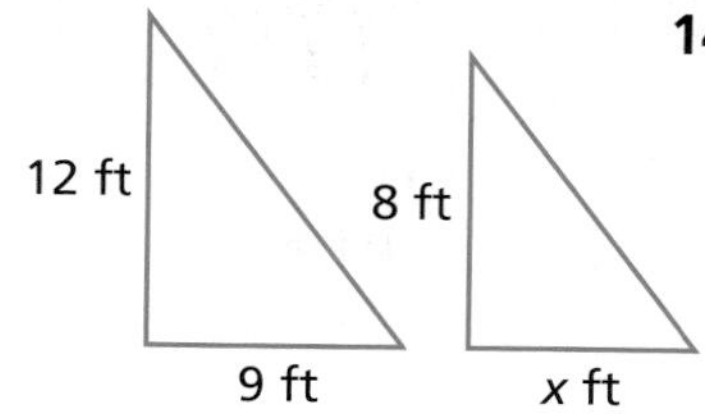

14.

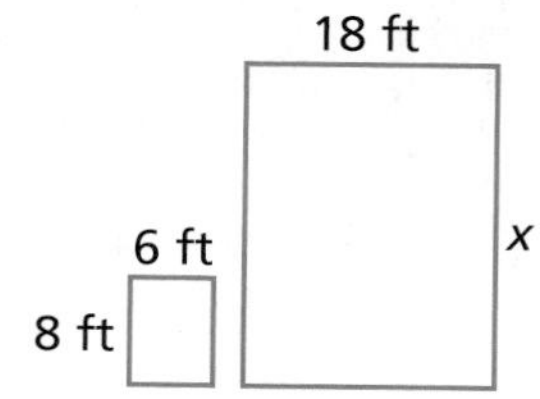

15. Art Helen is copying a printed reproduction of the Mona Lisa. The print is 24 in. wide and 36 in. tall. If Helen's canvas is 12 in. wide, how tall should her canvas be?

16. A rectangle is 16 cm long and 7 cm wide. A similar rectangle is 3.5 cm wide and x cm long. Find x.

17. Physical Science Will is 5 ft tall. He casts a 3 ft shadow at the same time that a tree casts a 9 ft shadow. Use similar triangles to find the height of the tree.

18. Write a Problem A drawing on a sheet of graph paper shows a rectangle 9 cm wide and 12 cm long. The width of the rectangle is labeled 3 ft. Write and solve a problem about the rectangle.

19. Write About It Consider the statement "All similar figures are congruent." Is this statement true or false? Explain.

20. Challenge In right triangle ABC, $\angle B$ is the right angle, $AB = 36$ cm, and $BC = 28$ cm. Right triangle ABC is similar to right triangle DEF. If $DE = 9$ cm, what is the area of triangle DEF?

Test Prep and Spiral Review

21. Multiple Choice An isosceles triangle has two sides that are each 4.5 centimeters long and a base that is 3 centimeters long. A similar triangle has a base that is 1.5 centimeters long. How long are each of the other two sides of the similar triangle?

Ⓐ 2.25 cm　Ⓑ 3.75 cm　Ⓒ 4.5 cm　Ⓓ 150 cm

22. Gridded Response A rectangle is 6 feet wide by 35 feet long. A similar rectangle has a width of 12 in. How many inches long is the similar rectangle?

Use each table of values to make an equation of the data. (Lesson 3-5)

23.

x	0	1	2	3	4	5
y	1	3	5	7	9	11

24.

x	0	1	2	3	4	5
y	0	3	6	9	12	15

Solve each proportion. (Lesson 5-4)

25. $\frac{6}{12} = \frac{9}{x}$　**26.** $\frac{4}{9} = \frac{2.4}{y}$　**27.** $\frac{44}{12} = \frac{w}{3}$　**28.** $\frac{18}{6} = \frac{15}{k}$

Hands-On LAB 5-6

Explore Dilations

Use with Lesson 5-6

go.hrw.com
Lab Resources Online
KEYWORD: MT7 Lab5

Activity 1

Triangle $A'B'D'$ is a dilation of triangle ABD. Point C is called the center of dilation.

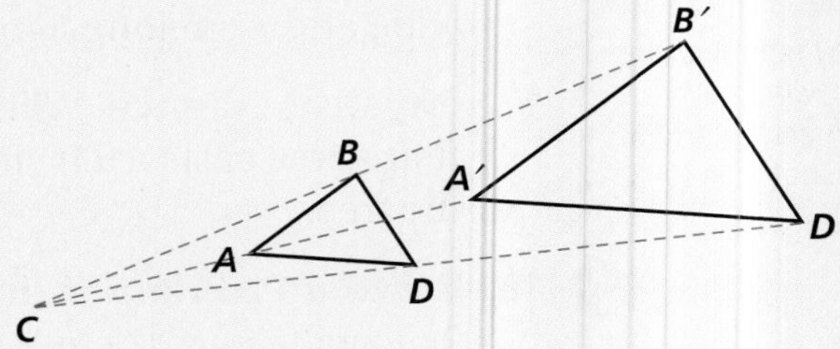

1. Use a ruler to measure segments CA' and CA to the nearest millimeter.
2. Calculate the ratio $\frac{\text{length of } CA'}{\text{length of } CA}$.
3. Repeat 1 and 2 for segments CB', CB, CD', and CD. Copy the table below and record your measurements.

CA'	CA	$\frac{CA'}{CA}$	CB'	CB	$\frac{CB'}{CB}$	CD'	CD	$\frac{CD}{CD'}$

Think and Discuss

1. What seems to be true about the ratios you calculated? Write a conjecture about the ratios of the segments you measured.
2. Measure segment AD and segment $A'D'$ to the nearest millimeter. What is the ratio of the length of $A'D'$ to the length of AD? How does this compare to the ratios you recorded in the table above?
3. If the corresponding angles of each triangle are congruent, can you conclude that triangles ABD and $A'B'D'$ are similar? Explain.

Try This

The center of dilation can be a point on the figure itself. In the figure at right, the center of dilation is point D.

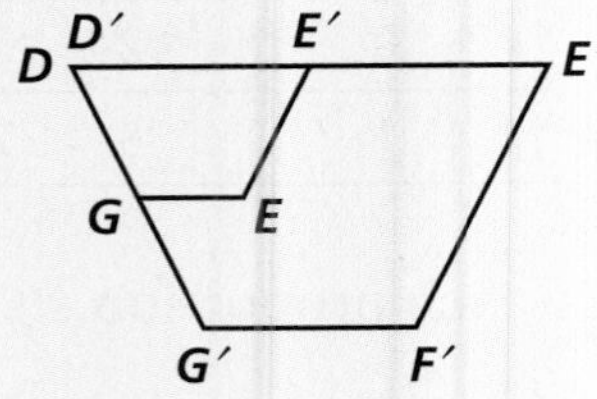

1. What seems to be true of the dilation of a point on a figure if that point is also the center of dilation?
2. Measure the lengths of the corresponding sides of quadrilaterals $DEFG$ and $D'E'F'G'$. Are the ratios of the corresponding sides in proportion? Can you conclude that the quadrilaterals are similar?

Activity 2

You can also graph dilations in the coordinate plane. Quadrilateral *P′Q′R′S′* is a dilation of *PQRS*. The origin is the center of dilation.

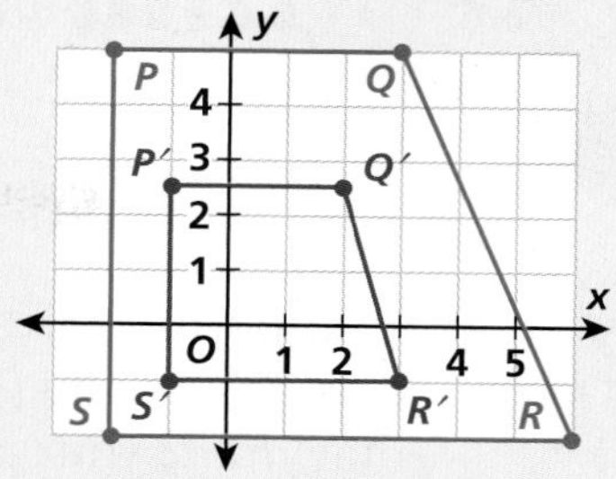

1. For each pair of corresponding vertices, record the *x*- and *y*-coordinates.
2. Calculate the ratio of the coordinates.
3. Copy and complete the table below. The first row of the table has been completed for you.

Vertex	*x*	*y*	Vertex	*x*	*y*	Ratio of *x*-coordinates (*P′Q′R′S′* ÷ *PQRS*)	Ratio of *y*-coordinates (*P′Q′R′S′* ÷ *PQRS*)
P′	−1	2.5	*P*	−2	5	$\frac{-1}{-2} = 0.5$	$\frac{2.5}{5} = 0.5$
Q′			*Q*				
R′			*R*				
S′			*S*				

Think and Discuss

1. What seems to be true about the ratios you calculated? Write a conjecture about the ratios of the coordinates of a dilation image to the coordinates of the original.
2. In Activity 1, triangle *A′B′D′* was larger than triangle *ABD*. How is the relationship between quadrilateral *P′Q′R′S′* and quadrilateral *PQRS* different?

Try This

Use what you learned from your observations above to create a dilation of each figure below. Use the origin as the center of dilation.

1.

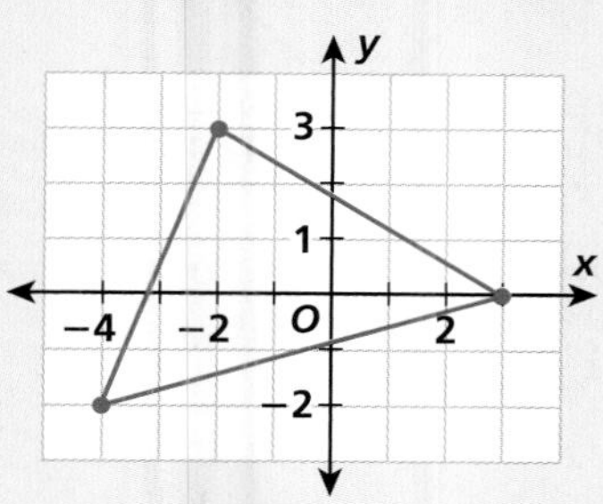

2.

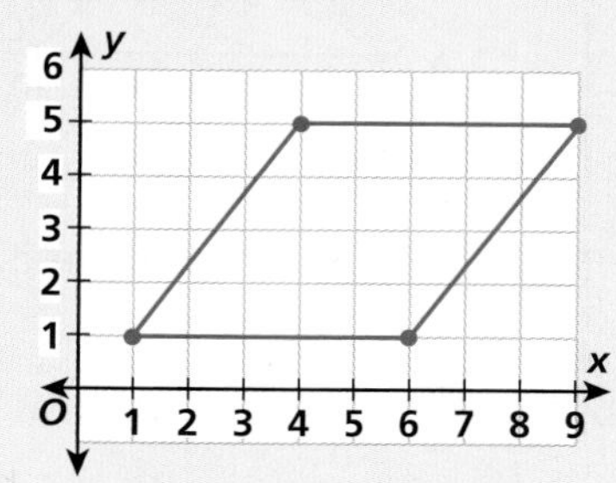

5-6 Dilations

Learn to identify and create dilations of plane figures.

Vocabulary

dilation

center of dilation

Your pupils are the black areas in the center of your eyes. When you go to the eye doctor, the doctor may *dilate* your pupils, which makes them larger.

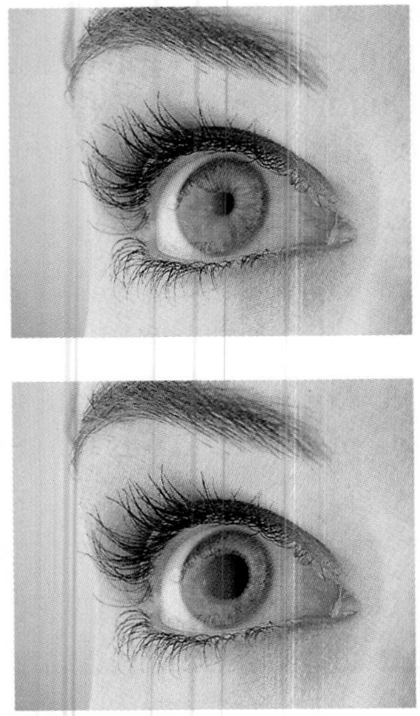

Your pupil works like a camera lens, dilating to let in more or less light.

Some transformations of geometric figures do not change the size or shape of a figure. A **dilation** is a transformation that changes the size, but not the shape, of a figure. A dilation can enlarge or reduce a figure.

Every dilation has a fixed point that is the *center of dilation*. To find the center of dilation, draw a line that connects each pair of corresponding vertices. The lines intersect at one point. This point is the **center of dilation**.

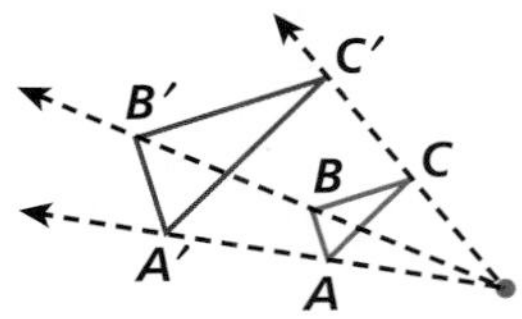

EXAMPLE 1 Identifying Dilations

Tell whether each transformation is a dilation.

A

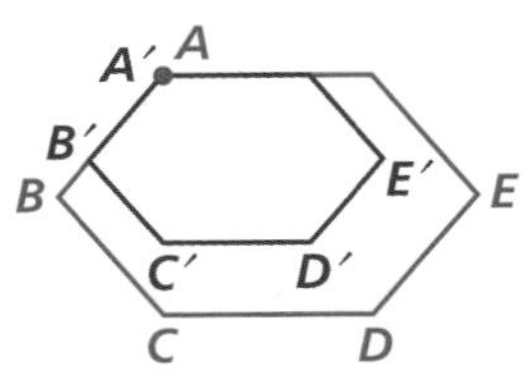

The transformation is a dilation.

B

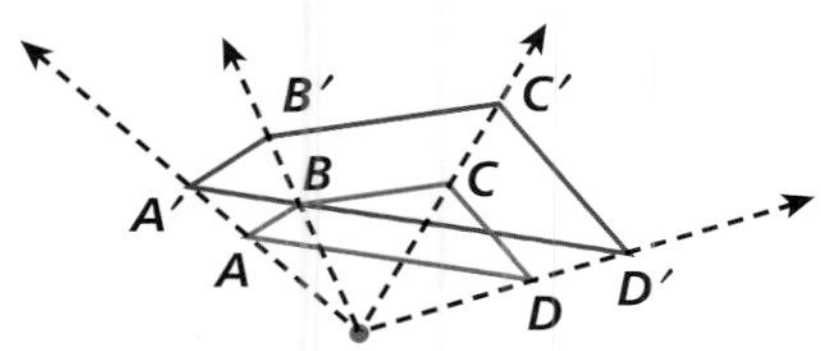

The transformation is a dilation.

C

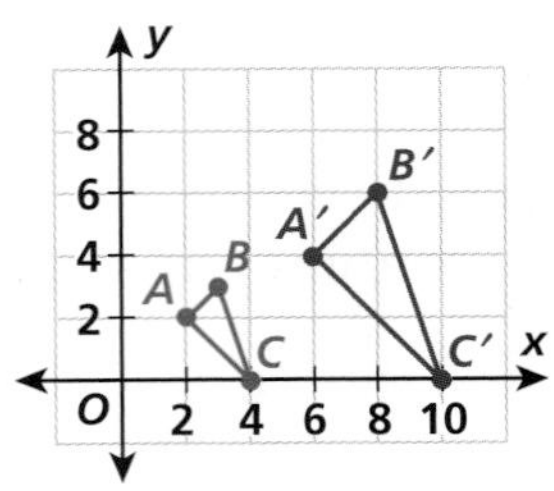

The transformation is a dilation.

D

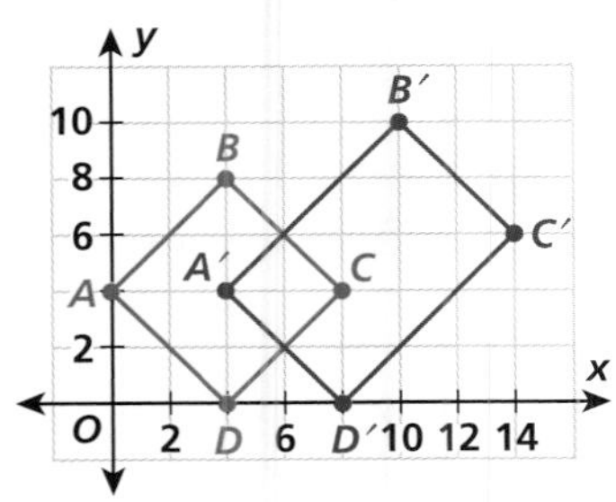

The transformation is *not* a dilation. The figure is distorted.

A scale factor describes how much a figure is enlarged or reduced. A scale factor can be expressed as a decimal, fraction, or percent. A 10% increase is a scale factor of 1.1, and a 10% decrease is a scale factor of 0.9.

EXAMPLE 2 Dilating a Figure

Dilate the figure by a scale factor of 0.2 with *P* as the center of dilation.

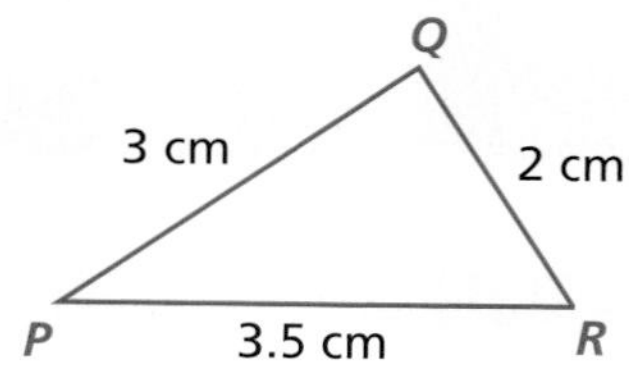

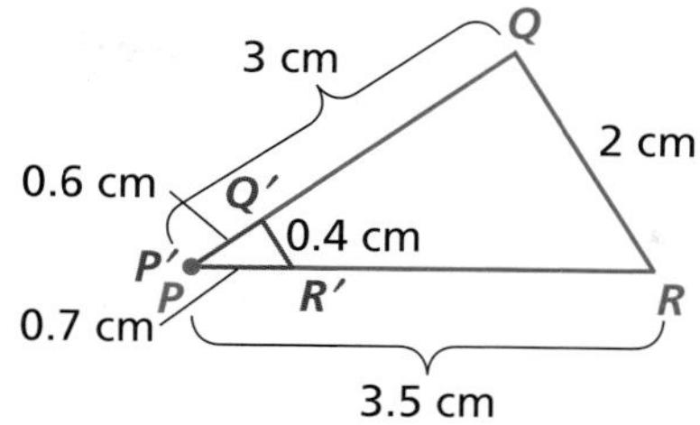

Multiply each side by 0.2.
P′ and P are the same point.

EXAMPLE 3 Using the Origin as the Center of Dilation

Helpful Hint

A scale factor between 0 and 1 reduces a figure. A scale factor greater than 1 enlarges it.

A **Dilate the figure by a scale factor of 2.5. What are the vertices of the image?**

Multiply the coordinates by 2.5 to find the vertices of the image.

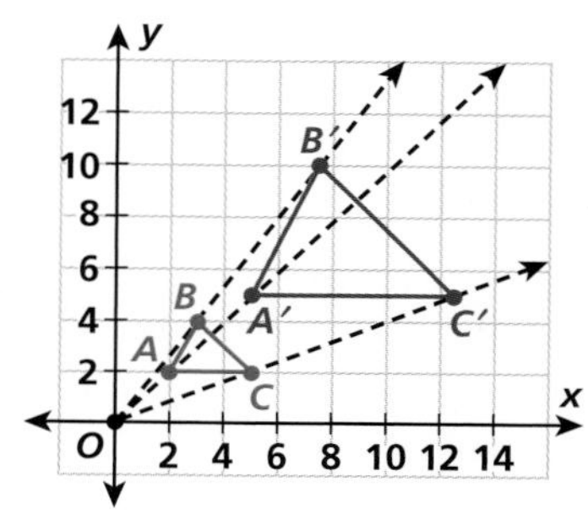

$\triangle ABC$		$\triangle A'B'C'$
$A(2, 2) \longrightarrow$	$A'(2 \cdot 2.5, 2 \cdot 2.5) \longrightarrow$	$\mathbf{A'(5, 5)}$
$B(3, 4) \longrightarrow$	$B'(3 \cdot 2.5, 4 \cdot 2.5) \longrightarrow$	$\mathbf{B'(7.5, 10)}$
$C(5, 2) \longrightarrow$	$C'(5 \cdot 2.5, 2 \cdot 2.5) \longrightarrow$	$\mathbf{C'(12.5, 5)}$

The vertices of the image are $A'(5, 5)$, $B'(7.5, 10)$, and $C'(12.5, 5)$.

B **Dilate the figure by a scale factor of $\frac{2}{3}$. What are the vertices of the image?**

Multiply the coordinates by $\frac{2}{3}$ to find the vertices of the image.

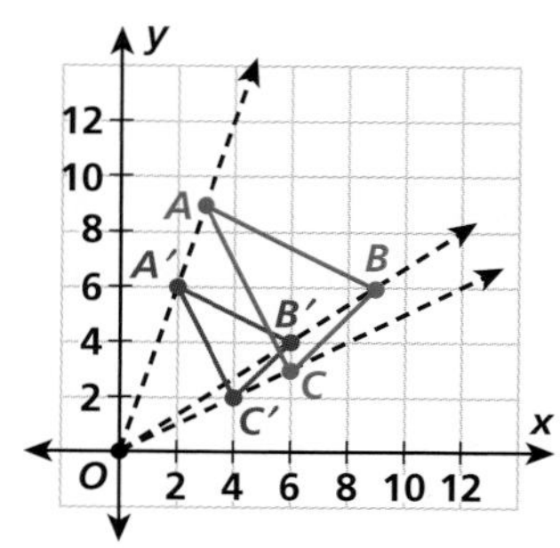

$\triangle ABC$		$\triangle A'B'C'$
$A(3, 9) \longrightarrow$	$A'\left(3 \cdot \frac{2}{3}, 9 \cdot \frac{2}{3}\right) \longrightarrow$	$\mathbf{A'(2, 6)}$
$B(9, 6) \longrightarrow$	$B'\left(9 \cdot \frac{2}{3}, 6 \cdot \frac{2}{3}\right) \longrightarrow$	$\mathbf{B'(6, 4)}$
$C(6, 3) \longrightarrow$	$C'\left(6 \cdot \frac{2}{3}, 3 \cdot \frac{2}{3}\right) \longrightarrow$	$\mathbf{C'(4, 2)}$

The vertices of the image are $A'(2, 6)$, $B'(6, 4)$, and $C'(4, 2)$.

Think and Discuss

1. **Describe** the image of a dilation with a scale factor of 1.
2. **Compare** a dilation with the origin as the center of dilation to a dilation with a vertex of the figure as the center of dilation.

5-6 Exercises

go.hrw.com
Homework Help Online
KEYWORD: MT7 5-6
Parent Resources Online
KEYWORD: MT7 Parent

GUIDED PRACTICE

See Example 1

Tell whether each transformation is a dilation.

1.

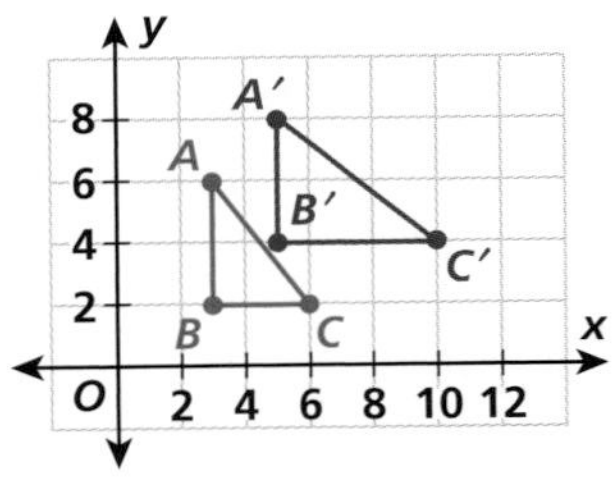

2.

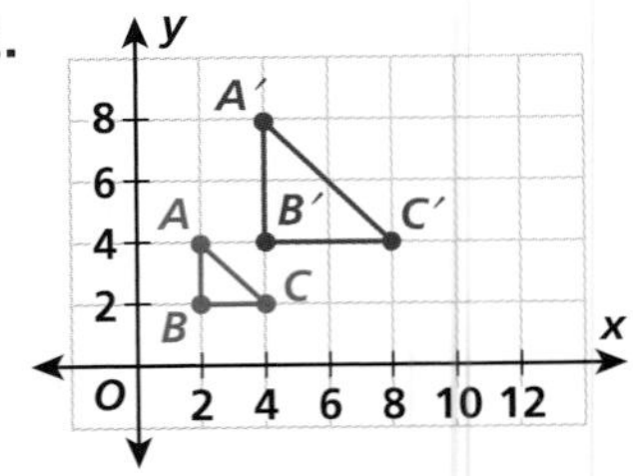

See Example 2

Dilate each figure by the given scale factor with P as the center of dilation.

3. Scale factor = 1.5

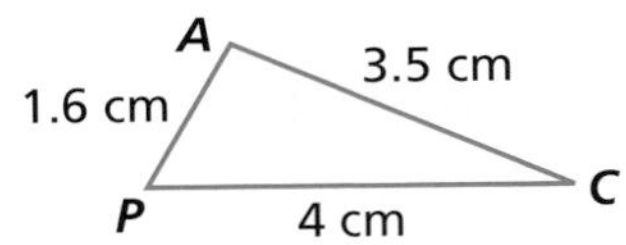

4. Scale factor = $\frac{1}{2}$

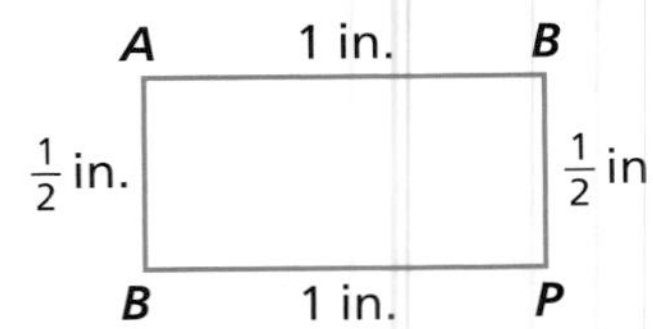

See Example 3

Dilate each figure by the given scale factor with the origin as the center of dilation. What are the vertices of the image?

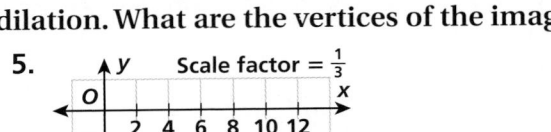

5. Scale factor = $\frac{1}{3}$

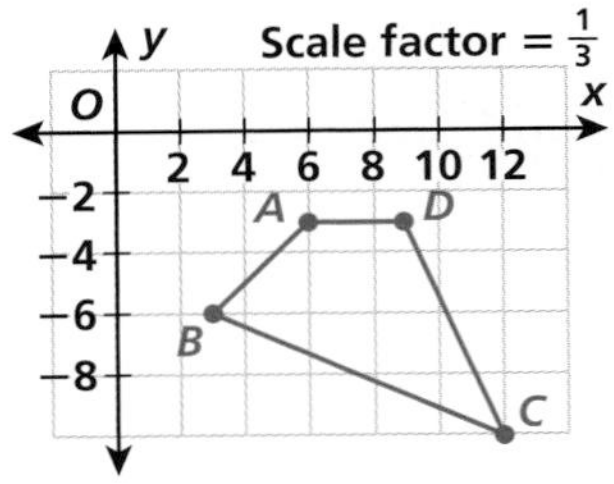

6. Scale factor = 4

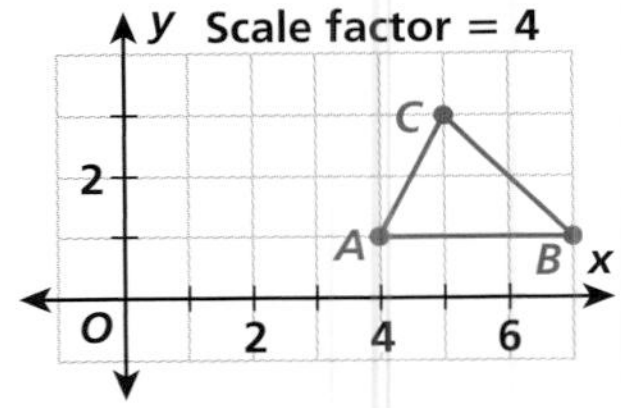

INDEPENDENT PRACTICE

See Example 1

Tell whether each transformation is a dilation.

7.

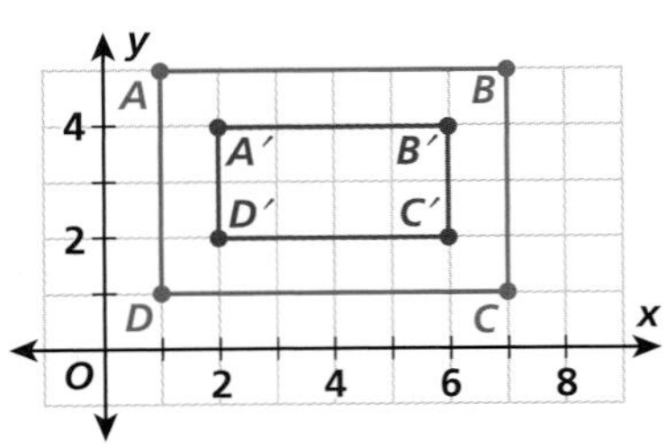

8.

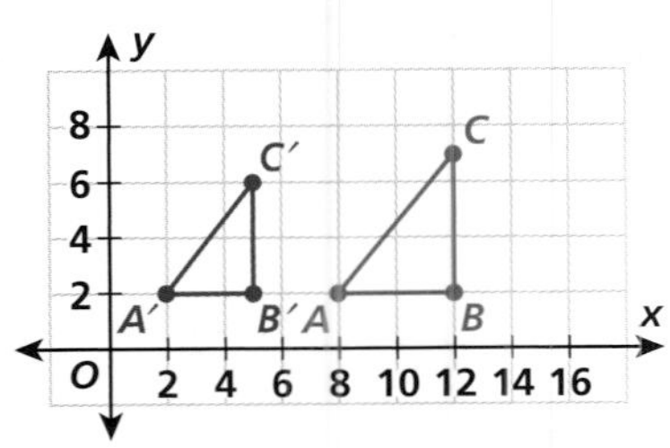

See Example 2

Dilate each figure by the given scale factor with P as the center of dilation.

9. Scale factor = 2

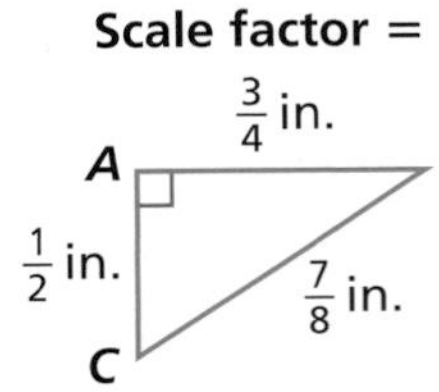

10. Scale factor = $\frac{1}{4}$

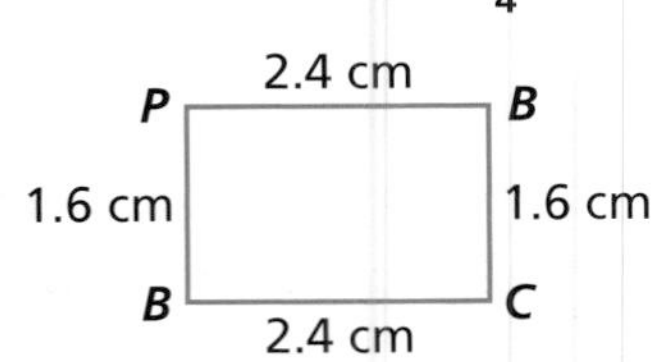

See Example 3

Dilate each figure by the given scale factor with the origin as the center of dilation. What are the vertices of the image?

11.

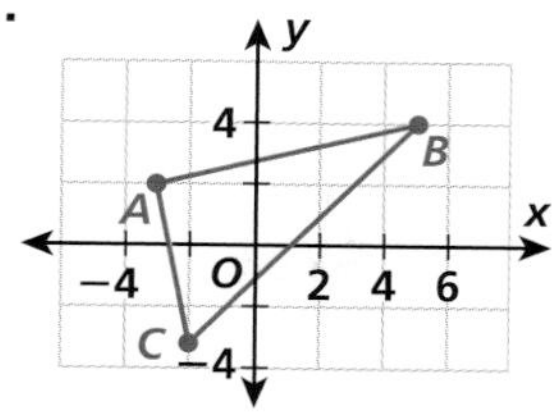

Scale factor = 3

12.

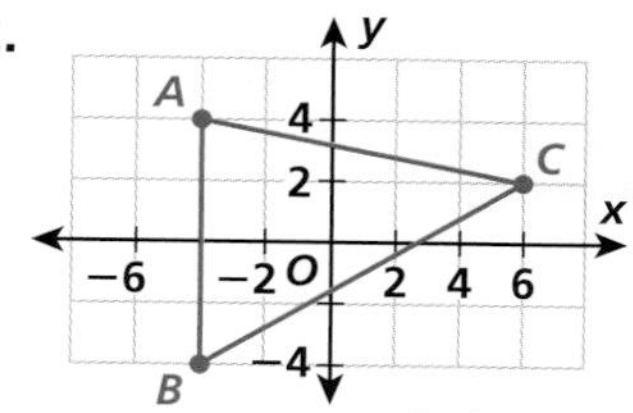

Scale factor = $\frac{1}{2}$

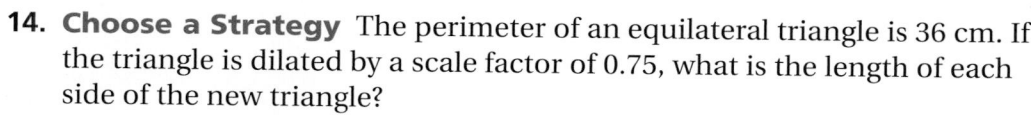

PRACTICE AND PROBLEM SOLVING

Extra Practice
See page 791.

13. A rectangle has vertices $A(2, 4)$, $B(7, 4)$, $C(7, 0)$, and $D(2, 0)$. Give the coordinates after dilating from the origin by a scale factor of 1.5.

14. Choose a Strategy The perimeter of an equilateral triangle is 36 cm. If the triangle is dilated by a scale factor of 0.75, what is the length of each side of the new triangle?

Ⓐ 3 cm Ⓑ 4 cm Ⓒ 9 cm Ⓓ 12 cm

LINK

Photography

In a camera lens, a larger aperture lets in more light than a smaller one.

15. Photography The aperture is the polygonal opening in a camera lens when a picture is taken. The aperture can be small or large. Is an aperture a dilation? Why or why not?

16. Write About It Explain how you can check the drawing of a dilation for accuracy.

17. Challenge What scale factor was used in the dilation of a triangle with vertices $A(4, -8)$, $B(10, 4)$, and $C(-2, 12)$, to the triangle with vertices $A'(-3, 6)$, $B'\left(-7\frac{1}{2}, -3\right)$, and $C'\left(1\frac{1}{2}, -9\right)$?

TEST PREP and Spiral Review

18. Multiple Choice An equilateral triangle has a perimeter of 18 centimeters. If the triangle is dilated by a factor of 0.5, what is the length of each side of the new triangle?

Ⓐ 36 cm Ⓑ 12 cm Ⓒ 9 cm Ⓓ 3 cm

19. Short Response A square has a side length of 4.8 feet. If the square is dilated by a factor of 4, what is the length of a side of the new square? What is its perimeter? What is its area?

Find the missing term in each sequence. (Lesson 3-6)

20. 5, 15, 25, ▢, 45, . . . **21.** 9, 3, −3, −9, ▢, . . . **22.** 3, 4.5, ▢, 7.5, 9, . . .

Find the length of the indicated side. (Lesson 5-5)

23. A rectangle has a length of 20 yd and a width of 12 yd. A similar rectangle has a length of x yd and a width of 9 yd. Find the length of the similar rectangle.

5-7 Indirect Measurement

Learn to find measures indirectly by applying the properties of similar figures.

Vocabulary

indirect measurement

A scout troop wants to make a temporary bridge across a river. To do this, they need to know how wide the river is.

Sometimes, distances cannot be measured directly. One way to find such a distance is to use **indirect measurement**, a way of using similar figures and proportions to find a measure.

The distance across the river can be found by using a pair of similar triangles.

EXAMPLE 1 ***Geography Application***

A scout troop wants to make a temporary bridge across the river. The diagram shows the measurements the troop knows. The triangles in the diagram are similar. How wide is the river where the troop wants to make the bridge?

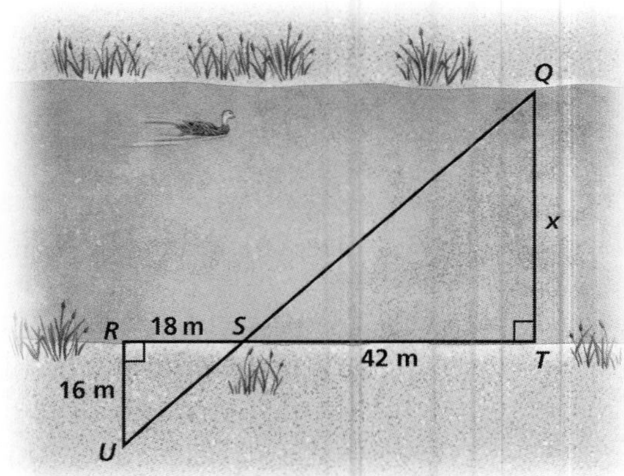

Triangles RSU and TSQ are similar.

$\frac{QT}{UR} = \frac{ST}{SR}$ *Set up a proportion.*

$\frac{x}{16} = \frac{42}{18}$ *Substitute 16 for UR, 42 for ST, and 18 for SR.*

$18x = 672$ *Find the cross products.*

$\frac{18x}{18} = \frac{672}{18}$ *Divide both sides by 18.*

$x \approx 37.\overline{3}$

The distance across the river is approximately 37.3 meters.

EXAMPLE 2 **PROBLEM SOLVING APPLICATION**

PROBLEM SOLVING

A flagpole casts a 32 ft shadow, while a 6 ft tall man standing nearby casts a 4.5 ft shadow. How tall is the pole?

1 Understand the Problem

The **answer** is the height of the flagpole.

List the important information:

- The length of the flagpole's shadow is 32 ft.
- The height of the man is 6 ft.
- The length of the man's shadow is 4.5 ft.

2 Make a Plan

Use the information to *draw a diagram.*

3 Solve

Draw a diagram. Then draw the dashed lines to form triangles. The flagpole and its shadow and the man and his shadow form similar right triangles.

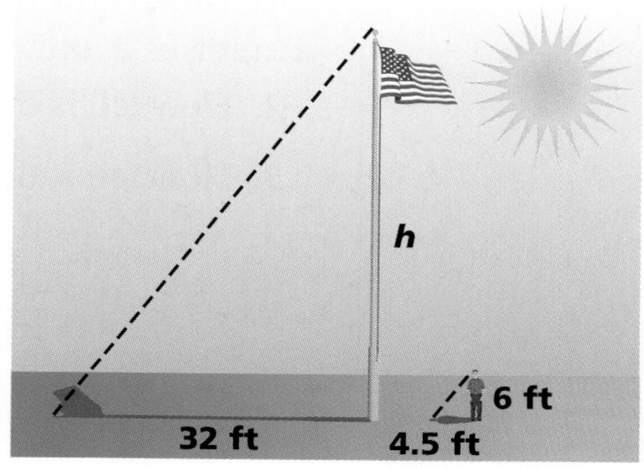

$\frac{6}{4.5} = \frac{h}{32}$ *Corresponding sides of similar figures are proportional.*

$4.5h = 192$ *Find the cross products.*

$\frac{4.5h}{4.5} = \frac{192}{4.5}$ *Divide both sides by 4.5.*

$h \approx 42.\overline{6}$

The height of the flagpole is approximately 42.7 ft.

4 Look Back

Since $\frac{4.5}{6} = \frac{3}{4}$, the man's shadow is $\frac{3}{4}$ of his height. So, the flagpole's shadow should also be $\frac{3}{4}$ of its height and $\frac{3}{4}$ of 42.7 is approximately 32.

Think and Discuss

1. **Explain** why it is easier to use triangles instead of other polygons for indirect measurement.
2. **Explain** how you can tell whether the terms of a proportion you have written are in the correct order.

5-7 Exercises

go.hrw.com
Homework Help Online
KEYWORD: MT7 5-7
Parent Resources Online
KEYWORD: MT7 Parent

GUIDED PRACTICE

See Example 1

1. Walter wants to know the width of the pond on his farm. He drew the diagram and labeled it with measurements he made. The triangles in the diagram are similar. How wide is the pond?

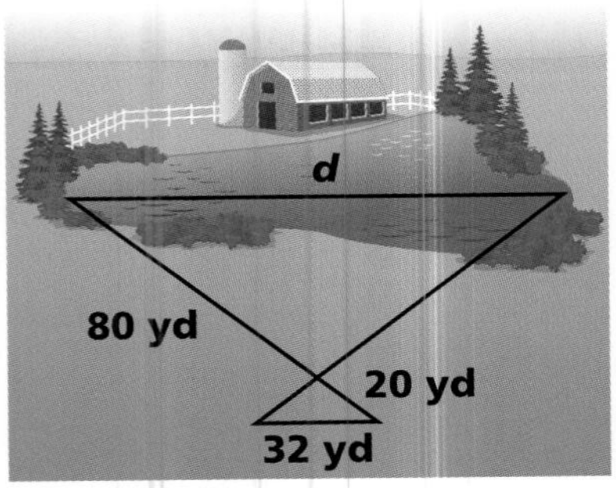

See Example 2

Use the diagram for Exercises 2 and 3.

2. How tall is the tree?
3. How tall is the girl?

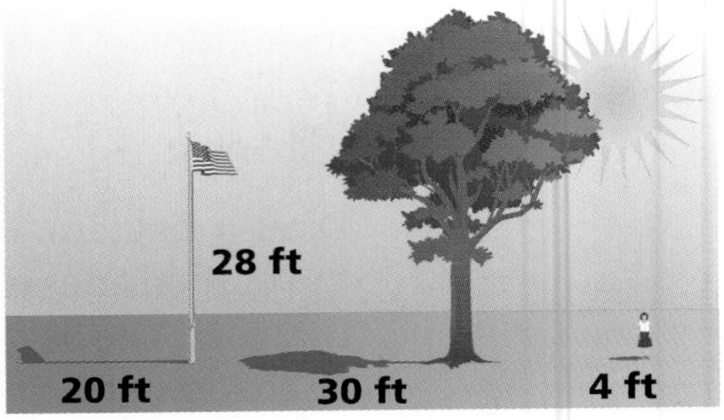

INDEPENDENT PRACTICE

See Example 1

4. The town council has decided to build a footbridge over a pond in the park. An engineer drew a diagram of the pond and labeled it with measurements she made. The triangles in the diagram are similar. How long will the footbridge be?

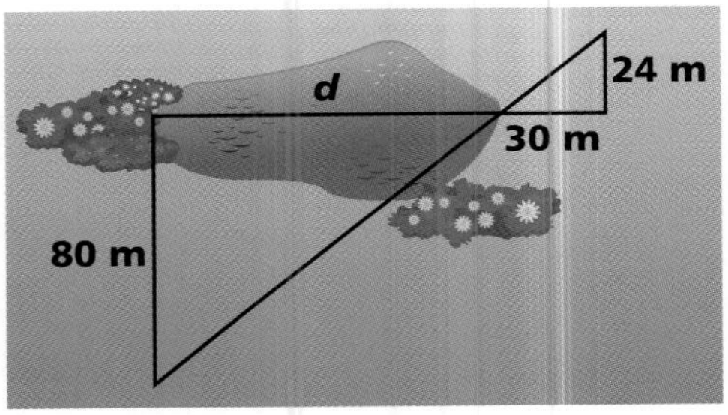

See Example 2

Use the diagram for Exercises 5 and 6.

5. How tall is the child?
6. The house is 19 ft tall. How long is its shadow?

PRACTICE AND PROBLEM SOLVING

Extra Practice
See page 791.

7. There is a 3 m tall vertical ladder from the ground to a ramp. The bottom of the ladder is 10 m from the base of the ramp. The distance along the ramp from the top of the ladder to the loading platform is 24 m. How high above the ground is the loading platform?

8. Brooke is 5 ft tall. She and her class are walking through a wooded area looking for a tree that is 50 ft tall. If the length of Brooke's shadow is 2 ft, how will the students know when they have found a 50 ft tree?

9. A ramp is built by putting a triangle on top of a trapezoid. How long is the ramp?

10. Estimation An 11 m tall sign casts a 19 m shadow when the shadow of a boy standing next to it is 3 m long. To the nearest tenth of a meter, approximately how tall is the boy?

11. A 40 ft tall monument casts a shadow that just reaches the base of a 4 ft tall parking meter. If the parking meter's shadow is 6.5 ft long, how far apart are the monument and the meter?

12. Write a Problem Write a problem using indirect measurement to measure an object at home or school.

13. Write About It Explain how you might use similar rectangles to measure indirectly.

14. Challenge Stanley is 6 ft tall. He wants to stand in the shade of a tree that is 35 ft tall. If the tree casts a 10 ft shadow, what is the farthest Stanley can stand from the tree and be completely in its shadow? Round your answer to the nearest tenth of a foot.

Test Prep and Spiral Review

15. Multiple Choice Triangles *ABC* and *DEF* are similar right triangles. If you know the lengths of sides *AB, AC, BC,* and *DE,* which other length(s) can you find?

Ⓐ Only *DF* Ⓑ Only *EF* Ⓒ *DF* and *EF* Ⓓ None of them

16. Short Answer At the same time that a tree casts a 44 ft shadow, a 3.5 ft girl standing next to the tree casts a 5 ft shadow. How much taller than the girl is the tree?

Multiply. Write each answer in simplest form. (Lesson 2-4)

17. $-\frac{1}{4}\left(\frac{4}{5}\right)$ **18.** $\frac{4}{7}\left(\frac{3}{8}\right)$ **19.** $-\frac{2}{3}\left(-\frac{1}{4}\right)$ **20.** $\frac{3}{8}\left(-\frac{2}{3}\right)$

Write in exponential form. (Lesson 4-1)

21. $3 \cdot 3 \cdot 3 \cdot 3$ **22.** -8 **23.** $(-2) \cdot (-2) \cdot (-2)$ **24.** $e \cdot e \cdot e \cdot e \cdot e$

5-8 Scale Drawings and Scale Models

Learn to make comparisons between and find dimensions of scale drawings, models, and actual objects.

Vocabulary

scale drawing

scale

scale model

reduction

enlargement

To get an idea of scale, notice the red tractor at the lower left.

Stan Herd is a crop artist and farmer who has created works of art that are as large as 160 square acres. Herd first makes a *scale drawing* of each piece, and then he determines the actual lengths of the parts that make up the art piece.

A **scale drawing** is a two-dimensional drawing that accurately represents an object. The scale drawing is mathematically similar to the object.

A **scale** gives the ratio of the dimensions in the drawing to the dimensions of the object. All dimensions are reduced or enlarged using the same scale.

Scale	Interpretation
1:20	1 unit on the drawing is 20 units.
1 cm:1 m	1 cm on the drawing is 1 m.
$\frac{1}{4}$ in. = 1 ft	$\frac{1}{4}$ in. on the drawing is 1 ft.

EXAMPLE 1 Using Proportions to Find Unknown Scales

Reading Math

The scale *a*:*b* is read "*a* to *b*." For example, the scale 1 cm:6 ft is read "one centimeter to six feet."

The length of an object on a scale drawing is 8 cm, and its actual length is 48 m. The scale is 1 cm:___ m. What is the scale?

$\frac{1 \text{ cm}}{x \text{ m}} = \frac{8 \text{ cm}}{48 \text{ m}}$ *Set up a proportion using* $\frac{\text{scale length}}{\text{actual length}}$.

$1 \cdot 48 = x \cdot 8$ *Find the cross products.*

$x = 6$ *Divide both sides by 8.*

The scale is 1 cm:6 m.

EXAMPLE 2 *Life Science Application*

Under a 1000:1 microscope view, a paramecium appears to have length 39 mm. What is its actual length?

$\frac{1000}{1} = \frac{39 \text{ mm}}{x \text{ mm}}$ *Set up a proportion using* $\frac{\text{scale length}}{\text{actual length}}$.

$1000 \cdot x = 1 \cdot 39$ *Find the cross products.*

$x = 0.039$ *Divide both sides by 1000.*

The actual length of the paramecium is 0.039 mm.

A **scale model** is a three-dimensional model that accurately represents a solid object. The scale model is mathematically similar to the solid object.

EXAMPLE 3 Finding Unknown Dimensions Given Scale Factors

Helpful Hint

Scales can use the same units or different units.

A model of a 36 ft tall house was made using the scale 3 in:2 ft. What is the height of the model?

$\frac{3 \text{ in.}}{2 \text{ ft}} = \frac{3 \text{ in.}}{24 \text{ in.}} = \frac{1 \cancel{\text{in.}}}{8 \cancel{\text{in.}}}$ *Find the scale factor.*

The scale factor for the model is $\frac{1}{8}$. Now set up a proportion.

$\frac{1}{8} = \frac{h \text{ in.}}{432 \text{ in.}}$ *Convert: 36 ft = 432 in.*

$432 = 8h$ *Find the cross products.*

$h = 54$ *Divide both sides by 8.*

The height of the model is 54 in.

EXAMPLE 4 *Life Science Application*

A DNA model was built using the scale 2 cm:0.0000001 mm. If the model of the DNA chain is 17 cm long, what is the length of the actual chain?

$\frac{2 \text{ cm}}{0.0000001 \text{ mm}} = \frac{20 \text{ mm}}{0.0000001 \text{ mm}} = 200{,}000{,}000$ *Find the scale factor.*

The scale factor for the model is 200,000,000. This means the model is 200 million times larger than the actual chain.

$\frac{200{,}000{,}000}{1} = \frac{17 \text{ cm}}{x \text{ cm}}$ *Set up a proportion.*

$200{,}000{,}000x = 17(1)$ *Find the cross products.*

$x = 0.000000085$ *Divide both sides by 200,000,000.*

The length of the DNA chain is 8.5×10^{-8} cm.

A scale drawing or model that is smaller than the actual object is called a **reduction**. A scale drawing or model that is larger than the object is called an **enlargement**.

Think and Discuss

1. **Describe** which scale would produce the largest drawing of an object: 1:20, 1 in. = 1 ft, or $\frac{1}{4}$ in. = 1 ft.
2. **Explain** why comparing models with different scale factors, such as the paramecium in Example 2 and the house in Example 3, can be misleading.

5-8 Exercises

go.hrw.com
Homework Help Online
KEYWORD: MT7 5-8
Parent Resources Online
KEYWORD: MT7 Parent

GUIDED PRACTICE

See Example 1
1. A 10 ft fence is 8 in. long on a scale drawing. What is the scale?

See Example 2
2. Under a 200:1 microscope, a microorganism appears to have a length of 0.75 in. How long is the microorganism?

See Example 3
3. A model of a 42 ft tall shopping mall was built using the scale 1 in:3 ft. What is the height of the model?

See Example 4
4. A molecular model uses the scale 2.5 cm:0.00001 mm. If the model is 7 cm long, how long is the molecule?

INDEPENDENT PRACTICE

See Example 1
5. What is the scale of a drawing where a 6 m wall is 4 cm long?

See Example 2
6. Under a 750:1 magnification microscope, a paramecium has a length of 19 mm. What is the actual length of the paramecium?

See Example 3
7. A model of a house was built using the scale 5 in:25 ft. If a window in the model is 1.5 in. wide, how wide is the actual window?

See Example 4
8. To create a model of an artery, a health teacher uses the scale 2.5 cm:0.75 mm. If the diameter of the artery is 2.7 mm, what is the diameter on the model?

PRACTICE AND PROBLEM SOLVING

Extra Practice
See page 791.

Tell whether each scale reduces, enlarges, or preserves the size of an actual object.

9. 10 ft:24 in.
10. 1 mi:5280 ft
11. 20 cm:1000 mm
12. 0.2 in:2 ft
13. 50 ft:1 in.
14. 250 cm:1 km

Change both measurements to the same unit of measure, and find the scale factor.

15. 1 ft model of a 1 in. fossil
16. 20 cm model of a 28 m rocket
17. 2 ft model of a 30 yd sports field
18. 3 ft model of a 5 yd whale
19. 30 cm model of a 6 m tree
20. 6 in. model of a 6 ft sofa
21. **Architecture** Maurice is building a 2 ft tall model of the Gateway Arch in St. Louis, Missouri. If he is using a 3 in:78.75 ft scale, how tall is the actual arch?
22. **Geography** The straight-line distances between Houston and several cities on a map of Texas are shown in the table. The scale is 2 cm:50 mi. Find the actual distances in miles.

City	Distance from Houston (cm)
Abilene	12.7
Austin	5.8
Dallas	9.0
Galveston	1.9

23. On a scale drawing, a fence is $6\frac{1}{4}$ in. tall. The scale factor is $\frac{1}{12}$. Find the height of the actual fence in feet.

Architecture LINK

The blueprint shows the design for the Anderson's new family room. Use a metric ruler to measure the width of the 36-inch-wide door on the blueprint and determine the scale factor.

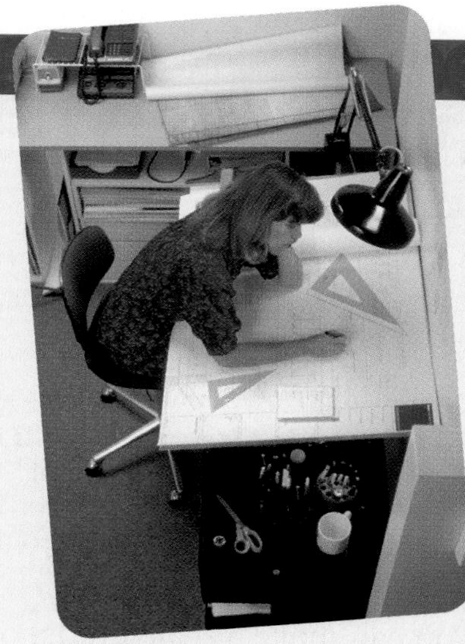

For Exercises 24–30, indicate the scale that you used.

24. How wide are the pocket doors (shown by the red line)?

25. What is the distance s between two interior studs?

26. How long is the oak mantle? (The right side ends just above the *B* in the word *BRICK*.)

27. What is the area of the tiled hearth in square inches? in square feet?

28. What is the area of the entire family room in square feet?

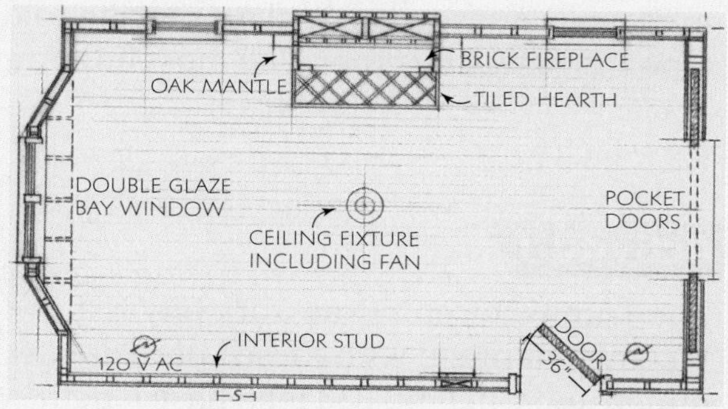

29. **Write About It** Could a 4 ft wide bookcase fit along the right-hand wall without blocking the pocket doors? Explain.

30. **Challenge** Suppose the architect used a $\frac{1}{8}$ in. = 1 ft scale.

a. What would the dimensions of the family room be?

b. Use the result from part **a** to find the area of the family room.

c. If the carpet the Andersons want costs \$4.99 per square foot, how much would it cost to carpet the family room?

go.hrw.com
Web Extra!
KEYWORD: MT7 Scale

TEST PREP and Spiral Review

31. **Multiple Choice** What scale factor was used to create a 10-inch-tall model of a 15-foot-tall statue?

Ⓐ 1:1.5　　Ⓑ 1:3　　Ⓒ 1:15　　Ⓓ 1:18

32. **Short Response** The height of a building on a $\frac{1}{4}$-inch scale drawing is 5 inches tall. How tall is the actual building? Explain.

State if the number is rational, irrational, or not a real number. (Lesson 4-7)

33. $\sqrt{9}$　　**34.** $\sqrt{-25}$　　**35.** $\sqrt{48}$　　**36.** $\sqrt{36}$　　**37.** $\frac{1}{\sqrt{4}}$

Find each unit rate. (Lesson 5-2)

38. \$90 for 8 hours of work　　**39.** 5 apples for \$0.85　　**40.** 24 players on 2 teams

Hands-On LAB 5-8

Make a Scale Model

Use with Lesson 5-8

REMEMBER
A scale such as 1 in. = 200 ft results in a smaller-scale model than a scale of 1 in. = 20 feet.

You can make a scale model of a solid object, such as a rectangular prism, in many ways; you can make a net and fold it, or you can cut card stock and tape the pieces together. The most important thing is to find a good scale.

Activity 1

The Trump Tower in New York City is a rectangular prism with these approximate dimensions: height, 880 feet; base length, 160 feet; base width, 80 feet.

1. Make a scale model of the Trump Tower.

   First determine the appropriate height for your model and find a good scale.

   To use $8\frac{1}{2}$ in. by 11 in. card stock, divide the longest dimension by 11 to find a scale.

   $$\frac{880 \text{ ft}}{11 \text{ in.}} = \frac{80 \text{ ft}}{1 \text{ in.}}$$

   Let 1 in. = 80 ft.

   The dimensions of the model using this scale are

   $\frac{880}{80} = 11$ in., $\frac{160}{80} = 2$ in., and $\frac{80}{80} = 1$ in.

   So you will need to cut the following:

   Two 11 in. × 2 in. rectangles

   Two 11 in. × 1 in. rectangles

   Two 2 in. × 1 in. rectangles

   Tape the pieces together to form the model.

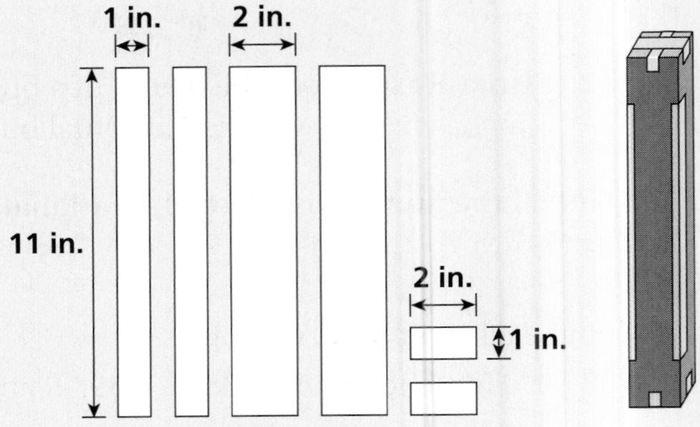

Think and Discuss

1. How tall would a model of a 500 ft tall building be if the same scale were used?
2. Why would a building stand more solidly than your model?
3. What could be another scale of the model if the numbers were without units?

Try This

1. Build a scale model of a four-wall handball court. The court is an open-topped rectangular prism 20 feet wide and 40 feet long. Three of the walls are 20 feet tall, and the back wall is 14 feet tall.

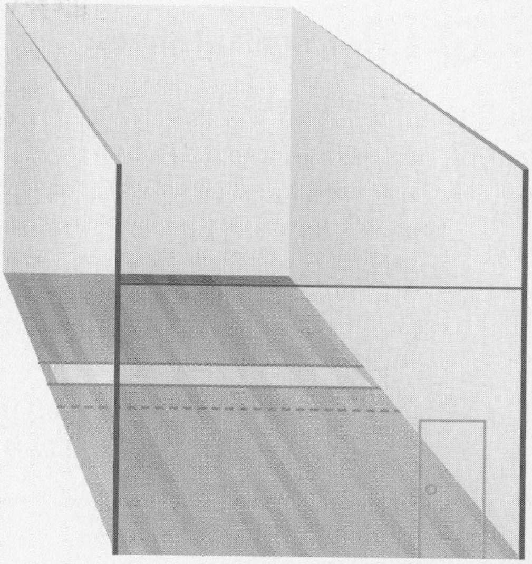

A scale model can also be used to make a model that is larger than the original object.

Activity 2

1 A size-AA battery has a diameter of about 0.57 inches and a height of about 2 inches. Make a scale model of a AA battery.

You can roll up paper or card stock to create a cylinder. Find the circumference of the battery: $0.57\pi \approx 1.8$ in.

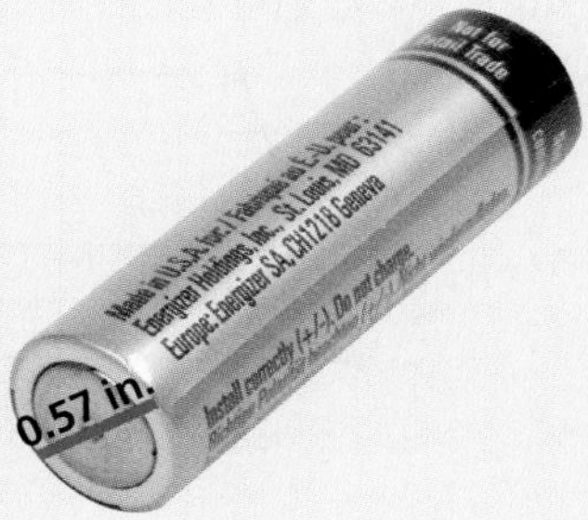

Note that the height is greater than the circumference, so use the height to find a scale.

$$\frac{\text{paper height}}{\text{battery height}} = \frac{11 \text{ in.}}{2 \text{ in.}} = 5.5$$

To use $8\frac{1}{2}$ in. by 11 in. paper or card stock, try multiplying the dimensions of the battery by 5.5.

$2(5.5) = 11$ in. $\qquad 1.8(5.5) = 9.9$ in.

Note that 9.9 in. by 11 in. is larger than an 8.5 in. by 11 in. piece of paper. If you use the width of the paper as the height of the scale model, you can find a smaller scale factor: $\frac{8.5 \text{ in}}{2 \text{ in.}} = 4.25$. Then use the smaller scale factor to find the corresponding circumference ($4.25 \cdot 1.8$ in. ≈ 7.7 in.) and diameter ($4.25 \cdot 0.57$ in. ≈ 2.4 in.). The pieces for the scale model are shown.

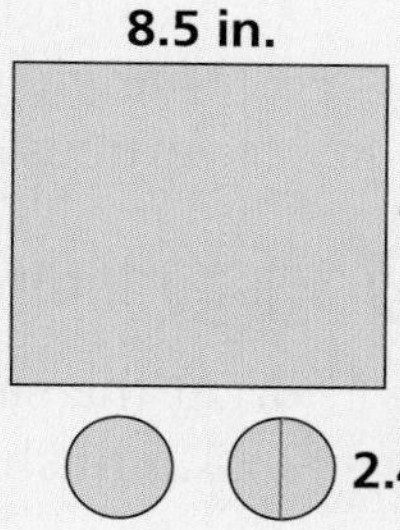

Think and Discuss

1. A salt crystal is a cube $\frac{1}{16}$ inch long on each side. What would a good scale be for a model of the crystal?

Try This

1. Measure the diameter and height of a can of soup. Determine a scale needed to use a $8\frac{1}{2}$ in. by 11 in. paper or card stock and make a scale model of the can.

READY TO GO ON?

SECTION 5B

Quiz for Lessons 5-5 Through 5-8

5-5 Similar Figures

Tell whether the triangles are similar.

1. $\triangle DEF$ and $\triangle JKL$

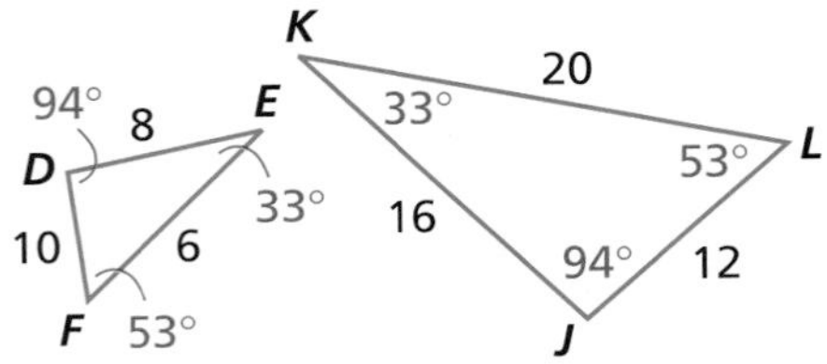

2. $\triangle PQR$ and $\triangle PRS$

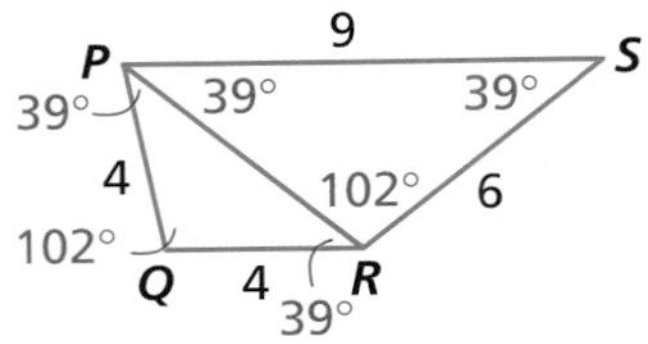

3. $\triangle UVW$ and $\triangle XYZ$

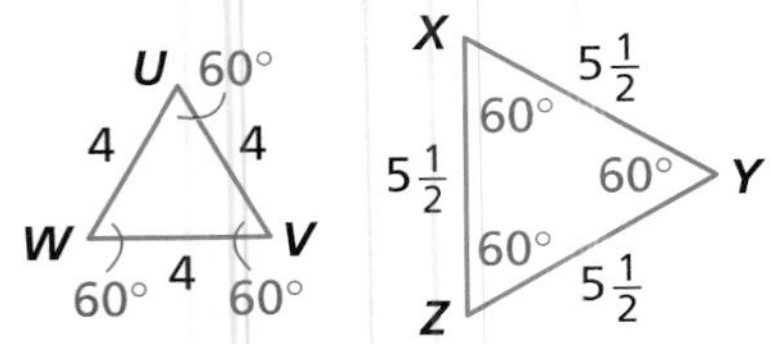

4. A picture 4 in. tall and 9 in. wide is to be scaled to 2.5 in. tall. How wide should the picture be for the two pictures to be similar?

5-6 Dilations

Tell whether each transformation is a dilation.

5.

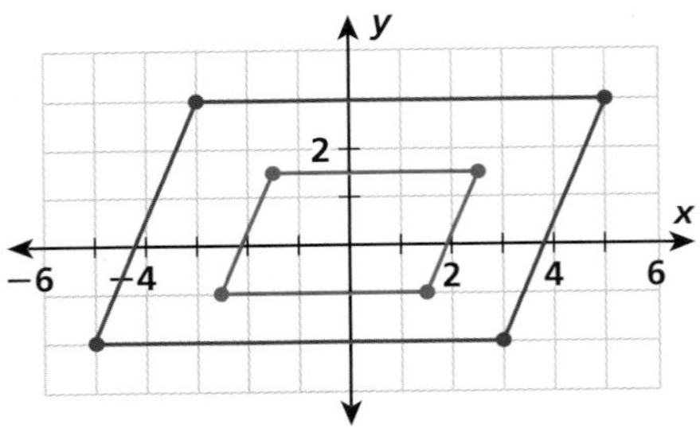

6.

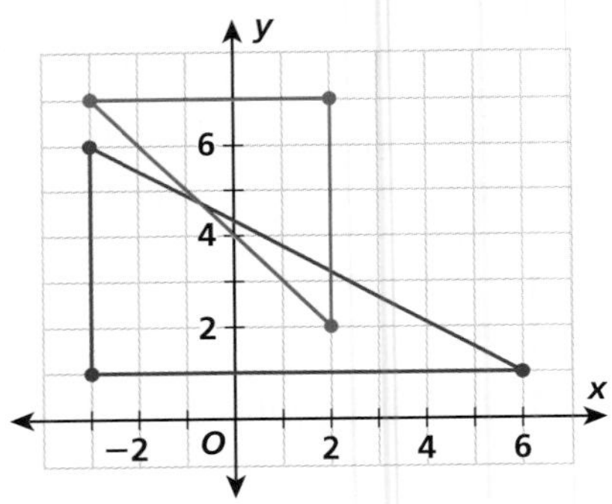

7. A triangle has vertices with coordinates (2, 0), (3, −1), and (−2, −5). If the triangle is dilated by a scale factor of 3, what are the coordinates of the vertices of the image?

5-7 Indirect Measurement

8. At the same time that a flagpole casts a 4.5 m shadow, a meter stick casts a 1.5 m shadow. How tall is the flagpole?

9. A tree casts a 30 foot shadow. Mi-Ling, standing next to the tree, casts a 13.5 foot shadow. If Mi-Ling is 5 ft tall, how tall is the tree?

5-8 Scale Drawings and Scale Models

10. $\frac{4}{20} = \frac{x}{16}$

11. $\frac{10}{4} = \frac{15}{x}$

12. $\frac{x}{3} = \frac{3}{12}$

13. $\frac{65}{x} = \frac{5}{15}$

14. The model of a 27 ft tall house was made using the scale 2 in:3 ft. What is the height of the model?

MULTI-STEP TEST PREP

CHAPTER 5

Javier Builds a Model Javier, an architect, builds a scale model of the new faculty center at the university. The diagram shows the scale model.

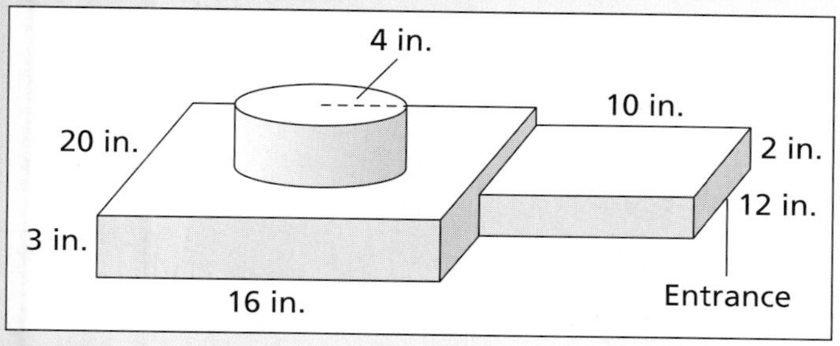

1. In the scale model, the entrance is 12 inches wide. If the entrance is actually 60 feet wide, what scale did Javier use to create the model? Explain your reasoning.
2. Find the actual dimensions of the new faculty center. Use the table to organize your work.

Model Dimensions	Actual Dimensions
2 in.	
3 in.	
4 in.	
10 in.	
12 in.	60 ft
16 in.	
20 in.	

3. Redraw the model and label its actual dimensions.
4. Javier makes a new model of the building using a scale of 1 in:10 ft. What is the width of the entrance in the new model?
5. How does the new model compare with the original one? Is it larger or smaller? Explain.

Multi-Step Test Prep

Game Time

Copy-Cat

You can use this method to copy a well-known work of art or any drawing. First, draw a grid over the work you want to copy, or draw a grid on tracing paper and tape it over the picture.

Next, on a separate sheet of paper draw a blank grid with the same number of squares. The squares do not have to be the same size. Copy each square from the original exactly onto the blank grid. Do not look at the overall picture as you copy. When you have copied all of the squares, the drawing on your finished grid should look just like the original work.

Suppose you are copying an image from a 12 in. by 18 in. print, and that you use 1-inch squares on the first grid.

1. If you use 3-inch squares on the blank grid, what size will your finished copy be?
2. If you want to make a copy that is 10 inches tall, what size should you make the squares on your blank grid? How wide will the copy be?
3. Choose a painting, drawing, or cartoon, and copy it using the method above.

Tic-Frac-Toe

Draw a large tic-tac-toe board. In each square, draw a blank proportion, $\frac{\square}{\square} = \frac{\square}{\square}$. Players take turns using a spinner with 12 sections or a 12-sided die. A player's turn consists of placing a number anywhere in one of the proportions. The player who correctly completes the proportion can claim that square. A square may also be blocked by filling in three parts of a proportion that cannot be completed with a number from 1 to 12. The first player to claim three squares in a row wins.

go.hrw.com
Game Time Extra
KEYWORD: MT7 Games

A complete copy of the gameboard is available online.

It's in the Bag!

FOLDNOTES

Materials
- wide duct tape
- ruler
- scissors
- 6 index cards (3 in. by 5 in.)
- markers

PROJECT A Worthwhile Wallet

Make a duct-tape wallet to carry index cards. The index cards will help you study ratios, proportions, and similarity.

Directions

1. Cut three strips of duct tape at least 9 inches long. Lay the strips next to each other, sticky side up, so that they overlap slightly. The total width should be about $5\frac{1}{2}$ inches. **Figure A**

2. Lay three more strips of duct tape on top of the first three, sticky side down. Trim the ends. This will make a sheet of duct-tape "fabric."

3. Fold up the fabric about $3\frac{1}{2}$ inches from the bottom to form a pocket. Use duct tape to seal the sides shut. **Figure B**

4. Fold the top down. Trim the corners of the flap. **Figure C**

A
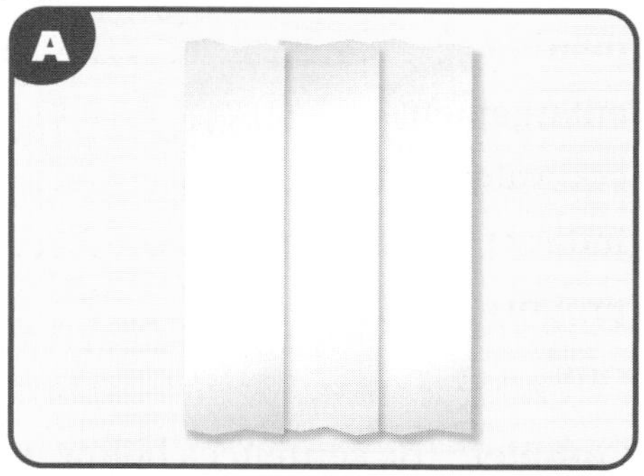

B

C
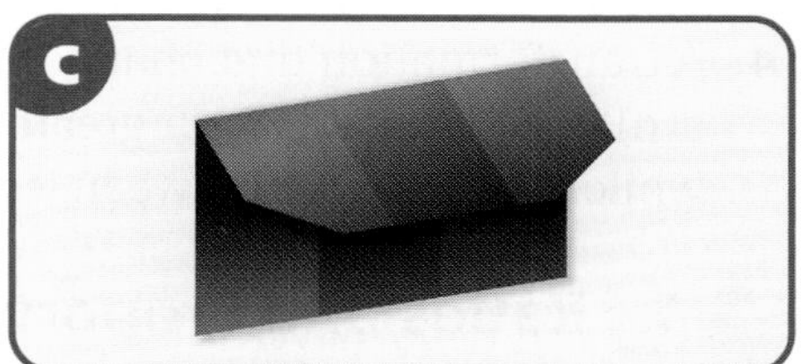

Taking Note of the Math

Review the chapter to identify key concepts. Then write vocabulary, examples, and practice problems on the index cards. Store the cards in the duct-tape wallet.

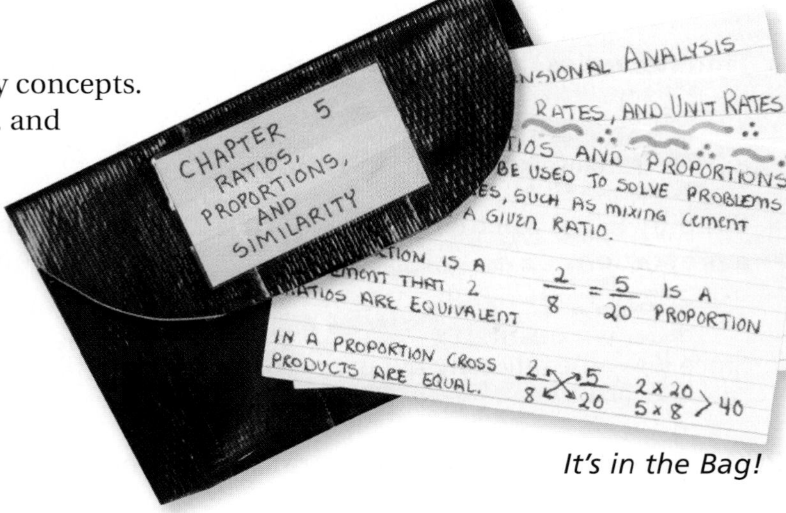

CHAPTER 5

Study Guide: Review

Vocabulary

center of dilation 244
congruent angles 238
conversion factor 224
cross product 229
dilation 244
enlargement 253
equivalent ratio 216
indirect measurement 248
proportion 216
rate 220
ratio 216
reduction 253
scale 252
scale drawing 252
scale factor 239
scale model 253
similar 238
unit price 221
unit rate 220

Complete the sentences below with vocabulary words from the list above. Words may be used more than once.

1. A(n) __?__ is a comparison of two quantities by division. Two ratios that are equivalent are said to be in __?__.
2. A(n) __?__ is a comparison of two quantities that have different units. A rate in which the second quantity is 1 is called a(n) __?__.
3. A scale drawing is mathematically __?__ to the actual object. All dimensions are reduced or enlarged using the same __?__.
4. A transformation that changes the size but not the shape of a figure is called a(n) __?__. A scale factor greater than 1 results in a(n) __?__ of the figure, while a scale factor between 0 and 1 results in a(n) __?__ of the figure.

5-1 Ratios and Proportions (pp. 216–219)

EXAMPLE

- **Find two ratios that are equivalent to $\frac{4}{12}$.**

$\frac{4 \cdot 2}{12 \cdot 2} = \frac{8}{24}$ $\qquad$ $\frac{4 \div 2}{12 \div 2} = \frac{2}{6}$

8:24 and 2:6 are equivalent to 4:12.

- **Simplify to tell whether $\frac{5}{15}$ and $\frac{6}{24}$ form a proportion.**

$\frac{5 \div 5}{15 \div 5} = \frac{1}{3}$ $\qquad$ $\frac{6 \div 6}{24 \div 6} = \frac{1}{4}$

Since $\frac{1}{3} \neq \frac{1}{4}$, the ratios are not in proportion.

EXERCISES

Find two ratios that are equivalent to each given ratio.

5. $\frac{8}{16}$
6. $\frac{9}{18}$
7. $\frac{35}{60}$

Simplify to tell whether the ratios form a proportion.

8. $\frac{8}{24}$ and $\frac{2}{6}$
9. $\frac{3}{12}$ and $\frac{6}{18}$
10. $\frac{25}{125}$ and $\frac{5}{25}$
11. $\frac{6}{8}$ and $\frac{9}{16}$

5-2 Ratios, Rates, and Unit Rates (pp. 220–223)

EXAMPLE

■ **Alex can buy a 4 pack of AA batteries for $2.99 or an 8 pack for $4.98. Which is the better buy?**

$\frac{\text{price per package}}{\text{number of batteries}} = \frac{\$2.99}{4} \approx \$0.75$ per battery

$\frac{\text{price per package}}{\text{number of batteries}} = \frac{\$4.98}{8} \approx \$0.62$ per battery

The better buy is the 8 pack for $4.98.

EXERCISES

Determine the better buy.

12. 50 formatted computer disks for $14.99 or 75 disks for $21.50

13. 6 boxes of 3-inch incense sticks for $22.50 or 8 boxes for $30

14. a package of 8 binder dividers for $23.09 or a 25 pack for $99.99

5-3 Dimensional Analysis (pp. 224–228)

EXAMPLE

■ **At a rate of 75 kilometers per hour, how many meters does a car travel in 1 minute?**

km to m: $\frac{1000\text{ m}}{1\text{ km}}$ h to min: $\frac{1\text{ h}}{60\text{ min}}$

$$\frac{75\not{\text{km}}}{1\not{\text{h}}} \cdot \frac{1000\text{ m}}{1\not{\text{km}}} \cdot \frac{1\not{\text{h}}}{60\text{ min}} = \frac{75 \cdot 1000\text{ m}}{60\text{ min}} = \frac{1250\text{ m}}{1\text{ min}}$$

The car travels 1250 meters in 1 minute.

EXERCISES

Use conversion factors to find each rate.

15. 90 km/h to m/h

16. 75 feet per second to feet per minute

17. 35 kilometers per hour to meters per minute

5-4 Solving Proportions (pp. 229–233)

EXAMPLE

■ **Solve the proportion $\frac{18}{12} = \frac{x}{2}$.**

$12x = 18 \cdot 2$ *Find the cross products.*

$\frac{12x}{12} = \frac{36}{12}$ *Divide both sides by 12.*

$x = 3$ *Simplify.*

EXERCISES

Solve each proportion.

18. $\frac{3}{5} = \frac{9}{x}$

19. $\frac{24}{h} = \frac{16}{4}$

20. $\frac{w}{6} = \frac{7}{2}$

21. $\frac{3}{8} = \frac{11}{y}$

5-5 Similar Figures (pp. 238–241)

EXAMPLE

■ **A stamp 1.2 in. tall and 1.75 in. wide is to be scaled to 4.2 in. tall. How wide should the new stamp be?**

$\frac{\text{scaled height}}{\text{original height}} = \frac{4.2}{1.2} = 3.5 = \text{scale factor}$

scaled width = original width · scale factor
= 1.75(3.5) = 6.125

The larger stamp should be 6.125 in. wide.

EXERCISES

22. A picture 3 in. wide by 5 in. tall is to be scaled to 7.5 in. wide to be put on a flyer. How tall should the flyer picture be?

23. A picture 8 in. wide by 10 in. tall is to be scaled to 2.5 in. wide to be put on an invitation. How tall should the invitation picture be?

5-6 Dilations (pp. 244–247)

EXAMPLE

■ **Dilate triangle ABC by a scale factor of 2 with $O(0, 0)$ as the center of dilation.**

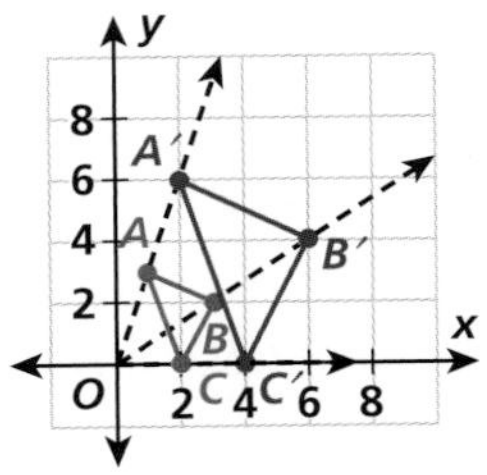

EXERCISES

Dilate each triangle ABC by the given scale factor with $O(0, 0)$ as the center of dilation.

24. $A(1, 0)$, $B(1, 2)$, $C(3, 1)$; scale factor = 3

25. $A(4, 6)$, $B(8, 4)$, $C(6, 2)$; scale factor = 0.5

26. $A(2, 2)$, $B(6, 2)$, $C(4, 4)$; scale factor = 1.5

5-7 Indirect Measurement (pp. 248–251)

EXAMPLE

■ **A telephone pole casts a 5 ft shadow at the same time that a man standing next to it casts a 1.5 ft shadow. If the man is 6 ft tall, how tall is the telephone pole?**

$\frac{1.5}{5} = \frac{6}{x}$ *Set up a proportion.*

$1.5x = 30$ *Find the cross products.*

$\frac{1.5x}{1.5} = \frac{30}{1.5}$ *Divide both sides by 1.5.*

$x = 20$ *Simplify.*

The telephone pole is 20 ft tall.

EXERCISES

27. A flagpole casts a 15 ft shadow at the same time Jon casts a 5 ft shadow. If Jon is 6 ft tall, how tall is the flagpole?

28. April casts a 16.5 ft shadow at the same time that Ron casts an 18.6 ft shadow. If April is 5.5 ft tall, how tall is Ron?

5-8 Scale Drawings and Scale Models (pp. 252–255)

EXAMPLE

■ **A length on a map is 4.2 in. The scale is 1 in:100 mi. Find the actual distance.**

$\frac{1 \text{ in.}}{100 \text{ mi}} = \frac{4.2 \text{ in.}}{x \text{ mi}}$ *Set up a proportion using* $\frac{\text{scale length}}{\text{actual length}}$

$1 \cdot x = 100 \cdot 4.2$ *Find the cross products.*

$x = 420$ mi *Simplify.*

The actual distance is 420 mi.

EXERCISES

29. A length on a scale drawing is 5.4 cm. The scale is 1 cm:12 m. Find the actual length.

30. A 79.2 ft length is to be scaled on a drawing with the scale 1 in:12 ft. Find the scaled length.

31. A locomotive of a model train is 5 inches long. If the actual locomotive is 80 feet long, what is the scale of the model?

The scale of a map is 1 in.:10 mi. How many actual miles does each measurement represent?

32. 4.6 in.

33. $5\frac{3}{4}$ in.

34. 15.3 in.

35. $7\frac{1}{4}$ in.

Study Guide: Review

CHAPTER TEST

CHAPTER 5

Simplify to tell whether the ratios form a proportion.

1. $\frac{4}{5}$ and $\frac{16}{20}$ **2.** $\frac{33}{60}$ and $\frac{11}{21}$ **3.** $\frac{7}{9}$ and $\frac{35}{45}$ **4.** $\frac{8}{20}$ and $\frac{4}{25}$

Estimate each unit rate.

5. \$3.59 for $\frac{1}{2}$ pound

6. 57 students in 3 classrooms

7. \$46.50 for 5 hours

8. 62 books on 5 shelves

9. You can buy one 10 pack of AAA batteries for \$5.49 and get one free, or buy two 4 packs for \$2.98. Which is the better buy?

Find the appropriate factor for each conversion.

10. gallons to quarts **11.** millimeters to centimeters **12.** hours to days

Use conversion factors to find each unit to the nearest hundredth.

13. Change 60 ounces to pounds.

14. Change 35 pounds to ounces.

15. Simon bought 5 cans of chili for \$10.95. At this rate, how much would 12 cans of chili cost?

Solve each proportion.

16. $\frac{6}{9} = \frac{n}{72}$ **17.** $\frac{18}{12} = \frac{3}{x}$ **18.** $\frac{0.7}{1.4} = \frac{z}{28}$ **19.** $\frac{12}{y} = \frac{32}{16}$

20. Fran scans a document that is 8.5 in. wide by 11 in. long into her computer. If she scales the length down to 7 in., how wide should the similar document be?

Tell whether each transformation is a dilation.

21.

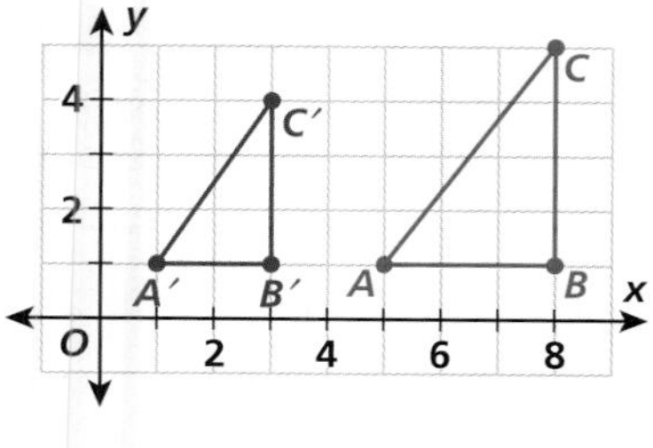

22.

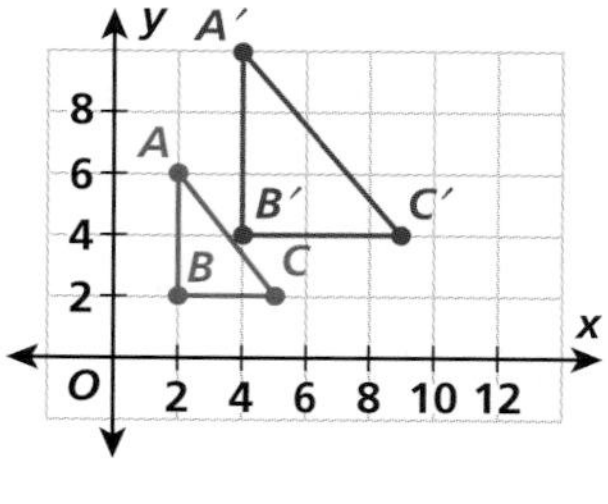

23. Wally has an 18 in. model of a 42 ft. dinosaur, *Tyrannosaurus rex*. What scale factor does this represent?

24. Margie's school building casts a 12.5 ft shadow at the same time that Margie casts a 2.875 ft shadow. If Margie is 5.75 ft tall, how tall is the school?

25. If a wall in a $\frac{1}{4}$ in. scale drawing is 3 in. tall, how tall is the actual wall?

CHAPTER 5

TEST TACKLER

Standardized Test Strategies

Short Response: Write Short Responses

To answer a short response test item completely, you must show how you solved the problem and explain your answer. Short response test items are scored using a 2-point scoring rubric. A sample scoring rubric is shown below.

EXAMPLE 1

Short Response A carpenter is pouring a concrete foundation for a garden planter in the shape of a right triangle. The length of one leg of the planter is 18 feet, and the length of the diagonal is 22 feet. What is the length of the other leg of the planter? Round your answer to the nearest tenth. Show all of your work.

Here are examples of how different responses were scored using the scoring rubric shown.

2-point response:

Let s = the length of the other leg.

$18^2 + s^2 = 22^2$ *Use the Pythagorean Theorem.*

$s^2 = 160$

$\sqrt{s} = \sqrt{160}$ *Find the square root.*

$s = 12.64911$ *Round to the nearest tenth.*

$s = 12.6$ *ft.*

The length of the other leg is 12.6 ft.

1-point response:

Let s = the length of the other leg.

$18^2 + s^2 = 22^2$

$324 + s^2 = 484$

$\sqrt{s} = \sqrt{160}$

$s = 13$ *ft*

The length of the other leg is 13 ft.

The student showed all of the work, but there was a minor computation error, which resulted in an incorrect answer.

0-point response:

$s = 12$

The student's answer is not rounded to the nearest tenth, and there is no explanation.

Scoring Rubric

2 points: The student demonstrates a thorough understanding of the concept, correctly answers the question, and provides a complete explanation.

1 point: The student correctly answers the question but does not show all work or does not provide an explanation.

1 point: The student makes minor errors, resulting in an incorrect solution, but shows an understanding of the concept through explanation.

0 points: The student gives a response showing no work or giving no explanation, or the student gives no response.

HOT TIP! Read short-response test items carefully. If you are allowed to write in the test booklet, underline or circle the parts of the question that tell you what your solution must include. Be sure to use complete sentences in your explanation.

Read each test item, and answer the questions that follow by using the scoring rubric on page 266.

Item A

Dilate the figure by a scale factor of $\frac{1}{4}$ with the origin as the center of dilation. What are the vertices of the image? Show all of your work.

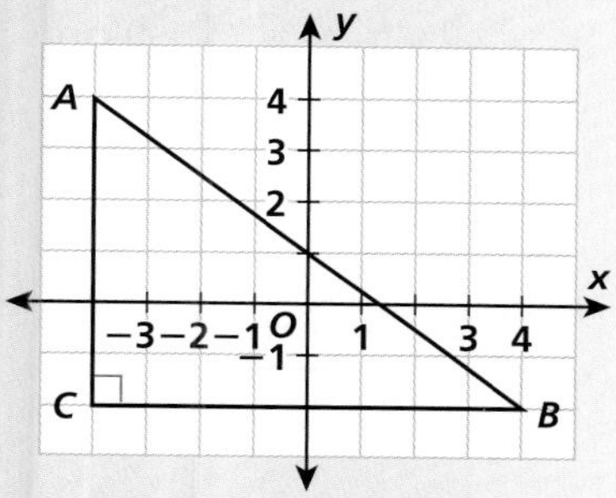

Student's Response

$A'(-1, 1)$, $B'\left(1, -\frac{1}{2}\right)$, $C'\left(-1, -\frac{1}{2}\right)$

1. What score should the student's response receive? Explain your reasoning.
2. What additional information, if any, should the student's answer include in order for the student to receive full credit?

Item B

The ratio of the length of a rectangular garden to its width is 12:5. If the width of the garden is 8 feet, find the area of the garden. Show all of your work.

Student's Response

$\frac{l}{w} = \frac{12}{5}$ *The ratio of the length to the width is 12:5.*

$\frac{12}{5} = \frac{8}{l}$; $12l = 40$; $l = 3.\overline{3}$ *The length is 3.3 ft.*

$A = lw$; $A = 3.3 \times 8 = 26.4$

The area is $26.4\ ft^2$.

3. What score should the student's response receive? Explain your reasoning.
4. What additional information, if any, should the student's answer include in order for the student to receive full credit?

Item C

An office supply store charges \$24 for 72 file folders. A student says that the unit price is \$3 per folder. What is the student's error? What is the correct unit price? Show all of your work.

Student's Response

The student divided wrong. The student should have divided 24 by 72, not 72 by 24.

5. What score should the student's response receive? Explain your reasoning.
6. What additional information, if any, should the student's answer include in order for the student to receive full credit?

STANDARDIZED TEST PREP

go.hrw.com
State Test Practice Online
KEYWORD: MT7 TestPrep

Cumulative Assessment, Chapters 1–5

Multiple Choice

1. Which inequality describes the graph?

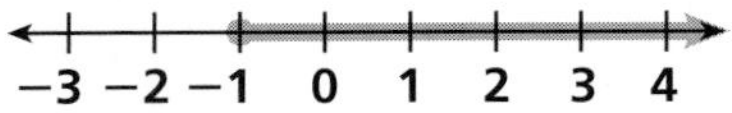

Ⓐ $x < -1$ Ⓒ $x \leq -1$

Ⓑ $x > -1$ Ⓓ $x \geq -1$

2. Which value of x is the solution of the equation $-6x = 48$?

Ⓕ $x = -8$ Ⓗ $x = 42$

Ⓖ $x = -6$ Ⓙ $x = 54$

3. Which two numbers both have an absolute value of 6?

Ⓐ 0 and 6 Ⓒ −3 and 3

Ⓑ −6 and 6 Ⓓ 5 and −1

4. What is the next number in this sequence? −1, −4, −7, −10, ▢ . . .

Ⓕ 16 Ⓗ −12

Ⓖ 13 Ⓙ −13

5. If a drinking glass holds $\frac{1}{16}$ gallon of water, how many gallons of water are contained in 8 drinking glasses?

Ⓐ $\frac{1}{8}$ gallon Ⓒ 2 gallons

Ⓑ $\frac{1}{2}$ gallon Ⓓ 64 gallons

6. A turnstile counted 1040 people who entered a zoo in a 4-hour period. Which proportion can be used to find how many people p entered in an 8-hour period at the same hourly rate?

Ⓕ $\frac{4}{1040} = \frac{p}{8}$ Ⓗ $\frac{4}{p} = \frac{8}{1040}$

Ⓖ $\frac{1040}{4} = \frac{p}{8}$ Ⓙ $\frac{4}{1040} = \frac{12}{p}$

7. Which ratio pairs are NOT in proportion?

Ⓐ $\frac{3}{7}$ and $\frac{9}{21}$ Ⓒ $\frac{3}{8}$ and $\frac{4}{9}$

Ⓑ $\frac{9}{4}$ and $\frac{18}{8}$ Ⓓ $\frac{2}{3}$ and $\frac{10}{15}$

8. Which figure is similar to the figure below?

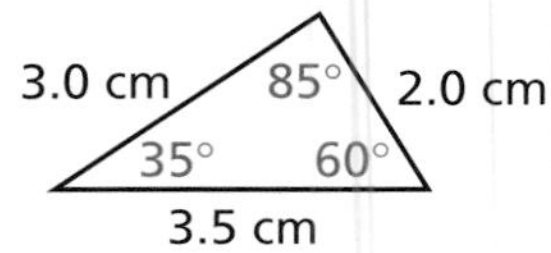

Ⓕ

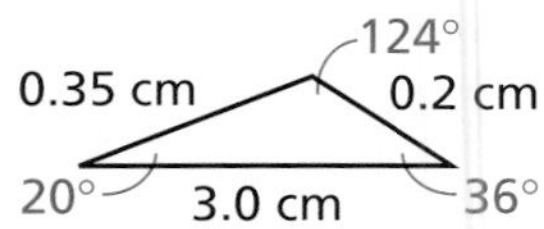

Ⓖ

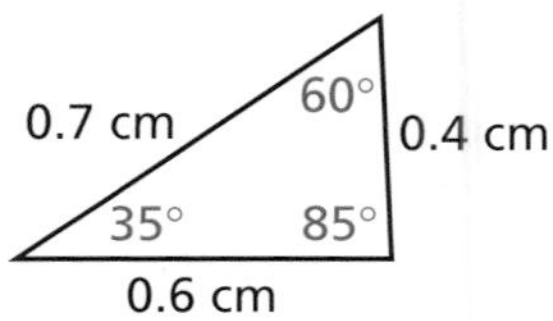

Ⓗ

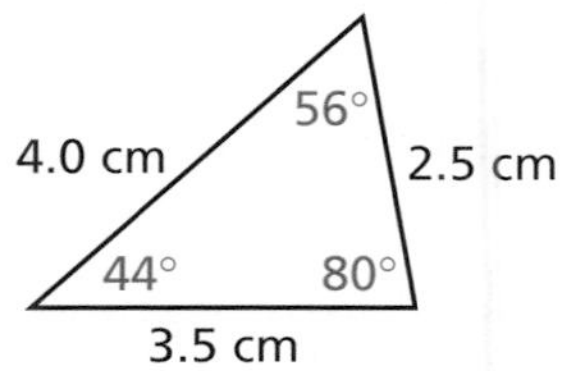

Ⓙ

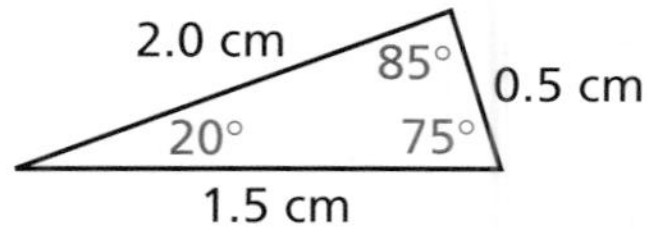

9. Which set of fractions are in order from least to greatest?

Ⓐ $\frac{3}{8}, \frac{1}{4}, \frac{2}{5}, \frac{1}{3}$ Ⓒ $\frac{1}{4}, \frac{1}{3}, \frac{2}{5}, \frac{3}{8}$

Ⓑ $\frac{1}{3}, \frac{1}{4}, \frac{2}{5}, \frac{3}{8}$ Ⓓ $\frac{1}{4}, \frac{1}{3}, \frac{3}{8}, \frac{2}{5}$

HOT TIP! It is helpful to draw or redraw a figure. Answers to geometry problems may become clearer as you redraw the figure.

10. The area of a square is 85 square feet. Which measurement best approximates a side length?

Ⓕ 8.8 ft   Ⓗ 9.2 ft

Ⓖ 9 ft   Ⓙ 9.9 ft

Gridded Response

11. A football team earns a first down when the team has moved the ball 10 yards forward. If a team has moved the ball forward 15 feet, what is the least number of yards the team needs to earn a first down?

12. A ballet class has a rule that all productions must have a ratio of 4 boys for every 5 girls. If there are 12 boys in a production, how many girls can be in the same production?

13. What is the length, in feet, of the base of the sail, *x*?

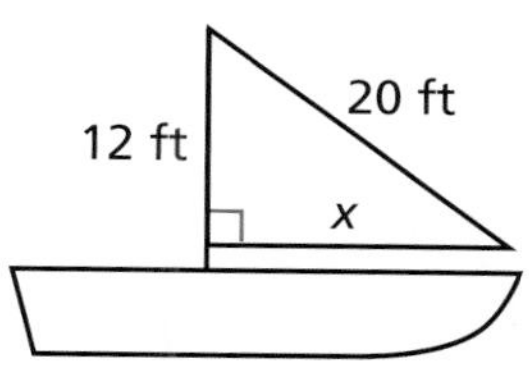

14. A 60-yard piece of string is divided into three pieces. The first piece is twice the length of the second piece, and the third piece is three times the length of the second piece. What is the length in yards of the longest piece?

15. If a snail moves 5 centimeters in 10 seconds, how fast in meters per minute can a snail move?

16. Three friends split the cost of a birthday present and a meal for another friend. The present cost $56.75, and the meal cost $23.65. Find the amount that each friend paid.

Short Response

17. At the student store, the ratio of notebooks sold to three-ring binders sold is 5 to 7.

a. At this rate, how many notebooks can you predict will be sold if 210 three-ring binders are sold? Show your work.

b. At the same rate, predict how many total notebooks and three-ring binders will be sold. Explain your reasoning.

18. While shopping for school supplies Sara finds boxes of pencils in two sizes. One box has 8 pencils for $0.89, and the other box has 12 pencils for $1.25.

a. Which box is the better bargain? Why? Round your answer to the nearest cent.

b. How much would it save to buy 48 pencils at the better rate? Show your work.

Extended Response

19. To build an accurate model of the solar system, choose a diameter for the model of the Sun. Then all distances and sizes of the planets can be calculated proportionally using the table below.

a. What is the diameter of Pluto in the model?

b. What is Pluto's distance from the Sun in the model?

c. What would Pluto's distance from the Sun be in the model if the Sun's diameter were changed to 2 ft?

	Sun	Mars	Jupiter	Pluto
Diameter (mi)	864,000	4200	88,640	1410
Distance from Sun (million mi)		141	483	3670

CHAPTER

6 Percents

6A Proportions and Percents
6-1 Relating Decimals, Fractions, and Percents
6-2 Estimate with Percents
6-3 Finding Percents
6-4 Finding a Number When the Percent Is Known
6B Applying Percents
6-5 Percent Increase and Decrease
6-6 Applications of Percents
6-7 Simple Interest
LAB Compute Compound Interest
MULTI-STEP TEST PREP

go.hrw.com
Chapter Project Online
KEYWORD: MT7 Ch6

Player	Age	At Bats	Home Runs	At Bats/Home Runs
Barry Bonds	40	9098	703	12.9
Sammy Sosa	36	8021	574	14.0
Ken Griffey Jr.	35	7376	501	14.7
Alex Rodriguez	29	5590	381	14.7

Career Sports Statistician

Statisticians are mathematicians who work with data, creating statistics, graphs, and tables that describe and explain the real world. Sports statisticians combine their love of sports with their ability to use mathematics.

Statistics not only explain what has happened, but can help you predict what may happen in the future. The table describes the home run hitting of some Major League baseball players as of the 2004 season.

ARE YOU READY?

Vocabulary

Choose the best term from the list to complete each sentence.

cross multiply
equivalent ratios
proportion
ratio

1. A(n) __?__ is a comparison of two quantities by division.
2. Ratios that make the same comparison are __?__.
3. Two ratios that are equivalent are in __?__.
4. To solve a proportion, you can __?__.

Complete these exercises to review skills you will need for this chapter.

Write Fractions as Decimals

Write each fraction as a decimal.

5. $\frac{3}{4}$ **6.** $\frac{5}{8}$ **7.** $\frac{2}{5}$ **8.** $\frac{2}{3}$

Write Decimals as Fractions

Write each decimal as a fraction in simplest form.

9. 0.7 **10.** 0.6 **11.** 0.25 **12.** 0.375

13. 0.2 **14.** 0.9 **15.** 0.86 **16.** 0.99

Solve Proportions

Solve each proportion.

17. $\frac{x}{3} = \frac{9}{27}$ **18.** $\frac{7}{8} = \frac{h}{4}$ **19.** $\frac{9}{n} = \frac{2}{3}$

20. $\frac{3}{8} = \frac{12}{t}$ **21.** $\frac{4}{5} = \frac{28}{z}$ **22.** $\frac{100}{p} = \frac{90}{45}$

Multiply with Fractions and Decimals

Multiply.

23. $\frac{12}{13} \times 8$ **24.** 18×0.45 **25.** $20 \times \frac{9}{10}$

26. 2.75×11 **27.** $\frac{1}{5} \times 12$ **28.** 6×0.08

29. $13 \times \frac{25}{26}$ **30.** 15.32×9 **31.** $\frac{2}{9} \times 78$

CHAPTER 6

Study Guide: Preview

Where You've Been

Previously, you

- compared and ordered integers and positive rational numbers.
- found solutions to application problems involving proportional relationships.

In This Chapter

You will study

- comparing and ordering rational numbers, including integers, percents, and positive and negative fractions and decimals.
- estimating and solving application problems involving percents.

Where You're Going

You can use the skills learned in this chapter

- to estimate tips.
- to find sales tax.
- to calculate discounts or markups.
- to find the amount of interest earned over a given time.

Key Vocabulary/Vocabulario

commission	comisión
compatible numbers	números compatibles
estimate	estimación
interest	interés
percent	por ciento
percent decrease	porcentaje de disminución
percent increase	porcentaje de aumento
principal	capital
sales tax	impuesto sobre la venta
simple interest	interés simple

Vocabulary Connections

To become familiar with some of the vocabulary terms in the chapter, consider the following. You may refer to the chapter, the glossary, or a dictionary if you like.

1. The word *principal* means "first." What do you suppose **principal** means when referring to interest?
2. The word **commission** has the Latin prefix *com-*, which means "with," and the Latin root *mis,* which means "send." What do you think these Latin parts mean together when referring to money?
3. The word *percent* contains the root word *cent,* which means "one hundred." What do you think a **percent** is?

Study Guide: Preview

Reading and Writing Math

CHAPTER 6

Reading Strategy: Read Problems for Understanding

When solving a word problem, first read the problem to identify exactly what the problems asks you to do. Then read the problem again, slowly and carefully, to break the problem into parts. Highlight or underline the key information. Then make a plan to solve the problem.

From Lesson 5-5

15. Art Helen is copying a printed reproduction of the *Mona Lisa*. The print is 24 in. wide and 36 in. tall. If Helen's canvas is 12 in. wide, how tall should her canvas be?

Slowly read the exercise again.

Step 1	**Identify exactly what the problem asks you to do.**	• Find the height of the canvas Helen should use.
Step 2	**Break the problem into parts. Highlight or underline the key information.**	• The print is **24 in. wide** and **36 in. tall.** • The canvas is **12 in. wide** • The **height** of the canvas is **unknown.** • The print and the copy are **similar rectangles.**
Step 3	**Make a plan to solve the problem.**	• Set up a proportion using the corresponding sides of the similar rectangles. • Find the cross products, and solve for x. • Check the answer by making sure the cross products are equal.

Try This

For the problem below,

a. identify exactly what the problem asks you to do.

b. break the problem into parts. Highlight or underline the key information.

c. Make a plan to solve the problem.

1. An 8-pound weight is positioned 2 feet from a fulcrum. Another weight is placed 12 feet from the fulcrum on the opposite end. For the scale to balance, how much should this second weight weigh?

6-1 Relating Decimals, Fractions, and Percents

Learn to compare and order decimals, fractions, and percents.

Vocabulary

percent

In an average day, a typical newborn baby sleeps 16 out of 24 hours. The part of a day the baby sleeps can be shown in several ways.

$$\frac{16}{24} = 0.66\overline{6} = 66.\overline{6}\%$$

So newborns sleep over 60% of the time.

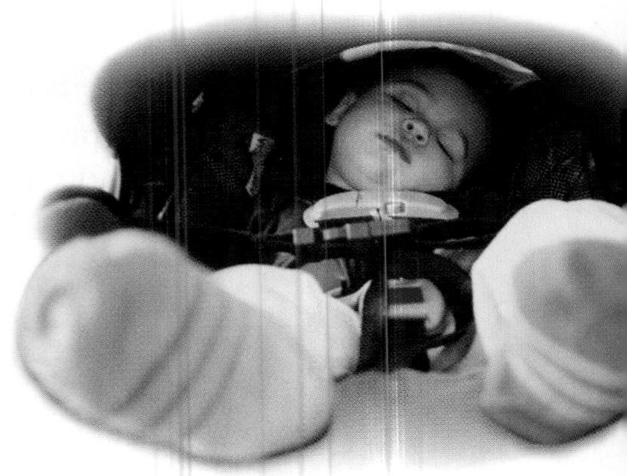

Percents are ratios that compare a number to 100.

Reading Math

Think of the % symbol as meaning per 100 or /100.
75% = 75/100 = 0.75

Ratio	Decimal	Percent
$\frac{3}{10} = \frac{30}{100}$	0.30	30%
$\frac{1}{2} = \frac{50}{100}$	0.50	50%
$\frac{3}{4} = \frac{75}{100}$	0.75	75%

To convert a fraction to a decimal, divide the numerator by the denominator.

$$\frac{1}{8} = 1 \div 8 = 0.125$$

To convert a decimal to a percent, multiply by 100 and insert the percent symbol.

$$0.125 \cdot 100 \rightarrow 12.5\%$$

```
   0.125
8)1.000
  8
  20
  16
   40
   40
    0
```

EXAMPLE 1 Finding Equivalent Ratios and Percents

Find the missing ratio or percent equivalent for each letter on the number line.

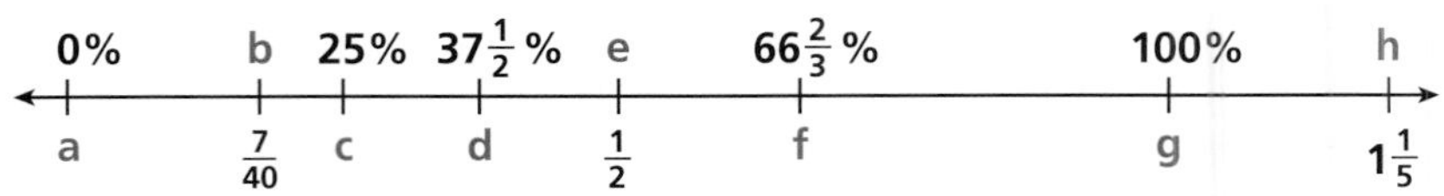

a: $0\% = \frac{0}{100} = 0$

b: $\frac{7}{40} = 0.175 = 17.5\% = 17\frac{1}{2}\%$

c: $25\% = \frac{25}{100} = \frac{5}{20} = \frac{1}{4}$

d: $37\frac{1}{2}\% = 0.375 = \frac{375}{1000} = \frac{3}{8}$

e: $\frac{1}{2} = 0.5 = 50\%$

f: $66\frac{2}{3}\% = 0.66\overline{6} = \frac{2}{3}$

g: $100\% = \frac{100}{100} = 1$

h: $1\frac{1}{5} = 1.2 = 120\%$

To compare and order fractions, decimals, and percents, write them in the same form first.

Remember!

When multiplying a decimal by 100, simply move the decimal point two spaces to the right.

EXAMPLE 2 Comparing Fractions, Decimals, and Percents

Compare. Write <, >, or =.

A $\frac{1}{2}$ ▢ 37%

$\frac{1}{2} = 0.50 = 50\%$ *Write as a percent.*

$50\% > 37\%$ *Compare.*

$\frac{1}{2} > 37\%$

B 0.125 ▢ 19%

$0.125 = 12.5\%$ *Write as a percent.*

$12.5\% < 19\%$ *Compare.*

$0.125 < 19\%$

EXAMPLE 3 Ordering Fractions, Decimals, and Percents

Write 0.25%, $\frac{13}{5}$, 0.57, and 300% in order from least to greatest.

$\frac{13}{5} = 2.6 = 260\%$ *Write as percents.*

$0.57 = 57\%$

$0.25\% < 57\% < 260\% < 300\%$ *Compare.*

0.25%, 0.57, $\frac{13}{5}$, 300%

EXAMPLE 4 *Physical Science Application*

The United States nickel was once made of 100% nickel. Today nickels are 3 parts copper and 1 part nickel. What percent of today's nickel is pure nickel?

$\frac{\text{parts pure nickel}}{\text{total parts}} \rightarrow \frac{1}{4}$ *Set up a ratio and simplify.*

$\frac{1}{4} = 1 \div 4 = 0.25 = 25\%$ *Find the percent.*

So today's nickel is 25% pure nickel.

Think and Discuss

1. **Give an example** of a real-world situation in which you would use (1) decimals, (2) fractions, and (3) percents.
2. **Show** 25 cents as a part of a dollar in terms of (1) a reduced fraction, (2) a percent, and (3) a decimal. Which is most common?
3. **Explain** how you can find a fraction, decimal, or percent when you have only one form of a number.

6-1 Exercises

go.hrw.com
Homework Help Online
KEYWORD: MT7 6-1
Parent Resources Online
KEYWORD: MT7 Parent

GUIDED PRACTICE

See Example 1 **Find the missing ratio or percent equivalent for each letter on the number line.**

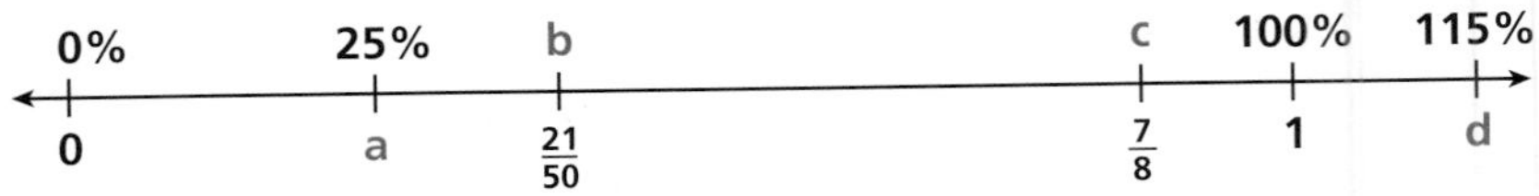

1. a **2.** b **3.** c **4.** d

See Example 2 **Compare. Write <, >, or =.**

5. $\frac{3}{4}$ ▒ 70% **6.** 42% ▒ $\frac{2}{5}$ **7.** 87.5% ▒ 0.875 **8.** 0.99 ▒ 100%

See Example 3 **Order the numbers from least to greatest.**

9. 36%, 0.3, $33\frac{1}{3}$%, $\frac{3}{8}$ **10.** $\frac{4}{5}$, −0.5, 500%, $66\frac{2}{3}$%

See Example 4 **11.** A molecule of water is made up of 2 atoms of hydrogen and 1 atom of oxygen. What percent of the atoms of a water molecule is oxygen?

INDEPENDENT PRACTICE

See Example 1 **Find the missing ratio or percent equivalent for each letter on the number line.**

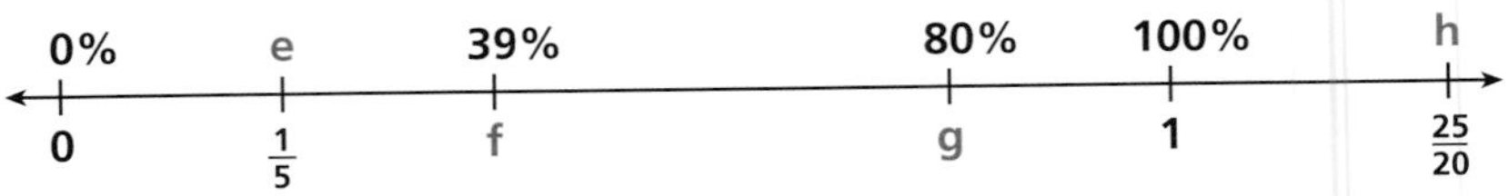

12. e **13.** f **14.** g **15.** h

See Example 2 **Compare. Write <, >, or =.**

16. $\frac{2}{3}$ ▒ 66% **17.** 37% ▒ $\frac{3}{8}$ **18.** 6% ▒ 0.6 **19.** 0.09 ▒ 9%

See Example 3 **Order the numbers from least to greatest.**

20. −6%, 0.6, $66\frac{1}{3}$%, $\frac{3}{6}$ **21.** $\frac{2}{5}$, 0.04, 42%, 70%

See Example 4 **22.** Sterling silver is an alloy combining 925 parts pure silver and 75 parts of another metal, such as copper. What percent of sterling silver is not pure silver?

PRACTICE AND PROBLEM SOLVING

Extra Practice
See page 792.

Write the labels from each circle graph as percents.

23.

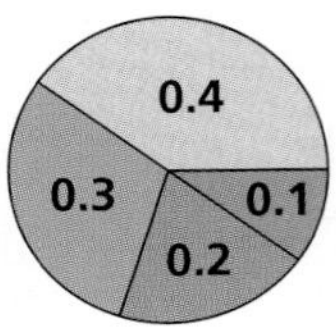

24.

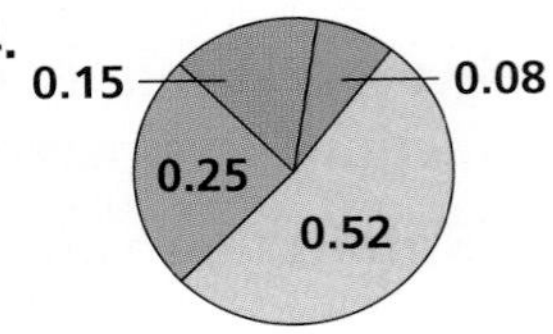

25.

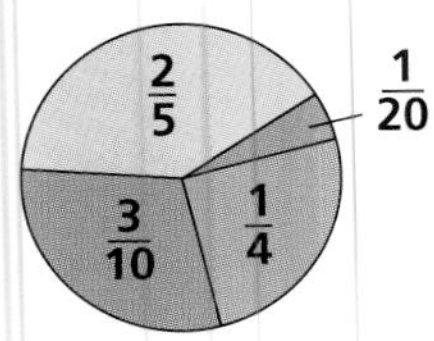

26. **Patterns** Find the next three numbers in this pattern. Then describe the pattern.

$\frac{1}{8}$, 25%, 0.375, $\frac{1}{2}$, 62.5%, 0.75

27. **Critical Thinking** Describe a situation when changing a fraction to a percent would be helpful.

28. **Geography** The graph shows the percents of the total U.S. land area taken up by the five largest states. The sixth section of the graph represents the area of the remaining 45 states.

Total Land by State in the United States

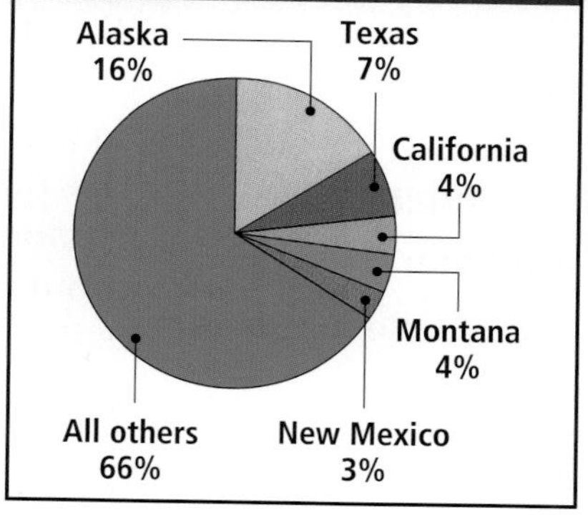

a. Alaska is the largest state in total land area. Write Alaska's portion of the total U.S. land area as a fraction and as a decimal.

b. What percent of the total U.S. land area is taken up by Alaska and Texas? How might you describe this percent?

29. **What's the Error?** An analysis showed that 0.06% of the T-shirts made by one company were defective. A student says this is 6 out of every 100. What is the student's error?

30. **Write About It** Explain the steps you would take to order $\frac{1}{3}$, 0.33, and 30% from least to greatest.

31. **Challenge** Wyatt and Allyson were asked to solve a percent problem using the numbers 13 and 38. Wyatt found 13% of 38, and Allyson found 38% of 13. Explain why they both got the same answer. Would this work for other numbers as well? Why or why not?

TEST PREP and Spiral Review

32. **Multiple Choice** Of the 32 students in Mr. Smith's class, 12 have jobs during the summer. What percent of the students have a summer job?

Ⓐ 12% Ⓑ 20% Ⓒ 37.5% Ⓓ 62.5%

33. **Multiple Choice** Claudia has 40 CDs. Of these, 14 are country music CDs. What percent of Claudia's CD collection is country music?

Ⓕ 40% Ⓖ 35% Ⓗ 14% Ⓙ 12%

Compare. Write <, >, =. (Lesson 2-2)

34. $\frac{4}{9}$ ■ $\frac{21}{25}$ 35. $\frac{3}{7}$ ■ $\frac{8}{9}$ 36. $-\frac{1}{3}$ ■ $-\frac{2}{5}$ 37. $-\frac{8}{14}$ ■ $-\frac{4}{7}$

Find the common difference in each sequence. (Lesson 3-6)

38. 1.2, 2.4, 3.6, 4.8, . . . 39. 27, 23, 19, 15, . . . 40. 0, −8, −16, −24, . . .

6-2 Estimate with Percents

Problem Solving Skill

Learn to estimate percents.

Vocabulary
estimate
compatible numbers
benchmark

Waiters, waitresses, and other restaurant employees depend upon tips for much of their income. Typically, a tip is 15% to 20% of the bill. Tips do not have to be calculated exactly, so estimation is often used. When the sales tax is about 8%, doubling the tax gives a good estimate for a tip.

Some problems require only an **estimate**. Estimates involving percents and fractions can be found by using **compatible numbers**, numbers that go well together because they have common factors.

$\frac{13}{24}$ *13 and 24 are not compatible numbers.*

$\frac{12}{24}$ *12 and 24 are compatible numbers because 12 is a common factor of 12 and 24*

$\frac{12}{24} = \frac{1}{2}$ *Simplify.*

$\frac{13}{24} \approx \frac{1}{2}$ *$\frac{13}{24}$ is nearly equivalent to $\frac{12}{24}$*

When estimating with percents, it helps to know some *benchmarks*. **Benchmarks** are common numbers that serve as points of reference. Some common benchmarks for percents are shown in the table.

Percent	Decimal	Fraction	Percent	Decimal	Fraction
5%	0.05	$\frac{1}{20}$	50%	0.5	$\frac{1}{2}$
10%	0.1	$\frac{1}{10}$	$66.\overline{6}$%	$0.\overline{6}$	$\frac{2}{3}$
25%	0.25	$\frac{1}{4}$	75%	0.75	$\frac{3}{4}$
$33.\overline{3}$%	$0.\overline{3}$	$\frac{1}{3}$	100%	1	1

EXAMPLE 1 Estimating with Percents

Estimate.

A **24% of 44**

$24\% \approx 25\%$ *Use a benchmark close to 24%.*

$\approx \frac{1}{4}$ *Write 25% as a fraction.*

$\frac{1}{4} \cdot 44 = 11$ *Use mental math: 44 ÷ 4.*

24% of 44 is about 11.

Estimate.

B **36% of 20**

$36\% \approx 35\%$	*Round.*
$\approx 25\% + 10\%$	*Break the percent into two benchmarks.*
$35\% \cdot 20 = (25\% + 10\%) \cdot 20$	*Set up an equation.*
$= 25\% \cdot 20 + 10\% \cdot 20$	*Use Distributive Property.*
$= 5 + 2$	*25% of 20 is 5, and 10% of 20 is 2.*

36% of 20 is about 7.

EXAMPLE 2 ***PROBLEM SOLVING APPLICATION***

PROBLEM SOLVING

Angelica ate lunch with a group of friends. The restaurant would not issue separate checks, so each friend had to calculate what she owed. Angelica's entrée, drink, and dessert cost a total of \$9.75. If the sales tax rate is 8.25% and Angelica wants to leave a 15% tip, about how much should she pay?

1 Understand the Problem

The **answer** is the total amount Angelica should pay for her lunch.

List the important information:

- Angelica's food and drink cost a total of \$9.75.
- The sales tax rate is 8.25%.
- Angelica wants to leave a 15% tip.

2 Make a Plan

Think: Sales tax and tip together are 23.25% of Angelica's food and drink total (8.25% + 15% = 23.25%). The numbers \$9.75 and 23.25% are difficult to work with. Use compatible numbers: \$9.75 is close to \$10.00; 23.25% is close to 25%.

3 Solve

$$\$10.00 \cdot 25\% = \$10.00 \cdot 0.25$$
$$= \$2.50$$

$\$9.75 + \$2.50 = \$12.25$

Angelica should pay \$12.25.

4 Look Back

To determine whether \$12.25 is a reasonable estimate of what Angelica should pay, use a calculator to find the tax and the tip for \$9.75.

$\$9.75 \cdot 1.2325 = \$12.02$, so \$12.25 is a reasonable estimate.

EXAMPLE 3 *Manufacturing Application*

A company has found that on average 9% of the radios it manufactures are defective. Out of a production run of 1523 radios, the plant manager assumes that 137 are defective. Estimate to see if the plant manager's number is reasonable. Explain.

$9\% \cdot 1523 \approx 10\% \cdot 1500$		*Use compatible numbers.*
$\approx 0.1 \cdot 1500$		*Write 10% as a decimal.*
≈ 150		*Multiply.*

Because 150 is close to 137, the plant manager's number is reasonable.

Think and Discuss

1. **Determine** the ratios that are nearly equivalent to each of the following percents: 23%, 53%, 65%, 12%, and 76%.
2. **Describe** how to find 35% of a number when you know 10% of the number.

6-2 Exercises

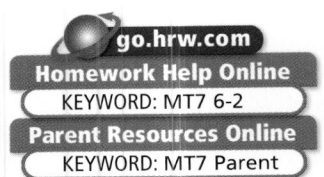

go.hrw.com
Homework Help Online
KEYWORD: MT7 6-2
Parent Resources Online
KEYWORD: MT7 Parent

GUIDED PRACTICE

See Example 1

Estimate.

1. 11% of 507
2. 26% of 99
3. 34% of 91
4. 48% of 124
5. 20% of 66
6. $12\frac{1}{2}\%$ of 87
7. $66\frac{2}{3}\%$ of 25
8. 47% of 80

See Example 2

9. Arnold ate breakfast at a restaurant. The total cost of his food, juice, and coffee was $6.45. If the sales tax rate is 8% and Arnold wants to leave a 20% tip, about how much should he pay?

See Example 3

10. Approximately 11% of each batch of yo-yos is defective. Mr. Andersen said that in a batch of 1500 yo-yos, 125 yo-yos would be defective. Estimate to determine if Mr. Andersen's number is reasonable. Explain.

INDEPENDENT PRACTICE

See Example 1

Estimate.

11. 48% of 202
12. 74% of 39
13. 101% of 6
14. 20% of 42
15. 40% of 81
16. $62\frac{1}{2}\%$ of 239
17. $33\frac{1}{3}\%$ of 26
18. 30% of 118

See Example 2

19. Inga wants to buy a new MP3 player that costs $119.99. If the sales tax is 6.35%, about how much should Inga expect to pay?

See Example 3

20. In a recent election, the leading candidate captured approximately 75% of the 24,082 total votes. The newspaper reported that the winner captured 18,039 votes. Estimate to determine if the newspaper report is reasonable. Explain.

PRACTICE AND PROBLEM SOLVING

Extra Practice
See page 792.

Choose the best estimate. Write A, B, or C.

21. 5% of 29.4
Ⓐ 0.15
Ⓑ 1.5
Ⓒ 15

22. 50% of 29.85
Ⓐ 3
Ⓑ 12
Ⓒ 15

23. 33.3% of 65
Ⓐ 2
Ⓑ 20
Ⓒ 30

24. 66% of $357.99
Ⓐ $120
Ⓑ $240
Ⓒ $360

25. 75% of $317.99
Ⓐ $24
Ⓑ $120
Ⓒ $240

26. 105% of $776.50
Ⓐ $80
Ⓑ $900
Ⓒ $800

Estimate.

27. 50% of 297 is about what number?
28. 75% of 76 is about what number?
29. 103% of 40 is about what number?
30. 103% of 885 is about what number?
31. 50% of 1611 is about what number?
32. 50% of 12.42 is about what number?
33. $33\frac{1}{3}$% of 87 is about what number?
34. 9.6% of 77 is about what number?
35. 24% of 402 is about what number?
36. 66% of 1.8 is about what number?

37. On a weekday, 911 cars passed through a city intersection. On Saturday, only 33% of that number passed through the intersection. Approximately how many cars passed through the intersection on the weekend?

38. A jury wants to give an award of about 9% of $695,531. What is a good estimate of the award?

LINK
Physical Science

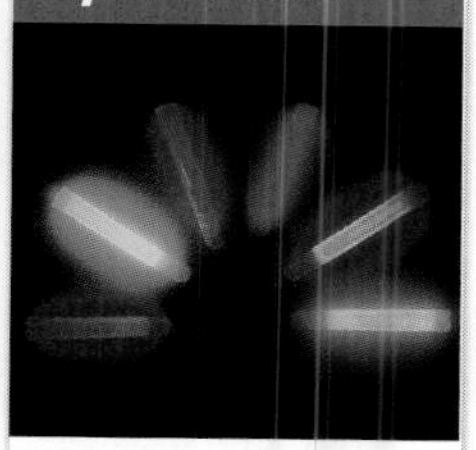

Freezing a light stick may make it glow longer, but not as brightly.

39. **Business** The daily circulation for a city newspaper was 498,739. After a six-month period, the circulation dropped 5.1%. Approximately what was the daily circulation at the end of the six-month period?

40. **Finance** Brooke earns $320 a week. After taxes, her paycheck is only 78% of her earnings. Approximately how much is her paycheck each week?

41. **Physical Science** When you snap a light stick, you break a barrier between two chemical compounds. This causes a reaction that releases energy as light. An improvement allows a 9-hour light stick to glow for 50% more time. Approximately how long does the improved light stick glow?

42. **Sports** In 2004, Barry Bonds reached base approximately 60% of his 617 plate appearances. Approximately how many times did he reach base?

43. **Social Studies** Alaska is the largest state in the United States in total land area, and Rhode Island is the smallest.

Area and Population: 2004		
	Total Land (mi^2)	Population
Alaska	571,949	655,435
Rhode Island	1045	1,080,632

Source: U.S. Census Bureau

a. The area of Rhode Island is approximately 2% the area of Alaska. Determine if this statement is reasonable. Explain.

b. Although Rhode Island is much smaller than Alaska, it has a larger population. Alaska has approximately 60% the population of Rhode Island. Determine if this statement is reasonable. Explain.

c. Estimate the number of people per square mile in Alaska and in Rhode Island.

44. **Write a Problem** Write a percent estimation problem using the following data: The equatorial circumference of Earth is approximately 40,075 km. The equatorial circumference of the moon is approximately 25% Earth's equatorial circumference.

45. **Write About It** Explain how you can estimate 1%, 10%, and 100% of 4027.

46. **Challenge** Explain two ways to estimate 20% of 82.

TEST PREP and Spiral Review

47. **Multiple Choice** 328% of 82 is about what number?

Ⓐ 246 Ⓑ 264 Ⓒ 287 Ⓓ 298

48. **Multiple Choice** Regina receives a 5% commission on the merchandise she sells. Last week, Regina sold $11,976.57 worth of merchandise. Approximately how much commission does she earn?

Ⓕ $600 Ⓖ $11,400 Ⓗ $550 Ⓙ $10,450

49. **Multiple Choice** Which is the best estimate for 20% of 703?

Ⓐ 14 Ⓑ 140 Ⓒ 1400 Ⓓ 14,000

Evaluate. (Lesson 4-1)

50. 2^5
51. $(-3)^2$
52. $(-7)^3$
53. -4^3
54. $(-2)^7$
55. 5^3
56. $(-4)^4$
57. 8^1

Find the percent, fraction, or decimal equivalent for each of the following. (Lesson 6-1)

58. $\frac{9}{10}$ as a percent
59. 46% as a fraction
60. $\frac{3}{8}$ as a decimal
61. $\frac{7}{14}$ as a decimal
62. 0.78 as a fraction
63. 52.5% as a decimal

6-3 Finding Percents

Learn to find percents.

The Nielsen Television Ratings monitor the popularity of television shows viewers watch at certain times. Statistics for these shows are reported as a percent of all American homes in which television is being watched at a given time.

© United Feature Syndicate, Inc.

EXAMPLE 1 Finding the Percent One Number Is of Another

What percent of 144 is 64?

Method 1: Set up a proportion to find the percent.

Think: What number is to 100 as 64 is to 144?

$\frac{\text{number}}{100} = \frac{\text{part}}{\text{whole}}$ *Set up a proportion.*

$\frac{n}{100} = \frac{64}{144}$ *Substitute.*

$n \cdot 144 = 100 \cdot 64$ *Find the cross products.*

$144n = 6400$ *Simplify.*

$\frac{144n}{144} = \frac{6400}{144}$ *Divide both sides by 144.*

$n \approx 44.4$ *Simplify.*

64 is approximately 44.4% of 144.

Method 2: Set up an equation to find the percent.

$p \cdot 144 = 64$ *Set up an equation.*

$\frac{144p}{144} = \frac{64}{144}$ *Divide both sides by 144.*

$p = 0.\overline{4}$, or approximately 0.444. *Simplify.*

64 is approximately 44.4% of 144. *0.44 is 44%*

Check

$44.4\% \cdot 144 \stackrel{?}{=} 64$ *Substitute 44.4% for p.*

$0.444 \cdot 144 \stackrel{?}{=} 64$ *Write a decimal and multiply.*

$63.936 \approx 64$ ✔ *44.4% of 144 is approximately 64.*

EXAMPLE 2 **Recreation Application**

A **A brother and three sisters built a treehouse in their backyard. Mary did $\frac{1}{4}$ of the work, Joshua did 0.28 of the work, Caroline did 30% of the work, and Laura did the rest. What percent of the work on the treehouse did Laura do?**

First, find what percent of the work Mary and Joshua did.

$\frac{1}{4} = 25\%$ and $0.28 = 28\%$

Next, subtract the percents you know from 100% to find the remaining percent.

$100\% - 25\% - 28\% - 30\% = 17\%$

Laura did 17% of the work.

B **Emma is planning a vegetable garden for her backyard. She knows that she wants $\frac{3}{8}$ of the garden to have squash, 0.25 to have tomatoes, 12.5% to have carrots, 15% to have cabbage, and the rest to have lettuce. What percent of the garden will have lettuce?**

First, find what percent of the garden will have squash and tomatoes.

$\frac{3}{8} = 37.5\%$ and $0.25 = 25\%$

Next, subtract the percents you know from 100% to find the remaining percent.

$100\% - 37.5\% - 25\% - 12.5\% - 15\% = 10\%$

10% of the garden will have lettuce.

EXAMPLE 3 **Finding the Percent of a Number**

A **A domestic pig can run about $33\frac{1}{3}\%$ of the speed of a giraffe. A giraffe can run about 32 mi/h. To the nearest tenth, how fast can a domestic pig run?**

Choose a method: Set up an equation.

Think: What speed is $33\frac{1}{3}\%$ of 32 mi/h?

$s = 33\frac{1}{3}\% \cdot 32$ *Set up an equation.*

$s = \frac{1}{3} \cdot 32$ *$33\frac{1}{3}\%$ is equivalent to $\frac{1}{3}$.*

$s = \frac{32}{3} = 10\frac{2}{3} = 10.\overline{6}$ *Simplify.*

$s \approx 10.7$ *Round to the nearest tenth.*

A domestic pig can run about 10.7 miles per hour.

B **Mt. Churchill, in Alaska, is about 15,638 feet high. The height of Mt. McKinley is approximately 130% of the height of Mt. Churchill. To the nearest foot, find the height of Mt. McKinley.**

Choose a method: Set up a proportion.

Think: 130 is to 100 as **what height** is to 15,638 ft?

$\frac{130}{100} = \frac{h}{15{,}638}$ *Set up a proportion.*

$130 \cdot 15{,}638 = 100 \cdot h$ *Find the cross products.*

$2{,}032{,}940 = 100h$ *Simplify.*

$\frac{2{,}032{,}940}{100} = \frac{100h}{100}$ *Divide both sides by 100.*

$20{,}329.4 = h$ *Simplify.*

$20{,}329 \approx h$ *Round to the nearest whole number.*

Mt. McKinley is about 20,329 feet high.

Helpful Hint

When solving a problem when the percent is greater than 100, look for the number that will be greater than the number given. In this case, it is 15,638.

Think and Discuss

1. **Show** why 5% of a number is less than $\frac{1}{10}$ of the number.
2. **Demonstrate** two ways to find 70% of a number.
3. **Name** fractions in simplest form that are the same as 40% and as 250%.

6-3 Exercises

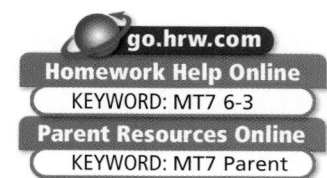

go.hrw.com
Homework Help Online
KEYWORD: MT7 6-3
Parent Resources Online
KEYWORD: MT7 Parent

GUIDED PRACTICE

See Example 1

1. What percent of 91 is 45?
2. What percent of 1270 is 375?
3. What percent of 240 is 180?
4. What percent of 186 is 75?

See Example 2

5. Four friends ordered a pizza. Christopher ate $\frac{1}{5}$, Emma ate 30%, Tanya ate 0.27, and Jamie ate the rest. What percent of the pizza did Jamie eat?

See Example 3

6. Elijah walks 2 miles to school. If Bailey's walk is 80% of the length of Elijah's walk, find the length of Bailey's walk.
7. Jay's term paper is 18 pages long. If Madison's paper is 175% of the length of Jay's paper, find the length of Madison's paper.
8. Of 109.6 million households, 19,508,800 watched the television show *CSI* during the week of October 3, 2005. What percent of American households watched *CSI* this week?

INDEPENDENT PRACTICE

See Example 1

9. What percent of 56 is 224?

10. What percent of 180 is 30?

11. 12.5 is what percent of 1250?

12. 115 is what percent of 40?

See Example 2

13. The Bishop family bought a case of water containing 24 bottles. During one week, Lydia drank $\frac{1}{8}$ of the bottles, Mitchell drank $33\frac{1}{3}\%$ of the bottles, Alexa drank 0.25 of the bottles, and Todd drank the rest. What percent of the case did Todd drink?

See Example 3

14. The tallest building in the United States is the Sears Tower in Chicago. The height of the Sears Tower is 1450 feet, which is 240% of the height of the Seattle Space Needle in Washington. Find the height of the Seattle Space Needle to the nearest foot.

15. In Arkansas, the highest elevation is Mount Magazine, and the lowest is the Ouachita River. Mount Magazine is 2753 ft above sea level, which is about 5098% of the elevation of the lowest portion of the state. Find the elevation of the Ouachita River area.

PRACTICE AND PROBLEM SOLVING

Extra Practice
See page 792.

Find each number to the nearest tenth.

16. What number is $33\frac{1}{3}\%$ of 30?

17. What number is $11\frac{1}{3}\%$ of 215?

18. What number is 77% of 9?

19. What number is $3\frac{1}{2}\%$ of 11,400?

20. What number is 166% of 300?

21. What number is $66\frac{2}{3}\%$ of 750?

Complete each statement.

22. Since 8 is 16% of 50,
   a. 16 is ▒% of 50.
   b. 24 is ▒% of 50.
   c. 80 is ▒% of 50.

23. Since 8 is 5% of 160,
   a. 8 is ▒% of 80.
   b. 8 is ▒% of 40.
   c. 8 is ▒% of 20.

24. Since 15 is 300% of 5,
   a. 15 is ▒% of 10.
   b. 15 is ▒% of 20.
   c. 15 is ▒% of 40.

Patterns Describe the patterns shown below.

25. 1% of 1200 = 12
2% of 600 = 12
4% of 300 = 12
8% of 150 =12
16% of 75 = 12

26. 400% of 320 = 1280
200% of 160 = 320
100% of 80 = 80
50% of 40 = 20
25% of 20 = 5

27. 400% of 5 = 20
200% of 15 = 30
100% of 45 = 45
50% of 135 = 67.5
25% of 405 = 101.25

28. **Social Studies** In 2003, 14% of the 50 largest U.S. cities were located in Texas. How many of the 50 largest U.S. cities were located in Texas in 2003?

29. **Geography** About 600 mi^2 of the 700 mi^2 of the Okefenokee Swamp is located in Georgia. If Georgia is 57,906 mi^2, find the percent of that area that is part of the Okefenokee Swamp.

30. **Language Arts** The Hawaiian words shown contain all of the letters of the Hawaiian alphabet. The ` is actually a consonant!

   a. What percent of the Hawaiian alphabet are vowels?

   b. To the nearest tenth, what percent of the letters in the English alphabet are also in the Hawaiian alphabet?

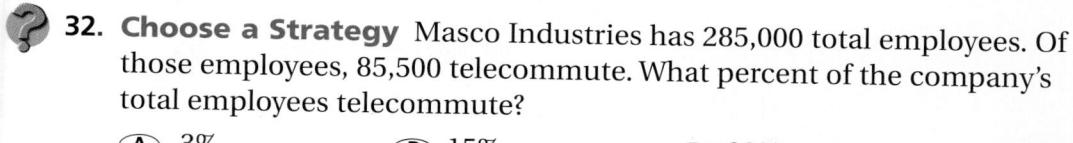

31. **Multi-Step** Joseph, Ana, Lena, and George chipped in money for a friend's gift. The gift cost \$45.99 plus \$3.45 sales tax. Joseph paid \$12.50, Ana paid $\frac{1}{4}$ of the total cost, Lena paid 24% of the total cost, and George paid the rest. Order the people from least amount paid to greatest amount paid.

32. **Choose a Strategy** Masco Industries has 285,000 total employees. Of those employees, 85,500 telecommute. What percent of the company's total employees telecommute?

   (A) 3% (B) 15% (C) 30% (D) 150%

33. **Write About It** A question on a math quiz asks, "What is 175% of 72?" Petra calculates 12.6 as the answer. Is this a reasonable answer? Explain.

34. **Challenge** Molly cut 10 ft 6 in. from a pipe measuring 8 yd 1 ft. What percent of the pipe's original length did Molly remove, and what is the length of the pipe that remains?

Test Prep and Spiral Review

35. **Multiple Choice** Currently, 96 students are enrolled in the Grove City Dance Center. Of those students, 54 study tap dance. The remaining students study ballet. What percentage of the students study ballet?

   (F) 42% (G) 43.75% (H) 54% (J) 56.25%

36. **Gridded Response** According to the 2003 U.S. Census, approximately 129 million Americans spend 3.4% of a 24-hour day commuting. How many minutes a day does a person in this group spend commuting?

Solve each proportion. (Lesson 5-4)

37. $\frac{x}{3} = \frac{8}{12}$
38. $\frac{7}{y} = \frac{49}{98}$
39. $\frac{10}{12} = \frac{b}{6}$
40. $\frac{12}{36} = \frac{4}{c}$
41. $\frac{b}{6} = \frac{42}{18}$
42. $\frac{8}{c} = \frac{64}{24}$
43. $\frac{11}{33} = \frac{3}{x}$
44. $\frac{14}{9} = \frac{y}{18}$

Estimate. (Lesson 6-2)

45. 26% of 398
46. 48% of 746
47. 39% of 99

6-4 Finding a Number When the Percent Is Known

Learn to find a number when the percent is known.

Carcharocles megalodon, a giant shark that became extinct almost 3 million years ago, had teeth as large as 7.25 inches along an edge. This is 240% bigger than the largest teeth of a modern great white shark.

When one number is known, and its relationship to another number is given by a percent, the other number can be found.

Carcharocles megalodon's jaw may have been 6 feet wide.

EXAMPLE 1 **Finding a Number When the Percent Is Known**

42 is 5% of what number?

Choose a method: Set up an equation to find the number.

$42 = 5\% \cdot n$ *Set up an equation.*

$42 = 0.05n$ $5\% = 0.05$

$\frac{42}{0.05} = \frac{0.05}{0.05}n$ *Divide both sides by 0.05.*

$840 = n$ *Simplify*

42 is 5% of 840.

EXAMPLE 2 ***Physical Science Application***

In a science lab, a sample of a compound contains 14.5 grams of magnesium. If 72.5% of the sample is magnesium, find the number of grams the entire sample weighs.

Choose a method: Set up a proportion to find the number.

Think: 72.5 is to 100 as 14.5 g is to **what mass**?

$\frac{72.5}{100} = \frac{14.5}{m}$ *Set up a proportion.*

$72.5 \cdot m = 100 \cdot 14.5$ *Find the cross products.*

$72.5m = 1450$ *Simplify.*

$\frac{72.5m}{72.5} = \frac{1450}{72.5}$ *Divide both sides by 72.5*

$m = 20$ *Simplify.*

The entire sample weighs 20 grams.

EXAMPLE 3 *Life Science Application*

Life Science LINK

Reticulated means "net-like" or "forming a network." The reticulated python is named for the pattern on its skin.

A **The king cobra can reach a length of 18 feet. This is only about 60% of the length of the largest reticulated python. Find the length of the largest reticulated python.**

Choose a method: Set up a proportion.

Think: 60 is to 100 as 18 ft is to **what length**?

$\frac{60}{100} = \frac{18}{\ell}$	*Set up a proportion.*
$60 \cdot \ell = 100 \cdot 18$	*Find the cross products.*
$\frac{60\ell}{60} = \frac{1800}{60}$	*Divide both sides by 60.*
$\ell = 30$	*Simplify.*

The largest reticulated python is 30 feet long.

B ***Carcharocles megalodon*** **had teeth as large as 7.25 inches along an edge. This is 240% of the maximum size of the teeth of a modern great white shark. To the nearest inch, find the maximum size of the teeth of a great white shark.**

Choose a method: Set up an equation.

Think: 7.25 in. is 240% of **what length**?

$7.25 = 2/40\% \cdot \ell$	*Set up an equation.*
$7.25 = 2.40 \cdot \ell$	*240% = 2.40*
$\frac{7.25}{2.40} = \frac{\ell}{2.40}$	*Divide both sides by 2.40.*
$3 \approx \ell$	*Simplify.*

The maximum size is about 3 inches along an edge.

You have now seen all three types of percent problems.

Percent Problem	Equation	Proportion
Finding the percent of a number	15% of 120 = n	$\frac{15}{100} = \frac{n}{120}$
Finding the percent one number is of another	p% of 120 = 18	$\frac{p}{100} = \frac{18}{120}$
Finding a number when the percent is known	15% of n = 18	$\frac{15}{100} = \frac{18}{n}$

Think and Discuss

1. **Compare** finding a number when a percent is known to finding the percent one number is of another number.
2. **Explain** whether a number is greater than or less than 36 if 22% of the number is 36.

6-4 Exercises

go.hrw.com
Homework Help Online
KEYWORD: MT7 6-4
Parent Resources Online
KEYWORD: MT7 Parent

GUIDED PRACTICE

See Example 1
Find each number to the nearest tenth.

1. 6.9 is $11\frac{1}{2}$% of what number?
2. 92 is $66\frac{2}{3}$% of what number?
3. 12% of what number is 20?
4. 30% of what number is 96?

See Example 2
5. How much water can a 7.4 oz piece of chalk absorb if it can absorb 32% of its weight?

See Example 3
6. At 2 P.M., a flag pole casts a shadow that is 155% of its actual height. If the shadow is 23.25 ft, what is the actual height of the pole?

INDEPENDENT PRACTICE

See Example 1
Find each number to the nearest tenth.

7. 90 is $66\frac{2}{3}$% of what number?
8. 63 is 15% of what number?
9. 0.75% of what number is 10?
10. 44% of what number is 37.4?

See Example 2
11. Isaac sold 58 of his baseball cards at a collectors' show. If this represented $14\frac{1}{2}$% of his total collection, how many baseball cards did Isaac have before he sold his cards?

See Example 3
12. When a tire is labeled "185/70/14," that means it is 185 mm wide, the sidewall height (from the rim to the road) is 70% of its width, and the wheel has a diameter of 14 in. What is the tire's sidewall height?

PRACTICE AND PROBLEM SOLVING

Extra Practice
See page 792.

Complete each statement.

13. Since 2% of 500 is 10,
    a. 4% of ▒ is 10.
    b. 8% of ▒ is 10.
    c. 16% of ▒ is 10.
14. Since 100% of 8 is 8,
    a. 50% of ▒ is 8.
    b. 25% of ▒ is 8.
    c. 10% of ▒ is 8.
15. Since 15% of 60 is 9,
    a. 30% of ▒ is 9.
    b. 45% of ▒ is 9.
    c. 60% of ▒ is 9.
16. In a survey of 175 students, 42 said that their favorite cookout food was hamburgers, and 61 said that their favorite was hot dogs. Give these numbers as percents.
17. **Life Science** The Congress Avenue bridge in Austin, Texas, is home to the largest urban bat colony in the world. Nearly 1.5 million Mexican free-tailed bats live under the bridge. This bat population is approximately 228.3% the population of Austin. What is the population of Austin to the nearest thousand people?

Social Studies LINK

The U.S. census collects information about state populations, economics, income and poverty levels, births and deaths, and so on. This information can be used to study trends and patterns. For Exercises 18–20, round answers to the nearest tenth.

2000 U.S. Census Data			
	Population	Male	Female
Alaska	626,932	324,112	302,820
New York	18,976,457	9,146,748	9,829,709
Age 34 and Under	139,328,990	71,053,554	68,275,436
Age 35 and Over	142,092,916	67,000,009	75,092,907
Total U.S.	281,421,906	138,053,563	143,368,343

18. What percent of New York's population is male?

19. What percent of the entire country's population, to the nearest tenth of a percent, is made up of people in New York?

20. Tell what percent of the U.S. population each represents.

a. people 34 and under **b.** people 35 and over **c.** male **d.** female

21. American Indians and Native Alaskans make up about 15.6% of Alaska's population. What is their population, to the nearest thousand?

22. ★ **Challenge** About 71% of the U.S. population age 85 and over is female. Of the fractions that round to 71% when rounded to the nearest percent, which has the least denominator?

go.hrw.com
Web Extra!
KEYWORD: MT7 Census

TEST PREP and Spiral Review

23. Multiple Choice There are 72 boys in the eighth-grade class at Lincoln Middle School. The other 55% of the class are girls. How many girls are there?

Ⓐ 55 Ⓑ 72 Ⓒ 88 Ⓓ 127

24. Gridded Response 25% of what number is 9.6?

Each square root is between two integers. Name the integers. (Lesson 4-6)

25. $\sqrt{35}$ **26.** $\sqrt{45}$ **27.** $\sqrt{55}$ **28.** $\sqrt{65}$ **29.** $\sqrt{140}$

30. $\sqrt{27}$ **31.** $\sqrt{101}$ **32.** $\sqrt{42}$ **33.** $\sqrt{222}$ **34.** $\sqrt{1011}$

Find the decimal equivalent of each. (Lesson 6-1)

35. $\frac{5}{8}$ **36.** 212% **37.** 71% **38.** $4\frac{1}{12}$ **39.** $-\frac{3}{4}$

40. $\frac{4}{5}$ **41.** 123% **42.** 26% **43.** $3\frac{1}{2}$ **44.** $27\frac{1}{5}$

CHAPTER 6

READY TO GO ON?

SECTION 6A

Quiz for Lessons 6-1 Through 6-4

6-1 Relating Decimals, Fractions, and Percents

Compare. Write <, >, or =.

1. $\frac{5}{6}$ ■ 83% **2.** $\frac{4}{9}$ ■ 45% **3.** 0.03 ■ 3% **4.** 6.5 ■ 65%

Order the numbers from least to greatest.

5. $\frac{1}{4}$, 0.1, 3%, 28% **6.** 130%, $\frac{3}{2}$, 1.25, 10% **7.** $\frac{2}{3}$, 72%, 0.6, $\frac{3}{4}$

8. A molecule of ferric oxide is made up of 2 atoms of iron and 3 atoms of oxygen. What percent of the atoms of a ferric oxide molecule is oxygen?

6-2 Estimate with Percents

Estimate.

9. 48% of 52 **10.** 33% of 613 **11.** $12\frac{1}{2}$% of 57 **12.** 60% of 26

Estimate the tip for each bill.

13. tip: 10% bill: $28.20 **14.** tip: 15% bill: $41.80

15. Approximately 9.6% of all daily shipments are returned. Ms. Kui said that in a daily shipment of 12,034 packages, approximately 120 would be returned. Estimate to determine if Ms. Kui's number is reasonable. Explain.

6-3 Finding Percents

16. What number is 32% of 8?

17. Of Canada's total area of 9,976,140 km^2, 755,170 km^2 is water. To the nearest tenth of a percent, what part of Canada is water?

6-4 Finding a Number When the Percent Is Known

18. 27 is 7.5% of what number?

19. 336 is 375% of what number?

20. The speed of sound in air at sea level at 32°F is 1088 ft/s. If that represents only 22.04% of the speed of sound in ice-cold water, what is the speed of sound in ice-cold water, to the nearest whole number?

Focus on Problem Solving

Make a Plan

• Do you need an estimate or an exact answer?

When you are solving a word problem, ask yourself whether you need an exact answer or whether an estimate is sufficient. For example, if the amounts given in the problem are approximate, only an approximate answer can be given. If an estimate is sufficient, you may wish to use estimation techniques to save time in your calculations.

For each problem below, explain whether an exact answer is needed or whether an estimate is sufficient. Then find the answer.

1. In a poll of 5000 registered voters in a certain district, 2800 favored a proposed new library. What percent favored the new library?

2. Albert needs to score 78% on his final exam to get a B in his math class. If the final is worth 300 points, how many points does he need?

3. Mai is trying to save about \$500 for a trip to Hawaii. If she has \$125 in an account that earns 7% interest and puts \$10 per month in the account, will she have enough in 3 years?

4. Esteban makes \$8.30 per hour at his job. If he receives a 3% raise, how much will he be making per hour?

5. Carmen is planning to tile her kitchen floor. The room is 215 square feet. It is recommended that she buy enough tiles for an area 25% greater than the actual kitchen floor space to account for breakage. How many square feet of tile should she buy?

6. There are about 1,032,000 known species of animals on Earth. Of these, about 751,000 are insects. What percent of known species are insects?

6-5 Percent Increase and Decrease

Learn to find percent increase and decrease.

Vocabulary

- percent change
- percent increase
- percent decrease

Many animals hibernate during the winter to survive harsh conditions and food shortages. While they sleep, their body temperatures drop, their breathing rates decrease, and their heart rates slow. They may even appear to be dead.

"He hums in his sleep."

© 2002. *The New Yorker* Collection from cartoonbank.com. All rights reserved.

Percents can be used to describe a change. **Percent change** is the ratio of the *amount of change* to the *original amount.*

$$\text{percent change} = \frac{\text{amount of change}}{\text{original amount}}$$

Percent increase describes how much the original amount increases. **Percent decrease** describes how much the original amount decreases.

EXAMPLE 1 Finding Percent Increase or Decrease

Find the percent increase or decrease from 36 to 45.

This is a percent increase.

$45 - 36 = 9$ — *First find the amount of change.*

Think: 9 is what percent of 36?

$\frac{\text{amount of increase}}{\text{original amount}} \rightarrow \frac{9}{36}$ — *Set up the ratio.*

$\frac{9}{36} = 0.25 = 25\%$ — *Find the decimal form. Write as a percent.*

From 36 to 45 is a 25% increase.

EXAMPLE 2 *Life Science Application*

A **The heart rate of a grizzly bear slows from 50 to 8 beats per minute during hibernation. What is the percent decrease?**

$50 - 8 = 42$ — *First find the amount of change.*

Think: 42 is what percent of 50?

$\frac{\text{amount of decrease}}{\text{original amount}} \rightarrow \frac{42}{50}$ — *Set up the ratio.*

$\frac{42}{50} = 0.84 = 84\%$ — *Find the decimal form. Write as a percent.*

The grizzly bear's heart rate decreases by 84% during hibernation.

B **According to the U.S. Census Bureau, 72.3 million children (aged 17 years and younger) lived in the United States in 2004. It is estimated that there will be 80.3 million children in 2020. What is the percent increase, to the nearest percent?**

$80.3 - 72.3 = 8$ *First find the amount of change.*

Think: 8 is what percent of 72.3?

$\frac{\text{amount of increase}}{\text{original amount}} = \frac{8}{72.3}$ *Set up the ratio.*

$\frac{8}{72.3} \approx 0.1107 \approx 11.07\%$ *Find the decimal form.*
Write as a percent.

From 2004 to 2020, the number of children in the United States is estimated to increase 11%.

EXAMPLE 3 Using Percent Increase or Decrease to Find Prices

A **Anthony bought an LCD monitor originally priced at \$750 that was reduced in price by 35%. What was the reduced price?**

$\$750 \cdot 35\%$ *First find 35% of \$750.*

$\$750 \cdot 0.35 = \$262.50$ *35% = 0.35*

The amount of decrease is \$262.50.

Think: The reduced price is \$262.50 *less than* \$750.

$\$750 - \$262.50 = \$487.50$ *Subtract the amount of decrease.*

The reduced price of the monitor was \$487.50.

B **Mr. Anzivino received a shipment of refrigerators that cost \$966 each. To set the retail price, he marks the price of each refrigerator up $66\frac{2}{3}\%$. What is the retail price of each refrigerator?**

$\$966 \cdot 66\frac{2}{3}\%$ *First find $66\frac{2}{3}\%$ of \$966.*

$\$966 \cdot \frac{2}{3} = \$644$ *$66\frac{2}{3}\% = \frac{2}{3}$*

The amount of increase is \$644.

Think: The retail price is \$644 *more than* \$966.

$\$966 + \$644 = \$1610$ *Add the amount of increase.*

The retail price of each refrigerator is \$1610.

Think and Discuss

1. Explain whether a 150% increase or a 150% decrease is possible.

2. Compare finding a 20% increase to finding 120% of a number.

6-5 Exercises

go.hrw.com
Homework Help Online
KEYWORD: MT7 6-5
Parent Resources Online
KEYWORD: MT7 Parent

GUIDED PRACTICE

See Example 1

Find each percent increase or decrease to the nearest percent.

1. from 40 to 59 **2.** from 85 to 30 **3.** from 85 to 170

See Example 2

4. A population of squirrels rose from 338 to 520 over a period of 3 years. What is the percent increase, to the nearest tenth of a percent?

See Example 3

5. An automobile dealer agrees to reduce the $10,288 sticker price of a new car by 5% for a customer. What is the price of the car for the customer?

INDEPENDENT PRACTICE

See Example 1

Find each percent increase or decrease to the nearest percent.

6. from 800 to 1500 **7.** from 0.76 to 0.59 **8.** from 35 to 19

See Example 2

9. The boiling point of water is lower at higher altitudes. Water boils at 212°F at sea level and 193.7°F at 10,000 ft. What is the percent decrease in the temperatures, to the nearest tenth of a percent?

See Example 3

10. Mr. Woodruff owns an automobile parts store and typically marks up merchandise 32% over warehouse cost. How much would he charge customers for a rotor that costs him $62.25?

PRACTICE AND PROBLEM SOLVING

Extra Practice
See page 793.

Find each percent increase or decrease to the nearest percent.

11. from $34.70 to $23.20 **12.** from $72 to $119 **13.** from $320 to $195

14. from $644 to $588 **15.** from $0.37 to $0.28 **16.** from $12.50 to $14.75

Find each missing number.

17. originally: $400
new price: ___
25% increase

18. originally: 140
new amount ___
50% increase

19. originally: ___
new amount: 210
75% increase

20. originally: ___
new price: $3.80
15% decrease

21. originally: 28
new amount: 42
___% increase

22. originally: $45
new price: $27
___% decrease

23. **Multi-Step** A pair of $195 boots are discounted 40%.

a. How much is the price decrease?

b. What is the sale price of the boots?

c. If the boots are reduced in price by an additional $66\frac{2}{3}$%, what will be the new sale price?

d. What percent decrease does this final sale price represent?

LINK

Literature

Harper Lee's *To Kill a Mockingbird* has sold over 10,000,000 copies worldwide and has been translated into more than 25 languages.

24. **Earth Science** After the Mount St. Helens volcano erupted in 1980, the elevation of the mountain decreased by about 13.6%. Its elevation had been 9677 ft. What was its elevation after the eruption?

25. **Literature** A signed hard-cover edition of Harper Lee's *To Kill a Mockingbird* is worth $1500. A paperback version of the novel sells for $6. What is the percent increase in price between the paperback version and the signed hard-cover version?

26. **Multi-Step** A video game console that is normally priced at $269.99 has been marked down to 70% of its original price. If sales tax is 8%, how much will Marcus pay for the discounted game console, to the nearest cent?

27. Last year, 12,932 people attended an annual convention. This year, 11,245 people are planning to attend. Does this represent a percent increase or a percent decrease? Find the percent change, to the nearest percent.

28. **Critical Thinking** Is the percent change the same when a DVD is marked up from $10 to $15 as when it is reduced from $15 to $10? Explain.

29. **Choose a Strategy** A digital camera originally sold for $249. Two months later, the price was reduced 40%. During a sale, the camera was discounted an additional 15% off the reduced price. What was the final price of the camera?

    (A) $14.94 (B) $22.41 (C) $126.99 (D) $136.95

30. **Write About It** Describe how you can use mental math to find the percent increase from 75 to 100 and the percent decrease from 100 to 75.

31. **Challenge** During a sale, the price of a cell phone was decreased by 20%. By what percent must the sale price be increased to restore the original price?

TEST PREP and Spiral Review

32. **Multiple Choice** A washing machine that usually sells for $459 is on sale for $379. What is the percent decrease, to the nearest tenth of a percent?

    (F) 17.4% (G) 21.1% (H) 32.8% (J) 82.6%

33. **Extended Response** Puzzle Place has discounted its puzzles 20%. A puzzle of a giraffe is priced at $20.95, and a puzzle of a mountain is priced at $16.50. How much will Thomas save on both puzzles? If the sales tax rate is 6%, what is the final cost of the puzzles?

34. A square has a perimeter of 56 cm. If the square is dilated by a scale factor of 0.2, what is the length of each side of the new square? (Lesson 5-6)

Find each percent or number. (Lesson 6-3)

35. What percent of 122 is 61?

36. What is 35% of 2340?

37. What is 145% of 215?

6-6 Applications of Percents

Learn to find commission, sales tax, and percent of earnings.

Vocabulary
commission
commission rate
sales tax

Car salespeople often work for *commission.* A **commission** is a fee paid to a person who makes a sale. It is usually a percent of the selling price. This percent is called the **commission rate** .

commission rate • sales = commission

Often salespeople are paid a commission plus a regular salary. The total pay is a percent of the sales they make plus a salary.

EXAMPLE 1 Multiplying by Percents to Find Commission Amounts

Julie is paid a monthly salary of $2100 plus commissions. Last month she sold one car for $39,500, earning a 4% commission on the sale. How much was her commission? What was her total pay for the month?

First find her commission.

$4\% \cdot \$39{,}500 = c$ *commission rate · sales = commission*

$0.04 \cdot 39{,}500 = c$ *Change the percent to a decimal.*

$1580 = c$ *Solve for c.*

She earned a commission of $1580 on the sale.

Now find her total pay for last month.

$\$1580 + \$2100 = \$3680$ *commission + salary = total pay*

Her total pay for last month was $3680.

Sales tax is the tax on the sale of an item or service. It is a percent of the purchase price and is collected by the seller.

EXAMPLE 2 Multiplying by Percents to Find Sales Tax Amounts

If the sales tax rate is 7.75%, how much tax would Meka pay if she bought a portable CD player for $45.80 and two CDs for $15.99 each?

CD player: 1 at $45.80 → $45.80
CDs: 2 at $15.99 → <u>$31.98</u>
$77.78 *Total price*

$0.0775 \cdot 77.78 = 6.02795$ *Write the tax rate as a decimal and multiply by the total price.*

Meka would pay $6.03 in sales tax.

EXAMPLE 3 Using Proportions to Find the Percent of Earnings

Jorge earns $36,000 yearly. Of that, he pays $12,240 for rent. What percent of Jorge's earnings goes to rent?

Think: What percent of $36,000 is $12,240?

$\frac{n}{100} = \frac{12,240}{36,000}$ *Set up a proportion.*

$n \cdot 36,000 = 100 \cdot 12,240$ *Find the cross products.*

$36,000n = 1,224,000$ *Simplify.*

$\frac{36,000n}{36,000} = \frac{1,224,000}{36,000}$ *Divide both sides by 36,000.*

$n = 34$ *Simplify.*

So 34% of Jorges's earnings goes to rent.

EXAMPLE 4 Dividing by Percents to Find Total Sales

Students in Salim's class sell gift wrap to raise funds for class trips. The class earns 11% on all sales. If the class earned $647.35 this year, how much were the total sales?

Think: 647.35 is 11% of what number?

Let s = total sales

$647.35 = 0.11 \cdot s$ *Set up an equation.*

$\frac{647.35}{0.11} = \frac{0.11s}{0.11}$ *Divide each side by 11.*

$5885 = s$ *Simplify.*

The total sales of gift wrap for Salim's class were $5885.

Think and Discuss

1. **Tell** how finding commission is similar to finding sales tax.
2. **Explain** whether adding 6% sales tax to a total gives the same result as finding 106% of the total.
3. **Explain** how to find the price of an item if you know the total cost after 5% sales tax.
4. **Explain** whether the sales tax on a $20 item would be double the sales tax on a $10 item. Justify your answer.

6-6 Exercises

go.hrw.com
Homework Help Online
KEYWORD: MT7 6-6
Parent Resources Online
KEYWORD: MT7 Parent

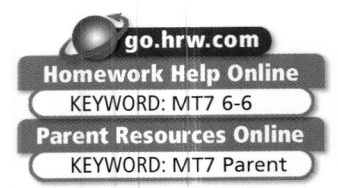

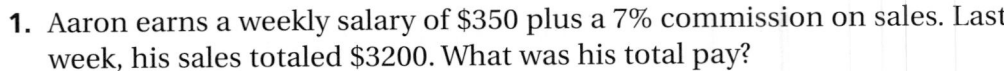

GUIDED PRACTICE

See Example 1
1. Aaron earns a weekly salary of $350 plus a 7% commission on sales. Last week, his sales totaled $3200. What was his total pay?

See Example 2
2. In a state with a sales tax rate of 7%, Hernando buys a radio for $59.99 and a CD for $13.99. How much is the sales tax?

See Example 3
3. Last year, Nadia earned $31,025. Of that amount, she spent $3612.59 on food. What percent of her income went to food, to the nearest tenth of a percent?

See Example 4
4. Shane works at a computer store. If he earns $20.93 from a 7% commission on the sale of a printer, what is the price of the printer?

INDEPENDENT PRACTICE

See Example 1
5. Kayla earns a weekly salary of $290 plus a 5.5% commission on sales at a gift shop. How much would she make in a week if she sold $5700 worth of merchandise?

See Example 2
6. The sales tax rate in Brad's town is 4.25%. If he buys 3 lamps for $22.49 each and a sofa for $829.99, how much sales tax does he owe?

See Example 3
7. Jada typically earns $1545 each month, of which $47.20 is spent on electricity. What percent of Jada's earnings are spent on electricity each month, to the nearest tenth of a percent?

See Example 4
8. Heather works in a clothes shop, where she earns a commission of 5% and no weekly salary. What will Heather's weekly sales have to be for her to earn $375 in one week?

PRACTICE AND PROBLEM SOLVING

Extra Practice
See page 793.

Find each sales tax to the nearest cent.

9. total sales: $210.13
   sales tax rate: 7.25%
10. total sales: $42.99
    sales tax rate: 9%
11. total sales: $895.75
    sales tax rate: 4.25%

Find the total sales to the nearest cent.

12. commission: $63.06
    commission rate: 5%
13. commission: $2842
    commission rate: 3.5%

14. **Consumer Economics** Roz takes home $1600 each month. She budgets 30% of her paycheck for rent, 20% for food, and 10% for utilities. The remainder is divided evenly among entertainment, clothes, transportation, savings, and charity. How much money does Roz budget each month for each category?

15. **Critical Thinking** Deborah can choose between a monthly salary of $1800 plus 6.5% of sales or $2100 plus 4% of sales. She expects sales between $5,000 and $10,000 a month. Which salary option should she choose? Explain.

Economics LINK

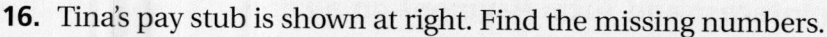

Tax brackets are used to determine how much income tax people pay. Depending upon a person's taxable income, tax is given by the formula base tax + tax rate (amount over). "Amount over" refers only to the income above the amount listed. Refer to the table for Exercises 16–18.

2005 IRS Income Tax Brackets (Single)

Taxable Income Range	Base Tax	Tax Rate	Amount Over
\$0–\$7,300	\$0	10%	\$0
\$7,300–\$29,700	\$730	15%	\$7,300
\$29,700–\$71,950	\$4,090	25%	\$29,700
\$71,950–\$150,150	\$14,652.50	28%	\$71,950
\$150,150–\$326,450	\$36,548.50	33%	\$150,150
\$326,450 and up	\$94,727.50	35%	\$326,450

Ellie's Flowers
Hours worked 24
Hourly rate ☐ per hour
Gross pay \$162.50
Federal income tax (10%) ☐
Other federal taxes (7.65%) ☐
NET PAY ☐

16. Tina's pay stub is shown at right. Find the missing numbers.

17. Anna earned \$71,458 total in 2005. She was able to deduct \$7250 for job-related expenses. This amount is subtracted from her total income to determine her taxable income.

a. What was Anna's taxable income in 2005?

b. How much income tax did she owe?

c. What percent of Anna's total income did the tax represent?

d. What percent of her taxable income did the tax represent?

18. ★ **Challenge** Charlena paid \$10,050 in taxes in 2005. How much taxable income did she earn that year?

TEST PREP and Spiral Review

19. **Short Answer** Gabrielle earned a weekly salary of \$235 plus 8% commission on sales over \$500. What was her weekly pay if she had \$6,250 in sales?

20. **Gridded Response** Rafael buys a video game for \$49.95. The sales tax rate is 6.5%. What is the total cost, including tax, to the nearest dollar?

Simplify to tell whether the ratios form a proportion. (Lesson 5-1)

21. $\frac{3}{7}$ and $\frac{6}{14}$ **22.** $\frac{5}{8}$ and $\frac{10}{4}$ **23.** $\frac{13}{4}$ and $\frac{52}{16}$ **24.** $\frac{22}{7}$ and $\frac{11}{3}$

Find each percent increase or decrease to the nearest percent. (Lesson 6-5)

25. from 600 to 300 **26.** from \$109.99 to \$94.99

6-7 Simple Interest

Learn to compute simple interest.

Vocabulary

interest

simple interest

principal

rate of interest

When you borrow money from a bank, you pay **interest** for the use of the bank's money. When you deposit money into a savings account, you are paid interest. **Simple interest** is one type of fee paid for the use of money.

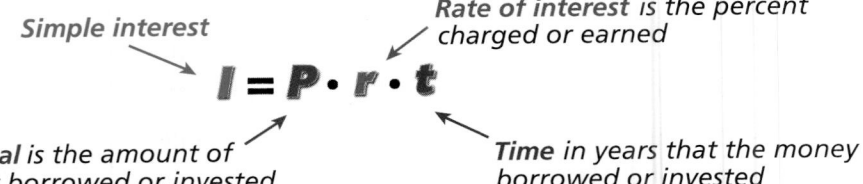

$$I = P \cdot r \cdot t$$

Simple interest (I)

Rate of interest (r) *is the percent charged or earned*

Principal (P) *is the amount of money borrowed or invested*

Time (t) *in years that the money is borrowed or invested*

EXAMPLE 1 Finding Interest and Total Payment on a Loan

Tristan borrowed \$14,500 from his brother and promised to pay him back over 5 years at an annual simple interest rate of 7%. How much interest will he pay if he pays off the entire loan at the end of the fifth year? What is the total amount he will repay?

First, find the interest he will pay.

$I = P \cdot r \cdot t$ — *Use the formula.*

$I = 14{,}500 \cdot 0.07 \cdot 5$ — *Substitute. Use 0.07 for 7%.*

$I = 5075$ — *Solve for I.*

Tristan will pay \$5075 in interest.

You can find the total amount A to be repaid on a loan by adding the principal P to the interest I.

$P + I = A$ — *principal + interest = amount*

$14{,}500 + 5075 = A$ — *Substitute.*

$19{,}575 = A$ — *Solve for A.*

Tristan will repay a total of \$19,575 on his loan.

EXAMPLE 2 Determining the Amount of Investment Time

Isaiah invested \$3500 in a mutual fund at a yearly rate of 6%. He earned \$945 in interest. For how long was the money invested?

$I = P \cdot r \cdot t$ — *Use the formula.*

$945 = 3500 \cdot 0.06 \cdot t$ — *Substitute.*

$945 = 210t$ — *Simplify.*

$4.5 = t$ — *Solve for t.*

The money was invested for 4.5 years, or 4 years and 6 months.

EXAMPLE 3 Computing Total Savings

Nadia's aunt deposited $3000 into a savings account as a college fund for Nadia. How much will be in this account after 5 years if the account earns a yearly simple interest rate of 3.5%?

$I = P \cdot r \cdot t$	*Use the formula.*
$I = 3000 \cdot 0.035 \cdot 5$	*Substitute. Use 0.035 for 3.5%.*
$I = 525$	*Solve for I.*

Now you can find the total.

$P + I = A$	*Use the formula.*
$3000 + 525 = A$	*Substitute.*
$3525 = A$	*Solve for A.*

Nadia will have $3525 in her savings account after 5 years.

EXAMPLE 4 Finding the Rate of Interest

To pay for her college expenses, Hannah borrows $7000. She plans to repay the loan in 5 years at simple interest. If Hannah repays a total of $9187.50, what is the interest rate?

$P + I = A$	*Use the formula.*
$7000 + I = 9187.5$	*Substitute.*
$-7000 \quad\quad -7000$	*Subtract 7000 from both sides.*
$I = 2187.5$	*Simplify.*

She paid $2187.50 in interest. Use the amount of interest to find the interest rate.

$I = P \cdot r \cdot t$	*Use the formula.*
$2187.5 = 7000 \cdot r \cdot 5$	*Substitute.*
$2187.5 = 35{,}000r$	*Simplify.*
$\frac{2187.5}{35{,}000} = \frac{35{,}000r}{35{,}000}$	*Divide both sides by 35,000.*
$0.0625 = r$	*Simplify.*

The simple annual rate is 6.25%, or $6\frac{1}{4}$%.

Think and Discuss

1. **Explain** the meaning of each variable in the interest formula.
2. **Tell** what value should be used for t when referring to 6 months.
3. **Name** the variables in the simple interest formula that represent dollar amounts.
4. **Demonstrate** that doubling the time while halving the interest rate results in the same amount of simple interest.

6-7 Exercises

go.hrw.com
Homework Help Online
KEYWORD: MT7 6-7
Parent Resources Online
KEYWORD: MT7 Parent

GUIDED PRACTICE

See Example 1

1. Nick borrowed $7150, to be repaid after 5 years at an annual simple interest rate of 6.25%. How much interest will be due after 5 years? How much will Nick have to repay?

See Example 2

2. Mr. Williams invested $4000 in a bond with a yearly interest rate of 4%. His total interest on the investment was $800. What was the length of the investment?

See Example 3

3. Paige deposited $1277 in a savings account. How much would she have in the account after 3 years at an annual simple interest rate of 4%?

See Example 4

4. Tom borrowed $35,000 to remodel his house. At the end of the 5-year loan, he had repaid a total of $46,375. At what simple interest rate did he borrow the money?

INDEPENDENT PRACTICE

See Example 1

5. A bank offers an annual simple interest rate of 7% on home improvement loans. How much would Billy owe if he borrowed $18,500 over a period of 3.5 years?

See Example 2

6. Eliza deposits $8500 in a college fund. If the fund earns an annual simple interest rate of 6.5%, how long must the money be in the fund to earn $9392.50 in interest?

See Example 3

7. Jessika gave a security deposit of $1200 to her landlord, Mr. Arce, 8 years ago. Mr. Arce now intends to give her the deposit back with simple interest of 2.85%. How much will he return to her?

See Example 4

8. Premier Bank loaned a construction company $275,000 at an annual simple interest rate. After 5 years, the company repaid the bank $350,625. What was the interest rate on the loan?

PRACTICE AND PROBLEM SOLVING

Extra Practice
See page 793.

Find the interest and the total amount to the nearest cent.

9. $315 at 6% per year for 5 years
10. $800 at 9% per year for 1 year
11. $4250 at 7% per year for 1.5 years
12. $550 at 5.5% per year for 3 years
13. $617 at 6% per year for 3 months
14. $2975 at 6% per year for 5 years
15. $900 at 7.25% per year for 3 years
16. $200 at 7% per year for 9 months

17. Jabari borrowed $1700 for 15 months at 16% annual simple interest rate. How much interest will he have to pay? What is the total amount he will repay?

18. Selena borrowed $9500 to buy a used car. The credit union charged 7% simple interest per year. She paid $3325 in interest. For what period of time did she borrow money?

LINK

Money

Many bank ATMs in Bangkok, Thailand, are located in sculptures to attract customers.

19. **Critical Thinking** Meghan and Sabrina compared the amount of interest they each earned on their savings accounts. Each had deposited \$1000, but Meghan earned \$140 interest and Sabrina earned \$157.50. Whose savings account had a higher interest rate? Explain.

20. **Money** The Smiths will borrow \$35,500 from a bank to start a business. They have two loan options. Option A is a 5-year loan; option B is a 4-year loan. Use the graph to answer the following questions.

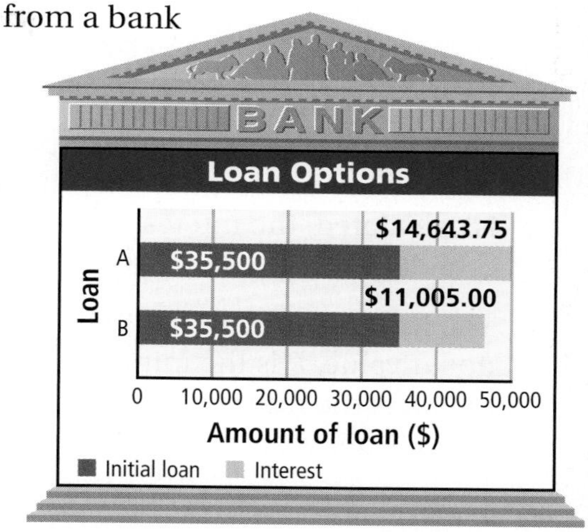

   a. What is the total amount the Smiths would pay under each loan option?
   b. What would be the interest rate under each loan option?
   c. What would be the monthly payment under each loan option?
   d. How much interest will the Smiths save by choosing loan option B?

21. **What's the Question?** Alice places \$700 in a savings account with a simple annual interest rate of 4%. When Alice withdraws the money, she has \$840. What is the question?

22. **Write About It** Which loan would cost a borrower less: \$3000 at 6% for 4 years or \$3000 at 7.5 for 3 years? How much interest would the borrower save by taking the cheaper loan?

23. **Challenge** How would the total payment on a 5-year loan at 3% annual simple interest compare with the total payment on a 5-year loan where one-twelfth of that simple interest, 0.25%, is calculated monthly? Give an example.

Test Prep and Spiral Review

24. **Multiple Choice** Sam invested \$2500 for 2 years in a savings account. The savings account paid an annual simple interest rate of 2.5% How much interest did Sam earn during the 2 years?

   (A) \$62.50 (B) \$125 (C) \$1250 (D) \$2625

25. **Multiple Choice** Toni invested \$250 in a savings account for 4 years. The total interest earned on the investment was \$125. What was the interest rate on the account?

   (F) 3.125% (G) 12.5% (H) 125% (J) 1125%

Find the appropriate factor for each conversion. (Lesson 5-3)

26. meters to millimeters
27. quarts to gallons
28. gallons to pints

Find each number. (Lesson 6-4)

29. 19 is 20% of what number?
30. 74% of what number is 481?

Technology LAB 6-7

Compute Compound Interest

Use with Lesson 6-7

go.hrw.com
Lab Resources Online
KEYWORD: MT7 Lab6

Compound interest is interest paid not only on the principal but also on any interest that has already been earned. Every time interest is calculated, the interest is added to the principal for future interest calculations.

The formula for compound interest is $A = P\left(1 + \frac{r}{k}\right)^{nk}$, where A is the final dollar value, P is the initial dollar investment, r is the annual interest rate, n is the number of years, and k is the number of compounding periods per year.

Activity 1

1 Use a calculator to find the value after 9 years of $1500 invested in a savings bank that pays 3% interest compounded annually.

The initial investment P is $1500. The rate r is 3% = 0.03. The interest period is one year. The number of interest periods n is 9, and $k = 1$.

$$A = 1500\left(1 + \frac{0.03}{1}\right)^{9 \cdot 1} = 1500(1.03)^9$$

On your graphing calculator, press

1500 [×] 1.03 [^] 9 [ENTER].

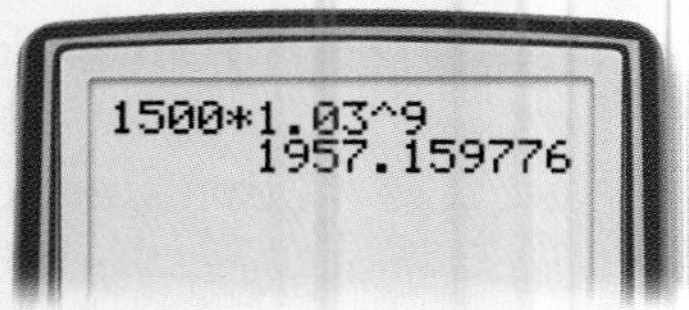

After 9 years, the initial investment of $1500 will be worth $1957.16 (rounded to the nearest cent).

2 Use a calculator to find the value after 9 years of $1500 invested in a savings bank that pays 6% interest compounded semi-annually (twice a year).

The initial investment P is $1500. Since $n = 9$ years and interest is compounded twice a year ($k = 2$), there are $9 \cdot 2 = 18$ interest periods in 9 years. The interest rate for each period r is 6% divided by 2, or 3% = 0.03.

$$A = 1500 \times \left(1 + \frac{0.06}{2}\right)^{9 \cdot 2} = 1500 \times (1.03)^{18}$$

On your calculator, press 1500 [×] 1.03 [^] 18 [ENTER].
You should find that $A = \$2553.65$.

Think and Discuss

1. Compare the value of an initial deposit of $1000 at 6% simple interest for 10 years with the same initial deposit at 6% annual compound interest for 10 years. Which is greater? Why?

Try This

1. Find the value of an initial investment of $2500 for the specified term and interest rate.

   a. 8 years, 5% compounded annually

   b. 20 years, 5% compounded monthly

Activity 2

1 Use a calculator to find the initial investment on an account that contains $3693.64 after earning 5% interest compounded annually for 8 years.

Using the formula for compound interest, you have $3693.64 = P\left(1 + \frac{0.05}{1}\right)^{8 \cdot 1} = P(1.05)^8$. To isolate P, divide both sides of the equation by $(1.05)^8$. This results in $P = 3693.64 \div (1.05)^8$.

On your graphing calculator, press

3693.64 [÷] 1.05 [^] 8 [ENTER].

The initial investment was $2500.00 (rounded to the nearest cent).

2 Use a calculator to check the answer from **1**.

If the initial investment was $2500, then $A = 2500\left(1 + \frac{0.05}{1}\right)^{8 \cdot 1} = 2500(1.05)^8$.

On your graphing calculator, press 2500 [×] 1.05 [^] 8 [ENTER]. You should find that A = $3693.638609, which rounds to $3693.64.

Think and Discuss

1. Can you think of a time when earning compound interest would be more advantageous than earning simple interest? When would simple interest be better?

Try This

1. Danielle's parents are investing in a college fund for her. They hope to have $10,000 when Danielle starts college in 18 years. If the money in the account earns 6.25% interest compounded semiannually, how much should their initial investment be? Check your answer.

2. Rodney put some money in an account that earned 8% interest compounded quarterly (four times per year) 4 years ago in order to save for a car. If the account now has $2247.58, what was Rodney's initial investment? Check your answer.

CHAPTER 6

READY TO GO ON?

SECTION 6B

Quiz for Lessons 6-5 Through 6-7

6-5 Percent Increase and Decrease

Find each percent increase or decrease to the nearest percent.

1. from 40 to 55
2. from 75 to 150
3. from 110 to 82
4. from 87 to 25

5. A population of geese rose from 234 to 460 over a period of two years. What is the percent increase, to the nearest tenth of a percent?
6. Mr. Simmons owns a hardware store and typically marks up merchandise by 28% over warehouse cost. How much would he charge a customer for a hammer that costs him $13.50?
7. A blouse and skirt that normally sell for $39.55 are on sale for 30% off the normal price. What is the sales price?

6-6 Applications of Percents

Find each commission or sales tax to the nearest cent.

8. total sales: $12,500
   commission rate: 3.25%
9. total sales: $14.23
   sales tax rate: 8.25%
10. total sales: $25,000
    commission rate: 2.75%
11. total sales: $251.50
    sales tax rate: 7.5%
12. total sales: $10,500
    commission rate: 4%
13. total sales: $75.99
    sales tax rate: 6.125%

14. Josh earns a weekly salary of $300 plus a 6% commission on sales. Last week, his sales totaled $3500. What was his total pay?

6-7 Simple Interest

Find the interest and the total amount to the nearest cent.

15. $225 at 5% per year for 3 years
16. $775 at 8% per year for 1 year

17. Leroy borrowed $8250 to be repaid after 3 years at an annual simple interest rate of 7.25%. How much interest will be due after 3 years? How much will Leroy have to repay?
18. Kim deposited $1422 in a savings account. How much would she have in the account after 5 years at an annual simple interest rate of 3%?
19. Hank borrowed $25,000 to remodel his house. At the end of 3 years, he had repaid a total of $29,125. At what simple interest rate did he borrow the money?
20. Akule borrowed $1500 at an annual simple interest rate of 12%. He paid $270 in interest. For what period of time did Akule borrow the money?

Multi-Step Test Prep

Get in Gear Mrs. Okendo's class is planning a camping trip. The students need to buy some camping gear. They use the advertisement from Mitchell's Sporting Goods to help them plan their purchases.

1. What is the discount on the lantern as a percent? How much do you save by buying the lantern during the sale?
2. Jake is looking for a tent for under $100. Explain how he can estimate the dollar amount of the discount on the tent at Mitchell's. Will Jake be able to buy his tent there?
3. Mitchell's advertises that all backpacks are discounted at least 25% during the spring sale. Is the statement true? Why or why not?
4. Li Ming needs to buy a sleeping bag, tent, and lantern. How much will these items cost if she buys them at Mitchell's? How much money will she save altogether?
5. Mrs. Okendo buys a set of 8 compasses for the class at Mitchell's. If the sales tax rate is 8.25%, what is the final cost for the compasses?

MITCHELL'S SPORTING GOODS
SPRING SALE!
18% OFF
COMPASS REG. PRICE $6
$13.75 OFF THE REGULAR PRICE
14% OFF
BACKPACK REG. PRICE $62.50
TENT REG. PRICE $119
10% OFF
2/5 OFF
SLEEPING BAG REG. PRICE $42
LANTERN REG. PRICE $15

Game Time

Percent Puzzlers

Prove your precision with these perplexing percent puzzlers!

1. A farmer is dividing his sheep among four pens. He puts 20% of the sheep in the first pen, 30% in the second pen, 37.5% in the third pen, and the rest in the fourth pen. What is the smallest number of sheep he could have?

2. Karen and Tina are on the same baseball team. Karen has hit in 35% of her 200 times at bat. Tina has hit in 30% of her 20 times at bat. If Karen hits in 100% of her next five times at bat and Tina hits in 80% of her next five times at bat, who will have the higher percentage of hits?

3. Joe was doing such a great job at work that his boss gave him a 10% raise! Then he made such a huge mistake that his boss gave him a 10% pay cut. What percent of his original salary does Joe make now?

4. Suppose you have 100 pounds of saltwater that is 99% water (by weight) and 1% salt. Some of the water evaporates so that the remaining liquid is 98% water and 2% salt. How much does the remaining liquid weigh?

Percent Tiles

Use cardboard or heavy paper to make 100 tiles with a digit from 0 through 9 (10 of each) on each tile, and print out a set of cards. Each player draws seven tiles. Lay four cards out on the table as shown. The object of the game is to collect as many cards as possible. To collect a card, use numbered tiles to correctly complete the statement on the card.

A complete set of the rules and game cards are available online.

go.hrw.com
Game Time Extra
KEYWORD: MT7 Games

It's in the Bag!

Materials
- 4-8 in. colored squares of paper
- 2-$4\frac{1}{2}$ in. squares of card stock
- about 12 in. of ribbon
- tape
- glue
- markers

PROJECT Origami Percents

Make this spectacular fold-and-hold origami notebook to record facts about percents.

Directions

1. Fold one of the colored squares of paper in half vertically and then horizontally. Unfold the paper. Then fold the square diagonally and unfold the paper. **Figure A**

2. Fold the diagonal crease back and forth so that it is easy to work with. Then bring the two ends of the diagonal together as shown in the figure. **Figure B**

3. Repeat steps 1 and 2 for all of the squares of paper, and set them aside.

4. Lay the squares of card stock in front of you so that they are about $\frac{1}{4}$ inch apart. Lay the ribbon across the squares as shown, and tape it down. **Figure C**

5. Glue one of the folded squares onto the piece of card stock on the left. Glue the next folded square onto the first one so that their sides match up and they open in the same direction. Continue with the remaining squares, gluing the last one onto the piece of card stock on the right.

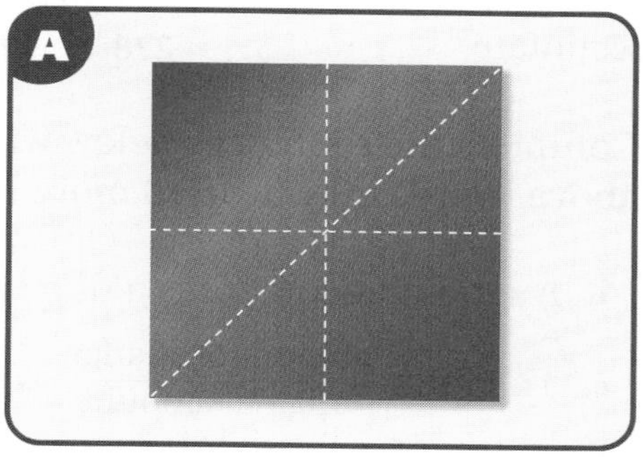
A

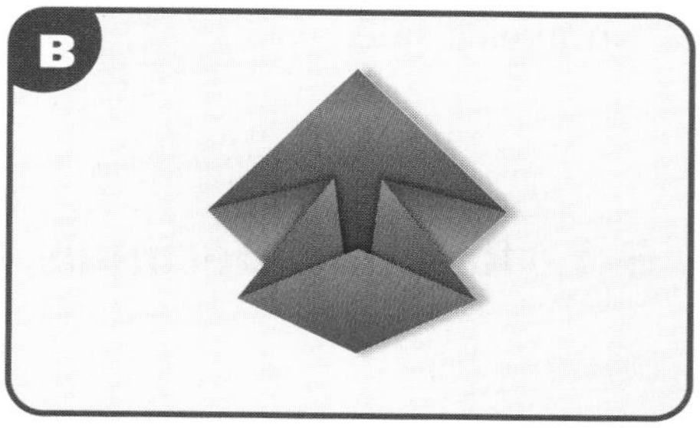
B

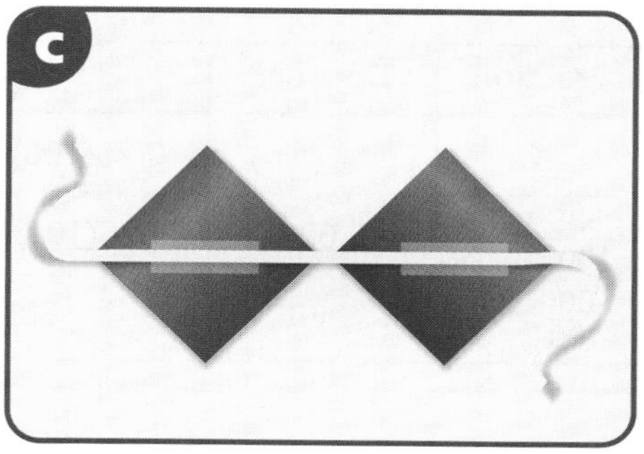
C

Taking Note of the Math

Write notes from the chapter on the various faces of the folded squares.

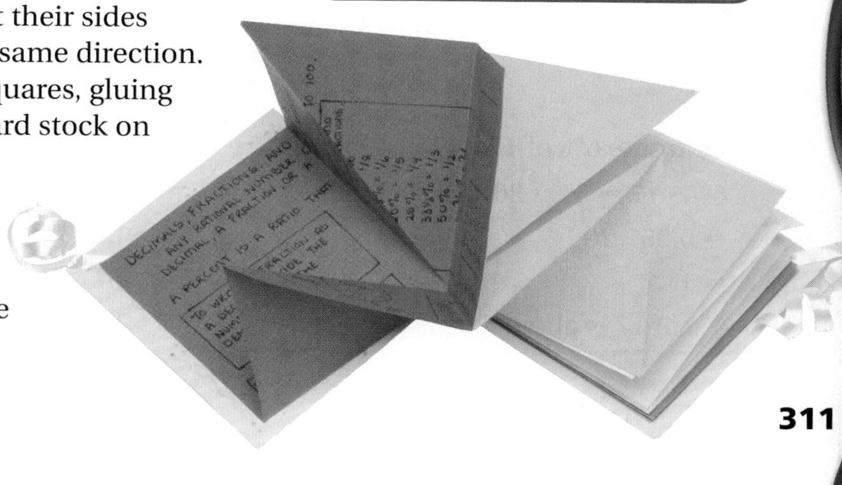

CHAPTER 6

Study Guide: Review

Vocabulary

benchmark	278	interest	302	principal	302
commission	298	percent	274	rate of interest	302
commission rate	298	percent change	294	sales tax	298
compatible numbers	278	percent decrease	294	simple interest	302
estimate	278	percent increase	294		

Complete the sentences below with vocabulary words from the list above. Words may be used more than once.

1. A ratio that compares a number to 100 is called a(n) __?__.
2. The ratio $\frac{\text{amount of change}}{\text{original amount}}$ is called the __?__.
3. Percent is used to calculate __?__, a fee paid to a person who makes a sale.

6-1 Relating Decimals, Fractions, and Percents (pp. 274–277)

EXAMPLE

■ **Complete the table.**

Fraction	Decimal	Percent
$\frac{3}{4}$	0.75	0.75(100) = 75%
$\frac{625}{1000} = \frac{5}{8}$	0.625	0.625(100) = 62.5%
$\frac{80}{100} = \frac{4}{5}$	0.80	80%

EXERCISES

Complete the table.

Fraction	Decimal	Percent
$\frac{7}{16}$	4. ■	5. ■
6. ■	1.125	7. ■
8. ■	9. ■	70%

6-2 Estimate with Percents (pp. 278–282)

EXAMPLE

■ **Estimate 6% of 17.**

$6\% \cdot 17 \approx 5\% \cdot 20$ *Use compatible numbers.*

$\approx 0.05 \cdot 20$ *Write 5% as a decimal.*

≈ 1 *Multiply.*

6% of 17 is about 1.

EXERCISES

Estimate.

10. 11% of 303
11. 102% of 62
12. $33\frac{1}{3}\%$ of 10
13. 60% of 34
14. a 15% tip for $48.90
15. a 20% tip for $82.75

6-3 Finding Percents (pp. 283–287)

EXAMPLE

- **A raw apple weighing 5.3 oz contains about 4.45 oz of water. What percent of an apple is water?**

$\frac{\text{number}}{100} = \frac{\text{part}}{\text{whole}}$ *Set up a proportion.*

$\frac{n}{100} = \frac{4.45}{5.3}$ *Substitute.*

$5.3n = 445$ *Cross multiply.*

$n = \frac{445}{5.3} \approx 83.96 \approx 84\%$

An apple is about 84% water.

EXERCISES

16. The length of a year on Mars is about 687 Earth days. The length of a year on Venus is about 225 Earth days. About what percent of the length of Mars's year is Venus's year?

17. The main span of the Brooklyn Bridge is 1595 feet long. The Golden Gate Bridge is about 263% the length of the Brooklyn Bridge. To the nearest hundred feet, how long is the Golden Gate Bridge?

6-4 Finding a Number When the Percent Is Known (pp. 288–291)

EXAMPLE

- **In 2003 the population of Fairbanks, Alaska, was 30,970. This was about 491% of the population of Kodiak, Alaska. To the nearest ten people, find the population of Kodiak in 2003.**

$\frac{491}{100} = \frac{30{,}970}{n}$ *Set up a proportion.*

$491n = 3{,}097{,}000$ *Cross multiply.*

$n = \frac{3{,}097{,}000}{491} \approx 6307.5356 \approx 6310$

The population of Kodiak was about 6310.

EXERCISES

18. The diameter at the equator of Saturn is 74,897 miles. This is about 945% of the diameter of Earth at its equator. To the nearest ten miles, find the diameter of Earth at its equator.

19. At the age of 20 weeks, Zoe weighed 16 lb 4 oz. Her birth weight was about $33\frac{1}{3}\%$ of her 20-week weight. To the nearest ounce, what was her birth weight?

6-5 Percent Increase and Decrease (pp. 294–297)

EXAMPLE

- **In 1990 there were 639,270 robberies reported in the United States. This number decreased in 2002 to 420,637. What was the percent decrease?**

$639{,}270 - 420{,}637 = 218{,}633$ *Amount of decrease*

$\frac{\text{amount of decrease}}{\text{original amount}} = \frac{218{,}633}{639{,}270}$

$\approx 0.3420 \approx 34.2\%$

The number of reported robberies decreased by 34.2%.

EXERCISES

20. On sale, a skirt was reduced from \$25 to \$21. Find the percent decrease.

21. In 1900 the U.S. public debt was \$1.2 billion dollars. This number increased to \$5674.2 billion dollars in 2000. Find the percent increase.

22. At the beginning of a 40-week medically supervised diet, Arnie weighed 276 lb. After the diet, Arnie weighed 181 lb. Find the percent decrease.

6-6 Applications of Percents (pp. 298–301)

EXAMPLE

- **As an appliance salesman, Gavin earns a base pay of $525 per week plus a 6% commission on his weekly sales. Last week, his sales totaled $3250. How much did he earn for the week?**

Find the amount of commission.

$6\% \cdot \$3250 = 0.06 \cdot \$3250 = \$195$

Add the commission amount to his base pay.

$\$195 + \$525 = \$720$

Last week Gavin earned $720.

EXERCISES

23. As a real estate agent, Kensho earns $4\frac{1}{2}\%$ commission on the houses he sells. In the first quarter of this year, he sold two houses, one for $175,000 and the other for $199,000. How much was Kensho's commission for this quarter?

24. If the sales tax is $8\frac{1}{4}\%$, how much tax would Luisa pay for a picture frame that costs $17.99 and a desk calendar that costs $24.99?

6-7 Simple Interest (pp. 302–305)

EXAMPLE

- **For home improvements, the Walters borrowed $10,000 for 3 years at simple interest. They repaid a total of $11,050. What was the interest rate of the loan?**

Find the amount of interest.

$P + I = A$		*Use the formula.*
$10{,}000 + I =$	$11{,}050$	*Substitute.*
$-10{,}000$	$-10{,}000$	*Subtract 10,000 from both sides.*
$I =$	1050	*Simplify.*

Substitute into the simple interest formula.

$I = P \cdot r \cdot t$	*Use the formula.*
$1050 = 10{,}000 \cdot r \cdot 3$	*Substitute.*
$1050 = 30{,}000r$	*Simplify.*
$\frac{1050}{30{,}000} = \frac{30{,}000r}{30{,}000}$	*Divide both sides by 30,000.*
$0.035 = r$	*Simplify.*

The interest rate of the loan was 3.5%.

EXERCISES

Using the simple interest formula, find the missing number.

25. interest = ▒; principal = $14,500; rate = $6\frac{1}{4}\%$ per year; time = $3\frac{1}{2}$ years

26. interest = $32; principal = ▒; rate = 2% per year; time = 4 years

27. interest = $367.50; principal = $1500; rate per year = ▒; time = $3\frac{1}{2}$ years

28. interest = $1787.50; principal = $55,000; rate = $6\frac{1}{2}\%$ per year; time = ▒

Which simple-interest loan would cost the borrower less? How much less?

29. $1000 at 3% for 4 years or $1000 at 3.75% for 3 years

Study Guide: Review

CHAPTER TEST

CHAPTER 6

Order the numbers from least to greatest.

1. $\frac{4}{5}$, 75%, 0.82, $\frac{17}{20}$ **2.** $\frac{8}{20}$, 0.35, 15%, 0.2 **3.** 75%, $\frac{7}{9}$, 0.8, $\frac{5}{6}$ **4.** 58%, $\frac{33}{60}$, 0.45, 49%

Estimate.

5. 17% of 42 **6.** 79% of 122 **7.** 32% of 511

8. 83% of 197 **9.** 4% of 1900 **10.** 27% of 80

11. a 15% tip on a \$37 bill **12.** a 19% tip on a \$53 bill **13.** a 17% tip on a \$23 bill

14. Of the 50 states in the Union, 32% have names that begin with either *M* or *N*. How many states have names beginning with either *M* or *N*?

15. 30 is 12.5% of what number? **16.** 244 is 250% of what number?

17. $7\frac{1}{2}$ is 5% of what number? **18.** 5.6 is 56% of what number

19. At 3 P.M., a chimney casts a shadow that is 135% its actual height. If the shadow is 37.8 ft, what is the actual height of the chimney?

Find each percent increase or decrease to the nearest percent.

20. from 125 to 75 **21.** from 20 to 62 **22.** from 236 to 125 **23.** from 11 to 98

24. from 0.5 to 2 **25.** from 12.2 to 6.1 **26.** from 18.4 to 3.2 **27.** from 0.2 to 6

28. The price for a share of XYZ stock went from \$32 to \$37 in one month. What was the percent increase to the nearest tenth of a percent?

Find each commission or sales tax to the nearest cent.

29. total sales: \$13,600
commission rate: 2.75%

30. total sales: \$135.50
sales tax rate: 8.25%

31. total sales: \$20,250
commission rate: 3.9%

32. Ms. Tan earns \$350 per week plus an 8% commission on her shoe sales. She sold \$560 last week. What was her total pay for the week?

33. George earns an annual salary of \$36,000. In addition to this, he earns a 3% commission on all sales he makes. If George had \$264,000 in sales last year, what was his total pay?

34. Dena borrowed \$7500 to buy a used car. The credit union charged 9% simple interest per year. She paid \$2025 in interest. For what period of time did she borrow the money?

35. At Thrift Bank, if you keep \$675 in a savings account for 12 years, your money will earn \$486 in interest. What annual simple interest rate doesthe bank offer?

CHAPTER 6

STANDARDIZED TEST PREP

go.hrw.com
State Test Practice Online
KEYWORD: MT7 TestPrep

Cumulative Assessment, Chapters 1–6

Multiple Choice

1. If the figures are similar, what is the scale factor?

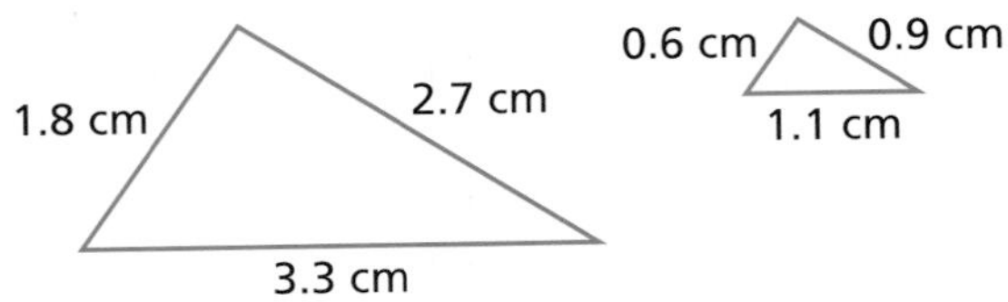

(A) 1:3 (C) 2:9

(B) 2:3 (D) 1:9

2. If the base of a right triangle is 24 centimeters and the hypotenuse is 40 centimeters, what is the area of the triangle?

(F) 384 cm^2 (H) 768 cm^2

(G) 480 cm^2 (J) 960 cm^2

3. Which situation corresponds to the graph?

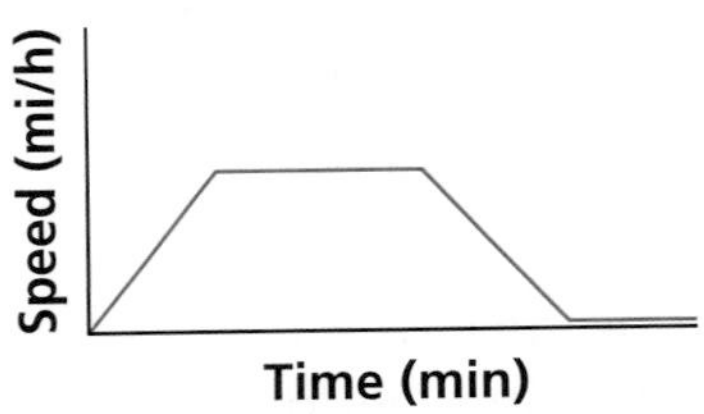

(A) Jill's dog chases a cat, stops and waits, and then runs down a hill.

(B) Joe's dog sits at his feet, sees a cat and darts off, and then comes back.

(C) Abe's dog chases a squirrel to a tree, runs circles around the tree, and then runs back to Abe and sits down.

(D) Amy's dog walks around the block, then runs to the house, and then sits.

4. Which equation is equivalent to the equation $\frac{1}{2}x + 8 = -10$?

(F) $\frac{1}{2}x = -2$ (H) $x + 8 = -20$

(G) $x + 8 = -5$ (J) $\frac{1}{2}x = -18$

5. Which situation corresponds to the inequality $x < 90$?

(A) Jerry has at least \$90 in his bank account.

(B) Jerry owes his mom no more than \$90 for his car insurance.

(C) Jerry rented more than 90 videos last year.

(D) Jerry works fewer than 90 hours each month at the newspaper.

6. A refrigerator that usually sells for \$879 goes on sale for \$649. What is the percent decrease, to the nearest tenth of a percent?

(F) 12.2% (H) 35.4%

(G) 26.2% (J) 173.8%

7. The human body is 65% water. Which is NOT an equivalent number?

(A) 0.65 (C) 6.5×10^{-1}

(B) $\frac{13}{20}$ (D) 6.50

8. One in every 3 girls plays a varsity sport in high school. In 1970, 1 in every 27 girls played a varsity sport. What is the percent increase, rounded to the nearest percent?

(F) 8% (H) 800%

(G) 88% (J) 888%

9. Gloria invests $158 in a simple interest account for 4 years at 2% interest. How many dollars did she earn in interest?

Ⓐ $170.64 Ⓒ $12.64

Ⓑ $126.40 Ⓓ $1.26

HOT TIP! **Underline key words, such as *at least, rounded to,* and *equivalent,* to help you focus on what is being asked.**

Gridded Response

10. Heidi, Mike, Brenda, and Luis won 120 tokens in all at a fair. Heidi won $\frac{1}{5}$ of the tokens, Mike won 0.4 of the tokens, Brenda won 25% of the tokens, and Luis won the rest. How many tokens did Luis win?

11. Yesenia, a real estate agent, has 32 houses on the market. If she sells 5 of the houses this month, what percent of the houses on the market will she sell? Grid your response as a decimal rounded to the nearest thousandth.

12. A recipe calls for 4 cups of strawberries for every 6 cups of whipped topping. If Gino uses 54 cups of whipped topping, how many cups of strawberries does he need?

13. Six more than $\frac{1}{4}$ of a number is $\frac{1}{3}$ of the number. What is the number?

14. What is the length of the hypotenuse after a dilation with a scale factor of $\frac{1}{2}$? Round your answer to the nearest hundredth.

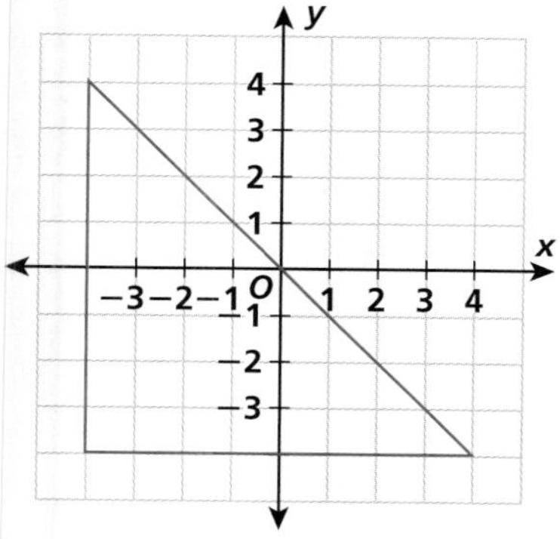

Short Response

15. If 10 kg of acid is added to 15 kg of water, what percent of the resulting solution is acid? Show your work.

16. In the chemistry laboratory, Jim is working with six large jars of capacities 5 L, 4 L, 3 L, 2 L, 1 L, and 10 L. The 5 L jar is filled with an acid mix, and the rest of the jars are empty. Jim uses the 5 L jar to fill the 4 L jar and pours the excess into the 10 L jar. Then he uses the 4 L jar to fill the 3 L jar and pours the excess into the 10 L jar. He repeats the process until all but the 1 L and 10 L jars are empty. What percent of the 10 L jar is now filled? Show your work.

17. Mr. Coluzzi bought a 5-pound bag of Granny Smith apples for $3.99. Individual apples cost $0.82 per pound. Justify whether Mr. Coluzzi made the better buy.

18. Four friends equally shared the cost of a $48.80 gift. They got a 20% discount and paid 7.25% sales tax. How much money did each person pay? Explain.

Extended Response

19. Amanda and Sergio each have $3000 to invest. Amanda invests with her local banker, while Sergio invests his money using an online service. They both invest at a 3% interest rate.

    a. Amanda's banker invests the money using a simple interest plan. If Amanda keeps her money in this plan for 5 years, how much interest will she earn?

    b. What is the value of Sergio's investment if he invests for 5 years compounded annually?

    c. What is the difference in the amount of money earned? Explain your reasoning.

    d. Who earns more money after 5 years?

Problem Solving on Location

PENNSYLVANIA

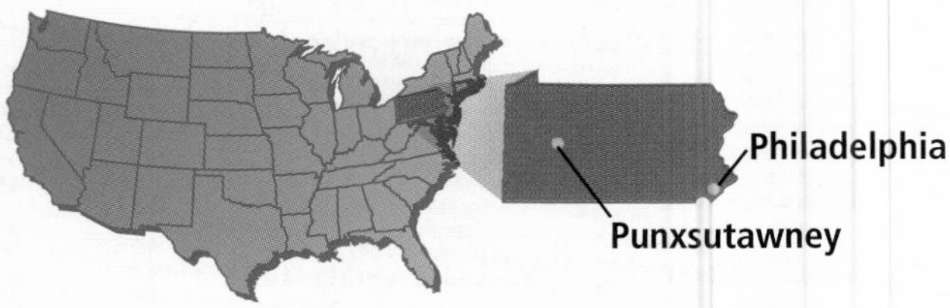

Punxsutawney Phil

Punxsutawney Phil is our country's most famous groundhog. Each year on Groundhog Day (February 2), thousands of visitors trek to Punxsutawney, Pennsylvania, to await his appearance. According to tradition, if Phil comes out of his hole and sees his shadow, there will be six more weeks of winter. If he doesn't see his shadow, there will be an early spring.

Choose one or more strategies to solve each problem.

1. During the 15-year period from 1970 to 1984, the number of times Phil did not see his shadow was 25% of the number of times he did see his shadow. How many times did he see his shadow during this period?

2. Groundhogs hibernate during the winter. While hibernating, their hearts beat at just 4% of their normal rate. A groundhog's normal heart rate is 139% that of a human's. Given that a typical human heart rate is 72 beats per minute, what is a groundhog's hibernating heart rate?

For 3, use the table.

3. The table shows some Groundhog Day results from past years. Assume that the percent of time Phil sees his shadow will remain the same in the future.

a. Predict the number of times Phil will *not* see his shadow from 2011 to 2018.

b. How many different ways are there to choose the years in which Phil does not see his shadow during this period?

Phil's Shadow sightings

1980	yes	1990	no
1981	yes	1991	yes
1982	yes	1992	yes
1983	no	1993	yes
1984	yes	1994	yes
1985	yes	1995	no
1986	no	1996	yes
1987	yes	1997	no
1988	no	1998	yes
1989	yes		

Problem Solving Strategies

- Draw a Diagram
- Make a Model
- Guess and Test
- Work Backward
- Find a Pattern
- Make a Table
- Solve a Simpler Problem
- Use Logical Reasoning
- Act It Out
- Make an Organized List

The Mural Arts Program

With more murals than any other U.S. city, Philadelphia is undoubtedly the Mural Capital of the United States. The city's mural arts program was founded in 1984 as a way to combat graffiti. Since then, the walls of more than 2400 buildings have been painted with murals.

Choose one or more strategies to solve each problem.

1. For the average mural, the ratio of the height to the width is 3:2. The sum of the height and width is 75 feet. What is the height of the average mural?

2. To create one of the city's murals, artist Don Gensler made a design on his computer and then projected sections of the image onto 5 ft by 5 ft pieces of cloth. The entire mural measured 35 ft by 125 ft. How many pieces of cloth were needed?

For 3 and 4, use the table.

3. An artist makes a $\frac{1}{2}$ in. scale drawing of the Jackie Robinson mural. To help make a grid on the drawing, she makes a small mark every 3 in. around its perimeter. How many marks does he make?

4. One of the murals in the table was created by students from McKinley Elementary School. Their mural has a height-to-width ratio that is less than 1. A scale drawing of their mural using a scale of 1:10 would be around 3 ft tall. Which mural was made by the students?

Philadelphia Murals

Title	Height (ft)	Width (ft)
Camilla's Dream	28	33
Common Threads	120	62.5
Philadelphia Muses	60	115
Jackie Robinson	30	24

CHAPTER 7

Foundations of Geometry

7A	**Two-Dimensional Geometry**
7-1	Points, Lines, Planes, and Angles
LAB	Bisect Figures
7-2	Parallel and Perpendicular Lines
LAB	Constructions
7-3	Angles in Triangles
7-4	Classifying Polygons
LAB	Exterior Angles of a Polygon
7-5	Coordinate Geometry
7B	**Patterns in Geometry**
7-6	Congruence
7-7	Transformations
LAB	Combine Transformations
7-8	Symmetry
7-9	Tessellations

MULTI-STEP TEST PREP

go.hrw.com
Chapter Project Online
KEYWORD: MT7 Ch7

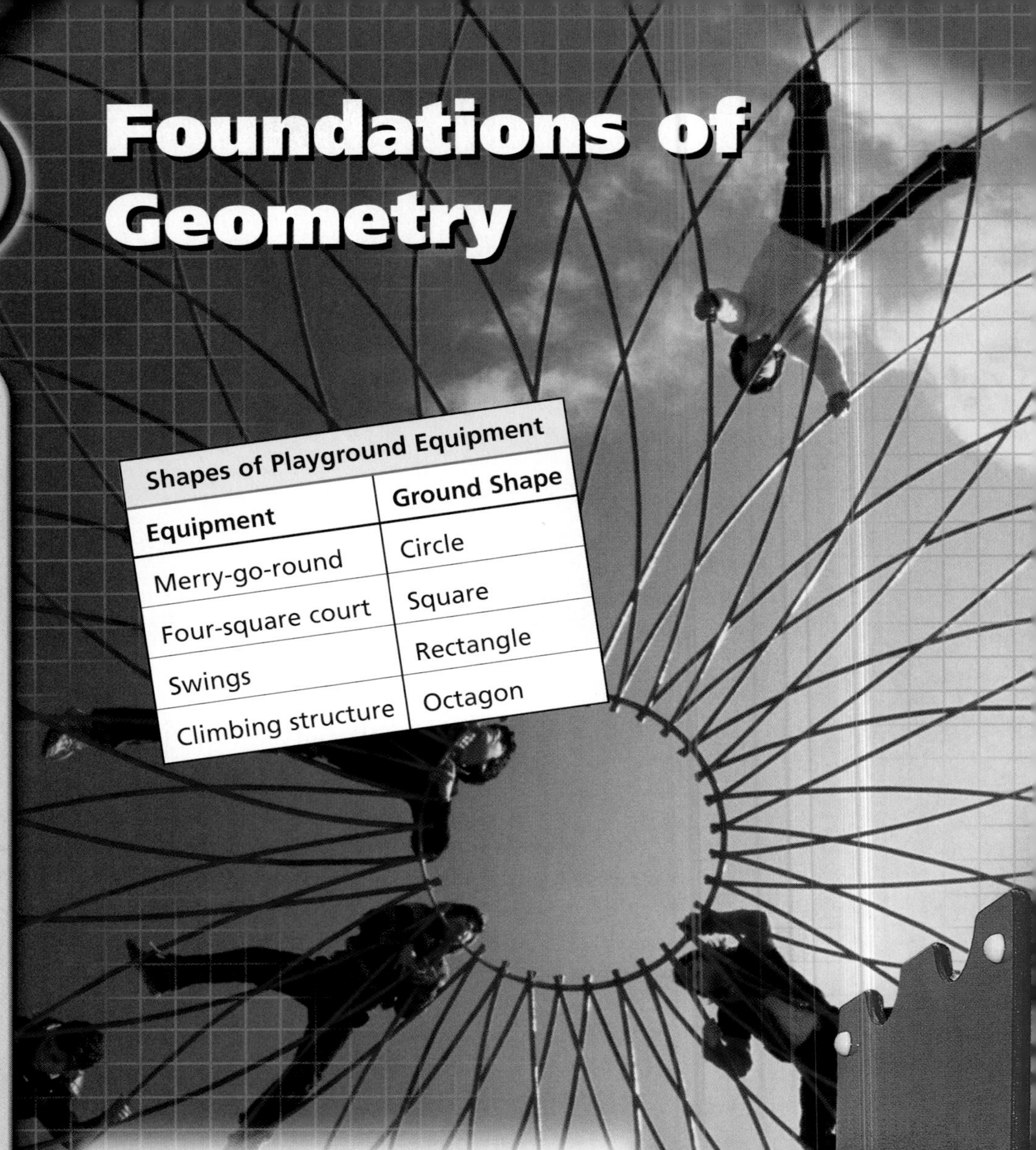

Shapes of Playground Equipment

Equipment	Ground Shape
Merry-go-round	Circle
Four-square court	Square
Swings	Rectangle
Climbing structure	Octagon

Career *Playground Equipment Designer*

Playground equipment must be attractive, safe, fun, and appropriate for the ages of the children who will use it. Years ago, designers used pencils, T-squares, and slide rules to create their designs. Designers now use computers, 3-D programs, and virtual reality to design playgrounds.

ARE YOU READY?

Vocabulary

Choose the best term from the list to complete each sentence.

1. In the ___?___ (4, −3), 4 is the ___?___, and −3 is the ___?___.
2. The ___?___ divide the ___?___ into four sections.
3. The point (0, 0) is called the ___?___.
4. The point (0, −3) lies on the ___?___, while the point (−2, 0) lies on the ___?___.

coordinate axes
coordinate plane
ordered pair
origin
***x*-axis**
***x*-coordinate**
***y*-axis**
***y*-coordinate**

Complete these exercises to review skills you will need for this chapter.

Ordered Pairs

Write the coordinates of the indicated points.

5. point A
6. point B
7. point C
8. point D
9. point E
10. point F
11. point G
12. point H

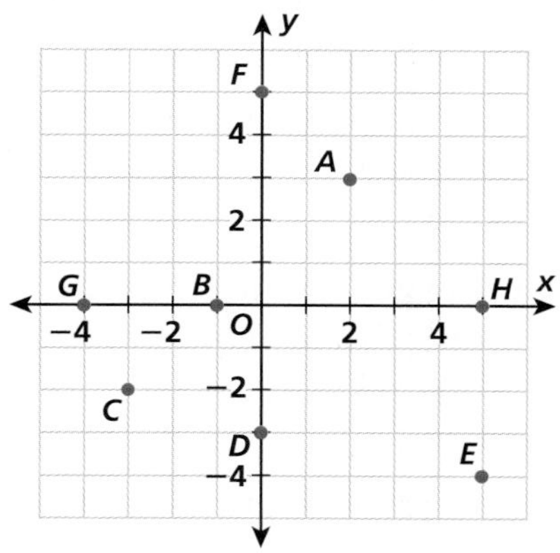

Similar Figures

Tell whether the figures in each pair appear to be similar.

13. 

14. 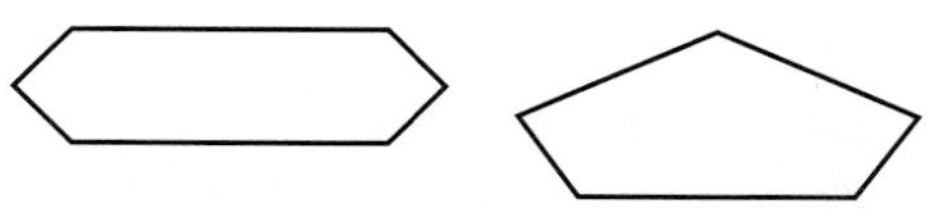

Equations

Solve each equation.

15. $2p = 18$
16. $7 + h = 21$
17. $\frac{x}{3} = 9$
18. $y - 6 = 16$
19. $4d + 1 = 13$
20. $-2q - 3 = 3$
21. $4(z - 1) = 16$
22. $x + 3 + 4x = 23$

Determine whether the given values are solutions of the given equations.

23. $\frac{2}{3}x + 1 = 7 \quad x = 9$
24. $2x - 4 = 6 \quad x = -1$
25. $8 - 2x = -4 \quad x = 5$
26. $\frac{1}{2}x + 5 = -2 \quad x = -14$

CHAPTER 7

Study Guide: Preview

Where You've Been

Previously, you

- located and named points on a coordinate plane.
- recognized geometric concepts and properties in fields such as art and architecture.
- used critical attributes to define similarity.

In This Chapter

You will study

- graphing translations and reflections on a coordinate plane.
- using geometric concepts and properties of geometry to solve problems in fields such as art and architecture.
- using critical attributes to define congruency.

Where You're Going

You can use the skills learned in this chapter

- to find angle measures by using relationships within figures.
- to create tessellations.
- to identify properties of geometry in art and architecture.

Key Vocabulary/Vocabulario

equilateral triangle	triángulo equilátero
line	línea
parallel lines	líneas paralelas
perpendicular lines	rectas perpendiculars
plane	plano
point	punto
polygon	polígono
reflection	reflexión
slope	pendiente
transformation	transformación
translation	translación
transversal	transversal

Vocabulary Connections

To become familiar with some of the vocabulary terms in the chapter, consider the following. You may refer to the chapter, the glossary, or a dictionary if you like.

1. The word *equilateral* contains the roots *equi,* which means "equal," and lateral, which means "of the side." What do you suppose an **equilateral triangle** is?
2. The Greek prefix *poly* means "many," and the root *gon* means "angle." What do you suppose a **polygon** is?
3. Think of what **slope** means when you are talking about a hill. How do you think this applies to lines on a coordinate plane?

Reading and Writing Math

Writing Strategy: Keep a Math Journal

By keeping a math journal, you can improve your writing and thinking skills. Use your journal to summarize key ideas and vocabulary from each lesson and to analyze any questions you may have about a concept or your homework.

Journal Entry: Read the entry a student made in her journal.

January 27

I'm having trouble with Lesson 6-5. I can find what percent one number is of another number, but I get confused about finding percent increase and decrease. My teacher helped me think it through:

Find the percent increase or decrease from 20 to 25.

- *First figure out if it is a percent increase or decrease. It goes from a smaller to a larger number, so it is a percent increase because the number is getting larger, or increasing.*
- *Then find the amount of increase, or the difference, between the two numbers.* $25 - 20 = 5$
- *Now find what percent the amount of increase, or difference, is of the original number.*

$$\frac{\text{amount of increase}}{\text{original number}} \rightarrow \frac{5}{20} = 0.25 = 25\%$$

So it is a 25% increase.

Try This

Begin a math journal. Write in it each day this week, using these ideas as starters. Be sure to date and number each page.

- In this lesson, I already know . . .
- In this lesson, I am unsure about . . .
- The skills I need to complete this lesson are . . .
- The challenges I encountered were . . .
- I handled these challenges by . . .
- In this lesson, I enjoyed/did not enjoy . . .

7-1 Points, Lines, Planes, and Angles

Learn to classify and name figures.

Points, lines, and planes are the building blocks of geometry. Segments, rays, and angles are defined in terms of these basic figures.

Vocabulary

point, line, plane, segment, ray, angle, right angle, acute angle, obtuse angle, complementary angles, supplementary angles, congruent, vertical angles

A **point** names a location.		point A
A **line** is perfectly straight and extends forever in both directions.	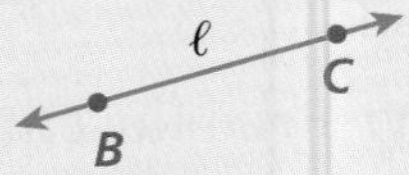	line ℓ, or $\overleftrightarrow{BC}$
A **plane** is a perfectly flat surface that extends forever in all directions.	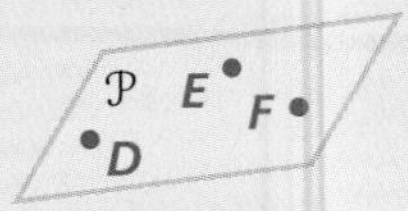	plane $\mathcal{P}$, or plane DEF
A **segment**, or line segment, is the part of a line between two points.		$\overline{GH}$
A **ray** is part of a line that starts at one point and extends forever in one direction.	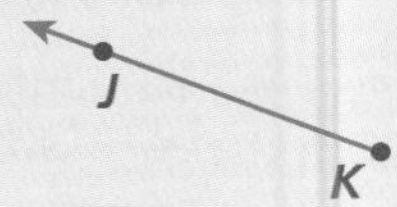	$\overrightarrow{KJ}$

$\overleftrightarrow{BC}$ is read "line BC." $\overline{GH}$ is read "segment GH." $\overrightarrow{KJ}$ is read "ray KJ." To name a ray, always write the endpoint first.

EXAMPLE 1 Naming Points, Lines, Planes, Segments, and Rays

Use the diagram to name each figure.

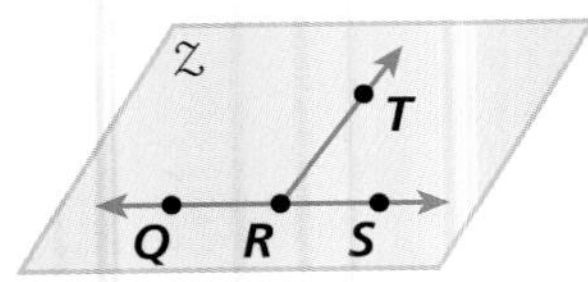

A four points

Q, R, S, T

B a line

Possible answers: $\overleftrightarrow{QS}$, $\overleftrightarrow{QR}$ or $\overleftrightarrow{RS}$ — *Any 2 points on the line can be used.*

C a plane

Possible answers: plane $\mathcal{Z}$ or plane QRT — *Any 3 points in the plane that form a triangle can name a plane.*

D four segments

Possible answers: $\overline{QR}$, $\overline{RS}$, $\overline{RT}$, $\overline{QS}$ — *Write the 2 points in any order, for example, $\overline{QR}$ or $\overline{RQ}$.*

E five rays

$\overrightarrow{RQ}$, $\overrightarrow{RS}$, $\overrightarrow{RT}$, $\overrightarrow{SQ}$, $\overrightarrow{QS}$ — *Write the endpoint first.*

An **angle** (∠) is formed by two rays with a common endpoint called the *vertex* (plural, *vertices*). Angles can be measured in degrees. m∠1 means the measure of ∠1. The angle can be named ∠*XYZ*, ∠*ZYX*, ∠1, or ∠*Y*. The vertex must be the middle letter.

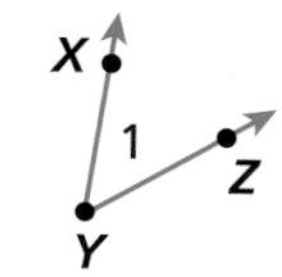

The measures of angles that fit together to form a straight line, such as ∠*FKG*, ∠*GKH*, and ∠*HKJ*, add to 180°.

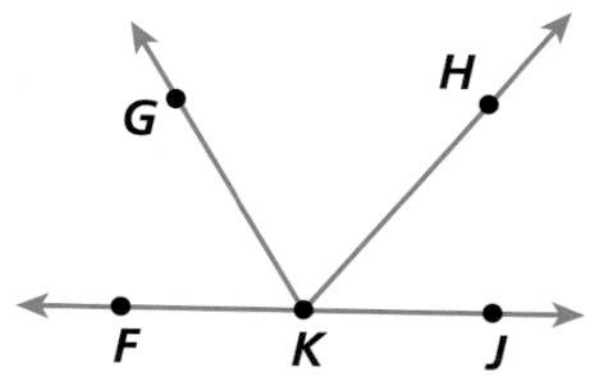

The measures of angles that fit together to form a complete circle, such as ∠*MRN*, ∠*NRP*, ∠*PRQ*, and ∠*QRM*, add to 360°.

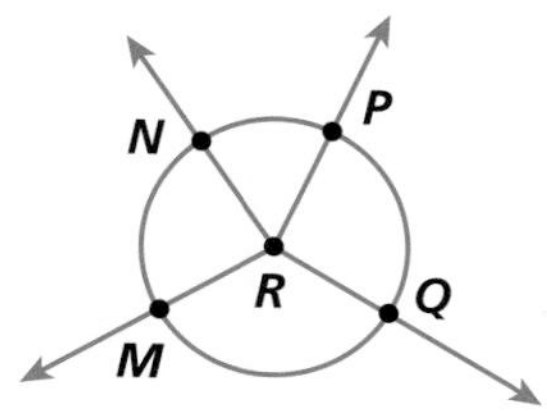

A **right angle** measures 90°. An **acute angle** measures greater than 0° and less than 90°. An **obtuse angle** measures greater than 90° and less than 180°. **Complementary angles** are two angles whose measures add to 90°. **Supplementary angles** are two angles whose measures add to 180°.

EXAMPLE 2 Classifying Angles

Use the diagram to name each figure.

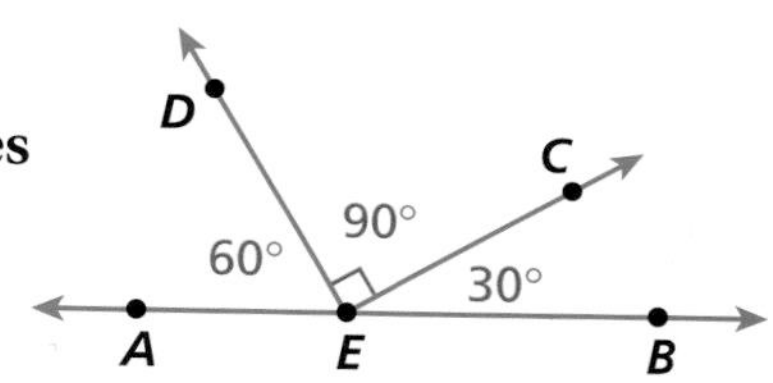

A a right angle

∠*DEC*

B two acute angles

∠*AED*, ∠*CEB*

C two obtuse angles

∠*AEC*, ∠*DEB* *m∠AEC = 150°; m∠DEB = 120°*

D a pair of complementary angles

∠*AED*, ∠*CEB* *m∠AED + m∠CEB = 60° + 30° = 90°*

E two pairs of supplementary angles

∠*AED*, ∠*DEB* *m∠AED + m∠DEB = 60° + 120° = 180°*

∠*AEC*, ∠*CEB* *m∠AEC + m∠CEB = 150° + 30° = 180°*

Reading Math

A right angle can be labeled with a small box at the vertex.

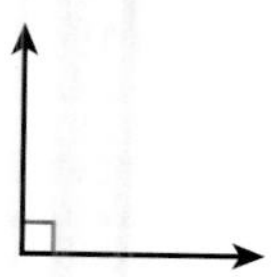

Congruent figures have the same size and shape.

- Segments that have the same length are congruent.
- Angles that have the same measure are congruent.
- The symbol for congruence is ≅, which is read "is congruent to."

Intersecting lines form two pairs of **vertical angles**. Vertical angles are always congruent, as shown in the next example.

EXAMPLE 3 Finding the Measures of Vertical Angles

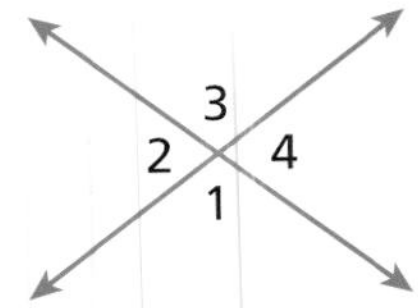

In the figure, ∠1 and ∠3 are vertical angles, and ∠2 and ∠4 are vertical angles.

A **If m∠2 = 75°, find m∠4.**

m∠1 = 180° − 75° — *∠2 and ∠1 are supplementary.*

= 105°

m∠4 = 180° − 105° — *∠1 and ∠4 are supplementary.*

= 75°

So m∠2 = m∠4, or ∠2 ≅ ∠4

B **If m∠3 = x°, find m∠1.**

m∠1 = 180° − m∠4 — *∠3 and ∠4 are supplementary.*

m∠1 = 180° − (180° − x°) — *Substitute 180° − x° for m∠4.*

= 180° − 180° + x° — *Distributive Property*

= x° — *Simplify.*

So m∠1 = m∠3, or ∠1 ≅ ∠3.

Think and Discuss

1. **Tell** which statements are correct if ∠X and ∠Y are congruent.
   a. ∠X = ∠Y **b.** m∠X = m∠Y **c.** ∠X ≅ ∠Y **d.** m∠X ≅ m∠Y
2. **Explain** why vertical angles must always be congruent.

7-1 Exercises

go.hrw.com
Homework Help Online
KEYWORD: MT7 7-1
Parent Resources Online
KEYWORD: MT7 Parent

GUIDED PRACTICE

See Example 1 **Use the diagram to name each figure.**

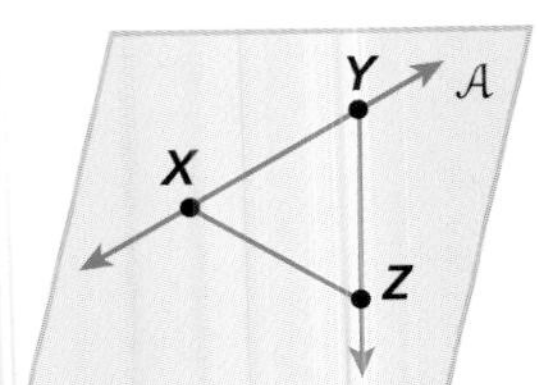

1. three points
2. a line
3. a plane
4. three segments
5. three rays

See Example 2 **Use the diagram to name each figure.**

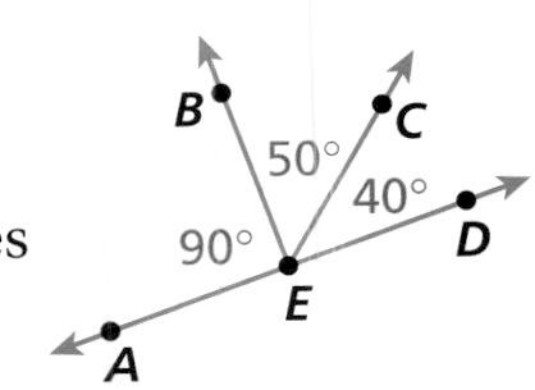

6. a right angle
7. two acute angles
8. an obtuse angle
9. a pair of complementary angles
10. two pairs of supplementary angles

See Example 3

In the figure, $\angle 1$ and $\angle 3$ are vertical angles, and $\angle 2$ and $\angle 4$ are vertical angles.

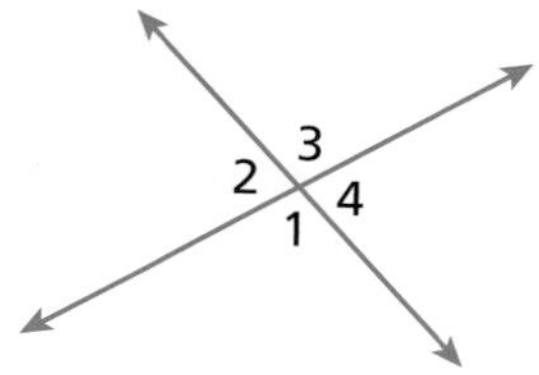

11. If $m\angle 3 = 105°$, find $m\angle 1$.

12. If $m\angle 2 = x°$, find $m\angle 4$.

INDEPENDENT PRACTICE

See Example 1

Use the diagram to name each figure.

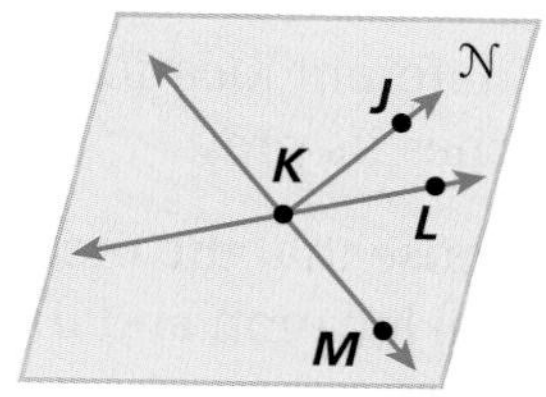

13. four points

14. two lines

15. a plane

16. three segments

17. five rays

See Example 2

Use the diagram to name each figure.

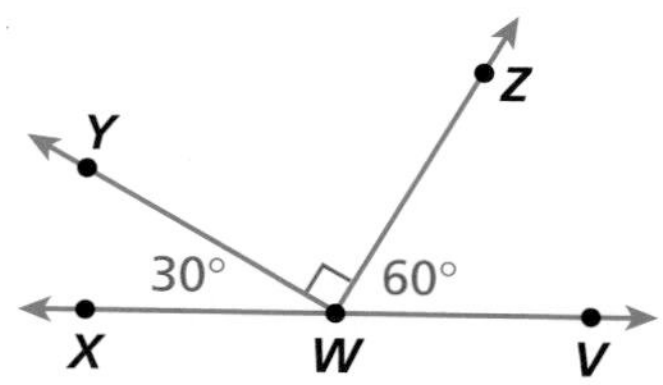

18. a right angle

19. two acute angles

20. two obtuse angles

21. a pair of complementary angles

22. two pairs of supplementary angles

See Example 3

In the figure, $\angle 1$ and $\angle 3$ are vertical angles, and $\angle 2$ and $\angle 4$ are vertical angles.

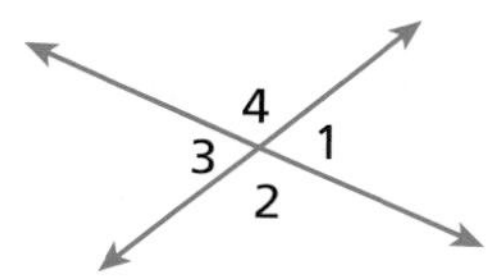

23. If $m\angle 2 = 126°$, find $m\angle 4$.

24. If $m\angle 1 = b°$, find $m\angle 3$.

PRACTICE AND PROBLEM SOLVING

Extra Practice
See page 794.

Use the figure for Exercises 25–34. Write *true* or *false*. If a statement is false, rewrite it so it is true.

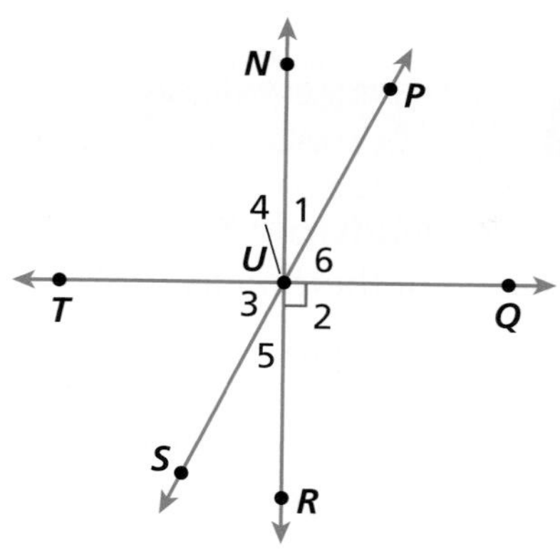

25. $\overleftrightarrow{NQ}$ is a line in the figure.

26. Rays $\overrightarrow{UQ}$ and $\overrightarrow{UT}$ make up line $\overleftrightarrow{TQ}$.

27. $\angle QUR$ is an obtuse angle.

28. $\angle 4$ and $\angle 2$ are supplementary.

29. $\angle 1$ and $\angle 6$ are supplementary.

30. $\angle 3$ and $\angle 1$ are complementary.

31. If $m\angle 1 = 35°$, then $m\angle 6 = 40°$.

32. If $m\angle SUN = 150°$, then $m\angle SUR = 150°$.

33. If $m\angle 1 = x°$, then $m\angle PUQ = 180° - x°$.

34. $m\angle 1 + m\angle 3 + m\angle 5 + m\angle 6 = 180°$.

35. Critical Thinking Two complementary angles have a ratio of 1:2. What is the measure of each angle?

Physical Science LINK

The archerfish can spit a stream of water up to 3 meters in the air to knock its prey into the water. This job is made more difficult by *refraction,* the bending of light waves as they pass from one substance to another. When you look at an object through water, the light between you and the object is refracted. Refraction makes the object appear to be in a different location. Despite refraction, the archerfish still catches its prey.

36. Suppose that the measure of the angle between the bug's actual location and the bug's apparent location is 35°.

a. Refer to the diagram. Along the fish's line of vision, what is the measure of the angle between the fish and the bug's apparent location?

b. What is the relationship of the angles in the diagram?

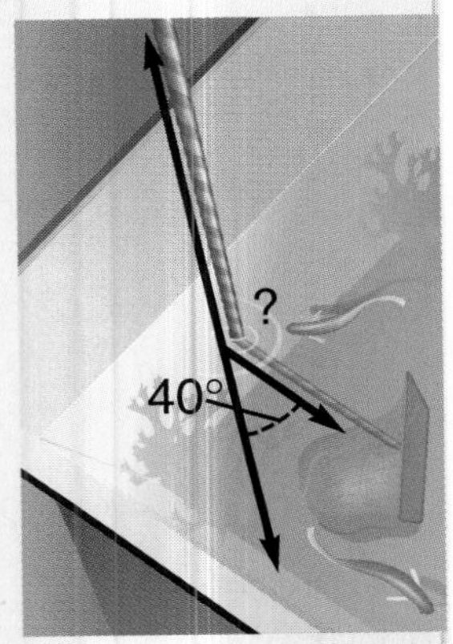

37. In the image, the underwater part of the net appears to be 40° to the right of where it actually is. What is the measure of the angle formed by the image of the underwater part of the net and the part of the net above the water?

38. **Write About It** Suppose an archerfish is directly below its prey. Explain why there would be little or no distortion.

39. **Challenge** A person on the shore is looking at a fish in the water. At the same time, the fish is looking at the person from below the surface. Describe what each observer sees, and where the person and the fish actually are in relation to where they appear to be.

Test Prep and Spiral Review

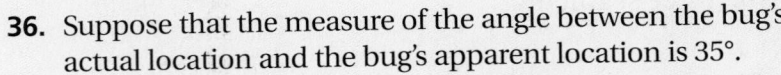

40. **Multiple Choice** When two angles are complementary, what is the sum of their measures?

Ⓐ 90° Ⓑ 180° Ⓒ 270° Ⓓ 360°

41. **Gridded Response** $\angle 1$ and $\angle 3$ are supplementary angles. If $m\angle 1 = 63°$, find $m\angle 3$.

Multiply. Write the product as one power. (Lesson 4-3)

42. $m^3 \cdot m^2$ **43.** $w \cdot w^6$ **44.** $7^8 \cdot 7^3$ **45.** $11^6 \cdot 11^9$

46. Callie made a 5 in. tall by 7 in. wide postcard. A company would like to sell a poster based on the postcard. The poster will be 2 ft tall. How wide will the poster be? (Lesson 5-5)

Hands-On LAB 7-1

Bisect Figures

Use with Lesson 7-1

go.hrw.com
Lab Resources Online
KEYWORD: MT7 Lab7

When you *bisect* a figure, you divide it into two congruent parts.

Activity

1 Follow the steps below to bisect a segment.

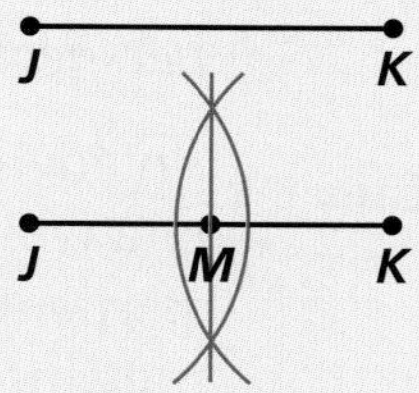

a. Draw $\overline{JK}$ on your paper. Place your compass point on J and draw an arc. Without changing your compass opening, place your compass point on K and draw an arc.

b. Connect the intersections of the arcs with a line. Measure $\overline{JM}$ and $\overline{KM}$. What do you notice?

2 Follow the steps below to bisect an angle.

a. Draw acute $\angle H$ on your paper.

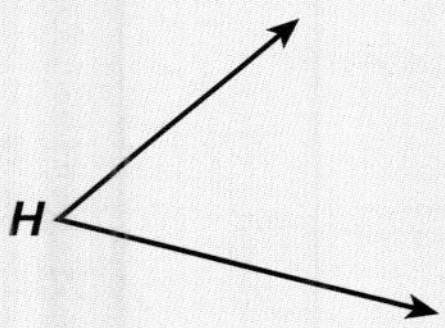

b. Place your compass point on H and draw an arc through both sides of the angle.

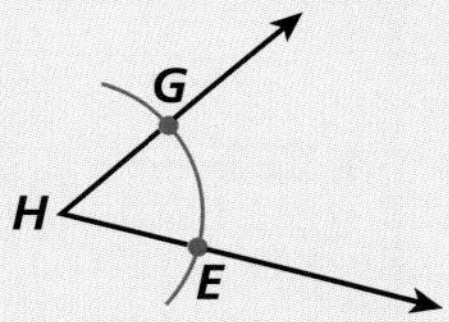

c. Without changing your compass opening, draw intersecting arcs from G and E. Label the intersection D.

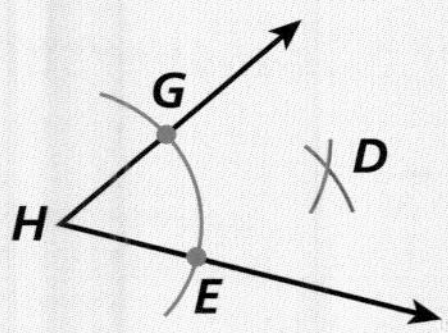

d. Draw $\overrightarrow{HD}$. Measure $\angle GHD$ and $\angle DHE$. What do you notice?

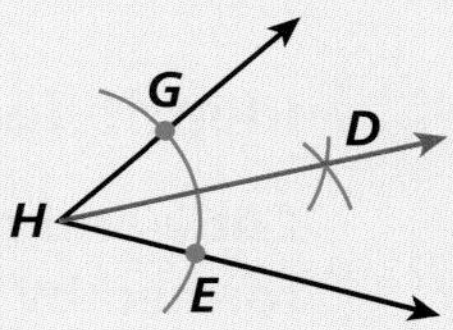

Think and Discuss

1. Explain how to use a compass and a straightedge to divide a segment into four congruent segments. Prove that the segments are congruent.

Try This

Draw each figure, and then use a compass and a straightedge to bisect it. Verify by measuring.

1. a 2-inch segment

2. a 0.5-inch segment

3. a 6-inch segment

4. a 48° angle

5. a 90° angle

6. a 110° angle

7-2 Parallel and Perpendicular Lines

Learn to identify parallel and perpendicular lines and the angles formed by a transversal.

Vocabulary

parallel lines

perpendicular lines

transversal

Parallel lines are lines in a plane that never meet, such as the opposite edges of a skyscraper's windows. The edges appear to get closer to each other because of *perspective.*

An edge and the bottom of a window are like **perpendicular lines**; that is, they intersect at 90° angles.

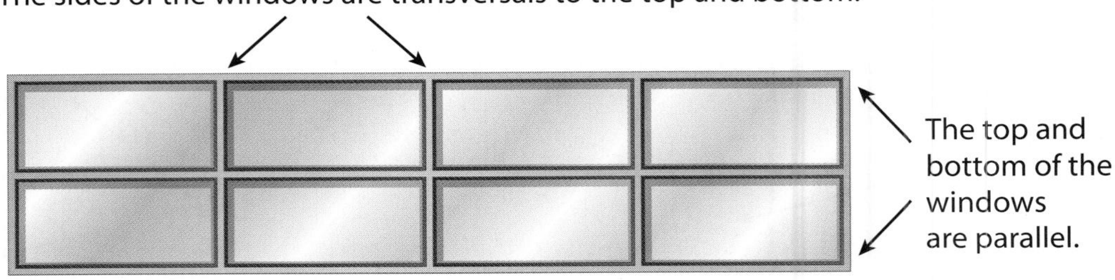

The sides of the windows are transversals to the top and bottom.
The top and bottom of the windows are parallel.

A **transversal** is a line that intersects two or more lines that lie in the same plane. Transversals to parallel lines form angles with special properties.

EXAMPLE 1 Identifying Congruent Angles Formed by a Transversal

Caution!

You cannot tell if angles are congruent by measuring because measurement is not exact.

Copy and measure the angles formed by the transversal and the parallel lines. Which angles seem to be congruent?

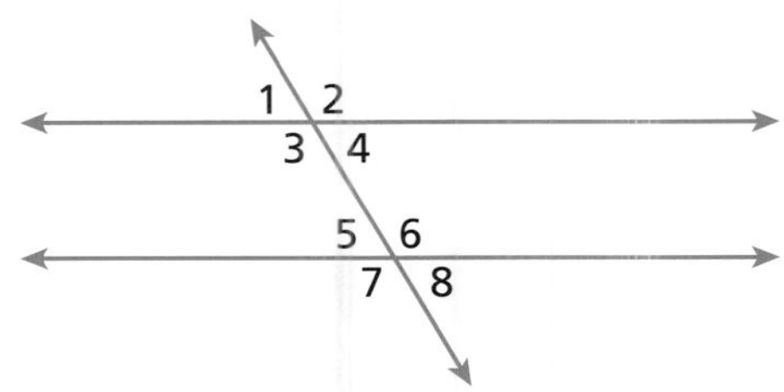

$\angle 1$, $\angle 4$, $\angle 5$, and $\angle 8$ all measure 60°.
$\angle 2$, $\angle 3$, $\angle 6$, and $\angle 7$ all measure 120°.

Angles marked in blue appear congruent to each other, and angles marked in red appear congruent to each other.
$\angle 1 \cong \angle 4 \cong \angle 5 \cong \angle 8$
$\angle 2 \cong \angle 3 \cong \angle 6 \cong \angle 7$

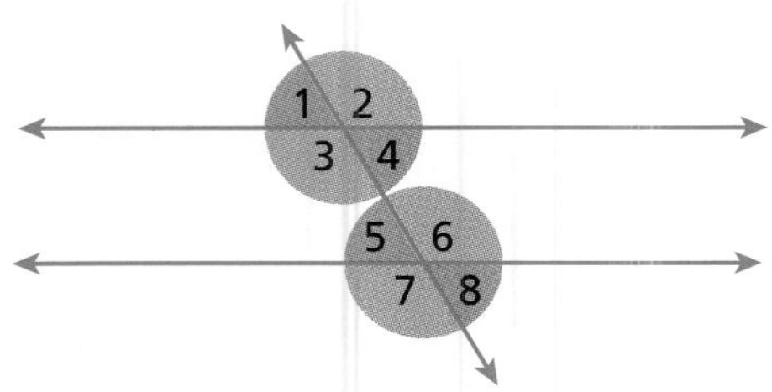

Some pairs of the eight angles formed by two parallel lines and a transversal have special names.

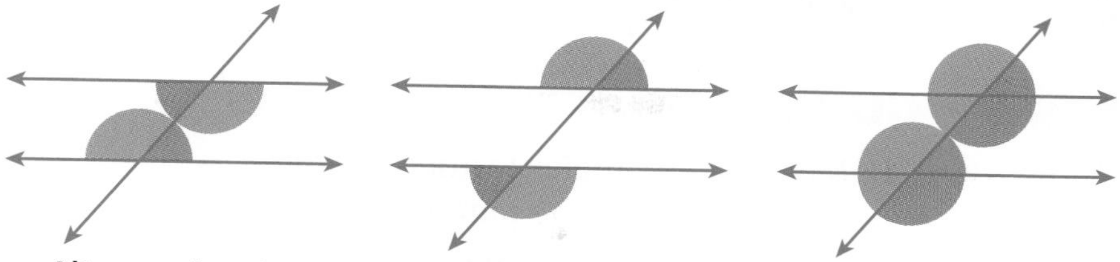

Alternate interior   Alternate exterior   Corresponding

PROPERTIES OF TRANSVERSALS TO PARALLEL LINES
If two parallel lines are intersected by a transversal, • corresponding angles are congruent, • alternate interior angles are congruent, • and alternate exterior angles are congruent. If the transversal is perpendicular to the parallel lines, all of the angles formed are congruent 90° angles.

EXAMPLE 2 **Finding Angle Measures of Parallel Lines Cut by Transversals**

In the figure, line *a* || line *b*. Find the measure of each angle.

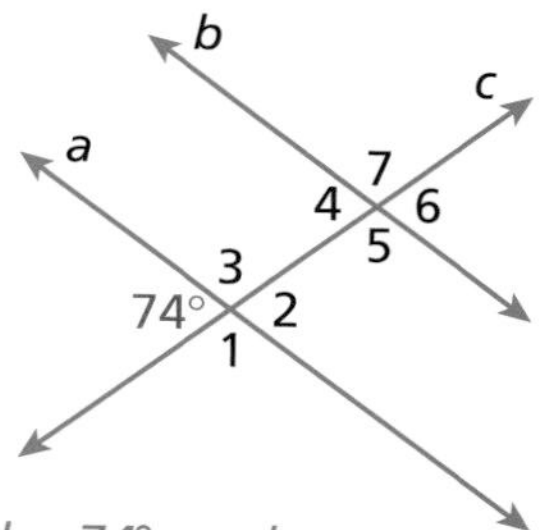

A $\angle 4$

$m\angle 4 = 74°$ *Corresponding angles are congruent.*

B $\angle 3$

$$\begin{aligned} m\angle 3 + 74° &= 180° && \text{∠3 is supplementary to the 74° angle.} \\ -74° &\quad -74° && \text{Subtract 74° from both sides.} \\ m\angle 3 &= 106° && \text{Simplify.} \end{aligned}$$

C $\angle 5$

$m\angle 5 = 106°$ *∠3 and ∠5 are alternate interior angles, so they are congruent.*

Writing Math

The symbol for parallel is ||. The symbol for perpendicular is ⊥.

Think and Discuss

1. **Tell** how many different angles would be formed by a transversal intersecting three parallel lines. How many different angle measures would there be?
2. **Explain** how a transversal could intersect two other lines so that corresponding angles are *not* congruent.

7-2 Exercises

go.hrw.com
Homework Help Online
KEYWORD: MT7 7-2
Parent Resources Online
KEYWORD: MT7 Parent

GUIDED PRACTICE

See Example 1

1. Measure the angles formed by the transversal and the parallel lines. Which angles seem to be congruent?

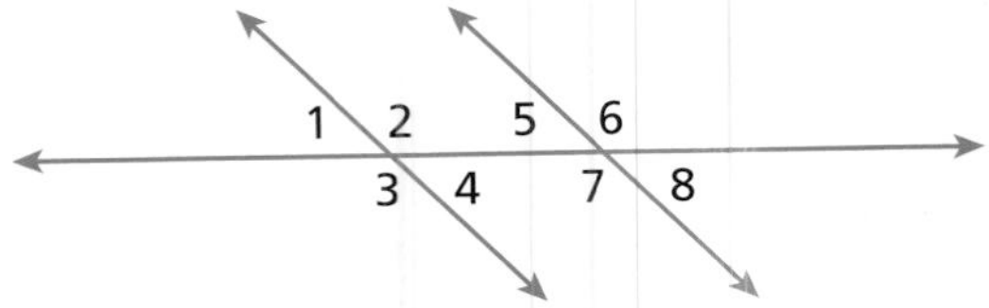

See Example 2

In the figure, line $m \parallel$ line n. Find the measure of each angle.

2. ∠1
3. ∠4
4. ∠6
5. ∠7

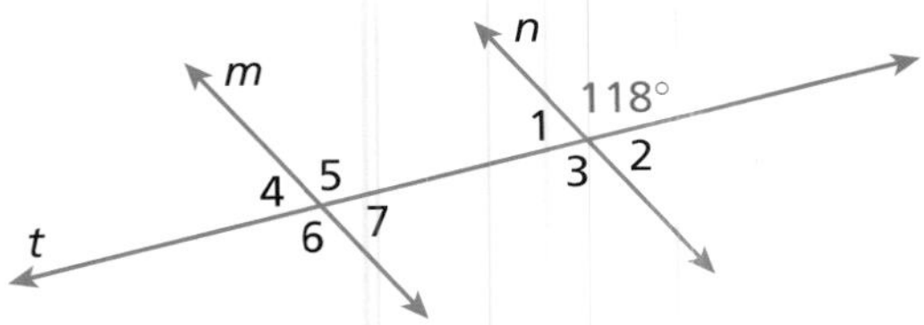

INDEPENDENT PRACTICE

See Example 1

6. Measure the angles formed by the transversal and the parallel lines. Which angles seem to be congruent?

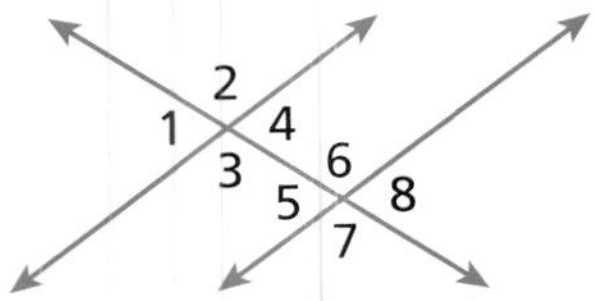

See Example 2

In the figure, line $p \parallel$ line q. Find the measure of each angle.

7. ∠1
8. ∠4
9. ∠6
10. ∠7

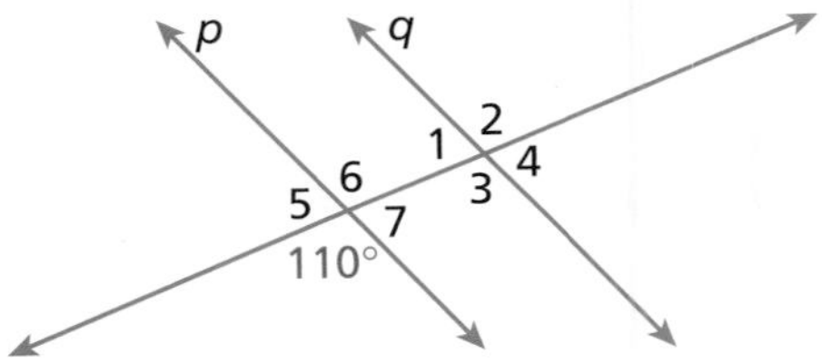

PRACTICE AND PROBLEM SOLVING

Extra Practice
See page 794.

In the figure, line $t \parallel$ line s.

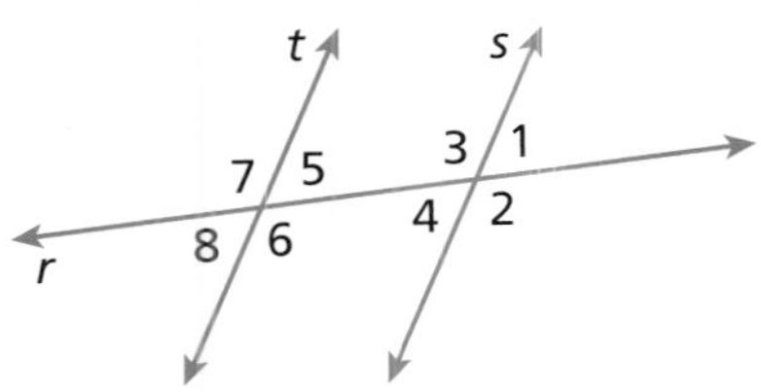

11. Name all angles congruent to ∠1.
12. Name all angles congruent to ∠2.
13. Name three pairs of supplementary angles.
14. Which line is the transversal?
15. If m∠4 is 51°, what is m∠2?
16. If m∠7 is 116°, what is m∠3?
17. If m∠5 is 91°, what is m∠2?

Draw a diagram to illustrate each of the following.

18. line $p \parallel$ line $q \parallel$ line r and line s transversal to lines p, q, and r
19. line $m \parallel$ line n and transversal h with congruent angles ∠1 and ∠3
20. line $h \parallel$ line j and transversal k with eight congruent angles

LINK

Physical Science

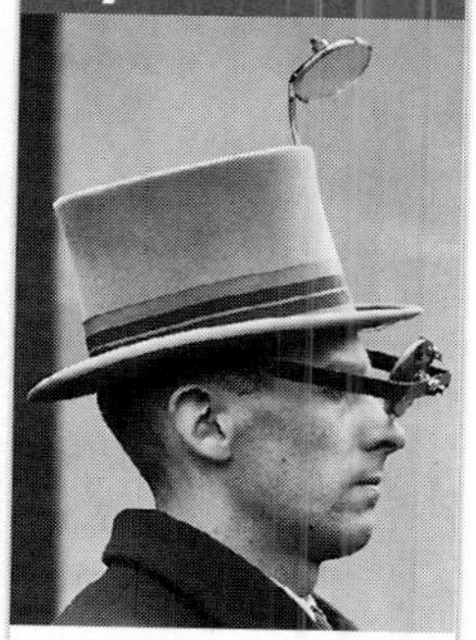

This hat from the 1937 British Industries Fair is equipped with a pair of parallel mirrors to enable the wearer to see above crowds.

go.hrw.com
Web Extra!
KEYWORD: MT7 Periscope

21. Critical Thinking Two parallel lines are cut by a transversal. Can you determine the measures of all the angles formed if given only one angle measure? Explain.

22. Physical Science A periscope contains two parallel mirrors that face each other. With a periscope, a person in a submerged submarine can see above the surface of the water.

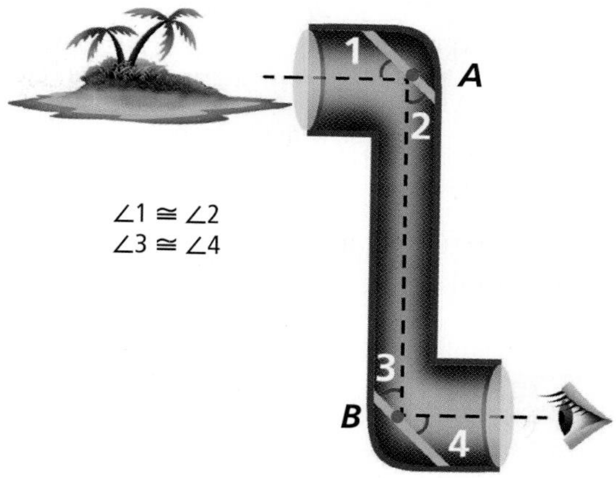

a. Name the transversal in the diagram.

b. If $m\angle 1 = 45°$, find $m\angle 2$, $m\angle 3$, and $m\angle 4$.

23. What's the Error? Line a is parallel to line b. Line c is perpendicular to line b. Line c forms a 60° angle with line a. Why is this figure impossible to draw?

24. Write About It Choose an example of abstract art or architecture with parallel lines. Explain how parallel lines, transversals, or perpendicular lines are used in the composition.

25. Challenge In the figure, ∠1, ∠4, ∠6, and ∠7 are all congruent, and ∠2, ∠3, ∠5, and ∠8 are all congruent. Does this mean that line s is parallel to line t? Explain.

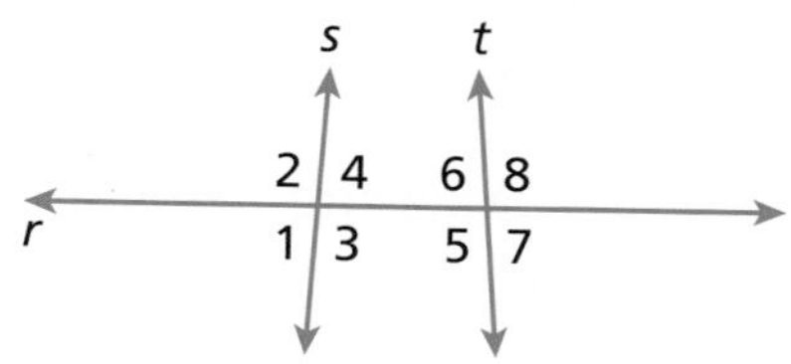

Test Prep and Spiral Review

26. Multiple Choice Two parallel lines are intersected by a transversal. The measures of two corresponding angles that are formed are each 54°. What are the measures of each of the angles supplementary to the corresponding angles?

Ⓐ 36°   Ⓑ 72°   Ⓒ 108°   Ⓓ 126°

27. Extended Response Suppose a transversal intersects two parallel lines. One angle that is formed is a right angle. What are the measures of the remaining angles? What is the relationship between the transversal and the parallel lines?

Find each number. (Lesson 6-3)

28. What is 15% of 96?

29. What is 146% of 12,500?

30. What is 0.5% of 1000?

31. What is 99.9% of 1500?

∠1 and ∠3 are vertical angles, and ∠2 and ∠4 are vertical angles. ∠1 and ∠2 are supplementary angles. (Lesson 7-1)

32. If $m\angle 1 = 25°$, find $m\angle 3$°.

33. If $m\angle 2 = 95°$, find $m\angle 3$.

Hands-On LAB 7-2

Constructions

Use with Lesson 7-2

go.hrw.com
Lab Resources Online
KEYWORD: MT7 Lab7

Constructing an angle is an important step in the construction of parallel lines.

Activity

1 Follow the steps below to construct an angle congruent to ∠B.

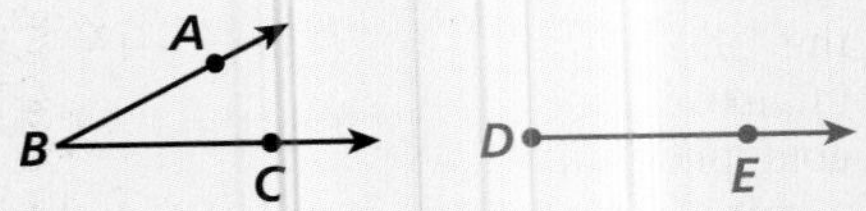

a. Draw acute ∠ABC on your paper. Draw $\overrightarrow{DE}$.

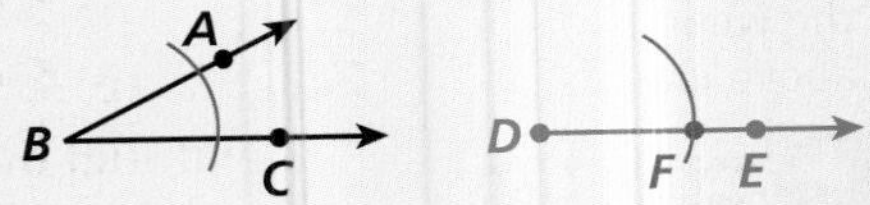

b. With your compass point on B, draw an arc through ∠ABC. With the same compass opening, place your compass point on D and draw an arc through $\overrightarrow{DE}$. Label the intersection point F.

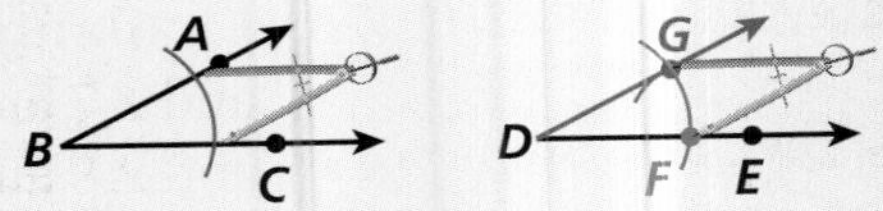

c. Adjust your compass to the width of the arc intersecting ∠ABC. Place your compass point on F and draw an arc that intersects the arc through $\overrightarrow{DE}$ at G. Draw $\overrightarrow{DG}$. Measure ∠ABC and ∠GDF.

2 Follow the steps below to construct parallel line segments.

1. Construct $\overline{QR}$ on your paper by placing the point of your compass on Q and the pencil on R below. Draw point Q on your paper and place the point of your compass on it. Make a short arc and draw a line from Q to the arc. The intersection of the point and the arc is R. Draw point S above or below $\overline{QR}$. Draw a line through point S that intersects $\overline{QR}$. Label the intersection T.

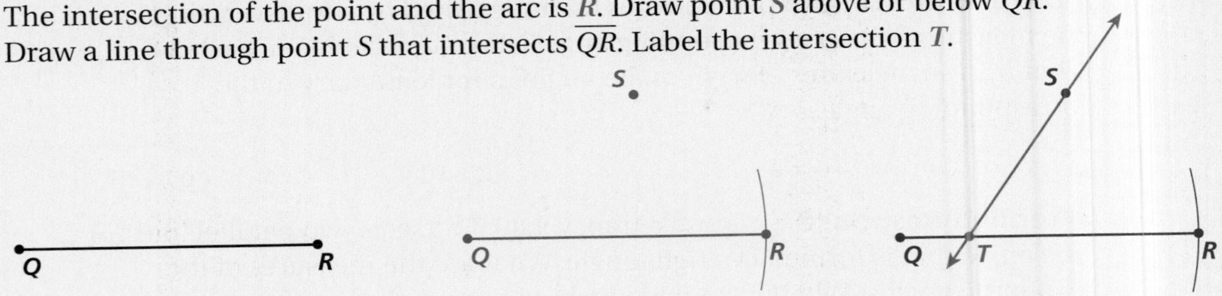

2. Construct an angle with its vertex at S congruent to ∠STR. Use the method described in **1**. How do you know the lines are parallel?

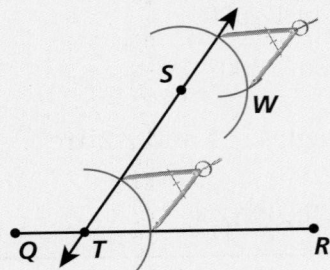

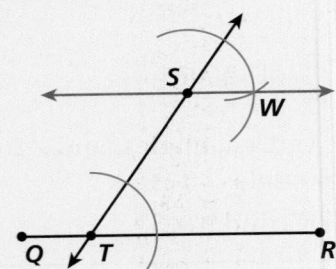

3 **Follow the steps below to construct perpendicular lines.**

a. Draw $\overleftrightarrow{MN}$ on your paper. Draw point P above or below $\overleftrightarrow{MN}$.

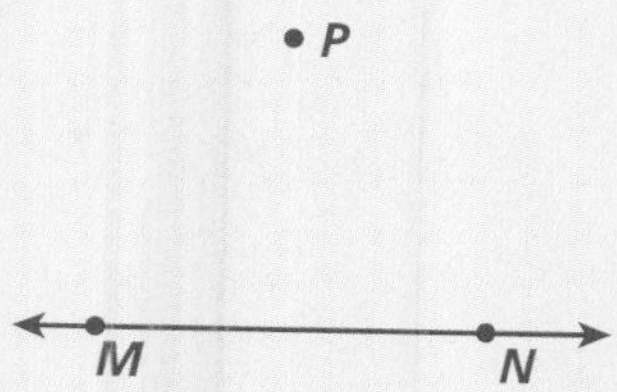

b. With your compass point at P, draw an arc intersecting $\overleftrightarrow{MN}$ at points Q and R.

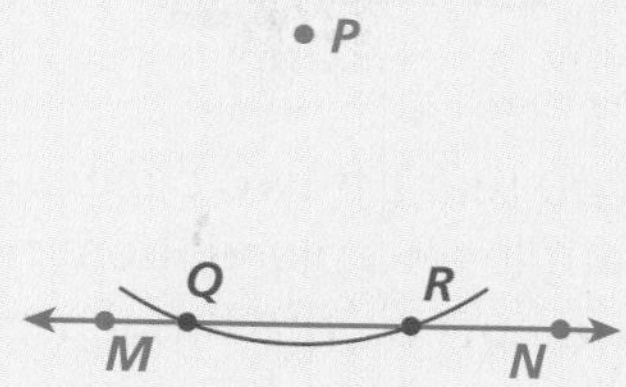

c. Draw arcs from points Q and R, using the same compass opening, that intersect at point S.

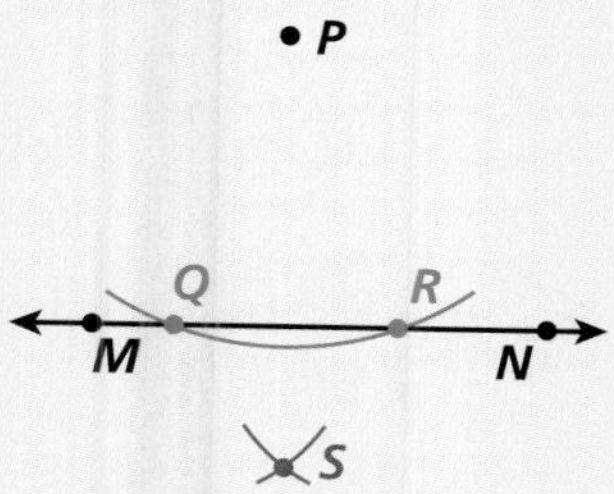

d. Draw $\overleftrightarrow{PS}$. What do you think is true about $\overleftrightarrow{MN}$ and $\overleftrightarrow{PS}$? Check your guess.

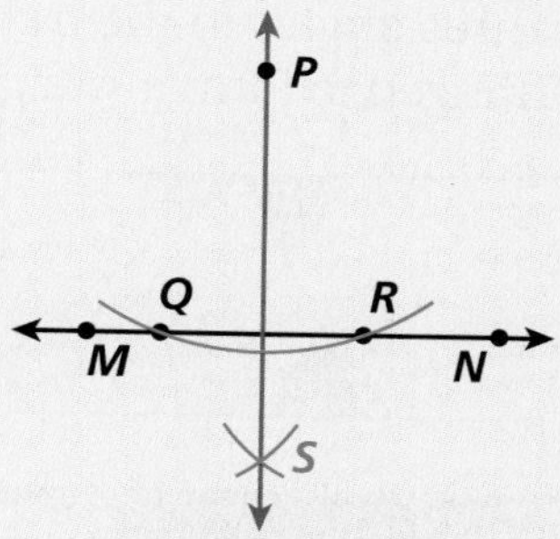

Think and Discuss

1. How many lines can be drawn that are perpendicular to a given line? Explain your answer.
2. Name three ways that you can determine if two lines are parallel.

Try This

Use a compass and a straightedge to construct each figure.

1. an angle congruent to $\angle LMN$

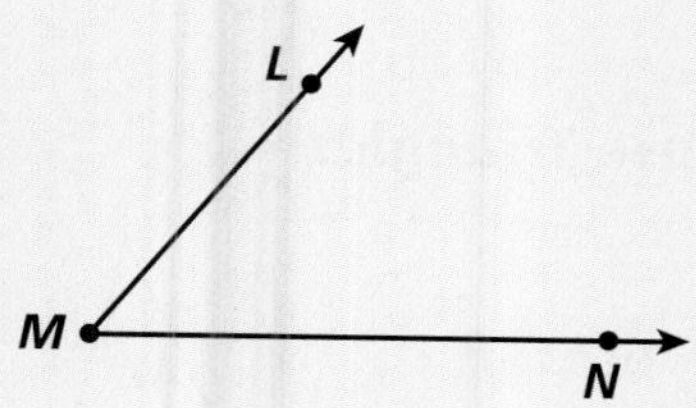

2. a line parallel to $\overleftrightarrow{ST}$

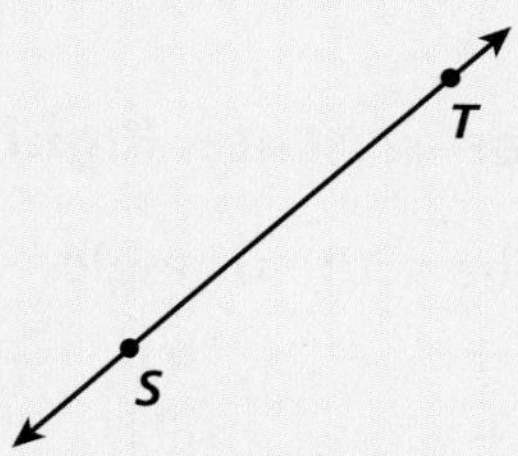

3. a line perpendicular to $\overleftrightarrow{GH}$

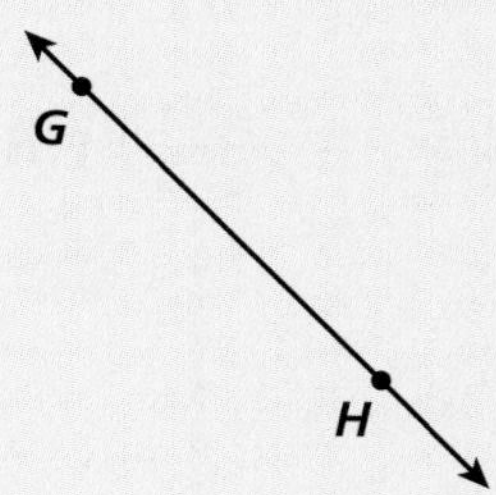

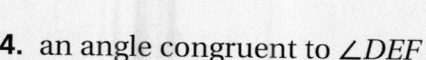

4. an angle congruent to $\angle DEF$

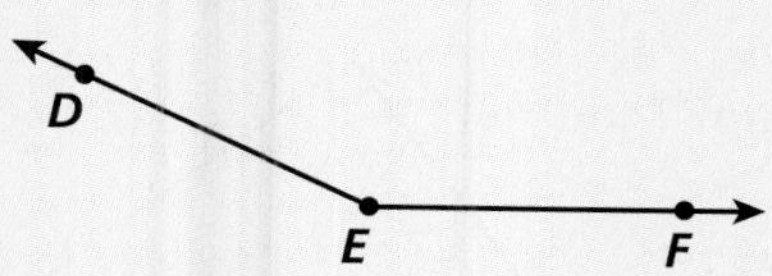

5. a line parallel to $\overleftrightarrow{AB}$

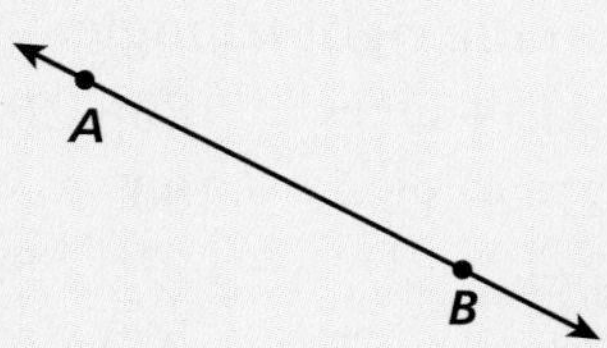

6. a line perpendicular to $\overleftrightarrow{CD}$

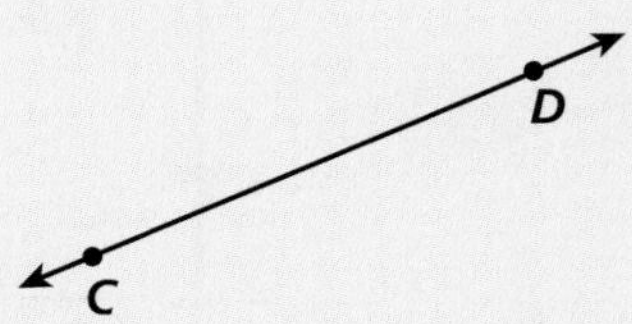

7-3 Angles in Triangles

Learn to find unknown angles in triangles.

Vocabulary

Triangle Sum Theorem

acute triangle

right triangle

obtuse triangle

equilateral triangle

isosceles triangle

scalene triangle

If you tear off two corners of a triangle and place them next to the third corner, the three angles seem to form a straight angle.

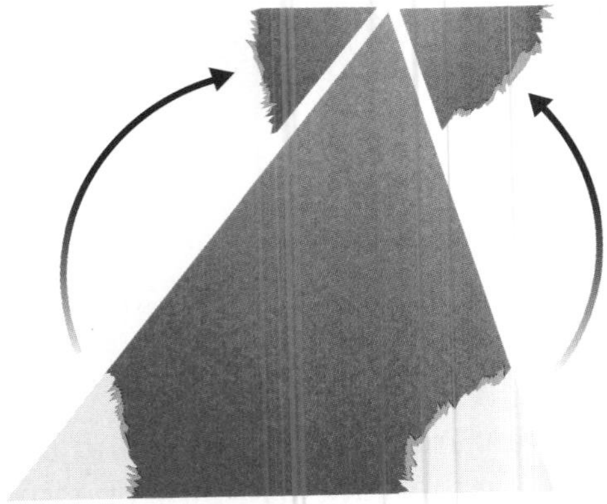

This torn triangle demonstrates an important geometry theorem called the Triangle Sum Theorem.

Draw a triangle and extend one side. Then draw a line parallel to the extended side, as shown.

The three angles in the triangle can be arranged to form a straight angle, or 180°.

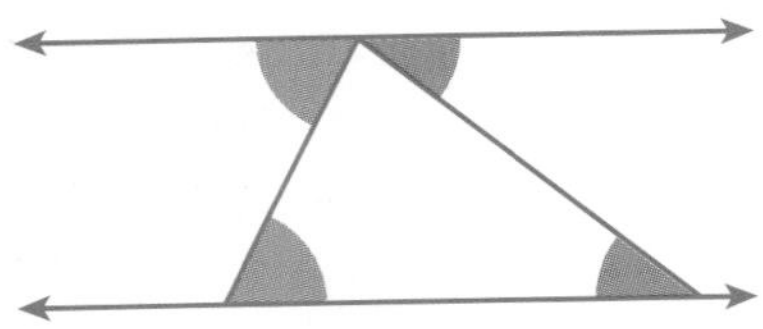

The sides of the triangle are transversals to the parallel lines.

TRIANGLE SUM THEOREM

Words	Numbers	Algebra
The angle measures of a triangle add to 180°.	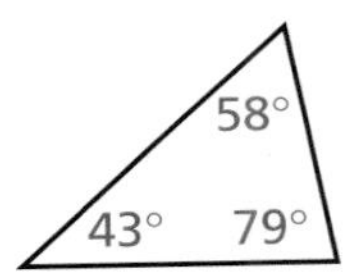 $43° + 58° + 79° = 180°$	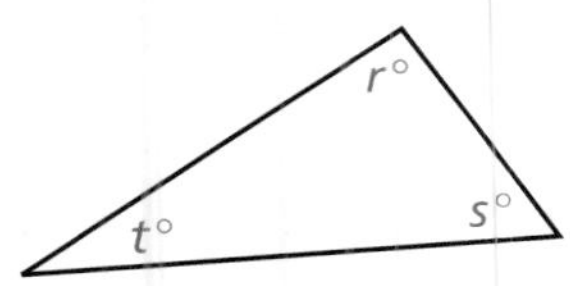 $r° + s° + t° = 180°$

An **acute triangle** has 3 acute angles. A **right triangle** has 1 right angle. An **obtuse triangle** has 1 obtuse angle.

EXAMPLE 1 Finding Angles in Acute, Right, and Obtuse Triangles

A **Find $x°$ in the acute triangle.**

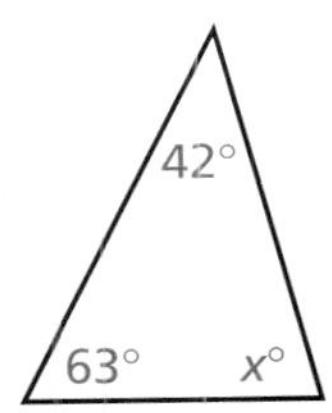

$63° + 42° + x° = 180°$ *Triangle Sum Theorem*

$105° + x° = 180°$

$-105° \quad -105°$ *Subtract 105° from both sides.*

$x° = 75°$

B **Find $y°$ in the right triangle.**

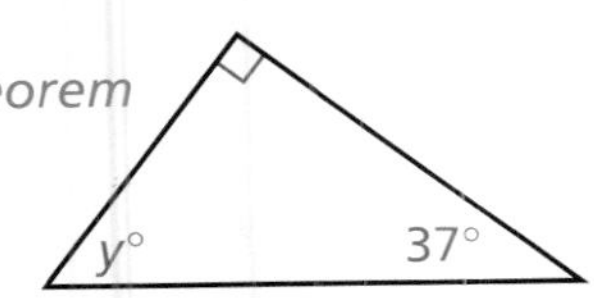

$37° + 90° + y° = 180°$ *Triangle Sum Theorem*

$127° + y° = 180°$

$-127° \quad -127°$ *Subtract 127° from both sides.*

$y° = 53°$

C **Find $z°$ in the obtuse triangle.**

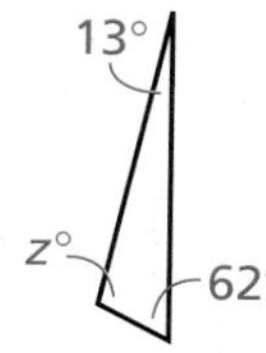

$$13° + 62° + z° = 180°$$ *Triangle Sum Theorem*

$$75° + z° = 180°$$

$$\underline{-\,75° \qquad -\,75°}$$ *Subtract 75° from both sides.*

$$z° = 105°$$

An **equilateral triangle** has 3 congruent sides and 3 congruent angles. An **isosceles triangle** has at least 2 congruent sides and 2 congruent angles. A **scalene triangle** has no congruent sides and no congruent angles.

EXAMPLE 2 Finding Angles in Equilateral, Isosceles, and Scalene Triangles

A **Find the angle measures in the equilateral triangle.**

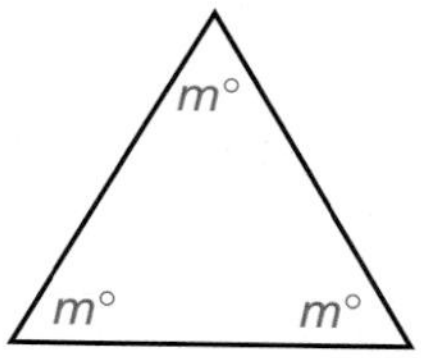

$$3m° = 180°$$ *Triangle Sum Theorem*

$$\frac{3m°}{3} = \frac{180°}{3}$$ *Divide both sides by 3.*

$$m° = 60°$$

All three angles measure **60°**.

B **Find the angle measures in the isosceles triangle.**

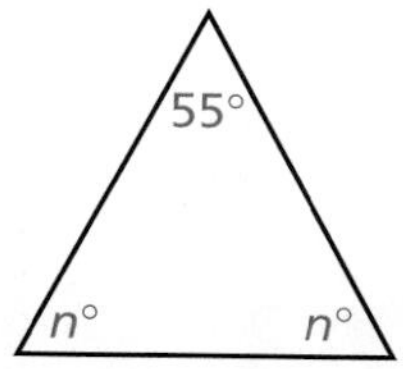

$$55° + n° + n° = 180°$$ *Triangle Sum Theorem*

$$55° + 2n° = 180°$$ *Simplify.*

$$\underline{-\,55° \qquad -\,55°}$$ *Subtract 55° from both sides.*

$$2n° = 125°$$

$$\frac{2n°}{2} = \frac{125°}{2}$$ *Divide both sides by 2.*

$$n° = 62.5°$$

The angles labeled $n°$ measure **62.5°**.

C **Find the angle measures in the scalene triangle.**

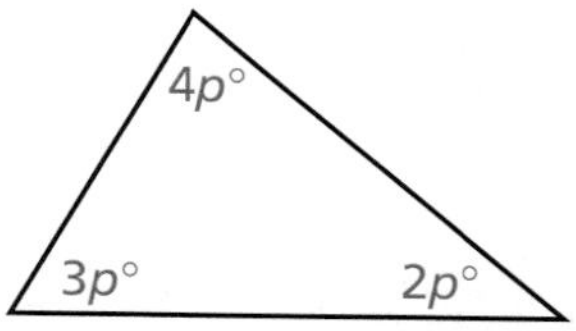

$$2p° + 3p° + 4p° = 180°$$ *Triangle Sum Theorem*

$$9p° = 180°$$ *Simplify.*

$$\frac{9p°}{9} = \frac{180°}{9}$$ *Divide both sides by 9.*

$$p° = 20°$$

The angle labeled $2p°$ measures $2(20°) = 40°$, the angle labeled $3p°$ measures $3(20°) = 60°$, and the angle labeled $4p°$ measures $4(20°) = 80°$.

EXAMPLE 3 Finding Angles in a Triangle That Meets Given Conditions

The second angle in a triangle is twice as large as the first. The third angle is half as large as the second. Find the angle measures and draw a possible figure.

Let $x°$ = first angle measure. Then $2x°$ = second angle measure, and $\frac{1}{2}(2x)° = x°$ = third angle measure.

$$x° + 2x° + x° = 180°$$ *Triangle Sum Theorem*

$$\frac{4x°}{4} = \frac{180°}{4}$$ *Simplify, then divide both sides by 4.*

$$x° = 45°$$

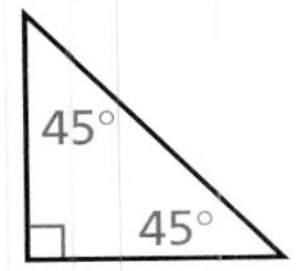

Two angles measure 45° and one angle measures 90°. The triangle has two congruent angles. The triangle is an isosceles right triangle.

Think and Discuss

1. **Explain** whether a right triangle can be equilateral. Can it be isosceles? scalene?
2. **Explain** whether a triangle can have 2 right angles. Can it have 2 obtuse angles?

7-3 Exercises

go.hrw.com
Homework Help Online
KEYWORD: MT7 7-3
Parent Resources Online
KEYWORD: MT7 Parent

GUIDED PRACTICE

See Example 1

1. Find $q°$ in the acute triangle.
2. Find $r°$ in the right triangle.
3. Find $s°$ in the obtuse triangle.

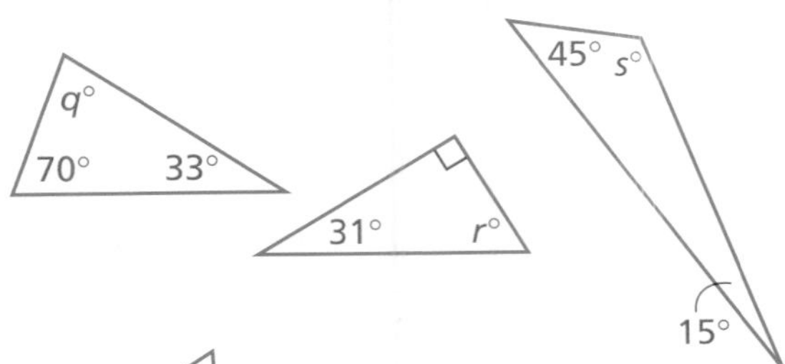

See Example 2

4. Find the angle measures in the equilateral triangle.
5. Find the angle measures in the isosceles triangle.
6. Find the angle measures in the scalene triangle.

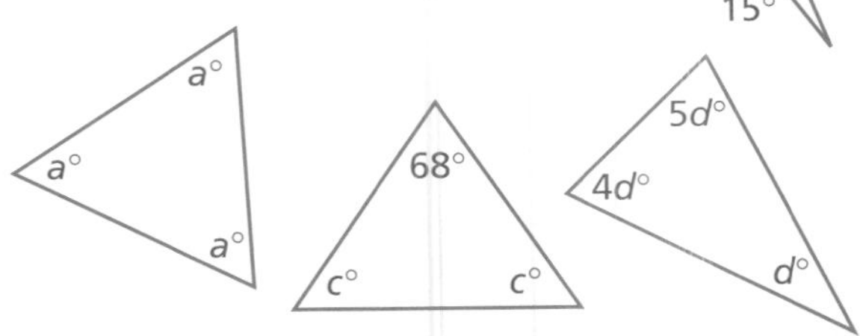

See Example 3

7. The second angle in a triangle is half as large as the first. The third angle is three times as large as the second. Find the angle measures and draw a possible picture.

INDEPENDENT PRACTICE

See Example 1

8. Find $r°$ in the acute triangle.

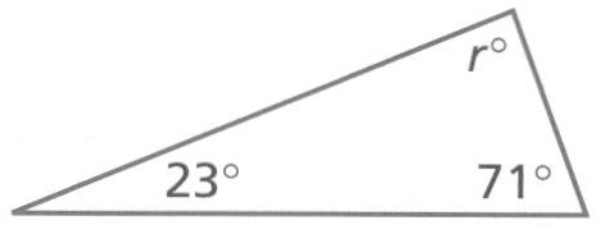

9. Find $s°$ in the right triangle.

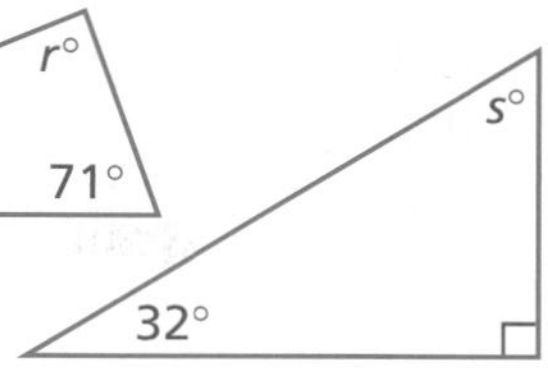

10. Find $t°$ in the obtuse triangle.

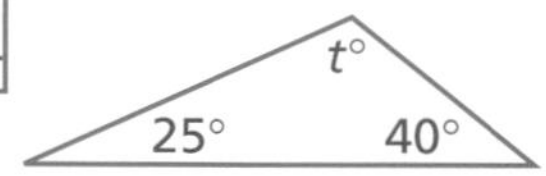

See Example 2

11. Find the angle measures in the equilateral triangle.

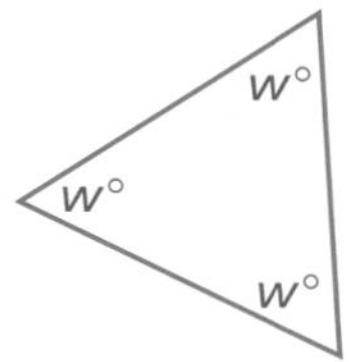

12. Find the angle measures in the isosceles triangle.

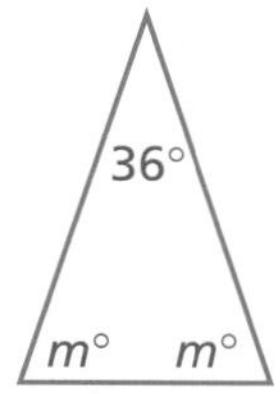

13. Find the angle measures in the scalene triangle.

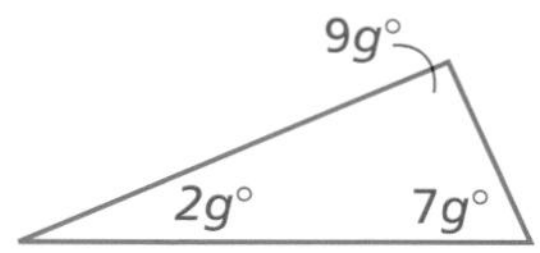

See Example 3

14. The second angle in a triangle is five times as large as the first. The third angle is two-thirds as large as the first. Find the angle measures and draw a possible picture.

PRACTICE AND PROBLEM SOLVING

Extra Practice
See page 794.

Find the value of each variable.

15.

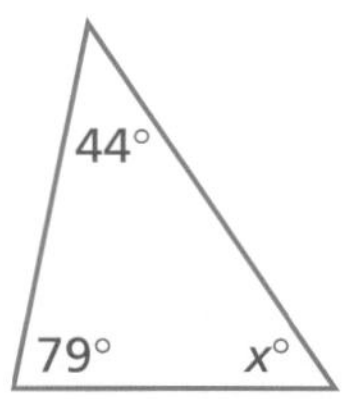

16.

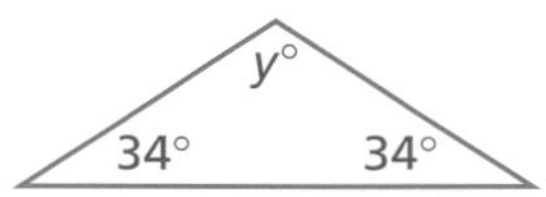

17.

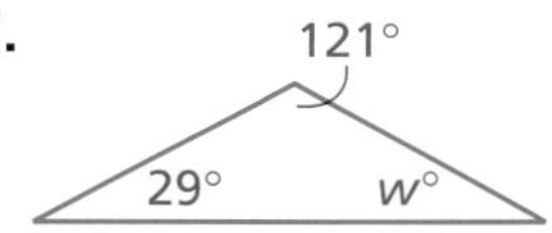

18.

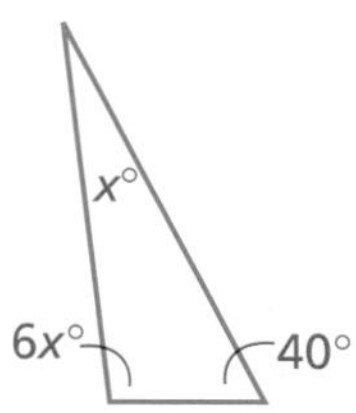

19.

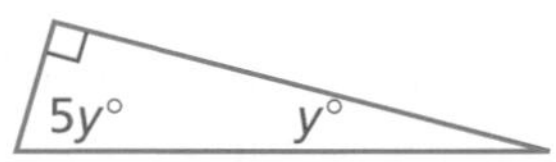

20.

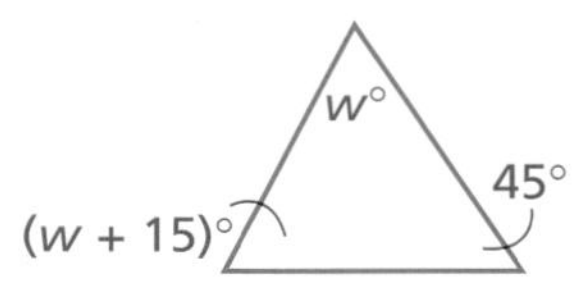

Sketch a triangle to fit each description. If no triangle can be drawn, write *not possible.*

21. acute scalene

22. obtuse equilateral

23. right scalene

24. right equilateral

25. obtuse scalene

26. acute isosceles

27. Triangle ABC is a right triangle and $m\angle A = 38°$. What does the third angle measure?

28. Can an acute isosceles triangle have two angles that measure 40°? Explain.

29. Triangle LMN is an obtuse triangle and $m\angle L = 25°$. $\angle M$ is the obtuse angle. What is the largest $m\angle N$ can be to the nearest whole degree?

30. **Social Studies** American Samoa is a territory of the United States made up of a group of islands in the Pacific Ocean, about halfway between Hawaii and New Zealand. The flag of American Samoa is shown.

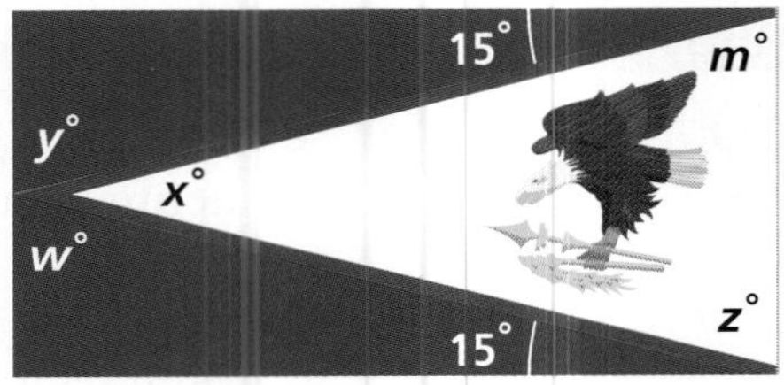

a. Find the measure of each angle in the blue triangles.

b. Use your answers to part **a** to find the angle measures in the white triangle.

c. Classify the triangles in the flag by their sides and angles.

31. **Choose a Strategy** Which of the following sets of angle measures can be used to create an isosceles triangle?

Ⓐ 45°, 45°, 95° Ⓑ 49°, 51°, 80° Ⓒ 27°, 27°, 126° Ⓓ 35°, 55°, 100°

32. **Write About It** Explain how to cut a square or an equilateral triangle in half to form two identical triangles. What are the angle measures in the resulting triangles in each case?

33. **Challenge** Find *x*, *y*, and *z*.

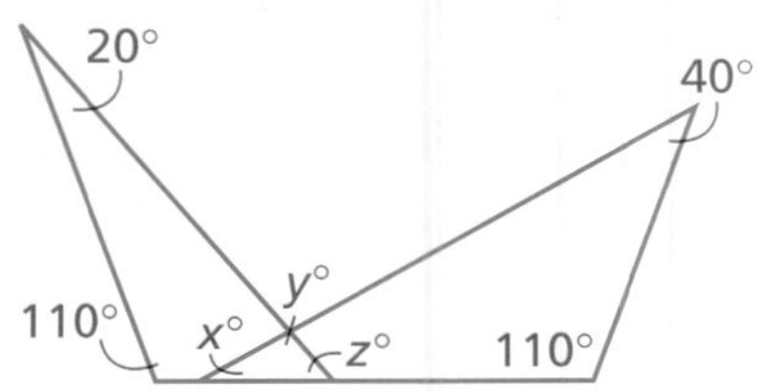

Test Prep and Spiral Review

34. **Multiple Choice** Which type of triangle can be constructed with a 50° angle between two 8-inch sides?

Ⓐ Equilateral Ⓑ Isosceles Ⓒ Scalene Ⓓ Obtuse

35. **Short Response** Two angles of a triangle are 45° and 30°. What is the measure of the third angle? Is the triangle acute, right, or obtuse?

Each square root is between two integers. Name the integers. (Lesson 4-6)

36. $\sqrt{42}$ 37. $\sqrt{71}$ 38. $\sqrt{35}$ 39. $\sqrt{296}$

In the figure, line *x* || line *y*. (Lesson 7-2)

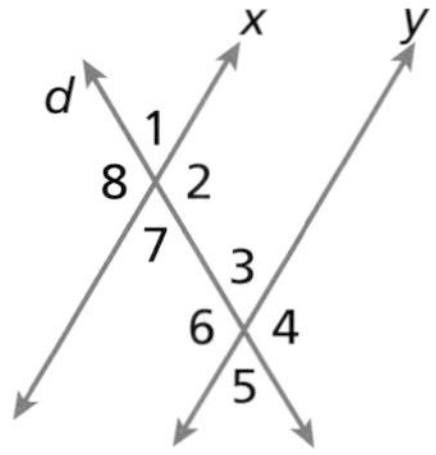

40. If $m\angle 1 = 34°$, what is $m\angle 7$?

41. If $m\angle 6 = 125°$, what is $m\angle 5$?

42. If $m\angle 1 = 34°$, what is $m\angle 4$?

43. If $m\angle 5 = 34°$, what is $m\angle 2$?

7-4 Classifying Polygons

Learn **to classify and find angles in polygons.**

Vocabulary

polygon
regular polygon
trapezoid
parallelogram
rectangle
rhombus
square

Kites have been around for over 3000 years, when the Chinese made them from bamboo and silk. The most common flat kite is in the shape of a diamond, a type of *quadrilateral* called a *kite.*

A **polygon** is a closed plane figure formed by three or more segments. A polygon is named by the number of its sides.

Polygon	Number of Sides
Triangle	3
Quadrilateral	4
Pentagon	5
Hexagon	6
Heptagon	7
Octagon	8
n-gon	n

Quadrilateral

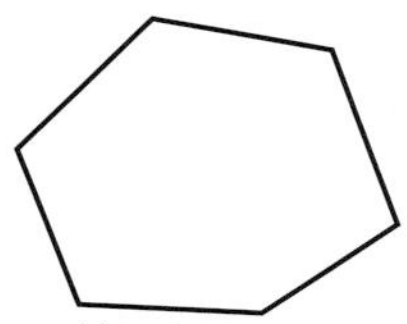

Hexagon

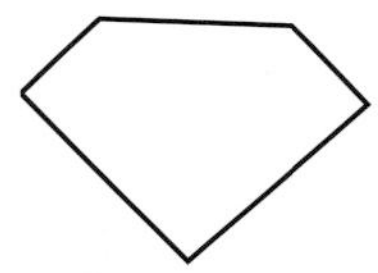

Pentagon

EXAMPLE 1 Finding Sums of the Angle Measures in Polygons

Find the sum of the angle measures in each figure.

A **Find the sum of the angle measures in a quadrilateral.**

Divide the figure into triangles.

$2 \cdot 180° = 360°$ *2 triangles*

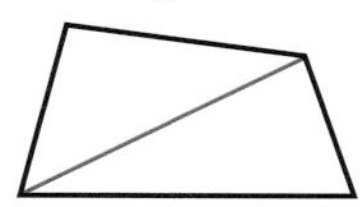

B **Find the sum of the angle measures in a pentagon.**

Divide the figure into triangles.

$3 \cdot 180° = 540°$ *3 triangles*

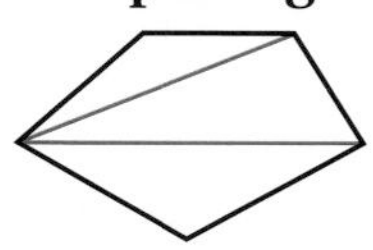

Look for a pattern between the number of sides and the number of triangles.

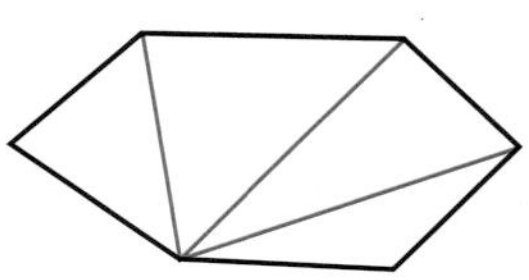

Hexagon:
6 sides
4 triangles

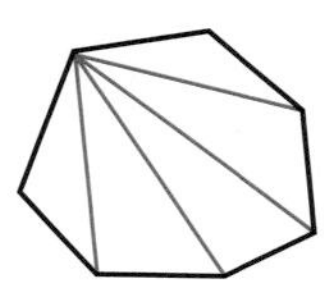

Heptagon:
7 sides
5 triangles

The pattern is that the number of triangles is always 2 less than the number of sides. So an n-gon can be divided into $n - 2$ triangles. The sum of the angle measures of any n-gon is $180°(n - 2)$.

All the sides and angles of a **regular polygon** have equal measures.

EXAMPLE 2 Finding the Measure of Each Angle in a Regular Polygon

Find the angle measures in each regular polygon.

A

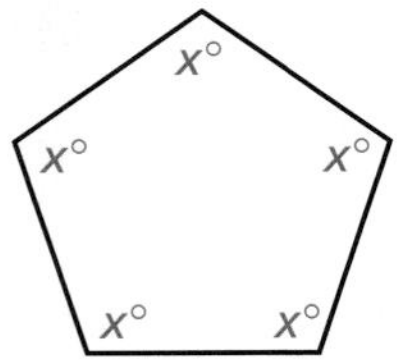

5 congruent angles

$5x° = 180°(5 - 2)$

$5x° = 180°(3)$

$5x° = 540°$

$\frac{5x°}{5} = \frac{540°}{5}$

$x° = 108°$

B

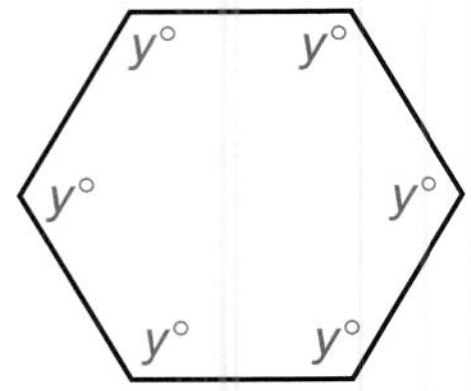

6 congruent angles

$6y° = 180°(6 - 2)$

$6y° = 180°(4)$

$6y° = 720°$

$\frac{6y°}{6} = \frac{720°}{6}$

$y° = 120°$

Quadrilaterals with certain properties are given additional names. A **trapezoid** has exactly 1 pair of parallel sides. A **parallelogram** has 2 pairs of parallel sides. A **rectangle** has 4 right angles. A **rhombus** has 4 congruent sides. A **square** has 4 congruent sides and 4 right angles.

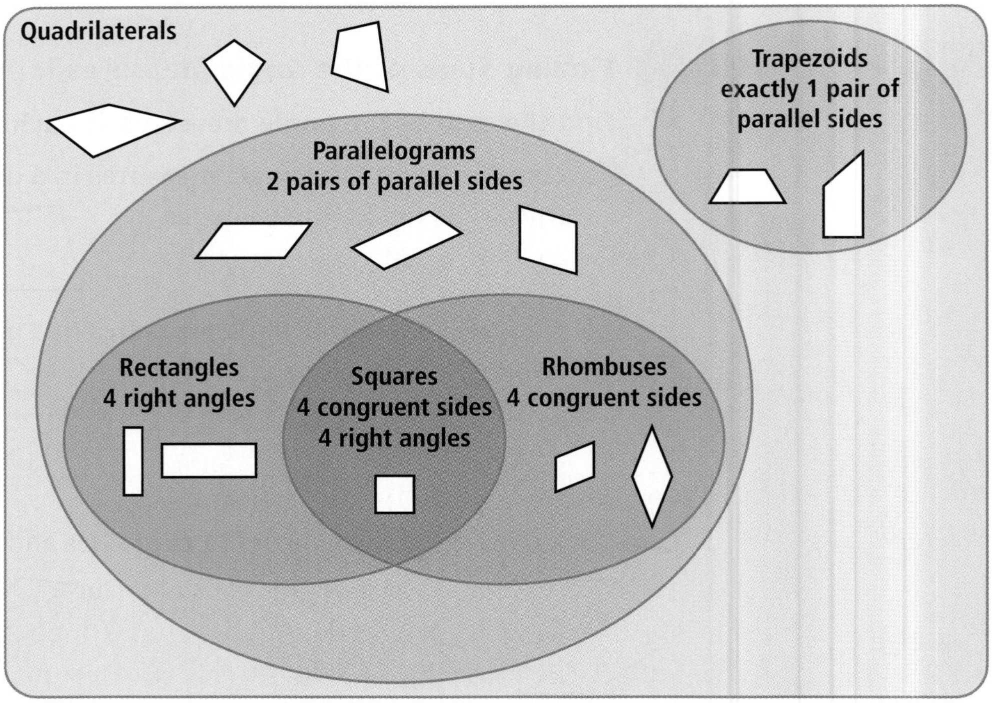

EXAMPLE 3 Classifying Quadrilaterals

Give all of the names that apply to each figure.

A

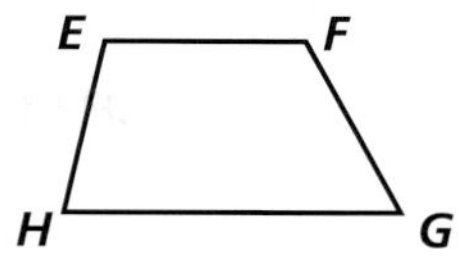

$\overline{EF} \parallel \overline{GH}$

quadrilateral — *Four-sided polygon*
trapezoid — *1 pair of parallel sides*

B

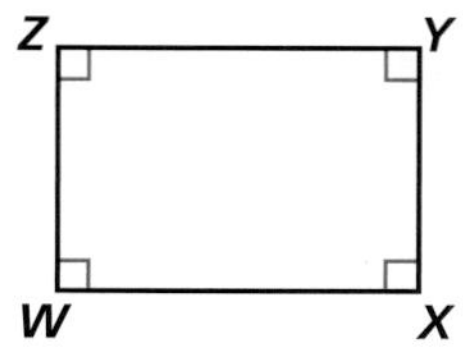

quadrilateral — *Four-sided polygon*
parallelogram — *2 pairs of parallel sides*
rectangle — *4 right angles*

Think and Discuss

1. Choose which is larger, an angle in a regular heptagon or an angle in a regular octagon. Justify your answer.

2. Explain why all rectangles are parallelograms and why all squares are rectangles.

7-4 Exercises

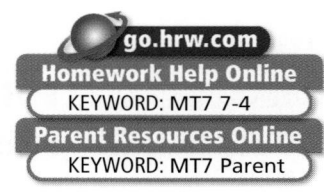

go.hrw.com
Homework Help Online
KEYWORD: MT7 7-4
Parent Resources Online
KEYWORD: MT7 Parent

GUIDED PRACTICE

See Example 1

Find the sum of the angle measures in each figure.

1.

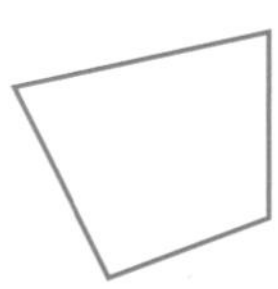

2.

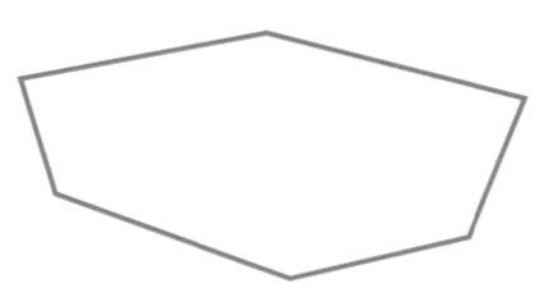

3.

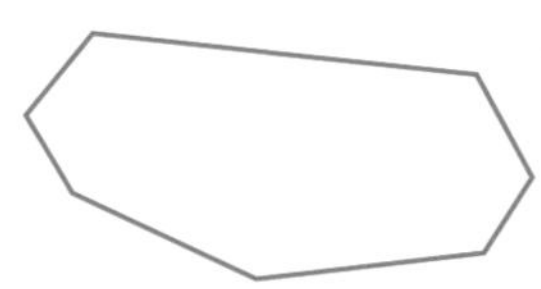

See Example 2

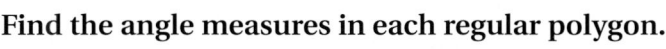

Find the angle measures in each regular polygon.

4.

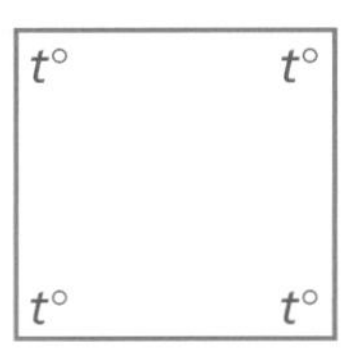

5.

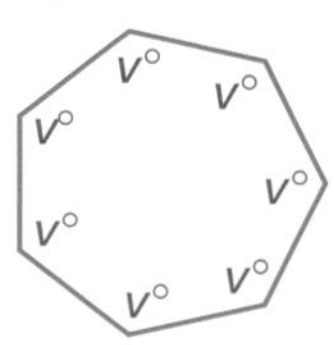

6.

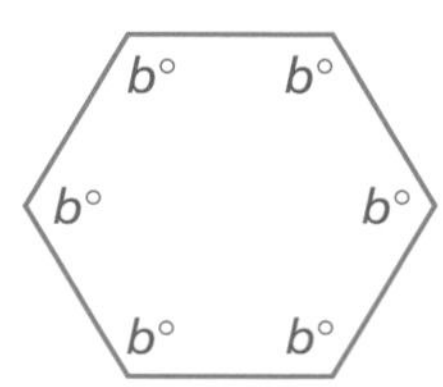

See Example 3
Give all of the names that apply to each figure.

7.
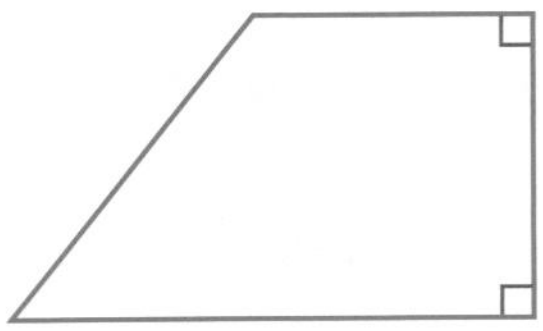

8.
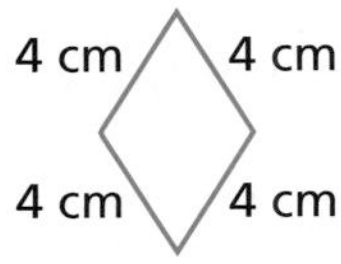

9.
 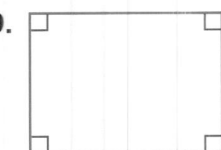

INDEPENDENT PRACTICE

See Example 1
Find the sum of the angle measures in each figure.

10.
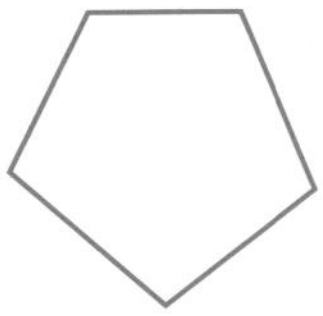

11.
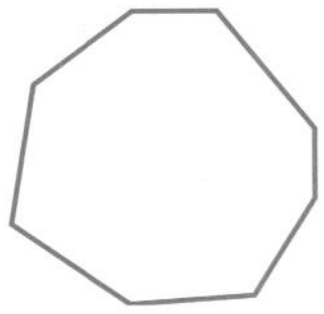

12.
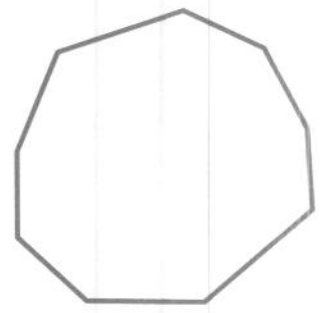

See Example 2
Find the angle measures in each regular polygon.

13.
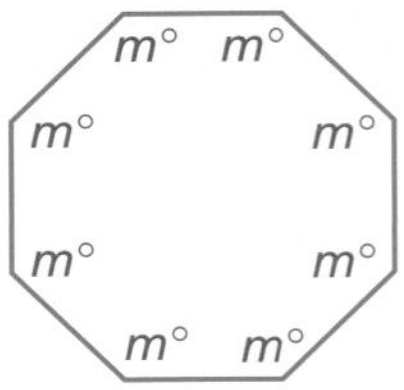

14.
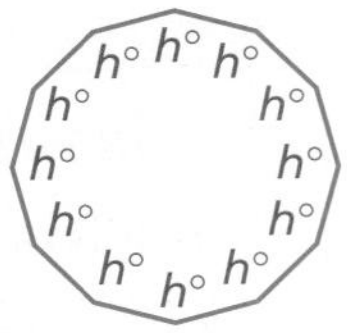

15.
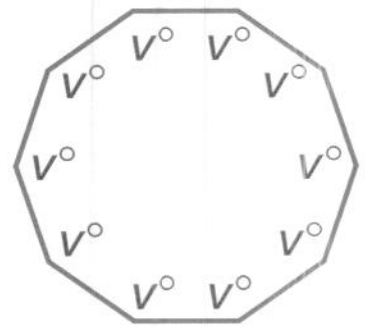

See Example 3
Give all of the names that apply to each figure.

16.
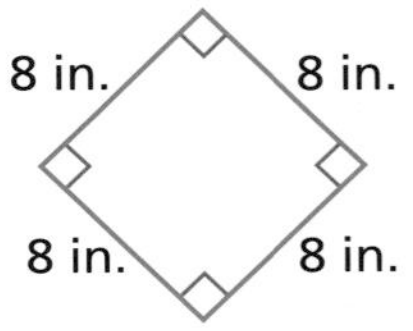

17.
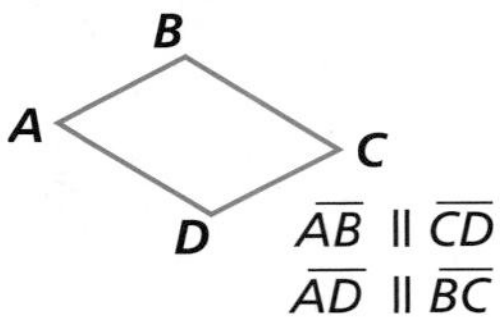

$\overline{AB} \parallel \overline{CD}$
$\overline{AD} \parallel \overline{BC}$

18.
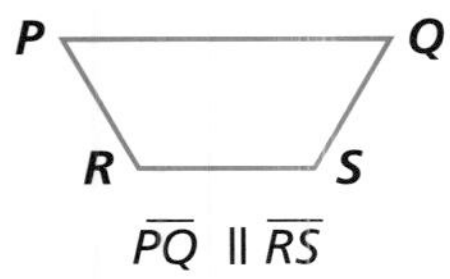

$\overline{PQ} \parallel \overline{RS}$

PRACTICE AND PROBLEM SOLVING

Extra Practice
See page 794.

Find the sum of the angle measures in each regular polygon. Then find the measure of each angle.

19. 20-gon **20.** 13-gon **21.** 60-gon **22.** pentagon **23.** 16-gon

Find the value of each variable.

24.
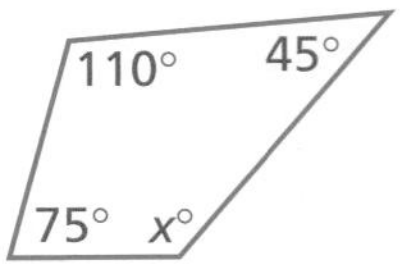

25.
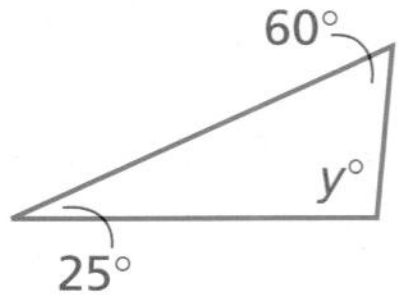

26.
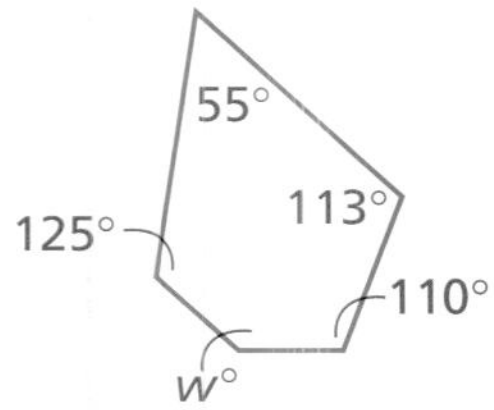

27.
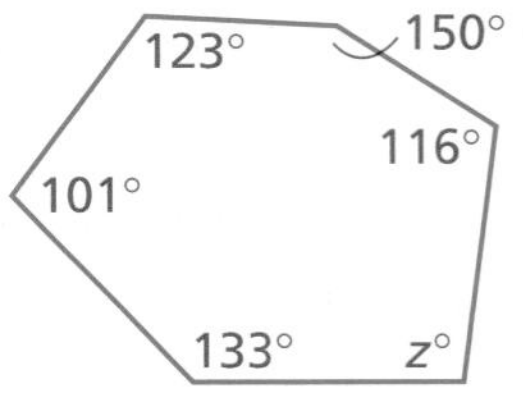

28.
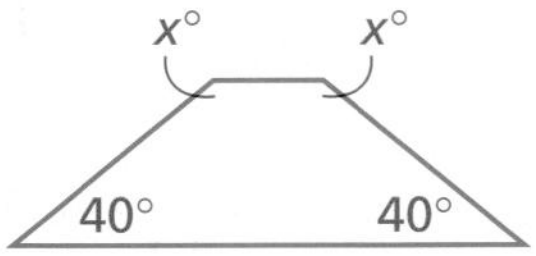

29.
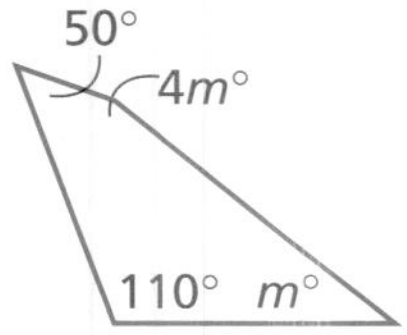

The sum of the angle measures of a polygon is given. Name the polygon.

30. 1080° **31.** 540° **32.** 360° **33.** 1620°

Graph the given vertices on a coordinate plane. Connect the points to draw a polygon and classify it by the number of its sides.

34. $A(0, 3)$, $B(1, 1)$, $C(4, 1)$, $D(5, 3)$, $E(4, 5)$, $F(1, 5)$

35. $A(-3, 2)$, $B(-3, -1)$, $C(1, -3)$, $D(4, 0)$, $E(1, 4)$

Sketch a quadrilateral to fit each description. If no quadrilateral can be drawn, write *not possible.*

36. a parallelogram that is not a rhombus

37. a square that is not a rectangle

LINK

Earth Science

The Imperial State Crown of Great Britain contains over 3000 precious stones, including 2800 diamonds.

38. Earth Science Precious stones are often cut in a *brilliant cut* to maximize the light they reflect. The best angles for a cut depend on the type of stone. The best angles for a diamond are shown.

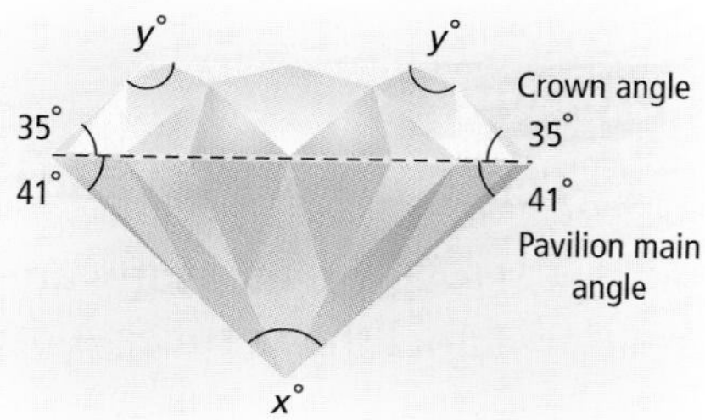

a. If the pavilion main angle is 41°, find x.

b. If the crown angle is 35°, find y.

39. Architecture Fernando is designing a house. He wants one room to be in the shape of an irregular heptagon with two corners that form right angles. What angle measures could the remaining five corners have?

40. What's the Error? A student said that all squares are rectangles, but not all squares are rhombuses. What was the error?

41. Write About It Why is it possible to find the sum of the angle measures of an n-gon using the formula $(180n - 360)°$?

42. Challenge Use a diagram and the properties of parallel lines to explain which angles in a parallelogram must be congruent.

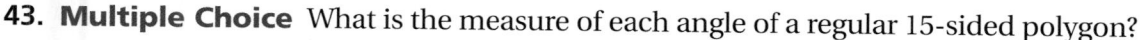

TEST PREP and Spiral Review

43. Multiple Choice What is the measure of each angle of a regular 15-sided polygon?

Ⓐ 146° Ⓑ 148° Ⓒ 150° Ⓓ 156°

44. Short Response The sum of the angle measures of a regular polygon is 720°. Name the regular polygon. What is the measure of each angle?

Subtract. (Lesson 1-5)

45. $-5 - 12$ **46.** $-25 - 25$ **47.** $34 - (-17)$ **48.** $-30 - 41$

49. The first angle in a triangle is less than 90°. The second angle is $\frac{3}{4}$ as large as the first angle. The third angle is $\frac{2}{3}$ as large as the second angle. Find the angle measures and draw a possible figure. (Lesson 7-3)

Technology LAB 7-4

Exterior Angles of a Polygon

Use with Lesson 7-4

go.hrw.com
Lab Resources Online
KEYWORD: MT7 Lab7

The *exterior angles* of a polygon are formed by extending the polygon's sides. Every exterior angle is supplementary to the angle next to it inside the polygon.

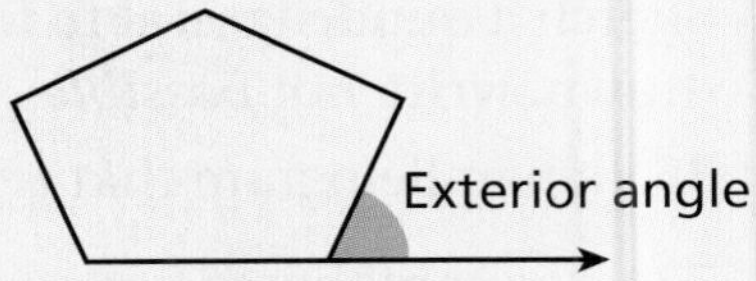

Activity

1 Follow the steps to find the sum of the exterior angle measures for a polygon.

a. Use geometry software to make a pentagon. Label the vertices *A* through *E*.

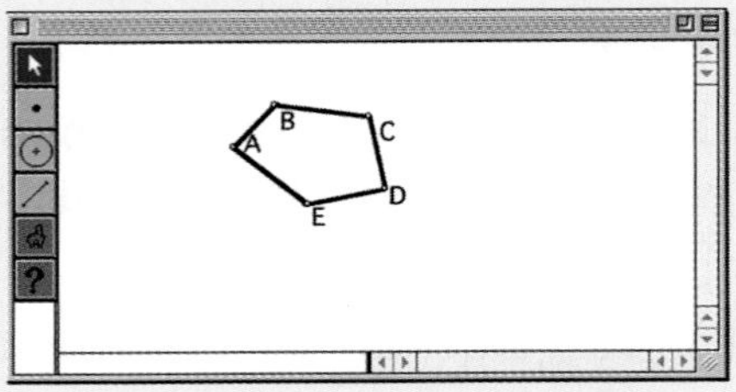

b. Use the **LINE-RAY** tool to extend the sides of the pentagon. Add points *F* through *J* as shown.

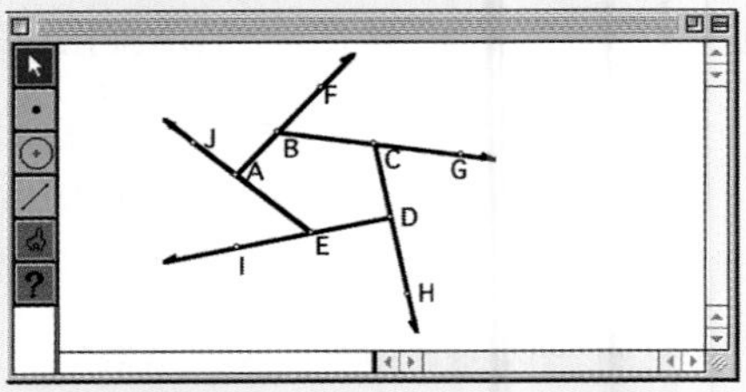

c. Use the **ANGLE MEASURE** tool to measure each exterior angle and the **CALCULATOR** tool to add the measures. Notice the sum.

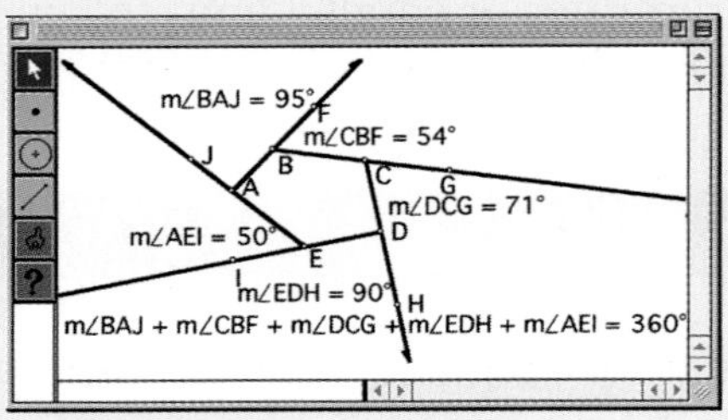

d. Drag vertices *A* through *E* and watch the sum. Notice that the sum of the angle measures is *always* 360°.

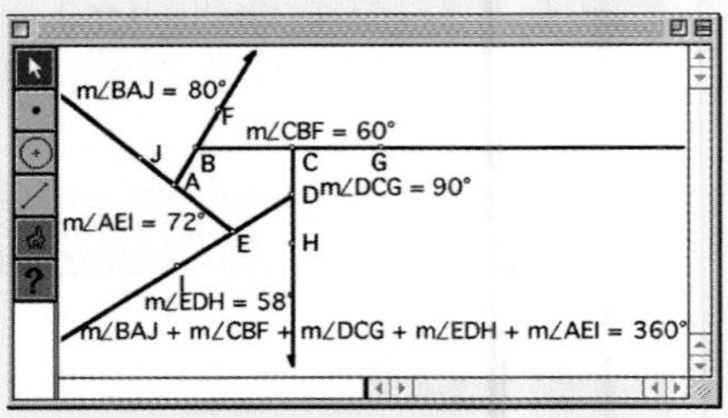

Think and Discuss

1. Suppose you were to drag the vertices of a polygon so that the polygon almost vanishes. How would this show that the sum of the exterior angle measures is 360°?

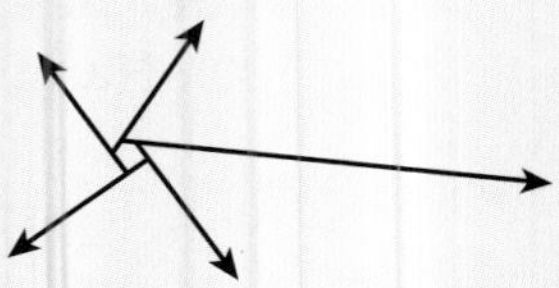

Try This

1. Use geometry software to draw any polygon. Find the sum of its exterior angle measures. Drag its vertices to check that the sum is always the same.

7-5 Coordinate Geometry

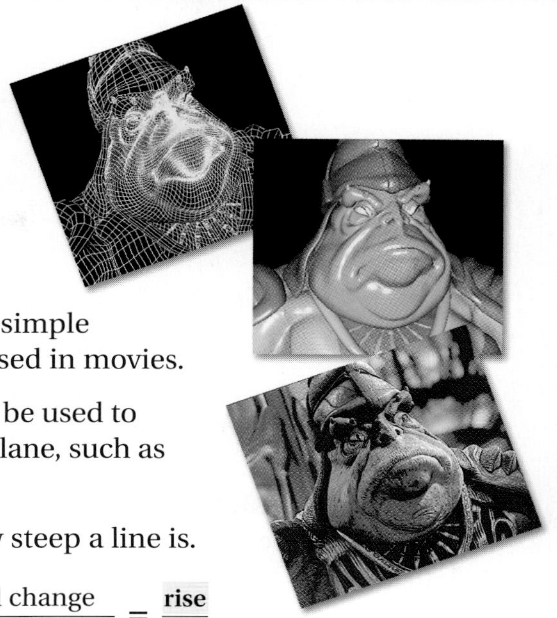

Learn to identify polygons in the coordinate plane.

Vocabulary

slope

rise

run

In computer graphics, a coordinate system is used to create images, from simple geometric figures to realistic figures used in movies.

Properties of the coordinate plane can be used to find information about figures in the plane, such as whether lines in the plane are parallel.

Slope is a number that describes how steep a line is.

$$\text{slope} = \frac{\text{vertical change}}{\text{horizontal change}} = \frac{\textbf{rise}}{\textbf{run}}$$

Positive slope

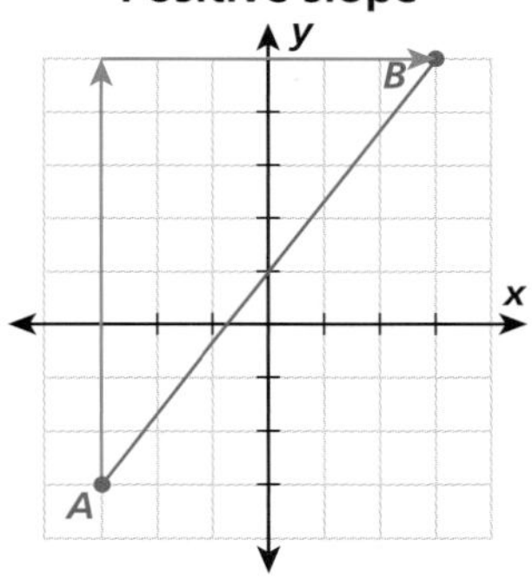

slope of $\overline{AB} = \frac{8}{6} = \frac{4}{3}$

slope of $\overline{CD} = \frac{-3}{6} = \frac{-1}{2}$

Negative slope

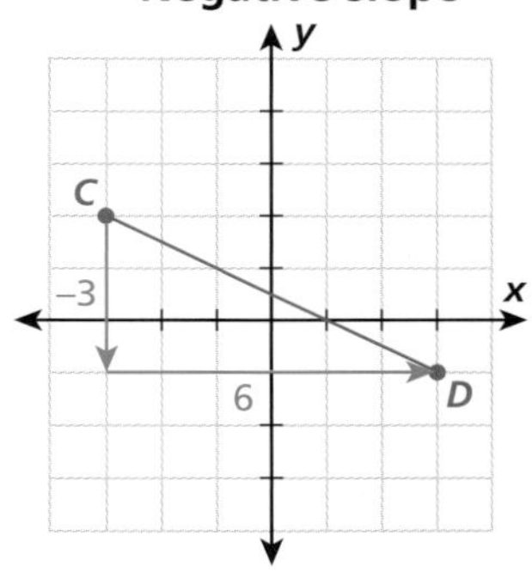

The slope of a horizontal line is 0. The slope of a vertical line is undefined.

EXAMPLE 1 Finding the Slope of a Line

Remember!

When a number is divided by zero, the quotient is undefined. There is no answer.

Determine if the slope of each line is positive, negative, 0, or undefined. Then find the slope of each line.

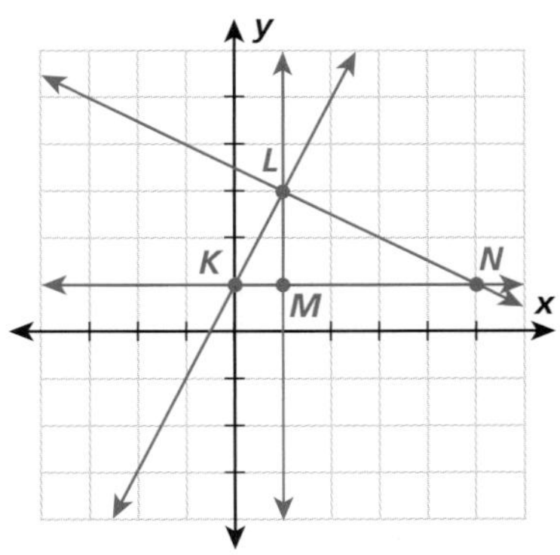

A $\overleftrightarrow{KL}$

positive; slope of $\overleftrightarrow{KL} = \frac{2}{1} = 2$

B $\overleftrightarrow{LM}$

undefined; slope of $\overleftrightarrow{LM} = \frac{1}{0}$

C $\overleftrightarrow{LN}$

negative; slope of $\overleftrightarrow{LN} = \frac{-2}{4} = -\frac{1}{2}$

D $\overleftrightarrow{KM}$

0; slope of $\overleftrightarrow{KM} = \frac{0}{1}$

Slopes of Parallel and Perpendicular Lines

Two lines with equal slopes are parallel.

Two lines whose slopes have a product of -1 are perpendicular.

EXAMPLE 2 Finding Perpendicular and Parallel Lines

Which lines are parallel?
Which lines are perpendicular?

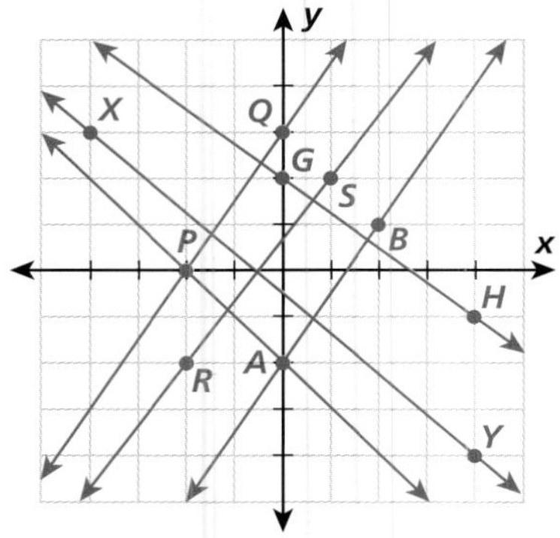

slope of $\overleftrightarrow{PQ} = \frac{3}{2}$

slope of $\overleftrightarrow{RS} = \frac{4}{3}$

slope of $\overleftrightarrow{AB} = \frac{3}{2}$

slope of $\overleftrightarrow{PA} = \frac{-2}{2}$ or -1

slope of $\overleftrightarrow{GH} = \frac{-3}{4}$

slope of $\overleftrightarrow{XY} = \frac{-7}{8}$

$\overleftrightarrow{PQ} \parallel \overleftrightarrow{AB}$ *The slopes are equal:* $\frac{3}{2} = \frac{3}{2}$

$\overleftrightarrow{RS} \perp \overleftrightarrow{GH}$ *The slopes have a product of* -1: $\frac{4}{3} \cdot \frac{-3}{4} = -1$

Helpful Hint

If a line has slope $\frac{a}{b}$, then a line perpendicular to it has slope $-\frac{b}{a}$.

EXAMPLE 3 Using Coordinates to Classify Quadrilaterals

Graph the quadrilaterals with the given vertices. Give all of the names that apply to each quadrilateral.

A $J(1, 2), K(4, 2), L(4, -1), M(1, -1)$

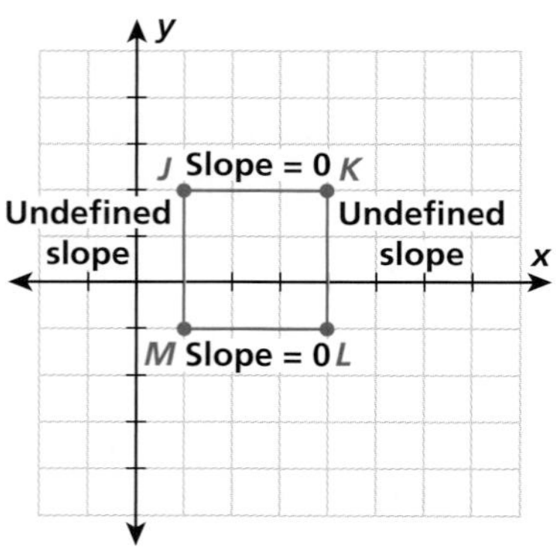

$\overline{JK} \parallel \overline{ML}$ and $\overline{MJ} \parallel \overline{LK}$
$\overline{JK} \perp \overline{LK}$, $\overline{JK} \perp \overline{MJ}$,
$\overline{ML} \perp \overline{LK}$ and $\overline{ML} \perp \overline{MJ}$
parallelogram, rectangle, square, rhombus

B $P(-1, 2), Q(2, 1), R(-1, -2), S(-3, 0)$

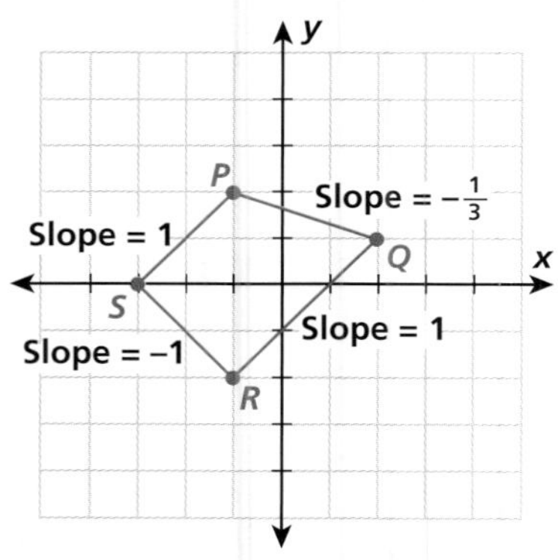

$\overline{SP} \parallel \overline{RQ}$
trapezoid

EXAMPLE 4 Finding the Coordinates of a Missing Vertex

Find the coordinates of the missing vertex of square *ABCD*.

Square $ABCD$ with $A(4, 0)$, $B(0, 4)$, and $C(-4, 0)$

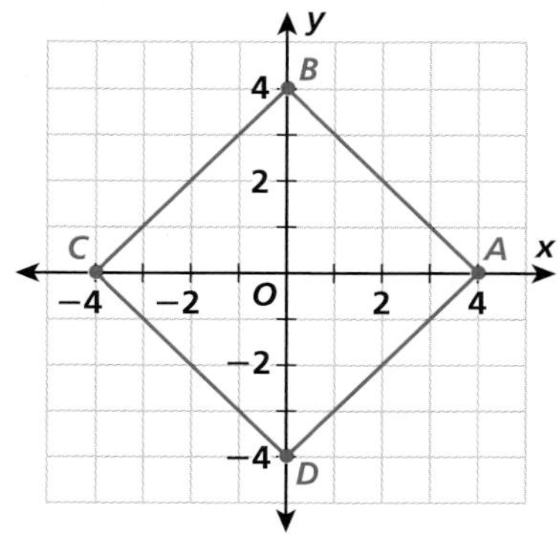

Step 1 Graph and connect the given points.

Step 2 Complete the figure to find the missing vertex. $\overline{AB}$ has a slope of -1, so $\overline{CD}$ has a slope of -1. $\overline{BC}$ has a slope of 1, so $\overline{AD}$ has a slope of 1.

The coordinates of D are $(0, -4)$.

Remember!

In a square opposite sides are parallel.

Think and Discuss

1. Explain how you can use slopes to classify a quadrilateral.

7-5 Exercises

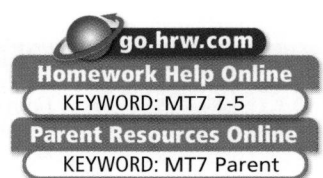

go.hrw.com
Homework Help Online
KEYWORD: MT7 7-5
Parent Resources Online
KEYWORD: MT7 Parent

GUIDED PRACTICE

See Example 1

Determine if the slope of each line is positive, negative, 0, or undefined. Then find the slope of each line.

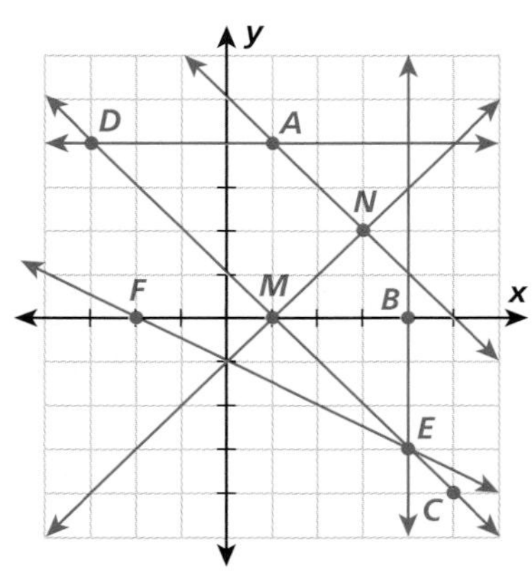

1. $\overleftrightarrow{AD}$
2. $\overleftrightarrow{BE}$
3. $\overleftrightarrow{MN}$
4. $\overleftrightarrow{EF}$

See Example 2

5. Which lines are parallel?
6. Which lines are perpendicular?

See Example 3

Graph the quadrilaterals with the given vertices. Give all of the names that apply to each quadrilateral.

7. $D(-3, -2)$, $E(-3, 3)$, $F(2, 3)$, $G(2, -2)$
8. $R(-4, -1)$, $S(-2, 2)$, $T(4, 2)$, $V(5, -1)$

See Example 4

Find the coordinates of the missing vertex.

9. rhombus $ABCD$ with $A(2, 3)$, $B(3, 1)$, and $D(1, 1)$
10. square $JKLM$ with $J(-3, 1)$, $K(0, 1)$, and $L(0, -2)$

INDEPENDENT PRACTICE

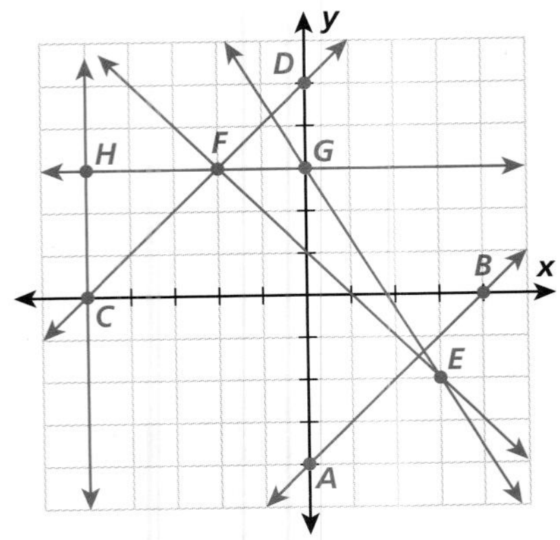

See Example 1

Determine if the slope of each line is positive, negative, 0, or undefined. Then find the slope of each line.

11. $\overleftrightarrow{AB}$

12. $\overleftrightarrow{EG}$

13. $\overleftrightarrow{HG}$

14. $\overleftrightarrow{CH}$

See Example 2

15. Which lines are parallel?

16. Which lines are perpendicular?

See Example 3

Graph the quadrilaterals with the given vertices. Give all of the names that apply to each quadrilateral.

17. $D(-4, 3)$, $E(4, 3)$, $F(4, -5)$, $G(-4, -5)$

18. $W(-2, 1)$, $X(-2, -2)$, $Y(4, 1)$, $Z(0, 2)$

See Example 4

Find the coordinates of the missing vertex.

19. rectangle *ABCD* with $A(-3, 3)$, $B(4, 3)$, and $D(-3, -1)$

20. trapezoid *JKLM* with $J(-1, 5)$, $K(2, 3)$, and $L(2, 1)$

PRACTICE AND PROBLEM SOLVING

Extra Practice
See page 794.

Draw the line through the given points and find its slope.

21. $A(1, 0)$, $B(2, 3)$

22. $C(-3, 0)$, $D(-3, -4)$

23. $G(4, -2)$, $H(-1, -2)$

24. $E(-2, 1)$, $F(3, -2)$

25. A line passes through the coordinates $P(1, 3)$ and $Q(-2, -3)$. Identify the slope of $\overleftrightarrow{PQ}$. Then name two coordinates and the slope of a line perpendicular to $\overleftrightarrow{PQ}$.

26. $\overleftrightarrow{AB} \parallel \overleftrightarrow{CD}$ and the slope of $\overleftrightarrow{AB}$ is undefined. What can you tell about the slope of $\overleftrightarrow{CD}$? Explain.

27. On a coordinate grid draw a line s with slope 0 and a line t with slope 1. Then draw three lines through the intersection of lines s and t that have slopes between 0 and 1.

28. On a coordinate grid draw a line m with slope 0 and a line n with slope -1. Then draw three lines through the intersection of lines m and n that have slopes between 0 and -1.

29. Critical Thinking Square *ABCD* has vertices at $(1, 2)$ and $(1, -2)$. Find the possible coordinates of the two missing vertices to create the square with the least area. Justify your solution.

30. Critical Thinking Triangle *LMN* has vertices at $L(-2, 2)$, $M(0, 0)$, and $N(-5, -1)$. What kind of triangle is it? Explain.

Tell if each statement is true or false. If it is false, give a counterexample.

31. Opposite sides of a rhombus have the same slope.

32. All of the adjacent sides of quadrilaterals have slopes with a product of -1.

33. All parallelograms have two pairs of lines with the same slope and adjacent sides that have slopes with a product of -1.

34. A trapezoid has two pairs of sides that have the same slope.

35. The slope of a horizontal line is always 0.

36. The slope of a line through the origin is always defined.

Identify and name each figure.

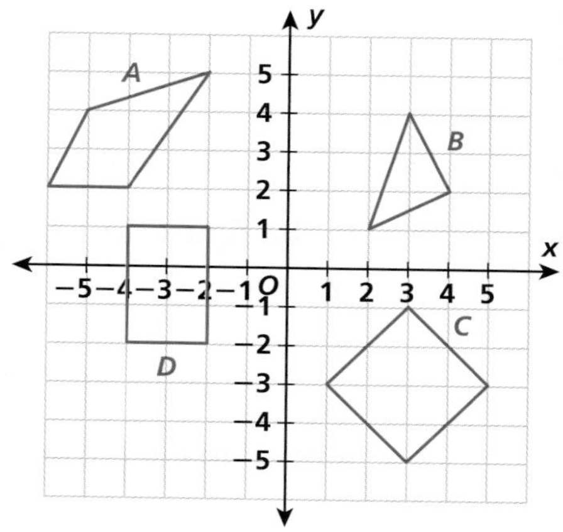

37. This figure has two sides with undefined slopes.

38. This figure has a side with a slope of -1.

39. This figure has a side with a slope of 3.

40. This figure has a side with a slope of $\frac{1}{3}$.

41. What's the Question? Points $P(3, 7)$, $Q(5, 2)$, $R(3, -3)$, and $S(1, 2)$ form the vertices of a polygon. The answer is that the segments are not perpendicular. What is the question?

42. Write About It Explain how using different points on a line to find the slope affects the answer.

43. Challenge Use a square in a coordinate plane to explain why a line with slope 1 makes a 45° angle with the x-axis.

Test Prep and Spiral Review

44. Multiple Choice A right triangle has vertices at (0, 0), (0,4), and (10, 4). What is the slope of the hypotenuse?

Ⓐ 2.5　　Ⓑ 2　　Ⓒ 1.8　　Ⓓ 0.4

45. Gridded Response Find the slope of the line that crosses through the points $A(2, 4)$ and $B(-1, 5)$.

Find each number. (Lesson 6-4)

46. 60% of what number is 12?

47. 112 is 80% of what number?

48. 30 is 2% of what number?

49. 90% of what number is 18?

Find the sum of the angle measures of each polygon. (Lesson 7-4)

50. 15-gon　　**51.** hexagon　　**52.** n-gon　　**53.** decagon

CHAPTER 7

READY TO GO ON?

SECTION 7A

Quiz for Lessons 7-1 Through 7-5

7-1 Points, Lines, Planes, and Angles

Use the diagram to name each figure.

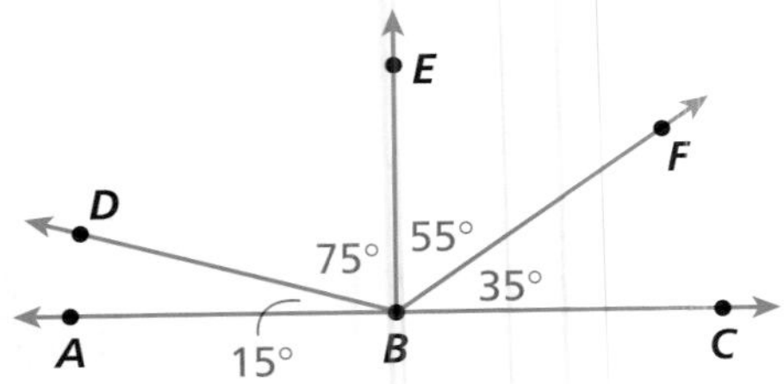

1. two pairs of complementary angles
2. three pairs of supplementary angles
3. two right angles

7-2 Parallel and Perpendicular Lines

In the figure, line $m \parallel$ line n. Find the measure of each angle.

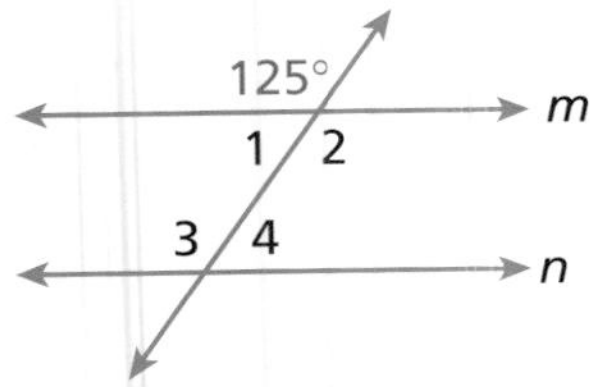

4. $\angle 1$
5. $\angle 2$
6. $\angle 3$

7-3 Angles in Triangles

Find $x°$ in each triangle.

7.

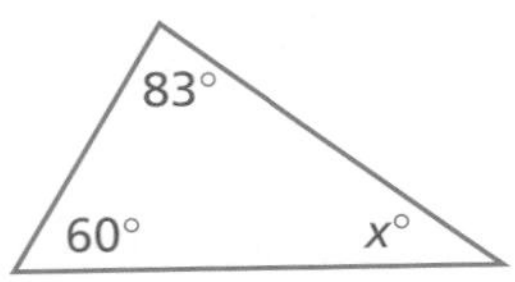

8.

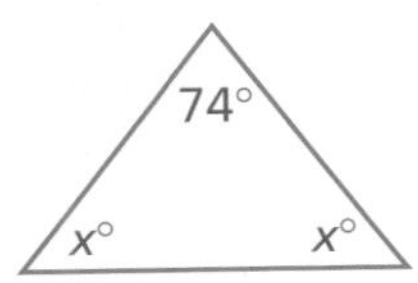

9. In $\triangle ABC$, $m\angle A = 57°$, and $\angle B$ is a right angle. What is $m\angle C$?

7-4 Classifying Polygons

Give all of the names that apply to each figure.

10.

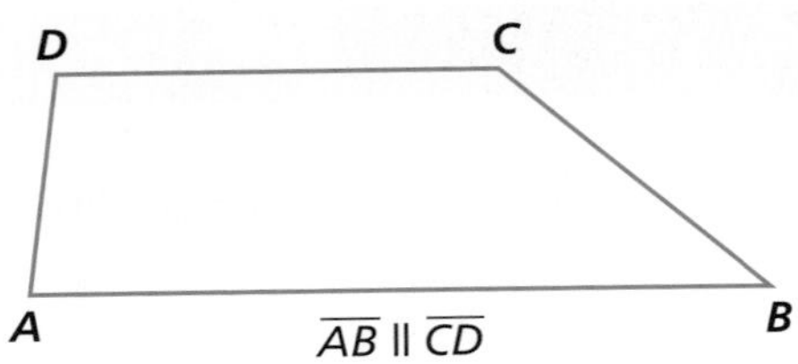

11.

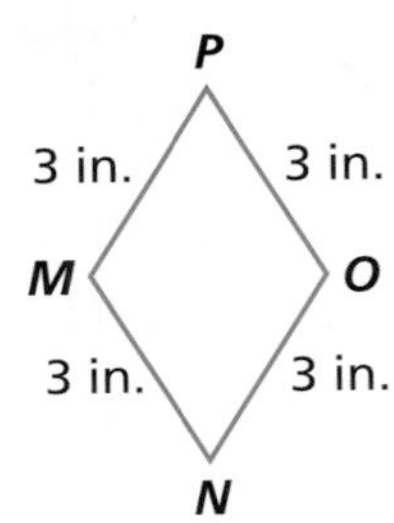

7-5 Coordinate Geometry

Graph the quadrilaterals with the given vertices. Give all of the names that apply to each quadrilateral.

12. $A(-2, 1)$, $B(3, 2)$, $C(2, 0)$, $D(-3, -1)$
13. $P(-3, 4)$, $Q(2, 4)$, $R(2, -1)$, $S(-3, -1)$

Find the coordinates of the missing vertex.

14. square $ABCD$ with $A(-1, 1)$, $B(2, 1)$, and $C(2, -2)$
15. parallelogram $PQRS$ with $P(3, 3)$, $Q(4, 2)$, and $R(2, -2)$

Ready to Go On?

Focus on Problem Solving

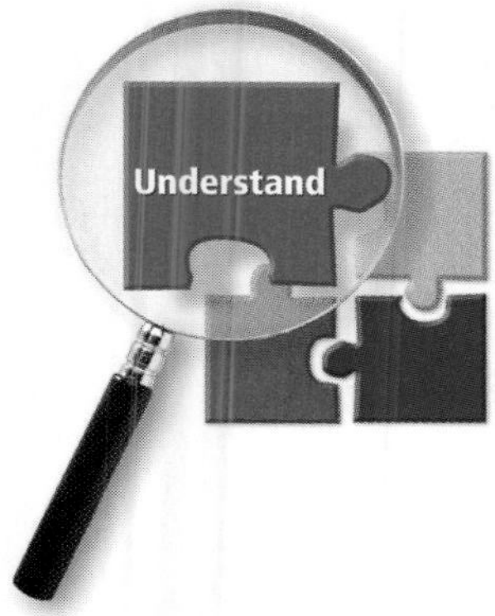

Understand the Problem

- **Restate the problem in your own words**

If you write a problem in your own words, you may understand it better. Before writing a problem in your own words, you may need to read it over several times—perhaps aloud, so you can hear yourself say the words.

Once you have written the problem in your own words, you may want to make sure you included all of the necessary information to solve the problem.

Write each problem in your own words. Check to make sure you have included all of the information needed to solve the problem.

1. In the figure, $\angle 1$ and $\angle 2$ are complementary, and $\angle 1$ and $\angle 5$ are supplementary. If $m\angle 1 = 60°$, find $m\angle 3 + m\angle 4$.

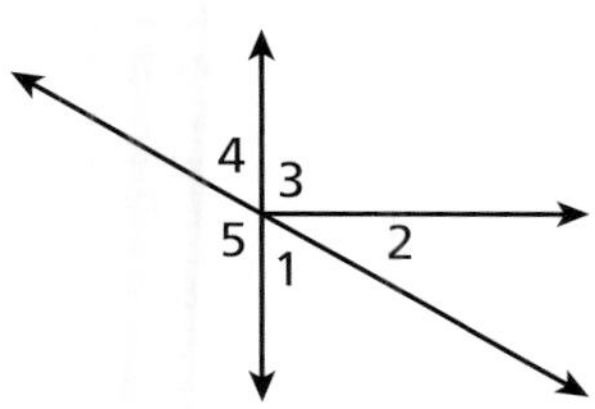

2. In triangle ABC, $m\angle A = 35°$ and $m\angle B = 55°$. Use the Triangle Sum Theorem to determine whether triangle ABC is a right triangle.

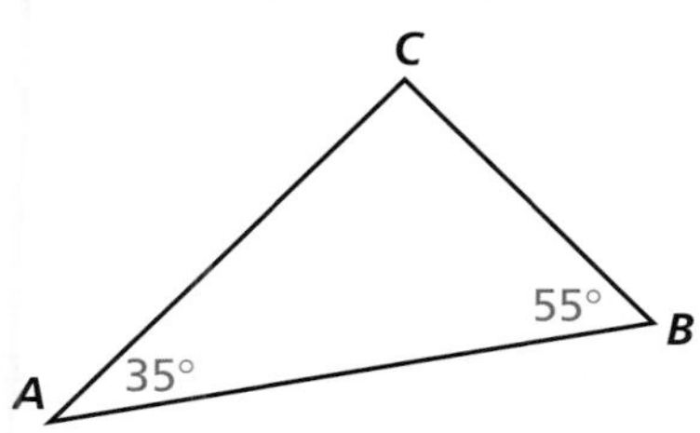

3. The second angle in a quadrilateral is eight times as large as the first angle. The third angle is half as large as the second. The fourth angle is as large as the first angle and the second angle combined. Find the angle measures in the quadrilateral.

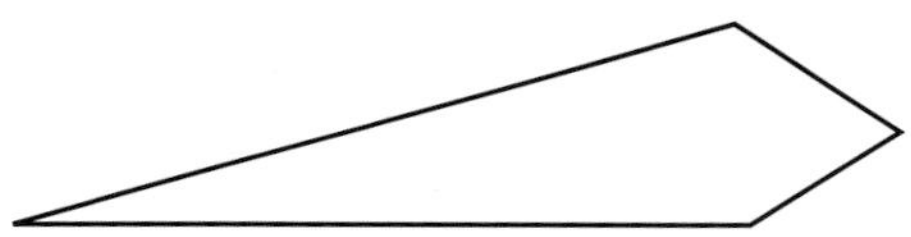

4. Parallel lines m and n are intersected by a transversal, line p. The acute angles formed by line m and line p measure 45°. Find the measure of the obtuse angles formed by the intersection of line n and line p.

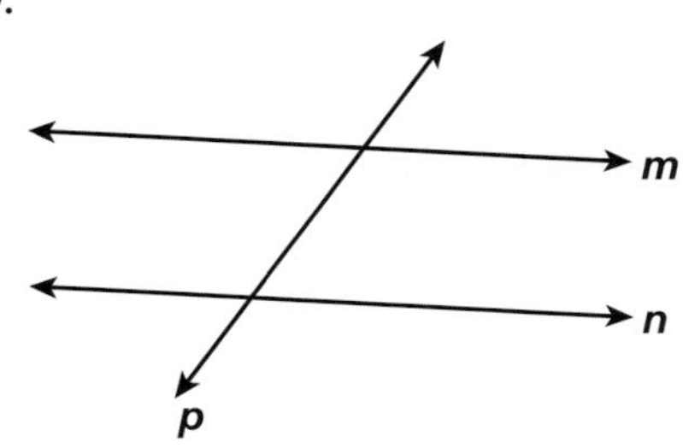

7-6 Congruence

Learn to use properties of congruent figures to solve problems.

Vocabulary
correspondence

Below are the DNA profiles of two pairs of twins. Twins A and B are identical twins. Twins C and D are fraternal twins.

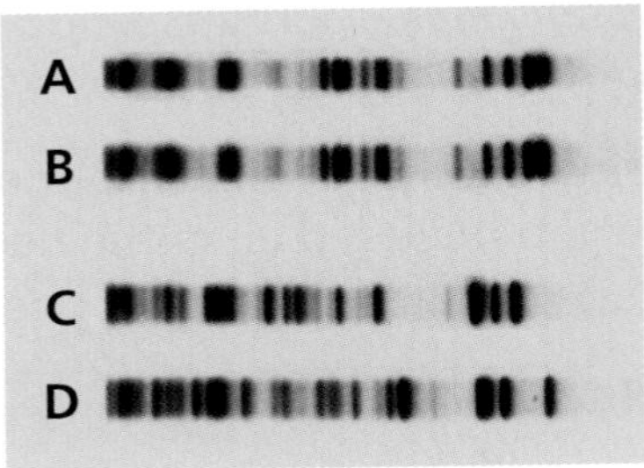

A **correspondence** is a way of matching up two sets of objects. The bands of DNA that are next to each other in each pair match up, or *correspond.* In the DNA of the identical twins, the corresponding bands are the same.

If two polygons are congruent, all of their corresponding sides and angles are congruent.

CONGRUENT TRIANGLES			
Diagram	Statement	Corresponding Angles	Corresponding Sides
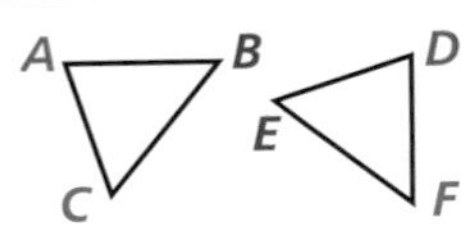	$\triangle ABC \cong \triangle DEF$	$\angle A \cong \angle D$ $\angle B \cong \angle E$ $\angle C \cong \angle F$	$\overline{AB} \cong \overline{DE}$ $\overline{BC} \cong \overline{EF}$ $\overline{AC} \cong \overline{DF}$

EXAMPLE 1 Writing Congruence Statements

Write a congruence statement for each pair of congruent polygons.

Helpful Hint

Marks on the sides of a figure can be used to show congruence.
$\overline{KM} \cong \overline{RS}$ (1 mark)
$\overline{KL} \cong \overline{RQ}$ (2 marks)
$\overline{ML} \cong \overline{SQ}$ (3 marks)

A

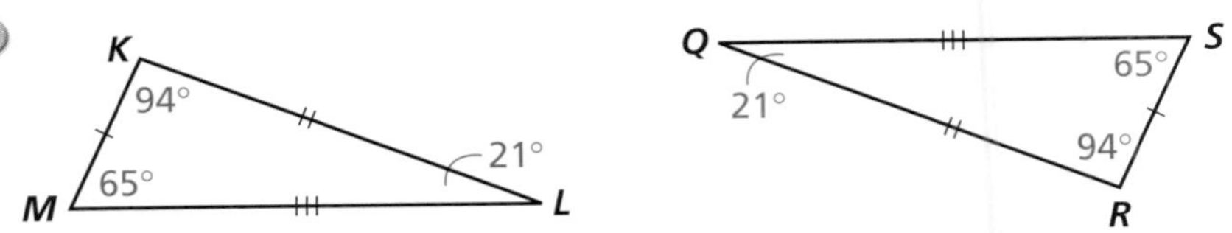

In a congruence statement, the vertices in the second triangle have to be written in order of correspondence with the first triangle.

$\angle K$ corresponds to $\angle R$. $\angle K \cong \angle R$
$\angle L$ corresponds to $\angle Q$. $\angle L \cong \angle Q$
$\angle M$ corresponds to $\angle S$. $\angle M \cong \angle S$

The congruence statement is triangle $KLM \cong$ triangle RQS.

Write a congruence statement for each pair of congruent polygons.

B

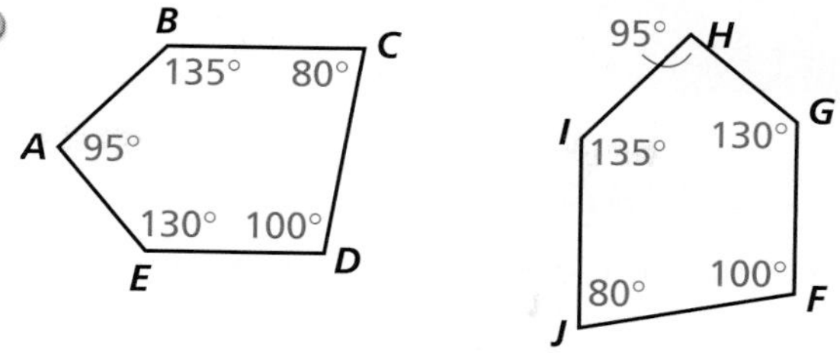

The vertices in the first pentagon are written in order around the pentagon starting at any vertex.

$\angle A$ corresponds to $\angle H$.	*$\angle A \cong \angle H$*
$\angle B$ corresponds to $\angle I$.	*$\angle B \cong \angle I$*
$\angle C$ corresponds to $\angle J$.	*$\angle C \cong \angle J$*
$\angle D$ corresponds to $\angle F$.	*$\angle D \cong \angle F$*
$\angle E$ corresponds to $\angle G$.	*$\angle E \cong \angle G$*

The congruence statement is pentagon $ABCDE \cong$ pentagon $HIJFG$.

EXAMPLE 2 Using Congruence Relationships to Find Unknown Values

In the figure, quadrilateral $PQSR \cong$ quadrilateral $WTUV$.

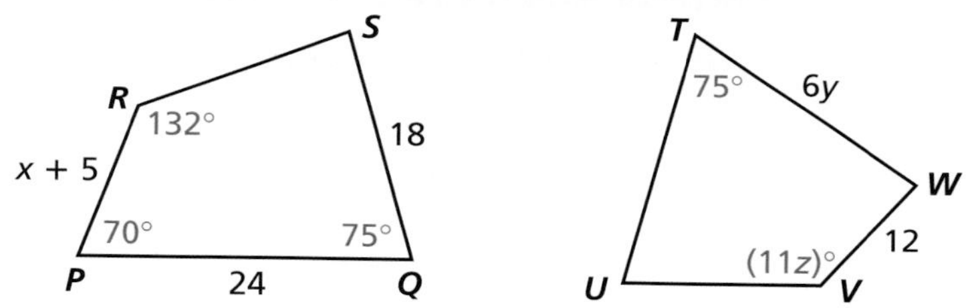

A Find x.

$x + 5 = 12$ *$\overline{PR} \cong \overline{WV}$*

$-5 = -5$ *Subtract 5 from both sides.*

$x = 7$

B Find y.

$6y = 24$ *$\overline{WT} \cong \overline{PQ}$*

$\frac{6y}{6} = \frac{24}{6}$ *Divide both sides by 6.*

$y = 4$

C Find z.

$132 = 11z$ *$\angle R \cong \angle V$*

$\frac{132}{11} = \frac{11z}{11}$ *Divide both sides by 11.*

$12 = z$

Think and Discuss

1. Explain what it means for two polygons to be congruent.

2. Tell how to write a congruence statement for two polygons.

7-6 Exercises

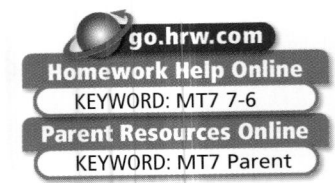

go.hrw.com
Homework Help Online
KEYWORD: MT7 7-6
Parent Resources Online
KEYWORD: MT7 Parent

GUIDED PRACTICE

See Example 1

Write a congruence statement for each pair of congruent polygons.

1.
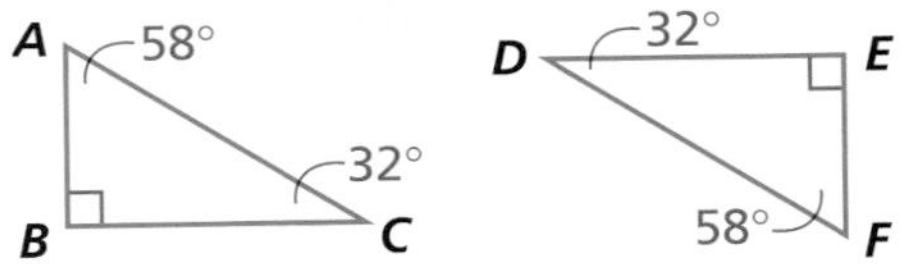

2.
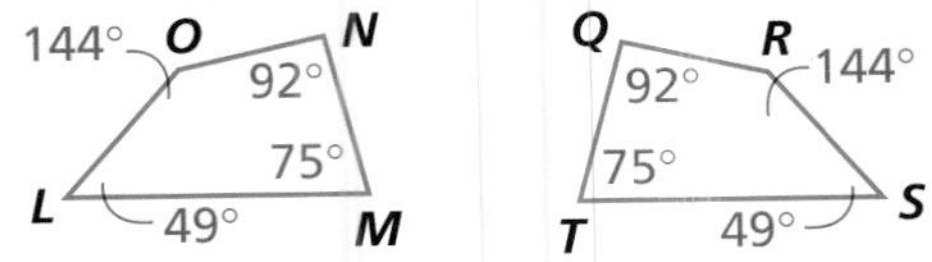

See Example 2

In the figure, triangle $ABC \cong$ triangle LMN.

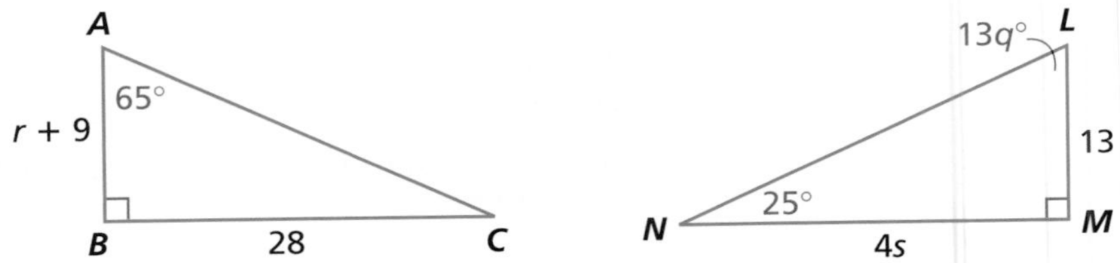

3. Find q.

4. Find r.

5. Find s.

INDEPENDENT PRACTICE

See Example 1

Write a congruence statement for each pair of congruent polygons.

6.
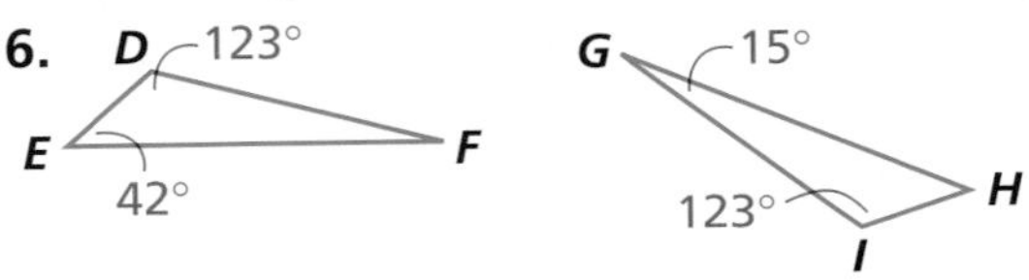

7.
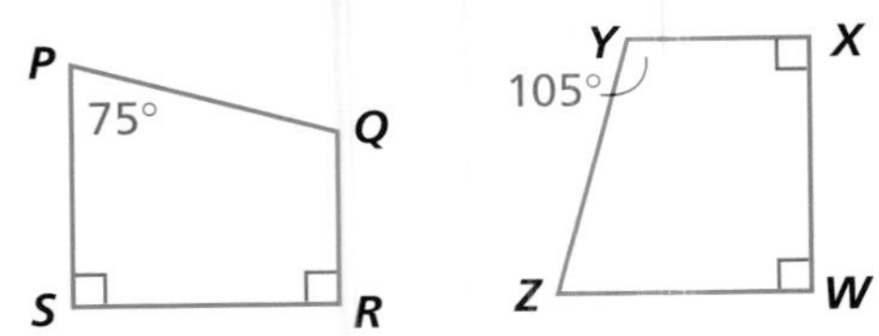

See Example 2

In the figure, quadrilateral $ABCD \cong$ quadrilateral $LMNO$.

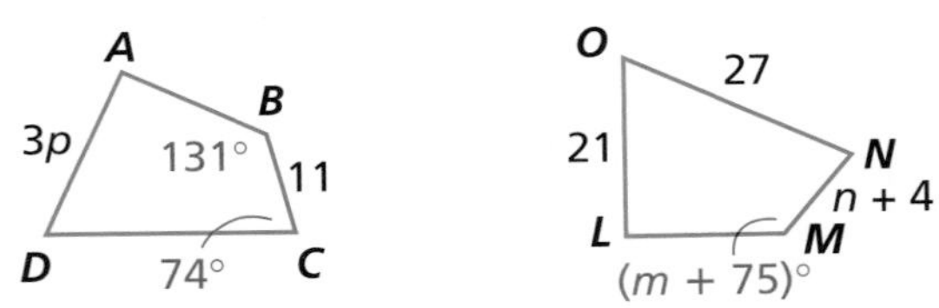

8. Find m.

9. Find n.

10. Find p.

PRACTICE AND PROBLEM SOLVING

Extra Practice
See page 795.

Find the value of each variable.

11. pentagon $ABCDE \cong$ pentagon $PQRST$

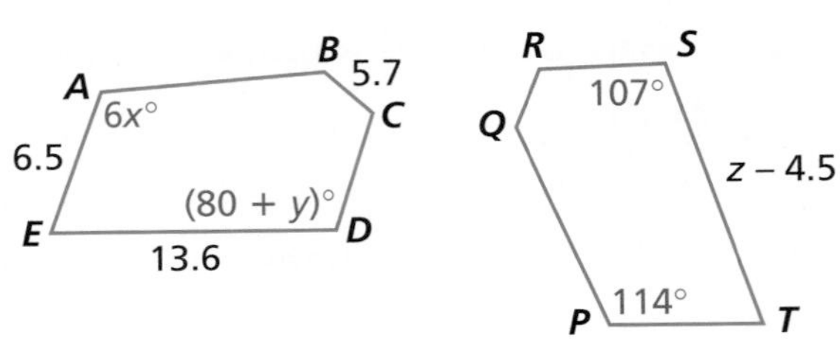

12. hexagon $ABCDEF \cong$ hexagon $LMNOPQ$

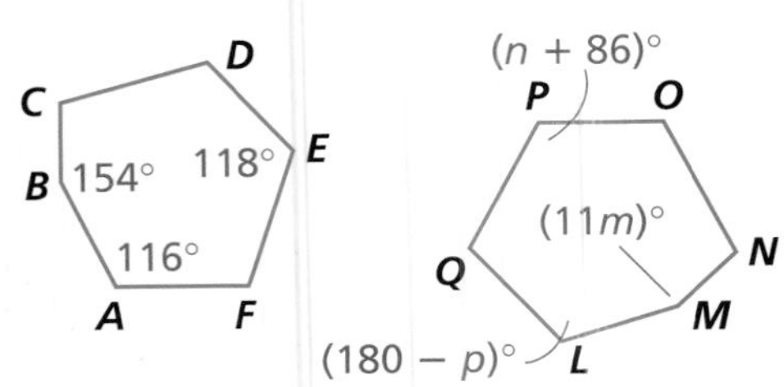

Find the value of each variable.

13. quadrilateral $ABCD \cong$ quadrilateral $EFGH$

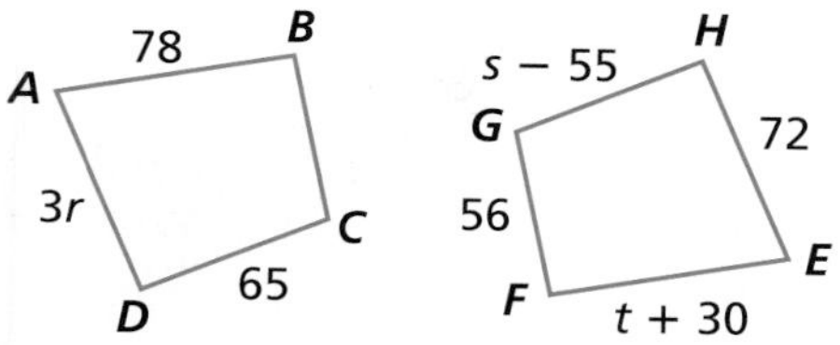

14. heptagon $ABCDEFG \cong$ heptagon $JKLMNOP$

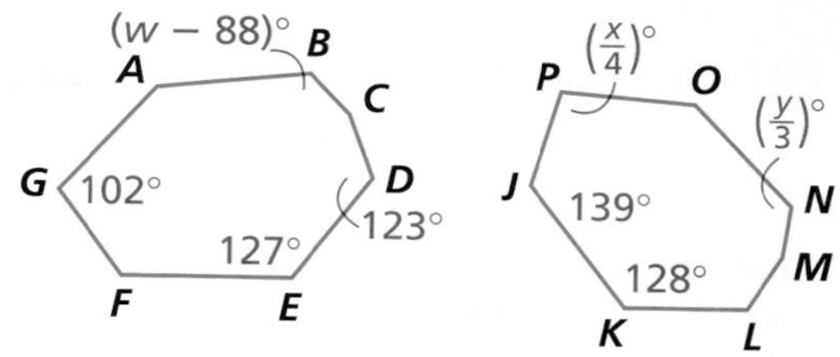

15. Right triangle $PQR \cong$ right triangle STU. $m\angle P = 28°$ and $m\angle U = 90°$. Find $m\angle Q$.

16. Write a Problem Write and solve a problem about the right triangles shown.

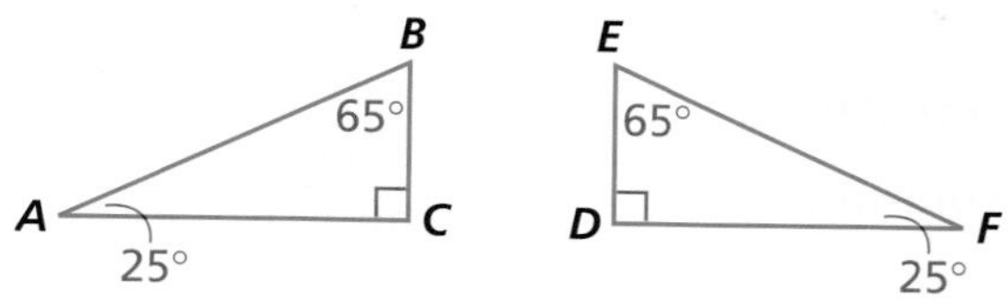

17. Write About It How can knowing two polygons are congruent help you find angle measures of the polygons?

18. Challenge Triangle $ABC \cong$ triangle LMN and $\overline{AE} \parallel \overline{BD}$. Find $m\angle ACD$.

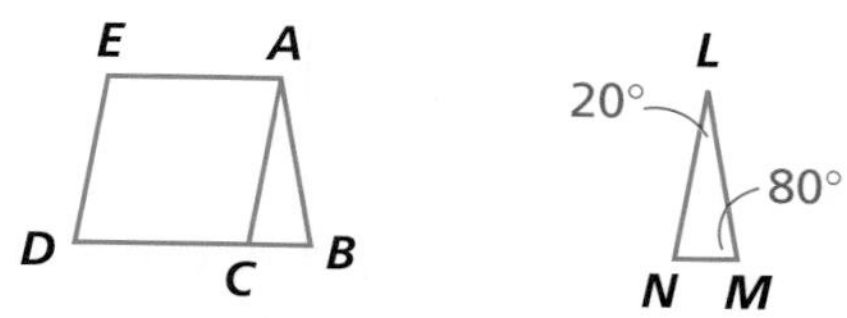

TEST PREP and Spiral Review

19. Multiple Choice Triangle $EFG \cong$ triangle JIH. Find the value of x.

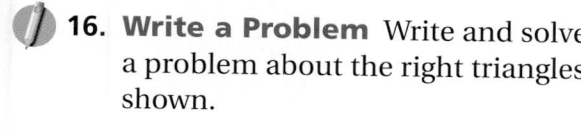

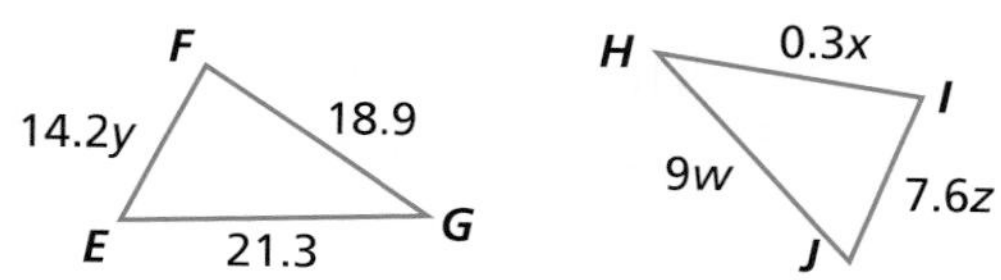

Ⓐ 5.67 Ⓑ 30 Ⓒ 63 Ⓓ 71

20. Multiple Choice Triangle $ABC \cong$ triangle JKL. $m\angle A = 30°$ and $m\angle B = 50°$. Find the $m\angle K$.

Ⓕ 30° Ⓖ 50° Ⓗ 80° Ⓙ 100°

21. Gridded Response Quadrilateral $ABCD \cong$ quadrilateral $WXYZ$. The length of $\overline{AB} = 21$ and the length of $\overline{WX} = 7m$. Find m.

Find the missing y-coordinate of each ordered pair that is a solution to $y = 4x - 2$. (Lesson 3-2)

22. $(0, y)$ **23.** $(1, y)$ **24.** $(3, y)$ **25.** $(7, y)$

The measures of two angles of a triangle are given. Find the measure of the third angle. (Lesson 7-3)

26. 45°, 45° **27.** 30°, 60° **28.** 21°, 82° **29.** 105°, 42°

7-7 Transformations

Learn to transform plane figures using translations, rotations, and reflections.

Vocabulary

transformation
translation
rotation
center of rotation
reflection
image

When you are on an amusement park ride, you are undergoing a *transformation*. A **transformation** is a change in a figure's position or size. Ferris wheels and merry-go-rounds are *rotations*. Free-fall rides and water slides are *translations*. Translations, rotations, and reflections are types of transformations.

Translation	Rotation	Reflection
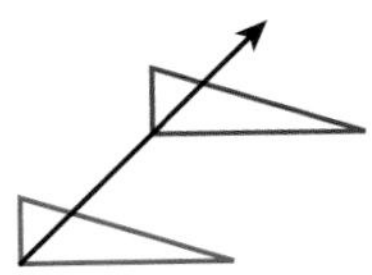	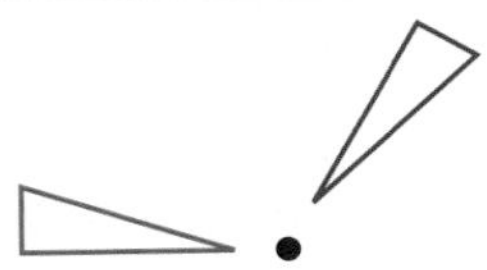	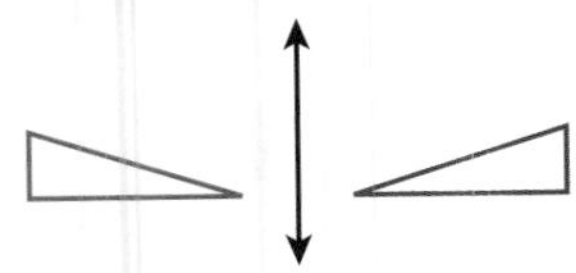
A **translation** slides a figure along a line without turning.	A **rotation** turns a figure around a point, called the **center of rotation**.	A **reflection** flips a figure across a line to create a mirror image.

The resulting figure, or **image**, of a translation, rotation, or reflection is congruent to the original figure.

EXAMPLE 1 Identifying Transformations

Identify each as a translation, rotation, reflection, or none of these.

A

translation

B

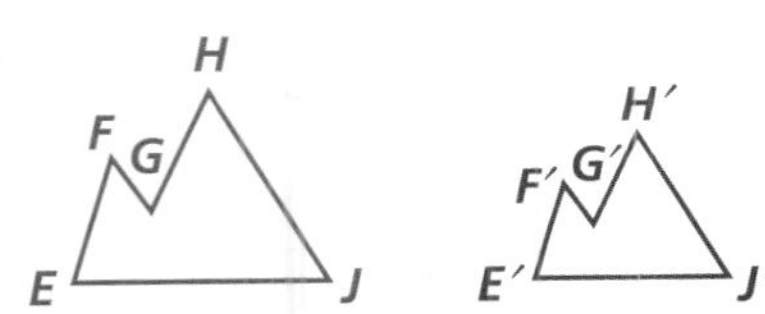

none of these

C

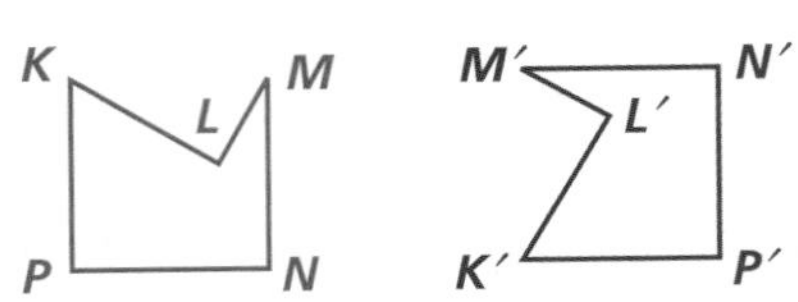

rotation

D

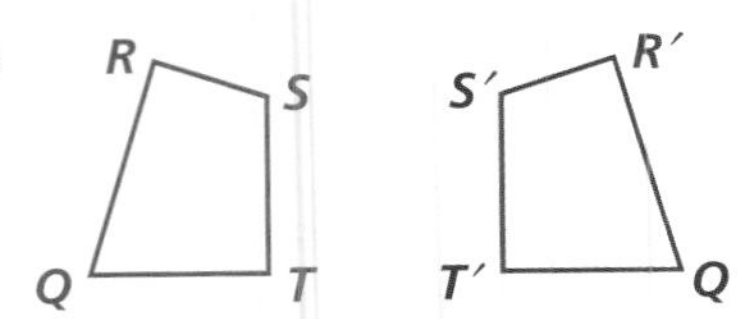

reflection

Reading Math

A′ is read "*A* prime." The point *A*′ is the image of point *A*.

EXAMPLE 2 Graphing Transformations

Draw the image of a triangle with vertices $A(1, 1)$, $B(1, 4)$, and $C(3, 4)$ after each transformation.

A translation 5 units down

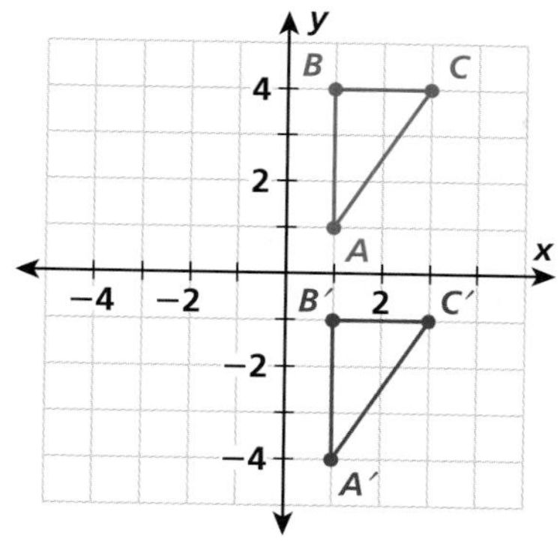

B reflection across the y-axis

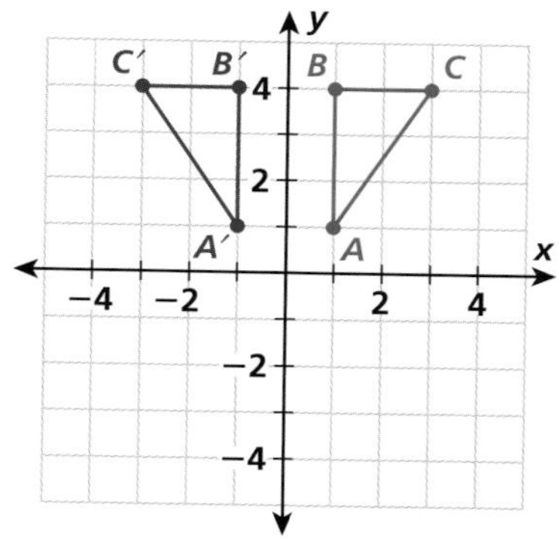

EXAMPLE 3 Describing Graphs of Transformations

Parallelogram $EFGH$ has vertices $E(-2, 1)$, $F(3, 1)$, $G(4, 4)$, and $H(-1, 4)$. Find the coordinates of the image of the indicated point after each transformation.

A translation 2 units down, point E

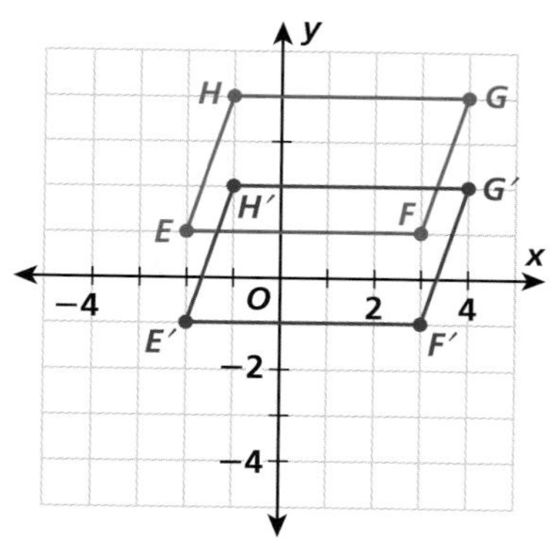

E' $(-2, -1)$

B 180° rotation around $(0, 0)$, point G

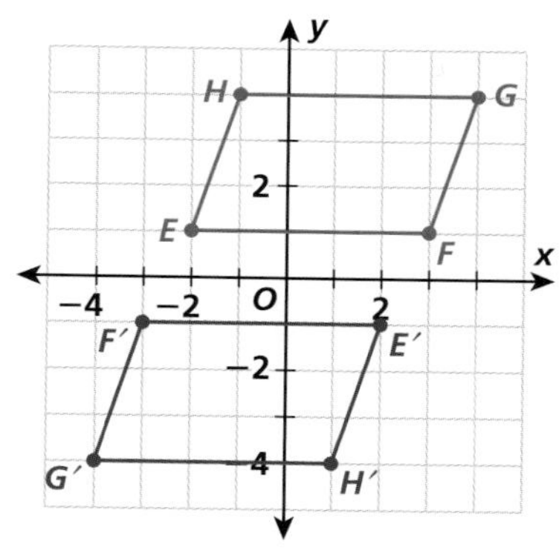

G' $(-4, -4)$

Think and Discuss

1. **Tell** whether the image of a vertical line is sometimes, always, or never vertical after a translation, a reflection, or a rotation.
2. **Describe** what happens to the x-coordinate and the y-coordinate after a point is reflected across the x-axis.

7-7 Exercises

go.hrw.com
Homework Help Online
KEYWORD: MT7 7-7
Parent Resources Online
KEYWORD: MT7 Parent

GUIDED PRACTICE

See Example 1

Identify each as a translation, rotation, reflection, or none of these.

1. 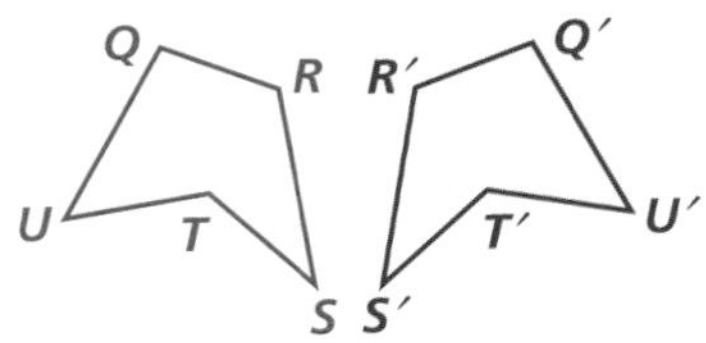

2. 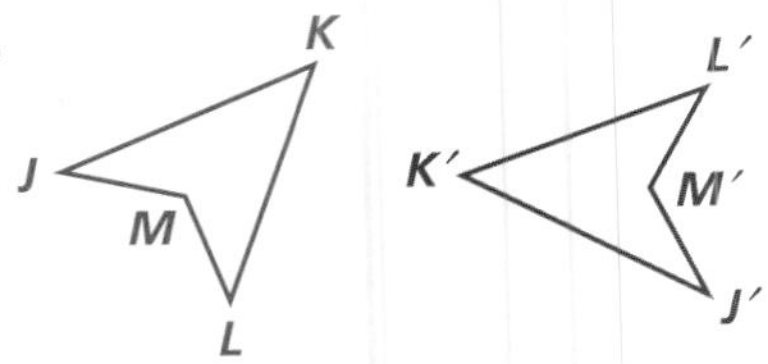

See Example 2

Draw the image of the parallelogram *ABCD* with vertices (−3, 0), (−4, 3), (1, 4), and (2, 1) after each transformation.

3. translation 1 unit up
4. reflection across the x-axis
5. reflection across the y-axis
6. 180° rotation around (0, 0)

See Example 3

Triangle *ABC* has vertices *A*(2, 1), *B*(3, 3), and *C*(1, 2). Find the coordinates of the image of the indicated point after each transformation.

7. translation 4 units down, point C
8. reflection across the x-axis, point B
9. reflection across the y-axis, point C
10. 180° rotation around (0,0), point A

INDEPENDENT PRACTICE

See Example 1

Identify each as a translation, rotation, reflection, or none of these.

11. 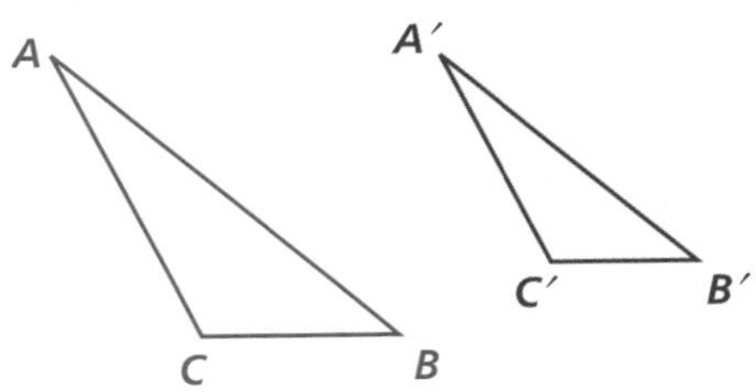

12. 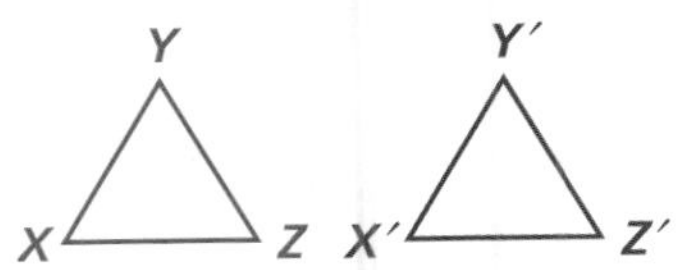

See Example 2

Draw the image of the quadrilateral *ABCD* with vertices (1, 1), (2, 4), (4, 5), and (5, 3) after each transformation.

13. translation 5 units down
14. reflection across the x-axis
15. reflection across the y-axis
16. 180° rotation around (0, 0)

See Example 3

Square *ABCD* has vertices *A*(−2, 2), *B*(2, 2), *C*(2, −2), and *D*(−2, −2). Find the coordinates of the image of the indicated point after each transformation.

17. translation 3 units to the left, point A
18. translation 4 units to the right, point B
19. reflection across the x-axis, point C
20. 180° rotation around (0, 0), point A

PRACTICE AND PROBLEM SOLVING

Extra Practice
See page 795.

Copy each figure and perform the given transformations.

21. Reflect across line m.

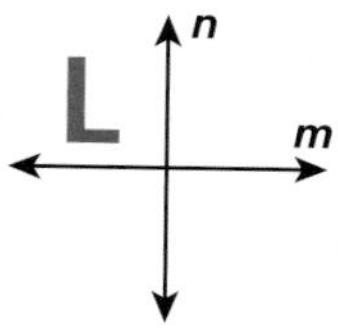

22. Reflect across line n

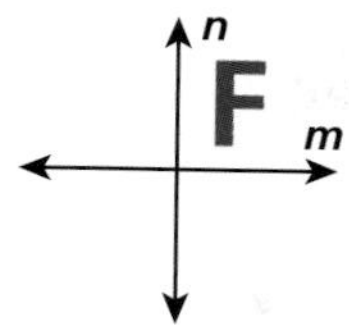

23. Rotate clockwise 90°.

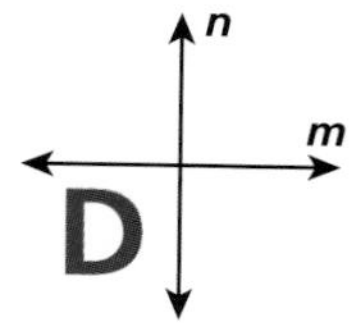

Give the coordinates of each point after a reflection across the given axis.

24. (1, 4); x-axis **25.** (−3, 2); x-axis **26.** (m, n); x-axis

27. (5, −2); y-axis **28.** (−2, 4); y-axis **29.** (m, n); y-axis

Give the coordinates of each point after a 180° rotation around (0, 0).

30. (1, 2) **31.** (−4, 5) **32.** (m, n)

33. Write a Problem Write a problem involving transformations on a coordinate grid that result in a pattern.

34. Write About It Explain how each type of transformation performed on the arrow would affect the direction the arrow is pointing.

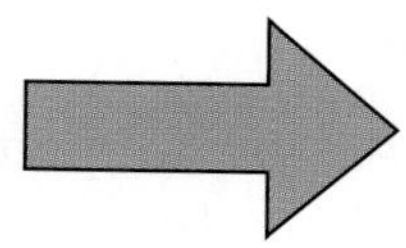

35. Challenge A triangle has vertices (2, 5), (3, 7), and (7, 5). After a reflection and a translation, the coordinates of the image are (7, −2), (8, −4), and (12, −2). Describe the transformations.

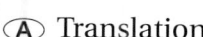

TEST PREP and Spiral Review

36. Multiple Choice Which best represents the transformation at right?

(A) Translation

(B) Rotation

(C) Reflection

(D) None of these

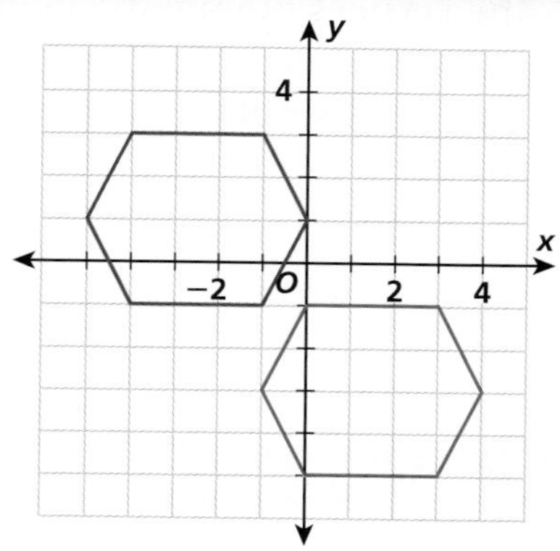

37. Short Response Draw the image of a triangle with vertices (−1, 2), (3, 3), and (1, −3) after a translation 2 units up and 2 units to the right.

Find each percent increase or decrease to the nearest percent. (Lesson 6-5)

38. from 75 to 90 **39.** from 1200 to 1400 **40.** from 44 to 21

Draw the line through the given points and find its slope. (Lesson 7-5)

41. $A(5, 2)$, $B(3, 2)$ **42.** $G(6, -3)$, $H(-4, -9)$ **43.** $C(3, 4)$, $D(0, 0)$

Hands-On LAB 7-7

Use with Lesson 7-7

Combine Transformations

go.hrw.com
Lab Resources Online
KEYWORD: MT7 Lab7

KEY

Pattern blocks =

triangle rhombus trapezoid

You can use a coordinate plane when transforming a geometric figure.

Activity 1

1 Follow the steps below to transform a figure.

a. Place a red pattern block on a coordinate plane. Trace the block, and label the vertices.

b. Translate the figure 3 units down and 5 units right, and then reflect the resulting figure across the x-axis. Draw the image and label the vertices.

c. Now place a green pattern block on the same coordinate plane. Trace the block and label the vertices. Rotate the figure 180° around the point (0, 0), and then translate it 4 units up and 3 units right. Draw the image and label the vertices.

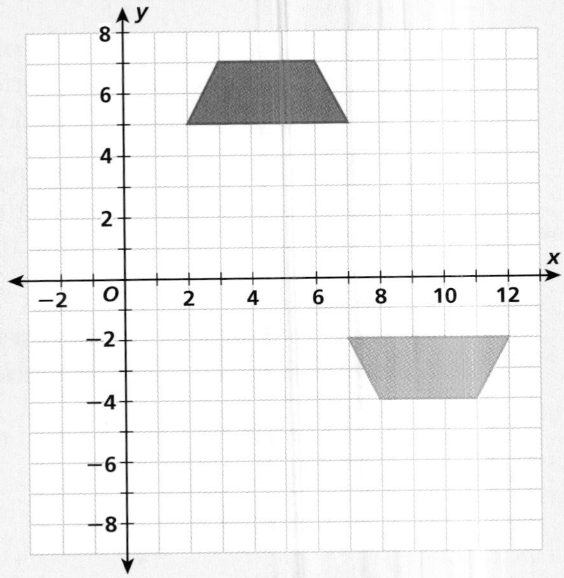

Think and Discuss

1. When you perform two or more transformations on a figure, does it matter in which order the transformations are performed? Explain.

Try This

1. Place a blue pattern block on a coordinate plane. Trace the block, and label the vertices. Perform two different transformations on the figure. Draw the image and label the vertices. Trade with a classmate. Describe the transformations your classmate used.

Activity 2

1 **Follow the steps below to transform a figure.**

a. Place a rhombus on a coordinate plane. Trace the rhombus, and label the vertices.

b. Rotate the figure 90° clockwise about the origin.

c. Reflect the resulting figure across the x-axis. Draw the image and label the vertices.

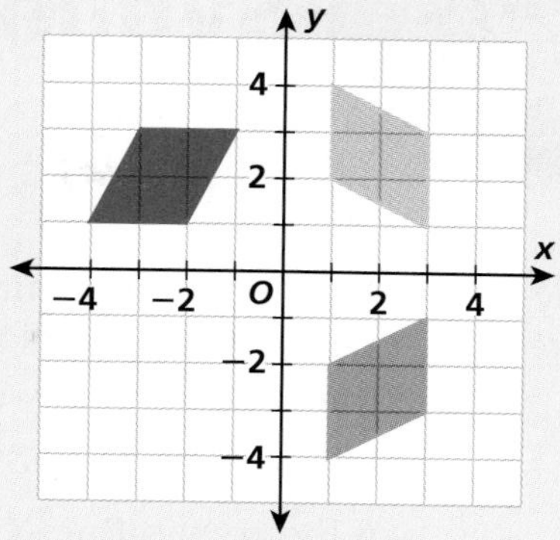

d. Now place a rhombus in the same position as the original figure. Reflect the figure across the line $y = x$.

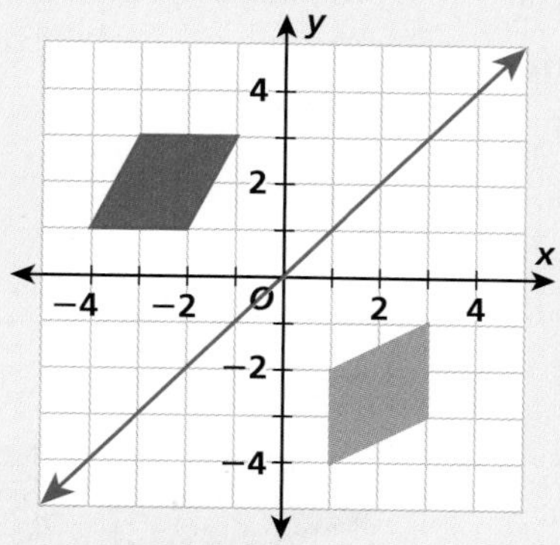

Think and Discuss

1. What do you notice about the images that result from the two transformations in parts **b** and **c** above and the image that results from the single transformation in part **d** above?

Try This

1. Place a pattern block on a coordinate plane. Trace the block and label the vertices. Perform two different transformations on the figure. Draw the image and label the vertices. Explain what single transformation of the original figure would result in the same image.

Describe two different ways to transform each figure from position A to position B.

2.

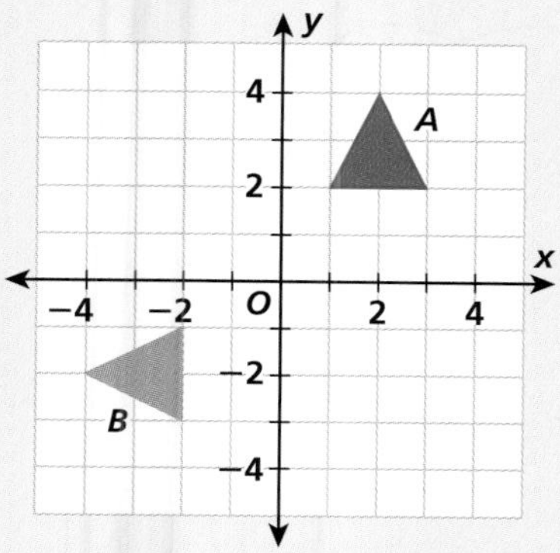

3.

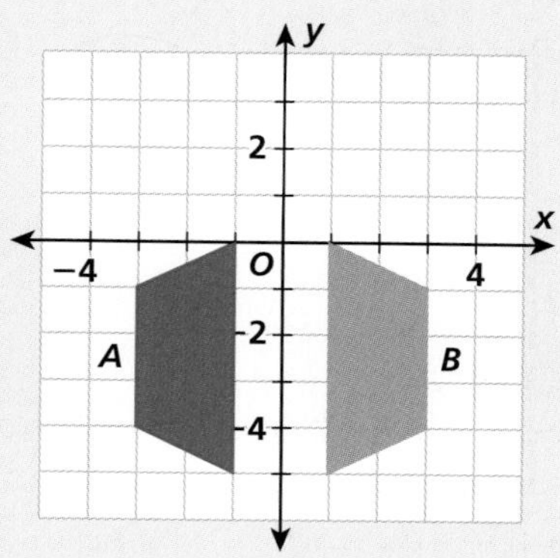

7-8 Symmetry

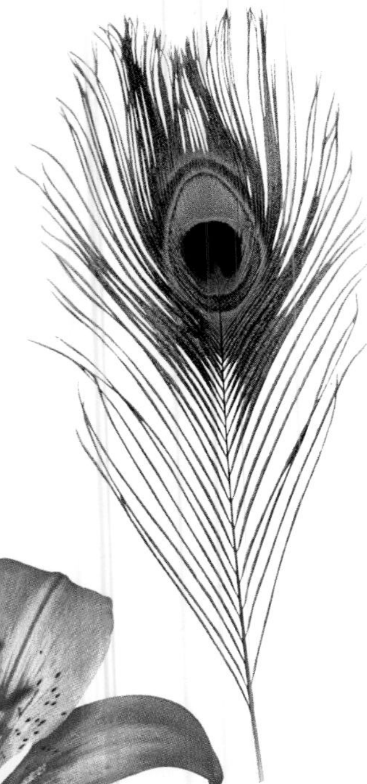

Learn to identify symmetry in figures.

Vocabulary

line symmetry

line of symmetry

rotational symmetry

Nature provides many beautiful examples of *symmetry*, such as the wings of a butterfly or the petals of a flower. Symmetric objects have parts that are congruent.

A figure has **line symmetry** if you can draw a line through it so that the two sides are mirror images of each other. The line is called the **line of symmetry**.

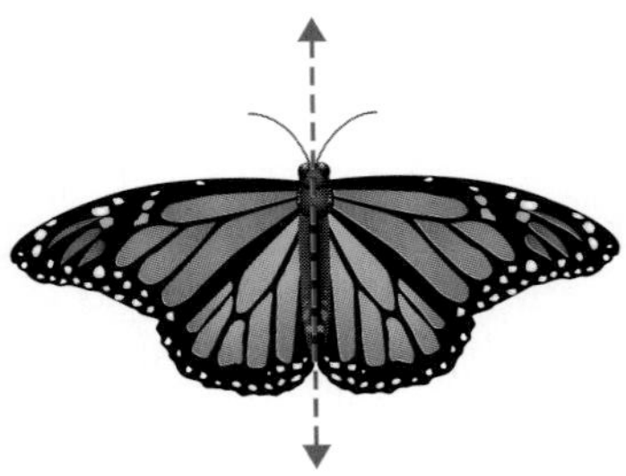

EXAMPLE 1 Drawing Figures with Line Symmetry

Complete each figure. The dashed line is the line of symmetry.

A

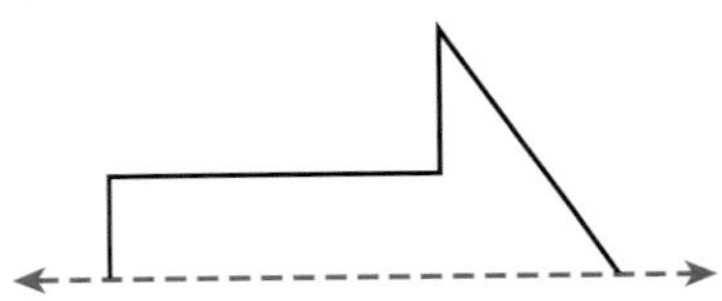

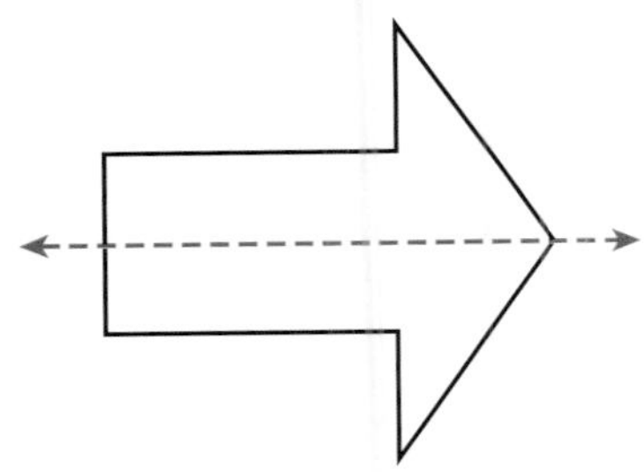

Helpful Hint

If you fold a figure on the line of symmetry, the halves match exactly.

B

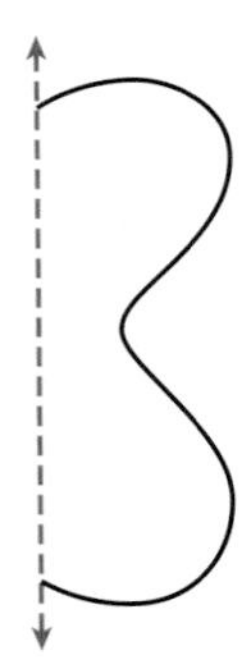

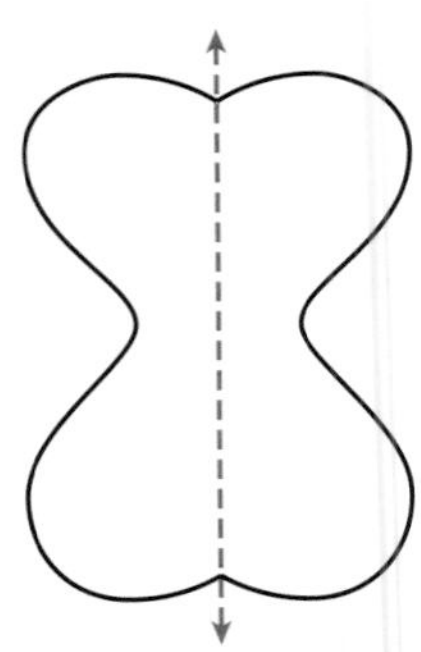

A figure has **rotational symmetry** if you can rotate the figure around some point so that it coincides with itself. The point is the center of rotation, and the amount of rotation must be less than one full turn, or 360°.

7-fold rotational symmetry

6-fold rotational symmetry

7-fold and 6-fold rotational symmetry mean that the figures coincide with themselves 7 times and 6 times respectively, within one full turn.

EXAMPLE 2 Drawing Figures with Rotational Symmetry

Complete each figure. The point is the center of rotation.

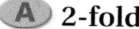

A 2-fold

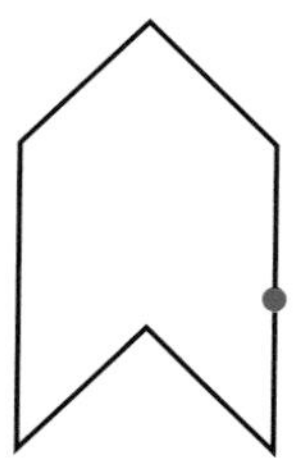

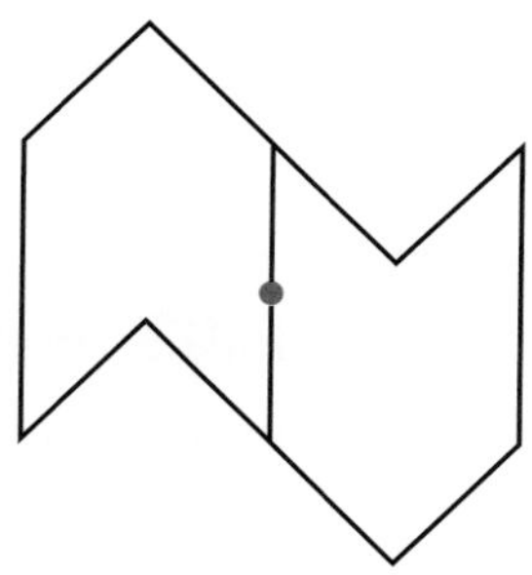

Figure coincides with itself twice every full turn.

B 8-fold

Figure coincides with itself 8 times every full turn.

Think and Discuss

1. **Explain** what it means for a figure to be symmetric.
2. **Tell** which letters of the alphabet have line symmetry.
3. **Tell** which letters of the alphabet have rotational symmetry.

7-8 Exercises

go.hrw.com
Homework Help Online
KEYWORD: MT7 7-8
Parent Resources Online
KEYWORD: MT7 Parent

GUIDED PRACTICE

See Example 1

Complete each figure. The dashed line is the line of symmetry.

1.

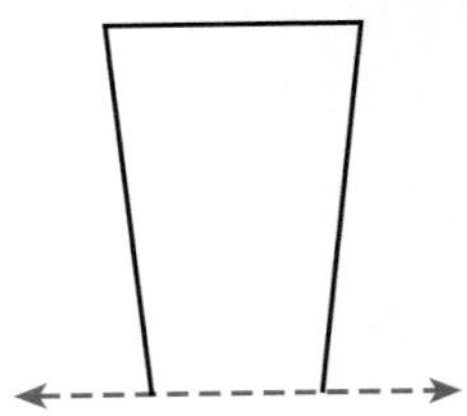

2.

3.

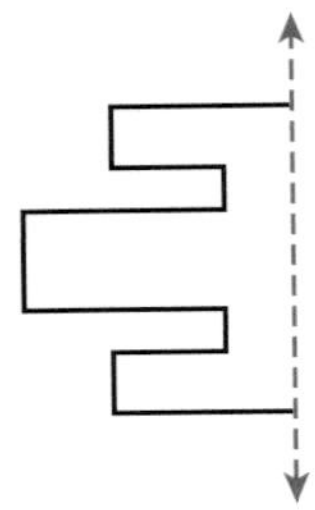

4.

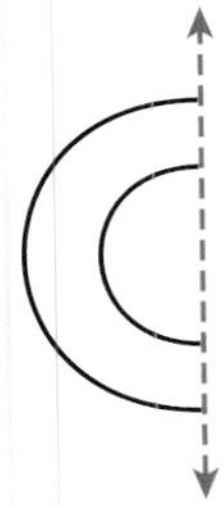

See Example 2

Complete each figure. The point is the center of rotation.

5. 4-fold

6. 6-fold

7. 3-fold

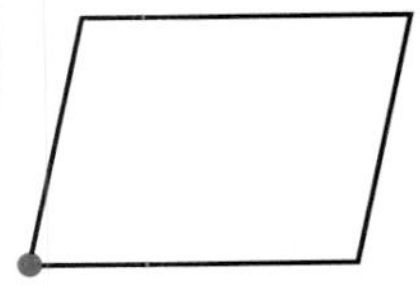

INDEPENDENT PRACTICE

See Example 1

Complete each figure. The dashed line is the line of symmetry.

8.

9.

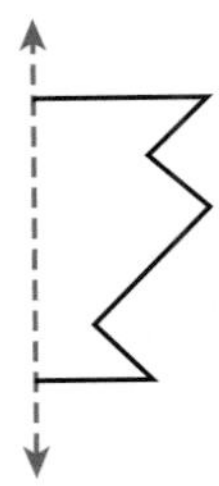

10.

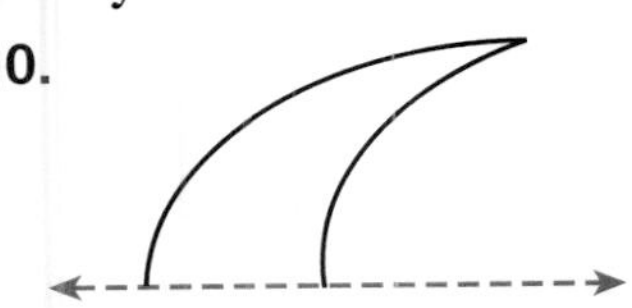

11.

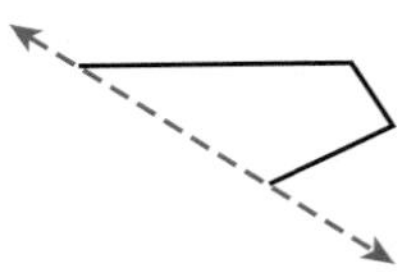

12.

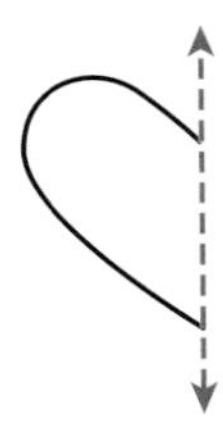

13.

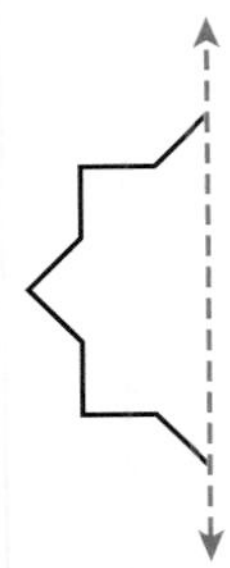

See Example 2

Complete each figure. The point is the center of rotation.

14. 4-fold

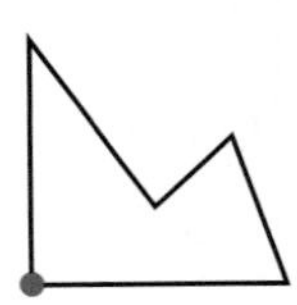

15. 5-fold

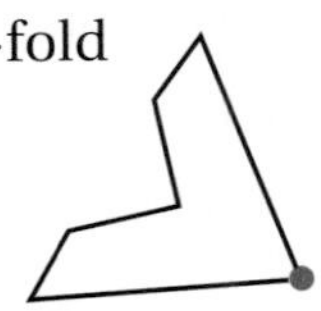

16. 2-fold

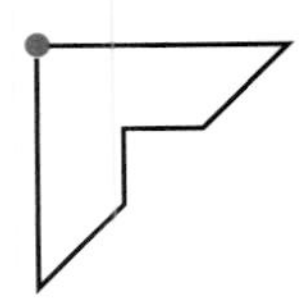

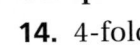

PRACTICE AND PROBLEM SOLVING

Extra Practice
See page 795.

Draw an example of a figure with each type of symmetry.

17. line and rotational symmetry

18. no symmetry

How many lines of symmetry do the following figures have?

19. square

20. rectangle

21. equilateral triangle

22. isosceles triangle

LINK Social Studies

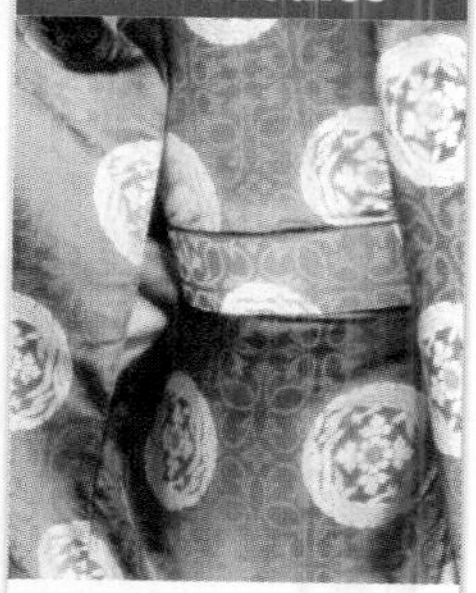

In Japan, a kimono that displays the wearer's family crest is worn for ceremonial occasions.

23. Social Studies Family crests called *ka-mon* have been in use in Japan for many centuries. Copy each crest below. Describe the symmetry, and draw any lines of symmetry or the center of rotation.

a. 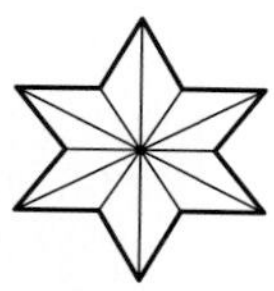
Kage Asa no ha

b. 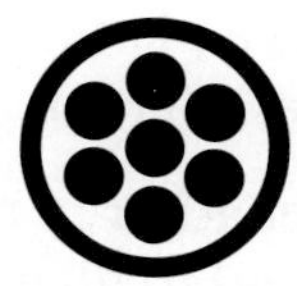
Maru ni shichiyo

c. 
Nito Nami

24. Write a Problem Signal flags are hung from lines of rigging on ships. Write a problem about the types of symmetry in the flags.

25. Write About It To complete a figure with n-fold rotational symmetry, explain how much you rotate each part.

26. Challenge The flag of Switzerland has 180° rotational symmetry. Identify at least three other countries that have flags with 180° rotational symmetry.

TEST PREP and Spiral Review

27. Short Answer Draw a figure that has line symmetry and rotational symmetry.

28. Multiple Choice Which figure has 90° rotational symmetry?

Ⓐ regular pentagon

Ⓑ square

Ⓒ regular hexagon

Ⓓ regular heptagon

Find each unit rate. (Lesson 5-2)

29. 20 bananas for $4.40

30. 496 miles in 16 hours

31. 20 oz for $3.20

In the figure, *ABCDE* ≅ *PQRST*. (Lesson 7-6)

32. Find j.

33. Find k.

34. Find m.

35. Find n.

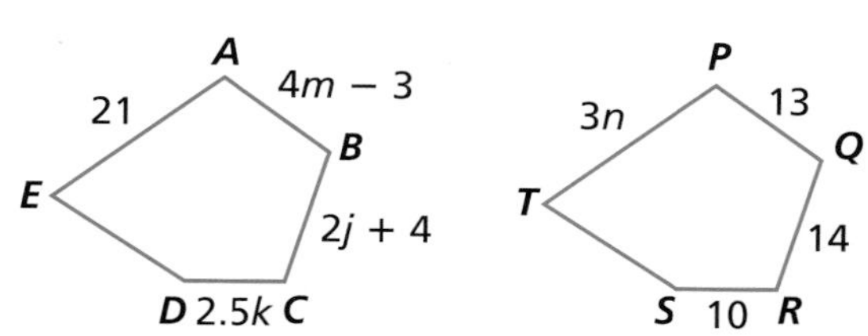

7-9 Tessellations

Learn to create tessellations.

Vocabulary

tessellation

regular tessellation

Fascinating designs can be made by repeating a figure or group of figures. These designs are often used in art and architecture.

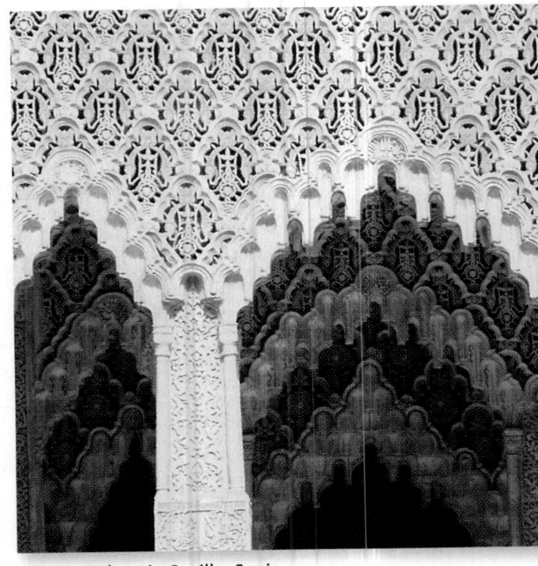

Alcazar Palace in Seville, Spain

A repeating pattern of plane figures that completely covers a plane with no gaps or overlaps is a **tessellation**.

In a **regular tessellation**, a regular polygon is repeated to fill a plane. The angle measures at each vertex must add to 360°, so only three regular tessellations exist.

Equilateral triangles

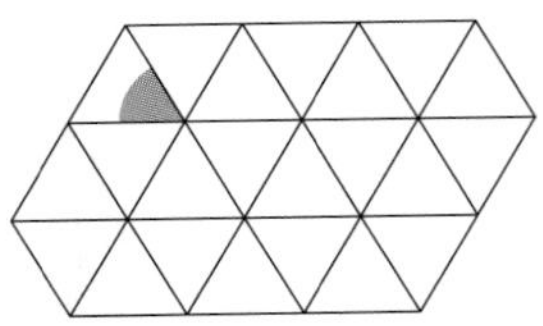

$6 \cdot 60° = 360°$

Squares

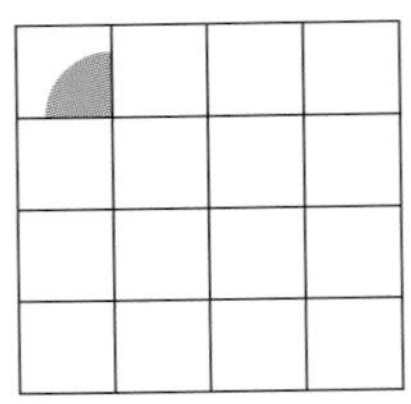

$4 \cdot 90° = 360°$

Regular hexagons

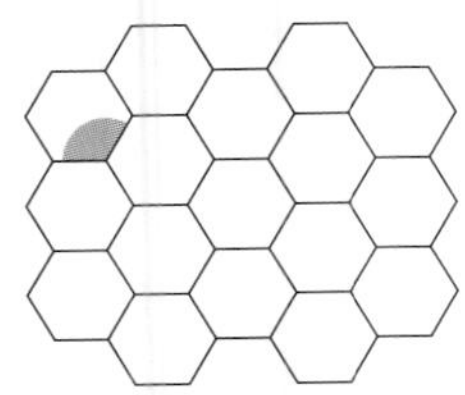

$3 \cdot 120° = 360°$

It is also possible to tessellate with polygons that are not regular. Since the angle measures of a triangle add to 180°, six triangles meeting at each vertex will tessellate. The angle measures of a quadrilateral add to 360°, so four quadrilaterals meeting at a vertex will tessellate.

EXAMPLE 1 Creating a Tessellation

Create a tessellation with quadrilateral *ABCD*.

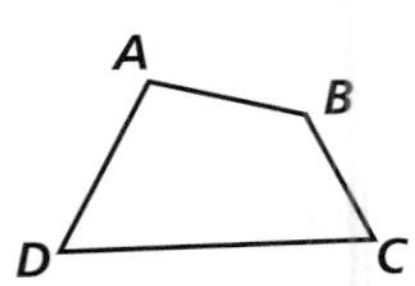

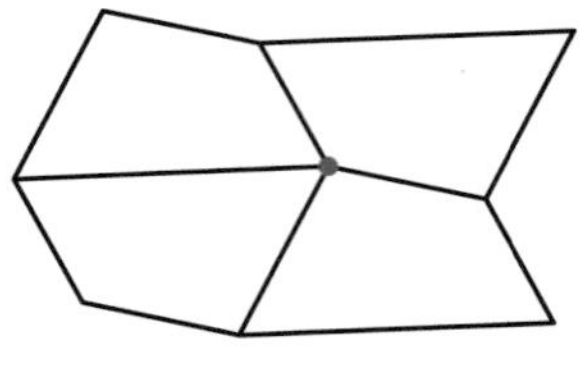

There must be a copy of each angle of quadrilateral ABCD at every vertex.

EXAMPLE 2 Creating a Tessellation by Transforming a Polygon

Use rotations to create a variation of the tessellation in Example 1.

Step 1: Find the midpoint of a side.

Step 2: Make a new edge for half of the side.

Step 3: Rotate the new edge around the midpoint to form the edge of the other half of the side.

Step 4: Repeat with the other sides.

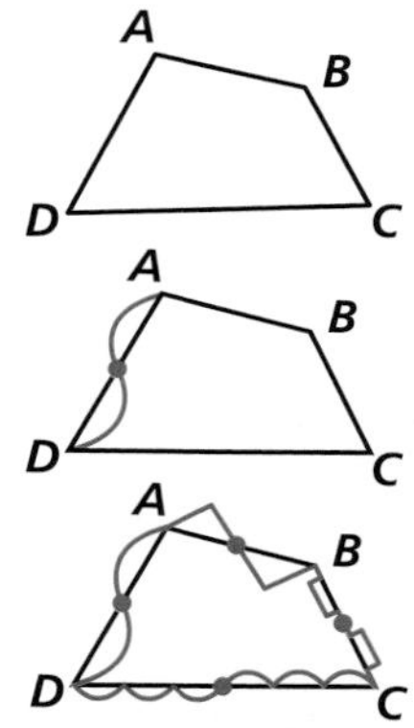

Step 5: Use the figure to make a tessellation.

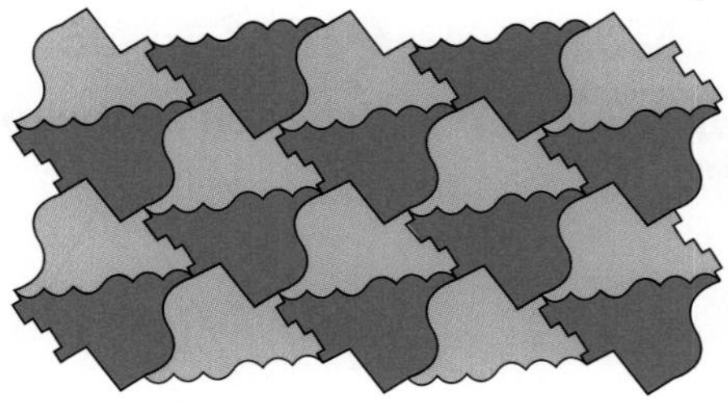

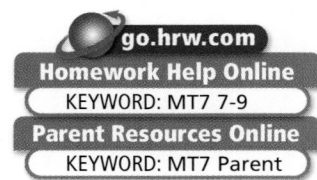

Think and Discuss

1. **Explain** why a regular pentagon cannot be used to create a regular tessellation.
2. **Describe** the transformations used to make the tessellation in Example 2.

7-9 Exercises

go.hrw.com
Homework Help Online
KEYWORD: MT7 7-9
Parent Resources Online
KEYWORD: MT7 Parent

GUIDED PRACTICE

See Example 1

1. Create a tessellation with quadrilateral *QRST*.

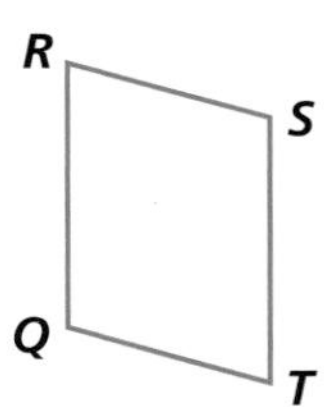

See Example 2

2. Use rotations to create a variation of the tessellation in Exercise 1.

INDEPENDENT PRACTICE

See Example 1

3. Create a tessellation with triangle *PQR*.

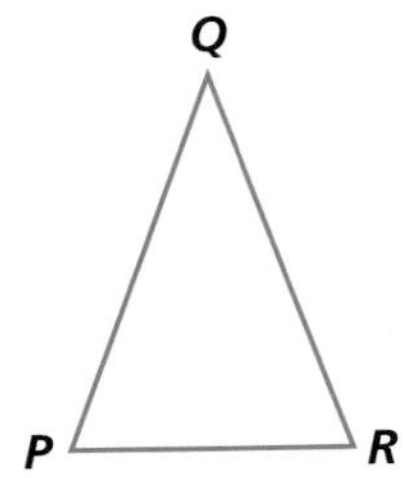

See Example 2

4. Use rotations to create a variation of the tessellation in Exercise 3.

PRACTICE AND PROBLEM SOLVING

Extra Practice
See page 795.

Use each shape to create a tessellation.

5.

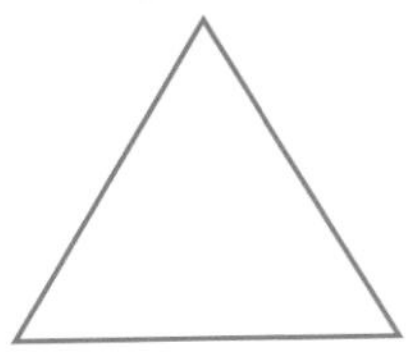

6.

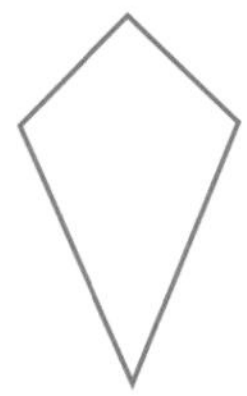

7.

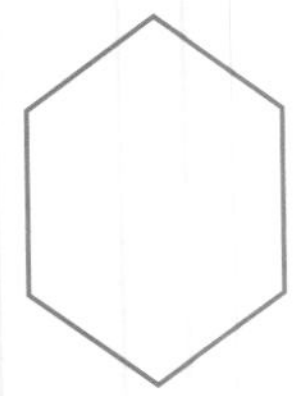

8.

9.

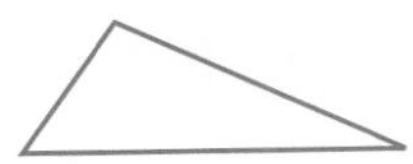

10.

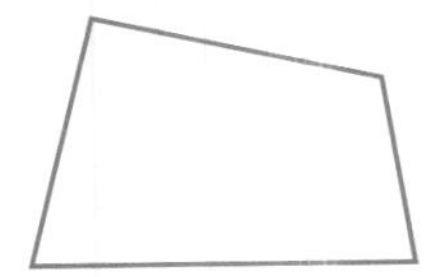

11. A piece is removed from one side of a rectangle and translated to the opposite side. Will this shape tessellate?

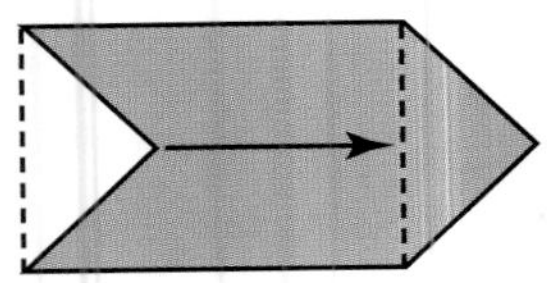

12. A piece is removed from one side of a trapezoid and translated to the opposite side. Will this shape tessellate?

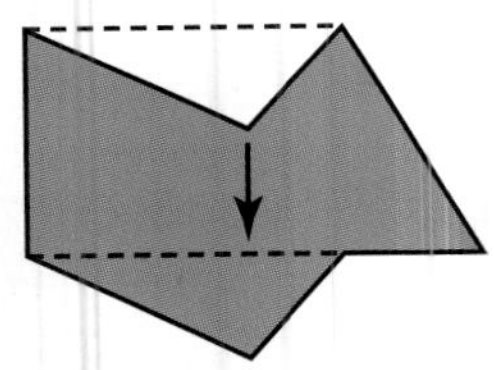

13. In a *semiregular tessellation,* two or more regular polygons are repeated to fill the plane and the vertices are all identical. Use each arrangement of regular polygons to create a semiregular tessellation.

a.

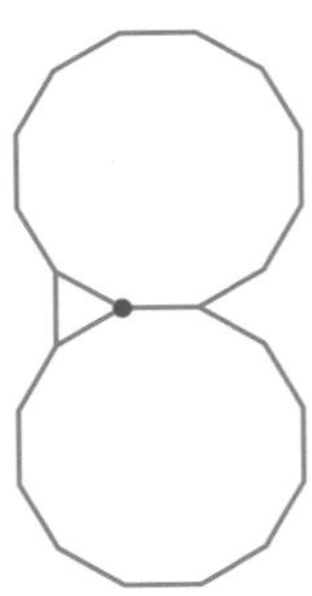

b.

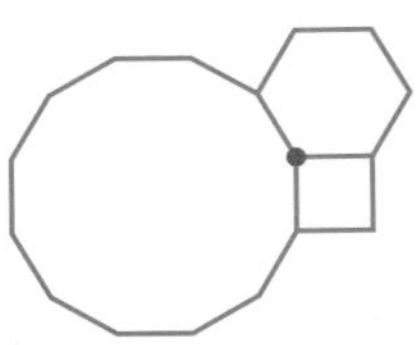

c.

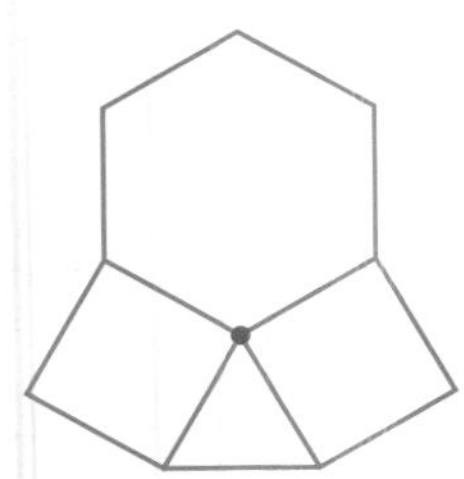

Art LINK

M. C. Escher created works of art by repeating interlocking shapes. He used both regular and nonregular tessellations. He often used what he called *metamorphoses,* in which shapes change into other shapes. Escher used his reptile pattern in many hexagonal tessellations. One of the most famous is entitled simply *Reptiles.*

Hand with reflecting sphere by M. C. Escher ©2004
Cordon Art-Baarn-Holland. All rights reserved.

14. The steps below show the method Escher used to make a bird out of a triangle. Use the bird to create a tessellation.

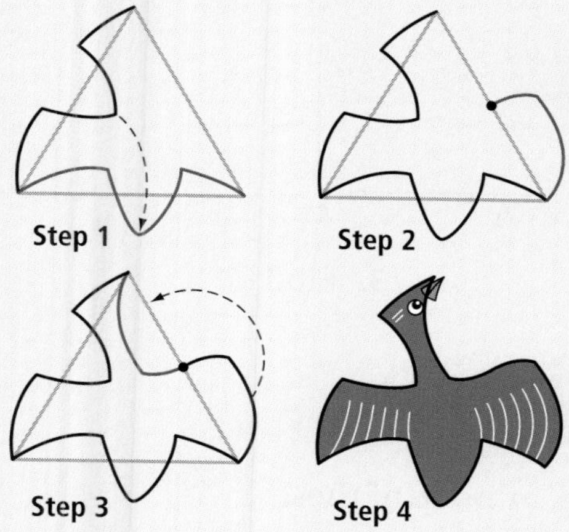

go.hrw.com
Web Extra!
KEYWORD: MT7 Escher

15. Critical Thinking What regular polygon do you think Escher used to begin *Reptiles*?

16. Challenge Create an Escher-like tessellation of your own design.

Symmetry Drawing E25 by M. C. Escher ©2004
Cordon Art-Baarn-Holland. All rights reserved.

Test Prep and Spiral Review

17. Multiple Choice Which of the following shapes will NOT form a regular tessellation?

18. Short Answer Which set of polygons will create a tessellation? Explain.

Write each number in scientific notation. (Lesson 4-4)

19. 3,400,000,000 **20.** 0.00000045 **21.** 28,000

Tell whether the two lines described in each exercise are parallel, perpendicular, or neither. (Lesson 7-5)

22. $\overleftrightarrow{PQ}$ has slope $\frac{3}{2}$. $\overleftrightarrow{EF}$ has slope $-\frac{2}{3}$.

23. $\overleftrightarrow{AB}$ has slope $\frac{9}{11}$. $\overleftrightarrow{CD}$ has slope $-\frac{3}{4}$.

READY TO GO ON?

Quiz for Lessons 7-6 Through 7-9

7-6 Congruence

In the figure, triangle $ABC \cong$ triangle LMN.

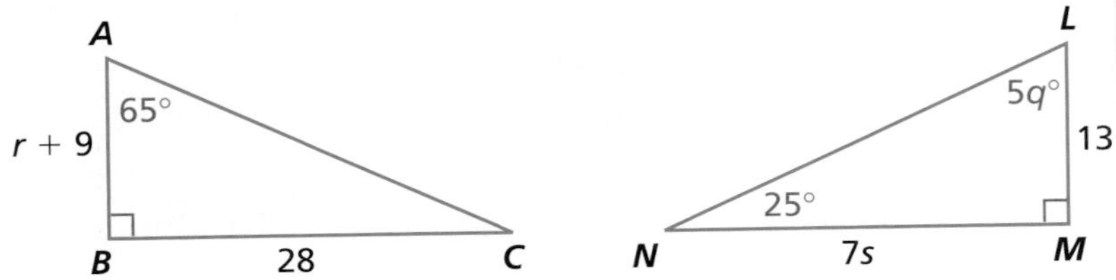

1. Find q.
2. Find r.
3. Find s.

7-7 Transformations

Identify each as a translation, rotation, reflection, or none of these.

4. 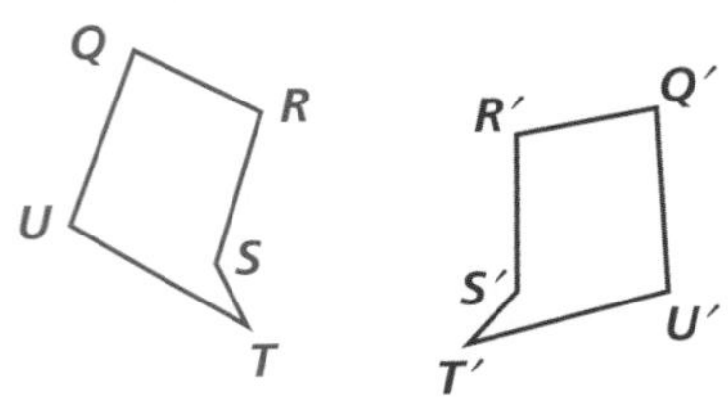

5. 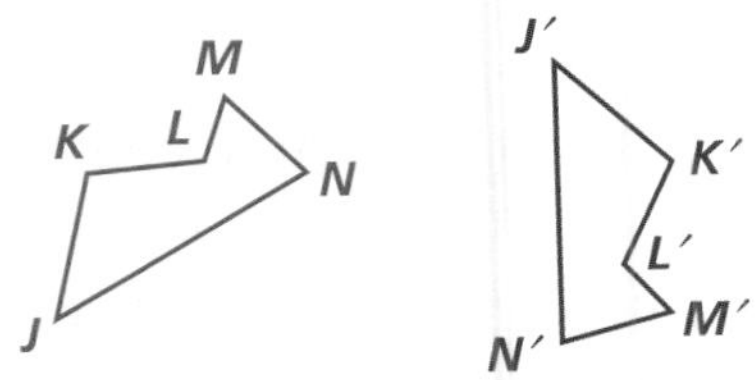

Quadrilateral $ABCD$ has vertices $A(-7, 5)$, $B(-4, 5)$, $C(-2, 3)$, and $D(-6, 2)$. Find the coordinates of the image of each point after each transformation.

6. translation 4 units down, point C
7. reflection across the y-axis, point A

7-8 Symmetry

8. Complete the figure. The dashed line is the line of symmetry.

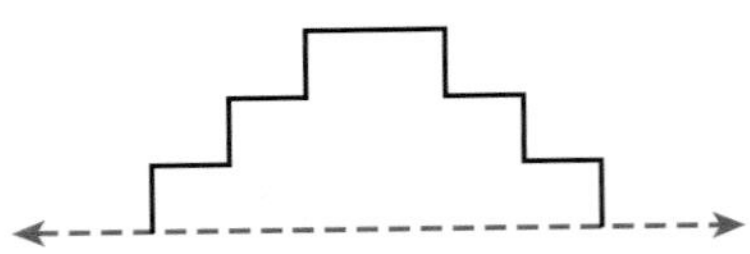

9. Complete the figure with 4-fold rotational symmetry. The point is the center of rotation.

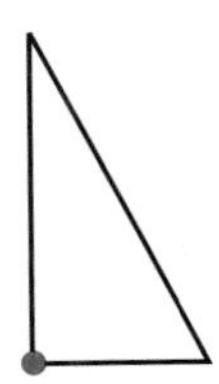

7-9 Tessellations

10. Copy the given figure and use it to create a tessellation.

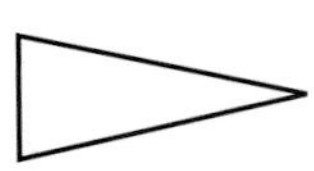

MULTI-STEP TEST PREP

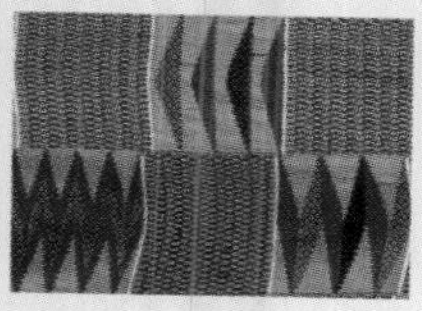

Cloth Creations The Asante people of Ghana are known for weaving Kente cloth, a colorful textile based on repeating geometric patterns. Susan is using a coordinate plane to design her own Kente cloth pattern.

1. Susan starts with triangle *ABC* as shown. Explain how she can use slopes to make sure the triangle is a right triangle.

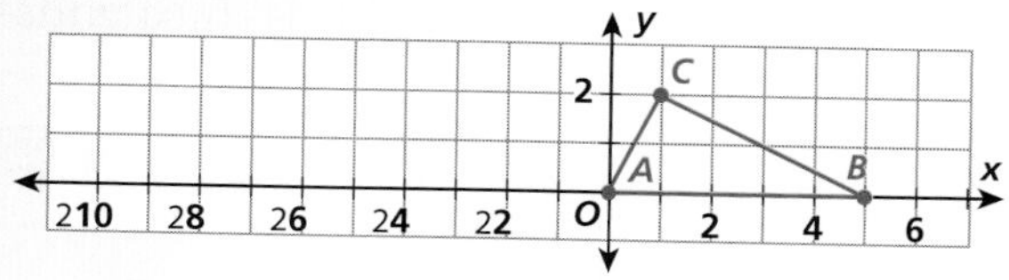

2. To begin the pattern, Susan uses transformations to make a row of triangles that are all congruent to triangle *ABC*. Describe the transformations she should use to make these triangles.

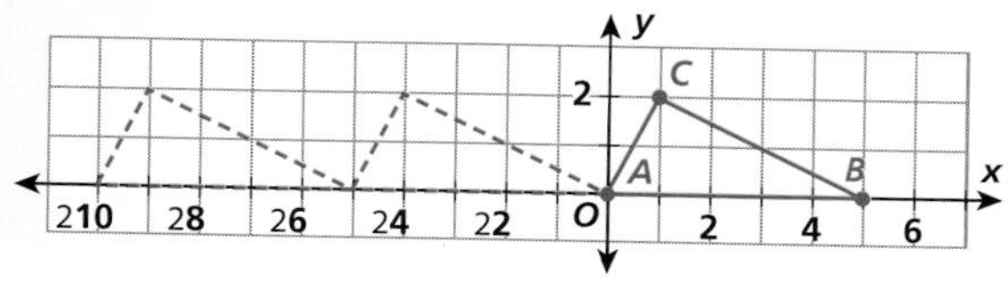

3. Next, she extends the pattern by making additional rows of triangles. The first triangle in Row 2 is shown. Complete the table by writing the coordinates of the top vertex of each triangle in the pattern.

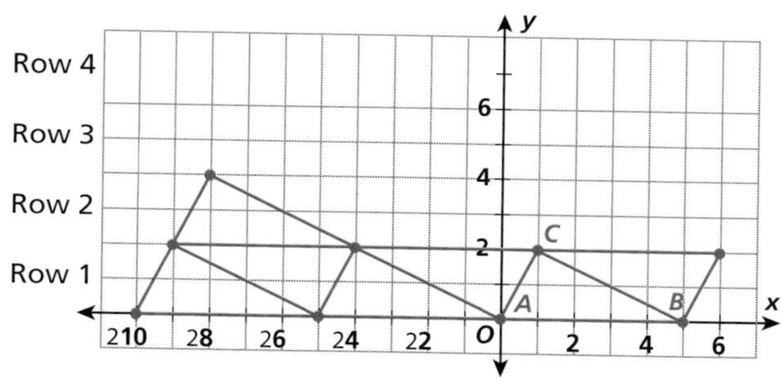

4. What patterns do you notice in the table?

5. Susan's Kente cloth pattern is a tessellation of what types of figures?

Row	Top Vertex of Triangles in Row			
Row 1	(−9, 2)	(−4, 2)	(1, 2)	(6, 2)
Row 2	(−8, 4)			
Row 3				
Row 4				

Game Time

Coloring Tessellations

Two of the three regular tessellations—triangles and squares—can be colored with two colors so that no two polygons that share an edge are the same color. The third—hexagons—requires three colors.

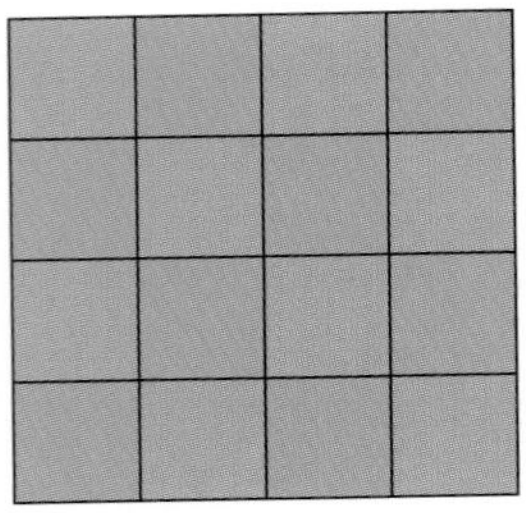
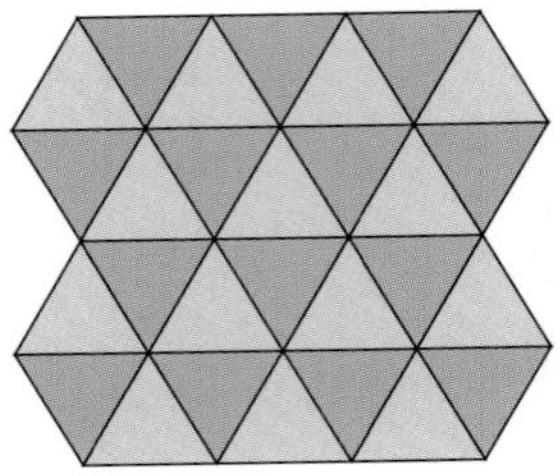
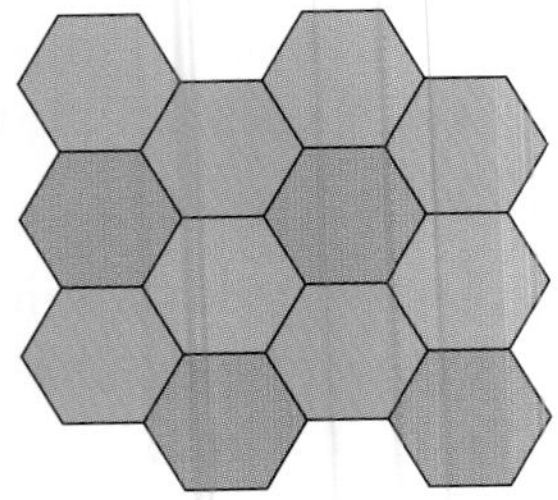

1. Determine if each semiregular tessellation can be colored with two colors. If not, tell the minimum number of colors needed.

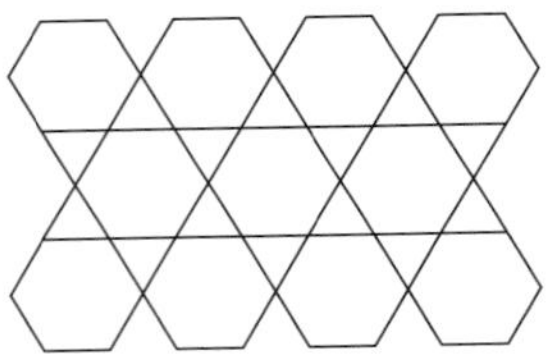
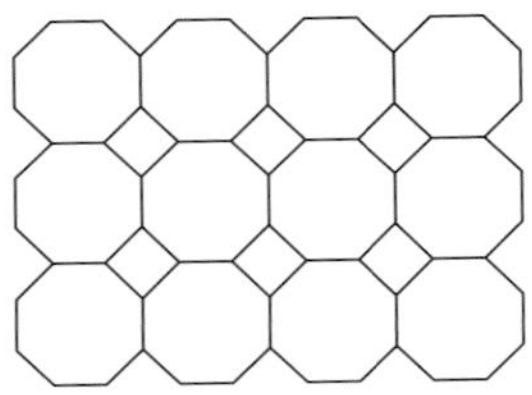
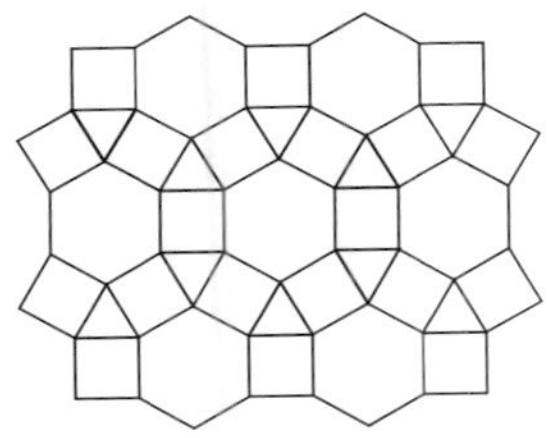

2. Try to write a rule about which tessellations can be colored with two colors.

Polygon Rummy

The object of this game is to create geometric figures. Each card in the deck shows a property of a geometric figure. To create a figure, you must draw a polygon that matches at least three cards in your hand. For example, if you have the cards "quadrilateral," "a pair of parallel sides," and "a right angle," you could draw a rectangle.

A complete set of rules and playing cards is available online.

go.hrw.com
Game Time Extra
KEYWORD: MT7 Games

FOLDNOTES

It's in the Bag!

Materials
- 3 sheets of white paper
- CD or CD-ROM
- scissors
- tape
- markers
- empty CD case

PROJECT

Project CD Geometry

Make your own CD to record important facts about plane geometry.

1. Fold a sheet of paper in half. Place a CD on top of the paper so that it touches the folded edge. Trace around the CD. **Figure A**

2. Cut out the CD shape, being careful to leave the folded edge attached. This will create two paper CDs that are joined together. Cut a hole in the center of each paper CD. **Figure B**

3. Repeat steps 1 and 2 with the other two sheets of paper.

4. Tape the ends of the paper CDs together to make a string of six CDs. **Figure C**

5. Accordion fold the CDs to make a booklet. Write the number and name of the chapter on the top CD. Store the CD booklet in an empty CD case.

A

B

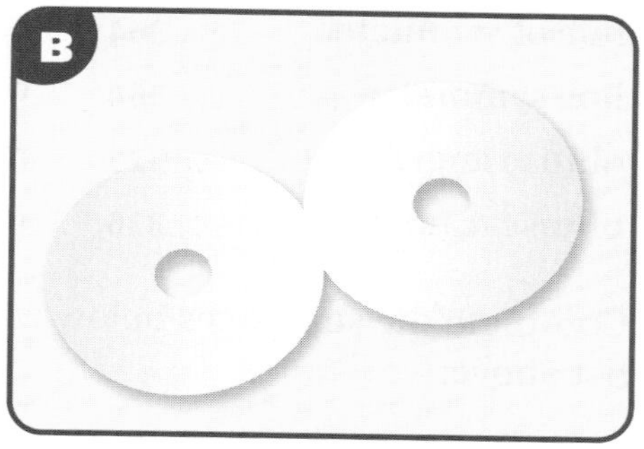

C

Taking Note of the Math

Use the blank pages in the CD booklet to take notes on the chapter. Be sure to include definitions and sample problems that will help you review essential concepts about plane geometry.

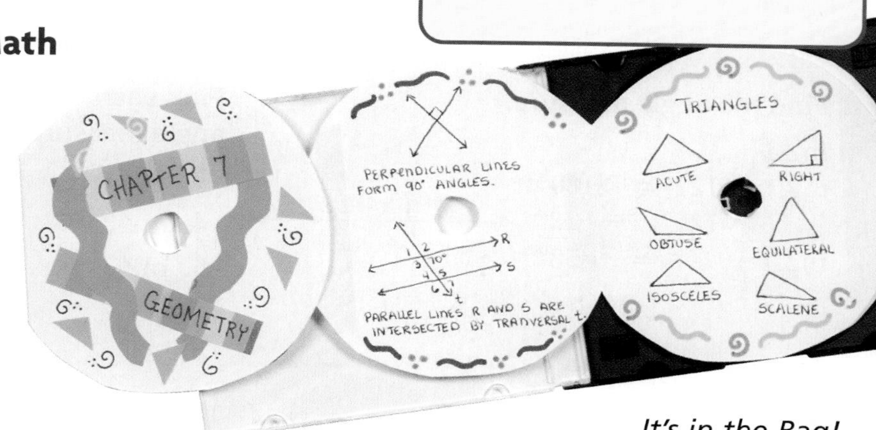

CHAPTER 7

Study Guide: Review

Vocabulary

- acute angle 325
- acute triangle 336
- angle 325
- center of rotation 358
- complementary angles . . 325
- congruent 325
- correspondence 354
- equilateral triangle 337
- image 358
- isosceles triangle 337
- line 324
- line of symmetry 364
- line symmetry 364
- obtuse angle 325
- obtuse triangle 336
- parallel lines 330
- parallelogram 342
- perpendicular lines 330
- plane 324
- point 324
- polygon 341
- ray 324
- rectangle 342
- reflection 358
- regular polygon 342
- regular tessellation 368
- rhombus 342
- right angle 325
- right triangle 336
- rise 347
- rotation 358
- rotational symmetry 365
- run 347
- scalene triangle 337
- segment 324
- slope 347
- square 342
- supplementary angles . . 325
- tessellation 368
- transformation 358
- translation 358
- transversal 330
- trapezoid 342
- Triangle Sum Theorem . 336
- vertical angles 325

Complete the sentences below with vocabulary words from the list above.

1. Lines in the same plane that never meet are called __?__. Lines that intersect at 90° angles are called __?__.

2. A quadrilateral with 4 congruent angles is called a __?__. A quadrilateral with 4 congruent sides is called a __?__.

7-1 Points, Lines, Planes, and Angles (pp. 324–328)

EXAMPLE

- **Find the angle measure.**

$m\angle 1$

$$m\angle 1 + 122° = 180°$$
$$-122° \quad -122°$$
$$m\angle 1 = 58°$$

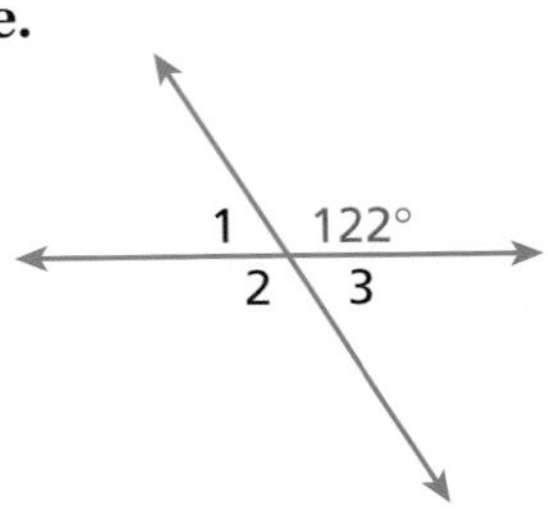

EXERCISES

Find each angle measure.

3. $m\angle 1$
4. $m\angle 2$
5. $m\angle 3$

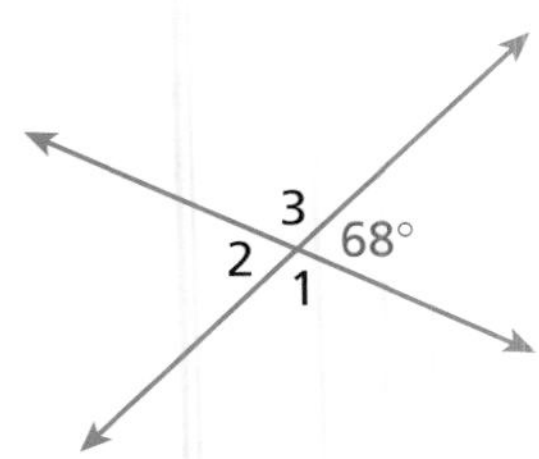

7-2 Parallel and Perpendicular Lines (pp. 330–333)

EXAMPLE

Line $j \parallel$ line k. Find each angle measure.

- $m\angle 1$

  $m\angle 1 = 143°$

- $m\angle 2$

$$\begin{aligned} m\angle 2 + 143° &= 180° \\ -143° \quad & \quad -143° \\ m\angle 2 &= 37° \end{aligned}$$

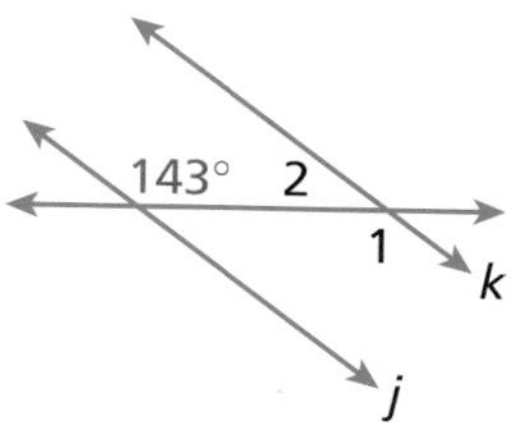

EXERCISES

Line $p \parallel$ line q. Find each angle measure.

6. $m\angle 1$

7. $m\angle 2$

8. $m\angle 3$

9. $m\angle 4$

10. $m\angle 5$

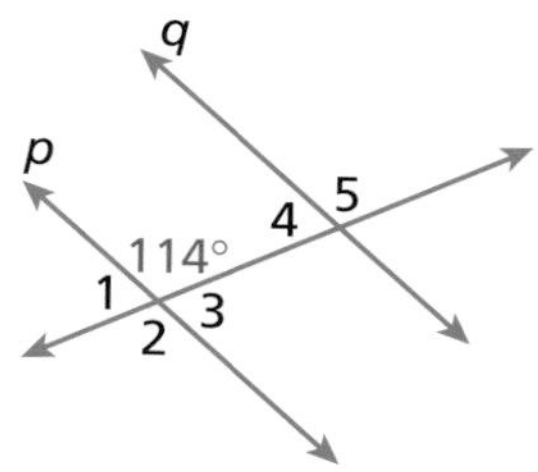

7-3 Angles in Triangles (pp. 336–340)

EXAMPLE

- **Find $n°$.**

$$\begin{aligned} n° + 50° + 90° &= 180° \\ n° + 140° &= 180° \\ -140° \quad & \quad -140° \\ n° &= 40° \end{aligned}$$

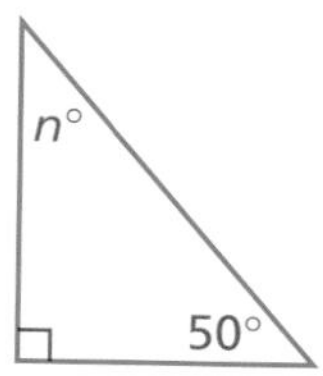

EXERCISES

11. Find $m°$.

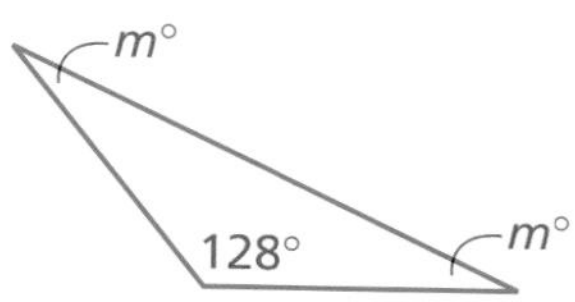

7-4 Classifying Polygons (pp. 341–345)

EXAMPLE

- **Find the angle measures in a regular 12-gon.**

$12x° = 180°(12 - 2)$

$12x° = 180°(10)$

$12x° = 1800°$

$x° = 150°$

EXERCISES

Find the angle measures in each regular polygon.

12. a regular octagon

13. a regular 11-gon

7-5 Coordinate Geometry (pp. 347–351)

EXAMPLE

- **Graph the quadrilateral with the given vertices. Give all the names that apply.**

  $D(-2, 1)$, $E(2, 3)$, $F(3, 1)$, $G(-1, -1)$

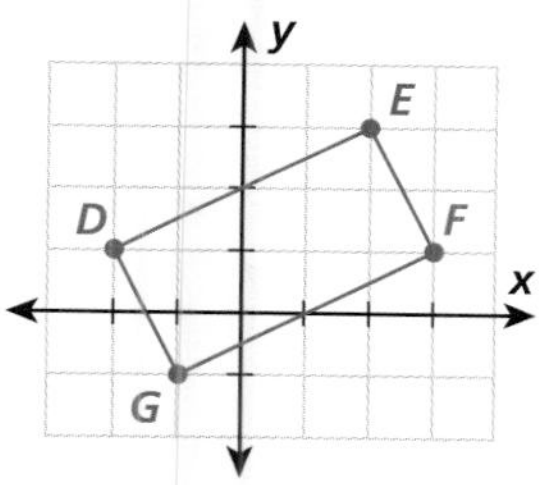

$\overline{DE} \parallel \overline{FG}$

$\overline{EF} \parallel \overline{GD}$

$\overline{DE} \perp \overline{EF}$

parallelogram, rectangle

EXERCISES

Graph the quadrilaterals with the given vertices. Give all the names that apply.

14. $Q(2, 0)$, $R(-1, 1)$, $S(3, 3)$, $T(8, 3)$

15. $K(2, 3)$, $L(3, 0)$, $M(2, -3)$, $N(1, 0)$

16. $W(2, 2)$, $X(2, -2)$, $Y(-1, -3)$, $Z(-1, 1)$

7-6 Congruence (pp. 354–357)

EXAMPLE

■ Triangle $ABC \cong$ triangle FDE. Find x.

$$\begin{aligned} x - 4 &= 4 \\ +4 & +4 \\ x &= 8 \end{aligned}$$

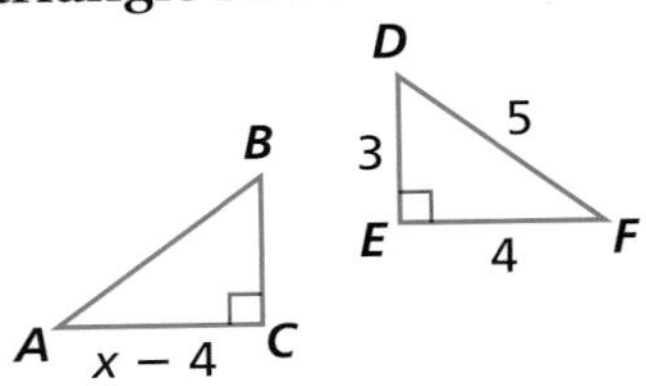

EXERCISES

Triangle $JQZ \cong$ triangle VTZ.

17. Find x.

18. Find t.

19. Find q.

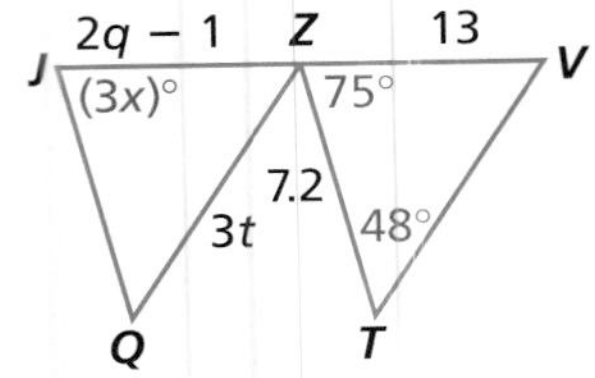

7-7 Transformations (pp. 358–361)

EXAMPLE

■ Draw the image of a triangle with vertices $(-2, 2)$, $(1, 1)$, and $(-3, -2)$ after a 180° rotation around $(0, 0)$.

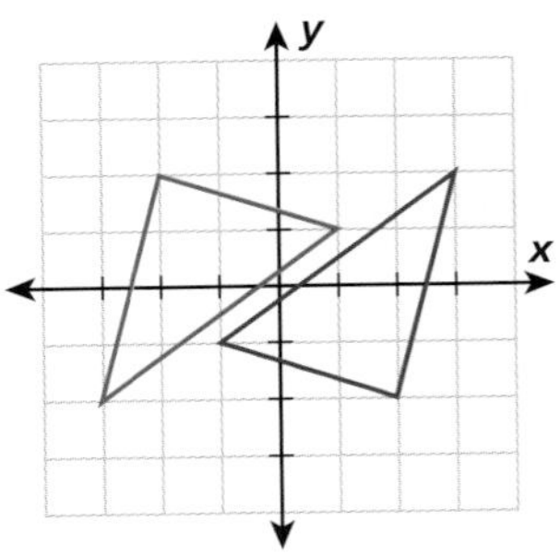

EXERCISES

Draw the image of a triangle ABC with vertices $(1, 1)$, $(1, 4)$, and $(3, 1)$ after each transformation.

20. reflection across the x-axis

21. translation 5 units left

22. 180° rotation around $(0, 0)$

7-8 Symmetry (pp. 364–367)

EXAMPLE

■ Complete the figure. The dashed line is the line of symmetry.

EXERCISES

Complete each figure.

23. 6-fold

24.

25.

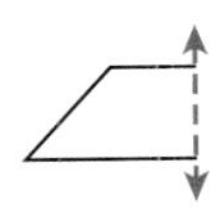

7-9 Tessellations (pp. 368–371)

EXAMPLE

■ Create a tessellation with the figure.

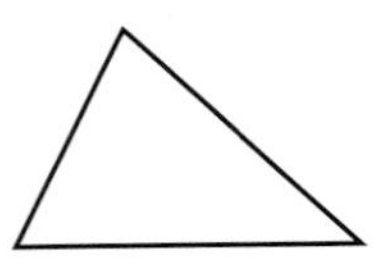

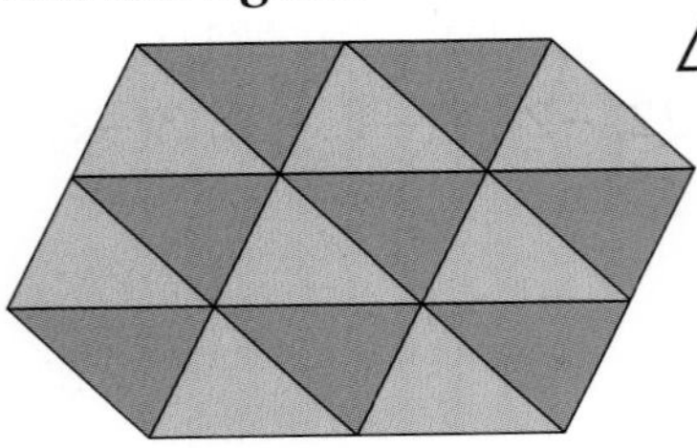

EXERCISES

Create a tessellation with each figure.

26.

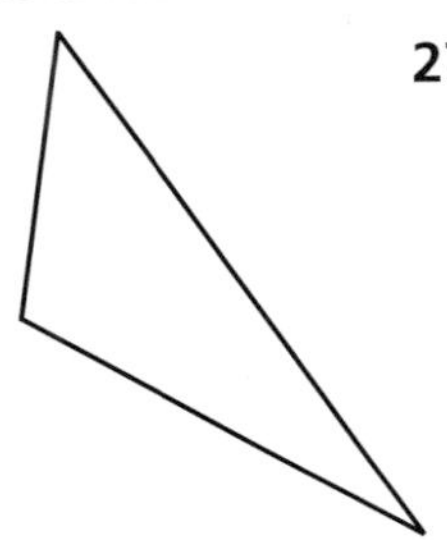

27.

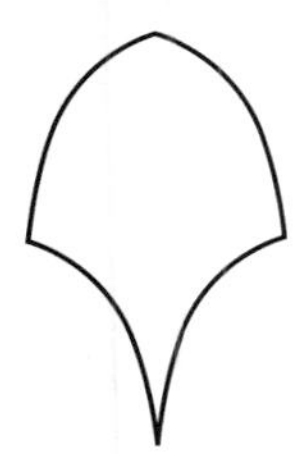

CHAPTER TEST

In the figure, line $m \parallel$ line n.

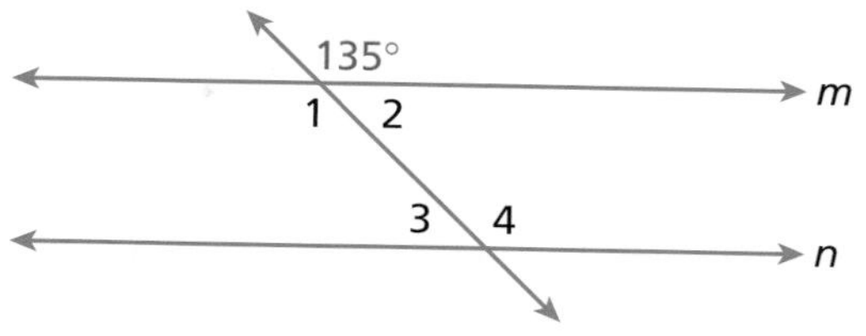

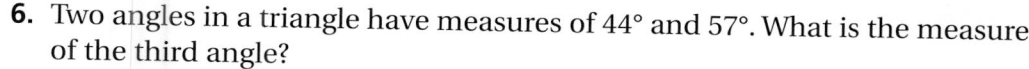

1. Name two pairs of supplementary angles.

2. Find the m∠1.

3. Find the m∠2.

4. Find the m∠3.

5. Find the m∠4.

6. Two angles in a triangle have measures of 44° and 57°. What is the measure of the third angle?

7. What are the measures of the congruent angles in an isosceles triangle if the measure of the third angle is 102°?

Give all of the names that apply to each figure.

8.

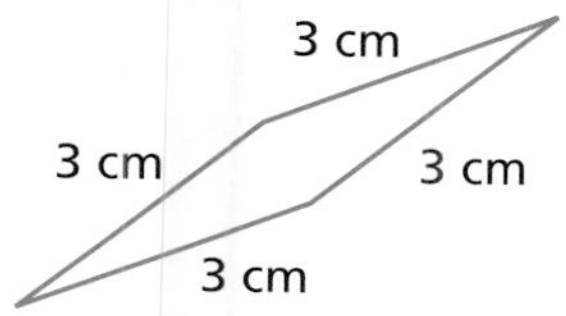

9.

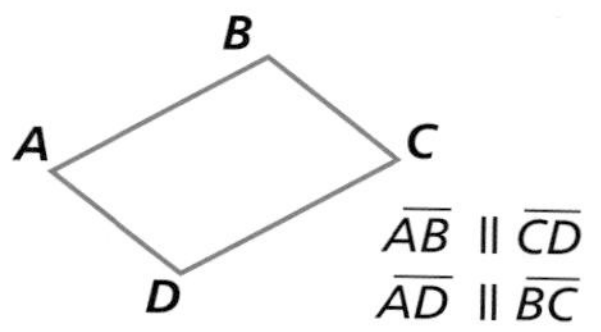

Graph the quadrilateral with the given vertices. Give all of the names that apply to each quadrilateral.

10. $A(3,4)$, $B(8,4)$, $C(5,0)$, $D(0,0)$

11. $K(-4,0)$, $L(-2,5)$, $M(2,5)$, $N(4,0)$

Find the coordinates of the missing vertex.

12. rectangle $PQRS$ with $P(0,0)$, $Q(0,4)$, $R(4,4)$

In the figure, quadrilateral $ABCD \cong$ quadrilateral $LMNO$.

13. Find m.

14. Find n.

15. Find p.

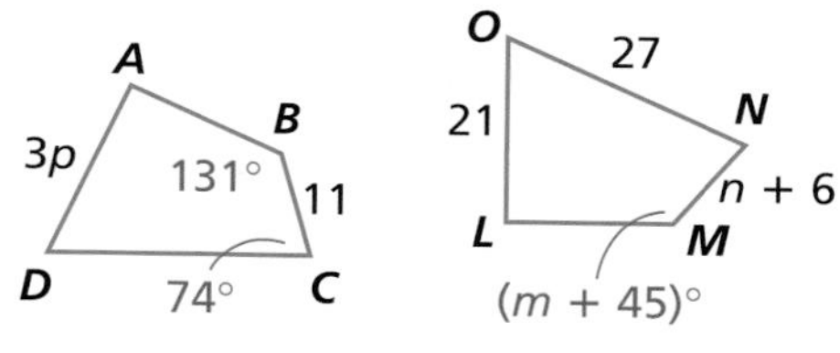

Pentagon $ABCDE$ has vertices $A(1, -2)$, $B(3, -1)$, $C(7, -2)$, $D(6, -4)$, and $E(2, -5)$. Find the coordinates of the image of each point after each transformation.

16. rotation 90° around the origin, point E

17. reflection across the x-axis, point C

18. translation 6 units up, point B

19. reflection across the y-axis, point A

20. Complete the figure. The dashed line is the line of symmetry.

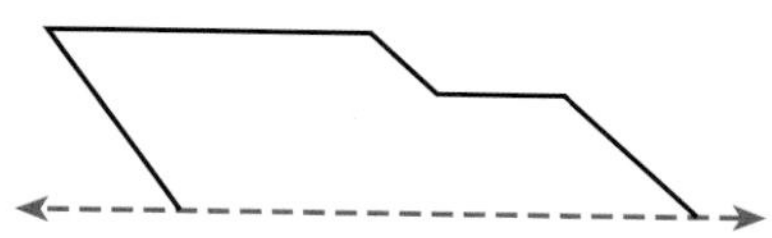

TEST TACKLER

Standardized Test Strategies

Extended Response: Write Extended Responses

Extended response test items often consist of multi-step problems to evaluate your understanding of a math concept. Extended response questions are scored using a 4-point scoring rubric.

Scoring Rubric

4 points: The student answers all parts of the question correctly, shows all work, and provides a complete and correct explanation.

3 points: The student answers all parts of the question, shows all work, and provides a complete explanation that demonstrates understanding, but the student makes minor errors in computation.

2 points: The student does not answer all parts of the question but shows all work and provides a complete and correct explanation for the parts answered, or the student correctly answers all parts of the question but does not show all work or does not provide an explanation.

1 point: The student gives incorrect answers and shows little or no work or explanation, or the student does not follow directions.

0 points: The student gives no response.

EXAMPLE 1

Extended Response Julianna bought a shirt marked down 20%. She had a coupon for an additional 20% off the sale price. Is this the same as getting 40% off the regular price? Explain your reasoning.

4-point response:

No, the prices are not the same. Suppose the shirt originally cost \$40.

20% off a 20% markdown: $\$40 \times 20\% = \$8$; $\$40 - \$8 = \$32$;
$\$32 \times 20\% = \$6.40$; $\$32 - \$6.40 = \underline{\$25.60}$

40% off: $\$40 \times 40\% = \$16$; $\$40 - \$16 = \underline{\$24}$

The student answers the question correctly and shows all work.

3-point response:

Yes, it is the same. If the shirt originally cost \$25, it would cost \$15 after taking 20% off of a 20% discount. A 40% discount off \$20 is \$15.

Shirt original price = \$25	
Shirt at 20% off = \$20	$\$25 \times 20\% = \$5$; $\$25 - \$5 = \$20$
Shirt at 20% off sales price = \$15	$\$20 \times 20\% = \$4$; $\$20 - \$4 = \$15$
Shirt at 40% off = \$15	$\$25 \times 40\% = \$10$; $\$25 - \$10 = \$15$

The student makes a minor computation error that results in an incorrect answer.

2-point response:

No, it is not the same. A \$30 shirt with 20% off and then an additional 20% off is \$6. A \$30 shirt at 40% off is \$12.

The student makes major computation errors and does not show all work.

1-point response:

It is the same.

The student shows no work and has the wrong answer.

HOT TIP! To receive full credit, make sure all parts of the problem are answered. Be sure to show all of your work and to write a neat and clear explanation.

Read each test item and answer the questions that follow.

Item A
Janell has two job offers. Job A pays $500 per week. Job B pays $200 per week plus 15% commission on her sales. She expects to make $7500 in sales per month. Which job pays better? Explain your reasoning.

1. A student wrote this response:

Job A pays better.

What score should the student's response receive? Explain your reasoning.

2. What additional information, if any, should the student's response include in order to receive full credit?

3. Add to the response so that it receives a score of 4-points.

4. How much would Janell have to make in sales per month for job A and job B to pay the same amount?

Item B
A new MP3 player normally costs $97.99. This week, it is on sale for 15% off its regular price. In addition to this, Jasmine receives an employee discount of 20% off the sale price. Excluding sales tax, what percent of the original price will Jasmine pay for the MP3 player?

5. What information needs to be included in a response to receive full credit?

6. Write a response that would receive full credit.

Item C
Three houses were originally purchased for $125,000. After each year, the value of each house either increased or decreased. Which house had the least value after the third year? What was the value of that house? Explain your reasoning.

		Percent Change in Value		
House	Original Cost ($)	Year 1	Year 2	Year 3
A	125,000	1%	1%	1%
B	125,000	4%	−2%	−1%
C	125,000	3%	−2%	2%

7. A student wrote this response:

House A increased 3% over three years. House B increased 1% over three years. House C increased 3% over three years. So, House B had the least value after the third year. Its value increased 1% of $125,000, or $1250, for a total value of $126,250.

What score should the student's response receive? Explain your reasoning.

8. What additional information, if any, should the student's response include in order to receive full credit?

Item D
Kara is trying to save $4500 to buy a used car. She has $3000 in an account that earns a yearly simple interest of 5%. Will she have enough money in her account after 3 years to buy a car? If not, how much more money will she need? Explain your reasoning.

9. What information needs to be included in a response to receive full credit?

10. Write a response that would receive full credit.

STANDARDIZED TEST PREP

go.hrw.com
State Test Practice Online
KEYWORD: MT7 TestPrep

Cumulative Assessment, Chapters 1–7

Multiple Choice

1. Which angle is a right angle?

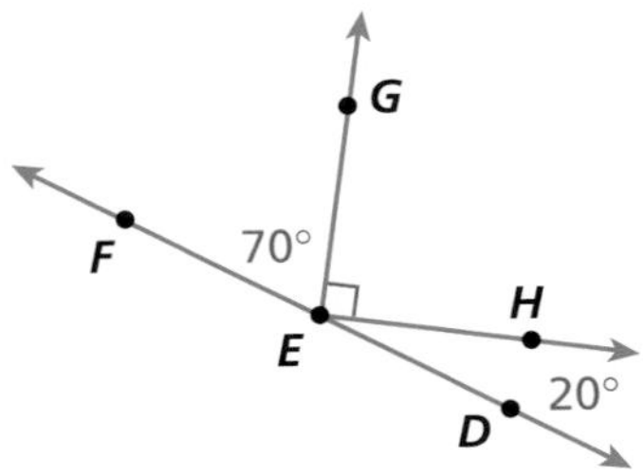

Ⓐ ∠FED
Ⓑ ∠FEG
Ⓒ ∠GEH
Ⓓ ∠GED

2. A jeweler buys a diamond for \$68 and resells it for \$298. What is the percent increase to the nearest percent?

Ⓕ 3%
Ⓖ 33%
Ⓗ 138%
Ⓙ 338%

3. A grocery store sells one dozen ears of white corn for \$2.40. What is the unit price for one ear of corn?

Ⓐ 0.05/ear of corn
Ⓑ \$0.20/ear of corn
Ⓒ \$1.30/ear of corn
Ⓓ \$2.40/ear of corn

4. The people of Ireland drink the most milk in the world. All together, they drink more than 602,000,000 quarts each year. What is this number written in scientific notation?

Ⓕ 60.2×10^5
Ⓖ 602×10^6
Ⓗ 6.02×10^8
Ⓙ 6.02×10^9

5. Cara is making a model of a car that is 14 feet long. What other information is needed to find the length of the model?

Ⓐ Car's width
Ⓑ Car's speed
Ⓒ Scale factor
Ⓓ Car's height

6. For which equation is the point a solution to the equation?

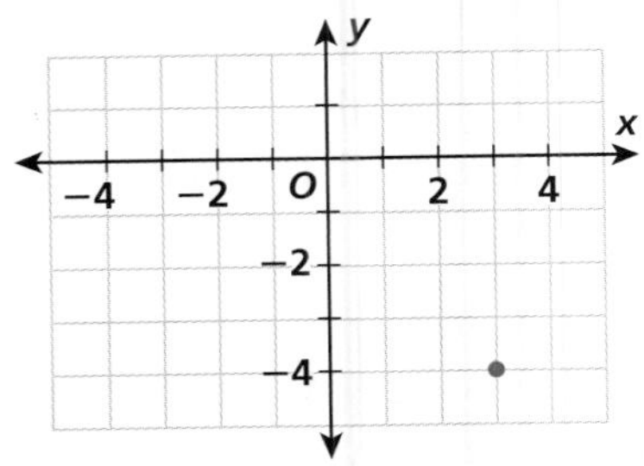

Ⓕ $y = 2x + 1$
Ⓖ $y = 2x - 2$
Ⓗ $y = -x + 1$
Ⓙ $y = -2x + 2$

7. What is q in the acute triangle?

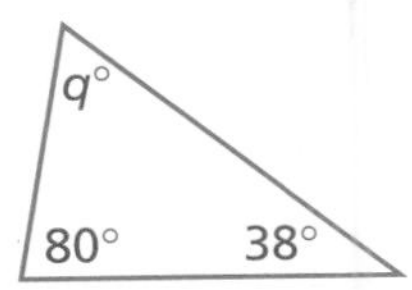

Ⓐ 62
Ⓑ 72
Ⓒ 118
Ⓓ 128

8. Which expression represents "twice the difference of a number and 5"?

Ⓕ $2(x + 5)$
Ⓖ $2x - 5$
Ⓗ $2(x - 5)$
Ⓙ $2x + 5$

9. For which equation is $x = -1$ the solution?

Ⓐ $3x + 8 = 11$
Ⓑ $8 - x = 9$
Ⓒ $-3x + 8 = 5$
Ⓓ $8 + x = 9$

10. Marcus bought a shirt that was on sale for 20% off its regular price. If Marcus paid $20 for the shirt, what what its regular price?

(F) $25 (H) $16

(G) $40 (J) $30

HOT TIP! **Use logic to eliminate answer choices that are incorrect. This will help you to make an educated guess if you are having trouble with the question.**

Gridded Response

Use the following figure for items 11 and 12. Line *p* is parallel to line *q*.

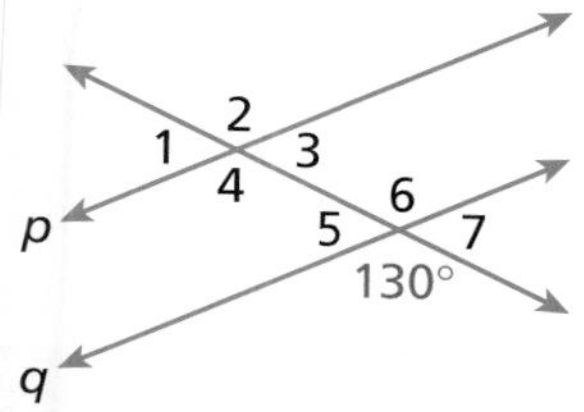

11. What is the measure of $\angle 4$, in degrees?

12. What is the sum of the measures of $\angle 2$ and $\angle 6$, in degrees?

13. Maryann bought a purse on sale for 25% off. She paid $36 for the purse before tax. How much did the purse cost originally?

14. What is the value of the expression $-2xy + y^2$, when $x = -1$ and $y = 4$?

15. A parallelogram has vertices at $A(-2, 4)$, $B(-1, -1)$, $C(1, 0)$, and $D(0, 5)$. What is the *x*-coordinate of *B* after the parallelogram is reflected over the *y*-axis?

16. Guillermo invests $180 at a 4% simple interest rate for 6 months. How much money will Guillermo earn in interest? Write your answer as a decimal to the nearest tenth.

Short Response

17. Triangle *ABC*, with vertices $A(2, 3)$, $B(4, -5)$, $C(6, 8)$, is reflected across the *x*-axis to form triangle $A'B'C'$.

    a. On a coordinate grid, draw and label triangle *ABC* and triangle $A'B'C'$.

    b. Give the new coordinates for triangle $A'B'C'$.

18. Complete the table to show the number of diagonals for the polygons with the numbers of sides listed.

Number of Sides	Number of Diagonals
3	0
4	
5	
6	
7	
n	

Extended Response

19. Four people are introduced to each other at a party, and they all shake hands.

    a. Explain in words how the diagram can be used to determine the number of handshakes exchanged at the party.

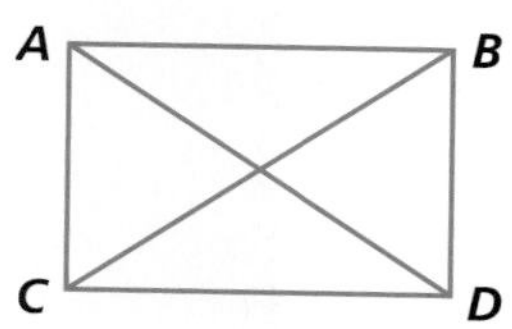

    b. How many handshakes are exchanged?

    c. Suppose that six people were introduced to each other at a party. Draw a diagram similar to the one shown that could be used to determine the number of handshakes exchanged.

CHAPTER

8

Perimeter, Area, and Volume

8A Perimeter and Area

8-1 Perimeter and Area of Rectangles and Parallelograms

LAB Explore the Effects of Changing Dimensions

8-2 Perimeter and Area of Triangles and Trapezoids

LAB Approximate *Pi* by Measuring

8-3 Circles

8B Three-Dimensional Geometry

LAB Construct Nets

8-4 Drawing Three-Dimensional Figures

LAB Find Volume of Prisms and Cylinders

8-5 Volume of Prisms and Cylinders

LAB Find Volume of Pyramids and Cones

8-6 Volume of Pyramids and Cones

LAB Find Surface Area of Prisms and Cylinders

8-7 Surface Area of Prisms and Cylinders

LAB Find Surface Area of Pyramids

8-8 Surface Area of Pyramids and Cones

8-9 Spheres

8-10 Scaling Three-Dimensional Figures

Ext Symmetry in Three Dimensions

MULTI-STEP TEST PREP

go.hrw.com
Chapter Project Online
KEYWORD: MT7 Ch8

Mystery Solid	Front View	Side View	Top View
A	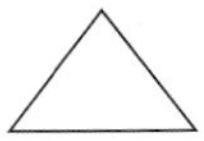	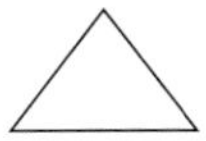	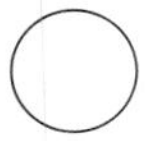
B			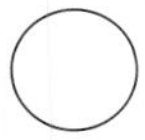
C		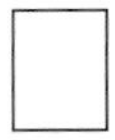	

Career ***Surgeon***

Today, some surgeons perform specialized operations known as laser surgery. With many laser surgeries, surgeons cannot actually see the three-dimensional area where they are operating; instead, they must rely on what they can see in two-dimensional images projected onto a screen to guide them. See if you can identify each three-dimensional "mystery solid" based on the two-dimensional views in the table.

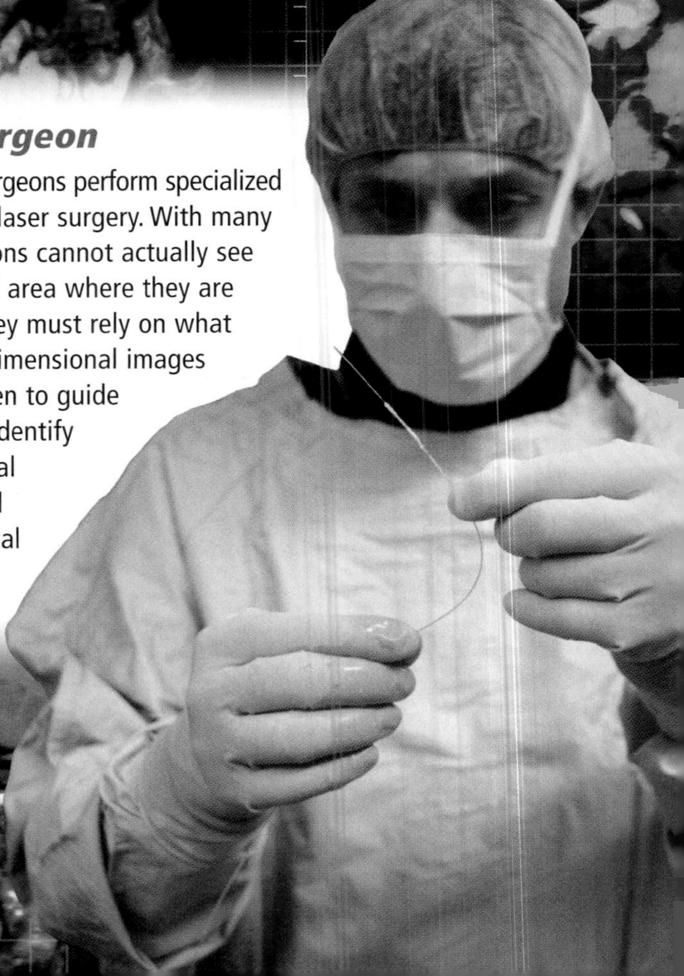

ARE YOU READY?

Vocabulary

Choose the best term from the list to complete each sentence.

decimal
denominator
fraction
tenths
hundredths
numerator

1. A(n) __?__ is a number that represents a part of a whole.
2. A(n) __?__ is another way of writing a fraction.
3. To multiply 7 by the fraction $\frac{2}{3}$, multiply 7 by the __?__ of the fraction and then divide the result by the __?__ of the fraction.
4. To round 7.836 to the nearest tenth, look at the digit in the __?__ place.

Complete these exercises to review skills you will need for this chapter.

Square and Cube Numbers

Evaluate.

5. 16^2 **6.** 9^3 **7.** $(4.1)^2$ **8.** $(0.5)^3$

9. $\left(\frac{1}{4}\right)^2$ **10.** $\left(\frac{2}{5}\right)^2$ **11.** $\left(\frac{1}{2}\right)^3$ **12.** $\left(\frac{2}{3}\right)^3$

Multiply with Fractions

Multiply.

13. $\frac{1}{2}(8)(10)$ **14.** $\frac{1}{2}(3)(5)$ **15.** $\frac{1}{3}(9)(12)$ **16.** $\frac{1}{3}(4)(11)$

17. $\frac{1}{2}(8^2)16$ **18.** $\frac{1}{2}(5^2)24$ **19.** $\frac{1}{2}(6)(3 + 9)$ **20.** $\frac{1}{2}(5)(7 + 4)$

Multiply with Decimals

Multiply. Write each answer to the nearest tenth.

21. $2(3.14)(12)$ **22.** $3.14(5^2)$ **23.** $3.14(4^2)(7)$ **24.** $3.14(2.3)^2(5)$

Multiply with Fractions and Decimals

Multiply. Write each answer to the nearest tenth.

25. $\frac{1}{3}(3.14)(5^2)(7)$ **26.** $\frac{1}{3}\left(3.14\right)(5^3)$

27. $\frac{1}{3}(3.14)(3.2)^2(2)$ **28.** $\frac{4}{3}(3.14)(2.7)^3$

29. $\frac{1}{5}\left(\frac{22}{7}\right)(4^2)(5)$ **30.** $\frac{4}{11}\left(\frac{22}{7}\right)(3.2^3)$

31. $\frac{1}{2}\left(\frac{22}{7}\right)(1.7)^2(4)$ **32.** $\frac{7}{11}\left(\frac{22}{7}\right)(9.5)^3$

CHAPTER 8

Study Guide: Preview

Study Guide: Preview

Where You've Been

Previously, you

- found the perimeter and area of polygons.
- sketched a three-dimensional figure when given the top, side, and front views.
- found the volume of prisms and cylinders.

In This Chapter

You will study

- describing the effects on perimeter and area when the dimensions of a figure change proportionally.
- drawing three-dimensional figures from different perspectives.
- describing the effect on volume when the dimensions of a solid change proportionally.
- finding the surface area and volume of various solids.

Where You're Going

You can use the skills learned in this chapter

- to determine the amount of materials needed to build a fence.
- to determine the amount of paint needed to paint a wall.

Key Vocabulary/Vocabulario

circle	círculo
circumference	circunferincia
cone	cono
cylinder	cilindro
diameter	diámetro
perimeter	perímetro
prism	prisma
pyramid	pirámide
sphere	esfera
surface area	área total

Vocabulary Connections

To become familiar with some of the vocabulary terms in the chapter, consider the following. You may refer to the chapter, the glossary, or a dictionary if you like.

1. The word **circumference** contains the prefix *circum-*, which means "around." What do you suppose the circumference of a circle is?
2. The Greek prefix *peri-* means "around," and the root *meter* means "means of measuring." What do you suppose **perimeter** means?
3. The Greek prefix *dia-* means "across." What do you suppose the **diameter** of a circle is?

Reading and Writing Math

Study Strategy: Concept Map

Concept maps are visual tools for organizing information. A concept map shows how key concepts are related and can help you summarize and analyze information in lessons or chapters.

Create a Concept Map

1. Give your concept map a title.
2. Identify the main idea of your concept map.
3. List the key concepts.
4. Link the concepts to show the relationships between the concepts and the main idea.

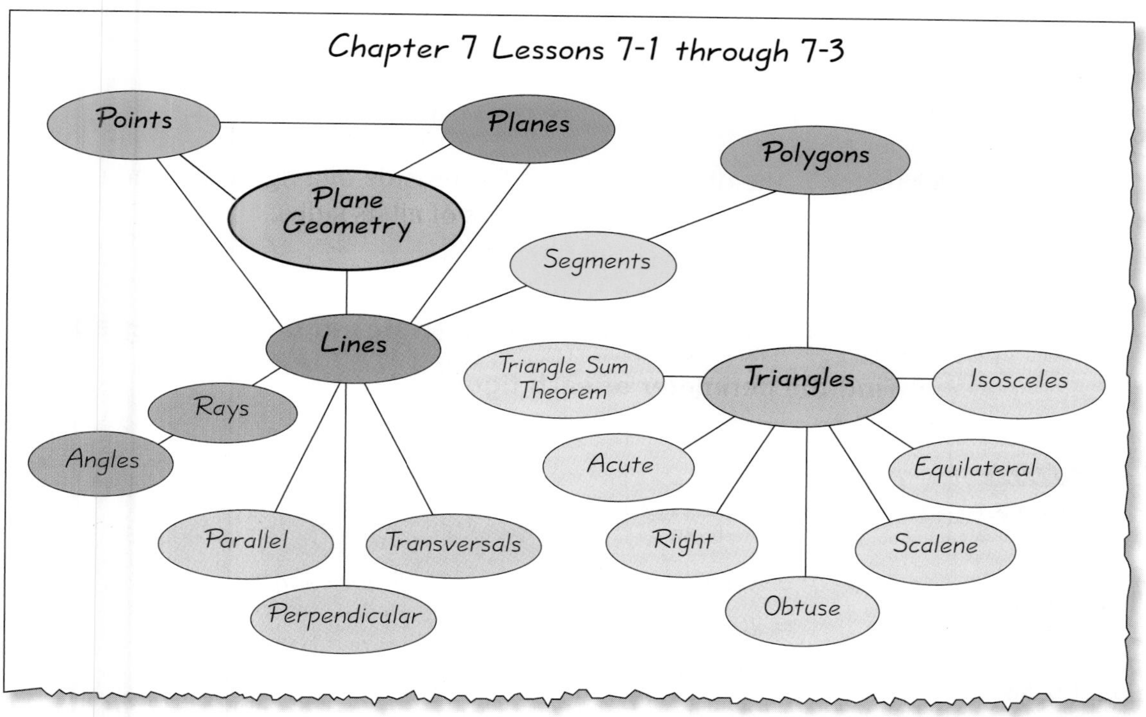

Try This

1. Complete the concept map above to include Lessons 7-4 and 7-5.
2. Create your own concept map for the concept of transformations.

8-1 Perimeter & Area of Rectangles & Parallelograms

Learn to find the perimeter and area of rectangles and parallelograms.

Vocabulary

perimeter

area

The NAMES Project Foundation's AIDS Memorial Quilt is a tribute to those who have died of AIDS. The quilt contains more than 82,800 names on more than 44,000 rectangular panels that measure 3 ft by 6 ft. To find the size of the entire quilt, you need to be able to find the perimeter and area of a rectangle.

Any side of a rectangle or parallelogram can be chosen as the base. The height is measured along a line perpendicular to the base.

Rectangle

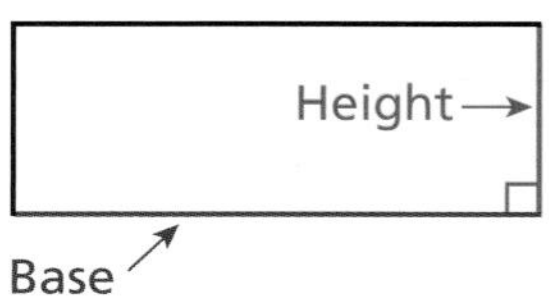

Parallelogram

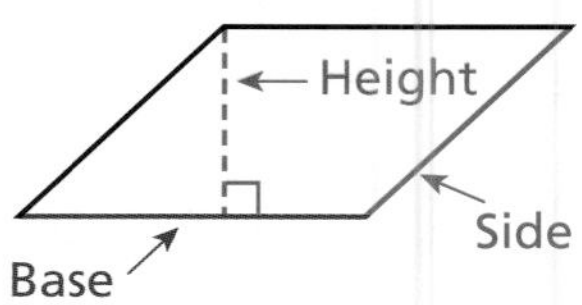

Perimeter is the distance around the outside of a figure. To find the perimeter of a figure, add the lengths of all its sides.

EXAMPLE 1 Finding the Perimeter of Rectangles and Parallelograms

Find the perimeter of each figure.

A

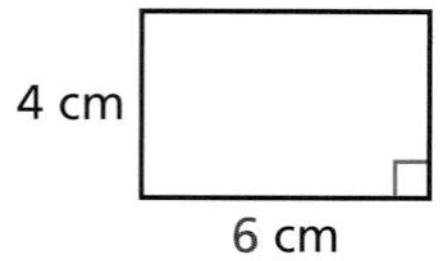

$P = 6 + 6 + 4 + 4$ *Add all side lengths.*

$= 20$ cm

or $P = 2b + 2h$ *Perimeter of rectangle*

$= 2(6) + 2(4)$ *Substitute 6 for b and 4 for h.*

$= 12 + 8 = 20$ cm

B

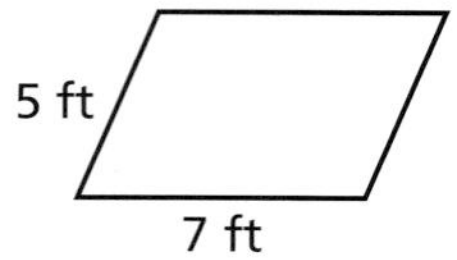

$P = 5 + 5 + 7 + 7 = 24$ ft *Add all side lengths.*

Caution!

When referring to the measurements of a rectangle, the terms *length* (ℓ) and *width* (w) are sometimes used in place of *base* (b) and *height* (h). So the formula for the perimeter of a rectangle can be written as $P = 2b + 2h = 2\ell + 2w = 2(\ell + w)$.

Area is the number of square units in a figure. A parallelogram can be cut and the cut piece shifted to form a rectangle with the same base length and height as the original parallelogram. So a parallelogram has the same area as a rectangle with the same base length and height.

Helpful Hint

The formula for the area of a rectangle can also be written as $A = \ell w$.

AREA OF RECTANGLES AND PARALLELOGRAMS

Words	Numbers		Formula
The area A of a rectangle or parallelogram is the base length b times the height h.	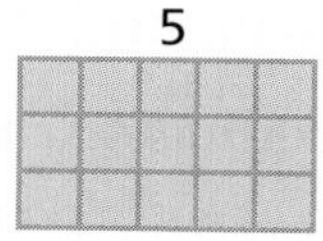 $5 \cdot 3 = 15$ units^2 **Rectangle**	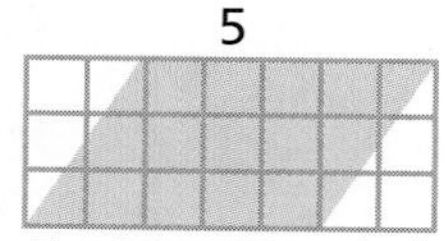 $5 \cdot 3 = 15$ units^2 **Parallelogram**	$A = bh$

EXAMPLE 2 Using a Graph to Find Area

Graph and find the area of each figure with the given vertices.

A $(-3, -2), (3, -2), (3, 1), (-3, 1)$

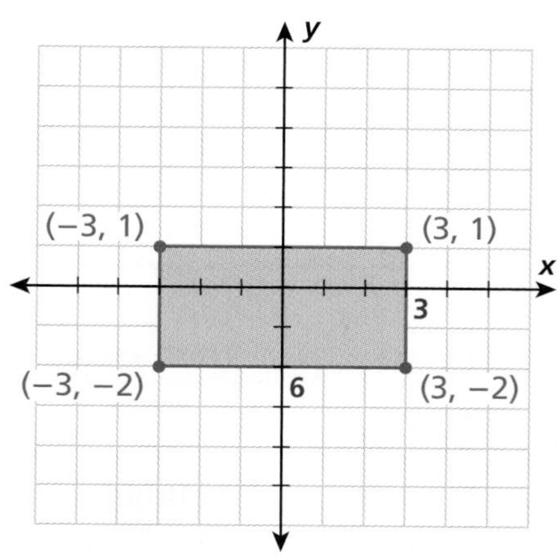

$A = bh$ *Area of rectangle*

$= 6 \cdot 3$ *Substitute 6 for b and 3 for h.*

$= 18$ units^2

Graph and find the area of each figure with the given vertices.

B $(-4, -4), (1, -4), (3, 0), (-2, 0)$

> **Caution!**
> The height of a parallelogram is not the length of its slanted side. The height of a figure is always perpendicular to the base.

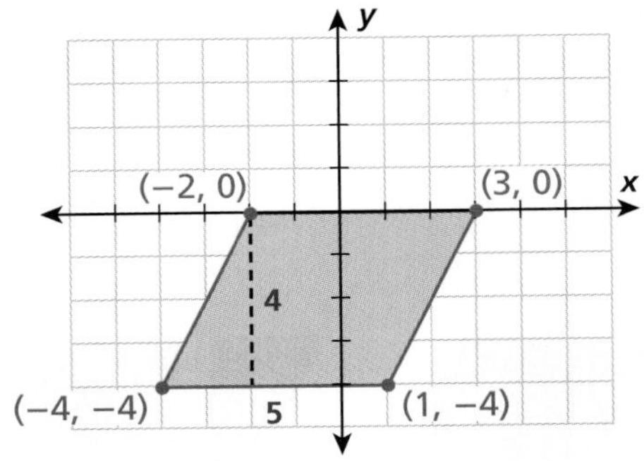

$A = bh$ *Area of rectangle*

$= 5 \cdot 4$ *Substitute 5 for b and 4 for h.*

$= 20 \text{ units}^2$

EXAMPLE 3 Finding Area and Perimeter of a Composite Figure

Find the perimeter and area of the figure.

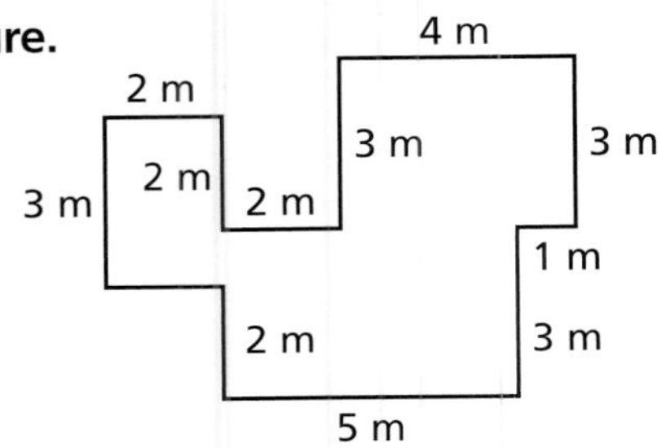

The length of the side that is not labeled is the same as the length of the opposite side, 2 m.

$P = 3 + 2 + 2 + 2 + 3 + 4 + 3 + 1 + 3$
$+ 5 + 2 + 2$
$= 32 \text{ m}$

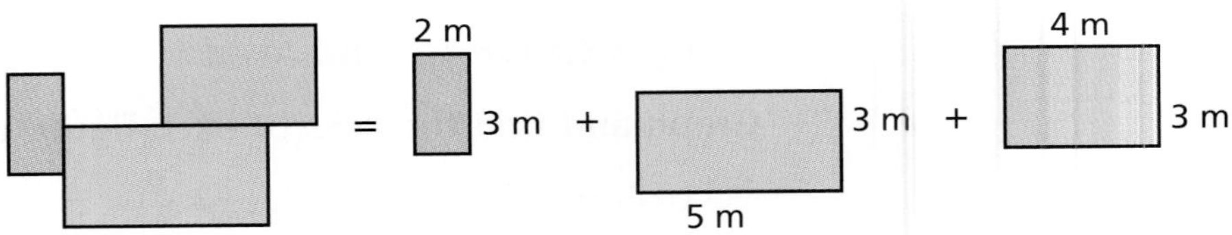

$A = (3 \cdot 2) + (5 \cdot 3) + (4 \cdot 3)$ *Add the areas together.*

$= 6 + 15 + 12$

$= 33 \text{ m}^2$

Think and Discuss

1. Compare the area of a rectangle with base b and height h with the area of a rectangle with base $2b$ and height $2h$.

2. Express the formulas for the area and perimeter of a square using s for the length of a side.

8-1 Exercises

go.hrw.com
Homework Help Online
KEYWORD: MT7 8-1
Parent Resources Online
KEYWORD: MT7 Parent

GUIDED PRACTICE

See Example 1

Find the perimeter of each figure.

1. 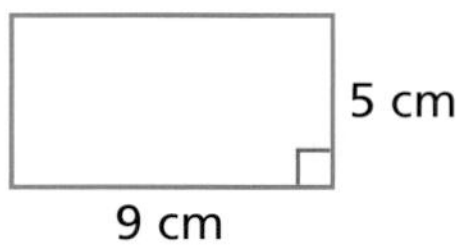

2. 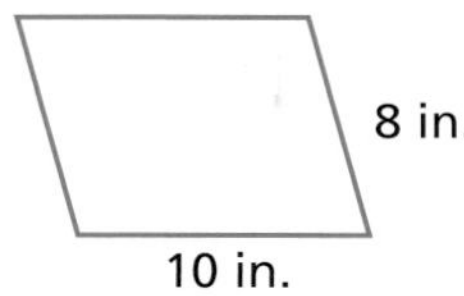

3. 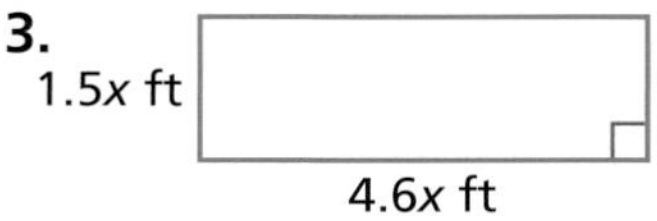

See Example 2

Graph and find the area of each figure with the given vertices.

4. $(-4, 3), (0, 3), (4, -1), (0, -1)$

5. $(-2, -3), (-2, 0), (4, 0), (4, -3)$

6. $(-6, -1), (-5, 2), (2, 2), (1, -1)$

7. $(-2, 3), (0, 3), (0, -4), (-2, -4)$

See Example 3

8. Find the perimeter and area of the figure.

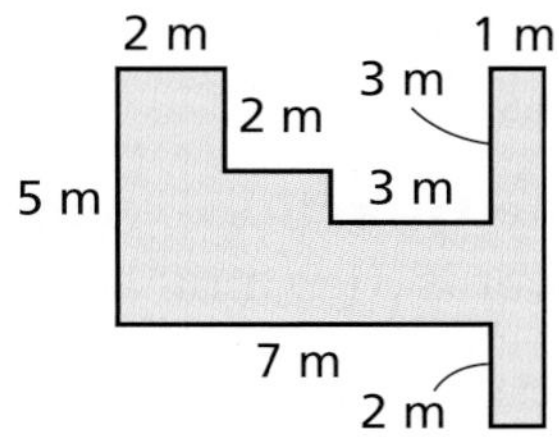

INDEPENDENT PRACTICE

See Example 1

Find the perimeter of each figure.

9. 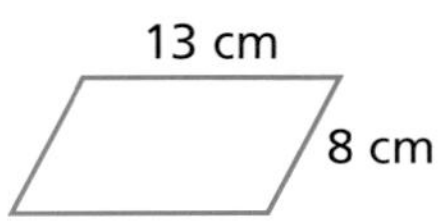

10. 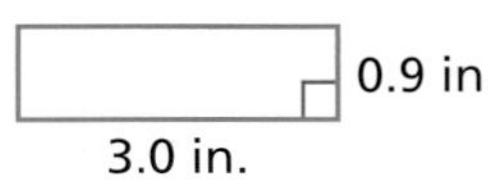

11. 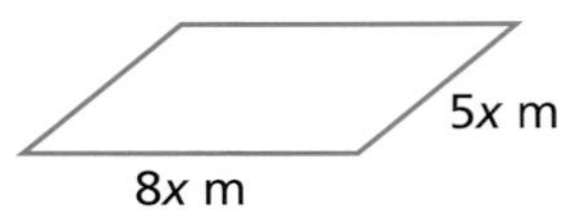

See Example 2

Graph and find the area of each figure with the given vertices.

12. $(-1, -1), (-1, -6), (2, -6), (2, -1)$

13. $(0, 3), (6, 3), (3, -1), (-3, -1)$

14. $(-1, -2), (-1, 4), (1, 5), (1, -1)$

15. $(3, -2), (6, -2), (6, 2), (3, 2)$

See Example 3

16. Find the perimeter and area of the figure.

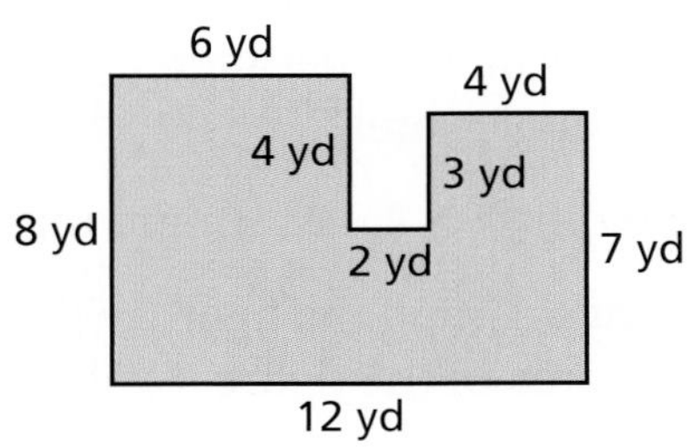

PRACTICE AND PROBLEM SOLVING

Extra Practice
See page 796.

Find the perimeter of each figure.

17. 

18. 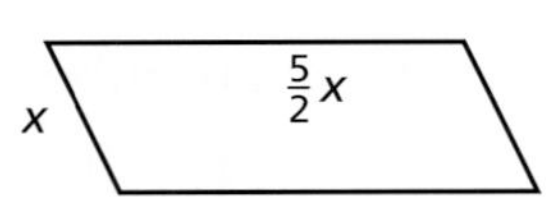

Find the perimeter and area of each figure.

19.

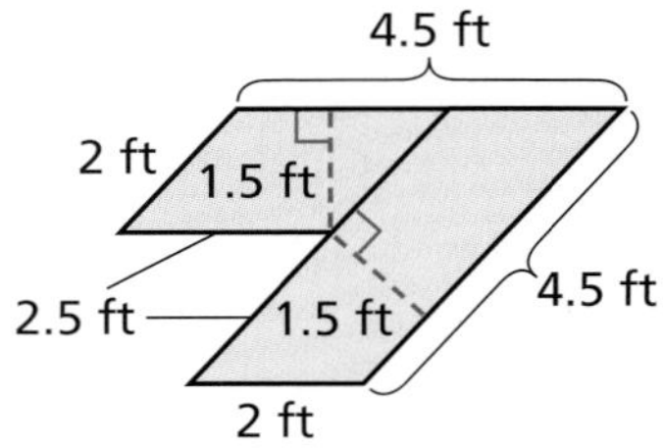

20.

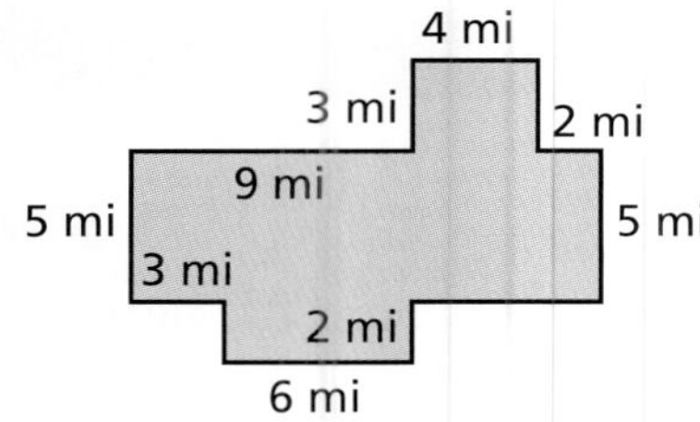

Multi-Step A rectangular ice-skating rink measures 50 ft by 75 ft.

21. It costs $13.50 per foot to install sheets of clear protective plastic around the rink. How much does it cost to enclose the rink with plastic sheets?

22. A machine can clear 750 ft^2 of ice per minute. How long will it take the machine to clear the entire rink?

23. Social Studies The state of Tennessee is shaped approximately like a parallelogram. Estimate the area of the state.

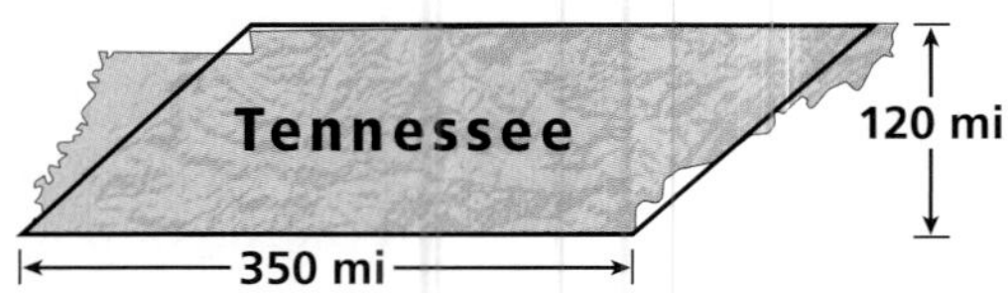

24. What's the Question? A rectangle has a base 6 mm and height 5.2 mm. If the answer is 31.2 mm^2, what is the question?

25. Write About It A rectangle and an identical rectangle with a smaller rectangle cut from the bottom and placed on top are shown. Do the two figures have the same area? Do they have the same perimeter? Explain.

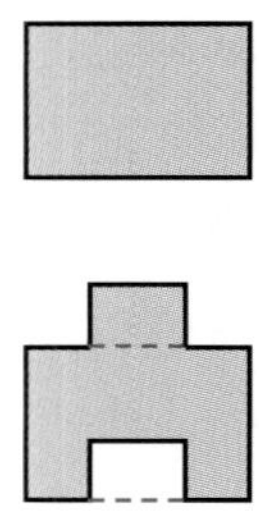

26. Challenge A ruler is 30 cm long by 5 cm wide. How many rulers this size can be cut from a 544 cm^2 rectangular piece of wood with base length 32 cm?

Test Prep and Spiral Review

27. Multiple Choice The lengths of the sides of a rectangle are whole numbers. If the rectangle's perimeter is 24 units, which of the following could NOT be the rectangle's area?

Ⓐ 27 square units Ⓑ 24 square units Ⓒ 20 square units Ⓓ 11 square units

28. Short Response Graph the figure with vertices (2, 5), (−3, 5), (−5, 1), and (0, 1). Find the area of the figure. Explain how you found the area.

Solve. Check your answer. (Lesson 2-8)

29. $5x + 2 = -18$ **30.** $\frac{b}{-6} + 12 = 5$ **31.** $\frac{a + 4}{11} = -3$ **32.** $\frac{1}{3}x - \frac{1}{4} = \frac{5}{12}$

State whether each number is rational, irrational, or not a real number. (Lesson 4-7)

33. -14 **34.** $\sqrt{13}$ **35.** $\frac{127}{46,191}$ **36.** $\sqrt{-\frac{5}{6}}$ **37.** $\frac{21}{0}$

Hands-On LAB 8-1

Explore the Effects of Changing Dimensions

Use with Lesson 8-1

go.hrw.com
Lab Resources Online
KEYWORD: MT7 Lab8

REMEMBER

For polygons to be similar,

- **Corresponding angles must be congruent.**
- **Corresponding sides must have lengths that form equivalent ratios.**

You can use grid paper to explore how changing the dimensions of a figure affects the figure's perimeter and area.

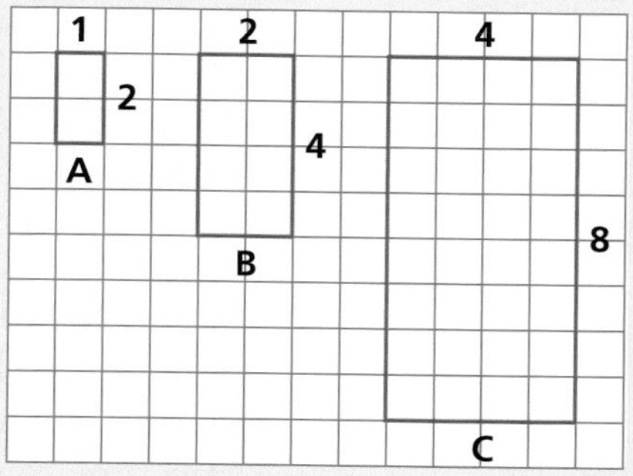

Activity

1 Make the following similar rectangles on grid paper.

Rectangle A: 1 × 2 units   Rectangle B: 2 × 4 units

Rectangle C: 4 × 8 units

Copy the table shown.

Fill in the missing information.

Rectangle	Base	Height	Perimeter	Area
A				
B				
C				

2 Make two more rectangles that are similar to the rectangles in Part 1. Call them *Rectangles E* and *F*.

a. Find the base, height, perimeter, and area of each rectangle.

b. Add this information to your table.

Think and Discuss

1. Look at rectangles B and C. How do the bases and heights compare? How do the perimeters and areas compare?

2. How does changing the width and length of the rectangle affect the perimeter? the area? Make a conjecture about the perimeters and areas of similar figures.

Try This

Use grid paper to make four similar figures to each figure given. Make a table of the bases, heights, perimeters, and areas of each. Does your conjecture hold true?

1. rectangle: 2 × 6 units

2. square: 3 × 3 units

3. rectangle: 2 × 8 units

8-2 Perimeter and Area of Triangles and Trapezoids

Learn to find the perimeter and area of triangles and trapezoids.

The figures show a *fractal* called the Koch snowflake. It is constructed by first drawing an equilateral triangle. Then triangles with sides one-third the length of the original sides are added to the middle of each side. The second step is then repeated over and over again.

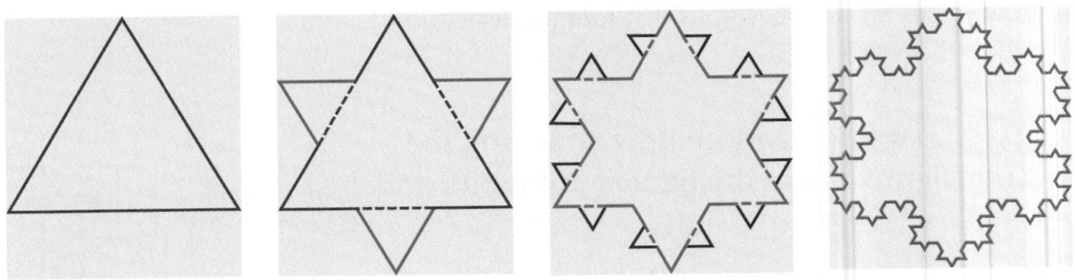

The area and perimeter of each figure is larger than that of the one before it. However, the area of any figure is never greater than the area of the shaded box, while the perimeters increase without bound. To find the area and perimeter of each figure, you must be able to find the area of a triangle..

EXAMPLE 1 Finding the Perimeter of Triangles and Trapezoids

Find the perimeter of each figure.

A

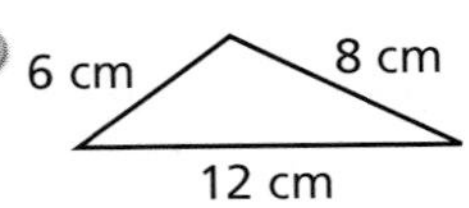

$$\begin{aligned} P &= 6 + 8 + 12 \\ &= 26 \text{ cm} \end{aligned}$$

Add all sides.

B

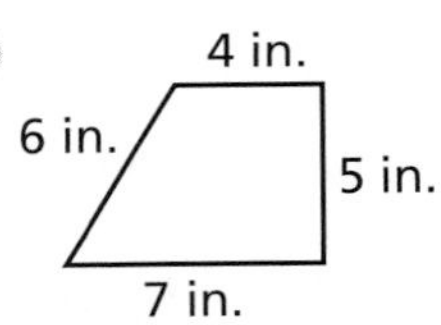

$$\begin{aligned} P &= 4 + 5 + 6 + 7 \\ &= 22 \text{ in.} \end{aligned}$$

Add all sides.

EXAMPLE 2 Finding a Missing Measurement

Find the missing measurement for the trapezoid with perimeter 92 cm.

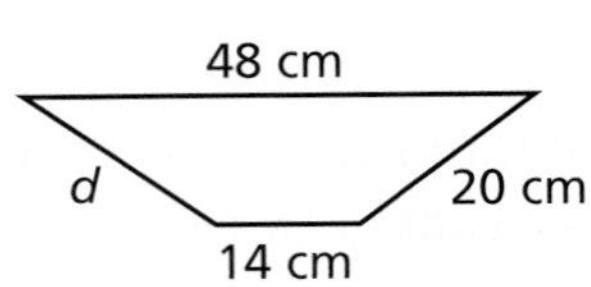

$$\begin{aligned} P &= 48 + 14 + 20 + d \\ 92 &= 82 + d && \text{Substitute 92 for } P. \\ -82 & \quad -82 && \text{Subtract 82 from both sides.} \\ 10 &= d \\ d &= 10 \text{ cm} \end{aligned}$$

EXAMPLE 3 *Multi-Step Application*

A farmer wants to fence a field that is in the shape of a right triangle. He knows that the two shorter sides of the field are 20 yards and 35 yards long. How long will the fence be to the nearest hundredth of a yard?

Find the length of the third side of the field using the Pythagorean Theorem.

$a^2 + b^2 = c^2$

$20^2 + 35^2 = c^2$ *Substitute 20 for a and 35 for b.*

$400 + 1225 = c^2$

$1625 = c^2$

$40.31 \approx c$ $\sqrt{1625} = \sqrt{c^2}$

Find the perimeter of the field.

$P = a + b + c$

$= 20 + 35 + 40.31$ *Add all sides.*

$= 95.31$

The fence will be 95.31 yards long.

A triangle or a trapezoid can be thought of as half of a parallelogram.

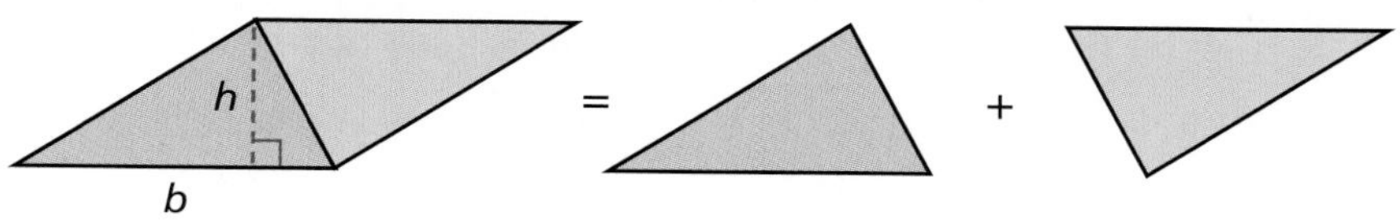

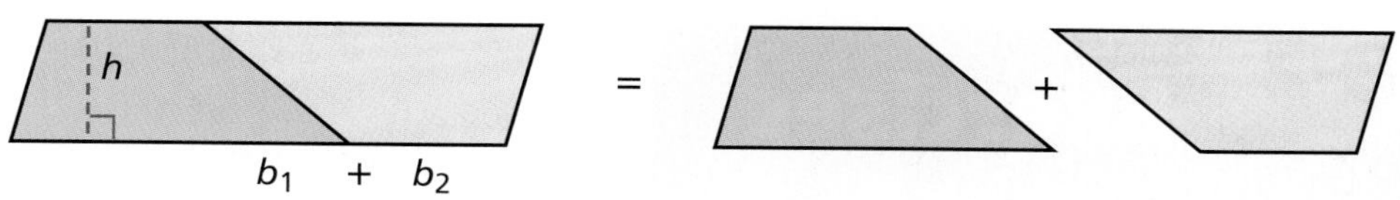

AREA OF TRIANGLES AND TRAPEZOIDS

Words	Numbers	Formula
Triangle: The area A of a triangle is one-half of the base length b times the height h.	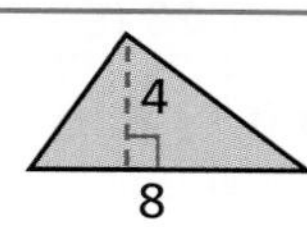 $A = \frac{1}{2}(8)(4)$ $= 16 \text{ units}^2$	$A = \frac{1}{2}bh$
Trapezoid: The area of a trapezoid is one-half the height h times the sum of the base lengths b_1 and b_2.	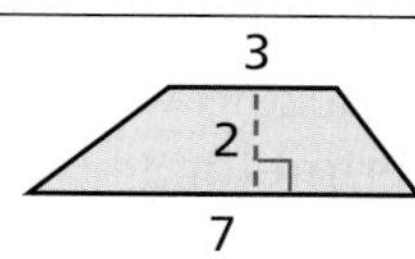 $A = \frac{1}{2}(2)(3 + 7)$ $= 10 \text{ units}^2$	$A = \frac{1}{2}h(b_1 + b_2)$

Reading Math

In the term b_1, the number 1 is called a *subscript*. It is read as "*b* one" or "*b* sub-one."

EXAMPLE 4 Finding the Area of Triangles and Trapezoids

Graph and find the area of the figure with vertices (−2, 2), (6, 2), (3, 7).

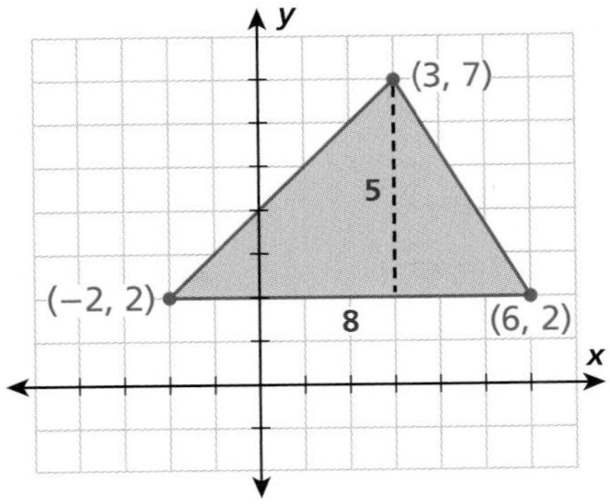

$A = \frac{1}{2}bh$ *Area of a triangle*

$= \frac{1}{2} \cdot \mathbf{8} \cdot \mathbf{5}$ *Substitute for b and h.*

$= 20 \text{ units}^2$

Think and Discuss

1. **Describe** what happens to the area of a triangle when the base is doubled and the height remains the same.
2. **Describe** what happens to the area of a trapezoid when the length of both bases are doubled but the height remains the same.

8-2 Exercises

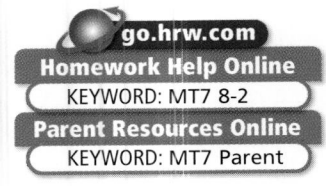

go.hrw.com
Homework Help Online
KEYWORD: MT7 8-2
Parent Resources Online
KEYWORD: MT7 Parent

GUIDED PRACTICE

See Example 1 **Find the perimeter of each figure.**

1.

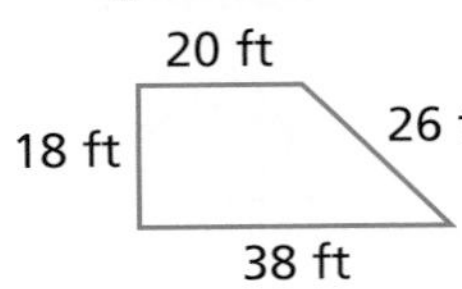

2.

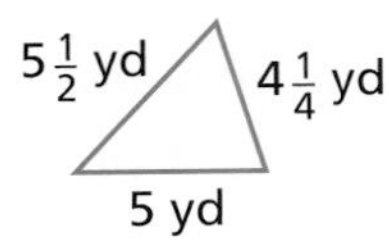

3.

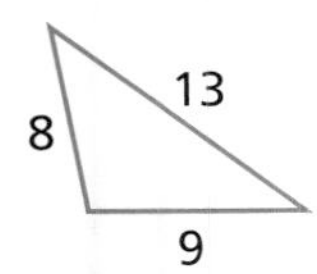

See Example 2 **Find the missing measurement for each figure with the given perimeter.**

4. trapezoid with perimeter 34.5 units

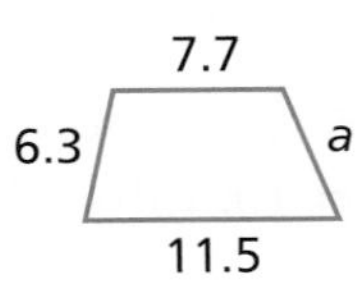

5. trapezoid with perimeter 84 units

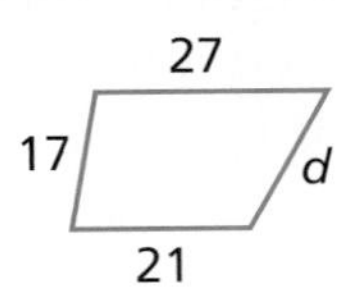

6. triangle with perimeter 18 units

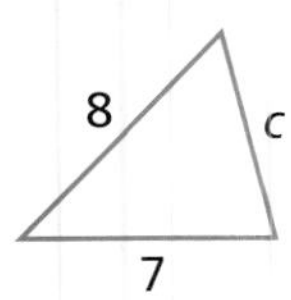

See Example 3

7. Jolene is putting trim around the edge of a triangle head scarf. The scarf forms a right triangle with legs that measure 15 inches each. Find how much trim Jolene needs to the nearest tenth of an inch.

See Example 4

Graph and find the area of each figure with the given vertices.

8. (−4, −2), (0, 5), (2, −2)

9. (−6, 2), (4, 2), (−2, 4), (−2, −4)

10. (−5, −4), (0, −4), (−3, 2)

11. (0, −1), (−7, −1), (−5, 4), (−2, 4)

INDEPENDENT PRACTICE

See Example 1

Find the perimeter of each figure.

12.

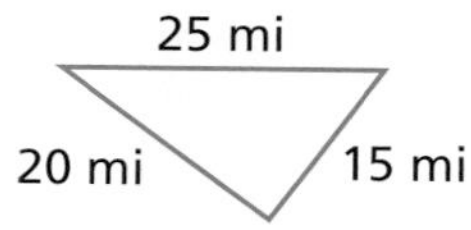

13.

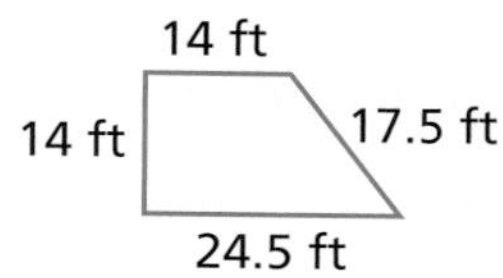

14.

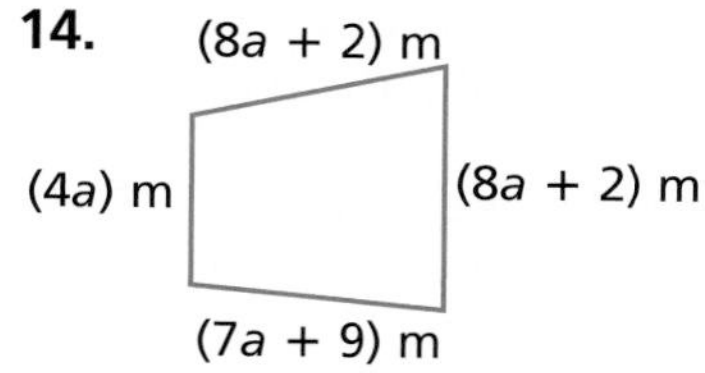

See Example 2

Find the missing measurement for each figure with the given perimeter.

15. triangle with perimeter 27 units

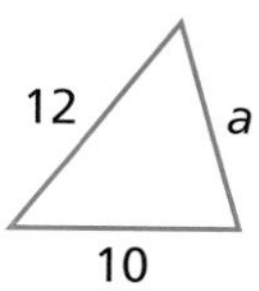

16. triangle with perimeter 34 units

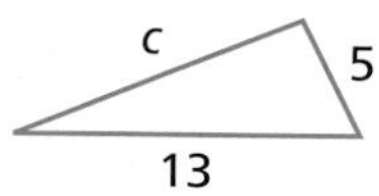

17. trapezoid with perimeter 71 units

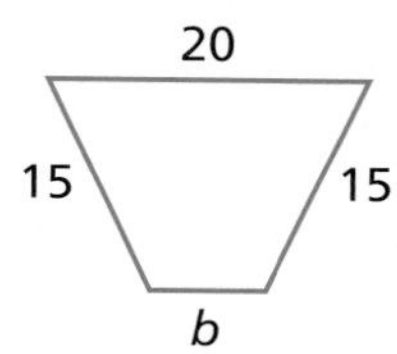

See Example 3

18. Miguel is making a stained glass window. He cuts a 12 cm square along the diagonal to create two right triangles. Find the perimeter of each triangle to the nearest tenth of a centimeter.

See Example 4

Graph and find the area of each figure with the given vertices.

19. (1, 5), (1, 1), (−3, 1), (−5, 1)

20. (−4, −1), (3, 5), (1, −2)

21. (−1, 2), (0, −4), (3, 2)

22. (−4, 3), (2, 1), (2, −3), (−4, −5)

PRACTICE AND PROBLEM SOLVING

Extra Practice
See page 796.

Find the area of each figure with the given dimensions.

23. triangle: $b = 10$, $h = 12$

24. trapezoid: $b_1 = 8$, $b_2 = 14$, $h = 7$

25. triangle: $b = 5x$, $h = 10$

26. trapezoid: $b_1 = 4.5$, $b_2 = 8$, $h = 6.7$

27. The perimeter of a triangle is 37.4 ft. Two of its sides measure 16.4 ft and 11.9 ft, respectively. What is the length of its third side?

28. The area of a triangle is 126 mm^2. Its height is 21 mm. What is the length of its base?

29. **Multi-Step** A right triangle has one leg that is 13 cm long. The hypotenuse is 27 cm long. Find the area of the triangle to the nearest tenth.

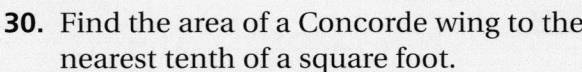

Physical Science LINK

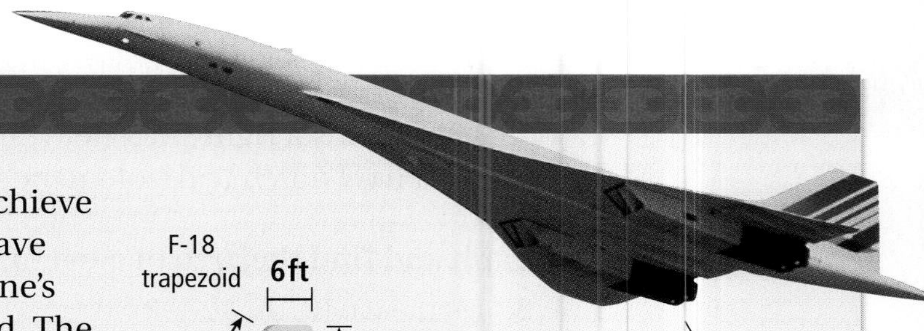

To fly, a plane must overcome gravity and achieve *lift*, the force that allows a flying object to have upward motion. The shape and size of a plane's wings affect the amount of lift that is created. The wings of high-speed airplanes are thin and usually angled back to give the plane more lift.

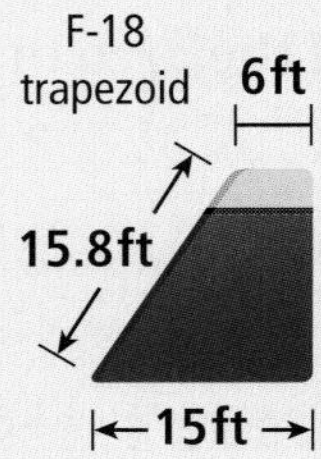

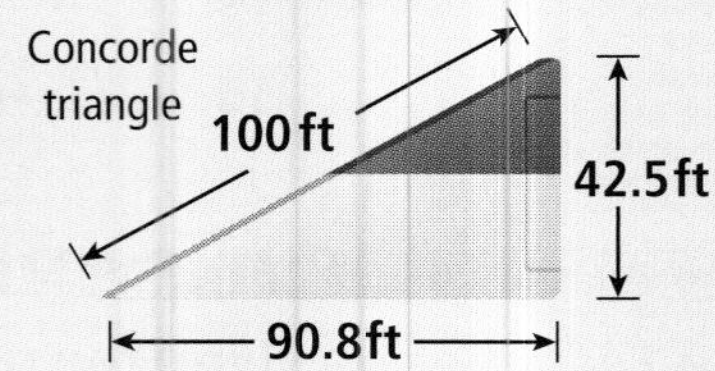

30. Find the area of a Concorde wing to the nearest tenth of a square foot.
31. Find the total perimeter of the two wings of a Concorde to the nearest tenth of a foot.
32. What is the area of a Boeing 747 wing to the nearest tenth of a square foot?
33. What is the perimeter of an F-18 wing to the nearest tenth of a foot?
34. What is the total area of the two wings of an F-18?
35. Find the area and perimeter of the wing of a space shuttle rounded to the nearest tenth.
36. **Challenge** The wing of the Wright brothers' plane is about half the length of a Boeing 747 wing. Compare the area of the Wright brothers' wing with the area of a Boeing 747 wing. Is the area of the Wright brothers' wing half the area of the 747 wing? Explain.

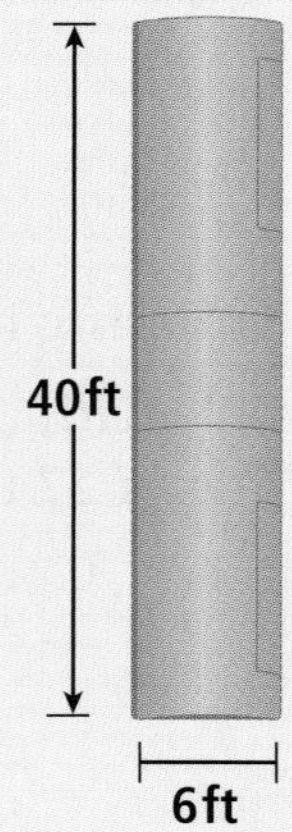

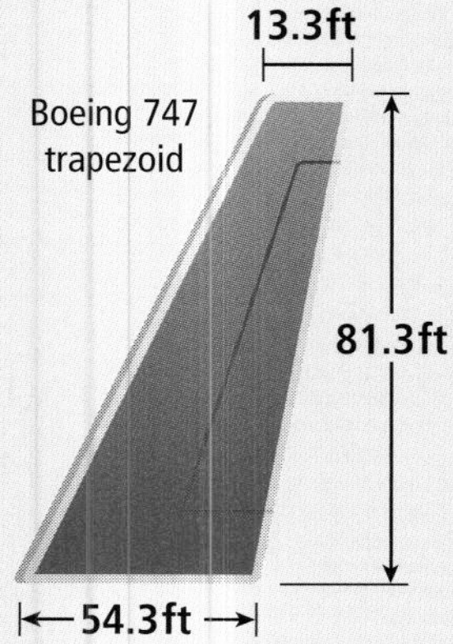

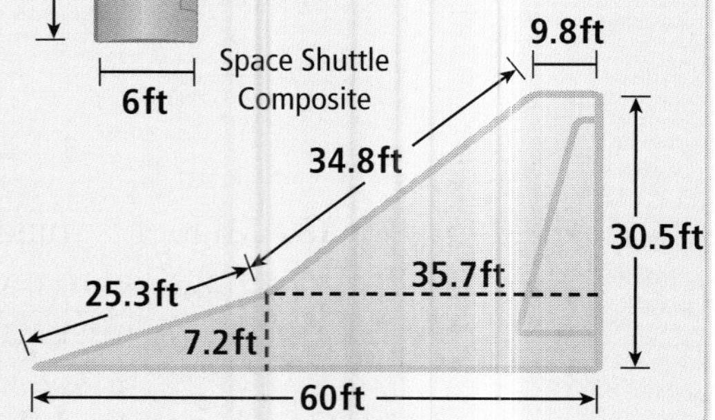

go.hrw.com
Web Extra!
KEYWORD: MT7 Lift

TEST PREP and Spiral Review

37. **Multiple Choice** Find the area of a trapezoid with the dimensions $b_1 = 4$, $b_2 = 6$, and $h = 4.6$.

Ⓐ 16.1 square units Ⓑ 18.4 square units Ⓒ 23 square units Ⓓ 46 square units

38. **Gridded Response** The perimeter of a triangle is 24.9 feet. The length of one side is 9.6 feet. Another side is 8.2 feet. Find the length, in feet, of the third side.

Find the appropriate factor for each conversion. (Lesson 5-3)

39. feet to inches
40. pints to quarts
41. grams to milligrams

Find the area of the quadrilateral with the given vertices. (Lesson 8-1)

42. (0, 0), (0, 9), (5, 9), (5, 0)
43. (−3, 1), (4, 1), (6, 3), (−1, 3)

Hands-On

LAB 8-3

Approximate *Pi* by Measuring

Use with Lesson 8-3

go.hrw.com
Lab Resources Online
KEYWORD: MT7 Lab8

You can use a ruler and string to measure circles.

Activity

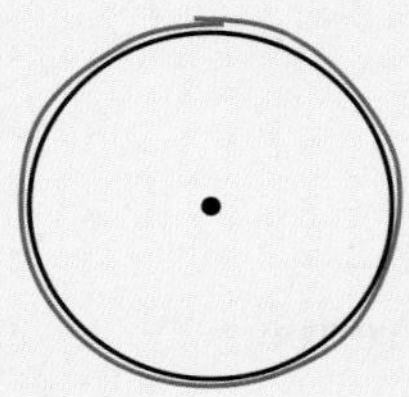

a. Find the distance around three different circular objects by wrapping a piece of string around each of them and using a marker to mark the string where it meets. Be sure that your mark shows on both overlapping parts of the string. Lay the string out straight and use a ruler to measure between the marks. Record the measurements for each object.

b. Measure the distance across each object. Be sure that you measure each circle at its widest point. Record the measurements for each object.

Object	Distance Around	Distance Across	$\frac{\text{Distance Around}}{\text{Distance Across}}$

c. Divide the distance around by the distance across for each object. Round each answer to the nearest hundredth and record it.

Think and Discuss

1. What do you notice about the ratios of the distance around each object to the distance across each object?

2. How could you estimate the distance around a circular object without measuring it if you know the distance across?

Try This

1. Choose three circular objects different from the objects you used in the activity.

a. Measure the distance across each object.

b. Estimate the distance around each object without measuring.

c. Measure the distance around each object and compare each measurement with the estimate from **b**.

8-3 Circles

Learn to find the circumference and area of circles.

Vocabulary
circle
radius
diameter
circumference

DOCTOR FUN

"I love a good G-force face!"

copyright © 2005 David Farley

The 20-G Centrifuge at NASA's Ames Research Center is used to study the effects of hypergravity on human and nonhuman subjects, as well as to evaluate flight hardware. Subjects or equipment are placed in one of the three cabs located on the rotating arm. Each time a cab returns to its starting position, it completes one *circumference* of the centrifuge.

A **circle** is the set of points in a plane that are a fixed distance from a given point, called the *center*. A **radius** connects the center to any point on the circle, and a **diameter** connects two points on the circle and passes through the center.

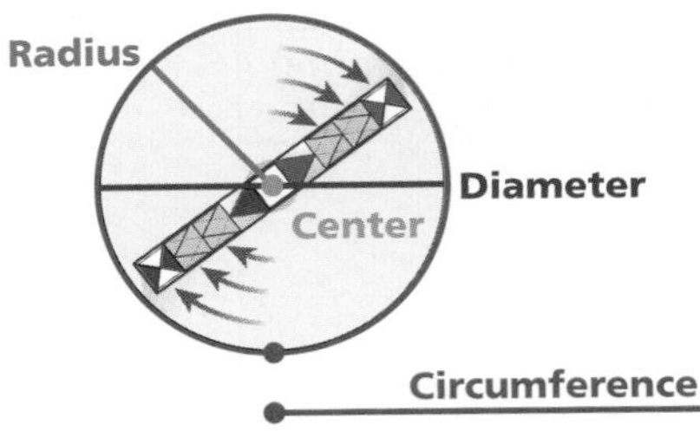

The diameter d is twice the radius r.

$$d = 2r$$

The **circumference** of a circle is the distance around the circle.

Remember!

Pi (π) is an irrational number that is often approximated by the rational numbers 3.14 and $\frac{22}{7}$.

CIRCUMFERENCE OF A CIRCLE

Words	Numbers	Formula
The circumference C of a circle is π times the diameter d, or 2π times the radius r.	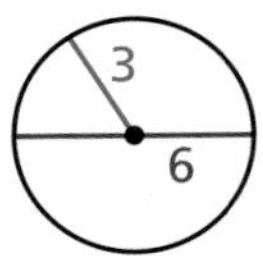 $C = \pi(6)$ $= 2\pi(3)$ ≈ 18.8 units	$C = \pi d$ or $C = 2\pi r$

EXAMPLE 1 Finding the Circumference of a Circle

Find the circumference of each circle, both in terms of π and to the nearest tenth. Use 3.14 for π.

A circle with radius 4 cm

$C = 2\pi r$
$= 2\pi(4)$
$= 8\pi \text{ cm} \approx 25.1 \text{ cm}$

B circle with diameter 4.5 in.

$C = \pi d$
$= \pi(4.5)$
$= 4.5\pi \text{ in.} \approx 14.1 \text{ in.}$

AREA OF A CIRCLE		
Words	**Numbers**	**Formula**
The area A of a circle is π times the square of the radius r.	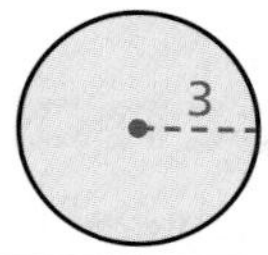 $A = \pi(3^2) = 9\pi \approx 28.3 \text{ units}^2$	$A = \pi r^2$

EXAMPLE 2 Finding the Area of a Circle

Find the area of each circle, both in terms of π and to the nearest tenth. Use 3.14 for π.

A **circle with radius 5 cm**

$A = \pi r^2 = \pi(5^2)$

$= 25\pi \text{ cm}^2 \approx 78.5 \text{ cm}^2$

B **circle with diameter 5.6 in.**

$A = \pi r^2 = \pi(2.8^2)$ *$\frac{d}{2} = 2.8$*

$= 7.84\pi \text{ in}^2 \approx 24.6 \text{ in}^2$

EXAMPLE 3 Finding Area and Circumference on a Coordinate Plane

Graph the circle with center (2, −2) that passes through (0, −2). Find the area and circumference, both in terms of π and to the nearest tenth. Use 3.14 for π.

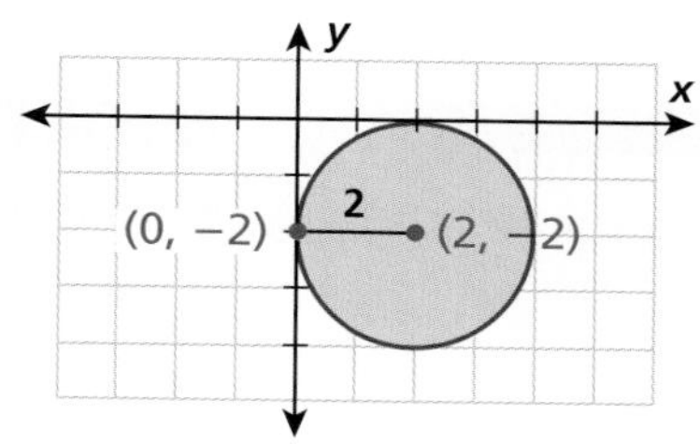

$A = \pi r^2$
$= \pi(2^2)$
$= 4\pi \text{ units}^2$
$\approx 12.6 \text{ units}^2$

$C = \pi d$
$= \pi(4)$
$= 4\pi \text{ units}$
$\approx 12.6 \text{ units}$

EXAMPLE 4 *Physical Science Application*

The radius of the 20-G Centrifuge at NASA's Ames Research Center is 29 ft. If a subject in one of the cabs at the end of the rotating arm remains in the centrifuge for 12 complete revolutions, how far does the subject travel? Use $\frac{22}{7}$ for π.

$C = 2\pi r = 2\pi(29) = \pi(58) \approx \frac{22}{7}\left(\frac{58}{1}\right) = \frac{1276}{7}$ *Find the circumference.*

The distance traveled is the circumference of the centrifuge times the number of revolutions, or about $\frac{1276}{7} \cdot 12 = \frac{15{,}312}{7} \approx 2187.4$ ft.

Think and Discuss

1. Give the formula for the area of a circle in terms of the diameter d.

8-3 Exercises

go.hrw.com
Homework Help Online
KEYWORD: MT7 8-3
Parent Resources Online
KEYWORD: MT7 Parent

GUIDED PRACTICE

See Example 1

Find the circumference of each circle, both in terms of π and to the nearest tenth. Use 3.14 for π.

1. circle with diameter 6 cm

2. circle with radius 3.2 in.

See Example 2

Find the area of each circle, both in terms of π and to the nearest tenth. Use 3.14 for π.

3. circle with radius 4.1 ft

4. circle with diameter 15 cm

See Example 3

5. Graph a circle with center $(-2, 1)$ that passes through $(-4, 1)$. Find the area and circumference, both in terms of π and to the nearest tenth. Use 3.14 for π.

See Example 4

6. A wheel has a diameter of 3.5 ft. Approximately how far does it travel if it makes 20 complete revolutions? Use $\frac{22}{7}$ for π.

INDEPENDENT PRACTICE

See Example 1

Find the circumference of each circle, both in terms of π and to the nearest tenth. Use 3.14 for π.

7. circle with radius 9 in.

8. circle with diameter 6.3 m

See Example 2

Find the area of each circle, both in terms of π and to the nearest tenth. Use 3.14 for π.

9. circle with diameter 32 cm

10. circle with radius 2.5 yd

See Example 3

11. Graph a circle with center $(1, 0)$ that passes through $(-3, 0)$. Find the area and circumference, both in terms of π and to the nearest tenth. Use 3.14 for π.

See Example 4

12. If the diameter of a wheel is 5 ft, about how many miles does the wheel travel if it makes 134 revolutions? Use $\frac{22}{7}$ for π. (*Hint:* 1 mi = 5280 ft.)

PRACTICE AND PROBLEM SOLVING

Extra Practice
See page 796.

Find the circumference and area of each circle to the nearest tenth. Use 3.14 for π.

13.

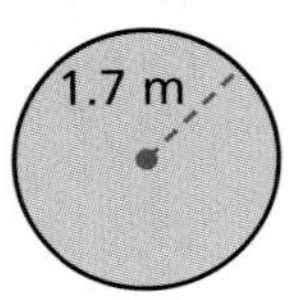

14.

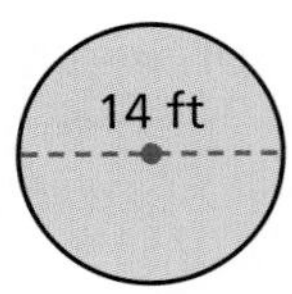

15.

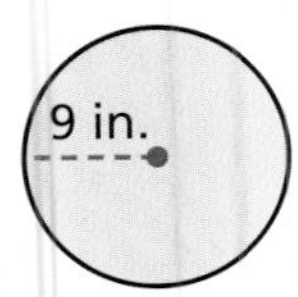

Find the radius of each circle with the given measurement.

16. $C = 26\pi$ in.

17. $C = 12.8\pi$ cm

18. $C = 15\pi$ ft

19. $A = 36\pi\ \text{cm}^2$

20. $A = 289\pi\ \text{in}^2$

21. $A = 136.89\pi\ \text{m}^2$

Find the shaded area to the nearest tenth. Use 3.14 for π.

22.

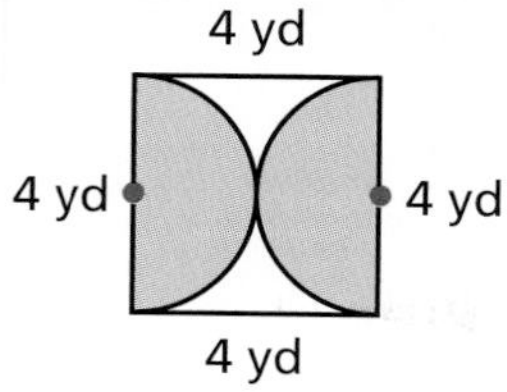

23.

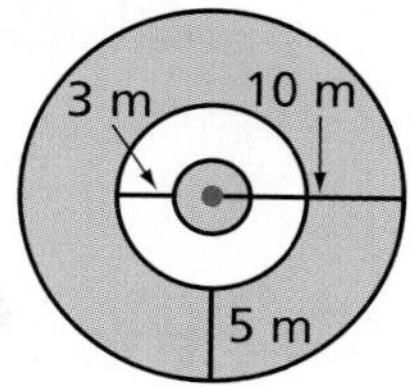

LINK

Entertainment

The London Eye takes its passengers on a 30-minute flight that reaches a height of 450 feet above the River Thames.

24. **Entertainment** The London Eye is an observation wheel with a diameter greater than 135 meters and less than 140 meters. Describe the range of the possible circumferences of the wheel to the nearest meter.

25. **Sports** The radius of a face-off circle on an NHL hockey rink is 15 ft. What are its circumference and area to the nearest tenth? Use 3.14 for π.

26. **Food** A pancake restaurant serves small silver dollar pancakes and regular-size pancakes.

a. What is the area of a silver dollar pancake to the nearest tenth?

b. What is the area of a regular pancake to the nearest tenth?

c. If 6 silver dollar pancakes are the same price as 3 regular pancakes, which is a better deal?

27. **What's the Error?** The area of a circle is 121π cm^2. A student says this means the diameter is 11 in. What is the error?

28. **Write About It** Explain how you would find the area of the composite figure shown. Then find the area.

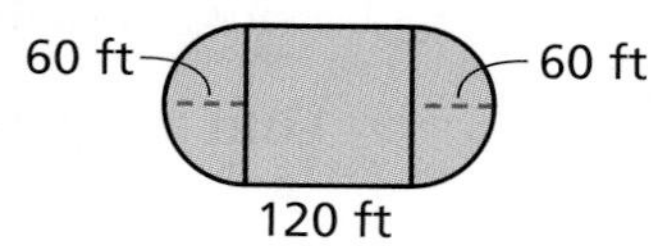

29. **Challenge** Graph the circle with center (1, 2) that passes through the point (4, 6). Find its area and circumference, both in terms of π and to the nearest tenth.

Test Prep and Spiral Review

30. **Multiple Choice** A circular flower bed has radius 22 inches. What is the circumference of the bed to the nearest tenth of an inch?

Ⓐ 69.1 inches Ⓑ 103.7 inches Ⓒ 138.2 inches Ⓓ 1519.8 inches

31. **Gridded Response** The first Ferris wheel was constructed for the 1893 World's Fair. It had a diameter of 250 feet. Find the circumference, to the nearest foot, of the Ferris wheel. Use 3.14 for π.

Find the missing angle measure for each triangle. (Lesson 7-3)

32. 70°, 80°, x° 33. 120°, 10°, x° 34. 50°, 20°, x° 35. 100°, 15°, x°

Graph and find the area of each figure with the given vertices. (Lesson 8-2)

36. (1, 0), (10, 0), (1, −6) 37. (5, 5), (2, 1), (11, 1), (8, 5)

Ready To Go On?

Quiz for Lessons 8-1 Through 8-3

8-1 Perimeter and Area of Rectangles and Parallelograms

Find the perimeter of each figure.

1.

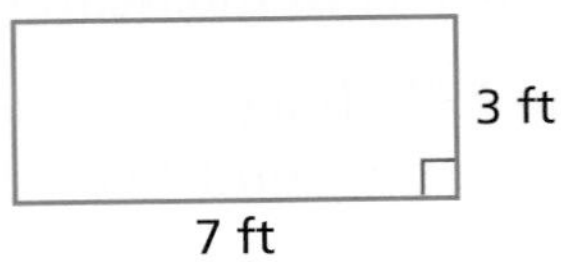

2.

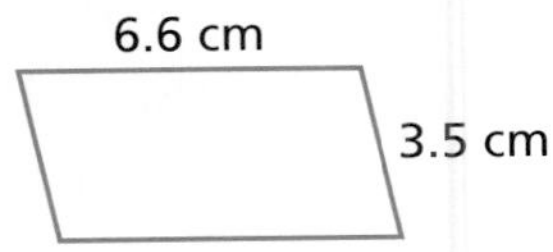

Graph and find the area of each figure with the given vertices.

3. $(-4, 4), (2, 4), (2, -3), (-4, -3)$

4. $(-2, 3), (-2, -1), (2, -1), (2, 4)$

5. $(-5, 0), (-1, 0), (-6, -3), (-2, -3)$

6. $(-3, 4), (1, 4), (-4, -3), (0, -3)$

7. Find the perimeter and area of the figure.

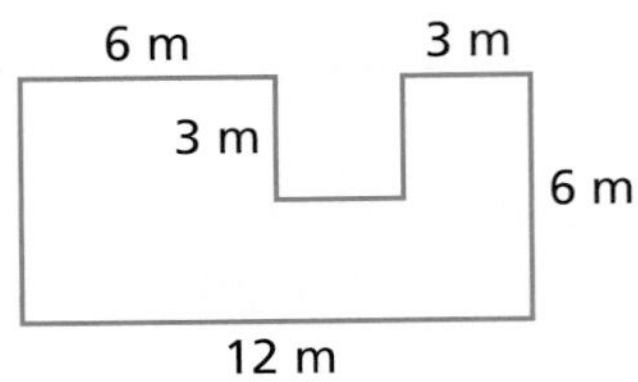

8-2 Perimeter and Area of Triangles and Trapezoids

Find the perimeter of each figure.

8.

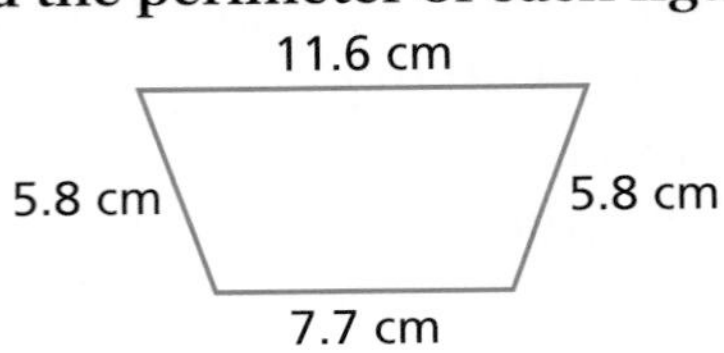

9.

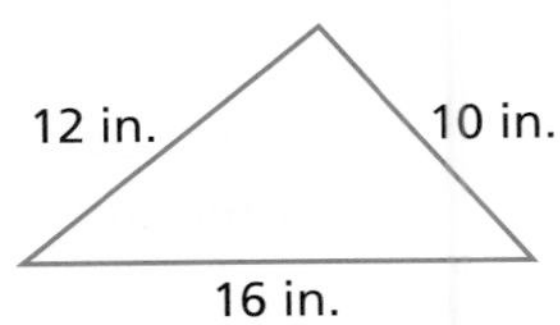

10. Kumiko wants to put a border around a flower garden shaped like a right triangle. The legs of the triangle measure 10 ft and 12 ft. Find how long the border will be to the nearest tenth of a foot.

Graph and find the area of each figure with the given vertices.

11. $(-6, -2), (4, -2), (-3, 3)$

12. $(-4, 0), (0, 0), (3, 3)$

13. $(2, -2), (3, 3), (-4, 3), (-3, -2)$

14. $(0, 3), (3, 4), (3, -2), (0, -2)$

8-3 Circles

Find the area and circumference of each circle, both in terms of π and to the nearest tenth. Use 3.14 for π.

15. radius $= 19$ cm

16. diameter $= 4.3$ ft

17. radius $= 7\frac{1}{2}$ ft

18. Graph a circle with center $(-3, 1)$ that passes through $(-1, 1)$. Find the area and circumference, both in terms of π and to the nearest tenth. Use 3.14 for π.

Focus on Problem Solving

Look Back

- **Does your solution answer the question?**

When you think you have solved a problem, think again. Your answer may not really be the solution to the problem. For example, you may solve an equation to find the value of a variable, but to find the answer the problem is asking for, the value of the variable may need to be substituted into an expression.

Write and solve an equation for each problem. Check to see whether the value of the variable is the answer to the question. If not, give the answer to the question.

1. Triangle *ABC* is an isosceles triangle. Find its perimeter.

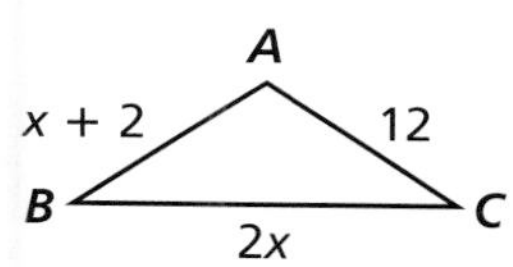

2. Find the measure of the smallest angle in triangle *DEF*.

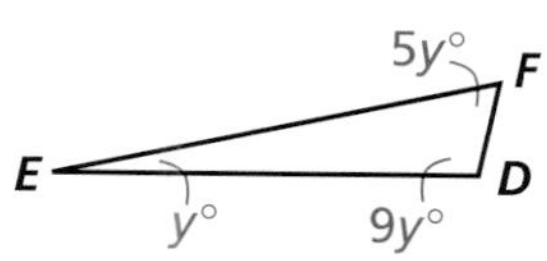

3. Find the measure of the largest angle in triangle *DEF*.

4. Find the area of right triangle *GHI*.

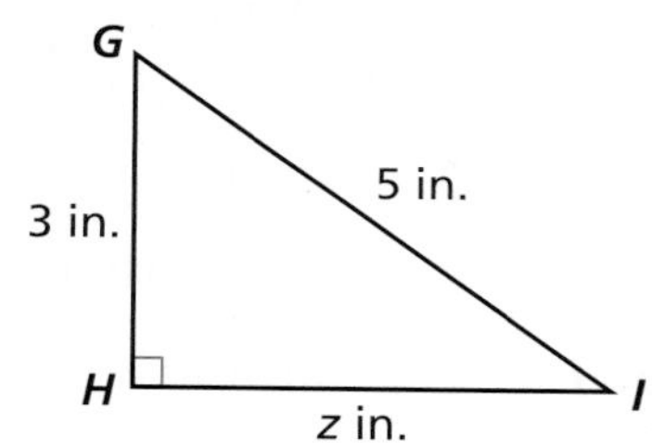

5. A *pediment* is a triangular space filled with statuary on the front of a building. The approximate measurements of an isosceles triangular pediment are shown below. Find the area of the pediment.

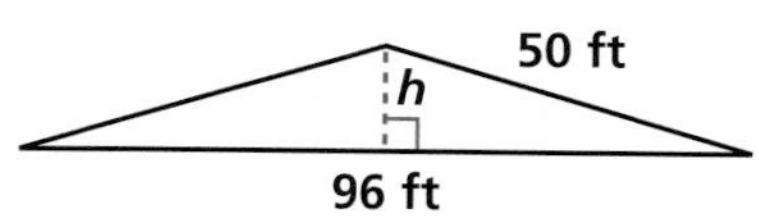

Hands-On LAB 8-4

Construct Nets

Use with Lesson 8-4

go.hrw.com
Lab Resources Online
KEYWORD: MT7 Lab8

REMEMBER
- A polygon is a closed plane figure formed by three or more line segments.
- Congruent polygons are the same size and shape.

You can explore the faces of a three-dimensional figure by making a *net*, an arrangement of two-dimensional figures that can be folded to form a three-dimensional figure.

Activity 1

Make a net of a box, such as a small cereal box.

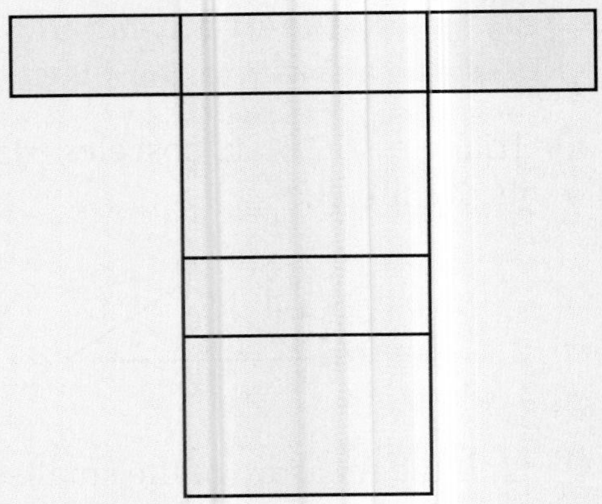

a. Lay one side of the box on paper and trace around it. Flip it on another side and trace around it. Continue flipping and tracing until you have traced around the top, bottom, and each side.

b. List the polygons you drew.

c. Identify any congruent polygons.

d. Cut out, fold, and tape your net to make a three-dimensional figure.

Think and Discuss

1. How many polygons make up a box?

2. What types of polygons are they?

3. Were any polygons congruent? If so, which ones?

Try This

1. Use your box from Activity 1 to make a different net by flipping it a different way. Are the polygons you drew the same? Cut out, fold, and tape your net. Does it still form the same three-dimensional figure?

2. Use what you have learned in this activity to describe a box. Use math terminology in your description.

3. Make a net of a cube. How many different nets can you make? Draw them. Then list the polygons you drew. Identify any congruent polygons. Use math terminology to describe a cube.

Activity 2

Make a net of a can.

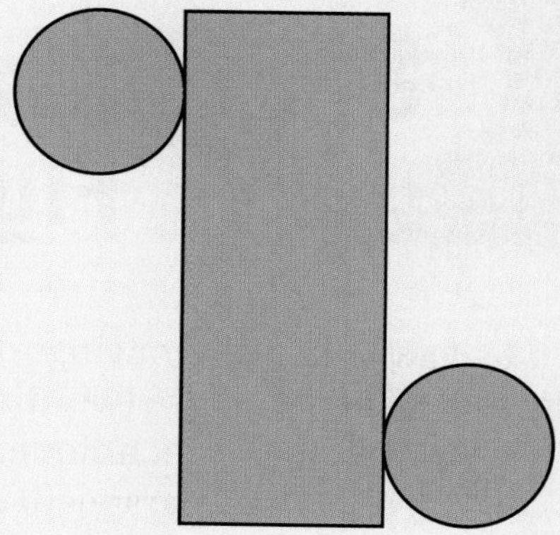

a. Lay the bottom of the can on paper and trace around it.

b. Tip the can onto its side. Mark the paper where the top and bottom of the can touches the paper.

c. Make a mark on the edge of the can where it touches the paper. Roll the can until the mark comes back to the original position.

d. Make a mark where the can touches the paper at the top and bottom, as you did in part **b**.

e. Connect the four marks you made in parts **b** and **c.**

f. Tip the can over to its top, and trace around it.

g. Cut out and tape your net to make a three-dimensional figure.

Think and Discuss

1. How many figures make up a can?
2. What types of figures are they?
3. Are any of the figures congruent? If so, which ones?

Try This

1. Use what you have learned in this activity to describe a can. Use math terminology in your description.

Activity 3

Make a figure like the one shown at right.

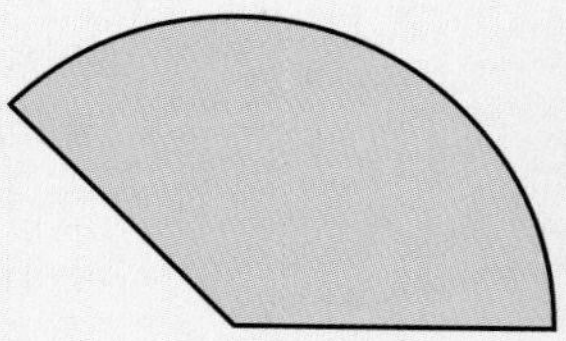

a. Use a compass to draw part of a circle.

b. Mark the point where you placed the compass, and connect this point with straight lines to the endpoints of the arc you drew in part **a.**

c. Cut out the figure and bend it so that the two straight edges are touching. Tape the two edges together.

Think and Discuss

1. What kind of figure did you make?
2. Is there a surface missing from the cone? What is the shape of the missing part?

Try This

1. Make a net of a pyramid. Cut out and tape the net to form a three-dimensional figure. Use math terminology to describe a pyramid.

8-4 Drawing Three-Dimensional Figures

Learn to draw and identify parts of three-dimensional figures.

Vocabulary
face
edge
vertex
orthogonal views

Drawings of three-dimensional objects are two-dimensional representations. Techniques such as shading and perspective are used to give the appearance of depth to these drawings.

Like the objects they represent, drawings of three-dimensional figures have *faces, edges,* and *vertices*. A **face** is a flat surface, an **edge** is where two faces meet, and a **vertex** is where three or more edges meet.

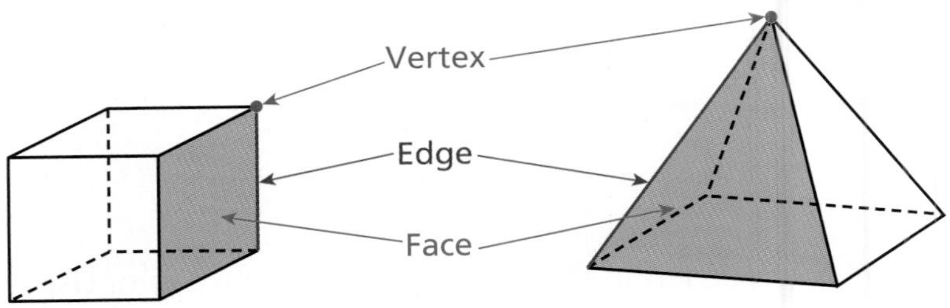

Since in a drawing of a three-dimensional object, you can only see up to three sides of a figure, you have to visualize how the figure looks from other angles. One way to do this is by drawing the *orthogonal views* of the figure. **Orthogonal views** show how the figure looks from different perspectives, such as the front, side, and top views. For figures constructed with cubes, the orthogonal views will be groups of squares.

EXAMPLE 1 Identifying Vertices, Edges, and Faces

Name the vertices, edges, and faces of the three-dimensional figure shown.

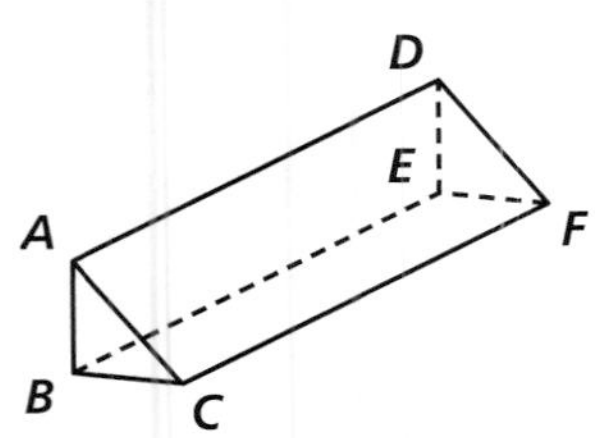

The vertices are *A, B, C, D, E,* and *F.*

The edges are $\overline{AB}$, $\overline{BC}$, $\overline{CA}$, $\overline{DE}$, $\overline{EF}$, $\overline{FD}$, $\overline{AD}$, $\overline{BE}$, and $\overline{CF}$.

The faces are triangles *ABC* and *DEF* and quadrilaterals *ADFC, ADEB,* and *BEFC.*

EXAMPLE 2 Drawing a Figure When Given Different Perspectives

Draw the figure shown in the front, top, and side views.

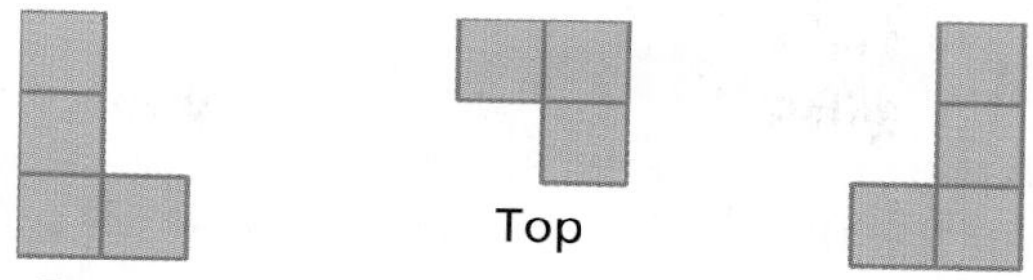

Front Top Side

From the front and side views, there appears to be one cube on the top level, in the back left corner. The top view shows that the bottom layer has three cubes.

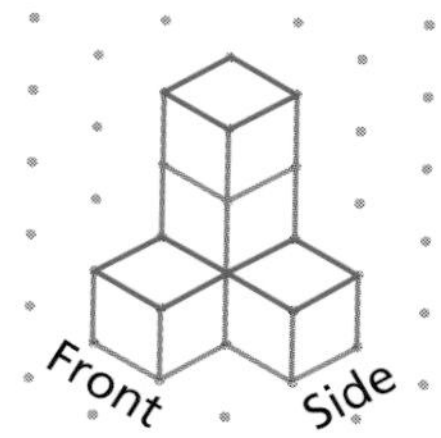

EXAMPLE 3 Drawing Different Perspectives of a Figure

Draw the front, top, and side views of the figure.

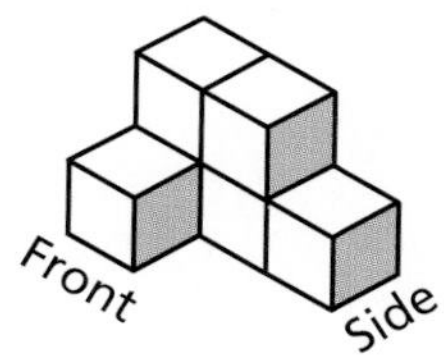

Front: The figure looks like 2 squares on top of three squares.

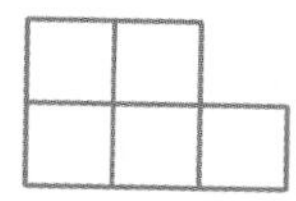

Front

Top: The figure looks like a row of 3 squares with 1 square below the left square.

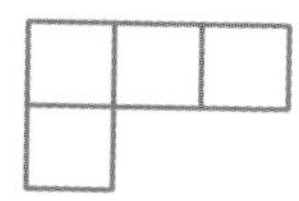

Top

Side: The figure looks like 1 square on top of two squares.

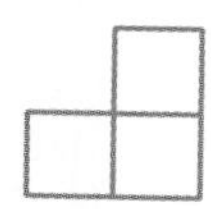

Side

When looking at a figure made of cubes, the bottom view is a mirror image of the top view, the back view is a mirror image of the front view, and the side views are mirror images of each other.

Think and Discuss

1. **Give** a situation in which the front and side views of a figure would be the same.
2. **Give** a situation in which all three views of a figure would be the same.
3. **Explain** whether it is possible for all of the views of a figure to be congruent rectangles.

8-4 Exercises

go.hrw.com
Homework Help Online
KEYWORD: MT7 8-4
Parent Resources Online
KEYWORD: MT7 Parent

GUIDED PRACTICE

See Example 1

1. Name the vertices, edges, and faces of the three-dimensional figure shown.

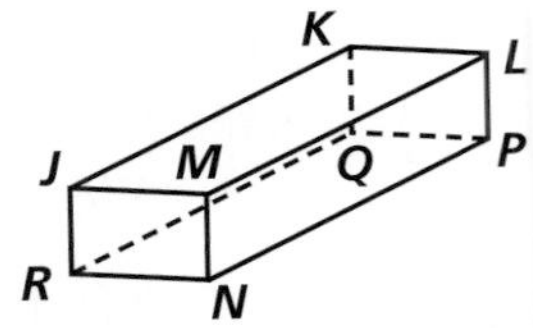

See Example 2

2. Draw the figure that has the following front, top, and side views.

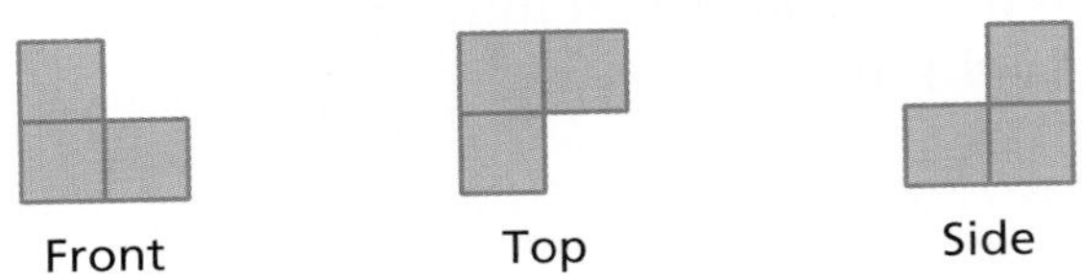

See Example 3

3. Draw the front, top, and side views of the figure.

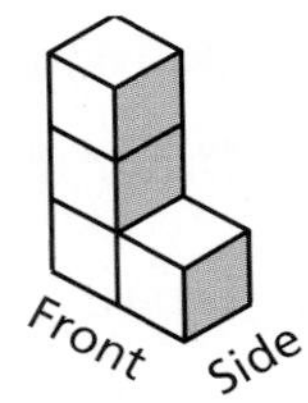

INDEPENDENT PRACTICE

See Example 1

4. Name the vertices, edges, and faces of the three-dimensional figure shown.

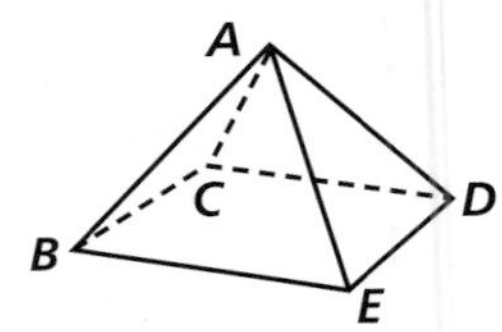

See Example 2

5. Draw the figure shown in the front, top, and side views.

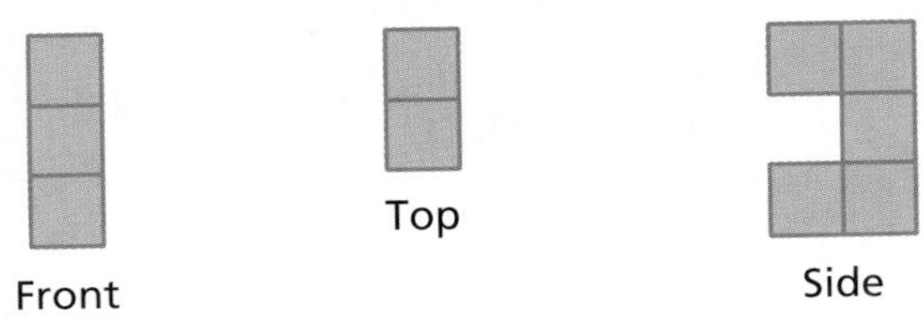

See Example 3

6. Draw the front, top, and side views of the figure.

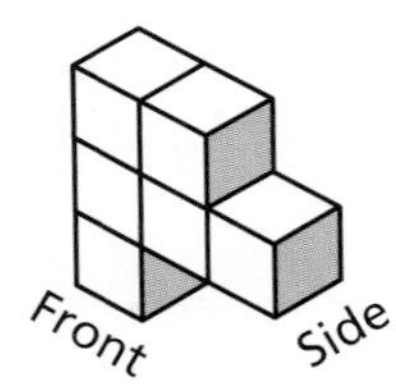

PRACTICE AND PROBLEM SOLVING

Extra Practice
See page 796.

Draw the front, top, and side views of each figure shown.

7.

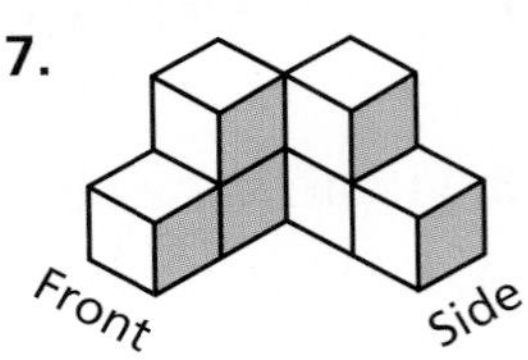

8.

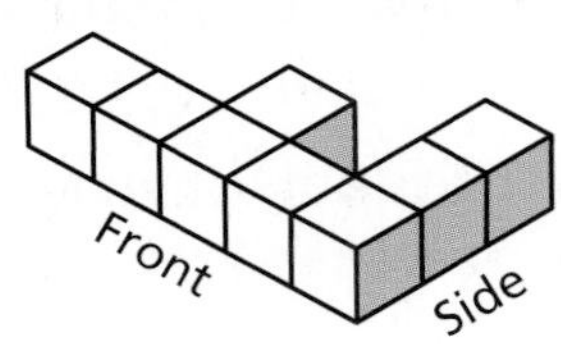

9.

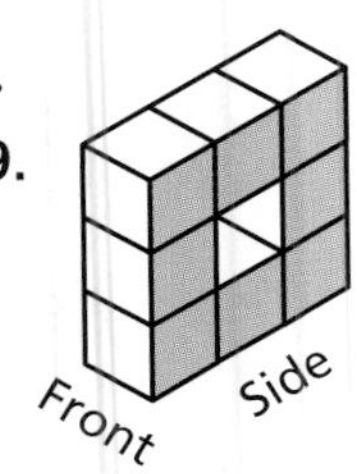

Draw the figure shown in the orthogonal views.

10. 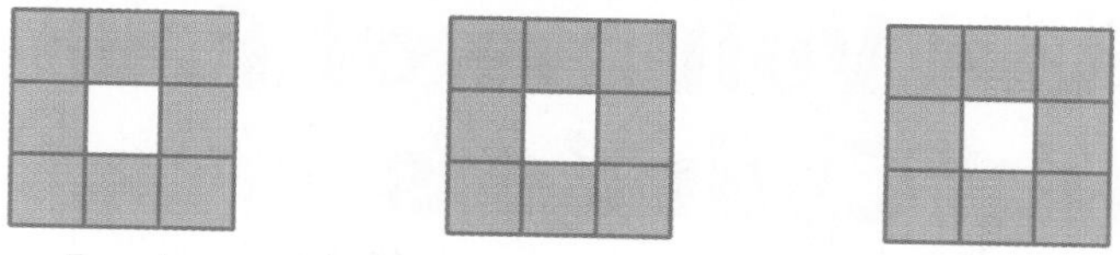

Use isometric dot paper to sketch each figure.

11. a cube 4 units on each side

12. a triangular box 5 units high

13. a rectangular box 2 units high, with a base 5 units by 7 units

14. **Art** The sculpture *123454321* by Sol LeWitt consists of 9 cubes of different sizes. Draw the front, top, and side views of the sculpture.

15. **Write About It** Describe a figure for which the top and front views would be the same.

16. **Challenge** The video game Tetris is played by stacking seven different configurations of four squares. Choose three different Tetris shapes and draw a figure made of cubes as if the Tetris shapes were the front, top, and side views of the figure. Do not use a single Tetris shape more than twice.

Test Prep and Spiral Review

17. **Multiple Choice** Which is the top view of the figure?

Ⓐ 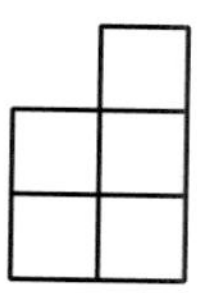

Ⓑ 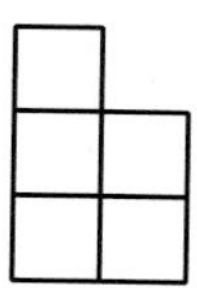

Ⓒ 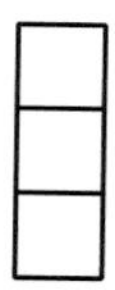

Ⓓ 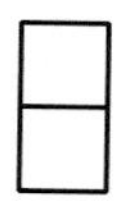

18. **Short Response** Draw the orthogonal views of the figure.

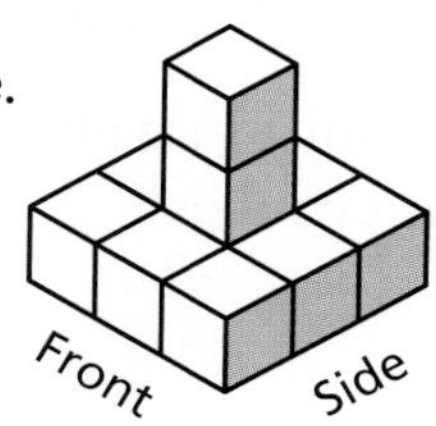

Find each commission to the nearest cent. (Lesson 6-6)

19. total sales: \$39.68
commission rate: 4.5%

20. total sales: \$475
commission rate: 3.75%

21. total sales: \$2,143
commission rate: 6%

Find the area of each circle to the nearest tenth. Use 3.14 for π. (Lesson 8-3)

22. circle with radius 7 ft

23. circle with diameter 17 in.

Hands-On LAB 8-5

Find Volume of Prisms and Cylinders

Use with Lesson 8-5

go.hrw.com
Lab Resources Online
KEYWORD: MT7 Lab8

You can use models to explore the volume of rectangular prisms and cylinders.

Activity

1 Use five different-sized rectangular prisms, such as empty cartons.

a. Cover the bottom of each prism with cubes to find the area of the prism's base. Record the information in a table.

b. Fill the prism with cubes. Find the height. Then count the cubes to find the prism's volume. Record the information in a table.

Object	
Area of Base	
Height	
Volume	

2 Use five different-sized cylinders, such as empty cans.

a. Measure the radius of each circular base and calculate its area. Record the information in a table.

b. Measure the height of each cylinder. Record the information in a table.

c. Fill each cylinder with popcorn kernels.

d. Use a measuring cup to find how much popcorn filled the cylinder.

e. Find the approximate volume of each cylinder. 1 cup = 14.4 in^3. Record the information in a table.

Think and Discuss

1. What do you notice about the relationship between the base, the height, and the volume of the rectangular prisms? of the cylinders?
2. Make a conjecture about how to find the volume of any rectangular prism or cylinder.

Try This

1. Use your conjecture to find the volume of a new rectangular prism. Check your conjecture by following the steps in Activity 1. Revise your conjecture as needed.
2. Use your conjecture to find the volume of a new cylinder. Check your conjecture by following the steps in Activity 2. Revise your conjecture as needed.

8-5 Volume of Prisms and Cylinders

Learn to find the volume of prisms and cylinders.

Vocabulary

cylinder

prism

The largest drum ever built measures 4.8 meters in diameter and is 4.95 meters deep. It was built by Asano Taiko Company in Japan. You can use these measurements to find the approximate volume of the drum, which is roughly a *cylinder*.

The circumference of the Taiko drum pictured is about half that of the largest drum ever made.

A **cylinder** is a three-dimensional figure that has two congruent circular bases. A **prism** is a three-dimensional figure named for the shape of its bases. The two bases are congruent polygons. All of the other faces are parallelograms.

Triangular prism **Rectangular prism** **Cylinder**

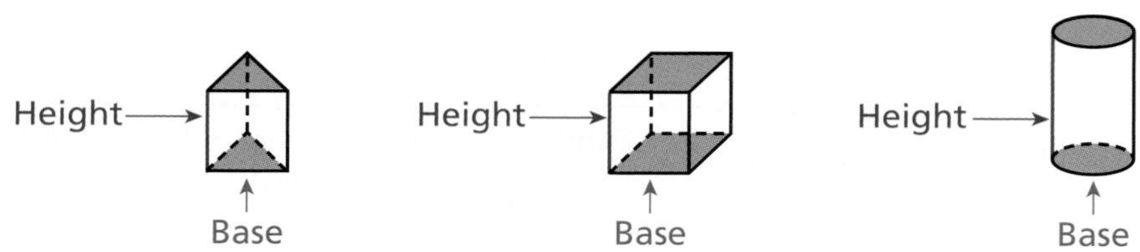

VOLUME OF PRISMS AND CYLINDERS

Words	Numbers		Formula
Prism: The volume V of a prism is the area of the base B times the height h.	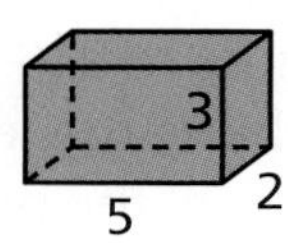	$B = 2(5)$ $= 10$ units^2 $V = (10)(3)$ $= 30$ units^3	$V = Bh$
Cylinder: The volume of a cylinder is the area of the base B times the height h.	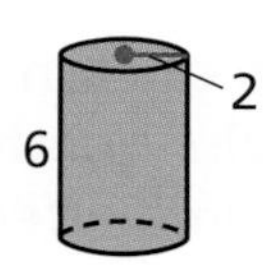	$B = \pi(2^2)$ $= 4\pi$ units^2 $V = (4\pi)(6) = 24\pi$ ≈ 75.4 units^3	$V = Bh$ $= (\pi r^2)h$

EXAMPLE 1 Finding the Volume of Prisms and Cylinders

Remember!

Area is measured in *square units.* Volume is measured in *cubic units.*

Find the volume of each figure to the nearest tenth. Use 3.14 for π.

A **A rectangular prism with base 2 m by 5 m and height 7 m.**

$B = 2 \cdot 5 = 10\text{ m}^2$ *Area of base*

$V = Bh$ *Volume of prism*

$= 10 \cdot 7 = 70\text{ m}^3$

Find the volume of each figure to the nearest tenth. Use 3.14 for π.

B

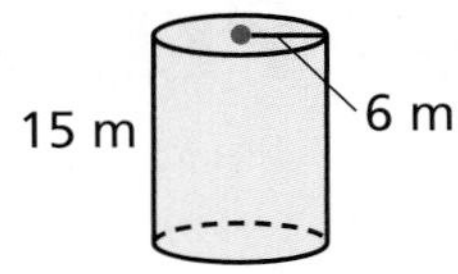

$B = \pi(6^2) = 36\pi \text{ m}^2$ *Area of base*

$V = Bh$ *Volume of a cylinder*

$= 36\pi \cdot 15$

$= 540\pi \approx 1695.6 \text{ m}^3$

C

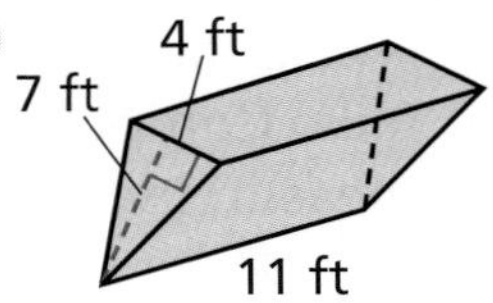

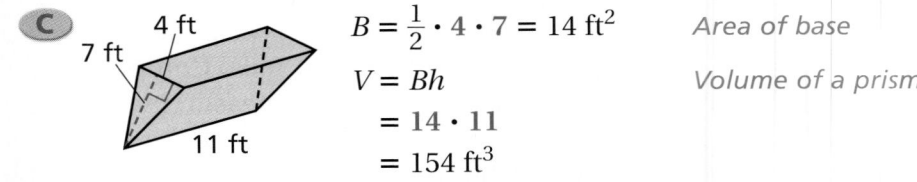

$B = \frac{1}{2} \cdot 4 \cdot 7 = 14 \text{ ft}^2$ *Area of base*

$V = Bh$ *Volume of a prism*

$= 14 \cdot 11$

$= 154 \text{ ft}^3$

The volume of a rectangular prism can be written as $V = \ell wh$, where ℓ is the length, w is the width, and h is the height.

EXAMPLE 2 Exploring the Effects of Changing Dimensions

A **A cereal box measures 6 in. by 2 in. by 9 in. Explain whether doubling the length, width, or height of the box would double the amount of cereal the box holds.**

Original Dimensions	Double the Length	Double the Width	Double the Height
$V = \ell wh$ $= 6 \cdot 2 \cdot 9$ $= 108 \text{ in}^3$	$V = (2\ell)wh$ $= 12 \cdot 2 \cdot 9$ $= 216 \text{ in}^3$	$V = \ell(2w)h$ $= 6 \cdot 4 \cdot 9$ $= 216 \text{ in}^3$	$V = \ell w(2h)$ $= 6 \cdot 2 \cdot 18$ $= 216 \text{ in}^3$

The original box has a volume of 108 in^3. You could double the volume to 216 in^3 by doubling any one of the dimensions. So doubling the length, width, or height would double the amount of cereal the box holds.

B **A can of corn has a radius of 2.5 in. and a height of 4 in. Explain whether doubling the height of the can would have the same effect on the volume as doubling the radius.**

Original Dimensions	Double the Height	Double the Radius
$V = \pi r^2 h$ $= 2.5^2\pi \cdot 4$ $= 25\pi \text{ in}^3$	$V = \pi r^2(2h)$ $= 2.5^2\pi \cdot 8$ $= 50\pi \text{ in}^3$	$V = \pi(2r)^2 h$ $= 5^2\pi \cdot 4$ $= 100\pi \text{ in}^3$

By doubling the height, you would double the volume. By doubling the radius, you would increase the volume four times the original.

EXAMPLE 3 *Music Application*

The Asano Taiko Company of Japan built the world's largest drum in 2000. The drum's diameter is 4.8 meters, and its height is 4.95 meters. Estimate the volume of the drum.

$d = 4.8 \approx 5,\ h = 4.95 \approx 5$

$r = \frac{d}{2} = \frac{5}{2} = 2.5$

$V = (\pi r^2)h$ — *Volume of a cylinder.*

$= (3.14)(2.5)^2 \cdot 5$ — *Use 3.14 for π.*

$= (3.14)(6.25)(5)$

$= 19.625 \cdot 5$

$= 98.125 \approx 98$

The volume of the drum is approximately 98 m^3.

To find the volume of a composite three-dimensional figure, find the volume of each part and add the volumes together.

EXAMPLE 4 Finding the Volume of Composite Figures

Find the volume of the figure.

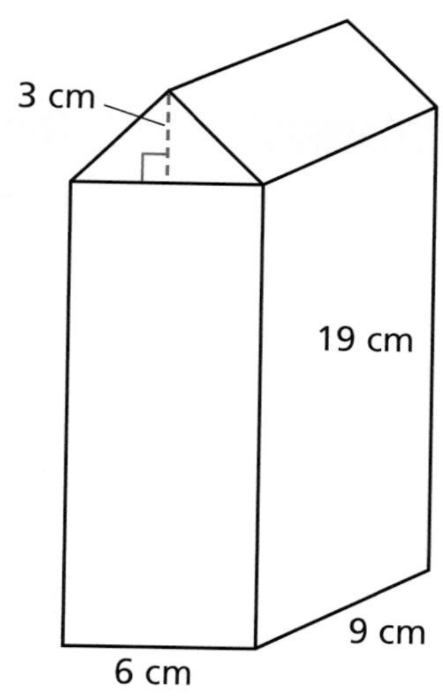

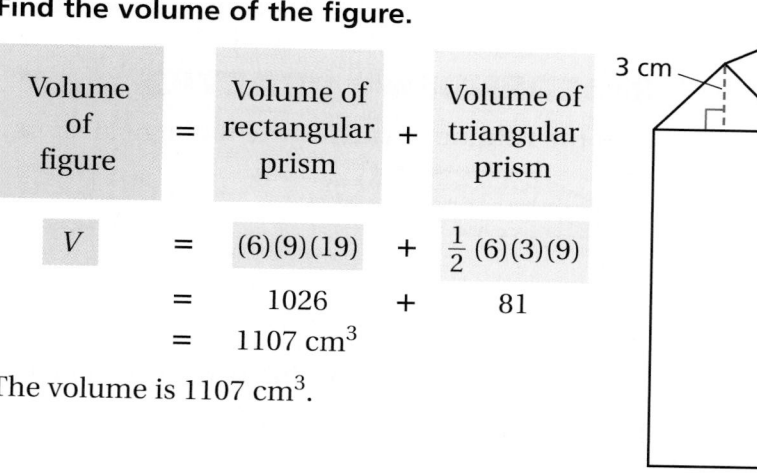

Volume of figure	=	Volume of rectangular prism	+	Volume of triangular prism
V	=	$(6)(9)(19)$	+	$\frac{1}{2}(6)(3)(9)$
	=	1026	+	81
	=	1107 cm^3		

The volume is 1107 cm^3.

Think and Discuss

1. **Use models** to show that two rectangular prisms can have different heights but the same volume.
2. **Apply** your results from Example 2 to make a conjecture about changing dimensions in a triangular prism.
3. **Use a model** to describe what happens to the volume of a cylinder when the diameter of the base is tripled.

8-5 Exercises

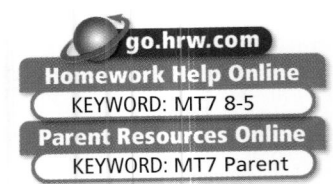

go.hrw.com
Homework Help Online
KEYWORD: MT7 8-5
Parent Resources Online
KEYWORD: MT7 Parent

GUIDED PRACTICE

See Example 1

Find the volume of each figure to the nearest tenth. Use 3.14 for π.

1.

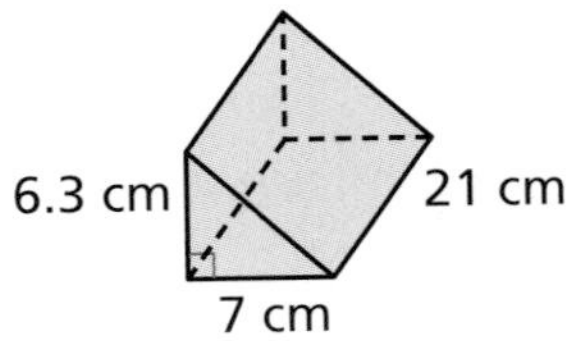

2.

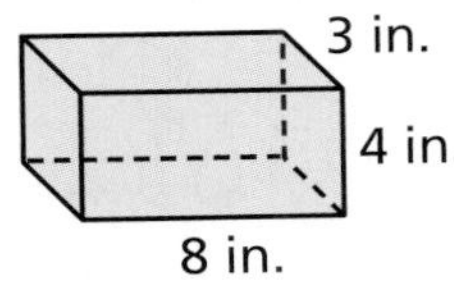

3.

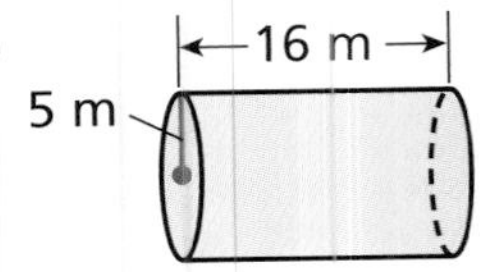

See Example 2

4. A can of juice has a radius 3 in. and a height 6 in. Explain whether tripling the radius would triple the volume of the can.

See Example 3

5. Grain is stored in cylindrical structures called *silos.* Estimate the volume of a silo with diameter 11.1 feet and height 20 feet.

See Example 4

6. Find the volume of the barn.

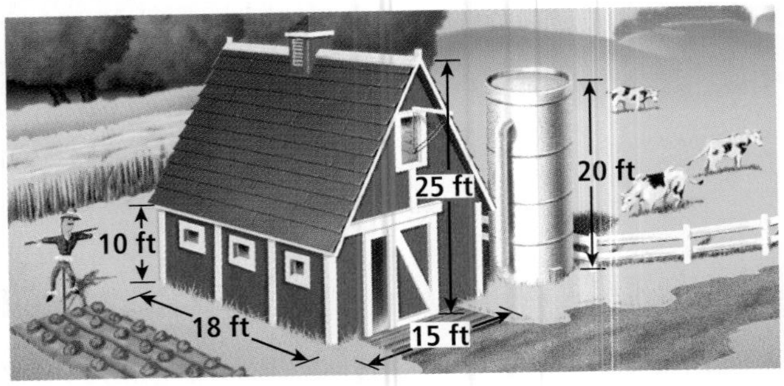

INDEPENDENT PRACTICE

See Example 1

Find the volume of each figure to the nearest tenth. Use 3.14 for π.

7.

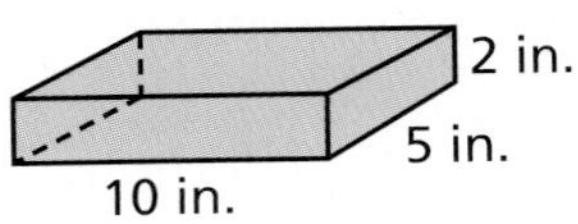

8.

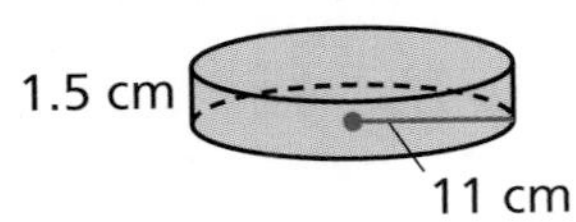

9.

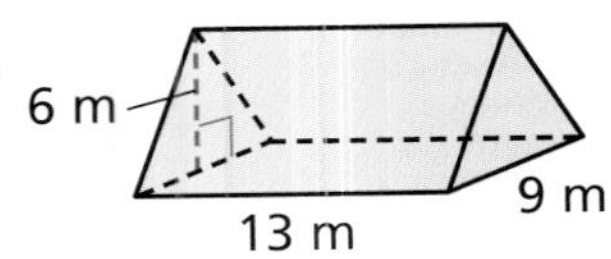

See Example 2

10. A jewelry box measures 7 in. by 5 in. by 8 in. Explain whether increasing the height 4 times, from 8 in. to 32 in., would increase the volume 4 times.

See Example 3

11. A toy box is 5.1 cm by 3.2 cm by 4.2 cm. Estimate the volume of the toy box.

See Example 4

12. Find the volume of the treehouse.

PRACTICE AND PROBLEM SOLVING

Extra Practice
See page 797.

13. While Karim was at camp, his father sent him a care package. The box measured 10.2 in. by 19.9 in. by 4.2 in.

a. Estimate the volume of the box.

b. What might be the measurements of a box with twice its volume?

LINK

Life Science

Through the 52 large windows of the Giant Ocean Tank, visitors can see 3000 corals and sponges as well as large sharks, sea turtles, barracudas, moray eels, and hundreds of tropical fishes.

14. Social Studies The tablet held by the Statue of Liberty is approximately a rectangular prism with volume 1,107,096 in^3. Estimate the thickness of the tablet.

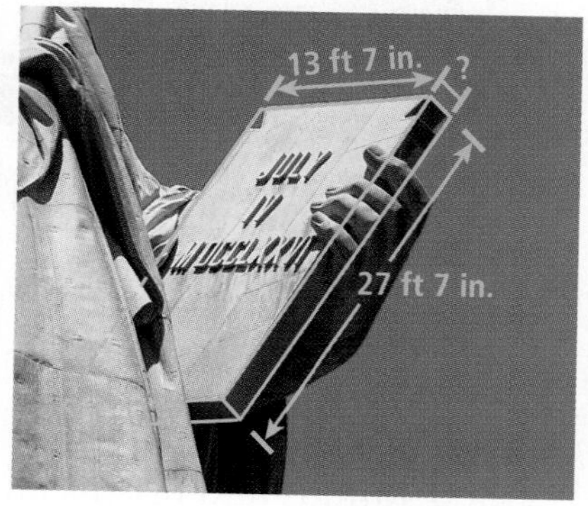

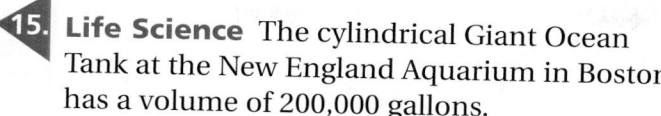

15. Life Science The cylindrical Giant Ocean Tank at the New England Aquarium in Boston has a volume of 200,000 gallons.

a. One gallon of water equals 231 cubic inches. How many cubic inches of water are in the Giant Ocean Tank?

b. Use your answer from part **a** as the volume. The tank is 24 ft deep. Find the radius in feet of the Giant Ocean Tank.

16. Life Science As many as 60,000 bees can live in 3 cubic feet of space. There are about 360,000 bees in a rectangular observation beehive that is 2 ft long by 3 ft high. What is the minimum possible width of the observation hive?

17. What's the Error? A student read this statement in a book: "The volume of a triangular prism with height 15 in. and base area 20 in. is 300 in^3." Correct the error in the statement.

18. Write About It Explain why 1 cubic yard equals 27 cubic feet.

19. Challenge A 5-inch section of a hollow brick measures 12 inches tall and 8 inches wide on the outside. The brick is 1 inch thick. Find the volume of the brick, not the hollow interior.

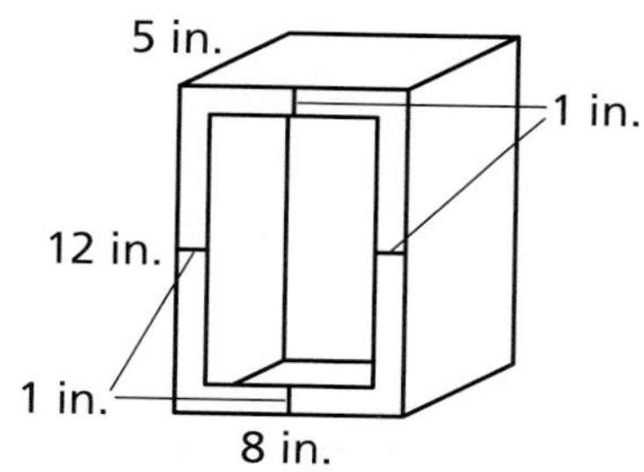

Test Prep and Spiral Review

20. Multiple Choice Cylinder A has radius 6 centimeters and height 14 centimeters. Cylinder B has radius half as long as cylinder A. What is the volume of cylinder B? Use 3.14 for π and round to the nearest tenth.

Ⓐ 393.5 cm^3　Ⓑ 395.6 cm^3　Ⓒ 422.3 cm^3　Ⓓ 791.3 cm^3

21. Multiple Choice A tractor trailer has dimensions of 13 feet by 53 feet by 8 feet. What is the volume of the trailer?

Ⓕ 424 ft^3　Ⓖ 689 ft^3　Ⓗ 2756 ft^3　Ⓙ 5512 ft^3

Give the coordinates of each point after a reflection across the given axis. (Lesson 7-7)

22. $(-3, 4)$; y-axis　**23.** $(5, 9)$; x-axis　**24.** $(6, -3)$; y-axis

25. Find the height of a rectangle with perimeter 14 inches and length 3 inches. What is the area of the rectangle? (Lesson 8-1)

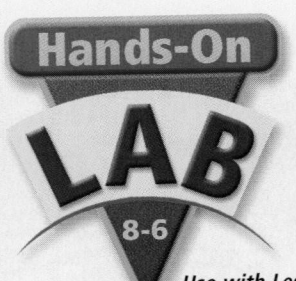

Hands-On LAB 8-6

Find Volume of Pyramids and Cones

Use with Lesson 8-6

go.hrw.com
Lab Resources Online
KEYWORD: MT7 Lab8

You can use containers to explore the relationship between the volumes of pyramids and prisms and the relationship between the volumes of cones and cylinders.

Activity 1

Find or make a hollow prism and a hollow pyramid that have congruent bases and heights.

a. Fill the pyramid with popcorn kernels. Make sure that the popcorn kernels are level with the opening of the pyramid, and then pour the kernels into the prism.

b. Repeat step **a** until the prism is full and the popcorn kernels are level with the top of the prism. Keep track of the number of full pyramids it takes to fill the prism.

Think and Discuss

1. How many full pyramids did it take to fill a prism with a congruent base and height?

2. Use a fraction to express the relationship between the volume of a pyramid and the volume of a prism with a congruent base and height.

3. If the volume of a prism is Bh, write a rule for the volume of a pyramid.

Try This

1. Use your rule from Think and Discuss 3 to find the volume of another pyramid. Check your rule by following the steps in Activity 1. Revise your rule as needed.

2. The volume of a pyramid is 31 in^3. What is the volume of a prism with the same base and height? Explain your reasoning.

3. The volume of a prism is 27 cm^3. What is the volume of a pyramid with the same base and height? Explain your reasoning.

4. A glass lantern filled with oil is shaped like a square pyramid. Each side of the base is 5 centimeters long, and the lantern is 11 centimeters tall. What is the volume of the lantern?

Activity 2

Find or make a hollow cylinder and a hollow cone that have congruent bases and heights.

a. Fill the cone with popcorn kernels. Make sure that the popcorn kernels are level with the opening of the cone, and then pour the kernels into the cylinder.

b. Repeat step **a** until the cylinder is full and the popcorn kernels are level with the top of the cylinder. Keep track of the number of full cones it takes.

Think and Discuss

1. How many full cones did it take to fill a cylinder with a congruent base and height?
2. Use a fraction to express the relationship between the volume of a cone and the volume of a cylinder with a congruent base and height.
3. If the volume of a cylinder is Bh or $\pi r^2 h$, write a rule for the volume of a cone.

Try This

1. Use your rule from Think and Discuss 3 to find the volume of another cone. Check your rule by following the steps in Activity 2. Revise your rule as needed.
2. The volume of a cone is 3.7 m^3. What is the volume of a cylinder with the same base and height? Explain your reasoning.
3. The volume of a cylinder is 228 ft^3. What is the volume of a cone with the same base and height? Explain your reasoning.
4. Evan is using a plastic cone to build a sand castle. The cone has a diameter of 10 inches and is 18 inches tall. What is the volume of the cone?
5. Aneesha has two paper cones. The first cone has a radius of 2 inches and a height of 3 inches. The second cone has the same base but is twice the height. Aneesha says that the second cone has twice the volume of the first cone. Is she correct? Explain your reasoning.

8-6 Volume of Pyramids and Cones

Learn to find the volume of pyramids and cones.

Vocabulary

pyramid

cone

Part of the Rock and Roll Hall of Fame building in Cleveland, Ohio, is a glass pyramid. The entire building was designed by architect I. M. Pei and has approximately 150,000 ft^2 of floor space.

A **pyramid** is a three-dimensional figure whose base is a polygon, and all of the other faces are triangles. It is named for the shape of its base. A **cone** has a circular base. The height of a pyramid or cone is measured from the highest point to the base along a line perpendicular to the base.

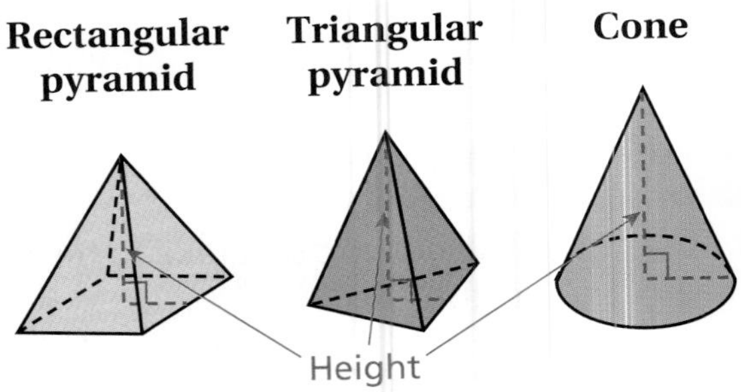

VOLUME OF PYRAMIDS AND CONES

Words	Numbers		Formula
Pyramid: The volume V of a pyramid is one-third of the area of the base B times the height h.	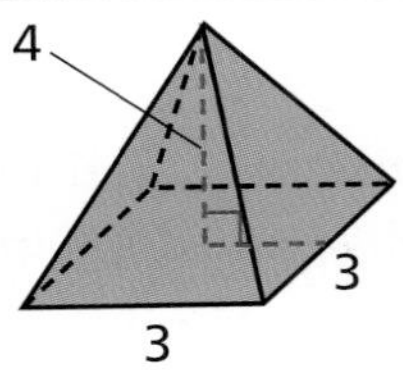	$B = 3(3)$ $= 9 \text{ units}^2$ $V = \frac{1}{3}(9)(4)$ $= 12 \text{ units}^3$	$V = \frac{1}{3}Bh$
Cone: The volume of a cone is one-third of the area of the circular base B times the height h.	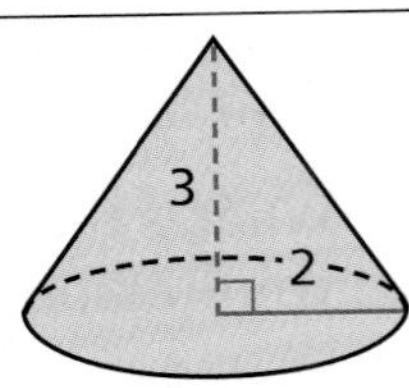	$B = \pi(2^2)$ $= 4\pi \text{ units}^2$ $V = \frac{1}{3}(4\pi)(3)$ $= 4\pi$ $\approx 12.6 \text{ units}^3$	$V = \frac{1}{3}Bh$ or $V = \frac{1}{3}\pi r^2 h$

EXAMPLE 1 Finding the Volume of Pyramids and Cones

Find the volume of each figure. Use 3.14 for π.

A

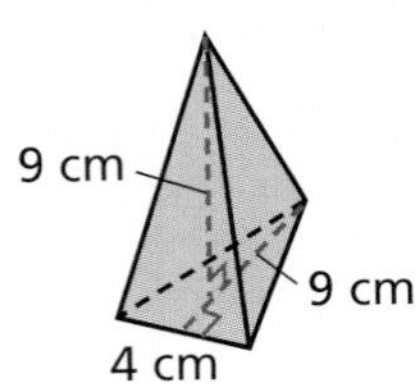

$B = \frac{1}{2}(4 \cdot 9) = 18 \text{ cm}^2$

$V = \frac{1}{3} \cdot 18 \cdot 9$ $\quad V = \frac{1}{3}Bh$

$V = 54 \text{ cm}^3$

Find the volume of each figure. Use 3.14 for π.

B

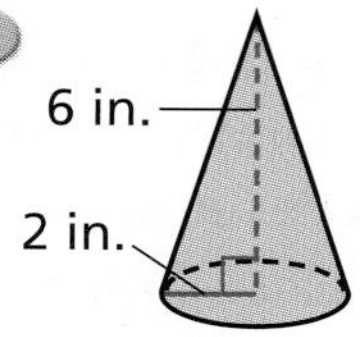

$B = \pi(2^2) = 4\pi \text{ in}^2$

$V = \frac{1}{3} \cdot 4\pi \cdot 6$ — *$V = \frac{1}{3}Bh$*

$V = 8\pi \approx 25 \text{ in}^3$ — *Use 3.14 for π.*

C

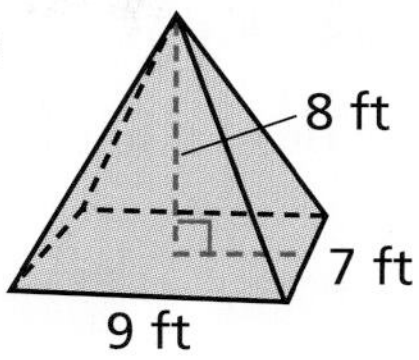

$B = 9 \cdot 7 = 63 \text{ ft}^2$

$V = \frac{1}{3} \cdot 63 \cdot 8$ — *$V = \frac{1}{3}Bh$*

$V = 168 \text{ ft}^3$

D

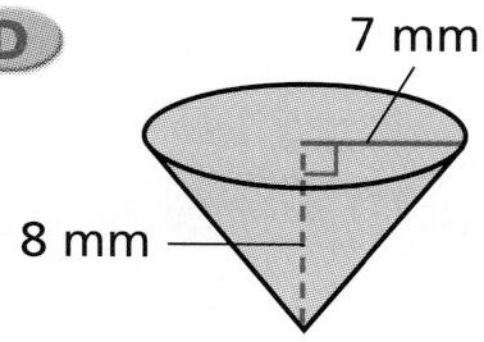

$B = \pi(7^2) = 49\pi \text{ mm}^2$

$V = \frac{1}{3} \cdot 49\pi \cdot 8$ — *$V = \frac{1}{3}Bh$*

$V = \frac{392}{3}\pi \approx 410.5 \text{ mm}^2$ — *Use 3.14 for π.*

EXAMPLE 2 Exploring the Effects of Changing Dimensions

A cone has radius 3 m and height 10 m. Explain whether doubling the height would have the same effect on the volume of the cone as doubling the radius.

Original Dimensions	Double the Height	Double the Radius
$V = \frac{1}{3}\pi r^2 h$	$V = \frac{1}{3}\pi r^2(2h)$	$V = \frac{1}{3}\pi(2r)^2 h$
$= \frac{1}{3}\pi(3^2)(10)$	$= \frac{1}{3}\pi(3^2)(2 \cdot 10)$	$= \frac{1}{3}\pi(2 \cdot 3)^2(10)$
$\approx 94.2 \text{ m}^3$	$\approx 188.4 \text{ m}^3$	$\approx 376.8 \text{ m}^3$

When the height of the cone is doubled, the volume is doubled. When the radius is doubled, the volume becomes 4 times the original volume.

EXAMPLE 3 *Social Studies Application*

Caution!

A lowercase b is used to represent the length of the base of a two-dimensional figure. A capital B is used to represent the area of the base of a solid figure.

The Great Pyramid of Giza is a square pyramid. Its height is 481 ft, and its base has 756 ft sides. Find the volume of the pyramid.

$B = 756^2 = 571{,}536 \text{ ft}^2$ — *$A = bh$*

$V = \frac{1}{3}(571{,}536)(481)$ — *$V = \frac{1}{3}Bh$*

$V = 91{,}636{,}272 \text{ ft}^3$

EXAMPLE 4 Using a Calculator to Find Volume

Some traffic pylons are shaped like cones. Use a calculator to find the volume of a traffic pylon to the nearest hundredth if the radius of the base is 5 inches and the height is 24 inches.

Use the *pi* button on your calculator to find the area of the base.

[2nd] [^] (π) [×] 5 [x^2] [ENTER] $B = \pi r^2$

Next, with the area of the base still displayed, find the volume of the cone.

[×] 24 [×] [(] 1 [÷] 3 [)] [ENTER] $V = \frac{1}{3}Bh$

The volume of the traffic pylon is approximately 628.32 in^3.

Think and Discuss

1. **Describe** two or more ways that you can change the dimensions of a rectangular pyramid to double its volume.
2. **Use a model** to compare the volume of a cube with 1 in. sides with a pyramid that is 1 in. high and has a 1 in. square base.

8-6 Exercises

go.hrw.com
Homework Help Online
KEYWORD: MT7 8-6
Parent Resources Online
KEYWORD: MT7 Parent

GUIDED PRACTICE

See Example 1

Find the volume of each figure to the nearest tenth. Use 3.14 for π.

1. 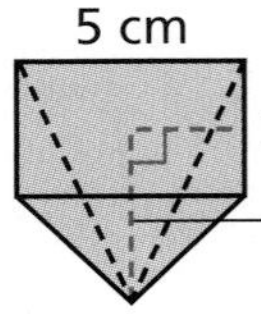

2. 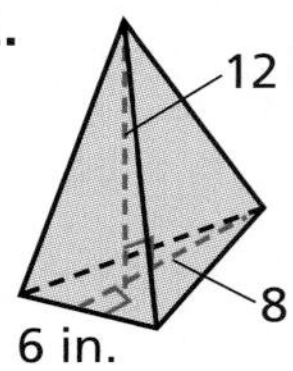

3. 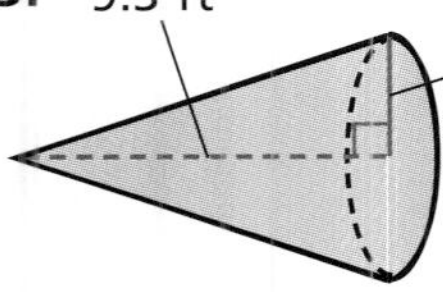

4. 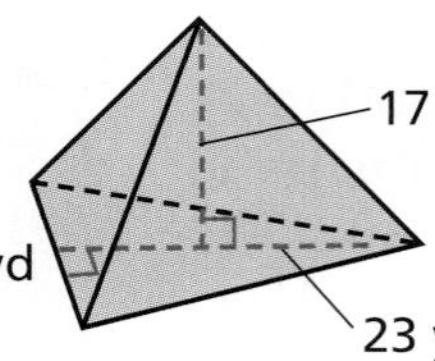

5. 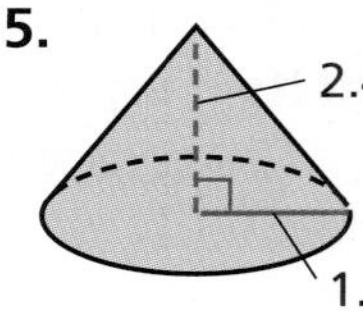

6. 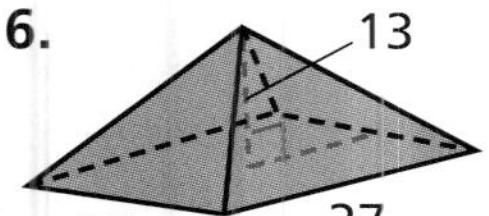

See Example 2

7. A square pyramid has height 6 m and a base that measures 2 m on each side. Explain whether doubling the height would double the volume of the pyramid.

See Example 3

8. The Transamerica Pyramid in San Francisco has a base area of 22,000 ft^2 and a height of 853 ft. What is the volume of the building?

See Example 4

9. Gretchen made a paper cone to hold a gift for a friend. The paper cone was 17 inches high and had a diameter of 6 inches. Use a calculator to find the volume of the paper cone to the nearest hundredth.

INDEPENDENT PRACTICE

See Example 1

Find the volume of each figure to the nearest tenth. Use 3.14 for π.

10.
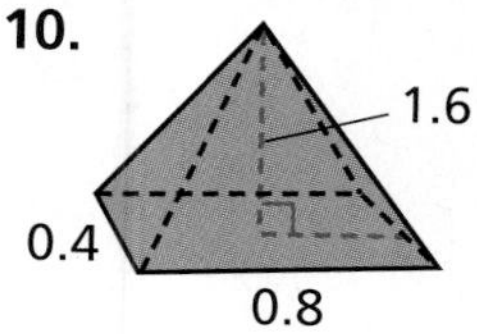

11.
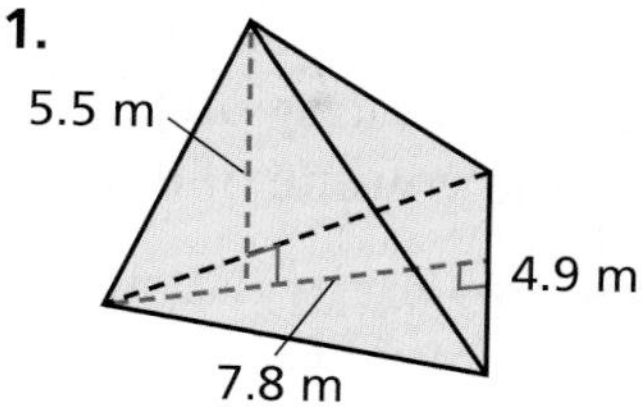

12.
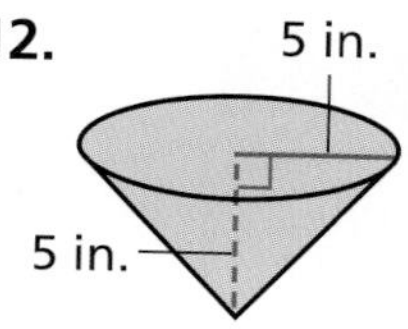

13.
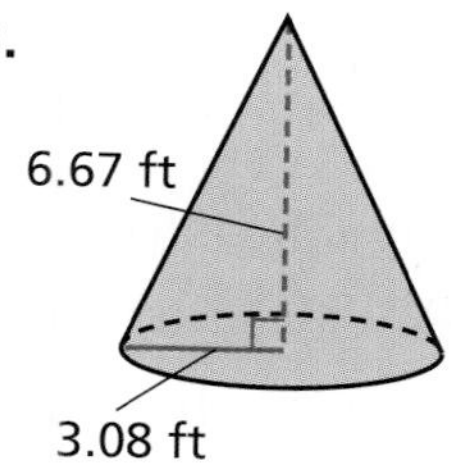

14.
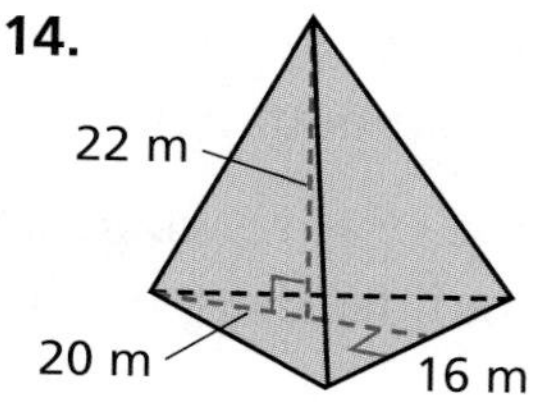

15.
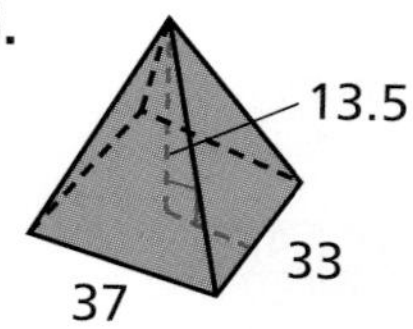

See Example 2

16. A triangular pyramid has a height of 12 in. The triangular base has a height of 12 in. and a width of 12 in. Explain whether doubling the height of the base would double the volume of the pyramid.

See Example 3

17. A cone-shaped building is commonly used to store sand. What would be the volume of a cone-shaped building with diameter 50 m and height 20 m to the nearest hundredth?

See Example 4

18. Antonio made mini waffle cones for a birthday party. Each waffle cone was 3 inches high and had a radius of $\frac{3}{4}$ inch. Use a calculator to find the volume of the waffle cone to the nearest hundredth.

PRACTICE AND PROBLEM SOLVING

Extra Practice
See page 797.

Find the missing measure to the nearest tenth. Use 3.14 for π.

19. cone:
radius = 4 in.
height = □
volume = 100.5 in^3

20. cylinder:
radius = □
height = 2.5 m
volume = 70.65 m^3

21. triangular pyramid:
base height = □
base width = 8 ft
height = 6 ft
volume = 88 ft^3

22. rectangular pyramid:
base length = 3 ft
base width = □
height = 7 ft
volume = 42 ft^3

23. **Estimation** Orange traffic cones come in a variety of sizes. Approximate the volume in cubic inches of a traffic cone with height 2 feet and diameter 10 inches by using 3 in place of π.

LINK

Architecture

I. M. Pei, designer of the Louvre Pyramid, has designed more than 50 buildings around the world and has won many major awards.

go.hrw.com
Web Extra!
KEYWORD: MT7 Pei

24. **Architecture** The Pyramid of the Sun, in Teotihuacán, Mexico, is about 65 m tall and has a square base with side length 225 m.
    a. What is the volume in cubic meters of the pyramid?
    b. How many cubic meters are in a cubic kilometer?
    c. What is the volume in cubic kilometers of the pyramid to the nearest thousandth?

25. **Architecture** The pyramid at the entrance to the Louvre in Paris has a height of 72 feet and a square base that is 112 feet long on each side. What is the volume of this pyramid?

26. **What's the Error?** A student says that the formula for the volume of a cylinder is the same as the formula for the volume of a pyramid, $\frac{1}{3}Bh$. What error did this student make?

27. **Write About It** How would a cone's volume be affected if you doubled the height? the radius? Use a model to help explain.

28. **Challenge** The diameter of a cone is x cm, the height is 18 cm, and the volume is 96π cm^3. What is x?

Test Prep and Spiral Review

29. **Multiple Choice** A pyramid has a rectangular base measuring 12 centimeters by 9 centimeters. Its height is 15 centimeters. What is the volume of the pyramid?

    Ⓐ 540 cm^3 Ⓑ 405 cm^3 Ⓒ 315 cm^3 Ⓓ 270 cm^3

30. **Multiple Choice** A cone has diameter 12 centimeters and height 9 centimeters. Using 3.14 for π, find the volume of the cone to the nearest tenth.

    Ⓕ 1,356.5 cm^3 Ⓖ 339.1 cm^3 Ⓗ 118.3 cm^3 Ⓙ 56.5 cm^3

31. **Gridded Response** Suppose a cone has a volume of 104.7 cubic centimeters and a radius of 5 centimeters. Find the height of the cone to the nearest whole centimeter. Use 3.14 for π.

Solve. (Lesson 1-7)

32. $9 + t = 18$
33. $t - 2 = 6$
34. $10 + t = 32$
35. $t + 7 = 7$

36. Draw the front, top, and side views of the figure. (Lesson 8-4)

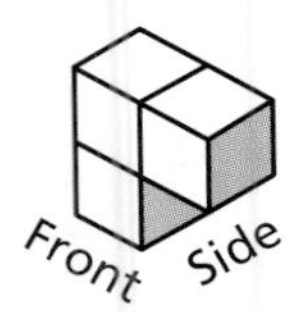

Hands-On LAB 8-7

Find Surface Areas of Prisms and Cylinders

Use with Lesson 8-7

go.hrw.com
Lab Resources Online
KEYWORD: MT7 Lab8

REMEMBER
- A net is an arrangement of two-dimensional figures that can fold to form a three-dimensional figure.

You can explore the surface area of prisms and cylinders using models and nets.

Activity 1

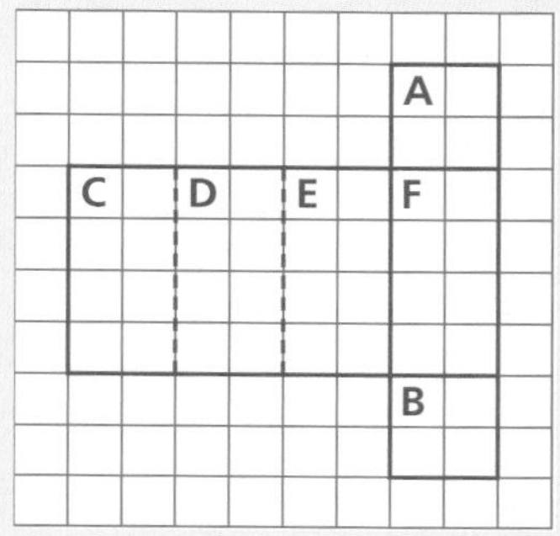

1 Find six different-sized rectangular and triangular prisms.

a. Make a net of the prism by tracing around each face on grid paper.

b. Label the bases A and B. Continue labeling the lateral faces.

c. Copy the tables shown. Fill in the information for each prism.

Rectangular Prism	
Face	**Area**
Base A	
Base B	
Lateral face C	
Lateral face D	
Lateral face E	
Lateral face F	
Total Surface Area	

Triangular Prism	
Face	**Area**
Base A	
Base B	
Lateral face C	
Lateral face D	
Lateral face E	
Total Surface Area	

2 For each prism from **1**, find the perimeter of a base. Then multiply the base's perimeter by the prism's height. Finally, find the total area of the lateral faces.

Think and Discuss

1. In **2**, how did the product of the base's perimeter and the prism's height compare with the sum of the areas of the lateral faces?

2. Write a rule for finding the surface area of any prism.

Try This

1. Use your rule from Think and Discuss 2 to find the surface area of two new prisms. Check your rule by following the steps in **1**. Revise your rule as needed.

Activity 2

1 Find six different-sized cylinders. Follow these steps to make a net for each cylinder.

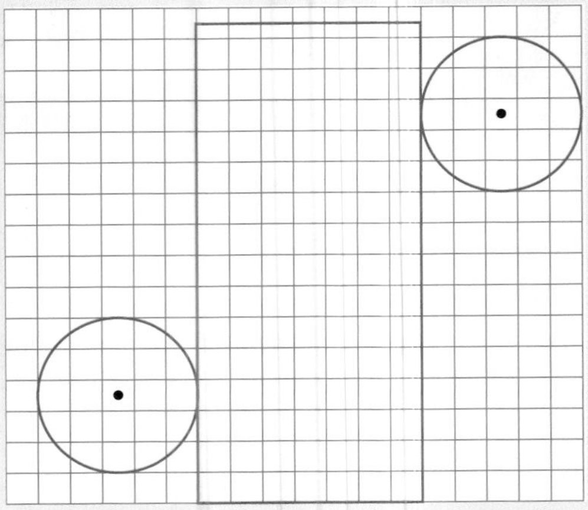

a. Trace around the top of the cylinder on grid paper.

b. Lay the cylinder on the grid paper so that it touches the circle, and mark its height. Then roll the cylinder one complete revolution, marking where the cylinder begins and ends. Draw a rectangle that has the same height as the cylinder and a width equal to one revolution of the cylinder.

c. Trace the bottom of the cylinder so that it touches the bottom of the rectangle.

d. Find the approximate area of each piece by counting squares.

e. Add the areas to find the total surface area of the cylinder.

f. Copy the table shown. Record the information in the table.

Cylinder		
Face	**Area by Counting Squares**	**Area by Using Formula**
Circular base A		
Circular base B		
Lateral face C		
Total Surface Area		

2 Follow these steps for each cylinder from **1**.

a. Tape your pieces together to make a cylinder.

b. Use area formulas to find the area of each base and the lateral face.

c. Add the areas to find the total surface area of your net.

d. Record the information in the table.

Think and Discuss

1. How did the area found by counting squares compare with the area found by using a formula?
2. How does the circumference of the base compare with the length of the lateral face?
3. Make a rule for finding the surface area of any cylinder.

Try This

1. Use your rule from Think and Discuss 3 to find the surface area of a new cylinder. Check your rule by following the steps in the activity. Revise your rule as needed.

8-7 Surface Area of Prisms and Cylinders

Learn to find the surface area of prisms and cylinders.

Vocabulary

surface area

lateral face

lateral surface

An *anamorphic image* is a distorted picture that becomes recognizable when reflected onto a cylindrical mirror.

Surface area is the sum of the areas of all surfaces of a figure. The **lateral faces** of a prism are parallelograms that connect the bases. The **lateral surface** of a cylinder is the curved surface.

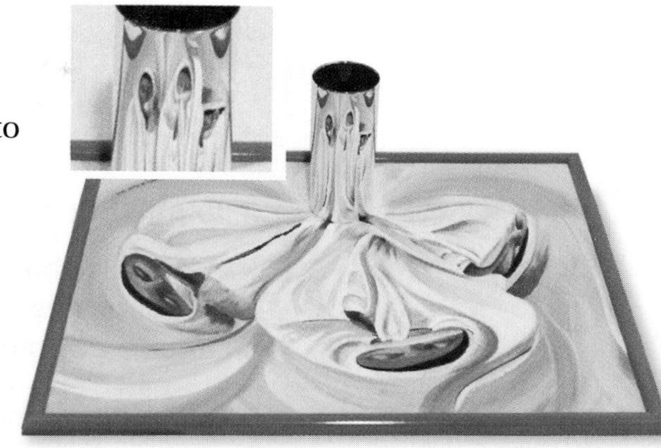

SURFACE AREA OF PRISMS AND CYLINDERS

Words	Numbers	Formula
Prism: The surface area S of a prism is twice the base area B plus the lateral area F. The lateral area is the base perimeter P times the height h.	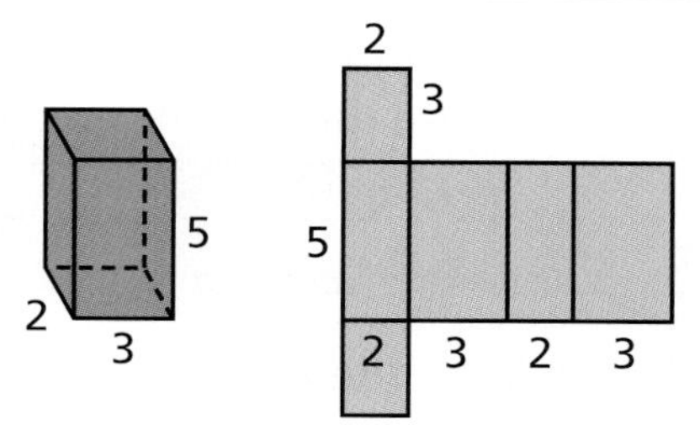 $S = 2(3 \cdot 2) + (10)(5) = 62$ units^2	$S = 2B + F$ or $S = 2B + Ph$
Cylinder: The surface area S of a cylinder is twice the base area B plus the lateral area L. The lateral area is the base circumference $2\pi r$ times the height h.	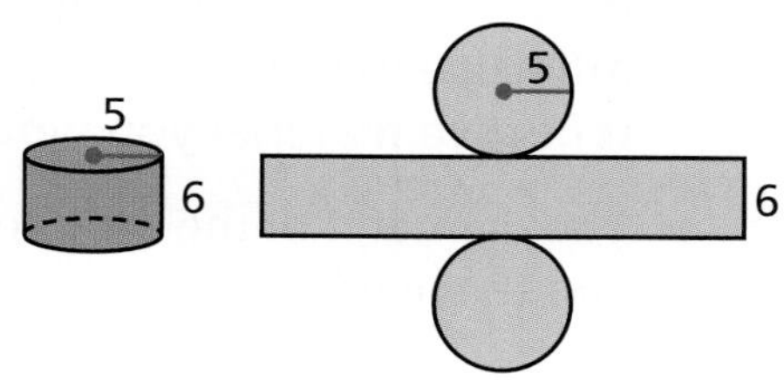 $S = 2\pi(5^2) + 2\pi(5)(6) \approx 345.4$ units^2	$S = 2B + L$ or $S = 2\pi r^2 + 2\pi rh$

EXAMPLE 1 Finding Surface Area

Find the surface area of each figure to the nearest tenth. Use 3.14 for π.

A

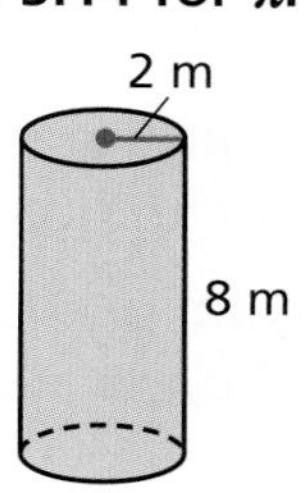

$$S = 2\pi r^2 + 2\pi rh$$
$$= 2\pi(2^2) + 2\pi(2)(8)$$
$$= 40\pi \text{ m}^2$$
$$\approx 125.6 \text{ m}^2$$

Find the surface area of each figure to the nearest tenth. Use 3.14 for π.

B

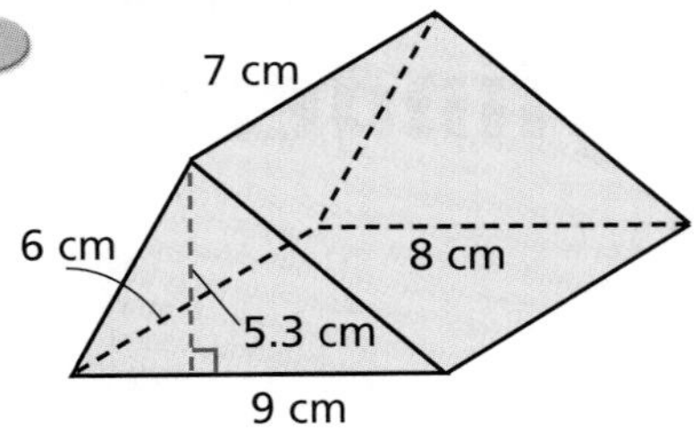

$S = 2B + Ph$

$= 2\left(\frac{1}{2} \cdot 9 \cdot 5.3\right) + (23)(7)$

$= 208.7 \text{ cm}^2$

EXAMPLE 2 Exploring the Effects of Changing Dimensions

A cylinder has diameter 10 in. and height 4 in. Explain whether doubling the height would have the same effect on the surface area as doubling the radius.

Original Dimensions	Double the Height	Double the Radius
$S = 2\pi r^2 + 2\pi rh$ $= 2\pi(5)^2 + 2\pi(5)(4)$ $= 90\pi \text{ in}^2 \approx 282.6 \text{ in}^2$	$S = 2\pi r^2 + 2\pi rh$ $= 2\pi(5)^2 + 2\pi(5)(8)$ $= 130\pi \text{ in}^2 \approx 408.2 \text{ in}^2$	$S = 2\pi r^2 + 2\pi rh$ $= 2\pi(10)^2 + 2\pi(10)(4)$ $= 280\pi \text{ in}^2 \approx 879.2 \text{ in}^2$

They would not have the same effect. Doubling the radius would increase the surface area more than doubling the height.

EXAMPLE 3 *Art Application*

A Web site advertises that it can turn your photo into an anamorphic image. To reflect the picture, you need to cover a cylinder that is 49 mm in diameter and 107 mm tall with reflective material. Estimate the amount of reflective material you would need.

The diameter of the cylinder is about 50 mm, and the height is about 100 mm.

$L = 2\pi rh$ — *Only the lateral surface needs to be covered.*

$= 2\pi(25)(100)$ — *diameter $\approx$ 50 mm, so $r \approx$ 25 mm*

$\approx 15{,}700 \text{ mm}^2$

Think and Discuss

1. **Explain** how finding the surface area of a cylindrical drinking glass would be different from finding the surface area of a cylinder.
2. **Compare** the amount of paint needed to cover a cube with 1 ft sides to the amount needed to cover a cube with 2 ft sides.

8-7 Exercises

go.hrw.com
Homework Help Online
KEYWORD: MT7 8-7
Parent Resources Online
KEYWORD: MT7 Parent

GUIDED PRACTICE

See Example 1

Find the surface area of each figure to the nearest tenth. Use 3.14 for π.

1.
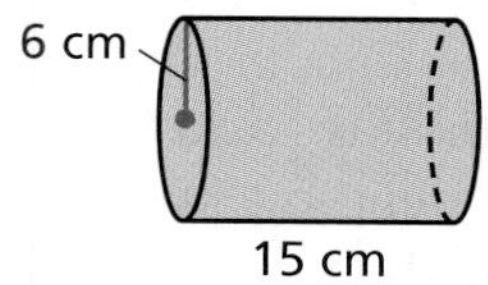

2.
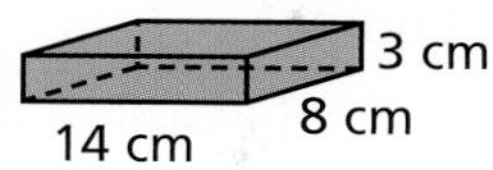

3.
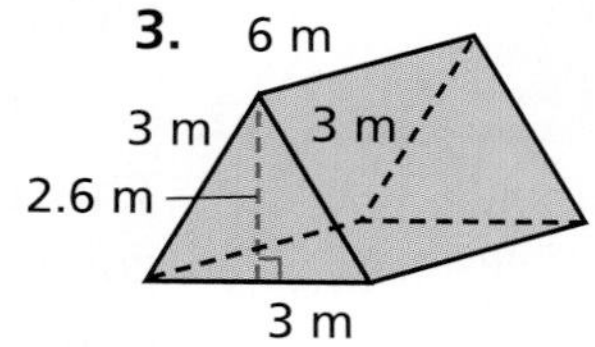

See Example 2

4. A rectangular prism is 3 ft by 4 ft by 7 ft. Explain whether doubling all of the dimensions would double the surface area.

See Example 3

5. Tilly is covering a can with contact paper, not including its top and bottom. The can measures 8 inches high and has a radius of 2 inches. Estimate the amount of contact paper she needs.

INDEPENDENT PRACTICE

See Example 1

Find the surface area of each figure to the nearest tenth. Use 3.14 for π.

6.
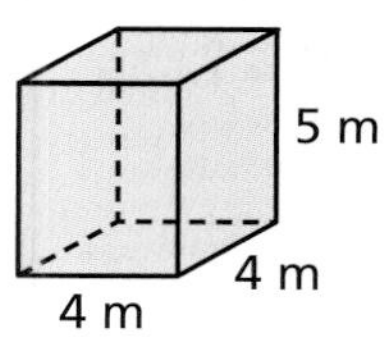

7.
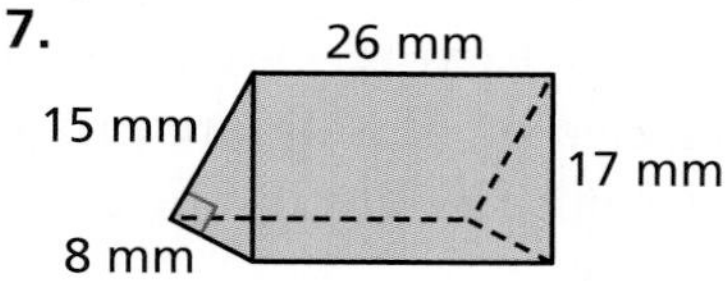

8.
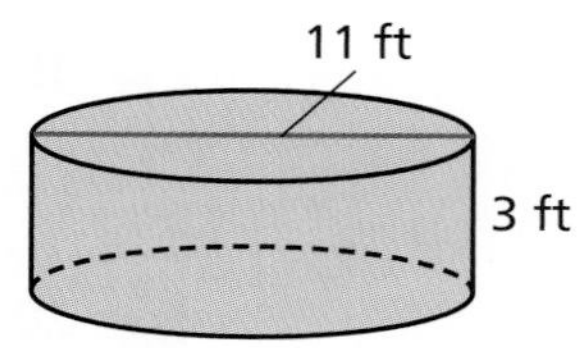

See Example 2

9. A cylinder has diameter 4 ft and height 9 ft. Explain whether halving the diameter has the same effect on the surface area as halving the height.

See Example 3

10. Frank is wrapping a present. The box measures 6.2 cm by 9.9 cm by 5.1 cm. Estimate the amount of wrapping paper, not counting overlap, that Frank needs.

PRACTICE AND PROBLEM SOLVING

Extra Practice
See page 797.

Find the surface area of each figure with the given dimensions to the nearest tenth. Use 3.14 for π.

11. cylinder: $d = 30$ mm, $h = 49$ mm

12. rectangular prism: $5\frac{1}{4}$ in. by 8 in. by 12 in.

Find the missing dimension in each figure with the given surface area.

13.
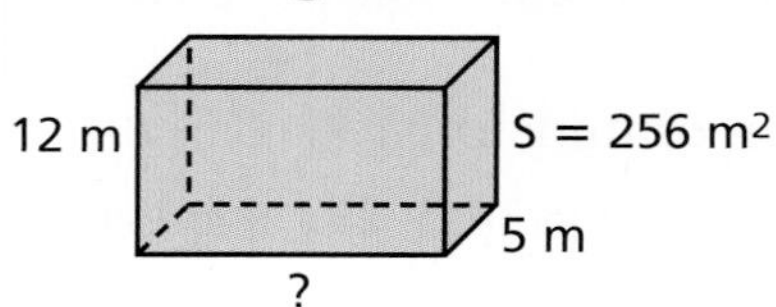

14.
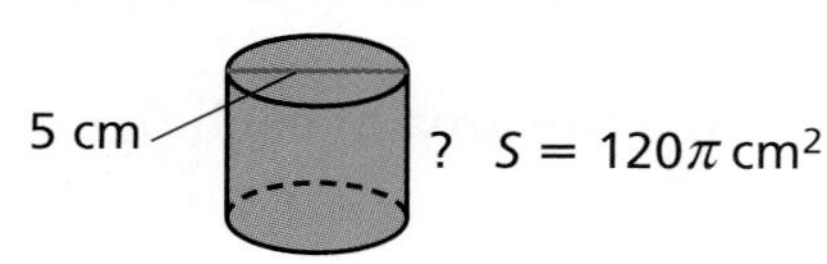

Sports

One machine used to shape the inside of a half-pipe is called the Pipe Dragon. Others are the Pipe Master, Turbo Grinder, Scorpion, and Pipe Magician.

15. **Multi-Step** Jesse makes rectangular glass aquariums measuring 12 in. by 6 in. by 8 in. Glass costs $0.08 per square inch. How much will the glass for one aquarium cost?

16. **Sports** In the snowboard half-pipe, competitors ride back and forth on a course shaped like a cylinder cut in half lengthwise. What is the surface area of this half-pipe course?

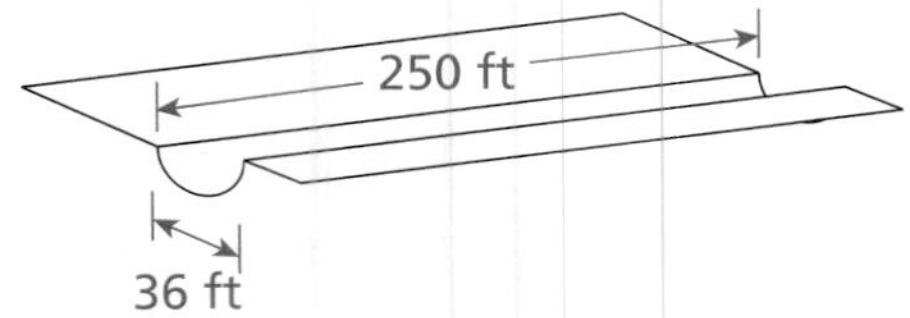

17. **Multi-Step** Olivia is painting the four sides and top of a large trunk. The trunk measures 5 ft long by 3.5 ft deep by 3 ft high. A gallon of paint covers approximately 300 square feet. She wants at least 15% extra paint for waste and overage. How many quarts of paint does she need?

18. **Choose a Strategy** Which of the following nets can be folded into the given three-dimensional figure?

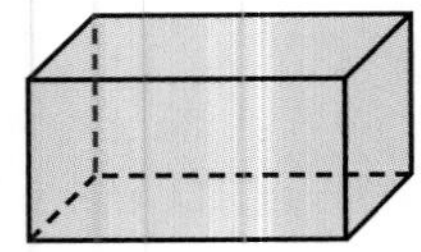

Ⓐ 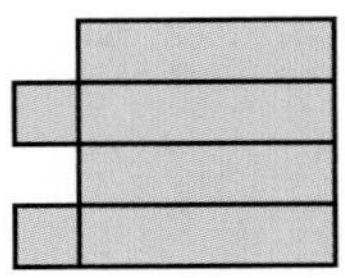 Ⓑ 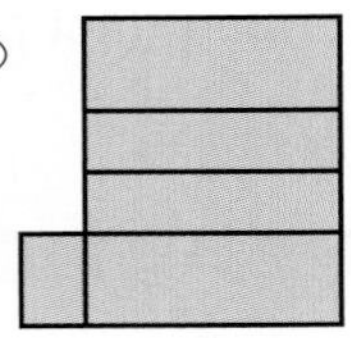 Ⓒ 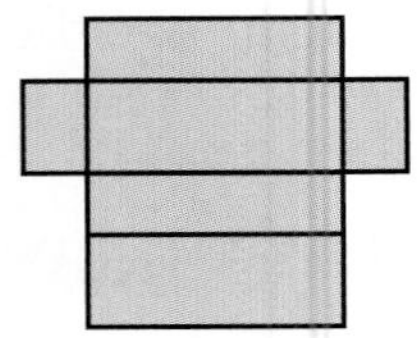 Ⓓ 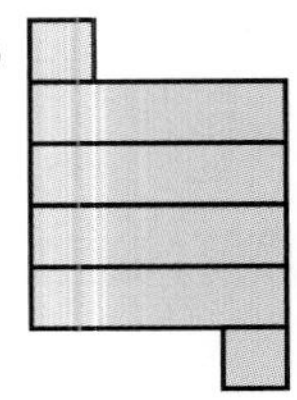

19. **Write About It** Describe the effect on the surface area of a square prism when you double the length of one of its sides.

20. **Challenge** A rectangular wood block that is 12 cm by 9 cm by 5 cm has a hole drilled through the center with diameter 4 cm. What is the total surface area of the wood block?

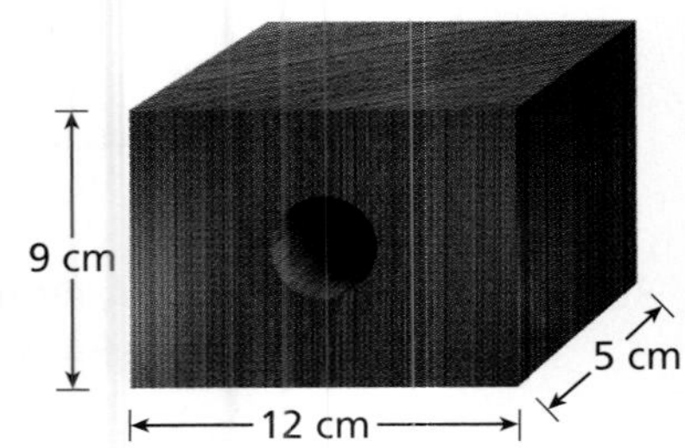

Test Prep and Spiral Review

21. **Multiple Choice** Find the surface area of a cylinder with radius 5 feet and height 3 feet. Use 3.14 for π.

Ⓐ 125.6 ft^2 Ⓑ 150.72 ft^2 Ⓒ 172.7 ft^2 Ⓓ 251.2 ft^2

22. **Gridded Response** A rectangular prism has dimensions 2 meters by 4 meters by 18 meters. Find the surface area, in square meters, of the prism.

Add or subtract. (Lesson 2-3)

23. $-0.4 + 0.7$ 24. $1.35 - 5.6$ 25. $-0.01 - 0.25$ 26. $-0.65 + (-1.12)$

Find the area of each figure with the given dimensions. (Lesson 8-2)

27. triangle: $b = 4, h = 6$ 28. triangle: $b = 3, h = 14$ 29. trapezoid: $b_1 = 3.4, b_2 = 6.6, h = 1.8$

Hands-On LAB 8-8

Find Surface Area of Pyramids

Use with Lesson 8-8

go.hrw.com
Lab Resources Online
KEYWORD: MT7 Lab8

You can explore the surface area of pyramids using models and nets.

Activity

1 Find six different pyramids. Follow these steps for each one.

a. Trace around each face on grid paper to make a net. Cut out the net.

b. Find the approximate area of each face by counting the squares, and add them to find the surface area of the pyramid.

c. Copy the table shown. Record your observations in the table.

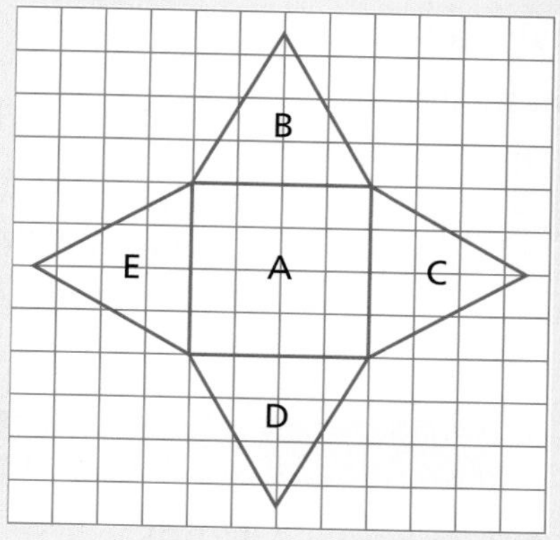

2 Follow these steps for each pyramid from Activity 1.

a. Fold and tape your net to make a pyramid.

b. Use area formulas to find the area of the base and each lateral face, and add them to find the surface area of your net.

c. Record your observations in the table.

Face	Pyramid: Area by Counting Squares	Pyramid: Area by Using Formula
Base A		
Lateral face B		
Lateral face C		
Lateral face D		
Lateral face E		
Total Surface Area		

Think and Discuss

1. How did the area found by counting compare with the area found by using a formula?
2. Find the product of a base's perimeter and the height of a triangular face, known as the slant height, ℓ. How does this compare with the total area of the triangular faces?
3. Make a rule for finding the surface area of any pyramid.

Try This

1. Use your rule from Think and Discuss 3 to find the surface area of a new pyramid. Check your rule by following the steps in the activity. Revise your rule as needed.

8-8 Surface Area of Pyramids and Cones

Learn to find the surface area of pyramids and cones.

Vocabulary

slant height

regular pyramid

right cone

The **slant height** of a pyramid or cone is measured along its lateral surface.

The base of a **regular pyramid** is a regular polygon, and the lateral faces are all congruent.

In a **right cone**, a line perpendicular to the base through the tip of the cone passes through the center of the base.

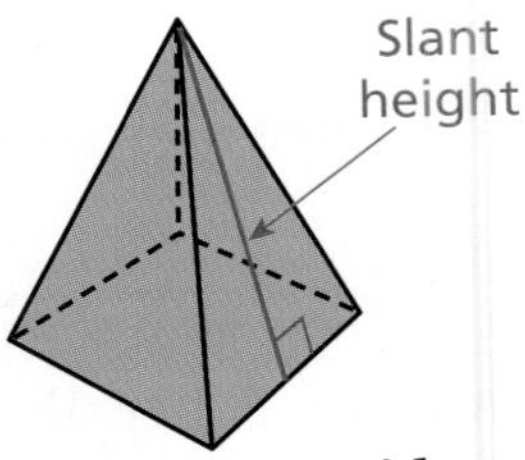

Regular pyramid

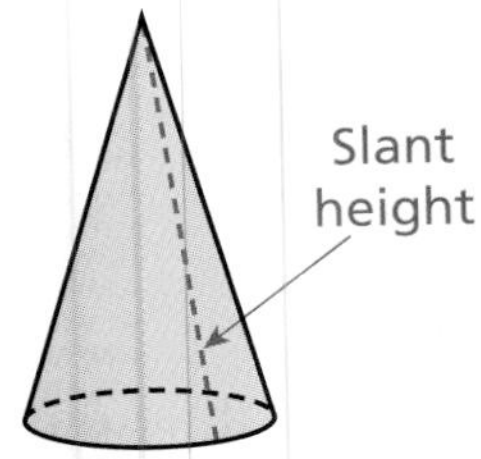

Right cone

SURFACE AREA OF PYRAMIDS AND CONES

Words	Numbers	Formula
Pyramid: The surface area S of a regular pyramid is the base area B plus the lateral area F. The lateral area is one-half the base perimeter P times the slant height ℓ.	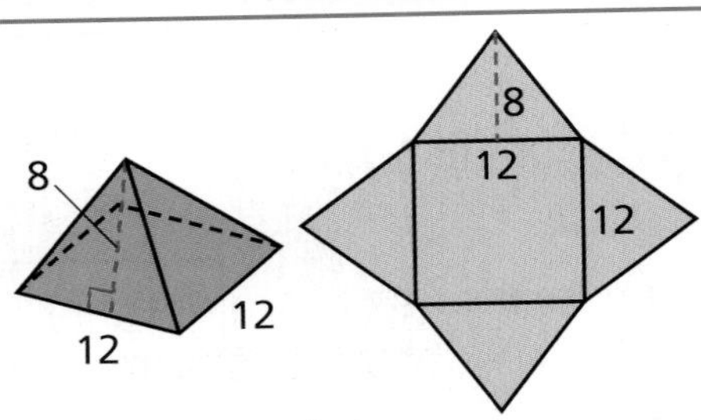 $S = (12 \cdot 12) + \frac{1}{2}(48)(8) = 336 \text{ units}^2$	$S = B + F$ or $S = B + \frac{1}{2}P\ell$
Cone: The surface area S of a right cone is the base area B plus the lateral area L. The lateral area is one-half the base circumference $2\pi r$ times the slant height ℓ.	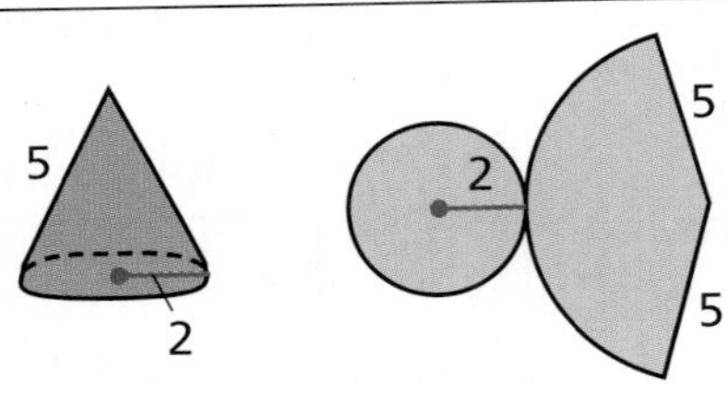 $S = \pi(2^2) + \pi(2)(5) = 14\pi \approx 43.98 \text{ units}^2$	$S = B + L$ or $S = \pi r^2 + \pi r\ell$

EXAMPLE 1 Finding Surface Area

Find the surface area of each figure to the nearest tenth. Use 3.14 for π.

A

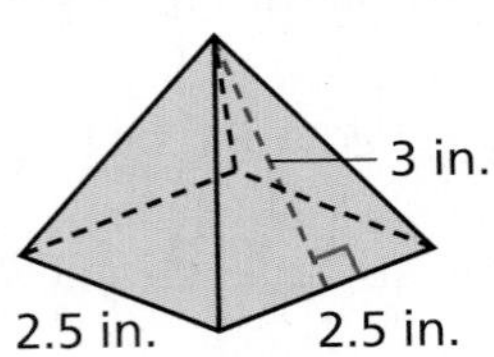

$S = B + \frac{1}{2}P\ell$

$= (2.5 \cdot 2.5) + \frac{1}{2}(10)(3)$

$= 21.25 \text{ in}^2$

Find the surface area of each figure to the nearest tenth. Use 3.14 for π.

B

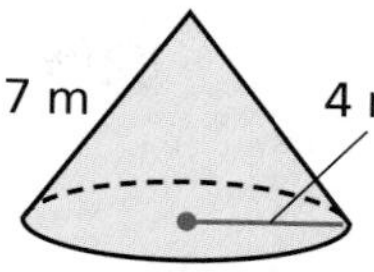

$$S = \pi r^2 + \pi r \ell$$
$$= \pi(4)^2 + \pi(4)(7)$$
$$= 44\pi \approx 138.2 \text{ m}^2$$

EXAMPLE 2 Exploring the Effects of Changing Dimensions

A cone has diameter 6 in. and slant height 4 in. Explain whether doubling the slant height would have the same effect on the surface area as doubling the radius. Use 3.14 for π.

Original Dimensions	Double the Slant Height	Double the Radius
$S = \pi r^2 + \pi r\ell$ $= \pi(3)^2 + \pi(3)(4)$ $= 21\pi \text{ in}^2 \approx 66.0 \text{ in}^2$	$S = \pi r^2 + \pi r(2\ell)$ $= \pi(3)^2 + \pi(3)(8)$ $= 33\pi \text{ in}^2 \approx 103.6 \text{ in}^2$	$S = \pi(2r)^2 + \pi(2r)\ell$ $= \pi(6)^2 + \pi(6)(4)$ $= 60\pi \text{ in}^2 \approx 188.4 \text{ in}^2$

They would not have the same effect. Doubling the radius would increase the surface area more than doubling the slant height.

EXAMPLE 3 *Life Science Application*

LINK

Life Science

Ant lions are the larvae of an insect similar to a dragonfly. They dig cone-shaped pits in the sand to trap ants and other crawling insects.

An ant lion pit is an inverted cone with the dimensions shown. What is the lateral surface area of the pit?

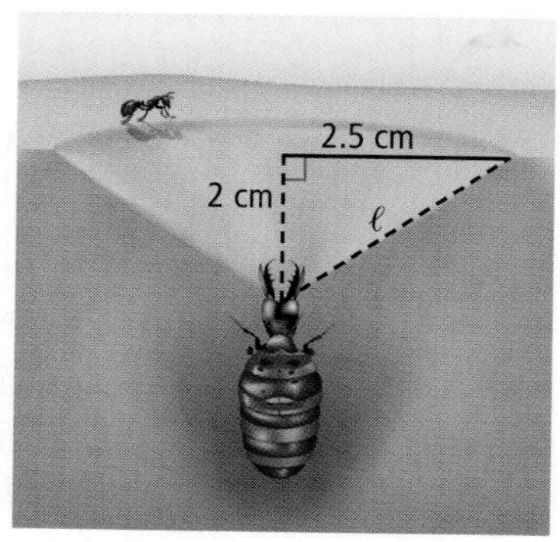

The slant height, radius, and depth of the pit form a right triangle.

$a^2 + b^2 = \ell^2$ *Pythagorean Theorem*

$(2.5)^2 + 2^2 = \ell^2$

$10.25 = \ell^2$

$\ell \approx 3.2$

$L = \pi r\ell$ *Lateral surface area*

$= \pi(2.5)(3.2) \approx 25.1 \text{ cm}^2$

Think and Discuss

1. Compare the formula for surface area of a pyramid to the formula for surface area of a cone.

2. Explain how you would find the slant height of a square pyramid with base edge length 6 cm and height 4 cm.

8-8 Exercises

go.hrw.com
Homework Help Online
KEYWORD: MT7 8-8
Parent Resources Online
KEYWORD: MT7 Parent

GUIDED PRACTICE

See Example 1

Find the surface area of each figure to the nearest tenth. Use 3.14 for π.

1.

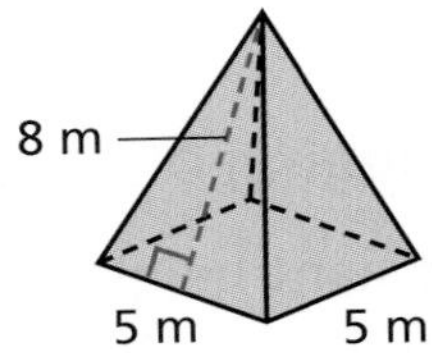

2.

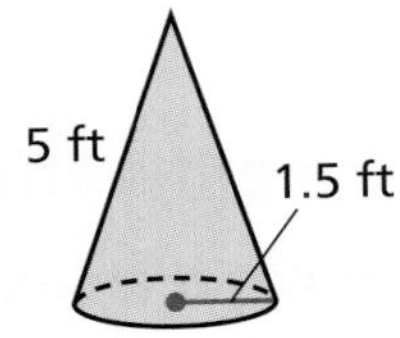

3.

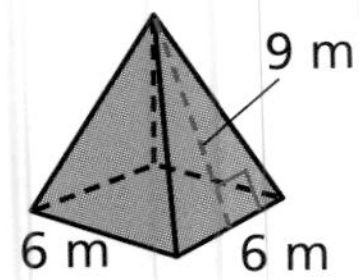

See Example 2

4. A cone has diameter 12 in. and slant height 9 in. Tell whether doubling both dimensions would double the surface area.

See Example 3

5. The rooms at the Wigwam Village Motel in Cave City, Kentucky, are cones about 20 ft high and have a diameter of about 20 ft. Estimate the lateral surface area of a room.

INDEPENDENT PRACTICE

See Example 1

Find the surface area of each figure to the nearest tenth. Use 3.14 for π.

6.

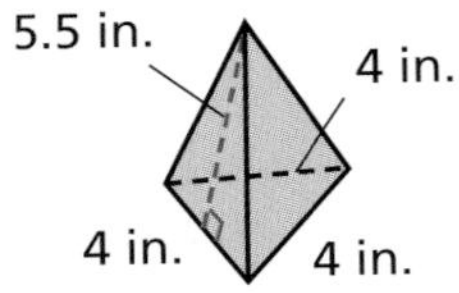

7.

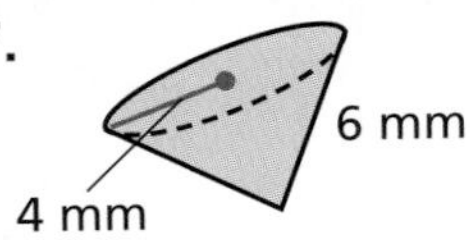

8.

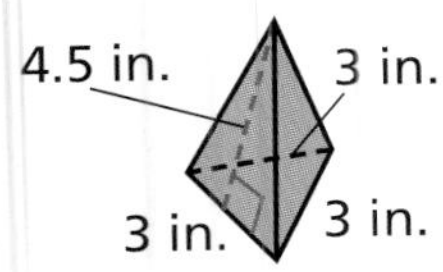

See Example 2

9. A regular square pyramid has a base with 12 yd sides and slant height 5 yd. Tell whether doubling both dimensions would double the surface area.

See Example 3

10. In the late 1400s, Leonardo da Vinci designed a parachute shaped like a pyramid. His design called for a tent-like structure made of linen, measuring 21 feet on each side and 12 feet high. Estimate how much material would be needed to make the parachute?

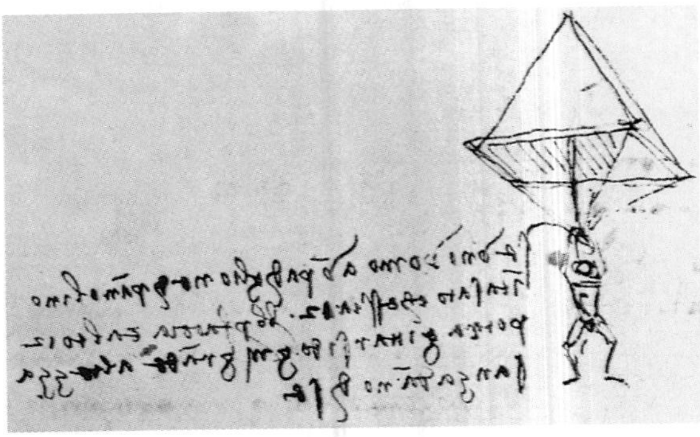

PRACTICE AND PROBLEM SOLVING

Extra Practice
See page 797.

Find the surface area of each figure with the given dimensions. Use 3.14 for π.

11. regular triangular pyramid:
base area = 0.06 km^2
base perimeter = 0.8 km
slant height = 0.3 km

12. cone: $r = 12\frac{1}{2}$ mi
slant height = $44\frac{1}{4}$ mi

13. **Earth Science** When the Moon is between the Sun and Earth, it casts a conical shadow called the *umbra*. If the shadow is 2140 mi in diameter and 260,955 mi along the edge, what is the lateral surface area of the umbra?

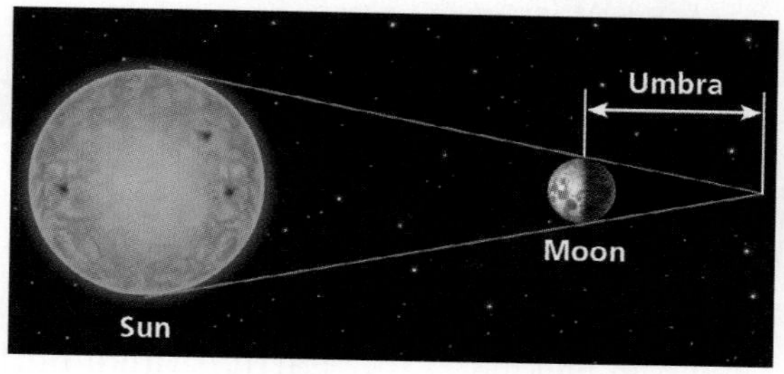

14. **Social Studies** The Pyramid Arena in Memphis, Tennessee, is 321 feet tall and has a square base with side length 200 yards. What is the lateral surface area of the pyramid in feet?

15. The table shows the dimensions of three square pyramids.
   a. Complete the table.
   b. Which pyramid has the least lateral surface area? What is its lateral surface area?
   c. Which pyramid has the greatest volume? What is its volume?

Dimensions of Giza Pyramids (ft)

Pyramid	Height	Slant Height	Side of Base
Khufu	■	612	756
Khafre	471	588	704
Menkaure	216	■	346

16. **Write a Problem** An ice cream cone has a diameter of 4 in. and a slant height of 11 in. Write and solve a problem about the ice cream cone.

17. **Write About It** The height and base dimensions of a cone are known. Explain how to find the slant height.

18. **Challenge** The oldest pyramid is said to be the Step Pyramid of King Zoser, built around 2650 B.C. in Saqqara, Egypt. The base is a rectangle that measures 358 ft by 411 ft, and the height of the pyramid is 204 ft. Find the lateral surface area of the pyramid.

Test Prep and Spiral Review

19. **Multiple Choice** Find the surface area of a triangular pyramid with base area 12 square meters, base perimeter 24 meters, and slant height 8 meters.

Ⓐ 72 m^2 Ⓑ 108 m^2 Ⓒ 204 m^2 Ⓓ 2304 m^2

20. **Gridded Response** What is the lateral surface area of a cone with diameter 12 centimeters and slant height 6 centimeters? Use 3.14 for π.

Simplify. (Lesson 1-6)

21. $-4(6 - 8)$
22. $3(-5 - 4)$
23. $-2(4 - 9)$
24. $-6(8 - 9)$

Find the volume of each rectangular prism. (Lesson 8-5)

25. length 5 ft, width 3 ft, height 8 ft
26. length 2.5 m, width 3.5 m, height 7 m

8-9 Spheres

Learn to find the volume and surface area of spheres.

Vocabulary
- sphere
- hemisphere
- great circle

Earth is not a perfect *sphere,* but it has been molded by gravitational forces into a spherical shape. Earth has a diameter of about 7926 miles and a surface area of about 197 million square miles.

A **sphere** is the set of points in three dimensions that are a fixed distance from a given point, the center. A plane that intersects a sphere through its center divides the sphere into two halves, or **hemispheres**. The edge of a hemisphere is a **great circle**.

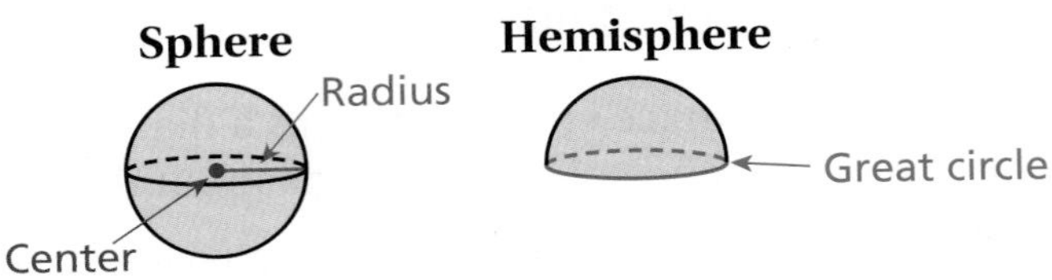

The volume of a hemisphere is exactly halfway between the volume of a cone and the volume of a cylinder with the same radius r and height equal to r.

VOLUME OF A SPHERE		
Words	**Numbers**	**Formula**
The volume V of a sphere is $\frac{4}{3}\pi$ times the cube of the radius r.	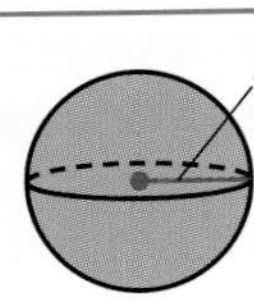 $V = \frac{4}{3}\pi(3^3)$ $= \frac{108}{3}\pi$ $= 36\pi$ $\approx 113.1 \text{ units}^3$	$V = \frac{4}{3}\pi r^3$

EXAMPLE 1 Finding the Volume of a Sphere

Find the volume of a sphere with radius 9 ft, both in terms of π and to the nearest tenth. Use 3.14 for π.

$V = \frac{4}{3}\pi r^3$ *Volume of a sphere*

$= \frac{4}{3}\pi(9)^3$ *Substitute 9 for r.*

$= 972\pi \text{ ft}^3 \approx 3052.1 \text{ ft}^3$

The surface area of a sphere is four times the area of a great circle.

SURFACE AREA OF A SPHERE

Words	Numbers	Formula
The surface area S of a sphere is 4π times the square of the radius r.	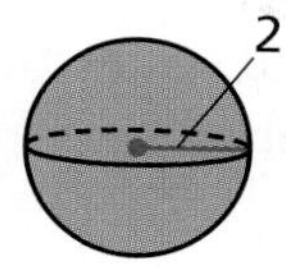 $S = 4\pi(2^2)$ $= 16\pi$ ≈ 50.3 units^2	$S = 4\pi r^2$

EXAMPLE 2 Finding Surface Area of a Sphere

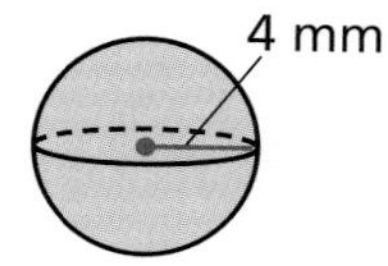

Find the surface area, both in terms of π and to the nearest tenth. Use 3.14 for π.

$S = 4\pi r^2$ — *Surface area of a sphere*

$= 4\pi(4^2)$ — *Substitute 4 for r.*

$= 64\pi \text{ mm}^2 \approx 201.1 \text{ mm}^2$

EXAMPLE 3 Comparing Volumes and Surface Areas

Compare the volume and surface area of a sphere with radius 42 cm with that of a rectangular prism measuring 56 × 63 × 88 cm.

Sphere:

$V = \frac{4}{3}\pi r^3 = \frac{4}{3}\pi(42)^3$

$\approx \left(\frac{4}{3}\right)\left(\frac{22}{7}\right)(74{,}088)$

$\approx 310{,}464 \text{ cm}^3$

$S = 4\pi r^2 = 4\pi(42)^2$

$= 7056\pi$

$\approx 7056\left(\frac{22}{7}\right) \approx 22{,}176 \text{ cm}^2$

Rectangular prism:

$V = \ell wh$

$= (56)(63)(88)$

$= 310{,}464 \text{ cm}^3$

$S = 2\ell w + 2\ell h + 2wh$

$= 2(56)(63) + 2(56)(88) + 2(63)(88)$

$= 28{,}000 \text{ cm}^2$

The sphere and the prism have approximately the same volume, but the prism has a larger surface area.

Think and Discuss

1. **Compare** the area of a great circle with the surface area of a sphere.
2. **Explain** which would hold the most water: a bowl in the shape of a hemisphere with radius r, a cylindrical glass with radius r and height r, or a conical drinking cup with radius r and height r.

8-9 Exercises

go.hrw.com
Homework Help Online
KEYWORD: MT7 8-9
Parent Resources Online
KEYWORD: MT7 Parent

GUIDED PRACTICE

See Example 1

Find the volume of each sphere, both in terms of π and to the nearest tenth. Use 3.14 for π.

1. $r = 3$ cm **2.** $r = 12$ ft **3.** $d = 3.4$ m **4.** $d = 10$ mi

See Example 2

Find the surface area of each sphere, both in terms of π and to the nearest tenth. Use 3.14 for π.

5.
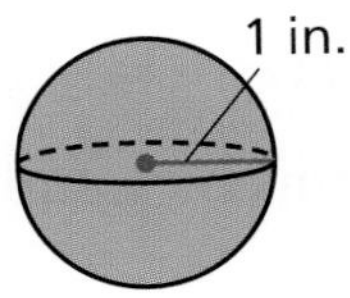

6.
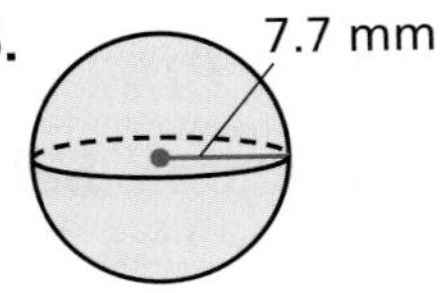

7.
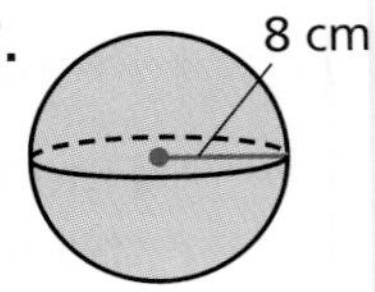

8.
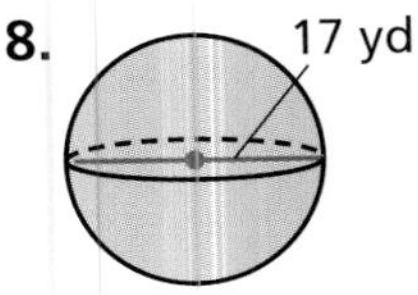

See Example 3

9. Compare the volume and surface area of a sphere with radius 4 in. with that of a cube with sides measuring 6.45 in.

INDEPENDENT PRACTICE

See Example 1

Find the volume of each sphere, both in terms of π and to the nearest tenth. Use 3.14 for π.

10. $r = 14$ ft **11.** $r = 5.7$ cm **12.** $d = 26$ mm **13.** $d = 2$ in.

See Example 2

Find the surface area of each sphere, both in terms of π and to the nearest tenth. Use 3.14 for π.

14.
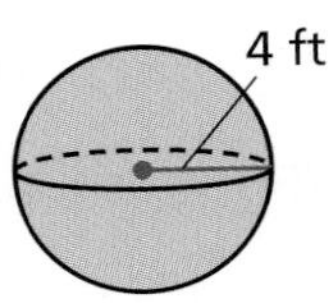

15.
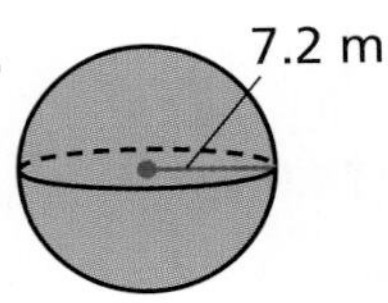

16.
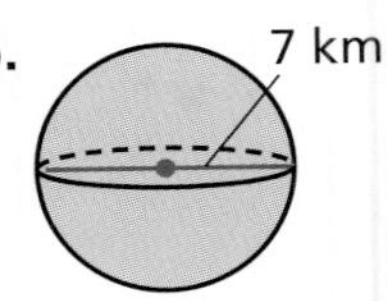

17.
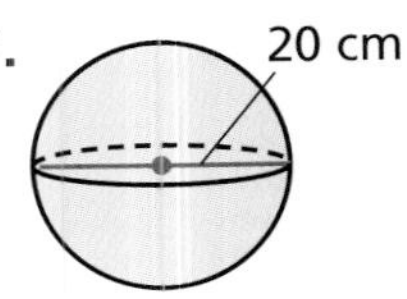

See Example 3

18. Compare the volume and surface area of a sphere with diameter 5 ft with that of a cylinder with height 2 ft and a base with radius 3 ft.

PRACTICE AND PROBLEM SOLVING

Extra Practice
See page 797.

Find the missing measurements of each sphere, both in terms of π and to the nearest hundredth. Use 3.14 for π.

19. radius = 6.5 in.
volume = ▢
surface area = 169π in^2

20. radius = 11.2 m
volume = 1873.24π m^3
surface area = ▢

21. diameter = 6.8 yd
volume = ▢
surface area = ▢

22. radius = ▢
diameter = 22 in.
surface area = ▢

23. Use models of a sphere, cylinder, and two cones. The sphere and cylinder have the same diameter and height. The cones have the same diameter and half the height of the sphere. Describe the relationship between the volumes of these shapes.

Life Science LINK

Eggs come in many different shapes. The eggs of birds that live on cliffs are often extremely pointed to keep the eggs from rolling. Other birds, such as great horned owls, have eggs that are nearly spherical. Turtles and crocodiles also have nearly spherical eggs, and the eggs of many dinosaurs were spherical.

24. To lay their eggs, green turtles travel hundreds of miles to the beach where they were born. The eggs are buried on the beach in a hole about 40 cm deep. The eggs are approximately spherical, with an average diameter of 4.5 cm, and each turtle lays an average of 113 eggs at a time. Estimate the total volume of eggs laid by a green turtle at one time.

25. Fossilized embryos of dinosaurs called titanosaurid sauropods have recently been found in spherical eggs in Patagonia. The eggs were 15 cm in diameter, and the adult dinosaurs were more than 12 m in length. Find the volume of an egg.

26. Hummingbirds lay eggs that are nearly spherical and about 1 cm in diameter. Find the surface area of an egg.

27. **Challenge** An ostrich egg has about the same volume as a sphere with a diameter of 5 inches. If the shell is about $\frac{1}{12}$ inch thick, estimate the volume of just the shell, not including the interior of the egg.

TEST PREP and Spiral Review

28. Multiple Choice The surface area of a sphere is 50.24 square centimeters. What is its diameter? Use 3.14 for π.

Ⓐ 1 cm Ⓑ 2 cm Ⓒ 2.5 cm Ⓓ 4 cm

29. Gridded Response Find the surface area, in square feet, of a sphere with radius 3 feet. Use 3.14 for π.

Simplify. (Lesson 4-5)

30. $\sqrt{144}$ **31.** $\sqrt{64}$ **32.** $\sqrt{169}$ **33.** $\sqrt{225}$ **34.** $\sqrt{1}$

Find the surface area of each figure to the nearest tenth. Use 3.14 for π. (Lesson 8-8)

35. a square pyramid with base 13 m by 13 m and slant height 7.5 m

36. a cone with a diameter 90 cm and slant height 125 cm

8-10 Scaling Three-Dimensional Figures

Learn to make scale models of solid figures.

Vocabulary

capacity

A packaging company sells boxes in a variety of sizes. It offers a supply of cube boxes that measure 1 ft × 1 ft × 1 ft, 2 ft × 2 ft × 2 ft, and 3 ft × 3 ft × 3 ft. What is the volume and surface area of each of these boxes?

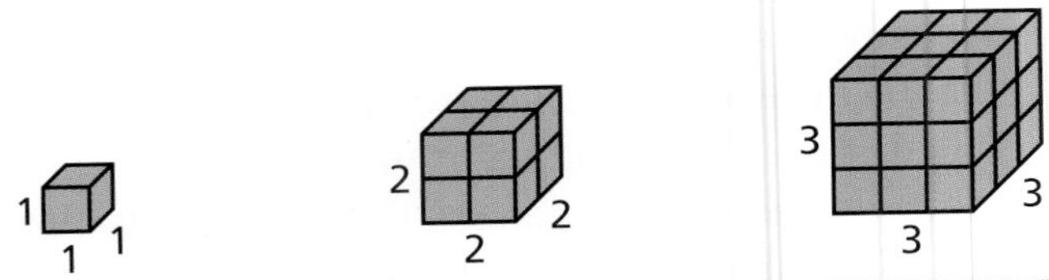

Edge Length	1 ft	2 ft	3 ft
Volume	$1 \times 1 \times 1 = 1$ ft^3	$2 \times 2 \times 2 = 8$ ft^3	$3 \times 3 \times 3 = 27$ ft^3
Surface Area	$6 \cdot 1 \times 1 = 6$ ft^2	$6 \cdot 2 \times 2 = 24$ ft^2	$6 \cdot 3 \times 3 = 54$ ft^2

Helpful Hint

Multiplying the linear dimensions of a solid by n creates n^2 as much surface area and n^3 as much volume.

Corresponding edge lengths of any two cubes are in proportion to each other because the cubes are similar. However, volumes and surface areas do not have the same scale factor as edge lengths.

Each edge of the 2 ft cube is 2 times as long as each edge of the 1 ft cube. However, the cube's volume, or **capacity**, is $2^3 = 8$ times as large, and its surface area is $2^2 = 4$ times as large as the 1 ft cube's.

EXAMPLE 1 Scaling Models That Are Cubes

A 6 cm cube is built from small cubes, each 2 cm on an edge. Compare the following values.

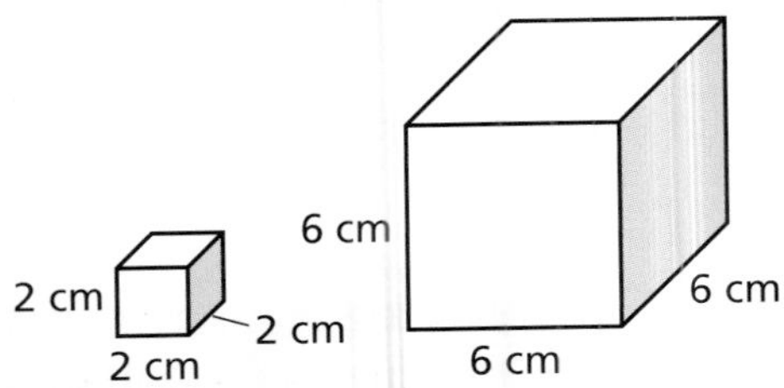

A **the edge lengths of the large and small cubes**

$\frac{\text{6 cm cube}}{\text{2 cm cube}} \rightarrow \frac{6\text{ cm}}{2\text{ cm}} = 3$ *Ratio of corresponding edges*

The edges of the large cube are 3 times as long as those of the small cube.

B **the surface areas of the two cubes**

$\frac{\text{6 cm cube}}{\text{2 cm cube}} \rightarrow \frac{216\text{ cm}^2}{24\text{ cm}^2} = 9$ *Ratio of corresponding areas*

The surface area of the large cube is $3^2 = 9$ times that of the small cube.

C **the volumes of the two cubes**

$\frac{\text{6 cm cube}}{\text{2 cm cube}} \rightarrow \frac{216\text{ cm}^3}{8\text{ cm}^3} = 27$ *Ratio of corresponding volumes*

The volume of the large cube is $3^2 = 27$ times that of the small cube.

EXAMPLE 2 Scaling Models That Are Other Solid Figures

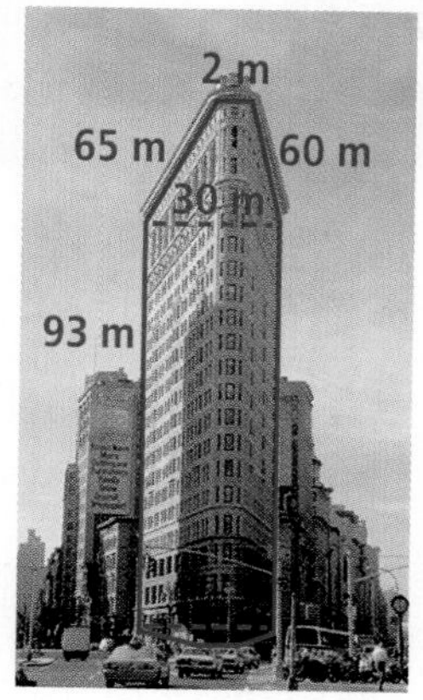

The Fuller Building in New York, also known as the Flatiron Building, can be modeled as a trapezoidal prism with the approximate dimensions shown. For a 10 cm tall model of the Fuller Building, find the following.

A **What is the scale factor of the model?**

$\frac{10 \text{ cm}}{93 \text{ m}} = \frac{10 \text{ cm}}{9300 \text{ cm}} = \frac{1}{930}$ *Convert and simplify.*

The scale factor of the model is 1:930.

B **What are the other dimensions of the model?**

left side: $\frac{1}{930} \cdot 65 \text{ m} = \frac{6500}{930} \text{ cm} \approx 6.99 \text{ cm}$

back: $\frac{1}{930} \cdot 30 \text{ m} = \frac{3000}{930} \text{ cm} \approx 3.23 \text{ cm}$

right side: $\frac{1}{930} \cdot 60 \text{ m} = \frac{6000}{930} \text{ cm} \approx 6.45 \text{ cm}$

front: $\frac{1}{930} \cdot 2 \text{ m} = \frac{200}{930} \text{ cm} \approx 0.22 \text{ cm}$

The trapezoidal base has side lengths 6.99 cm, 3.23 cm, 6.45 cm, and 0.22 cm.

EXAMPLE 3 *Business Application*

A machine fills a cube box that has edge lengths of 1 ft with shampoo samples in 3 seconds. How long does it take the machine to fill a cube box that has edge lengths of 4 ft?

$V = 4 \text{ ft} \cdot 4 \text{ ft} \cdot 4 \text{ ft} = 64 \text{ ft}^3$ *Find the volume of the larger box.*

$\frac{3}{1 \text{ ft}^3} = \frac{x}{64 \text{ ft}^3}$ *Set up a proportion and solve.*

$3 \cdot 64 = x$ *Cross multiply.*

$192 = x$ *Calculate the fill time.*

It takes 192 seconds to fill the larger box.

Think and Discuss

1. **Describe** how the volume of a model compares to the original object if the linear scale factor of the model is 1:2.
2. **Explain** one possible way to double the surface area of a rectangular prism.

8-10 Exercises

go.hrw.com
Homework Help Online
KEYWORD: MT7 8-10
Parent Resources Online
KEYWORD: MT7 Parent

GUIDED PRACTICE

See Example 1

An 8 in. cube is built from small cubes, each 2 in. on a side. Compare the following values.

1. the side lengths of the large and small cubes
2. the surface areas of the two cubes
3. the volumes of the two cubes

See Example 2

4. The dimensions of a basketball arena are 500 ft long, 375 ft wide, and 125 ft high. The scale model used to build the arena is 40 in. long. Find the width and height of the model.

See Example 3

5. A 3 ft by 1 ft by 1 ft fish tank in the shape of a rectangular prism drains in 3 min. How long would it take a 7 ft by 4 ft by 4 ft fish tank to drain at the same rate?

INDEPENDENT PRACTICE

See Example 1

A 6 m cube is built from small cubes, each 3 m on a side. Compare the following values.

6. the side lengths of the large and small cubes
7. the surface areas of the two cubes
8. the volumes of the two cubes

See Example 2

9. The Great Pyramid of Giza has a square base measuring 230 m on each side and a height of about 147 m. Nathan is building a model of the pyramid with a 50 cm square base. What is the height to the nearest centimeter of Nathan's model?

See Example 3

10. An aboveground pool 5 ft tall with a diameter of 40 ft is filled with water in 50 minutes. How long will it take to fill an aboveground pool that is 6 ft tall with a diameter of 36 ft?

PRACTICE AND PROBLEM SOLVING

Extra Practice
See page 797.

For each cube, a reduced scale model is built using a scale factor of $\frac{1}{2}$. Find the length of the model and the number of 1 cm cubes used to build it.

11. a 2 cm cube
12. a 6 cm cube
13. an 18 cm cube
14. a 4 cm cube
15. a 14 cm cube
16. a 16 cm cube
17. What is the volume in cubic centimeters of a 1 m cube?
18. An insulated lunch box measures 7 in. by 9.5 in. by 5 in. A larger version of the lunch box is available. Its dimensions are greater by a linear factor of 1.1. How much greater is the volume of the larger lunch box than the smaller one? What is the volume of the larger lunch box?
19. **Art** A sand castle requires 3 pounds of sand. How much sand would be required to double all the dimensions of the sand castle?

20. **Recreation** If it took 100,000 Lego® blocks to build a cylindrical monument with a 5 m diameter, about how many Legos would be needed to build a monument with an 8 m diameter and the same height?

21. A kitchen sink measures 21 in. by 16 in. by 8 in. It takes 4 minutes 30 seconds to fill with water. A smaller kitchen sink takes 4 min 12 seconds to fill with water.

    a. What is the volume of the smaller kitchen sink?

    b. About how many gallons of water does the smaller kitchen sink hold? (*Hint:* 1 gal = 231 in^3)

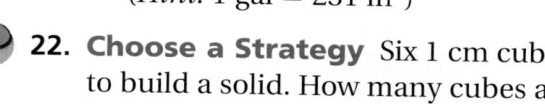

Legoland, in Billund, Denmark, contains Lego models of the Taj Mahal, Mount Rushmore, other monuments, and visitors, too.

22. **Choose a Strategy** Six 1 cm cubes are used to build a solid. How many cubes are used to build a scale model of the solid with a linear scale factor of 2 to 1? Describe the tools and techniques you used.

    (A) 12 cubes (B) 24 cubes (C) 48 cubes (D) 144 cubes

23. **Write About It** If the linear scale factor of a model is $\frac{1}{5}$, what is the relationship between the volume of the original object and the volume of the model?

24. **Challenge** To double the volume of a rectangular prism, what number is multiplied by each of the prism's linear dimensions? Give your answer to the nearest hundredth.

Test Prep and Spiral Review

25. **Multiple Choice** A 9-inch cube is created from small cubes, each 1 inch on a side. What is the ratio of the volume of the larger cube to the volume of the smaller cube?

    (A) 1:9 (B) 9:1 (C) 81:1 (D) 729:1

26. **Extended Response** A 5-inch cube is created from small cubes, each 1 inch on a side. Compare the side lengths, surface area, and volume of the larger to the smaller cube.

Solve. (Lesson 1-7)

27. $3 + x = 11$ 28. $y - 6 = 8$ 29. $13 = w + 11$ 30. $5.6 = b - 4$

Find the surface area of each sphere to the nearest tenth. Use $\pi = 3.14$. (Lesson 8-9)

31. radius 5 mm 32. radius 12.2 ft 33. diameter 4 in. 34. diameter 20 cm

CHAPTER 8

READY TO GO ON?

SECTION 8B

Quiz for Lessons 8-4 Through 8-10

8-4 Drawing Three-Dimensional Figures

1. Draw the front, top, and side views of the figure.

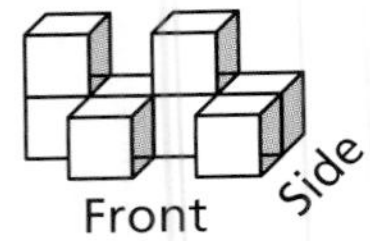

8-5 Volume of Prisms and Cylinders

Find the volume of each figure to the nearest tenth. Use 3.14 for π.

2.

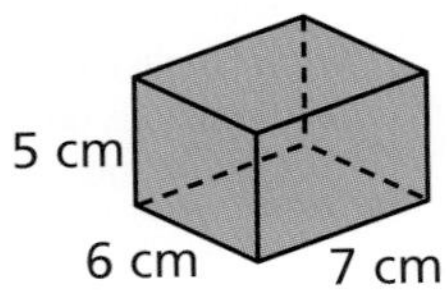

3.

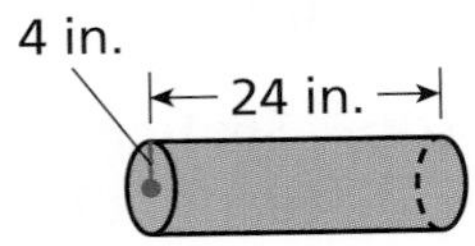

4.

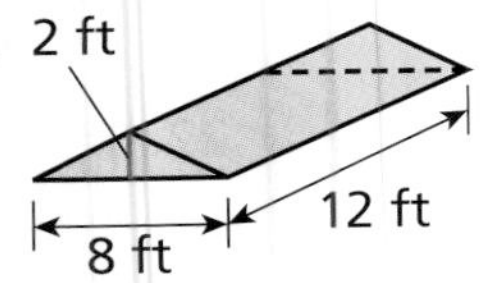

8-6 Volume of Pyramids and Cones

Find the volume of each figure to the nearest tenth. Use 3.14 for π.

5.

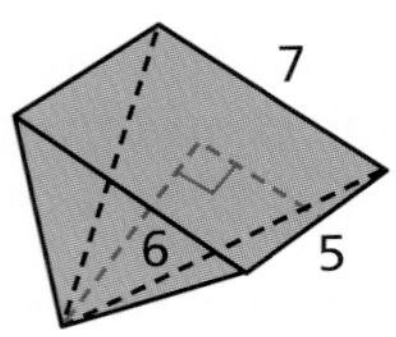

6.

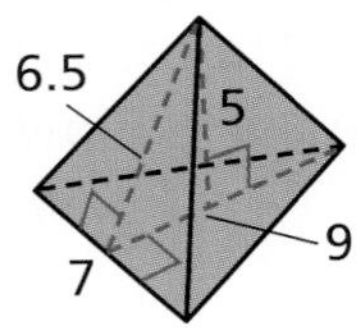

7.

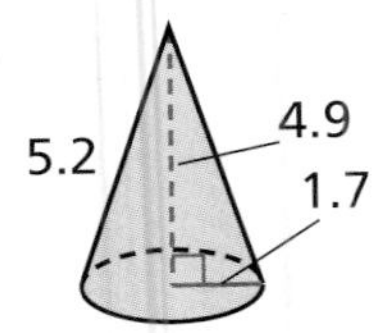

8-7 Surface Area of Prisms and Cylinders

Find the surface area of the indicated figure to the nearest tenth. Use 3.14 for π.

8. the prism from Exercise 2

9. the cylinder from Exercise 3

8-8 Surface Area of Pyramids and Cones

Find the surface area of the indicated figure to the nearest tenth. Use 3.14 for π.

10. the pyramid from Exercise 6

11. the cone from Exercise 7

8-9 Spheres

Find the surface area and volume of each sphere with the given measurements, both in terms of π and to the nearest tenth. Use 3.14 for π.

12. radius 6.6 mm

13. radius 9 cm

14. diameter 15 yd

8-10 Scaling Three-Dimensional Figures

15. The dimensions of a skating arena are 400 ft long, 280 ft wide, and 100 ft high. The scale model used to build the arena is 20 in. long. Find the width and height of the model.

MULTI-STEP TEST PREP

Home on the Range Many rural areas in the United States are configured in sections. A section is one square mile, which is equal to 640 acres. A family owns the 4-section farm shown in the diagram. They are preparing information about the farm for their tax return.

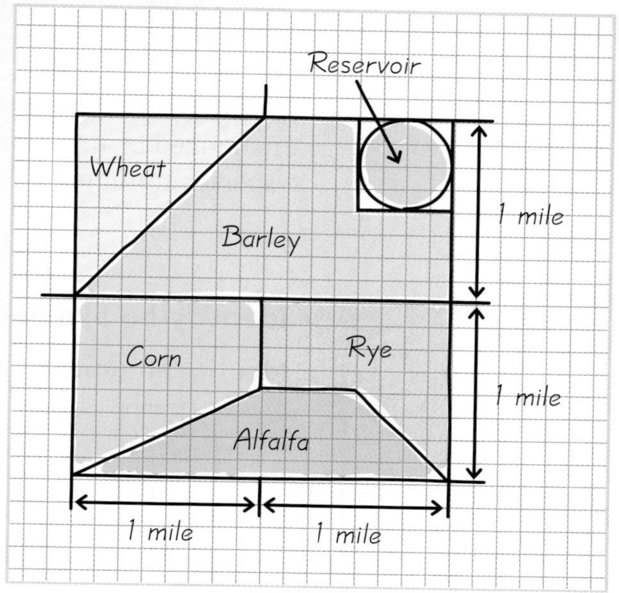

1. What is the area in square miles for each of the five crops on the farm?
2. What is the area in acres for each of the crops?
3. A road goes around the perimeter of the field that is planted with barley. What is the length of the road to the nearest tenth of a mile? Explain how you made your calculation.
4. The farm includes a circular reservoir. What is the area of the reservoir to the nearest tenth of a square mile? Use 3.14 for π.
5. How many acres of unused land are there in the square plot that surrounds the reservoir?
6. The reservoir is a cylinder 15 feet deep. How many cubic feet of water does the reservoir hold? Use 3.14 for π. (*Hint:* 1 mile = 5280 feet)

EXTENSION Symmetry in Three Dimensions

Learn to identify types of symmetry in three dimensions.

Vocabulary
bilateral symmetry
cross section

Solid figures can have different kinds of symmetry.

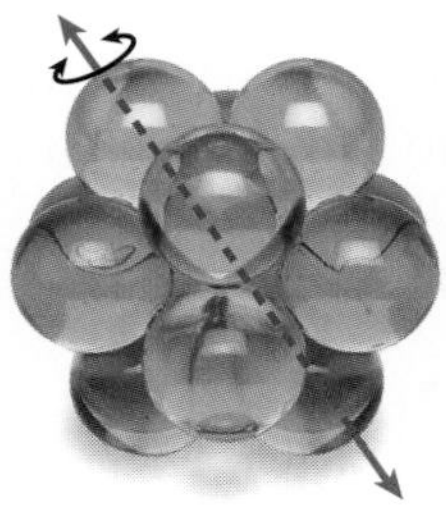

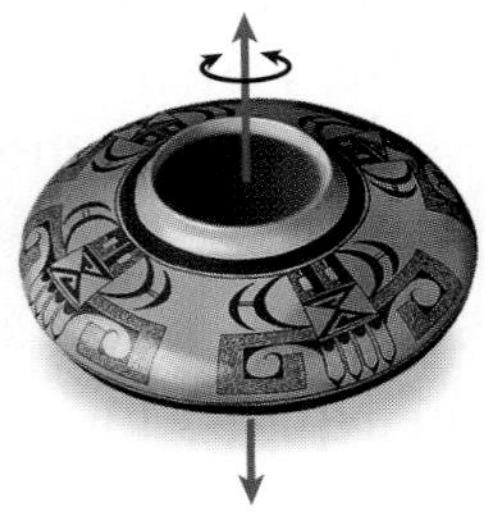

A solid figure with *rotational symmetry* is unchanged in appearance when it is turned a specific number of degrees about a line.

A solid figure with **bilateral symmetry** has two-sided symmetry, or *reflection symmetry*, across a plane.

EXAMPLE 1 Identifying Symmetry in a Solid Figure

Identify all types of symmetry in each figure.

A

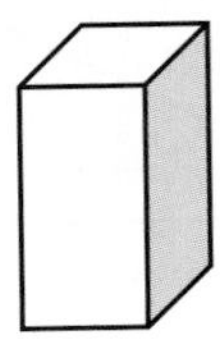

This rectangular prism has both rotational symmetry and bilateral symmetry.

B

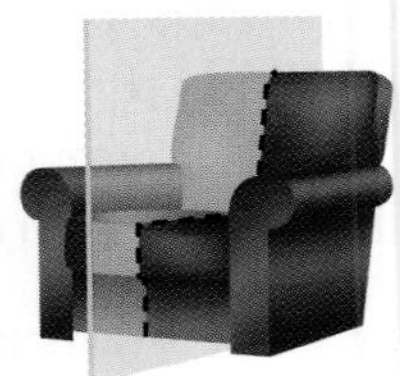

This chair has only bilateral symmetry.

When a solid and a plane intersect, the intersection is called a **cross section** .

EXAMPLE 2 Drawing a Cross Section

Draw the cross section and describe its symmetry.

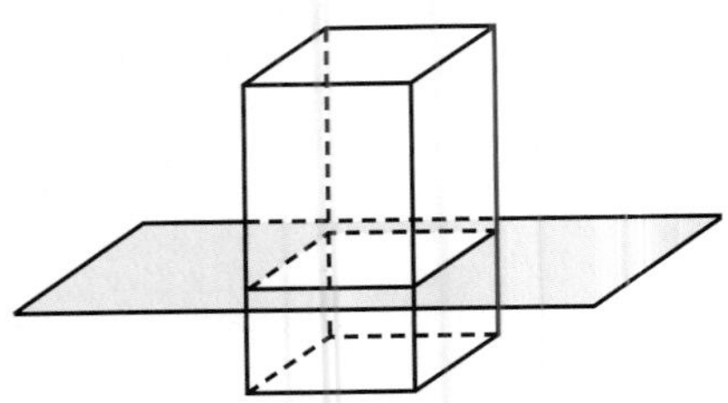

The cross-section is a square, which has four-fold rotational symmetry and line symmetry. There are four lines of symmetry, two from the midpoints of each side to the midpoints of the opposite side and two from the vertices to the corresponding opposite vertices.

EXTENSION Exercises

Identify all types of symmetry in each figure.

1. 

2. 

3. 

Draw the cross section and describe its symmetry.

4. 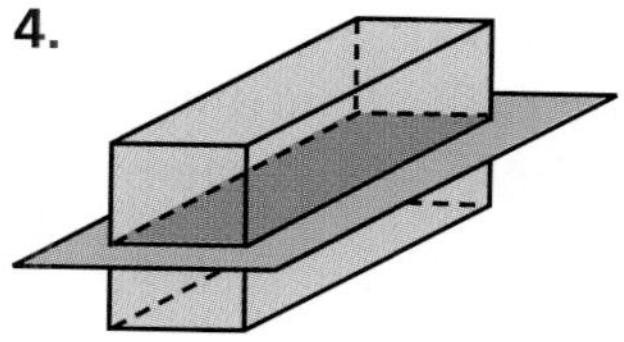

5. 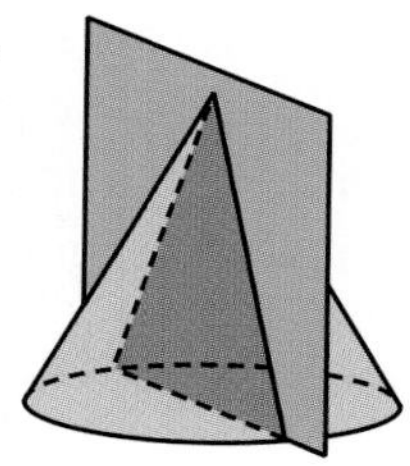

6. 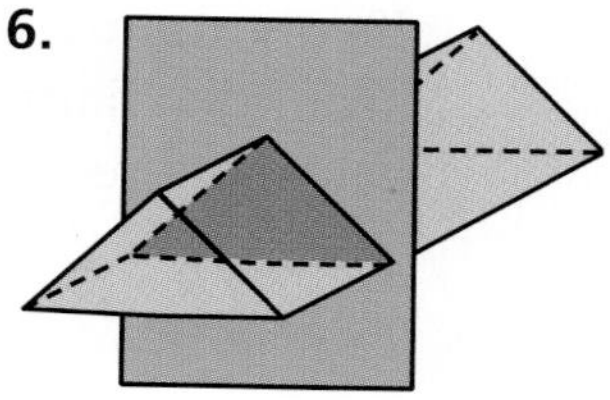

Identify all types of symmetry in each figure.

7. 

8. 

9. 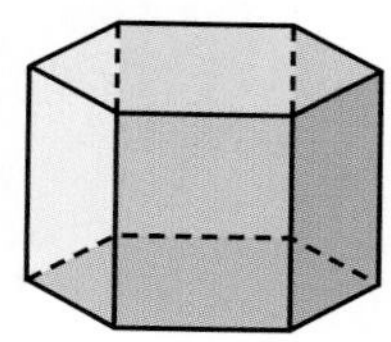

Draw the cross section and describe its symmetry.

10. 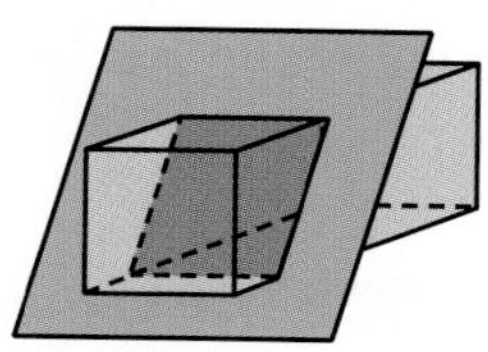

11. 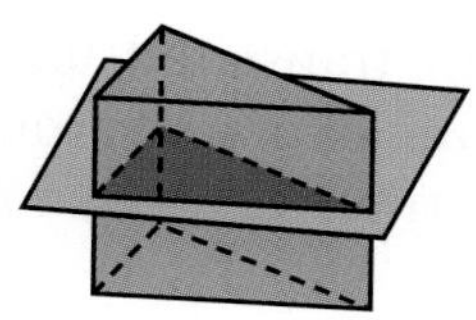

12. The Transamerica Pyramid in San Francisco is a square pyramid. Each floor is a horizontal cross section of the pyramid. What is the shape of such a cross section? How is the size of each floor related to the size of the floor below it?

13. When a plane and a cone intersect, is it possible for the cross-section to be a three-sided figure? Explain.

14. Describe the possible cross sections of a sphere.

15. When a plane and a cylinder intersect, is it possible for the cross-section to be a square? Explain.

Game Time

Planes in Space

Some three-dimensional figures can be generated by plane figures.

Experiment with a circle first. Move the circle around. See if you recognize any three-dimensional shapes.

If you rotate a circle around a diameter, you get a sphere.

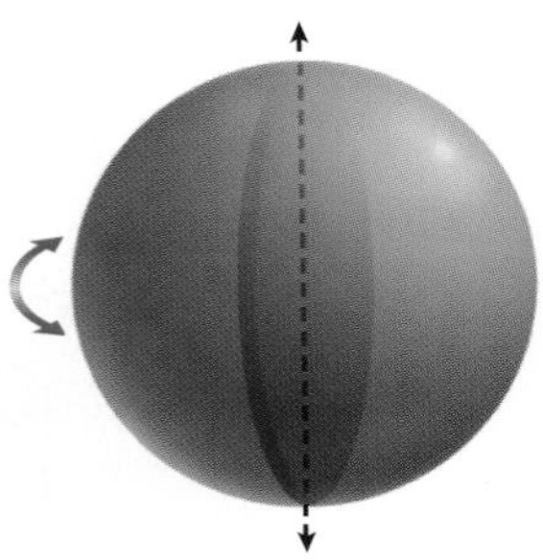

If you translate a circle up along a line perpendicular to the plane that the circle is in, you get a cylinder.

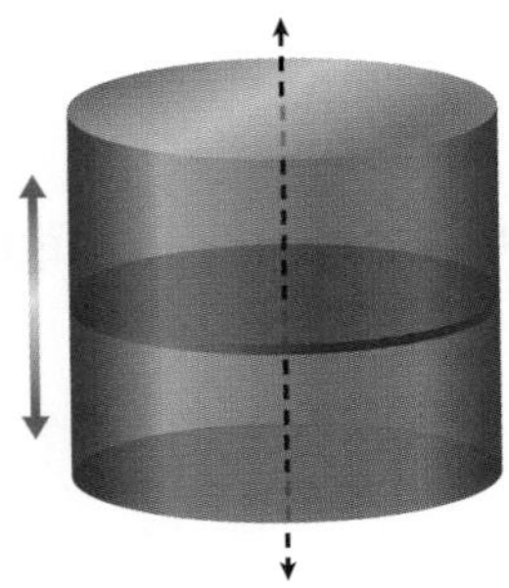

If you rotate a circle around a line outside the circle but in the same plane as the circle, you get a donut shape called a *torus*.

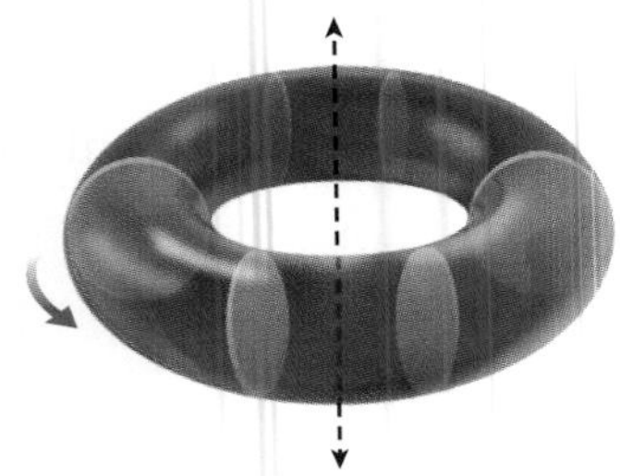

Draw or describe the three-dimensional figure generated by each plane figure.

1. a square translated along a line perpendicular to the plane it is in
2. a rectangle rotated around one of its edges
3. a right triangle rotated around one of its legs

Triple Concentration

The goal of this game is to form *Pythagorean triples,* which are sets of three whole numbers *a*, *b*, and *c* such that $a^2 + b^2 = c^2$. A set of cards with numbers on them are arranged face down. A turn consists of drawing 3 cards to try to form a Pythagorean triple. If the cards do not form a Pythagorean triple, they are replaced in their original positions.

go.hrw.com
Game Time Extra
KEYWORD: MT7 Games

A complete set of rules and cards are available online.

It's in the Bag!

FOLDNOTES

Materials
- white paper
- scissors
- decorative paper
- stapler
- hole punch
- twine or yarn
- cardboard tube
- glue
- markers

PROJECT The Tube Journal

Use this journal to take notes on perimeter, area, and volume. Then roll up the journal and store it in a tube for safekeeping!

Directions

1. Start with several sheets of paper that measure $8\frac{1}{2}$ inches by 11 inches. Cut an inch off the end of each sheet so they measure $8\frac{1}{2}$ inches by 10 inches.

2. Stack the sheets and fold them in half lengthwise to form a journal that is approximately $4\frac{1}{4}$ inches by 10 inches. Cover the outside of the journal with decorative paper, trim it as needed, and staple everything together along the edge. **Figure A**

3. Punch a hole through the journal in the top left corner. Tie a 6-inch piece of twine or yarn through the hole. **Figure B**

4. Use glue to cover a cardboard tube with decorative paper. Then write the name and number of the chapter on the tube.

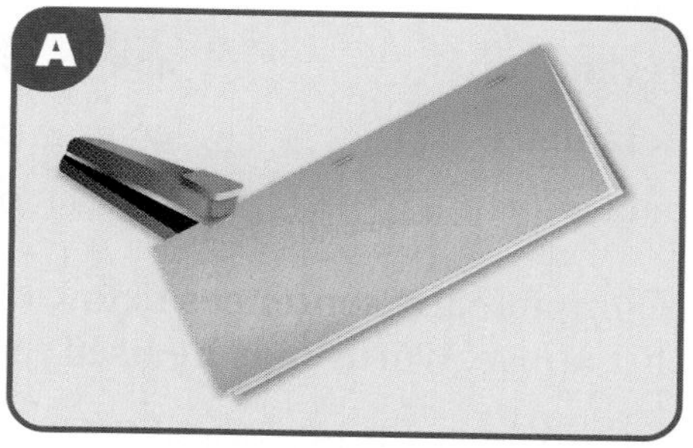

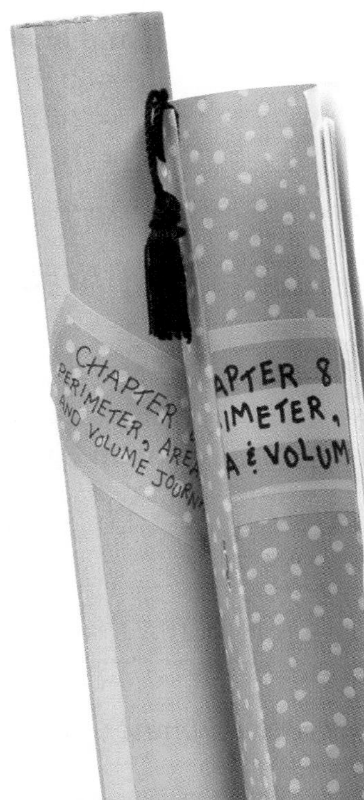

Taking Note of the Math

Use your journal to take notes on perimeter, area, and volume. Then roll up the journal and store it in the cardboard tube. Be sure the twine hangs out of the tube so that the journal can be pulled out easily.

CHAPTER 8

Study Guide: Review

Vocabulary

area	389	face	408	pyramid	420
capacity	440	great circle	436	radius	400
circle	400	hemisphere	436	regular pyramid	432
circumference	400	lateral face	427	right cone	432
cone	420	lateral surface	427	slant height	432
cylinder	413	orthogonal views	408	sphere	436
diameter	400	perimeter	388	surface area	427
edge	408	prism	413	vertex	408

Complete the sentences below with vocabulary words from the list above. Words may be used more than once.

1. In a two-dimensional figure, __?__ is the distance around the outside of the figure, while __?__ is the number of square units in the figure.

2. In a three-dimensional figure, a(n) __?__ is where two faces meet, and a(n) __?__ is where three or more edges meet.

8-1 Perimeter and Area of Rectangles and Parallelograms (pp. 388–392)

EXAMPLE

■ **Find the area and perimeter of a rectangle with base 2 ft and height 5 ft.**

$A = bh$ | $P = 2l + 2w$
$= 5(2)$ | $= 2(5) + 2(2)$
$= 10 \text{ ft}^2$ | $= 10 + 4 = 14 \text{ ft}$

EXERCISES

Find the area and perimeter of each figure.

3. a rectangle with base $1\frac{2}{3}$ in. and height $4\frac{1}{3}$ in.
4. a parallelogram with base 18 m, side length 22 m, and height 11 m.

8-2 Perimeter and Area of Triangles and Trapezoids (pp. 394–398)

EXAMPLE

■ **Find the area and perimeter of a right triangle with base 6 cm and height 3 cm.**

$A = \frac{1}{2}bh = \frac{1}{2}(6)(3) = 9 \text{ cm}^2$

$6^2 + 3^2 = c^2$

$6.71 \approx c$

$P = 6 + 3 + 6.71 = 15.71 \text{ cm}$

EXERCISES

Find the area and perimeter of each figure.

5. a triangle with base 6 cm, sides 2.1 cm and 6.1 cm, and height 3 cm
6. trapezoid $ABCD$ with $AB = 3.5$ in., $BC = 8.1$ in., $CD = 12.5$ in., and $AD = 2.2$ in., where $\overline{AB} \parallel \overline{CD}$ and $h = 2.0$ in.

8-3 Circles (pp. 400–403)

EXAMPLE

- **Find the area and circumference of a circle with radius 3.1 cm. Use 3.14 for π.**

$A = \pi r^2$ $\quad$ $C = 2\pi r$

$= \pi(3.1)^2$ $\quad$ $= 2\pi(3.1)$

$= 9.61\pi \approx 30.2 \text{ cm}^2$ $\quad$ $= 6.2\pi \approx 19.5 \text{ cm}$

EXERCISES

Find the area and circumference of each circle, both in terms of π and to the nearest tenth. Use 3.14 for π.

7. $r = 12$ in.
8. $r = 4.2$ cm
9. $d = 6$ m
10. $d = 1.2$ ft

8-4 Drawing Three-Dimensional Figures (pp. 408–411)

EXAMPLE

- **Draw the top view of the figure.**

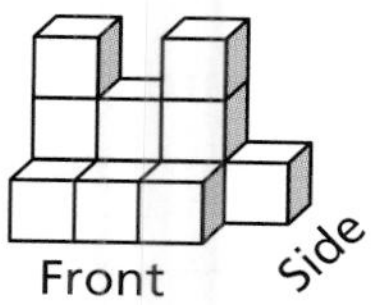

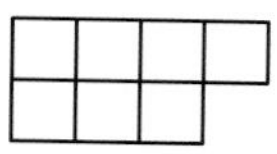

EXERCISES

Draw the top view of each figure.

11.

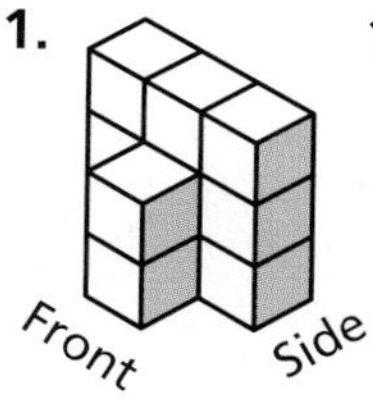

12.

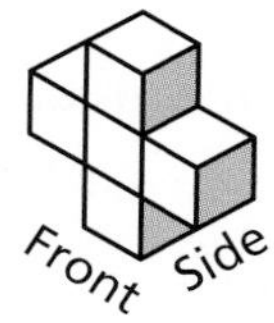

13.

8-5 Volume of Prisms and Cylinders (pp. 413–417)

EXAMPLE

- **Find the volume.**

$V = Bh = (\pi r^2)h$

$= \pi(4^2)(6)$

$= (16\pi)(6) = 96\pi \text{ cm}^3$

$\approx 301.6 \text{ cm}^3$

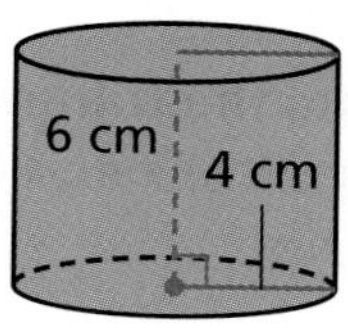

EXERCISES

Find the volume of each figure.

14.

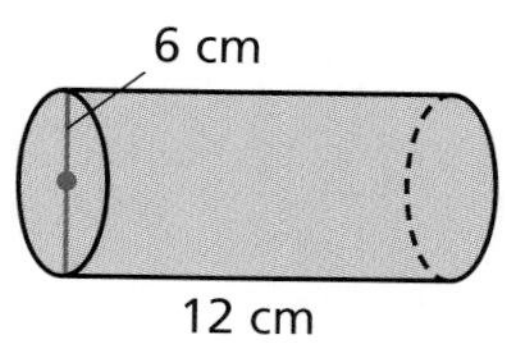

15.

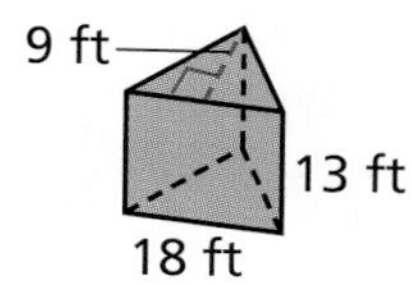

8-6 Volume of Pyramids and Cones (pp. 420–424)

EXAMPLE

- **Find the volume.**

$V = \frac{1}{3}Bh = \frac{1}{3}(6)(4)(8)$

$= \frac{1}{3}(24)(8) = 64 \text{ in}^3$

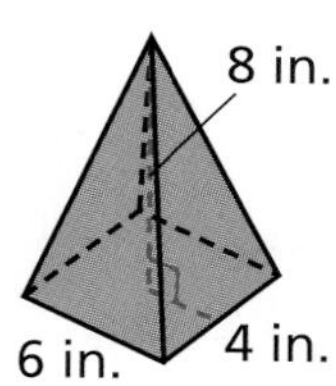

EXERCISES

Find the volume of each figure. Use 3.14 for π.

16.

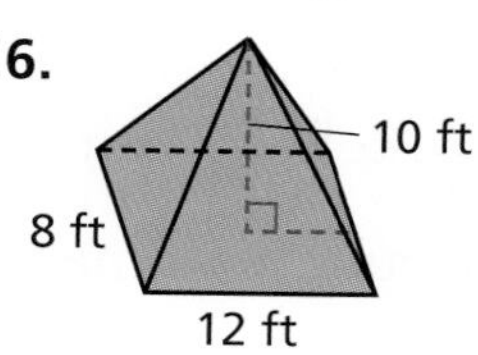

17.

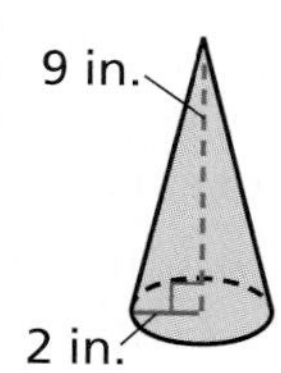

8-7 Surface Area of Prisms and Cylinders (pp. 427–430)

EXAMPLE

- **Find the surface area.**

$S = 2B + Ph$
$= 2(6) + (10)(4)$
$= 52 \text{ in}^2$

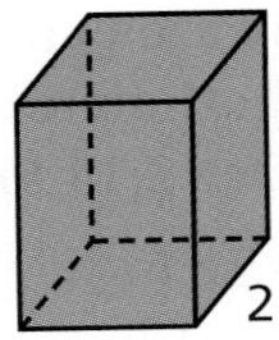

EXERCISES

Find the surface area of the figure.

18.

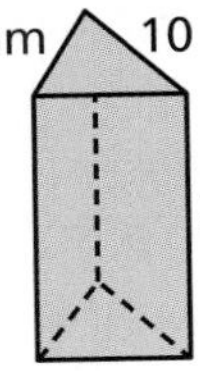

8-8 Surface Area of Pyramids and Cones (pp. 432–435)

EXAMPLE

- **Find the surface area.**

$S = B + \frac{1}{2}P\ell$
$= 16 + \frac{1}{2}(16)(5)$
$= 56 \text{ in}^2$

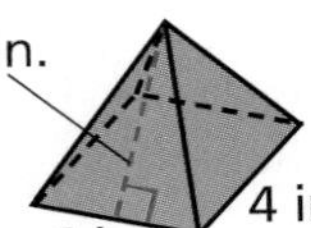

EXERCISES

Find the surface area of each figure.

19.

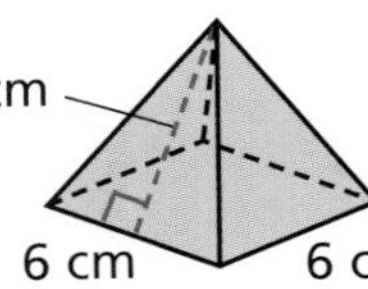

20.

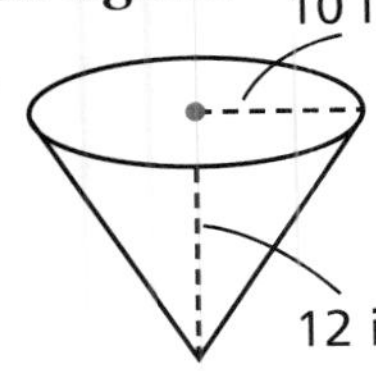

8-9 Spheres (pp. 436–439)

EXAMPLE

- **Find the volume of a sphere of radius 12 cm.**

$V = \frac{4}{3}\pi r^3 = \frac{4}{3}\pi(12^3)$
$= 2304\pi \text{ cm}^3 \approx 7234.6 \text{ cm}^3$

EXERCISES

Find the volume of each sphere, both in terms of π and to the nearest tenth. Use 3.14 for π.

21. $r = 6$ in.

22. $d = 36$ m

8-10 Scaling Three-Dimensional Figures (pp. 440–443)

EXAMPLE

- **A 4 in. cube is built from small cubes, each 2 in. on a side. Compare the volumes of the large cube and the small cube.**

$$\frac{\text{vol. of large cube}}{\text{vol. of small cube}} = \frac{4^3 \text{ in}^3}{2^3 \text{ in}^3} = \frac{64 \text{ in}^3}{8 \text{ in}^3} = 8$$

The volume of the large cube is 8 times that of the small cube.

EXERCISES

A 9 ft cube is built from small cubes, each 3 ft on a side. Compare the indicated measures of the large cube and the small cube.

23. side lengths

24. surface areas

25. volumes

CHAPTER TEST

Find the perimeter of each figure.

1.

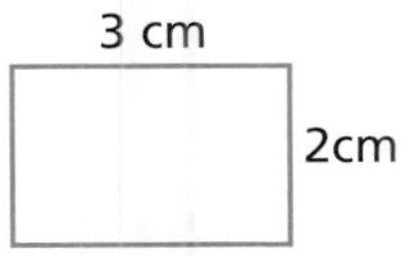

2.

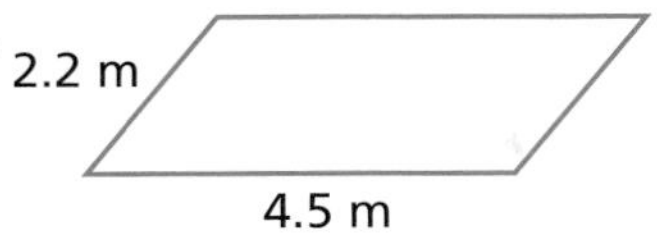

3.

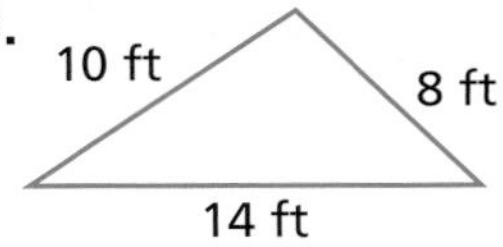

Graph and find the area of each figure with the given vertices.

4. $(-3, 2), (-3, -2), (5, -2), (5, 2)$

5. $(2, 4), (7, 4), (5, 0), (0, 0)$

6. $(-5, 0), (0, 0), (4, 4)$

7. $(0, 4), (3, 6), (3, -3), (0, -3)$

Find the area and circumference of each circle, both in terms of π and to the nearest tenth. Use 3.14 for π.

8. radius = 15 cm

9. diameter = 6.5 ft

10. radius = 2.2 m

11. Draw the front, top, and side views of the figure.

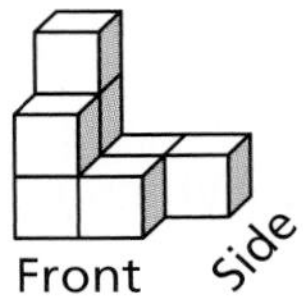

Find the volume of each figure to the nearest tenth. Use 3.14 for π.

12. a cube of side length 8 ft

13. a cylinder of height 5 cm and radius 2 cm

14. a cone of diameter 12 in. and height 18 in.

15. a sphere of radius 9 cm

16. a rectangular prism with base 5 m by 3 m and height 6 m

17. a pyramid with a 3 ft by 3 ft square base and height 4 ft

Find the surface area of each figure to the nearest tenth. Use 3.14 for π.

18.

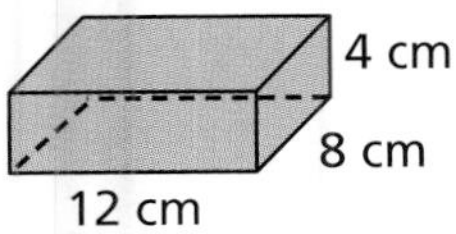

19.

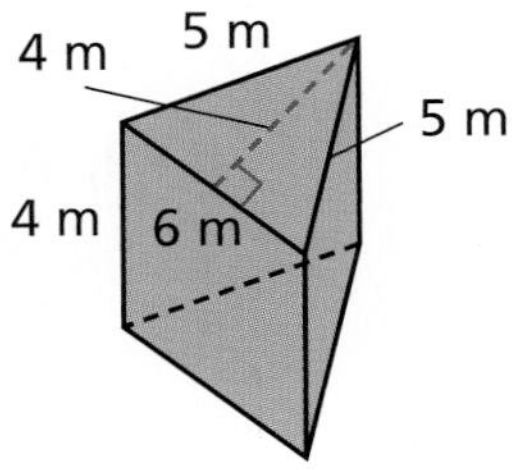

20.

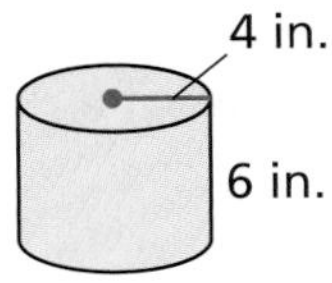

21.

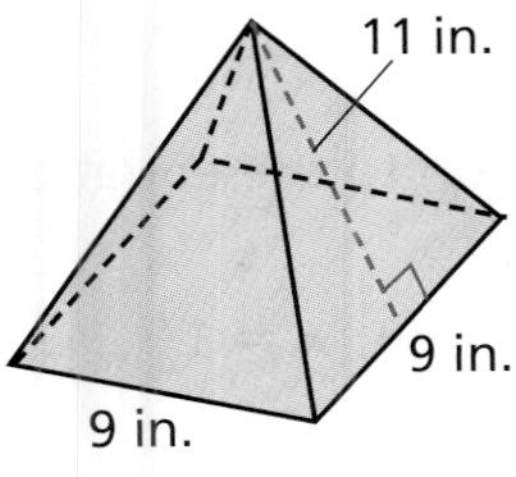

22.

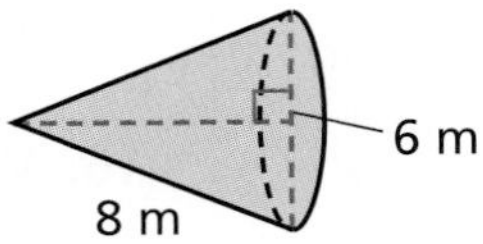

23.

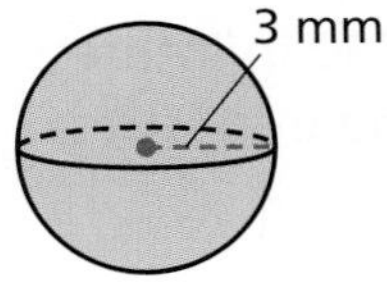

24. The dimensions of a history museum are 400 ft long, 200 ft wide, and 75 ft tall. The scale model used to build the museum is 40 in. long. Find the width and height of the model.

CHAPTER 8

STANDARDIZED TEST PREP

go.hrw.com
State Test Practice Online
KEYWORD: MT7 TestPrep

Cumulative Assessment, Chapters 1–8

Multiple Choice

1. Which addition equation represents the number line diagram below?

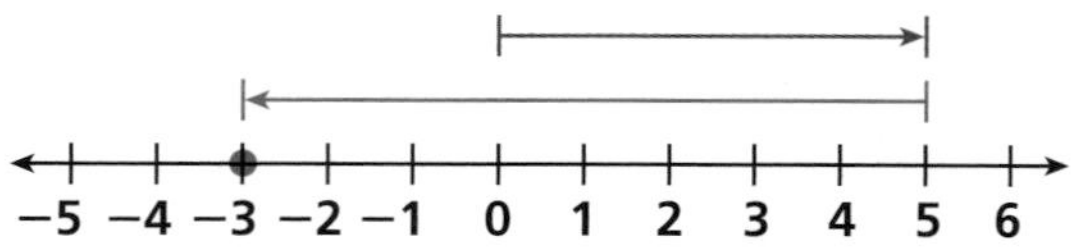

Ⓐ $5 + (-8)$
Ⓑ $5 + 8$
Ⓒ $-5 + 8$
Ⓓ $-5 + (-8)$

2. Jerome has to replace the tile in his bathroom. Which of the following shapes would NOT cover his bathroom walls with a tessellation?

Ⓕ
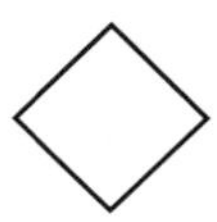

Ⓗ
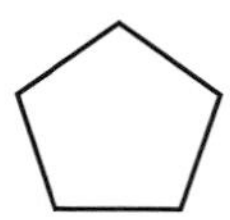

Ⓖ

Ⓙ

3. If $\frac{g^x}{g^5} = g^{-8}$ and $g^{-3} \cdot g^y = g^{12}$, what is the value of $x + y$?

Ⓐ −9
Ⓑ −3
Ⓒ 12
Ⓓ 15

4. Eduardo invests his savings at 3% simple interest for 5 years and earns $150 in interest. How much money did Eduardo invest?

Ⓕ $10
Ⓖ $22.50
Ⓗ $1000
Ⓙ $2250

5. A triangle has angle measures of 78°, $m°$, and $m°$. What is the value of m?

Ⓐ 12
Ⓑ 51
Ⓒ 102
Ⓓ 141

6. Which word does NOT describe the number $\sqrt{16}$?

Ⓕ rational
Ⓖ integer
Ⓗ whole
Ⓙ irrational

7. For which positive radius, r, is the circumference of a circle the same as the area of a circle?

Ⓐ $r = 1$
Ⓑ $r = 2$
Ⓒ $r = 3$
Ⓓ $r = 4$

8. Which equation describes the graph?

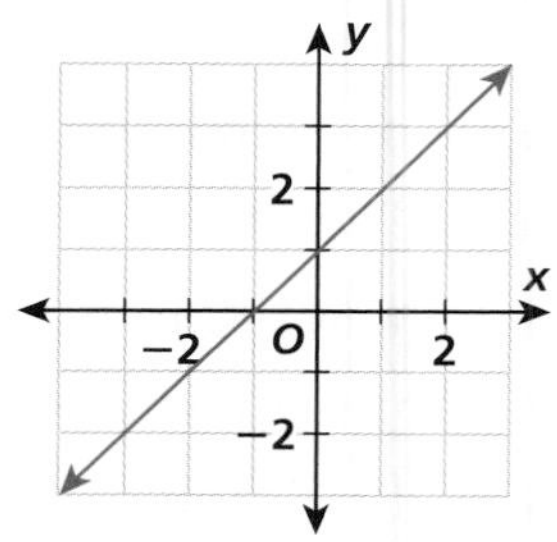

Ⓕ $y = x - 1$
Ⓖ $y = x + 1$
Ⓗ $y = 2x + 1$
Ⓙ $y = x + 2$

9. Armen rollerblades at a rate of 12 km/h. What is Armen's rate in meters per second?

Ⓐ 200 m/s
Ⓑ $3\frac{1}{3}$ m/s
Ⓒ $\frac{1}{3}$ m/s
Ⓓ $\frac{3}{10}$ m/s

10. What is the solution to the equation $\frac{2}{3}x + \frac{1}{6} = 1$?

Ⓕ $x = \frac{5}{9}$
Ⓖ $x = \frac{4}{5}$
Ⓗ $x = 1\frac{1}{4}$
Ⓙ $x = 3\frac{2}{3}$

11. Suzanne plans to install a fence around the perimeter of her land. How much fencing does she need?

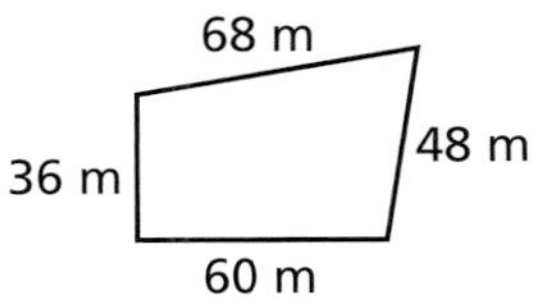

Ⓐ 212 m
Ⓑ 368 m
Ⓒ 2448 m
Ⓓ 2800 m

HOT TIP! **When a variable is used more than one time in an expression or an equation, it always has the same value.**

12. The Cougars, the Wildcats, and the Broncos won a total of 18 games during the football season. The Cougars won 2 more games than the Wildcats. The Broncos won $\frac{2}{3}$ as many games as the Wildcats. How many games did the Wildcats win?

Ⓕ 2
Ⓖ 4
Ⓗ 6
Ⓙ 8

Gridded Response

13. A cone-shaped cup has a height of 3 in. and a volume of 9 in^3. What is the length in inches of the diameter of the cone? Round your answer to the nearest hundredth.

14. Shaunda measures the diameter of a ball as 12 in. How many cubic inches of air does this ball hold? Round your answer to the nearest tenth.

15. What is the *y*-coordinate of the point (−3, 6) that has been translated down 4 units?

16. Given the obtuse triangle, what is the measure of angle *x*, in degrees?

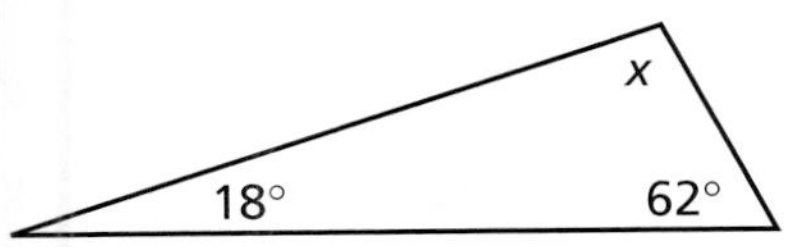

Short Response

17. Draw a rectangle with base length 7 cm and height 4 cm. Then draw a rectangle with base length 14 cm and height 1 cm. Which rectangle has the larger area? Which rectangle has the larger perimeter? Show your work or explain in words how you determined your answers.

18. A cylinder with a height of 6 in. and a diameter of 4 in. is filled with water. A cone with height 6 in. and diameter 2 in. is placed in the cylinder, point down, with its base even with the top of the cylinder. Draw a diagram to illustrate the situation described, and then determine how much water is left in the cylinder. Show your work.

19. An airplane propeller is 37 inches from its tip to the center axis of its rotation. Suppose the propeller spins at a rate of 2500 revolutions per minute. How far will a point on the tip of the propeller travel in one minute? How far will the point on the tip travel in one hour? Show your work or explain in words how you determined your answers.

Extended Response

20. A *geodesic dome* is constructed of triangles. The surface is approximately spherical.

   a. A pattern for a geodesic dome that approximates a hemisphere uses 30 triangles with base 8 ft and height 5.63 ft and 75 triangles with base 8 ft and height 7.13 ft. Find the surface area of the dome.

   b. The base of the dome is approximately a circle with diameter 41 ft. Use a hemisphere with this diameter to estimate the surface area of the dome.

   c. Compare your answer from part **a** with your estimate from part **b**. Explain the difference.

Problem Solving on Location

NEVADA

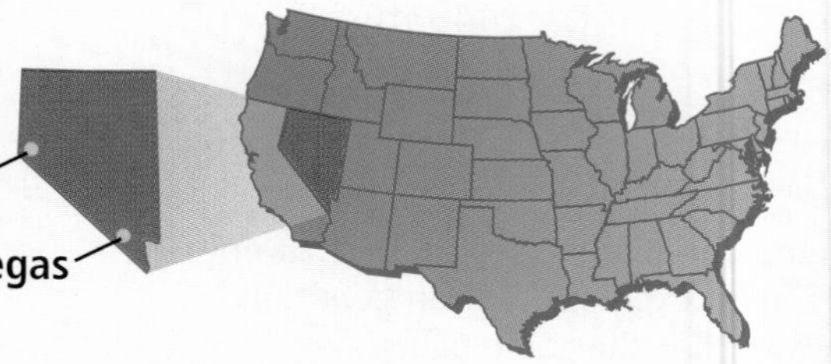

The Nevada State Capitol

In 1864 Carson City became the capital of Nevada, then the newest state in the union. Six years later, construction was completed on the State Capitol. To this day the building remains the only state capitol with a silver-colored dome. It is only fitting, given that Nevada mines supply more than 40% of the nation's silver.

Choose one or more strategies to solve each problem.

1. The Nevada State Capitol's library is in the shape of a regular octagon. For an upcoming banquet, a string of lights will be hung from each corner of the library's ceiling to each of the other non-adjacent corners. How many strings of lights will be needed?

2. The State Capitol's dome is approximately a hemisphere with a radius of 15 feet. Silver paint for the dome comes in large containers that hold enough paint to cover 600 ft^2 and in small containers that hold enough paint to cover 250 ft^2. How many of each type of 7container should be purchased in order to repaint the outside of the dome?

For 3 and 4, use the table.

3. The length of the original State Capitol was 3 times its width. What were the length and width of the original building?

4. In 1914, two rectangular wings were added to the building. The length of each wing is 10 feet more than the width. What is the length and width of each wing?

Nevada State Capitol	
Structure	Area (per story)
Original building (1870)	7500 ft^2
North wing (1914)	3000 ft^2
South wing (1914)	3000 ft^2

Problem Solving Strategies

Draw a Diagram
Make a Model
Guess and Test
Work Backward
Find a Pattern
Make a Table
Solve a Simpler Problem
Use Logical Reasoning
Act It Out
Make an Organized List

The Luxor Hotel

With more than 4,400 rooms, the Luxor is the second-largest hotel in the United States. The pyramid-shaped building is an unmistakable part of the Las Vegas skyline. Inside, the hotel features nine restaurants, an IMAX theater, a shopping bazaar, and a full-size replica of an Egyptian temple.

Choose one or more strategies to solve each problem.

1. The base of the hotel is a square with a perimeter of 2,600 feet. Along one side, the hotel is lit with lighting fixtures at each corner and every 50 feet in between. How many fixtures are there?

2. Each side of the pyramid is a triangle. The two angles at the base of the triangle have the same measure. The angle at the top of the triangle is 12° greater than the angles at the base. What are the measures of the angles in each triangle?

For 3 and 4, use the diagram.

3. The hotel's Egyptian Ballroom can be subdivided into several smaller rooms, as shown. Rooms A, B, C, E, F, and G are all congruent. What is the length and width of Room G?

4. If the area of the Egyptian Ballroom is 15,680 ft^2, what are the dimensions of Room D? Round your answer to the nearest tenth of a foot.

Egyptian Ballroom

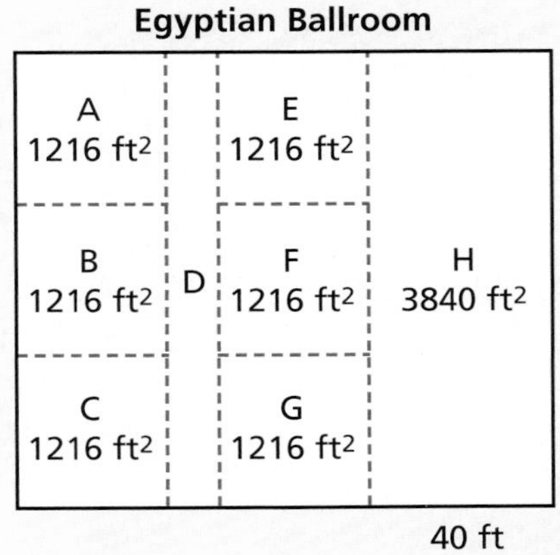

CHAPTER 9

Data and Statistics

9A Collecting and Describing Data

9-1 Samples and Surveys

LAB Explore Samples

9-2 Organizing Data

9-3 Measures of Central Tendency

9-4 Variability

LAB Create Box-and-Whisker Plots

9B Displaying Data

LAB Make a Circle Graph

9-5 Displaying Data

LAB Create Histograms

9-6 Misleading Graphs and Statistics

9-7 Scatter Plots

LAB Create a Scatter Plot

9-8 Choosing the Best Representation of Data

LAB Use a Spreadsheet to Create Graphs

MULTI-STEP TEST PREP

go.hrw.com
Chapter Project Online
KEYWORD: MT7 Ch9

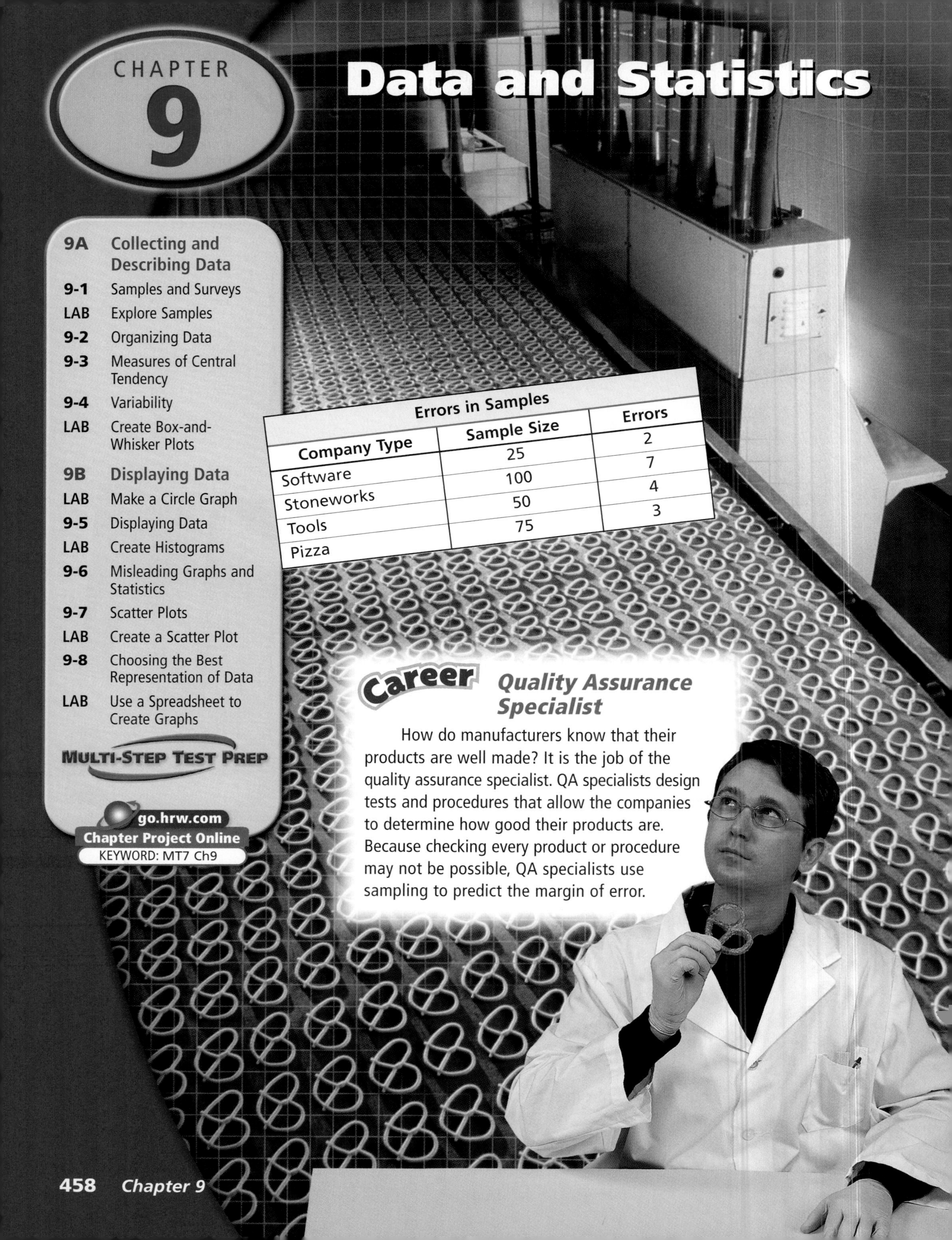

Errors in Samples

Company Type	Sample Size	Errors
Software	25	2
Stoneworks	100	7
Tools	50	4
Pizza	75	3

Career *Quality Assurance Specialist*

How do manufacturers know that their products are well made? It is the job of the quality assurance specialist. QA specialists design tests and procedures that allow the companies to determine how good their products are. Because checking every product or procedure may not be possible, QA specialists use sampling to predict the margin of error.

ARE YOU READY?

Vocabulary

Choose the best term from the list to complete each sentence.

coordinate grid
place value
rounding
scale

1. A __?__ is a uniform measure where equal distances are marked to represent equal amounts.
2. __?__ is the process of approximating to a given __?__.
3. Ordered pairs of numbers are graphed on a __?__.

Complete these exercises to review skills you will need for this chapter.

Round Decimals

Round each number to the indicated place value.

4. 34.7826; nearest tenth
5. 137.5842; nearest whole number
6. 287.2872; nearest thousandth
7. 362.6238; nearest hundred

Compare and Order Decimals

Order each sequence of numbers from greatest to least.

8. 3.005, 3.05, 0.35, 3.5
9. 0.048, 0.408, 0.0408, 0.48
10. 5.01, 5.1, 5.011, 5.11
11. 1.007, 0.017, 1.7, 0.107

Place Value of Whole Numbers

Write each number in standard form.

12. 1.3 million
13. 7.59 million
14. 4.6 billion
15. 2.83 billion

Read a Table

Use the table for problems 16–18.

16. Which activity experienced the greatest change in participation from 2000 to 2001?
17. Which activity experienced the greatest positive change in participation from 2000 to 2001?
18. Which activity experienced the least change in participation from 2000 to 2001?

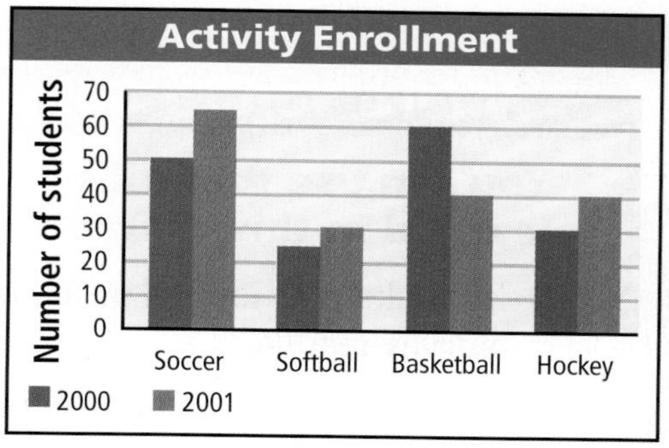

CHAPTER 9

Study Guide: Preview

Where You've Been

Previously, you

- used an appropriate representation for displaying relationships among collected data.
- described a set of data using mean, median, mode, and range.
- made inferences based on analysis of data.

In This Chapter

You will study

- selecting an appropriate representation for displaying relationships among collected data.
- selecting the appropriate measure of central tendency to describe data.
- making predictions and analyzing trends in scatter plots.
- recognizing misuses of graphical information.

Where You're Going

You can use the skills learned in this chapter

- to make predictions based on survey results.
- to conduct advanced research studies in science and social studies courses.

Key Vocabulary/Vocabulario

histogram	histograma
line plot	diagrama de acumulación
mean	media
median	mediana
mode	moda
population	población
sample	muestra
scatter plot	diagrama de dispersión

Vocabulary Connections

To become familiar with some of the vocabulary terms in the chapter, consider the following. You may refer to the chapter, the glossary, or a dictionary if you like.

1. The *population* of an area is the total number of people living in that area. What might **population** mean in the process of gathering data?
2. The word *median* is derived from the Latin word *medius*, meaning "middle." What might the **median** value in a set of data be?
3. When you *sample* a food, you taste a small portion. What might a **sample** be in data collection?

Reading and Writing Math

Reading Strategy: Interpret Graphics

Knowing how to interpret figures, diagrams, charts, and graphs will help you gather the information you need to solve the problem.

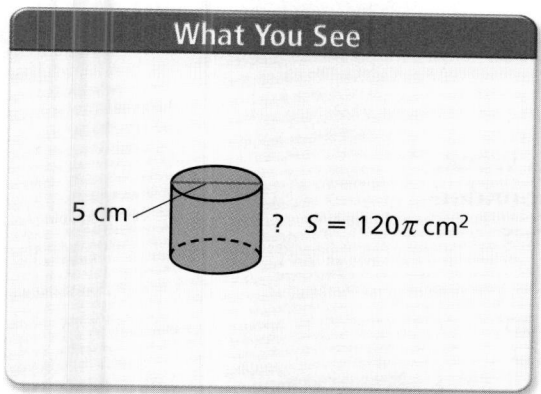

What You See

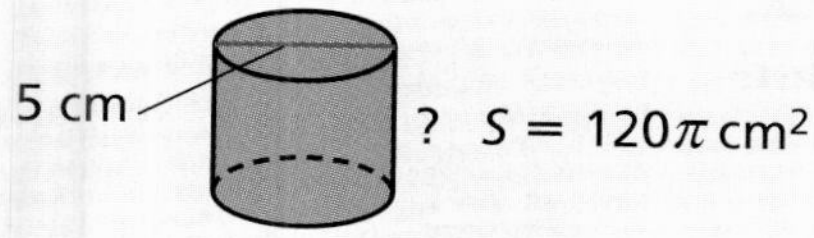

How to Interpret

✔ **Read all labels.**

Diameter = 5 cm
Surface Area = $120\pi\ cm^2$
The height of the cylinder is unknown.

✘ **Do not assume anything**

The height of the cylinder appears to be about the same as the diameter, but you can't know this without calculating the height.

What You See

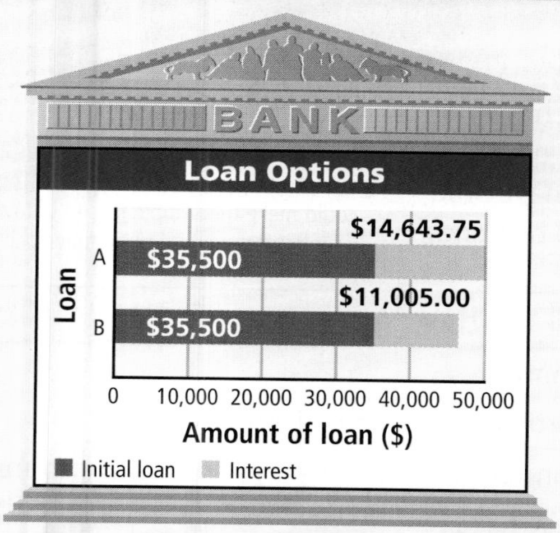

How to Interpret

✔ **Read the title.**

"Loan Options"

✔ **Read each axis label.**

horizontal — Indicates the amounts of the loans measured in dollars

Vertical — Indicates the loan options

✔ **Determine what information is represented.**

The amounts of principal and interest for two loans are shown.

Try This

Look up each exercise in the text and answer the corresponding questions.

1. Lesson 1-6 Exercise 36: What is the title of the graph? How deep is the deepest trench?
2. Lesson 2-3 Exercises 38 and 39: What does each number in the graph represent? What source provided the most energy?
3. Lesson 8-8 Exercise 2: What is the slant height of the cone? What is the radius of the base of the cone?

9-1 Samples and Surveys

Learn to identify sampling methods and to recognize biased samples.

Vocabulary

population

sample

random sample

systematic sample

stratified sample

convenience sample

voluntary-response sample

biased sample

A fitness magazine printed a readers' survey. Statements 1, 2, and 3 are interpretations of the results. Which do you think the magazine would use?

1. **The average American exercises 3 times a week.**
2. **The average reader of this magazine exercises 3 times a week.**
3. **The average reader who responded to the survey exercises 3 times a week.**

People who read fitness magazines are likely to be interested in exercise. This could make the sample biased in favor of people who exercise more times per week.

The **population** is the entire group being considered for a survey. The **sample** is the part of the population being surveyed.

To get accurate information, it is important to use a good sampling method. In a **random sample**, each member of the population has an equal chance of being selected. A random sample is best, but other methods can also be used.

Sampling Method	How Members are Chosen
Random	By chance
Systematic	According to a rule or formula
Stratified	At random from randomly chosen subgroups
Convenience	Easiest to reach
Voluntary-response	Members choose to be in the sample

EXAMPLE 1 Identifying Sampling Methods

Identify the sampling method used.

A **An exit poll taken of every tenth voter.**

Systematic *The rule is to question every tenth voter.*

B **Listeners are invited to call in to a radio show to voice their opinions.**

Voluntary-response *Callers choose to participate.*

Identify the sampling method used.

C **In a statewide survey, five counties are randomly chosen, and 100 people are randomly chosen from each county.**

Stratified — *The five counties are the random subgroups. People are chosen randomly from within the counties.*

Sometimes, these sampling methods result in *biased samples.* A **biased sample** does not accurately represent the population. The data collected from biased samples is not reliable.

EXAMPLE 2 Identifying Biased Samples

Identify the population and sample. Give a reason the sample could be biased.

A **A radio station manager chooses 1500 names from the local phone book to survey people about their listening habits.**

Population	Sample	Possible Bias
People in the local area	Up to 1500 people who take the survey	Not all people are in the phone book.

B **An advice columnist asks her readers to write in with their opinions about how to hang the toilet paper on the roller.**

Population	Sample	Possible Bias
Readers of the column	Readers who write in	Only readers with strong opinions write in.

C **Surveyors in a mall choose shoppers to ask about product preferences.**

Population	Sample	Possible Bias
All shoppers in the mall	The people who are polled	Not all of the shoppers in the mall will be near the surveyors.

Think and Discuss

1. Describe ways to eliminate the possible bias in Example 2C.

2. Decide which sampling method would be best to find the number of times a week the average student in your school exercises.

9-1 Exercises

go.hrw.com
Homework Help Online
KEYWORD: MT7 9-1
Parent Resources Online
KEYWORD: MT7 Parent

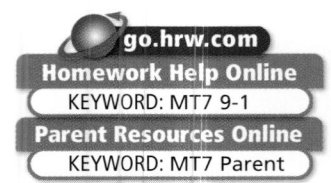

GUIDED PRACTICE

See Example 1

Identify the sampling method used.

1. People whose house number ends with a 1 are polled.
2. Students sitting at the same lunch table are polled.

See Example 2

Identify the population and sample. Give a reason the sample could be biased.

3. A pet store owner surveys 100 customers to find out which brand of dog food is most frequently purchased.

INDEPENDENT PRACTICE

See Example 1

Identify the sampling method used.

4. A surveyor flips through the phone book and selects 30 names.
5. A newspaper columnist asks readers to write in with their 10 favorite restaurants.

See Example 2

Identify the population and sample. Give a reason the sample could be biased.

6. A deli owner asks Sunday's customers to choose their favorite mustard.
7. A baseball team asks season ticket holders their preference of concession stands.

PRACTICE AND PROBLEM SOLVING

Extra Practice
See page 798.

Identify the sampling method used.

8. Every fifth name is called from a list of voters.
9. The customers in a hair salon are surveyed.
10. Each student writes a question on a slip of paper and puts it in a box. The teacher draws one question to discuss.
11. A Web site asks visitors to fill out a survey.
12. Fifteen classes are randomly chosen. Ten students are randomly chosen from each class.

Identify the population and sample. Give a reason the sample could be biased.

13. A teacher asks students who buy lunch if they like the cafeteria food.
14. An architecture firm asks people attending a city council meeting which design for a new city hall they prefer.
15. A biologist studying trees samples blossoms of trees along the river.

LINK

Business

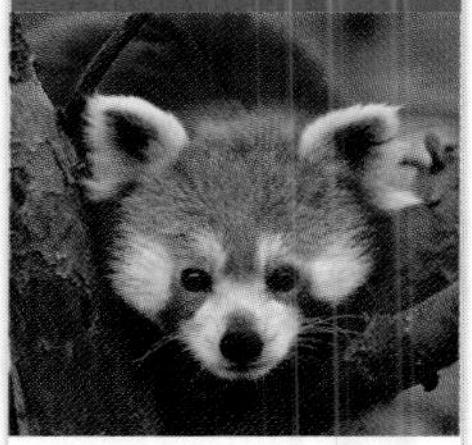

The Cincinnati Zoo has more than 500 animal and 3000 plant species on display.

16. **Recreation** Marvin looked through the baseball cards he collected 20 years ago. Most of the baseball players began their careers in the 1980s.
    a. What is the population of this survey?
    b. Give a reason why the sample could be biased.

17. **Business** For an advertising campaign, Jared needs to survey people to find out why they like to visit the Cincinnati Zoo.
    a. How can he select an unbiased sample for the survey?
    b. How can he make the sampling method systematic?
    c. Why would surveying only families with children be biased?

18. **What's the Error?** Kyla wanted to use a stratified sample to find out the most ordered food product at restaurants. She surveyed every tenth customer from five randomly chosen restaurants. Why is this not a stratified sample?

19. **Write About It** To plan your class picnic, you survey students about where they want to have the picnic. Choose a sampling method. Explain your choice.

20. **Challenge** The diagrams show the locations where soil samples will be taken to test for pollution. Identify the sampling method used for each diagram.

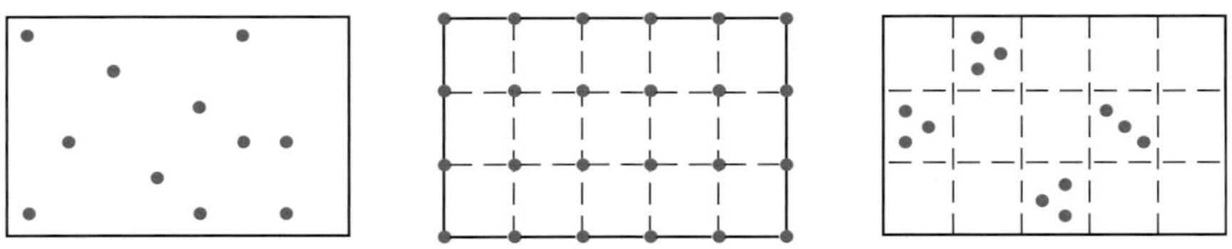

Test Prep and Spiral Review

21. **Multiple Choice** Every fifth person standing in line is asked a question. Identify the sampling method used.

    (A) Convenience (B) Random (C) Stratified (D) Systematic

22. **Short Response** At a baseball game, a market researcher randomly asks 100 people to name their favorite sport. Identify the population and sample. Give a reason why the sample could be biased.

Use a number line to find each sum. (Lesson 1-4)

23. $-6 + 11$ 24. $-31 + (-31)$ 25. $-8 + 14$

Multiply. Write the product as one power. (Lesson 4-3)

26. $3^6 \cdot 3^7$ 27. $7^2 \cdot 7^4$ 28. $12^4 \cdot 14^5$ 29. $x^3 \cdot x^5$

Hands-On LAB 9-1

Explore Samples

Use with Lesson 9-1

go.hrw.com
Lab Resources Online
KEYWORD: MT7 Lab9

REMEMBER
- Be organized before starting.
- Be sure that your sample reflects your population.

You can predict data about a population by collecting data from a representative sample.

Activity

Your school district has been discussing the possibility of school uniforms. Each school will get to choose its uniform and colors. Your class has been chosen to make the selection for your school. To be fair, you want the other students in the school to have some input. You conduct a survey to see what the majority of students in your school want.

1 Model the survey by following the steps below.

a. Choose your population.
- every student in the school
- all girls
- only your class
- all boys
- all 8th grade students
- teachers

b. Choose two different sampling methods. Discuss the pros and cons of each method listed.
- random
- systematic
- stratified
- convenience
- voluntary response

c. Decide what colors and what uniform choices to present to your sample.
- pants
- navy blue
- sweaters
- skirts
- school colors
- vests
- shorts
- forest green
- jackets

Think and Discuss

1. Explain why choosing the teachers as your population might not be the best choice.

2. How did you decide which colors to present to your sample?

Try This

1. Create forms for your survey listing the different options. Then survey your sample. Make a table of your results. Explain what your table tells you about the population.

9-2 Organizing Data

Learn to organize data in tables and stem-and-leaf plots.

Vocabulary

line plot
stem-and-leaf plot
back-to-back stem-and-leaf plot
Venn diagram

An eighth-grade class participated in a month-long fitness challenge. Below are the numbers of miles each student ran, walked, or biked during the first week.

7 5 6 5 5 10 9 9 9 3 3 10 1 0 8
6 8 2 3 1 5 0 4 6 4 8 9 3 4 4

Organizing raw data can help you see patterns and trends. One way to organize data is to use a *line plot*. A **line plot** uses a number line to show how often a value occurs in a data set.

EXAMPLE 1 Organizing Data in Line Plots

Use a line plot to organize the data for the eighth-grade fitness challenge.

Find the least value, 0, and the greatest value, 10, in the data set. Then draw a number line from 0 to 10. Place an "**x**" above each number on the number line for each time it appears in the data set

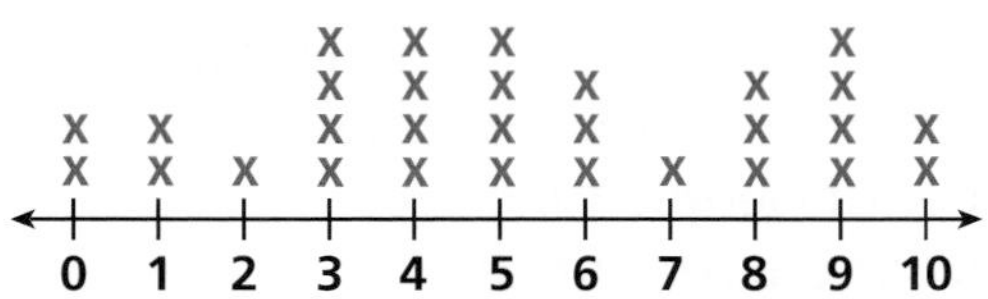

There are 30 numbers in the data set and 30 x's above the number line.

A **stem-and-leaf plot** is a graph used to organize and display data to compare frequencies. Each leaf on the plot represents the right-hand digit in a data value. Each stem represents the remaining left-hand digits.

Stem = first digit(s)

$2 \mid 5 = 25$

Leaf = last digit

EXAMPLE 2 Reading Stem-and-Leaf Plots

List the data values in the stem-and-leaf plot.

0	2 5
1	3 3 7 8
2	0 2 6
3	1 7

Key: 3 | 1 means 31

The data values are 2, 5, 13, 13, 17, 18, 20, 22, 26, 31, and 37.

A **back-to-back stem-and-leaf plot** can be used to compare two sets of data. The stems are in the center, and the left leaves are read in reverse.

EXAMPLE 3 Organizing Data in Back-to-Back Stem-and-Leaf Plots

Use the given data to make a back-to-back stem-and-leaf plot.

Super Bowl Scores, 1995–2005											
	1995	**1996**	**1997**	**1998**	**1999**	**2000**	**2001**	**2002**	**2003**	**2004**	**2005**
Winning	49	27	35	31	34	23	34	20	48	32	24
Losing	26	17	21	24	19	16	7	17	21	29	21

Losses		Wins
7	0	
9 7 7 6	1	
9 6 4 1 1 1	2	0 3 4 7
	3	1 2 4 4 5
	4	8 9

Key: |3|1 *means 31 points*
1|2| *means 21 points*

Venn diagrams are used to show relationships between sets.

EXAMPLE 4 Organizing Data in Venn Diagrams

In a survey, the genders and ages of people who completed the questions is shown at right. Make a Venn diagram to show the number of people who are female and over age 30.

Survey Results			
Gender	**Age**	**Gender**	**Age**
M	18	M	16
F	30	M	35
F	25	F	28
M	50	F	45
M	60	F	35
F	17	M	38
F	42	F	29
F	30	F	46
M	27	M	32
F	48	F	25

Draw two circles. Label one circle "Female" and the other circle "Over 30." The region that overlaps represents the characteristics that are shared by both sets of data.

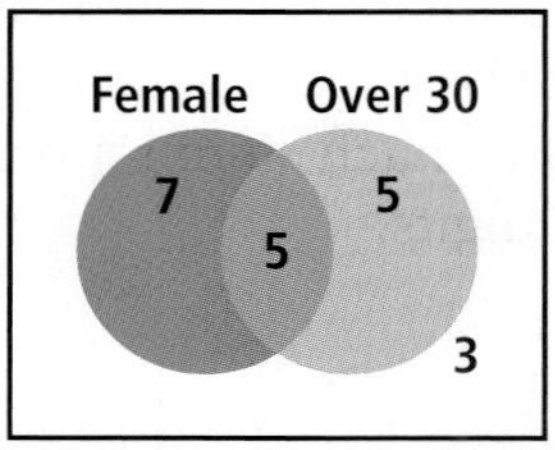

Think and Discuss

1. Explain what the overlapping region represents in a Venn diagram.

9-2 Exercises

go.hrw.com
Homework Help Online
KEYWORD: MT7 9-2
Parent Resources Online
KEYWORD: MT7 Parent

GUIDED PRACTICE

See Example 1

1. Use a line plot to organize the data of ages of children visiting a park.

5 7 8 2 3 3 4 5 8 2
9 10 9 10 8 8 7 6 6 5

See Example 2

List the data values in the stem-and-leaf plot.

2.

0	2 3 3 7
1	1 3 7 7 8
2	0 0 7
3	4 4 5 5

Key: 3 | 5 means 35

3.

6	3 6 8
7	3 3 5 7
8	0 0 1 1
9	0 4 5 9

Key: 9 | 9 means 99

See Example 3

4. Use the given data to make a back-to-back stem-and-leaf plot.

Political Divisions of the U.S. Senate

Congress	89th	90th	91st	92nd	93rd	94th	95th	96th	97th	98th
Democrats	68	64	57	54	56	61	61	58	46	46
Republicans	32	36	43	44	42	37	38	41	53	54

See Example 4

5. Make a Venn diagram to show how many eighth-grade female students responded to a recent survey.

Survey Results

Grade	6th	5th	8th	6th	7th	8th	7th	8th	6th	5th
Gender	M	F	M	F	M	F	M	F	F	M

INDEPENDENT PRACTICE

See Example 1

6. Use a line plot to organize the data of the number of books read by students over the summer.

3 0 3 6 0 1 2 5 5 5 2
3 0 0 1 6 0 7 8 6 5 6

See Example 2

List the data values in the stem-and-leaf plot.

7.

5	0 1 4 8
6	2 6 7
7	1 4 5 6 6
8	2

Key: 6 | 2 means 62

8.

0	1 5 7
1	2 4 6 8
2	0 1 7 9
3	3 3 4 6

Key: 2 | 1 means 21

See Example 3

9. Use the data given in the map to make a back-to-back stem-and-leaf plot.

Extreme November Temperatures

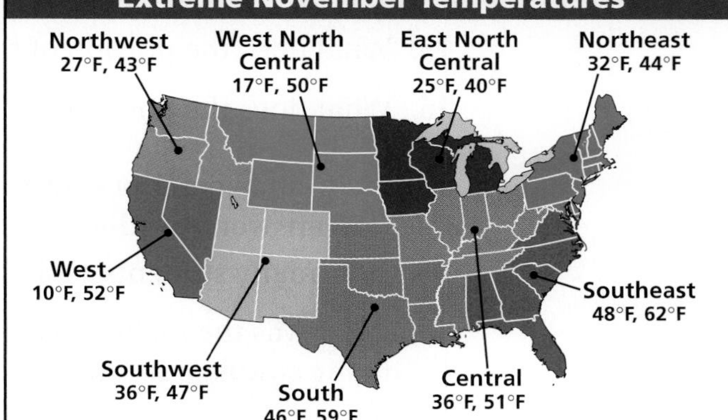

See Example 4

10. Make a Venn diagram to show how many unemployed college graduates responded to a recent survey.

Survey Results												
College Graduate	yes	no	yes	yes	yes	yes	no	yes	no	yes	yes	no
Employed	yes	yes	no	no	yes	no	yes	yes	yes	no	yes	no

PRACTICE AND PROBLEM SOLVING

Extra Practice
See page 798.

11. **Use the given data to make a back-to-back stem-and-leaf plot.**

Miles per Gallon Ratings of a Car Company's Models										
Model	A	B	C	D	E	F	G	H	I	J
City Miles	11	17	28	19	18	15	18	22	14	20
Highway Miles	15	24	36	28	26	20	23	25	17	29

12. The ages of 20 middle school students are shown in the line plot. List the ages in order from the most frequent to the least frequent.

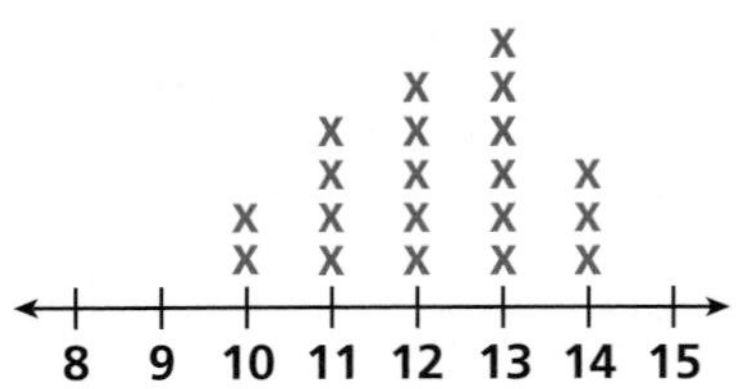

Use the Venn diagram to answer questions 13–16.

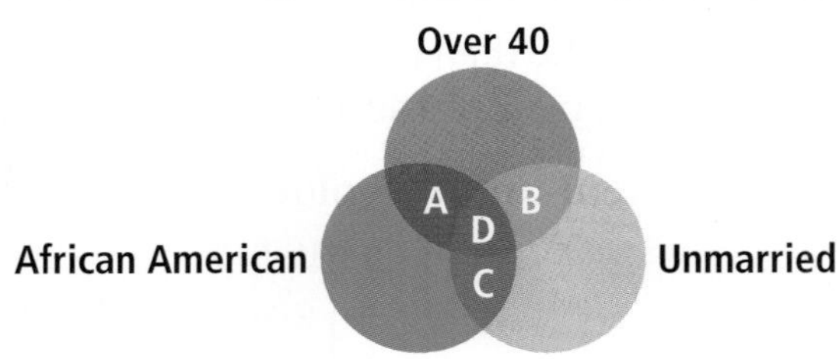

13. What does the portion of the Venn diagram labeled "A" represent?

14. What does the portion of the Venn diagram labeled "B" represent?

15. What does the portion of the Venn diagram labeled "C" represent?

16. What does the portion of the Venn diagram labeled "D" represent?

The stem-and-leaf plot shows the scores for a recent math test. Use it to answer questions 17–19.

17. How many students took the test?

18. What was the highest score received? How many students received the highest score?

19. What was the lowest score received?

Boys		Girls
1 5	6	9
6 8 8 9	7	1 5 5 5
1 1 1 5 9	8	2 2 8
1 8 9	9	1 2 2 7 9

Language Arts LINK

An author's writing style is as unique as a fingerprint. Punctuation, spelling, and word usage can be used to determine authorship.

Don Foster used this fact to analyze the 350-year-old poem "A Funeral Elegy." The analysis confirmed that the poem of previously unknown authorship was actually written by William Shakespeare.

Don Foster's methods have also been used to analyze ransom notes and evidence in court cases.

20. Act 5 of Shakespeare's *A Midsummer Night's Dream* has the following references to numbers: 1 nine times, 2 three times, 3 six times, 10 two times, 12 one time, and 14 one time. Use the data to make a line plot.

21. **Challenge** Select two paragraphs from a work by your favorite author and a third paragraph by a different author. Compare word choices or punctuation use in the three paragraphs. Explain the similarities and differences. Use a line plot or back-to-back stem-and-leaf plot to support your argument.

	Verse													
	1	2	3	4	5	6	7	8	9	10	11	12	13	14
,	4	8	6	8	10	12	15	10	7	3	5	5	5	11
—	1	1	3	0	1	2	2	0	0	0	1	1	2	2
!	0	0	1	0	0	1	3	1	0	0	0	0	0	1
.	1	1	1	1	1	1	2	1	1	2	2	3	2	1

TEST PREP and Spiral Review

22. **Multiple Choice** For which set of data would it NOT be appropriate to make a stem-and-leaf plot?

Ⓐ Scores of a baseball league's games
Ⓑ Average high temperatures
Ⓒ Prices of fruit at a local market
Ⓓ Instruments played in the band

23. **Short Response** Use the data to make a back-to-back stem-and-leaf plot of the ages of people who visited an art exhibit. Men: 32, 45, 61, 33, 41, 61; women: 31, 44, 55, 32, 55, 64

Solve each proportion. (Lesson 5-4)

24. $\frac{9}{10} = \frac{x}{15}$ **25.** $\frac{2}{w} = \frac{8}{12}$ **26.** $\frac{6}{1} = \frac{d}{3}$ **27.** $\frac{r}{4} = \frac{36}{3}$

Identify the sampling method used. (Lesson 9-1)

28. Shoppers at a store grand opening place their names in a box. One shopper is chosen at random.

29. Every fourth customer at the grand opening receives a gift certificate.

9-3 Measures of Central Tendency

Learn to find appropriate measures of central tendency.

Vocabulary

mean
median
mode
range
outlier

Measures of central tendency are used to describe the middle of a data set. Mean, median, and mode are measures of central tendency.

Measures of Central Tendency and Range	
	Description
Mean	To find the mean (average), add the values in the data set. Then divide by the number of values in the set. Use when the data does not have any outliers.
Median	The middle value, or the mean of the two middle values, in an ordered set of data. Use when the data does have outliers.
Mode	The value(s) that occur most frequently. A data set may have no mode, one mode, or several modes. Use when you want to show which value(s) occur most often.
Range	The difference between the least and the greatest values in a data set. Use when you want to show the spread of the data.

An **outlier** is a value that is either far less than or far greater than the rest of the values in the data.

EXAMPLE 1 Finding Measures of Central Tendency and Range

Find the mean, median, mode, and range of the data set.

9, 6, 91, 5, 7, 6, 8, 8, 7, 9

mean: $9 + 6 + 91 + 5 + 7 + 6 + 8 + 8 + 7 + 9 = 156$

$\frac{156}{10} = 15.6$ *Divide by 10.*

median: $5\ 6\ 6\ 7\ 7\ 8\ 8\ 9\ 9\ 91$ *Order the values.*

5 values | 5 values

$\frac{7 + 8}{2} = 7.5$ *Average the two middle values.*

mode: 6, 7, 8, 9 *Four values occur twice each.*

range: $91 - 5 = 86$

EXAMPLE 2 Choosing the Best Measure of Central Tendency

Determine and find the most appropriate measure of central tendency or range for each situation. Justify your answer.

A **The students in an 8th grade math class received the following scores on a test: 98, 79, 75, 90, 85, 90, 79, 88, 99, 100, 90, 72, 83, 90, 95, 98, 85, 69, 90, 82, 97, and 90. What score occurred most often?**

Find the mode.

69, 72, 75, 79, 79, 82, 83, 85, 85, 88, 90, 90, 90, 90, 90, 90, 95, 97, 98, 98, 99, 100

List the scores in order. Underline the scores that appear more than once.

Ninety appears most frequently. The mode is 90.

B **For the 2004 NFL season, the top four player salaries were \$35,037,700, \$19,004,000, \$16,536,500, and \$16,000,000. What number best describes these salaries?**

\$35,037,700 is an outlier because it is much greater than the other salaries. Find the median.

\$16,000,000, \$16,536,500, \$19,004,000, \$35,037,700

$$\frac{16{,}536{,}500 + 19{,}004{,}000}{2} = 17{,}770{,}250$$

The median of the top four NFL salaries is \$17,770,250.

Sometimes you may want to choose a measure of central tendency or range in order to give a certain message about a group of data.

EXAMPLE 3 *Business Application*

A store had sales of \$1025, \$974, \$993, \$1001, \$1027, \$1657, and \$1471 during one week. Which measure of data would make the store's sales for the week look the best?

Find each measure of central tendency and the range of the data.

mean: $\frac{1025 + 974 + 993 + 1001 + 1027 + 1657 + 1471}{7} = 1164$

median: 974, 996, 1001, 1025, 1027, 1471, 1657; 1025

mode: There is no mode.

range: $1471 - 974 = 497$

The mean makes the sales for the week appear the greatest.

Think and Discuss

1. Explain how the range is affected by outliers.

2. Give a data set with the same mean, median, and mode.

9-3 Exercises

go.hrw.com
Homework Help Online
KEYWORD: MT7 9-3
Parent Resources Online
KEYWORD: MT7 Parent

GUIDED PRACTICE

See Example 1

Find the mean, median, mode, and range of each data set.

1. 35, 21, 34, 44, 36, 42, 29
2. 2.0, 4.4, 6.2, 3.2, 4.4, 6.2
3. 7, 5, 4, 6, 8, 3, 5, 2, 5
4. 23, 13, 45, 56, 72, 44, 89, 92, 67

See Example 2

Determine and find the most appropriate measure of central tendency or range for each situation.

5. The ages of the people attending the Harris family reunion are shown in the table. What was the spread in ages?

63	60	38	35	59	57	40	38	9	4	35
35	15	12	10	30	59	59	3	12	4	31

6. The scores on a math test were 80, 79, 90, 95, 85, 82, 96, 94, 81, 49, 92, and 87. What number best describes these scores?

See Example 3

7. The weekly salaries of the employees of a hair salon are $1025, $975, $823, $750, $1400, $823, $1000, and $823. Which measure of data would make the salaries seem the highest?

INDEPENDENT PRACTICE

See Example 1

Find the mean, median, mode, and range of each data set.

8. 5, 2, 12, 7, 13, 9, 8
9. 92, 88, 84, 86, 88
10. 6, 8, 6, 7, 9, 2, 4, 22
11. 4.3, 1.3, 4.5, 8.6, 9, 3, 2.1, 14

See Example 2

Determine and find the most appropriate measure of central tendency or range for each situation.

12. The ages of the students in a middle school choir are 10, 11, 12, 11, 12, 11, 10, 11, 13, 12, 13, 12, 11, 13, 14, 12, 14, 12, 11, and 12. What age appears most often in the list?
13. The number of customers each day at a deli was 62, 50, 63, 58, 61, 122, and 70. What number best describes this data?

See Example 3

14. The students in one middle school homeroom received the following scores on their achievement test: 32, 87, 89, 96, 96, 85, 79, 96, 90, 85, 78, 72, 96, 99, 91, 82, 77, 82, and 81. Which measure of data would make the scores appear the highest?

PRACTICE AND PROBLEM SOLVING

Extra Practice
See page 798.

Which measure of central tendency gives the lowest value for each data set?

15. 20, 17, 42, 26, 27, 12, 31
16. 8, 5, 3, 75, 7, 3, 4, 7, 9, 8, 2, 8, 5, 7, 8
17. 3.3, 4.0, 3.3, 5.6, 4.6, 3.3, 5.6
18. 15, 10, 12, 10, 13, 13, 13, 10, 3, 13

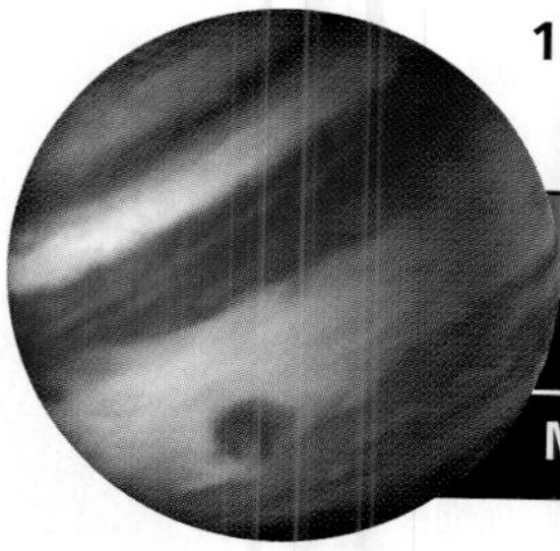

19. **Astronomy** The table shows the approximate distance each planet is from the Sun.

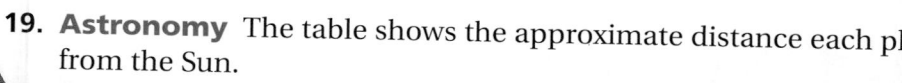

Distance from the Sun									
Planet	Mercury	Venus	Earth	Mars	Jupiter	Saturn	Uranus	Neptune	Pluto
Miles (million)	36	67	93	141	484	887	1784	2796	3661

a. Find the range of the data.

b. Which measure of central tendency makes the planets appear to be closer to the Sun?

20. **School** Teresa has taken three tests worth 100 points each. Her scores are 85, 93, and 88. She has one test left to take. What score must she get on her last test to get an average of 90?

21. **Write a Problem** Use your test scores from one course to write a problem about central tendency.

22. **Write About It** If six friends went to dinner and split the check equally, what measure of central tendency would describe the amount each person paid? Explain.

23. **Challenge** If $4\left(\frac{x + y + z}{3}\right) = 8$, what is the mean of x, y, and z?

Test Prep and Spiral Review

24. **Multiple Choice** Which measure of central tendency has the smallest value for the data set: 11, 11, 4, 15, 18, 22, 24, 7?

Ⓐ Mean Ⓑ Median Ⓒ Mode Ⓓ They are all equal.

25. **Gridded Response** Kelly recorded the number of sit-ups she did each day in the table below. Find the mean number of sit-ups Kelly did per day.

Mon	Tue	Wed	Thur	Fri
34	45	66	75	82

Find each number to the nearest tenth. (Lesson 6-3)

26. What number is 55% of 240?

27. What number is $66\frac{2}{3}\%$ of 847?

Identify the population and sample. Give a reason why the sample could be biased. (Lesson 9-1)

28. In December, a store owner asks every third shopper whether they are buying items for themselves or as gifts.

29. A market researcher pays a group of shoppers at a mall to fill out a questionnaire about products they are shown.

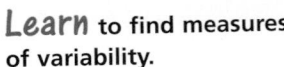

9-4 Variability

Learn to find measures of variability.

Vocabulary

variability

quartile

box-and-whisker plot

The table below summarizes a veterinarian's records for kitten litters born in a given year.

Litter Size	2	3	4	5	6
Number of Litters	1	6	8	11	1

The term *box-and-whisker plot* may remind you of a box of kittens. But it is a way to display data.

While central tendency describes the middle of a data set, **variability** describes how spread out the data is.

Quartiles divide a data set into four equal parts. The third quartile minus the first quartile is the range for the middle half of the data.

Kitten Data

Lower half — *Upper half*

(2 3 3 3 3 3 (3) 4 4 4 4 4 4) (4) (4 5 5 5 5 5 (5) 5 5 5 5 5 6)

First quartile: 3 median of lower half

Median: 4 (second quartile)

Third quartile: 5 median of upper half

EXAMPLE 1 **Finding Measures of Variability**

Find the first and third quartiles for each data set.

A **85, 92, 78, 88, 90, 88, 89**

(78 (85) 88) 88 (89 (90) 92) *Order the values.*

first quartile: 85

third quartile: 90

B **13, 14, 16, 18, 18, 21, 12, 21, 11, 19, 15, 13**

(11, 12, (13, 13), 14, 15) (16, 18, (18, 19), 21, 21) *Order the values.*

first quartile: $\frac{13 + 13}{2} = 13$

third quartile: $\frac{18 + 19}{2} = 18.5$

A **box-and-whisker plot** shows the distribution of data. The middle half of the data is represented by a "box" with a vertical line at the median. The lower fourth and upper fourth are represented by "whiskers" that extend to the smallest and largest values.

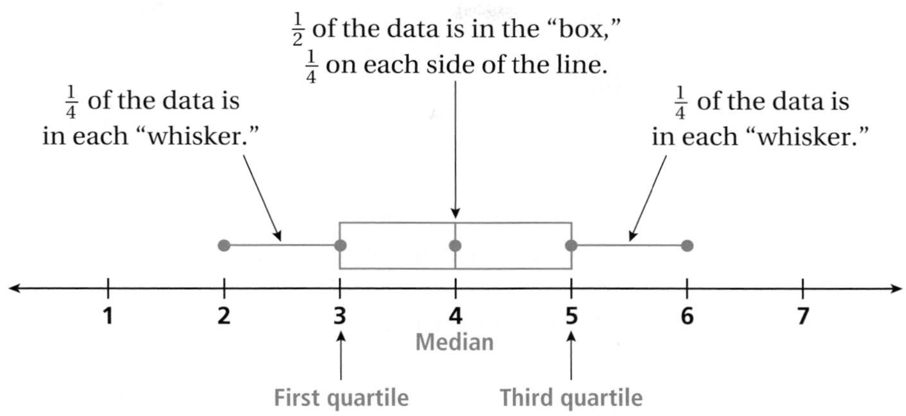

EXAMPLE 2 **Making a Box-and-Whisker Plot**

Use the given data to make a box-and-whisker plot.

23 16 51 23 56 22 63 51 22 15 19 42 44 50 38 31 47

Step 1: Order the data and find the smallest value, first quartile, median, third quartile, and largest value.

15, 16, 19, 22, 22, 23, 23, 31, 38, 42, 44, 47, 50, 51, 51, 56, 63

smallest value: 15

first quartile: $\frac{22 + 22}{2} = 22$

median: 38

third quartile: $\frac{50 + 51}{2} = 50.5$

largest value: 63

Step 2: Draw a number line and plot a point above each value from Step 1.

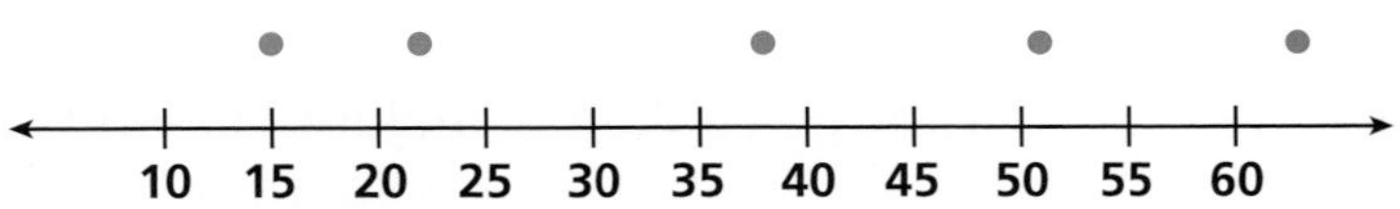

Step 3: Draw the box and whiskers.

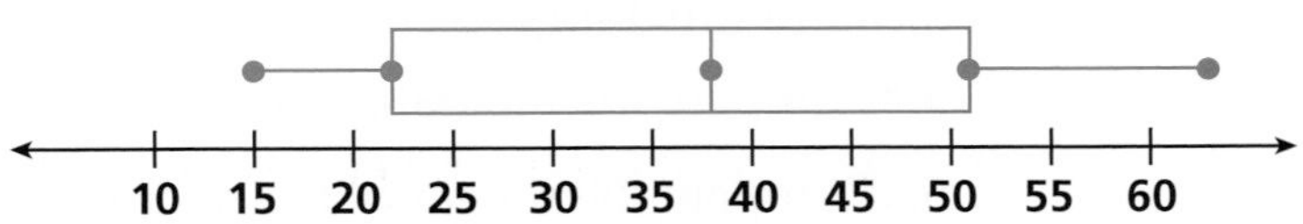

EXAMPLE 3 Comparing Data Sets Using Box-and-Whisker Plots

The number of touchdown passes that Brett Favre and Dan Marino threw during the first 14 years of their careers is shown in the box-and-whisker plots at right.

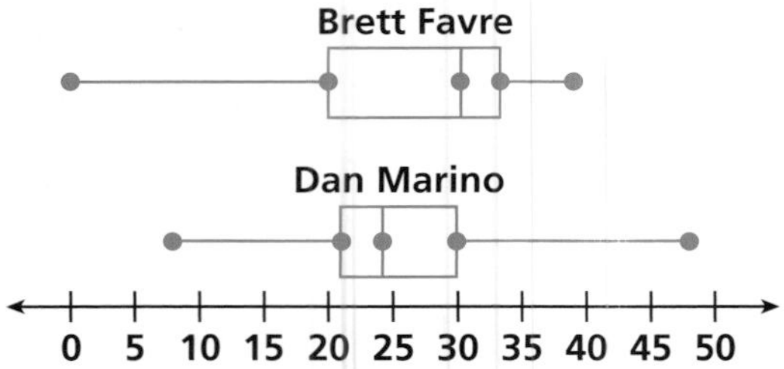

A Compare the medians and ranges.

Brett Favre's median is greater than Dan Marino's.

Dan Marino's range is greater than Brett Favre's.

B Compare the ranges of the middle half of the data for each.

The range of the middle of each data set is the length of the "box". So, the range of the middle half of the data is greater for Brett Favre.

Think and Discuss

1. **Explain** why the data must first be ordered from smallest to largest before making a box-and-whisker plot.
2. **Compare** the number of data values in the box with the number of data values in the whiskers.

9-4 Exercises

go.hrw.com
Homework Help Online
KEYWORD: MT7 9-4
Parent Resources Online
KEYWORD: MT7 Parent

GUIDED PRACTICE

See Example 1 **Find the first and third quartiles for each data set.**

1. 52, 75, 55, 30, 70, 56, 66
2. 4, 1, 3, 0, 6, 3, 5, 4, 3, 2, 6, 2

See Example 2 **Use the given data to make a box-and-whisker plot.**

3. 32, 47, 42, 33, 23, 59, 29, 19, 34
4. 41, 11, 26, 58, 54, 32, 38, 56, 21

See Example 3 **Use the box-and-whisker plots to compare the data sets.**

5. Compare the medians and ranges.
6. Compare the ranges of the middle half of the data for each set.

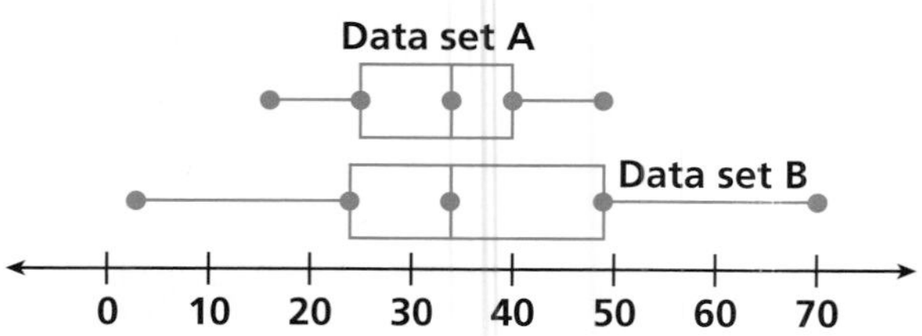

INDEPENDENT PRACTICE

See Example 1

Find the first and third quartiles for each data set.

7. 48, 72, 43, 42, 69, 50, 56, 48, 52

8. 18, 17, 13, 7, 6, 25, 55, 3, 6

See Example 2

Use the given data to make a box-and-whisker plot.

9. 50, 68, 85, 54, 80, 75, 68

10. 7, 4, 5.7, 1.4, 6.8, 6.3, 11, 3.2

See Example 3

Use the box-and-whisker plots to compare the data sets.

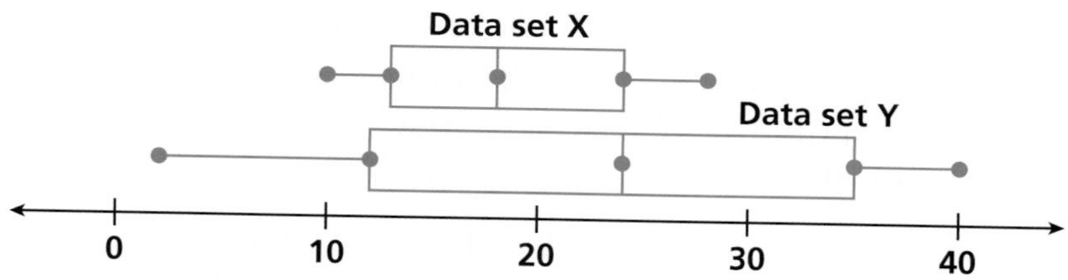

11. Compare the medians and ranges.

12. Compare the ranges of the middle half of the data for each set.

PRACTICE AND PROBLEM SOLVING

Extra Practice
See page 798.

Find the first and third quartiles for each data set.

13. 88, 78, 85, 74, 66, 82, 68

14. 9, 2, 8, 6, 1, 7, 3, 11

15. 46, 53, 67, 29, 35, 54, 49, 61, 35

16. 3.5, 3.4, 3.7, 3.5, 3.4, 3.3, 3.4, 3.4

Use the given data to make a box-and-whisker plot.

17. 87, 79, 95, 99, 67, 71, 83, 91

18. 16, 3, 9.3, 11.3, 14, 7, 7, 4.2, 4.5

19. 0, 2, 5, 2, 1, 3, 5, 2, 4, 3, 5, 4

20. 6.4, 8.0, 6.5, 3.0, 5.4, 2.2, 5.3

21. Earth Science Hurricanes and tropical storms form in all seven ocean basins. Use a box-and-whisker plot to compare the number of tropical storms in every ocean basin per year with the number of hurricanes in every ocean basin per year.

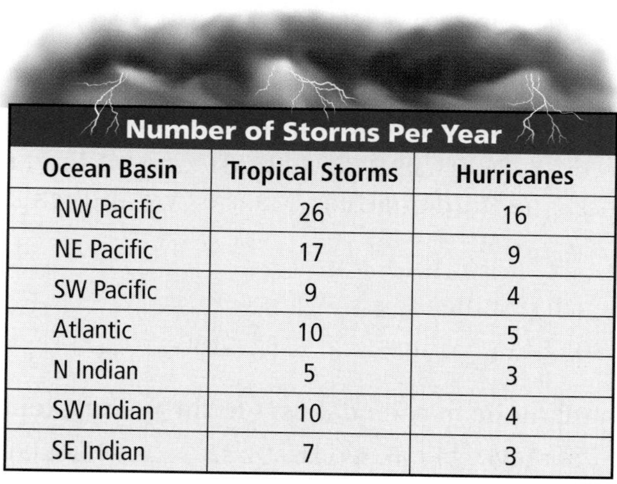

Number of Storms Per Year

Ocean Basin	Tropical Storms	Hurricanes
NW Pacific	26	16
NE Pacific	17	9
SW Pacific	9	4
Atlantic	10	5
N Indian	5	3
SW Indian	10	4
SE Indian	7	3

22. Match each set of data with a box-and-whisker plot.

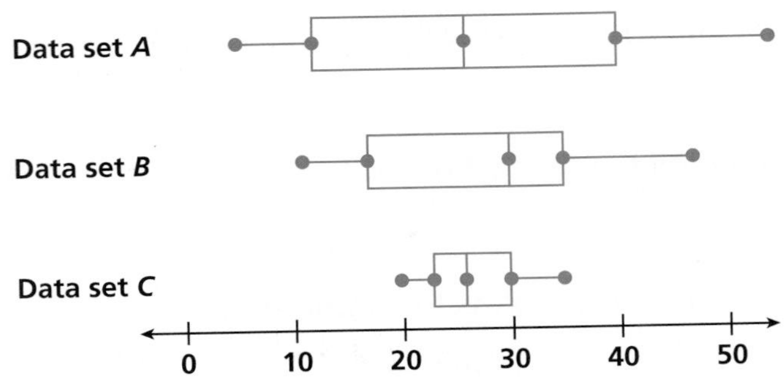

a. range: 49
first quartile: 7
third quartile: 35

b. range: 15
first quartile: 18
third quartile: 25

c. range: 36
first quartile: 12
third quartile: 30

23. **Critical Thinking** Make a box-and-whisker plot of the following data: 18, 16, 21, 10, 15, 25, 13, 22, 25, 13, 15, 10. Add 50 to the list of data and make a new box-and-whisker plot. How did the addition of an outlier affect the box-and-whisker plot?

24. **What's the Error?** A student wrote that the data set 33, 28, 29, 56, 27, 43, 33, 25, 40, 65 has a range of 32. What's the error?

25. **Write About It** What do box-and-whisker plots tell you about data that measures of central tendency do not?

26. **Challenge** What would an exceptionally short box with extremely long whiskers tell you about a data set?

Test Prep and Spiral Review

27. **Multiple Choice** Find the first quartile for the data set shown in the box-and-whisker plot.

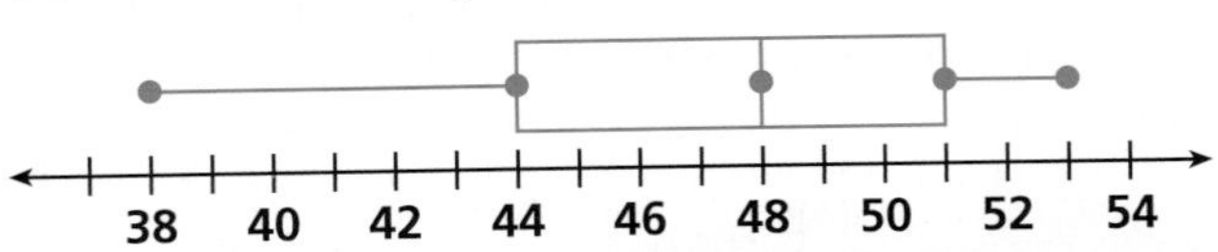

Ⓐ 38 Ⓑ 44 Ⓒ 46 Ⓓ 48

28. **Extended Response** Ken recorded his golf scores during a three week period. His scores were: 85, 76, 83, 99, 83, 74, 75, 81, and 87. Find the range, median, and first and third quartiles. Make a box-and-whisker plot of the data.

Find the square roots of each number. (Lesson 4-5)

29. 16 30. 81 31. 100 32. 1

Find the mean, median, and mode of each data set to the nearest tenth. (Lesson 9-3)

33. 3, 5, 5, 6, 9, 3, 5, 2, 5 34. 17, 15, 14, 16, 18, 13 35. 100, 75, 48, 75, 48, 63, 45

Technology LAB 9-4

Create Box-and-Whisker Plots

Use with Lesson 9-4

go.hrw.com
Lab Resources Online
KEYWORD: MT7 Lab9

The data below are the heights in inches of the 15 girls in Mrs. Lopez's 8th-grade class.

57, 62, 68, 52, 53, 56, 58, 56, 57, 50, 56, 59, 50, 63, 52

Activity

Graph the heights of the 15 girls in Mrs. Lopez's class on a box-and-whisker plot.

Press STAT **Edit** to enter the values into List 1 (**L1**). If necessary, press the up arrow and then CLEAR ENTER to clear old data. Enter the data from the class into **L1**. Press ENTER after each value.

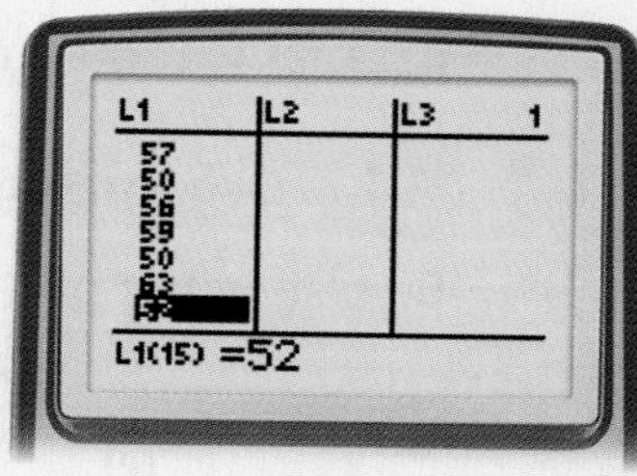

Use the **STAT PLOT** editor to obtain the plot setup menu.

Press 2nd Y= (STAT PLOT) ENTER. Use the arrow keys and ENTER to select **On** and then the fifth type. **Xlist** should be **L1** and **Freq** should be 1, as shown. Press ZOOM **9:ZoomStat**.

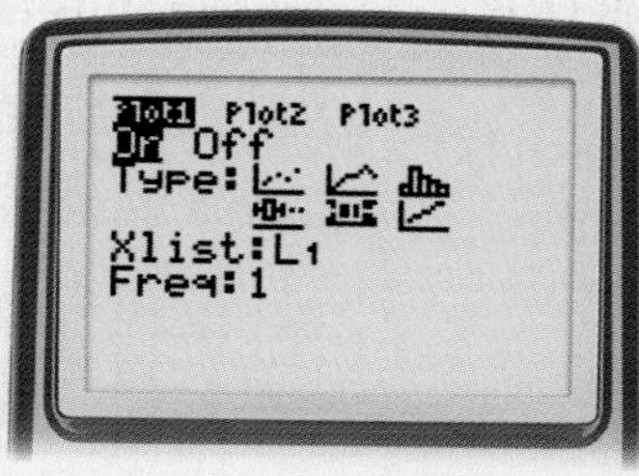

Use the TRACE key and the ◀ and ▶ keys to see all five summary statistical values (minimum: **MinX**, first quartile: **Q1**, median: **MED**, third quartile: **Q3**, and maximum: **MaxX**). The minimum value in the data set is 50 in., the first quartile is 52 in., the median is 56 in., the third quartile is 59 in., and the maximum is 68 in.

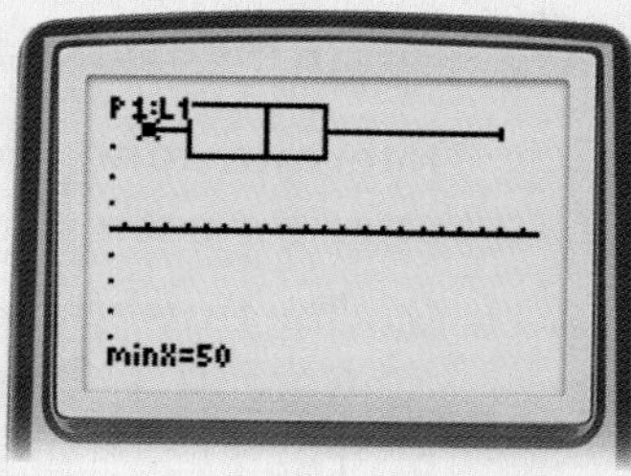

Think and Discuss

1. Explain how the box-and-whisker plot gives information that is hard to see by just looking at the numbers.

Try This

1. The data below shows the number of hours slept one night for ach of the 11 boys from Mrs. Lopez's 8th-grade class.

7.5, 6.5, 5, 6, 8, 7.25, 6.5, 7, 7, 8, 6.75

Make a box-and-whisker plot of this data. What are the minimum, first quartile, median, third quartile, and maximum values of the data set?

CHAPTER 9

READY TO GO ON?

SECTION 9A

Quiz for Lessons 9-1 Through 9-4

9-1 Samples and Surveys

Identify the sampling method used.

1. Every third student is called from a class roster.
2. Fifty customers are chosen by chance from five random grocery stores.

Identify the population and sample. Give a reason the sample could be biased.

3. A restaurant owner asks Friday's customers to choose a favorite salsa.
4. A DVD rental manager asks people who rent dramas what their favorite movie is.

9-2 Organizing Data

5. Use a line plot to organize the data of the ages of people playing bridge.

72	78	76	75	79	70	74	80	72	78
71	69	70	72	68	70	69	75	75	74

6. Use the given data to make a back-to-back stem-and-leaf plot.

Greatest Number of Home Runs by a Player, 2000–2004					
	2000	2001	2002	2003	2004
American League	47	52	57	47	43
National League	50	73	49	47	48

7. Make a Venn diagram to show how many 2-year-old, male cats were adopted.

Gender	F	M	M	F	M	M	M	F	F	M
Age (y)	1	1	2	3	1	1	2	3	2	2

9-3 Measures of Central Tendency

Determine and find the most appropriate measure of central tendency or range for each situation.

8. The finishing times in minutes for a 5-kilometer run by a group of friends were 21.1, 20.6, 19.7, 20.3, 17.7, and 22.6. What was the spread of the times?
9. The week's average high temperatures in degrees Fahrenheit were 70, 72, 72, 74, 76, 75, and 74. What number best describes the temperatures?

9-4 Variability

Use the given data to make a box-and-whisker plot.

10. 43, 36, 25, 22, 34, 40, 18, 32, 43
11. 21, 51, 36, 38, 45, 52, 28, 16, 41

Ready to Go On?

Focus on Problem Solving

Make a Plan

- **Identify too much/too little information**

When you read a problem, you must decide if the problem has too much or too little information. If the problem has too much information, you must decide what information to use to solve the problem. If the problem has too little information, then you should determine what additional information you need to solve the problem.

Read the problems below and decide if there is too much or too little information in each problem. If there is too much information, tell what information you would use to solve the problem. If there is too little information, tell what additional information you would need to solve the problem.

1. On Monday, 20 students took an exam. There were 10 students who scored above 85 and 10 students who scored below 85. What was the average score?

2. The average elevation in California is about 2900 ft above sea level. The highest point, Mt. Whitney, has an elevation of 14,494 ft above sea level. The lowest point, Death Valley, has an elevation of 282 ft below sea level. What is the range of elevations in California?

3. Use the table to find the median number of marriages per year in the United States for the years between 1940 and 2000.

4. Aishya is cross-training for a marathon. She ran for 50 minutes on Monday, 70 minutes on Wednesday, and 45 minutes on Friday. On Tuesday and Thursday, she lifted weights at the gym for 45 minutes each day. She swam for 45 minutes over the weekend. What was the average amount of time per day Aishya spent running last week?

Number of Marriages in the United States

Year	1940	1950	1960	1970	1980	1990	2000
Number (thousands)	1596	1667	1523	2159	2390	2443	2329

Source: National Center for Health Statistics

Hands-On LAB 9-5

Make a Circle Graph

Use with Lesson 9-5

go.hrw.com
Lab Resources Online
KEYWORD: MT7 Lab9

WHAT YOU NEED:
- Compass
- Ruler
- Protractor
- Paper

REMEMBER
- A circle measures 360°.
- Percent compares a number to 100.

Activity

Skunks are legal pets in some states but not in most. Use the information from the table to make a circle graph showing the percents for each category.

Skunks as Pets by State

Legality	Number of States
Legal (no restrictions)	6
Legal with permit	12
Legal in some areas	2
Illegal	27
Other conditions	3

a. Use a compass to draw a large circle. Use a ruler to draw a vertical radius.

b. Extend the table to show the percent of states with each category of legality.

c. Use the percents to determine the angle measure of each sector of the graph.

d. Use a protractor to draw each angle clockwise from the radius.

e. Label the graph and each sector. Color the sectors.

Legality	Number of States	Percent of States	Angle of Section
Legal (no restrictions)	6	$\frac{6}{50} = 12\%$	$\frac{12}{100} \cdot 360 = 43.2°$
Legal with permit	12	$\frac{12}{50} = 24\%$	$\frac{24}{100} \cdot 360 = 86.4°$
Legal in some areas	2	$\frac{2}{50} = 4\%$	$\frac{4}{100} \cdot 360 = 14.4°$
Illegal	27	$\frac{27}{50} = 54\%$	$\frac{54}{100} \cdot 360 = 194.4°$
Other conditions	3	$\frac{3}{50} = 6\%$	$\frac{6}{100} \cdot 360 = 21.6°$

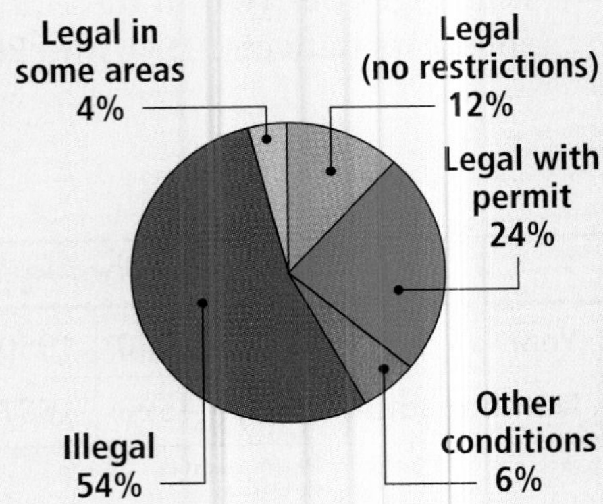

Think and Discuss

1. How many states would need to legalize skunks for the largest sector to be 180°?

Try This

1. Make a circle graph to show only the states where skunks are not illegal.

9-5 Displaying Data

Learn to display data in bar graphs, histograms, and line graphs.

Vocabulary

double-bar graph
frequency table
histogram
double-line graph

In 1990, the United States qualified for the soccer World Cup for the first time in 40 years. Since then, popularity in youth soccer in the United States has grown tremendously.

A **double-bar graph** is used to display and compare two sets of data. You can organize data using a **frequency table** by listing items according to the number of times that the items occur.

EXAMPLE 1 **Displaying Data in a Double-Bar Graph**

Make a double-bar graph.

The following are the ages when a randomly chosen soccer group of 20 boys and 20 girls began playing in a local youth soccer league.

Age	4	5	6	7	8
Boys	5	10	3	2	0
Girls	2	11	5	1	1

The frequencies are the heights of the bars in the bar graph. Use a different color to represent each gender.

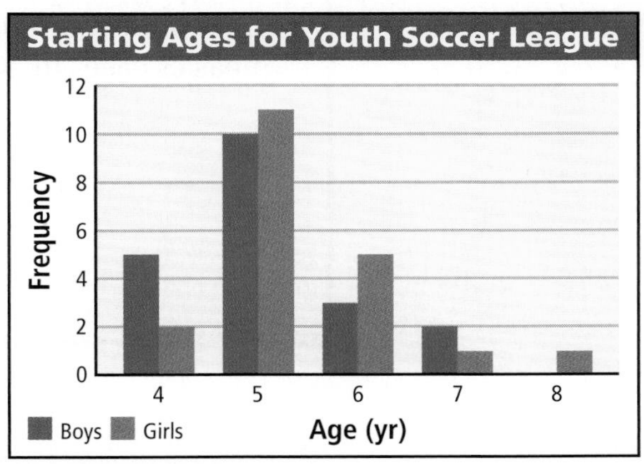

A **histogram** is a bar graph that shows the frequency of data within equal intervals.

EXAMPLE 2 Displaying Data in a Histogram

Edwina asked 10 classmates how many minutes of sleep they had the previous night. Use the data to make a histogram.

460 400 425 440 490 365 435 500 380 505

Make a frequency table with 30-minute intervals. Then make a histogram.

Helpful Hint

Histograms do not have spaces between the bars.

Minutes	Frequency
360–389	2
390–419	1
420–449	3
450–479	1
480–509	3

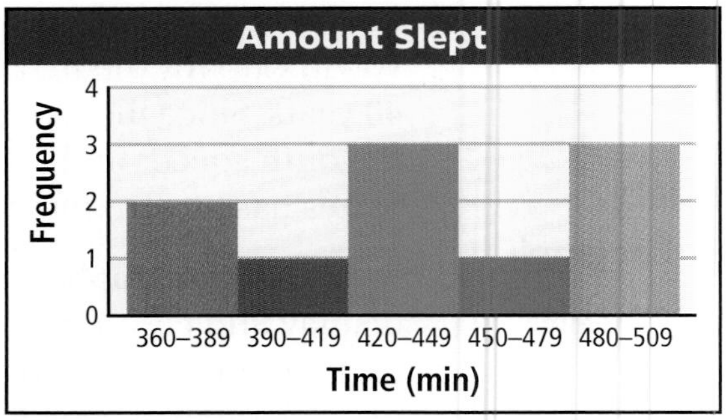

A **double-line graph** is used to show how two related sets of data change over time.

EXAMPLE 3 Displaying Data in a Line Graph

Make a double-line graph of the given data. Use the graph to estimate the number of measles cases and whooping cough cases in 2002.

Number of Worldwide Cases		
Year	Measles	Whooping Cough
1992	1,481,971	255,475
1996	870,989	141,445
2000	836,407	186,198
2004	504,742	235,740

Plot the data. The graph shows about 200,000 whooping cough cases and about 650,000 measles cases in 2002.

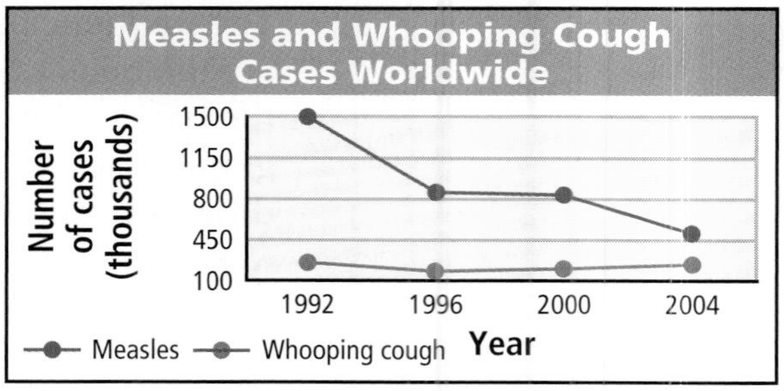

Think and Discuss

1. Describe the difference between a bar graph and a histogram.

9-5 Exercises

go.hrw.com
Homework Help Online
KEYWORD: MT7 9-5
Parent Resources Online
KEYWORD: MT7 Parent

GUIDED PRACTICE

See Example 1

1. Make a double-bar graph.
   Data Set 1: 11 10 13 11 12 13 13 9 10 11 12 10
   Data Set 2: 13 11 12 12 11 9 10 11 12 10 9 11

See Example 2

2. The Freshman National Merit Scholars and their schools are listed for 2004. Use the data to make a histogram with intervals of 50.

   Vanderbilt, 144; Princeton, 192; Duke, 90; Stanford, 217; Yale, 224; Northwestern, 152; Rice University, 173; Cal Tech, 51; University of Chicago, 198; M.I.T., 134; University of Texas-Austin, 242; Washington University, 197

See Example 3

3. Make a double-line graph of the given data. Use the graph to estimate the life expectancies of a male and a female born in 1997.

Life Expectancy by Birth Year (U.S.)

Year	1980	1985	1990	1995	2000
Age Male	70.0	71.1	71.8	72.5	74.3
Age Female	77.4	78.2	78.8	78.9	79.7

Source: National Center for Health Statistics

INDEPENDENT PRACTICE

See Example 1

4. Make a double-bar graph.

Temperature °F	10	15	20	25	30	35	40
Data Set 1	2	6	9	7	4	2	1
Data Set 2	5	7	8	5	4	2	0

See Example 2

5. Restaurants sometimes organize their menus by the number of items in each price range. Use the entrée prices to make a histogram with intervals of $10.
   $9 $11 $22 $22 $30 $24 $13 $16 $17 $21 $18 $25 $17 $25
   $17 $21 $19 $21 $14 $19 $15 $15 $10 $16 $12 $21 $19 $17

See Example 3

6. Make a double-line graph of the given data. Use the graph to estimate the populations of Philadelphia and San Francisco in 1995.

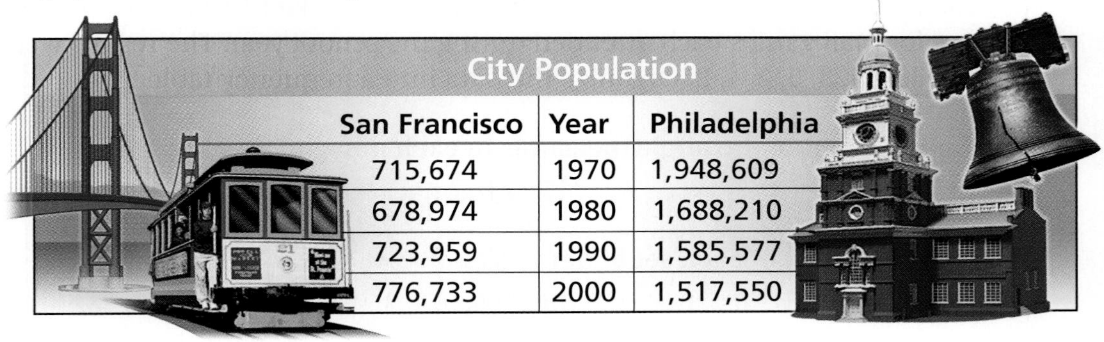

City Population

San Francisco	Year	Philadelphia
715,674	1970	1,948,609
678,974	1980	1,688,210
723,959	1990	1,585,577
776,733	2000	1,517,550

PRACTICE AND PROBLEM SOLVING

Extra Practice
See page 799.

7. Organize the data into a frequency table and make a double-bar graph.
Data set 1: 1 6 3 1 4 6 4 5 6 1 2 5 5 4 2 3 1 6 2 2
Data set 2: 3 1 3 4 2 1 5 6 1 2 6 5 1 6 4 3 3 2 1 5

8. Make a histogram of honey yield per colony with intervals of 4.

Honey-Producing Colonies

Year	1999	2000	2001	2002	2003	2004
Yield per Colony (pounds)	76.3	83.9	74.0	67.8	70.0	71.8

Source: USDA

9. Write a Problem You are given the heights of the players on a soccer team. Determine the number of four different-size jerseys to order. Write a problem using a histogram that would help you find this information.

10. Write About It Which kind of graph would you use to compare the average salaries of professional basketball players and professional hockey players from 1995 to 2005?

11. Challenge Determine the size of the interval used in the histogram using the data below.

Time needed to heat a frozen dinner in the microwave (min)

4:30	5:30	7:00	4:45	5:20	8:00
3:45	2:30	6:40	6:00	4:30	5:25

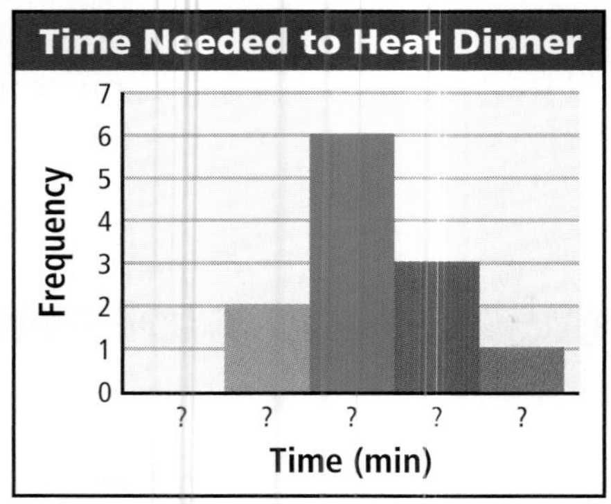

Test Prep and Spiral Review

12. Multiple Choice Which data display is most appropriate to show the change in sales over a four-month period?

Ⓐ Bar graph Ⓑ Frequency table Ⓒ Line graph Ⓓ Stem-and-leaf plot

13. Short Response A middle school principal asked 12 students the number of football games each attended during the school year. The results were 1, 3, 5, 2, 4, 4, 4, 3, 5, 2, 4, 2. Organize the data into a frequency table.

Find the sum of the angle measures in each polygon. (Lesson 7-4)

14. 18-gon **15.** 24-gon **16.** heptagon

Find the range of each set of data. (Lesson 9-4)

17. 16, 32, 1, 54, 30, 28 **18.** 105, 969, 350, 87, 410 **19.** 0.2, 0.8, 0.65, 0.7, 1.6, 1.1

Technology LAB 9-5

Create Histograms

Use with Lesson 9-5

go.hrw.com
Lab Resources Online
KEYWORD: MT7 Lab9

You can use a graphing calculator to make a histogram.

Activity

The frequency table shows the length of the feet of students in Mrs. Alvarez's math class. Use a graphing calculator to make a histogram of the data.

Foot Length (in.)	Number of Students
Less than 5	0
5 to less than 6	1
6 to less than 7	4
7 to less than 8	11
8 to less than 9	7
9 to less than 10	4
10 or greater	1

To enter the data, press STAT .

Then press ENTER to select 1:Edit.

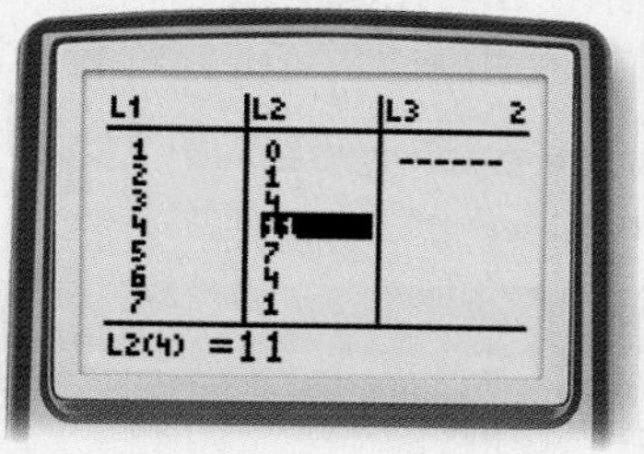

Under L1, enter 1, 2, 3, 4, 5, 6, and 7 to represent the seven intervals. Interval 1 corresponds to "Less than 5," while interval 7 corresponds to "10 or greater."

In L2, enter the number of students for each interval.

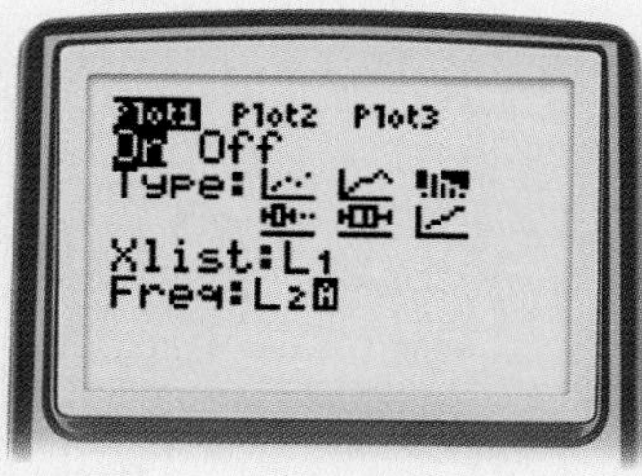

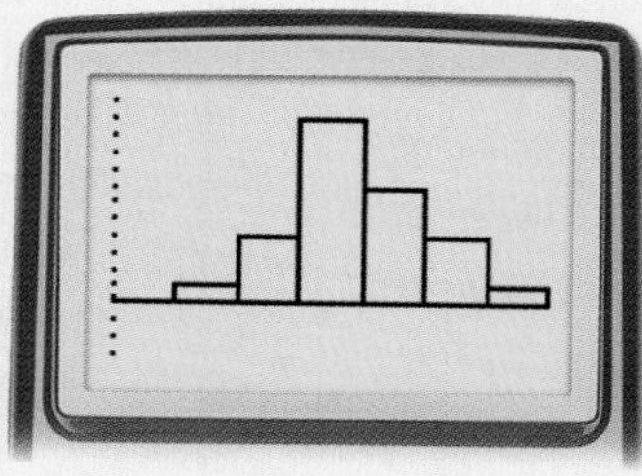

To see a histogram of the data, press 2nd Y= ENTER to select "STAT PLOTS 1:"

Scroll and press ENTER to select "On" and the histogram icon.

Then scroll to "Freq:" and press 2nd 2 to paste the data from L2.

Press ZOOM 9 to view the histogram. Press TRACE and the arrow keys to read the histogram.

Think and Discuss

1. How would the histogram change if the first interval is left out? Draw the histogram.

2. Explain how you can use the histogram to find the total number of students who have feet that are at least 7 inches long.

Try This

1. Measure the lengths of the right arms of everyone in your classroom. Divide the data into 5 equal intervals. Use a graphing calculator to make a histogram of the data.

9-6 Misleading Graphs and Statistics

Learn to recognize misleading graphs and statistics.

Graphs and statistics are often used to make advertisements visually appealing. Some advertisements, however, use art to mislead consumers.

EXAMPLE 1 Identifying Misleading Graphs

Explain why each graph is misleading.

A

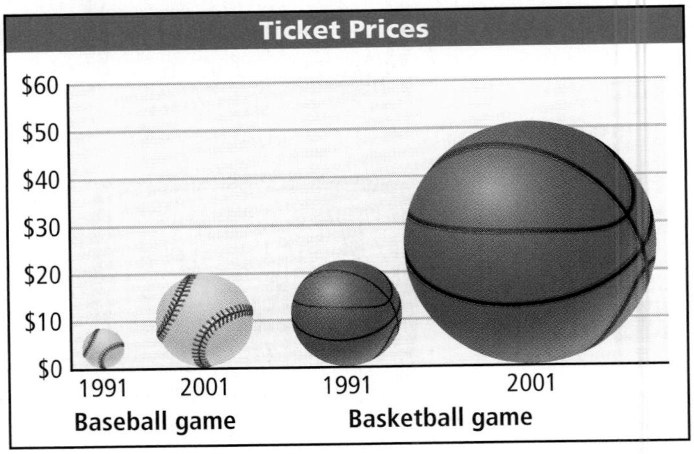

The heights of the balls are used to represent the ticket prices. However, the areas of the circles and volumes of the balls distort the comparison. The basketball prices are only about $2\frac{1}{2}$ times greater than the baseball prices, but they look like much more.

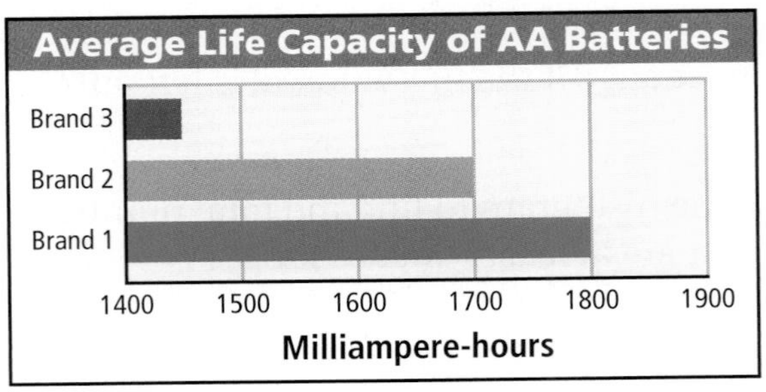

B Since the horizontal scale does not start at 0, the bar for Brand 1 appears to be four times as long as the bar for Brand 3. In fact, the capacity of Brand 1 is only 20% more than Brand 3.

Explain why the graph is misleading.

C

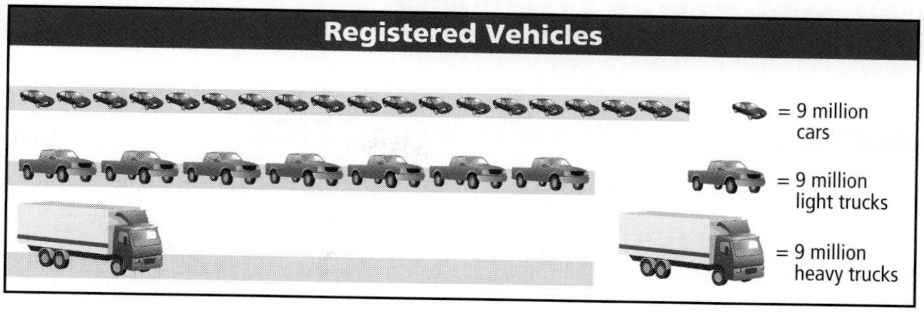

Different-sized icons represent the same number of vehicles. The number of light trucks looks like it is close to the number of cars, but it is really less than half. The number of heavy trucks is less than 5% of the total, but it appears much greater.

EXAMPLE 2 Identifying Misleading Statistics

Explain why each statistic is misleading.

A **A housing development features 5 home models with the starting prices of \$475,000, \$500,000, \$225,000, \$480,000, and \$510,000. The developer places an ad that reads:**

"New homes—average price \$438,000"

Although \$438,000 is the average price, only one model sells below that price. It is likely that a new home owner will pay more than the advertised price of \$438,000.

B **A movie previews for 12 selected viewers. Eight viewers rate the movie highly. The producer tells the production studio:**

"The movie will be a hit because test audiences rate the movie favorably at a rate of 2 to 1."

The sample size is too small. Twice as many people liked the movie, but the difference between 4 and 8 people is not meaningful.

C **The revenue for Ski Resort A for November and December was \$6,600,000. The revenue for Ski Resort B for January and February was \$8,300,000.**

The revenues are measured at different times of the year. Weather conditions can change dramatically from month to month, affecting revenue.

Think and Discuss

1. **Give an example** of a graph that starts at zero but is still misleading.
2. **Explain** how a statistic can be accurate but still misleading.

9-6 Exercises

go.hrw.com
Homework Help Online
KEYWORD: MT7 9-6
Parent Resources Online
KEYWORD: MT7 Parent

GUIDED PRACTICE

See Example 1 **Explain why each graph is misleading.**

1.

2.
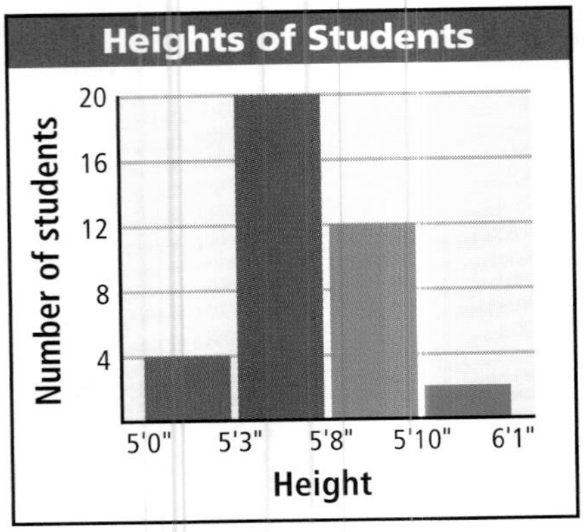

See Example 2 **Explain why each statistic is misleading.**

3. A stalk of broccoli has 477 mg of potassium. A large carrot has 230 mg of potassium. A small head of cauliflower has 803 mg of potassium.

4. The total number of life jackets sold by Water Sports World from April 1 to September 1 was 619. The total number of life jackets sold by Boats and More from July 1 to September 1 was 153.

INDEPENDENT PRACTICE

See Example 1 **Explain why each graph is misleading.**

5.
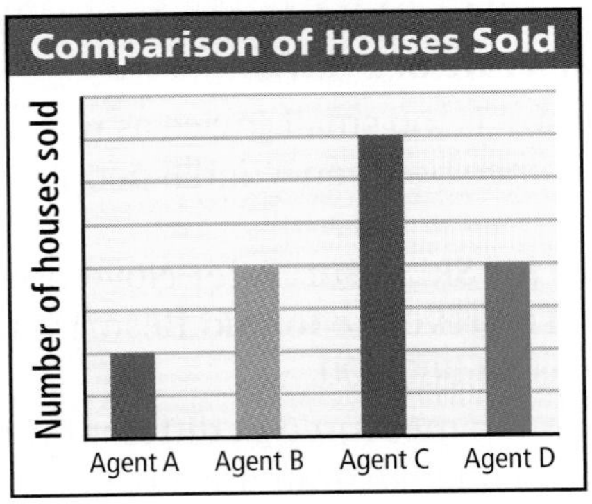

6.
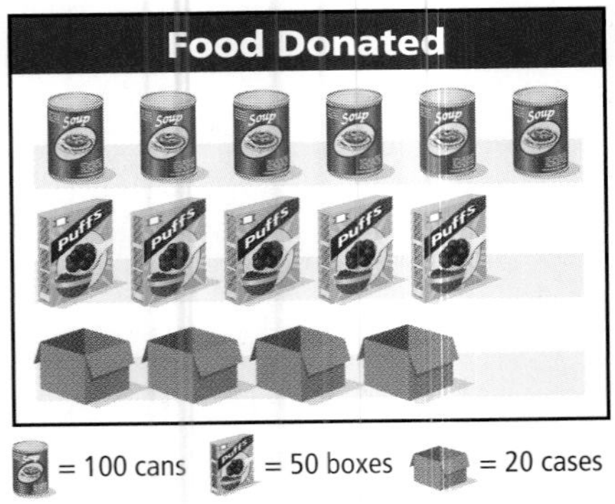

See Example 2 **Explain why each statistic is misleading.**

7. A survey of 1000 college students found that 110 majored in engineering and 112 majored in the social sciences. A magazine article reports that students prefer the social sciences over engineering.

8. A reporter asked 90 students if they participate in organized athletics. Of the 50 who responded "yes," 26 played on school teams, 14 played in community leagues, and 10 competed in individual competitions. The reporter said, "Half of all students play on school teams."

PRACTICE AND PROBLEM SOLVING

Extra Practice
See page 799.

Explain why each graph is misleading.

9.

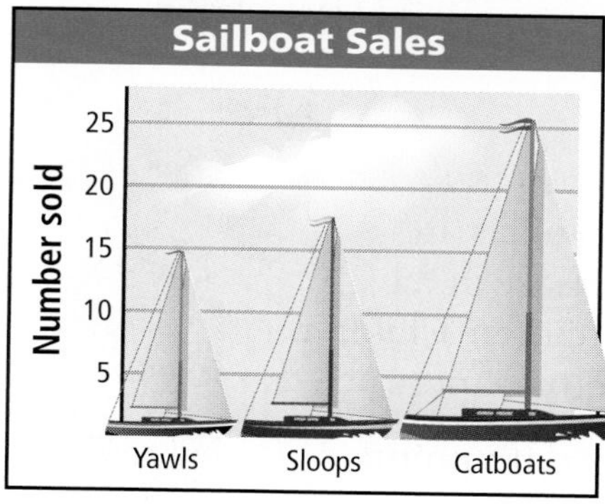

10.

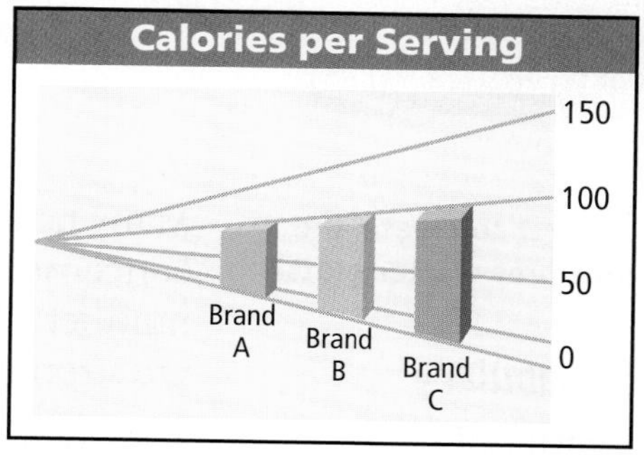

11. Write About It When might you want to use a scale on a graph that does not start at 0?

12. Challenge The two graphs show the recent performance of two companies' stocks, A and B. Which graph should be shown to the stockholders of company A?

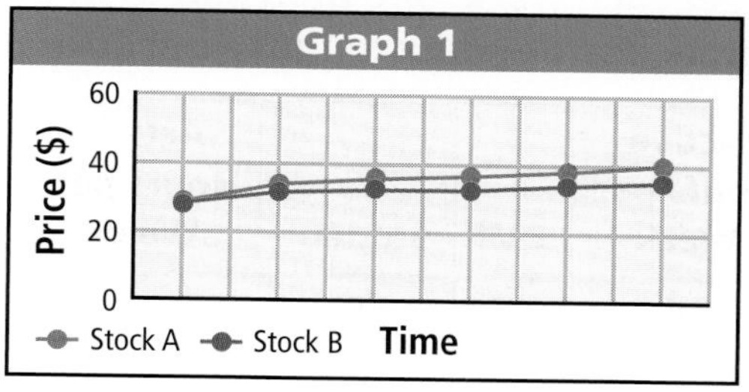

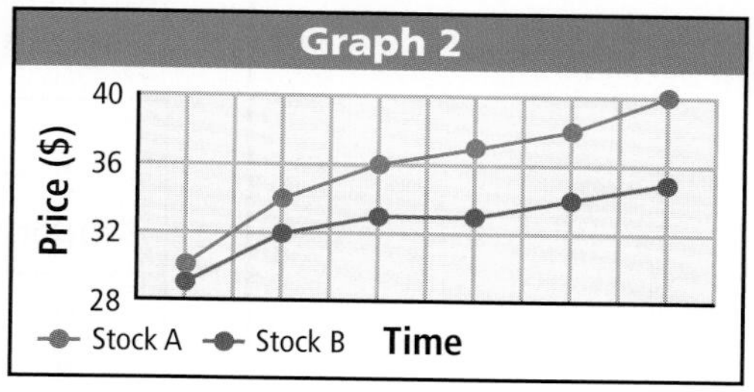

TEST PREP and Spiral Review

13. Multiple Choice Six dentists are surveyed regarding toothpaste. Four dentists recommended Brand X. An ad for Brand X states: "Recommended by 2 out of 3 dentists." Explain why the statement is misleading.

Ⓐ The sample was too large.

Ⓑ The sample was too small.

Ⓒ The sample should have included construction workers.

Ⓓ The statement should say "Recommended by 1 out of 2 dentists."

14. Short Response A salesman earns the following commissions: December $965; January $125; February $170; March $100; April $110; May $120. He tells his friends that he averages $265 per month in commission. Explain why the statistic is misleading.

Find the area of each figure with the given dimensions. (Lesson 8-2)

15. trapezoid: $b_1 = 3$, $b_2 = 5$, $h = 8$

16. triangle: $b = 16$, $h = 9$

17. People responding to a survey had the following ages: 30, 21, 20, 26, 23, 30, 23, 23, 21, 20, 27, 20, 24, 23, and 30. Use the data to make a line plot. (Lesson 9-2)

9-7 Scatter Plots

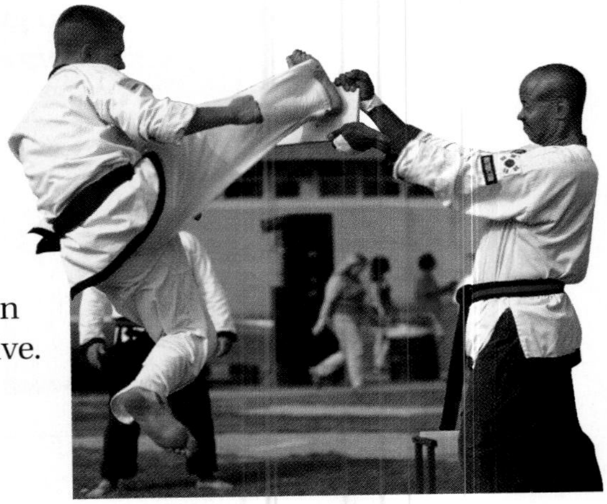

Learn to create and interpret scatter plots.

Vocabulary
scatter plot
correlation
line of best fit

Many health care professionals are concerned about the increase in the number of overweight children. Children are strongly encouraged to be more active.

A **scatter plot** is a graph with points plotted to show a relationship between two sets of data.

EXAMPLE 1 Making a Scatter Plot of a Data Set

A teacher surveyed her students about the amount of physical activity they get each week. She then had their body mass index (BMI) measured. Use her data to make a scatter plot.

Student	Active Hours per Week	BMI	Student	Active Hours per Week	BMI
A	10	16	F	8	18
B	3	25	G	7	21
C	6	24	H	2	28
D	8	20	I	19	9
E	10	16	J	14	12

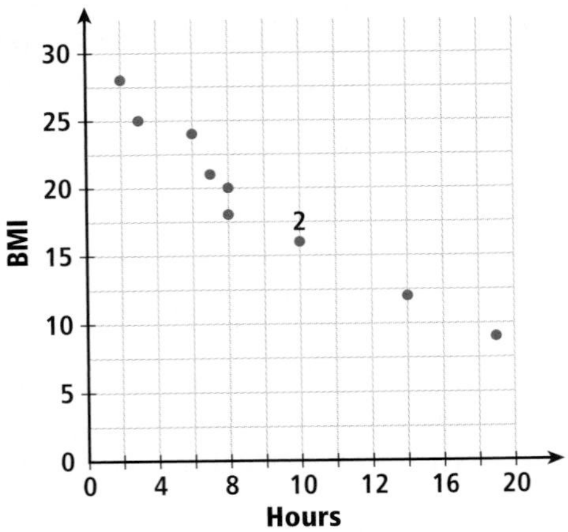

The points on the scatter plot are (10, 16), (3, 25), (6, 24), (8, 20), (10, 16), (8, 18), (7, 21), (2, 28), (19, 9), and (14, 12). The **2** *at (10, 16) indicates that the point occurs twice.*

Correlation describes the relationship between two data sets.
A **line of best fit** is a straight line that comes closest to the points on a scatter plot. One way to estimate a line of best fit is to lay a ruler's edge over the graph and adjust it until it looks closest to all the points.

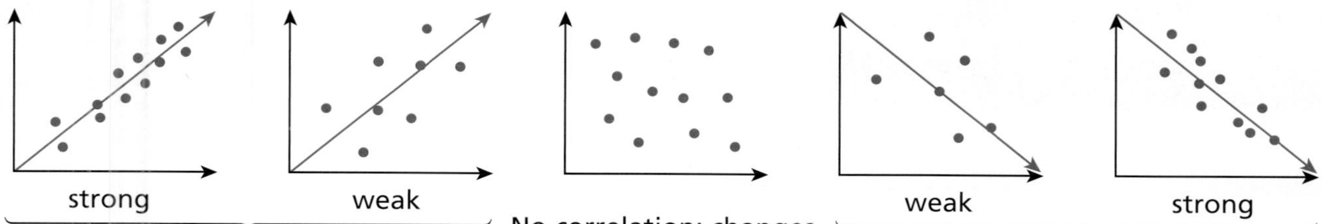

Positive correlation: both data sets increase together.

No correlation: changes in one data set do not affect the other data set.

Negative correlation: as one data set increases, the other decreases.

EXAMPLE 2 Identifying the Correlation of Data

Do the data sets have a positive, a negative, or no correlation?

Helpful Hint

A strong correlation does not mean there is a cause-and-effect relationship. For example, your age and the price of a regular movie ticket are both increasing, so they are positively correlated.

A The number of hours a plane is in flight and the number of miles flown

Positive correlation: The longer a plane is in flight, the more miles it flies.

B The number of hours in flight and the number of passengers

No correlation: The number of hours in flight does not affect the number of passengers on the plane.

C The number of hours in flight and the gallons of fuel remaining

Negative correlation: The longer a plane is in flight, the less fuel it has.

EXAMPLE 3 Using a Scatter Plot to Make Predictions

Use the data to predict the exam grade for a student who studies 10 hours per week.

Hours Studied	5	9	3	12	1
Exam Grade	80	95	75	98	70

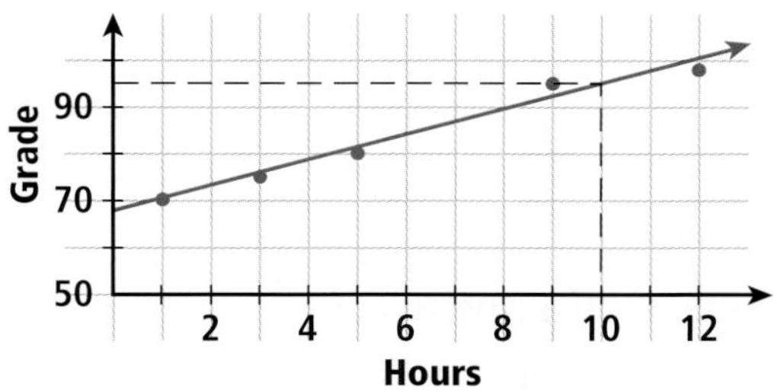

According to the graph, a student who studies 10 hours per week should earn a score of about 95.

Think and Discuss

1. Compare a scatter plot to a line graph.

2. Give an example of each type of correlation.

9-7 Exercises

go.hrw.com
Homework Help Online
KEYWORD: MT7 9-7
Parent Resources Online
KEYWORD: MT7 Parent

GUIDED PRACTICE

See Example 1

1. Use the given data to make a scatter plot.

Country	Area (mi^2)	Population
Guatemala	42,467	12,335,580
Honduras	43,715	5,997,327
El Salvador	8,206	5,839,079
Nicaragua	50,503	4,717,132
Costa Rica	19,929	3,674,490
Panama	30,498	2,778,526

See Example 2

Do the data sets have a positive, a negative, or no correlation?

2. The square footage of a house in a given neighborhood and its price
3. The age of a house and the number of people living in the house

See Example 3

4. Use the data to predict the wind chill at 35 mi/h.

Apparent Temperature Due to Wind at 15°F						
Wind speed (mi/h)	10	20	30	40	50	60
Wind Chill (°F)	2.7	−2.3	−5.5	−7.9	−9.8	−11.4

INDEPENDENT PRACTICE

See Example 1

5. Use the given data to make a scatter plot.

Car Brand	Cost ($1000)	Fuel Economy (mi/gal)
A	25	19
B	19	31
C	34	15
D	28	23
E	22	33

See Example 2

Do the data sets have a positive, a negative, or no correlation?

6. The number of weeks a CD has been out and weekly sales
7. The number of weeks a CD has been out and total sales

See Example 3

8. Use the data to predict the apparent temperature at 70% humidity.

Temperature Due to Humidity at a Room Temperature of 72°F						
Humidity (%)	0	20	40	60	80	100
Apparent Temperature (°F)	64	67	70	72	74	76

Life Science LINK

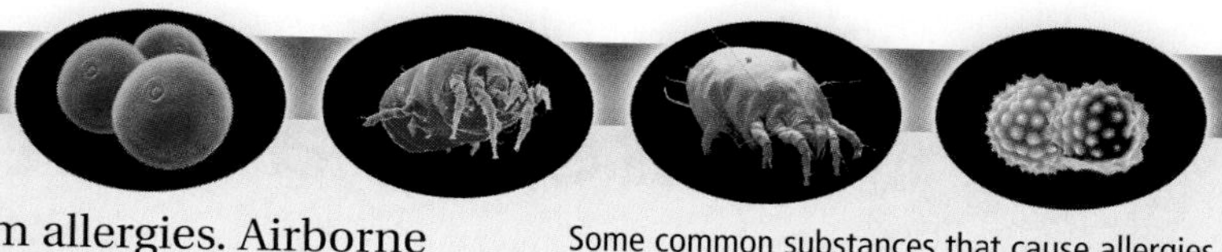

Some common substances that cause allergies include pollens, dust mites, and mold spores.

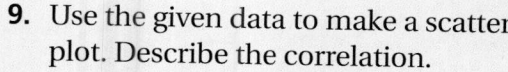

About 50 million Americans suffer from allergies. Airborne pollen generated by trees, grasses, plants, and weeds is a major cause of illness and disability. Because pollen grains are small and light, they can travel through the air for hundreds of miles. Pollen levels are measured in grains per cubic meter.

9. Use the given data to make a scatter plot. Describe the correlation.

Pollen Levels

Day	Weed Pollen	Grass Pollen
1	350	16
2	51	1
3	49	9
4	309	3
5	488	29
6	30	3
7	65	12

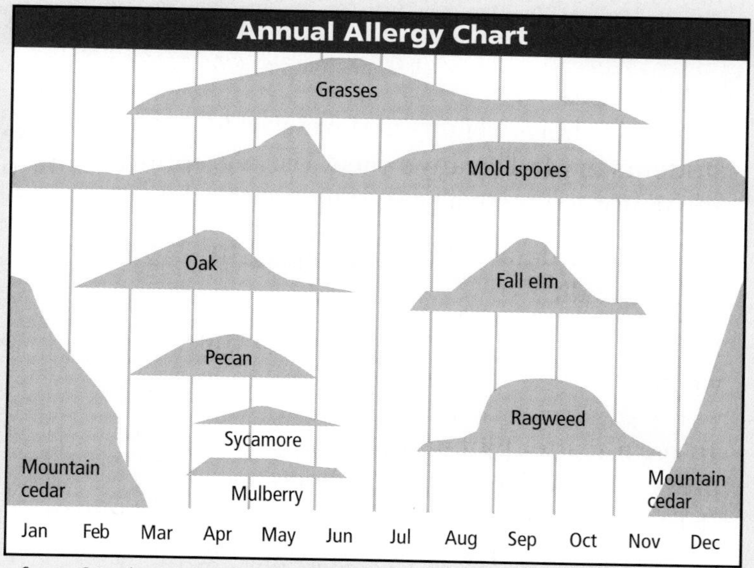

Source: Central Texas Allergy and Asthma Center

10. Explain how the pollens are compared in the chart at right.

Use the chart at right to determine if the pollens have a positive, a negative, or no correlation.

11. mountain cedar, grass

12. fall elm, ragweed

13. **Challenge** Use the allergy chart to explain the difference between correlation and a cause-and-effect relationship.

go.hrw.com
Web Extra!
KEYWORD: MT7 Pollen

Test Prep and Spiral Review

14. Multiple Choice Does the size of a box of cereal and the price of the cereal have a positive, negative, or no correlation?

Ⓐ Positive Ⓑ Negative Ⓒ Scatterplot Ⓓ No

15. Short Response What type of correlation exists between a person's birthday and his or her height? Explain.

Determine the number of lines of symmetry for each polygon. (Lesson 7-8)

16. square

17. equilateral triangle

18. regular pentagon

19. A bookstore sells 2 copies of *Sail Away* and 4 copies of *Race Car Mania*. The bookstore owner concludes that his customers are twice as likely to buy racing books than sailing books. Identify why this statistic is misleading. (Lesson 9-6)

Technology LAB 9-7

Create a Scatter Plot

Use with Lesson 9-7

go.hrw.com
Lab Resources Online
KEYWORD: MT7 Lab9

You can use a graphing calculator to make a scatter plot.

Activity 1

The table shows heights and weights of students in Mr. Devany's class. Use a graphing calculator to create a scatter plot of the data.

Height (in.)	Weight (lb)
41	92
43	111
46	105
50	120
51	110
55	107
60	125
62	125
62	125
66	152
69	175
70	210

To enter the data, press STAT ENTER to select "1:Edit"

In L1, enter the heights. In L2, enter the weights.

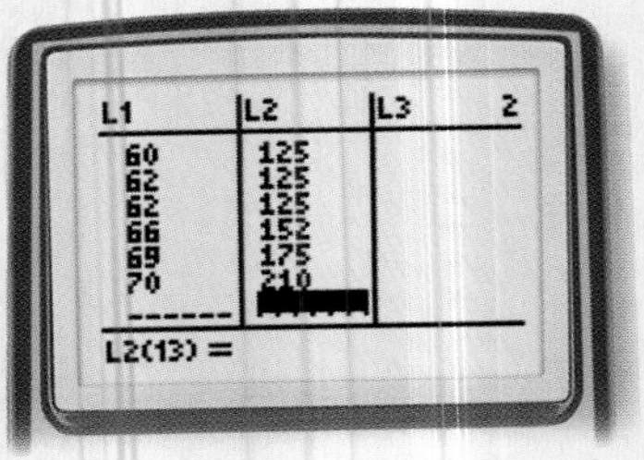

To see a scatter plot of the data, press 2nd Y= ENTER to select "STAT PLOTS 1:"

Scroll and press ENTER to select "On" and the scatter plot icon. Scroll to "Xlist=" and press 2nd 1.
Scroll to "Ylist=" and press 2nd 2. Finally, scroll to "Mark:" and choose the box.

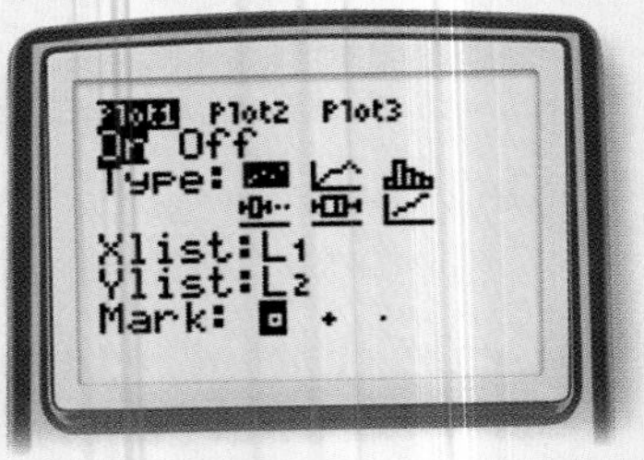

To view the scatter plot, press ZOOM 9.
Press TRACE and the arrow keys to read the histogram.

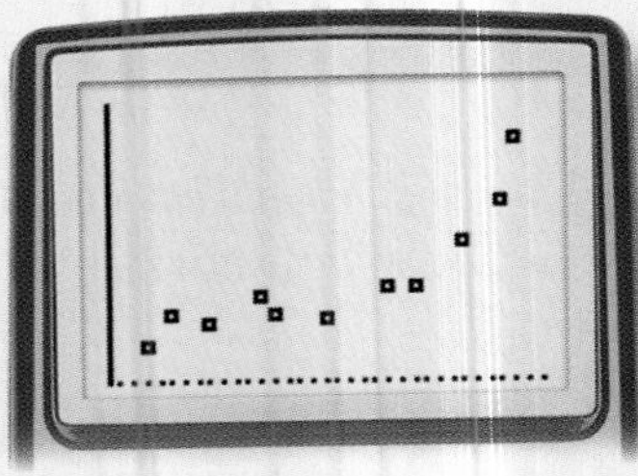

Think and Discuss

1. Explain what happens when you change the window to [0, 100] by [0, 500].
2. Suppose you added a third category: boy or girl. How could the height, weight, and gender data be displayed?

Try This

Use a graphing calculator to create a scatter plot of the data.

1.

x	41	43	46	50	51	55	60	62	66	69	70
y	92	111	105	120	110	107	125	142	152	175	210

Activity 2

You can use a graphing calculator to find a line of best fit on a scatter plot.

Create a scatter plot of the data shown. Use a line of best fit to predict the value of y when $x = 11$.

Follow the steps in Activity 1 to make a scatter plot of the data.

x	y
2	26.1
4	21.5
6	17.4
8	13.2
10	11.7
12	8.5
14	4.2
16	1.9

To find a line of best fit, press STAT ▶ 4 to choose "LinReg(ax+b)."

Press 2nd 1 , 2nd 2 , VARS ENTER ENTER ENTER.

Your calculator will display the y-intercept and slope of the line of best fit.

Press ZOOM 9 to see the scatter plot and the line of best fit.

You can press Y= to see an equation of the line.

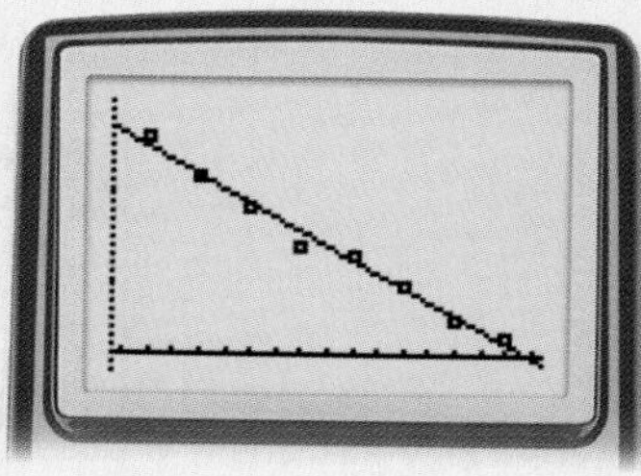

To find y when $x = 11$, press 2nd TRACE ENTER 11 ENTER. The screen shows that $y = 9.68$ when $x = 11$.

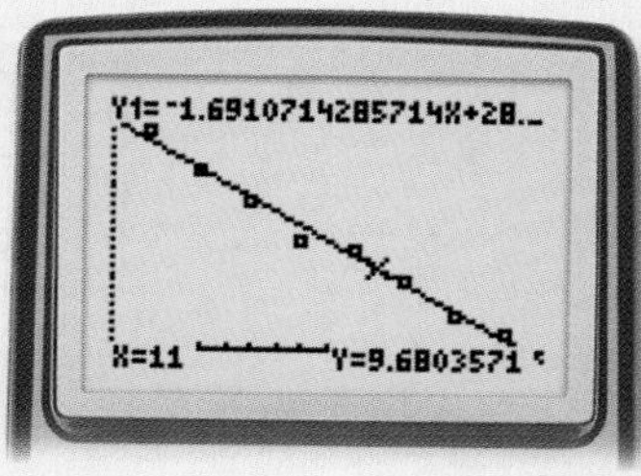

Think and Discuss

1. What uses might a line of best fit have in the real world?
2. What type of correlation does the data have in Activity 2? How do you know?

Try This

Collect at least 6 pieces of string with different lengths. Measure the length of each piece of string and record the values in L1. Form a square with each piece of string. Measure the length of one side of each square and record the values in L2. Make a scatter plot of the data and find the line of best fit.

1. What should the slope be? (*Hint*: What is the relationship between the perimeter of a square and the length of one side?)
2. What is the slope of the line of best fit you found on your calculator?
3. Explain why the slope of your line might not match the slope you predicted.

9-8 Choosing the Best Representation of Data

Learn **to select the best representation for a set of data.**

In a survey, students were asked, "About how many hours a year do you volunteer?" The responses are shown in the table.

Hours Spent Volunteering	
Fewer than 20	15%
20–39	35%
40–59	13%
60–79	7%
80 or more	30%

Data can be represented in several different ways, depending both on the type of data and the message to be conveyed.

Type of Graph	Common Use
Line graph	Shows change in data over time.
Bar graph	Shows relationships or comparisons between groups.
Circle graph	Compares parts to a whole.
Histogram	Shows the frequency of data divided into equal groups.
Box-and-whisker plot	Shows the distribution and spread of data.
Line plot	Shows the distribution of data.
Scatter plot	Shows the relationship of two data sets.

EXAMPLE 1 Selecting a Data Display

A **Which graph is a better display of the data on students volunteering?**

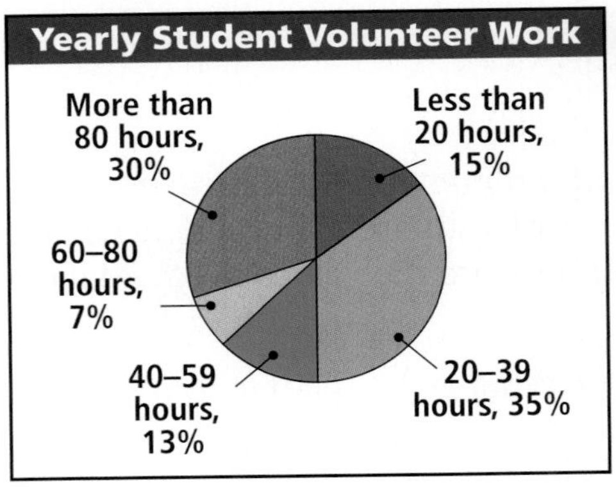

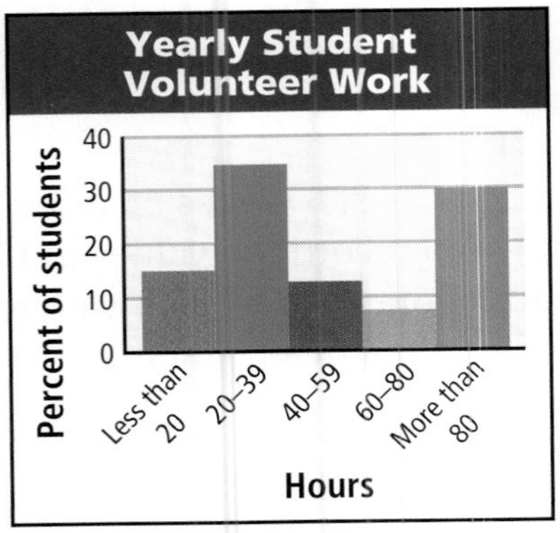

The data shows how groups of people who responded to the survey compare to the whole. The circle graph is the better representation.

B **Which graph shows the distribution of test scores better?**

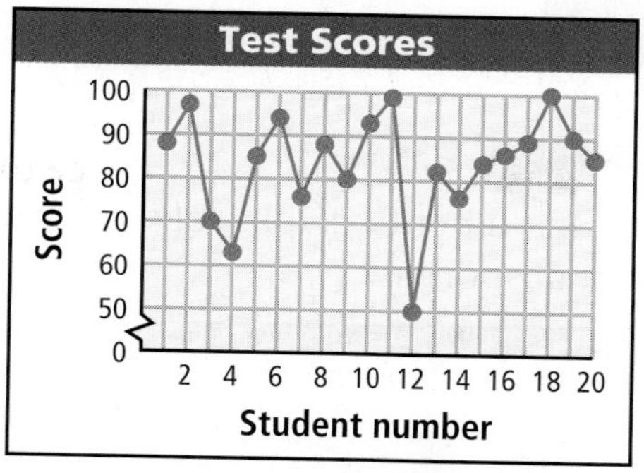

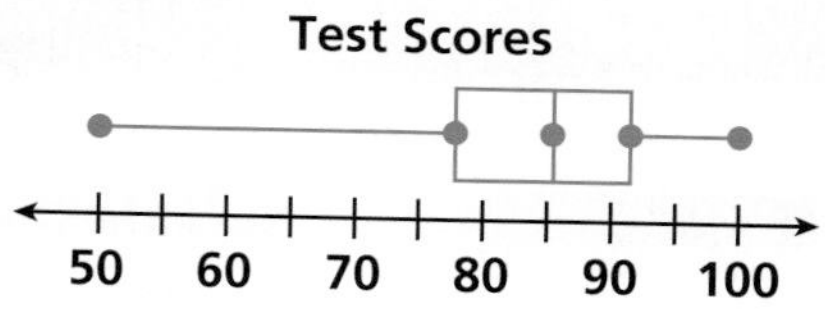

Since the question asks about the distribution of the data, the box-and-whisker plot is the better representation.

EXAMPLE **2** **PROBLEM SOLVING APPLICATION**

PROBLEM SOLVING

José spent a week camping and hiking. The data of each hike is recorded in the table. Choose an appropriate data display. Draw the graph. About how long would it have taken José to hike 12 km?

Time (h)	1	1.5	2	3	4.5	6	7
Distance (km)	3.2	4.8	8	10.5	11.2	13.7	15.6

1 Understand the Problem

You are looking for the best data display and the estimated time for a 12 km hike.

2 Make a Plan

You need to find the relationship between time and distance. Since the data can be written as ordered pairs, plot them in a scatter plot.

3 Solve

Plot the data points on the scatter plot. To estimate the time needed for a 12 km hike, draw the line of best fit. Then find t when $d = 12$. The line of best fit indicates that a 12 km hike would take about 5 hours.

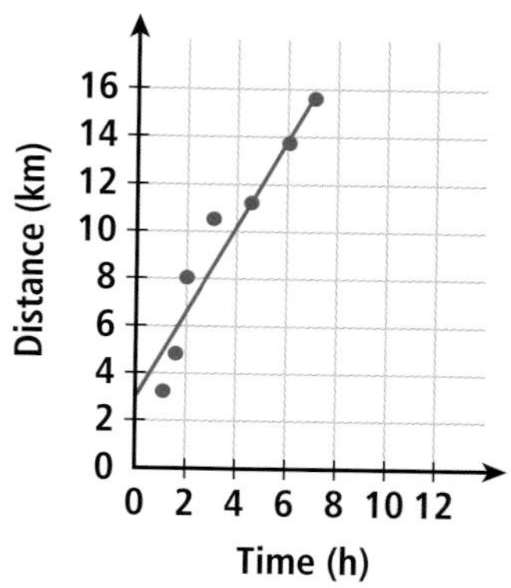

4 Look Back

Look at the table. An 11.2 km hike took 5.5 h and a 13.7 km hike took 6 h, so 5 h for a 12 km hike is reasonable.

Think and Discuss

1. Describe the kind of data that is best represented by a bar graph.

2. Give a situation in which you would use a line graph to display data.

9-8 Exercises

go.hrw.com
Homework Help Online
KEYWORD: MT7 9-8
Parent Resources Online
KEYWORD: MT7 Parent

GUIDED PRACTICE

See Example 1

1. Which graph is a better display of the numbers of students participating in high school sports?

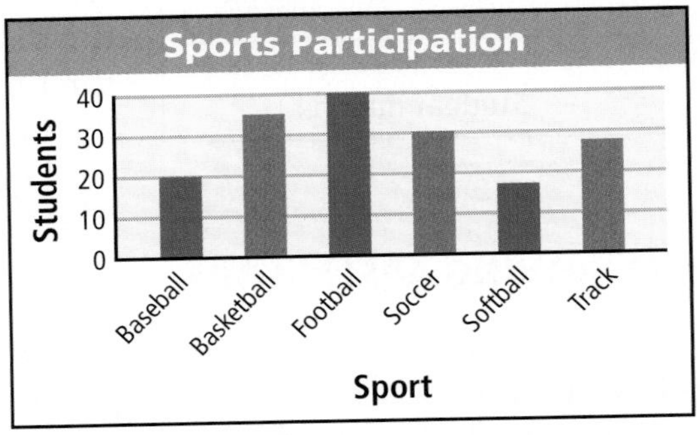

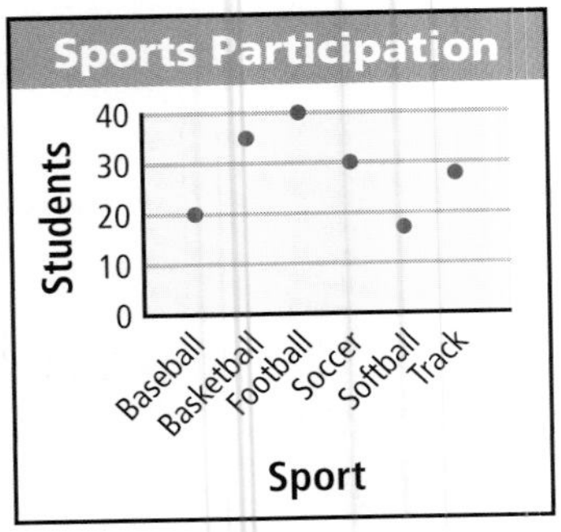

See Example 2

2. The highest elevations for several states are listed in the table. Choose an appropriate data display and draw the graph. Which of the states shown in the graph has the third highest elevation?

State	Highest Elevation
Alaska	6194 m
California	4421 m
Colorado	4399 m
Washington	4392 m

INDEPENDENT PRACTICE

See Example 1

3. Which graph is a better display of the percent of times a coin comes up heads and tails in 80 tosses?

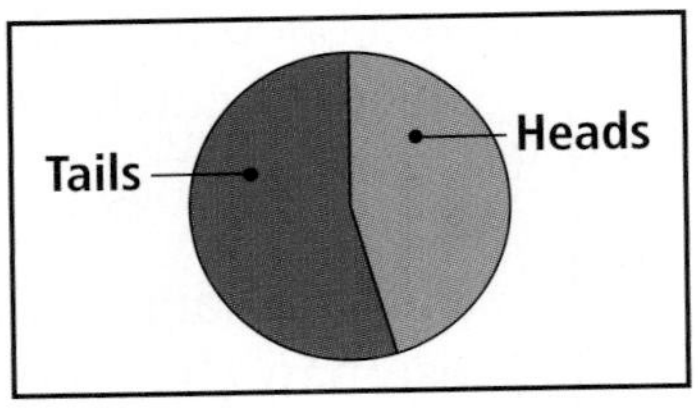

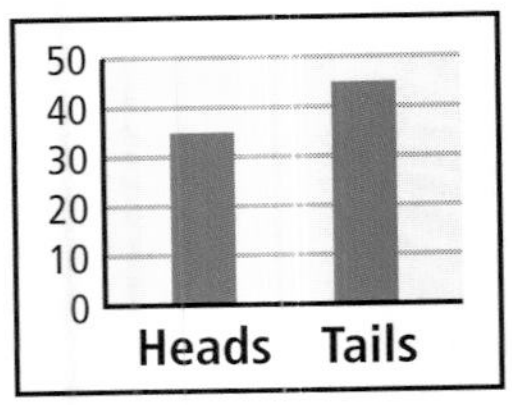

See Example 2

4. Ann spent the day shopping and running errands. The table shows her distance from home at various times during the day. Choose an appropriate data display and draw the graph. Approximately how far was Ann from home at 11:00 AM?

Time	Distance (mi)
8:00 AM	0
10:00 AM	5
12:00 noon	12
2:00 PM	8
4:00 PM	3

PRACTICE AND PROBLEM SOLVING

Extra Practice
See page 799.

Choose the best data display for each situation. Explain.

5. height of a child over time

6. class sizes at a middle school

7. amount of time spent on different tasks during a day

8. comparison of people's shoe sizes to their ages

LINK

Sports

In 2003, 7000 athletes from 150 countries competed in the Special Olympics World Summer Games.

9. Fitness A survey of exercise habits was conducted. The ages of respondents and the number of minutes they reported exercising weekly are shown. Choose and construct a better display for the data.

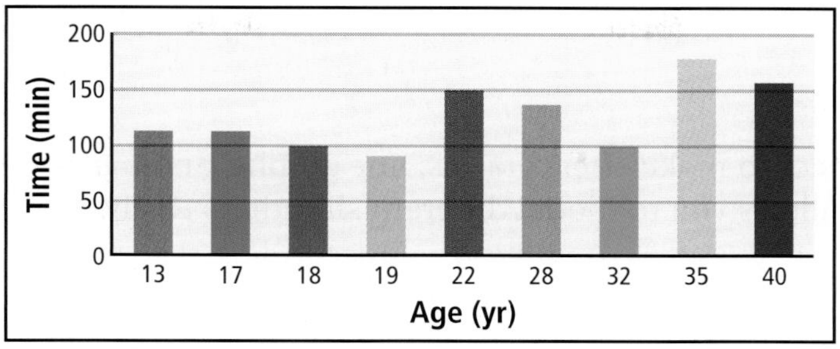

Age	Time (min)
13	120
17	120
18	100
19	90
22	150
28	135
32	100
35	180
40	160

10. Sports What kind of graph would best show the increase in the number of participants in the Special Olympics World Summer Games since it was founded in 1968?

11. Write a Problem Write a survey question for which a circle graph would best represent the data. Then collect the data and make the circle graph.

12. Write About It Explain how you would decide if a line graph or a scatter plot were a better representation of data.

13. Challenge An appliance store sells four brands of televisions. The table shows how many of each brand were sold last month. Which two kinds of graphs could be used to display this data? What message would each kind of graph give about the data?

Brand	Number Sold
A	120
B	130
C	100
D	95

Test Prep and Spiral Review

14. Multiple Choice What type of display would you least likely construct from data of test scores for a class?

Ⓐ circle graph　Ⓑ line graph　Ⓒ histogram　Ⓓ bar graph

15. Short Answer Find the mean, median, mode, and range of the data in the stem-and-leaf plot. If any of the measures cannot be found, give the reason.

0	1 4 9
1	3 3 4 7
2	1 2 2 2 3 3

Find the area of each circle. Round to the nearest tenth, if necessary. Use 3.14 for π. (Lesson 8-3)

16. circle with diameter 10 cm

17. circle with radius 5.2 yd

18. A 9 cm cube is built from 1 cm cubes. Compare the ratio of the length of an edge of the large cube to the length of an edge of a small cube. (Lesson 8-10)

Technology LAB 9-8

Use with Lesson 9-8

Use a Spreadsheet to Create Graphs

go.hrw.com
Lab Resources Online
KEYWORD: MT7 Lab9

You can use a spreadsheet to make circle graphs, line graphs, and bar graphs. A spreadsheet allows you to model different situations easily.

Activity

1. Suppose a farmer has 22 pigs, 2 milk cows, 4 goats, 3 sheep, and 6 chickens. You can use a spreadsheet to make a circle graph of the data.

	A	B	C	D	E	F	G
1							
2		pig	cow	goat	sheep	chicken	
3		22	2	4	3	6	
4							

In row 2, enter the type of animal.

In row 3, enter the number of each type of animal.

Select the data by clicking in cell B2 and dragging over to cell F3.

Chart Wizard icon

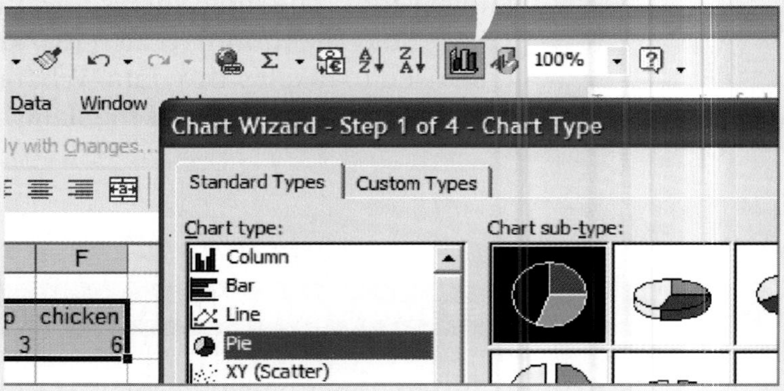

Click the Chart Wizard icon in the top toolbar.

Click "Pie" under Chart Type in the Chart Wizard window. (*Pie chart* is another name for a circle graph.)

Click the top left circle graph under the Chart Sub-Type.

Click "Next" until the Finish button appears. Click "Finish."

Now change the number of pigs to 12 and the number of goats to 11. Notice how the circle graph changes to reflect the new data.

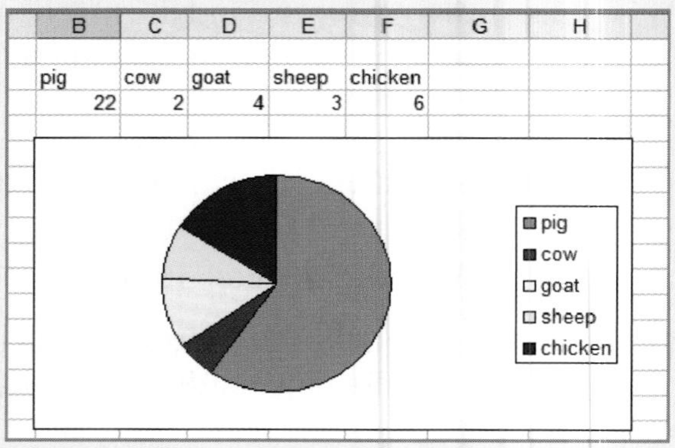

2. Use the spreadsheet to draw a line graph of the data.

Right click on the graph and select "Chart Type . . ."

Click "Line" and make sure that the top left graph is selected.

Click "OK."

Now change the number of animals. Notice how the line graph changes to reflect the new data.

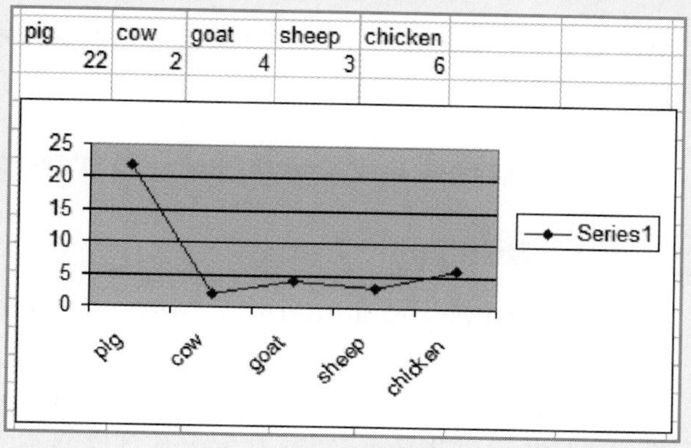

3. Use the spreadsheet to make a bar graph of the data.

Right click on the graph and select "Chart Type . . ."

Click "Column" and make sure that the top left graph is selected.

Click "OK."

Now change the number of animals. Notice how the line graph changes to reflect the new data.

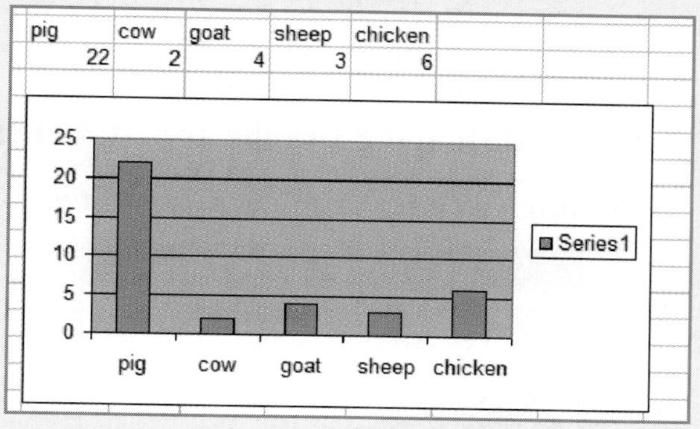

Think and Discuss

1. Compare the three types of graphs. When might you prefer using one type over the others? Which is the best representation of the animal data? Explain.

2. Explain the value of spreadsheets for modeling different situations.

3. Describe a situation when you would want to use a spreadsheet to make a circle graph.

Try This

1. Take a walk in your neighborhood and record the color of the first 30 cars you see. Use a spreadsheet to make a circle graph, a line graph, and a bar graph of your data. Which represents the data best? Explain.

2. Now record the color of the next 30 cars you see. Modify your data from Try This 1. How did each graph change?

CHAPTER 9

READY TO GO ON?

SECTION 9B

Quiz for Lessons 9-5 Through 9-8

9-5 Displaying Data

1. Organize the data into a frequency table and make a double-bar graph.

   Data set 1: 3, 5, 4, 2, 5, 2, 3, 3, 6, 5, 3, 3, 4, 2, 1
   Data set 2: 2, 5, 4, 3, 2, 5, 4, 6, 3, 4, 3, 2, 2, 4, 5

Value	1	2	3	4	5	6
Data Set 1	1	3	5	2	3	1
Data Set 2	0	4	3	4	3	1

2. A fitness group calculated the average number of minutes they exercised each day. Use the data to make a histogram with intervals of 10.

   29 31 42 42 50 44 33 36 37 41 38 45 37 45
   37 41 39 41 34 39 35 35 30 36 32 41 39 37

9-6 Misleading Graphs and Statistics

Explain why each graph is misleading.

3. 

4. 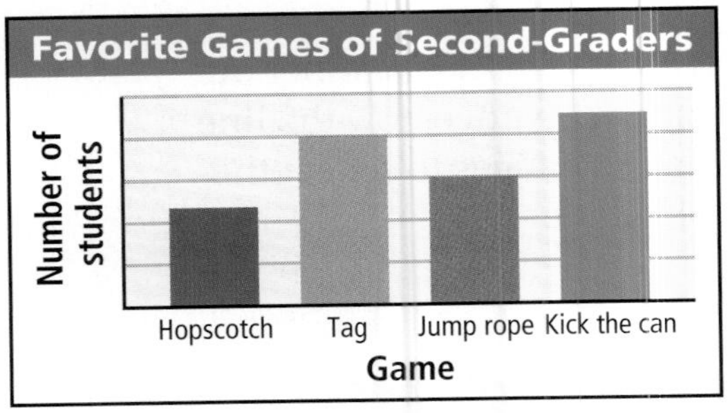

5. A survey found 39% of students like tacos best, 32% like pizza best, and 29% like hamburgers best. The survey concludes that most students at the middle school like tacos the best. Explain why the statistic is misleading.

9-7 Scatter Plots

6. Use the given data of the estimated U.S. population to make a scatter plot.

Year	1998	1999	2000	2001	2002	2003	2004
Population (in millions)	270.2	272.7	282.2	285.1	287.9	290.8	293.7

Does the data set have a positive, a negative, or no correlation?

7. The number of miles on a used car and the price of the used car

9-8 Choosing the Best Representation of Data

8. The eighth-grade chorus had 10 altos, 16 sopranos, 4 bass vocalists, and 10 tenors. Choose an appropriate data display and draw the graph. What percent of the chorus were the altos and tenors?

MULTI-STEP TEST PREP

CHAPTER 9

Bowled Over A group of middle school students forms a bowling club. The table shows the number of years each student has been bowling and the scores from the group's first trip to the bowling alley.

1. The club's president prepares a newsletter describing the "typical" student in the club. Choose a measure of central tendency to describe the typical number of years that the club members have been bowling. Choose a measure of central tendency to describe their typical score. Justify your choices.
2. Make a stem-and-leaf plot of the scores. What can you say about the scores based on the stem-and-leaf plot?
3. Brian is making a graph showing his score and those of his friends Jessica and Kendall. He wants to make it seem like his score was much greater than those of his friends. Show how he can make a misleading graph.
4. Make a scatter plot of the data.
5. A new student joins the club. She has been bowling for 5 years. Use your scatter plot to predict her score the next time the group goes bowling.

Student	Years Bowling	Score
Jessica	3	90
Brian	3	100
Chandra	2	81
Roberto	7	128
Lee	1	84
Flora	3	92
Mike	4	102
Hisako	3	90
Isabel	6	135
Warren	1	65
Kendall	2	90
Mei	1	77

Game Time

Distribution of Primes

Remember that a prime number is only divisible by 1 and itself. There are infinitely many prime numbers, but there is no algebraic formula to find them. The largest known prime number, discovered on November 14, 2001, is $2^{13,466,917} - 1$. In standard form, this number would have 4,053,946 digits.

Sieve of Eratosthenes

One way to find prime numbers is called the sieve of Eratosthenes. Use a list of whole numbers in order. Cross off 1. The next number, 2, is prime. Circle it. Then cross off all multiples of 2, because they are not prime. Circle the next number on the list. Cross off all of its multiples. Repeat this step until all of the numbers are circled or crossed off. The circled numbers will all be primes.

~~1~~	(2)	3	~~4~~	5	~~6~~	7	~~8~~	9	~~10~~
11	~~12~~	13	~~14~~	15	~~16~~	17	~~18~~	19	~~20~~
21	~~22~~	23	~~24~~	25	~~26~~	27	~~28~~	29	~~30~~
31	~~32~~	33	~~34~~	35	~~36~~	37	~~38~~	39	~~40~~
41	~~42~~	43	~~44~~	45	~~46~~	47	~~48~~	49	~~50~~

1. Use the sieve of Eratosthenes to find all prime numbers less than 50.
2. Create a scatter plot of the first 15 prime numbers. Use the prime numbers as the x-coordinates and their positions in the sequence as the y-coordinates; 2 is the 1st prime, 3 is the 2nd prime, and so on.

Prime Number	2	3	5	7											
Position in Sequence	1	2	3	4	5	6	7	8	9	10	11	12	13	14	15

3. Estimate the line of best fit and use it to estimate the number of primes under 100. Use the sieve of Eratosthenes to check your estimate.

Math in the Middle

This game can be played by two or more players. On your turn, roll 5 number cubes. The number of spaces you move is your choice of the mean, rounded to the nearest whole number; the median; or the mode, if it exists. The winner is the first player to land on the *Finish* square by exact count.

A complete set of rules and a game board are available online.

go.hrw.com
Game Time Extra
KEYWORD: MT7 Games

FOLDNOTES

It's in the Bag!

Materials
- **5 paper plates**
- **scissors**
- **glue**
- **decorative paper**
- **markers**

PROJECT Data Pop-Ups

Here is a way to take notes on collecting, displaying, and analyzing data that is guaranteed to pop out!

1. Cut one paper plate in half. You will use the two halves later to make covers for your pop-up book.

2. Fold each of the remaining paper plates in half. Cut two 1-inch slits in the middle of the folded edge of each plate. The slits should be about 1 inch apart. **Figure A**

3. Bend the paper between the slits back and forth, and then push it inward as you unfold the plate. This will create a pop-up tab. **Figure B**

4. Fold the paper plates shut. Glue the bottom of one paper plate to the top of the next paper plate to form a book. Make covers by gluing one of the paper-plate halves onto the front of the book and the other onto the back of the book.

5. Cut out four small rectangles of decorative paper. After taking notes on these rectangles, you will glue them onto the pop-up tabs in your book. **Figure C**

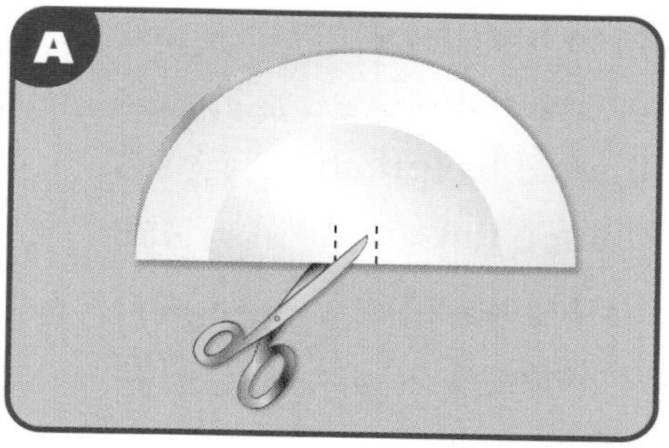
A

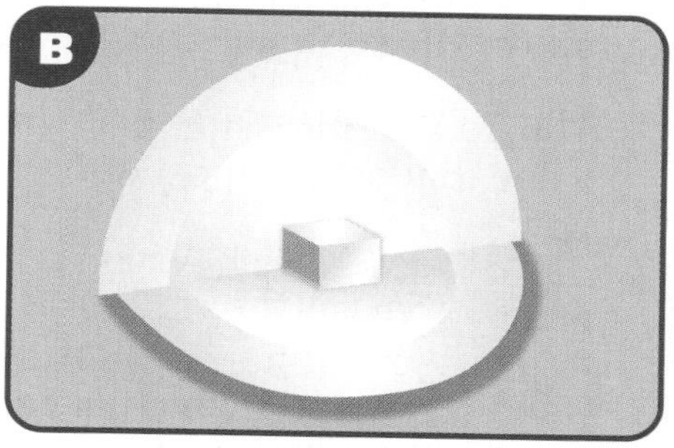
B

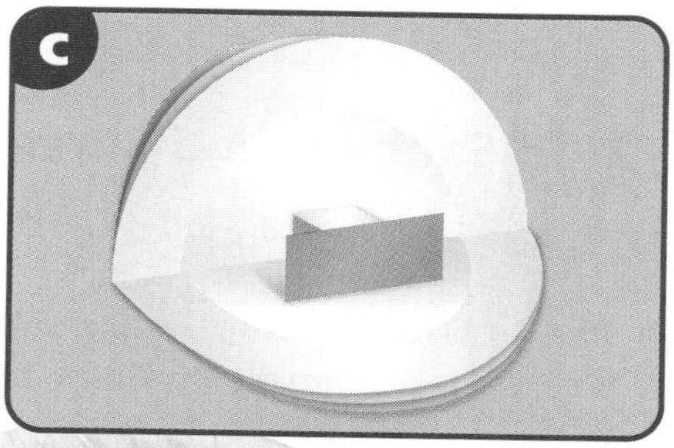
C

Taking Note of the Math

Use the rectangles of decorative paper to take notes on collecting, displaying, and analyzing data. Then glue the rectangles to the pop-up tabs inside the book. You can also take notes by writing directly on the paper plates.

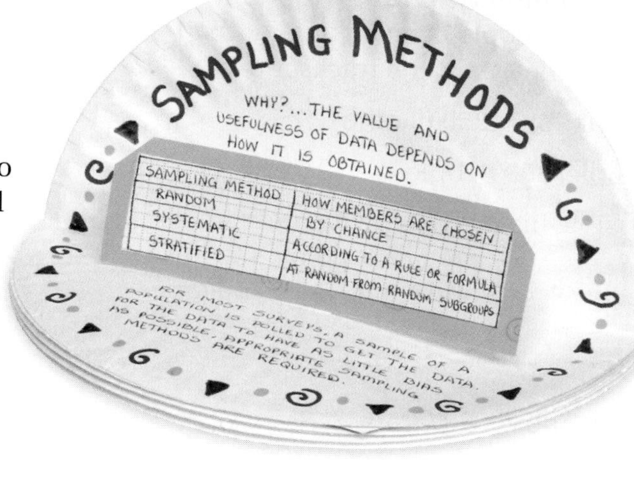

CHAPTER 9

Study Guide: Review

Vocabulary

back-to-back stem-and-leaf plot 467	line of best fit 494	sample 462
biased sample 463	line plot 467	scatter plot 494
box-and-whisker plot ..477	mean 472	stem-and-leaf plot 467
convenience sample ...462	median 472	stratified sample 462
correlation 494	mode 472	systematic sample 462
double-bar graph 485	outlier 472	variability 476
double-line graph 486	population 462	Venn diagram 468
frequency table 485	quartile 476	voluntary-response sample 462
histogram 485	random sample 462	
	range 472	

Complete the sentences below with vocabulary words from the list above.

1. The __?__ of a data set is the middle value, while the __?__ is the value that occurs most often.
2. __?__ describes how spread out a data set is. One measure of __?__ is the __?__.
3. The __?__ is the line that comes closest to all the points on a(n) __?__. __?__ describes the type of relationship between two data sets.

9-1 Samples and Surveys (pp. 462–465)

EXAMPLE

■ **Identify the population and sample. Give a reason the sample could be biased.**

In a community of 1250 people, a pollster asks 250 people living near a railroad track if they want the tracks moved.

Population: 1250 people

Sample: 250 people

Possible bias: People living near tracks are annoyed by the noise and want tracks moved.

EXERCISES

Identify the population and sample. Give a reason the sample could be biased.

4. Out of the 125 people in line for a *Star Wars* movie, 25 are asked to name their favorite type of movie.
5. A pollster surveyed 100 people who owned cell phones about whether they felt it was safe to use cell phones while driving.
6. Fifty parents of children attending local preschools are asked if the community should build a new playground.

9-2 Organizing Data (pp. 467–471)

EXAMPLE

■ **Use a line plot to organize the data.**

7	10	6	9	7	4	8	9
3	8	2	10	5	9	7	

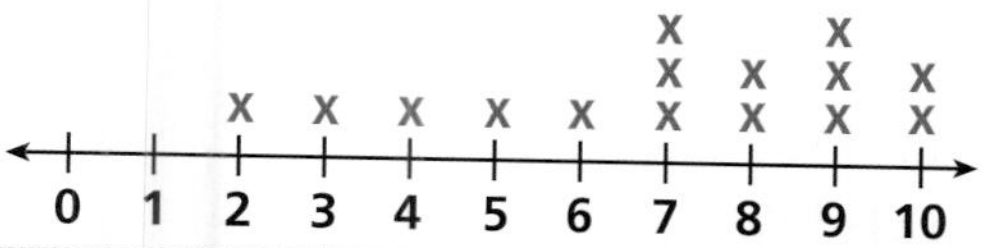

EXERCISE

Use a line plot to organize the data.

7.

Ages of People at a Skate Park					
12	13	13	14	12	11
14	15	13	13	12	13

9-3 Measures of Central Tendency (pp. 472–475)

EXAMPLE

■ **The numbers of people to swim in a public pool each day one week were 50, 65, 72, 3, 85, 105, and 120. Explain which measure of central tendency best describes the middle of these numbers and find it.**

Because there is an outlier, the median is the best measure of central tendency.
5, 50, 65, (72), 85, 105, 120

EXERCISE

Explain which measure of central tendency is the most appropriate for the situation and find it.

8. The prices of the cars sold in one month were $17,500; $15,300; $16,800; $65,900; $12,800; $16,300. What number best describes the middle of these numbers?

9-4 Variability (pp. 476–480)

EXAMPLE

■ **Use the given data to make a box-and-whisker plot.**

7, 10, 14, 16, 17, 17, 18, 20, 20

7 (10 14) 16 | 17 | 17 (18 20) 20

smallest value: 7

first quartile: $\frac{10 + 14}{2} = 12$

median: 17

third quartile: $\frac{18 + 20}{2} = 19$

largest value: 20

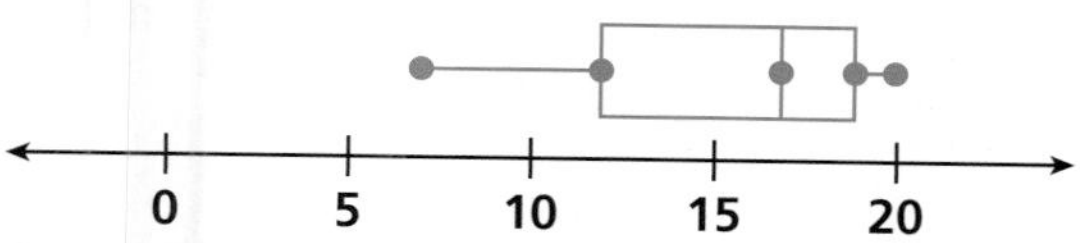

EXERCISES

Use the given data to make a box-and-whisker plot.

9. 56, 56, 56, 59, 63, 68, 68, 73, 73, 73

10. 87, 87, 80, 72, 85, 82, 53, 65, 65

11. 80, 80, 80, 82, 85, 87, 87, 90, 90, 90

9-5 Displaying Data (pp. 485–488)

EXAMPLE

■ **Make a histogram of the data set.**

72, 64, 56, 60, 66, 72, 48, 66, 58, 60, 60, 50, 68, 72, 68, 62, 72, 58, 60, 68

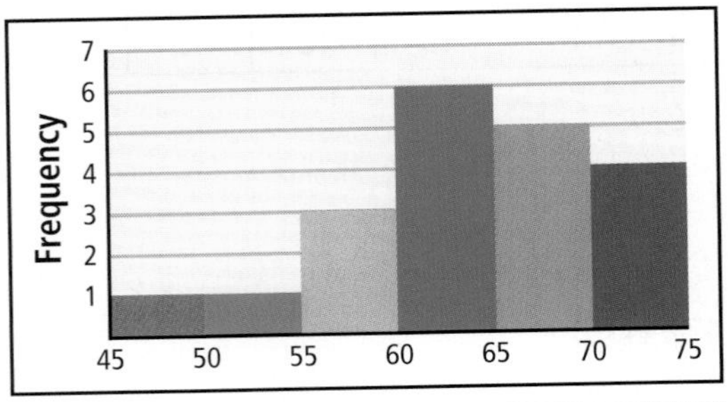

EXERCISES

Make a histogram of each data set.

12.

Weight (lb)	Frequency
91–100	5
101–110	7
111–120	10
121–130	4
131–140	2
141–150	3

13. Computer usage (h/week): 8, 3, 5, 10, 11, 12, 10, 7, 8, 7, 7, 22, 13, 15, 18, 6, 3

9-6 Misleading Graphs and Statistics (pp. 490–493)

EXAMPLE

■ **Explain why the graph is misleading.**

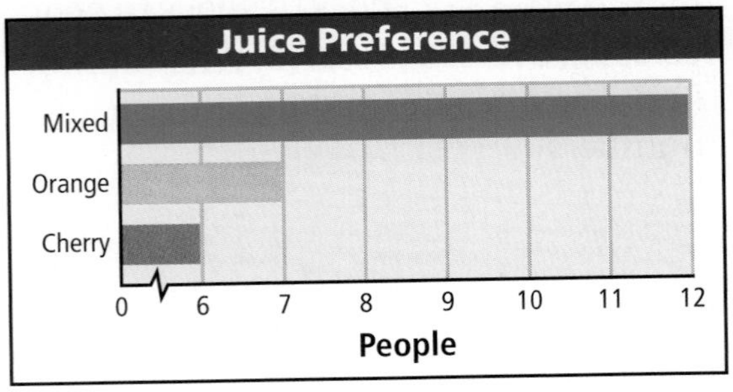

The bar for mixed juice is 7 times longer than the bar for cherry juice, but it is only preferred by 2 times as many people.

EXERCISE

14. Explain why the graph is misleading.

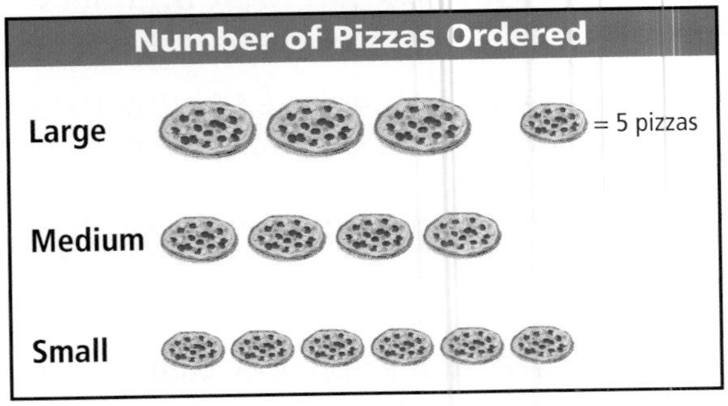

9-7 Scatter Plots (pp. 494–497)

EXAMPLE

■ **Does the age of a battery in a flashlight and the intensity of the flashlight beam have a positive, a negative, or no correlation? Explain.**

Negative: The older the battery is, the less intense the flashlight beam will be.

■ **Choose the best display to compare children's shoe sizes to their heights.**

A scatter plot would be the best display because you are comparing two sets of data.

EXERCISES

Does the data set have a positive, a negative, or no correlation? Explain.

15. the number of miles on a car's odometer and the size of the gas tank

Choose the best data display for the situation below. Explain your answer.

16. the amount of money spent in each category of a budget

CHAPTER TEST

Identify the sampling method used.

1. Twenty U.S. cities are randomly chosen and 100 people are randomly chosen from each city.
2. A telemarketer flips through the phone book and selects 30 names.
3. A chef asks the first five customers who order the new dessert if they like it. Identify the population and the sample. Why might the sample be biased?
4. The scores on a history test were 79, 82, 85, 100, 82, 83, 78, 84, 80, 82, and 77. What number best describes the middle of these scores?

Use the given data to make a box-and-whisker plot.

5. 62, 60, 77, 66, 92, 87, 62, 60, 64
6. 2.2, 6.8, 6.4, 8, 6.5, 4.2, 6.5, 5, 8
7. A middle school class calculated the average number of minutes they spent on the phone each day. Use the data to make a histogram with intervals of 10.

18	31	32	42	50	34	33	36	27	41	5	35	27	15
37	12	9	31	24	29	10	25	20	66	22	31	9	3

Explain why each graph is misleading.

8.

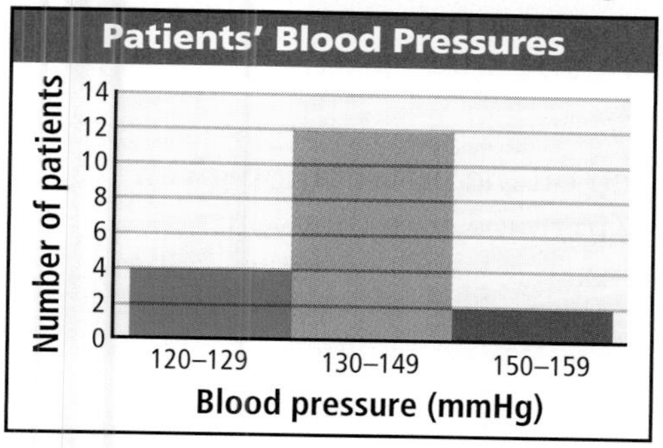

9.

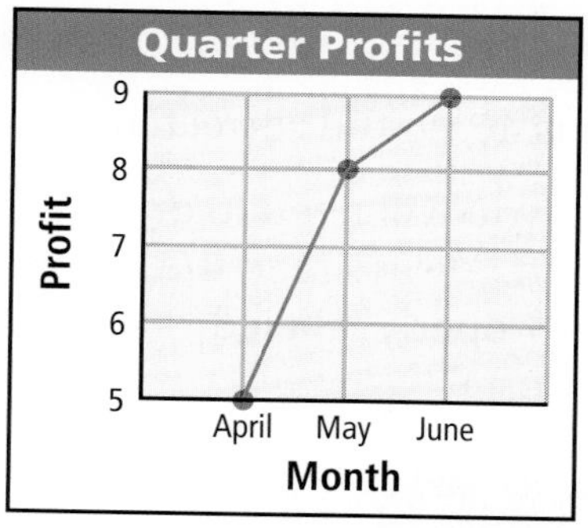

10. Use the given data to make a scatter plot.

Food	Pizza	Hamburger	Taco	Hot Dog	Caesar Salad	Taco Salad
Fat (g)	11	13	14	12	4	21
Calories	374	310	220	270	90	410

11. In a randomly chosen group of 100 people, 38 have type O positive blood, 7 have O negative, 34 have A positive, 6 have A negative, 9 have B positive, 2 have B negative, 3 have AB positive, and 1 has AB negative. Choose an appropriate data display and draw the graph. About what fraction of the population has type O blood?

TEST TACKLER

Standardized Test Strategies

All Types: Using a Graphic

Sometimes a graph or a picture is given with a test item. Look carefully at any drawings on a test. Keep in mind that figures are not always drawn to scale and can be misleading.

EXAMPLE 1

Multiple Choice The box-and-whisker plot shows the number of sales for the year. What is the range?

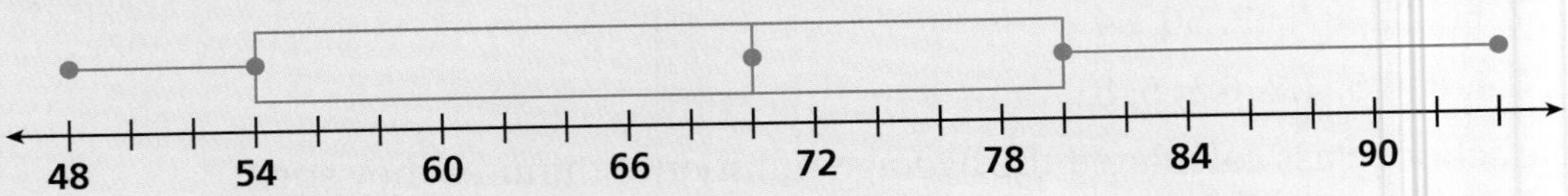

Ⓐ 46 Ⓑ 54 Ⓒ 68 Ⓓ 80

- Look at the box-and-whisker plot. The whiskers extend to the smallest and largest values. The range is the difference between these values.

  $94 - 48 = 46$ *Find the difference.*

- The range is 46, so the correct answer is choice A.
- Sometimes you will need to draw a diagram based on the information given in a test item. Always read the question carefully to make sure that your diagram is properly labeled.

EXAMPLE 2

Short Answer An ice rink has an area of 3750 ft^2 and length of 75 ft. What is the perimeter of the ice rink? Explain your reasoning and show your work.

Draw a diagram to help you visualize the problem.

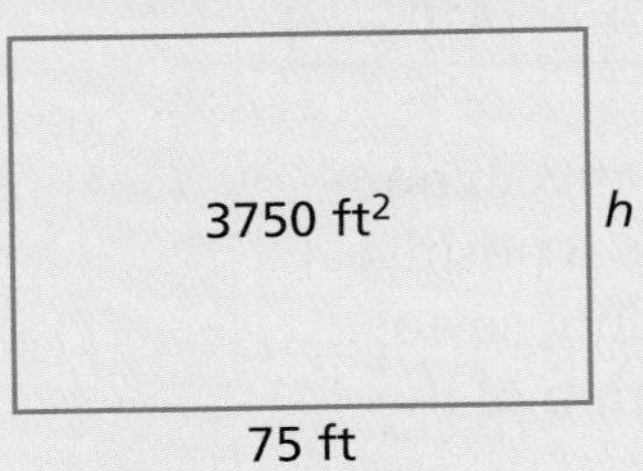

$A = bh$ *You know the area and base. You need to find the height.*

$3750 = 75h$

$50 = h$

$P = 2(b + h)$ *Use the formula for perimeter.*

$P = 2(75 + 50)$ *Substitute the known values.*

$P = 2(125)$

$P = 250$

The perimeter of the ice rink is 250 ft.

HOT TIP! Draw a diagram if one is not provided to help you visualize the problem.

Read each test problem and answer the questions that follow.

Item A
A pizza restaurant sells a 12-inch small pizza, a 14-inch medium pizza, and a 16-inch large pizza. How much more pizza do you get for a large pizza than a small pizza? Explain your reasoning and show your work.

1. Draw a diagram to help you visualize the problem.
2. Use information from your diagram to solve the problem.

Item B
A middle school has 1000 students. According to the circle graph, how many students are in track?

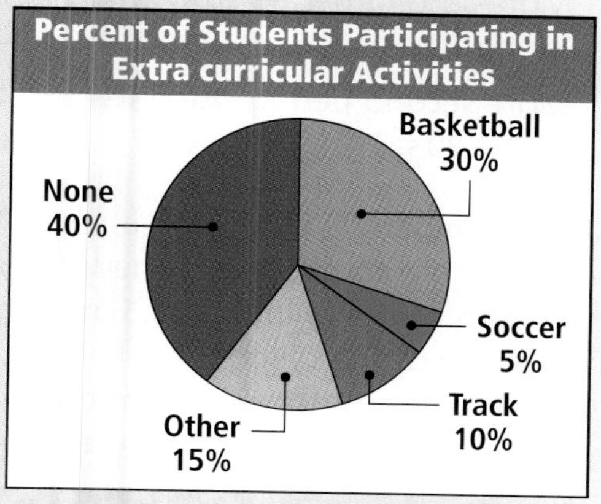

Ⓕ 400 Ⓖ 300 Ⓗ 100 Ⓙ 30

3. What percent of the students are in track? How do you know?
4. How do you find the number of students who are in track?

Item C
When a rectangle is divided into thirds, three squares are formed, each with a perimeter of 9.6 cm. What is the perimeter of the original rectangle?

5. Draw a diagram to visualize the problem.
6. What information from your diagram do you need to solve the problem?
7. If your answer is a decimal, what do you need to remember to do on the grid?
8. Show how you would grid your response below.

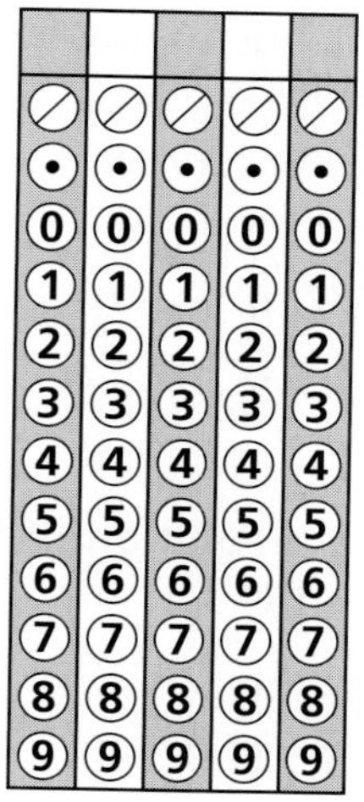

Item D
A 10 cm section of plastic pipe has an inner diameter 12 cm and an outer diameter 16 cm. What is the volume of the solid plastic pipe to the nearest tenth?

Ⓐ 879.2 cm^3 Ⓑ 1130.4 cm^3 Ⓒ 2009.6 cm^3 Ⓓ 3140 cm^3

9. Draw a diagram to help you visualize the problem.
10. Use information from your diagram to solve the problem.

STANDARDIZED TEST PREP

go.hrw.com
State Test Practice Online
KEYWORD: MT7 TestPrep

Cumulative Assessment, Chapters 1–9

Multiple Choice

1. Which is NOT true for this data set?
10, 10, 10.5, 9, 9.5

(A) mean < mode

(B) median > mean

(C) median = mean

(D) median = mode

2. In order to participate in after-school activities, a student needs to have a grade point average, *g*, of 2.0 or better. Which inequality represents this requirement?

(F) $g \geq 2.0$

(G) $g \leq 2.0$

(H) $g > 2.0$

(J) $g < 2.0$

3. Which ordered pair is a solution to the equation $2x + 4y = -18$?

(A) (0, −9)

(B) (6, 0)

(C) (−11, 1)

(D) (−3, −4)

4. Which expression is ***NOT*** equivalent to $4 \cdot 4 \cdot 4 \cdot 4 \cdot 4$?

(F) $\frac{1}{4^{-5}}$

(G) 20

(H) $4^2 \cdot 4^3$

(J) 1024

5. A 6-inch model is made to represent a 30-foot plane. What is the scale?

(A) 1 in. = 5 ft

(B) 5 in. = 1 ft

(C) 6 in. = 5 ft

(D) 30 in. = 5 ft

6. The stem-and-leaf plot shows test scores for a teacher's first and second periods. What can you conclude?

1st period		2nd period
7	6	5 8
6 4 2	7	5 6 9
9 8 6 4 2 0	8	1 3 5 7 7 8 8
9 7 7 2 1	9	0 6 7 8 9

Key: |9|0 *means 90*
7|6| *means 67*

(F) More first period students scored in the 90's.

(G) Fewer first period students scored 80 or below.

(H) More second period students scored in the 70's.

(J) More second period students scored in the 80's.

7. A soup company is producing a cylindrical can to package its new soup. The radius of the cylinder is 1.5 in. and the volume of the cylinder has to be 14 in^3. What must the height of the can be, rounded to the nearest whole inch?

(A) 1 inch

(B) 2 inches

(C) 3 inches

(D) 4 inches

8. Emma buys a refrigerator on sale for \$665. This is 30% off the original price. What is the original price of the refrigerator?

(F) \$200

(G) \$950

(H) \$1995

(J) \$2217

9. Which is a solution to the equation $-10 + 5x = -25$?

(A) $x = -15$
(B) $x = -7$
(C) $x = -3$
(D) $x = -1$

10. If triangle $JQZ \cong$ triangle VTZ, what is the value of r?

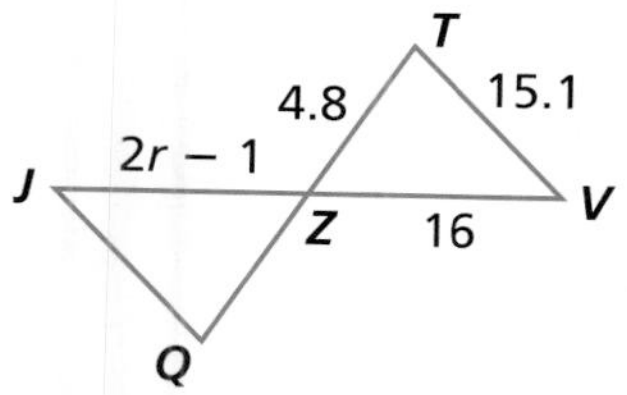

(F) 7.5
(G) 8.5
(H) 9
(J) 33

Read a graph or diagram as closely as you do the actual question. These visual aids contain important information.

Gridded Response

11. The function $f(t) = -16t^2 + 180$ models the distance an object falls when it is dropped from the top of a building 180 ft tall in t seconds. How many feet does the stone fall after 2 seconds?

Use the box-and-whisker plot to answers questions 12 and 13.

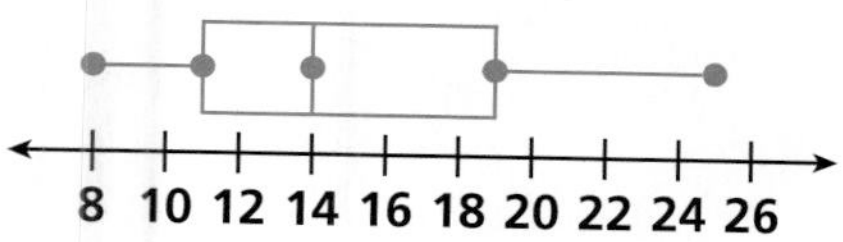

12. What is the range of the data?

13. What is the first quartile of the data?

14. Monica scored 85, 83, 81, 80, and 81 on her last five assignments. What would Monica need to earn on her next assignment to bring her average to an 85?

Short Response

15. Name two ordered pairs (x, y) that satisfy these conditions: The mean of 0, x, and y is twice the median; $0 < x < y$; and $y = nx$ (y is a multiple of x). What is the value of n? Show your work or explain in words how you determined your answer.

16. Explain why the graph is misleading and then redraw it so that it better represents the data.

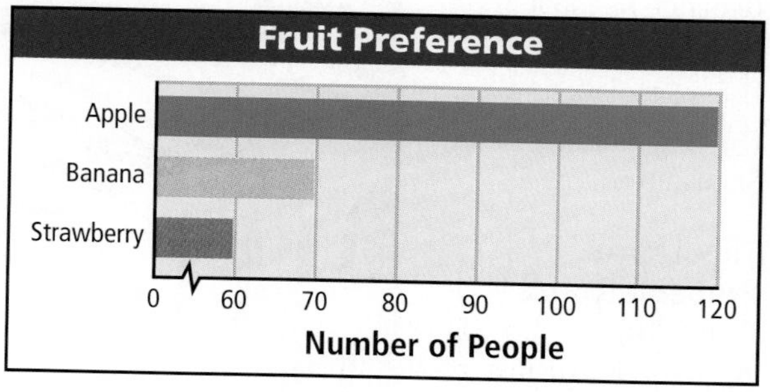

Extended Response

17. Twenty students in a gym class kept a record of their jogging. The results are shown in the scatter plot.

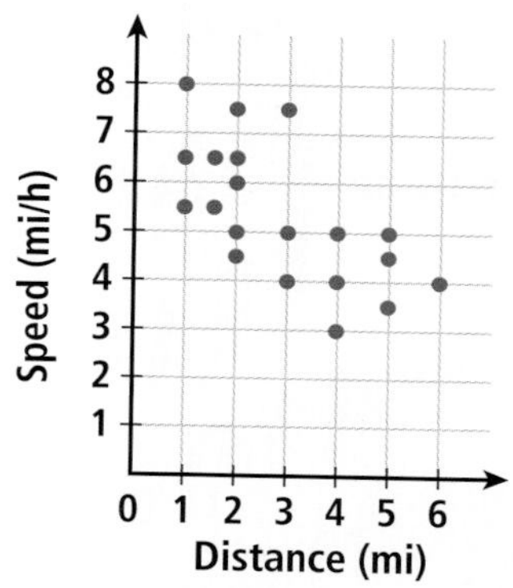

a. Describe the correlation of the data in the scatter plot.

b. Find the average speeds of joggers who run 1, 2, 3, 4, 5, and 6 miles.

c. Explain the relationship between your answer from part **a** and your answers from part **b**.

Standardized Test Prep

CHAPTER 10

Probability

10A Experimental Probability

10-1 Probability

10-2 Experimental Probability

LAB Generate Random Numbers

10-3 Use a Simulation

LAB Use Different Models for Simulations

10B Theoretical Probability and Counting

10-4 Theoretical Probability

10-5 Independent and Dependent Events

10-6 Making Decisions and Predictions

10-7 Odds

10-8 Counting Principles

10-9 Permutations and Combinations

MULTI-STEP TEST PREP

go.hrw.com
Chapter Project Online
KEYWORD: MT7 Ch10

Letter	Code
A	1000001
E	1000101
H	1001000
I	1001001
L	1001100
M	1001101
O	1001111
T	1010100
V	1010110

Career *Cryptographer*

1001001100110010011111010110
10001011001101100000110101001001000

Is this pattern of zeros and ones some kind of message or secret code? A cryptographer could find out. Cryptographers create and break codes by assigning number values to letters of the alphabet.

Almost all text sent over the Internet is encrypted to ensure security for the sender. Codes made up of zeros and ones, or *binary codes*, are frequently used in computer applications.

Use the table to break the code above.

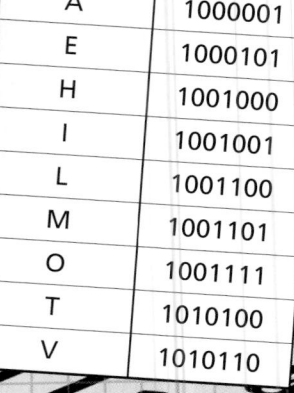

ARE YOU READY?

Vocabulary

Choose the best term from the list to complete each sentence.

fraction
percent
range
ratio

1. The term __?__ means "per hundred."
2. A __?__ is a comparison of two numbers.
3. In a set of data, the __?__ is the greatest value minus the least value.
4. A __?__ is in simplest form when its numerator and denominator have no common factors other than 1.

Complete these exercises to review skills you will need for this chapter.

Simplify Ratios

Write each ratio in simplest form.

5. 5:50 **6.** 95 to 19 **7.** $\frac{20}{100}$ **8.** $\frac{192}{80}$

Write Fractions as Decimals

Write each fraction as a decimal.

9. $\frac{52}{100}$ **10.** $\frac{7}{1000}$ **11.** $\frac{3}{5}$ **12.** $\frac{2}{9}$

Write Fractions as Percents

Write each fraction as a percent.

13. $\frac{19}{100}$ **14.** $\frac{1}{8}$ **15.** $\frac{5}{2}$ **16.** $\frac{2}{3}$

17. $\frac{3}{4}$ **18.** $\frac{9}{20}$ **19.** $\frac{7}{10}$ **20.** $\frac{2}{5}$

Operations with Fractions

Add. Write each answer in simplest form.

21. $\frac{3}{8} + \frac{1}{4} + \frac{1}{6}$ **22.** $\frac{1}{6} + \frac{2}{3} + \frac{1}{9}$ **23.** $\frac{1}{8} + \frac{1}{4} + \frac{1}{8} + \frac{1}{2}$ **24.** $\frac{1}{3} + \frac{1}{4} + \frac{2}{5}$

Multiply. Write each answer in simplest form.

25. $\frac{3}{8} \cdot \frac{1}{5}$ **26.** $\frac{2}{3} \cdot \frac{6}{7}$ **27.** $\frac{3}{7} \cdot \frac{14}{27}$ **28.** $\frac{13}{52} \cdot \frac{3}{51}$

29. $\frac{4}{5} \cdot \frac{11}{4}$ **30.** $\frac{5}{2} \cdot \frac{3}{4}$ **31.** $\frac{27}{8} \cdot \frac{4}{9}$ **32.** $\frac{1}{15} \cdot \frac{30}{9}$

CHAPTER 10

Study Guide: Preview

Where You've Been

Previously, you

- found the probability of independent events.
- constructed sample spaces for simple or composite experiments.
- made inferences based on analysis of given or collected data.

In This Chapter

You will study

- finding the probabilities of independent and dependent events.
- selecting and using different models to simulate an event.
- using theoretical probabilities and experimental results to make predictions.

Where You're Going

You can use the skills learned in this chapter

- to make predictions based on theoretical and experimental probabilities in science courses like biology.
- to learn how to create more advanced simulations for use in fields like computer science and meteorology.

Key Vocabulary/Vocabulario

combination	combinación
dependent events	sucesos dependientes
experimental probability	probabilidad experimental
independent events	sucesos independientes
mutually exclusive	mutuamente excluyentes
outcome	resultado
permutation	permutación
probability	probabilidad
simulation	simulación
theoretical probability	probabilidad teórica

Vocabulary Connections

To become familiar with some of the vocabulary terms in the chapter, consider the following. You may refer to the chapter, the glossary, or a dictionary if you like.

1. The word *dependent* means "determined by another." What do you think **dependent events** are?
2. The prefix *in-* means "not." What do you suppose **independent events** are?
3. The word *simulation* comes from the Latin root *simulare,* which means "to represent." What do you think a **simulation** is in probability?

Reading and Writing Math

Reading Strategy: Learn Math Vocabulary

Mathematics has a vocabulary all its own. To learn and remember new vocabulary words, use the following study strategies.

- Try to figure out the meanings of new words based on their context.
- Use a dictionary to look up root words or prefixes.
- Relate the new word to familiar everyday words.
- Use mnemonics or memory tricks to remember the definition.

Once you know what a word means, write its definition in your own words.

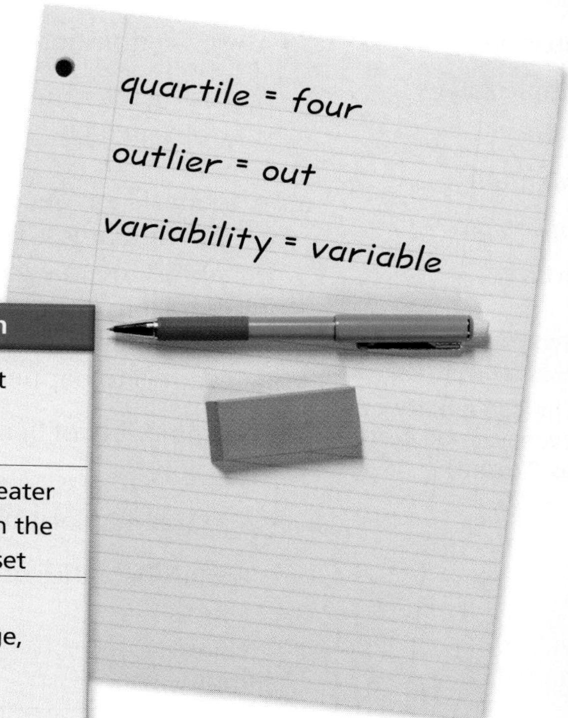

Term	Study Notes	Definition
Quartile	The root word quart- means "four."	Three values that divide a data set into fourths
Outlier	Relate it to the word out, which means "away from a place."	A value much greater or much less than the others in a data set
Variability	Relate it to the word variable, which is a value that can change.	The spread, or amount of change, of values in a set of data

Try This

Complete the table below.

	Term	Study Notes	Definition
1.	Systematic sample		
2.	Median		
3.	Quartile		
4.	Frequency table		

10-1 Probability

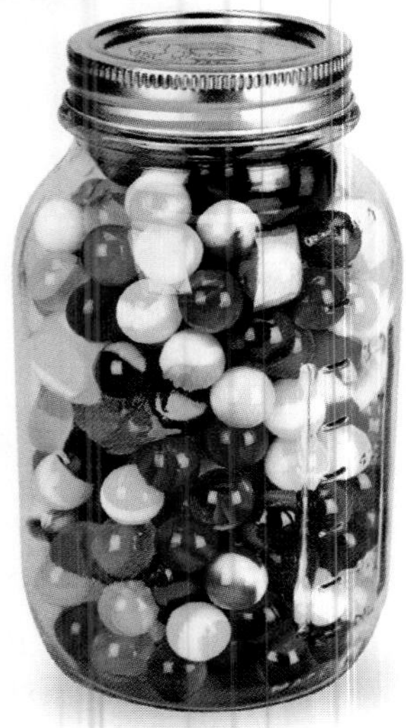

Learn to find the probability of an event by using the definition of probability.

Vocabulary

experiment
trial
outcome
sample space
event
probability
impossible
certain

An **experiment** is an activity in which results are observed. Each observation is called a **trial**, and each result is called an **outcome**. The **sample space** is the set of all possible outcomes of an experiment.

Experiment	Sample space
• flipping a coin	• heads, tails
• rolling a number cube	• 1, 2, 3, 4, 5, 6
• guessing the number of marbles in a jar	• whole numbers

An **event** is any set of one or more outcomes. The **probability** of an event is a number from 0 (or 0%) to 1 (or 100%) that tells you how likely the event is to happen.

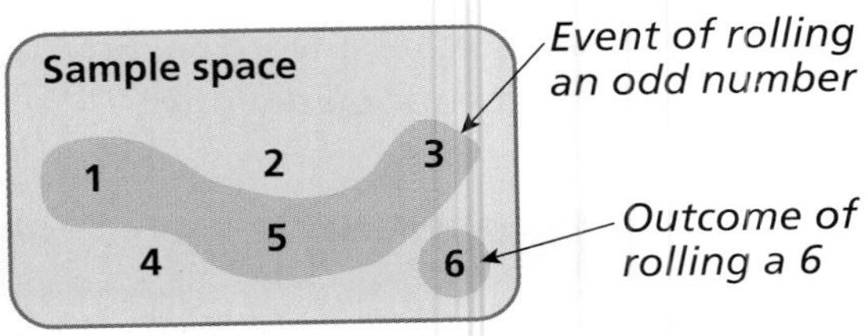

Writing Math

The probability of an event can be written as *P*(event).

- A probability of 0 means the event is **impossible**, or can never happen.
- A probability of 1 means the event is **certain**, or has to happen.
- The probabilities of all the outcomes in the sample space add up to 1.

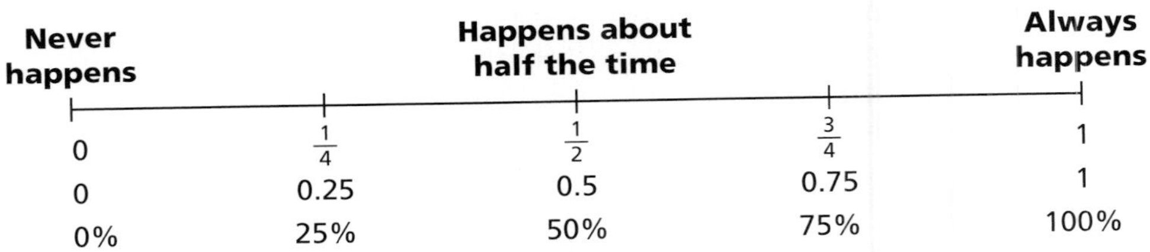

EXAMPLE 1 Finding Probabilities of Outcomes in a Sample Space

Give the probability for each outcome.

A The weather forecast shows a 30% chance of snow.

Outcome	Snow	No snow
Probability		

The probability of snow is $P(\text{snow}) = 30\% = 0.3$. The probabilities must add to 1, so the probability of no snow is $P(\text{no snow}) = 1 - 0.3 = 0.7$, or 70%.

Give the probability for each outcome.

B

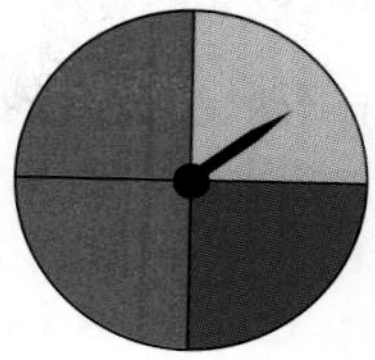

Outcome	Red	Yellow	Blue
Probability	▩	▩	▩

One-half of the spinner is red, so a reasonable estimate of the probability that the spinner lands on red is $P(\text{red}) = \frac{1}{2}$.
One-fourth of the spinner is yellow, so a reasonable estimate of the probability that the spinner lands on yellow is $P(\text{yellow}) = \frac{1}{4}$.
One-fourth of the spinner is blue, so a reasonable estimate of the probability that the spinner lands on blue is $P(\text{blue}) = \frac{1}{4}$.

Check The probabilities of all the outcomes must add to 1.

$\frac{1}{2} + \frac{1}{4} + \frac{1}{4} = 1$ ✔

To find the probability of an event, add the probabilities of all the outcomes included in the event.

EXAMPLE 2 Finding Probabilities of Events

A quiz contains 3 multiple-choice questions and 2 true-false questions. Suppose you guess randomly on every question. The table below gives the probability of each score.

Score	0	1	2	3	4	5
Probability	0.105	0.316	0.352	0.180	0.043	0.004

A **What is the probability of guessing 4 or more correct?**

The event "4 or more correct" consists of the outcomes 4 and 5.

$P(\text{four or more correct}) = 0.043 + 0.004$
$= 0.047$, or 4.7%

B **What is the probability of guessing fewer than 3 correct?**

The event "fewer than 3 correct" consists of the outcomes 0, 1, and 2.

$P(\text{fewer than 3 correct}) = 0.105 + 0.316 + 0.352$
$= 0.773$, or 77.3%

C **What is the probability of failing the quiz (getting 0, 1, 2, or 3 correct) by guessing?**

The event "failing the quiz" consists of the outcomes 0, 1, 2, and 3.

$P(\text{failing the quiz}) = 0.105 + 0.316 + 0.352 + 0.18$
$= 0.953$, or 95.3%

EXAMPLE 3 **PROBLEM SOLVING APPLICATION**

PROBLEM SOLVING

Six students are running for class president. Jin's probability of winning is $\frac{1}{8}$. Jin is half as likely to win as Monica. Petra has the same chance to win as Monica. Lila, Juan, and Marc all have the same chance of winning. Create a table of probabilities for the sample space.

1 Understand the Problem

The **answer** will be a table of probabilities. Each probability will be a number from 0 to 1. The probabilities of all outcomes add to 1. List the **important information:**

- $P(\text{Jin}) = \frac{1}{8}$
- $P(\text{Monica}) = 2P(\text{Jin}) = 2 \cdot \frac{1}{8} = \frac{1}{4}$
- $P(\text{Petra}) = P(\text{Monica}) = \frac{1}{4}$
- $P(\text{Lila}) = P(\text{Juan}) = P(\text{Marc})$

2 Make a Plan

You know the probabilities add to 1, so use the strategy **write an equation**. Let p represent the probability for Lila, Juan, and Marc.

$$P(\text{Jin}) + P(\text{Monica}) + P(\text{Petra}) + P(\text{Lila}) + P(\text{Juan}) + P(\text{Marc}) = 1$$

$$\frac{1}{8} + \frac{1}{4} + \frac{1}{4} + p + p + p = \frac{5}{8} + 3p = 1$$

3 Solve

$$\frac{5}{8} + 3p = 1$$

$$-\frac{5}{8} \qquad -\frac{5}{8} \qquad \textit{Subtract } \tfrac{5}{8} \textit{ from both sides.}$$

$$3p = \frac{3}{8}$$

$$\frac{1}{3} \cdot 3p = \frac{1}{3} \cdot \frac{3}{8} \qquad \textit{Multiply both sides by } \tfrac{1}{3}.$$

$$p = \frac{1}{8}$$

Outcome	Jin	Monica	Petra	Lila	Juan	Marc
Probability	$\frac{1}{8}$	$\frac{1}{4}$	$\frac{1}{4}$	$\frac{1}{8}$	$\frac{1}{8}$	$\frac{1}{8}$

4 Look Back

Check that the probabilities add to 1.

$$\frac{1}{8} + \frac{1}{4} + \frac{1}{4} + \frac{1}{8} + \frac{1}{8} + \frac{1}{8} = 1 \checkmark$$

Think and Discuss

1. **Give** a probability for each of the following: usually, sometimes, always, never. Compare your values with the rest of your class.
2. **Explain** the difference between an outcome and an event.

10-1 Exercises

go.hrw.com
Homework Help Online
KEYWORD: MT7 10-1
Parent Resources Online
KEYWORD: MT7 Parent

GUIDED PRACTICE

See Example 1

1. The weather forecast calls for a 60% chance of rain. Give the probability for each outcome.

Outcome	Rain	No rain
Probability	▒	▒

See Example 2

A game consists of randomly selecting 4 colored ducks from a pond and counting the number of green ducks. The table gives the probability of each outcome.

Number of Green Ducks	0	1	2	3	4
Probability	0.043	0.248	0.418	0.248	0.043

2. What is the probability of selecting at most 1 green duck?
3. What is the probability of selecting more than 1 green duck?

See Example 3

4. There are 4 teams in a school tournament. Team A has a 25% chance of winning. Team B has the same chance as Team D. Team C has half the chance of winning as Team B. Create a table of probabilities for the sample space.

INDEPENDENT PRACTICE

See Example 1

5. Give the probability for each outcome.

Outcome	Red	Blue	Yellow	Green
Probability	▒	▒	▒	▒

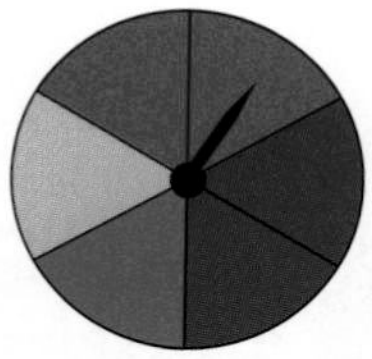

See Example 2

Customers at Pizza Palace can order up to 5 toppings on a pizza. The table gives the probabilities for the number of toppings ordered on a pizza.

Number of Toppings	0	1	2	3	4	5
Probability	0.205	0.305	0.210	0.155	0.123	0.002

6. What is the probability that at least 2 toppings are ordered?
7. What is the probability that fewer than 3 toppings are ordered?

See Example 3

8. Five students are trying out for the lead role in a school play. Kim and Sasha have the same chance of being chosen. Kris has a 30% chance of being chosen, and Lei and Denali are both half as likely to be chosen as Kris. Create a table of probabilities for the sample space.

PRACTICE AND PROBLEM SOLVING

Extra Practice

See page 800.

Use the table to find the probability of each event.

Outcome	A	B	C	D	E
Probability	0.306	0	0.216	0.115	0.363

9. A, C, or E occurring

10. B or D occurring

11. A, B, D, or E occurring

12. A not occurring

13. Consumer A cereal company puts "prizes" in some of its boxes to attract shoppers. There is a 0.005 probability of getting two tickets to a movie theater, $\frac{1}{8}$ probability of finding a watch, 12.5% probability of getting an action figure, and 0.2 probability of getting a sticker. What is the probability of not getting any prize?

14. Critical Thinking You are told there are 4 possible events that may occur. Event A has a 25% chance of occurring, event B has a probability of $\frac{1}{5}$ and events C and D have an equal likelihood of occurring. What steps would you take in order to find the probabilities of events C and D?

15. Give an example of an event that has 0 probability of occurring.

16. What's the Error? Two people are playing a game. One of them says, "Either I will win or you will. The sample space contains two outcomes, so we each have a probability of one-half." What is the error?

17. Write About It Suppose an event has a probability of p. What can you say about the value of p? What is the probability that the event will not occur? Explain.

18. Challenge List all possible events in the sample space with outcomes A, B, and C.

TEST PREP and Spiral Review

19. Multiple Choice The local weather forecaster said there is a 30% chance of rain tomorrow. What is the probability that it will NOT rain tomorrow?

Ⓐ 0.7 Ⓑ 0.3 Ⓒ 70 Ⓓ 30

20. Gridded Response A sports announcer states that a runner has an 84% chance of winning a race. Give the probability, as a fraction in lowest terms, that the runner will NOT win the race.

Evaluate the powers of 10. (Lesson 4-2)

21. 10^{-4} **22.** 10^{-1} **23.** 10^{-5} **24.** 10^{-7}

Find the slope of the line through the given points. (Lesson 7-5)

25. $A(-2, 5), B(-2, 4)$ **26.** $G(4, -3), H(5, 2)$ **27.** $R(8, 4), S(10, 1)$ **28.** $J(3, 2), K(-1, 2)$

10-2 Experimental Probability

Learn to estimate probability using experimental methods.

Vocabulary

experimental probability

Despite the rising price of gasoline, sports utility vehicles (SUV's) remain popular. The public perception of the safety of SUV's varies widely. The accident rate of SUV's is about the same as with other vehicles, but SUV's tend to have a higher rate among accidents involving fatalities. Insurance companies estimate the probability of accidents by studying accident rates for different types of vehicles.

In **experimental probability**, the likelihood of an event is estimated by repeating an experiment many times and observing the number of times the event happens. That number is divided by the total number of trials. The more the experiment is repeated, the more accurate the estimate is likely to be.

$$\text{probability} \approx \frac{\text{number of times the event occurs}}{\text{total number of trials}}$$

EXAMPLE 1 Estimating the Probability of an Event

A **After 1000 spins of the spinner, the following information was recorded. Estimate the probability of the spinner landing on red.**

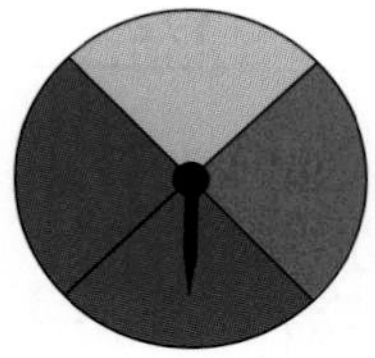

Outcome	Blue	Red	Yellow
Spins	448	267	285

$$\text{probability} \approx \frac{\text{number of spins that landed on red}}{\text{total number of spins}} = \frac{267}{1000} = 0.267$$

The probability of landing on red is about 0.267, or 26.7%.

B **A marble is randomly drawn out of a bag and then replaced. The table shows the results after 100 draws. Estimate the probability of drawing a yellow marble.**

Outcome	Green	Red	Yellow	Blue	White
Draws	12	35	21	18	14

$$\text{probability} \approx \frac{\text{number of yellow marbles drawn}}{\text{total number of draws}} = \frac{21}{100} = 0.21$$

The probability of drawing a yellow marble is about 0.21, or 21%.

C **A researcher has been observing the types of vehicles passing through an intersection. Of the last 50 cars, 29 were sedans, 9 were trucks, and 12 were SUV's. Estimate the probability that the next vehicle through the intersection will be an SUV.**

Outcome	Sedan	Truck	SUV
Observations	29	9	12

$$\text{probability} \approx \frac{\text{number of SUV's}}{\text{total number of vehicles}} = \frac{12}{50} = 0.24 = 24\%$$

The probability that the next vehicle through the intersection will be an SUV is about 0.24, or 24%.

EXAMPLE 2 *Safety Application*

Use the table to compare the probability of being involved in a fatal traffic crash in an SUV with being in a fatal traffic crash in a mid-size car.

Traffic Crashes in Ohio, 2004

Vehicle Class	**Number of Fatal Crashes**	**Total Number of Crashes**
Sub-compact cars	23	7, 962
Compact cars	266	110,598
Mid-size cars	464	200,433
Full-size cars	161	76,570
Minivan	97	45,043
SUV's	172	75,593

Source: Ohio Department of Public Safety

$$\text{probability} \approx \frac{\text{number of fatal crashes}}{\text{total number of crashes}}$$

$$\text{probability of SUV} \approx \frac{172}{75{,}593} \approx 0.0023$$

$$\text{probability of mid-size car} \approx \frac{464}{200{,}433} \approx 0.0023$$

In 2004, an SUV was just as likely to be involved in a fatal traffic crash as a mid-size car.

Think and Discuss

1. **Compare** the probability in Example 1A of the spinner landing on red to what you think the probability should be.
2. **Give** a possible number of marbles of each color in the bag in Example 1B. Explain your reasoning.

10-2 Exercises

go.hrw.com
Homework Help Online
KEYWORD: MT7 10-2
Parent Resources Online
KEYWORD: MT7 Parent

GUIDED PRACTICE

See Example 1

1. A game spinner was spun 500 times. It was found that A was spun 170 times, B was spun 244 times, and C was spun 86 times. Estimate the probability that the spinner will land on A.

2. A coin was randomly drawn from a bag and then replaced. After 300 draws, it was found that 45 pennies, 76 nickels, 92 dimes, and 87 quarters had been drawn. Estimate the probability of drawing a quarter.

See Example 2

3. Use the table to compare the probability that a student walks to school to the probability that a student bikes to school.

4. Use the table to compare the probability that a student takes the bus to school to the probability that a student rides in a car to school.

Mode of Transportation	Number of Students
Bus	265
Car	313
Walk	105
Bike	87

INDEPENDENT PRACTICE

See Example 1

5. A researcher polled 260 students at a university and found that 83 of them owned a laptop computer. Estimate the probability that a randomly selected college student owns a laptop computer.

6. Keisha made 12 out of her last 58 shots on goal. Estimate the probability that she will make her next shot on goal.

See Example 2

7. Stefan polled 113 students about the number of siblings they have. Use the table to compare the probability that a student has one sibling to the probability that a student has two siblings.

8. Use the table to compare the probability that a student has no siblings to the probability that a student has three siblings.

Number of Siblings	Number of Students
0	14
1	45
2	27
3	15
4+	12

PRACTICE AND PROBLEM SOLVING

Extra Practice
See page 800.

Use the table for Exercises 7–11.
Estimate the probability of each event.

9. A batter hits a single.
10. A batter hits a double.
11. A batter hits a triple.
12. A batter hits a home run.
13. A batter makes an out.

Result	Number
Single	20
Double	12
Triple	2
Home run	8
Walk	10
Out	28
Total	**80**

Earth Science LINK

The strength of an earthquake is measured on the Richter scale. A *major* earthquake measures between 7 and 7.9 on the Richter scale, and a *great* earthquake measures 8 or higher. The table shows the number of major and great earthquakes per year worldwide from 1985 to 2004.

14. Estimate the probability that there will be more than 15 major earthquakes next year.

15. Estimate the probability that there will be fewer than 12 major earthquakes next year.

16. Estimate the probability that there will be no great earthquakes next year.

17. **Challenge** Estimate the probability that there will be more than one major earthquake in the next month.

Number of Earthquakes Worldwide

Year	Major	Great	Year	Major	Great
1985	13	1	1995	22	3
1986	5	1	1996	14	1
1987	11	0	1997	16	0
1988	8	0	1998	11	1
1989	6	1	1999	18	0
1990	12	0	2000	14	1
1991	11	0	2001	15	1
1992	23	0	2002	13	0
1993	15	1	2003	14	1
1994	13	2	2004	14	2

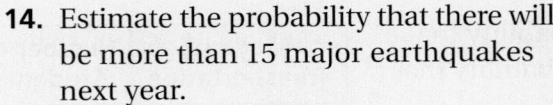

go.hrw.com
Web Extra!
KEYWORD: MT7 Quake

TEST PREP and Spiral Review

18. **Multiple Choice** A spinner was spun 220 times. The outcome was red 58 times. Estimate the probability of the spinner landing on red.

Ⓐ about 0.126 Ⓑ about 0.225 Ⓒ about 0.264 Ⓓ about 0.32

19. **Short Response** A researcher observed students buying lunch in a cafeteria. Of the last 50 students, 22 bought an apple, 17 bought a banana, and 11 bought a pear. If 150 more students buy lunch, estimate the number of students who will buy a banana. Explain.

Evaluate each expression for the given value of the variable. (Lesson 2-3)

20. $45.6 + x$ for $x = -11.1$ **21.** $17.9 - b$ for $b = 22.3$ **22.** $r + (-4.9)$ for $r = 31.8$

A spinner is divided into 8 equal sections. There are 3 red sections, 4 blue, and 1 green. Give the probability of each outcome. (Lesson 10-1)

23. red **24.** blue **25.** green

Technology LAB 10-3

Generate Random Numbers

Use with Lesson 10-3

go.hrw.com
Lab Resources Online
KEYWORD: MT7 Lab10

A spreadsheet can be used to generate random decimal numbers that are greater than or equal to 0 but less than 1. By using formulas, you can shift these numbers into a useful range.

Activity

1 Use a spreadsheet to generate five random decimal numbers that are between 0 and 1. Then convert these numbers to integers from 1 to 10.

a. Type **=RAND()** into cell A1 and press **ENTER**. A random decimal number appears.

	A
1	0.063515
2	

b. Click to highlight cell A1. Go to the **Edit** menu and **Copy** the contents of A1. Then click and drag to highlight cells A2 through A5. Go to the **Edit** menu and use **Paste** to fill cells A2 through A5.

	A
1	0.20589
2	0.837083
3	0.445334
4	0.939134
5	0.993354
6	

Notice that the random number in cell A1 changed when you filled the other cells.

RAND() gives a decimal number greater than or equal to 0, but less than 1. To generate random integers from 1 to 10, you need to do the following:

- Multiply **RAND()** by 10 (to give a number greater than or equal to 0 but less than 10).
- Use the **INT** function to drop the decimal part of the result (to give an integer from 0 to 9).
- Add 1 (to give an integer from 1 to 10).

c. Change the formula in A1 to **=INT(10*RAND()) + 1** and press **ENTER.** Repeat the process in part **b** to fill cells A2 through A5.

A2 = =INT(10*RAND()) + 1

	A	B	C	D
1	9			
2	1			
3	7			
4	7			
5	6			
6				

The formula **=INT(10*RAND()) + 1** generates random integers from 1 to 10.

Think and Discuss

1. Explain how **INT(10*RAND()) + 1** generates random integers from 1 to 10.

Try This

1. Use a spreadsheet to simulate 3 spins of a spinner with 4 equal regions.

10-3 Use a Simulation

Problem Solving Strategy

Learn to use a simulation to estimate probability.

Vocabulary

simulation

random numbers

In football, many factors are used to evaluate how good a quarterback is. One important factor is the quarterback's ability to complete passes.

If a quarterback has a completion percentage of 64%, he completes about 64 of every 100 passes he throws. What is the probability that he will complete at least 6 of 10 passes thrown? A simulation can help you estimate this probability.

A **simulation** is a model of a real situation. In a set of **random numbers**, each number has the same probability of occurring, and no pattern can be used to predict the next number. Random numbers can be used to simulate random events in real situations. The table is a set of 280 random digits.

During the 2004 season, Indianapolis's Peyton Manning had a completion percentage of 67.6%.

87244	11632	85815	61766	19579	28186	18533	42633
74681	65633	54238	32848	87649	85976	13355	46498
53736	21616	86318	77291	24794	31119	48193	44869
86585	27919	65264	93557	94425	13325	16635	28584
18394	73266	67899	38783	94228	23426	76679	41256
39917	16373	59733	18588	22545	61378	33563	65161
96916	46278	78210	13906	82794	01136	60848	98713

EXAMPLE 1 **PROBLEM SOLVING APPLICATION**

PROBLEM SOLVING

A quarterback has a completion percentage of 64%. Estimate the probability that he will complete at least 6 of his next 10 passes.

1 Understand the Problem

The **answer** will be the probability that he will complete at least 6 of his next 10 passes. It must be a number between 0 and 1. List the **important information**:

- The probability that the quarterback will complete a pass is 0.64.

2 Make a Plan

Use a simulation to model the situation. Use digits from the table, grouped in pairs. The numbers 01–64 represent completed passes, and the numbers 65–00 represent incomplete passes. Each group of 20 digits represents one trial. You can start anywhere on the table.

3 Solve

The first 20 digits in the table are shown below.
87244 11632 85815 61766

The digits can be grouped in ten pairs, as shown below.
87 24 41 16 32 85 81 56 17 66
This represents 6 of 10 completed passes.

If you continue using the table, the next nine trials are as follows.

19	57	92	81	86	18	53	34	26	33	*7 completed passes*
74	68	16	56	33	54	23	83	28	48	*7 completed passes*
87	64	98	59	76	13	35	54	64	98	*6 completed passes*
53	73	62	16	16	86	31	87	72	91	*5 completed passes*
24	79	43	11	19	48	19	34	48	69	*8 completed passes*
86	58	52	79	19	65	26	49	35	57	*7 completed passes*
94	42	51	33	25	16	63	52	85	84	*7 completed passes*
18	39	47	32	66	67	89	93	87	83	*4 completed passes*
94	22	82	34	26	76	67	94	12	56	*5 completed passes*

Out of the 10 trials, 7 represented 6 or more completed passes. Based on this simulation, the probability of completing at least 6 of 10 passes is about 0.70, or 70%.

4 Look Back

A completion percentage of 64% means the quarterback completes about 64 of every 100 passes. This ratio is equivalent to 6.4 out of 10 passes, so he should make at least 6 passes most of the time. The answer is reasonable.

Helpful Hint

Calculators and computers can generate sets of approximately random numbers. A formula is used to generate the numbers, so they are not truly random, but they work for most simulations.

Think and Discuss

1. Explain why a random number generator on a computer or calculator is useful for estimating probability by simulation.

2. Tell how you could use a simulation to estimate the probability that a quarterback who has a completion percentage of 50% will make at least 7 of 10 passes.

10-3 Exercises

go.hrw.com
Homework Help Online
KEYWORD: MT7 10-3
Parent Resources Online
KEYWORD: MT7 Parent

GUIDED PRACTICE

See Example 1

Use the table of random numbers to simulate each situation. Use at least 10 trials for each simulation.

49064	12830	66783	14965	81537	24935	69675	32681
42893	42668	70963	58827	17354	42190	36165	29827
21705	89446	38703	21274	90049	19036	37971	05322
52737	40117	54132	11152	02985	82873	28197	89796

1. Liza makes free throws at a rate of 81%. If she takes 8 free throws during a game, estimate the probability that she will make at least 6 free throws.
2. During the summer, a city has a 15% chance of a day with a temperature over 90°F. Estimate the probability that at least 3 days have a temperature over 90°F during the last week in August.
3. Customers at a carnival game win about 25% of the time. Estimate the probability that no more than 1 of the next 6 customers will win the game.
4. Marcelo completes a sale with approximately 32% of the customers he meets. If he has 6 customer appointments tomorrow, estimate the probability that he will complete at least 3 sales.

INDEPENDENT PRACTICE

See Example 1

Use the table of random numbers to simulate each situation. Use at least 10 trials for each simulation.

63415	12776	31960	42974	36444	23826	46320	48308
41591	43536	64118	53147	23544	61352	12954	57628
26446	12734	22435	42612	24834	21961	12526	22832
16522	33043	21997	15738	25788	33205	55699	33357
53040	39923	29591	64384	58166	39164	54474	38970

5. Veronica gets a hit 32% of the time she bats. Estimate the probability that she will get at least 5 hits in her next 10 at bats.
6. At a local fast-food restaurant, about 83% of the customers order their food to go. Estimate the probability that 6 of the next 7 customers will order their food to go.
7. A local radio station is having a contest. Each time you call in, your chances of winning are 6%. If you call in 10 times, estimate the probability that you will win more than once.
8. Kyle works at a juice bar. He knows about 45% of the customers by name. Estimate the probability that he will know the names of at least 7 of the next 9 customers.

PRACTICE AND PROBLEM SOLVING

Extra Practice
See page 800.

LINK
Life Science

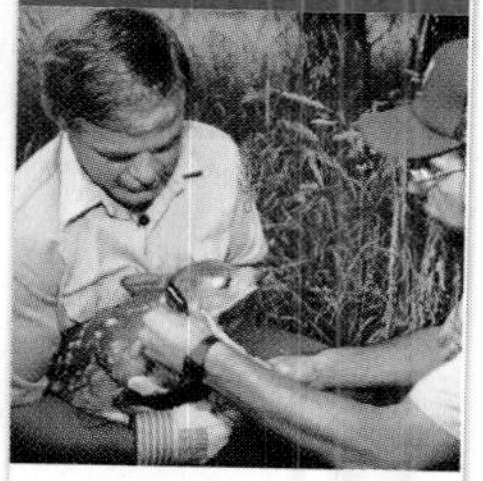

The capture-release-recapture method uses ratios to estimate the size of wild populations.

Use the table of random numbers for Exercises 9 and 10. Use at least 10 trials to simulate each situation.

19067	26149	88557	80696	88246	56652	73023	56838
98048	26387	65953	94163	66233	57325	65618	76782
32958	47253	24960	32052	16921	54925	44766	33115
89164	06342	98577	44523	72304	38221	33506	63923

9. **Entertainment** A radio station plays a song from the 1980s about 60% of the time. What is the probability that at least 4 of the next 5 songs are from the 1980s?

10. **Life Science** About 7% of the deer population in an area was captured, tagged, and released. If 8 deer were randomly captured later, estimate the probability that at least 1 deer would have a tag.

11. **Write About It** A silk screener checks the prints on T-shirts. If 2% of the T-shirts were defective, how could you estimate the probability that no more than 1 T-shirt in each case of 144 would be defective?

12. **Challenge** A box of tulip bulbs has bulbs in 5 colors. The probabilities for each color are given below. Vijay likes red and yellow best. Rosa likes blue and red best. If each chooses 6 bulbs randomly, estimate the probability that they will each get at least one of their favorites.

Color	Red	Yellow	Blue	Orange	Pink
Probability	0.3	0.1	0.3	0.2	0.1

TEST PREP and Spiral Review

13. **Multiple Choice** Diego hit a home run 25% of his times at bat. He wants to estimate his probability of hitting at least 3 home runs during his next 10 at bats. Using a random number table, he performs 10 trials. Of the 10 trials, 2 represented 3 or more home runs. What is the probability that Diego will hit 3 home runs during his next 10 at bats?

(A) 2% (B) 20% (C) 25% (D) 30%

14. **Short Response** In a certain area, 11% of the wolf population is tagged and released. Describe how to use a random number table to determine the probability that at least 2 out of the next 10 wolves caught will be tagged.

Find the appropriate factor for each conversion. (Lesson 5-3)

15. quarts to pints
16. inches to yards
17. millimeters to meters

A spinner was spun 400 times. It landed on red 192 times, blue 144 times, and green 64 times. Estimate the probability of each event. (Lesson 10-2)

18. spinner landing on red
19. spinner landing on green
20. spinner landing on blue

Hands-On LAB 10-3

Use Different Models for Simulations

Use with Lesson 10-3

go.hrw.com
Lab Resources Online
KEYWORD: MT7 Lab10

You can use a simulation to model an experiment that would be difficult to perform.

Activity 1

A cereal company discovered that 1 out of 6 boxes did not contain a prize. Suppose you buy 10 boxes of the cereal. What is the probability that you will buy a cereal box without a prize?

Use a number cube to simulate buying a box of cereal. Let 6 represent a box without a prize and 1–5 represent a box with a prize.

Number Rolled	Frequency
1 (prize)	
2 (prize)	
3 (prize)	
4 (prize)	
5 (prize)	
6 (no prize)	

a. Copy the table. Then roll the number cube 10 times to represent buying 10 boxes of cereal. Tally your results.

b. Find the experimental probability of buying a box without a prize.

Think and Discuss

1. What other methods could you use to simulate this situation? Which methods are best? Explain.

Try This

1. Roll the number cube 100 times. What is the experimental probability of buying a box without a prize? How does this probability compare with your earlier result?

Activity 2

Each Thursday, a radio station randomly plays new releases 50% of the time. What is the probability that 6 of the next 10 songs will be new releases on any given Thursday?

You can use a coin to simulate playing a new release. Let heads represent a new release and tails represent a song that is not a new release.

Trial	Heads (new)	Tails (not new)
1		
2		
3		
4		
5		

a. Copy the table. For each trial, toss the coin 10 times to represent playing 10 songs. Tally your results. Complete 5 trials.

b. In how many trials did heads appear 6 or more times?

c. Find the experimental probability that 6 of the next 10 songs on any given Thursday will be new releases.

Think and Discuss

1. Why is tossing a coin a good way to simulate this situation?
2. What other methods could you use to simulate this situation? Which methods are best? Explain.

Try This

1. Toss the coin 100 times. What is the experimental probability that 6 of the next 10 songs are new releases? How does this probability compare with your earlier result?

Activity 3

Belinda makes 80% of her free throws. What is the probability that she will make 8 out of her next 10 free throws?

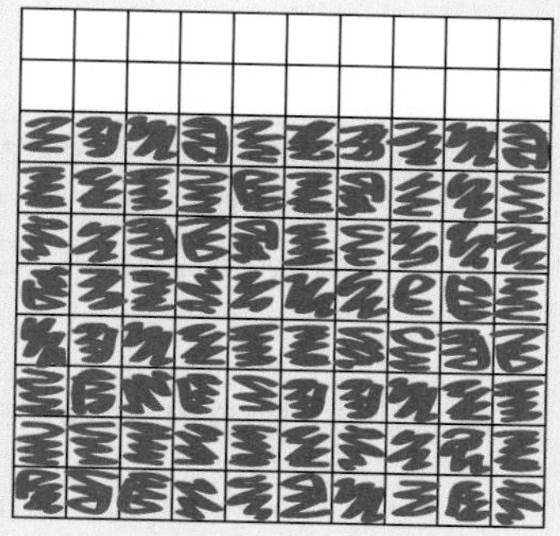

1. You can use an area model to simulate Belinda's shooting a free throw. Color 80 squares on a sheet of 10-by-10 grid paper to represent free throws made. The remaining 20 blank squares will represent free throws missed.
   a. For each trial, flip a dime 10 times onto the grid paper. Do not count a result if the dime does not land completely within the grid. Flip the dime again. If the dime lands completely within the shaded area, count it as a free throw made. If the dime lands in the unshaded area or partly in both the shaded and unshaded areas, count it as a free throw missed. Tally your results. Complete 10 trials.
   b. Find the experimental probability of Belinda's making 8 out of the next 10 free throws.

Think and Discuss

1. What other methods could you use to simulate this situation?
2. Why are 80 squares filled in and 20 squares left blank? Does it matter which 80 squares are filled in? Explain.

Try This

Select and conduct a simulation to find the experimental probability. Explain which method you chose and why.

1. Raul works for a pet groomer. He knows about 70% of the pets from previous visits. Estimate the probability that he will know at least 6 of the next 8 pets that arrive.
2. At a local restaurant, about 50% of the customers order dessert. Estimate the probability that 4 out of the next 10 customers will order dessert.

CHAPTER 10

READY TO GO ON?

SECTION 10A

Quiz for Lessons 10-1 Through 10-3

10-1 Probability

Use the table to find the probability of each event.

Outcome	A	B	C	D
Probability	0.3	0.1	0.4	0.2

1. *P*(C)
2. *P*(not B)
3. *P*(A or D)
4. *P*(A, B, or C)
5. There are 4 students in a race. Jennifer has a 30% chance of winning. Anjelica has the same chance as Jennifer. Debra and Yolanda have equal chances. Create a table of probabilities for the sample space.

10-2 Experimental Probability

A colored chip is randomly drawn from a box and then replaced. The table shows the results after 400 draws.

Outcome	Red	Green	Blue	Yellow
Draws	76	172	84	68

6. Estimate the probability of drawing a red chip.
7. Estimate the probability of drawing a green chip.
8. Use the table to compare the probability of drawing a blue chip to the probability of drawing a yellow chip.

10-3 Use a Simulation

Use the table of random numbers to simulate each situation. Use at least 10 trials for each simulation.

93840	03363	31168	57602	19464	52245	98744	61040
68395	76832	56386	45060	57512	38816	51623	23252
16805	92120	74443	49176	49898	62042	65847	15380
85178	78842	16598	28335	84837	76406	53436	45043

9. At a local school, 58% of the tenth-grade students play a musical instrument. Estimate the probability that at least 6 out of 8 randomly selected tenth-grade students play a musical instrument.
10. Kayla has a package of 100 multicolored beads that contains 15 purple beads. If she randomly selects 8 beads to make a friendship bracelet, estimate the probability that she will get more than 1 purple bead.

Ready to Go On?

Focus on Problem Solving

Understand the Problem

• Understand the words in the problem

Words that you don't understand can make a simple problem seem difficult. Before you try to solve a problem, you will need to know the meaning of the words in it.

If a problem gives a name of a person, place, or thing that is difficult to understand, such as *Eulalia*, you can use another name or a pronoun in its place. You could replace *Eulalia* with *she*.

Read the problems so that you can hear yourself saying the words.

Copy each problem, and circle any words that you do not understand. Look up each word and write its definition, or use context clues to replace the word with a similar word that is easier to understand.

1. A point in the circumscribed triangle is chosen randomly. What is the probability that the point is in the circle?

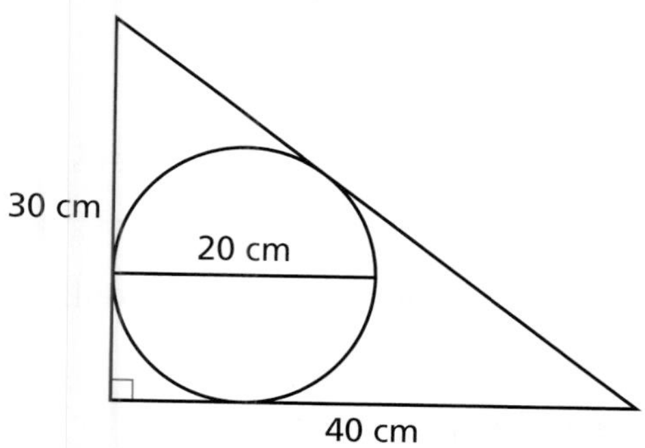

2. A chef observed the number of people ordering each antipasto from the evening's specials. Estimate the probability that the next customer will order gnocchi al veneta.

Antipasto	Saltimbocca Alla Romana	Gnocchi Al Veneta	Galleto Alla Griglia
Number Ordered	16	21	13

3. Evelina and Ilario play chess 3 times a week. They have had 6 stalemates in the last 10 weeks. Estimate the probability that Evelina and Ilario will have a stalemate the next time they play chess.

4. A pula has a coat of arms on the obverse and a running zebra on the reverse. If a pula is tossed 150 times and lands with the coat of arms facing up 70 times, estimate the probability of its landing with the zebra facing up.

10-4 Theoretical Probability

Learn to estimate probability using theoretical methods.

Vocabulary
- theoretical probability
- equally likely
- fair
- mutually exclusive
- disjoint events

In the game of Monopoly®, you can get out of jail if you roll doubles, but if you roll doubles three times in a row, you have to go to jail. Your turn is decided by the probability that both dice will be the same number.

Theoretical probability is used to estimate probabilities by making certain assumptions about an experiment. Suppose a sample space has 5 outcomes that are **equally likely**, that is, they all have the same probability, x. The probabilities must add to 1.

$$x + x + x + x + x = 1$$
$$5x = 1$$
$$x = \frac{1}{5}$$

THEORETICAL PROBABILITY FOR EQUALLY LIKELY OUTCOMES

Suppose there are n equally likely outcomes in the sample space of an experiment.
- The probability of each outcome is $\frac{1}{n}$.
- The probability of an event is $\frac{\text{number of outcomes in the event}}{n}$.

A coin, die, or other object is called **fair** if all outcomes are equally likely.

EXAMPLE 1 Calculating Theoretical Probability

An experiment consists of rolling a fair number cube. Find the probability of each event.

A $P(5)$

The number cube is fair, so all 6 outcomes in the sample space are equally likely: 1, 2, 3, 4, 5, and 6.

$$P(5) = \frac{\text{number of outcomes for 5}}{6} = \frac{1}{6}$$

B **P(even number)**

There are 3 possible even numbers: 2, 4, and 6.

$$P(\text{even number}) = \frac{\text{number of possible even numbers}}{6} = \frac{3}{6} = \frac{1}{2}$$

Suppose you roll two fair number cubes. Are all outcomes equally likely? It depends on how you consider the outcomes. You could look at the number on each number cube or at the total shown on the number cubes.

If you look at the total, all outcomes are not equally likely. For example, there is only one way to get a total of 2, 1 + 1, but a total of 5 can be 1 + 4, 2 + 3, 3 + 2, or 4 + 1.

EXAMPLE 2 Calculating Probability for Two Fair Number Cubes

An experiment consists of rolling two fair number cubes. Find the probability of each event.

A ***P*(total shown = 1)**

First find the sample space that has all outcomes equally likely.

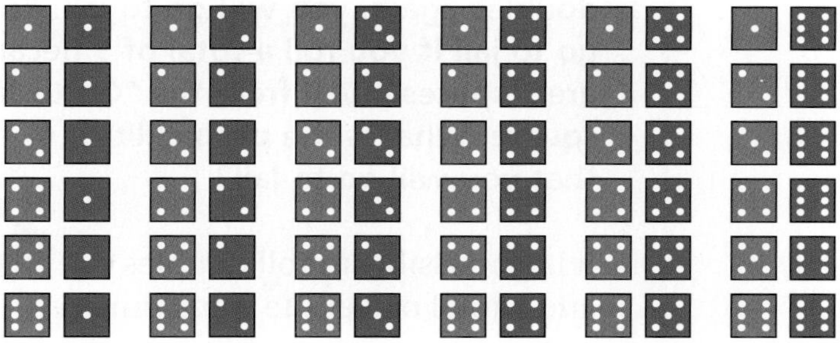

There are 36 possible outcomes in the sample space. Then find the number of outcomes in the event "total shown = 1." There is no way to get a total of 1, so $P(\text{total shown} = 1) = \frac{0}{36} = 0$.

B ***P*(at least one 6)**

There are 11 outcomes in the event rolling "at least one 6":

$P(\text{at least one } 6) = \frac{11}{36}$

Writing Math

You can write the outcome of a red 3 and a blue 6 as the ordered pair (3, 6).

EXAMPLE 3 Altering Probability

A bag contains 5 blue chips and 8 green chips. How many yellow chips should be added so that the probability of drawing a green chip is $\frac{2}{5}$?

Adding chips to the bag will increase the number of possible outcomes. Let x equal the number of yellow chips.

$\frac{8}{13 + x} = \frac{2}{5}$	*Set up a proportion.*
$2(13 + x) = 8(5)$	*Find the cross products.*
$26 + 2x = 40$	*Multiply.*
$-26 \qquad -26$	*Subtract 26 from both sides.*
$\frac{2x}{2} = \frac{14}{2}$	*Divide both sides by 2.*
$x = 7$	

Seven yellow chips should be added to the bag.

Two events are **mutually exclusive**, or **disjoint events**, if they cannot both occur in the same trial of an experiment. For example, rolling a 5 and an even number on a number cube are mutually exclusive events because they cannot both happen at the same time. Suppose A and B are two mutually exclusive events.

- $P(\text{both } A \text{ and } B \text{ will occur}) = 0$
- $P(\text{either } A \text{ or } B \text{ will occur}) = P(A) + P(B)$

EXAMPLE 4

Finding the Probability of Mutually Exclusive Events

Suppose you are playing a game of Monopoly and have just rolled doubles two times in a row. If you roll doubles again, you will go to jail. You will also go to jail if you roll a total of 3 because you are 3 spaces away from the "Go to Jail" square. What is the probability that you will go to jail?

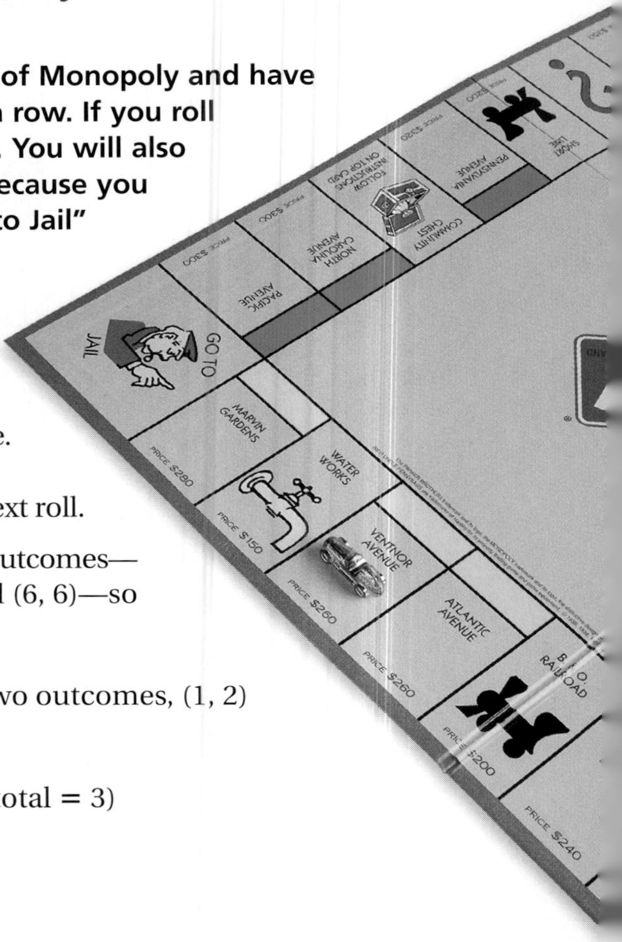

It is impossible to roll doubles and a total of 3 at the same time, so the events are mutually exclusive. Add the probabilities to find the probability of going to jail on the next roll.

The event "doubles" consists of six outcomes—(1, 1), (2, 2), (3, 3), (4, 4), (5, 5), and (6, 6)—so $P(\text{doubles}) = \frac{6}{36}$.

The event "total = 3" consists of two outcomes, (1, 2) and (2, 1), so $P(\text{total of } 3) = \frac{2}{36}$.

$$\begin{aligned} P(\text{going to jail}) &= P(\text{doubles}) + P(\text{total} = 3) \\ &= \frac{6}{36} + \frac{2}{36} \\ &= \frac{8}{36} \end{aligned}$$

The probability of going to jail is $\frac{8}{36} = \frac{2}{9}$, or about 22.2%.

Think and Discuss

1. **Describe** a sample space for tossing two coins that has all outcomes equally likely.
2. **Give an example** of an experiment in which it would not be reasonable to assume that all outcomes are equally likely.

10-4 Exercises

go.hrw.com
Homework Help Online
KEYWORD: MT7 10-4
Parent Resources Online
KEYWORD: MT7 Parent

GUIDED PRACTICE

See Example 1
An experiment consists of rolling a fair number cube. Find the probability of each event.

1. P(odd number)
2. P(2 or 4)

See Example 2
An experiment consists of rolling two fair number cubes. Find the probability of each event.

3. P(total shown = 10)
4. P(rolling two 2's)
5. P(rolling two odd numbers)
6. P(total shown > 8)

See Example 3
7. What color should you shade the blank region so that the probability of the spinner landing on that color is $\frac{1}{2}$?

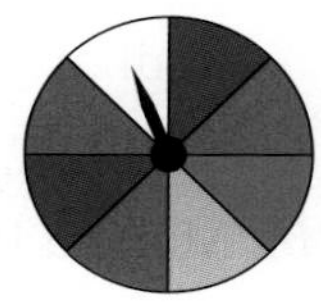

See Example 4
8. Suppose you are playing a game in which two fair dice are rolled. To make the first move, you need to roll doubles or a sum of 3 or 11. What is the probability that you will be able to make the first move?

INDEPENDENT PRACTICE

See Example 1
An experiment consists of rolling a fair number cube. Find the probability of each event.

9. $P(9)$
10. P(not 6)
11. $P(< 5)$
12. $P(> 3)$

See Example 2
An experiment consists of rolling two fair number cubes. Find the probability of each event.

13. P(total shown = 3)
14. P(at least one even number)
15. P(total shown > 0)
16. P(total shown < 9)

See Example 3
17. A bag contains 20 pennies, 25 nickels, and 15 quarters. How many dimes should be added so that the probability of drawing a quarter is $\frac{1}{6}$?

See Example 4
18. Suppose you are playing a game in which two fair dice are rolled. You need 9 to land on the finish by an exact count or 3 to land on a "roll again" space. What is the probability of landing on the finish or rolling again?

PRACTICE AND PROBLEM SOLVING

Extra Practice
See page 800.

Three fair coins are tossed: a penny, a dime, and a quarter. Find the sample space with all outcomes equally likely. Then find each probability.

19. P(TTH)
20. P(THH)
21. P(dime heads)
22. P(exactly 2 tails)
23. P(0 tails)
24. P(at most 1 tail)

Life Science LINK

What color are your eyes? Can you roll your tongue? These traits are determined by the genes you inherited from your parents. A *Punnett square* shows all possible gene combinations for two parents whose genes are known.

To make a Punnett square, draw a two-by-two grid. Write the genes of one parent above the top row and the other parent along the side. Then fill in the grid as shown.

	B	*b*
b	*Bb*	*bb*
b	*Bb*	*bb*

25. In the Punnett square above, one parent has the gene combination *Bb*, which represents one gene for brown eyes and one gene for blue eyes. The other parent has the gene combination *bb*, which represents two genes for blue eyes. If all outcomes in the Punnett square are equally likely, what is the probability of a child with the gene combination *bb*?

26. Make a Punnett square for two parents who both have the gene combination *Bb*.

a. If all outcomes in the Punnett square are equally likely, what is the probability of a child with the gene combination *BB*?

b. The gene combinations *BB* and *Bb* will result in brown eyes, and the gene combination *bb* will result in blue eyes. What is the probability that the couple will have a child with brown eyes?

27. **Challenge** The combinations *Tt* and *TT* represent the ability to roll your tongue, while *tt* means you cannot roll your tongue. Draw a Punnett square that results in a probability of $\frac{1}{2}$ that the child can roll his or her tongue. Explain whether the parents can roll their tongues.

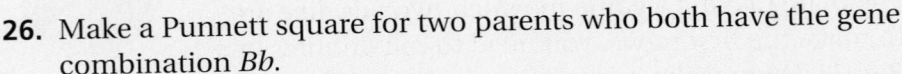

TEST PREP and Spiral Review

28. **Multiple Choice** A bag has 3 red marbles and 6 blue marbles in it. What is the probability of drawing a red marble?

Ⓐ 1 Ⓑ $\frac{2}{3}$ Ⓒ $\frac{1}{3}$ Ⓓ $\frac{1}{2}$

29. **Gridded Response** On a fair number cube, what is the probability, written as a fraction, of rolling a 2 or higher?

Determine whether each ordered pair is a solution of $y = 3x - 2$. (Lesson 3-1)

30. (3, 11) **31.** (0, −2) **32.** (−1, −5) **33.** (−4, 10)

34. Wallace completed 27 of his last 38 passes. Estimate the probability that he will complete his next pass. (Lesson 10-2)

10-5 Independent and Dependent Events

Learn to find the probabilities of independent and dependent events.

Vocabulary

compound event

independent events

dependent events

Skydivers carry two *independent* parachutes. One parachute is the primary parachute, and the other is for emergencies.

A compound **event** is made up of two or more separate events. To find the probability of a compound event, you need to know if the events are independent or dependent.

Events are **independent events** if the occurrence of one event does not affect the probability of the other. Events are **dependent events** if the occurrence of one does affect the probability of the other.

EXAMPLE 1 Classifying Events as Independent or Dependent

Determine if the events are dependent or independent.

A **a coin landing heads on one toss and tails on another toss**

The result of one toss does not affect the result of the other, so the events are independent.

B **drawing a 6 and then a 7 from a deck of cards**

Once one card is drawn, the sample space changes. The events are dependent.

FINDING THE PROBABILITY OF INDEPENDENT EVENTS

If A and B are independent events, then $P(A \text{ and } B) = P(A) \cdot P(B)$.

EXAMPLE 2 Finding the Probability of Independent Events

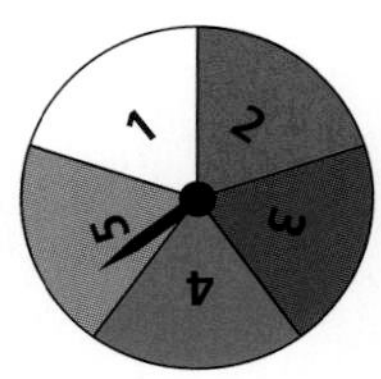

An experiment consists of spinning the spinner 3 times.

A **What is the probability of spinning a 2 all 3 times?**

The result of each spin does not affect the results of the other spins, so the spin results are independent.

For each spin, $P(2) = \frac{1}{5}$.

$P(2, 2, 2) = \frac{1}{5} \cdot \frac{1}{5} \cdot \frac{1}{5} = \frac{1}{125} = 0.008$ *Multiply.*

An experiment consists of spinning the spinner 3 times. For each spin, all outcomes are equally likely.

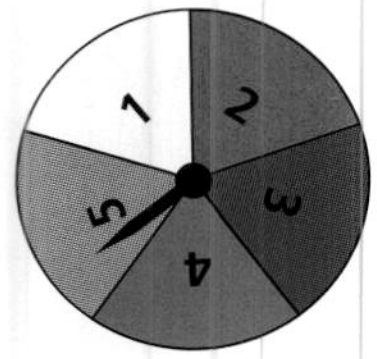

B **What is the probability of spinning an even number all 3 times?**

For each spin, $P(\text{even}) = \frac{2}{5}$.

$P(\text{even, even, even}) = \frac{2}{5} \cdot \frac{2}{5} \cdot \frac{2}{5} = \frac{8}{125} = 0.064$ *Multiply.*

C **What is the probability of spinning a 2 at least once?**

Think: $P(\text{at least one 2}) + P(\text{not 2, not 2, not 2}) = 1$.

For each spin, $P(\text{not 2}) = \frac{4}{5}$.

$P(\text{not 2, not 2, not 2}) = \frac{4}{5} \cdot \frac{4}{5} \cdot \frac{4}{5} = \frac{64}{125} = 0.512$ *Multiply.*

Subtract from 1 to find the probability of spinning at least one 2.

$1 - 0.512 = 0.488$

To calculate the probability of two dependent events occurring, do the following:

1. Calculate the probability of the first event.
2. Calculate the probability that the second event would occur if the first event had already occurred.
3. Multiply the probabilities.

FINDING THE PROBABILITY OF DEPENDENT EVENTS

If A and B are dependent events, then $P(A \text{ and } B) = P(A) \cdot P(B \text{ after } A)$.

Suppose you draw 2 marbles without replacement from a bag that contains 3 purple and 3 orange marbles. On the first draw,

$P(\text{purple}) = \frac{3}{6} = \frac{1}{2}$.

The sample space for the second draw depends on the first draw.

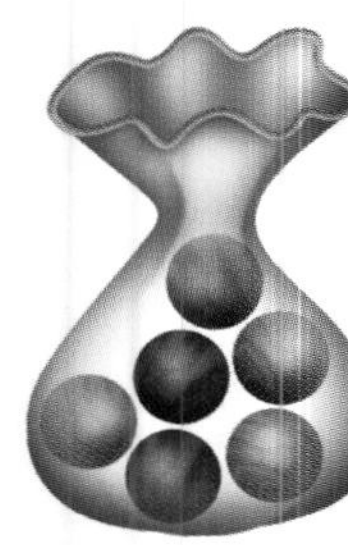

Before first draw

Outcome of first draw	Purple	Orange
Sample space for second draw	2 purple 3 orange	3 purple 2 orange

If the first draw was purple, then the probability of the second draw being purple is

$P(\text{purple}) = \frac{2}{5}$.

So the probability of drawing two purple marbles is

$P(\text{purple, purple}) = \frac{1}{2} \cdot \frac{2}{5} = \frac{1}{5}$.

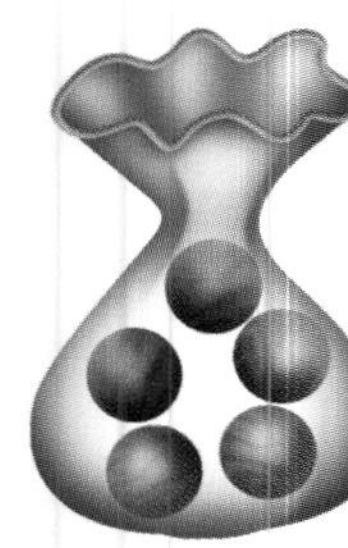

After first draw

EXAMPLE 3 Finding the Probability of Dependent Events

A jar contains 16 quarters and 10 nickels.

A **If 2 coins are chosen at random, what is the probability of getting 2 quarters?**

Because the first coin is not replaced, the sample space is different for the second coin, so the events are dependent. Find the probability that the first coin chosen is a quarter.

$P(\text{quarter}) = \frac{16}{26} = \frac{8}{13}$

If the first coin chosen is a quarter, then there would be 15 quarters and a total of 25 coins left in the jar. Find the probability that the second coin chosen is a quarter.

$P(\text{quarter}) = \frac{15}{25} = \frac{3}{5}$

$\frac{8}{13} \cdot \frac{3}{5} = \frac{24}{65}$ *Multiply.*

The probability of getting two quarters is $\frac{24}{65}$.

B **If 2 coins are chosen at random, what is the probability of getting 2 coins that are the same?**

There are two possibilities: 2 quarters or 2 nickels. The probability of 2 quarters was calculated in Example 3A. Now find the probability of getting 2 nickels.

$P(\text{nickel}) = \frac{10}{26} = \frac{5}{13}$ *Find the probability that the second coin chosen is a nickel.*

If the first coin chosen is a nickel, there are now only 9 nickels and 25 total coins in the jar.

$P(\text{nickel}) = \frac{9}{25}$ *Find the probability that the second coin chosen is a nickel.*

$\frac{5}{13} \cdot \frac{9}{25} = \frac{9}{65}$ *Multiply.*

The events of 2 quarters and 2 nickels are mutually exclusive, so you can add their probabilities.

$\frac{24}{65} + \frac{9}{65} = \frac{33}{65}$ *P(quarters) + P(nickels)*

The probability of getting 2 coins the same is $\frac{33}{65}$.

Remember!

Two mutually exclusive events cannot both happen at the same time.

Think and Discuss

1. **Give an example** of a pair of independent events and a pair of dependent events.
2. **Tell** how you could make the events in Example 1B independent events.

10-5 Exercises

go.hrw.com
Homework Help Online
KEYWORD: MT7 10-5
Parent Resources Online
KEYWORD: MT7 Parent

GUIDED PRACTICE

See Example 1

Determine if the events are dependent or independent.

1. drawing a red and a blue marble at the same time from a bag containing 6 red and 4 blue marbles
2. drawing a heart from a deck of cards and a coin landing on tails

See Example 2

An experiment consists of spinning each spinner once.

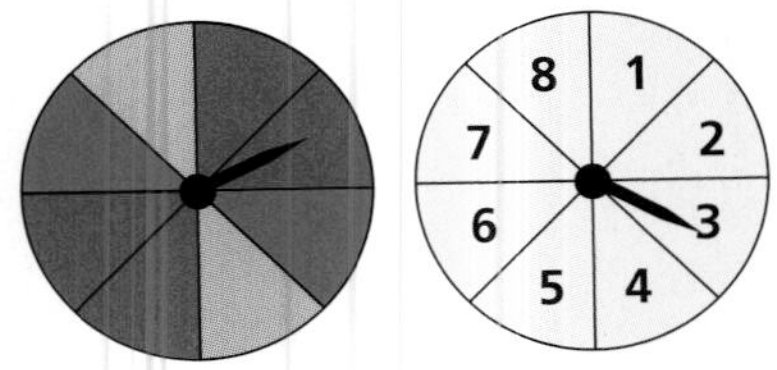

3. Find the probability that the first spinner lands on yellow and the second spinner lands on 8.

See Example 3

A sock drawer contains 10 white socks, 6 black socks, and 8 blue socks.

4. If 2 socks are chosen at random, what is the probability of getting a pair of white socks?
5. If 3 socks are chosen at random, what is the probability of getting first a black sock, then a white sock, and then a blue sock?

INDEPENDENT PRACTICE

See Example 1

Determine if the events are dependent or independent.

6. drawing the name Roberto from a hat without replacing it and then drawing the name Paulo from the hat
7. rolling 2 fair number cubes and getting both a 1 and a 6

See Example 2

An experiment consists of tossing 2 fair coins, a penny and a nickel.

8. Find the probability of heads on the penny and tails on the nickel.
9. Find the probability that both coins will land the same way.

See Example 3

A box contains 4 berry, 3 cinnamon, 4 apple, and 5 carob granola bars.

10. If Dawn randomly selects 2 bars, what is the probability that they will both be cinnamon?
11. If two bars are selected randomly, what is the probability that they will be the same kind?

PRACTICE AND PROBLEM SOLVING

Extra Practice
See page 801.

A box contains 6 red marbles, 4 blue marbles, and 8 yellow marbles.

12. Find *P*(yellow then red) if a marble is selected, and then a second marble is selected without replacing the first marble.
13. Find *P*(yellow then red) if a marble is selected, and replaced, and then a second marble is selected.

14. You roll a fair number cube twice. What is the probability of rolling two 3's if the first roll is a 5? Explain.

15. School On a quiz, there are 5 true-false questions. A student guesses on all 5 questions. What is the probability that the student gets all 5 questions right?

Games

This giant Scrabble game was held on the 50th anniversary of Scrabble. Each tile was 100 times the size of a standard tile, and the board was nearly 100 ft by 100 ft.

16. Games The table shows the Scrabble® tiles available at the start of a game. There are 100 tiles: 42 vowels, 56 consonants, and 2 blanks. To begin play, each player draws a tile. The player with the tile closest to the beginning of the alphabet goes first. A blank tile beats any letter.

Scrabble Letter Distribution		
A-9	B-2	C-2
D-4	E-12	F-2
G-3	H-2	I-9
J-1	K-1	L-4
M-2	N-6	O-8
P-2	Q-1	R-6
S-4	T-6	U-4
V-2	W-2	X-1
Y-2	Z-1	blank-2

a. If you draw first, what is the probability that you will select an *A*?

b. If you draw first and do not replace the tile, what is the probability that you will select an *E* and your opponent will select an *I*?

c. If you draw first and do not replace the tile, what is the probability that you will select an *E* and your opponent will win the first turn?

17. Write a Problem Write a problem about the probability of an event in a board game, and then solve it.

18. Write About It In an experiment, two cards are drawn from a deck. How is the probability different if the first card is replaced before the second card is drawn than if the first card is not replaced?

19. Challenge Suppose you deal yourself 7 cards from a standard 52-card deck. What is the probability that you will deal all red cards?

Test Prep and Spiral Review

20. Multiple Choice If *A* and *B* are independent events such that $P(A) = 0.14$ and $P(B) = 0.28$, what is the probability that both *A* and *B* will occur?

Ⓐ 0.0392 Ⓑ 0.0784 Ⓒ 0.24 Ⓓ 0.42

21. Gridded Response A bag contains 8 red marbles and 2 blue marbles. What is the probability, written as a fraction, of choosing a red marble and a blue marble from the bag at the same time?

Find the first and third quartiles for each data set. (Lesson 9-4)

22. 19, 24, 13, 18, 21, 8, 11

23. 56, 71, 84, 66, 52, 11, 80

24. An experiment consists of rolling two fair number cubes. Find the probability of rolling a total of 14. (Lesson 10-4)

10-6 Making Decisions and Predictions

Learn to use probability to make decisions and predictions.

Aliza works for a store that sells socks. She conducted a survey to learn about color preferences. She recorded the colors of the last 100 pairs of socks sold. Aliza can use the results of her survey to decide how many pairs of socks of each color to order from the maker.

Probability can be used to make decisions or predictions. Use the probability of an event's occurring to set up a proportion to find the number of times an event is likely to occur.

EXAMPLE 1 Using Probability to Make Decisions and Predictions

A The table shows the colors of the last 100 pairs of socks sold. Aliza plans to place an order for 1200 pairs of socks. How many blue pairs of socks should she order?

Pairs of Socks Sold	
Color	**Number**
Black	9
Blue	20
Gold	6
Green	22
Purple	25
Red	18

$\frac{\text{number of blue pairs of socks sold}}{\text{total number of pairs of socks sold}} = \frac{20}{100}, \text{ or } \frac{1}{5}$ *Find the probability of selling a blue pair of socks.*

$\frac{1}{5} = \frac{n}{1200}$ *Set up a proportion.*

$1 \cdot 1200 = 5n$ *Find the cross products.*

$\frac{1200}{5} = \frac{5n}{5}$ *Divide both sides by n.*

$240 = n$

Aliza should order 240 blue pairs of socks.

B **At a carnival, a spinner is used to determine a player's prize. If the spinner lands on red, the player gets a stuffed animal. Suppose the spinner is spun 160 times. What is the best prediction of the number of stuffed animals that will be given away?**

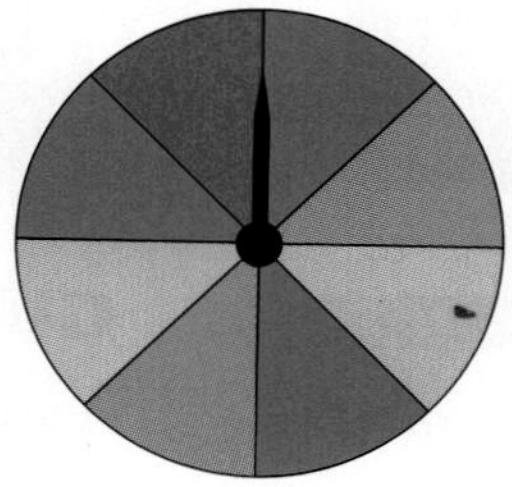

$\frac{\text{number of possible red outcomes}}{\text{total possible outcomes}} = \frac{1}{8}$ — *Find the theoretical probability of spinning red.*

$\frac{1}{8} = \frac{n}{160}$ — *Set up a proportion.*

$1 \cdot 160 = 8n$ — *Find the cross products.*

$\frac{160}{8} = \frac{8n}{8}$ — *Divide both sides by 8.*

$20 = n$

Approximately 20 stuffed animals will be given away.

Probability is often used to determine whether a game is fair. A game involving chance is fair if each player is equally likely to win.

EXAMPLE 2 Deciding Whether a Game Is Fair

In a game, two players each roll two fair dice and add the two numbers. Player A wins with a sum of 6 or less. Otherwise player B wins. Decide whether the game is fair.

List all possible outcomes.

$1 + 1 = 2$	$2 + 1 = 3$	$3 + 1 = 4$	$4 + 1 = 5$	$5 + 1 = 6$	$6 + 1 = 7$
$1 + 2 = 3$	$2 + 2 = 4$	$3 + 2 = 5$	$4 + 2 = 6$	$5 + 2 = 7$	$6 + 2 = 8$
$1 + 3 = 4$	$2 + 3 = 5$	$3 + 3 = 6$	$4 + 3 = 7$	$5 + 3 = 8$	$6 + 3 = 9$
$1 + 4 = 5$	$2 + 4 = 6$	$3 + 4 = 7$	$4 + 4 = 8$	$5 + 4 = 9$	$6 + 4 = 10$
$1 + 5 = 6$	$2 + 5 = 7$	$3 + 5 = 8$	$4 + 5 = 9$	$5 + 5 = 10$	$6 + 5 = 11$
$1 + 6 = 7$	$2 + 6 = 8$	$3 + 6 = 9$	$4 + 6 = 10$	$5 + 6 = 11$	$6 + 6 = 12$

Find the theoretical probability of each player's winning.

$P(\text{player A winning}) = \frac{15}{36}$ — *There are 15 combinations with a sum of 6 or less*

$P(\text{player B winning}) = \frac{21}{36}$ — *There are 21 combinations with a sum greater than 6.*

Since $\frac{15}{36} \neq \frac{21}{36}$, the game is not fair.

Think and Discuss

1. Give an example of a game that is fair. Explain how you know.

10-6 Exercises

go.hrw.com
Homework Help Online
KEYWORD: MT7 10-6
Parent Resources Online
KEYWORD: MT7 Parent

GUIDED PRACTICE

See Example 1

A store sells cases to hold CDs. The table shows the capacities of the last 200 cases sold. The store is going to order 1500 more CD cases. Use probability to decide how many of each type of case to order.

CD Cases Sold	
Capacity	**Number**
24 CDs	70
32 CDs	13
64 CDs	24
96 CDs	52
160 CDs	41

1. 24-CD case
2. 96-CD case
3. Players use a spinner to move around a game board. Suppose the spinner is spun 40 times. Predict how many times the spinner will land on "Get a Clue!"

See Example 2

Decide whether each game is fair.

4. Roll two fair number cubes labeled 1–6. Add the two numbers. Player A wins if the sum is odd. Player B wins if the sum is even.
5. Toss three fair coins. Player A wins if exactly 2 heads land up. Otherwise Player B wins.

INDEPENDENT PRACTICE

See Example 1

6. In her last ten 10K runs, Celia had the following times in minutes: 50:30, 50:37, 48:29, 50:46, 51:12, 49:19, 49:50, 51:19, 53:39, and 53:54. Based on these results, what is the best prediction of the number of times Celia will run faster than 50 minutes in her next 30 runs?
7. Football games begin with a coin toss to decide who kicks off and who receives. The Cougars won the coin toss in their first 2 games. Predict how many coin tosses the Cougars will win in their next 10 games.

See Example 2

Decide whether each game is fair.

8. Roll two fair number cubes labeled 1–6. Add the two numbers. Player A wins if the sum is a multiple of 3. Otherwise Player B wins.
9. A spinner is divided evenly into 8 sections. There are 4 blue sections, 2 red, 1 green, and 1 yellow. Player A wins if the spinner lands on blue. Otherwise Player B wins.

PRACTICE AND PROBLEM SOLVING

Extra Practice
See page 801.

A fair number cube is labeled 1–6. Predict the number of outcomes for the given number of rolls.

10. outcome: 3
    number of rolls: 36
11. outcome: even number
    number of rolls: 50
12. outcome: not 2
    number of rolls: 72
13. outcome: greater than 6
    number of rolls: 100

14. **School** Before a school election, a sample of voters gave Karim 28 votes, Marisol 41, and Richard 11. Based on these results, predict the number of votes for each candidate if 1600 students vote.

15. **Critical Thinking** Jack suggested the following game to Charlie: "Let's roll two dice. We'll subtract the smaller number from the larger. If the difference is 0, 1, or 2, I get a point. If the difference is 3, 4, or 5, you get a point." Charlie thought the game sounded fair. Decide whether Charlie was correct. If he was not, describe a way to make the game fair.

16. **Estimation** An ice-skating rink inspects 23 pairs of skates and finds 2 pairs to be defective. Estimate the probability that a pair of skates chosen at random will be defective. The rink has 121 pairs of ice skates. Estimate the number of pairs that are likely to be defective.

17. **School** There are 540 students in Marla's school. In her classroom, there are 2 left-handed students and 18 right-handed students. Predict the number of left-handed students in the whole school.

18. **Write a Problem** Use sports statistics from the newspaper or Internet to write a prediction problem using probability.

19. **Write About It** If you make a prediction based on experimental probability, how accurate will your prediction be?

20. **Challenge** A bag contains 10 number tiles labeled 1–10. Which 2 number tiles would you remove from the bag to increase the chances of the following events: drawing an even tile, drawing a multiple of 3, and drawing a number less than 5? Explain.

Test Prep and Spiral Review

21. **Multiple Choice** In a survey of 500 potential voters, Susan Wilson was picked by 182 people, Anthony Altimuro by 96, Laura Carson by 128, and Paul Johannson by 94. In the actual election, which is the best estimate of the percent of votes Anthony Altimuro can expect to receive?

    (A) 19% (B) 24% (C) 48% (D) 96%

22. **Short Answer** A game consists of spinning the spinner twice and adding the results. Player A wins if the sum is 4. Otherwise Player B wins. Decide whether the game is fair.

Find the area of each figure with the given dimensions. (Lesson 8-2)

23. triangle: $b = 26$, $h = 16$

24. trapezoid: $b_1 = 14$, $b_2 = 18$, $h = 9$

25. triangle: $b = 10m$, $h = 8$

26. trapezoid: $b_1 = 6.2$, $b_2 = 11$, $h = 5.4$

27. A company manufactures a toy cube that is 4 in. on each edge. If the length of each edge is doubled, what will be the effect on the volume of the cube? (Lesson 8-5)

10-7 Odds

Learn to convert between probabilities and odds.

Vocabulary

odds in favor

odds against

Schools often sell raffle tickets as a way to raise money. Family and friends buy the tickets and have a chance to win a prize. The odds of winning depend on the number of tickets sold and the number of prizes raffled.

The **odds in favor** of an event is the ratio of favorable outcomes to unfavorable outcomes. The **odds against** an event is the ratio of unfavorable outcomes to favorable outcomes.

odds in favor	$a:b$	a = number of favorable outcomes b = number of unfavorable outcomes $a + b$ = total number of outcomes
odds against	$b:a$	

EXAMPLE 1 Finding Odds

Jordan Middle School sold 552 raffle tickets for the chance to be a teacher for the day. Minnie bought 6 raffle tickets.

A **What are the odds in favor of Minnie's winning the raffle?**

The number of favorable outcomes is 6, and the number of unfavorable outcomes is $552 - 6 = 546$. Minnie's odds in favor of winning the raffle are 6 to 546, or 1 to 91.

B **What are the odds against Minnie's winning the raffle?**

The odds in favor of Minnie's winning are 1 to 91, so the odds against her winning are 91 to 1.

Probability and odds are related. The odds in favor of rolling a two on a fair number cube are 1:5. There is 1 way to get a two and 5 ways not to get a two. The sum of the numbers in the ratio is the denominator of the probability, $\frac{1}{6}$.

CONVERTING ODDS TO PROBABILITIES

If the odds in favor of an event are $a:b$, then the probability of the event's occurring is $\frac{a}{a + b}$.

EXAMPLE 2 Converting Odds to Probabilities

A **If the odds in favor of winning movie passes are 1:10, what is the probability of winning movie passes?**

$P(\text{movie passes}) = \frac{1}{1 + 10} = \frac{1}{11}$

On average, there is 1 win for every 10 losses, so someone wins 1 out of every 11 times.

B **If the odds against winning a flat-screen television are 39,999:1, what is the probability of winning a flat-screen television?**

If the odds against winning the television are 39,999:1, then the odds in favor of winning the television are 1:39,999.

$P(\text{television}) = \frac{1}{1 + 39{,}999} = \frac{1}{40{,}000} = 0.000025$

Suppose that the probability of an event is $\frac{1}{3}$. This means that, on average, it will happen in 1 out of every 3 trials, and it will not happen in 2 out of every 3 trials. The odds in favor of the event are 1:2, and the odds against the event are 2:1.

CONVERTING PROBABILITIES TO ODDS

If the probability of an event is $\frac{m}{n}$, then the odds in favor of the event are $m{:}(n - m)$ and the odds against the event are $(n - m){:}m$.

EXAMPLE 3 Converting Probabilities to Odds

A **The probability of winning a CD player is $\frac{1}{75}$. What are the odds in favor of winning a CD player?**

On average, 1 out of every 75 people wins, and the other 74 people lose. The odds in favor of winning the CD player are 1:(75 − 1), or 1:74.

B **The probability of winning an electric scooter is $\frac{1}{125{,}000}$. What are the odds against winning a scooter?**

On average, 1 out of every 125,000 people wins, and the other 124,999 people lose. The odds against winning the scooter are (125,000 − 1):1, or 124,999:1.

Think and Discuss

1. Explain the difference between probability and odds.

2. Compare the odds in favor of an event with the odds against it.

10-7 Exercises

go.hrw.com
Homework Help Online
KEYWORD: MT7 10-7
Parent Resources Online
KEYWORD: MT7 Parent

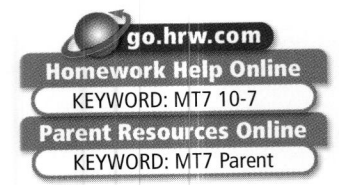

GUIDED PRACTICE

See Example 1

Monroe Middle School is holding a raffle for a new bicycle. Jonathan bought 7 of the 945 tickets that were sold.

1. What are the odds in favor of Jonathan's winning the raffle?
2. What are the odds against Jonathan's winning the raffle?

See Example 2

3. If the odds in favor of winning a trip for two to Hawaii are 1:141,999, what is the probability of winning the trip?
4. If the odds against winning a digital camera are 25,999:1, what is the probability of winning the camera?

See Example 3

5. The probability of winning a CD is $\frac{1}{80}$. What are the odds in favor of winning the CD?
6. The probability of winning a vacation is $\frac{1}{22{,}750}$. What are the odds against winning the vacation?

INDEPENDENT PRACTICE

See Example 1

A teachers' convention is giving away a new computer as a door prize. Each of the 2240 attendees is given 5 tickets for chances to win the computer.

7. What are the odds in favor of winning the computer?
8. What are the odds against winning the computer?

See Example 2

9. If the odds in favor of winning a new portable music player are 1:8999, what is the probability of winning the player?
10. If the odds against being randomly selected for a committee are 19:1, what is the probability of being selected?

See Example 3

11. The probability of winning a gift certificate is $\frac{1}{620}$. What are the odds in favor of winning the gift certificate?
12. The probability of winning a portable DVD player is $\frac{1}{12{,}000}$. What are the odds against winning the player?

PRACTICE AND PROBLEM SOLVING

Extra Practice
See page 801.

You roll two fair number cubes. Find the odds in favor of and against each event.

13. rolling two 1's
14. rolling a total of 6
15. rolling a total of 4
16. rolling doubles
17. rolling an odd and an even number
18. rolling a 5 and a 3
19. The probability of choosing a black card from a standard deck is 50%. What are the odds in favor of choosing a black card?

20. **Earth Science** A newspaper reports that there is a 70% probability of an earthquake of magnitude 6.7 or greater striking the San Francisco Bay Area by 2030. What are the odds in favor of the earthquake's happening?

21. Ruben and Manuel play dominoes twice a week. Over the last 12 weeks, Ruben has won 16 times. Estimate the odds in favor of Manuel's winning the next match.

22. **Business** To promote sales, a cereal company is putting game pieces inside 2,000,000 of its cereal boxes. Of these pieces, 50 win a DVD player, and 10 win a trip to New York City.
    a. What are the odds in favor of winning a DVD player?
    b. What is the probability of winning a prize in the contest?
    c. What are the odds against winning a prize in the contest?

23. **Critical Thinking** Suppose you are in two contests that are independent of each other. You are given the odds of winning one at 1:4 and the odds of winning the other at 3:20. How would you find the odds of winning both?

24. **What's the Error?** A company receives 6 applications for one job. All of the candidates are equally likely to be selected for the job. One of the candidates figures that the odds in favor of her being selected are 1:6. What error has the candidate made?

25. **Write About It** A computer randomly selects a digit from 0 to 9. Describe how to determine the odds that the number selected will be greater than 6.

26. **Challenge** A spinner has three outcomes, regions A, B, or C. Region A is twice as large as regions B or C. Regions B and C have the same size. Find the odds in favor of the spinner landing on A.

Test Prep and Spiral Review

27. **Multiple Choice** The probability of winning a raffle is $\frac{1}{1200}$. What are the odds in favor of winning the raffle?

    (A) 1:1200 (B) 1:1199 (C) 1199:1 (D) 1200:1

28. **Gridded Response** The odds of winning a bicycle is 1:149. What is the probability, written as a fraction, of winning a bicycle?

Find the interest and the total amount to the nearest cent. (Lesson 6-7)

29. \$300 at 5% per year for 2 years
30. \$750 at 4.5% per year for 4 years

31. Toss two fair coins. Player A wins if the coins land with two heads or two tails facing up. Otherwise, Player B wins. Decide whether the game is fair.

10-8 Counting Principles

Learn to find the number of possible outcomes in an experiment.

Vocabulary

Fundamental Counting Principle

tree diagram

Addition Counting Principle

© Scott Adams/Dist. by United Feature Syndicate, Inc.

The demand for new telephone numbers is exploding as people are using extra phone lines, cellular phones, pagers, computer modems, and fax machines. To meet the demand, state regulators are adding new area codes.

Phone numbers have ten digits beginning with the three-digit area code. This results in over a billion possible phone numbers!

THE FUNDAMENTAL COUNTING PRINCIPLE

If there are m ways to choose a first item and n ways to choose a second item after the first item has been chosen, then there are $m \cdot n$ ways to choose all the items.

EXAMPLE 1 Using the Fundamental Counting Principle

A telephone company is assigned a new area code and can issue new 7-digit phone numbers. All phone numbers are equally likely.

A **Find the number of possible 7-digit phone numbers.**

Use the Fundamental Counting Principle.

first digit	second digit	third digit	fourth digit	fifth digit	sixth digit	seventh digit
?	?	?	?	?	?	?
10 choices	10 choices	10 choices	10 choices	10 choices	10 choices	10 choices

$10 \cdot 10 \cdot 10 \cdot 10 \cdot 10 \cdot 10 \cdot 10 = 10{,}000{,}000$

The number of possible 7-digit phone numbers is 10,000,000.

B **Find the probability of being assigned the phone number 555-1234.**

$$P(555\text{-}1234) = \frac{1}{\text{number of possible phone numbers}}$$

$$= \frac{1}{10{,}000{,}000}$$

$$= 0.0000001$$

A telephone company is assigned a new area code and can issue new 7-digit phone numbers. All phone numbers are equally likely.

C **Find the probability of a phone number that does not contain an 8.**

First use the Fundamental Counting Principle to find the number of phone numbers that do not contain an 8.

$9 \cdot 9 \cdot 9 \cdot 9 \cdot 9 \cdot 9 \cdot 9 = 4{,}782{,}969$ possible phone numbers without an 8

There are 9 choices for any digit except 8.

$$P(\text{no } 8) = \frac{4{,}782{,}969}{10{,}000{,}000} \approx 0.478$$

The Fundamental Counting Principle tells you only the *number* of outcomes in some experiments, not what the outcomes are. A **tree diagram** is a way to show all of the possible outcomes.

EXAMPLE 2 Using a Tree Diagram

You pack 2 pairs of pants, 3 shirts, and 2 sweaters for your vacation. Describe all of the outfits you can make if each outfit consists of a pair of pants, a shirt, and a sweater.

You can find all of the possible outcomes by making a tree diagram. There should be $2 \cdot 3 \cdot 2 = 12$ different outfits.

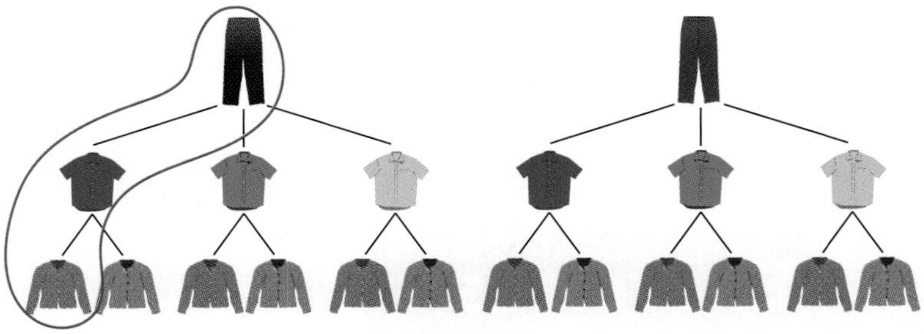

Each "branch" of the tree diagram represents a different outfit. The outfit shown in the circled branch could be written as (black, red, gray). The other outfits are as follows:
(black, red, tan), (black, green, gray), (black, green, tan),
(black, yellow, gray), (black, yellow, tan),
(blue, red, gray), (blue, red, tan), (blue, green, gray),
(blue, green, tan), (blue, yellow, gray), (blue, yellow, tan).

THE ADDITION COUNTING PRINCIPLE

If one group contains m objects and a second group contains n objects, and the groups have no objects in common, then there are $m + n$ total objects to choose from.

EXAMPLE 3 Using the Addition Counting Principle

How many items can you choose from Bergen's Deli menu?

Bergen's Deli Menu		
Sandwiches	**Salads**	**Soups**
Turkey Ham Roast Beef Rueben	Cobb Salad Taco Salad Grilled Chicken Salad	Tomato Chicken Noodle Split Pea

None of the lists contains identical items, so use the Addition Counting Principle.

Total Choices = **Sandwiches** + **Salads** + **Soups**

$$T = 4 + 3 + 3 = 10$$

There are 10 items to choose from.

Think and Discuss

1. **Suppose** in Example 2 you could pack one more item. Which would you bring, another shirt or another pair of pants? Explain.

10-8 Exercises

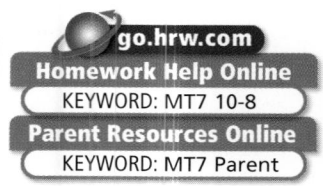

go.hrw.com
Homework Help Online
KEYWORD: MT7 10-8
Parent Resources Online
KEYWORD: MT7 Parent

GUIDED PRACTICE

See Example 1

Employee identification codes at a company contain 2 letters followed by 3 digits. All codes are equally likely.

1. Find the number of possible identification codes.
2. Find the probability of being assigned the ID *AB*123.
3. Find the probability that an ID code does not contain the number 5.

See Example 2

4. The soup choices at a restaurant are clam chowder, baked potato, and split pea. The sandwich choices are egg salad, roast beef, and pastrami. Describe all of the different soup and sandwich options available.

See Example 3

5. Fahti checked out 3 mysteries, 3 historical fiction books, and 2 biographies from the library. How many choices of books does she have to read?

INDEPENDENT PRACTICE

See Example 1

License plates in a certain state contain 3 letters followed by 4 digits. Assume that all combinations are equally likely.

6. Find the number of possible license plates.
7. Find the probability of not being assigned a plate containing *C* or *D*.
8. Find the probability of receiving a plate containing no vowels (*A, E, I, O, U*).

See Example 2

9. A clothing catalog offers a shirt in red, blue, yellow, or green, with a choice of petite or regular, and in small, medium, or large sizes. Describe all of the different shirts that are available.
10. There are 3 ways to travel from Los Angeles to San Francisco (car, train, or plane) and 2 ways to travel from San Francisco to Honolulu (plane or boat). Describe all the ways a person can travel from Los Angeles to Honolulu with a stopover in San Francisco.

See Example 3

11. A company makes cell phone face plates. It offers 6 solid colors, 6 prints, and 6 transparent colors. How many different face plates does the company offer?

PRACTICE AND PROBLEM SOLVING

Extra Practice
See page 801.

Find the number of possible outcomes.

12. dogs: terrier, retriever, hound, poodle
toys: bone, ball
13. sausage: Polish, bratwurst, chicken apple
condiment: ketchup, mustard, relish
14. car: sedan, coupe, minivan
color: red, blue, white, black
15. destinations: Paris, London, Rome
months: May, June, July, August
16. An airline confirmation code is 6 letters that can repeat. How many confirmation codes are possible?
17. A personal code for an online account must be 6 characters, either letters or numbers, which can repeat. How many codes are possible?
18. A car model is sold in 6 colors, with or without air conditioning, with or without a moon roof, and with either automatic or standard transmission. In how many different ways can this car model be sold?
19. Sarah needs to register for one course in each of the six subject areas. The school offers 5 math courses, 4 foreign language courses, 3 science courses, 3 English courses, 5 social studies courses, and 6 elective courses. In how many ways can she register?
20. A computer password consists of 4 letters. The password is case sensitive, which means upper-case and lower-case letters are different characters. What is the probability of randomly being assigned the password YarN?

LINK

Technology

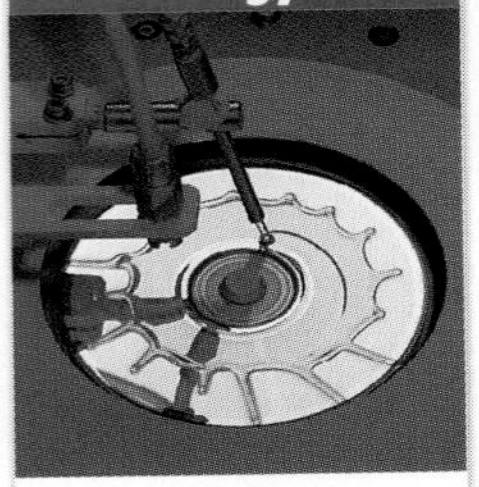

In the process of spin-coating a CD-ROM, the disc is rotated at high speeds. This process is used to apply layers as thin as $\frac{1}{8}$ of a micron, which is 640 times thinner than a human hair.

21. **Technology** Tim is buying a new computer from an online store. His options are shown at right. He can choose a color, one software package, and one hardware option.
    a. How many computer choices are available?
    b. Tim decides he wants a red computer. Describe all of the choices available to him.

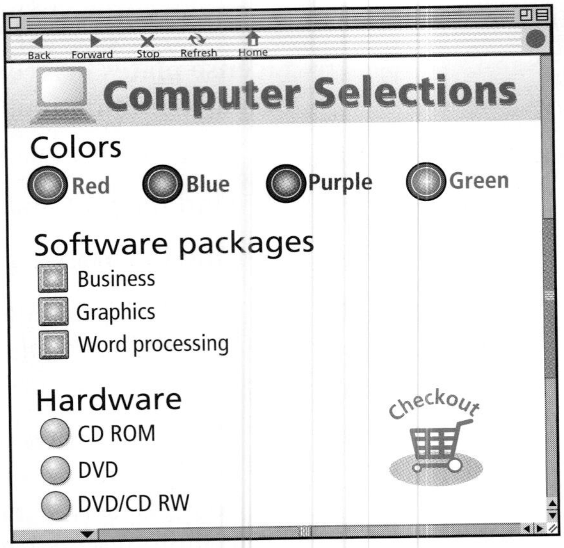

22. **Write About It** Describe when you would want to use the Fundamental Counting Principle instead of a tree diagram. Describe when a tree diagram would be more useful than the Fundamental Counting Principle.

23. **Challenge** A password can have letters, numerals, or 32 other special symbols in each of its 6-character spaces. There are two restrictions. The password cannot begin with a special symbol or 0, and it cannot end with a vowel (*A, E, I, O, U*). Find the total number of passwords.

TEST PREP and Spiral Review

24. **Multiple Choice** Lynnwood High School requires all staff members to have a 6-character computer password that contains 2 letters and 4 numbers. Find the number of possible passwords.

    (A) 2,600,000 (B) 6,760,000 (C) 17,576,000 (D) 45,697,600

25. **Gridded Response** A password contains 3 letters from the alphabet and 2 digits (0–9). Find the probability, written as a decimal, of NOT having a password with a *B* or *D*.

Evaluate each expression. (Lesson 4-5)

26. $\sqrt{121} + \sqrt{25}$ 27. $(4 + 3)^2$ 28. $\overline{\sqrt{441}}$ 29. $\sqrt{5^2 + 12^2}$

Use the table of random numbers to answer the following question. Use at least 10 trials to simulate the situation. (Lesson 10-3)

82	78	3	56	86	14	96	96	46	23	62	28	75	61	64	6	30
4	12	62	54	98	30	94	11	46	22	24	55	89	92	41	79	15
58	69	73	19	73	95	45	26	39	37	91	57	90	19	7	38	44

30. At a local restaurant, 45% of the customers order spaghetti. Estimate the probability that 6 of the next 10 customers will order spaghetti.

10-9 Permutations and Combinations

Learn to find permutations and combinations.

Vocabulary
factorial
permutation
combination

Most MP3 players have a shuffle feature that allows you to play songs in a random order. You can use *factorials* to find out how many song orders are possible.

The **factorial** of a number is the product of all the whole numbers from the number down to 1. The factorial of 0 is defined to be 1.

$$5! = 5 \cdot 4 \cdot 3 \cdot 2 \cdot 1 = 120$$

EXAMPLE 1 **Evaluating Expressions Containing Factorials**

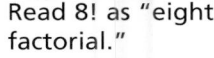

Reading Math
Read 8! as "eight factorial."

Evaluate each expression.

A **8!**

$8 \cdot 7 \cdot 6 \cdot 5 \cdot 4 \cdot 3 \cdot 2 \cdot 1 = 40{,}320$

B $\frac{7!}{4!}$

$\frac{7 \cdot 6 \cdot 5 \cdot \cancel{4} \cdot \cancel{3} \cdot \cancel{2} \cdot \cancel{1}}{\cancel{4} \cdot \cancel{3} \cdot \cancel{2} \cdot \cancel{1}}$ *Write out each factorial and simplify.*

$7 \cdot 6 \cdot 5 = 210$ *Multiply remaining factors.*

C $\frac{14!}{(11 - 4)!}$ *Subtract within parentheses.*

$\frac{14!}{7!}$

$\frac{14 \cdot 13 \cdot 12 \cdot 11 \cdot 10 \cdot 9 \cdot 8 \cdot \cancel{7} \cdot \cancel{6} \cdot \cancel{5} \cdot \cancel{4} \cdot \cancel{3} \cdot \cancel{2} \cdot \cancel{1}}{\cancel{7} \cdot \cancel{6} \cdot \cancel{5} \cdot \cancel{4} \cdot \cancel{3} \cdot \cancel{2} \cdot \cancel{1}}$

$14 \cdot 13 \cdot 12 \cdot 11 \cdot 10 \cdot 9 \cdot 8 = 17{,}297{,}280$

A **permutation** is an arrangement of things in a certain order.

If no letter can be used more than once, there are 6 permutations of the first 3 letters of the alphabet: *ABC, ACB, BAC, BCA, CAB,* and *CBA.*

first letter		second letter		third letter
?		?		?
3 choices	$\cdot$	2 choices	$\cdot$	1 choice

The product can be written as a factorial.

$3 \cdot 2 \cdot 1 = 3! = 6$

If no letter can be used more than once, there are 60 permutations of the first 5 letters of the alphabet, when taken 3 at a time: *ABC, ABD, ABE, ACD, ACE, ADB, ADC, ADE,* and so on.

first letter		second letter		third letter
?		?		?
5 choices	·	4 choices	·	3 choices = 60 permutations

Notice that the product can be written as a quotient of factorials.

$$60 = 5 \cdot 4 \cdot 3 = \frac{5 \cdot 4 \cdot 3 \cdot 2 \cdot 1}{2 \cdot 1} = \frac{5!}{2!}$$

PERMUTATIONS

The number of permutations of n things taken r at a time is

$$_nP_r = \frac{n!}{(n-r)!}.$$

EXAMPLE 2 **Finding Permutations**

There are 7 swimmers in a race.

A **Find the number of orders in which all 7 swimmers can finish.**

The number of swimmers is 7.

$$_7P_7 = \frac{7!}{(7-7)!} = \frac{7!}{0!} = \frac{7 \cdot 6 \cdot 5 \cdot 4 \cdot 3 \cdot 2 \cdot 1}{1} = 5040$$

All 7 swimmers are taken at a time.

There are 5040 permutations. This means there are 5040 orders in which 7 swimmers can finish.

Remember!

By definition, 0! = 1.

B **Find the number of ways the 7 swimmers can finish first, second, and third.**

The number of swimmers is 7.

$$_7P_3 = \frac{7!}{(7-3)!} = \frac{7!}{4!} = \frac{7 \cdot 6 \cdot 5 \cdot \cancel{4} \cdot \cancel{3} \cdot \cancel{2} \cdot \cancel{1}}{\cancel{4} \cdot \cancel{3} \cdot \cancel{2} \cdot \cancel{1}} = 210$$

The top 3 places are taken at a time.

There are 210 permutations. This means that the 7 swimmers can finish in first, second, and third in 210 ways.

A **combination** is a selection of things in any order.

If no letter can be used more than once, there is only 1 combination of the first 3 letters of the alphabet. *ABC, ACB, BAC, BCA, CAB,* and *CBA* are considered to be the same combination of *A, B,* and *C* because the order does not matter.

If no letter is used more than once, there are 10 combinations of the first 5 letters of the alphabet, when taken 3 at a time. To see this, look at the list of permutations below.

These 6 permutations are all the same combination.

ABC	ABD	ABE	ACD	ACE	ADE	BCD	BCE	BDE	CDE
ACB	ADB	AEB	ADC	AEC	AED	BDC	BEC	BED	CED
BAC	BAD	BAE	CAD	CAE	DAE	CBD	CBE	DBE	DCE
BCA	BDA	BEA	CDA	CEA	DEA	CDB	CEB	DEB	DEC
CAB	DAB	EAB	DAC	EAC	EAD	DCB	EBC	EBD	ECD
CBA	DBA	EBA	DCA	ECA	EDA	DBC	ECB	EDB	EDC

In the list of 60 permutations, each combination is repeated 6 times. The number of combinations is $\frac{60}{6} = 10$.

COMBINATIONS

The number of combinations of n things taken r at a time is

$$_nC_r = \frac{_nP_r}{r!} = \frac{n!}{r!(n-r)!}.$$

EXAMPLE 3 Finding Combinations

A gourmet pizza restaurant offers 10 topping choices.

A Find the number of 3-topping pizzas that can be ordered.

10 possible toppings

$$_{10}C_3 = \frac{10!}{3!(10-3)!} = \frac{10!}{3!7!} = \frac{10 \cdot 9 \cdot 8 \cdot \cancel{7} \cdot \cancel{6} \cdot \cancel{5} \cdot \cancel{4} \cdot \cancel{3} \cdot \cancel{2} \cdot \cancel{1}}{(3 \cdot 2 \cdot 1)(\cancel{7} \cdot \cancel{6} \cdot \cancel{5} \cdot \cancel{4} \cdot \cancel{3} \cdot \cancel{2} \cdot \cancel{1})} = 120$$

3 toppings chosen at a time

There are 120 combinations. This means that there are 120 different 3-topping pizzas that can be ordered.

B Find the number of 6-topping pizzas that can be ordered.

10 possible toppings

$$_{10}C_6 = \frac{10!}{6!(10-6)!} = \frac{10!}{6!4!} = \frac{10 \cdot 9 \cdot 8 \cdot 7 \cdot \cancel{6} \cdot \cancel{5} \cdot \cancel{4} \cdot \cancel{3} \cdot \cancel{2} \cdot \cancel{1}}{(\cancel{6} \cdot \cancel{5} \cdot \cancel{4} \cdot \cancel{3} \cdot \cancel{2} \cdot \cancel{1})(4 \cdot 3 \cdot 2 \cdot 1)} = 210$$

6 toppings chosen at a time

There are 210 combinations. This means that there are 210 different 6-topping pizzas.

Think and Discuss

1. **Explain** the difference between a combination and a permutation.
2. **Give an example** of an experiment where order is important and one where order is not important.

10-9 Exercises

go.hrw.com
Homework Help Online
KEYWORD: MT7 10-9
Parent Resources Online
KEYWORD: MT7 Parent

GUIDED PRACTICE

See Example 1

Evaluate each expression.

1. $6!$
2. $\frac{7!}{3!}$
3. $\frac{9!}{(7-3)!}$
4. $\frac{5!}{(4-1)!}$

See Example 2

There are 11 runners in a race.

5. In how many possible orders can all 11 runners finish the race?
6. How many ways can the 11 runners finish first, second, and third?

See Example 3

A group of 8 people are forming several committees.

7. Find the number of different 3-person committees that can be formed.
8. Find the number of different 6-person committees that can be formed.

INDEPENDENT PRACTICE

See Example 1

Evaluate each expression.

9. $4!$
10. $\frac{8!}{2!}$
11. $\frac{4!}{(3-2)!}$
12. $\frac{9!}{(8-5)!}$

See Example 2

Ann has 7 books she wants to put on her bookshelf.

13. How many possible arrangements of books are there?
14. Suppose Ann has room on the shelf for only 4 of the 7 books. In how many ways can she arrange the books now?

See Example 3

If Dena joins a CD club, she gets 8 free CDs.

15. If Dena can select from a list of 32 CDs, how many groups of 8 different CDs are possible?
16. If Dena can select from a list of 48 CDs, how many groups of 8 different CDs are possible?

PRACTICE AND PROBLEM SOLVING

Extra Practice
See page 801.

Evaluate each expression.

17. $\frac{8!}{(8-3)!}$
18. $\frac{11!}{6!(11-6)!}$
19. ${}_{10}P_{10}$
20. ${}_{8}C_{3}$
21. ${}_{15}C_{15}$
22. ${}_{10}C_{7}$
23. $\frac{12!}{10!}$
24. ${}_{8}P_{4}$

Simplify each expression.

25. ${}_{n}C_{n}$
26. $\frac{n!}{(n-1)!}$
27. ${}_{n}C_{0}$
28. ${}_{n}C_{n-1}$
29. ${}_{n}P_{0}$
30. ${}_{n}P_{n}$
31. ${}_{n}C_{1}$
32. ${}_{n}P_{1}$

33. **Sports** How many ways can a coach choose the first, second, third, and fourth runners in a relay race from a team of 10 runners?

Art

Josef Albers used the simple design of nested squares to investigate color relationships. He did not mix colors, but instead created hundreds of variations using paint straight from the tube.

34. Cooking Cole is making a fruit salad. He can choose from the following fruits: oranges, apples, pears, peaches, grapes, strawberries, cantaloupe, and honeydew melon. If he wants to have 4 different fruits, how many possible fruit salads can he make?

35. Art An artist is making a painting of three squares, one inside the other. He has 12 different colors to choose from. How many different paintings could he make if the squares are all different colors?

36. Sports At a track meet, there are 5 athletes competing in the decathlon.

a. Find the number of orders in which all 5 athletes can finish.

b. Find the number of orders in which the 5 athletes can finish in first, second, and third places.

37. Life Science There are 11 different species of birds in a forest. In how many ways can researchers capture, tag, and release birds of 6 different species?

38. What's the Question? There are 12 different items available at a buffet. Customers can choose up to 4 of these items. If the answer is 495, what is the question?

39. Write About It Explain how you could use combinations and permutations to find the probability of an event.

40. Challenge How many ways can a local chapter of the Mathematical Association of America schedule 4 speakers for 4 different meetings in one day if all of the speakers are available on any of 3 dates?

TEST PREP and Spiral Review

41. Multiple Choice In how many ways can 8 students form a single-file line if each student's place in line must be considered?

Ⓐ 40,320 Ⓑ 5040 Ⓒ 8 Ⓓ 1

42. Short Response A group of 15 people are forming committees. Find the number of different 4-person committees that can be formed. Then find the number of different 5-person committees that can be formed. Show your work.

43. Draw the front, top, and side views of the figure at right. (Lesson 8-4)

Describe the number of different combinations that can be made using one item from each category. (Lesson 10-8)

44. 3 shirts
4 pairs of shorts
7 pairs of socks

45. 4 kinds of bread
5 kinds of meat
3 kinds of chips

CHAPTER 10

READY TO GO ON?

SECTION 10B

Quiz for Lessons 10-4 Through 10-9

10-4 Theoretical Probability

An experiment consists of rolling two fair number cubes. Find the probability of each event.

1. $P(\text{total shown} = 7)$ **2.** $P(\text{two 5's})$ **3.** $P(\text{two even numbers})$

10-5 Independent and Dependent Events

4. An experiment consists of tossing 2 fair coins, a penny and a nickel. Find the probability of tails on the penny and heads on the nickel.

5. A jar contains 5 red marbles, 2 blue marbles, 4 yellow marbles, and 4 green marbles. If two marbles are chosen at random, what is the probability that they will be the same color?

10-6 Making Decisions and Predictions

6. Players use the spinner shown to move around a game board. Suppose the spinner is spun 50 times. Predict how many times it will land on "Lose your turn."

7. A spinner is divided evenly into 6 sections. There are 3 blue sections, 2 red, and 1 white. Player A wins if the spinner lands on blue. Otherwise Player B wins. Decide whether the game is fair.

10-7 Odds

8. If the odds in favor of winning a trip for two to New York City are 1:259,999, what is the probability of winning the trip?

10-8 Counting Principles

Family identification codes at a preschool contain 3 letters followed by 3 digits. All codes are equally likely.

9. Find the probability of being assigned the ID *BCD*352.

10. A catalog company offers backpacks in 5 solid colors, 4 prints, and 4 cartoon characters. How many choices of backpacks are there?

10-9 Permutations and Combinations

Evaluate each expression.

11. $7!$ **12.** $5!$ **13.** $\frac{6!}{2!}$ **14.** $\frac{8!}{(6-3)!}$

15. There are 10 cross-country skiers in a race. In how many possible orders can all 10 skiers finish the race?

Ready to Go On?

MULTI-STEP TEST PREP

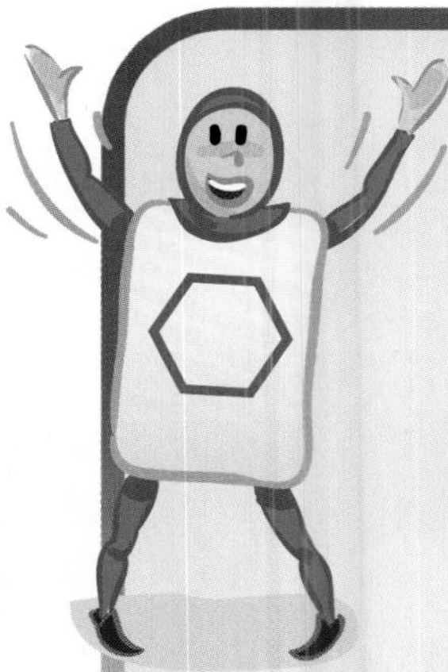

Perplexing Polygons In Mrs. Mac's class, each student is given a set of polygon cards to cut out along the dotted lines. Each student places the cards in his or her own brown paper bag.

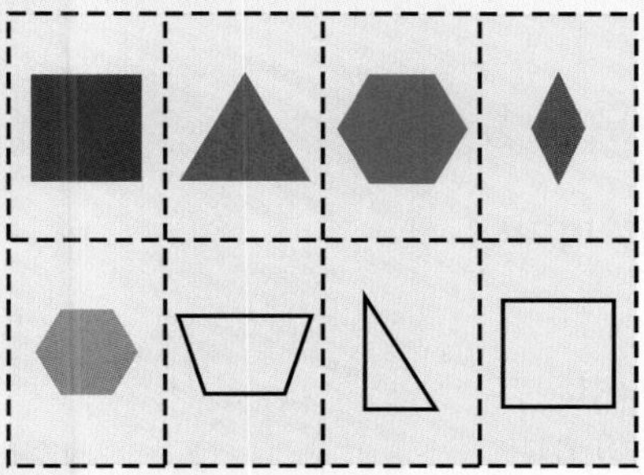

1. Juan draws a polygon from his bag at the same time that Monica draws a polygon from her bag. They do this experiment 50 times and replace the polygons each time before drawing again. How many times would Juan be expected to draw a shaded polygon at the same time that Monica draws a triangle?
2. Kyle draws twice from his bag of polygons. After the first draw, he does not put the polygon back in the bag. Predict the number of times he might draw a square and then a triangle if he conducts this experiment 24 times.
3. Eight students place all of their polygons into a hat. What is the probability of drawing a hexagon?
4. The students are asked to remove 16 polygons from the hat. How can they do this so that the probability of drawing a hexagon remains the same?
5. Eight of the students place all of their polygons into a single bag. Describe how to remove polygons from this bag so that the probability of drawing a hexagon is $\frac{1}{5}$.

Game Time

The Paper Chase

Stephen's desk has 8 drawers. When he receives a paper, he usually chooses a drawer at random to put it in. However, 2 out of 10 times he forgets to put the paper away, and it gets lost.

The probability that a paper will get lost is $\frac{2}{10}$, or $\frac{1}{5}$.

- What is the probability that a paper will get put into a drawer?
- If all drawers are equally likely to be chosen, what is the probability that a paper will get put in drawer 3?

When Stephen needs a document, he looks first in drawer 1 and then checks each drawer in order until the paper is found or until he has looked in all the drawers.

1. If Stephen checked drawer 1 and didn't find the paper he was looking for, what is the probability that the paper will be found in one of the remaining 7 drawers?
2. If Stephen checked drawers 1, 2, and 3, and didn't find the paper he was looking for, what is the probability that the paper will be found in one of the remaining 5 drawers?
3. If Stephen checked drawers 1–7 and didn't find the paper he was looking for, what is the probability that the paper will be found in the last drawer?

Try to write a formula for the probability of finding a paper.

Permutations

Use a set of Scrabble™ tiles, or make a similar set of lettered cards. Draw 2 vowels and 3 consonants, and place them face up in the center of the table. Each player tries to write as many permutations as possible in 60 seconds. Score 1 point per permutation, with a bonus point for each permutation that forms an English word.

A complete copy of the rules is available online.

go.hrw.com
Game Time Extra
KEYWORD: MT7 Games

FOLDNOTES

It's in the Bag!

Materials
- 7 large sticky notes
- glue
- markers

PROJECT Probability Post-Up

Fold sticky notes into an accordion booklet. Then use the booklet to record notes about probability.

Directions

1. Make a chain of seven overlapping sticky notes by placing the sticky portion of one note on the bottom portion of the previous note. **Figure A**

2. Glue the notes together to make sure they stay attached.

3. Accordion-fold the sticky notes. The folds should occur at the bottom edge of each note in the chain. **Figure B**

4. Write the name and number of the chapter on the first sticky note.

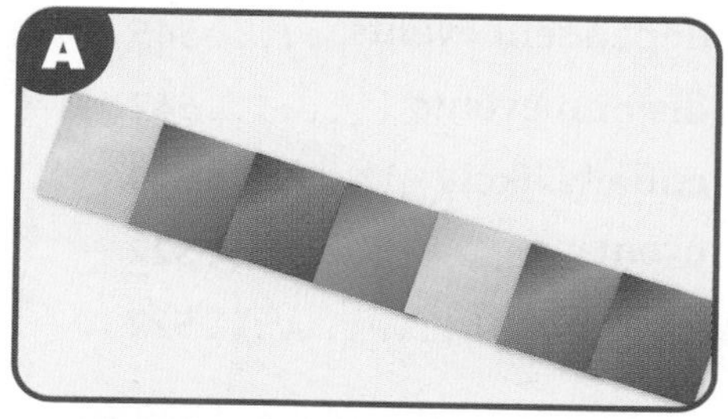
A

B

Taking Note of the Math

Use the sticky-note booklet to record key information from the chapter. Be sure to include definitions, examples of probability experiments, and anything else that will help you review the material in the chapter.

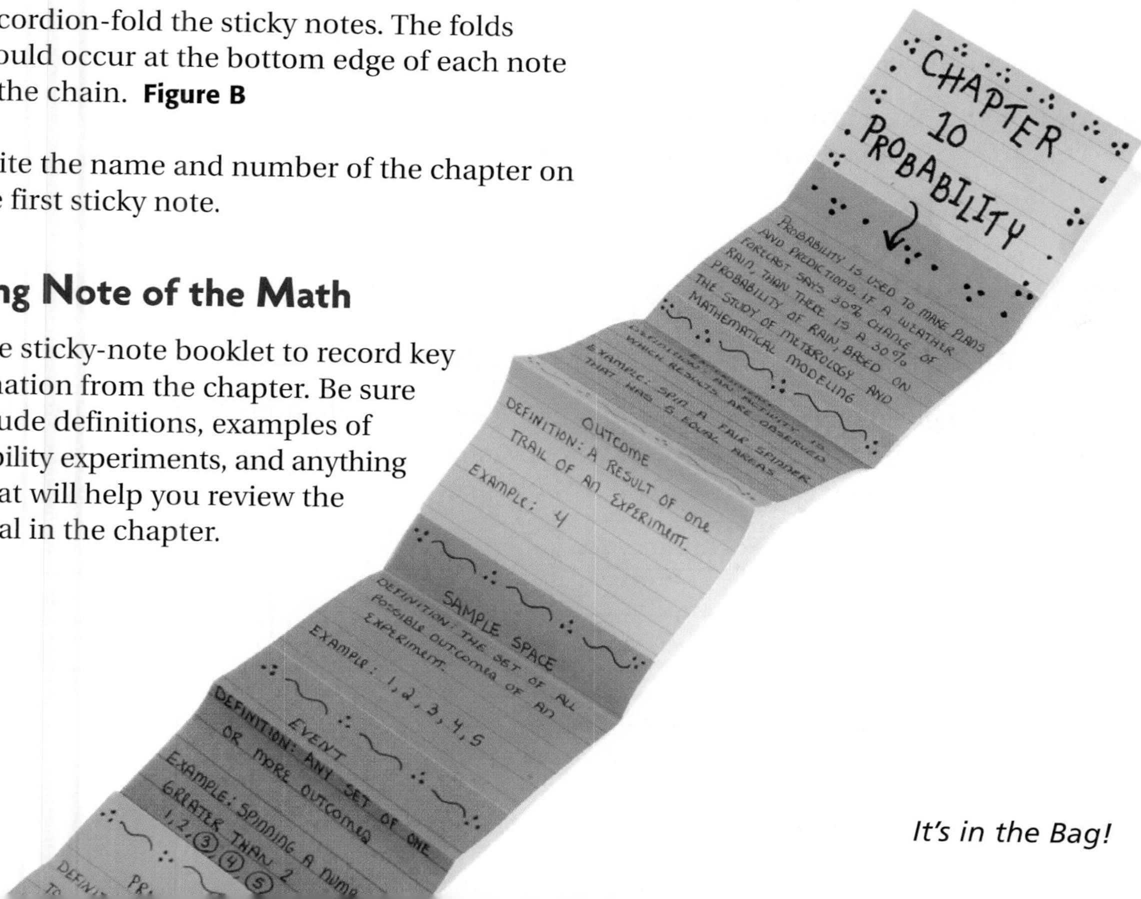

CHAPTER 10

Study Guide: Review

Vocabulary

Addition Counting Principle ... 559	experimental probability ... 527	odds in favor ... 554
certain ... 522	factorial ... 563	outcome ... 522
combination ... 564	fair ... 540	permutation ... 563
dependent events ... 545	Fundamental Counting Principle ... 558	probability ... 522
disjoint events ... 542	impossible ... 522	random numbers ... 532
equally likely ... 540	independent events ... 545	sample space ... 522
event ... 522	mutually exclusive ... 542	simulation ... 532
experiment ... 522	odds against ... 554	theoretical probability ... 540
		tree diagram ... 559
		trial ... 522

Complete the sentences below with vocabulary words from the list above. Words may be used more than once.

1. The __?__ of an event tells you how likely the event is to happen.
   - A probability of 0 means it is __?__ for the event to occur.
   - A probability of 1 means it is __?__ that the event will occur.
2. The set of all possible outcomes of an experiment is called the __?__.
3. A(n) __?__ is an arrangement where order is important.
   A(n) __?__ is an arrangement where order is not important.

10-1 Probability (pp. 522–526)

EXAMPLE

■ **Of the garbage collected in a city, it is expected that about $\frac{1}{5}$ of the garbage will be recycled.**

Outcome	Recycled	Not Recycled
Probability	■	■

$P(\text{recycled}) = \frac{1}{5} = 0.2 = 20\%$

$P(\text{not recycled}) = 1 - \frac{1}{5} = \frac{4}{5} = 0.8 = 80\%$

EXERCISES

Give the probability for each outcome.

4. About 85% of the people attending a band's CD signing have already heard the CD.

Outcome	Heard	Not Heard
Probability	■	■

10-2 Experimental Probability (pp. 527–530)

EXAMPLE

- **The table shows the results of spinning a spinner 72 times. Estimate the probability of the spinner landing on red.**

Outcome	White	Red	Blue	Black
Spins	18	28	12	14

probability $\approx \frac{28}{72} = \frac{7}{18} \approx 0.389 = 38.9\%$

EXERCISES

5. The table shows the result of rolling a number cube 80 times. Estimate the probability of rolling a 4.

Outcome	1	2	3	4	5	6
Rolls	13	15	10	12	5	25

10-3 Use a Simulation (pp. 532–535)

EXAMPLE

- **At a local school, 75% of the students study a foreign language. If 5 students are chosen randomly, estimate the probability that at least 4 study a foreign language. Use the random number table to make a simulation with at least 4 trials.**

08	57	09	92	75	27	37	87	52	36
16	73	29	39	73	78	65	88	02	42

The probability is about $\frac{3}{4}$, or 75%.

EXERCISES

08570	99275	27378	75236	16732
93973	78658	80242	53191	86579

6. On an assembly line, 20% of the items are rejected. Estimate the probability that at least 3 of the next 6 items are rejected. Use the random number table to make a simulation with at least 4 trials.

10-4 Theoretical Probability (pp. 540–544)

EXAMPLE

- **A fair number cube is rolled once. Find the probability of getting a 4.**

$P(4) = \frac{1}{6}$

EXERCISES

7. A marble is drawn at random from a box that contains 8 red, 15 blue, and 7 white marbles. What is the probability of getting a red marble?

10-5 Independent and Dependent Events (pp. 545–549)

EXAMPLE

- **Two marbles are drawn from a jar containing 5 blue marbles and 4 green. What is *P*(blue, green) if the first marble is not replaced?**

	P(blue)	*P*(green)	*P*(blue, green)
Not replaced	$\frac{5}{9}$	$\frac{4}{8}$	$\frac{20}{72} \approx 0.28$

EXERCISES

8. A fair number cube is rolled four times. What is the probability of getting a 6 all four times?

9. Two cards are drawn at random from a deck that has 26 red and 26 black cards. What is the probability that the first card is red and the second card is black?

Study Guide: Review

10-6 Making Decisions and Predictions (pp. 550–553)

EXAMPLE

- **A director needs to order 600 T-shirts. Last summer she gave out 210 blue and 150 red T-shirts. Approximately how many red T-shirts should she order?**

$\frac{150}{360} = \frac{5}{12}$ *Find the probability of red.*

$\frac{5}{12} = \frac{n}{600}$ *Set up a proportion.*

$12n = 3000$ *Solve for n.*

$n = 250$

She should order 250 red T-shirts.

EXERCISES

10. The speeds of each of 10 laps by a NASCAR racer were measured. The approximate speeds in miles per hour were 188.2, 188.8, 191.2, 191.4, 189.1, 187.6, 186.3, 191.1, 190.3, and 189.5. If the driver goes 50 more laps, what is the best prediction of the number of laps that will be at a speed greater than 190 miles per hour?

10-7 Odds (pp. 554–557)

EXAMPLE

- **A digit from 1 to 9 is selected at random. What are the odds in favor of selecting an even number?**

favorable ⟶ 4:5 ⟵ *unfavorable*

EXERCISES

11. A letter is selected at random from the alphabet. What are the odds in favor of getting a letter in the word *RANDOM*?

10-8 Counting Principles (pp. 558–562)

EXAMPLE

- **A code contains 4 letters. How many possible codes are there?**

$26 \cdot 26 \cdot 26 \cdot 26 = 456{,}976$ codes

EXERCISES

ID codes contain 1 letter followed by 5 digits. All codes are equally likely.

12. Find the number of possible ID codes.

13. Find the probability that a code does not contain the digit 0.

10-9 Permutations and Combinations (pp. 563–567)

EXAMPLE

- **Blaire has 5 plants to arrange on a shelf that will hold 3 plants. How many ways are there to arrange the plants if the order is important? if the order is not important?**

important: ${}_5P_3 = \frac{5!}{(5-3)!} = \frac{5!}{2!} = 60$ ways

not important: ${}_5C_3 = \frac{5!}{3!\,(5-3)!} = 10$ ways

EXERCISES

14. Five children are arranged in a row of swings. How many different arrangements are possible?

15. A school's mock trial team has 10 members. A team of 6 students will be chosen to represent the school at a competition. How many different teams are possible?

CHAPTER TEST

Use the table to find the probability of each event.

1. $P(\text{D})$
2. $P(\text{not A})$
3. $P(\text{B or C})$

Outcome	A	B	C	D
Probability	0.2	0.2	0.1	0.5

4. There are 4 cyclists in a race. Kyle has a 50% chance of winning. Lance has the same chance as Miguel. Eddie has a $\frac{1}{5}$ chance of winning. Create a table of probabilities for the sample space.

A coin is randomly drawn from a box and then replaced. The table shows the results.

5. Estimate the probability of each outcome.
6. Estimate $P(\text{penny or nickel})$.
7. Estimate $P(\text{not dime})$.

Outcome	Penny	Nickel	Dime	Quarter
Probability	26	35	19	20

8. In Eastwood neighborhood, 37% of the families have a cat. Each block has 16 families, 8 on each side. Estimate the probability that 3 or more families on one side of a given block have a cat. Use the random number table to make a simulation with at least 10 trials.

97120	08320	17871	21826	74838	37240	36810	20423
12562	45677	88983	94930	31599	76585	61429	05379
34628	46304	66531	96270	21309	31567	30762	47240
30883	71946	25948	97988	26267	21350	59356	43952

An experiment consists of rolling two fair number cubes. Find the probability of each event.

9. $P(\text{total shown} = 3)$
10. $P(\text{rolling two 6's})$
11. $P(\text{total} < 2)$
12. A jar contains 6 red tiles, 2 blue, 3 yellow, and 5 green. If two tiles are chosen at random, what is the probability that they both will be green?
13. A spinner is divided evenly into 9 sections. They are numbered 1 to 9. Player A wins if the spinner lands on odd. Otherwise Player B wins. Decide whether the game is fair.
14. The probability of winning a new widescreen TV is $\frac{1}{1{,}000{,}000}$. What are the odds against winning the TV?
15. A code contains 4 letters and 2 numbers. How many possible codes are there?
16. There are 8 swimmers in a race. In how many possible orders can all 8 swimmers finish the race?

STANDARDIZED TEST PREP

go.hrw.com
State Test Practice Online
KEYWORD: MT7 TestPrep

Cumulative Assessment, Chapters 1–10

Multiple Choice

1. In a box containing marbles, 78 are blue, 24 are orange, and the rest are green. If the probability of selecting a green marble is $\frac{2}{5}$, how many green marbles are in the box?

Ⓐ 30 Ⓑ 68 Ⓒ 102 Ⓓ 150

2. In the chart below, the amount represented by each shaded square is twice that represented by each unshaded square. What is the ratio of gold to silver?

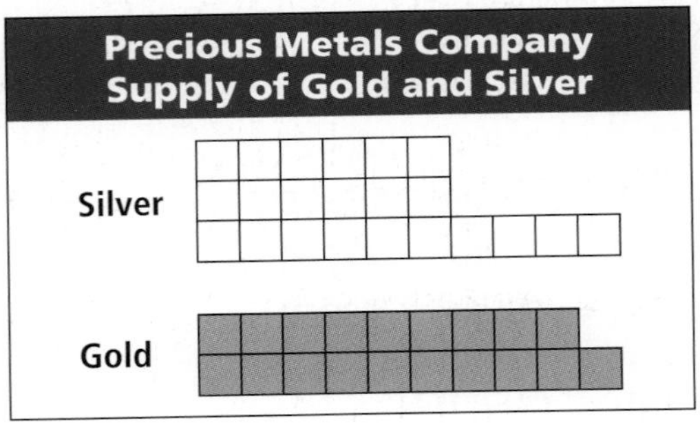

Ⓕ $\frac{19}{22}$ Ⓖ $\frac{13}{19}$ Ⓗ $\frac{22}{19}$ Ⓙ $\frac{19}{11}$

3. For which set of data are the mean, median, and mode all the same?

Ⓐ 3, 1, 3, 3, 5 Ⓑ 1, 1, 2, 5, 6 Ⓒ 2, 1, 1, 1, 5 Ⓓ 10, 1, 3, 5, 1

4. What is the value of $(-2 - 4)^3 + 3^0$?

Ⓕ −215 Ⓖ −8 Ⓗ 217 Ⓙ 219

5. About what percent of 75 is 55?

Ⓐ 25% Ⓑ 66% Ⓒ 75% Ⓓ 135%

6. Which does NOT describe $\frac{\sqrt{25}}{-5}$?

Ⓕ real Ⓖ rational Ⓗ integer Ⓙ median

7. The figure formed by the vertices (−2, 5), (2, 5), (4, −1), and (0, −1) can be best described by which type of quadrilateral?

Ⓐ square Ⓑ rectangle Ⓒ parallelogram Ⓓ trapezoid

8. How many vertices are in the prism below?

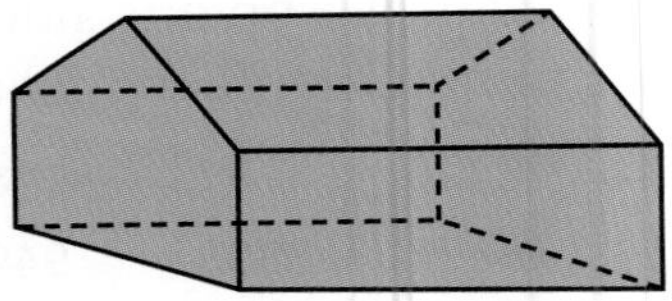

Ⓕ 7 Ⓖ 8 Ⓗ 10 Ⓙ 12

9. The triangular reflecting pool has an area of 350 ft². If the height of the triangle is 25 ft, what is the length of the hypotenuse to the nearest tenth?

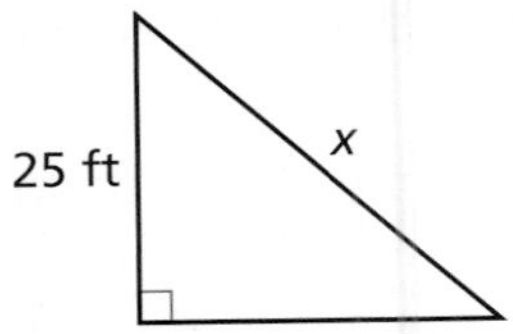

Ⓐ 28.7 ft Ⓑ 37.5 ft Ⓒ 38.9 ft Ⓓ 42.3 ft

10. If the probability of selecting a red marble is $\frac{1}{14}$, what are the odds in favor of selecting a red marble?

Ⓕ $\frac{13}{14}$ Ⓖ $\frac{2}{13}$ Ⓗ $\frac{1}{13}$ Ⓙ $\frac{1}{15}$

11. If the diameter of the dartboard is 10 in., what is the area of the 50-point portion, to the nearest tenth of a square inch?

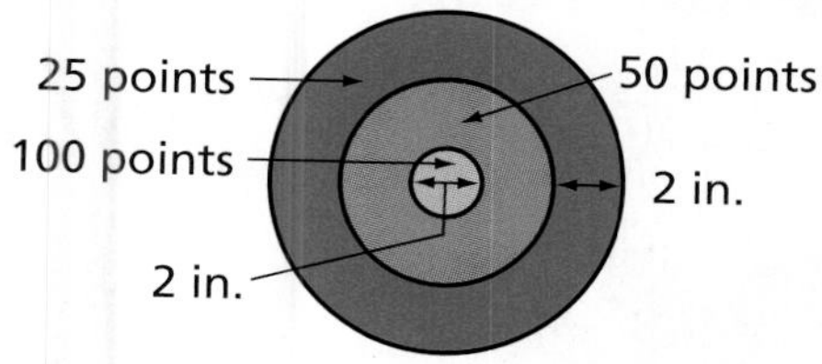

Ⓐ 3.1 in^2 Ⓒ 9.4 in^2

Ⓑ 6.3 in^2 Ⓓ 25.1 in^2

HOT TIP! Draw a picture to help you see if your answer is reasonable.

Gridded Response

Use the following graph for items 12 and 13.

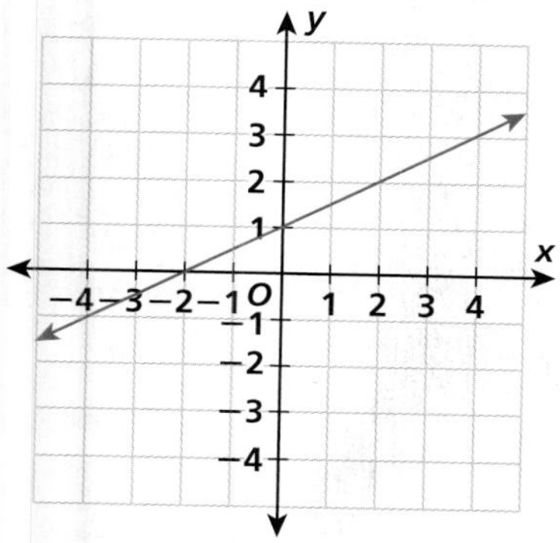

12. Find the x-coordinate of the ordered pair whose y-coordinate is 1.

13. Determine the value of y when $x = 6$.

14. What is the probability of rolling an even number on a number cube and tossing a heads on a coin?

15. Teresa has to create a password that contains 1 digit and 2 letters. Find the number of possible passwords.

16. What is the value of x for the equation $7 = \frac{2}{3}x - 3$?

Short Response

17. A dart thrown at the square board shown lands in a random spot. What is the probability that it lands in the blue square? Show your work.

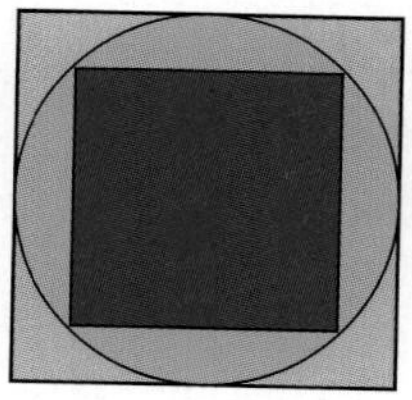

18. The pilot of a hot-air balloon is trying to land in a 2 km square field. There is a large tree in each corner. The ropes will tangle in a tree if the balloon lands within $\frac{1}{7}$ km of the tree's trunk. What is the probability the balloon will land without getting caught in a tree? Express your answer to the nearest tenth of a percent. Show your work.

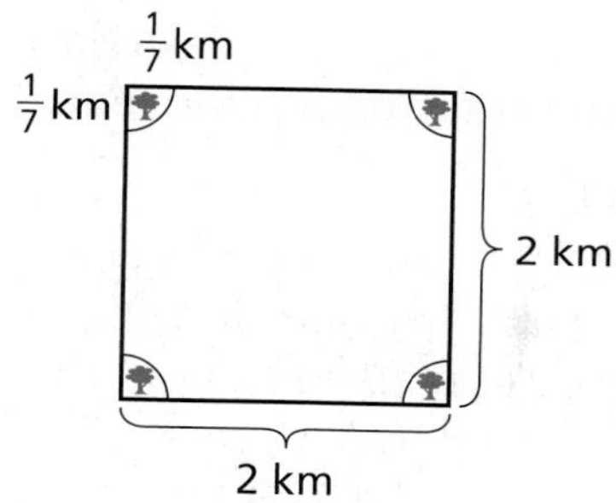

Extended Response

19. Students are choosing a new mascot and color. The mascot choices are a bear, a lion, a jaguar, or a tiger. The color choices are red, orange, or blue.

a. How many different combinations do the students have to choose from? Show your work.

b. If a second school color is added, either gold or silver, how many different combinations do the students have to choose from? Show your work.

c. How would adding a choice from among n names change the number of combinations to choose from?

Standardized Test Prep

Problem Solving on Location

SOUTH CAROLINA

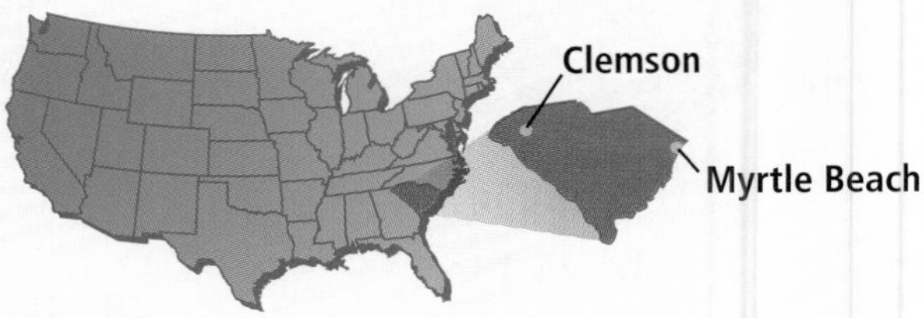

Clemson Tigers Football

For the past two decades, Clemson University's football team has been one of the sport's greatest success stories. Since 1985, the Clemson Tigers have appeared in 16 bowl games, placing them among the nation's most consistently winning teams during that period.

Choose one or more strategies to solve each problem.

1. The Clemson Tigers' team colors are orange, purple, and white. The players' jerseys and pants are available in all three colors. How many different uniforms can the team make by choosing a color for the jersey and a color for the pants?

2. The entrance to the team's locker room has an enormous photo of the university's stadium. The perimeter of the photo is 78 feet. The length is 21 feet greater than the width. What are the length and width of the photo?

For 3, use the graph.

3. During the 1998 season, the Tigers scored 104 fewer points than during the 1999 season. During the 1999 season, they scored 43 fewer points than the median of the seasons shown in the graph. How many points did the Tigers score during the 1998 season?

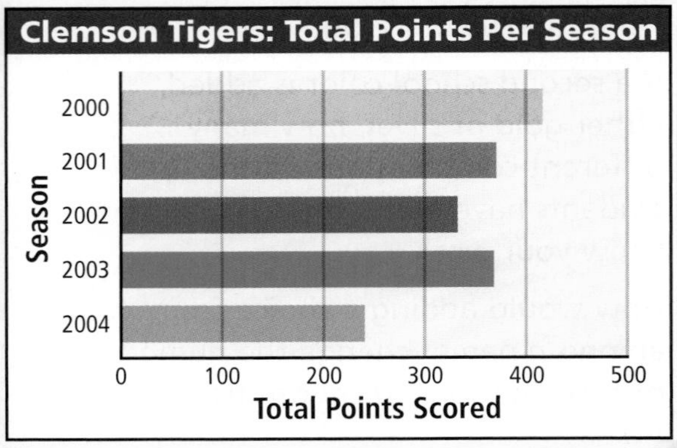

Problem Solving Strategies

- Draw a Diagram
- Make a Model
- Guess and Test
- Work Backward
- Find a Pattern
- Make a Table
- Solve a Simpler Problem
- Use Logical Reasoning
- Act It Out
- Make an Organized List

The South Carolina Hall of Fame

What do President Andrew Jackson, jazz musician Dizzy Gillespie, and athlete Lucile Godbold have in common? All of them were born in South Carolina, and all have been inducted into the South Carolina Hall of Fame. Located in Myrtle Beach, the hall honors citizens of the state who have made lasting contributions in a wide range of fields.

Choose one or more strategies to solve each problem.

1. Each year, 10 living nominees and 10 deceased nominees are selected for induction into the hall. The judges pick one from each group. How many different pairs of possible inductees are there?
2. The hall includes five inductees from the field of medicine. Their portraits are to be lined up next to each other. In how many different ways can the portraits be arranged?

For 3 and 4, use the graph.

3. The graph shows the total number of inductees in the South Carolina Hall of Fame. Assume that new inductees continue to be added to the hall at the same rate. Predict the total number of inductees in 2020.
4. In what year will there be more than 100 inductees for the first time?

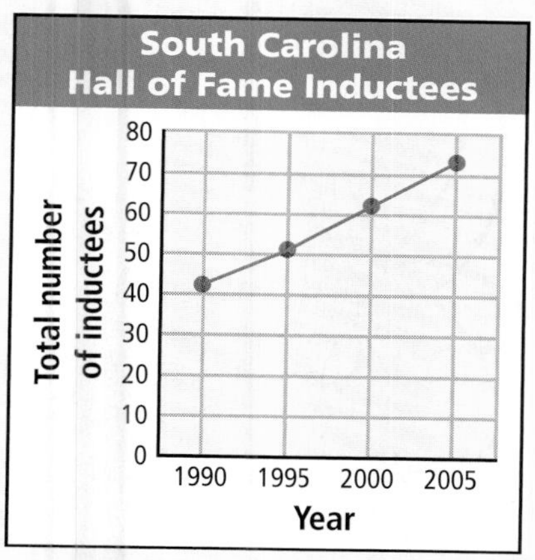

CHAPTER 11

Multi-Step Equations and Inequalities

11A Solving Linear Equations

- **11-1** Simplifying Algebraic Expressions
- **11-2** Solving Multi-Step Equations
- LAB Model Equations with Variables on Both Sides
- **11-3** Solving Equations with Variables on Both Sides

11B Solving Equations and Inequalities

- **11-4** Solving Inequalities by Multiplying or Dividing
- **11-5** Solving Two-Step Inequalities
- **11-6** Systems of Equations

MULTI-STEP TEST PREP

go.hrw.com
Chapter Project Online
KEYWORD: MT7 Ch11

River	Location	Discharge (m^3/s)
Colorado	Glen Canyon Dam, CO	314.6
Snake	Hells Canyon Dam, ID	726.04
Missouri	St. Joseph, MO	1751.4
Columbia	The Dalles, OR	6331.65

Career *Hydrologist*

Hydrologists measure water flow between rivers, streams, lakes, and oceans. They map their results to record locations and movement of water above and below the earth's surface.

Hydrologists are involved in projects such as water-resource studies, field irrigation, flood management, soil-erosion prevention, and the study of water discharge from creeks, streams, and rivers. The table shows the rate of water discharge for four U.S. rivers.

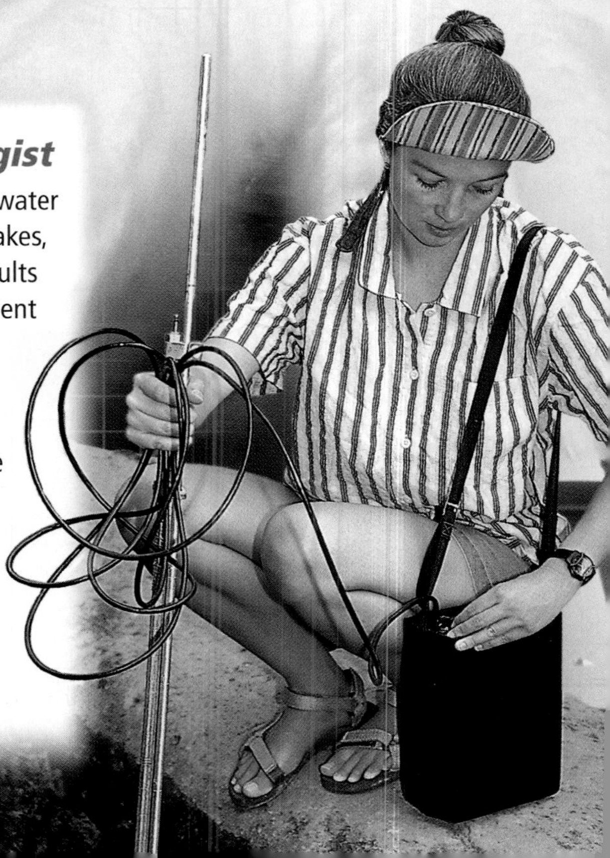

ARE YOU READY?

Vocabulary

Choose the best term from the list to complete each sentence.

algebraic expression
Distributive Property
like terms
terms
variable

1. A letter that represents a value that can change is called a(n) __?__.
2. A(n) __?__ has one or more variables.
3. The algebraic expression $5x^2 - 3y + 4x^2 + 7$ has four __?__. Because they have the same variable raised to the same power, $5x^2$ and $4x^2$ are __?__.
4. When you individually multiply the numbers inside the parentheses by the factor outside the parentheses, you are applying the __?__.

Complete these exercises to review skills you will need for this chapter.

Distribute Multiplication

Replace each ▢ with a number so that each equation illustrates the Distributive Property.

5. $6 \cdot (11 + 8) = 6 \cdot 11 + 6 \cdot$ ▢
6. $7 \cdot (14 + 12) =$ ▢ $\cdot\, 14 +$ ▢ $\cdot 12$
7. $9 \cdot (6 -$ ▢ $) = 9 \cdot 6 - 9 \cdot 2$
8. $14 \cdot ($ ▢ $- 7) = 14 \cdot 20 - 14 \cdot 7$

Simplify Algebraic Expressions

Simplify each expression by applying the Distributive Property and combining like terms.

9. $3(x + 2) + 7x$
10. $4(y - 3) + 8y$
11. $2(z - 1) - 3z$
12. $-4(t - 6) - t$
13. $-(r - 3) - 8r$
14. $-5(4 - 2m) + 7$

Connect Words and Equations

Write an equation to represent each situation.

15. The perimeter P of a rectangle is the sum of twice the length ℓ and twice the width w.
16. The volume V of a rectangular prism is the product of its three dimensions: length ℓ, width w, and height h.
17. The surface area S of a sphere is the product of 4π and the square of the radius r.
18. The cost c of a telegram of 18 words is the cost f of the first 10 words plus the cost a of each additional word.

CHAPTER 11

Study Guide: Preview

Where You've Been

Previously, you

- used models to solve equations.
- solved inequalities by adding or subtracting.
- determined if an ordered pair is a solution to an equation.

In This Chapter

You will study

- finding solutions to application problems using algebraic equations.
- solving multi-step equations.
- solving inequalities by multiplying or dividing.
- determining if an ordered pair is a solution to a system of equations.
- solving a system of equations.

Where You're Going

You can use the skills learned in this chapter

- to calculate profits or losses generated by the number of items a business produces.
- to solve complex application problems involving systems of equations and systems of inequalities in higher-level math courses.

Key Vocabulary/Vocabulario

equivalent expression	expresiónes equivalents
like term	términos semejantes
simplify	simplificar
solution of a system of equations	soluciones de un sistema de ecuaciones
system of equations	sistema de ecuaciones
term	término

Vocabulary Connections

To become familiar with some of the vocabulary terms in the chapter, consider the following. You may refer to the chapter, the glossary, or a dictionary if you like.

1. The word *equivalent* contains the same root as the word *equal*. What do you think **equivalent expressions** are?
2. The word *simplify* means "make less complicated." What do you think it means to **simplify** an expression?
3. The adjective *like* means "alike." What do you suppose **like terms** are?
4. A *system* is a group of related objects. What do you think a **system of equations** is?

Study Guide: Preview

Reading and Writing Math

Writing Strategy: Write to Justify

The icon appears throughout the book. This icon identifies questions that require you to write a problem or an explanation. Being able to justify your answer is proof that you have an understanding of the concept. You can use a four-step method to write a justification for your solution.

From Lesson 10-4

8. **Write About It** Suppose you are playing a game in which two fair dice are rolled. To make the first move, you need to roll doubles or a sum of 3 or 11. What is the probability that you will be able to make the first move?

Step 1 **Rewrite the problem statement in your own words.**

Find the probability of rolling a double or a sum of 3 or 11.

Step 2 **Make a table or other graphic to help explain your thinking.**

1, 1	1, 2	1, 3	1 ,4	1, 5	1, 6
2, 1	2, 2	2, 3	2, 4	2, 5	2, 6
3, 1	3, 2	3, 3	3, 4	3, 5	3, 6
4, 1	4, 2	4, 3	4, 4	4, 5	4, 6
5, 1	5, 2	5, 3	5, 4	5, 5	5, 6
6, 1	6, 2	6, 3	6, 4	6, 5	6, 6

Highlight the number of ways you can roll a double or a sum of 11 or 3.

Step 3 **Give evidence that you have answered the question.**

The probability of rolling a double is $\frac{6}{36}$.

The probability of rolling a sum of 3 is $\frac{2}{36}$.

The probability of rolling a sum of 11 is $\frac{2}{36}$.

Step 4 **Write a complete response.**

The events are mutually exclusive, so you add the probabilities. The probability that you will roll a double or a sum of 11 or 3 is $\frac{6}{36} + \frac{2}{36} + \frac{2}{36} = \frac{10}{36} = \frac{5}{18}$ or approximately 28%.

Try This

Describe a situation using two fair number cubes where the probability that two mutually exclusive events will occur is $\frac{1}{4}$. Justify your answer.

11-1 Simplifying Algebraic Expressions

Learn to combine like terms in an expression.

Vocabulary

term

like term

equivalent expression

simplify

Roosevelt High School holds an Academic Challenge each year. Local high school teams compete in four subject areas: math, English, history, and science. Students from each grade level have rated their strongest subject.

Students from different grades who chose the same subject are similar to *like terms* in an expression. **Terms** in an expression are separated by plus or minus signs.

$$7x + 5 - 3y + 2x$$

Helpful Hint

Constants such as 4, 0.75, and 11 are like terms because none of them have a variable.

Like terms, such as $7x$ and $2x$ in the expression above, can be grouped together because they have the same variable raised to the same power. Often, like terms have different coefficients. When you combine like terms, you change the way an expression looks but not the value of the expression. **Equivalent expressions** have the same value for all values of the variables.

EXAMPLE 1 Combining Like Terms to Simplify

Combine like terms.

A $7x + 2x$ — *Identify like terms.*

$9x$ — *Combine coefficients: 7 + 2 = 9.*

B $5m - 2m + 8 - 3m + 6$ — *Identify like terms.*

$0m + 14$ — *Combine coefficients.*

14 — *Simplify.*

EXAMPLE 2 Combining Like Terms in Two-Variable Expressions

Combine like terms.

A $7a + 4a + 3b + 5$

$\boxed{7a} + \boxed{4a} + (3b) + 5$ — *Identify like terms.*

$11a + 3b + 5$ — *Combine coefficients: 7 + 4 = 11.*

B $k + 3n - 2n + 4k$

$\boxed{1k} + (3n) - (2n) + \boxed{4k}$ — *Identify like terms; the coefficient of k is 1 because 1k = k.*

$5k + n$ — *Combine coefficients.*

C $3f - 9g + 15$

$\boxed{3f} - (9g) + 15$ — *No like terms*

To **simplify** an expression, perform all possible operations, including combining like terms.

EXAMPLE 3 Using the Distributive Property to Simplify

Remember!

The Distributive Property states that $a(b + c) = ab + ac$ for all real numbers a, b, and c. For example, $2(3 + 5) = 2(3) + 2(5)$.

Simplify $6(y + 8) - 5y$.

$6(y + 8) - 5y$	
$6(y) + 6(8) - 5y$	*Distributive Property*
$6y + 48 - 5y$	*Multiply.*
$1y + 48$	*Combine coefficients: 6 − 5 = 1.*
$y + 48$	*1y = y*

EXAMPLE 4 Combining Like Terms to Solve Algebraic Equations

Solve $9x - x = 136$.

$9x - x = 136$	*Identify like terms. The coefficient of x is 1.*
$8x = 136$	*Combine coefficients: 9 − 1 = 8.*
$\frac{8x}{8} = \frac{136}{8}$	*Divide both sides by 8.*
$x = 17$	*Simplify.*

Think and Discuss

1. **Describe** the first step in simplifying the expression $2 + 8(3y + 5) - y$.
2. **Tell** how many sets of like terms are in the expression in Example 1B. What are they?

11-1 Exercises

go.hrw.com
Homework Help Online
KEYWORD: MT7 11-1
Parent Resources Online
KEYWORD: MT7 Parent

GUIDED PRACTICE

See Example 1 **Combine like terms.**

1. $9x - 4x$
2. $2z + 5 + 3z$
3. $6f + 3 - 4f + 5 + 10f$
4. $9g + 8g$
5. $7p - 9 - p$
6. $3x + 5 - x + 3 + 4x$

See Example 2
7. $6x + 4y - x + 4y$
8. $4x + 5y - y + 3x$
9. $5x + 3y + 4x - 2y$
10. $6p + 3p + 7z - 3z$
11. $7g + 5h - 12$
12. $3h + 4m + 7h - 4m$

See Example 3 **Simplify.**

13. $4(r + 3) - 3r$
14. $7(3 + x) + 2x$
15. $7(t + 8) - 5t$

See Example 4 **Solve.**

16. $6n - 4n = 68$
17. $y + 5y = 90$
18. $5p - 2p = 51$

INDEPENDENT PRACTICE

See Example 1 **Combine like terms.**

19. $7y + 6y$
20. $4z - 5 - 2z$
21. $3a + 6 - 2a + 9 + 5a$
22. $5z - z$
23. $9x + 3 - 4x$
24. $9b + 6 - 3b - 3 - b$
25. $14p - 5p$
26. $7a + 8 - 3a$
27. $3x + 9 + 3x - 4 + 7x$

See Example 2
28. $3z + 4z + b - 5$
29. $5a + a + 4z - 3z$
30. $9x + 8y + 2x - 8 - 4y$
31. $6x + 2 + 3x + 6q$
32. $7d - d + 3e + 12$
33. $16a + 7c + 5 - 7a + c$

See Example 3 **Simplify.**

34. $5(y + 2) - y$
35. $2(3y - 7) + 6y$
36. $3(x + 6) + 8x$
37. $3(4y + 5) + 8$
38. $6(2x - 8) - 9x$
39. $4(4x - 4) + 3x$

See Example 4 **Solve.**

40. $7x - x = 72$
41. $9p - 4p = 30$
42. $p + 3p = 16$
43. $3y + 5y = 64$
44. $a + 6a = 98$
45. $8x - 3x = 60$

PRACTICE AND PROBLEM SOLVING

Extra Practice
See page 802.

46. Hobbies Charlie has x state quarters. Ty has 3 more quarters than Charlie has. Vinnie has 2 times as many quarters as Ty has. Write and simplify an expression to show how many state quarters they have in all.

47. Geometry A rectangle has length $5x$ and width x. Write and simplify an expression for the perimeter of the rectangle.

Simplify.

48. $6(4\ell + 7k) - 16\ell + 14$
49. $5d + 7 + 4d - 2d - 6$

Solve.

50. $13(g + 2) = 78$

51. $2(3x - 7) = 76$

Write and simplify an expression for each situation.

52. Business A promoter charges $7 for each adult ticket, plus an additional $2 per ticket for tax and handling. What is the total cost of x tickets?

53. Sports Use the information below to find how many medals of each kind were won by the four countries in the 2004 Summer Olympics.

United States	Great Britain	Brazil	Lithuania
35 Gold	9 Gold	4 Gold	1 Gold
39 Silver	9 Silver	3 Silver	2 Silver
29 Bronze	12 Bronze	3 Bronze	0 Bronze

54. Business A homeowner ordered 14 square yards of carpet for part of the first floor of a new house and 12 square yards of carpet for the basement. The total cost of the order was $832 before taxes. Write and solve an equation to find the price of each square yard of carpet before taxes.

55. What's the Error? A student said that $3x + 4y$ can be simplified to $7xy$ by combining like terms. What error did the student make?

56. Write About It Write an expression that can be simplified by combining like terms. Then write an expression that cannot be simplified, and explain why it is already in simplest form.

57. Challenge Simplify and solve $3(5x + 4 - 2x) + 5(3x - 3) = 45$.

Test Prep and Spiral Review

58. Multiple Choice Terrance bought 3 markers. His sister bought 5 markers. Terrance and his sister spent a total of $16 on the markers. What was the price of each marker?

Ⓐ $16 Ⓑ $8 Ⓒ $4 Ⓓ $2

59. Gridded Response Simplify $3(2x + 7) + 10x$. What is the coefficient of x?

Give the quadrant of each point. (Lesson 3-2)

60. (6, 8) **61.** (4, −3) **62.** (−9, 2)

Find each percent increase or decrease to the nearest percent. (Lesson 6-5)

63. from $125 to $160 **64.** from $241 to $190 **65.** from $21.95 to $34.50

11-2 Solving Multi-Step Equations

Learn to solve multi-step equations.

To solve a multi-step equation, you may have to simplify the equation first by combining like terms.

EXAMPLE 1 Solving Equations That Contain Like Terms

Solve.

$$3x + 5 + 6x - 7 = 25$$

$$3x + 5 + 6x - 7 = 25$$

$$9x - 2 = 25 \quad \textit{Combine like terms.}$$

$$\underline{+2} \quad \underline{+2} \quad \textit{Add 2 to both sides.}$$

$$9x = 27$$

$$\frac{9x}{9} = \frac{27}{9} \quad \textit{Divide both sides by 9.}$$

$$x = 3$$

Check

$$3x + 5 + 6x - 7 = 25$$

$$3(3) + 5 + 6(3) - 7 \stackrel{?}{=} 25 \quad \textit{Substitute 3 for x.}$$

$$9 + 5 + 18 - 7 \stackrel{?}{=} 25 \quad \textit{Multiply.}$$

$$25 \stackrel{?}{=} 25 \checkmark$$

If an equation contains fractions, it may help to multiply both sides of the equation by the least common denominator (LCD) to clear the fractions before you isolate the variable.

EXAMPLE 2 Solving Equations That Contain Fractions

Solve.

A $\frac{3y}{7} + \frac{5}{7} = -\frac{1}{7}$

$$7\left(\frac{3y}{7} + \frac{5}{7}\right) = 7\left(-\frac{1}{7}\right) \quad \textit{Multiply both sides by 7.}$$

$${}^{1}\cancel{7}\left(\frac{3y}{\cancel{7}_1}\right) + {}^{1}\cancel{7}\left(\frac{5}{\cancel{7}_1}\right) = {}^{1}\cancel{7}\left(-\frac{1}{\cancel{7}_1}\right) \quad \textit{Distributive Property}$$

$$3y + 5 = -1$$

$$\underline{-5} \quad \underline{-5} \quad \textit{Subtract 5 from both sides.}$$

$$3y = -6$$

$$\frac{3y}{3} = \frac{-6}{3} \quad \textit{Divide both sides by 3.}$$

$$y = -2$$

Remember!

The least common denominator (LCD) is the smallest number that each of the denominators will divide into.

Solve.

B $\frac{4p}{9} + \frac{p}{3} - \frac{1}{2} = \frac{11}{6}$

The LCD is 18.

$$18\left(\frac{4p}{9} + \frac{p}{3} - \frac{1}{2}\right) = 18\left(\frac{11}{6}\right)$$ *Multiply both sides by 18.*

$$^{2}\cancel{18}\left(\frac{4p}{\cancel{9}_1}\right) + {}^{6}\cancel{18}\left(\frac{p}{\cancel{3}_1}\right) - {}^{9}\cancel{18}\left(\frac{1}{\cancel{2}_1}\right) = {}^{3}\cancel{18}\left(\frac{11}{\cancel{6}_1}\right)$$ *Distributive Property*

$$8p + 6p - 9 = 33$$

$$14p - 9 = 33$$ *Combine like terms.*

$$\underline{\quad +9 \quad +9}$$ *Add 9 to both sides.*

$$14p = 42$$

$$\frac{14p}{14} = \frac{42}{14}$$ *Divide both sides by 14.*

$$p = 3$$

EXAMPLE 3 ***Travel Application***

On the first day of her vacation, Carly rode her motorcycle *m* miles in 4 hours. On the second day, she rode twice as far in 7 hours. If her average speed for the two days was 62.18 mi/h, how far did she ride on the first day? Round your answer to the nearest tenth of a mile.

Carly's average speed is her combined speeds for the two days divided by 2.

$$\frac{\text{Day 1 speed} + \text{Day 2 speed}}{2} = \text{average speed}$$

$$\frac{\frac{m}{4} + \frac{2m}{7}}{2} = 62.18$$ *Substitute $\frac{m}{4}$ for Day 1 speed and $\frac{2m}{7}$ for Day 2 speed.*

$$^{1}\cancel{2}\left(\frac{\frac{m}{4} + \frac{2m}{7}}{\cancel{2}_1}\right) = 2(62.18)$$ *Multiply both sides by 2.*

$$28\left(\frac{m}{4} + \frac{2m}{7}\right) = 28(124.36)$$ *Multiply both sides by the LCD 28.*

$$7m + 8m = 3482.08$$ *Simplify.*

$$\frac{15m}{15} = \frac{3482.08}{15}$$ *Combine like terms. Divide both sides by 15.*

$$m \approx 232.14$$

Carly rode approximately 232.1 miles on the first day.

Think and Discuss

1. List the steps required to solve $3x - 4 + 2x = 7$.

2. Tell how you would clear the fractions in $\frac{3x}{4} - \frac{2x}{3} + \frac{5}{8} = 1$.

11-2 Exercises

go.hrw.com
Homework Help Online
KEYWORD: MT7 11-2
Parent Resources Online
KEYWORD: MT7 Parent

GUIDED PRACTICE

See Example 1 **Solve.**

1. $7d - 12 + 2d + 3 = 18$
2. $3y + 4y + 6 = 20$
3. $10e - 2e - 9 = 39$
4. $4c - 5 + 14c = 67$
5. $5h + 6 + 8h - 3h = 76$
6. $7x - 2x + 3 = -32$

See Example 2

7. $\frac{4x}{13} + \frac{3}{13} = -\frac{1}{13}$
8. $\frac{y}{2} - \frac{5y}{6} + \frac{1}{3} = \frac{1}{2}$
9. $\frac{4}{5} - \frac{2p}{5} = \frac{6}{5}$
10. $\frac{15}{8}z + \frac{1}{4} = 4$

See Example 3

11. **Travel** Barry's family drove 843 mi to see his grandparents. On the first day, they drove 483 mi. On the second day, how long did it take to reach Barry's grandparents' house if they averaged 60 mi/h?

INDEPENDENT PRACTICE

See Example 1 **Solve.**

12. $5n + 3n - n + 5 = 26$
13. $-81 = 7k + 19 + 3k$
14. $36 - 4c - 3c = 22$
15. $12 + 5w - 4w = 15$
16. $37 = 15a - 5a - 3$
17. $30 = 7y - 35 + 6y$

See Example 2

18. $\frac{3}{8} + \frac{p}{8} = 3\frac{1}{8}$
19. $\frac{7h}{12} - \frac{4h}{12} = \frac{18}{12}$
20. $\frac{4g}{16} - \frac{3}{8} - \frac{g}{16} = \frac{3}{16}$
21. $\frac{7}{12} = \frac{3m}{6} - \frac{m}{3} + \frac{1}{4}$
22. $\frac{4}{13} = -\frac{2b}{13} + \frac{6b}{26}$
23. $\frac{3x}{4} - \frac{21x}{32} = -1\frac{1}{8}$

See Example 3

24. **Recreation** Lydia rode 243 miles in a three-day bike trip. On the first day, Lydia rode 67 miles. On the second day, she rode 92 miles. How many miles per hour did she average on the third day if she rode for 7 hours?

PRACTICE AND PROBLEM SOLVING

Extra Practice
See page 802.

Solve and check.

25. $\frac{5n}{8} - \frac{1}{2} = \frac{3}{4}$
26. $4n + 11 - 7n = -13$
27. $7b - 2 - 12b = 63$
28. $\frac{x}{2} + \frac{2}{3} = \frac{5}{6}$
29. $-2x - 7 + 3x = 10$
30. $\frac{3r}{4} - \frac{4}{5} = \frac{7}{10}$
31. $4y - 3 - 9y = 32$
32. $7n - 10 - 9n = -13$
33. **Finance** Alessia is paid 1.4 times her normal hourly rate for each hour she works over 30 hours in a week. Last week she worked 35 hours and earned \$436.60. What is her normal hourly rate?

LINK

Sports

You can estimate the weight in pounds of a fish that is L inches long and G inches around at the thickest part by using the formula $W \approx \frac{LG^2}{800}$.

34. **Geometry** The obtuse angle of an isosceles triangle measures 120°. Write and solve an equation to find the measure of the base angles.

35. **Critical Thinking** The sum of two consecutive numbers is 63. What are the two numbers? Explain your solution.

36. **Sports** The average weight of the top 5 fish at a fishing tournament was 12.3 pounds. The weights of the second-, third-, fourth-, and fifth-place fish are shown in the table. What was the weight of the heaviest fish?

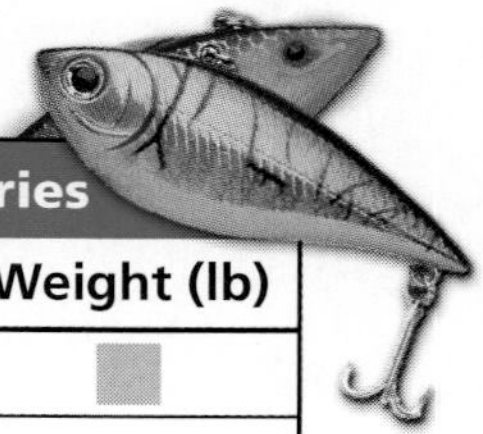

Winning Entries

Caught by	Weight (lb)
Wayne S.	
Carla P.	12.8
Deb N.	12.6
Virgil W.	11.8
Brian B.	9.7

37. **Physical Science** The formula $K = \frac{F-32}{1.8} + 273$ is used to convert a temperature from degrees Fahrenheit to kelvins. Water boils at 373 kelvins. Use the formula to find the boiling point of water in degrees Fahrenheit.

38. **What's the Error?** A student's work in solving an equation is shown. What error has the student made, and what is the correct answer?

$$\frac{1}{5}x + 5x = 13$$
$$x + 5x = 65$$
$$6x = 65$$
$$x = \frac{65}{6}$$

39. **Write About It** Compare the steps used to solve the following.

$$4x - 8 = 16 \qquad\qquad 4(x - 2) = 16$$

40. **Challenge** List the steps you would use to solve the following equation.

$$\frac{4\left(\frac{1}{3}x - \frac{1}{4}\right) + \frac{4}{3}x}{3} + 1 = 6$$

Test Prep and Spiral Review

41. **Multiple Choice** Solve $4k - 7 + 3 + 5k = 59$.

Ⓐ $k = 6$ Ⓑ $k = 6.6$ Ⓒ $k = 7$ Ⓓ $k = 11.8$

42. **Gridded Response** Antonio's first four test grades were 85, 92, 91, and 80. What must he score on the next test to have an 88 test average?

Find the volume of each figure to the nearest tenth. Use 3.14 for π. (Lesson 8-5)

43. cube with side length 3 in.

44. cylinder with $d = 14$ ft and $h = 7.8$ ft

Combine like terms. (Lesson 11-1)

45. $9m + 8 - 4m + 7 - 5m$

46. $6t + 3k - 15$

47. $5a + 3 - b + 1$

Hands-On LAB 11-3

Model Equations with Variables on Both Sides

Use with Lesson 11-3

go.hrw.com
Lab Resources Online
KEYWORD: MT7 Lab11

KEY

Algebra tiles

[+] = x [−] = $-x$

[−] = 1 [+] = −1

REMEMBER

It will not change the value of an expression if you add or remove zero.

[+] + [−] = 0 [+] + [−] = 0

To solve an equation with the same variable on both sides of the equal sign, you must first add or subtract to eliminate the variable term from one side of the equation.

Activity

1 Model and solve the equation $-x + 2 = 2x - 4$.

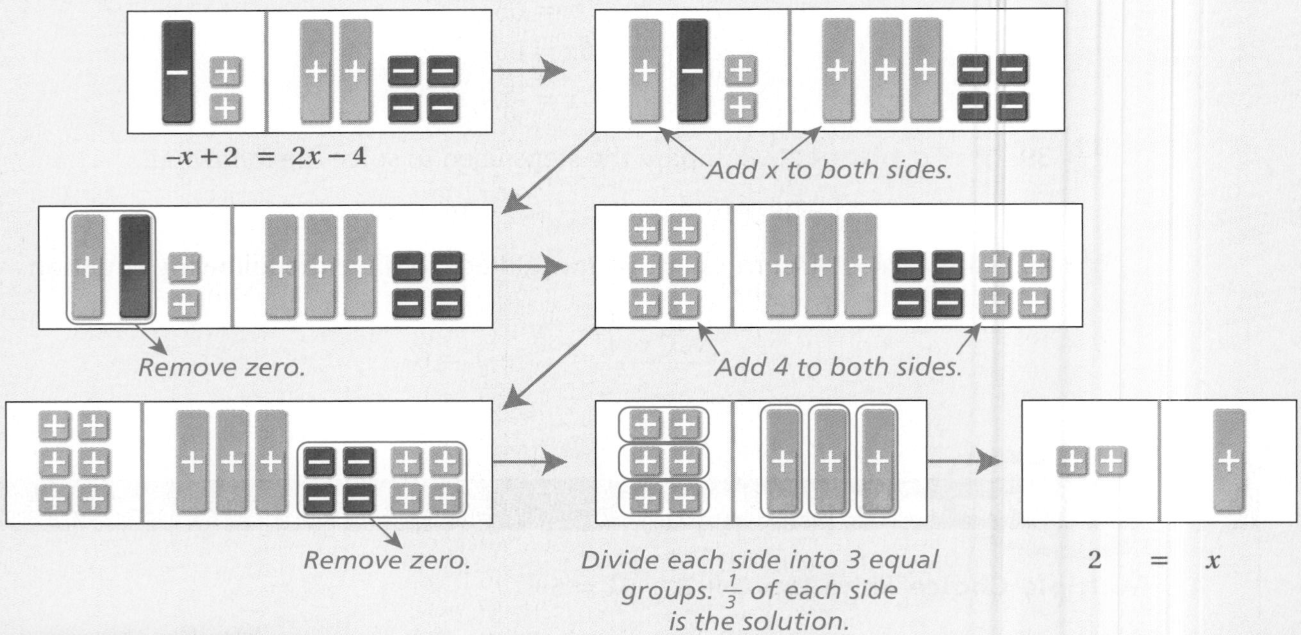

$-x + 2 = 2x - 4$
Add x to both sides.
Remove zero.
Add 4 to both sides.
Remove zero.
Divide each side into 3 equal groups. $\frac{1}{3}$ of each side is the solution.
$2 = x$

Think and Discuss

1. How would you check the solution to $-x + 2 = 2x - 4$ using algebra tiles?
2. Why must you isolate the variable terms by having them on only one side of the equation?

Try This

Model and solve each equation.

1. $x + 3 = -x - 3$ 2. $3x = -3x + 18$ 3. $6 - 3x = -4x + 8$ 4. $3x + 3x + 2 = x + 17$

11-3 Solving Equations with Variables on Both Sides

Learn to solve equations with variables on both sides of the equal sign.

Some problems produce equations that have variables on both sides of the equal sign. For example, Happy Paws, a dog-sitting service, charges a flat fee of \$19.00 plus \$1.50 per hour. A rival service, Woof Watchers, charges a flat fee of \$15.00 plus \$2.75 per hour. Find the number of hours for which the cost will be the same for both dog-sitting services.

Expression for Happy Paws $19.00 + 1.5h$ $15.00 + 2.75h$ *Expression for Woof Watchers*

$$19.00 + 1.5h = 15.00 + 2.75h$$

The variable h in these expressions represents the number of hours. The two expressions are equal when the cost is the same.

Solving an equation with variables on both sides is similar to solving an equation with a variable on only one side. You can add or subtract a term containing a variable on both sides of an equation.

EXAMPLE 1 Solving Equations with Variables on Both Sides

Solve.

A $2a + 3 = 3a$

$$\begin{aligned} 2a + 3 &= 3a \\ -2a \quad &\quad -2a \\ 3 &= a \end{aligned}$$

Subtract 2a from both sides.

B $3v - 8 = 7 + 8v$

$$\begin{aligned} 3v - 8 &= 7 + 8v \\ -3v \quad &\quad -3v \\ -8 &= 7 + 5v \end{aligned}$$

Subtract 3v from both sides.

$$\begin{aligned} -7 \quad &\quad -7 \\ -15 &= 5v \end{aligned}$$

Subtract 7 from both sides.

$$\frac{-15}{5} = \frac{5v}{5}$$

Divide both sides by 5.

$$-3 = v$$

Helpful Hint

Check your solution by substituting the value back into the original equation. For example, $2(3) + 3 = 3(3)$ or $9 = 9$.

Helpful Hint

If the variables in an equation are eliminated and the resulting statement is false, the equation has no solution.

Solve.

C $g + 7 = g - 3$

$$\begin{aligned} g + 7 &= g - 3 \\ -g \quad & \quad -g \\ 7 &\neq -3 \end{aligned}$$

Subtract g from both sides.

There is no solution. There is no number that can be substituted for the variable g to make the equation true.

To solve multi-step equations with variables on both sides, first combine like terms and clear fractions. Then add or subtract variable terms to both sides so that the variable occurs on only one side of the equation. Then use properties of equality to isolate the variable.

EXAMPLE 2 Solving Multi-Step Equations with Variables on Both Sides

Solve.

A $2c + 4 - 3c = -9 + c + 5$

$$2c + 4 - 3c = -9 + c + 5$$

$$-c + 4 = -4 + c \qquad \textit{Combine like terms.}$$

$$\underline{+c} \qquad \underline{+c} \qquad \textit{Add c to both sides.}$$

$$4 = -4 + 2c$$

$$\underline{+4} \qquad \underline{+4} \qquad \textit{Add 4 to both sides.}$$

$$8 = 2c$$

$$\frac{8}{2} = \frac{2c}{2} \qquad \textit{Divide both sides by 2.}$$

$$4 = c$$

B $\frac{2w}{3} - \frac{5w}{6} + \frac{1}{4} = w + \frac{11}{9}$

$$\frac{2w}{3} - \frac{5w}{6} + \frac{1}{4} = w + \frac{11}{9}$$

$$36\left(\frac{2w}{3} - \frac{5w}{6} + \frac{1}{4}\right) = 36\left(w + \frac{11}{9}\right) \qquad \textit{Multiply by LCD, 36.}$$

$$\overset{12}{\cancel{36}}\left(\frac{2w}{\cancel{3}_1}\right) - \overset{6}{\cancel{36}}\left(\frac{5w}{\cancel{6}_1}\right) + \overset{9}{\cancel{36}}\left(\frac{1}{\cancel{4}_1}\right) = 36(w) + \overset{4}{\cancel{36}}\left(\frac{11}{\cancel{9}_1}\right) \qquad \textit{Distributive Property}$$

$$24w - 30w + 9 = 36w + 44$$

$$-6w + 9 = 36w + 44 \qquad \textit{Combine like terms.}$$

$$\underline{+6w} \qquad \underline{+6w} \qquad \textit{Add 6w to both sides.}$$

$$9 = 42w + 44$$

$$\underline{-44} \qquad \underline{-44} \qquad \textit{Subtract 44 from both sides.}$$

$$-35 = 42w$$

$$\frac{-35}{42} = \frac{42w}{42} \qquad \textit{Divide both sides by 42.}$$

$$-\frac{5}{6} = w$$

EXAMPLE 3 Business Application

Happy Paws charges a flat fee of $19.00 plus $1.50 per hour to keep a dog during the day. A rival service, Woof Watchers, charges a flat fee of $15.00 plus $2.75 per hour. Find the number of hours for which you would pay the same total fee to both services.

$19.00 + 1.5h = 15.00 + 2.75h$ *Let h represent the number of hours.*

$-1.5h = -1.5h$ *Subtract 1.5h from both sides.*

$19.00 = 15.00 + 1.25h$

$-15.00 = -15.00$ *Subtract 15.00 from both sides.*

$4.00 = 1.25h$

$\frac{4.00}{1.25} = \frac{1.25h}{1.25}$ *Divide both sides by 1.25*

$3.2 = h$

The two services cost the same when used for 3.2 hours.

EXAMPLE 4 Multi-Step Application

Elaine runs the same distance every day. On Mondays, Fridays, and Saturdays, she runs 3 laps on the track and then runs 5 more miles. On Tuesdays and Thursdays, she runs 4 laps on the track and then runs 2.5 more miles. On Wednesdays, she just runs laps. How many laps does she run on Wednesdays?

First solve for the distance around the track.

$3x + 5 = 4x + 2.5$ *Let x represent the distance around the track.*

$-3x = -3x$ *Subtract 3x from both sides.*

$5 = x + 2.5$

$-2.5 = -2.5$ *Subtract 2.5 from both sides.*

$2.5 = x$ *The track is 2.5 miles around.*

Now find the total distance Elaine runs each day.

$3x + 5$ *Choose one of the original expressions.*

$3(2.5) + 5 = 12.5$ *Elaine runs 12.5 miles each day.*

Find the number of laps Elaine runs on Wednesdays.

$2.5n = 12.5$ *Let n represent the number of 2.5-mile laps.*

$\frac{2.5n}{2.5} = \frac{12.5}{2.5}$ *Divide both sides by 2.5.*

$n = 5$

Elaine runs 5 laps on Wednesdays.

Caution!

The value of the variable is not necessarily the answer to the question.

Think and Discuss

1. Explain how you would solve the equation $3x + 4 - 2x = 6x + 2 - 5x + 2$. What do you think the solution means?

11-3 Exercises

go.hrw.com
Homework Help Online
KEYWORD: MT7 11-3
Parent Resources Online
KEYWORD: MT7 Parent

GUIDED PRACTICE

See Example 1

Solve.

1. $6x + 3 = x + 8$
2. $5a - 5 = 7 + 2a$
3. $2x + 7 = 10x - 9$
4. $4y - 2 = 6y + 6$
5. $13x + 15 = 11x - 25$
6. $5t - 5 = 5t + 7$

See Example 2

7. $5x - 2 + 3x = 17 + 12x - 23$
8. $\frac{3n}{4} + \frac{n}{12} - 6 = 5 + 2n - 18$
9. $\frac{5}{12} + \frac{11d}{12} - 3 = 3d + 7 - 4d$
10. $4(x - 5) + 2 = x + 3$

See Example 3

11. A long-distance phone company charges \$0.027 per minute and a \$2 monthly fee. Another long-distance phone company charges \$0.035 per minute with no monthly fee. Find the number of minutes for which the charges for both companies would be the same.

See Example 4

12. June has a set of folding chairs. If she arranges the chairs in 5 rows, she has 2 chairs left over. If she arranges them in 3 rows of the same length, she has 14 left over. How many chairs does she have?

INDEPENDENT PRACTICE

See Example 1

Solve.

13. $3n + 16 = 7n$
14. $8x - 3 = 11 - 6x$
15. $5n + 3 = 14 - 6n$
16. $3(2x + 11) = 6x + 33$
17. $6x + 3 = x + 8$
18. $7y - 8 = 5y + 4$

See Example 2

19. $\frac{3p}{8} + \frac{7p}{16} - \frac{3}{4} = \frac{1}{4} + \frac{p}{16} + \frac{1}{2}$
20. $4(x - 5) - 5 = 6x + 7.4 - 4x$
21. $\frac{1}{2}(2n + 6) = 5n - 12 - n$
22. $\frac{a}{26} - 5.5 + 2a = \frac{9}{13} + \frac{20a}{13} + \frac{4}{13}$

See Example 3

23. Al's Rentals charges \$25 per hour to rent a Windsurfer™ and a wet suit. Wendy's charges \$20 per hour plus \$15 extra for a wet suit. Find the number of hours for which the total charges for both would be the same.

See Example 4

24. Sean and Laura have the same number of action figures in their collections. Sean has 6 complete sets plus 2 individual figures, and Laura has 3 complete sets plus 20 individual figures. How many figures are in a complete set?

PRACTICE AND PROBLEM SOLVING

Extra Practice
See page 802.

Solve and check.

25. $3y - 1 = 13 - 4y$
26. $4n + 8 = 9n - 7$
27. $5n + 20n = 5(n + 20)$
28. $3(4x - 2) = 12x$
29. $100(x - 3) = 450 - 50x$
30. $2p - 12 = 12 - 2p$

LINK

Physical Science

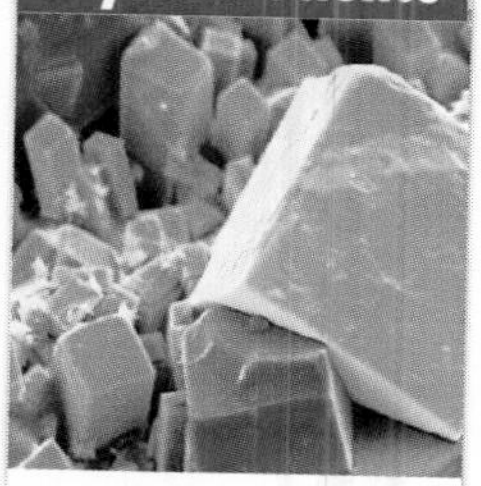

Sodium and chlorine bond together to form sodium chloride, or salt. The atomic structure of sodium chloride causes it to form cubes.

Both figures have the same perimeter. Find each perimeter.

31.

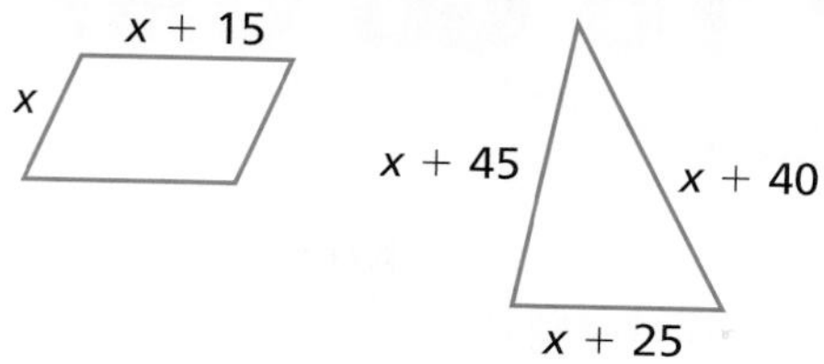

32.

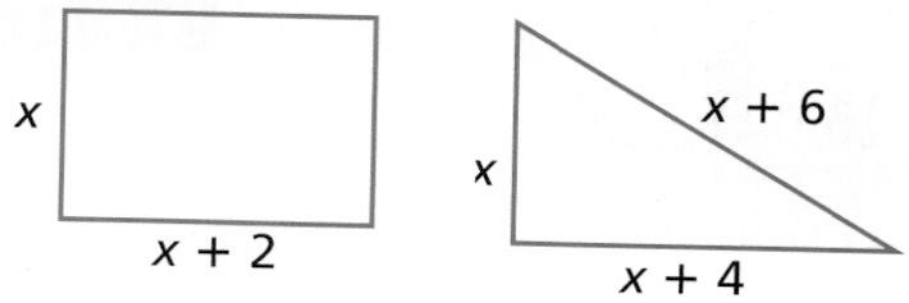

33. Find two consecutive whole numbers such that $\frac{3}{4}$ of the first number is 5 more than $\frac{1}{2}$ the second number. (*Hint:* Let n represent the first number. Then $n + 1$ represents the next consecutive whole number.)

34. **Physical Science** An atom of chlorine (Cl) has 6 more protons than an atom of sodium (Na). The atomic number of chlorine is 5 less than twice the atomic number of sodium. The atomic number of an element is equal to the number of protons per atom.

a. How many protons are in an atom of chlorine?

b. What is the atomic number of sodium?

35. **Business** George and Aaron work for different car dealerships. George earns a monthly salary of $2500 plus a 5% commission on his sales. Aaron earns a monthly salary of $3000 plus a 3% commission on his sales. How much must both sell to earn the same amount in a month?

36. **Choose a Strategy** Solve the following equation for t. How can you determine the solution once you have combined like terms?

$3(t - 24) = 7t - 4(t + 18)$

37. **Write About It** Two cars are traveling in the same direction. The first car is going 45 mi/h, and the second car is going 60 mi/h. The first car left 2 hours before the second car. Explain how you could solve an equation to find how long it will take the second car to catch up to the first car.

38. **Challenge** Solve the equation $\frac{x+2}{8} = \frac{6}{7} + \frac{x-1}{2}$.

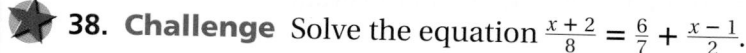

Test Prep and Spiral Review

39. **Multiple Choice** Find three consecutive integers so that the sum of the first two integers is 10 more than the third integer.

Ⓐ −7, −6, −5 Ⓑ 4, 5, 6 Ⓒ 11, 12, 13 Ⓓ 35, 36, 37

40. **Multiple Choice** Solve $6w - 15 = 9w$.

Ⓕ $w = 3$ Ⓖ $w = 0$ Ⓗ $w = -1$ Ⓙ $w = -5$

Write each number in scientific notation. (Lesson 4-4)

41. 0.00000064 **42.** 7,390,000,000 **43.** −0.0000016 **44.** −4,100,000

Solve. (Lesson 11-2)

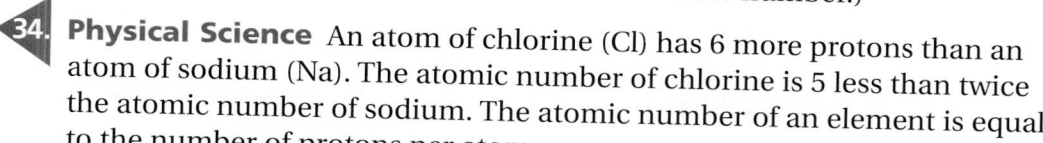

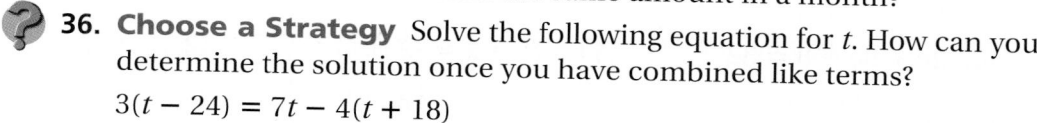

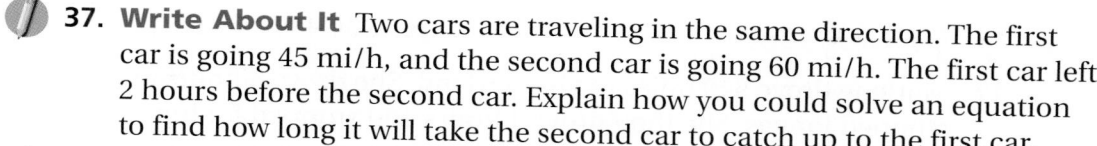

45. $6x - 3 + x = 4$ **46.** $32 = 13 - 4x + 21$ **47.** $5x + 14 - 2x = 23$

READY TO GO ON?

Quiz for Lessons 11-1 Through 11-3

11-1 Simplifying Algebraic Expressions

Simplify.

1. $5x + 3x$
2. $6p - 6 - p$
3. $2t + 3 - t + 4 + 5t$
4. $3x + 4y - x + 2y$
5. $4n + 2m + 8n - 2m$
6. $5b + 5c - 10$
7. $2(r + 1) - r$

Solve.

8. $9y - 5y = 8$
9. $7x + 2x = 45$

11-2 Solving Multi-Step Equations

Solve.

10. $2c + 6c + 8 = 32$
11. $\frac{3x}{7} - \frac{2}{7} = \frac{10}{7}$
12. $\frac{t}{4} + \frac{t}{3} = \frac{7}{12}$
13. $\frac{4m}{3} - \frac{m}{6} = \frac{7}{2}$
14. $\frac{3}{4}b - \frac{1}{5}b = 11$
15. $\frac{r}{3} + 7 - \frac{r}{5} = -3$
16. $30k + 88 = 163$
17. Marlene drove 540 miles to visit a friend. She drove 3 hours and stopped for gas. She then drove 4 hours and stopped for lunch. How many more hours did she drive if her average speed for the trip was 60 miles per hour?

11-3 Solving Equations with Variables on Both Sides

Solve.

18. $4x + 11 = x + 2$
19. $q + 5 = 2q + 7$
20. $6n + 21 = 4n + 57$
21. $2m + 6 = 2m - 1$
22. $9w - 2w + 8 = 4w + 38$
23. $-4a - 2a + 11 = 6a - 13$
24. $\frac{7}{12}y - \frac{1}{4} = 2y - \frac{5}{3}$
25. The rectangle and the triangle have the same perimeter. Find the perimeter of each figure.

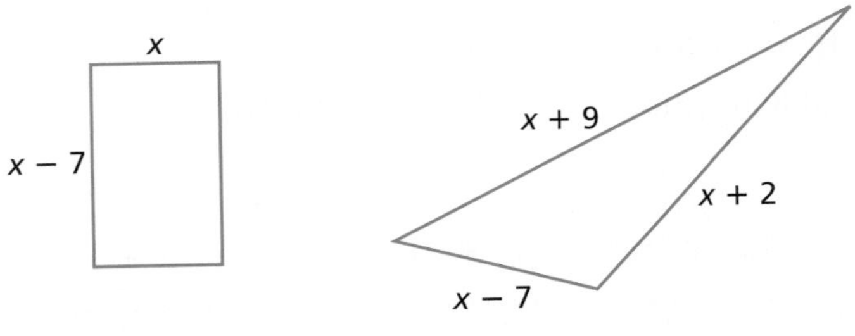

Focus on Problem Solving

Make a Plan

• Write an equation

Several steps may be needed to solve a problem. It often helps to write an equation that represents the steps.

Example:

Juan's first 3 exam scores are 85, 93, and 87. What does he need to score on his next exam to average 90 for the 4 exams?

Let x be the score on his next exam. The average of the exam scores is the sum of the 4 scores, divided by 4. This amount must equal 90.

$$\text{Average of exam scores} = 90$$
$$\frac{85 + 93 + 87 + x}{4} = 90$$
$$\frac{265 + x}{4} = 90$$
$$4\left(\frac{265 + x}{4}\right) = 4(90)$$
$$265 + x = 360$$
$$\underline{-265} \qquad \underline{-265}$$
$$x = 95$$

Juan needs a 95 on his next exam.

Read each problem and write an equation that could be used to solve it.

1. The average of two numbers is 34. The first number is three times the second number. What are the two numbers?

2. Nancy spends $\frac{1}{3}$ of her monthly salary on rent, 0.1 on her car payment, $\frac{1}{12}$ on food, and 20% on other bills. She has $680 left for other expenses. What is Nancy's monthly salary?

3. A vendor at a concert sells new and used CDs. The new CDs cost 2.5 times as much as the old CDs. If 4 used CDs and 9 new CDs cost $159, what is the price of each item?

4. Amanda and Rick have the same amount to spend on school supplies. Amanda buys 4 notebooks and has $8.60 left. Rick buys 7 notebooks and has $7.55 left. How much does each notebook cost?

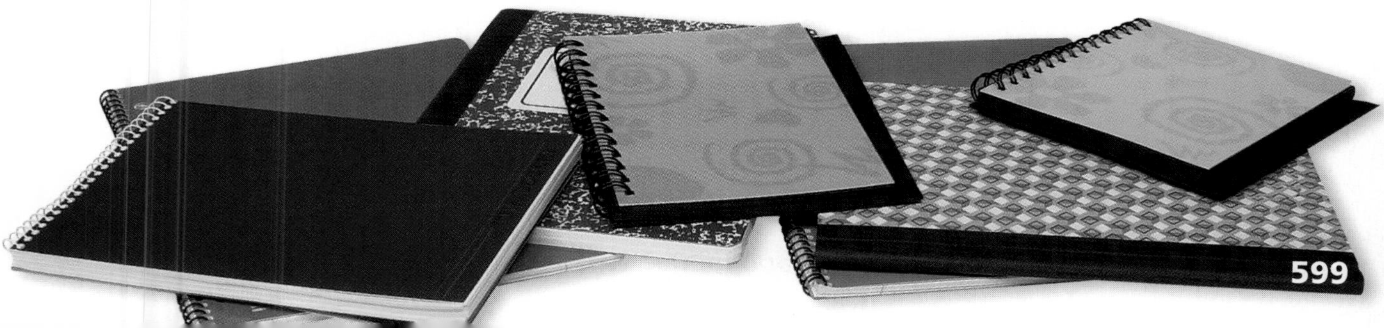

11-4 Solving Inequalities by Multiplying or Dividing

Learn to solve and graph inequalities by using multiplication or division.

Laid end to end, the paper used by personal computer printers each year would circle the earth more than 800 times. To find out how many sheets of paper this is, you can solve an inequality by dividing.

The steps for solving inequalities by multiplying or dividing are the same as for solving equations, with one exception. If both sides of an inequality are multiplied or divided by a negative number, the inequality symbol must be reversed.

EXAMPLE 1 Solving Inequalities by Multiplying or Dividing

Solve and graph.

A $24 > \frac{h}{5}$

$5 \cdot 24 > 5 \cdot \frac{h}{5}$ *Multiply both sides by 5.*

$120 > h$, or $h < 120$

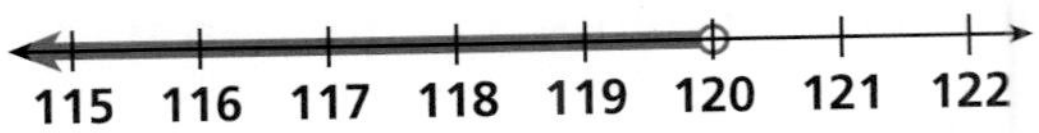

Check

According to the graph, 119 should be a solution because $119 < 120$, and 121 should not be a solution because $121 > 120$.

$24 > \frac{h}{5}$

$24 \overset{?}{>} \frac{119}{5}$ *Substitute 119 for h.*

$24 \overset{?}{>} 23.8$ ✔

So 119 is a solution.

$24 > \frac{h}{5}$

$24 \overset{?}{>} \frac{121}{5}$ *Substitute 121 for h.*

$24 \overset{?}{>} 24.2$ ✘

So 121 is not a solution.

B $-7x \geq 42$

$\frac{-7x}{-7} \leq \frac{42}{-7}$ *Divide both sides by −7; ≥ changes to ≤.*

$x \leq -6$

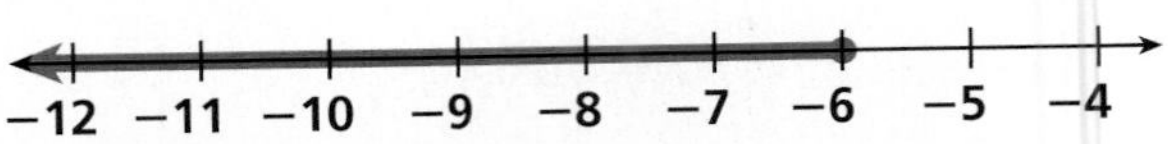

Remember!

When graphing an inequality on a number line, an open circle means that the point is not part of the solution and a closed circle means that the point is part of the solution.

EXAMPLE 2 **PROBLEM SOLVING APPLICATION**

PROBLEM SOLVING

If all the sheets of paper used by personal computer printers each year were laid end to end, they would circle the earth more than 800 times. The earth's circumference is about 25,120 mi (1,591,603,200 in.), and one letter-size sheet of paper is 11 in. long. How many sheets of paper are used each year?

1 Understand the Problem

The **answer** is the number of sheets of paper used by personal computer printers in one year. **List the important information:**

- The amount of paper would circle the earth *more than* 800 times.
- Once around the earth is 1,591,603,200 in.
- One sheet of paper is 11 in. long.

Show the relationship of the information:

the number of sheets of paper · **the length of one sheet** > **800** · **the distance around the earth**

2 Make a Plan

Use the relationship to *write an inequality.* Let x represent the number of sheets of paper.

$$x \cdot 11 \text{ in.} > 800 \cdot 1{,}591{,}603{,}200 \text{ in.}$$

3 Solve

$$11x > 800 \cdot 1{,}591{,}603{,}200$$

$$11x > 1{,}273{,}282{,}560{,}000 \qquad \textit{Simplify.}$$

$$\frac{11x}{11} > \frac{1{,}273{,}282{,}560{,}000}{11} \qquad \textit{Divide both sides by 11.}$$

$$x > 115{,}752{,}960{,}000$$

More than 115,752,960,000 sheets of paper are used by personal computer printers in one year.

4 Look Back

To circle the earth once takes $\frac{1{,}591{,}603{,}200}{11} = 144{,}691{,}200$ sheets of paper; to circle it 800 times would take $800 \cdot 144{,}691{,}200 = 115{,}752{,}960{,}000$ sheets.

Think and Discuss

1. Give all the symbols that make $5 \cdot -3$ ___ 15 true. Explain.

2. Explain how you would solve the inequality $-4x \leq 24$.

11-4 Exercises

go.hrw.com
Homework Help Online
KEYWORD: MT7 11-4
Parent Resources Online
KEYWORD: MT7 Parent

GUIDED PRACTICE

See Example 1

Solve and graph.

1. $\frac{r}{3} > 6$
2. $-4w > 12$
3. $20 \geq \frac{j}{6}$
4. $6r \leq 30$
5. $10 \leq \frac{a}{-4}$
6. $-36 < -2m$
7. $\frac{r}{-3} < 21$
8. $-20 \geq 5x$

See Example 2

9. The owner of a sandwich shop is selling the special of the week for $5.90. At this price, he makes a profit of $3.85 on each sandwich sold. To make a total profit of at least $400 from the special, what is the least number of sandwiches he must sell?

INDEPENDENT PRACTICE

See Example 1

Solve and graph.

10. $-16 < 2r$
11. $15 < \frac{x}{5}$
12. $-18w \geq -54$
13. $11 \leq \frac{p}{-7}$
14. $\frac{t}{9} > 4$
15. $9h > 108$
16. $\frac{a}{-7} < 14$
17. $-16q \leq 64$

See Example 2

18. **Social Studies** A bill in the U.S. House of Representatives passed because at least $\frac{2}{3}$ of the members present voted in favor of it. If the bill received 284 votes, at least how many members of the House of Representatives were present for the vote?

PRACTICE AND PROBLEM SOLVING

Extra Practice
See page 803.

Solve and graph.

19. $-18 < -3r$
20. $27 < \frac{x}{-3}$
21. $17w \geq -51$
22. $101 \leq \frac{p}{-7}$
23. $\frac{t}{-19} > -5$
24. $3h > 108$
25. $\frac{a}{10} < 12$
26. $-6q \leq -72$

Write and solve an algebraic inequality.

27. Nine times a number is less than 99.
28. The quotient of a number and 6 is at least 8.
29. The product of -7 and a number is no more than -63.
30. The quotient of some number and 3 is greater than 18.

Write and solve an algebraic inequality. Then explain the solution.

31. A school receives a shipment of books. There are 60 cartons, and each carton weighs 42 pounds. The school's elevator can hold 2200 pounds. What is the greatest number of cartons that can be carried on the elevator at one time if no people ride with them?
32. Each evening, Marisol spends at least twice as much time reading as she spends doing homework. If Marisol works on her homework for 40 minutes, how much time can she spend reading?

Choose the graph that represents each inequality.

33. $-2y < 14$

Ⓐ 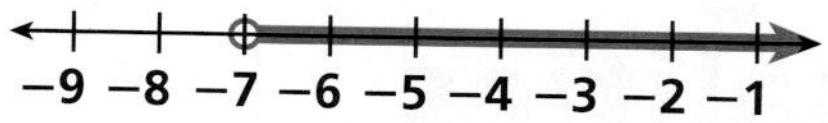

Ⓑ 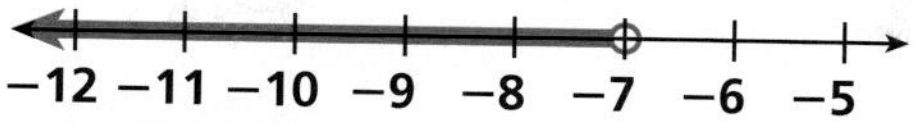

Ⓒ 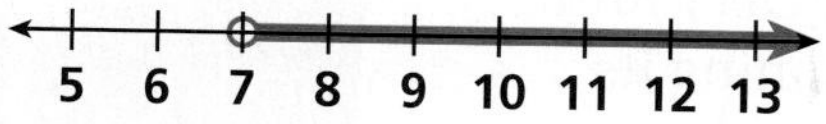

34. $6 \geq \frac{h}{5}$

Ⓐ 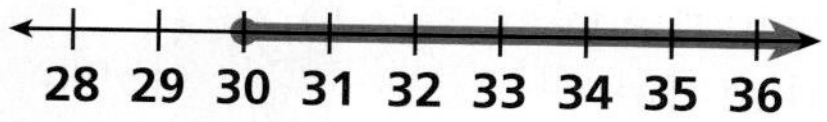

Ⓑ 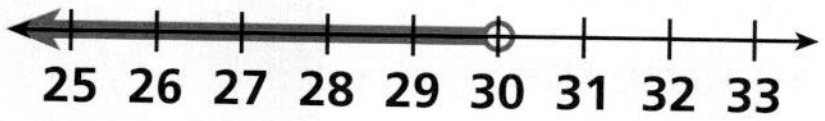

Ⓒ 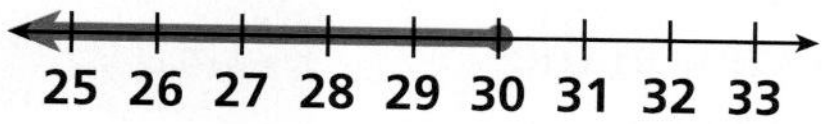

35. What's the Error? Connie solved $x \div 3 \geq 12$ and got an answer of $x \leq 36$. What error did Connie make?

36. Write About It The expressions *no more than, at most,* and *less than or equal to* all indicate the same relationship between values. Write a problem that uses this relationship. Write the problem using each of the three expressions.

37. Challenge Angel weighs 5 times as much as his dog. When they stand on a scale together, it gives a reading of less than 163 pounds. If both their weights are whole numbers, what is the most each can weigh?

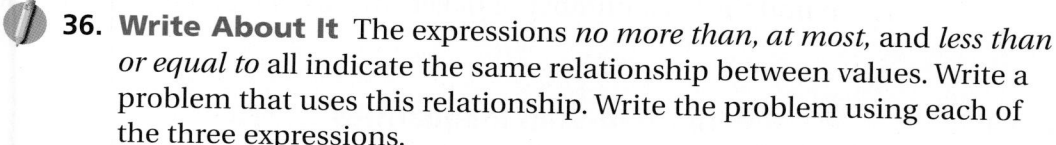

Test Prep and Spiral Review

38. Multiple Choice Which inequality is shown by the graph?

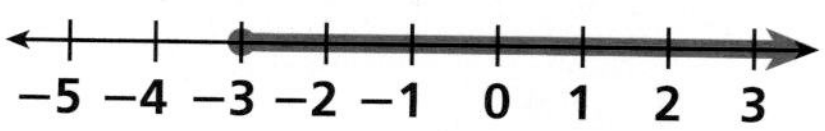

Ⓐ $w \leq -3$ Ⓑ $w > -3$ Ⓒ $w \geq -3$ Ⓓ $-3 < w$

39. Gridded Response In order to have the $200 he needs for a bike, Kevin plans to put money away each week for the next 15 weeks. What is the minimum amount in dollars that Kevin will need to average each week in order to reach his goal?

An experiment consists of rolling two fair number cubes. Find each probability. (Lesson 10-4)

40. $P(\text{total shown} > 10)$ **41.** $P(\text{two odd numbers})$ **42.** $P(\text{two 6's})$

43. In a chess tournament, 8 students will play against each other once. How many games will there be in all? (Lesson 10-6)

11-5 Solving Two-Step Inequalities

Learn to solve two-step inequalities and graph the solutions of an inequality on a number line.

The drama club at Deer Run High School is planning its annual spring musical. They have \$610.75 left from fund-raising earlier in the year, but they estimate that the costumes and sets will cost \$1100.00. In order to raise the extra money they will need and at least break even on the production, the drama club is planning to sell tickets to the musical for \$4.75 each. You can set up and solve a two-step inequality to find the least number of tickets the drama club will need to sell.

EXAMPLE 1 Solving Two-Step Inequalities

Solve and graph.

A $7y - 4 > 24$

$$\begin{aligned} 7y - 4 &> 24 \\ \underline{\quad +4} &\quad \underline{+4} \\ 7y &> 28 \end{aligned}$$ *Add 4 to both sides.*

$$\frac{7y}{7} > \frac{28}{7}$$ *Divide both sides by 7.*

$$y > 4$$

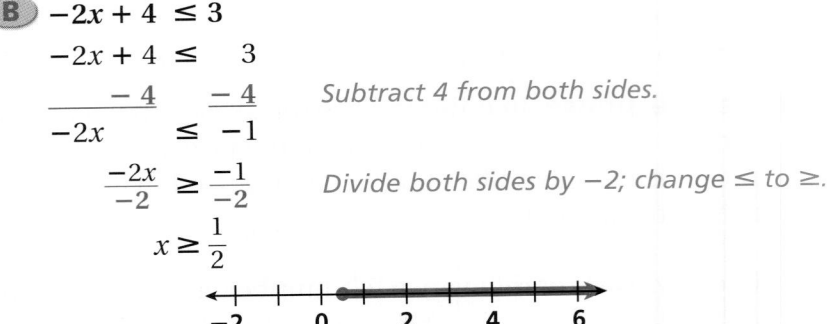

B $-2x + 4 \leq 3$

$$\begin{aligned} -2x + 4 &\leq 3 \\ \underline{\quad -4} &\quad \underline{-4} \\ -2x &\leq -1 \end{aligned}$$ *Subtract 4 from both sides.*

$$\frac{-2x}{-2} \geq \frac{-1}{-2}$$ *Divide both sides by −2; change ≤ to ≥.*

$$x \geq \frac{1}{2}$$

Remember!

If both sides of an inequality are multiplied or divided by a negative number, the inequality symbol must be reversed.

Recall that when an equation or an inequality contains fractions, it is often easier to multiply both sides by the LCD to clear the fractions.

EXAMPLE 2 Solving Inequalities That Contain Fractions

Solve $\frac{-3x}{8} + \frac{5}{6} \leq \frac{7}{12}$ and graph the solution.

$$24\left(\frac{-3x}{8} + \frac{5}{6}\right) \leq 24\left(\frac{7}{12}\right)$$ *Multiply by the LCD, 24.*

$$24\left(\frac{-3x}{8}\right) + 24\left(\frac{5}{6}\right) \leq 24\left(\frac{7}{12}\right)$$ *Distributive Property*

$$-9x + 20 \leq 14$$

$$\underline{\quad -20 \quad} \quad \underline{-20}$$ *Subtract 20 from both sides.*

$$-9x \leq -6$$

$$\frac{-9x}{-9} \geq \frac{-6}{-9}$$ *Divide both sides by −9; change ≤ to ≥.*

$$x \geq \frac{6}{9}$$

$$x \geq \frac{2}{3}$$ *Simplify.*

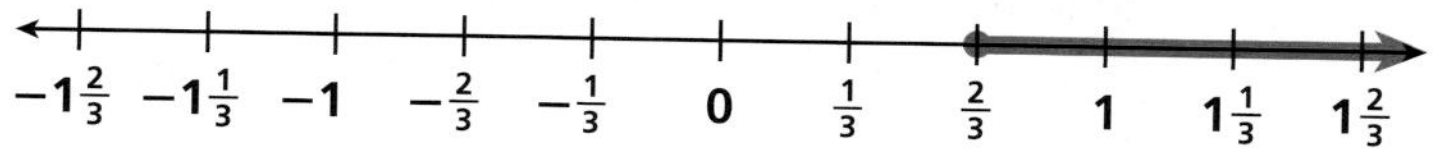

EXAMPLE 3 *School Application*

The drama club plans to present its annual spring musical. They have \$610.75 left from fund-raising, but they estimate that the entire production will cost \$1100.00. If they sell tickets for \$4.75 each, how many must they sell to at least break even?

In order to at least break even, ticket sales plus the money in the budget must be greater than or equal to the cost of the production.

$$4.75t + 610.75 \geq 1100.00$$

$$\underline{\quad -610.75 \quad} \quad \underline{-610.75}$$ *Subtract 610.75 from both sides.*

$$4.75t \geq 489.25$$

$$\frac{4.75t}{4.75} \geq \frac{489.25}{4.75}$$ *Divide both sides by 4.75.*

$$t \geq 103$$

The drama club must sell at least 103 tickets in order to break even.

Think and Discuss

1. **Compare** solving a multi-step equation with solving a multi-step inequality.
2. **Describe** two situations in which you would have to reverse the inequality symbol when solving a multi-step inequality.

11-5 Exercises

go.hrw.com
Homework Help Online
KEYWORD: MT7 11-5
Parent Resources Online
KEYWORD: MT7 Parent

GUIDED PRACTICE

See Example 1

Solve and graph.

1. $3k + 5 > 11$
2. $2z - 29.5 \leq 10.5$
3. $6y + 12 < -36$
4. $-4x + 6 \geq 14$
5. $2y + 2.5 \geq 16.5$
6. $3k - 2 > 13$

See Example 2

7. $\frac{x}{15} + \frac{1}{5} < \frac{2}{5}$
8. $\frac{b}{10} - \frac{3}{5} \geq -\frac{1}{2}$
9. $\frac{h}{3} - 2 \leq -\frac{5}{3}$
10. $\frac{c}{8} + \frac{1}{2} > \frac{3}{4}$
11. $\frac{1}{2} + \frac{d}{6} < \frac{1}{3}$
12. $\frac{2}{3} \geq \frac{6m}{9}$

See Example 3

13. The chess club is selling caps to raise $425 for a trip. They have $175 already. If the club members sell caps for $12 each, at least how many caps do they need to sell to make enough money for their trip?

INDEPENDENT PRACTICE

See Example 1

Solve and graph.

14. $8k - 6 > 18$
15. $5x + 3 > 23$
16. $3p + 3 \geq -36$
17. $13 \geq 11q - 9$
18. $3.6 + 7.2n < 25.2$
19. $-7x - 15 \geq 34$

See Example 2

20. $\frac{p}{15} + \frac{4}{5} < \frac{1}{3}$
21. $\frac{a}{9} + \frac{2}{3} \geq \frac{1}{3}$
22. $-\frac{1}{3} + \frac{n}{12} > -\frac{1}{4}$
23. $-\frac{2}{3} \leq \frac{1}{18}k - \frac{5}{6}$
24. $\frac{4}{7} + \frac{n}{14} \leq -\frac{3}{7}$
25. $\frac{1}{3} + \frac{r}{18} < \frac{1}{2}$

See Example 3

26. Josef is on the planning committee for the eighth-grade party. The food, decoration, and entertainment costs a total of $350. The committee has $75 already. If the committee sells the tickets for $5 each, at least how many tickets must be sold to cover the remaining cost of the party?

PRACTICE AND PROBLEM SOLVING

Extra Practice
See page 803.

Solve and graph.

27. $3p - 11 \leq 11$
28. $9n + 10 > -17$
29. $3 - 5w < 8$
30. $-6x - 18 \geq 6$
31. $12a + 4 > 10$
32. $-4y + 3 \geq 17$
33. $3q - 5q > -12$
34. $\frac{3m}{4} > \frac{5}{8}$
35. $4b - 3.2 < 7.6$
36. $3k + 6 \geq 4$
37. $\frac{90}{4} \leq -\frac{5}{6}f$
38. $-\frac{5}{9}v \geq -\frac{1}{3}$

39. **Critical Thinking** What is the least whole number that is a solution of $2r - 4.4 > 8.6$?

40. **Entertainment** A speech is being given in a gymnasium that can hold no more than 650 people. A permanent bleacher will seat 136 people. The event organizers are setting up 25 rows of chairs. At most, how many chairs can be in each row?

41. Katie and April are making a string of beads for *pi* day (March 14). The string already has 70 beads. If there are only 30 more days until *pi* day, and they want to string 1000 beads by then, at least how many beads do they have to string each day?

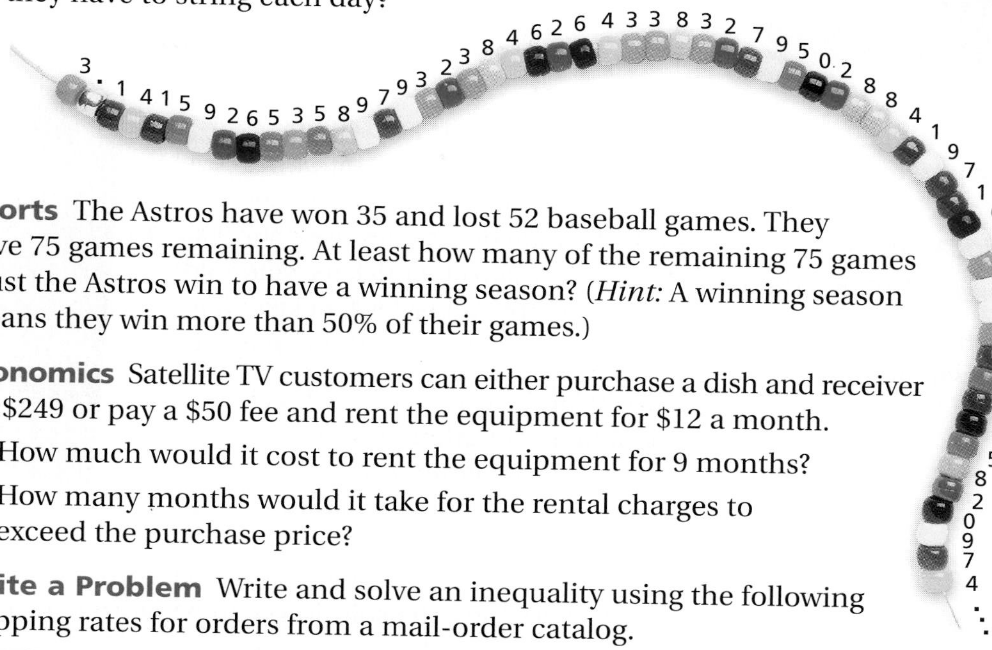

42. **Sports** The Astros have won 35 and lost 52 baseball games. They have 75 games remaining. At least how many of the remaining 75 games must the Astros win to have a winning season? (*Hint:* A winning season means they win more than 50% of their games.)

43. **Economics** Satellite TV customers can either purchase a dish and receiver for \$249 or pay a \$50 fee and rent the equipment for \$12 a month.

a. How much would it cost to rent the equipment for 9 months?

b. How many months would it take for the rental charges to exceed the purchase price?

44. **Write a Problem** Write and solve an inequality using the following shipping rates for orders from a mail-order catalog.

Mail-Order Shipping Rates					
Merchandise Amount	\$0.01–\$25.00	\$25.01–50.00	\$50.01–75.00	\$75.01–125.00	\$125.01 and over
Shipping Cost	\$3.95	\$5.95	\$7.95	\$9.95	\$11.95

45. **Write About It** Describe two ways to solve the inequality $-3x - 4 < x$.

46. **Challenge** Solve the inequality $\frac{x}{5} - \frac{x}{6} \geq \frac{1}{15}$.

Test Prep and Spiral Review

47. **Multiple Choice** Solve $3g - 6 > 18$.

Ⓐ $g > 21$ Ⓑ $g > 8$ Ⓒ $g > 6$ Ⓓ $g > 4$

48. **Short Response** Solve and graph $\frac{5x}{6} + \frac{1}{2} < \frac{2}{3}$.

Complete each figure. The dashed line is the line of symmetry. (Lesson 7-8)

49. 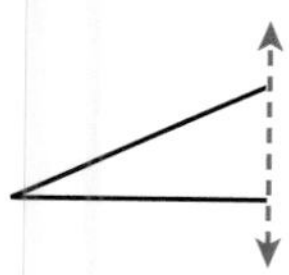

50. 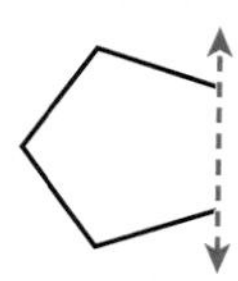

51. 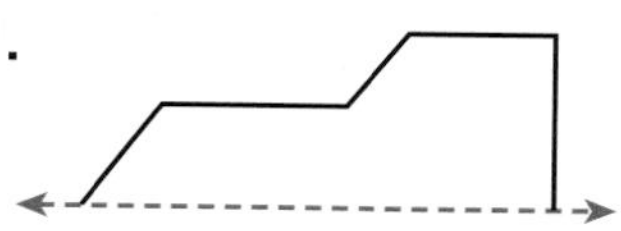

Solve. (Lesson 11-3)

52. $4w + 3 = w$

53. $13a + 10 = 70 - 2a$

54. $2x - 5 = 9x + 9$

11-6 Systems of Equations

Learn to solve systems of equations.

Vocabulary

system of equations

solution of a system of equations

Tickets for a concert are \$40 for main-floor seats and \$25 for upper-level seats. A total of 2000 concert tickets were sold. The total ticket sales were \$62,000. How many main-floor tickets were sold and how many upper-level tickets were sold? You can solve this problem using two equations.

A **system of equations** is a set of two or more equations that contain two or more variables. A **solution of a system of equations** is a set of values that are solutions of all of the equations. If the system has two variables, the solutions can be written as ordered pairs.

EXAMPLE 1 Solving Systems of Equations

Solve each system of equations.

A $y = x + 3$

$y = 2x + 5$

The expressions $x + 3$ and $2x + 5$ both equal y. So by the Transitive Property they equal each other.

$$y = x + 3 \qquad y = 2x + 5$$

$$x + 3 = 2x + 5$$

Solve the equation to find x.

$$\begin{aligned} x + 3 &= 2x + 5 \\ -x \quad &\quad -x & &\text{Subtract } x \text{ from both sides.} \\ 3 &= x + 5 \\ -5 \quad &\quad -5 & &\text{Subtract 5 from both sides.} \\ -2 &= x \end{aligned}$$

To find y, substitute -2 for x in one of the original equations.

$y = x + 3 = -2 + 3 = 1$

The solution is $(-2, 1)$.

Caution!

When solving systems of equations, remember to find values for all of the variables.

B $y = 3x + 8$

$y = -7 + 3x$

$$\begin{aligned} 3x + 8 &= -7 + 3x & &\text{Transitive Property} \\ -3x \quad &\quad -3x & &\text{Subtract } 3x \text{ from both sides.} \\ 8 &\neq -7 \end{aligned}$$

The system of equations has no solution.

To solve a general system of two equations with two variables, you can solve both equations for x or both for y.

EXAMPLE 2 Solving Systems of Equations by Solving for a Variable

Solve the system of equations.

A $x - y = 3$
$x + 5y = 39$

Solve both equations for x.

$$\begin{aligned} x - y &= 3 \\ +y \quad &\quad +y \\ x &= 3 + y \end{aligned} \qquad \begin{aligned} x + 5y &= 39 \\ -5y \quad &\quad -5y \\ x &= 39 - 5y \end{aligned}$$

$$3 + y = 39 - 5y$$

$$+5y \qquad +5y$$ *Add 5y to both sides.*

$$3 + 6y = 39$$

$$-3 \qquad -3$$ *Subtract 3 from both sides.*

$$6y = 36$$

$$\frac{6y}{6} = \frac{36}{6}$$ *Divide both sides by 6.*

$$y = 6$$

$$x = 3 + y$$

$$= 3 + 6 = 9$$ *Substitute 6 for y.*

The solution is (9, 6).

B $3x + y = 8$
$6x + 2y = 16$

Solve both equations for y.

$$\begin{aligned} 3x + y &= 8 \\ -3x \quad &\quad -3x \\ y &= 8 - 3x \end{aligned} \qquad \begin{aligned} 6x + 2y &= 16 \\ -6x \quad &\quad -6x \\ 2y &= 16 - 6x \\ \frac{2y}{2} &= \frac{16}{2} - \frac{6x}{2} \\ y &= 8 - 3x \end{aligned}$$

$$8 - 3x = 8 - 3x$$

$$+3x \qquad +3x$$ *Add 3x to both sides.*

$$8 = 8$$

Since $8 = 8$ is always true, the system of equations has an infinite number of solutions.

Helpful Hint

You can solve for either variable. It is usually easiest to solve for a variable that has a coefficient of 1.

Think and Discuss

1. **Compare** an equation to a system of equations.
2. **Describe** how you would know whether (−1, 0) is a solution of the system of equations below.

$$x + 2y = -1$$
$$-3x + 4y = 3$$

11-6 Exercises

go.hrw.com
Homework Help Online
KEYWORD: MT7 11-6
Parent Resources Online
KEYWORD: MT7 Parent

GUIDED PRACTICE

See Example 1

Solve each system of equations.

1. $y = x + 1$
   $y = 2x - 1$
2. $y = -2x + 3$
   $y = 5x - 4$
3. $y = 3x - 5$
   $y = 6x + 7$
4. $y = 6x - 12$
   $y = -9x + 3$
5. $y = 5x + 7$
   $y = -3x + 7$
6. $y = 3x + 5$
   $y = 3x - 10$

See Example 2

7. $2x + 2y = 16$
   $2x + 6y = 28$
8. $x + y = 20$
   $x = y - 4$
9. $x + 2y = 21$
   $-x + 3y = 29$
10. $5x - 2y = 4$
    $11x + 4y = -8$
11. $x = -3y$
    $7x - 2y = -69$
12. $-4x - 5y = -7$
    $11y = 2x + 37$

INDEPENDENT PRACTICE

See Example 1

Solve each system of equations.

13. $y = -2x - 1$
    $y = 2x + 3$
14. $y = 3x + 6$
    $y = x + 2$
15. $y = 5x - 3$
    $y = -3x + 13$
16. $y = x + 6$
    $y = -2x - 12$
17. $y = 3x - 1$
    $y = -2x + 9$
18. $y = -2x - 6$
    $y = 3x + 29$

See Example 2

19. $3x + 3y = 15$
    $3x - 6y = -12$
20. $2x + y = 11$
    $-x + 2y = 2$
21. $y = 5x - 2$
    $4x + 3y = 13$
22. $5x - 9y = 11$
    $3x + 7y = 19$
23. $12x + 18y = 30$
    $4x - 13y = 67$
24. $-14x - 11y = 97$
    $-12y + 11x = 27$

PRACTICE AND PROBLEM SOLVING

Extra Practice
See page 803.

25. **Crafts** Robin cross-stitches bookmarks and wall hangings. A bookmark takes her $1\frac{1}{2}$ days, and a wall hanging takes her 4 days. Robin recently spent 18 days cross-stitching 7 items. Solve the system of equations to find the number of bookmarks and the number of wall hangings that Robin cross-stitched.

$$1\frac{1}{2}b + 4w = 18$$
$$b + w = 7$$

Solve each system of equations.

26. $y = 3x - 2$
    $y = x + 2$
27. $y = -11x + 5$
    $y = 10x - 37$
28. $5x + 5y = -5$
    $5x - 5y = 25$
29. $3x - y = 5$
    $x - 4y = -2$
30. $2x + 6y = 1$
    $4x - 3y = 0$
31. $x + 1.5y = 7.4$
    $3x - 0.5y = -6.8$
32. $\frac{1}{5}x + \frac{3}{8}y = \frac{1}{2}$
    $2x + 3.75y = 5$
33. $0.25x + 0.6y = 2.5$
    $\frac{1}{4}x - \frac{3}{5}y = 3\frac{3}{7}$
34. $3x + 2y = -44$
    $-3x + 4y = 2$

LINK

Entertainment

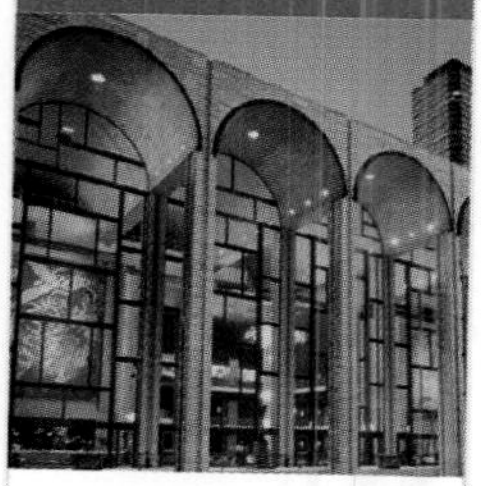

The Metropolitan Opera House in New York has 6 levels and 3500 seats.

go.hrw.com
Web Extra!
KEYWORD: MT7 Music

35. Gustav has 35 dimes and quarters that total \$5.00. Solve the system of equations to find how many dimes and how many quarters he has.

$$d + q = 35$$
$$0.1d + 0.25q = 5$$

36. Entertainment Tickets for a concert are \$40 for main-floor seats and \$25 for upper-level seats. A total of 2000 concert tickets were sold. The ticket sales were \$62,000. Let m represent the number of main-floor tickets and u represent the number of upper-level tickets.

a. Write an equation about the total number of tickets sold.

b. Write an equation about the total ticket sales.

c. Solve the system of equations to find how many main-floor tickets were sold and how many upper-level tickets were sold.

37. Geometry The perimeter of the rectangle is 114 units. The perimeter of the triangle is 63 units. Find x and y.

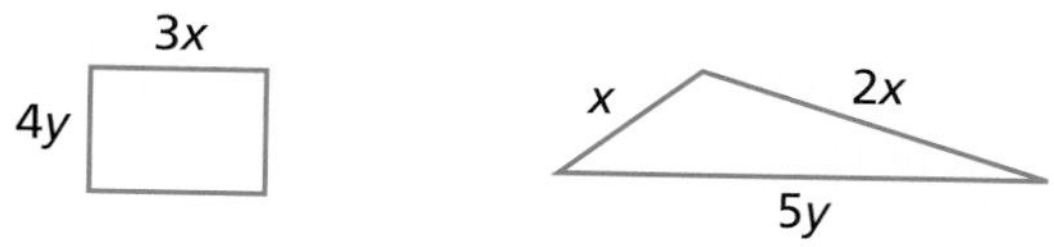

38. Write a Problem Write a word problem that requires using a system of equations to solve. Solve the problem.

39. Write About It List the steps you would use to solve the system of equations. Explain which variable you would solve for and why.

$$x + 2y = 7$$
$$2x + y = 8$$

40. Challenge Solve the system of equations

$$5x - y - 12z = 61$$
$$-2x + 11y + 8z = 4$$
$$-12x - 8y + 12z = -24$$

Test Prep and Spiral Review

41. Multiple Choice Carlos has \$3.35 in dimes and quarters. If he has a total of 23 coins, how many dimes does he have?

Ⓐ 9 Ⓑ 11 Ⓒ 16 Ⓓ 18

42. Gridded Response Solve the system of equations. What is the y-value?

$$2x + 3y = 10$$
$$x + 5y = 26$$

Solve each proportion. (Lesson 5-4)

43. $\frac{2}{3} = \frac{x}{6}$ **44.** $\frac{3}{4} = \frac{d}{28}$ **45.** $\frac{5}{1} = \frac{r}{7}$ **46.** $\frac{10}{3} = \frac{40}{w}$

Solve. (Lesson 11-2)

47. $4z - 2z = 23 + 17$ **48.** $3p + 5p + 15 = 39$ **49.** $20y - 7 + 11y = 2$

CHAPTER 11

READY TO GO ON?

SECTION 11B

Quiz for Lessons 11-4 Through 11-6

11-4 Solving Inequalities by Multiplying or Dividing

Solve and graph.

1. $-5x > 15$
2. $\frac{t}{4} > 8$
3. $9 \geq \frac{k}{3}$
4. $7r \leq 49$
5. $8 \leq \frac{b}{-2}$
6. $-32 < -4n$
7. $\frac{y}{-4} < 4$
8. $-24 \geq 6m$
9. $8 < -2a$
10. $-n > -10$
11. $\frac{h}{2} \leq -42$
12. $3d \geq -15$
13. Rachael is serving lemonade from a pitcher that holds 60 ounces. What are the possible numbers of 7-ounce juice glasses she can fill from one pitcher?

11-5 Solving Two-Step Inequalities

Solve and graph.

14. $2k + 4 > 10$
15. $0.5z - 5.5 \leq 4.5$
16. $5y + 10 < -25$
17. $\frac{3x}{5} - \frac{9}{15} \leq \frac{3}{5}$
18. $\frac{2h}{3} + \frac{7}{6} \geq -\frac{1}{6}$
19. $\frac{1}{2} + \frac{3c}{8} > \frac{1}{4}$
20. $\frac{1}{3} + \frac{t}{9} < -2$
21. $\frac{1}{3} - \frac{3x}{4} \geq \frac{5}{6}$
22. $\frac{3}{7} + \frac{m}{14} \leq -\frac{2}{7}$
23. Jillian must average at least 90 on two quiz scores before she can move to the next skill level. Jillian got a 92 on her first quiz. What scores could Jillian get on her second quiz in order to move to the next skill level?

11-6 Systems of Equations

Solve each system of equations.

24. $y = -3x + 2$
    $y = 4x - 5$
25. $y = 5x - 3$
    $y = 2x + 6$
26. $y = -2x + 6$
    $y = 3x - 9$
27. $x + y = 8$
    $x + 3y = 14$
28. $2x + y = 12$
    $3x - y = 13$
29. $4x - 3y = 33$
    $x = -4y - 25$
30. The sum of two numbers is 18. Their difference is 8.
    a. If the numbers are x and y, write a system of equations to describe their sum and their difference.
    b. Solve the system to find the numbers

Ready to Go On?

MULTI-STEP TEST PREP

Skate Away Ms. Lucinda wants to treat her class of 30 students to a skating party to celebrate the end of the school year.

Item	Cost
Rink rental	\$50 plus \$25 per hour
Skate rental (per person)	\$1.50 plus \$0.50 per hour
Refreshments (per person)	\$3.50

1. Ms. Lucinda considers renting the rink at Skate Away. How much would it cost to rent the rink for x hours?
2. Another rink, Skate Palace, charges \$100 plus \$15 per hour to rent the rink. Write and solve an equation to find the number of hours for which the cost of renting the rink at Skate Palace is the same as the cost of renting the rink at Skate Away.
3. Ms. Lucinda decides to take the class to Skate Away. How much will it cost to rent skates for 30 students for x hours? How much will it cost to buy refreshments for 30 students?
4. Ms. Lucinda has budgeted \$400 for the party. Write and solve an inequality to find the maximum number of hours the class can have its party at Skate Away. Be sure to include the cost of the rink, the skates, and the refreshments.
5. The final bill for the party was \$380. How long did the party last?

Game Time

Trans-Plants

Solve each equation below. Then use the values of the variables to decode the answer to the question.

$3a + 17 = -25$

$2b - 25 + 5b = 7 - 32$

$2.7c - 4.5 = 3.6c - 9$

$\frac{5}{12}d + \frac{1}{6}d + \frac{1}{3}d + \frac{1}{12}d = 6$

$4e - 6e - 5 = 15$

$420 = 29f - 73$

$2(g + 6) = -20$

$2h + 7 = -3h + 52$

$96i + 245 = 53$

$3j + 7 = 46$

$\frac{1}{2}k = \frac{3}{4}k - \frac{1}{2}$

$30l + 240 = 50l - 160$

$4m + \frac{3}{8} = \frac{67}{8}$

$24 - 6n = 54$

$8.4o - 6.8 = 14.2 + 6.3o$

$4p - p + 8 = 2p + 5$

$16 - 3q = 3q + 40$

$4 + \frac{1}{3}r = r - 8$

$\frac{2}{3}s - \frac{5}{6}s + \frac{1}{2} = -\frac{3}{2}$

$4 - 15 = 4t + 17$

$45 + 36u = 66 + 23u + 31$

$6v + 8 = -4 - 6v$

$4w + 3w - 6w = w + 15 + 2w - 3w$

$x + 2x + 3x + 4x + 5 = 75$

$\frac{4 - y}{5} = \frac{2 - 2y}{8}$

$-11 = 25 - 4.5z$

What happens to plants that live in a math classroom?

−7, 9, −10, −11   −16, 18, 10, 15   12, −4, 4, −14, 18, −10   18, 10, 10, −7, 12

24 Points

This traditional Chinese game is played using a deck of 52 cards numbered 1–13, with four of each number. The cards are shuffled, and four cards are placed face up in the center. The winner is the first player who comes up with an expression that equals 24, using each of the numbers on the four cards once.

Complete rules and a set of game cards are available online.

go.hrw.com
Game Time Extra
KEYWORD: MT7 Games

It's in the Bag!

FOLDNOTES

Materials
- magazine
- glue
- scissors
- index cards

PROJECT Picture Envelopes

Make these picture-perfect envelopes in which to store your notes on the lessons of this chapter.

Directions

1. Flip through a magazine and carefully tear out six pages with full-page pictures that you like.
2. Lay one of the pages in front of you with the picture face down. Fold the page into thirds as shown, and then unfold the page. **Figure A**
3. Fold the sides in, about 1 inch, and then unfold. Cut away the four rectangles at the corners of the page. **Figure B**
4. Fold in the two middle flaps. Then fold up the bottom and glue it onto the flaps. **Figure C**
5. Cut the corners of the top section at an angle to make a flap. **Figure D**
6. Repeat the steps to make five more envelopes. Label them so that there is one for each lesson of the chapter.

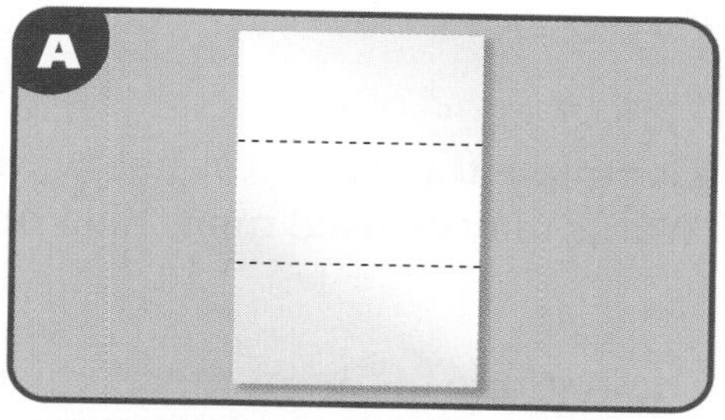

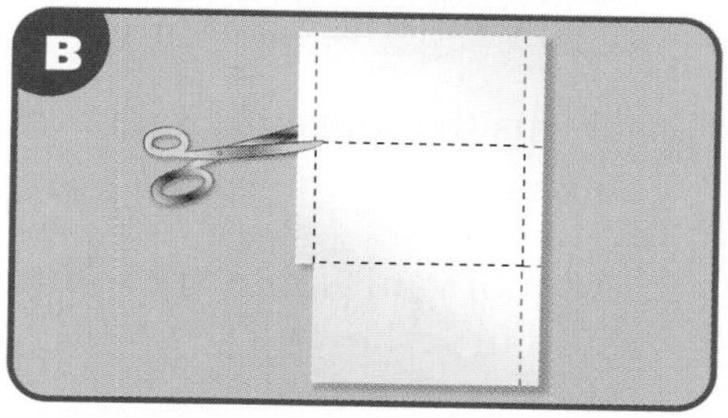

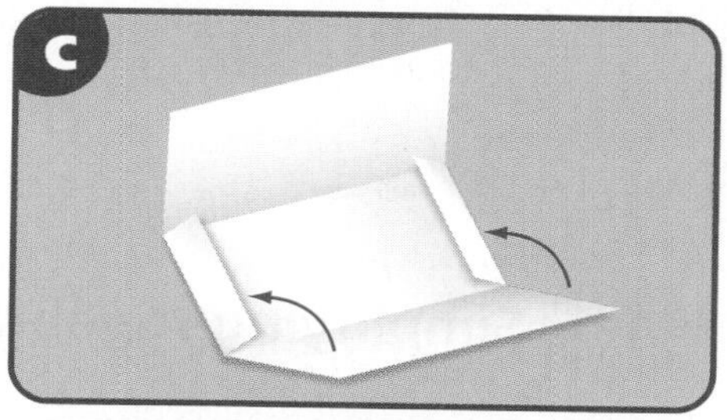

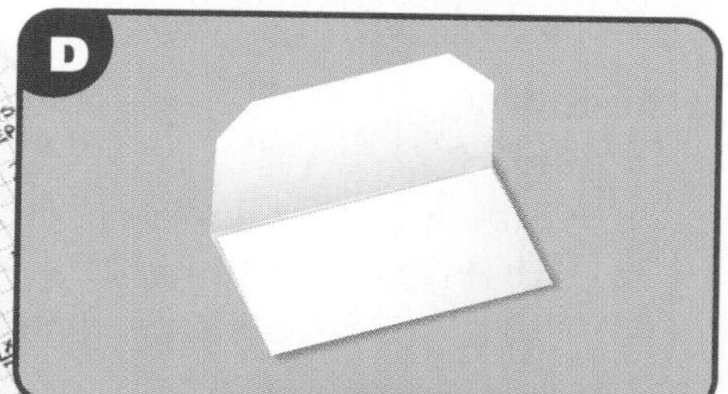

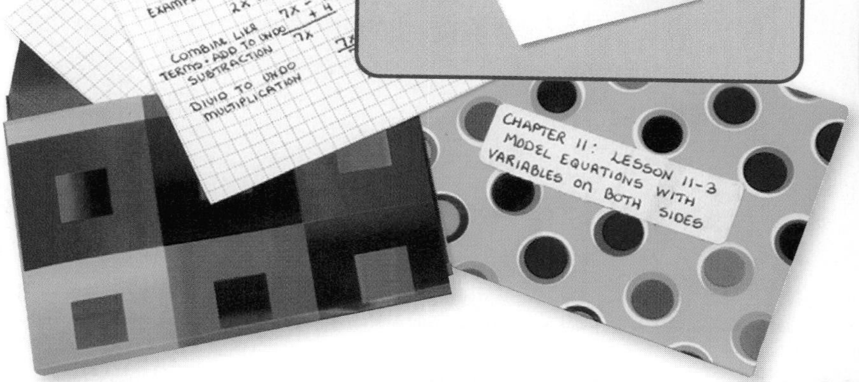

Taking Note of the Math

Use index cards to take notes on the lessons of the chapter. Store the cards in the appropriate envelopes.

CHAPTER 11

Study Guide: Review

Vocabulary

equivalent expression 584

like term 584

simplify 585

solution of a system of equations 608

system of equations 608

term 584

Complete the sentences below with vocabulary words from the list above. Words may be used more than once.

1. A group of two or more equations that contain two or more variables is called a(n) __?__.
2. Terms that have the same variable raised to the same power are __?__.
3. A set of values that are solutions of all the equations of a system is the __?__.
4. __?__ in an expression are set apart by plus or minus signs.

Study Guide: Review

11-1 Simplifying Algebraic Expressions (pp. 584–587)

EXAMPLE

■ **Simplify.**

$3(z - 6) + 2z$

$3z - 3(6) + 2z$ *Distributive Property*

$3z - 18 + 2z$ *3z and 2z are like terms.*

$5z - 18$ *Combine coefficients.*

■ **Solve.**

$14p - 8p = 54$

$6p = 54$ *Combine like terms.*

$\frac{6p}{6} = \frac{54}{6}$ *Divide both sides by 6.*

$p = 9$

EXERCISES

Simplify.

5. $5(3m - 2) + 4m$
6. $12w + 2(w + 3)$
7. $4x + 3y - 2x$
8. $2t^2 - 4t + 3t^3$

Solve.

9. $7y + y = 48$
10. $8z - 2z = 42$
11. $6y + y = 35$
12. $9z - 3z = 48$

11-2 Solving Multi-Step Equations (pp. 588–591)

EXAMPLE

■ **Solve.**

$\frac{5x}{9} - \frac{x}{6} + \frac{1}{3} = \frac{3}{2}$

$18\left(\frac{5x}{9} - \frac{x}{6} + \frac{1}{3}\right) = 18\left(\frac{3}{2}\right)$ *Multiply both sides by 18.*

$18\left(\frac{5x}{9}\right) - 18\left(\frac{x}{6}\right) + 18\left(\frac{1}{3}\right) = 18\left(\frac{3}{2}\right)$ *Distributive Property*

$10x - 3x + 6 = 27$ *Simplify.*

$7x + 6 = 27$ *Combine like terms.*

$\underline{\quad -6 \quad\; -6}$ *Subtract 6 from both sides.*

$7x = 21$

$\frac{7x}{7} = \frac{21}{7}$ *Divide both sides by 7.*

$x = 3$

EXERCISES

Solve.

13. $3y + 6 + 4y - 7 = -8$
14. $5h - 6 - h + 10 = 12$
15. $\frac{2t}{3} + \frac{1}{3} = -\frac{1}{3}$
16. $\frac{2r}{5} - \frac{4}{5} = \frac{2}{5}$
17. $\frac{z}{3} - \frac{3z}{4} + \frac{1}{2} = -\frac{1}{3}$
18. $\frac{3a}{8} - \frac{a}{12} + \frac{7}{2} = 7$

11-3 Solving Equations with Variables on Both Sides (pp. 593–597)

EXAMPLE

■ **Solve.**

$3x + 5 - 5x = -12 + x + 2$

$-2x + 5 = -10 + x$ *Combine like terms.*

$\underline{+2x} \qquad \underline{+2x}$ *Add 2x to both sides.*

$5 = -10 + 3x$

$\underline{+10 \quad +10}$ *Add 10 to both sides.*

$15 = 3x$

$\frac{15}{3} = \frac{3x}{3}$ *Divide both sides by 3.*

$5 = x$

EXERCISES

Solve.

19. $12s = 8 + 2(5s + 3)$
20. $\frac{5c}{8} - \frac{c}{3} = \frac{5c}{6} - 13$
21. $4 - 5x = 3 + x$
22. $4 - 2y = 4y$
23. $2n + 8 = 2n - 5$
24. $\frac{2z}{3} - \frac{3}{2} = \frac{3z}{2} - \frac{17}{3}$

11-4 Solving Inequalities by Multiplying or Dividing (pp. 600–603)

EXAMPLE

■ **Solve and graph.**

$\frac{z}{-13} \le -10$

$(-13)\frac{z}{-13} \ge (-13)-10$ *Multiply both sides by −13. Change ≤ to ≥.*

$z \ge 130$

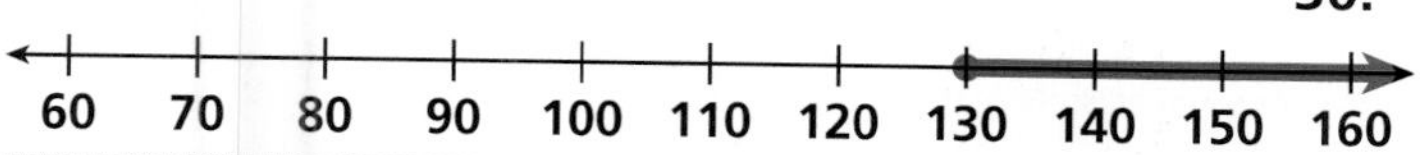

EXERCISES

Solve and graph.

25. $\frac{m}{6} \ge 3$
26. $4n \le -12$
27. $-8 < \frac{t}{2}$
28. $-5p > 15$
29. $9 \ge -\frac{b}{3}$
30. $-6a < -48$

11-5 Solving Two-Step Inequalities (pp. 604–607)

EXAMPLE

■ **Solve and graph.**

$$-3x - 3 < 9$$

$$\begin{aligned} -3x - 3 &< 9 \\ \underline{\quad +3} &\quad \underline{+3} \\ -3x &< 12 \end{aligned}$$ *Add 3 to both sides.*

$$\frac{-3x}{-3} > \frac{12}{-3}$$ *Divide both sides by −3. Change < to >.*

$$x > -4$$

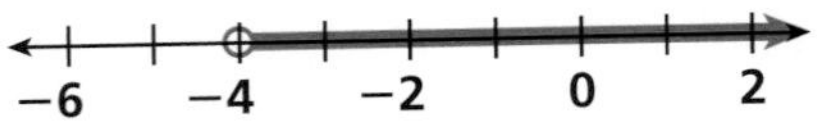

EXERCISES

Solve and graph.

31. $5z - 12 > -7$

32. $2h - 7 \geq 5$

33. $10 > \frac{a}{3} + 2$

34. $\frac{x}{3} - 8 \geq -10$

35. $5 - 3k < -4$

36. $2y + \frac{3}{4} > 1$

11-6 Systems of Equations (pp. 608–611)

EXAMPLE

■ **Solve the system of equations.**

$$4x + y = 3$$
$$x + y = 12$$

Solve both equations for y.

$$\begin{aligned} 4x + y &= 3 \\ \underline{-4x \quad} &\quad \underline{-4x} \\ y &= -4x + 3 \end{aligned} \qquad \begin{aligned} x + y &= 12 \\ \underline{-x \quad} &\quad \underline{-x} \\ y &= -x + 12 \end{aligned}$$

$$\begin{aligned} -4x + 3 &= -x + 12 \\ \underline{+4x \quad} &\quad \underline{+4x \quad} \\ 3 &= 3x + 12 \end{aligned}$$ *Add 4x to both sides.*

$$\begin{aligned} \underline{-12} &\quad \underline{\quad -12} \\ -9 &= 3x \end{aligned}$$ *Subtract 12 from both sides.*

$$\frac{-9}{3} = \frac{3x}{3}$$ *Divide both sides by 3.*

$$-3 = x$$

$$\begin{aligned} y &= -4x + 3 \\ &= -4(-3) + 3 \\ &= 12 + 3 \\ &= 15 \end{aligned}$$ *Substitute −3 for x.*

The solution is $(-3, 15)$.

EXERCISES

Solve each system of equations.

37. $y = x + 3$
$y = 2x + 5$

38. $2x - y = -2$
$x + y = 8$

39. $4x + 3y = 27$
$2x - y = 1$

40. $4x + y = 10$
$x - 2y = 7$

41. $y = x - 2$
$-x + y = 2$

42. $y = 3x + 1$
$3x - y = -1$

43. The sum of two numbers is 32. Twice the first number is equal to six times the second number. Find each number.

a. Use a different variable to represent each number and write an equation for each of the first two sentences.

b. Solve the system of equations.

c. Check your answer.

CHAPTER TEST

Simplify.

1. $7x + 5x$
2. $m + 3m - 3$
3. $6n + 1 - n + 5n$
4. $2y + 2z + 2$
5. $3(s + 2) - s$
6. $10b + 8(b - 1)$

Solve.

7. $10x - 2x = 16$
8. $\frac{3y + 5y}{3} = 8$
9. $6t + 4t = 120$
10. $4c + 6 + 2c = 24$
11. $\frac{2x}{5} - \frac{3}{5} = \frac{11}{5}$
12. $\frac{2}{5}b - \frac{1}{4}b = 3$
13. $15 - 6g + 8 = 19$
14. $93 + 50k = 218$
15. $\frac{w}{4} - \frac{w}{5} - \frac{1}{3} = \frac{16}{15}$
16. On her last three quizzes, Elise scored 84, 96, and 88. What grade must she get on her next quiz to have an average of 90 for all four quizzes?

Solve.

17. $3x + 13 = x + 1$
18. $q + 7 = 2q + 5$
19. $8n + 24 = 3n + 59$
20. $m + 5 = m - 3$
21. $-3a + 9 = 3a - 9$
22. $\frac{3z}{2} - \frac{17}{3} = \frac{2z}{3} - \frac{3}{2}$
23. The square and the equilateral triangle have the same perimeter. Find the perimeter of each figure.

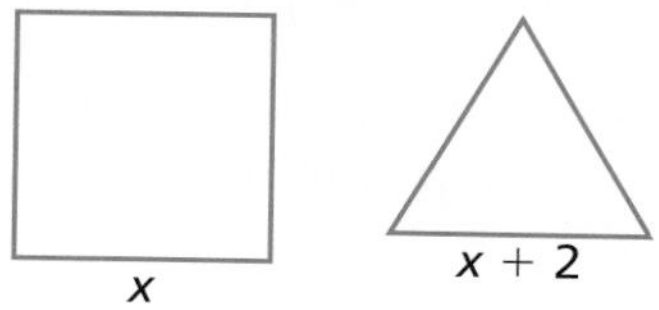

Solve and graph.

24. $\frac{t}{3} > 8$
25. $-5w > 30$
26. $12 \geq \frac{h}{4}$
27. $-36 \leq 6y$
28. $-56 < -7m$
29. $\frac{b}{-4} < 8$
30. $-12q \geq 48$
31. $\frac{g}{4} \leq -5$
32. Glenda has a \$40 gift certificate to a café that sells her favorite tuna sandwich for \$3.75 after tax. What are the possible numbers of tuna sandwiches that Glenda can buy with her gift certificate?

Solve and graph.

33. $6m + 4 > 2$
34. $8 - 3p > 14$
35. $4z + 4 \geq -8$
36. $\frac{x}{10} + \frac{1}{2} \geq \frac{2}{5}$
37. $\frac{3}{4} - \frac{c}{8} < \frac{1}{2}$
38. $\frac{2}{3} > \frac{1}{2} - \frac{d}{6}$

Solve each system of equations.

39. $x - 2y = 16$; $x - y = 8$
40. $y = 2x + 6$; $y = 2x - 3$
41. $x + 5y = 11$; $4x - y = 2$
42. $2y + x = 6$; $3y + 4x = 4$
43. $y = 5x + 10$; $y = x - 2$
44. $x - 5y = 4$; $-2x + 10y = -8$

TEST TACKLER

Standardized Test Strategies

Multiple Choice: Answering Context-Based Test Items

For some test items, you cannot answer just by reading the problem statement. You will need to read each option carefully to determine the correct response. Review each option and eliminate those that are false.

EXAMPLE 1

Multiple Choice

Which statement is true for the given spinner?

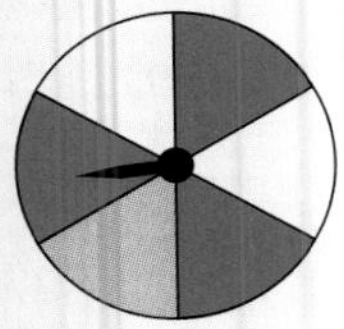

(A) The probability of spinning green is $\frac{1}{3}$.

(B) The probability of spinning blue is $\frac{1}{6}$.

(C) The probability of spinning white is the same as the probability of spinning green.

(D) The probability of spinning green is the same as the probability of spinning yellow or white.

Read each option carefully. Eliminate options that are false.

Option A: Find the probability of spinning green.

$P(\text{green}) = \frac{3}{6}$, or $\frac{1}{2}$ Option A is false.

Option B: Find the probability of spinning blue.

$P(\text{blue}) = \frac{0}{6}$, or 0 Option B is false.

Option C: Find the probabilities and compare.

$P(\text{white}) = \frac{2}{6}$, or $\frac{1}{3}$ $P(\text{green}) = \frac{3}{6}$, or $\frac{1}{2}$

$\frac{1}{3} \neq \frac{1}{2}$, so $P(\text{white}) \neq P(\text{green})$

Option C is false.

Option D: Find the probabilities and compare.

$P(\text{green}) = \frac{3}{6}$, or $\frac{1}{2}$ $P(\text{white or yellow}) = \frac{2}{6} + \frac{1}{6} = \frac{3}{6}$, or $\frac{1}{2}$

$\frac{1}{2} = \frac{1}{2}$, $P(\text{green}) = P(\text{white or yellow})$

Option D is true. It is the correct response.

HOT TIP! Be sure to review all of the answer options carefully before you make your choice.

Read each test item and answer the questions that follow.

Item A
Which equation has a solution of $x = 3$?

Ⓐ $2x - 6 = 3(x - 1)$

Ⓑ $-2x - 6 = \frac{3}{2}(-2x - 2)$

Ⓒ $2(x - 6) = 3x - 1$

Ⓓ $-2(x - 6) = x - 3$

1. What property do you have to use to solve each equation?

2. What two methods could you use to determine if $x = 3$ is a solution of one of the equations?

3. Which is the correct option? Explain.

Item B
An experiment consists of rolling a fair number cube labeled 1 to 6. Which statement is true?

Ⓕ $P(\text{odd}) = P(\text{even})$

Ⓖ $P(\text{multiple of } 3) > P(\text{multiple of } 2)$

Ⓗ $P(7) = 1$

Ⓙ $P(\text{less than } 4) = P(\text{greater than } 5)$

4. What does *multiple* mean? What are multiples of 3? What are multiples of 2?

5. How many numbers are less than 4 on the number cube? How many numbers are greater than 5?

6. Which is the correct option? Explain.

Item C
Which inequality has 0 as a part of its solution set?

Ⓐ $-3y < -6$

Ⓑ $8a + 3 > 7$

Ⓒ $4 - 9y < 13$

Ⓓ $-\frac{5t}{6} > 5$

7. What must you remember to do if you multiply or divide both sides of an inequality by a negative number?

8. Which is the correct option? Explain.

Item D
A poll was taken at Jefferson Middle School. Which statement is true for the given data?

Favorite Type of Movie	Number of Students
Drama	25
Comedy	40
Science fiction	28
Action	32

Ⓕ The probability that a student at Jefferson Middle School does *not* like dramas best is $\frac{4}{5}$.

Ⓖ The odds in favor of a student liking comedies best are 8:25.

Ⓗ Out of a population of 1200 students, you can predict that 280 students will like science fiction movies best.

Ⓙ The odds against a student liking action movies best are 125:32.

9. How can you find the probability of an event not occurring?

10. How can you use probability to make a prediction?

11. Which is the correct option? Explain.

STANDARDIZED TEST PREP

go.hrw.com
State Test Practice Online
KEYWORD: MT7 TestPrep

Cumulative Assessment, Chapters 1–11

Multiple Choice

1. Clarissa has 6 red socks, 4 black socks, 10 white socks, and 2 blue socks in a drawer. If Clarissa chooses one sock at a time, what is the probability that she will choose 2 black socks?

   (A) $\frac{7}{22}$ (C) $\frac{3}{121}$

   (B) $\frac{2}{11}$ (D) $\frac{7}{22}$

2. Which situation describes the graph?

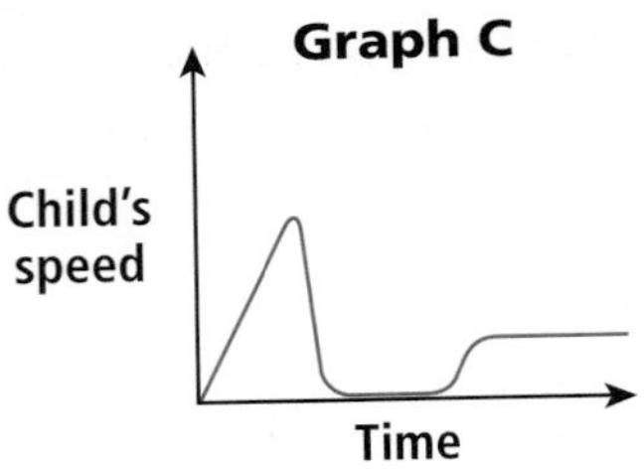

   (F) Linda sits on her bike.
   Linda runs to see the neighbor's dog.
   Linda sits and pets the dog.

   (G) Jim climbs on the jungle gym.
   Jim slides down the pole.
   Jim lies in the sand and rests.

   (H) Carlos runs to answer the phone.
   Carlos sits and talks on the phone.
   Carlos walks into another room.

   (J) Juan walks to his friend's house.
   Juan knocks on the door.
   Juan leaves his friend's house.

3. Which ordered pair is the solution of the following system of equations?

$$y = 2x + 6$$
$$x + y = 27$$

   (A) (3, 12) (C) (7, 20)

   (B) (10, 26) (D) (20, 7)

4. At lunch, each student writes his or her name on a piece of paper and puts the paper in a barrel. The principal draws five names for a free lunch. What type of sampling method is this?

   (F) stratified (H) random

   (G) systematic (J) biased

5. A trapezoid has two bases b_1 and b_2 and height h. For which values of b_1, b_2, and h is the area of a trapezoid equal to 32 in^2?

   (A) $b_1 = 9$ in., $b_2 = 7$ in., $h = 2$ in.

   (B) $b_1 = 5$ in., $b_2 = 3$ in., $h = 4$ in.

   (C) $b_1 = 2$ in., $b_2 = 8$ in., $h = 4$ in.

   (D) $b_1 = 9$ in., $b_2 = 7$ in., $h = 4$ in.

6. Between which two integers does $-\sqrt{67}$ lie?

   (F) −7 and −6 (H) −10 and −11

   (G) −9 and −8 (J) −8 and −7

7. What is the sum of the angle measures of this polygon?

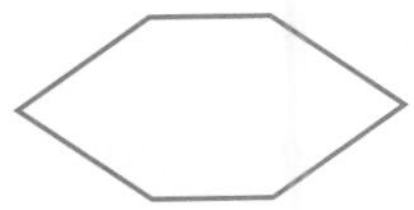

   (A) 180° (C) 720°

   (B) 360° (D) 1080°

8. If Serena buys a $96 bracelet for 20% off, how much money does Serena save?

   (F) $1.92 (H) $19.20

   (G) $9.60 (J) $76.80

9. Which value of x is the solution of the equation $\frac{3x}{8} - \frac{3}{4} = \frac{1}{6}$?

(A) $x = \frac{9}{22}$

(B) $x = \frac{5}{9}$

(C) $x = 1\frac{5}{9}$

(D) $x = 2\frac{4}{9}$

HOT TIP! **When finding the solution to an equation on a multiple-choice test, work backward by substituting the answer choices provided into the equation.**

Gridded Response

10. To prepare for her final exam, Sheyla studied 4 hours on Monday, 3 hours on Tuesday, 1 hour on Wednesday, and 3 hours on Thursday. What is the difference between the median and the mean of the number of hours Sheyla studied?

11. Zina has 10 coins consisting of nickels and dimes in her pocket. She calculates that she has \$0.70 altogether. If Zina has two more nickels than dimes, how many nickels does she have?

12. In a school of 1575 students, there are 870 females. What is the ratio of females to males in simplest form?

13. An $8\frac{1}{2}$ in. × 11 in. photograph is being cropped to fit into a special frame. One-fourth of an inch will be cropped from all sides of the photo. What is the area, in square inches, of the photograph that will be seen in the frame?

14. The perimeters of the two figures have the same measure. What is the perimeter of either figure?

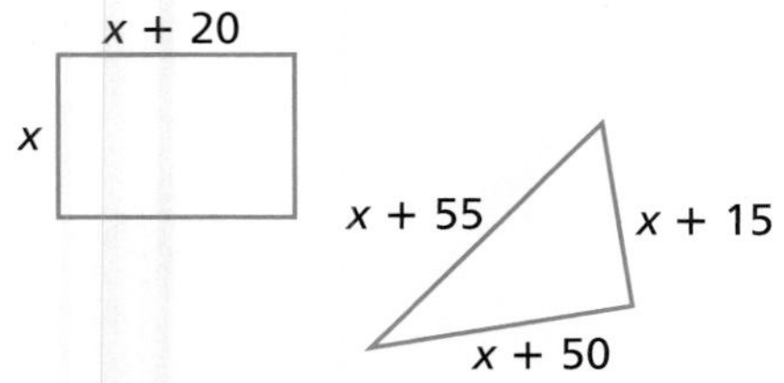

Short Response

15. Two numbers have a sum of 58. Twice the first number is 8 more than the second number.
    a. Write a system of equations that can be used to find the two numbers.
    b. What are the two numbers? Show your work.

16. Alfred and Eugene each spent \$62 on campsite and gasoline expenses during their camping trip. Each campsite they used had the same per-night charge. Alfred paid for 4 nights of campsites and \$30 of gasoline. Eugene paid for 2 nights of campsites and \$46 of gasoline. Write an equation that could be used to determine the cost of one night's stay at a campsite. What was the cost of one night's stay at a campsite?

Extended Response

17. You are designing a house to fit on a rectangular lot that has 90 feet of lake frontage and is 162 feet deep. The building codes require that the house not be built closer than 10 feet to the lot boundary lines.
    a. Write an inequality and solve it to find how long the front of the house facing the lake can be.
    b. If you want the house to cover no more than 20% of the lot, what would be the maximum square footage of the house?
    c. If you want to spend a maximum of \$100,000 building the house, to the nearest whole dollar, what would be the maximum you could spend per square foot for a 1988-square-foot house?

Standardized Test Prep

CHAPTER 12

Graphing Lines

12A Linear Equations
- **12-1** Graphing Linear Equations
- **12-2** Slope of a Line
- **12-3** Using Slopes and Intercepts
- **LAB** Graph Equations in Slope-Intercept Form
- **12-4** Point-Slope Form

12B Linear Relationships
- **12-5** Direct Variation
- **12-6** Graphing Inequalities in Two Variables
- **12-7** Lines of Best Fit
- **Ext** Solving Systems of Equations by Graphing

MULTI-STEP TEST PREP

go.hrw.com
Chapter Project Online
KEYWORD: MT7 Ch12

Whooping Crane Population

Year	1940	1960	1980	2000
Cranes	15	36	79	202

Career *Wildlife Ecologist*

Whatever happened to the Carolina parakeet and the passenger pigeon, two species of birds that once inhabited the United States? They are now as extinct as *Tyrannosaurus rex.* The primary focus of wildlife ecologists is to keep other animals from becoming extinct.

They have been successful with the whooping crane, the largest wild bird in North America. The table shows how the whooping crane has come back from the brink of extinction.

ARE YOU READY?

Vocabulary

Choose the best term from the list to complete each sentence.

1. The expression $4 - 3$ is an example of a(n) __?__ expression.

2. When you divide both sides of the equation $2x = 20$ by 2, you are __?__.

3. An example of a(n) __?__ is $3x > 12$.

4. The expression $7 - 6$ can be rewritten as the __?__ expression $7 + (-6)$.

addition
equation
inequality in one variable
solving for the variable
subtraction

Complete these exercises to review skills you will need for this chapter.

Operations with Integers

Simplify.

5. $\frac{7-5}{-2}$ **6.** $\frac{-3-5}{-2-3}$ **7.** $\frac{-8+2}{-2+8}$ **8.** $\frac{-16}{-2}$ **9.** $\frac{-22}{2}$ **10.** $-12 + 9$

Evaluate Expressions

Evaluate each expression for the given value of the variable.

11. $3x - 2$ for $x = -2$ **12.** $4y - 8 + \frac{1}{2}y$ for $y = 2$

13. $3(x + 1)$ for $x = -2$ **14.** $-3(y + 2) - y$ for $y = -1$

Equations

Solve.

15. $3p - 4 = 8$ **16.** $2(a + 3) = 4$ **17.** $9 = -2k + 27$

18. $3s - 4 = 1 - 3s$ **19.** $7x + 1 = x$ **20.** $4m - 5(m + 2) = 1$

Determine whether each ordered pair is a solution to $-\frac{1}{2}x + 3 = y$.

21. (4, 1) **22** $\left(-\frac{8}{2}, 2\right)$ **23** (0, 5) **24.** (−4, 5)

25. (8, 1) **26.** (2, 2) **27.** (–2, 4) **28.** (0, 1)

Solve Inequalities in One Variable

Solve and graph each inequality.

29. $x + 4 > 2$ **30.** $-3x < 9$ **31.** $x - 1 \leq -5$

CHAPTER 12

Study Guide: Preview

Where You've Been

Previously, you

- located and named points on a coordinate plane using ordered pairs of integers.
- graphed data to demonstrate relationships between sets of data.

In This Chapter

You will study

- locating and naming points on a coordinate plane using ordered pairs of rational numbers.
- generating different representations of data using tables, graphs, and equations.
- graphing linear equations using slope and *y*-intercept.
- graphing inequalities involving two variables on a coordinate plane.

Where You're Going

You can use the skills learned in this chapter

- to predict the distance a car needs to come to a complete stop, given its speed.
- to estimate the maximum distance a robotic vehicle can travel during a given period of time.

Key Vocabulary/Vocabulario

boundary line	línea de limíte
constant of proportionality	constante de proporcionalidad
direct variation	variación directa
linear equation	ecuación lineal
linear inequality	desigualdad lineal
point-slope form	forma punto-pendiente
slope-intercept form	forma pendiente-intersección
x-intercept	intersección con el eje de las *x*
y-intercept	intersección con el eje de las *y*

Vocabulary Connections

To become familiar with some of the vocabulary terms in the chapter, consider the following. You may refer to the chapter, the glossary, or a dictionary if you like.

1. The word *linear* means "relating to a line." What do you think the graph of a **linear equation** looks like?
2. The word *intercept* can mean "to interrupt a course or path." Where on a graph do you think you should look to find the ***y*-intercept** of a line?
3. The adjective *direct* can mean "passing in a straight line." What do you suppose the graph of an equation with **direct variation** looks like?
4. A *boundary* is a limit. What do you think the **boundary line** represents in a graph of a linear inequality?

Reading and Writing Math

Writing Strategy: Use Your Own Words

Explaining a concept in your own words will help you better understand it. For example, learning to solve two-step inequalities might seem difficult if the textbook does not use the same words that you would use.

As you work through each lesson, do the following:

- Identify the important concepts.
- Use your own words to explain the concepts.
- Use examples to help clarify your thoughts.

What Miguel Reads

Solving a two-step inequality uses the same inverse operations as solving a two-step equation.

Multiplying or dividing an inequality by a negative number reverses the inequality symbol.

What Miguel Writes

Solve a two-step inequality like a two-step equation. Use operations that undo each other.

When you multiply or divide by a negative number, switch the inequality symbol so that it faces the opposite direction.

$-4y > 8$ *Divide by −4 and*
$y < -2$ *switch the symbol.*

Try This

Rewrite each statement in your own words.

1. Like terms can be grouped together because they have the same variable raised to the same power.
2. If an equation contains fractions, consider multiplying both sides of the equation by the least common denominator (LCD) to clear the fractions before you isolate the variable.
3. To solve multi-step equations with variables on both sides, first combine like terms and then clear fractions. Then add or subtract variable terms on both sides so that the variable occurs on only one side of the equation. Then use properties of equality to isolate the variable.

12-1 Graphing Linear Equations

Learn to identify and graph linear equations.

Vocabulary

linear equation

Light travels faster than sound. That's why you see lightning before you hear thunder. The *linear equation* $d = 0.2s$ expresses the approximate distance, d, in miles of a thunderstorm for a given number of seconds, s, between the lightning flash and the thunder rumble.

A **linear equation** is an equation whose solutions fall on a line on the coordinate plane. All solutions of a particular linear equation fall on the line, and all the points on the line are solutions of the equation. To find a solution that lies between two points (x_1, y_1) and (x_2, y_2), choose an x-value between x_1 and x_2 and find the corresponding y-value.

Reading Math

Read x_1 as "x sub one" or "x one."

If an equation is linear, a constant change in the x-value corresponds to a constant change in the y-value. The graph shows an example where each time the **x-value increases by 3,** the **y-value increases by 2.**

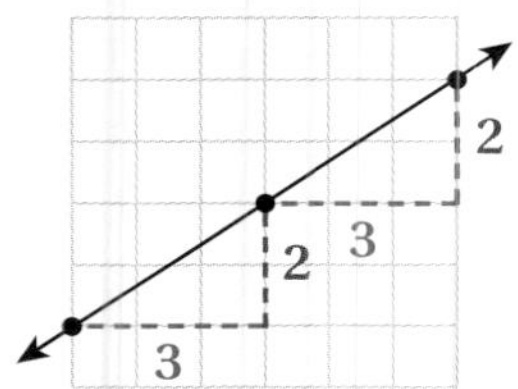

EXAMPLE 1 Graphing Equations

Graph each equation and tell whether it is linear.

A $y = 3x - 4$

x	3x − 4	y	(x, y)
0	3(0) − 4	−4	(0, −4)
1	3(1) − 4	−1	(1, −1)
2	3(2) − 4	2	(2, 2)
3	3(3) − 4	5	(3, 5)

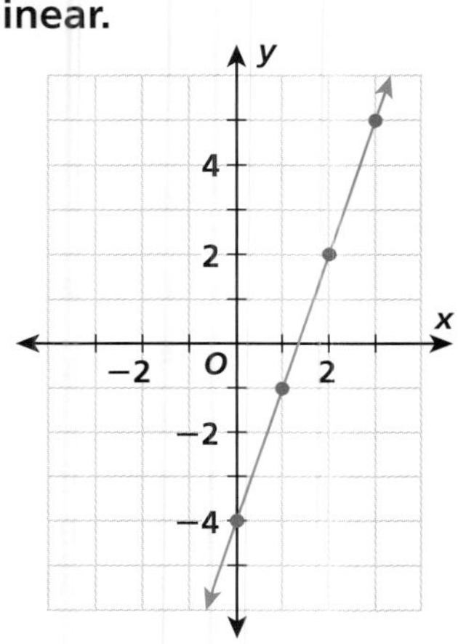

The equation $y = 3x - 4$ is a linear equation because it is the graph of a straight line, and each time x increases by 1 unit, y increases by 3 units.

Caution!

Be careful when graphing each ordered pair. Double check each point you plot.

Graph each equation and tell whether it is linear.

B $y = -x^2$

x	$-x^2$	y	(x, y)
−2	$-(-2)^2$	−4	(−2, −4)
−1	$-(-1)^2$	−1	(−1, −1)
0	$-(0)^2$	0	(0, 0)
1	$-(1)^2$	−1	(1, −1)
2	$-(2)^2$	−4	(2, −4)

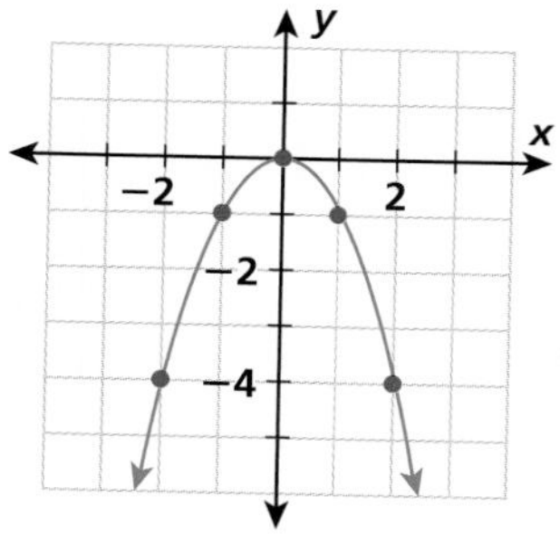

The equation $y = -x^2$ is not a linear equation because its graph is not a straight line. Also notice that as x increases by a constant of 1, the change in y is not constant.

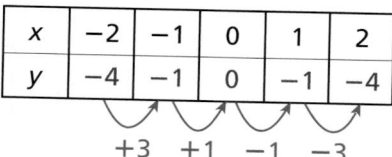

x	−2	−1	0	1	2
y	−4	−1	0	−1	−4

+3 +1 −1 −3

C $y = -\frac{3x}{4}$

x	$-\frac{3x}{4}$	y	(x, y)
−2	$-\frac{3(-2)}{4}$	$\frac{3}{2}$	$\left(-2, \frac{3}{2}\right)$
−1	$-\frac{3(-1)}{4}$	$\frac{3}{4}$	$\left(-1, \frac{3}{4}\right)$
0	$-\frac{3(0)}{4}$	0	(0, 0)
1	$-\frac{3(1)}{4}$	$-\frac{3}{4}$	$\left(1, -\frac{3}{4}\right)$
2	$-\frac{3(2)}{4}$	$-\frac{3}{2}$	$\left(2, -\frac{3}{2}\right)$

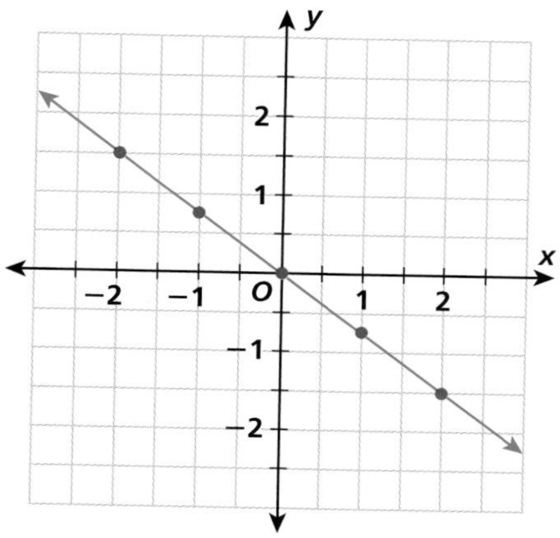

The equation $y = -\frac{3x}{4}$ is a linear equation because the points form a straight line. Each time the value of x increases by 1, the value of y decreases by $\frac{3}{4}$, or y decreases by 3 each time x increases by 4.

D $y = -3$

x	-3	y	(x, y)
−2	−3	−3	(−2, −3)
−1	−3	−3	(−1, −3)
0	−3	−3	(0, −3)
1	−3	−3	(1, −3)
2	−3	−3	(2, −3)

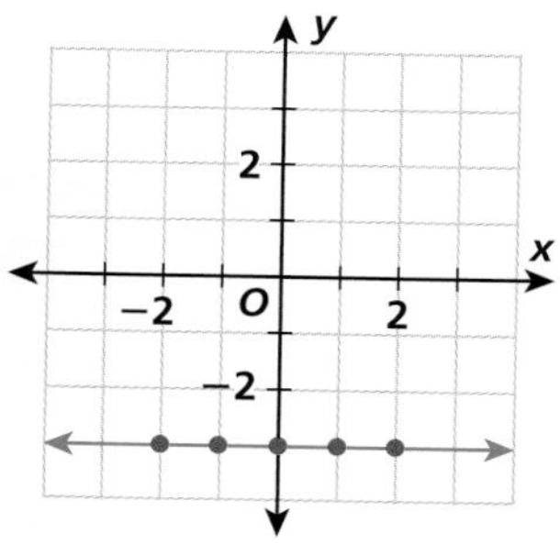

For any value of x, y = −3.

The equation $y = -3$ is a linear equation because the points form a straight line. As the value of x increases, the value of y has a constant change of 0.

EXAMPLE 2 *Physical Science Application*

The equation $d = 0.2s$ represents the approximate distance, d, in miles of a thunderstorm when s seconds pass between a flash of lightning and the sound of thunder. About how far is the thunderstorm from each student listed in the table? Draw a graph that represents the relationship between the time between lightning and thunder and the distance of the storm from the student.

Student	Time Between Flash and Thunder (s)
Sandy	5
Diego	9
Ted	4
Cecilia	11
Massoud	8

s	$d = 0.2s$	d	(s, d)
5	$d = 0.2(5)$	1.0	(5, 1)
9	$d = 0.2(9)$	1.8	(9, 1.8)
4	$d = 0.2(4)$	0.8	(4, 0.8)
11	$d = 0.2(11)$	2.2	(11, 2.2)
8	$d = 0.2(8)$	1.6	(8, 1.6)

The approximate distances are Sandy, 1 mile; Diego, 1.8 miles; Ted, 0.8 mile; Cecilia, 2.2 miles; and Massoud, 1.6 miles. This is a linear equation because when s increases by 10 seconds, d increases by 2 miles.

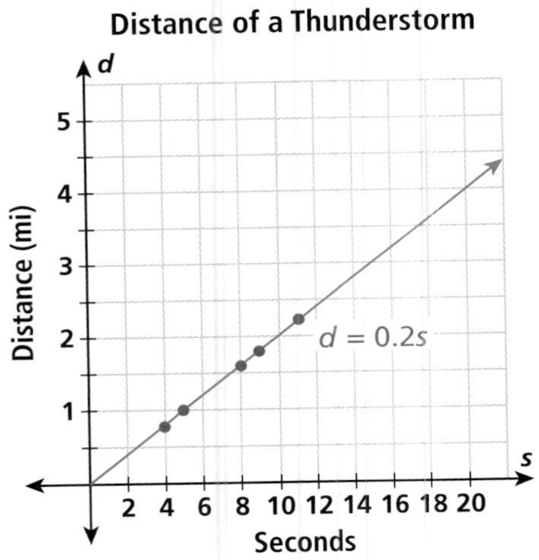

Think and Discuss

1. **Explain** whether an equation is linear if three ordered-pair solutions lie on a straight line but a fourth does not.
2. **Compare** the equations $y = 3x + 2$ and $y = 3x^2$. Without graphing, explain why one of the equations is not linear.
3. **Describe** why neither number in the ordered pair can be negative in Example 2.

12-1 Exercises

go.hrw.com
Homework Help Online
KEYWORD: MT7 12-1
Parent Resources Online
KEYWORD: MT7 Parent

GUIDED PRACTICE

See Example 1

Graph each equation and tell whether it is linear.

1. $y = x + 1$
2. $y = -3x$
3. $y = x^3$

See Example 2

4. **Life Science** *Tyrannosaurus rex* was one of the largest meat-eaters that ever lived. By 14 years of age, a *T. rex* was growing about 4 pounds every day. If you found a *T. rex* that was 14 years old, the equation $w = 4d + 5110$ would represent the weight w of the animal d days later. How much would it weigh after 2 days? after 3.5 days? after 5 days? Graph the equation and tell whether it is linear?

INDEPENDENT PRACTICE

See Example 1

Graph each equation and tell whether it is linear.

5. $y = \frac{1}{4}x - 1$
6. $y = -5$
7. $y = \frac{1}{3}x^2$
8. $x = 4$
9. $y = x^2 - 12$
10. $y = 3x + 2$

See Example 2

11. **Business** A charter bus service charges a \$125 transportation fee plus \$8.50 for each passenger. This is represented by the equation $C = 8.5p + 125$, where C is the total cost based on p passengers. What is the total cost of transportation for the following numbers of passengers: 50, 100, 150, 200, and 250? Graph the equation and tell whether it is linear.

PRACTICE AND PROBLEM SOLVING

Extra Practice
See page 804.

12. The minute hand of a clock moves $\frac{1}{10}$ degree every second. If you look at the clock when the minute hand is 10 degrees past the 12, you can use the equation $y = \frac{1}{10}x + 10$ to find how many degrees past the 12 the minute hand is after x seconds. Graph the equation and tell whether it is linear.

13. **Physical Science** The force exerted on an object by Earth's gravity is given by the formula $F = 9.8m$, where F is the force in newtons and m is the mass of the object in kilograms. How many newtons of gravitational force are exerted on a student with mass 52 kg?

14. **Consumer Math** At a rate of \$0.08 per kilowatt-hour, the equation $C = 0.08t$ gives the cost of a customer's electric bill for using t kilowatt-hours of energy. Complete the table of values and graph the energy cost equation for t ranging from 0 to 1000.

Kilowatt-hours (*t*)	540	580	620	660	700	740
Cost in Dollars (C)						

LINK

Transportation

France's *Train à Grande Vitesse* has served over 1,000,000,000 passengers since it began service in 1981.

Evaluate each equation for $x = -1, 0,$ and 1. Then graph the equation.

15. $y = 2x$

16. $y = 3x + 4$

17. $y = 5x - 1$

18. $y = x - 8$

19. $y = 2x - 3$

20. $y = 2x + 4$

21. $y = 2x - 4$

22. $y = x + 6$

23. $y = 2x + 3.5$

24. Transportation France's high-speed train, *Train à Grande Vitesse* (TGV), has a best-average speed of 254 kilometers per hour. Write an equation that gives the distance the train travels in h hours. Is this a linear equation? Explain.

25. Entertainment A driving range charges \$3 to rent a golf club plus \$2.25 for every bucket of golf balls you drive. Write an equation that shows the total cost of driving b buckets of golf balls. Graph the equation. Is it linear?

26. Critical Thinking A movie theater charges \$6.50 per ticket. For groups of 20 or more, tickets are reduced to \$4.50 each. Graph the total cost for groups consisting of between 5 and 30 people. Is the relationship linear? Explain your reasoning.

27. What's the Question? The equation $C = 7.5n + 1275$ gives the total cost of producing n engines. If the answer is \$16,275, what is the question?

28. Write About It Explain how you could show that $y = 6x + 2$ is a linear equation.

29. Challenge Three solutions of an equation are (2, 2), (4, 4), and (6, 6). Draw one possible graph that would show that the equation is not a linear equation.

TEST PREP and Spiral Review

30. Multiple Choice A landscaping company charges \$35 for a consultation fee, plus \$50 per hour. How much would it cost to hire the company for 3 hours?

Ⓐ \$225 Ⓑ \$185 Ⓒ \$150 Ⓓ \$135

31. Multiple Choice Perfect Pizza charges \$15 per pizza, plus a \$4.50 delivery charge per order. How much would it cost to have 8 pizzas delivered in one order?

Ⓕ \$124.50 Ⓖ \$120 Ⓗ \$51 Ⓙ \$36

32. Short Response Evaluate the equation $y = 3x - 5$ for $x = -1, 0, 1$. Then graph the equation.

Simplify. Write the product or quotient as one power. (Lesson 4-3)

33. $3^4 \cdot 3^{-2}$

34. $\frac{2^5}{2^9}$

35. $10^5 \cdot 10^2$

36. $\frac{10^{-3}}{5^3}$

37. The scores on a spelling test were 80, 90, 85, 95, 85, 80, 95, 100, 90, 80, 80, 80, and 85. What number best describes the middle of these scores? (Lesson 9-3)

12-2 Slope of a Line

Learn to find the slope of a line and use slope to understand and draw graphs.

Remember!

You looked at slope on the coordinate plane in Lesson 7-5 (p. 347).

In skiing, *slope* refers to a slanted mountainside. The steeper a slope is, the higher its difficulty rating will be. In math, slope defines the "slant" of a line. The larger the absolute value of the slope is, the "steeper," or more vertical, the line will be.

Linear equations have constant slope.
For a line on the coordinate plane, slope is the following ratio:

$$\text{slope} = \frac{\text{vertical change}}{\text{horizontal change}} = \frac{\text{change in } y}{\text{change in } x}$$

This ratio is often called $\frac{\text{rise}}{\text{run}}$, or "rise over run,"where *rise* is the number of units moved up or down and *run* is the number of units moved left or right. Slope can be positive, negative, zero, or undefined.

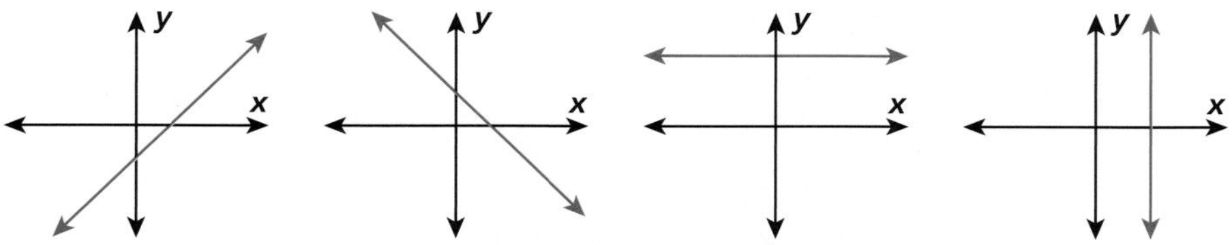

Positive slope **Negative slope** **Zero slope** **Undefined slope**

If you know any two points on a line, or two solutions of a linear equation, you can find the slope of the line without graphing.
The slope of a line through the points (x_1, y_1) and (x_2, y_2) is as follows:

$$\frac{y_2 - y_1}{x_2 - x_1}$$

EXAMPLE 1 Finding Slope, Given Two Points

Find the slope of the line that passes through (1, 7) and (9, 1).

Let (x_1, y_1) be (1, 7) and (x_2, y_2) be (9, 1).

$$\frac{y_2 - y_1}{x_2 - x_1} = \frac{1 - 7}{9 - 1}$$ *Substitute 1 for y_2, 7 for y_1, 9 for x_2, and 1 for x_1.*

$$= \frac{-6}{8} = -\frac{3}{4}$$

The slope of the line that passes through (1, 7) and (9, 1) is $-\frac{3}{4}$.

Slope measures the rate of change in an algebraic relationship. Linear equations have constant rates of change. This means that the rate of change is always the same. This is shown in a graph by a straight line.

Nonlinear equations have variable rates of change. This means that the rate of change is different between different values. This is shown in a graph by a curved line.

EXAMPLE 2 Identifying Constant and Variable Rates of Change in Graphs

Determine whether each graph shows a constant or variable rate of change. Explain your reasoning.

A

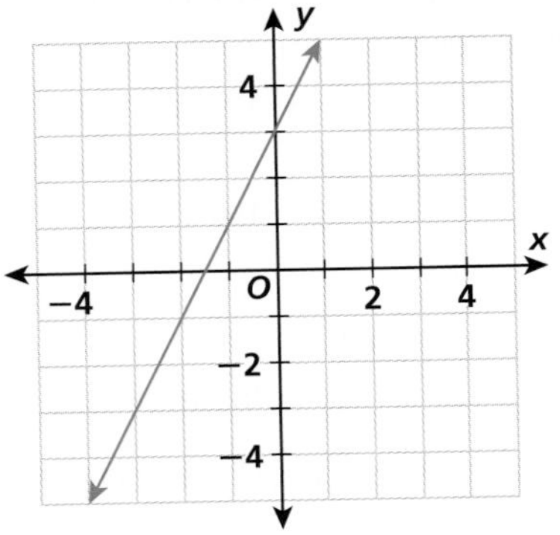

The graph shows a constant rate of change. The slope between any two points is always the same.

B

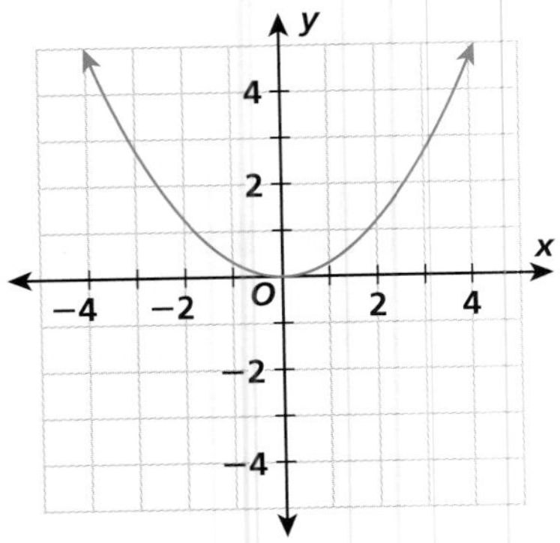

The graph shows a variable rate of change. The slope is negative in Quadrant II and positive in Quadrant I.

EXAMPLE 3 *Physical Science Application*

Helpful Hint

You can use any two points to find the slope of the line.

The table shows the volume of water released by Hoover Dam over a certain period of time. Use the data to make a graph. Find the slope of the line and explain what it shows.

Water Released from Hoover Dam	
Time (s)	Volume of Water (m^3)
5	75,000
10	150,000
15	225,000
20	300,000

Graph the data.

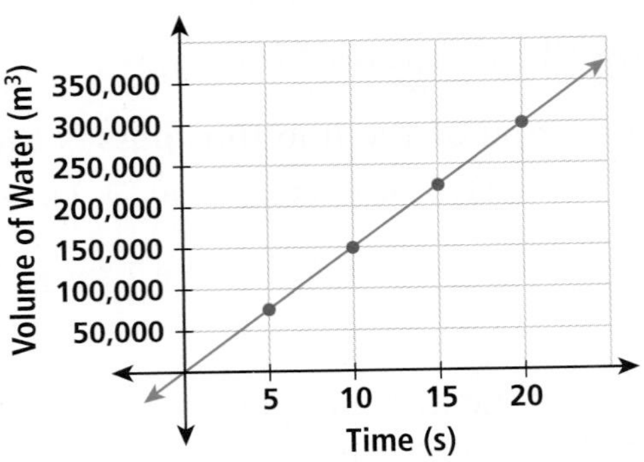

Find the slope of the line.

$$\frac{y_2 - y_1}{x_2 - x_1} = \frac{150{,}000 - 75{,}000}{10 - 5}$$

$$= \frac{75{,}000}{5} = 15{,}000$$

The slope of the line is 15,000. This means that for every second that passed, 15,000 m^3 of water was released from Hoover Dam.

Think and Discuss

1. **Explain** why it does not matter which point you choose as (x_1, y_1) and which point you choose as (x_2, y_2) when finding slope.
2. **Give an example** of two pairs of points from each of two parallel lines.

12-2 Exercises

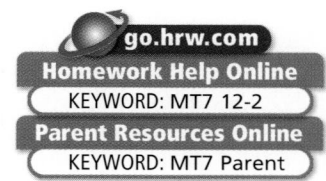

go.hrw.com
Homework Help Online
KEYWORD: MT7 12-2
Parent Resources Online
KEYWORD: MT7 Parent

GUIDED PRACTICE

See Example 1 **Find the slope of the line that passes through each pair of points.**

1. (2, 5) and (3, 6)
2. (2, 6) and (0, 2)
3. (−2, 4) and (6, 6)

See Example 2 **Determine whether each graph shows a constant or variable rate of change. Explain your reasoning.**

4.

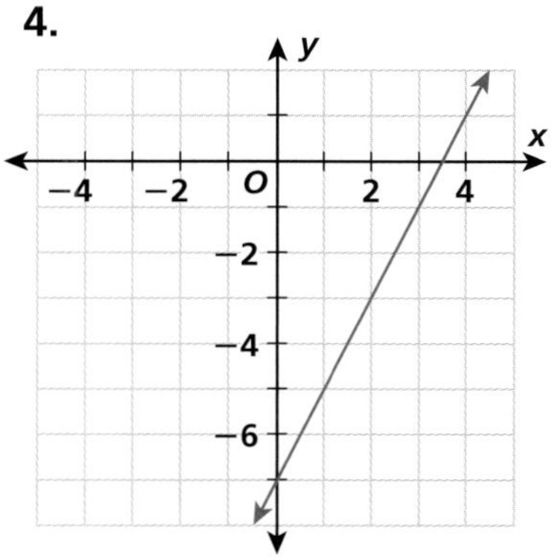

5.

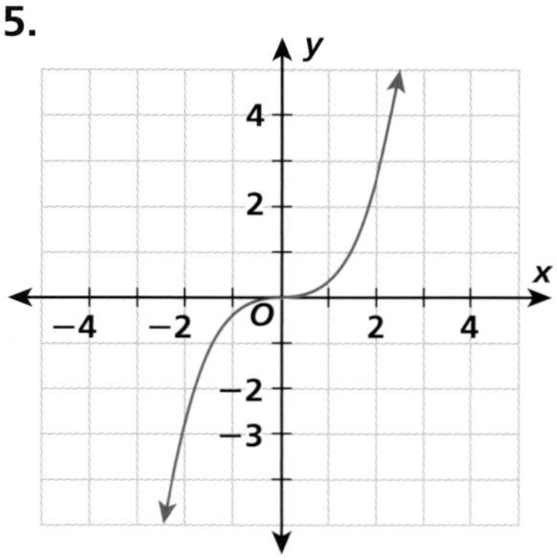

6.

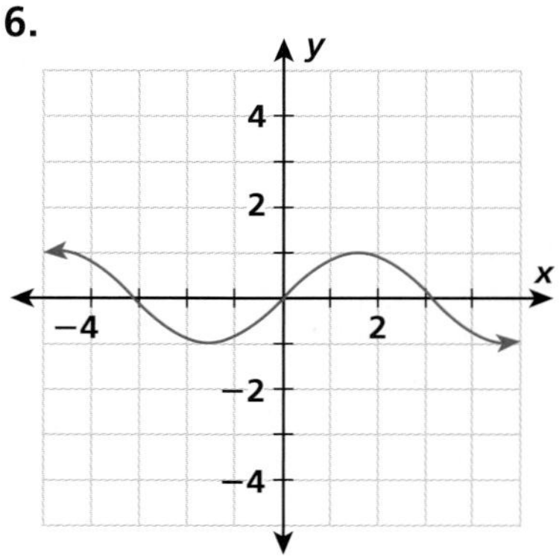

See Example 3

7. The table shows how much money Marvin earned while helping his mother with yard work one weekend. Use the data to make a graph. Find the slope of the line and explain what it shows.

Time (h)	Money Earned
3	\$15
5	\$25
7	\$35
9	\$45

INDEPENDENT PRACTICE

See Example 1 **Find the slope of the line that passes through each pair of points.**

8. (−2, −2) and (−4, 1)
9. (0, 0) and (4, −2)
10. (3, −6) and (2, −1)
11. (4, 2) and (0, 5)
12. (−2, −3) and (2, 4)
13. (0, −4) and (−7, 2)

See Example 2

Determine whether each graph shows a constant or variable rate of change. Explain your reasoning.

14.

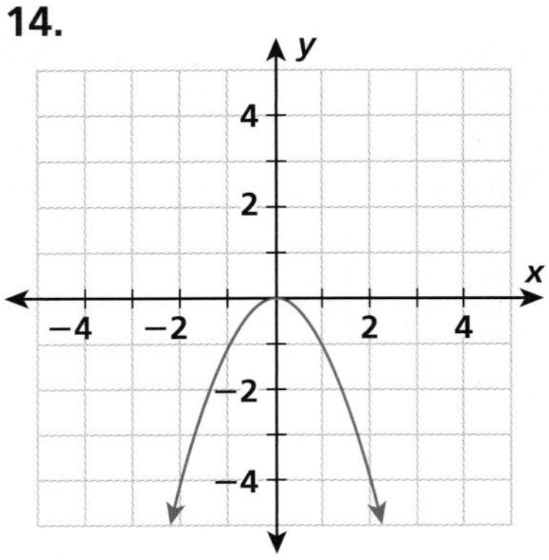

15.

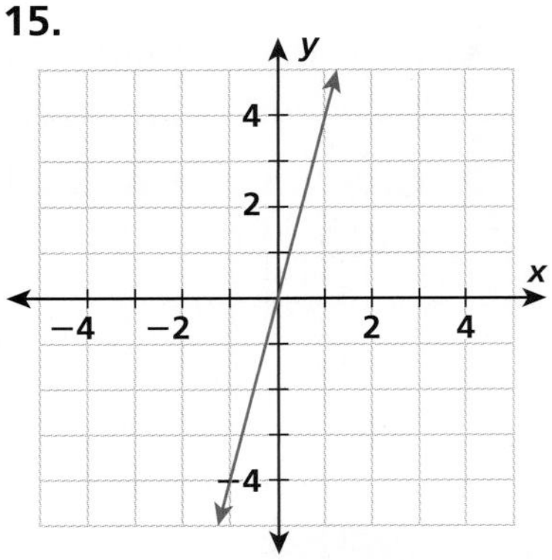

16.

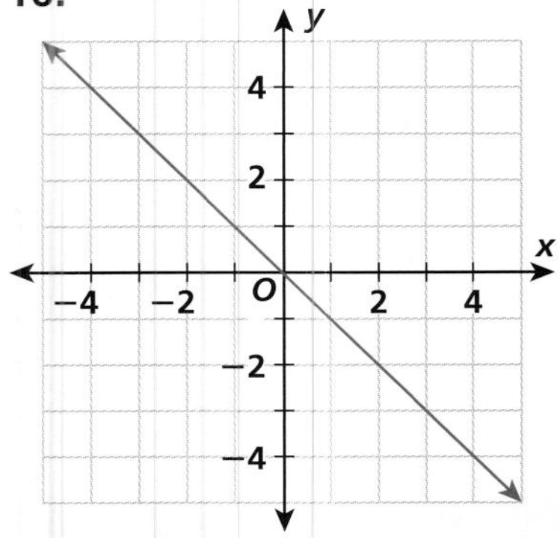

See Example 3

17. The table shows how much water was in a swimming pool as it was being filled. Use the data to make a graph. Find the slope of the line and explain what it shows.

Time (min)	Amount of Water (gal)
10	40
13	52
16	64
19	76

PRACTICE AND PROBLEM SOLVING

Extra Practice
See page 804.

For Exercises 18–21, match each graph with the situation described. Tell whether the rate of change is positive, negative, zero, or undefined.

Ⓐ

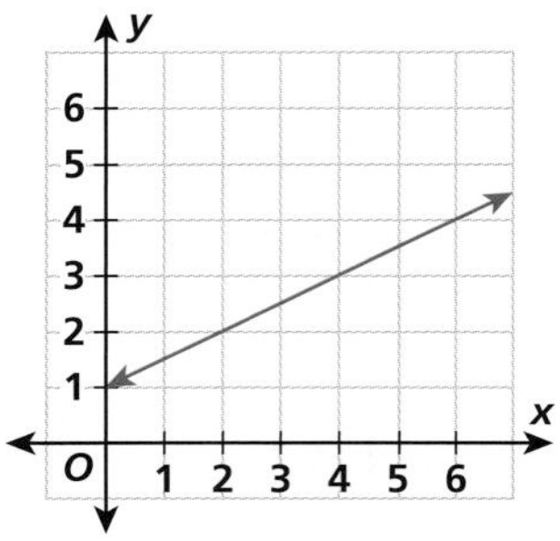

Ⓑ

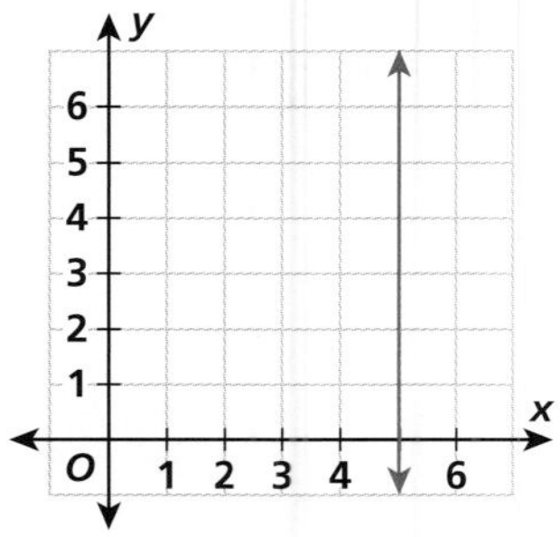

Ⓒ

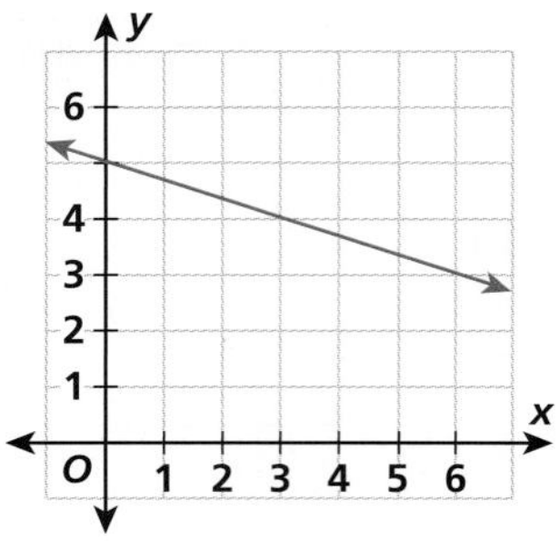

Ⓓ

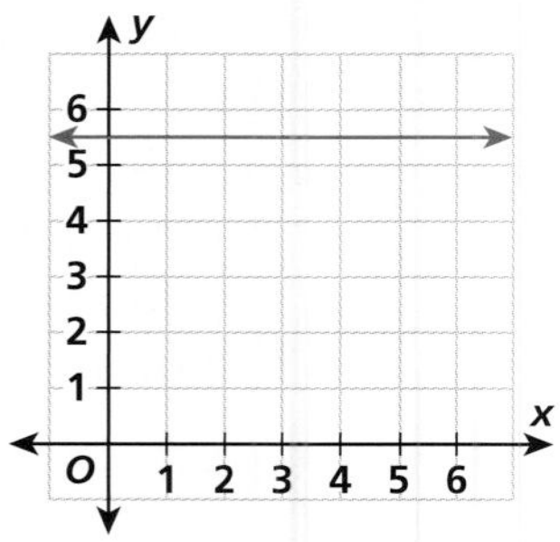

18. A car travels at a constant speed for a number of hours.

19. A bicyclist pedals up a hill over time.

20. The descent of an airplane as it lands at the airport.

21. The path of a rocket as it takes off from the ground.

22. **Safety** A wheelchair ramp rises 1.5 feet for every 18 feet of horizontal distance it covers. Find the rate of change of the ramp.

23. **Architecture** The Luxor Hotel in Las Vegas, Nevada, has a 350-foot-tall glass pyramid. The elevator of the pyramid moves at an incline such that its rate of change is -4 feet in the vertical direction for every 5 feet in the horizontal direction. Graph the line that describes the path it travels. (*Hint:* The point (0, 350) is the top of the pyramid.)

24. A large container holds 5 gallons of water. It begins leaking at a constant rate. After 10 minutes, the container has 3 gallons of water left. At what rate is the water leaking? After how many minutes will the container be empty?

25. **Construction** The angle, or pitch, of a roof is the number of inches it rises vertically for every 12 inches it extends horizontally. Morgan's roof has a pitch of 0. What does this mean?

26. **Manufacturing** A factory produces widgets at a constant rate. After 3 hours, 2520 widgets have been produced. After 8 hours, 6720 widgets have been produced. At what rate are the widgets being produced? How long will it take to produce 10,080 widgets?

27. **What's the Error?** The slope of the line through the points (2, 5) and $(-2, -5)$ is $\frac{2-(-2)}{5-(-5)} = \frac{2}{5}$. What is the error in this statement?

28. **Write About It** The equation of a vertical line is $x = a$, where a is any number. Explain why the slope of a vertical line is undefined, using a specific vertical line.

29. **Challenge** Graph the equations $y = 3x - 4$, $y = -\frac{1}{3}x$, and $y = 3x + 2$ on one coordinate plane. Identify the rate of change of each line. Explain how to tell whether a graph has a constant or variable rate of change.

TEST PREP and Spiral Review

30. **Multiple Choice** Which best describes the slope of the line that passes through points $(4, -4)$ and $(9, -4)$?

Ⓐ positive　Ⓑ negative　Ⓒ zero　Ⓓ undefined

31. **Gridded Response** What is the slope of the line that passes through points $(-5, 4)$ and $(-7, -2)$?

Do the data sets have a positive, a negative, or no correlation? (Lesson 9-7)

32. The number of weeks a book has been published and weekly sales

33. The number of weeks a book has been published and total sales

Graph each equation and tell whether it is linear. (Lesson 12-1)

34. $y = 2x + 3$　35. $y = 3x^2$　36. $y = -6$

12-3 Using Slopes and Intercepts

Learn to use slopes and intercepts to graph linear equations.

Vocabulary

x-intercept

y-intercept

slope-intercept form

The Java Cafe sells \$25 gift cards. A medium coffee costs \$2.50. The linear equation $y = -2.50x + 25$ relates the number of dollars y remaining on the card to the number of medium coffees x that a customer buys.

You can graph a linear equation easily by finding the *x-intercept* and the *y-intercept*. The **x-intercept** of a line is the value of x where the line crosses the x-axis (where $y = 0$). The **y-intercept** of a line is the value of y where the line crosses the y-axis (where $x = 0$).

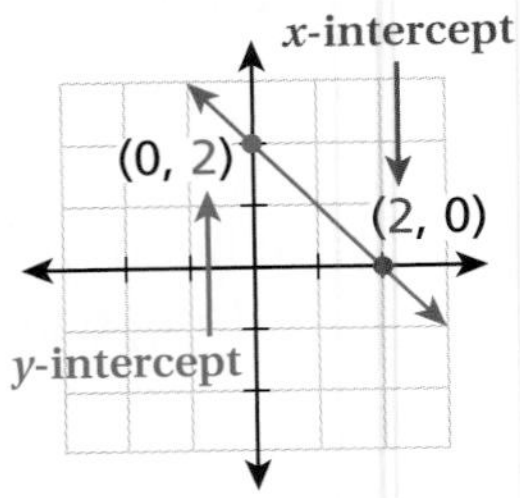

Graph of the line $y = -x + 2$

EXAMPLE 1 Finding x-intercepts and y-intercepts to Graph Linear Equations

Helpful Hint

The form $Ax + By = C$, where A, B, and C are real numbers, is called the Standard Form of a Linear Equation.

Find the x-intercept and y-intercept of the line $3x + 4y = 12$. Use the intercepts to graph the equation.

Find the x-intercept ($y = 0$).

$$3x + 4y = 12$$
$$3x + 4(0) = 12$$
$$3x = 12$$
$$\frac{3x}{3} = \frac{12}{3}$$
$$x = 4$$

The x-intercept is 4.

Find the y-intercept ($x = 0$).

$$3x + 4y = 12$$
$$3(0) + 4y = 12$$
$$4y = 12$$
$$\frac{4y}{4} = \frac{12}{4}$$
$$y = 3$$

The y-intercept is 3.

The graph of $3x + 4y = 12$ is the line that crosses the x-axis at the point (4, 0) and the y-axis at the point (0, 3).

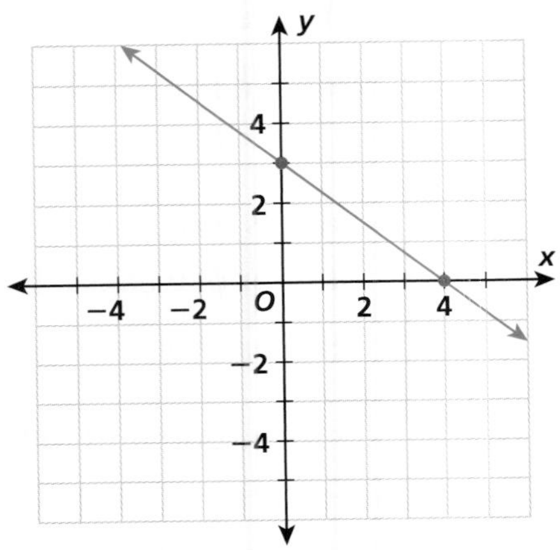

In an equation written in **slope-intercept form**, $y = mx + b$, m is the slope and b is the y-intercept.

Slope → m; y-intercept → b

$$y = mx + b$$

EXAMPLE 2 **Using Slope-Intercept Form to Find Slopes and y-intercepts**

Write each equation in slope-intercept form, and then find the slope and y-intercept.

> **Helpful Hint**
>
> For an equation such as $y = x - 6$, write it as $y = x + (-6)$ to read the y-intercept, -6.

A $y = x$

$y = x$

$y = 1x + 0$ *Rewrite the equation to show each part.*

$m = 1$ $\quad b = 0$

The slope of the line $y = x$ is 1, and the y-intercept is 0.

B $8x = 5y$

$8x = 5y$

$5y = 8x$ *Reflexive Property*

$\frac{5y}{5} = \frac{8x}{5}$ *Divide both sides by 5 to solve for y.*

$y = \frac{8}{5}x + 0$ *The equation is in slope-intercept form.*

$m = \frac{8}{5}$ $\quad b = 0$

The slope of the line $8x = 5y$ is $\frac{8}{5}$, and the y-intercept is 0.

C $3x + 7y = 9$

$3x + 7y = 9$

$\underline{-3x \qquad\qquad -3x}$ *Subtract 3x from both sides.*

$7y = 9 - 3x$

$7y = -3x + 9$ *Rewrite to match slope-intercept form.*

$\frac{7y}{7} = \frac{-3x}{7} + \frac{9}{7}$ *Divide both sides by 7.*

$y = -\frac{3}{7}x + \frac{9}{7}$ *The equation is in slope-intercept form.*

$m = -\frac{3}{7}$ $\quad b = \frac{9}{7}$

The slope of the line $3x + 7y = 9$ is $-\frac{3}{7}$, and the y-intercept is $\frac{9}{7}$.

EXAMPLE 3 Consumer Application

Helpful Hint

The *y*-intercept represents the initial amount on the card (\$25). The slope represents the rate of change (−\$2.50 per medium coffee).

The cash register deducts \$2.50 from a \$25 Java Cafe gift card for every medium coffee the customer buys. The linear equation $y = -2.50x + 25$ represents the number of dollars *y* on the card after *x* medium coffees. Graph the equation using the slope and *y*-intercept.

$y = -2.50x + 25$ *The equation is in slope-intercept form.*

$m = -2.50$ $b = 25$

The slope of the line is −2.50, and the *y*-intercept is 25. The line crosses the *y*-axis at (0, 25) and moves down 2.5 units for every 1 unit it moves right.

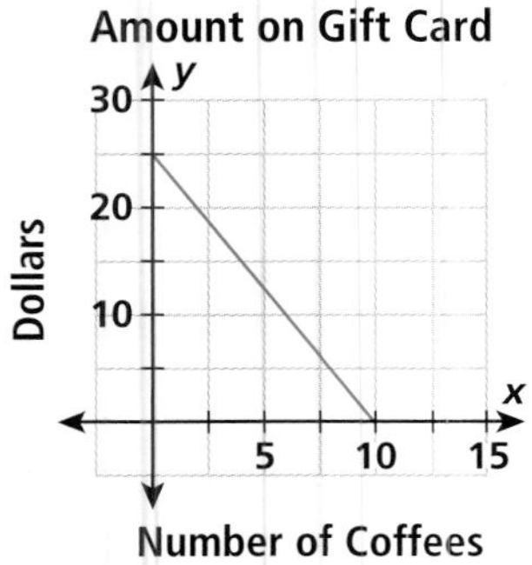

EXAMPLE 4 Writing Slope-Intercept Form

Write the equation of the line that passes through (−3, 1) and (2, −1) in slope-intercept form.

Find the slope.

$$\frac{y_2 - y_1}{x_2 - x_1} = \frac{-1 - 1}{2-(-3)}$$

$$= \frac{-2}{5} = -\frac{2}{5}$$ *The slope is $-\frac{2}{5}$.*

Substitute either point and the slope into the slope-intercept form and solve for *b*.

$y = mx + b$

$-1 = -\frac{2}{5}(2) + b$ *Substitute 2 for x, −1 for y, and $-\frac{2}{5}$ for m.*

$-1 = -\frac{4}{5} + b$ *Simplify.*

$+\frac{4}{5} \quad +\frac{4}{5}$ *Add $\frac{4}{5}$ to both sides.*

$-\frac{1}{5} = b$

Write the equation of the line, using $-\frac{2}{5}$ for *m* and $-\frac{1}{5}$ for *b*.

$y = -\frac{2}{5}x + \left(-\frac{1}{5}\right)$, or $y = -\frac{2}{5}x - \frac{1}{5}$

Think and Discuss

1. **Describe** the line represented by the equation $y = -5x + 3$.
2. **Give** a real-life example with a graph that has a slope of 5 and a *y*-intercept of 30.

12-3 Exercises

go.hrw.com
Homework Help Online
KEYWORD: MT7 12-3
Parent Resources Online
KEYWORD: MT7 Parent

GUIDED PRACTICE

See Example 1

Find the x-intercept and y-intercept of each line. Use the intercepts to graph the equation.

1. $x - y = 4$ **2.** $3x + 5y = 15$ **3.** $2x + 3y = -12$ **4.** $-5x + 2y = 10$

See Example 2

Write each equation in slope-intercept form, and then find the slope and y-intercept.

5. $3x = 9y$ **6.** $3x - y = 14$ **7.** $2x - 8y = 32$ **8.** $x + 4y = 12$

See Example 3

9. A freight company charges $25 plus $4.50 per pound to ship an item that weighs n pounds. The total shipping charges are given by the equation $C = 4.5n + 25$. Identify the slope and y-intercept, and use them to graph the equation for n between 0 and 50 pounds.

See Example 4

Write the equation of the line that passes through each pair of points in slope-intercept form.

10. $(-2, -7)$ and $(3, 8)$ **11.** $(0, 3)$ and $(2, -5)$ **12.** $(3, 5)$ and $(6, 6)$

INDEPENDENT PRACTICE

See Example 1

Find the x-intercept and y-intercept of each line. Use the intercepts to graph the equation.

13. $4y = 24 - 12x$ **14.** $5x = 15 + 3y$ **15.** $-y = 12 - 4x$ **16.** $2x + y = 7$

See Example 2

Write each equation in slope-intercept form, and then find the slope and y-intercept.

17. $-y = 3x$ **18.** $5y + 3x = 10$ **19.** $-4y - 8x = 8$ **20.** $3y + 6x = -15$

See Example 3

21. A computer salesperson receives a weekly salary of $250 plus a commission of $12 for each computer sold. Total weekly pay is given by the equation $P = 12n + 250$, where n is the number of computers he sells. Identify the slope and y-intercept, and use them to graph the equation for n between 0 and 50 computers.

See Example 4

Write the equation of the line that passes through each pair of points in slope-intercept form.

22. $(0, -6)$ and $(3, 15)$ **23.** $(-1, 1)$ and $(3, -3)$ **24.** $(-5, -4)$ and $(15, 0)$

PRACTICE AND PROBLEM SOLVING

Extra Practice
See page 804.

Use the x-intercept and y-intercept of each line to graph the equation.

25. $y = 2x - 10$ **26.** $y = \frac{1}{2}x + 3$ **27.** $y = 5x - 1.5$ **28.** $y = -\frac{3}{4}x + 10$

29. Write an equation that has the same y-intercept as $y = 2x + 4$.

Life Science LINK

Acute Mountain Sickness (AMS) occurs if you ascend in altitude too quickly without giving your body time to adjust. It usually occurs at altitudes over 10,000 feet above sea level. To prevent AMS you should not ascend more than 1,000 feet per day. And every time you climb a total of 3,000 feet, your body needs two nights to adjust.

Often people will get sick at high altitudes because there is less oxygen and lower atmospheric pressure.

30. The map shows a team's plan for climbing Long's Peak in Rocky Mountain National Park.

a. Make a graph of the team's plan of ascent and find the slope of the line. (Day number should be your x-value, and altitude should be your y-value.)

b. Find the y-intercept and explain what it means.

c. Write the equation of the line in slope-intercept form.

d. Does the team run a high risk of getting AMS?

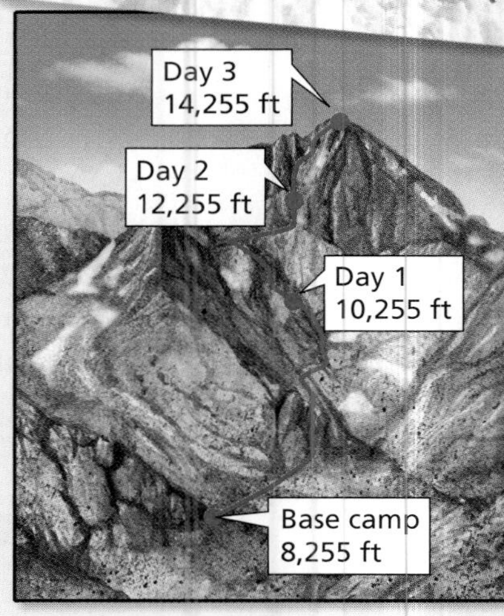

31. The equation that describes a mountain climber's ascent up Mount McKinley in Alaska is $y = 955x + 16{,}500$, where x is the day number and y is the altitude at the end of the day. What are the slope and y-intercept? What do they mean in terms of the climb?

32. **Challenge** Make a graph of the ascent of a team that follows the rules to avoid AMS exactly and spends the minimum number of days climbing from base camp (17,600 ft) to the summit of Mount Everest (29,035 ft). Can you write a linear equation describing this trip? Explain your answer.

Test Prep and Spiral Review

33. **Multiple Choice** What is the equation in slope-intercept form of the line that passes through points (1, 6) and (−1, −2)?

Ⓐ $y = 2x + 4$ Ⓑ $y = -3x + 6$ Ⓒ $y = 4x - 2$ Ⓓ $y = 4x + 2$

34. **Extended Response** Write the equation $9x + 7y = 63$ in slope-intercept form. Then identify m and b. Graph the line.

Find each unit rate. (Lesson 5-2)

35. \$31.75 for 5 hours **36.** 24 carts for 12 classrooms **37.** \$44 for 8 beef burritos

Find the slope of the line that passes through each pair of points. (Lesson 12-2)

38. (2, 3), (4, 8) **39.** (3, −1), (7, 4) **40.** (−6, 1), (−7, 7) **41.** (5, 4), (−11, 0)

Technology LAB 12-3

Graph Equations in Slope-Intercept Form

Use with Lesson 12-3

go.hrw.com
Lab Resources Online
KEYWORD: MT7 Lab12

To graph $y = x + 1$, a linear equation in slope-intercept form, in the standard graphing calculator window, press **Y=** ; enter the right side of the equation, **X,T,θ,n** **+** 1; and press **ZOOM** **6:ZStandard.**

From the slope-intercept equation, you know that the slope of the line is 1. Notice that the standard window distorts the screen, and the line does not appear to have a great enough slope.

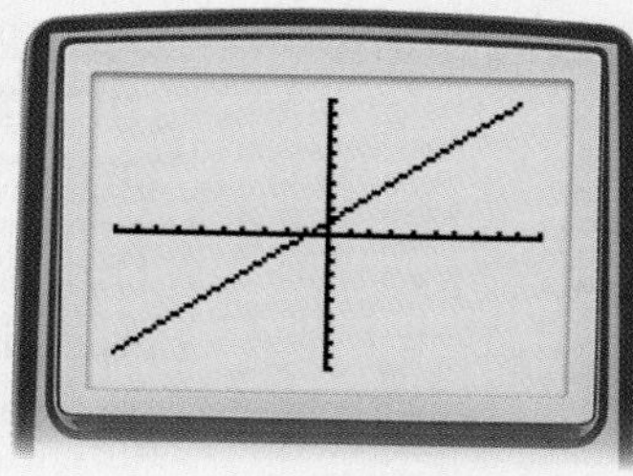

Press **ZOOM** **5:ZSquare**. This changes the scale for x from -10 to 10 to -15.16 to 15.16. The graph is shown at right. Or press **ZOOM** **8:ZInteger** **ENTER** . This changes the scale for x to -47 to 47 and the scale for y to -31 to 31.

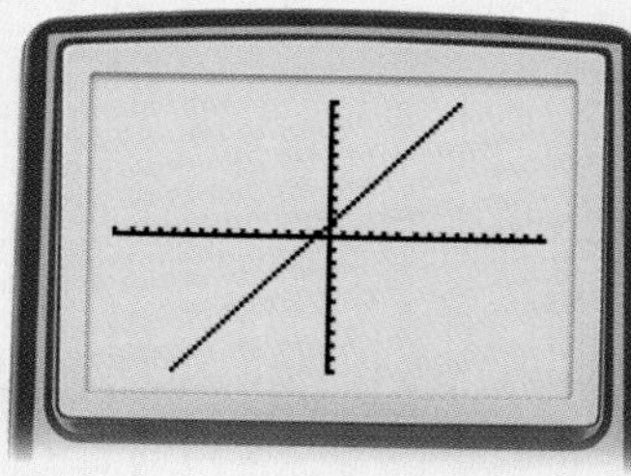

Activity

1 Graph $2x + 3y = 36$ in the integer window. Find the x- and y-intercepts of the graph.

First solve $3y = -2x + 36$ for y.

$y = \frac{-2x + 36}{3}$, so $y = -\frac{2}{3}x + 12$.

Press **Y=** ; enter the right side of the equation, **(** **(−)** 2 **÷** 3 **)** **X,T,θ,n** **+** 12; and press **ZOOM** **8:ZInteger** **ENTER** .

Press **TRACE** to see the equation of the line and the y-intercept. The graph in the **ZInteger** window is shown.

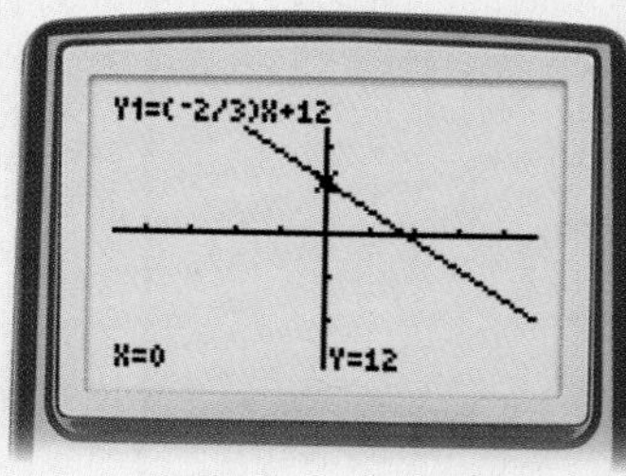

Think and Discuss

1. How do the ratios of the range of y to the range of x in the **ZSquare** and **ZInteger** windows compare?

Try This

Graph each equation in a square window.

1. $y = 3x$

2. $3y = x$

3. $3y - 6x = 15$

4. $2x + 5y = 40$

12-4 Point-Slope Form

Learn to find the equation of a line given one point and the slope.

Vocabulary

point-slope form

Lasers aim light along a straight path. If you know the destination of the light beam (a point on the line) and the slant of the beam (the slope), you can write an equation in *point-slope form* to calculate the height at which the laser is positioned.

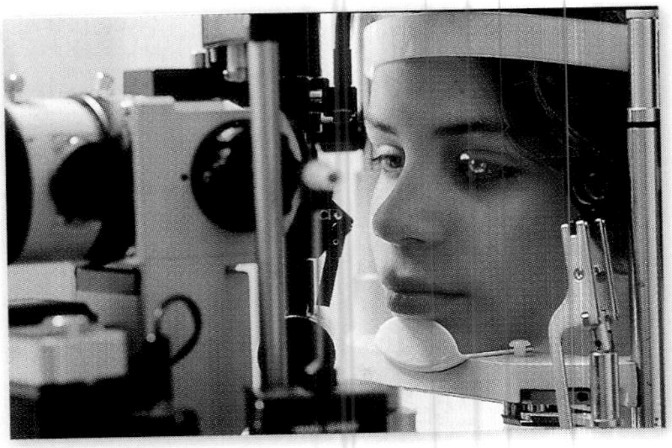

The **point-slope form** of an equation of a line with slope m passing through (x_1, y_1) is $y - y_1 = m(x - x_1)$.

Point on the line	Point-slope form
(x_1, y_1)	$y - y_1 = m(x - x_1)$
	Slope (m)

EXAMPLE 1 Using Point-Slope Form to Identify Information About a Line

Use the point-slope form of each equation to identify a point the line passes through and the slope of the line.

A $y - 9 = -\frac{2}{3}(x - 21)$

$y - y_1 = m(x - x_1)$

$y - 9 = -\frac{2}{3}(x - 21)$ — *The equation is in point-slope form.*

$m = -\frac{2}{3}$ — *Read the value of m from the equation.*

$(x_1, y_1) = (21, 9)$ — *Read the point from the equation.*

The line defined by $y - 9 = -\frac{2}{3}(x - 21)$ has slope $-\frac{2}{3}$, and passes through the point (21, 9).

B $y - 2 = 3(x + 8)$

$y - y_1 = m(x - x_1)$

$y - 2 = 3(x + 8)$

$y - 2 = 3[x - (-8)]$ — *Rewrite using subtraction instead of addition.*

$m = 3$

$(x_1, y_1) = (-8, 2)$

The line defined by $y - 2 = 3(x + 8)$ has slope 3, and passes through the point (−8, 2).

EXAMPLE 2 Writing the Point-Slope Form of an Equation

Write the point-slope form of the equation with the given slope that passes through the indicated point.

A **the line with slope –2 passing through (4, 1)**

$y - y_1 = m(x - x_1)$

$\mathbf{y - 1 = -2(x - 4)}$ *Substitute 4 for x_1, 1 for y_1, and −2 for m.*

The equation of the line with slope −2 that passes through (4, 1) in point-slope form is $y - 1 = -2(x - 4)$.

B **the line with slope 5 passing through (−2, 4)**

$y - y_1 = m(x - x_1)$

$\mathbf{y - 4 = 5[x - (-2)]}$ *Substitute −2 for x_1, 4 for y_1, and 5 for m.*

$y - 4 = 5(x + 2)$

The equation of the line with slope 5 that passes through (−2, 4) in point-slope form is $y - 4 = 5(x + 2)$.

EXAMPLE 3 *Medical Application*

Suppose that laser eye surgery is modeled on a coordinate grid. The laser is positioned at the *y*-intercept so that the light shifts down 1 mm for each 40 mm it shifts to the right. The light reaches the center of the cornea of the eye at (125, 0). Write the equation of the light beam in point-slope form, and find the height of the laser.

As x increases by 40, y decreases by 1, so the slope of the line is $-\frac{1}{40}$. The line must pass through the point (125, 0).

$y - y_1 = m(x - x_1)$

$\mathbf{y - 0 = -\frac{1}{40}(x - 125)}$ *Substitute 125 for x_1, 0 for y_1, and $-\frac{1}{40}$ for m.*

The equation of the line the laser beam travels along, in point-slope form, is $y = -\frac{1}{40}(x - 125)$. Substitute 0 for x to find the y-intercept.

$y = -\frac{1}{40}(0 - 125)$

$y = -\frac{1}{40}(-125)$

$y = 3.125$

The y-intercept is 3.125, so the laser is at a height of 3.125 mm.

Think and Discuss

1. **Describe** the line, using the point-slope equation, that has a slope of 2 and passes through (−3, 4).
2. **Tell** how you find the point-slope form of the line when you know the coordinates of two points.

12-4 Exercises

go.hrw.com
Homework Help Online
KEYWORD: MT7 12-4
Parent Resources Online
KEYWORD: MT7 Parent

GUIDED PRACTICE

See Example 1

Use the point-slope form of each equation to identify a point the line passes through and the slope of the line.

1. $y - 2 = -3(x + 6)$
2. $y - 8 = 7(x - 14)$
3. $y + 3.7 = 3.2(x - 1.7)$
4. $y + 1 = 11(x - 1)$
5. $y + 6 = -4(x - 8)$
6. $y - 7 = 4(x + 3)$

See Example 2

Write the point-slope form of the equation with the given slope that passes through the indicated point.

7. the line with slope 5 passing through (0, 6)
8. the line with slope −8 passing through (−11, 7)

See Example 3

9. A basement filled with water from a rainstorm is drained at a rate of 10.5 liters per minute. After 40 minutes, there are 840 liters of water remaining. Write the equation of a line in point-slope form that models the situation. How long does it take to drain the basement?

INDEPENDENT PRACTICE

See Example 1

Use the point-slope form of each equation to identify a point the line passes through and the slope of the line.

10. $y - 2 = \frac{3}{4}(x + 9)$
11. $y + 9 = 4(x + 5)$
12. $y - 2 = -\frac{1}{6}(x - 11)$
13. $y - 13 = 16(x - 4)$
14. $y - 5 = -1.4(x - 6.7)$
15. $y + 9 = 1(x - 3)$

See Example 2

Write the point-slope form of the equation with the given slope that passes through the indicated point.

16. the line with slope −5 passing through (−3, −5)
17. the line with slope 6 passing through (−3, 0)

See Example 3

18. A stretch of highway has a 5% grade, so the road rises 1 ft for each 20 ft of horizontal distance. The beginning of the highway ($x = 0$) has an elevation of 2344 ft. Write an equation in point-slope form, and find the highway's elevation 7500 ft from the beginning.

PRACTICE AND PROBLEM SOLVING

Extra Practice
See page 805.

Write the point-slope form of each line described below.

19. the line parallel to $y = 4x - 5$ that passes through (−2, 3)
20. the line perpendicular to $y = -3x$ that passes through (8, −2)
21. the line perpendicular to $y = x + 2$ that passes through (−5, −7)
22. the line parallel to $y = -10x - 5$ that passes through (−3, 0)
23. **Critical Thinking** Compare finding the equation of a line using two known points to finding it using one known point and the slope of the line.

LINK

Earth Science

Mount Etna, a volcano in Sicily, Italy, has been erupting for over half a million years. It is one of the world's most active volcanoes. When it erupted in 1669 it almost completely destroyed the city of Catania.

go.hrw.com
Web Extra!
KEYWORD: MT7 Etna

24. Life Science An elephant's tusks grow throughout its life. Each month, an elephant tusk grows about 1 cm. Suppose you started observing an elephant when its tusks were 12 cm long. Write an equation in point-slope form that describes the length of the elephant's tusks after m months of observation.

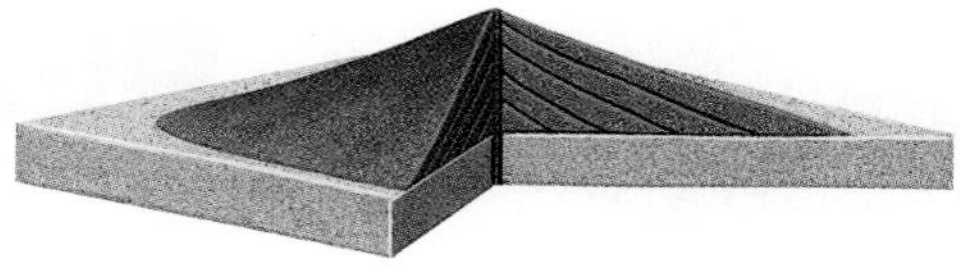

Shield volcano typical slope: 0.03–0.17

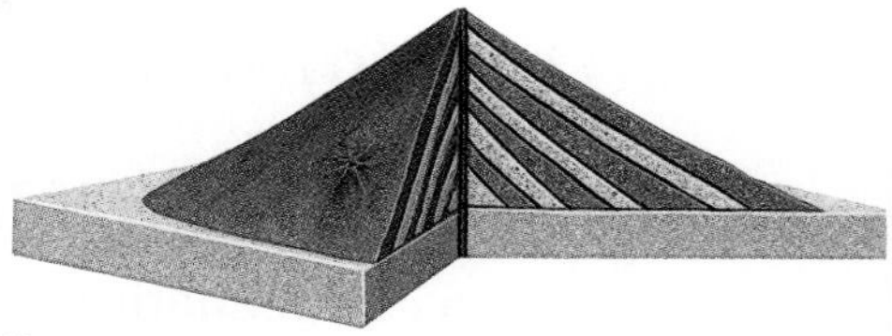

Composite volcano typical slope: 0.17–0.5

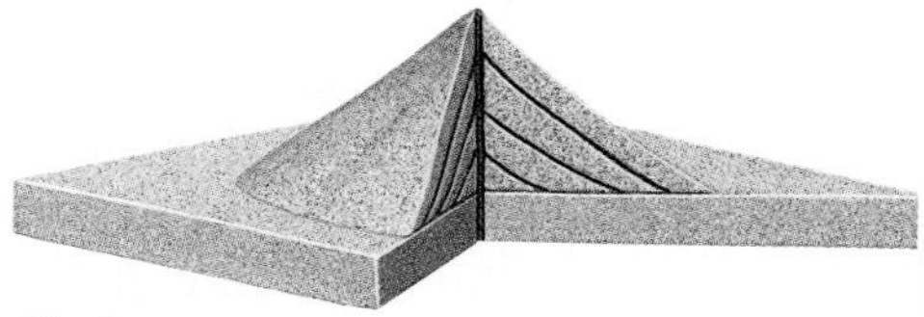

Cinder cone volcano typical slope: 0.5–0.65

25. Earth Science Jorullo is a cinder cone volcano in Mexico. Suppose Jorullo is 315 m tall, 50 m from the center of its base. Use the slope of a cinder cone to write a possible equation in point-slope form that approximately models the height of the volcano, x meters from the center of its base.

26. Write a Problem Write a problem about the point-slope form of an equation using the data on a car's fuel economy.

Fuel Economy		
Gas Tank Capacity	City Efficiency	Highway Efficiency
14 gal	26 mi/gal	34 mi/gal

27. Write About It Explain how you could convert an equation in point-slope form to slope-intercept form.

28. Challenge The value of one line's x-intercept is the opposite of the value of its y-intercept. The line contains the point $(9, -3)$. Find the point-slope form of the equation.

TEST PREP and Spiral Review

29. Multiple Choice What is the point-slope form of a line that is parallel to $y = \frac{3}{4}x - 5$ and passes through the point $(-16, 5)$?

Ⓐ $y - 5 = \frac{3}{4}(x - 16)$

Ⓒ $y - 5 = \frac{3}{4}(x + 16)$

Ⓑ $y - 5 = -\frac{4}{3}(x + 16)$

Ⓓ $y - 5 = -\frac{4}{3}(x - 16)$

30. Gridded Response Use the point-slope form of the equation $y - 6 = 8(x + 1)$. What is the y-value of the y-intercept?

Combine like terms. (Lesson 11-1)

31. $7x - 5y + 18$

32. $3x + y + 5y - 2x$

33. $8y - 2x - 8y - 2x$

Write each equation in slope-intercept form, and then find the slope and y-intercept. (Lesson 12-3)

34. $2x = 8y$

35. $x - y = 5$

36. $4x + 4y = 4$

READY TO GO ON?

Quiz for Lessons 12-1 Through 12-4

12-1 Graphing Linear Equations

Graph each equation and tell whether it is linear.

1. $y = 2 - 4x$
2. $x = 2$
3. $y = 3x^2$
4. At Maggi's Music, the equation $u = \frac{3}{4}n + 1$ represents the price for a used CD u with a selling price n when the CD was new. How much will a used CD cost for each of the listed new prices? Graph the equation and tell whether it is linear.

New Price	Used Price
\$8	
\$12	
\$14	
\$20	

12-2 Slope of a Line

Find the slope of the line that passes through each pair of points.

5. (6, 3) and (2, 4)
6. (1, 4) and (−1, −3)
7. (0, −3) and (−4, 0)
8. Determine whether the graph shows a constant or variable rate of change.

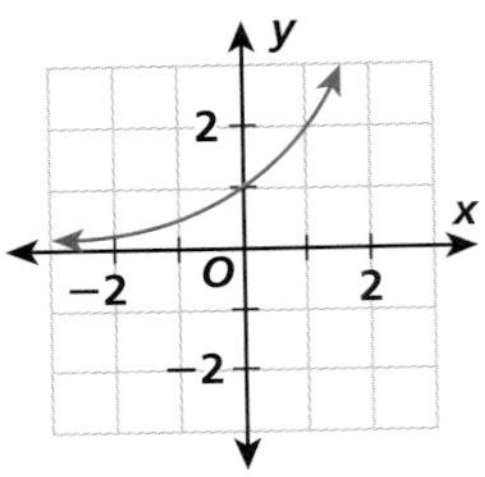

12-3 Using Slopes and Intercepts

9. A camp charges families \$625 per month for one child and then \$225 per month for each additional child. The linear equation $y = 225x + 625$ represents the amount a family would pay for x additional children. Identify the slope and y-intercept, and use them to graph the equation.

Write the equation of the line that passes through each pair of points in slope-intercept form.

10. (−4, 3) and (−2, 1)
11. (2, 7) and (5, 2)
12. (4, 2) and (2, −5)

12-4 Point-Slope Form

Use the point-slope form of each equation to identify a point the line passes through and the slope of the line.

13. $y + 5 = -3(x - 2)$
14. $y = -(x + 3)$
15. $y - 7 = -3x$

Write the point-slope form of the equation with the given slope that passes through the indicated point.

16. slope −3, passing through (7, 2)
17. slope 2, passing through (−5, 3)

Focus on Problem Solving

Understand the Problem

• Identify important details in the problem

When you are solving word problems, you need to find the information that is important to the problem.

You can write the equation of a line if you know the slope and one point on the line or if you know two points on the line.

Example:

A school bus carrying 40 students is traveling toward the school at **30 mi/hr**. After **15 minutes**, it has **20 miles to go.** How far away from the school was the bus when it started?

You can write the equation of the line in point-slope form.

$$\begin{aligned} y - y_1 &= m(x - x_1) \\ y - (-20) &= 30(x - 0.25) \\ y + 20 &= 30x - 7.5 \\ -20 &\quad\;\; -20 \\ y &= 30x - 27.5 \end{aligned}$$

The slope is the rate of change, or 30.
15 minutes = 0.25 hours
(0.25, −20) is a point on the line.

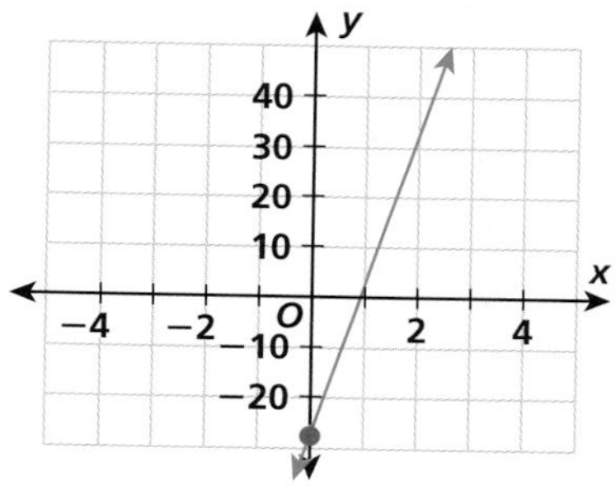

The y-intercept of the line is −27.5. At 0 minutes, the bus had 27.5 miles to go.

Read each problem, and identify the information needed to write the equation of a line. Give the slope and one point on the line, or give two points on the line.

1. At sea level, water boils at 100°C. At an altitude of 600 m, water boils at 95°C. If the relationship is linear, estimate the temperature that water would boil at an altitude of 1800 m.

2. Omar earns a weekly salary of $560, plus a commission of 8% of his total sales. How many dollars in merchandise does he have to sell to make $600 in one week?

3. A community activities group has a goal of passing out 5000 fliers advertising a charity run. On Saturday, the group passed out 2000 fliers. If the group can pass out 600 fliers per week, how long will it take them to pass out the remaining fliers to the community?

4. Kayla rents a booth at a craft fair. If she sells 50 bracelets, her profit is $25. If she sells 80 bracelets, her profit is $85. What would her profit be if she sold 100 bracelets?

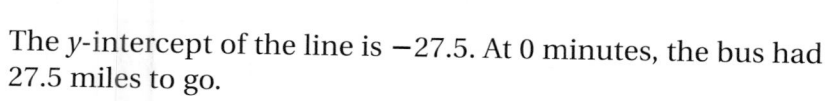

12-5 Direct Variation

Learn to recognize direct variation by graphing tables of data and checking for constant ratios.

Vocabulary

direct variation

constant of proportionality

An amplifier can create 125 watts of sound from an input signal with 1 watt of power. The same amplifier, with the same settings, will create 625 watts of sound with a 5-watt input, 5000 watts of sound with a 40-watt input, and so on.

The ratio of watts of sound to watts of power is constant. The amplifier creates 125 watts of sound for every 1 watt of power.

$$\frac{\text{watts of sound}}{\text{watts of power}} = \frac{125}{1} = \frac{625}{5} = \frac{5000}{40}$$

DIRECT VARIATION		
Words	**Numbers**	**Algebra**
For **direct variation**, two variable quantities are related proportionally by a constant positive ratio. The ratio is called the **constant of proportionality**.	$8 = k$ $16 = 2k$ $24 = 3k$	$y = kx$ $k = \frac{y}{x}$

The number of watts of sound the amplifier puts out *varies directly* with the watts of power and is represented by the equation $y = kx$. The constant ratio k is 125.

EXAMPLE 1 Determining Whether a Data Set Varies Directly

Helpful Hint

The graph of a direct-variation equation is always linear *and* always contains the point (0, 0). The variables x and y either increase together or decrease together.

Determine whether the data sets show direct variation.

A

Shoe Sizes					
U.S. Size	7	8	9	10	11
European Size	39	41	43	44	45

Make a graph that shows the relationship between the U.S. sizes and the European sizes. The graph is not linear.

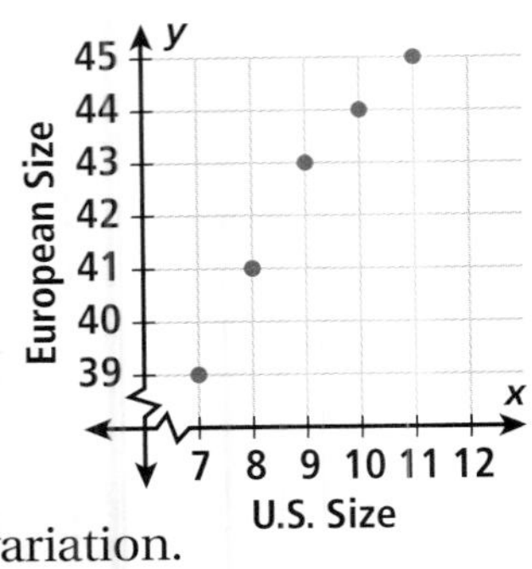

You can also compare ratios to see if a direct variation occurs.

$\frac{39}{7} \neq \frac{45}{11}$ → 315, 429

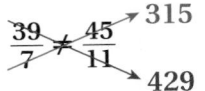

315 ≠ 429
The ratios are not proportional.

The relationship of the data is not a direct variation.

Determine whether the data sets show direct variation.

B

Number of Watts of Sound for Watts of Power					
Input Signal Power (W)	6	8	12	20	28
Output Sound Intensity $\left(\frac{W}{m^2}\right)$	4.5	6	9	15	21

Make a graph that shows the relationship between the input power and the output intensity.

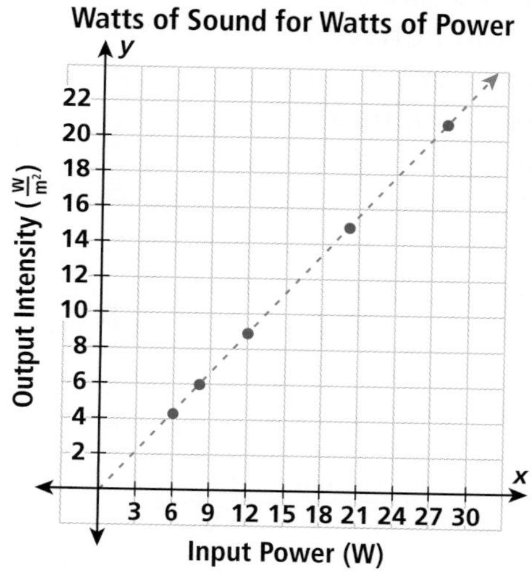

Plot the points.
The points lie in a straight line.
(0, 0) is on the line.

You can also compare ratios to see if direct variation occurs.

$\frac{6}{4.5} = \frac{8}{6} = \frac{12}{9} = \frac{20}{15} = \frac{28}{21}$ *Compare ratios. The ratio is constant.*

The ratios are proportional. The relationship is a direct variation.

EXAMPLE 2 Finding Equations of Direct Variation

Find each equation of direct variation, given that y varies directly with x.

A **y is 48 when x is 3**

$y = kx$	*y varies directly with x.*
$48 = k \cdot 3$	*Substitute for x and y.*
$16 = k$	*Solve for k.*
$y = 16x$	*Substitute 16 for k in the original equation.*

B **y is 15 when x is 10**

$y = kx$	*y varies directly with x.*
$15 = k \cdot 10$	*Substitute for x and y.*
$\frac{3}{2} = k$	*Solve for k.*
$y = \frac{3}{2}x$	*Substitute $\frac{3}{2}$ for k in the original equation.*

EXAMPLE 3 *Physical Science Application*

When a driver applies the brakes, a car's total stopping distance is the sum of the reaction distance and the braking distance. The reaction distance is the distance the car travels before the driver presses the brake pedal. The braking distance is the distance the car travels after the brakes have been applied.

Determine whether there is a direct variation between either data set and speed. If so, find the equation of direct variation.

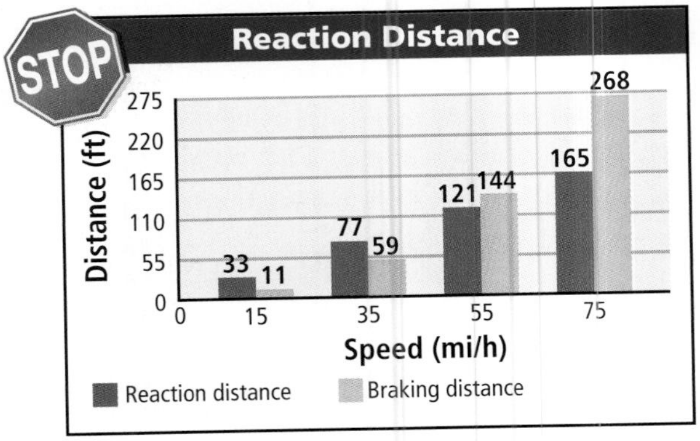

A **reaction distance and speed**

$\frac{\text{reaction distance}}{\text{speed}} = \frac{33}{15} = 2.2$ $\qquad$ $\frac{\text{reaction distance}}{\text{speed}} = \frac{77}{35} = 2.2$

The first two pairs of data result in a common ratio. In fact, all of the reaction distance to speed ratios are equivalent to 2.2.

$$\frac{\text{reaction distance}}{\text{speed}} = \frac{33}{15} = \frac{77}{35} = \frac{121}{55} = \frac{165}{75} = 2.2$$

The variables are related by a constant ratio of 2.2 to 1, and (0, 0) is included. The equation of direct variation is $y = 2.2x$, where x is the speed, y is the reaction distance, and 2.2 is the constant of proportionality.

B **braking distance and speed**

$\frac{\text{braking distance}}{\text{speed}} = \frac{11}{15} = 0.7\overline{3}$ $\qquad$ $\frac{\text{braking distance}}{\text{speed}} = \frac{59}{35} = 1.69$

$0.7\overline{3} \neq 1.69$

If any of the ratios are not equal, then there is no direct variation. It is not necessary to compute additional ratios.

Think and Discuss

1. **Describe** the slope and the y-intercept of a direct variation equation.
2. **Compare** and contrast proportional and non-proportional linear relationships.

12-5 Exercises

go.hrw.com
Homework Help Online
KEYWORD: MT7 12-5
Parent Resources Online
KEYWORD: MT7 Parent

GUIDED PRACTICE

See Example 1

Make a graph to determine whether the data sets show direct variation.

1. The table shows an employee's pay per number of hours worked.

Hours Worked	0	1	2	3	4	5	6
Pay ($)	0	9.50	19.00	28.50	38.00	47.50	57.00

See Example 2

Find each equation of direct variation, given that y varies directly with x.

2. y is 12 when x is 3
3. y is 18 when x is 6
4. y is 10 when x is 12
5. y is 5 when x is 10
6. y is 360 when x is 3
7. y is 4 when x is 36

See Example 3

8. The table shows how many hours it takes to travel 600 miles, depending on your speed in miles per hour. Determine whether there is direct variation between the two data sets. If so, find the equation of direct variation.

Speed (mi/h)	5	6	7.5	10	15	30	60
Time (h)	120	100	80	60	40	20	10

INDEPENDENT PRACTICE

See Example 1

Make a graph to determine whether the data sets show direct variation.

9. The table shows the amount of current flowing through a 12-volt circuit with various resistances.

Resistance (ohms)	48	24	12	6	4	3	2
Current (amps)	0.25	0.5	1	2	3	4	6

See Example 2

Find each equation of direct variation, given that y varies with x.

10. y is 3.5 when x is 3.5
11. y is 3 when x is 9
12. y is 96 when x is 4
13. y is 4 when x is 26
14. y is 48 when x is 3
15. y is 5 when x is 50

See Example 3

16. The table shows how many hours it takes to drive certain distances at a speed of 30 miles per hour. Determine whether there is direct variation between the two data sets. If so, find the equation of direct variation.

Distance (mi)	15	30	60	90	120	150	180
Time (h)	0.5	1	2	3	4	5	6

PRACTICE AND PROBLEM SOLVING

Extra Practice

See page 805.

Tell whether each equation represents direct variation between x and y.

17. $y = 217x$ **18.** $y = -3x^2$ **19.** $y = \frac{k}{x}$ **20.** $y = 4\pi x$

21. Critical Thinking Is every linear relationship a direct variation? Is every direct variation a linear relation? Explain.

LINK

Life Science

Although snakes shed their skins all in one piece, most reptiles shed their skins in much smaller pieces.

22. Life Science The weight of a person's skin is related to body weight by the equation $s = \frac{1}{16}w$, where s is skin weight and w is body weight.

a. Does this equation show direction variation between body weight and skin weight?

b. If a person calculates skin weight as $9\frac{3}{4}$ lb, what is the person's body weight?

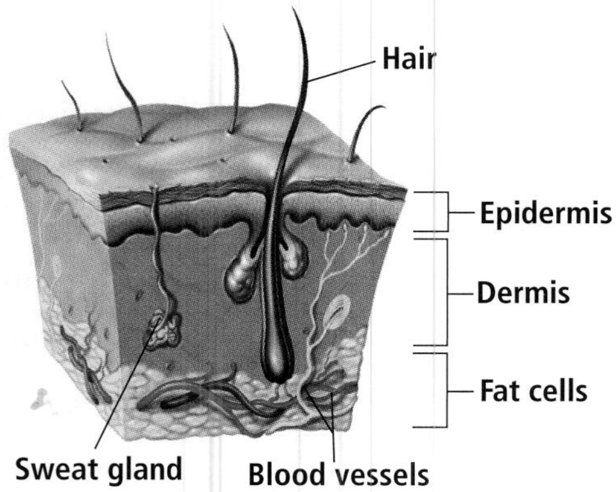

23. Write a Problem The perimeter P of a square varies directly with the length l of a side. Write a direct variation problem about the perimeter of a square.

24. Write About It Describe how the constant of proportionality k affects the appearance of the graph of a direct variation equation.

25. Challenge Watermelons are being sold at 79¢ a pound. What condition would have to exist for the price paid and the number of watermelons sold to represent a direct variation?

Test Prep and Spiral Review

26. Multiple Choice Given that y varies directly with x, what is the equation of direct variation if y is 16 when x is 20?

Ⓐ $y = 1\frac{1}{5}x$ Ⓑ $y = \frac{5}{4}x$ Ⓒ $y = \frac{4}{5}x$ Ⓓ $y = 0.6x$

27. Gridded Response If y varies directly with x, what is the value of x when $y = 14$ and $k = \frac{1}{2}$?

Explain why the statistic is misleading. (Lesson 9-6)

28. A market researcher surveyed 100 people. Of the 100 people surveyed, 60 own a car. Of the 60 people who own a car, 20 own a white car. The market researcher proclaimed: "One-third of all people own a white car."

Find the slope and y-intercept of each equation. (Lesson 12-3)

29. $y = 4x - 2$ **30.** $y = -2x + 12$ **31.** $y = -0.25x$ **32.** $y = -x - 4$

12-6 Graphing Inequalities in Two Variables

Learn to graph inequalities on the coordinate plane.

Vocabulary

boundary line

linear inequality

Graphing can help you visualize the relationship between a summer camp's growing capacity and the number of years that have passed.

A graph of a linear equation separates the coordinate plane into three parts: the points on one side of the line, the points on the **boundary line**, and the points on the other side of the line.

Each point in the coordinate plane makes one of these three statements true:

Equality ⟶ $y = x + 2$

Inequality ⟶ $y > x + 2$; ⟶ $y < x + 2$

When the equality symbol is replaced in a linear equation by an inequality symbol, the statement is a **linear inequality**. Any ordered pair that makes the linear inequality true is a solution.

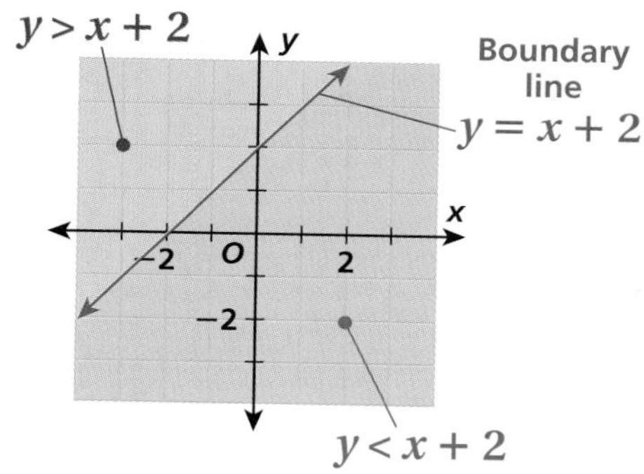

EXAMPLE 1 Graphing Inequalities

Graph each inequality.

A $y > x + 3$

First graph the boundary line $y = x + 3$. Since no points that are on the line are solutions of $y > x + 3$, make the line *dashed*. Then determine on which side of the line the solutions lie.

(0, 0)	*Test a point not on the line.*
$y > x + 3$	
$0 \overset{?}{>} 0 + 3$	*Substitute 0 for x and 0 for y.*
$0 \overset{?}{>} 3$	

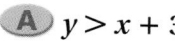

Since $0 > 3$ is not true, (0, 0) is not a solution of $y > x + 3$. Shade the side of the line that does not include (0, 0).

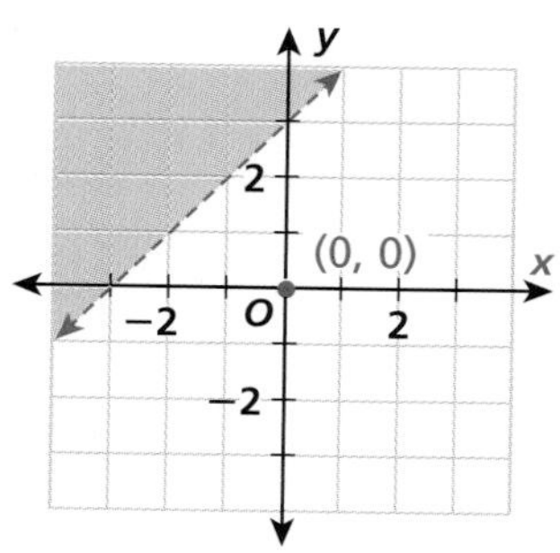

Helpful Hint

Any point on the line $y = x + 3$ is not a solution of $y > x + 3$ because the inequality symbol $>$ means only "greater than" and does not include "equal to."

Graph each inequality.

B $y \leq x + 1$

First graph the boundary line $y = x + 1$. Since points that are on the line are solutions of $y \leq x + 1$, make the line ***solid.*** Then shade the part of the coordinate plane in which the rest of the solutions of $y \leq x + 1$ lie.

$(2, 1)$	*Choose any point not on the line.*
$y \leq x + 1$	
$1 \overset{?}{\leq} 2 + 1$	*Substitute 2 for x and 1 for y.*
$1 \overset{?}{\leq} 3$ ✔	

Since $1 \leq 3$ is true, $(2, 1)$ is a solution of $y \leq x + 1$. Shade the side of the line that includes the point $(2, 1)$.

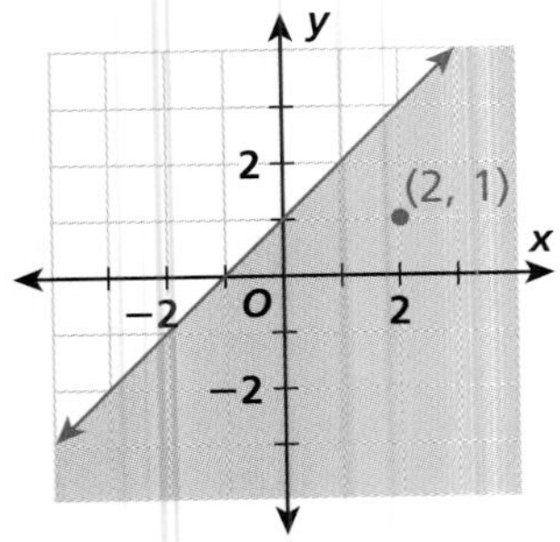

Helpful Hint

Any point on the line $y = x + 1$ is a solution of $y \leq x + 1$. This is because the inequality symbol $\leq$ means "less than *or equal to.*"

C $6y + 3x \leq 12$

First write the inequality in slope-intercept form.

$6y + 3x \leq 12$	
$6y \leq -3x + 12$	*Subtract 3x from both sides.*
$y \leq -\frac{1}{2}x + 2$	*Divide both sides by 6.*

Then graph the line $y = -\frac{1}{2}x + 2$. Since points that are on the line are solutions of $y \leq -\frac{1}{2}x + 2$, make the line ***solid.*** Then shade the part of the coordinate plane in which the rest of the solutions of $y \leq -\frac{1}{2}x + 2$ lie.

$(0, 0)$	*Choose any point not on the line.*
$6y + 3x \leq 12$	
$6(0) + 3(0) \overset{?}{\leq} 12$	*Substitute 0 for x and 0 for y.*
$0 \overset{?}{\leq} 12$ ✔	

Since $0 \leq 2$ is true, $(0, 0)$ is a solution of $y \leq -\frac{1}{2}x + 2$. Shade the side of the line that includes the point $(0, 0)$.

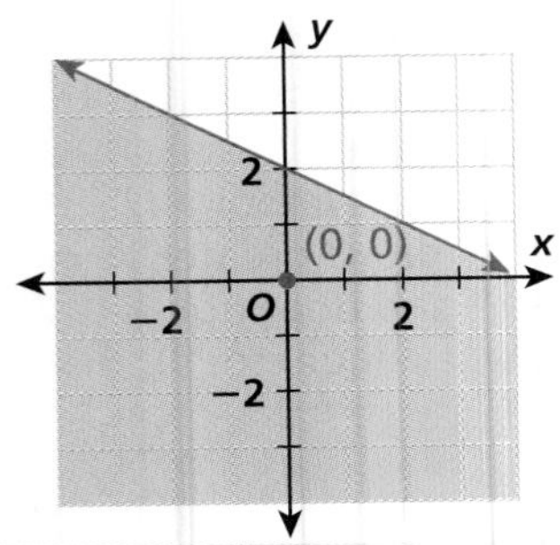

EXAMPLE 2 *Social Studies Application*

Helpful Hint

The phrase "up to 300" can be translated as "less than or equal to 300."

Camp Wakatobi opened in 2000 with room for up to 300 middle school students. Since then, the camp has increased its capacity by 60 students every 2 years. Graph the relationship between the years elapsed and the camp's capacity. If Camp Wakatobi continues to grow at the same rate, will it have enough room for 750 students in the year 2012?

First find the equation of the line that corresponds to the inequality. The year 2000 is year 0, 2001 is year 1, and so on.

In year 0, the camp capacity was 300. ⟶ point (0, 300)

In year 2, the camp capacity was 360. ⟶ point (2, 360)

$m = \frac{360 - 300}{2 - 0} = \frac{60}{2} = 30$ — *With two known points, find the slope.*

$y = 30x + 300$ — *The y-intercept is 300.*

Graph the boundary line $y = 30x + 300$. Since points on the line are solutions of $y \leq 30x + 300$, make the line ***solid***.

Shade the part of the coordinate plane in which the rest of the solutions of $y \leq 30x + 300$ lie.

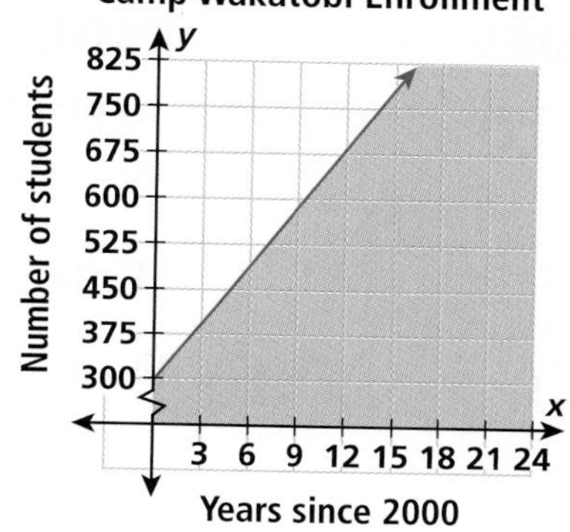

(5, 0) — *Choose any point not on the line.*

$y \leq 30x + 300$

$0 \overset{?}{\leq} 30(5) + 300$ — *Substitute 5 for x and 0 for y.*

$0 \overset{?}{\leq} 450$ ✔

Since $0 \leq 450$ is true, (5, 0) is a solution of $y \leq 30x + 300$. Shade the part on the side of the line that includes point (5, 0).

The point (12, 750) is not included in the shaded area, so the camp would not have room for 750 students in the year 2012.

Think and Discuss

1. **Describe** the graph of $5x + y < 15$. Tell how it would change if $<$ were changed to $\geq$.
2. **Compare and contrast** the use of an open circle, a closed circle, a dashed line, and a solid line when graphing inequalities.
3. **Explain** how you can tell if a point on the line is a solution of the inequality.
4. **Name** a linear inequality for which the graph is a horizontal dashed line and all points below it.

12-6 Exercises

go.hrw.com
Homework Help Online
KEYWORD: MT7 12-6
Parent Resources Online
KEYWORD: MT7 Parent

GUIDED PRACTICE

See Example 1

Graph each inequality.

1. $y < x + 3$
2. $y \geq 3x - 2$
3. $y > -2x + 1$
4. $5x + y \leq 2$
5. $y \leq \frac{3}{4}x + 4$
6. $\frac{1}{3}x - \frac{1}{6}y < -1$

See Example 2

7. **a.** The organizers of a bicycle trip have a budget of \$450 to buy spare tires and tire repair kits. They can buy spare tires for \$18 each and repair kits for \$15 each. Write and graph an inequality showing the different ways the organizers can spend their budget.
   b. Can the organizers of the bicycle trip buy 15 spare tires and 10 tire repair kits and still be within their budget?

INDEPENDENT PRACTICE

See Example 1

Graph each inequality.

8. $y \leq -\frac{1}{2}x - 4$
9. $y < -2.5x + 1.5$
10. $-3(4x + y) \geq -6$
11. $2x - \frac{2}{3}y > -3$
12. $3x - 5y > 7$
13. $4\left(\frac{3}{4}x + \frac{1}{4}y\right) \leq -4$

See Example 2

14. **a.** To avoid the bends, a diver should ascend no faster than 30 feet per minute. Write and graph an inequality showing the relationship between the depth of a diver and the time required to ascend to the surface.
    b. If a diver who begins at a depth of 77 ft ascends to the surface in 2.6 minutes, is the diver in danger of developing the bends?

PRACTICE AND PROBLEM SOLVING

Extra Practice
See page 805.

15. **a.** Graph the inequality $y \geq x + 4$.
    b. Name an ordered pair that is a solution of the inequality.
    c. Is (2, 4) a solution of $y \geq x + 4$? Explain how to check your answer.
    d. Which side of the line $y = x + 4$ is shaded?
    e. Name an ordered pair that is a solution of $y < x + 4$.

16. **Food** The school cafeteria needs to buy no more than 28 pounds of apples. A supermarket sells 4-pound and 7-pound bags of apples. Write and graph an inequality showing the number of 4-pound and 7-pound bags of apples the cafeteria can buy.

17. **Estimation** The amount of money Natasha spends for her birthday party is a function of the number of people who attend the party. This can be expressed by the inequality $y \geq \frac{14}{3}x + 20$ for x people. Graph an inequality showing the possible numbers of people x for a party that costs y dollars. If Natasha wants to invite 10 people, approximately how much money will she spend?

LINK

Earth Science

Neoprene weather balloons can rise to altitudes of 90,000 ft to measure wind, temperature, pressure, and humidity.

Tell whether the given ordered pair is a solution of each inequality shown.

18. $y \leq 2x + 4$, (2, 1)

19. $y > -5x + 2$, (−2, 12)

20. $y \geq 4x - 4$, (4, 15)

21. $y > -x + 12$, (0, 14)

22. $y \geq 3.2x + 1.8$, (6, 23)

23. $y \leq 5(x - 2)$, (2, 2)

24. **Earth Science** A weather balloon can ascend at a rate of up to 800 feet per minute.

a. Write an inequality showing the relationship between the distance the balloon can ascend and the number of minutes.

b. Graph the inequality for time between 0 and 30 minutes.

c. Can the balloon ascend to a height of 2 miles within 15 minutes? (*Hint:* 1 mile is equal to 5280 feet.)

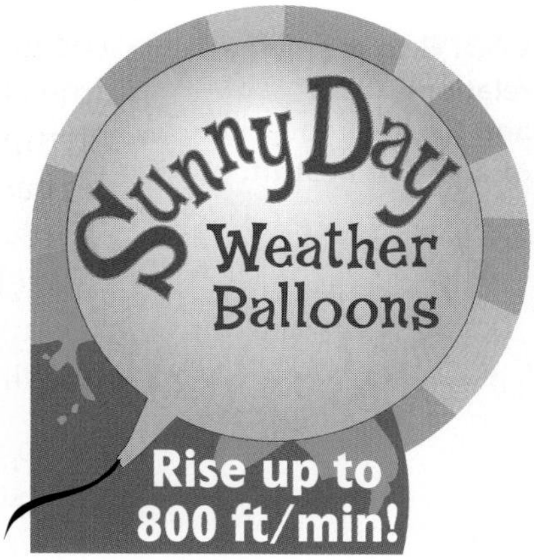

25. **Choose a Strategy** Which of the following ordered pairs is NOT a solution of the inequality $3x + 8y \leq 111$? Describe the tools and techniques you used.

Ⓐ (0, 0) Ⓑ (−5, 16) Ⓒ (−3, −14) Ⓓ (6, 9)

26. **Write About It** When you graph a linear inequality that is solved for y, when do you shade above the boundary line and when do you shade below it? When do you use a dashed line?

27. **Challenge** Graph the region that satisfies all three inequalities: $x \geq -3$, $y \geq 2$, and $y < -\frac{1}{3}x + 3$.

Test Prep and Spiral Review

28. **Multiple Choice** On a local highway, a car can travel no faster than 55 miles per hour. Which of the following is an inequality showing the relationship between the distance driven by the car and the number of hours?

Ⓕ $d \leq \frac{t}{55}$ Ⓖ $d \leq \frac{55}{t}$ Ⓗ $d \leq 55t$ Ⓙ $d \geq 55t$

29. **Short Response** Graph the inequality $y > 3x - 1$. Is the ordered pair (4, −2) a solution of the inequality?

Solve. (Lesson 11-2)

30. $4n - 3 + 5n + 2 = 8$

31. $6m + 2 - m = -28$

32. $1.4p + 7 - 3.9p = -2$

Write the point-slope form of each equation with the given slope that passes through the indicated point. (Lesson 12-4)

33. slope 5, passing through (4, 1)

34. slope −2, passing through (6, −6)

12-7 Lines of Best Fit

Learn to recognize relationships in data and find the equation of a line of best fit.

The graph shows the winning times for the women's 3000 meter Olympic speed skating event. As is the case with many Olympic sports, the athletes keep improving and setting new records, so there is a correlation between the year and the winning time.

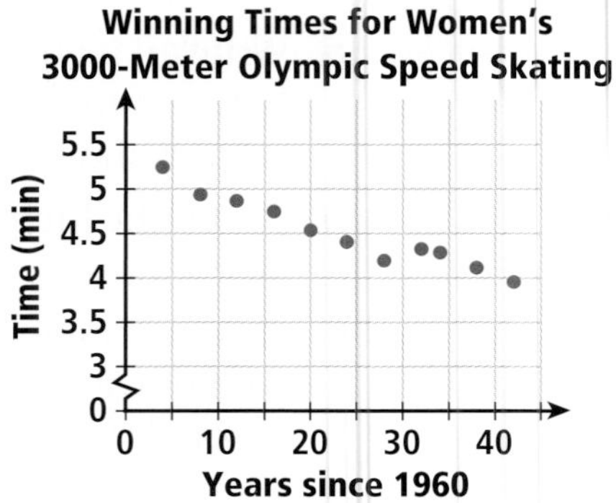

When data show a correlation, you can estimate and draw a *line of best fit* that approximates a trend for a set of data and use it to make predictions.

To estimate the equation of a line of best fit:

- calculate the means of the x-coordinates and y-coordinates: (x_m, y_m).
- draw the line through (x_m, y_m) that appears to best fit the data.
- estimate the coordinates of another point on the line.
- find the equation of the line.

EXAMPLE 1 Finding a Line of Best Fit

Plot the data and find a line of best fit.

x	2	4	5	1	3	8	6	7
y	4	3	6	2	5	8	7	5

Plot the data points and find the mean of the x- and y-coordinates.

$x_m = \frac{2+4+5+1+3+8+6+7}{8} = 4.5 \qquad y_m = \frac{4+3+6+2+5+8+7+5}{8} = 5$

$(x_m, y_m) = (\mathbf{4.5}, \mathbf{5})$

Draw a line through (4.5, 5) that best represents the data.

Estimate and plot the coordinates of another point on that line, such as (2, 3). Find the equation of the line.

$m = \frac{5-3}{4.5-2} = \frac{2}{2.5} = \mathbf{0.8}$ *Find the slope.*

$y - y_1 = m(x - x_1)$ *Use point-slope form.*

$y - \mathbf{5} = \mathbf{0.8}(x - \mathbf{4.5})$ *Substitute.*

$y - 5 = 0.8x - 3.6$

$y = 0.8x + 1.4$

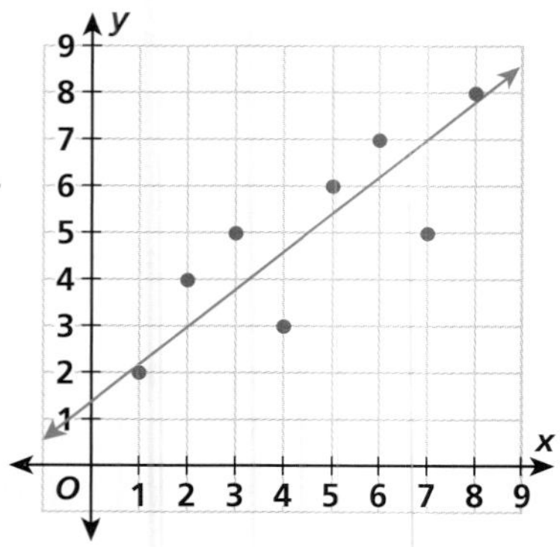

The equation of a line of best fit is $y = 0.8x + 1.4$.

Remember!

A line of best fit is a line that comes close to all the points on a scatter plot. Try to draw the line so that about the same number of points are above the line as below the line.

EXAMPLE 2 *Sports Application*

Find a line of best fit for the women's 3000-meter speed skating. Use the equation of the line to predict when the winning time will be 0 minutes. Is it reasonable to make this prediction? Explain.

Year	1964	1968	1972	1976	1980	1984	1988	1992	1994	1998	2002
Winning Time (min)	5.25	4.94	4.87	4.75	4.54	4.41	4.20	4.33	4.29	4.12	3.96

Let 1960 represent year 0. The first point is then (4, 5.25), and the last point is (42, 3.96). Plot the data points and find the mean of the x- and y-coordinates.

$$x_m = \frac{4 + 8 + 12 + 16 + 20 + 24 + 28 + 32 + 34 + 38 + 42}{11} \approx 23.5$$

$$y_m = \frac{5.25 + 4.94 + 4.87 + 4.75 + 4.54 + 4.41 + 4.20 + 4.33 + 4.29 + 4.12 + 3.96}{11} \approx 4.5$$

$$(x_m, y_m) = (\mathbf{23.5}, \mathbf{4.5})$$

Draw a line through (23.5, 4.5) that best represents the data.

Estimate and plot the coordinates of another point on that line, (8, 5).

Find the equation of that line.

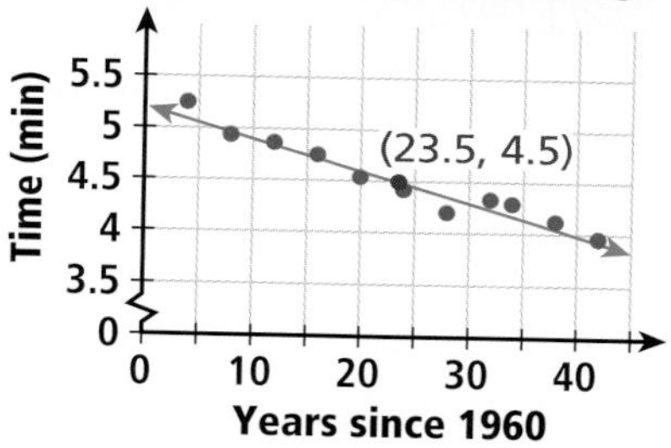

$$m = \frac{5 - 4.5}{8 - 23.5} = \frac{0.5}{-15.5} \approx \mathbf{-0.03}$$

$$y - y_1 = m(x - x_1)$$

$$y - \mathbf{4.5} = \mathbf{-0.03}(x - \mathbf{23.5})$$

$$y - 4.5 = -0.03x + 0.7 \quad \textit{Round 0.705 to 0.7.}$$

$$y = -0.03x + 5.2$$

The equation of a line of best fit is $y = -0.03x + 5.2$.

The winning time is 0 minutes at the x-intercept, when $y = 0$.

$0 = -0.03x + 5.2$ *Substitute.*

$-5.2 = -0.03x$ *Solve for x, which represents the number of years since 1960.*

$173.\overline{3} = x$

$1960 + 173 = 2133$ *Add to find the year.*

The winning time will be 0 in 2133. It is not reasonable to make this prediction because it is impossible for the winning time to be 0.

Caution!

Remember that x represents the number of years since 1960. It does not represent the year 173, which would be unreasonable.

Think and Discuss

1. **Describe** what a line of best fit can tell you.
2. **Tell** whether a line of best fit must include one or more points in the data.

12-7 Exercises

go.hrw.com
Homework Help Online
KEYWORD: MT7 12-7
Parent Resources Online
KEYWORD: MT7 Parent

GUIDED PRACTICE

See Example 1

Plot the data and find a line of best fit.

1.

x	2	3	5	1	7	4	6
y	6	8	11	4	14	8	12

2.

x	20	80	30	50	110	60	90
y	13	75	20	40	100	54	82

See Example 2

3. Life Science Find a line of best fit for the life expectancy data. Use the equation of the line to predict when the life expectancy will be 200 years of age. Is it reasonable to make this prediction? Explain.

Year	1993	1994	1995	1996	1997	1998	1999	2000	2001	2002
Life Expectancy: Age (*y*)	75.5	75.7	75.8	76.1	76.5	76.7	76.7	77.0	77.2	77.3

INDEPENDENT PRACTICE

See Example 1

Plot the data and find a line of best fit.

4.

x	10	25	5	30	20	15	35
y	35	87	17	105	70	52	122

5.

x	0.1	0.5	0.2	0.4	0.6	0.3	0.7
y	8	5	7	4	3	5	3

See Example 2

6. Consumer Math Find a line of best fit for the used-car data. Use the equation of the line to predict what the car's value will be when it is 15 years old. Is it reasonable to make this prediction? Explain.

Age of Car (*y*)	1	2	3	4	5	6	7	8	9
Value ($)	$12,500	$10,500	$9,200	$8,200	$5,800	$5,000	$4,200	$3,500	$3,000

PRACTICE AND PROBLEM SOLVING

Extra Practice
See page 805.

Tell whether a line of best fit for each scatter plot would have a positive or negative slope. If a line of best fit would not be appropriate for the data, write *neither*.

7.

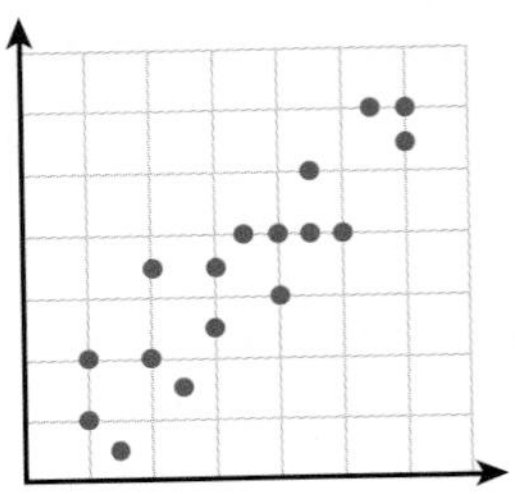

8.

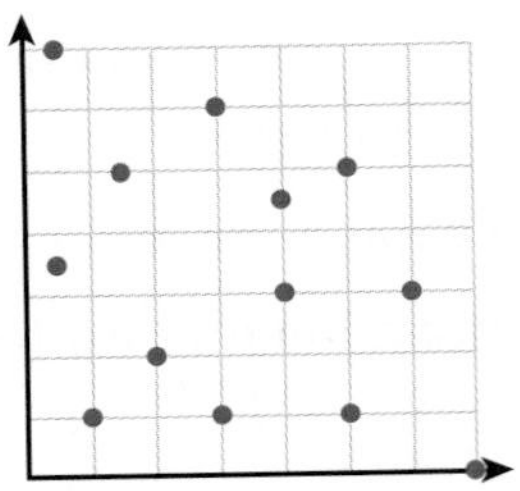

9.

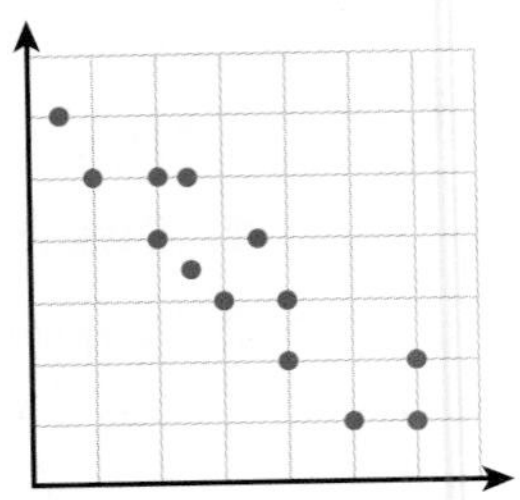

10.

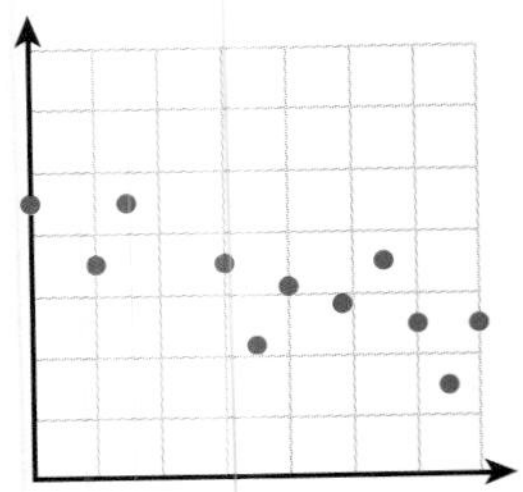

Economics LINK

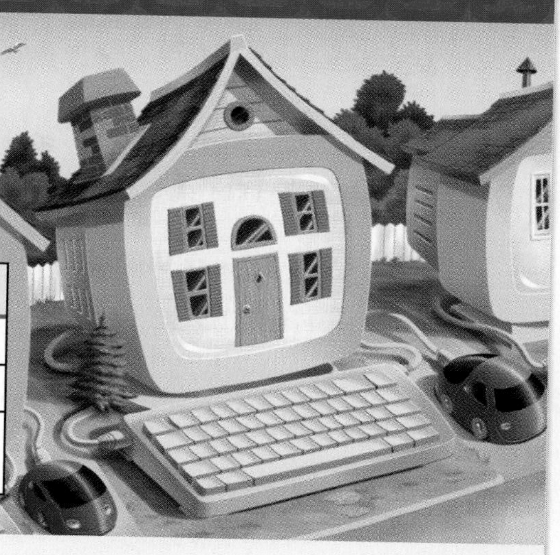

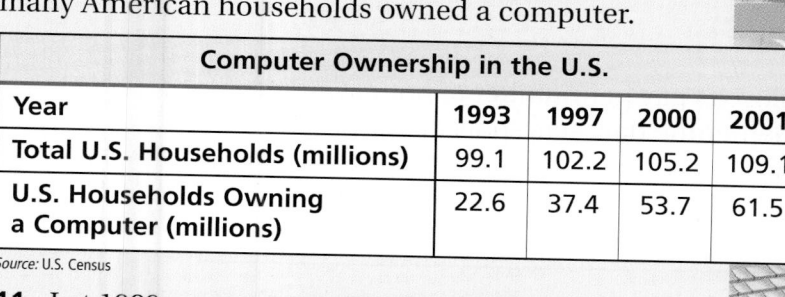

Economic analysts study trends in data dealing with how and what people buy. They often make predictions about future markets based on these economic trends. The table shows data on how many American households owned a computer.

Computer Ownership in the U.S.

Year	1993	1997	2000	2001
Total U.S. Households (millions)	99.1	102.2	105.2	109.1
U.S. Households Owning a Computer (millions)	22.6	37.4	53.7	61.5

Source: U.S. Census

11. Let 1989 represent year 0 along the *x*-axis.

a. What is the mean number of years for the data shown?

b. Find the percent of U.S. households owning a computer for each year shown in the table, to the nearest tenth. Then find the mean.

12. Let *y* represent the percent of U.S. households that owned a computer between 1989 and 2001. Find a line of best fit, and plot it on the same graph as the data points. Use the point (7, 36) to write the equation of the line of best fit.

13. Predict the percent of U.S. households owning a computer in the year 2010. Justify your prediction.

14. **Challenge** What information does the slope of the line of best fit give you? What would a negative slope mean?

go.hrw.com
Web Extra!
KEYWORD: MT7 Economy

TEST PREP and Spiral Review

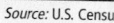

15. **Multiple Choice** What type of slope would a line of best fit for the scatter plot at right have? If a line of best fit would not be appropriate, choose neither.

Ⓐ positive Ⓑ negative Ⓒ zero Ⓓ neither

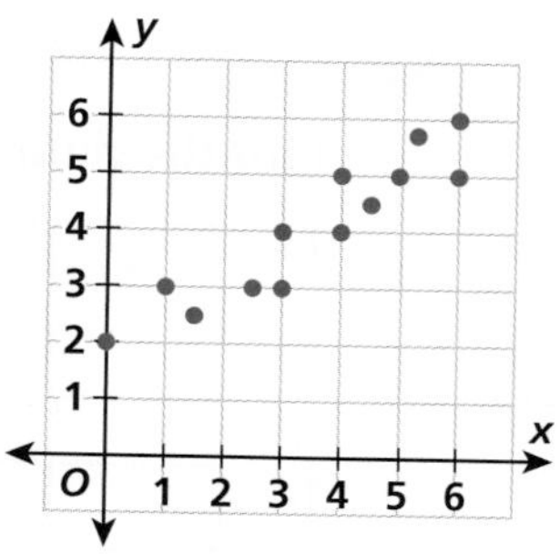

16. **Short Response** Plot the data and find a line of best fit.

x	0	0.5	1	1.5	1.75	2	2.5
y	4	3.5	1	1.5	1	0	0

Solve each inequality. (Lesson 11-5)

17. $4x + 3 - x > 15$ **18.** $3 - 7x \leq 24$ **19.** $3x + 9 < -3$ **20.** $1 - x \geq 11$

Find the *x*-intercept and *y*-intercept of each line. (Lesson 12-3)

21. $3x - 8y = 48$ **22.** $5y - 15x = -45$ **23.** $13x + 2y = 26$ **24.** $9x + 27y = 81$

CHAPTER 12

READY TO GO ON?

SECTION 12B

Quiz for Lessons 12-5 Through 12-7

12-5 Direct Variation

1. The table shows an employee's pay per number of hours worked. Make a graph to determine whether the data sets show direct variation.

Hours Worked	0	1	2	3	4	5	6
Pay ($)	0	8.50	17.00	25.50	34.00	42.50	51.00

Find each equation of direct variation, given that y varies directly with x.

2. y is 10 when x is 2
3. y is 16 when x is 4
4. y is 2.5 when x is 2.5
5. y is 2 when x is 8

12-6 Graphing Inequalities in Two Variables

Graph each inequality.

6. $y > -3x + 2$
7. $4x + y \leq 1$
8. $y \leq \frac{2}{3}x + 3$
9. $\frac{1}{2}x - \frac{1}{4}y < -1$
10. $y < -1.5x + 2.5$
11. $-4(2x + y) \geq -8$
12. **a.** The organizers of a fishing outing have a prize budget of $150 to buy shirts and hats for the participants. They can buy shirts for $10 each and hats for $12 each. Write and graph an inequality showing the different ways the organizers can spend their prize budget.

    b. Can the organizers of the fishing outing purchase 7 hats and 6 shirts and still be within their prize budget?

12-7 Lines of Best Fit

Plot the data and find a line of best fit.

13.

x	2	7	3	4	6	1	9	5
y	4	13	7	8	11	2	17	10

14.

x	0.4	0.5	0.3	0.7	0.2	0.8	0.1	0.6
y	5	5	6	2	8	1	8	3

15. Find a line of best fit for the price of a retailer's stock. Use the equation of the line to predict the stock price in 2008. Is it reasonable to make this prediction? Explain.

Year	1999	2000	2001	2002	2003	2004	2005
Stock Price ($)	11.70	11.95	12.28	12.54	12.77	13.00	13.26

MULTI-STEP TEST PREP

Talk, Talk, Talk Mrs. Kim decides to buy a cell phone for her son, Jason. As shown in the table, Mrs. Kim found two companies that offer special rates for students. Unlike many of their competitors, these companies do not round the time to the nearest minute; they charge only for the exact amount of time each customer uses.

Cell Phone Plans	
Talk Cheap	No monthly fee; $0.55 per minute
Talk Easy	$35 monthly fee; $0.15 per minute

1. Build a table, make a graph, and write an equation to represent the cost of cellular service for each company.
2. If price is the only factor, which plan is better? Explain.
3. Which company should Mrs. Kim choose if Jason never uses more than 30 minutes of phone time in a month?
4. If Jason knows the cost of each plan for 30 minutes, can he double this cost to find the cost for 60 minutes? Explain your answer.

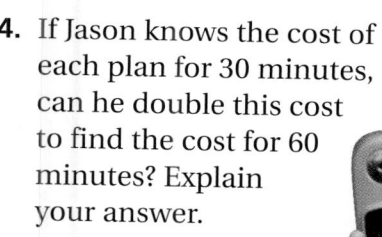

EXTENSION

Solving Systems of Equations by Graphing

Learn to solve a system of equations by graphing.

Recall that two or more equations considered together form a system of equations. You've solved systems of equations using substitution. You can also use graphing to help you solve a system.

When you graph a system of linear equations in the same coordinate plane, their point of intersection is the solution of the system.

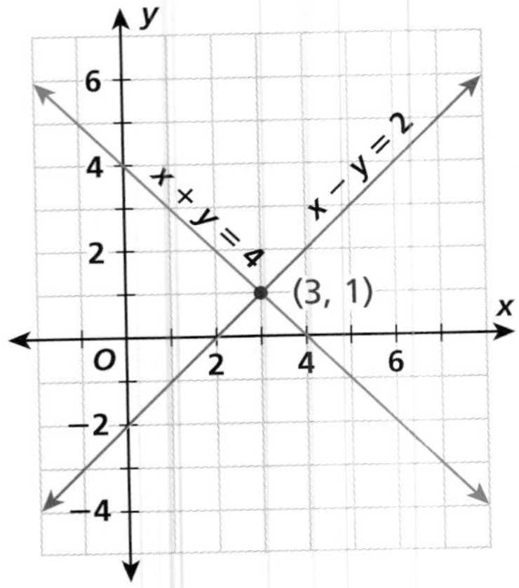

EXAMPLE 1 **Using a Graph to Solve a System of Linear Equations**

Solve the system graphically, and check your answer algebraically.

$$3x + y = 5$$
$$y - x = 1$$

Write each equation in slope-intercept form.

$3x + y = 5$

$y = -3x + 5$

slope $= -3$, y-intercept $= 5$

$y - x = 1$

$y = x + 1$

slope $= 1$, y-intercept $= 1$

Use each slope and y-intercept to graph the equations. The point of intersection of the graphs appears to be (1, 2), which is the solution of the system.

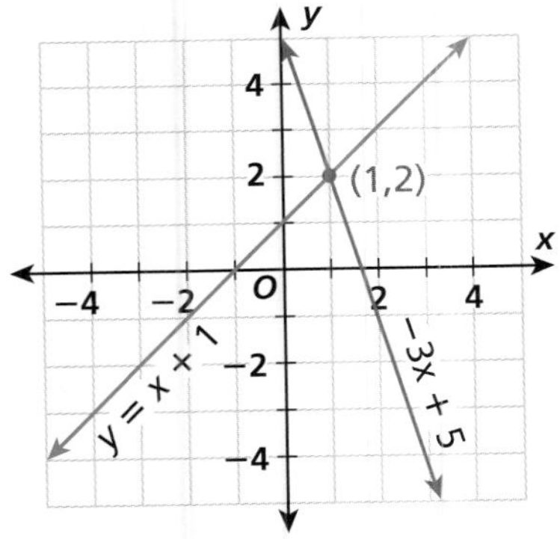

Check by substituting $x = 1$ and $y = 2$ into each of the *original* equations in the system.

Check

$$3x + y = 5$$
$$3(1) + 2 \stackrel{?}{=} 5$$
$$3 + 2 \stackrel{?}{=} 5$$
$$5 \stackrel{?}{=} 5 \checkmark$$

$$y - x = 1$$
$$2 - 1 \stackrel{?}{=} 1$$
$$1 \stackrel{?}{=} 1 \checkmark$$

The ordered pair (1, 2) checks in the original system of equations, so (1, 2) is the solution.

EXAMPLE 2 Graphing a System of Linear Equations to Solve a Problem

A plane left Tokyo traveling at 500 mi/h. After the plane had traveled 3000 miles, a second plane started along the same route, flying at 700 mi/h. How many hours after leaving Tokyo will the second plane catch up with the first plane?

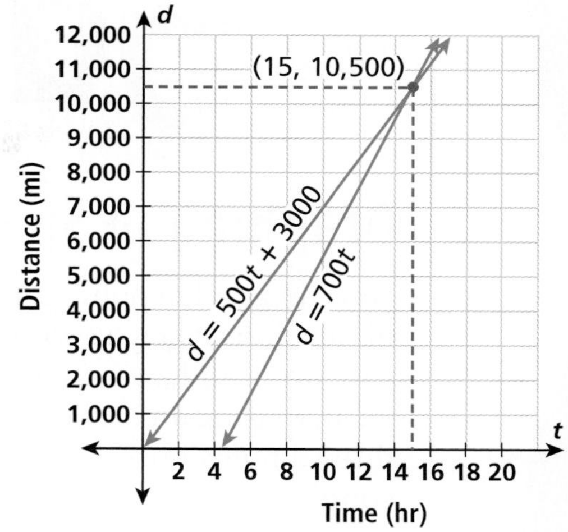

Let t = the number of hours and d = the distance in miles.

For plane 1, $d = 500t + 3000$.
For plane 2, $d = 700t$.

Graph each equation. The point of intersection appears to be (15, 10,500).

Check

$10{,}500 \stackrel{?}{=} 500(15) + 3000$ $\quad$ $10{,}500 \stackrel{?}{=} 700(15)$

$10{,}500 \stackrel{?}{=} 10{,}500$ ✔ $\quad$ $10{,}500 \stackrel{?}{=} 10{,}500$ ✔

Plane 2 will catch up with plane 1 after 15 hours in flight, 10,500 miles from Tokyo.

EXTENSION Exercises

Tell whether the ordered pair is the solution of each given system.

1. (5, 11) $\quad y = 3x - 4$, $\; y = 2x + 1$

2. (0, 2) $\quad y = 3x + 2$, $\; y = 4x$

3. (4, −7) $\quad 2x + y = 1$, $\; -3x + y = -9$

Solve each system graphically, and check your answer algebraically.

4. $y = 2x$, $\; y = 3x - 3$

5. $y = -3x + 2$, $\; y = \frac{1}{3}x + 2$

6. $y - x = -3$, $\; x - 3y = 9$

7. A bicyclist is racing toward the finish line. The finish line is 550 meters from a second bicyclist. The first bicyclist is pedaling at 120 meters per minute, and the second bicyclist races behind him at 150 meters per minute. If the first bicyclist had a 105-meter head start, will the second bicyclist catch him in time to tie the race?

8. Melissa has a choice of two phone plans. The first plan has a monthly fee of \$4.95 and charges 7 cents per minute. The second plan has no monthly fee, but charges 9 cents per minute. If Melissa averages about 260 minutes of calls per month, which plan is better for her?

Game Time

Graphing in Space

You can graph a point in two dimensions using a coordinate plane with an x- and a y-axis. Each point is located using an ordered pair (x, y). In three dimensions, you need three coordinate axes, and each point is located using an ordered triple (x, y, z).

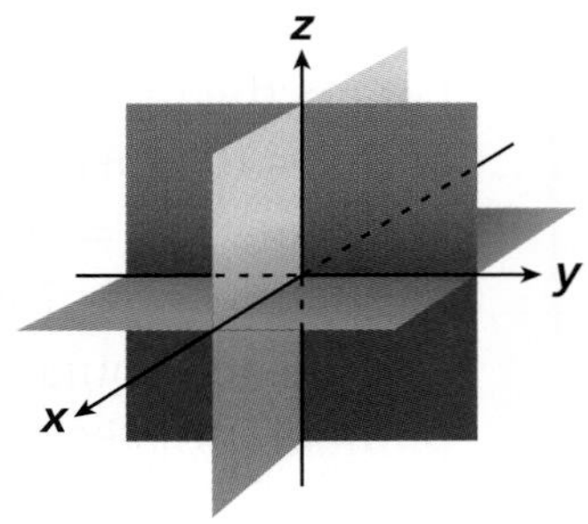

To graph a point, move along the x-axis the number of units of the x-coordinate. Then move left or right the number of units of the y-coordinate. Then move up or down the number of units of the z-coordinate.

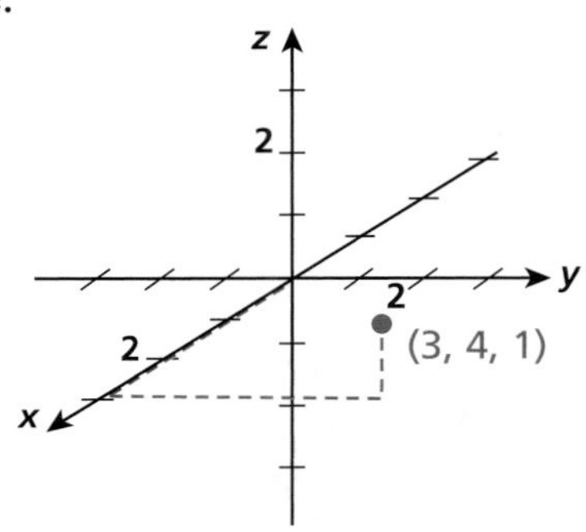

Plot each point in three dimensions.

1. (1, 2, 5)
2. (−2, 3, −2)
3. (4, 0, 2)

The graph of the equation $y = 2$ in three dimensions is a plane that is perpendicular to the y-axis and is two units to the right of the origin.

Describe the graph of each plane in three dimensions.

4. $x = 3$
5. $z = 1$
6. $y = -1$

Line Solitaire

Roll a red and a blue number cube to generate the coordinates of points on a coordinate plane. The x-coordinate of each point is the number on the red cube, and the y-coordinate is the number on the blue cube. Generate seven ordered pairs and plot the points on the coordinate plane. Then try to write the equations of three lines that divide the plane into seven regions so that each point is in a different region.

A complete copy of the rules is available online.

go.hrw.com
Game Time Extra
KEYWORD: MT7 Games

FOLDNOTES

It's in the Bag!

Materials
- small paper bag
- scissors
- tape
- graph paper
- stapler

PROJECT Graphing Tri-Fold

Use this organizer to hold notes, vocabulary, and practice problems related to graphing.

Directions

1. Hold the bag flat with the flap facing you at the bottom. Fold up the flap. Cut off the part of the bag above the flap. **Figure A**

2. Unfold the bag. Cut down the middle of the top layer of the bag until you get to the flap. Then cut across the bag just above the flap, again cutting only the top layer of the bag. **Figure B**

3. Open the bag. Cut away the sides at the bottom of the bag. These sections are shaded in the figure. **Figure C**

4. Unfold the bag. There will be three equal sections at the bottom of the bag. Fold up the bottom section and tape the sides to create a pocket. **Figure D**

5. Trim several pieces of graph paper to fit in the middle section of the bag. Staple them to the bag to make a booklet.

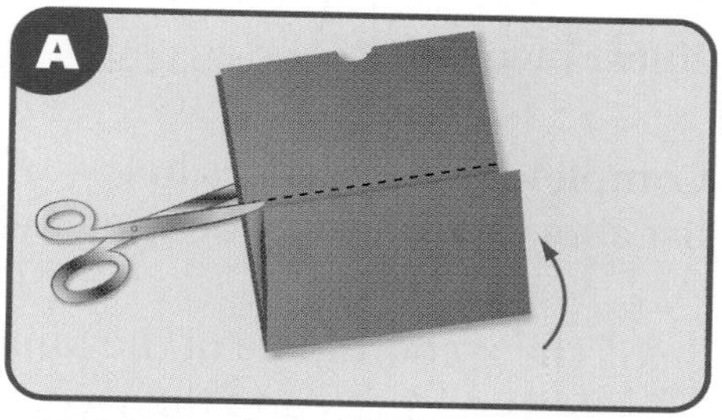
A

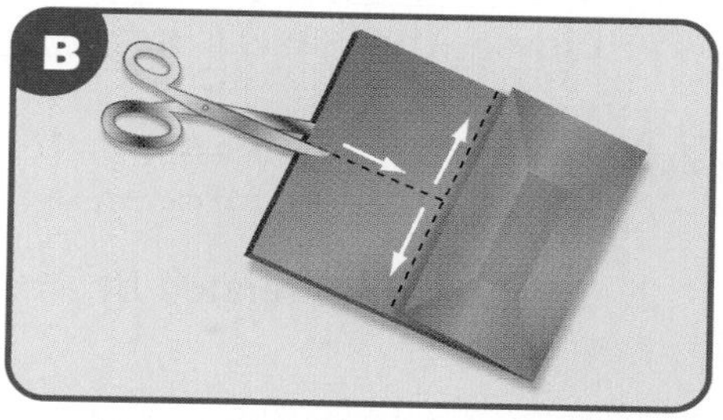
B

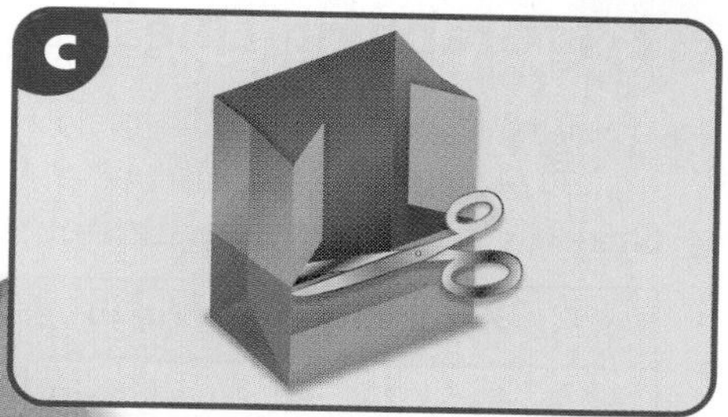
C

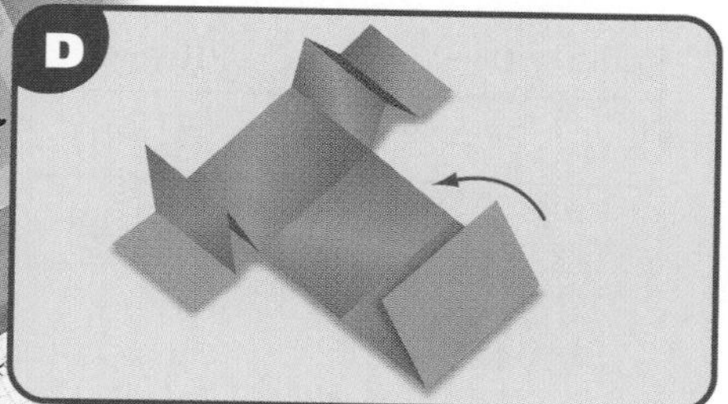
D

Taking Note of the Math

Write definitions of vocabulary words behind the "doors" at the top of your organizer. Graph sample linear equations on the graph paper. Use the pocket at the bottom of the organizer to store notes on the chapter.

CHAPTER 12

Study Guide: Review

Vocabulary

boundary line 655

constant of proportionality 650

direct variation 650

linear equation 628

linear inequality 655

point-slope form 644

slope-intercept form 639

x-intercept 638

y-intercept 638

Complete the sentences below with vocabulary words from the list above. Words may be used more than once.

1. The x-coordinate of the point where a line crosses the x-axis is its ___?___, and the y-coordinate of the point where the line crosses the y-axis is its ___?___.

2. $y = mx + b$ is the ___?___ of a line, and $y - y_1 = m(x - x_1)$ is the ___?___ .

3. Two variables related by a constant ratio are in ___?___.

12-1 Graphing Linear Equations (pp. 628–632)

EXAMPLE

- **Graph $y = x - 2$. Tell whether it is linear.**

x	x − 2	y	(x, y)
−1	−1 − 2	−3	(−1, −3)
0	0 − 2	−2	(0, −2)
1	1 − 2	−1	(1, −1)
2	2 − 2	0	(2, 0)

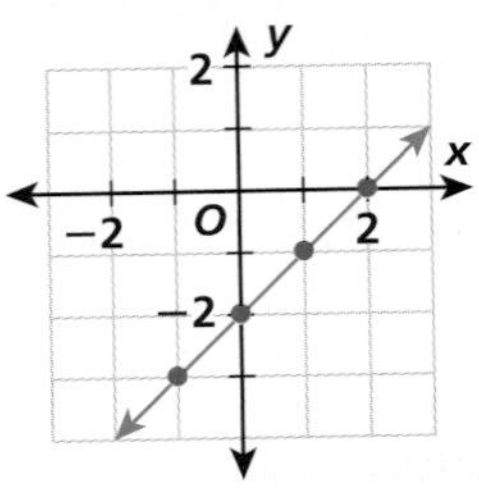

$y = x - 2$ is linear; its graph is a straight line.

EXERCISES

Graph each equation and tell whether it is linear.

4. $y = 4x - 2$
5. $y = 2 - 3x$
6. $y = -2x^2$
7. $y = 2x^3$
8. $y = -x^3$
9. $y = 2x$
10. $y = \frac{12}{x}$ for $x \neq 0$
11. $y = -\frac{10}{x}$ for $x \neq 0$

12-2 Slope of a Line (pp. 633–637)

EXAMPLE

- **Find the slope of the line that passes through (−1, 2) and (1, 3).**

  Let (x_1, y_1) be $(-1, 2)$ and (x_2, y_2) be $(1, 3)$.

  $$\frac{y_2 - y_1}{x_2 - x_1} = \frac{3 - 2}{1 - (-1)} = \frac{1}{2}$$

  The slope of the line that passes through $(-1, 2)$ and $(1, 3)$ is $\frac{1}{2}$.

EXERCISES

Find the slope of the line that passes through each pair of points.

12. (4, 2) and (8, 5)

13. (4, 3) and (5, −1)

14. (3, 3) and (−2, −3)

15. (−1, 2) and (5, −4)

16. (−3, −3) and (−4, −2)

17. (−2, −3) and (0, 0)

18. (−5, 7) and (−1, −2)

12-3 Using Slopes and Intercepts (pp. 638–642)

EXAMPLE

- **Write $3x + 4y = 12$ in slope-intercept form. Identify the slope and y-intercept.**

  $3x + 4y = 12$

  $4y = -3x + 12$ *Subtract 3x from both sides.*

  $\frac{4y}{4} = \frac{-3x}{4} + \frac{12}{4}$ *Divide both sides by 4.*

  $y = -\frac{3}{4}x + 3$ *slope-intercept form*

  $m = -\frac{3}{4}$ and $b = 3$

EXERCISES

Write each equation in slope-intercept form. Identify the slope and y-intercept.

19. $3y = 4x + 15$

20. $5y = 6x - 10$

21. $2x + 3y = 12$

22. $4y - 7x = 12$

Write the equation of the line that passes through each pair of points in slope-intercept form.

23. (0, 4) and (−1, 1)

24. (−1, 5) and (2, −4)

25. (6, 5) and (−3, 8)

26. (3, −1) and (−1, −3)

12-4 Point-Slope Form (pp. 644–647)

EXAMPLE

- **Write the point-slope form of the line with slope −4 that passes through (3, −2).**

  $y - y_1 = m(x - x_1)$

  $y - (-2) = -4(x - 3)$ *Substitute 3 for x_1,*

  $y + 2 = -4(x - 3)$ *−2 for y_1, −4 for m.*

  In point-slope form, the equation of the line with slope −4 that passes through (3, −2) is $y + 2 = -4(x - 3)$.

EXERCISES

Write the point-slope form of each line with the given conditions.

27. slope 2, passes through (3, 4)

28. slope −4, passes through (−2, 3)

29. slope $-\frac{5}{6}$, passes through (0, −3)

30. slope $\frac{2}{7}$, passes through (0, 0)

Study Guide: Review

12-5 Direct Variation (pp. 650–654)

EXAMPLE

- *y* varies directly with *x*, and *y* is 32 when *x* is 4. Write the equation of direct variation.

$y = kx$	*y varies directly with x.*
$32 = k \cdot 4$	*Substitute 4 for x and 32 for y.*
$8 = k$	*Solve for k.*
$y = 8x$	*Substitute 8 for k in the original equation.*

EXERCISES

y varies directly with *x*. Write the equation of direct variation for each set of conditions.

31. y is 42 when x is 7

32. y is 78 when x is 6

33. y is 8 when x is 56

12-6 Graphing Inequalities in Two Variables (pp. 655–659)

EXAMPLE

- Graph the inequality $y > x - 4$.

Graph $y = x - 4$ as a dashed line. Test (0, 0) in the inequality; $0 > -4$ is true, so shade the side of the line that contains (0, 0).

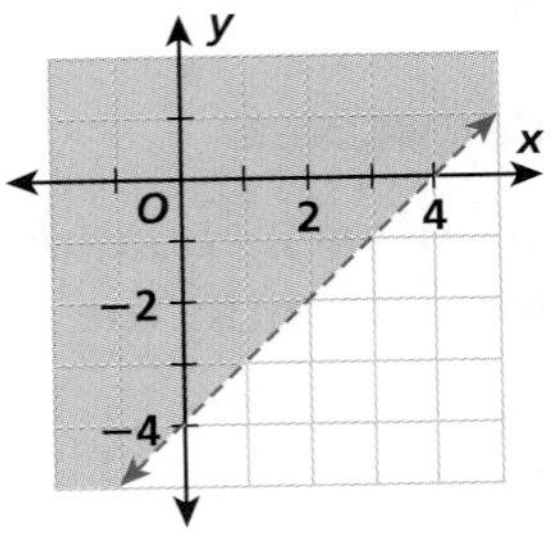

EXERCISES

Graph each inequality.

34. $y \leq x + 3$

35. $3y \geq 4x + 12$

36. $2x + 5y > 10$

37. $2y - 3x < 6$

38. Jon can input up to 55 data items per minute. Graph the relationship between the number of minutes and the number of data items he inputs.

12-7 Lines of Best Fit (pp. 660–663)

EXAMPLE

- Plot the data and find a line of best fit.

x	3	4	5	5	6	7
y	4	2	4	5	7	5

Calculate the means of *x* and *y*.

$x_m = \frac{30}{6} = 5 \qquad y_m = \frac{27}{6} = 4.5$

Draw a line through (5, 4.5) to fit the data. Estimate another point on the line, (3, 3). Find the slope, 0.75, and use point-slope form to write an equation of the line.

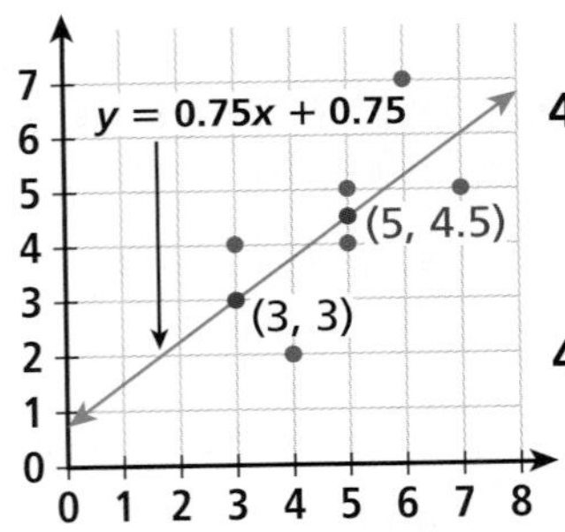

$y - 3 = 0.75(x - 3)$

$y = 0.75x + 0.75$ is a line of best fit.

EXERCISES

Plot the data and find a line of best fit.

39.

x	2	3	3	5	5	6
y	2	5	7	5	8	6

40.

x	1	3	4	4	6	7
y	2	1	4	7	6	7

41.

x	10	20	30	40	50	60
y	7	18	32	38	54	61

42.

x	10	25	40	55	70	85
y	67	58	41	29	28	20

CHAPTER TEST

Graph each equation and tell whether it is linear.

1. $y = x + 2$ **2.** $y = -2x$ **3.** $y = -2x^2$ **4.** $y = 0.5x + 1$

Find the slope of the line that passes through each pair of points.

5. (0, −8) and (−1, −10) **6.** (0, −2) and (−5, 0) **7.** (3, 1) and (0, 3)

8. Determiine whether the graph shows a constant or variable rate of change.

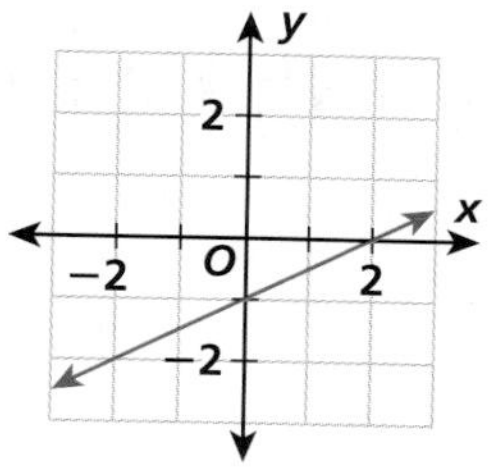

Write the equation of the line that passes through each pair of points in slope-intercept form.

9. (−1, −6) and (2, 6) **10.** (0, 5) and (3, −1) **11.** (−6, −3) and (12, 0)

Use the point-slope form of each equation to identify a point the line passes through and the slope of the line.

12. $y - 4 = -2(x + 7)$ **13.** $y + 2.4 = 2.1(x - 1.8)$ **14.** $y + 8 = -6(x - 9)$

Write the point-slope form of the equation with the given slope that passes through the indicated point.

15. slope −2, passing through (−4, 1) **16.** slope 3, passing through (2, 0)

Find each equation of direct variation, given that *y* varies directly with *x*.

17. *y* is 225 when *x* is 25 **18.** *y* is 0.1875 when *x* is 0.25 **19.** *x* is 13 when *y* is 91

Graph each inequality.

20. $y > x + 3$ **21.** $3y \leq x - 6$ **22.** $2y + 3x \geq 12$ **23.** $y < 4x + \frac{1}{2}$

24. a. A dragonfly beats its wings up to 30 times per second. Write and graph an inequality showing the relationship between flying time and the number of times the dragonfly beats its wings.

b. Is it possible for a dragonfly to beat its wings 1000 times in half a minute?

Plot the data and find a line of best fit.

25.

x	10	25	5	40	30	20	15	35
y	25	62	13	100	75	48	39	88

26.

x	0	2	2	3	4	7
y	6	6	5	2	1	1

STANDARDIZED TEST PREP

go.hrw.com
State Test Practice Online
KEYWORD: MT7 TestPrep

Cumulative Assessment, Chapters 1–12

Multiple Choice

1.

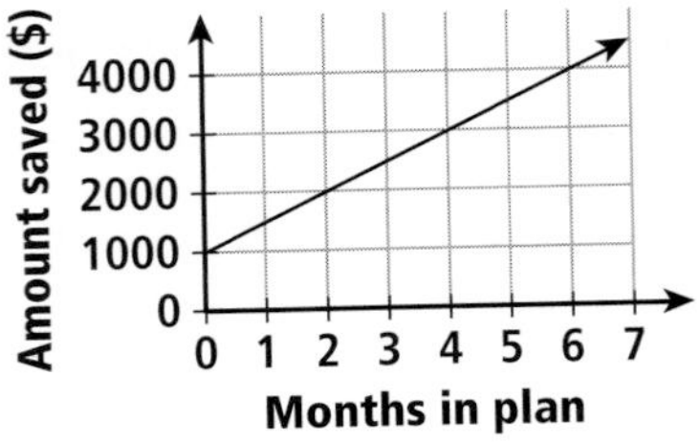

The line graph shows the activity of a savings account. What does the y-intercept represent?

(A) Every month \$1000 is deposited.

(B) The initial deposit is \$1000.

(C) There is no initial deposit.

(D) After the second month, there is \$2000 in the savings account.

2. Which of the following is NOT a rational number?

(F) $-\sqrt{196}$ (H) $-\sqrt{10}$

(G) $-5.8\overline{3}$ (J) $-\frac{2}{3}$

3. What is the volume of a sphere whose surface area is 200.96 cm^2? Use 3.14 for π.

(A) 50.24 cm^3 (C) 267.95 cm^3

(B) 133.98 cm^3 (D) 803.84 cm^3

4. Which inequality describes the graph?

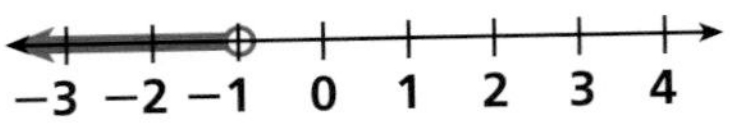

(F) $x < -1$ (H) $x \leq -1$

(G) $x > -1$ (J) $x \geq -1$

5. The rectangle and the triangle have the same area. What is the perimeter of the rectangle?

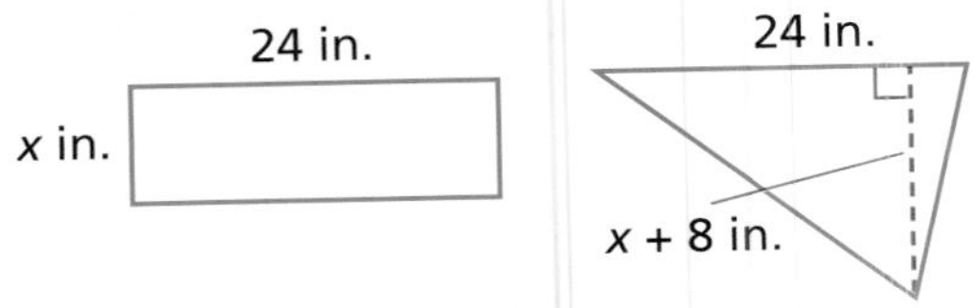

(A) 192 in. (C) 56 in.

(B) 64 in. (D) 32 in.

6. There are 36 dogs in an animal shelter that houses 144 animals. Which percent represents the portion of the animals that are dogs?

(F) 10% (H) 75%

(G) 25% (J) 400%

7. In the box-and-whisker plot below, what is the difference between the first and third quartiles?

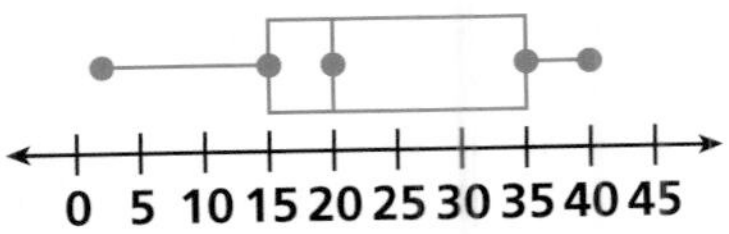

(A) 5 (C) 20

(B) 12.5 (D) 28.5

8. A cell phone store offers 10 different colors, 4 different face plates, and 6 different ring tones. How many different phones does a customer have to choose from?

(F) 240 (H) 64

(G) 120 (J) 20

9. Which figure has line symmetry, but not rotational symmetry?

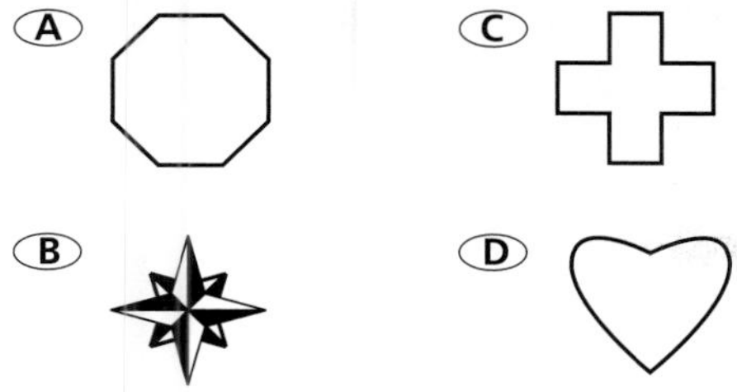

HOT TIP! Remember that you can write both fractions and terminating decimals as answers for gridded-response test questions.

Gridded Response

10. What is the value of x so that the slope of the line passing through the points $(-1, 4)$ and $(x, 1)$ is $-\frac{3}{4}$?

11. If $\triangle JKL$ and $\triangle MNP$ are similar, what is the perimeter of $\triangle JKL$?

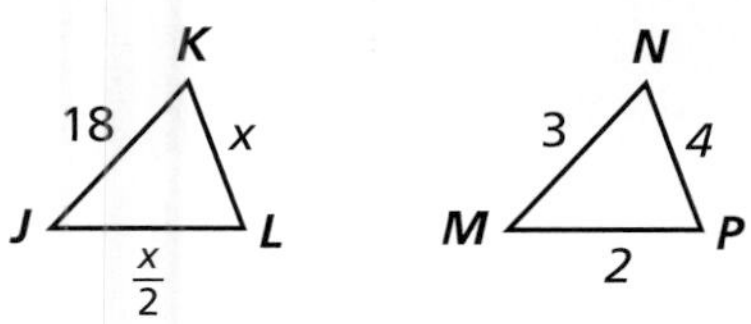

12. What is the slope of a line perpendicular to the line $y - 6 = -4(x + 8)$?

13. What is $f(-2)$ for the function $f(x) = -\frac{2}{3}x - \frac{7}{8}$?

14. In a school with 1248 students, there are 24 students whose last name is Perez. What is the probability that a student whose last name is Perez will be chosen at random? Write your answer as a fraction in simplest form.

15. Maya ran every day for a week. She ran 3 miles on Sunday and increased her distance $\frac{1}{2}$ mile each day. What was the mean distance, in miles, that Maya ran for the week?

Short Response

16. Scientists have found that a linear equation can be used to model the relation between the outdoor temperature and the number of chirps per minute crickets make. If a snowy tree cricket makes 100 chirps/min at 63°F and 178 chirps/min at 77°F, at what approximate temperature does the cricket make 126 chirps/min? Show your work.

17. Plot the points $A(-5, -4)$, $B(1, -2)$, $C(2, 3)$, and $D(-4, 1)$. Use straight segments to connect the four points in order. Then find the slope of each line segment. What special kind of quadrilateral is $ABCD$? Explain.

18. Write an equation in slope-intercept form that has the same slope as $-6x - 3y = 3$ and the same y-intercept as $-3y + 5 = 9x + 5$. Tell whether your equation is a direct variation. Explain.

Extended Response

19. Paul Revere had to travel 3.5 miles to Charlestown from Boston by boat. Assume that from Charlestown to Lexington, he was able to ride a horse that traveled at a rate of $\frac{1}{8}$ mile per minute. His total distance traveled y is the sum of the distance to Charlestown and the distance from Charlestown to Lexington.

- **a.** Write a linear equation that could be used to find the distance y Paul Revere traveled in x minutes.
- **b.** What does the slope of the line represent?
- **c.** What does the y-intercept of the line represent?
- **d.** Graph your equation from part **a** on a coordinate plane.

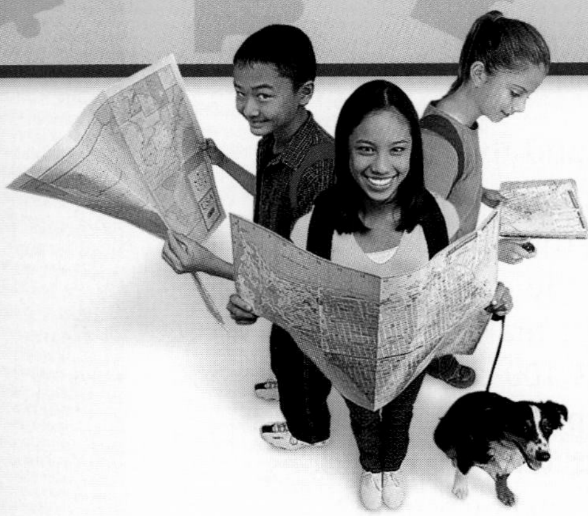

Problem Solving on Location

MARYLAND

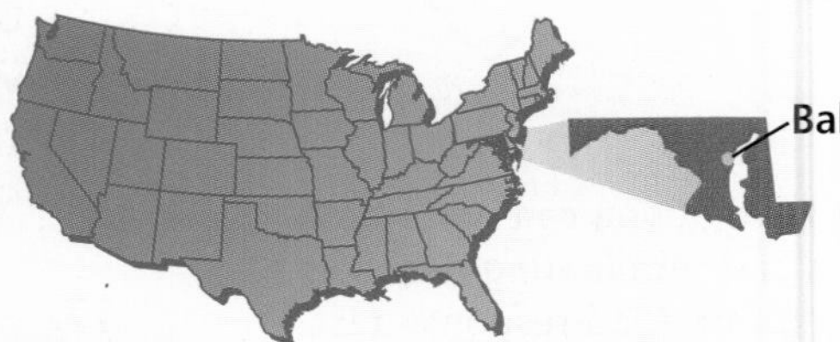

The Chesapeake Bay Bridge

The Chesapeake Bay Bridge is actually two bridges in one. The original two-lane structure opened to traffic in 1952. In 1973, construction was completed on a second span alongside the first. Today, the side-by-side bridges carry more than 25 million vehicles per year, and the 4.3-mile crossing has become world famous for its spectacular views.

Choose one or more strategies to solve each problem.

1. When the bridge opened in 1952, the toll for each vehicle was \$1.40, plus \$0.25 per passenger other than the driver. On opening day, the driver of a bus paid a toll of \$3.15. How many people were in the bus?

2. In 2001, about 24 million vehicles crossed the Chesapeake Bay Bridge. In 2004, about 26 million vehicles crossed the bridge. Suppose the number of crossings continues to increase by 2 million vehicles every 3 years. In what year will the number of crossings reach 34 million?

For 3, use the graph.

3. The bridge's westbound span has three lanes, while the eastbound span has only two. This means the westbound span can carry more vehicles per hour, as shown in the graph. In a 24-hour period, how many more vehicles can cross the westbound span than the eastbound span?

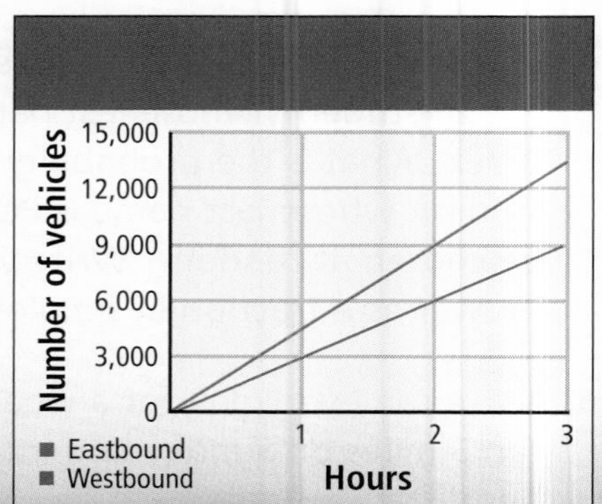

Problem Solving Strategies

- Draw a Diagram
- Make a Model
- Guess and Test
- Work Backward
- Find a Pattern
- Make a Table
- Solve a Simpler Problem
- Use Logical Reasoning
- Act It Out
- Make an Organized List

The Baltimore Kinetic Sculpture Race

The annual Baltimore Kinetic Sculpture Race is a 15-mile race over land and sea that involves sculptures powered by humans. In recent years, entries in the madcap race have included a nine-seat platypus, a floating teapot, and a giant sea turtle built from old bicycle parts.

Choose one or more strategies to solve each problem.

1. Each team in the race consists of pilots and a pit crew. The entry fee for pilots is \$25 and the entry fee for pit-crew members is \$15. A team of seven paid an entry fee of \$135. How many pilots were on the team?

2. A team completes the first 2 miles of the race in 1 hour. They complete the first 4 miles of the race in 2 hours. If they continue at this rate, how long will it take the team to complete the entire course?

For 3, use the table.

3. If a team breaks one of the rules of the race, a penalty is added to their total time. The table shows the penalties for various violations of the rules. A team had five different violations, for a total penalty of 6 hours and 30 minutes. Which rules did the team break?

Baltimore Kinetic Sculpture Race: Penalties

Violation	Penalty
A. Lost safety equipment	1 hour
B. Pilot gets wet	30 minutes
C. Sculpture is pushed or pulled	3 hours
D. Sculpture goes off course	2 hours
E. Sculpture drifts out of bounds in harbor	1 hour
F. Team gets help from a motor vehicle	1 hour

CHAPTER 13

Sequences and Functions

13A Sequences
- **13-1** Terms of Arithmetic Sequences
- **13-2** Terms of Geometric Sequences
- **LAB** Explore the Fibonacci Sequence
- **13-3** Other Sequences

13B Functions
- **13-4** Linear Functions
- **13-5** Exponential Functions
- **13-6** Quadratic Functions
- **LAB** Explore Cubic Functions
- **13-7** Inverse Variation

MULTI-STEP TEST PREP

go.hrw.com
Chapter Project Online
KEYWORD: MT7 Ch13

Growth Rates of *E. coli* Bacteria

Conditions	Doubling Time (min)
Optimum temperature (30°C) and growth medium	20
Low temperature (below 30°C)	40
Low nutrient growth medium	60
Low temperature and low nutrient growth medium	120

Career *Bacteriologist*

Bacteriologists study the growth and characteristics of microorganisms. They generally work in the fields of medicine and public health.

Bacteria colonies grow very quickly. The rate at which bacteria multiply depends upon temperature, nutrient supply, and other factors. The table shows growth rates of an *E. coli* bacteria colony under different conditions.

ARE YOU READY?

Vocabulary

Choose the best term from the list to complete each sentence.

	linear equation
	point-slope form
	slope
	***x*-intercept**
	***y*-intercept**

1. An equation whose solutions fall on a line on a coordinate plane is called a(n) __?__.
2. When the equation of a line is written in the form $y = mx + b$, m represents the __?__ and b represents the __?__.
3. To write an equation of the line that passes through (1, 3) and has slope 2, you might use the __?__ of the equation of a line.

Complete these exercises to review skills you will need for this chapter.

Number Patterns

Find the next three numbers. Then describe the pattern.

4. $\frac{1}{-3}, \frac{3}{-4}, \frac{5}{-5}, \ldots$
5. 2, 3, 6, 11, 18, . . .
6. −11, −8, −5, . . .
7. $4, 2\frac{1}{2}, 1, \ldots$

Evaluate Expressions

Evaluate each expression for the given values of the variables.

8. $a + (b - 1)c$ for $a = 6, b = 3, c = -4$
9. $a \cdot b^c$ for $a = -2, b = 4, c = 2$
10. $(ab)^c$ for $a = 3, b = -2, c = 2$
11. $-(a + b) + c$ for $a = -1, b = -4, c = -10$

Graph Linear Equations

Use the slope and the *y*-intercept to graph each line.

12. $y = \frac{2}{3}x + 4$
13. $y = -\frac{1}{2}x - 2$
14. $y = 3x + 1$
15. $2y = 3x - 8$
16. $3y + 2x = 6$
17. $x - 5y = 5$

Simplify Ratios

Write each ratio in simplest form.

18. $\frac{3}{9}$
19. $\frac{21}{5}$
20. $\frac{-12}{4}$
21. $\frac{27}{45}$
22. $\frac{3}{-45}$
23. $\frac{20}{-8}$

CHAPTER 13

Study Guide: Preview

Where You've Been

Previously, you

- described the relationship between the terms in a sequence and their positions in the sequence.
- graphed data to demonstrate relationships in familiar concepts.

In This Chapter

You will study

- finding and evaluating an algebraic expression to determine any term in an arithmetic sequence.
- using function rules to describe patterns in sequences.
- determining if a sequence can be arithmetic, geometric, or neither.

Where You're Going

You can use the skills learned in this chapter

- to use interest rates to predict the interest earned on money invested in a savings account.
- to understand and explore topics in physics, such as waves, cycles, and frequencies.

Key Vocabulary/Vocabulario

common ratio	razón común
exponential function	función exponencial
geometric sequence	sucesión geométrica
inverse variation	variación inversa
linear function	función lineal
parabola	parábola
quadratic function	función cuadrática

Vocabulary Connections

To become familiar with some of the vocabulary terms in the chapter, consider the following. You may refer to the chapter, the glossary, or a dictionary if you like.

1. The word *exponential* means "relating to an exponent." What do you think makes a function an **exponential function**?
2. The word *inverse* means "opposite." If two variables are related by an **inverse variation**, what do you think happens to the value of the second variable as the value of the first variable increases?

Reading and Writing Math

Study Strategy: Use Multiple Representations

By using multiple representations to introduce a math concept, you can understand the concept more clearly. As you study, take note of the use of the tables, lists, graphs, diagrams, symbols, and words to help clarify concepts.

Equation

EXAMPLE 2 ***Physical Science Application***

The equation $d = 0.2s$ represents the approximate distance, d, in miles of a thunderstorm when s seconds pass between a flash of lightning and the sound of thunder. About how far is the thunderstorm from each student listed in the table?

Student	Time Between Flash and Thunder (s)
Sandy	5
Diego	9
Ted	4
Cecilia	11
Massoud	8

Draw a graph that represents the relationship between the time between lightning and thunder and the distance of the storm from the student.

Table

s	$d = 0.2s$	d	(s, d)
5	$d = 0.2(5)$	1.0	(5, 1)
9	$d = 0.2(9)$	1.8	(9, 1.8)
4	$d = 0.2(4)$	0.8	(4, 0.8)
11	$d = 0.2(11)$	2.2	(11, 2.2)
8	$d = 0.2(8)$	1.6	(8, 1.6)

The approximate distances are Sandy, 1 mile; Diego, 1.8 miles; Ted, 0.8 mile; Cecilia, 2.2 miles; and Massoud, 1.6 miles. This is a linear equation because when s increases by 10 units, d increases by 2 units.

Graph

Distance of a Thunderstorm

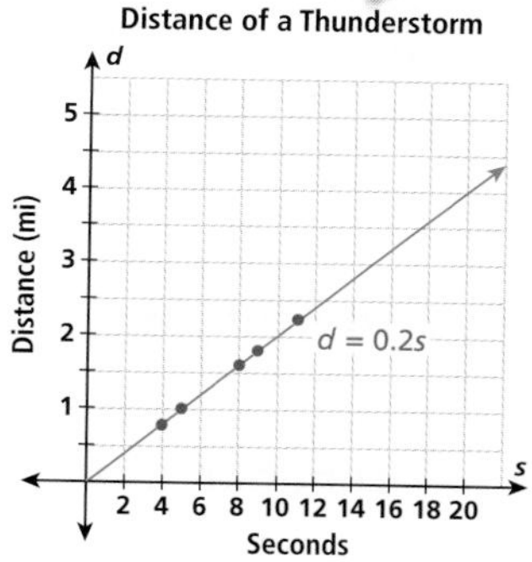

Try This

Find a different representation for each relationship.

1. The area A of a certain rectangle is 48 cm^2. The base is 3 times longer than the height. What are the dimensions of the rectangle?

2.

x	−2	−1	0
y	0	1	2

3. $x = -2$

13-1 Terms of Arithmetic Sequences

Learn to find terms in an arithmetic sequence.

Ruben recently joined a preferred-customer club at a local bookstore. He received 200 points for joining and gets an additional 50 points each time he buys a book. The points can then be used to get free merchandise.

The number of points Ruben has in his account is 250 after buying 1 book, 300 after buying 2 books, 350 after buying 3 books, and so on.

After 1 book	After 2 books	After 3 books	After 4 books
250	300	350	400

Difference $300 - 250 = 50$

Difference $350 - 300 = 50$

Difference $400 - 350 = 50$

In Chapter 3, you learned that in an arithmetic sequence, the difference between one term and the next is always the same and is called the *common difference.* The number of points in Ruben's account after each book purchased forms an arithmetic sequence with a common difference of 50.

EXAMPLE 1 **Identifying Arithmetic Sequences**

Determine if each sequence could be arithmetic. If so, give the common difference.

Caution!

You cannot tell if a sequence is arithmetic by looking at a finite number of terms because the next term might not fit the pattern. This is why we say a sequence *could be* arithmetic.

A **7, 11, 15, 19, 23, . . .**

7 11 15 19 23, . . .

4 4 4 4

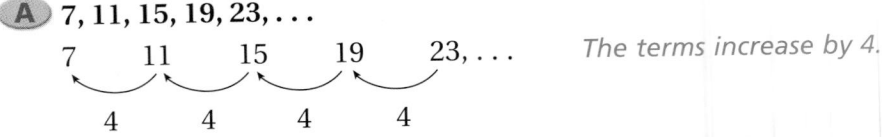

The terms increase by 4.

The sequence could be arithmetic with a common difference of 4.

B **1, 3, 9, 27, 81, . . .**

1 3 9 27 81, . . .

2 6 18 54

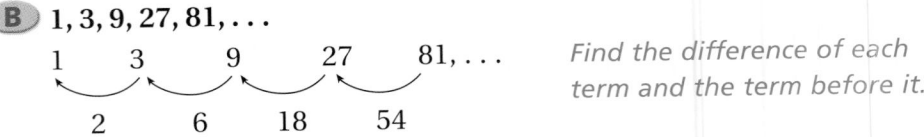

Find the difference of each term and the term before it.

The sequence is not arithmetic since it does not have a common difference.

Determine if each sequence could be arithmetic. If so, give the common difference.

C **200, 191, 182, 173, 164, . . .**

200 191 182 173 164, . . . *The terms decrease by 9.*

−9 −9 −9 −9

The sequence could be arithmetic with a common difference of −9.

D $1, \frac{5}{4}, \frac{3}{2}, \frac{7}{4}, 2, \ldots$

$1 \quad \frac{5}{4} \quad \frac{3}{2} \quad \frac{7}{4} \quad 2, \ldots$ *The terms increase by* $\frac{1}{4}$.

$\frac{1}{4} \quad \frac{1}{4} \quad \frac{1}{4} \quad \frac{1}{4}$

The sequence could be arithmetic with a common difference of $\frac{1}{4}$.

E **6, 1, −4, −9, −14, . . .**

6 1 −4 −9 −14, . . . *The terms decrease by 5.*

−5 −5 −5 −5

The sequence could be arithmetic with a common difference of −5.

Suppose you wanted to know the 100th term of the arithmetic sequence 5, 7, 9, 11, 13, ... If you do not want to find the first 99 terms, look for a pattern in the terms of the sequence.

Helpful Hint

Subscripts are used to show the positions of terms in the sequence. The first term is a_1, read "*a* sub one," the second is a_2, and so on.

Term Number	a_1	a_2	a_3	a_4	a_5
Term	5	7	9	11	13
Pattern	5 + 0(2)	5 + 1(2)	5 + 2(2)	5 + 3(2)	5 + 4(2)

The common difference d is 2. For the 2nd term, **one** 2 is added to a_1, which is 5. For the 3rd term, **two** 2's are added to 5. The pattern shows that for each term, the **number of 2's added** is one less than the term number, or $(n - 1)$.

The 100th term is the first term, 5, plus **99** times the common difference, 2.

$$a_{100} = 5 + 99(2) = 5 + 198 = 203$$

FINDING THE *n*th TERM OF AN ARITHMETIC SEQUENCE

The nth term a_n of an arithmetic sequence with common difference d and first term a_1 is

$$a_n = a_1 + (n - 1)d.$$

EXAMPLE 2 Finding a Given Term of an Arithmetic Sequence

Find the given term in each arithmetic sequence.

A 16th term: 4, 7, 10, 13, . . .

$a_n = a_1 + (n - 1)d$
$a_{16} = 4 + (16 - 1)3$
$a_{16} = 49$

B 22nd term: 28, 23, 18, 13, . . .

$a_n = a_1 + (n - 1)d$
$a_{22} = 28 + (22 - 1)(-5)$
$a_{22} = -77$

C 11th term: −7, −2, 3, 8, . . .

$a_n = a_1 + (n - 1)d$
$a_{11} = -7 + (11 - 1)5$
$a_{11} = 43$

D 30th term: $a_1 = 4, d = 12$

$a_n = a_1 + (n - 1)d$
$a_{30} = 4 + (30 - 1)12$
$a_{30} = 352$

You can use the formula for the *n*th term of an arithmetic sequence to solve for other variables.

EXAMPLE 3 *Consumer Application*

Ruben recently joined a preferred-customer club at a bookstore. He received 200 points for signing up and he will get 50 points for every book he buys. How many books does he have to buy to collect 1000 points?

Identify the arithmetic sequence: 250, 300, 350, . . .

$a_1 = 250$ — *$a_1 = 250$ = number of points after the first book*
$d = 50$ — *$d = 50$ = common difference*
$a_n = 1000$ — *$a_n = 1000$ = number of points needed*

Let *n* represent the number of books that will earn him a total of 1000 points. Use the formula for arithmetic sequences.

$a_n = a_1 + (n - 1)d$ — *Solve for n.*
$1000 = 250 + (n - 1)50$ — *Substitute the given values.*
$1000 = 250 + 50n - 50$ — *Distributive Property*
$1000 = 200 + 50n$ — *Combine like terms.*
$800 = 50n$ — *Subtract 200 from both sides.*
$16 = n$ — *Divide both sides by 50.*

After buying 16 books, Ruben will have collected 1000 points.

Think and Discuss

1. **Explain** how to determine if a sequence might be an arithmetic sequence.
2. **Compare** your answers for the 10th term of the arithmetic sequence 5, 7, 9, 11, 13, . . . by finding all of the first 10 terms and by using the formula.

13-1 Exercises

go.hrw.com
Homework Help Online
KEYWORD: MT7 13-1
Parent Resources Online
KEYWORD: MT7 Parent

GUIDED PRACTICE

See Example 1

Determine if each sequence could be arithmetic. If so, give the common difference.

1. 4, 6, 8, 10, 12, . . .
2. 16, 14, 13, 11, 10, . . .
3. $\frac{2}{9}, \frac{1}{3}, \frac{4}{9}, \frac{5}{9}, \frac{2}{3}, \ldots$
4. 87, 78, 69, 60, 51, . . .
5. $\frac{1}{3}, \frac{1}{9}, \frac{1}{27}, \frac{1}{81}, \frac{1}{243}, \ldots$
6. 6, 4, 2, 0, −2, . . .

See Example 2

Find the given term in each arithmetic sequence.

7. 17th term: 5, 7, 9, 11, . . .
8. 26th term: 3, 8, 13, 18, . . .
9. 31st term: −2, −5, −8, −11, . . .
10. 40th term: $a_1 = 13, d = 4$

See Example 3

11. Postage for a first-class letter costs \$0.39 for the first ounce and \$0.24 for each additional ounce. If a letter costs \$1.59 to mail, how many ounces is it?

INDEPENDENT PRACTICE

See Example 1

Determine if each sequence could be arithmetic. If so, give the common difference.

12. $\frac{1}{3}, \frac{2}{3}, 1, 1\frac{1}{3}, 1\frac{2}{3}, \ldots$
13. 5, 3, 1, −1, −3, . . .
14. $\frac{1}{5}, \frac{3}{5}, \frac{4}{5}, 1\frac{1}{5}, 1\frac{2}{5}, \ldots$
15. 6, 29, 52, 75, 98, . . .
16. $\frac{4}{7}, 1\frac{2}{7}, 2, 2\frac{5}{7}, 3\frac{2}{7}, \ldots$
17. 0.1, 0.4, 0.7, 1, 1.3, . . .

See Example 2

Find the given term in each arithmetic sequence.

18. 12th term: 4, 2, 0, −2, . . .
19. 23rd term: 0.1, 0.15, 0.2, 0.25
20. 25th term: $a_1 = 1, d = 5$
21. 16th term: $a_1 = 38.5, d = -2.5$

See Example 3

22. Oscar received 50 tokens for entering a race, plus 7 tokens each hour. If his total number of tokens was 113, for how many hours did he race?

PRACTICE AND PROBLEM SOLVING

Extra Practice
See page 806.

Find the next three terms of each arithmetic sequence.

23. 11, 14, 17, 20, . . .
24. −16, −9, −2, 5, . . .
25. 103, 90, 77, 64, . . .

26. The 6th term of an arithmetic sequence is 142. The common difference is 12. What are the first four terms of the arithmetic sequence?

Find the first five terms of each arithmetic sequence.

27. $a_1 = 1, d = 2$
28. $a_1 = 2, d = 8$
29. $a_1 = 0, d = 0.25$

30. The 1st term of an arithmetic sequence is 7. The common difference is 9. What position in the sequence is the term 160?

31. **Fitness** Marissa cuts 7 seconds off her time for every lap she runs around the track. At noon, the stopwatch read 11:53. Write the first four terms of an arithmetic sequence modeling the situation. ($a_1 = 11{:}53$)

32. **Recreation** The rates for a mini grand-prix course are shown in the flyer.

   a. What are the first 5 terms of the arithmetic sequence that represents the fees for the course?

   b. What would the rate be for 9 laps?

   c. If the cost of a license plus n laps is $11, find n.

33. **Critical Thinking** One law firm charges an administrative fee of $75, plus a $52.50 fee for each half hour of consultation. A second law firm charges an administrative fee of $50, plus a $65.50 fee for each half hour of consultation. What are the first 4 terms of the arithmetic sequences that represent the rates of the law firms? Which law firm charges less for 4 half-hour consultations?

34. **Write a Problem** Write an arithmetic sequence problem using $a_5 = -25$ and $d = 5.5$.

35. **Write About It** Explain how to find the common difference of an arithmetic sequence. What can you say about the terms of a sequence if the common difference is positive? if the common difference is negative?

36. **Challenge** The 1st term of an arithmetic sequence is 3, and the common difference is 6. Find two consecutive terms of the sequence that have a sum of 108. What positions are the terms in the sequence?

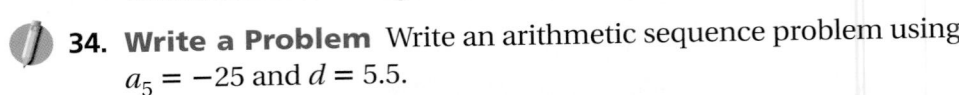

Test Prep and Spiral Review

37. **Multiple Choice** Use of an Internet service at a hotel costs $2.50 plus $0.25 per minute. Rebecca was charged $14.25 for one usage. For how many minutes did she use the Internet service?

   Ⓐ 5.7 Ⓑ 46 Ⓒ 47 Ⓓ 57

38. **Gridded Response** What is the 20th term in the arithmetic sequence 2, 6, 10, 14, . . .?

Solve. (Lesson 2-7)

39. $x + \frac{1}{6} = -\frac{5}{6}$ 40. $\frac{y}{2.4} = -3$ 41. $k - 11.6 = -21$ 42. $23\frac{5}{7} = c + 24$

Identify the population and sample. (Lesson 9-1)

43. A cable company surveys customers whose last names begin with an “s.”

44. The principal asks every other busload of students if their ride was comfortable.

13-2 Terms of Geometric Sequences

Learn to find terms in a geometric sequence.

Vocabulary

geometric sequence

common ratio

Joey mows his family's yard every week. His mother offers him a choice of \$10 per week, or 1¢ the first week, 2¢ the second week, 4¢ the third week, and so on.

Week 1	Week 2	Week 3	Week 4
1¢	2¢	4¢	8¢

Ratio $\frac{2}{1} = 2$ *Ratio* $\frac{4}{2} = 2$ *Ratio* $\frac{8}{4} = 2$

The weekly amounts Joey would get paid in this plan form a geometric sequence. In a **geometric sequence**, the ratio of one term to the next is always the same. This ratio is called the **common ratio**. The common ratio is multiplied by each term to get the next term.

EXAMPLE 1 Identifying Geometric Sequences

Determine if each sequence could be geometric. If so, give the common ratio.

A **162, 54, 18, 6, 2, . . .**

162   54   18   6   2, . . .   *Divide each term by the term before it.*

$\frac{1}{3}$ $\frac{1}{3}$ $\frac{1}{3}$ $\frac{1}{3}$ *Simplify.*

The sequence could be geometric with a common ratio of $\frac{1}{3}$.

B **7, −7, 7, −7, 7, . . .**

7   −7   7   −7   7, . . .   *Divide each term by the term before it.*

−1   −1   −1   −1   *Simplify.*

The sequence could be geometric with a common ratio of −1.

C **2, 5, 8, 11, 14, . . .**

2   5   8   11,   14, . . .   *Divide each term by the term before it.*

$\frac{5}{2}$ $\frac{8}{5}$ $\frac{11}{8}$ $\frac{14}{11}$

The sequence is not geometric since it does not have a common ratio.

Determine if each sequence could be geometric. If so, give the common ratio.

D **2, −5, 12.5, −31.52, 78.125, . . .**

2	−5	12.5	−31.25	78.125, . . .	*Divide each term by the term before it.*
	−2.5	−2.5	−2.5	−2.5	*Simplify.*

The sequence could be geometric with a common ratio of −2.5.

Suppose you wanted to find the 15th term of the geometric sequence 2, 6, 18, 54, 162, ... If you do not want to find the first 14 terms, look for a pattern in the terms of the sequence.

Term Number	a_1	a_2	a_3	a_4	a_5
Term	2	6	18	54	162
Pattern	$2(3)^0$	$2(3)^1$	$2(3)^2$	$2(3)^3$	$2(3)^4$

The common ratio r is 3. For the 2nd term, a_1, or 2, is multiplied by 3 **once**. For the 3rd term, 2 is multiplied by 3 **twice**. The pattern shows that for each term, the **number of times 3 is multiplied** is one less than the **term number**, or **(n − 1)**.

The 15th term is the first term, 2, times the common ratio, 3, raised to the 14th power.

$$a_{15} = 2(3)^{14} = 2(4{,}782{,}969) = 9{,}565{,}938$$

FINDING THE *n*th TERM OF A GEOMETRIC SEQUENCE

The nth term a_n of a geometric sequence with common ratio r is

$$a_n = a_1 r^{n-1}.$$

EXAMPLE 2 Finding a Given Term of a Geometric Sequence

Find the given term in each geometric sequence.

A **14th term: 3, 12, 48, 192, . . .**

$r = \frac{12}{3} = 4$

$a_{14} = 3(4)^{13} = 201{,}326{,}592$

B **49th term: 2, −2, 2, −2, 2, . . .**

$r = \frac{-2}{2} = -1$

$a_{49} = 2(-1)^{48} = 2$

C **7th term: 7, $\frac{7}{3}, \frac{7}{9}, \frac{7}{27}, \frac{7}{81}, \ldots$**

$r = \frac{\frac{7}{3}}{7} = \frac{1}{3}$

$a_7 = 7\left(\frac{1}{3}\right)^6 = \frac{7}{129}$

D **20th term: 500, 300, 180, 208, . . .**

$r = \frac{300}{500} = 0.6$

$a_{20} = 500(0.6)^{19} \approx 0.03$

EXAMPLE 3 *Money Application*

For mowing his family's yard every week, Joey has two options for payment: (1) \$10 per week or (2) 1¢ the first week, 2¢ the second week, 4¢ the third week, and so on, where he makes twice as much each week as he made the week before. If Joey will mow the yard for 15 weeks, which option should he choose?

If Joey chooses \$10 per week, he will get a total of 15(\$10) = \$150.

If Joey chooses the second option, his payment for just the 15th week will be more than the total of all the payments in option 1.

$$a_{15} = (\$0.01)(2)^{14} = (\$0.01)(16{,}384) = \$163.84$$

Option 1 gives Joey more money in the beginning, but option 2 gives him a larger total amount.

Think and Discuss

1. **Compare** arithmetic sequences with geometric sequences.
2. **Describe** how you find the common ratio in a geometric sequence.

13-2 Exercises

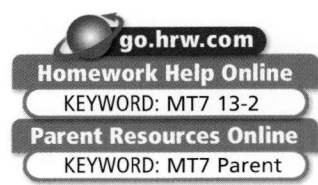

go.hrw.com
Homework Help Online
KEYWORD: MT7 13-2
Parent Resources Online
KEYWORD: MT7 Parent

GUIDED PRACTICE

See Example 1

Determine if each sequence could be geometric. If so, give the common ratio.

1. $-6, -3, 0, 3, 6, \ldots$
2. $3, 6, 12, 24, 48, \ldots$
3. $\frac{2}{3}, -\frac{2}{3}, \frac{2}{3}, -\frac{2}{3}, \frac{2}{3}, \ldots$
4. $1, 2.5, 6.25, 15.625, \ldots$
5. $\frac{4}{81}, \frac{4}{27}, \frac{4}{9}, \frac{4}{3}, \ldots$
6. $-2, -4, -8, -16, \ldots$

See Example 2

Find the given term in each geometric sequence.

7. 12th term: $3, 6, 12, 24, 48, \ldots$
8. 91st term: $\frac{1}{5}, -\frac{1}{5}, \frac{1}{5}, -\frac{1}{5}, \frac{1}{5}, \ldots$
9. 15th term: 531,441; 177,147; 59,049; 19,683; 6561
10. 7th term: $1, 5, 25, 125, 625, \ldots$

See Example 3

11. Heather makes \$5.50 per hour. Every 4 months, she is eligible for a 3% raise. How much will she make after 3 years if she gets a raise every 4 months?

INDEPENDENT PRACTICE

See Example 1

Determine if each sequence could be geometric. If so, give the common ratio.

12. 81, 27, 9, 3, 1, ...

13. $\frac{1}{3}, \frac{1}{27}, \frac{1}{9}, \frac{1}{81}, \ldots$

14. 2, 5, 8, 11, ...

15. 784, 392, 196, 98, ...

16. 1, −2, 4, −8, 16, ...

17. $6, 2, \frac{2}{3}, \frac{2}{9}, \ldots$

See Example 2

Find the given term in each geometric sequence.

18. 6th term: $\frac{1}{2}, 1, 2, 4, \ldots$

19. 7th term: 2401, 2058, 1764, 1512, ...

20. 6th term: $16, -4, 1, -\frac{1}{4}, \ldots$

21. 8th term: 2, 6, 18, 54, ...

22. 21st term: $\frac{1}{28}, \frac{1}{14}, \frac{1}{7}, \frac{2}{7}, \ldots$

23. 5th term: 1, 2.5, 6.25, 15.625, ...

See Example 3

24. A video game displays 55,000 points after the first level is completed. One fifth of the total points are added at the end of each level. How many points are there at the end of the fifth level?

PRACTICE AND PROBLEM SOLVING

Extra Practice

See page 806.

Find the next three terms of each geometric sequence.

25. $a_1 = 54$, common ratio $= \frac{1}{3}$

26. $a_1 = 5$, common ratio $= 3$

27. $a_1 = \frac{1}{81}$, common ratio $= -3$

28. $a_1 = 6$, common ratio $= 1.5$

Find the first five terms of each geometric sequence.

29. $a_1 = 2, r = 1$

30. $a_1 = 5, r = -1$

31. $a_1 = 30, r = 2.1$

32. $a_1 = 32, r = \frac{5}{2}$

33. $a_1 = 10, r = 0.25$

34. $a_1 = 56, r = -5$

35. Find the 1st term of a geometric sequence with 5th term $\frac{81}{5}$ and common ratio 3.

36. Find the 4th term of a geometric sequence with 10th term 64 and common ratio −2.

37. Find the 1st term of a geometric sequence with 3rd term $\frac{32}{147}$ and common ratio $\frac{4}{7}$.

38. Find the 1st term of a geometric sequence if $a_4 = 28$ and $r = 2$.

39. Find the 6th term of a geometric sequence with 4th term 12 and 5th term 18.

40. Sports In the women's NCAA volleyball tournament, 64 teams compete in the first round. There are 32 teams remaining in the second round, 16 teams remaining in the third round, and so on. How many teams are remaining in the sixth round?

41. Life Science Under controlled conditions, a culture of bacteria triples in size every 3 days. How many cells of the bacteria are in the culture after 3 weeks if there were originally 28 cells?

LINK

Physical Science

Introduced in 1965, the Super Ball® bounced to a height almost 90% of its starting height.

42. **Economics** A car that was originally valued at \$14,000 depreciates at the rate of 20% per year. This means that after each year, the car is worth 80% of its worth the previous year. What is the value of the car after 7 years? Round to the nearest dollar.

43. **Physical Science** A rubber ball is dropped from a height of 256 ft. After each bounce, the height of the ball is recorded.

Height of Bouncing Ball					
Number of Bounces	1	2	3	4	5
Height (ft)	192	144	108	81	60.75

a. Could the heights in the table form a geometric sequence? If so, what is the common ratio?

b. Estimate the height of the ball after the 8th bounce. Round your answer to the nearest foot.

44. **Multi-Step** Town A has a population of 600 and is growing at a rate of 2% per year. Town B has a population of 500 and is growing at a rate of 4% per year. If these rates continue, which town will have the greater population after 10 years? Explain.

45. **What's the Error?** A student is asked to find the next three terms of the geometric sequence with $a_1 = 15$ and common ratio 5. His answer is 3, $\frac{3}{5}$, $\frac{3}{25}$. What error has the student made, and what is the correct answer?

46. **Write About It** Compare a geometric sequence with $a_1 = 3$ and $r = 4$ with a geometric sequence with $a_1 = 4$ and $r = 3$.

47. **Challenge** The 4th term in a geometric sequence is 923. The 9th term is 224,289. Find the 6th term.

Test Prep and Spiral Review

48. **Multiple Choice** A tank holds 40,800 gallons of gasoline. One-half of the gasoline remaining in the tank is sold each day. How many gallons of gasoline are left in the tank after the 6th day?

Ⓐ 12 Ⓑ 127 Ⓒ 1,275 Ⓓ 12,750

49. **Short Response** Determine if the sequence 10, 5, $\frac{5}{2}$, $\frac{5}{4}$, $\frac{5}{8}$, . . . could be geometric. If so, give the common ratio. If not, explain why not.

Solve. (Lesson 1-8)

50. $\frac{m}{-3} = 4$ 51. $64 = 4x$ 52. $\frac{x}{-6} = -2$

Simplify. (Lesson 11-1)

53. $3(p + 7) - 5p$ 54. $4x + 5(2x - 9)$ 55. $8 + 7(y + 5) - 3$

Hands-On LAB 13-3

Explore the Fibonacci Sequence

Use with Lesson 13-3

go.hrw.com
Lab Resources Online
KEYWORD: MT7 Lab13

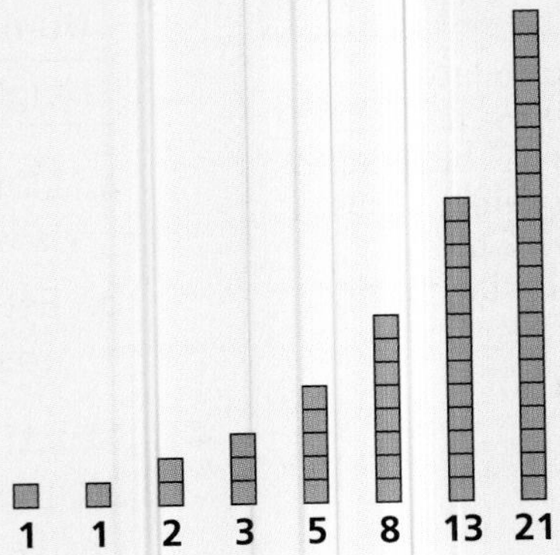

Activity

Use square tiles to model the following numbers:

1 1 2 3 5 8 13 21

Place the first stack of tiles on top of the second stack of tiles. What do you notice?

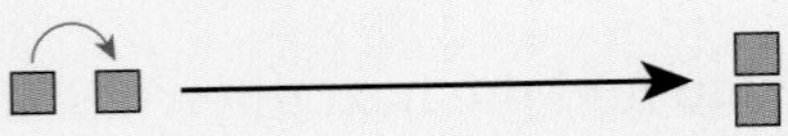

The first two stacks added together are equal in height to the third stack.

Place the second stack of tiles on top of the third stack of tiles. What do you notice?

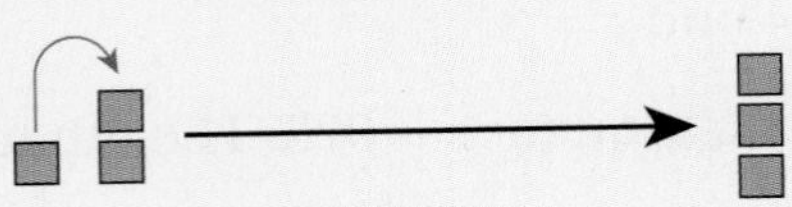

The second stack and the third stack added together are equal in height to the fourth stack.

This sequence is called the **Fibonacci sequence.** By adding two successive numbers, you get the next number in the sequence. The sequence will go on forever.

Think and Discuss

1. If there were a term before the 1 in the sequence, what would it be? Explain your answer.
2. Could the numbers 377, 610, and 987 be part of the Fibonacci sequence? Explain.

Try This

1. Use your square tiles to find the next two numbers in the sequence. What are they?
2. The 20th and 21st terms of the Fibonacci sequence are 6765 and 10,946. What is the 22nd term?

13-3 Other Sequences

Learn to find patterns in sequences.

Vocabulary
- first differences
- second differences
- Fibonacci sequence

The first five *triangular numbers* are shown below.

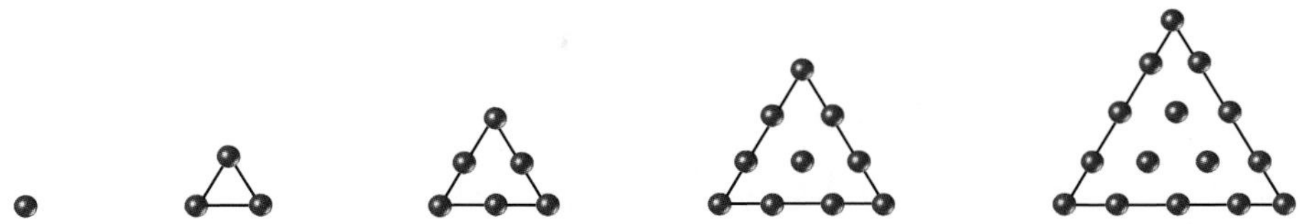

1 3 6 10 15

To continue the sequence, you can draw the triangles, or you can look for a pattern. If you subtract every term from the one after it, the **first differences** create a new sequence. If you do not see a pattern, you can repeat the process and find the **second differences**.

Term	1	2	3	4	5	6	7
Triangular Number	1	3	6	10	15	21	28

First differences: 2 3 4 5 6 7

Second differences: 1 1 1 1 1

EXAMPLE 1 Using First and Second Differences

Use first and second differences to find the next three terms in each sequence.

Remember!
The second difference is the difference between the first differences.

A 1, 7, 22, 46, 79, 121, 172, . . .

Sequence	1	7	22	46	79	121	172	232	301	379
1st Differences	6	15	24	33	42	51	60	69	78	
2nd Differences	9	9	9	9	9	9	9	9		

The next 1st difference in the table is going to be 9 more than the one before it, or 60. This means that the next number in the sequence is 60 more than 172. So the next three terms are 232, 301, and 379.

B 5, 5, 7, 13, 25, 45, 75, . . .

Sequence	5	5	7	13	25	45	75	117	173	245
1st Differences	0	2	6	12	20	30	42	56	72	
2nd Differences	2	4	6	8	10	12	14	16		

The next three terms are 117, 173, and 245.

By looking at the sequence 1, 2, 3, 4, 5, . . . , you would probably assume that the next term is 6. In fact, the next term could be any number. If no rule is given, you should use the simplest recognizable pattern in the given terms.

EXAMPLE 2 Finding a Rule Given Terms of a Sequence

Give the next three terms in each sequence using the simplest rule you can find.

A $\frac{1}{2}, \frac{1}{3}, \frac{1}{4}, \frac{1}{5}, \frac{1}{6}, \ldots$ 4

The next three terms are $\frac{1}{7}$, $\frac{1}{8}$, and $\frac{1}{9}$.

Add 1 to the denominator of the previous term. This could be written as the algebraic rule $a_n = \frac{1}{n+1}$.

B $1, -1, 3, -3, 5, -5, \ldots$

The next three terms are 7, −7, and 9.

Each positive term is followed by its opposite, and the next term is 2 more than the previous positive term.

C $2, 4, 8, 16, 32, 64, \ldots$

The next three terms are 128, 256, and 512.

Multiply the previous term by 2. This could be written as the algebraic rule $a_n = 2^n$.

D $1, 4, 9, 16, 25, 36, \ldots$

The next three terms are 49, 64, and 81.

The terms could be perfect squares. This could be written as the algebraic rule $a_n = n^2$.

Sometimes an algebraic rule is used to define a sequence.

EXAMPLE 3 Finding Terms of a Sequence Given a Rule

Find the first five terms of the sequence defined by $a_n = \frac{n+1}{n+2}$.

$$a_1 = \frac{1+1}{1+2} = \frac{2}{3}$$

$$a_2 = \frac{2+1}{2+2} = \frac{3}{4}$$

$$a_3 = \frac{3+1}{3+2} = \frac{4}{5}$$

$$a_4 = \frac{4+1}{4+2} = \frac{5}{6}$$

$$a_5 = \frac{5+1}{5+2} = \frac{6}{7}$$

The first five terms are $\frac{2}{3}$, $\frac{3}{4}$, $\frac{4}{5}$, $\frac{5}{6}$, and $\frac{6}{7}$.

A famous sequence called the **Fibonacci sequence** is defined by the following rule: Add the two previous terms to find the next term.

1, 1, 2, 3, 5, 8, 13, 21, . . .

$1 + 1 = 2$ $1 + 2 = 3$ $2 + 3 = 5$ $3 + 5 = 8$ $5 + 8 = 13$ $8 + 13 = 21$

EXAMPLE 4 Using the Fibonacci Sequence

Suppose *a, b, c,* and *d* are four consecutive numbers in the Fibonacci sequence. Complete the following table and guess the pattern.

a, b, c, d	*bc*	*ad*
1, 1, 2, 3	1(2) = 2	1(3) = 3
3, 5, 8, 13	5(8) = 40	3(13) = 39
13, 21, 34, 55	21(34) = 714	13(55) = 715
55, 89, 144, 233	89(144) = 12,816	55(233) = 12,815

The product of the two middle terms is either one more or one less than the product of the two outer terms.

Think and Discuss

1. Find the first and second differences for the sequence of pentagonal numbers: 1, 5, 12, 22, 35, 51, 70, ...

13-3 Exercises

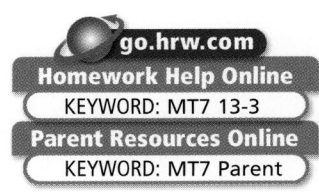

go.hrw.com
Homework Help Online
KEYWORD: MT7 13-3
Parent Resources Online
KEYWORD: MT7 Parent

GUIDED PRACTICE

See Example 1

Use first and second differences to find the next three terms in each sequence.

1. 1, 6, 20, 43, 75, 116, 166, . . .

2. 5, 10, 30, 65, 115, 180, . . .

3. 10, 10, 13, 22, 40, 70, 115, . . .

4. 4, 6, 16, 42, 92, 174, 296, . . .

See Example 2

Give the next three terms in each sequence using the simplest rule you can find.

5. $\frac{1}{3}, \frac{3}{5}, \frac{5}{7}, \frac{7}{9}, \frac{9}{11}, \frac{11}{13}, \ldots$

6. 3, −4, 5, −6, 7, −8, 9, . . .

7. 2, 3, 4, 2, 3, 4, 2, . . .

8. 1, 4, 9, 16, 25, . . .

See Example 3 **Find the first five terms of each sequence defined by the given rule.**

9. $a_n = \frac{2n}{n+4}$ **10.** $a_n = (n+1)(n+2)$ **11.** $a_n = \frac{2-n}{n} + 1$

See Example 4 **12.** Suppose *a*, *b*, and *c* are three consecutive numbers in the Fibonacci sequence. Complete the following table and guess the pattern.

a, b, c	ac	b^2
1, 1, 2	■	■
3, 5, 8	■	■
13, 21, 34	■	■
55, 89, 144	■	■

INDEPENDENT PRACTICE

See Example 1 **Use first and second differences to find the next three terms in each sequence.**

13. 12, 24, 37, 51, 66, 82, 99, . . .

14. −13, −9, 0, 14, 33, 57, 86, . . .

15. 22, 23, 26, 32, 42, 57, 78, . . .

16. 0.01, 0.02, 0.08, 0.24, 0.55, . . .

See Example 2 **Give the next three terms in each sequence using the simplest rule you can find.**

17. 1, −1, 2, −2, 3, −3, . . .

18. 1, 4, 3, 6, 5, 8, 7, . . .

19. 2.2, 2.02, 2.002, 2.0002, . . .

20. $1, \frac{1}{8}, \frac{1}{27}, \frac{1}{64}, \frac{1}{125}, \frac{1}{216}, \ldots$

See Example 3 **Find the first five terms of each sequence defined by the given rule.**

21. $a_n = \frac{n-2}{n+2}$ **22.** $a_n = n(n-1) - 2n$ **23.** $a_n = \frac{3n}{n+1}$

See Example 4 **24.** Suppose *a*, *b*, *c*, *d*, and *e* are five consecutive numbers in the Fibonacci sequence. Complete the following table and guess the pattern.

a, b, c, d, e	ae	bd	c^2
1, 1, 2, 3, 5	■	■	■
3, 5, 8, 13, 21	■	■	■
13, 21, 34, 55, 89	■	■	■

PRACTICE AND PROBLEM SOLVING

Extra Practice

See page 806.

The first 14 terms of the Fibonacci sequence are 1, 1, 2, 3, 5, 8, 13, 21, 34, 55, 89, 144, 233, and 377.

25. Where in this part of the sequence are the even numbers? Where do you think the next four even numbers will occur?

26. Where in this part of the sequence are the multiples of 3? Where do you think the next four multiples of 3 will occur?

27. **Geometry** What are the next three numbers in the sequence of rectangular numbers: 2, 6, 12, 20, 30, . . . ?

Music LINK

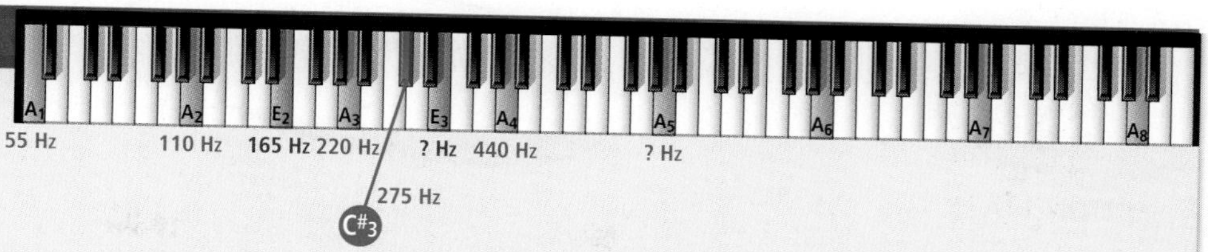

Pitch is the frequency of a musical note, measured in units called *hertz* (Hz). A pitch is named by its octave. A_4 is in the 4th octave on the piano keyboard and is often called middle A.

28. What kind of sequence is represented by the frequencies of $A_1, A_2, A_3, A_4, \ldots$? Write a rule to calculate these frequencies.

When a string of an instrument is played, its vibrations create many different frequencies. These varying frequencies are called *harmonics.*

Frequencies of Harmonics on A_1					
Harmonic	Fundamental (1st)	2nd	3rd	4th	5th
Note	A_1	A_2	E_2	A_3	$C^{\#}_3$

29. What is the frequency of the note E_3 if it is the 6th harmonic on A_1?

go.hrw.com
Web Extra!
KEYWORD: MT7 Pitch

30. **Write About It** Describe the sequence represented by the frequencies of different harmonics. Write a rule to calculate these frequencies.

31. **Challenge** In music, an important interval is a *fifth.* As you progress around the circle of fifths, the pitch frequencies are approximately as shown (rounded to the nearest tenth). What type of sequence do the frequencies form in clockwise order from C? Write the rule for the sequence. If the rule holds all the way around the circle, what would the frequency of the note F be?

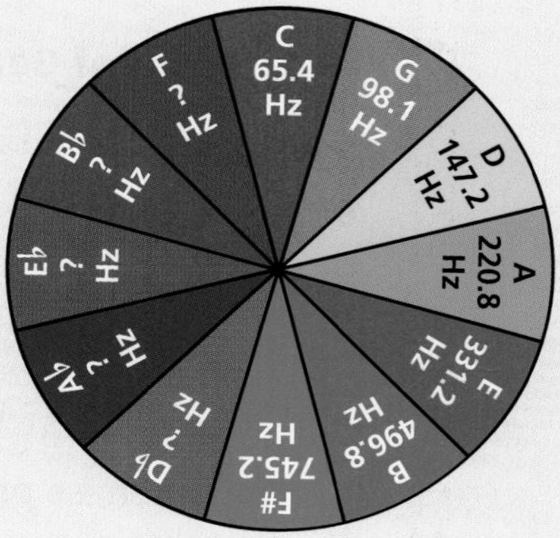

TEST PREP and Spiral Review

32. **Multiple Choice** What is the 11th term of a sequence defined by $a_n = \frac{n-1}{n}$?

Ⓐ $\frac{1}{11}$ Ⓑ $-\frac{10}{11}$ Ⓒ $\frac{10}{11}$ Ⓓ $\frac{11}{12}$

33. **Gridded Response** What is the 4th term of a sequence defined by $a_n = \frac{n+1}{n+2}$?

Write each number in standard notation. (Lesson 4-4)

34. 8.21×10^5 **35.** 2.07×10^{-7} **36.** -1.4×10^3

Determine if each sequence could be geometric. If so, give the common ratio. (Lesson 13-2)

37. 5, 10, 15, 20, 25, . . . **38.** 3, 6, 12, 24, 48, . . . **39.** 1, −3, 9, −27, 81, . . .

CHAPTER 13

READY TO GO ON?

SECTION 13A

Quiz for Lessons 13-1 Through 13-3

13-1 Terms of Arithmetic Sequences

Determine if each sequence could be arithmetic. If so, give the common difference.

1. 12, 13, 15, 17, . . .

2. 13, 26, 39, 52, . . .

3. 19, 60, 101, 174, . . .

Find the given term in each arithmetic sequence.

4. 8th term: 5, 8, 11, 14, . . .

5. 16th term: 9, 8.8, 8.6, . . .

6. 14th term: 7, $7\frac{1}{3}$, $\frac{2}{3}$, . . .

7. 7th term: $a_1 = 26$, $d = 11$,

8. Carmen makes 20 bracelets during the first week to sell at next year's fair. Each week, she makes 4 more than the previous week. In which week will she make 100 bracelets?

13-2 Terms of Geometric Sequences

Determine if each sequence could be geometric. If so, give the common ratio.

9. 1, −4, 16, −64, . . .

10. 3, −3, −9, −15, . . .

11. 50, 10, 2, 0.4, . . .

Find the given term in each geometric sequence.

12. 5th term: 11, 44, 176, . . .

13. 9th term: 36, 12, 4, . . .

14. 12th term: $-\frac{4}{3}$, 4, −12, . . .

15. 17th term: 10,000; 1000; 100; . . .

16. The purchase price of a machine at a factory was $500,000. Each year, the value of the machine depreciates by 5%. To the nearest dollar, what is the value of the machine after 6 years?

13-3 Other Sequences

Use first and second differences to find the next three terms in each sequence.

17. 7, 7, 9, 13, 19, . . .

18. 2, 10, 22, 38, 58, . . .

19. −5, −9, −10, −8, −3, . . .

Give the next three terms in each sequence using the simplest rule you can find.

20. $\frac{1}{2}, \frac{4}{5}, \frac{7}{8}, \frac{10}{11}, \ldots$

21. 1, 16, 81, 256, . . .

Find the first five terms of each sequence defined by the given rule.

22. $a_n = 4n - 7$

23. $a_n = 2^{n-1}$

24. $a_n = (-1)^n \cdot 2n$

25. $a_n = (n + 2)^2 - 2$

Ready to Go On?

Focus on Problem Solving

Make a Plan

- **Choose a method of computation**

When solving problems, you must decide which calculation method is best: paper and pencil, calculator, or mental math. Your decision will be based on many factors, such as the problem context, the numbers involved, and your own number sense. Use the following table as a guideline.

Paper and Pencil	Calculator	Mental Math
Use when solving multi-step problems so you can see how the steps relate.	Use when working complex operations.	Use when performing basic operations or generating simple estimates.

For each problem, tell whether you would use a calculator, mental math, or pencil and paper. Justify your choice, and then solve the problem.

1. The local high school radio station has 500 CDs. Each week, the music manager gets 25 new CDs. How many CDs will the station have in 8 weeks?

2. There are 360 deer in a forest. The population each year is 10% more than the previous year. How many deer will there be after 3 years?

3. Heidi works 8-hour shifts frosting cakes. She has frosted 12 cakes so far, and she thinks she can frost 4 cakes an hour during the rest of her shift. How many more hours will it take for her to frost a total of 32 cakes?

4. Kai has $170 in a savings account that earns 3% simple interest each year. How much interest will he have earned in 14 years?

5. A company's logo is in the shape of an isosceles triangle. When appearing on the company's stationery, the logo has a base of 5.1 cm and legs measuring 6.9 cm each. When appearing on a company poster, the similar logo has a base of 14.79 cm. Estimate the length of each leg of the logo on the poster.

6. Margo and her friends decided to hike the Wildcat Rock trail. After hiking $\frac{1}{4}$ of the way, they turned back because it began to rain. How far did they hike in all?

Trail	Distance (mi)
Meadowlark	$5\frac{3}{8}$
Key Lake	$4\frac{1}{2}$
Wildcat Rock	$6\frac{1}{4}$
Eagle Lookout	8

13-4 Linear Functions

Learn to identify linear functions.

Vocabulary

linear function

function notation

When filled, a space shuttle's main fuel tank holds about 529,000 gallons of liquid hydrogen and liquid oxygen. During lift-off, this fuel flows to the engines at a rate of 1035 gallons per second.

Fuel Remaining in Tank					
Time (s)	0	1	2	3	4
Fuel (gal)	529,000	527,965	526,930	525,895	524,860

Notice that the fuel amounts form an arithmetic sequence with common difference of −1035. Also, the data can be plotted on a coordinate plane as a line with slope −1035 and y-intercept 529,000.

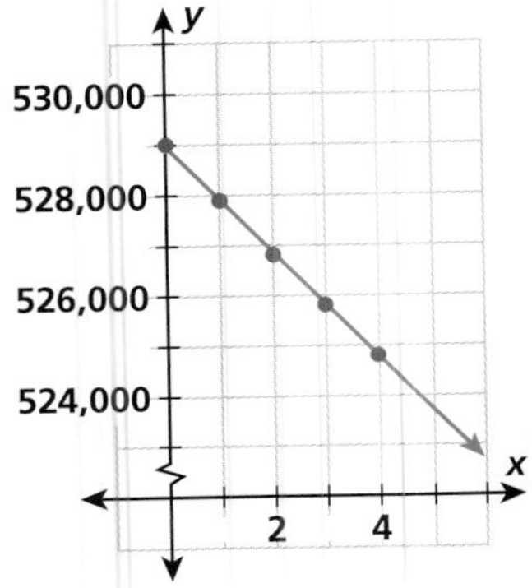

A **linear function** can be described by a linear equation. You can use **function notation** to show that the output value of the function f, written $f(x)$, corresponds to the input value x.

Reading Math

$f(x)$ is read "f of x."
$f(1)$ is read "f of 1."

$f(x) = 2x$ *The output y is the rule of f applied to x.*

$f(1) = 2(1)$ *f(1) means evaluate f(x) for x = 1.*

The graph of a linear function is a line. The linear function $f(x) = mx + b$ has a **slope** of m and a **y-intercept** of b.

EXAMPLE 1 Identifying Linear Functions

Determine whether $f(x) = 2x - 2$ is linear.

$f(x) = 2x - 2$

Graph the function.

$f(x) = 2x - 2$ does represent a linear function because its graph is a straight line. It has a slope of 2 and a y-intercept of −2.

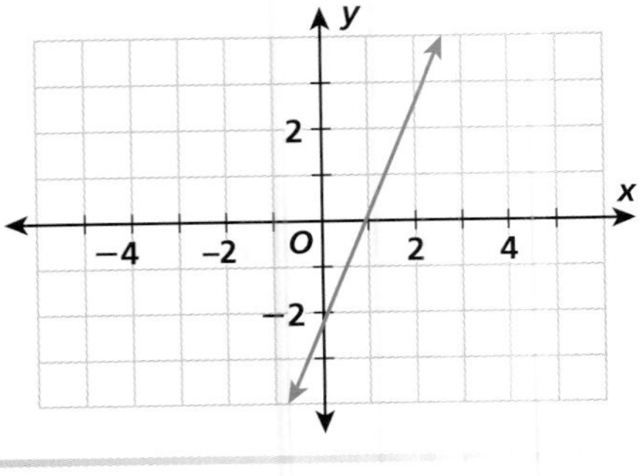

EXAMPLE 2 Writing the Equation for a Linear Function

Write a rule for each linear function.

A

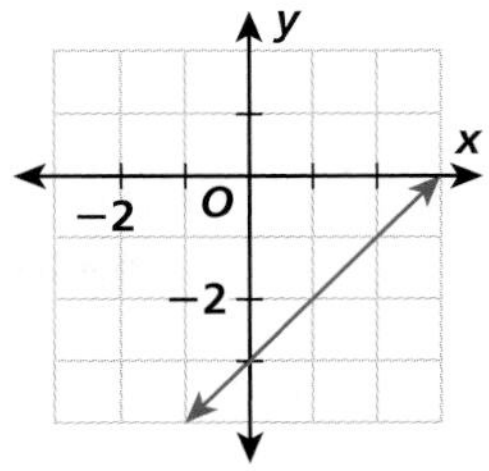

Step 1 Identify the y-intercept b from the graph.

$b = -3$

Step 2 Locate another point (x, y).

$(1, -2)$

Step 3 Substitute the x- and y-values into the equation $f(x) = mx + b$, and solve for m.

$-2 = m(1) + -3$

$1 = m$

The rule is $f(x) = 1x + (-3)$ or $f(x) = x - 3$.

B

x	y
−2	−16
−1	−13
1	−7
2	−4

Step 1 Locate two points.

$(1, -7)$ and $(2, -4)$

Step 2 Find the slope m.

$$m = \frac{y_2 - y_1}{x_2 - x_1} = \frac{-4 - (-7)}{2 - 1} = 3$$

Step 3 Substitute the x- and y-values into the equation $f(x) = mx + b$, and solve for m.

$-7 = 3(1) + b$

$-10 = b$

The rule is $f(x) = 3x + (-10)$ or $f(x) = 3x - 10$.

EXAMPLE 3 *Physical Science Application*

At lift-off, the space shuttle's main fuel tank contains about 529,000 gallons of liquid hydrogen and liquid oxygen. This fuel flows to the engines at a rate of 1035 gallons per second. Find a rule for the linear function that describes the amount remaining in the tank. Use it to find out how much fuel is left after 8 minutes.

$f(x) = mx + 529{,}000$ — *The y-intercept is the volume of fuel at lift-off, 529,000 gal.*

$527{,}965 = m(1) + 529{,}000$ — *At 1 s after lift-off, there are 529,000 − 1035, or 527,965, gal remaining.*

$527{,}965 = m + 529{,}000$

$\underline{-529{,}000} \qquad \underline{-529{,}000}$

$-1035 = m$

The rule for the function is $f(x) = -1035x + 529{,}000$.

After 8 minutes, or 480 seconds, there will be $f(480) = -1035(480) + 529{,}000 = 32{,}200$ gal.

Think and Discuss

1. **Describe** how to use a graph to find the equation of a linear function.

13-4 Exercises

go.hrw.com
Homework Help Online
KEYWORD: MT7 13-4
Parent Resources Online
KEYWORD: MT7 Parent

GUIDED PRACTICE

See Example 1

Determine whether each function is linear.

1. $f(x) = x + 3$
2. $f(x) = x^3 + 1$
3. $f(x) = 6x - 3$

See Example 2

Write a rule for each linear function.

4.

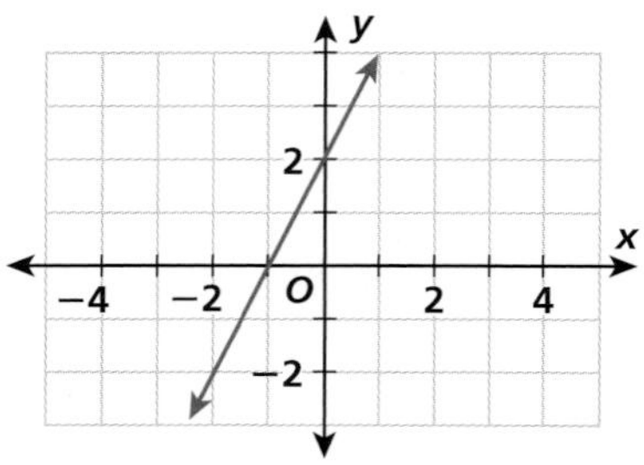

5.

x	y
−1	6
0	4
1	2
2	0

See Example 3

6. Liza earns \$480 per week for 40 hours of work. If she works overtime, she makes \$18 per overtime hour. Find a rule for the linear function that describes her weekly salary if she works x hours of overtime. Use it to find how much Liza earns if she works 6 hours of overtime.

INDEPENDENT PRACTICE

See Example 1

Determine whether each function is linear.

7. $f(x) = -4x + 8$
8. $f(x) = -\frac{3}{4}x - 5$
9. $f(x) = \frac{7}{x}$

See Example 2

Write a rule for each linear function.

10.

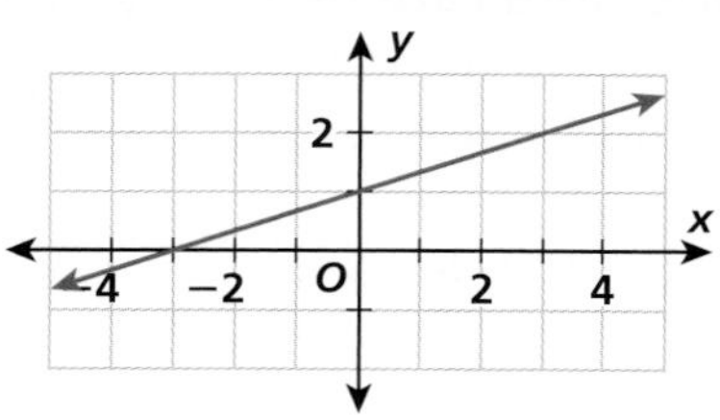

11.

x	y
−1	−11
0	−5
1	1
2	7

See Example 3

12. A swimming pool contains 1500 gallons of water. The pool is being drained for the season at a rate of 35 gallons per minute. Find a rule for the linear function that describes the amount of water in the tank. Use it to determine how much will be in the tank after 25 minutes.

PRACTICE AND PROBLEM SOLVING

Extra Practice
See page 807.

13. **Estimation** Suppose a baby weighed 8 pounds at birth, and gained about 1.2 pounds each month during the first year of life. To the nearest pound, approximately what was the weight of the baby during the seventh month?

LINK

Recreation

The volume of a typical hot air balloon is between 65,000 and 105,000 cubic feet. Most hot air balloons fly at altitudes of 1000 to 1500 feet.

go.hrw.com
Web Extra!
KEYWORD: MT7 Balloons

14. **Economics** *Linear depreciation* means that the same amount is subtracted each year from the value of an item. Suppose a car valued at \$17,440 depreciates \$1375 each year for x years.
    a. Write a linear function for the car's value after x years.
    b. What will the car's value be in 7 years?

15. **Recreation** A hot air balloon at a height of 1245 feet above sea level is ascending at a rate of 5 feet per second.
    a. Write a linear function that describes the balloon's height after x seconds.
    b. What will the balloon's height be in 5 minutes? How high will it have climbed from its original starting point?

16. **Business** The table shows a carpenter's cost for wood and the price the carpenter charges the customer for the wood.

Carpenter Cost	\$45	\$52	\$60.50	\$80
Selling Price	\$54	\$62.40	\$72.60	\$96

    a. Write a linear function for the selling price of wood that costs the carpenter x dollars.
    b. If the cost to the carpenter is \$340, what is the customer's cost?

17. **What's the Question?** Consider the function $f(x) = -2x + 6$. If the answer is -4, what is the question?

18. **Write About It** Explain how you can determine whether a function is linear without graphing it or making a table of values.

19. **Challenge** What is the only kind of line on a coordinate plane that is not a linear function? Give an example of such a line.

TEST PREP and Spiral Review

20. **Multiple Choice** The function $f(x) = 12{,}800 - 1100x$ gives the value of a car x years after it was purchased. What will the car's value be in 8 years?

    Ⓐ \$4000 Ⓑ \$5100 Ⓒ \$6200 Ⓓ \$7300

21. **Extended Response** A swimming pool contains 1800 gallons of water. It is being drained at a rate of 50 gallons per minute. Find a rule for the linear function that describes the amount of water in the pool. Use the rule to determine the amount of water in the pool after 30 minutes. After how many minutes will the pool be empty?

Multiply. Write each answer in simplest form. (Lesson 2-4)

22. $-8\left(3\frac{3}{4}\right)$ 23. $\frac{6}{7}\left(\frac{7}{19}\right)$ 24. $-\frac{5}{8}\left(-\frac{6}{15}\right)$ 25. $-\frac{9}{10}\left(\frac{7}{12}\right)$

Use a calculator to find each value. Round to the nearest tenth. (Lesson 4-6)

26. $\sqrt{35}$ 27. $\sqrt{45}$ 28. $\sqrt{55}$ 29. $\sqrt{65}$

13-5 Exponential Functions

Learn to identify and graph exponential functions.

Vocabulary

exponential function

exponential growth

exponential decay

Many computer viruses spread automatically by sending copies of themselves to all of the contacts in a computer user's e-mail address book. Suppose a certain computer virus is sent to 15 computers and infects 60 computers in 2 hours, 240 computers in 4 hours, 960 computers in 6 hours, and so on. The number of computers infected would form a geometric sequence.

A function rule that describes the pattern is $f(x) = 15(4)^x$, where 15 is a_1, the starting number, and 4 is r the common ratio. This type of function is an **exponential function**.

FORM OF AN EXPONENTIAL FUNCTION

An exponential function has the form $f(x) = a_1 \cdot r^x$, where $a_1 \neq 0$, $r > 0$, and $r \neq 1$.

In an exponential function, the **y-intercept** is $f(0) = a_1$. The expression r^x is defined for all values of x, so the domain of $f(x) = a_1 \cdot r^x$ is all real numbers.

EXAMPLE 1 Graphing Exponential Functions

Create a table for each exponential function, and use it to graph the function.

A $f(x) = \frac{1}{2} \cdot 2^x$

x	y	
−2	$\frac{1}{8}$	$\frac{1}{2} \cdot 2^{-2} = \frac{1}{2} \cdot \frac{1}{4}$
−1	$\frac{1}{4}$	$\frac{1}{2} \cdot 2^{-1} = \frac{1}{2} \cdot \frac{1}{2}$
0	$\frac{1}{2}$	$\frac{1}{2} \cdot 2^{0} = \frac{1}{2} \cdot 1$
1	1	$\frac{1}{2} \cdot 2^{v} = \frac{1}{2} \cdot 2$
2	2	$\frac{1}{2} \cdot 2^{2} = \frac{1}{2} \cdot 4$

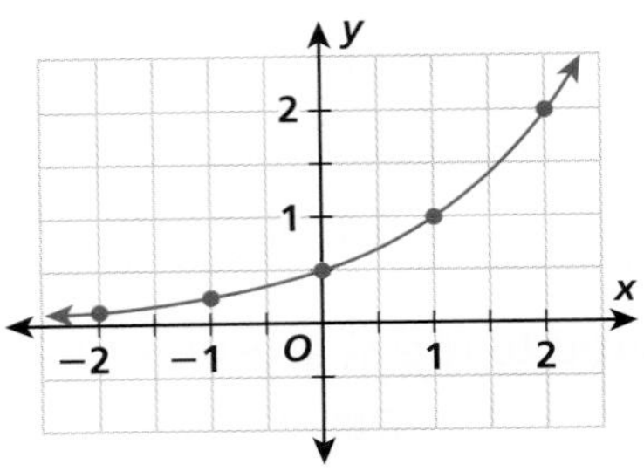

B $f(x) = 2 \cdot \left(\frac{1}{2}\right)^x$

x	y	
−2	8	$2 \cdot \left(\frac{1}{2}\right)^{-2} = 2 \cdot 4$
−1	4	$2 \cdot \left(\frac{1}{2}\right)^{-1} = 2 \cdot 2$
0	2	$2 \cdot \left(\frac{1}{2}\right)^{0} = 2 \cdot 1$
1	1	$2 \cdot \left(\frac{1}{2}\right)^{1} = 2 \cdot \frac{1}{2}$
2	$\frac{1}{2}$	$2 \cdot \left(\frac{1}{2}\right)^{2} = 2 \cdot \frac{1}{4}$

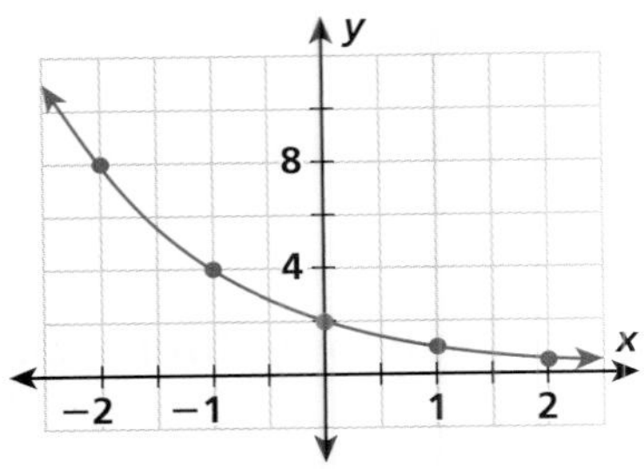

In the exponential function $f(x) = a_1 \cdot r^x$ if $r > 1$, the output gets larger as the input gets larger. In this case, f is called an **exponential growth** function.

EXAMPLE 2 Using an Exponential Growth Function

An e-mail computer virus was initially sent to 15 different computers. After 2 hours, it had infected 60 computers, after 4 hours, 240 computers, and after 6 hours, 960 computers. If this trend continues, how many computers will be infected after 24 hours?

Hours Elapsed	0	2	4	6
Number of Two-Hour Intervals	0	1	2	3
Computers Infected	15	60	240	960

$f(x) = a_1 \cdot r^x$ *Write the function.*

$f(x) = 15 \cdot r^x$ *$f(0) = a_1$*

$f(x) = 15 \cdot 4^x$ *The common ratio is 4.*

24 hours is 12 two-hour intervals, so let $x = 12$.

$f(12) = 15 \cdot 4^{12} = 251{,}658{,}240$ *Substitute 12 for x.*

251,658,240 computers will be infected in 24 hours.

In the exponential function $f(x) = a_1 \cdot r^x$, if $r < 1$, the output gets smaller as x gets larger. In this case, f is called an **exponential decay** function.

EXAMPLE 3 Using an Exponential Decay Function

Technetium-99m has a *half-life* of 6 hours, which means it takes 6 hours for half of the substance to decompose. Find the amount of technetium-99m remaining from a 100 mg sample after 90 hours.

Hours	0	6	12	18	24
Number of Half-lives x	0	1	2	3	4
Technetium-99m $f(x)$ (mg)	100	50	25	12.5	6.25

$f(x) = a_1 \cdot r^x$ *Write the function.*

$f(x) = 100 \cdot r^x$ *$f(0) = a_1$*

$f(x) = 100 \cdot \left(\frac{1}{2}\right)^x$ *The common ratio is $\frac{1}{2}$.*

Divide 90 hours by 6 hours to find the number of half-lives: $x = 15$.

$f(15) = 100 \cdot \left(\frac{1}{2}\right)^{15} \approx 0.003$ *Substitute 15 for x.*

There is approximately 0.003 mg left after 90 hours.

LINK

Physical Science

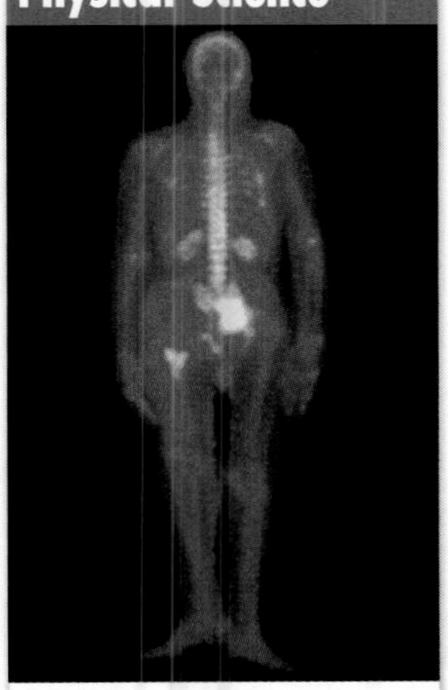

Technetium-99m is used to diagnose diseases in humans and animals.

Think and Discuss

1. **Compare** the graphs of exponential growth and decay functions.

13-5 Exercises

go.hrw.com
Homework Help Online
KEYWORD: MT7 13-5
Parent Resources Online
KEYWORD: MT7 Parent

GUIDED PRACTICE

See Example 1

Create a table for each exponential function, and use it to graph the function.

1. $f(x) = 2^x$
2. $f(x) = 50 \cdot \left(\frac{1}{3}\right)^x$
3. $f(x) = 2 \cdot 3^x$
4. $f(x) = 0.02 \cdot 4^x$
5. $f(x) = 5 \cdot -(2^x)$
6. $f(x) = \frac{1}{2} \cdot 3^x$

See Example 2

7. At the beginning of an experiment, a bacteria colony has a mass of 3×10^{-7} grams. If the mass of the colony triples every 10 hours, predict what the mass of the colony will be after 50 hours.

See Example 3

8. Radioactive glucose is used in cancer detection. It has a half-life of 100 minutes. Predict how much of a 100 mg sample remains after 24 hours.

INDEPENDENT PRACTICE

See Example 1

Create a table for each exponential function, and use it to graph the function.

9. $f(x) = 2 \cdot 3^x$
10. $f(x) = -4(0.4)^x$
11. $f(x) = \left(\frac{3}{4}\right)^x$
12. $f(x) = 12\left(\frac{1}{6}\right)^x$
13. $f(x) = 1 \cdot 7^x$
14. $f(x) = 2.3 \cdot 5.1^x$

See Example 2

15. A group of environmentalists preserved 300 exotic birds at a wildlife sanctuary. The population will triple every 6 years. Write an exponential function to calculate the number of birds that will be at the sanctuary at the end of each 6-year period. What will the predicted population be in 18 years?

See Example 3

16. Cesium-137 is a radioactive element with a half-life of 30 years. It is used to study soil erosion. Predict how much of a 60 mg sample of cesium-137 would remain after 210 years.

PRACTICE AND PROBLEM SOLVING

Extra Practice
See page 807.

For each exponential function, find $f(-3)$, $f(0)$, and $f(3)$.

17. $f(x) = 2^x$
18. $f(x) = 0.3^x$
19. $f(x) = 10^x$
20. $f(x) = 200 \cdot \left(\frac{1}{2}\right)^x$

Write the equation of the exponential function that passes through the given points. Use the form $f(x) = p \cdot a^x$.

21. (0, 3) and (1, 6)
22. (0, 6) and (1, 2)
23. (0, 1) and (2, 16)

Graph the exponential function of the form $f(x) = p \cdot a^x$.

24. $p = 5, a = 3$
25. $p = -1, a = \frac{1}{4}$
26. $p = 100, a = 0.01$

27. **Physical Science** The current in a circuit dies off exponentially, losing half its strength every 2.5 milliseconds. Predict what percent of the original current remains after 15 milliseconds.

Health LINK

The half-life of a substance in the body is the amount of time it takes for your body to metabolize half of the substance. An exponential decay function can be used to model the amount of the substance in the body.

Acetaminophen is the active ingredient in many pain and fever medications. Use the table for Exercises 28–30.

Acetaminophen Levels in the Body				
Elapsed Time (hr)	0	3	5	6
Substance Remaining (mg)	160	80	50.4	40

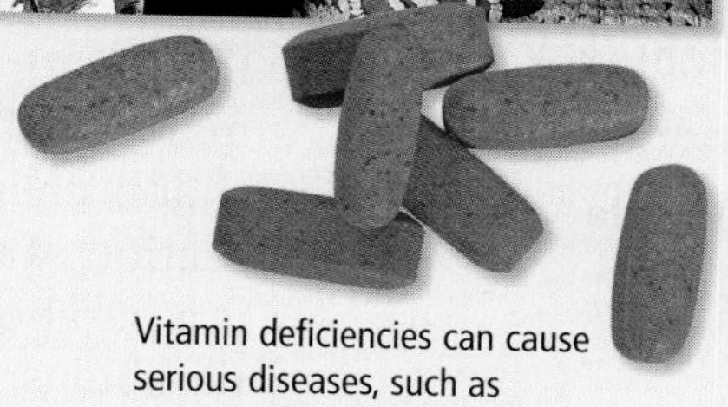

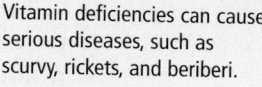

Vitamin deficiencies can cause serious diseases, such as scurvy, rickets, and beriberi.

28. How much acetaminophen was present initially?

29. Find the half-life of acetaminophen. Write an exponential function that describes the level of acetaminophen in the body.

30. If you take 500 mg of acetaminophen, what percent of that amount will be in your system after 9 hours?

31. **Write About It** The half-life of vitamin C is about 6 hours. If you take a 60 mg vitamin C tablet at 9:00 A.M., how much of the vitamin will still be present in your system at 9:00 P.M.? Explain.

Sources of caffeine include coffee, sodas, and some pain medications.

32. **Challenge** In children, the half-life of caffeine is about 3 hours. If a child has a 12 oz soft drink containing 40 mg caffeine at noon and another at 6:00 P.M., about how much caffeine will be present at 10:00 P.M.?

TEST PREP and Spiral Review

33. **Multiple Choice** The half-life of a particular radioactive isotope of thorium is 8 minutes. If 160 grams of the isotope are initially present, how many grams will remain after 40 minutes?

Ⓐ 1.25 grams Ⓑ 2.5 grams Ⓒ 5 grams Ⓓ 10 grams

34. **Gridded Response** Use the exponential function $f(x) = 5^x$. What is the value of $f(4)$?

Find the volume of each cone to the nearest cubic unit. (Lesson 8-6)

35. radius 10 mm; height 12 mm

36. diameter 4 ft; height 5.7 ft

Two fair number cubes are rolled. Find the probability of each event. (Lesson 10-4)

37. P(two odd numbers)

38. P(a two and a prime number)

13-6 Quadratic Functions

Learn to identify and graph quadratic functions.

Vocabulary

quadratic function

parabola

A **quadratic function** contains a variable that is squared. In the quadratic function

$$f(x) = ax^2 + bx + c$$

the *y*-intercept is *c*. The graphs of all quadratic functions have the same basic shape, called a **parabola**. The cross section of the large mirror in a telescope is a parabola. Because of a property of parabolas, starlight that hits the mirror is reflected toward a single point, called the *focus*.

The mirror of this telescope is made of liquid mercury that is rotated to form a parabolic shape.

EXAMPLE 1 **Graphing Quadratic Functions**

Create a table for each quadratic function, and use it to graph the function.

A $f(x) = x^2 - 3$

x	$f(x) = x^2 - 3$
−3	$(-3)^2 - 3 = 6$
−2	$(-2)^2 - 3 = 1$
−1	$(-1)^2 - 3 = -2$
0	$(0)^2 - 3 = -3$
1	$(1)^2 - 3 = -2$
2	$(2)^2 - 3 = 1$
3	$(3)^2 - 3 = 6$

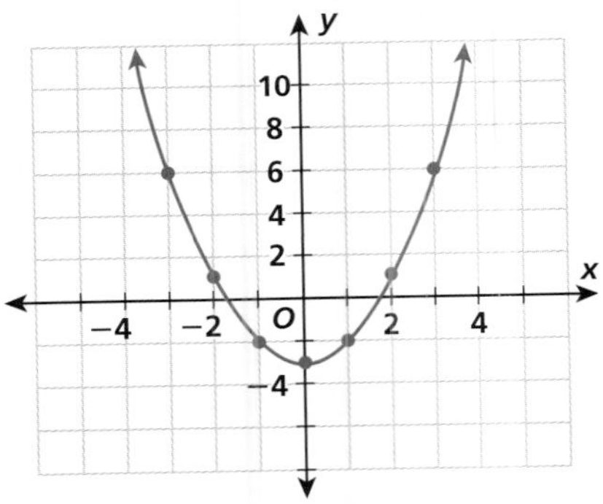

Plot the points and connect them with a smooth curve.

B $f(x) = x^2 + x - 2$

x	$f(x) = x^2 + x - 2$
−3	$(-3)^2 + (-3) - 2 = 4$
−2	$(-2)^2 + (-2) - 2 = 0$
−1	$(-1)^2 + (-1) - 2 = -2$
0	$(0)^2 + 0 - 2 = -2$
1	$(1)^2 + 1 - 2 = 0$
2	$(2)^2 + 2 - 2 = 4$
3	$(3)^2 + 3 - 2 = 10$

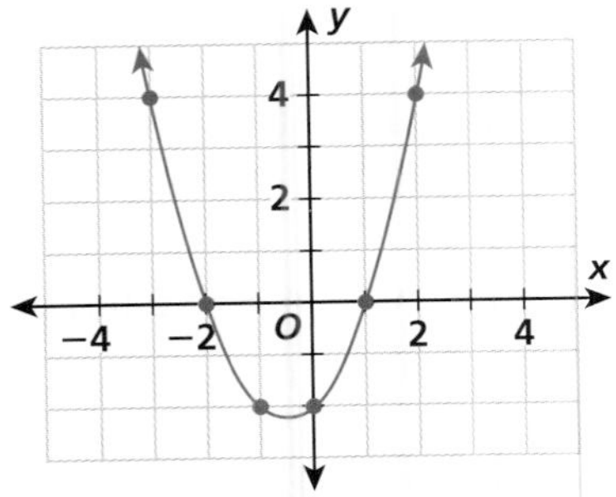

Plot the points and connect them with a smooth curve.

EXAMPLE 2 *Astronomy Application*

In a *liquid mirror,* a container of liquid mercury is rotated around an axis. Gravity and centrifugal force cause the liquid to form a parabolic shape. The cross section of a liquid mirror that rotates at 10 revolutions per minute is approximated by the graph of $f(x) = 0.027x^2$. If the diameter of the mirror is 3 m, about how much higher are the sides than the center?

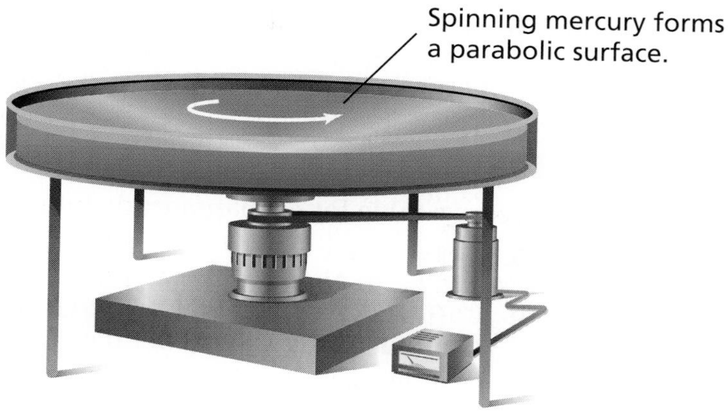

First create a table of values. Then graph the cross section.

x	$f(x)$
-2	$0.027(-2)^2 = 0.108$
-1	$0.027(-1)^2 = 0.027$
0	$0.027(0)^2 = 0$
1	$0.027(1)^2 = 0.027$
2	$0.027(2)^2 = 0.108$

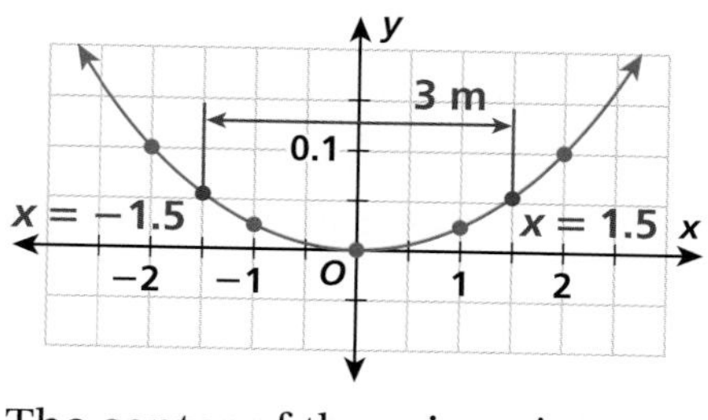

The center of the mirror is at $x = 0$, and the height is 0 m. If the diameter of the mirror is 3 m, the highest point on the sides is at $x = 1.5$. The height is $f(1.5) = 0.027(1.5)^2 \approx 0.06$ m. The sides are about 0.06 m higher than the center.

Think and Discuss

1. Compare the graphs of $f(x) = x^2$ and $f(x) = x^2 + 1$.

2. Describe the shape of a parabola.

13-6 Exercises

go.hrw.com
Homework Help Online
KEYWORD: MT7 13-6
Parent Resources Online
KEYWORD: MT7 Parent

GUIDED PRACTICE

See Example 1

Create a table for each quadratic function, and use it to graph the function.

1. $f(x) = x^2 + 5$
2. $f(x) = x^2 - 3$
3. $f(x) = x^2 + 1.5x$

See Example 2

4. **Sports** The function $f(t) = -0.15t^2 + 2.4t + 5.1$ gives the height in feet of a baseball t seconds after it was thrown. What was the height of the baseball when it was initially thrown ($t = 0$)?

INDEPENDENT PRACTICE

See Example 1

Create a table for each quadratic function, and use it to graph the function.

5. $f(x) = x^2 + x + 2$
6. $f(x) = -x^2 + 2$
7. $f(x) = 3x^2 - 2$

See Example 2

8. **Manufacturing** The function $f(x) = 2x^2 - 300x + 14{,}450$ gives the cost of manufacturing x items per day. Which number of items will give the lowest cost per day: 40, 75, or 90? What will the cost be?

PRACTICE AND PROBLEM SOLVING

Extra Practice
See page 817.

Find $f(-3)$, $f(0)$, and $f(3)$ for each quadratic function.

9. $f(x) = x^2 + 6$
10. $f(x) = \frac{1}{2}x^2$
11. $f(x) = x^2 + 3x$
12. $f(x) = x^2 + 9$
13. $f(x) = 3x^2 - x + 7$
14. $f(x) = \frac{x^2}{3} - 1$

Create a table for each quadratic function, and use it to find the x-intercepts.

15. $f(x) = (x - 4)(x + 12)$
16. $f(x) = (x - 2)(x - 5)$
17. $f(x) = (x - 1)(x + 3)$
18. $f(x) = x\,(x - 9)$

19. The sum of two numbers is 12. The sum of their squares is given by the function $f(x) = x^2 + (12 - x)^2$. Create a table of values using $x = 4, 5, 6, 7,$ and 8. Which pair of numbers gives the least sum of squares? What is the sum of their squares?

20. **Hobbies** The height of a model airplane launched from the top of a 24 ft hill is given by the function $f(t) = -0.08t^2 + 2.6t + 24$. Find the height of the airplane after 4, 8, and 16 seconds. Round to the nearest tenth of a foot. What can you tell about the direction of the airplane?

21. **Physical Science** The height of a toy rocket launched straight up with an initial velocity of 48 feet per second is given by the function $f(t) = 48t - 16t^2$. The time t is in seconds.
    a. Graph the function for $t = 0, 0.5, 1, 1.5, 2, 2.5,$ and 3.
    b. When is the rocket at its highest point? What is its height?
    c. How many seconds does it take for the rocket to land?

22. Describe the difference between a linear function and a quadratic function in terms of their graphs and their function equations.

23. Business A store owner can sell 30 digital cameras a week at a price of $150 each. For every $5 drop in price, she can sell 2 more cameras a week. If x is the number of $5 price reductions, the weekly sales function is $f(x) = (30 + 2x)(150 - 5x)$.

Predicted Sales			
Price	$150	$145	$140
Number Sold	30	32	34
Weekly Sales	$4500	$4640	$4760

a. Find $f(x)$ for $x = 3, 4, 5, 6$, and 7.

b. How many $5 price reductions will result in the highest weekly sales?

24. Critical Thinking The height of an object dropped from the top of a 16 ft ladder is given by the function $f(t) = -t^2 + 16$. Find $f(4)$. What does this tell you about $t = 4$ seconds? Does this equation seem more realistic for dropping a rock or a feather? Explain.

25. Choose a Strategy Suppose the function $f(x) = -5x^2 + 300x + 1250$ gives a company's profit for producing x items. How many items should be produced to maximize profit?

Ⓐ 25 Ⓑ 30 Ⓒ 35 Ⓓ 40

26. Write About It Which will grow faster as x gets larger, $f(x) = x^2$ or $f(x) = 2^x$? Check by testing each function for several values of x.

27. Challenge Create a table of values for the quadratic function $f(x) = -3(x^2 + 1)$, and then graph it. What are the x-intercepts of the function?

Test Prep and Spiral Review

28. Multiple Choice The height of a tennis ball thrown straight up with an initial velocity of 64 meters per second is given by the function $f(t) = 64t - 16t^2$. The time t is in seconds. How many seconds does it take for the tennis ball to land?

Ⓕ 0 s Ⓖ 4 s Ⓗ 16 s Ⓙ 64 s

29. Gridded Response What is the positive x-intercept of the quadratic function $f(x) = x^2 + 2x - 36$?

The scale of a drawing is 2 in. = 3 ft. Find the actual measurement for each length in the drawing. (Lesson 5-8)

30. 1 in. **31.** 5 in. **32.** 12 in. **33.** 8.5 in.

Find the first and third quartiles for each data set. (Lesson 9-4)

34. 55, 60, 40, 45, 70, 65, 35, 40, 75, 50, 60, 80

35. 52, 22, 18, 30, 41, 23, 31, 23, 39, 37

Technology LAB 13-6

Explore Cubic Functions

Use with Lesson 13-6

go.hrw.com
Lab Resources Online
KEYWORD: MT7 Lab13

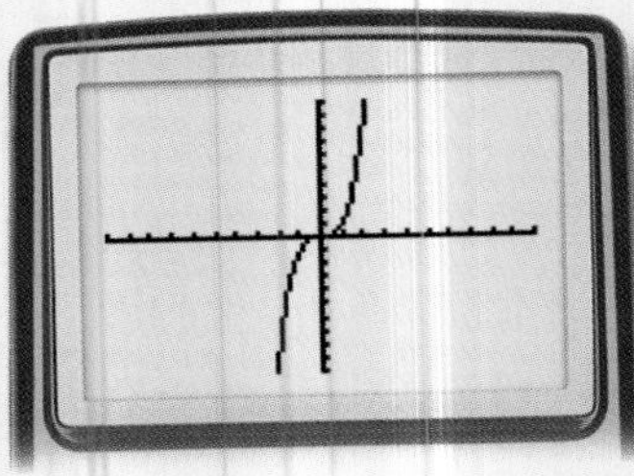

You can use your graphing calculator to explore cubic functions. To graph the cubic equation $y = x^3$ in the standard graphing calculator window, press [Y=]; enter the right side of the equation, [X,T,θ,n] [^] 3; and press [ZOOM] **6:ZStandard.**
Notice that the graph goes from the lower left to the upper right and crosses the x-axis once, at $x = 0$.

Activity 1

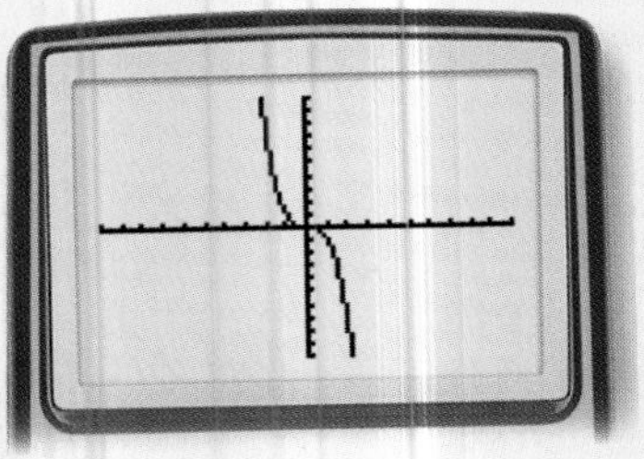

1 Graph $y = -x^3$. Describe the graph.

Press [Y=], and enter the right side of the equation, [(−)] [X,T,θ,n] [^] 3.

The graph goes from the upper left to the lower right and crosses the x-axis once.

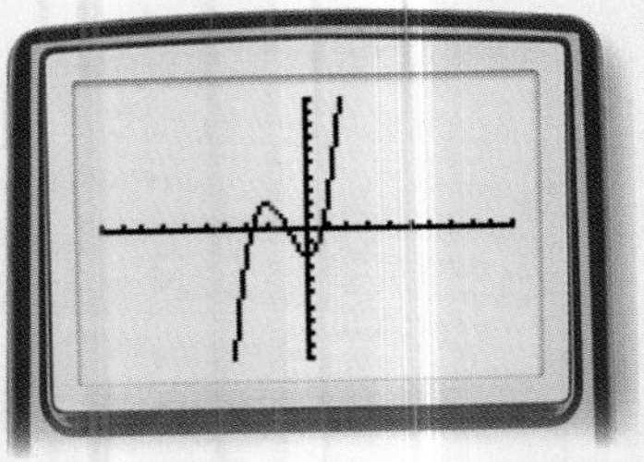

2 Graph $y = x^3 + 3x^2 - 2$. Describe the graph.

Press [Y=]; enter the right side of the equation, [X,T,θ,n] [^] 3 [+] 3 [X,T,θ,n] [x^2] [−] 2; and press [ZOOM] **6:ZStandard.**

The graph goes from the lower left to the upper right and crosses the x-axis three times.

Think and Discuss

1. How does the sign of the x^3-term affect the graph of a cubic function?

2. How could you find the value of 8^3 from the graph of $y = x^3$?

Try This

Graph each function and describe the graph.

1. $y = x^3 - 3$ **2.** $y = x^3 + 4x^2 - 3$ **3.** $y = (x - 3)^3$ **4.** $y = 6 - x^3$

Activity 2

1 Compare the graphs of $y = x^3$ and $y = x^3 + 3$.

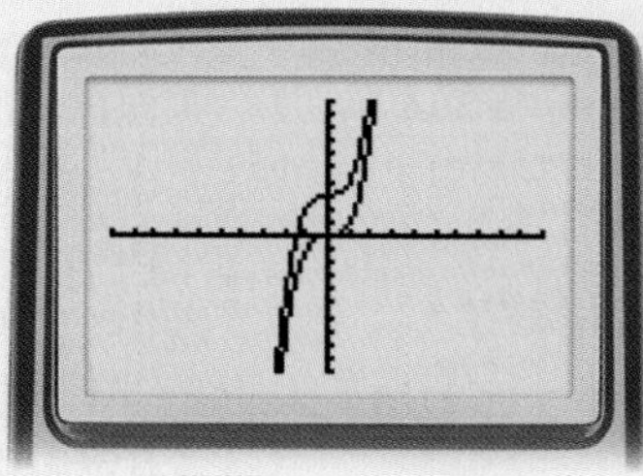

Graph **Y$_1$=X^3** and **Y$_2$=X^3+3** on the same screen, as shown. Use the TRACE button and the ◄ and ► buttons to trace to any integer value of x. Then use the ▲ and ▼ keys to move from one function to the other to compare the values of y for both functions for the value of x. You can also press 2nd GRAPH (TABLE) to see a table of values for both functions.

The graph of $y = x^3 + 3$ is translated up 3 units from the graph of $y = x^3$.

2 Compare the graphs of $y = x^3$ and $y = (x + 3)^3$.

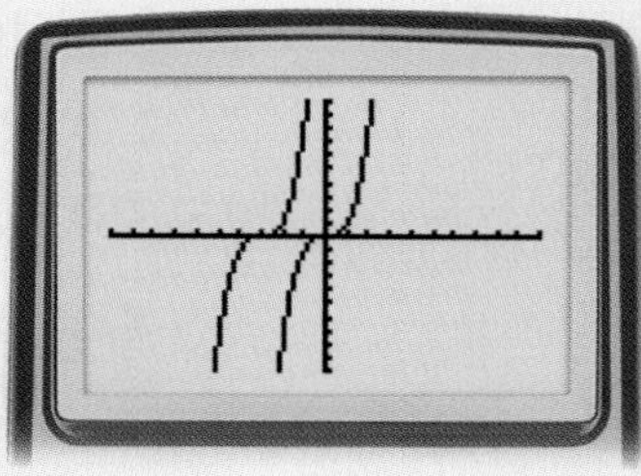

Graph **Y$_1$=X^3** and **Y$_2$=(X+3)^3** on the same screen. Notice that the graph of $y = (x + 3)^3$ is the graph of $y = x^3$ moved left 3 units. Press 2nd GRAPH (TABLE) to see a table of values. The graph of $y = (x + 3)^3$ is translated left 3 units from the graph of $y = x^3$.

3 Compare the graphs of $y = x^3$ and $y = 2x^3$.

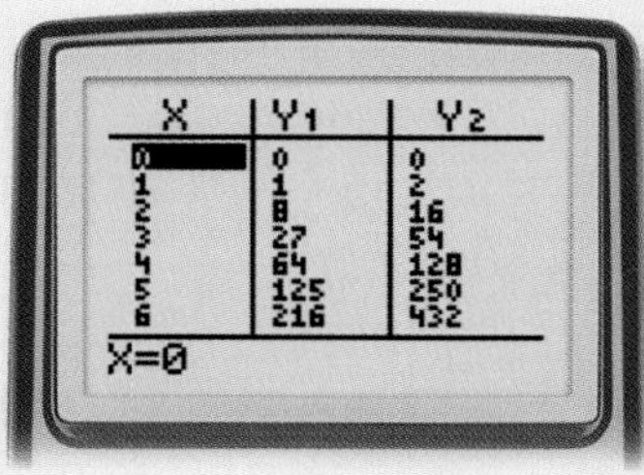

Graph **Y$_1$=X^3** and **Y$_2$=2X^3** on the same screen. Use the TRACE button and the arrow keys to see the values of y for any value of x. Press 2nd GRAPH (TABLE) to see a table of values.

The graph of $y = 2x^3$ is stretched upward from the graph of $y = x^3$. The y-value for $y = 2x^3$ increases twice as fast as it does for $y = x^3$. The table of values is shown.

Think and Discuss

1. What function would translate $y = x^3$ right 5 units?
2. Do you think that the methods shown of translating a cubic function would have the same result on a quadratic function? Explain.

Try This

Compare the graph of $y = x^3$ to the graph of each function.

1. $y = x^3 - 3$ **2.** $y = (x - 8)^3$ **3.** $y = \left(\frac{1}{3}\right)x^3$ **4.** $y = 7 - x^3$

13-7 Inverse Variation

Learn to recognize inverse variation by graphing tables of data.

Vocabulary

inverse variation

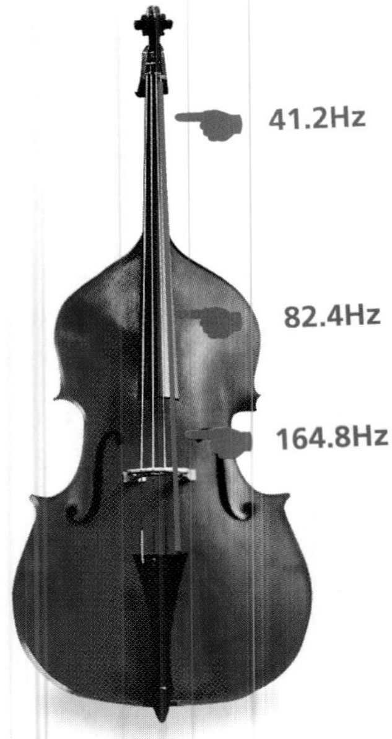

The frequency of a string on a double bass is related to its length. You can double a string's frequency by placing your finger at the halfway point of the string. The lowest note on a standard double bass is E_1. As you place your fingers at various fractions of the string's length, the frequency will *vary inversely*.

Full length: **41.2 Hz**
$\frac{1}{2}$ the length: **82.4 Hz**
$\frac{1}{4}$ the length: **164.8 Hz**

The fraction of the string length times the frequency is always 41.2.

INVERSE VARIATION		
Words	**Numbers**	**Algebra**
An **inverse variation** is a relationship in which one variable quantity increases as another variable quantity decreases. The product of the variables is a **constant**.	$y = \frac{120}{x}$ $xy = 120$	$y = \frac{k}{x}$ $xy = k$ $(k \neq 0)$

EXAMPLE 1 Identifying Inverse Variation

Determine whether each relationship is an inverse variation.

Helpful Hint

To determine if a relationship is an inverse variation, check if the product of x and y is always the same number.

A **The table shows the number of days needed to build a house based on the size of the work crew.**

Crew Size	3	4	6	12	24
Days of Construction	56	42	28	14	7

$3(56) = 168$; $4(42) = 168$; $6(28) = 168$; $12(14) = 168$; $24(7) = 168$
$xy = 168$ *The product is always the same.*
The relationship shows an inverse variation: $y = \frac{168}{x}$.

B **The table shows the number of CDs produced in a given time.**

CDs Produced	52	78	104	130	143	169
Time (min)	4	6	8	10	11	13

$52(4) = 208$; $78(6) = 468$ *The product is not always the same.*
The relationship is not an inverse variation.

In the inverse variation relationship $y = \frac{k}{x}$, where $k \neq 0$, y is a function of x. The function is not defined for $x = 0$, so the domain is all real numbers except 0.

EXAMPLE 2 Graphing Inverse Variations

Create a table. Then graph each inverse variation function.

A $f(x) = \frac{1}{x}$

x	y
-3	$-\frac{1}{3}$
-2	$-\frac{1}{2}$
-1	-1
$-\frac{1}{2}$	-2
$\frac{1}{2}$	2
1	1
2	$\frac{1}{2}$
3	$\frac{1}{3}$

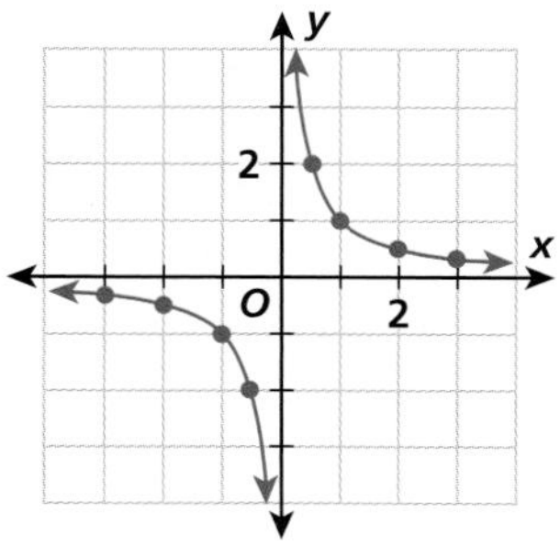

B $f(x) = \frac{-2}{x}$

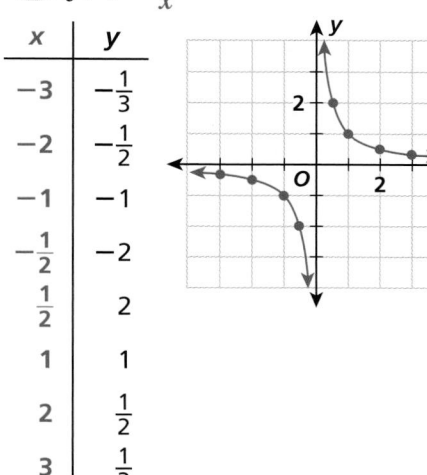

x	y
-3	$\frac{2}{3}$
-2	1
-1	2
$-\frac{1}{2}$	4
$\frac{1}{2}$	-4
1	-2
2	-1
3	$-\frac{2}{3}$

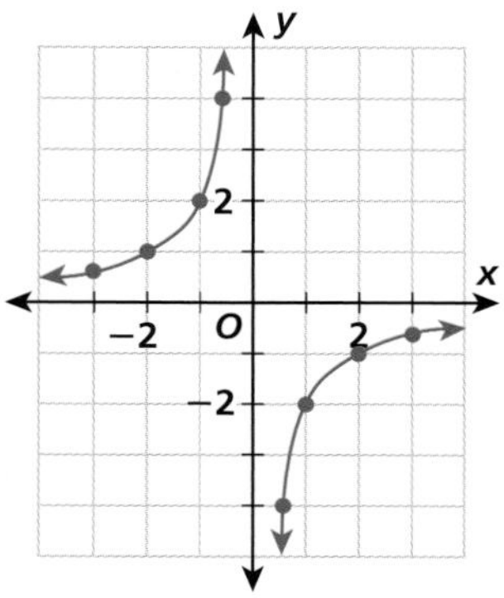

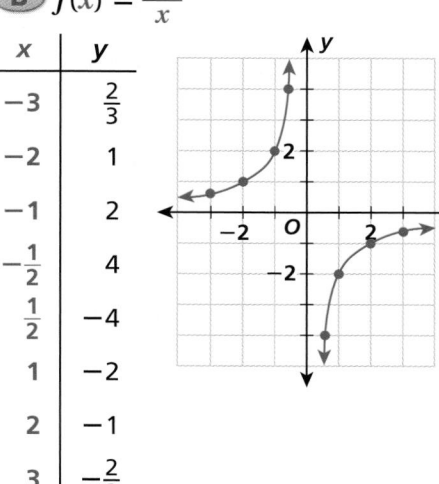

EXAMPLE 3 *Music Application*

The frequency of a double bass string changes according to the fraction of its length that is allowed to vibrate. Find the inverse variation function, and use it to find the resulting frequency when $\frac{1}{16}$ of the string E_1 is allowed to vibrate.

Frequency of E_1 by Fraction of the Original String Length				
Frequency (Hz)	41.2	82.4	164.8	329.6
Fraction of the Length	1	$\frac{1}{2}$	$\frac{1}{4}$	$\frac{1}{8}$

You can see from the table that $xy = 41.2(1) = 41.2$. So $y = \frac{41.2}{x}$. If the string is reduced to $\frac{1}{16}$ of its length, then its frequency will be $y = 41.2 \div \left(\frac{1}{16}\right) = 41.2 \cdot 16 = 659.2$ Hz. This note is called E_5.

Think and Discuss

1. **Identify** k in the inverse variation $y = \frac{3}{x}$.
2. **Describe** how you know if a relationship is an inverse variation.

13-7 Exercises

go.hrw.com
Homework Help Online
KEYWORD: MT7 13-7
Parent Resources Online
KEYWORD: MT7 Parent

GUIDED PRACTICE

See Example 1

Determine whether each relationship is an inverse variation.

1. The table shows the number of soccer balls produced in a given time.

Soccer Balls Produced	56	98	122	168	210
Time (min)	4	7	8	12	15

2. The table shows the painting time of a new house based on the number of workers.

Painting Time (hr)	6	7	10.5	21	42
Number of Workers	7	6	4	2	1

See Example 2

Create a table. Then graph each inverse variation function.

3. $f(x) = \frac{4}{x}$ **4.** $f(x) = \frac{3}{x}$ **5.** $f(x) = \frac{1}{3x}$ **6.** $f(x) = \frac{2}{3x}$

See Example 3

7. Ohm's law relates the current in a circuit to the resistance. Find the inverse variation function, and use it to find the current in a 12-volt circuit with 16 ohms of resistance.

Current (amps)	0.15	0.2	1	3	6
Resistance (ohms)	80	60	12	4	2

INDEPENDENT PRACTICE

See Example 1

Determine whether each relationship is an inverse variation.

8. The table shows the time it takes a model car to travel a certain distance, depending on the speed of the car.

Speed of Car (ft/s)	40	48	60	80	120
Time (s)	3	2.5	2	1.5	1

9. The table shows the number of miles bicycled in a given time.

Miles Bicycled	1	2	2.5	5	6
Time (min)	6	12	15	30	36

See Example 2

Create a table. Then graph each inverse variation function.

10. $f(x) = -\frac{2}{x}$ **11.** $f(x) = \frac{1}{4x}$ **12.** $f(x) = -\frac{1}{3x}$ **13.** $f(x) = -\frac{4}{5x}$

See Example 3

14. According to Boyle's law, when the volume of a gas decreases, the pressure increases. Find the inverse variation function, and use it to find the pressure of the gas if the volume is decreased to 8 liters.

Volume (L)	2	4	25	40	50
Pressure (atm)	20	10	1.6	1	0.8

PRACTICE AND PROBLEM SOLVING

Extra Practice
See page 807.

Find the inverse variation equation, given that x and y vary inversely.

15. $y = 3$ when $x = 3$ **16.** $y = 10$ when $x = 2$ **17.** $y = 13$ when $x = 2$

18. If y varies inversely with x and $y = 24$ when $x = 4$, find k.

19. The height of a triangle with area 72 cm^2 varies inversely with the length of its base. If $b = 48$ cm when $h = 3$ cm, find b when $h = 12$ cm.

20. Physical Science If a constant force of 20 newtons (N) is applied to an object, the mass of the object varies inversely with its acceleration. The table contains data for several objects of different sizes.

Mass (kg)	2	5	20	10	4
Acceleration (m/s^2)	10	4	1	2	5

a. Use the table to write an inverse variation function.

b. What is the mass of an object if its acceleration is 8 m/s^2?

21. Finance Mr. Anderson wants to earn \$50 in interest over a 1-year period from a savings account. The principal he must deposit varies inversely with the interest rate of the account. If the interest rate is 5%, he must deposit \$1000. If the interest rate is 3.125%, how much must he deposit?

22. Write a Problem Write a problem that can be solved using inverse variation. Use facts and formulas from your science book.

23. Write About It Explain the difference between direct variation and inverse variation.

24. Challenge The resistance of a 100 ft piece of wire varies inversely with the square of its diameter. If the diameter of the wire is 3 in., it has a resistance of 3 ohms. What is the resistance of a wire with a diameter of 1 in.?

TEST PREP and Spiral Review

25. Multiple Choice If y varies inversely with x and $y = 16$ when $x = 8$, what is k?

Ⓐ 2 Ⓑ 4 Ⓒ 64 Ⓓ 128

26. Gridded Response If y varies inversely with x and $y = 24$ when $x = 3$, what is the value of x when $y = 18$?

Solve. (Lesson 2-7)

27. $x - \frac{3}{2} = \frac{7}{2}$ **28.** $-\frac{3}{4}x + 6 = 8$ **29.** $\frac{1}{2}x - \frac{2}{3} = 6$

Solve each inequality. (Lesson 11-5)

30. $12x - 4 > 3x + 14$ **31.** $6p + 11 < 10 + 5p$ **32.** $5 + 4k \geq 18 + 2k$

CHAPTER 13

READY TO GO ON?

SECTION 13B

Quiz for Lessons 13-4 Through 13-7

13-4 Linear Functions

Determine whether each function is linear.

1. $f(x) = 2x^3$
2. $f(x) = 3x + 1$
3. $f(x) = \frac{2}{3}x - 2$
4. Write a rule for the linear function.

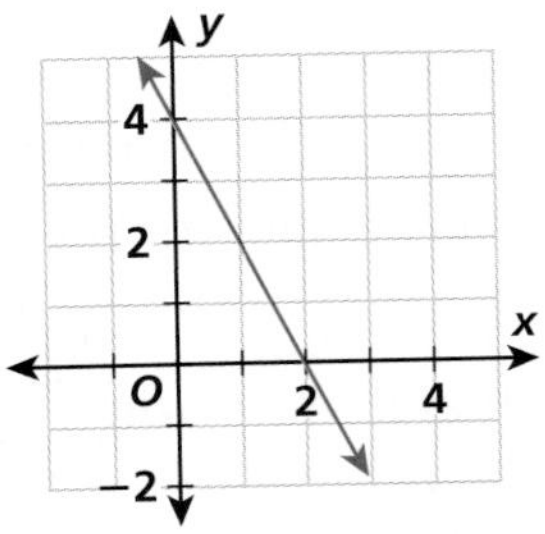

5. Kayo earns \$560 per week. If she works overtime, she makes \$21 per overtime hour. Find a rule for the linear function that describes her weekly salary if she works x hours of overtime. Use the rule to find how much Kayo earns if she works 8 hours of overtime.

13-5 Exponential Functions

Create a table for each exponential function, and use it to graph the function.

6. $f(x) = 3^x$
7. $f(x) = 0.01 \cdot 5^x$
8. $f(x) = \left(\frac{2}{3}\right)^x$
9. Ernio invested \$500 in an account where his balance will double every 8 years. Write an exponential function to calculate his account balance. What will his balance be in 32 years?

13-6 Quadratic Functions

Create a table for each quadratic function, and use it to graph the function.

10. $f(x) = x^2 + 4$
11. $f(x) = x^2 + 2.5x$
12. The function $f(x) = 2x^2 - 300x + 14{,}450$ gives the cost of manufacturing x items per day. Which number of items will give the lowest cost per day: 50, 70, or 85? What will the cost be?

13-7 Inverse Variation

Create a table. Then graph each inverse variation function.

13. $f(x) = \frac{2}{x}$
14. $f(x) = \frac{1}{2x}$
15. $f(x) = \frac{1}{x}$

Ready to Go On?

MULTI-STEP TEST PREP

CHAPTER 13

Beset by Beavers Greg and Maria are wildlife biologists. They are studying beaver population trends in a national forest. There are currently 200 beavers in the forest. The table shows Greg's and Maria's predictions for the beaver population in future years.

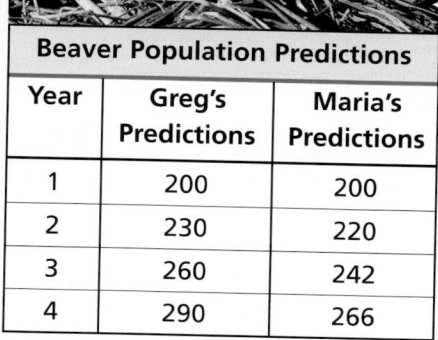

1. Write a rule based on Greg's prediction that gives the beaver population in year n. Then use the rule to find the population in year 8.
2. According to Greg's predictions, in what year will the beaver population be 500? Explain.
3. Write a rule based on Maria's prediction that gives the beaver population in year n. Then use the rule to find the population in year 8.
4. A third biologist, Amir, makes his predictions using the function $f(x) = 5x^2 + 195$, where x is the year. Use the function to find the beaver population that Amir predicts in year 8.
5. Which of the three biologists predicts the greatest beaver population in year 12? What is this population?

Beaver Population Predictions

Year	Greg's Predictions	Maria's Predictions
1	200	200
2	230	220
3	260	242
4	290	266

Game Time

Squared Away

How many squares can you find in the figure at right?

Did you find 30 squares?

There are four different-sized squares in the figure.

Size of Square	Number of Squares
4 × 4	1
3 × 3	4
2 × 2	9
1 × 1	16
	Total 30

3 × 3 squares

2 × 2 squares

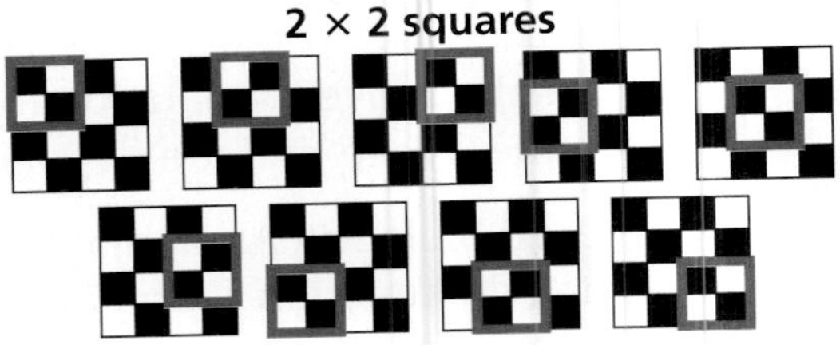

The total number of squares is $1 + 4 + 9 + 16 = 1^2 + 2^2 + 3^2 + 4^2$.

Draw a 5×5 grid and count the number of squares of each size. Can you see a pattern?

What is the total number of squares on a 6×6 grid? a 7×7 grid? Can you come up with a general formula for the sum of squares on an $n \times n$ grid?

What's Your Function?

One member from the first of two teams draws a function card from the deck, and the other team tries to guess the rule of the function. The guessing team gives a function input, and the card holder must give the corresponding output. Points are awarded based on the type of function and number of inputs required.

Complete rules and function cards are available online.

go.hrw.com
Game Time Extra
KEYWORD: MT7 Games

It's in the Bag!

Materials
- decorative paper
- glue
- markers

PROJECT Springboard to Sequences

Make this springy organizer to record notes on sequences and functions.

Directions

1. Cut out four squares of decorative paper that are 6 inches by 6 inches.
2. Fold one of the squares of paper in half vertically and then horizontally. Unfold the paper. Then fold the square diagonally and unfold the paper. **Figure A**
3. Fold the diagonal crease back and forth so that it is easy to work with. Then bring the two ends of the diagonal together as shown. **Figure B**
4. Fold the other squares of paper in the same way.
5. Insert one folded square into another—one facing up, the next facing down—so that a pair of inner faces match up. Glue the matching faces together. **Figure C**
6. Do the same with the remaining squares to complete the springboard.

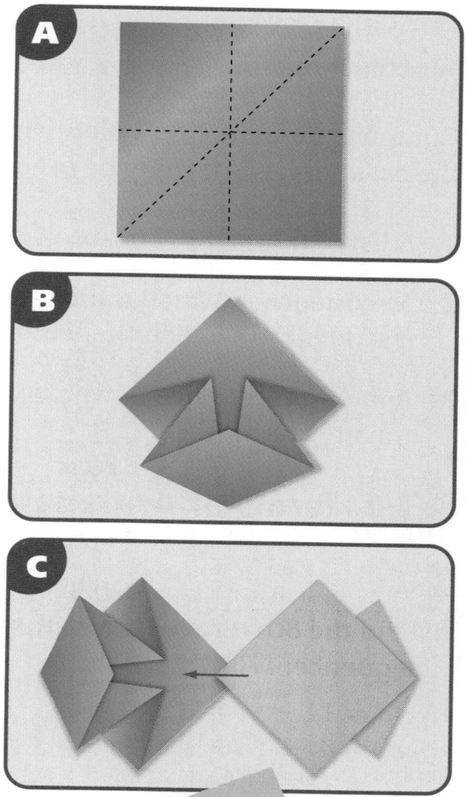

Taking Note of the Math

Write notes about sequences and functions on the various sections of the springboard.

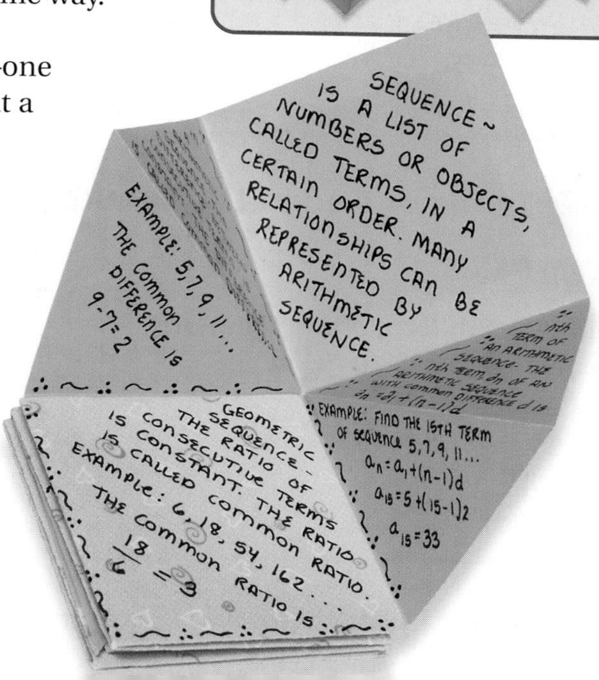

CHAPTER 13

Study Guide: Review

Vocabulary

common ratio 687
exponential decay 705
exponential function 704
exponential growth 705
Fibonacci sequence 695
first differences 693
function notation 700
geometric sequence 687
inverse variation 714
linear function 700
parabola 708
quadratic function 708
second differences 693

Complete the sentences below with vocabulary words from the list above. Words may be used more than once.

1. A list of numbers or terms in a certain order is called a(n) ___?___.
2. A sequence in which there is a common difference is a(n) ___?___; a sequence in which there is a common ratio is a(n) ___?___.
3. A famous sequence in which you add the two previous terms to find the next term is the ___?___.

13-1 Terms of Arithmetic Sequences (pp. 682–686)

EXAMPLE

- **Find the 8th term of the arithmetic sequence: 17, 14, 11, 8, ...**

$$d = 14 - 17 = -3$$
$$a_n = a_1 + (n-1)d$$
$$a_8 = 17 + (8-1)(-3)$$
$$a_8 = 17 - 21$$
$$a_8 = -4$$

EXERCISES

Find the given term in each arithmetic sequence.

4. 6th term: 4, 9, 14, . . .
5. 5th term: 0.05, 0.25, 0.45, . . .
6. 7th term: $\frac{1}{3}, \frac{5}{6}, \frac{4}{3}, \ldots$

13-2 Terms of Geometric Sequences (pp. 687–691)

EXAMPLE

- **Find the 8th term of the geometric sequence: 9, 18, 36, 72, ...**

$$r = \frac{18}{9} = 2$$
$$a_n = a_1 r^{n-1}$$
$$a_8 = 9(2)^{8-1} = 1152$$

EXERCISES

Find the given term in each geometric sequence.

7. 6th term: 3, −12, 48, −192, . . .
8. 5th term: $\frac{1}{4}, \frac{1}{5}, \frac{4}{25}, \ldots$
9. 40th term: 2, −2, 2, −2, . . .

13-3 Other Sequences (pp. 693–697)

EXAMPLE

- **Find the first four terms of the sequence defined by $a_n = -3(-1)^{n-1} - 2$.**

$a_1 = -3(-1)^{1-1} - 2 = -5$

$a_2 = -3(-1)^{2-1} - 2 = 1$

$a_3 = -3(-1)^{3-1} - 2 = -5$

$a_4 = -3(-1)^{4-1} - 2 = 1$

The first four terms are -5, 1, -5, and 1.

EXERCISES

Find the first four terms of each sequence defined by the given rule.

10. $a_n = 5n + 2$

11. $a_n = n^2 + 3$

12. $a_n = 6(-1)^n + 3n$

13. $a_n = n! + 1$

13-4 Linear Functions (pp. 700–703)

EXAMPLE

Write the rule for each linear function.

-

x	y
−2	−10
−1	−3
0	4
1	11

The y-intercept is $f(0) = 4$.

$f(x) = mx + 4$ $f(x) = mx + b$

Substitute and solve for m.

$11 = m(1) + 4$ $(x, y) = (1, 11)$

$7 = m$

$f(x) = 7x + 4$

- 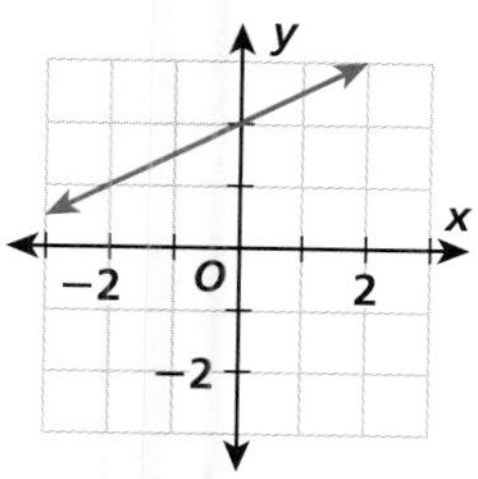

From the graph, $b = 2$.

$f(x) = mx + 2$

For point (2, 3):

$3 = m \cdot 2 + 2$

$-2 \qquad -2$

$\frac{1}{2} = \frac{m \cdot 2}{2}$

$\frac{1}{2} = m$

$f(x) = \frac{1}{2}m + 2$

EXERCISES

Write the equation for each linear function.

14.

x	y
−2	−3
−1	−2
0	−1
1	0

15.

x	y
−4	2
−2	3
0	4
2	5

16.

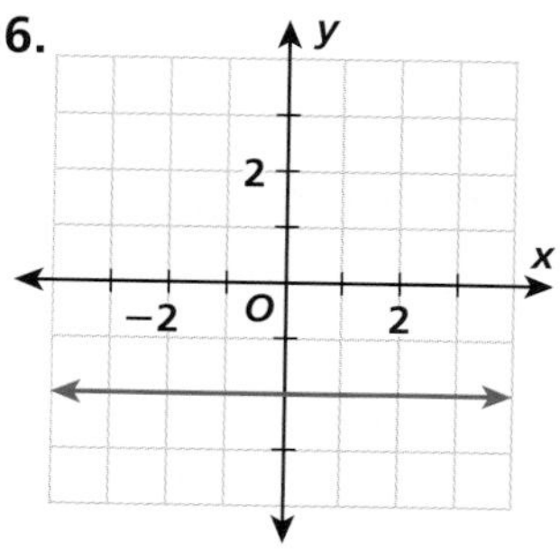

13-5 Exponential Functions (pp. 704–707)

EXAMPLE

■ **Graph the exponential function.**
$f(x) = 0.1 \cdot 4^x$

x	f(x)
−2	0.00625
−1	0.025
0	0.1
1	0.4
2	1.6

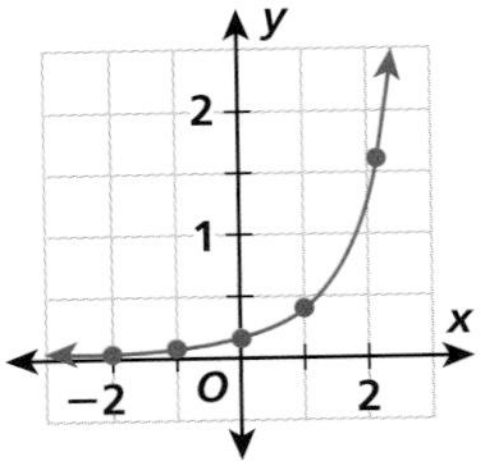

EXERCISES

Graph each exponential function.

17. $f(x) = 0.3 \cdot 4^x$

18. $f(x) = 6 \cdot \left(\frac{1}{3}\right)^x$

19. $f(x) = 3^x$

20. $f(x) = -3 \cdot 12^x$

13-6 Quadratic Functions (pp. 708–711)

EXAMPLE

■ **Graph the quadratic function.**
$f(x) = x^2 + 2x - 1$

x	f(x)
−3	2
−2	−1
−1	−2
0	−1
1	2
2	7
3	14

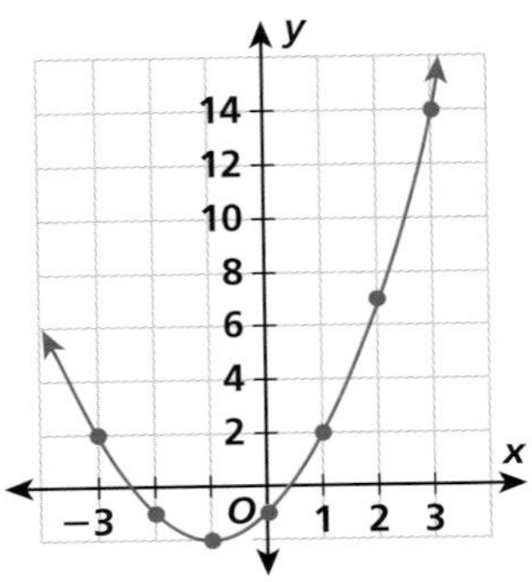

EXERCISES

Graph each quadratic function.

21. $f(x) = 2x^2$

22. $f(x) = x^2 + 3$

23. $f(x) = 2x^2 - x$

24. $f(x) = x^2 + 5x + 6$

13-7 Inverse Variation (pp. 714–717)

EXAMPLE

■ **Graph the inverse variation function.**
$f(x) = \frac{6}{x}$

x	y
−3	−2
−2	−3
−1	−6
1	6
2	3
3	2

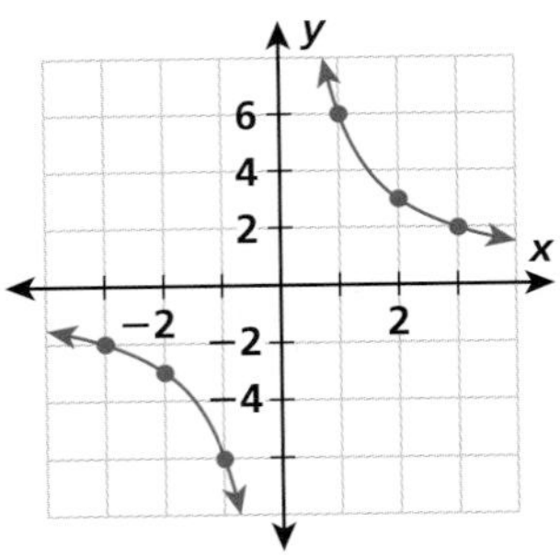

EXERCISES

Graph each inverse variation function.

25. $f(x) = \frac{10}{x}$

26. $f(x) = \frac{14}{x}$

27. $f(x) = -\frac{6}{x}$

28. $f(x) = -\frac{2}{x}$

CHAPTER TEST

Find the given term in each arithmetic sequence.

1. 21st term: $-4, -8, -12, -16, \ldots$
2. 13th term: $7, 7\frac{1}{5}, 7\frac{2}{5}, \ldots$
3. 24th term: $2, 6, 10, 14, \ldots$
4. 30th term: $a_1 = 11, d = 5$

Find the given term in each geometric sequence.

5. 7th term: $8, 32, 128, \ldots$
6. 101st term: $\frac{1}{3}, -\frac{1}{3}, \frac{1}{3}, -\frac{1}{3}, \ldots$
7. A tank contains 54,000 gallons of water. One-third of the water remaining in the tank is removed each day. How much water is left in the tank on the 15th day?

Find the first five terms of each sequence, defined by the given rule.

8. $a_n = 6n - 2$
9. $a_n = \frac{4n}{n + 2}$
10. $a_n = (n + 2)(n + 3)$

Write a rule for each linear function.

11.

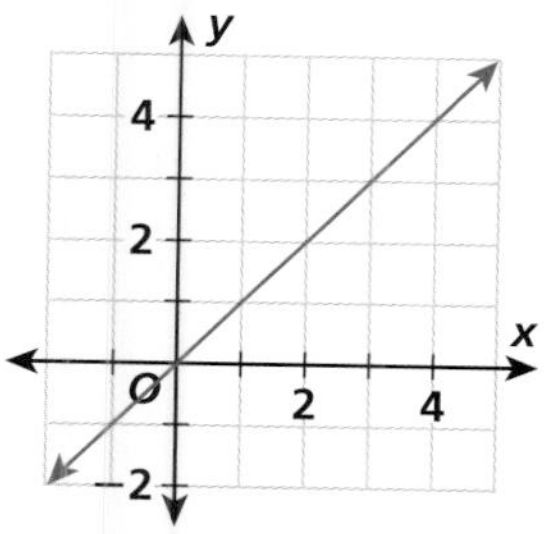

12.

x	y
−8	−7
−4	−4
0	−1
4	2

13. A small pool contains 1200 gallons of water. The pool is being drained at a rate of 45 gallons per minute. Find a rule for the linear function that describes the amount of water in the pool, and use the rule to determine how much water will be in the pool after 15 minutes.

Create a table for each exponential function, and use it to graph the function.

14. $f(x) = -2 \cdot (0.2)^x$
15. $f(x) = 10 \cdot \left(\frac{1}{5}\right)^x$
16. $f(x) = 4^x$

Create a table for each quadratic function, and use it to graph the function.

17. $f(x) = x^2 + x + 3$
18. $f(x) = 2x^2 - 1$
19. $f(x) = x^2 - x + 1$

Create a table. Then graph each inverse variation function.

20. $f(x) = \frac{6}{x}$
21. $f(x) = \frac{10}{x}$
22. $f(x) = -\frac{1}{2x}$

CHAPTER 13

TEST TACKLER

Standardized Test Strategies

Multiple Choice: Work Backward

When you do not know how to solve a multiple-choice test item, use the answer choices and work backward to make a guess. Try each option in the test item to see if it is correct and reasonable.

EXAMPLE 1

If $a_n = 2 + 6(n - 1)$, which term n results in $a_n = 26$?

(A) -5 (B) 4 (C) 5 (D) 6

Use the answer choices to work backward to find the value of n that makes the equation true.

Option A: If $n = -5$, then $26 = 2 + 6(-5 - 1)$ would be true.
$2 + 6(-5 - 1) = 2 + 6(-6) = 2 + (-36) = -34$. $-34 \neq 26$, so $n \neq -5$.

Option B: If $n = 4$, then $26 = 2 + 6(4 - 1)$ would be true.
$2 + 6(4 - 1) = 2 + 6(3) = 2 + 18 = 20$. $20 \neq 26$, so $n \neq 4$.

Option C: If $n = 5$, then $26 = 2 + 6(5 - 1)$ would be true.
$2 + 6(5 - 1) = 2 + 6(4) = 2 + 24 = 26$. $26 = 26$, so $n = 5$.

Option C is the correct response.

EXAMPLE 2

What is the equation of the line that passes through the points $(-1, -1)$ and $(1, 3)$?

(F) $y = 2x$ (G) $y = x$ (H) $y = x + 1$ (J) $y = 2x + 1$

Substitute for x and y to find a true equation.

Option F: Try $(-1, -1)$. $y = 2x$; $-1 \stackrel{?}{=} 2(-1)$; $-1 \neq -2$
Option F is not the correct response.

Option G: Try $(-1, -1)$. $y = x$; $-1 = -1$; The first point is true.
Now try $(1, 3)$: $1 \neq 3$. Option G is not the correct response.

Option H: Try $(-1, -1)$. $y = x + 1$; $-1 \stackrel{?}{=} -1 + 1$; $-1 \neq 0$
Option H is not the correct response.

Option J: The other three options are false.

Try $(-1, -1)$. $y = 2x + 1$; $-1 \stackrel{?}{=} 2(-1) + 1$; $-1 = -1$

Try $(1, 3)$. $y = 2x + 1$; $3 \stackrel{?}{=} 2(1) + 1$; $3 = 3$

HOT TIP! Before answering a test item, check if you can eliminate any of the options immediately.

Read each test item and answer the questions that follow.

ITEM A

What are the next three terms in the sequence 3, 8, 18, 38, . . . ?

(A) 48, 58, 68

(B) 76, 156, 316

(C) 58, 78, 98

(D) 78, 158, 318

1. Explain which option you can eliminate because it is not reasonable.
2. Explain how to work backward to find the correct response.

ITEM B

The 6th term of an arithmetic sequence is 18. The common difference is 3. What is the 1st term of the sequence?

(F) 1

(G) 2

(H) 3

(J) 4

3. Describe how to use mental math to eliminate at least one option.
4. Describe how you know by working backward that options F and G are incorrect.

ITEM C

The 3rd term of a geometric sequence is 12. The common ratio is 2. What is the 1st term of the sequence?

(A) $\frac{1}{3}$

(B) 1

(C) 3

(D) 8

5. Options A and D are distracters. Explain how these options were generated.
6. Explain how to work backward to find the correct response.

ITEM D

Which equation best describes the graph of the quadratic equation?

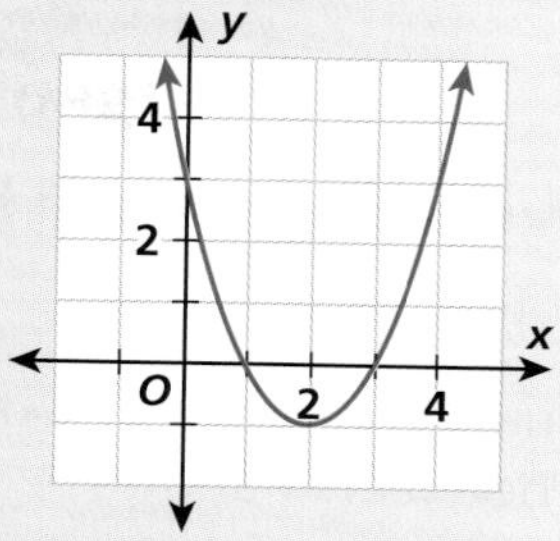

(F) $f(x) = x^2 + 4x - 3$

(G) $f(x) = x^2 - 4x + 3$

(H) $f(x) = x^2 - 3$

(J) $f(x) = x^2 + 4x + 3$

7. Can any of the options be eliminated immediately? Explain.
8. Explain how to work backward to find the correct response.

ITEM E

Which graph represents the equation $y = \frac{3}{x}$?

(A)

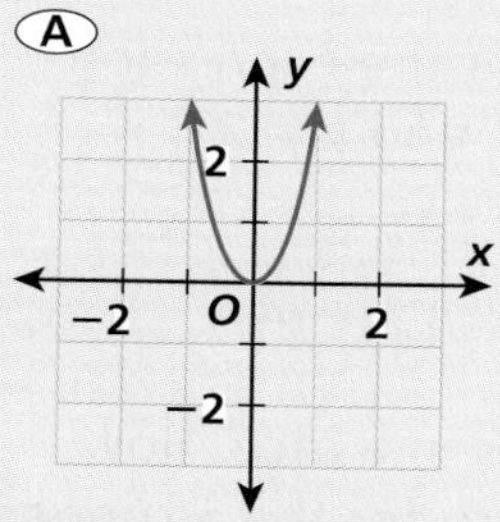

(C)

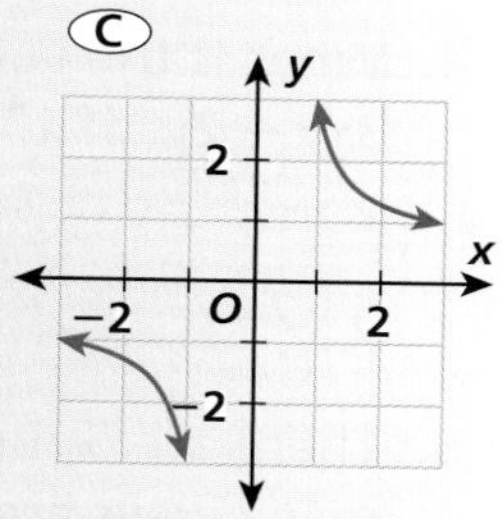

(B)

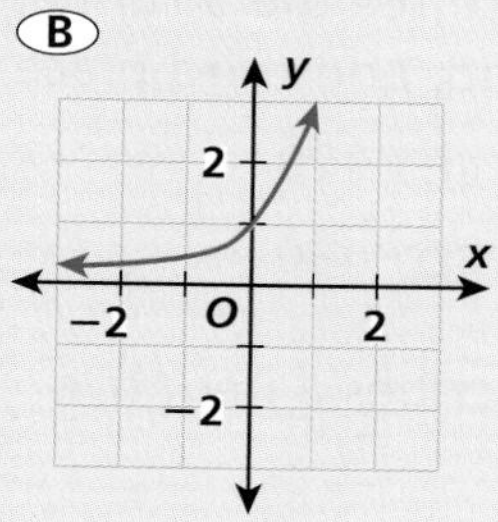

(D)

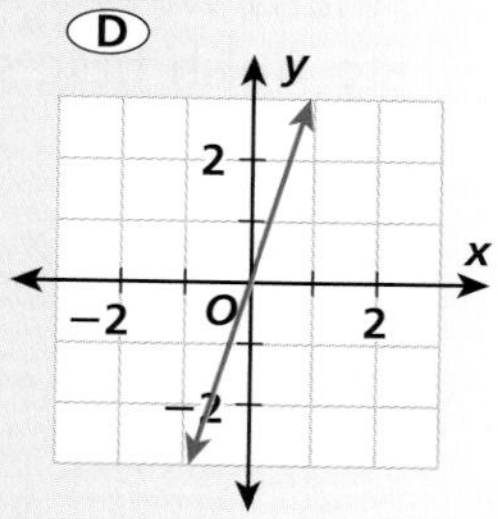

9. Explain which options you can eliminate because they are not reasonable.
10. Describe how to work backward to find the correct response.

STANDARDIZED TEST PREP

go.hrw.com
State Test Practice Online
KEYWORD: MT7 TestPrep

Cumulative Assessment, Chapters 1–13

Multiple Choice

1. Which equation represents a direct variation between x and y?

(A) $y = x + 2$

(B) $y = \frac{2}{x}$

(C) $y = 2x$

(D) $y = 2 - x$

2. The sum of two numbers is 304 and their difference is 112. What is the greater of the two numbers?

(F) 96

(G) 192

(H) 208

(J) 416

3. What is the 1st term of the geometric sequence with 8th term $\frac{1}{16}$ and common ratio $\frac{1}{2}$?

(A) $\frac{1}{2048}$

(B) $\frac{1}{56}$

(C) 4

(D) 8

4. What is the value of the expression $3xy - 2y^2$ if $x = -1$ and $y = 2$?

(F) 14

(G) 2

(H) -2

(J) -14

5. There are 5 runners in a race. How many ways are there for the 5 runners to finish first, second, and third place?

(A) 30

(B) 60

(C) 120

(D) 180

6. Which data set describes a negative correlation?

(F) a person's eye color and height

(G) a person's height and weight

(H) the distance traveled and the time it takes to travel

(J) the age of a light bulb and the intensity of the light beam

7. Which expression represents the perimeter of the figure?

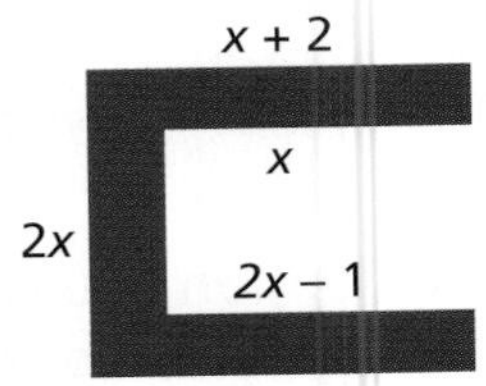

(A) $10x$

(B) $10x + 2$

(C) $6x + 1$

(D) $10x^2 + 4$

8. In the histogram below, which interval contains the median score?

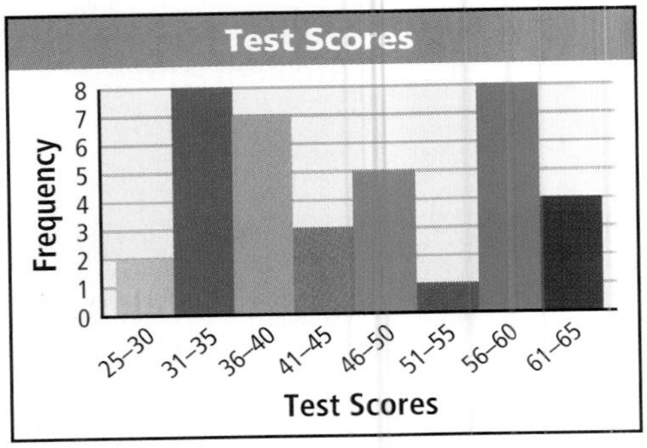

(F) 31–35

(G) 36–40

(H) 41–45

(J) 46–50

9. A triangle has two angles whose measures are 70° each. Which description fits this triangle?

(A) acute

(B) obtuse

(C) scalene

(D) equilateral

10. The rotational speed of a gear varies inversely as the number of teeth on the gear. A gear with 15 teeth has a rotational speed of 48 rpm. How many teeth are on a gear that has a rotational speed of 40 rpm?

(F) 13 teeth

(G) 18 teeth

(H) 58 teeth

(J) 128 teeth

11. An animal shelter needs to find homes for 40 dogs and 60 cats. If 15% of the dogs are female and 25% of the cats are female, what percent of the animals are female?

Ⓐ 21%
Ⓑ 22%
Ⓒ 40%
Ⓓ 42%

HOT TIP! **When trying to find the pattern in a sequence, find the first and second differences to see if there is a common difference.**

Gridded Response

Use the graph for items 12 and 13.

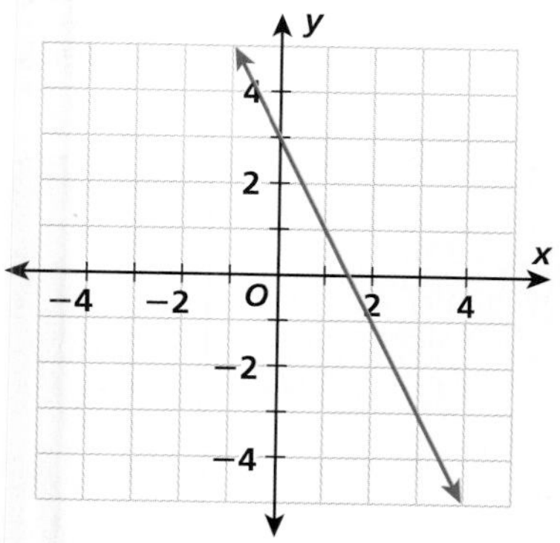

12. What is the slope of a line perpendicular to the line graphed?

13. What is the *y*-intercept of the line perpendicular to the line graphed that passes through the point (2, 2)?

14. If $3^{3x-2} = 81$, what is the value of *x*?

15. If *y* varies inversely with *x* and $y = \frac{2}{9}$ when $x = \frac{1}{3}$, what is the constant of variation?

16. What is the *x*-intercept of the function $f(x) = 4x^2 - 20x + 25$?

17. The length of a rectangle is one-third the width. If the perimeter of the rectangle is 56 units, what is the area in square units?

Short Response

18. Write out the next three terms of the sequence.

$$\sqrt{2}, \sqrt{2+\sqrt{2}}, \sqrt{2+\sqrt{2+\sqrt{2}}}, \sqrt{2+\sqrt{2+\sqrt{2+\sqrt{2}}}}, \ldots$$

Use your calculator to evaluate each term of the sequence. Describe what seems to be happening to the terms of the sequence.

19. A basketball player throws a basketball in a path defined by the function $f(x) = -16x^2 + 20x + 7$, where *x* is the time in seconds and $f(x)$ is the height in feet. Graph the function, and estimate how long it would take the basketball to reach its maximum height.

20. When playing the trombone, a musician produces different notes by changing the effective length of the tube by moving it in and out. This movement produces a sequence of lengths that form a geometric sequence. If the length is 119.3 inches in the 2nd position and 134.0 inches in the 4th position, what is the length in the 3rd position? Write a rule that would describe this relationship.

Extended Response

21. Consider the sequence 3, 4, 6, 9, 13, . . .
   a. Determine whether the sequence is arithmetic, geometric, or neither. Explain your answer.
   b. Find the difference between each pair of consecutive terms. What pattern do you notice?
   c. How many differences do you have to find before there is a common difference? Use your pattern to find the next three terms.

CHAPTER

14 Polynomials

14A Introduction to Polynomials

14-1 Polynomials

LAB Model Polynomials

14-2 Simplifying Polynomials

14B Polynomial Operations

LAB Model Polynomial Addition

14-3 Adding Polynomials

LAB Model Polynomial Subtraction

14-4 Subtracting Polynomials

14-5 Multiplying Polynomials by Monomials

LAB Multiply Binomials

14-6 Multiplying Binomials

EXT Dividing Polynomials by Monomials

MULTI-STEP TEST PREP

go.hrw.com
Chapter Project Online
KEYWORD: MT7 Ch14

CD Production Costs

Fixed		Variable (for each CD produced)		
Setup	Overhead	Blank CD	Packaging	Maintenance
\$100	\$97	51¢	19¢	18¢

Career *Financial Analyst*

Financial analysts can be found in many business settings. They can help determine the cost of each product a company makes. The table lists one company's costs of producing multiple copies of audio CDs. Financial analysts use polynomials to calculate the relationships between production costs, selling price, total sales, and profits.

ARE YOU READY?

Vocabulary

Choose the best term from the list to complete each sentence.

Associative Property

coefficient

Distributive Property

like terms

1. ___?___ have the same variables raised to the same powers.
2. In the expression $4x^2$, 4 is the ___?___.
3. $5 + (4 + 3) = (5 + 4) + 3$ by the ___?___.
4. $3 \cdot 2 + 3 \cdot 4 = 3(2 + 4)$ by the ___?___.

Complete these exercises to review skills you will need for this chapter.

Subtract Integers

Subtract.

5. $12 - 4$ **6.** $8 - 10$ **7.** $14 - (-4)$

8. $-9 - 5$ **9.** $-9 - (-5)$ **10.** $9 - (-5)$

Exponents

Multiply. Write each product as one power.

11. $3^4 \cdot 3^6$ **12.** $10^2 \cdot 10^3$ **13.** $x \cdot x^5$ **14.** $5^5 \cdot 5^5$

15. $y^2 \cdot y^6$ **16.** $z^3 \cdot z^3$ **17.** $a^2 \cdot a$ **18.** $b \cdot b$

Distributive Property

Rewrite using the Distributive Property.

19. $5(7 + 8)$ **20.** $3(x + y)$ **21.** $(a + b)6$ **22.** $(r + s)4$

Area

Find the area of the shaded portion in each figure.

23.
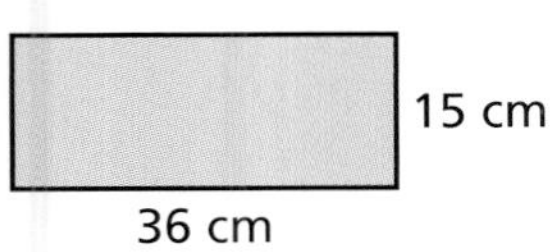

24.
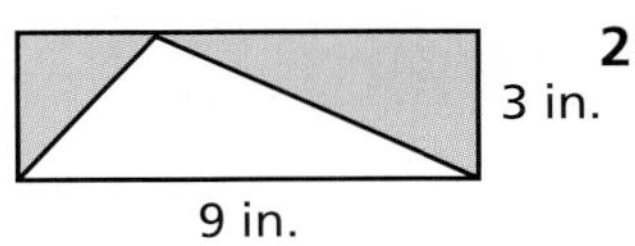

25.
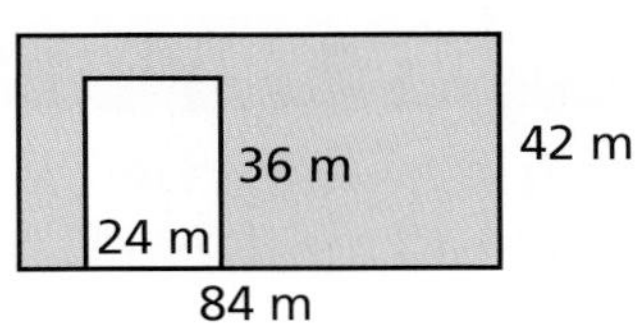

26.
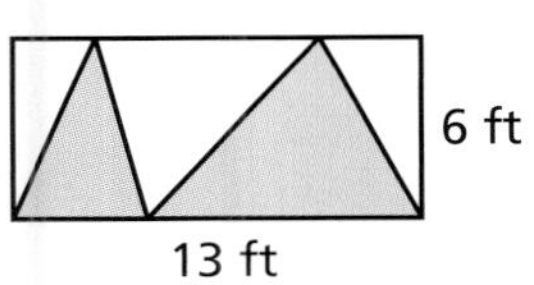

27.
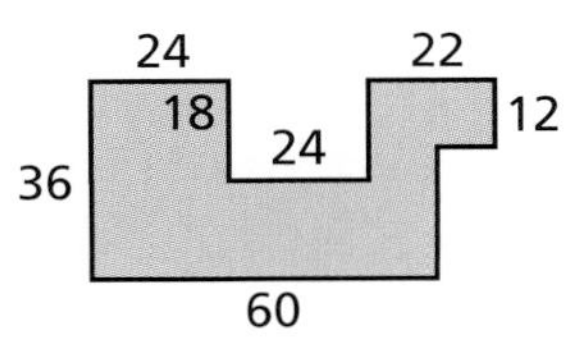

28.
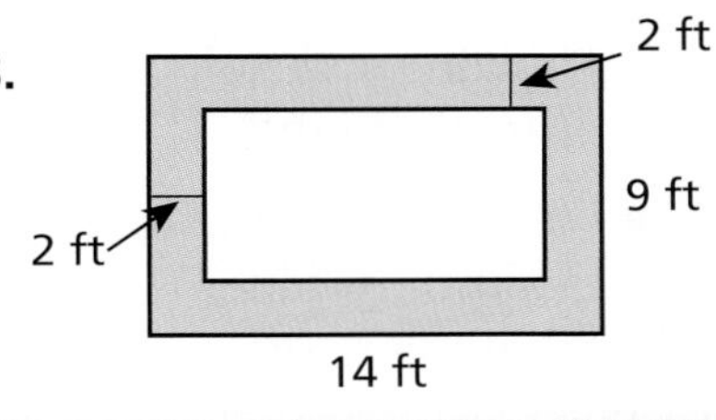

CHAPTER 14

Study Guide: Preview

Where You've Been

Previously, you

- classified figures by their characteristics.
- simplified numerical expressions.
- added, subtracted, and multiplied rational numbers.
- found the GCF of two or more numbers.

In This Chapter

You will study

- classifying polynomials by the number of terms.
- simplifying polynomial expressions by combining like terms.
- adding, subtracting, and multiplying monomials and binomials.
- using GCF to factor and divide polynomials.

Where You're Going

You can use the skills learned in this chapter

- to use polynomials to find the height of a projectile given its time in flight.
- to solve complex area and volume problems in higher math courses.

Key Vocabulary/Vocabulario

binomial	binomio
degree of a polynomial	grado de un polinomio
monomial	monomio
polynomial	polinomio
trinomial	trinomio

Vocabulary Connections

To become familiar with some of the vocabulary terms in the chapter, consider the following. You may refer to the chapter, the glossary, or a dictionary if you like.

1. The root of the words *monomial, binomial,* and *trinomial* is *-nomial,* which tells you how many different terms with exponents are in an algebraic expression. How many terms with exponents do you think there are in a **monomial**? in a **binomial**? in a **trinomial**?
2. The prefix *poly-* means "many." Knowing what you do about how the word *polygon* relates to the words *pentagon, hexagon,* and *octagon,* how do you think the word **polynomial** relates to the words *monomial, binomial,* and *trinomial*?

Reading and Writing Math

Study Strategy: Study for a Final Exam

A cumulative final exam will cover material you have learned over the course of the year. You must be prepared if you want to be successful. It may help you to make a study timeline like the one below.

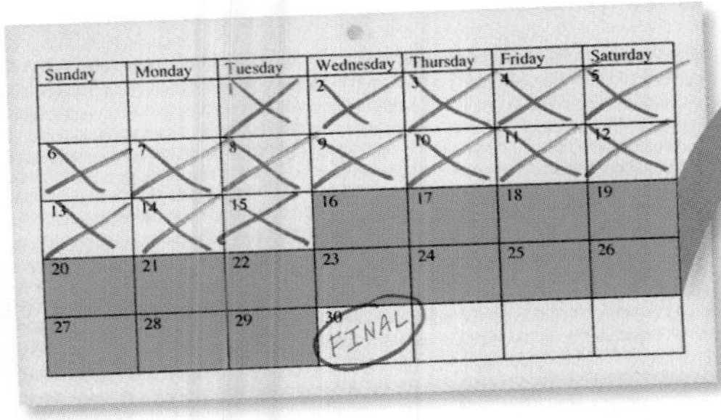

2 weeks before the final:

- *Look at previous exams and homework to determine areas I need to focus on; rework problems that were incorrect or incomplete.*
- *Make a list of all formulas I need to know for the final.*
- *Create a practice exam using problems from the book that are similar to problems from each exam.*

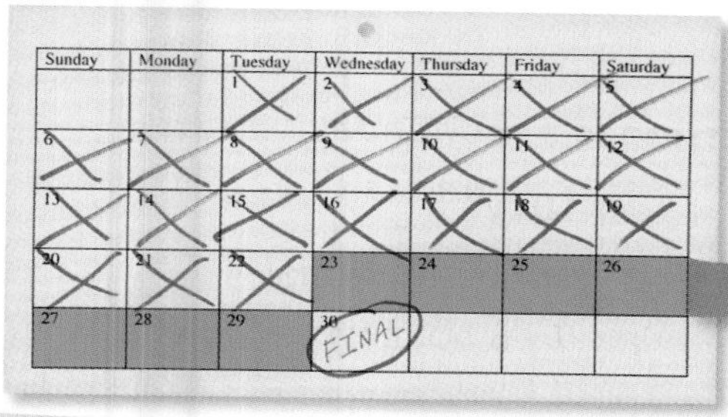

1 week before the final:

- *Take the practice exam and check it. For each problem I miss, find two or three similar problems and work those.*
- *Work with a friend in the class to quiz each other on formulas from my list.*

1 day before the final:

- *Make sure I have pencils and a calculator. (Check the batteries!)*

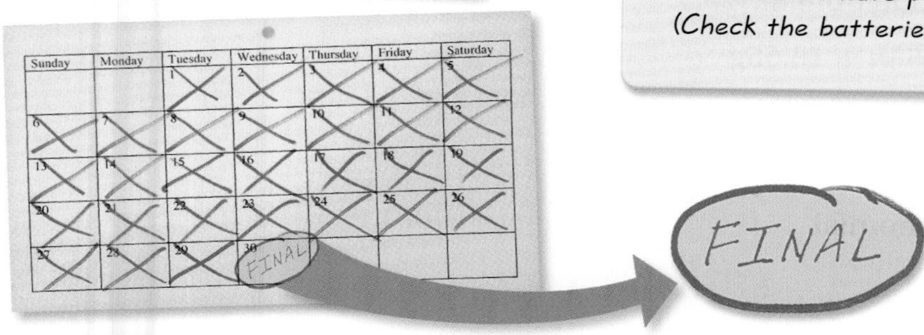

Try This

Complete the following to help you prepare for your cumulative test.

1. Create a timeline that you will use to study for your final exam.

14-1 Polynomials

Learn to classify polynomials by degree and by the number of terms.

Vocabulary

monomial

polynomial

binomial

trinomial

degree of a polynomial

Some fireworks shows are synchronized to music for dramatic effect. *Polynomials* are used to compute the exact height of each firework when it explodes.

The simplest type of polynomial is called a *monomial.* A **monomial** is a number or a product of numbers and variables with exponents that are whole numbers.

Monomials	$2n$, x^3, $4a^4b^3$, 7
Not monomials	$p^{2.4}$, 2^x, $\sqrt{x}$, $\frac{5}{g^2}$

EXAMPLE 1 Identifying Monomials

Determine whether each expression is a monomial.

A $\frac{1}{3}x^4y^7$

monomial

4 and 7 are whole numbers.

B $10xy^{0.3}$

not a monomial

0.3 is not a whole number.

A **polynomial** is one monomial or the sum or difference of monomials. Polynomials can be classified by the number of terms. A monomial has 1 term, a **binomial** has 2 terms, and a **trinomial** has 3 terms.

EXAMPLE 2 Classifying Polynomials by the Number of Terms

Classify each expression as a monomial, a binomial, a trinomial, or not a polynomial.

A $35.55h + 19.55g$

binomial — *Polynomial with 2 terms*

B $-2x^3y$

monomial — *Polynomial with 1 term*

C $6x^2 - 4xy + \frac{2}{x}$

not a polynomial — *A variable is in the denominator.*

D $7mn + 4m - 5n$

trinomial — *Polynomial with 3 terms*

The *degree of a term* is the sum of the exponents of the variables in the term. A polynomial can be classified by its degree. The **degree of a polynomial** is the same as the term with the greatest degree.

$$\underbrace{\underbrace{4x^2}_{\text{Degree 2}} + \underbrace{2x^5}_{\text{Degree 5}} + \underbrace{xy}_{\text{Degree 2}} + \underbrace{5}_{\text{Degree 0}}}_{\text{Degree 5}}$$

EXAMPLE 3 Classifying Polynomials by Their Degrees

Find the degree of each polynomial.

A $6x^2 + 3x + 4$

$$\underset{\textit{Degree 2}}{6x^2} + \underset{\textit{Degree 1}}{3x} + \underset{\textit{Degree 0}}{4}$$

The greatest degree is 2, so the degree of $6x^2 + 3x + 4$ is 2.

B $6 + 3m^2 + 4m^5$

$$\underset{\textit{Degree 0}}{6} + \underset{\textit{Degree 2}}{3m^2} + \underset{\textit{Degree 5}}{4m^5}$$

The greatest degree is 5, so the degree of $6 + 3m^2 + 4m^5$ is 5.

EXAMPLE 4 *Physics Application*

The height in feet of a firework launched straight up into the air from *s* feet off the ground at velocity *v* after *t* seconds is given by the polynomial $-16t^2 + vt + s$. Find the height of a firework launched from a 10 ft platform at 200 ft/s after 5 seconds.

$-16t^2 + vt + s$	*Write the polynomial expression for height.*
$-16(5)^2 + 200(5) + 10$	*Substitute 5 for t, 200 for v, and 10 for s.*
$-400 + 1000 + 10$	*Simplify.*
610	

The firework is 610 ft high 5 seconds after launching.

Social Studies LINK

These colorfully decorated fireworks are part of a traditional Chinese New Year celebration.

Think and Discuss

1. **Describe** two ways you can classify a polynomial. Give a polynomial with three terms, and classify it two ways.
2. **Explain** why $-5x^2 - 3$ is a polynomial but $-5x^{-2} - 3$ is not.

14-1 Exercises

go.hrw.com
Homework Help Online
KEYWORD: MT7 14-1
Parent Resources Online
KEYWORD: MT7 Parent

GUIDED PRACTICE

See Example 1 **Determine whether each expression is a monomial.**

1. $-2x^2y$
2. $\frac{4}{3x}$
3. $\sqrt{3x}$
4. 9

See Example 2 **Classify each expression as a monomial, a binomial, a trinomial, or not a polynomial.**

5. $\frac{3}{4}x + y$
6. $5r - 3r^2 + 6$
7. $\frac{3}{x^2} + 2x$
8. 2

See Example 3 **Find the degree of each polynomial.**

9. $-7m^5 + 3m^8$
10. $x^4 - 4$
11. 52

See Example 4

12. The trinomial $-16t^2 + 24t + 72$ describes the height in feet of a ball thrown straight up from a 72 ft platform with a velocity of 24 ft/s after t seconds. What is the ball's height after 2 seconds?

INDEPENDENT PRACTICE

See Example 1 **Determine whether each expression is a monomial.**

13. $5.2x^3$
14. $-3x^{-4}$
15. $\frac{5y^4}{6x}$
16. $\frac{4}{7}x^4y^2$
17. 210
18. 3^x

See Example 2 **Classify each expression as a monomial, a binomial, a trinomial, or not a polynomial.**

19. $-9m^2n^6$
20. $6g^{\frac{1}{3}}h^2$
21. $4x^3 + 2x^5 + 3$
22. $-a + 3$
23. $2\sqrt{x}$
24. $5v^3s$

See Example 3 **Find the degree of each polynomial.**

25. $2x^2 - 7x + 1$
26. $-3m^2 + 4m^3 - 2$
27. $-2 + 3x + 4x^4$
28. $6p^4 + 7p^2$
29. $n + 2$
30. $3y^8$

See Example 4

31. The volume of a box with height x, length $x + 2$, and width $3x - 5$ is given by the trinomial $3x^3 - x^2 - 10x$. What is the volume of the box if its height is 2 inches?

PRACTICE AND PROBLEM SOLVING

Extra Practice
See page 808.

32. **Transportation** The distance in feet required for a car traveling at r mi/h to come to a stop can be approximated by the binomial $\frac{r^2}{20} + r$. About how many feet will be required for a car to stop if it is traveling at 70 mi/h?

Classify each expression as a monomial, a binomial, a trinomial, or not a polynomial. If it is a polynomial, give its degree.

33. $4x^3$ **34.** $7x^{0.7} + 3x$ **35.** $-\frac{5}{6}x + \frac{3}{5}x^2$ **36.** $7y^2 - 6y$

37. $2f^3 + 5f^5 - f$ **38.** $3 - \frac{2}{x}$ **39.** $6x + 4\sqrt{x}$ **40.** $6x^{-4}$

41. $3b^2 - 9b - 8b^3$ **42.** $4 + 5x$ **43.** $2x^{\frac{1}{2}} - 3x^4 + 5$ **44.** 5

45. Transportation Gas mileage at speed s can be estimated using the given polynomials. Evaluate the polynomials to complete the table.

		Gas Mileage (mi/gal)		
		40 mi/h	50 mi/h	60 mi/h
Compact	$-0.025s^2 + 2.45s - 30$			
Midsize	$-0.015s^2 + 1.45s - 13$			
Van	$-0.03s^2 + 2.9s - 53$			

46. Critical Thinking Without solving, tell which of the following binomials has the greatest value when $x = 10$. Explain what method you used.

Ⓐ $3x^5 + 8$ Ⓑ $3x^8 + 8$ Ⓒ $3x^2 + 8$ Ⓓ $3x^6 + 8$

47. What's the Error? A student says that the degree of the polynomial $4b^5 - 7b^9 + 6b$ is 5. What is the error?

48. Write About It Give some examples of words that start with *mono-*, *bi-*, *tri-*, and *poly-*, and relate the meaning of each to polynomials.

49. Challenge The base of a triangle is described by the binomial $x + 2$, and its height is described by the trinomial $2x^2 + 3x - 7$. What is the area of the triangle if $x = 5$?

TEST PREP and Spiral Review

50. Multiple Choice The height in feet of a soccer ball kicked straight up into the air from s feet off the ground at velocity v after t seconds is given by the trinomial $-16t^2 + vt + s$. What is the height of the soccer ball kicked from 2 feet off the ground at 90 ft/s after 3 seconds?

Ⓕ 3 ft Ⓖ 15 ft Ⓗ 90 ft Ⓙ 128 ft

51. Gridded Response What is the degree of the polynomial $6 + 7k^4 - 8k^9$?

Write each number in scientific notation. (Lesson 4-4)

52. 4,080,000 **53.** -0.000035 **54.** 5,910,000,000

Solve. (Lesson 11-1)

55. $15x - 8x = 91$ **56.** $3j + 14 = 5j$ **57.** $4m - 1000 = -6m$

Hands-On LAB 14-1

Model Polynomials

Use with Lesson 14-1

go.hrw.com
Lab Resources Online
KEYWORD: MT7 Lab14

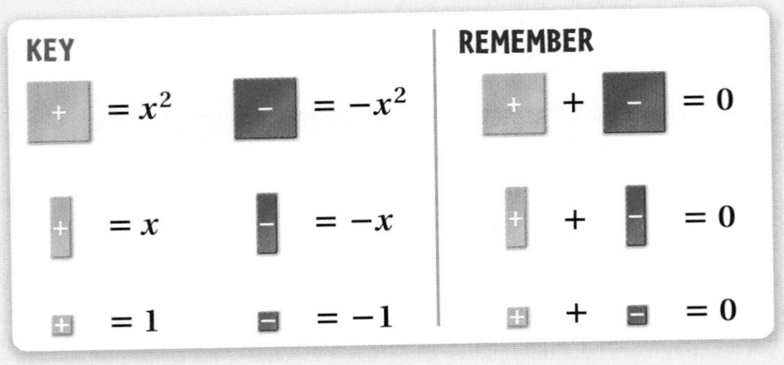

You can use algebra tiles to model polynomials. To model the polynomial $4x^2 + x - 3$, you need four x^2-tiles, one x-tile, and three -1-tiles.

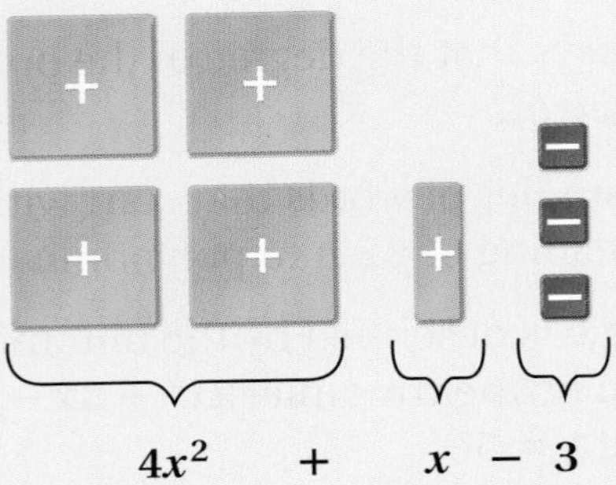

Activity 1

1 Use algebra tiles to model the polynomial $2x^2 + 4x + 6$.

All signs are positive, so use all yellow tiles.

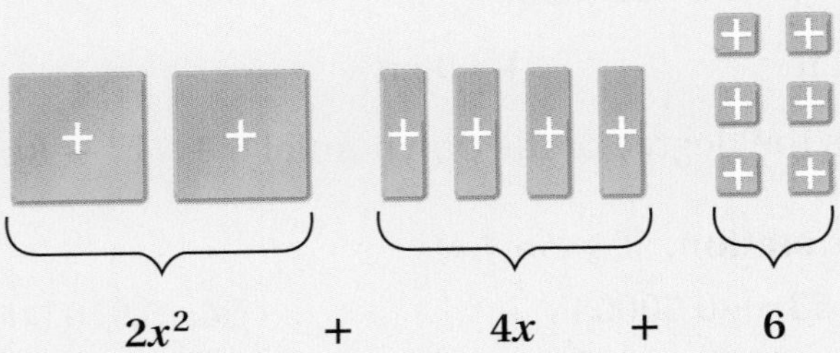

2 Use algebra tiles to model the polynomial $-x^2 + 6x - 4$.

Modeling $-x^2 + 6x - 4$ is similar to modeling $2x^2 + 4x + 6$. Remember to use red tiles for negative values.

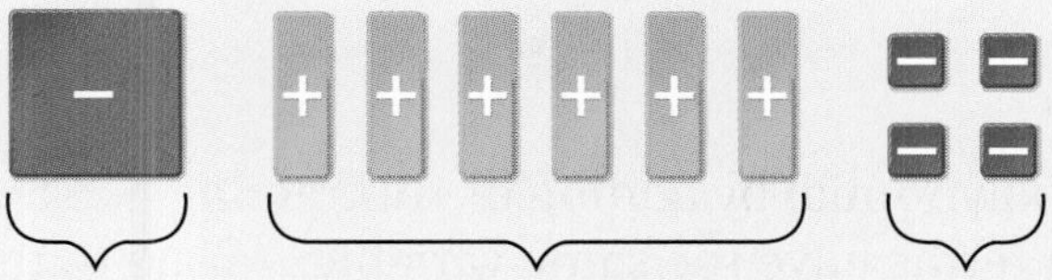

$-x^2 \quad + \quad 6x \quad - \quad 4$

Think and Discuss

1. How do you know when to use red tiles?

Try This

Use algebra tiles to model each polynomial.

1. $2x^2 + 3x - 5$ **2.** $-4x^2 + 5x - 1$ **3.** $5x^2 - x + 9$

Activity 2

1 Write the polynomial modeled by the tiles below.

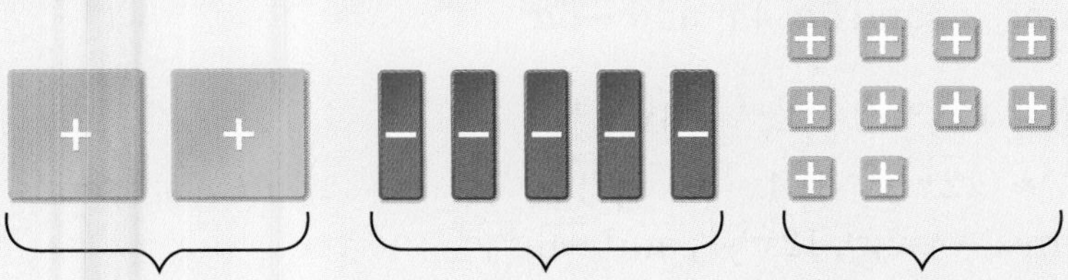

$2x^2 \quad - \quad 5x \quad + \quad 10$

The polynomial modeled by the tiles is $2x^2 - 5x + 10$.

Think and Discuss

1. How do you know the coefficient of the x^2 term in Activity 2?

Try This

Write a polynomial modeled by each group of algebra tiles.

1.

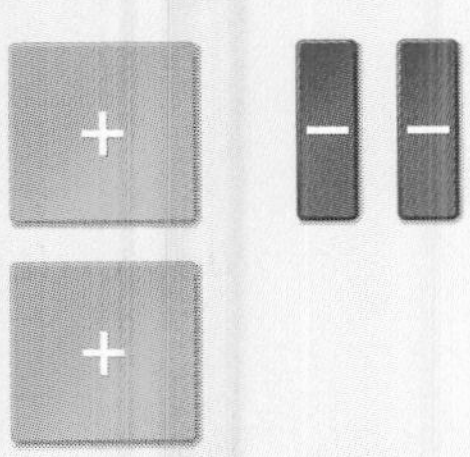

2.

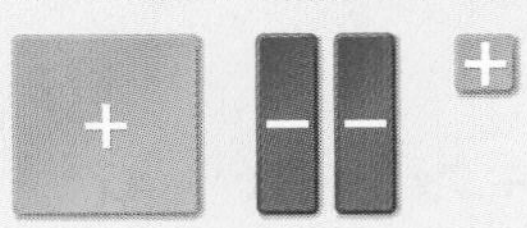

3.

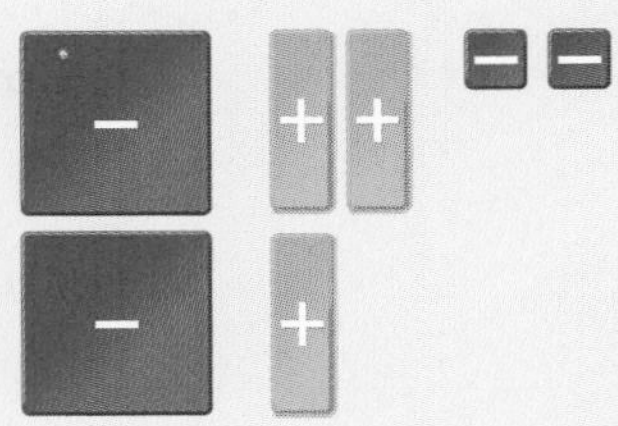

14-2 Simplifying Polynomials

Learn **to simplify polynomials.**

You can simplify a polynomial by adding or subtracting like terms. Remember that like terms have the same variables raised to the same powers.

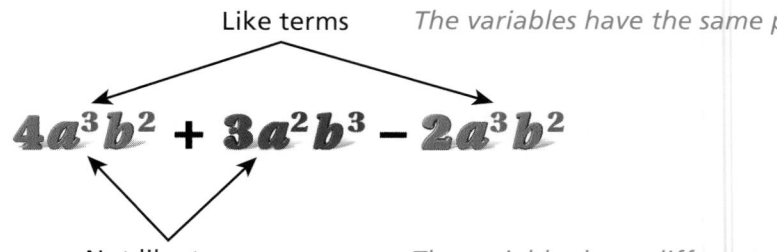

Like terms *The variables have the same powers.*

$$4a^3b^2 + 3a^2b^3 - 2a^3b^2$$

Not like terms *The variables have different powers.*

EXAMPLE 1 Identifying Like Terms

Identify the like terms in each polynomial.

A $\mathbf{2a + 4a^2 - 3 + 5a - 6a^2}$

$2a + 4a^2 - 3 + 5a - 6a^2$ *Identify like terms.*

Like terms: $2a$ and $5a$, $4a^2$ and $-6a^2$

B $\mathbf{-4x^5y^3 + 12x^5y^3 - 4x^3 - 6x^5y^3}$

$-4x^5y^3 + 12x^5y^3 - 4x^3 - 6x^5y^3$ *Identify like terms.*

Like terms: $-4x^5y^3$, $12x^5y^3$, and $-6x^5y^3$

C $\mathbf{5m^2 - 3mn + 4m}$

$5m^2 - 3mn + 4m$ *Identify like terms.*

There are no like terms.

To simplify a polynomial, combine like terms. It may be easier to arrange the terms in *descending* order (highest degree to lowest degree) before combining like terms.

EXAMPLE 2 Simplifying Polynomials by Combining Like Terms

Simplify.

A $\mathbf{x^2 + 5x^4 - 6 + 7x^2 + 3x^4 - 4x^2}$

$5x^4 + 3x^4 + x^2 + 7x^2 - 4x^2 - 6$ *Arrange in descending order.*

$5x^4 + 3x^4 + x^2 + 7x^2 - 4x^2 - 6$ *Identify like terms.*

$8x^4 + 4x^2 - 6$ *Combine coefficients:* *$5 + 3 = 8$ and $1 + 7 - 4 = 4$*

Simplify.

B $-5a^2b + 12ab^2 - 4a^2b - ab^2 + 3ab$

$-5a^2b + 12ab^2 - 4a^2b - ab^2 + 3ab$ *Identify like terms.*

$-9a^2b + 11ab^2 + 3ab$ *Combine coefficients: $-5 - 4 = -9$ and $12 - 1 = 11$*

Sometimes you may need to use the Distributive Property to simplify a polynomial.

EXAMPLE 3 Simplifying Polynomials by Using the Distributive Property

Simplify.

A $4(3x^2 + 5x)$

$4(3x^2 + 5x)$ *Distributive Property*

$4 \cdot 3x^2 + 4 \cdot 5x$

$12x^2 + 20x$

B $2(4ab^2 - 5b) + 3ab^2 + 6$

$2(4ab^2 - 5b) + 3ab^2 + 6$ *Distributive Property*

$2 \cdot 4ab^2 - 2 \cdot 5b + 3ab^2 + 6$

$8ab^2 - 10b + 3ab^2 + 6$

$11ab^2 - 10b + 6$ *Combine like terms.*

EXAMPLE 4 *Business Application*

A *board foot* is 1 ft by 1 ft by 1 in. of lumber. The amount of lumber that can be harvested from a tree with diameter d in. is approximately $20 + 0.005(d^3 - 30d^2 + 300d - 1000)$ board feet. Use the Distributive Property to write an equivalent expression.

$$20 + 0.005(d^3 - 30d^2 + 300d - 1000) = 20 + 0.005d^3 - 0.15d^2 + 1.5d - 5$$
$$= 15 + 0.005d^3 - 0.15d^2 + 1.5d$$

Think and Discuss

1. **Tell** how you know when you can combine like terms.
2. **Give** an example of an expression that you could simplify by using the Distributive Property and an expression that you could simplify by combining like terms.

14-2 Exercises

go.hrw.com
Homework Help Online
KEYWORD: MT7 14-2
Parent Resources Online
KEYWORD: MT7 Parent

GUIDED PRACTICE

See Example 1
Identify the like terms in each polynomial.

1. $-3b^2 + 5b + 4b^2 - b + 6$
2. $7mn - 5m^2n^2 + 8m^2n + 4m^2n^2$

See Example 2
Simplify.

3. $2x^2 - 3x + 5x^2 + 7x - 5$
4. $6 - 3b + 2b^4 - 7b^2 + 9 + 4b - 3b^2$

See Example 3
5. $4(3x - 8)$
6. $7(2x^2 + 4x)$
7. $5(3a^2 - 5a) + 2a^2 + 4a$

See Example 4
8. The level of nitric oxide emissions, in parts per million, from a car engine is approximated by the polynomial $-40{,}000 + 5x(800 - x^2)$, where x is the air-fuel ratio. Use the Distributive Property to write an equivalent expression.

INDEPENDENT PRACTICE

See Example 1
Identify the like terms in each polynomial.

9. $-t + 4t^2 - 5t^2 + 5t - 2$
10. $8rs - 3r^2s^2 + 5r^2s^2 + 2rs - 5$

See Example 2
Simplify.

11. $2p - 3p^2 + 5p + 12p^2$
12. $3fg + f^2g - fg^2 - 3fg + 4f^2g + 6fg^2$

See Example 3
13. $5(x^2 - 5x) + 4x^2 - 7x$
14. $2(b - 3) + 5b - 3b^2$
15. $\frac{1}{2}(6y^3 - 8) + 3y^3$

See Example 4
16. The concentration of a certain medication in an average person's bloodstream h hours after injection can be estimated using the expression $6(0.03h - 0.002h^2 - 0.01h^3)$. Use the Distributive Property to write an equivalent expression.

PRACTICE AND PROBLEM SOLVING

Extra Practice
See page 808.

Simplify.

17. $2s^2 - 3s + 10s^2 + 5s - 3$
18. $5gh^2 + 4g^2h + 2g^2h - g^2h$
19. $2(x^2 - 5x + 4) - 3x + 7$
20. $5(x - x^5 + x^3) - 3x$
21. $4(2m - 3m^2) + 7(3m^2 - 4m)$
22. $6b^4 + 2b^2 + 3(b^2 - 6)$
23. $5mn - 3m^3n^2 + 3(m^3n^2 + 4mn)$
24. $3(4x + y) + 2(3x - 2y)$

25. **Life Science** The rate of flow in cm/s of blood in an artery at d cm from the center is given by the polynomial $1000(0.04 - d^2)$. Use the Distributive Property to write an equivalent expression.

Art LINK

Abstract artists often use geometric shapes, such as cubes, prisms, pyramids, and spheres, to create sculptures.

26. Suppose the volume of a sculpture is approximately $s^3 + 0.52s^3 + 0.18s^3 + 0.33s^3$ cm^3 and the surface area is approximately $6s^2 + 3.14s^2 + 7.62s^2 + 3.24s^2$ cm^2.
    a. Simplify the polynomial expression for the volume of the sculpture, and find the volume of the sculpture for $s = 5$.
    b. Simplify the polynomial expression for the surface area of the sculpture, and find the surface area of the sculpture for $s = 5$.

Balanced/Unbalanced O by Fletcher Benton

Pyramid Balancing Cube and Sphere, artist unknown

27. A sculpture features a large ring with an outer lateral surface area of about $44xy$ in^2, an inner lateral surface area of about $38xy$ in^2, and 2 bases, each with an area of about $41y$ in^2. Write and simplify a polynomial that expresses the surface area of the ring.

28. **Challenge** The volume of the ring on the sculpture from Exercise 27 is $49\pi xy^2 - 36\pi xy^2$ in^3. Simplify the polynomial, and find the volume for $x = 12$ and $y = 7.5$. Give your answer both in terms of π and to the nearest tenth.

go.hrw.com
Web Extra!
KEYWORD: MT7 Art

TEST PREP and Spiral Review

29. **Multiple Choice** Simplify the expression $4x^2 + 8x^3 - 9x^2 + 2x$.

    Ⓐ $8x^3 - 5x^4 + 2x$ Ⓑ $8x^3 + 13x^2 + 2x$ Ⓒ $8x^3 - 5x^2 + 2x$ Ⓓ $5x^3$

30. **Short Response** Identify the like terms in the polynomial $3x^4 + 5x^2 - x^4 + 4x^2$. Then simplify the polynomial.

Find each percent to the nearest tenth. (Lesson 6-3)

31. What percent of 82 is 42?

32. What percent of 195 is 126?

Create a table for each quadratic function, and use it to make a graph. (Lesson 13-6)

33. $f(x) = -x^2 + 1$

34. $f(x) = x^2 + 2x - 1$

CHAPTER 14

READY TO GO ON?

SECTION 14A

Quiz for Lessons 14-1 Through 14-2

14-1 Polynomials

Determine whether each expression is a monomial.

1. $\frac{1}{5x^2}$
2. $\frac{1}{3}x^2 - x^3$
3. $7c^2d^8$

Classify each expression as a monomial, a binomial, a trinomial, or not a polynomial.

4. $\frac{1}{x} + x^2$
5. $a^3 + 2a - 17$
6. $y + 2$

Find the degree of each polynomial.

7. $u^6 + 7$
8. $3c^2 + c^5 + c + 1$
9. 43

10. The depth, in feet below the ocean surface, of a submerging exploration submarine after y minutes can be approximated by the polynomial $0.001y^4 - 0.12y^3 + 3.6y^2$. Estimate the depth after 45 minutes.

Ready to Go On?

14-2 Simplifying Polynomials

Identify the like terms in each polynomial.

11. $-5x^2y^2 + 4xy + x^2y^2$
12. $-z^2 + 7z + 4z^2 - z + 9$
13. $t + 8 - 2t - 6$
14. $8ab + 3ac + 5bc - 4ac + 6ab$

Simplify.

15. $6 + 3b^5 - 2b^3 + 7 - 5b^3$
16. $6y^2 + y + 7y^2 - 4y - 5$
17. $6(x^2 - 7x) + 2x^2 + 7x$
18. $y + 5 - 5y - 4(5y + 2)$

Solve.

19. The area of one face of a cube is given by the expression $3s^2 + 5s$. Write a polynomial to represent the total surface area of the cube.
20. The area of each lateral face of a regular square pyramid is given by the expression $\frac{1}{2}b^2 + 2b$. Write a polynomial to represent the lateral surface area of the pyramid.

Focus on Problem Solving

Look Back

- **Estimate to check that your answer is reasonable**

Before you solve a word problem, you can often read through the problem and make an estimate of the correct answer. Make sure your answer is reasonable for the situation in the problem. After you have solved the problem, compare your answer with the original estimate. If your answer is not close to your estimate, check your work again.

Each problem below has an incorrect answer given. Explain why the answer is not reasonable, and give your own estimate of the correct answer.

1 The perimeter of rectangle *ABCD* is 48 cm. What is the value of x?

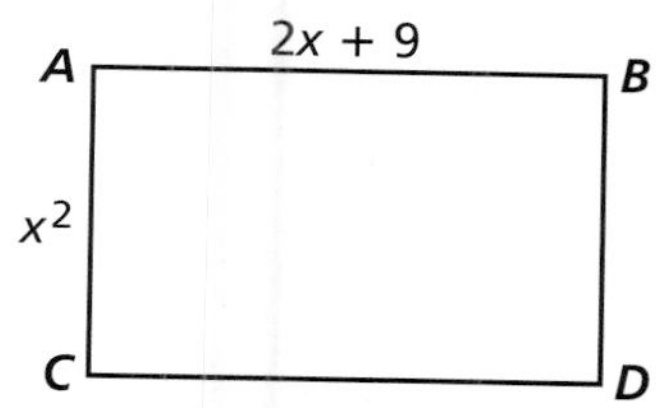

Answer: $x = -5$

2 A patio layer can use $4x + 6y$ ft of accent edging to divide a patio into three sections measuring x ft long by y ft wide. If each section must be at least 15 ft long and have an area of at least 165 ft^2, what is the minimum amount of edging needed for the patio?

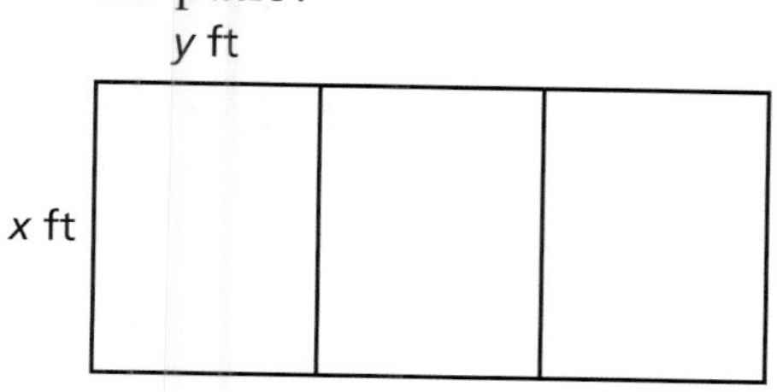

Answer: 52 ft

3 A baseball is thrown straight up from a height of 3 ft at 30 mi/h. The height of the baseball in feet after t seconds is $-16t^2 + 44t + 3$. How long will it take the baseball to reach its maximum height?

Answer: 5 minutes

4 Jacob deposited \$2000 in a savings account that earns 6% simple interest. The amount of money he has in his account after t years is $P + Prt$, where P is the initial amount of money in the account and r is the interest rate expressed as a decimal. How much money will he have in the account after 7 years?

Answer: \$1925

Hands-On LAB 14-3

Model Polynomial Addition

Use with Lesson 14-3

go.hrw.com
Lab Resources Online
KEYWORD: MT7 Lab14

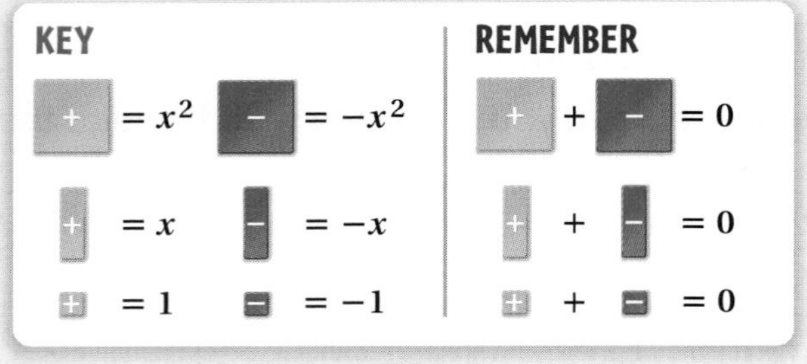

You can use algebra tiles to model polynomial addition.

Activity

1 Use algebra tiles to find the sum $(2x^2 - 2x + 3) + (x^2 + x - 5)$.

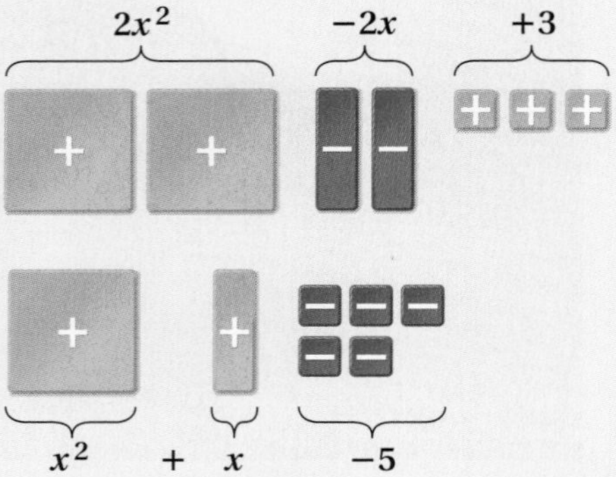

Use tiles to represent all terms from both expressions.

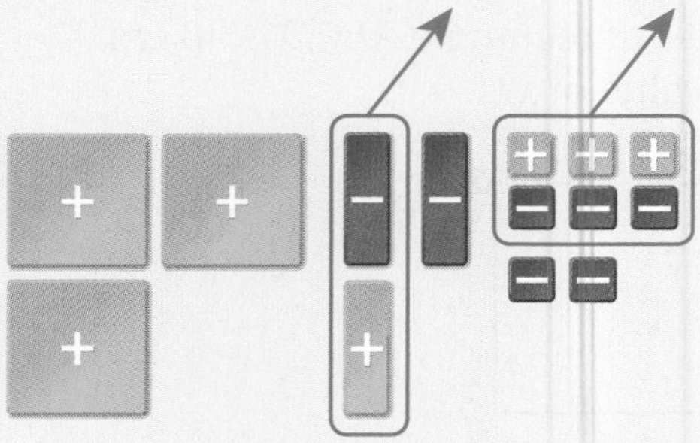

Remove any zero pairs.

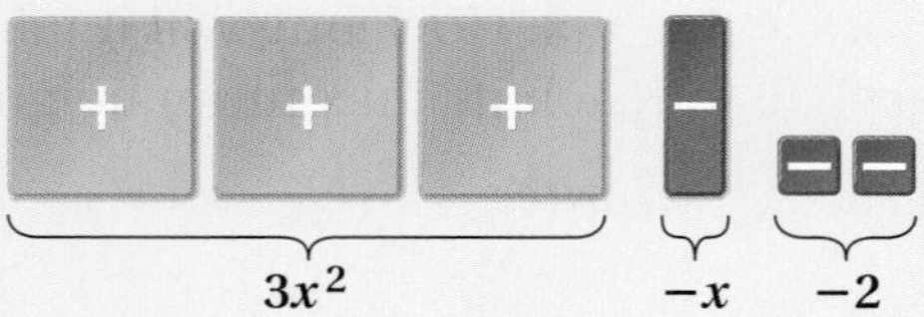

The remaining tiles represent the sum $3x^2 - x - 2$.

Think and Discuss

1. Explain what happens when you add the x-terms in $(-2x + 5) + (2x - 4)$.

Try This

Use algebra tiles to find each sum.

1. $(3m^2 + 2m + 6) + (4m^2 + m + 3)$

2. $(-5b^2 + 4b - 1) + (b - 1)$

14-3 Adding Polynomials

Learn to add polynomials.

Mina wants to put a mat and a frame around a picture that is 11 inches by 14 inches. If m is the width of the mat and f is the width of the frame, you can add polynomials to find an expression for the amount of framing material Mina needs.

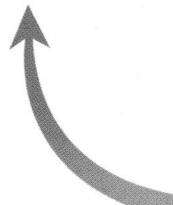

Remember, the Associative Property of Addition states that for any values of a, b, and c, $a + b + c = (a + b) + c = a + (b + c)$. You can use this property to add polynomials.

EXAMPLE 1 Adding Polynomials Horizontally

Add.

A $(6x^2 - 3x + 4) + (7x - 6)$

$(6x^2 - 3x + 4) + (7x - 6)$

$6x^2 - 3x + 4 + 7x - 6$ *Associative Property*

$6x^2 + 4x - 2$ *Combine like terms.*

B $(-4cd^2 - 3cd + 6) + (7cd - 6cd^2 - 6)$

$(-4cd^2 - 3cd + 6) + (7cd - 6cd^2 - 6)$

$-4cd^2 - 3cd + 6 + 7cd - 6cd^2 - 6$ *Associative Property*

$-10cd^2 + 4cd$ *Combine like terms.*

C $(ab^2 + 4a) + (3ab^2 + 4a - 3) + (a + 5)$

$(ab^2 + 4a) + (3ab^2 + 4a - 3) + (a + 5)$

$ab^2 + 4a + 3ab^2 + 4a - 3 + a + 5$ *Associative Property*

$4ab^2 + 9a + 2$ *Combine like terms.*

You can also add polynomials in a vertical format. Write the second polynomial below the first one, lining up the like terms. If the terms are rearranged, remember to keep the correct sign with each term.

EXAMPLE 2 Adding Polynomials Vertically

Add.

A $(5a^2 + 4a + 2) + (4a^2 + 3a + 1)$

$$\begin{array}{rl} 5a^2 + 4a + 2 & \\ +\ 4a^2 + 3a + 1 & \textit{Place like terms in columns.} \\ \hline 9a^2 + 7a + 3 & \textit{Combine like terms.} \end{array}$$

B $(2xy^2 + 3x - 4y) + (8xy^2 - 2x + 3)$

$$\begin{array}{rl} 2xy^2 + 3x - 4y & \\ +\ 8xy^2 - 2x + 3 & \textit{Place like terms in columns.} \\ \hline 10xy^2 + x - 4y + 3 & \textit{Combine like terms.} \end{array}$$

C $(4a^2b^2 + 3a^2 - 6ab) + (-4ab + a^2 - 5) + (3 + 7ab)$

$$\begin{array}{rl} 4a^2b^2 + 3a^2 - 6ab & \\ a^2 - 4ab - 5 & \\ +\ 7ab + 3 & \textit{Place like terms in columns.} \\ \hline 4a^2b^2 + 4a^2 - 3ab - 2 & \textit{Combine like terms.} \end{array}$$

EXAMPLE 3 *Art Application*

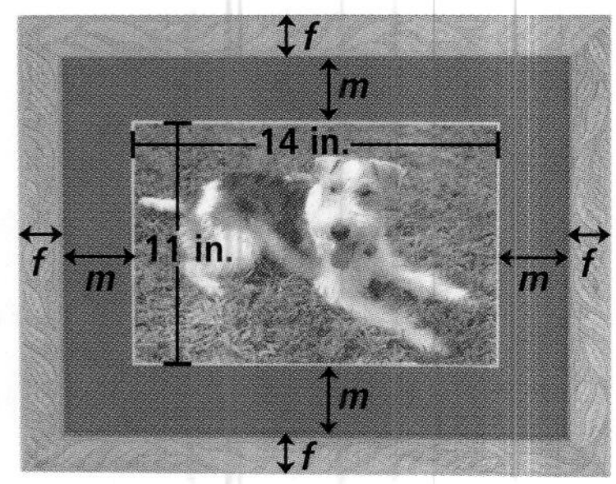

Mina is putting a mat of width *m* and a frame of width *f* around an 11-inch by 14-inch picture. Find an expression for the amount of framing material she needs.

The amount of material Mina needs equals the perimeter of the outside of the frame. Draw a diagram to help you determine the outer dimensions of the frame.

$\text{Base} = 14 + m + m + f + f$
$\quad = 14 + 2m + 2f$

$\text{Height} = 11 + m + m + f + f$
$\quad = 11 + 2m + 2f$

$P = (11 + 2m + 2f) + (14 + 2m + 2f) + (11 + 2m + 2f) + (14 + 2m + 2f)$
$\quad = 11 + 2m + 2f + 14 + 2m + 2f + 11 + 2m + 2f + 14 + 2m + 2f$
$\quad = 50 + 8m + 8f$ *Combine like terms.*

She will need $50 + 8m + 8f$ inches of framing material.

Think and Discuss

1. **Compare** adding $(5x^2 + 2x) + (3x^2 - 2x)$ vertically with adding it horizontally.
2. **Explain** why you can remove parentheses from polynomials to add the polynomials.

14-3 Exercises

go.hrw.com
Homework Help Online
KEYWORD: MT7 14-3
Parent Resources Online
KEYWORD: MT7 Parent

GUIDED PRACTICE

See Example 1

Add.

1. $(5x^3 + 6x - 1) + (-3x + 7)$
2. $(22x - 6) + (14x - 3)$
3. $(r^2s + 3rs) + (4r^2s - 8rs) + (6r^2s + 14rs)$

See Example 2

4. $(4b^2 - 5b + 10) + (6b^2 + 7b - 8)$
5. $(9ab^2 - 5ab + 6a^2b) + (8ab - 12a^2b + 6) + (6ab^2 + 5a^2b - 14)$
6. $(h^4j - hj^3 + hj - 6) + (5hj^3 + 5) + (6h^4j - 7hj)$

See Example 3

7. Colette is putting a mat of width $3w$ and a frame of width w around a 16-inch by 48-inch poster. Find an expression for the amount of frame material she needs.

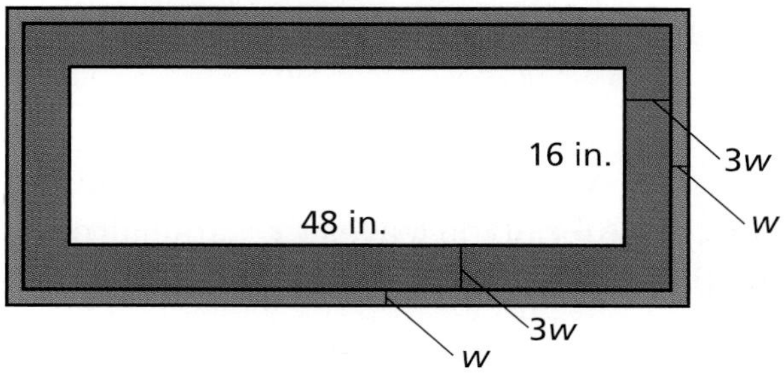

INDEPENDENT PRACTICE

See Example 1

Add.

8. $(5x^2y - 4xy + 3) + (7xy - 3x^2y)$
9. $(5g - 9) + (7g^2 - 4g + 8)$
10. $(6bc - 2b^2c^2 + 8bc^2) + (6bc - 3bc^2)$
11. $(9h^4 + 5h - 4h^6) + (h^6 - 6h + 3h^4)$
12. $(4pq - 5p^2q + 9pq^2) + (6p^2q - 11pq^2) + (2pq^2 - 7pq + 6p^2q)$

See Example 2

13. $(8t^2 + 4t + 3) + (5t^2 - 8t + 9)$
14. $(5b^3c^2 - 3b^2c + 2bc) + (8b^3c^2 - 3bc + 14) + (b^2c - 5bc - 9)$
15. $(w^2 - 3w + 5) + (-2w - 3w^2 - 1) + (w^2 + w - 6)$

See Example 3

16. Each side of an equilateral triangle has length $w + 3$. Each side of a square has length $4w - 2$. Write an expression for the sum of the perimeter of the equilateral triangle and the perimeter of the square.

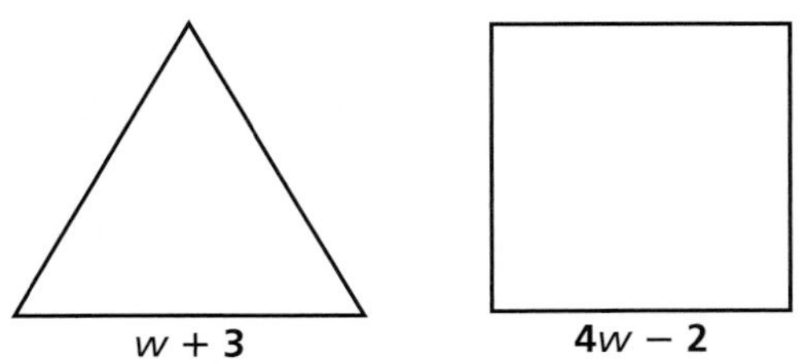

PRACTICE AND PROBLEM SOLVING

Extra Practice
See page 808.

LINK

Business

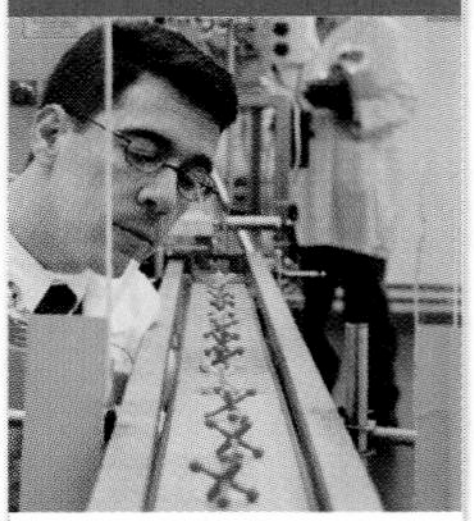

According to the Toy Industry Association, \$24.6 billion was spent on toys worldwide in 2000.

go.hrw.com
Web Extra!
KEYWORD: MT7 Toys

Add.

17. $(3w^2y + 3wy^2 - 4wy) + (5wy - 2wy^2 + 7w^2y) + (wy^2 - 5wy - 3w^2y)$

18. $(2p^2t - 3pt + 5) + (p^2t + 2pt^2 - 3pt) + (1 - 5pt^2 + p^2t)$

19. **Geometry** Write and simplify an expression for the combined volumes of a sphere with volume $\frac{4}{3}\pi r^3$, a cube with volume r^3, and a prism with volume $r^3 + 4r^2 + 5r + 2$. Use 3.14 for π.

20. **Business** The cost of producing n toys at a factory is given by the polynomial $0.5n^2 + 3n + 12$. The cost of packaging is $0.25n^2 + 5n + 4$. Write and simplify an expression for the total cost of producing and packaging n toys.

21. **Critical Thinking** Two airplanes depart from the same airport, traveling in opposite directions. After 2 hours, one airplane is $x^2 + 2x + 400$ miles from the airport, and the other airplane is $3x^2 - 50x + 100$ miles from the airport. How could you determine the distance between the two planes? Explain.

22. Write two polynomials whose sum is $3m^2 + 4m + 6$.

23. **Choose a Strategy** What is the missing term?
$(-6x^2 + 4x - 3) + (3x^2 + \square - 5) = -3x^2 - 6x - 8$

Ⓐ $2x$ Ⓑ $-2x$ Ⓒ $-10x$ Ⓓ $10x$

24. **Write a Problem** A plane leaves an airport heading north at $x + 3$ mi/h. At the same time, another plane leaves the same airport, heading south at $x + 4$ mi/h. Write a problem using the speeds of both planes.

25. **Write About It** Explain how to add polynomials.

26. **Challenge** What polynomial would have to be added to $6x^2 - 4x + 5$ so that the sum is $3x^2 + 4x - 7$?

TEST PREP and Spiral Review

27. **Multiple Choice** Debbie is putting a deck of width $5w$ around her 20 foot by 80 foot pool. Which is the expression for the perimeter of the pool and deck combined?

Ⓕ $100 + 10w$ Ⓖ $150 + 15w$ Ⓗ $200 + 20w$ Ⓙ $250 + 25w$

28. **Gridded Response** What is the sum of $(-10x^3 + 4x^4 - 3x^5 - 10)$, $(9x^3 - 8x^4 + 20x^5 + 15)$, and $(x^3 + 4x^2 - 17x^5 + 2)$?

Using the scale 1 in. = 6 ft, find the height or length of each object. (Lesson 5-8)

29. a 14 in. tall model of an office building

30. a 2.5 in. long model of a train

31. a 7 in. tall model of a billboard

32. a 4.5 in. long model of an airplane

Find the fraction equivalent of each decimal or percent. (Lesson 6-1)

33. 1.1 **34.** 58% **35.** 0.24 **36.** 300%

Hands-On LAB 14-4

Model Polynomial Subtraction

Use with Lesson 14-4

go.hrw.com
Lab Resources Online
KEYWORD: MT7 Lab14

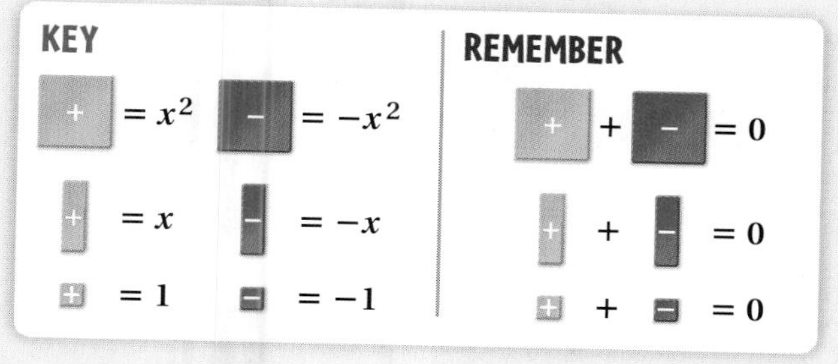

You can use algebra tiles to model polynomial subtraction.

Activity

1 Use algebra tiles to find the difference $(2x^2 - 2x + 3) - (x^2 + x - 3)$.

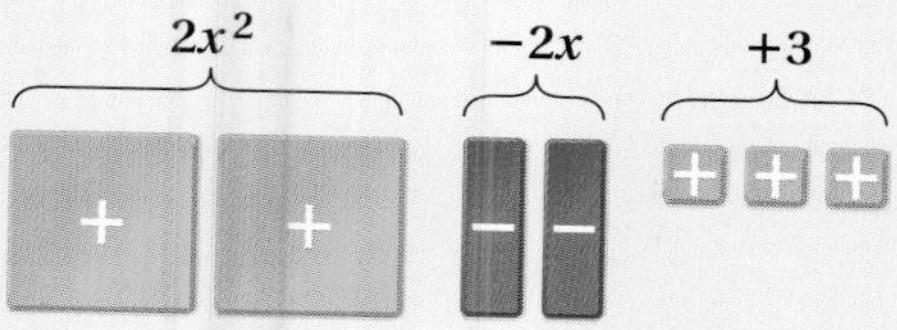

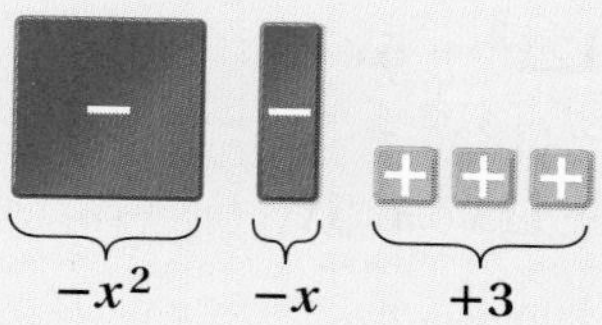

Remember, subtracting is the same as adding the opposite. Use the opposite of each term in $x^2 + x - 3$.

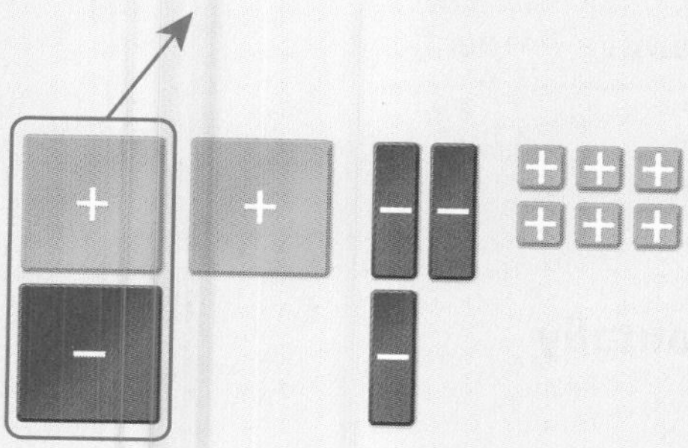

Remove any zero pairs.

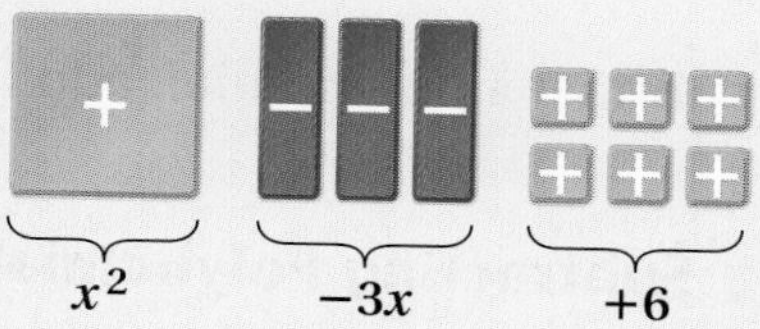

The remaining tiles represent the difference $x^2 - 3x + 6$.

Think and Discuss

1. Why do you have to add the opposite when subtracting?

Try This

Use algebra tiles to find each difference.

1. $(6m^2 + 2m) - (4m^2)$

2. $(-5b^2 - 9) - (b - 9)$

14-4 Subtracting Polynomials

Learn to subtract polynomials.

Manufacturers can use polynomials to estimate the cost of making a product and the revenue from sales. To estimate profits, they would subtract these polynomials.

Subtraction is the opposite of addition. To subtract a polynomial, you need to find its opposite.

EXAMPLE 1 Finding the Opposite of a Polynomial

Find the opposite of each polynomial.

A $8x^3y^6z$

$-(8x^3y^6z)$

$-8x^3y^6z$

B $12x^2 - 5x$

$-(12x^2 - 5x)$

$-12x^2 + 5x$ *Distributive Property*

C $-3ab^2 - 4ab + 3$

$-(-3ab^2 - 4ab + 3)$

$3ab^2 + 4ab - 3$ *Distributive Property*

To subtract a polynomial, add its opposite.

EXAMPLE 2 Subtracting Polynomials Horizontally

Subtract.

A $(n^3 - n + 5n^2) - (7n - 4n^2 + 9)$

$= (n^3 - n + 5n^2) + (-7n + 4n^2 - 9)$ *Add the opposite.*

$= n^3 - n + 5n^2 - 7n + 4n^2 - 9$ *Associative Property*

$= n^3 + 9n^2 - 8n - 9$ *Combine like terms.*

B $(-2cd^2 + cd + 4) - (-7cd^2 + 2 - 5cd)$

$= (-2cd^2 + cd + 4) + (7cd^2 - 2 + 5cd)$ *Add the opposite.*

$= -2cd^2 + cd + 4 + 7cd^2 - 2 + 5cd$ *Associative Property*

$= 5cd^2 + 6cd + 2$ *Combine like terms.*

You can also subtract polynomials in a vertical format. Write the second polynomial below the first one, lining up the like terms.

EXAMPLE 3 Subtracting Polynomials Vertically

Subtract.

A $(x^3 + 4x + 1) - (6x^3 + 3x + 5)$

$$\begin{array}{rcrl} (x^3 + 4x + 1) & & x^3 + 4x + 1 & \\ \underline{-\ (6x^3 + 3x + 5)} & \longrightarrow & \underline{+\ -6x^3 - 3x - 5} & \textit{Add the opposite.} \\ & & -5x^3 + \ \ x - 5 & \end{array}$$

B $(4m^2n - 3mn - 4m) - (-8m^2n - 6mn + 3)$

$$\begin{array}{rcrl} (4m^2n - 3mn - 4m) & & 4m^2n - 3mn - 4m & \\ \underline{-\ (-8m^2n - 6mn + 3)} & \longrightarrow & \underline{+\ \ 8m^2n + 6mn \qquad\quad - 3} & \textit{Add the} \\ & & 12m^2n + 3mn - 4m - 3 & \textit{opposite.} \end{array}$$

C $(4x^2y^2 + xy - 6x) - (7x + 5xy - 6)$

$$\begin{array}{rcrl} (4x^2y^2 + \ xy - 6x) & & 4x^2y^2 + \ xy - \ 6x & \\ \underline{-\ (7x \ + 5xy - 6)} & \longrightarrow & \underline{+ \qquad\quad - 5xy - \ 7x + 6} & \textit{Rearrange terms} \\ & & 4x^2y^2 - 4xy - 13x + 6 & \textit{as needed.} \end{array}$$

EXAMPLE 4 *Business Application*

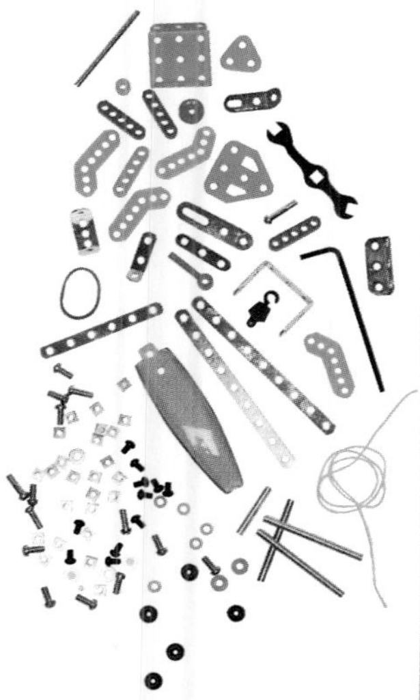

Suppose the cost in dollars of producing x model kits is given by the polynomial 400,000 + 3x and the revenue generated from sales is given by the polynomial 20x − 0.00004x^2. Find a polynomial expression for the profit from making and selling x model kits, and evaluate the expression for x = 200,000.

$20x - 0.00004x^2 - (400{,}000 + 3x)$	*revenue − cost*
$20x - 0.00004x^2 + (-400{,}000 - 3x)$	*Add the opposite.*
$20x - 0.00004x^2 - 400{,}000 - 3x$	*Associative Property*
$17x - 0.00004x^2 - 400{,}000$	*Combine like terms.*

The profit is given by the polynomial $17x - 0.00004x^2 - 400{,}000$. For $x = 200{,}000$,

$$17(200{,}000) - 0.00004(200{,}000)^2 - 400{,}000 = 1{,}400{,}000$$

The profit is $1,400,000, or $1.4 million.

Think and Discuss

1. **Explain** how to find the opposite of a polynomial.
2. **Compare** subtracting polynomials with adding polynomials.

14-4 Exercises

go.hrw.com
Homework Help Online
KEYWORD: MT7 14-4
Parent Resources Online
KEYWORD: MT7 Parent

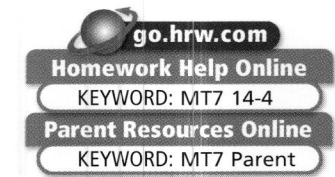

GUIDED PRACTICE

See Example 1

Find the opposite of each polynomial.

1. $4x^2y$
2. $-5x + 4xy^5$
3. $3x^2 - 8x + 5$
4. $-5y^2 - 2y + 4$
5. $-8x^3 + 5x - 6$
6. $6xy^2 + 4y + 2$

See Example 2

Subtract.

7. $(2b^3 + 5b^2 - 8) - (4b^3 + b - 12)$
8. $7b - (4b^2 + 3b - 12)$
9. $(4m^2n - 7mn + 3mn^2) - (-5mn - 4m^2n)$

See Example 3

10. $(8x^2 - 4x + 1) - (5x^2 + 2x + 3)$
11. $(-2x^2y - xy + 3x - 4) - (4xy - 7x + 4)$
12. $(-5ab^2 + 4ab - 3a^2b) - (7 - 5ab + 3ab^2 + 4a^2b)$

See Example 4

13. The volume of a rectangular prism, in cubic inches, is given by the expression $x^3 + 3x^2 - 5x + 7$. The volume of a smaller rectangular prism is given by the expression $5x^3 - 6x^2 + 7x - 14$. How much greater is the volume of the larger rectangular prism?

INDEPENDENT PRACTICE

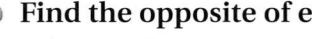

See Example 1

Find the opposite of each polynomial.

14. $-4rn^2$
15. $3v - 5v^2$
16. $4m^2 - 6m + 2$
17. $4xy^2 + 2xy$
18. $-8n^6 + 5n^3 - n$
19. $-9b^2 - 2b - 9$

See Example 2

Subtract.

20. $(6w^2 + 3w + 6) - (3w^2 + 4w - 5)$
21. $(14a + a^2) - (8 + a^2 + 9a)$
22. $(7r^2s^2 - 5rs^2 + 6r^2s + 7rs) - (3rs^2 - 3r^2s + 8rs)$

See Example 3

23. $(4x^2 + 6x - 1) - (3x^2 + 9x - 5)$
24. $(3a^2b^2 - 4ab - 2a - 4) - (4a^2b^2 + 5a - 3b + 6)$
25. $(4pt^2 - 6p^3 + 5p^2t^2) - (5p^2 - 6pt^2 + 7p^2t^2)$

See Example 4

26. The current in an electrical circuit at t seconds is $4t^3 - 5t^2 + 2t + 200$ amperes. The current in another electrical circuit is $3t^3 - 2t^2 + 5t + 100$ amperes. Write an expression to show the difference in the two currents.

PRACTICE AND PROBLEM SOLVING

Extra Practice
See page 809.

Subtract.

27. $(6a + 3b - 5ab) - (6a + 5b - 7ab)$

28. $(4pq^2 - 6p^2q + 3pq) - (7pq^2 + 7p^2q - 3pq)$

29. $(9y^2 - 5x^2y + x^2) - (3y^2 + 7x^2y - 4x^2)$

30. The area of the rectangle is $2a^2 - 4a + 5$ cm^2. The area of the square is $a^2 - 2a - 6$ cm^2. What is the area of the shaded region?

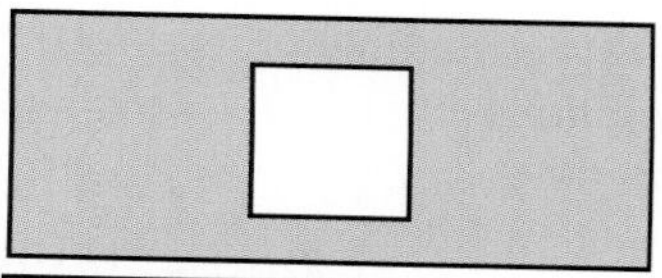

31. The area of the square is $4x^2 - 2x - 6$ in^2. The area of the triangle is $2x^2 + 4x - 5$ in^2. What is the area of the shaded region?

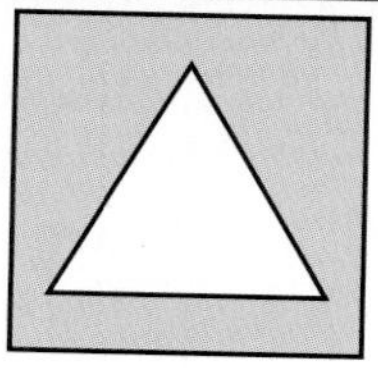

32. Business The price in dollars of one share of stock after y years is modeled by the expression $3y^3 - 6y + 4.25$. The price of one share of another stock is modeled by $3y^3 + 24y + 25.5$. What expression shows the difference in price of the two stocks after y years?

33. Choose a Strategy Which polynomial has the greatest value when $x = 6$?

Ⓐ $x^2 - 3x + 8$

Ⓑ $2x^4 + 7x + 14$

Ⓒ $-x^3 - 30x - 200$

Ⓓ $x^5 - 100x^4 + 10$

34. Write About It Explain how to subtract the polynomial $5x^3 - 3x - 6$ from $4x^3 + 7x + 1$.

35. Challenge Find the values of a, b, c, and d that make the equation true.
$(2t^3 - at^2 - 4bt - 6) - (ct^3 + 4t^2 + 7t + 1) = 4t^3 - 5t^2 - 15t + d$

TEST PREP and Spiral Review

36. Multiple Choice What is the opposite of the polynomial $-4a^2b - 3ab^2 + 5ab$?

Ⓕ $4a^2b + 3ab^2 + 5ab$

Ⓖ $4a^2b - 3ab^2 + 5ab$

Ⓗ $-4a^2b - 3ab^2 - 5ab$

Ⓙ $4a^2b + 3ab^2 - 5ab$

37. Extended Response A square has an area of $x^2 + 10x + 25$. A triangle inside the square has an area of $x^2 - 4$. Create an expression for the area of the square minus the area of the triangle. Evaluate the expression for $x = 8$.

Find the two square roots of each number. (Lesson 4-5)

38. 49 **39.** 9 **40.** 81 **41.** 169

Simplify. (Lesson 14-2)

42. $x^3y^2 - 2x^2y - 4x^3y^2$ **43.** $4(zy^3 - 2zy) + 3zy - 5zy^3$ **44.** $6(3x^2 - 6x - 1)$

14-5 Multiplying Polynomials by Monomials

Learn to multiply polynomials by monomials.

Chrystelle is making a square planter box in her woodworking class. The box's height is to be 3 inches more than the side length of its base. The volume of the box is found by multiplying a polynomial by a monomial.

Remember that when you multiply two powers with the same bases, you add the exponents. To multiply two monomials, multiply the coefficients and add the exponents of the variables that are the same.

$(5m^2n^3)(6m^3n^6) = 5 \cdot 6 \cdot m^{2+3}n^{3+6} = 30m^5n^9$

EXAMPLE 1 Multiplying Monomials

Multiply.

A $(4r^3s^4)(6r^5s^6)$

$4 \cdot 6 \cdot r^{3+5} \cdot s^{4+6}$ *Multiply coefficients and add exponents.*

$24r^8s^{10}$

B $(9x^2y)(-2x^3yz^6)$

$9 \cdot -2 \cdot x^{2+3} \cdot y^{1+1} \cdot z^6$ *Multiply coefficients and add exponents.*

$-18x^5y^2z^6$

To multiply a polynomial by a monomial, use the Distributive Property. Multiply every term of the polynomial by the monomial.

EXAMPLE 2 Multiplying a Polynomial by a Monomial

Multiply.

A $\frac{1}{4}x(y + z)$

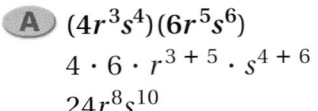

$\frac{1}{4}x(y + z)$ *Multiply each term in the parentheses by $\frac{1}{4}x$.*

$\frac{1}{4}xy + \frac{1}{4}xz$

B $-5a^2b(3a^4b^3 + 6a^2b^3)$

$-5a^2b(3a^4b^3 + 6a^2b^3)$ *Multiply each term in the parentheses by $-5a^2b$.*

$-15a^6b^4 - 30a^4b^4$

Helpful Hint

When multiplying a polynomial by a negative monomial, be sure to distribute the negative sign.

Multiply.

C $5rs^2(r^2s^4 + 3rs^3 - 4rst)$

$5rs^2(r^2s^4 + 3rs^3 - 4rst)$

$5r^3s^6 + 15r^2s^5 - 20r^2s^3t$

Multiply each term in the parentheses by $5rs^2$.

EXAMPLE 3 PROBLEM SOLVING APPLICATION

PROBLEM SOLVING

Chrystelle is making a planter box with a square base. She wants the height of the box to be 3 inches more than the side length of the base. If she wants the volume of the box to be 6804 in^3, what should the side length of the base be?

1 Understand the Problem

If the side length of the base is s, then the height is $s + 3$. The volume is $s \cdot s \cdot (s + 3) = s^2(s + 3)$. The **answer** will be a value of s that makes the volume of the box equal to 6804 in^3.

2 Make a Plan

You can make a table of values for the polynomial to try to find the value of s. Use the Distributive Property to write the expression $s^2(s + 3)$ another way. Use substitution to complete the table.

3 Solve

$s^2(s + 3) = s^3 - 3s^2$ *Distributive Property*

s	15	16	17	18
$s^3 + 3s^2$	$15^3 + 3(15)^2 = 4050$	$16^3 + 3(16)^2 = 4864$	$17^3 + 3(17)^2 = 5780$	$18^3 + 3(18)^2 = 6804$

The side length of the base should be 18 inches.

4 Look Back

If the side length of the base were 18 inches and the height were 3 inches more, or 21 inches, then the volume would be $18 \cdot 18 \cdot 21 = 6804$ in^3. The answer is reasonable.

Think and Discuss

1. **Compare** multiplying two monomials with multiplying a polynomial by a monomial.

14-5 Exercises

go.hrw.com
Homework Help Online
KEYWORD: MT7 14-5
Parent Resources Online
KEYWORD: MT7 Parent

GUIDED PRACTICE

See Example 1

Multiply.

1. $(-5s^2t^2)(3st^3)$ **2.** $(x^2y^3)(6x^4y^3)$ **3.** $(5h^2j^4)(-7h^4j^6)$

4. $6m(4m^5)$ **5.** $7p^3r(5pr^4)$ **6.** $13g^5h^3(10g^5h^2)$

See Example 2

7. $2h(3m - 4h)$ **8.** $4ab(a^2b - ab^2)$

9. $-3x(x^2 - 5x + 10)$ **10.** $6c^2d(3cd^3 - 5c^3d^2 + 4cd)$

See Example 3

11. The formula for the area of a trapezoid is $A = \frac{1}{2}h(b_1 + b_2)$, where h is the trapezoid's height and b_1 and b_2 are the lengths of its bases. Use the Distributive Property to simplify the expression. Then use the expression to find the area of a trapezoid with height 12 in. and base lengths 9 in. and 7 in.

INDEPENDENT PRACTICE

See Example 1

Multiply.

12. $(6x^2y^5)(-3xy^4)$ **13.** $(-gh^3)(-2g^2h^5)$ **14.** $(4a^2b)(2b^3)$

15. $(-s^4t^3)(2st)$ **16.** $12x^9y^7\left(\frac{1}{2}x^3y\right)$ **17.** $2.5j^3(3h^5j^7)$

See Example 2

18. $(3m^3n^4)(1 - 5mn^5)$ **19.** $3z(5z^2 - 4z)$

20. $-3h^2(6h + 3h^3)$ **21.** $-3cd(2c^3d^2 - 4cd^2)$

22. $-2b(4b^4 - 7b + 10)$ **23.** $-3s^2t^2(4s^2t + 5st - 2s^2t^2)$

See Example 3

24. A rectangle has a base of length $3x^2y$ and a height of $2x^3 - 4xy - 3$. Write and simplify an expression for the area of the rectangle. Then find the area of the rectangle if $x = 2$ and $y = 1$.

PRACTICE AND PROBLEM SOLVING

Extra Practice
See page 809.

Multiply.

25. $(-3b^2)(8b^4)$ **26.** $(4m^2n)(2mn^4)$

27. $(-2a^2b^2)(-3ab^4)$ **28.** $7g(g - 5)$

29. $-3m^2(m^3 - 5m)$ **30.** $2ab(3a^2b + 3ab^2)$

31. $x^4(x - x^3y^5)$ **32.** $m(x + 3)$

33. $f^2g^2(3 + f - g^3)$ **34.** $x^2(x^2 - 4x + 9)$

35. $(4m^2p^4)(5m^2p^4 - 3mp^3 + 6m^2p)$ **36.** $-3wz(5w^4z^2 + 4wz^2 - 6w^2z^2)$

37. Felix is building a cylindrical-shaped storage container. The height of the container is $x^3 - y^3$. Write and simplify an expression for the volume using the formula $V = \pi r^2h$. Then find the volume with $r = 1\frac{1}{2}$ feet, $x = 3$, and $y = -1$.

38. **Health** The table gives some formulas for finding the target heart rate for a person of age a exercising at p percent of his or her maximum heart rate.

	Target Heart Rate	
	Male	Female
Nonathletic	$p(220 - a)$	$p(226 - a)$
Fit	$\frac{1}{2}p(410 - a)$	$\frac{1}{2}p(422 - a)$

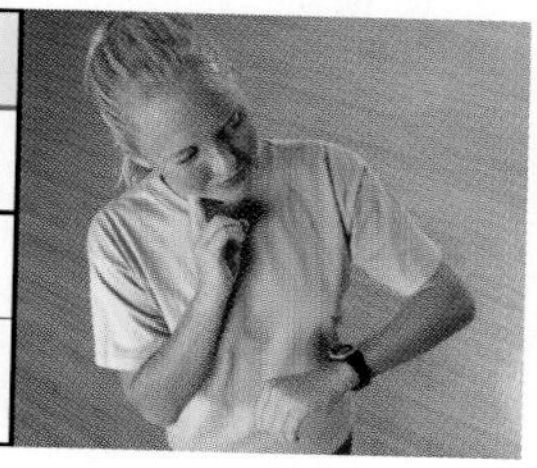

a. Use the Distributive Property to simplify each expression.

b. Use your answer from part **a** to write an expression for the difference between the target heart rate for a fit male and for a fit female. Both people are age a and are exercising at p percent of their maximum heart rates.

39. **What's the Question?** A square prism has a base area of x^2 and a height of $3x + 4$. If the answer is $3x^3 + 4x^2$, what is the question? If the answer is $14x^2 + 16x$, what is the question?

40. **Write About It** If a polynomial is multiplied by a monomial, what can you say about the number of terms in the answer? What can you say about the degree of the answer?

41. **Challenge** On a multiple-choice test, if the probability of guessing each question correctly is p, then the probability of guessing two or more correctly out of four is $6p^2(1 - 2p - p^2) + 4p^3(1 - p) + p^4$. Simplify the expression. Then write an expression for the probability of guessing fewer than two out of four correctly.

Test Prep and Spiral Review

42. **Multiple Choice** The width of a rectangle is 13 feet less than twice its length. What is the width of the rectangle if the area is 24 ft^2?

Ⓐ 3 ft Ⓑ 8 ft Ⓒ 9 ft Ⓓ 13 ft

43. **Short Response** A triangle has base $10cd^2$ and height $3c^2d^2 - 4cd^2$. Write and simplify an expression for the area of the triangle. Then evaluate the expression for $c = 2$ and $d = 3$.

Find the surface area of each figure to the nearest tenth. Use 3.14 for π. (Lesson 8-7)

44. a rectangular prism with base 4 in. by 3 in. and height 2.5 in.

45. a cylinder with radius 10 cm and height 7 cm

Find the inverse variation equation, given that x and y vary inversely. (Lesson 13-7)

46. $y = 4$ when $x = 12$

47. $y = 16$ when $x = 4$

48. $y = 9$ when $x = 5$

Hands-On LAB 14-6

Multiply Binomials

Use with Lesson 14-6

go.hrw.com
Lab Resources Online
KEYWORD: MT7 Lab14

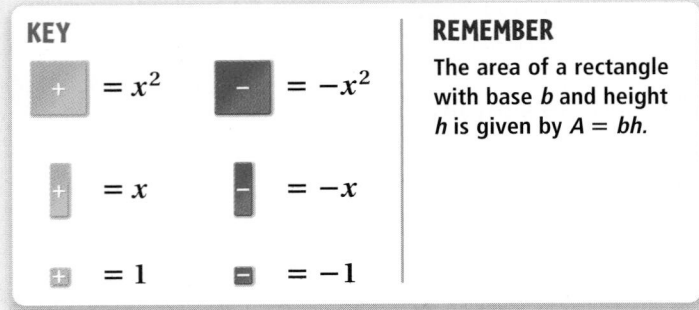

KEY

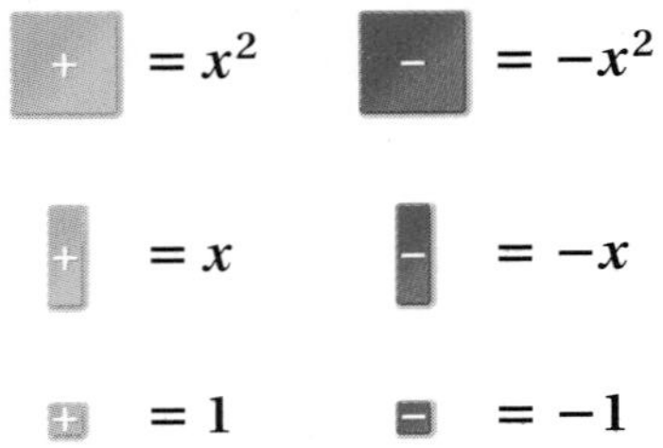

REMEMBER

The area of a rectangle with base *b* and height *h* is given by $A = bh$.

You can use algebra tiles to find the product of two binomials.

Activity 1

1 To model the product of $(x + 3)(2x + 1)$ with algebra tiles, make a rectangle with base $x + 3$ and height $2x + 1$.

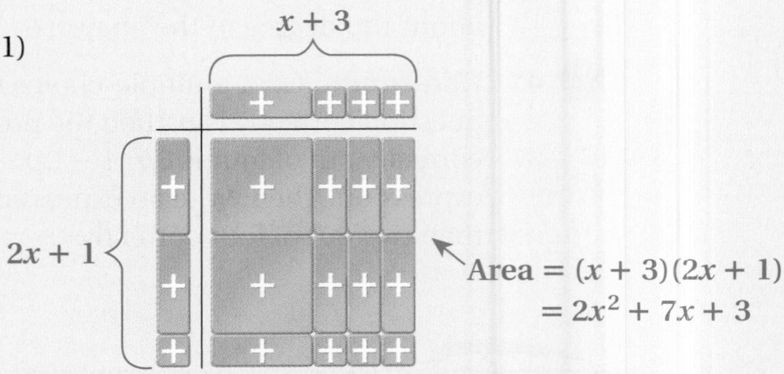

2 Use algebra tiles to find the product of $(x - 2)(-x + 1)$.

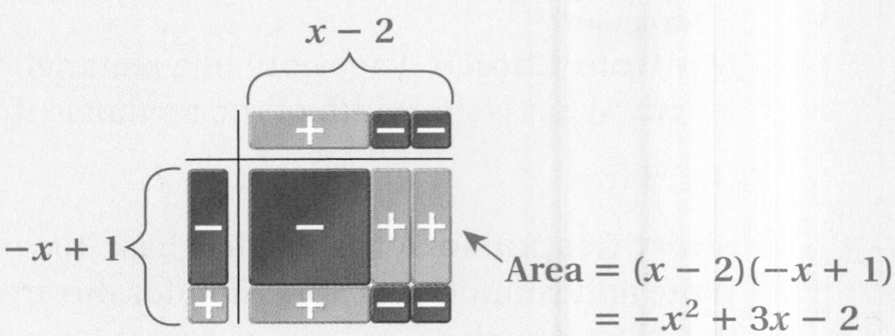

Think and Discuss

1. Explain how to determine the signs of each term in the product when you are multiplying $(x - 3)(x - 2)$.
2. How can you use algebra tiles to find $(x + 3)(x - 3)$?

Try This

Use algebra tiles to find each product.

1. $(x + 4)(x - 4)$ **2.** $(x - 3)(x + 2)$ **3.** $(x - 5)(-x + 3)$

Activity 2

Write two binomials whose product is modeled by the algebra tiles below, and then write the product as a polynomial expression.

The base of the rectangle is $x - 5$ and the height is $x - 2$, so the binomial product is $(x - 5)(x - 2)$.

The model shows one x^2-tile, seven $-x$-tiles, and ten 1-tiles, so the polynomial expression is $x^2 - 7x + 10$.

Think and Discuss

1. Write an expression modeled by the algebra tiles below. How many zero pairs are modeled? Describe them.

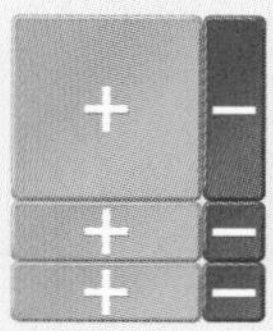

Try This

Write two binomials whose product is modeled by each set of algebra tiles below, and then write the product as a polynomial expression.

1. 

2. 

3. 

14-6 Multiplying Binomials

Learn to multiply binomials.

Vocabulary
FOIL

Jordan Middle School is designing a cactus garden. One raised bed will measure 12 ft by 5 ft. There will be a bark covered walkway of width x feet around the raised flower bed. To find the area of the bark walkway, you need to multiply two binomials.

You can use the Distributive Property to multiply two binomials.

$$(x + y)(x + z) = x(x + z) + y(x + z) = x^2 + xz + xy + yz$$

The product can be simplified using the **FOIL** method: the **F**irst terms, the **O**uter terms, the **I**nner terms, and the **L**ast terms of the binomials.

First   Last

$$(x + y)(x + z) = x^2 + xz + xy + yz$$

Inner
Outer

EXAMPLE 1 Multiplying Two Binomials

Multiply.

A $(p + 2)(3 - q)$

$(p + 2)(3 - q)$ *FOIL*

$3p - pq + 6 - 2q$

B $(m + n)(p + q)$

$(m + n)(p + q)$

$mp + mq + np + nq$

C $(x + 2)(x + 5)$

$(x + 2)(x + 5)$ *FOIL*

$x^2 + 5x + 2x + 10$

$x^2 + 7x + 10$ *Combine like terms.*

D $(3m + n)(m - 2n)$

$(3m + n)(m - 2n)$

$3m^2 - 6mn + mn - 2n^2$

$3m^2 - 5mn - 2n^2$

Helpful Hint

When you multiply two binomials, you will get four products. Then combine like terms.

EXAMPLE 2 Multi-Step

Find the area of a bark walkway of width x ft around a 12 ft by 5 ft raised flower bed.

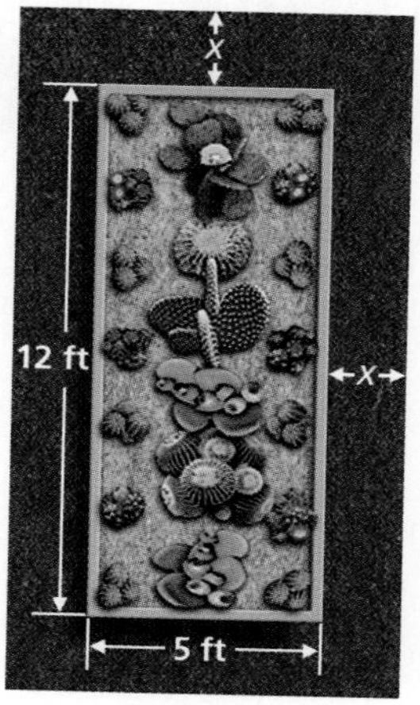

Area of Walkway =	Total Area	− Area of Flower Bed
	$= (5 + 2x)(12 + 2x)$	$- (5)(12)$
	$= 60 + 10x + 24x + 4x^2$	$- 60$
	$4x^2 + 34x$	

The walkway area is $34x + 4x^2$ ft^2.

Binomial products of the form $(a + b)^2$, $(a - b)^2$, and $(a + b)(a - b)$ are often called *special products*.

EXAMPLE 3 Special Products of Binomials

Multiply.

A $(x - 3)^2$

$(x - 3)(x - 3)$

$x^2 - 3x - 3x + 3^2$

$x^2 - 6x + 9$

B $(a + b)^2$

$(a + b)(a + b)$

$a^2 + ab + ab + b^2$

$a^2 + 2ab + b^2$

C $(n + 3)(n - 3)$

$(n + 3)(n - 3)$

$n^2 - 3n + 3n - 3^2$

$n^2 - 9$ *$-3n + 3n = 0$*

Special Products of Binomials
$(a + b)^2 = a^2 + ab + ab + b^2 = a^2 + 2ab + b^2$
$(a - b)^2 = a^2 - ab - ab + b^2 = a^2 - 2ab + b^2$
$(a + b)(a - b) = a^2 - ab + ab - b^2 = a^2 - b^2$

Think and Discuss

1. **Give an example** of a product of two binomials that has 4 terms, one that has 3 terms, and one that has 2 terms.

14-6 Exercises

go.hrw.com
Homework Help Online
KEYWORD: MT7 14-6
Parent Resources Online
KEYWORD: MT7 Parent

GUIDED PRACTICE

See Example 1

Multiply.

1. $(x - 5)(y + 4)$ **2.** $(x - 3)(x + 7)$ **3.** $(3m - 5)(4m + 9)$

4. $(h + 2)(3h + 4)$ **5.** $(m - 2)(m - 7)$ **6.** $(b + 3c)(4b + c)$

See Example 2

7. A courtyard is constructed in a 20 ft by 30 ft space. There is a walkway of width x all the way around the courtyard. Find the area of the walkway.

See Example 3

Multiply.

8. $(x + 2)^2$ **9.** $(b - 3)(b + 3)$ **10.** $(x - 4)^2$ **11.** $(3x + 5)^2$

INDEPENDENT PRACTICE

See Example 1

Multiply.

12. $(x + 4)(x - 3)$ **13.** $(v - 1)(v + 5)$ **14.** $(w + 6)(w + 2)$

15. $(3x - 5)(x + 6)$ **16.** $(4m - 1)(3m + 2)$ **17.** $(3b - c)(4b + 5c)$

18. $(3t - 1)(t + 1)$ **19.** $(3r + s)(4r - 5s)$ **20.** $(5n - 3b)(n + 2b)$

See Example 2

21. **Construction** The Gonzalez family is having a pool to swim laps built in their backyard. The pool will be 25 yards long by 5 yards wide. There will be a cement deck of width x yards around the pool. Find the total area of the pool and the deck.

See Example 3

Multiply.

22. $(x - 5)^2$ **23.** $(b + 3)^2$ **24.** $(x - 4)(x + 4)$

25. $(2x + 3)(2x - 3)$ **26.** $(4x - 1)^2$ **27.** $(a + 7)^2$

PRACTICE AND PROBLEM SOLVING

Extra Practice
See page 809.

Multiply.

28. $(m - 6)(m + 6)$ **29.** $(b - 5)(b + 12)$ **30.** $(q + 6)(q + 5)$

31. $(t - 9)(t - 4)$ **32.** $(g + 3)(g - 3)$ **33.** $(3b + 7)(b - 4)$

34. $(3t - 1)(6t + 7)$ **35.** $(4m - n)(m + 3n)$ **36.** $(3a + 6b)^2$

37. $(r + 5)(r - 5)$ **38.** $(5q - 2)^2$ **39.** $(3r - 2s)(5r - 4s)$

40. A metalworker makes a box from a 15 in. by 20 in. piece of tin by cutting a square with side length x out of each corner and folding up the sides. Write and simplify an expression for the area of the base of the box.

Life Science LINK

A. V. Hill (1886–1977) was a biophysicist and pioneer in the study of how muscles work. He studied muscle contractions in frogs and came up with an equation relating the force generated by a muscle to the speed at which the muscle contracts. Hill expressed this relationship as

$$(P + a)(V + b) = c,$$

where P is the force generated by the muscle, a is the force needed to make the muscle contract, V is the speed at which the muscle contracts, b is the smallest contraction rate of the muscle, and c is a constant.

41. Use the FOIL method to simplify Hill's equation.

42. Suppose the force a needed to make the muscle contract is approximately $\frac{1}{4}$ the maximum force the muscle can generate. Use Hill's equation to write an equation for a muscle generating the maximum possible force M. Simplify the equation.

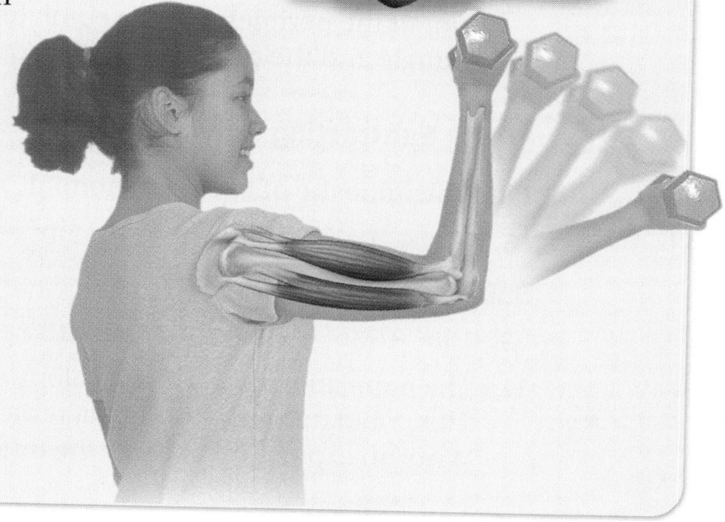

43. **Write About It** In Hill's equation, what happens to V as P increases? What happens to P as V increases? (*Hint:* You can substitute the value of 1 for a, b, and c to help you see the relationship between P and V.)

44. **Challenge** Solve Hill's equation for P. Assume that no variables equal 0.

Test Prep and Spiral Review

45. **Multiple Choice** Which polynomial shows the result of using the FOIL method to find $(x - 2)(x + 6)$?

Ⓐ $x^2 - 12$ Ⓑ $x^2 + 6x - 2x - 12$ Ⓒ $2x - 2x - 12$ Ⓓ $x^2 + 4$

46. **Gridded Response** Multiply $(3a - 2b)$ and $(5a + 8b)$. What is the coefficient of ab?

Find the scale factor that relates each model to the actual object. (Lesson 5-8)

47. 14 in. model, 70 in. object

48. 8 cm model, 16 cm object

49. 4 in. model, 6 ft 8 in. object

50. 2 cm model, 50 cm object

Simplify. (Lesson 14-2)

51. $-4(m^2 - 3m + 6)$

52. $3(a^2b - 4a + 3ab) - 2ab$

53. $x^2y + 4(xy^2 - 3x^2y + 4xy)$

CHAPTER 14

READY TO GO ON?

SECTION 14B

Quiz for Lessons 14-3 Through 14-6

14-3 Adding Polynomials

Add.

1. $(8x^3 + 6x - 3) + (-2x + 6)$
2. $(30x - 7) + (12x - 5)$
3. $(7b^3c^2 - 6b^2c + 3bc) + (8b^3c^2 - 5bc + 13) + (4b^2c - 5bc - 9)$
4. $(2w^2 - 4w + 6) + (-3w - 4w^2 - 5) + (w^2 + 4 - 4)$
5. Each side of an equilateral triangle has length $w + 2$. Each side of a square has length $3w - 4$. Write an expression for the sum of the perimeter of the equilateral triangle and the perimeter of the square.

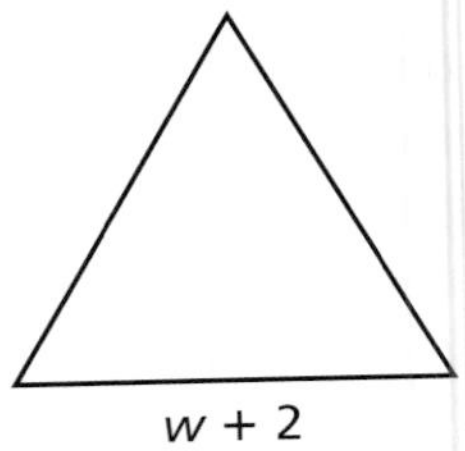

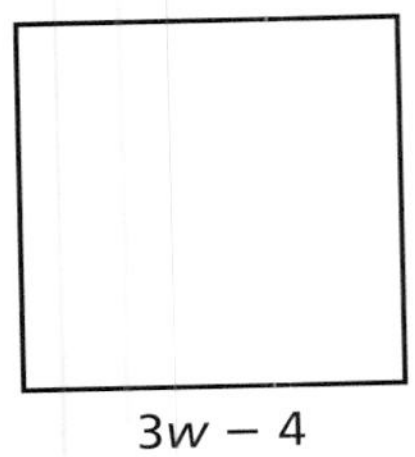

14-4 Subtracting Polynomials

Find the opposite of each polynomial.

6. $-3x + 4xy^3$
7. $2m^2 - 6m + 3$
8. $5v - 7v^2$

Subtract.

9. $10b^2 - (3b^2 + 6b - 8)$
10. $(13a + a^2) - (9 + a + 7a)$
11. $(6x^2 + 6x) - (3x^2 + 7x)$
12. The population of a bacteria colony after h hours is $4h^3 - 5h^2 + 2h + 200$. The population of another bacteria colony is $3h^3 - 2h^2 + 5h + 200$. Write an expression to show the difference between the two populations.

14-5 Multiplying Polynomials and Monomials

Multiply.

13. $(4x^3y^3)(-3xy^6)$
14. $(-s^2t^3)(st)$
15. $(3hj^5)(-6h^4j^5)$
16. $5c^2d(3cd^3 - 2c^3d^2 + 4cd)$
17. $-4s^2t^2(4s^2t + 3st - s^2t^2)$
18. A triangle has a base of length $2x^2y$ and a height of $x^3 - xy - 2$. Write and simplify an expression for the area of the triangle. Then find the area of the triangle if $x = 2$ and $y = 1$.

14-6 Multiplying Binomials

Multiply.

19. $(x - 2)(x + 6)$
20. $(3m - 4)(2m + 8)$
21. $(n - 5)(n - 3)$
22. $(x - 6)^2$
23. $(x - 5)(x + 5)$
24. $(3x + 2)(3x - 2)$
25. A rug is placed in a 10 ft × 20 ft room so that there is an uncovered strip of width x all the way around the rug. Find the area of the rug.

MULTI-STEP TEST PREP

Cooking Up a New Kitchen

Javier is a contractor who remodels kitchens. He drew the figure to help calculate the dimensions of a countertop surrounding a sink that is x inches long and y inches wide.

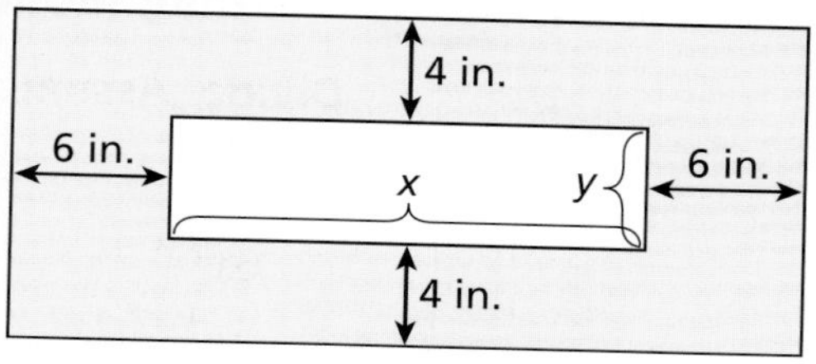

1. Write a polynomial that Javier can use to find the perimeter of the outer edge of the countertop.
2. Someone orders a countertop for a sink that is 18 inches long and 12 inches wide. Javier puts tape around the outer edge of the countertop to protect it while it is being moved. Use the polynomial to determine how many inches of tape are needed.
3. Write a polynomial that Javier can use to find the area of the countertop for any size sink.
4. The marble for the countertop costs \$1.25 per square inch. Write a polynomial that gives the cost of the countertop.
5. Find the cost of the countertop for the 18-inch by 12-inch sink. Explain your answer.

EXTENSION

Dividing Polynomials by Monomials

Learn to divide polynomials by monomials.

Remember that when you divide a monomial by a monomial, you subtract the exponents of variables that are in the denominator from the exponents of the like variables that are in the numerator.

EXAMPLE 1 Dividing Monomials by Monomials

Divide. Assume that no denominator equals zero.

A $\frac{12x^7}{2x^3}$

$6x^{7-3}$ — *Divide coefficients. Subtract exponents of like variables.*

$6x^4$

B $\frac{8x^7y^4}{6x^5y^3}$

$\frac{4}{3}x^{7-5}y^{4-3}$ — *Divide coefficients. Subtract exponents of like variables.*

$\frac{4}{3}x^2y^1 = \frac{4}{3}x^2y$

When you divide a polynomial by a monomial, you divide each term of the polynomial by the monomial.

EXAMPLE 2 Dividing Polynomials by Monomials

Remember!

For any nonzero number x, $x^0 = 1$.

Divide. Assume that no denominator equals zero.

A $(x^4 + 3x^3 - 5x^2) \div x^2$

$\frac{x^4 + 3x^3 - 5x^2}{x^2}$ — *Write the expression as a fraction.*

$\frac{x^4}{x^2} + \frac{3x^3}{x^2} - \frac{5x^2}{x^2}$ — *Divide each term of the numerator by the denominator.*

$x^{4-2} + 3x^{3-2} - 5x^{2-2}$

$x^2 + 3x^1 - 5x^0$

$x^2 + 3x - 5$ — *Simplify.*

B $(x^6y^2 - x^3y^5 - 3x^2y^7) \div x^2y$

$\frac{x^6y^2 - x^3y^5 - 3x^2y^7}{x^2y}$ — *Write the expression as a fraction.*

$\frac{x^6y^2}{x^2y} - \frac{x^3y^5}{x^2y} - \frac{3x^2y^7}{x^2y}$ — *Divide each term of the numerator by the denominator.*

$x^{6-2}y^{2-1} - x^{3-2}y^{5-1} - 3x^{2-2}y^{7-1}$

$x^4y - xy^4 - 3y^6$ — *Simplify.*

You can sometimes use division to factor a polynomial into a product of a monomial and a polynomial. The monomial is the product of the GCF of the coefficients and the lowest power of each variable in the polynomial.

EXAMPLE 3 Factoring Polynomials

Factor each polynomial.

A $3x^3 + 9x^5 - 6x^2$

The GCF of the coefficients is 3, and the lowest power of the variable is x^2, so factor out $3x^2$.

$$\frac{3x^3 + 9x^5 - 6x^2}{3x^2} = x + 3x^3 - 2$$

Write the polynomial as a product.

$3x^3 + 9x^5 - 6x^2 = 3x^2(x + 3x^3 - 2)$

B $16a^4b + 12a^3b$

The GCF of the coefficients is 4, and the lowest powers of the variables are a^3 and b, so factor out $4a^3b$.

$$\frac{16a^4b + 12a^3b}{4a^3b} = 4a + 3$$

Write the polynomial as a product.

$16a^4b + 12a^3b = 4a^3b(4a + 3)$

EXTENSION Exercises

Divide. Assume that no denominator equals zero.

1. $\frac{12a^5}{4a^2}$
2. $\frac{32m^5}{8m^3}$
3. $\frac{12a^4b^2}{2a^2b}$
4. $\frac{-12x^2y}{x^2y}$
5. $\frac{36a^5b^5c^7}{12a^4bc^3}$
6. $\frac{30x^7y^8z^6}{14x^7y^7z^3}$
7. $\frac{6x^5 + 9x^2}{3x}$
8. $\frac{15a^8 + 9a^6 + 12a^5}{3a^3}$
9. $\frac{13p^9q^6 - 52p^7q^4}{13p^5q^3}$
10. $\frac{j^4k^3 - 4j^6k^5}{3j^3k}$
11. $\frac{27a^6b^{13} - 18a^{12}b^8}{9a^3b^8}$
12. $\frac{12x^5 + 9x^4 + 15x^2}{x}$

Factor each polynomial.

13. $4m^2n^3 - 6m^3n$
14. $x^2y^3 + x^3y^2$
15. $15z^3 + 25z^6$
16. $5p^3q^4 + 15p^2q^3 + 5pq^2$
17. $15a^2 + 10a^3 + 5a^7$
18. $r^5s^3 + r^7s^4 + r^6s^8$
19. $4x^4y^8 + 16x^3y^2 - 8xy$
20. $36d + 12f$
21. $-3n + 3n^2$

Game Time

Short Cuts

You can use properties of algebra to explain many arithmetic shortcuts. For example, to square a two-digit number that ends in 5, multiply the first digit by one more than the first digit, and then place a 25 at the end.

To find 35^2, multiply the first digit, 3, by one more than the first digit, 4. You get $3 \cdot 4 = 12$. Place a 25 at the end, and you get 1225. So $35^2 = 1225$.

Why does this shortcut work? You can use FOIL to multiply 35 by itself:

$$\begin{aligned} 35^2 = 35 \cdot 35 = (30 + 5)(30 + 5) &= 900 + 150 + 150 + 25 \\ &= 900 + 300 + 25 \\ &= 1200 + 25 \qquad 1200 = 30 \cdot 40 \\ &= 1225 \end{aligned}$$

First use the shortcut to find each square. Then use FOIL to multiply the number by itself.

1. 15^2 **2.** 45^2 **3.** 85^2 **4.** 65^2 **5.** 25^2

6. Can you explain why the shortcut works?

Use FOIL to multiply each pair of numbers.

7. $11 \cdot 14$ **8.** $12 \cdot 16$ **9.** $13 \cdot 15$ **10.** $14 \cdot 17$ **11.** $18 \cdot 19$

12. Write a shortcut for multiplying two-digit numbers with a first digit of 1.

Rolling for Tiles

For this game, you will need a number cube, a set of algebra tiles, and a game board. Roll the number cube, and draw an algebra tile:

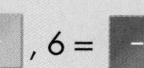

1 = , 2 = , 3 = , 4 = , 5 = , 6 = .

The goal is to model expressions that can be added, subtracted, multiplied, or divided to equal the polynomials on the game board.

A complete set of rules and a game board are available online.

go.hrw.com
Game Time Extra
KEYWORD: MT7 Games

It's in the Bag!

FOLDNOTES

Materials
- 3 sheets of decorative paper
- ruler
- compass
- scissors
- glue
- markers

PROJECT Polynomial Petals

Pick a petal and find a fact about polynomials!

Directions

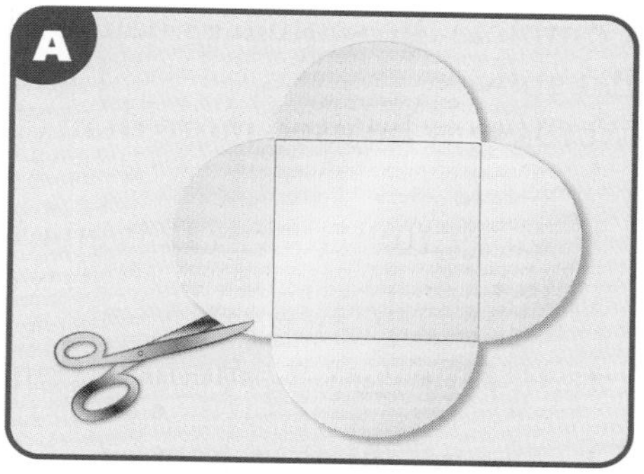

A

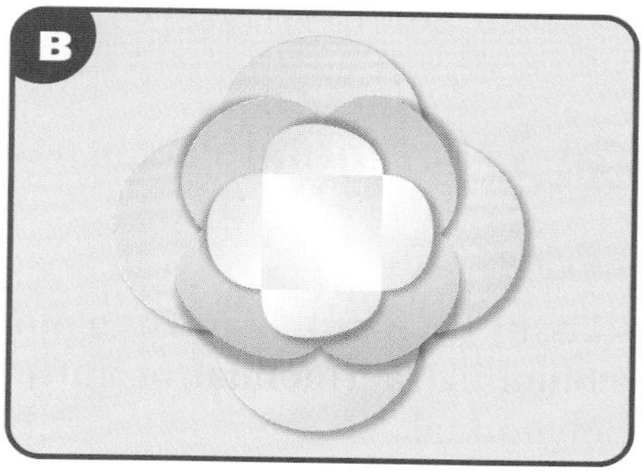

B

1. Draw a 5-inch square on a sheet of decorative paper. Use a compass to make a semicircle on each side of the square. Cut out the shape. **Figure A**

2. Draw a $3\frac{1}{2}$-inch square on another sheet of decorative paper. Use a compass to make a semicircle on each side of the square. Cut out the shape.

3. Draw a $2\frac{1}{2}$-inch square on the last sheet of decorative paper. Use a compass to make a semicircle on each side of the square. Cut out the shape.

4. Glue the medium square onto the center of the large square so that the squares are at a 45° angle to each other. **Figure B**

5. Glue the small square onto the center of the medium square in the same way.

Taking Note of the Math

Write examples of different types of polynomials on the petals. Then use the remaining petals to take notes on the key concepts from the chapter. When you're done, fold up the petals.

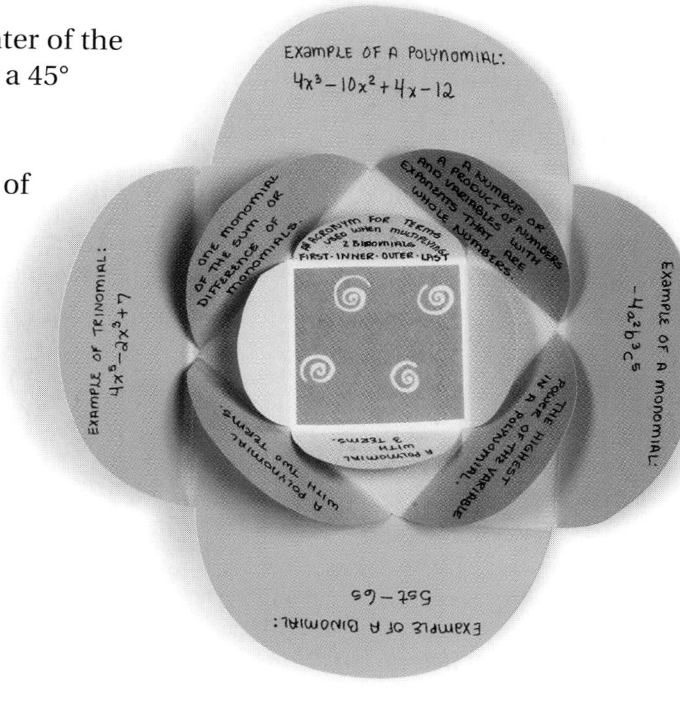

CHAPTER 14

Study Guide: Review

Vocabulary

binomial 734
degree of a polynomial 735
FOIL 762
monomial 734
polynomial 734
trinomial 734

Complete the sentences below with vocabulary words from the list above.
Words may be used more than once.

1. $4x^3 - 10x^2 + 4x - 12$ is an example of a __?__ whose __?__ is 3.

2. Use the __?__ method to find the product of two __?__.

3. A polynomial with 2 terms is called a __?__. A polynomial with 3 terms is called a __?__.

14-1 Polynomials (pp. 734–737)

EXAMPLE

Classify each expression as a monomial, a binomial, a trinomial, or not a polynomial.

- $4x^5 - 2x^3 + 7$
  trinomial
- $4xy - \frac{3}{x^4} + 7x^2y^4$
  not a polynomial

Find the degree of each polynomial.

- $x^3 - 2x + 1$
  degree 3
- $n + 3n^4 + 16n^2$
  degree 4

EXERCISES

Classify each expression as a monomial, a binomial, a trinomial, or not a polynomial.

4. $-5t^2 + 7t - 8$
5. $r^{-4} + 3r^{-2} + 5$
6. $12g + 7g^3 - \frac{5}{g^2}$
7. $-4a^2b^3c^5$
8. $\sqrt{x} - 2\sqrt{xy}$
9. $6st - 7s$

Find the degree of each polynomial.

10. $-3x^5 - 6x^8 + 5x$
11. $x^4 - 4x^2 + 3x - 1$
12. $14 + 8r^2 - 9r^3$
13. $\frac{1}{3}m^3 - \frac{1}{6}m^5 + \frac{7}{9}m^2$
14. $-3x^6 + 5x^5 - 9x$

14-2 Simplifying Polynomials (pp. 740–743)

EXAMPLE

Simplify.

- $\mathbf{5x^2 - 2x + 4 - 5x - 3 + 4x^2}$

  $5x^2 - 2x + 4 - 5x - 3 + 4x^2$

  $9x^2 - 7x + 1$

- $\mathbf{4(2x - 7) - 5x + 4}$

  $8x - 28 - 5x + 4$

  $3x - 24$

EXERCISES

Simplify.

15. $4t^2 - 6t + 3t - 4t^2 + 7t^2 + 1$
16. $4gh - 5g^2h + 7gh - 4g^2h$
17. $4(5mn - 3m)$
18. $4(2a^2 - 4b) + 6b$
19. $5(4st^2 - 6t) + 16st^2 + 7t$

14-3 Adding Polynomials (pp. 747–750)

EXAMPLE

Add.

- $\mathbf{(3x^2 - 2x) + (5x^2 + 3x + 2)}$

  $3x^2 - 2x + 5x^2 + 3x + 2$ *Identify like terms.*

  $8x^2 + x + 2$ *Combine like terms.*

- $\mathbf{(8t^3 + 4t + 6) + (4t^2 - 7t - 2)}$

$$\begin{array}{r} 8t^3 \qquad\quad + 4t + 6 \\ + \qquad 4t^2 - 7t - 2 \\ \hline 8t^3 + 4t^2 - 3t + 4 \end{array}$$

Place like terms in columns.

Combine like terms.

EXERCISES

Add.

20. $(4x^2 + 3x - 7) + (2x^2 - 5x + 12)$
21. $(5x^4 - 3x^2 + 4x - 2) + (4x^2 - 5x + 9)$
22. $(5h + 5) + (2h^2 + 3) + (3h - 1)$
23. $(3xy^2 - 5x^2y - 4xy) + (3x^2y + 6xy - xy^2)$
24. $(4n^2 + 6) + (3n^2 - 2) + (8 + 6n^2)$

14-4 Subtracting Polynomials (pp. 752–755)

EXAMPLE

- **Subtract.**

  $\mathbf{(6x^2 - 4x + 5) - (7x^2 - 8x + 2)}$

  $6x^2 - 4x + 5 + (-7x^2 + 8x - 2)$ *Add the opposite.*

  $6x^2 - 4x + 5 - 7x^2 + 8x - 2$ *Associative Property*

  $-x^2 + 4x + 3$ *Combine like terms.*

EXERCISES

Subtract.

25. $(x^2 - 4) - (4 - 5x^2)$
26. $(w^2 - 4w + 6) - (2w^2 + 8w - 8)$
27. $(3x^2 + 8x - 9) - (7x^2 - 8x + 5)$
28. $(4ab^2 - 5ab + 7a^2b) - (3a^2b + 6ab)$
29. $(3p^3q^2 - 4p^2q^2) - (2pq^2 + 4p^3q^2)$

14-5 Multiplying Polynomials by Monomials (pp. 756–759)

EXAMPLE

Multiply.

■ $(3x^2y^3)(2xy^2)$

$(3x^2y^3)(2xy^2)$

$3 \cdot 2 \cdot x^{2+1}y^{3+2}$

$6x^3y^5$

Multiply the coefficients and add the exponents.

■ $(-2ab^2)(4a^2b^2 - 3ab + 6a - 8)$

$(-2ab^2)(4a^2b^2 - 3ab + 6a - 8)$

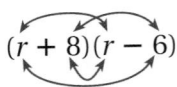

$-8a^3b^4 + 6a^2b^3 - 12a^2b^2 + 16ab^2$

EXERCISES

Multiply.

30. $(4st^3)(s - 3st + 8)$

31. $-6a^2b(-2a^2b^2 - 5ab^2 + 6a - 4b)$

32. $2m(m^2 - 8m + 1)$

33. $-5h(3gh^4 - 2g^3h^2 + 6h - 4g)$

34. $\frac{1}{2}j^3k^2(4j^2k - 3jk^2 + 2j^3k^3)$

35. $3x^2y^5(-5x^4y^7 + 6x^5y^9 - 8xy + 4xy^2)$

14-6 Multiplying Binomials (pp. 762–765)

EXAMPLE

Multiply.

■ $(r + 8)(r - 6)$

$(r + 8)(r - 6)$ *FOIL*

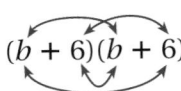

$r^2 - 6r + 8r - 48$ *Combine like terms.*

$r^2 + 2r - 48$

■ $(b + 6)^2$

$(b + 6)(b + 6)$ *FOIL*

$b^2 + 6b + 6b + 36$ *Combine like terms.*

$b^2 + 12b + 36$

EXERCISES

Multiply.

36. $(p - 6)(p - 2)$

37. $(b + 4)(b + 6)$

38. $(3r - 1)(r + 4)$

39. $(3a + 4b)(a - 5b)$

40. $(m - 7)^2$

41. $(3t - 6)(3t + 6)$

42. $(3b - 7t)(2b + 4t)$

43. $(10 - 3x)(4 + x)$

44. $(y - 11)^2$

CHAPTER TEST

CHAPTER 14

Classify each expression as a monomial, a binomial, a trinomial, or not a polynomial.

1. $t^2 + 2t^{0.5} - 4$
2. $-\frac{1}{2}a^3b^6$
3. $4m^4 - 5m + 8$

Find the degree of each polynomial.

4. $6 - 9b + 2m^4$
5. 54
6. $4 + y$
7. The volume of a cube with side length $x + 2$ is given by the polynomial $x^3 + 6x^2 + 12x + 8$. What is the volume of the cube if $x = 3$?

Simplify.

8. $2a - 4b - 5b + 6a - 2b$
9. $3(x^2 - 6x + 10)$
10. $-2x^2y + 3xy^2 - 4x^2y + 2x^2y$
11. $6(4b^2 - 7b) + 3b^2 + 5b$
12. The area of one face of a cube is given by the expression $2s^2 + 9s$. Write a polynomial to represent the total surface area of the cube.

Add.

13. $(4x^2 + 2x - 1) + (-2x + 5)$
14. $(12x - 5) + (9x - 5)$
15. $(3bc - b^2c^2 + 5bc^2) + (2bc - bc^2)$
16. $(6h^5 + 3h^3 - 2h^6) + (h^6 - 2h + 5h^4)$
17. $(b^3c^2 - 8b^2c + 5bc) + (6b^3c^2 - 4bc + 3) + (b^2c - 3bc - 11)$
18. Harold is placing a mat of width $w + 4$ around a 16 in. by 20 in. portrait. Write an expression for the perimeter of the outer edge of the mat.

Subtract.

19. $(4m^2n - 5mn + mn^2) - (-2mn + 4m^2n)$
20. $(12a + a^2) - (6 + a^2 + 8a)$
21. $(3a^2b - 5a^2b^2 + 6ab^2) - (2a^2b^2 - 7a^2b)$
22. $(j^4 + 7j^2 - 4j) - (5j^3 - 2j^2 - 6j + 1)$
23. A circle whose area is $2x^2 + 3x - 4$ is cut from a rectangular piece of plywood with area $4x^2 + 3x - 1$ and discarded. Write an expression for the area of the remaining plywood.

Multiply.

24. $(3x)(5x^4)$
25. $(4x^2y)(-5xy^3)$
26. $(2a^2b^4)(5a^4b^5)$
27. $a(a^3 - 4a + 5)$
28. $3m^3n^4(2m^3n^4 - 5m^2n^2)$
29. $3a^3(ab^2 - 2ab + 8a)$
30. $(x + 2)(x + 12)$
31. $(x + 2)(x - 4)$
32. $(a - 3)(a - 7)$
33. A student forms a box from a 10 in. by 15 in. piece of cardboard by cutting a square with side length x out of each corner and folding up the sides. Write and simplify an expression for the area of the base of the box.

STANDARDIZED TEST PREP

go.hrw.com
State Test Practice Online
KEYWORD: MT7 TestPrep

Cumulative Assessment, Chapters 1–14

Multiple Choice

1. The school's drama club sells tickets for their performance. Student tickets cost \$6 and non-student tickets cost \$10. If they sold 680 tickets for a total of \$5280, how many student tickets did they sell?

Ⓐ 680 tickets Ⓒ 300 tickets
Ⓑ 380 tickets Ⓓ 260 tickets

2. What is the measure of $\angle GJH$?

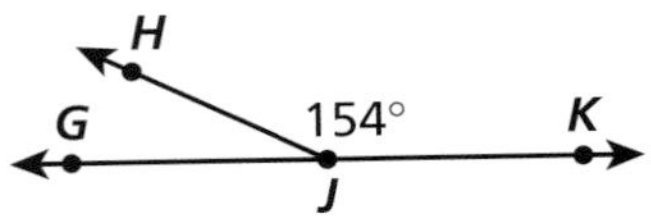

Ⓕ 26° Ⓗ 64°
Ⓖ 36° Ⓙ 206°

3. Giancarlo is using a paper cone as a drinking cup. How much water can the cup hold? Use 3.14 for π.

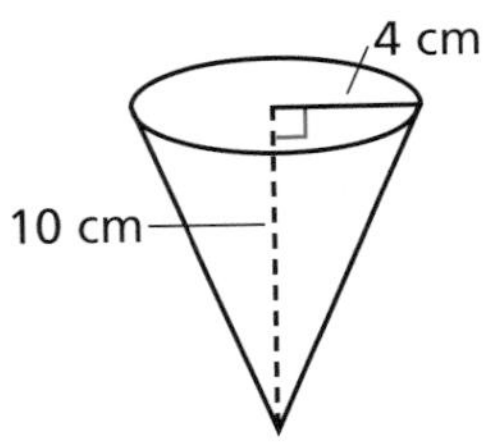

Ⓐ 41.9 cm^3 Ⓒ 167.47 cm^3
Ⓑ 502.4 cm^3 Ⓓ 1507.2 cm^3

4. Twenty-two percent of the sales of a general store are due to snack sales. If the store sold \$1350 worth of goods, how much of the total was due to snack sales?

Ⓕ \$167 Ⓗ \$1053
Ⓖ \$297 Ⓙ \$2970

5. If rectangle *MNQP* is similar to rectangle *ABDC*, then what is the area of rectangle *ABDC*?

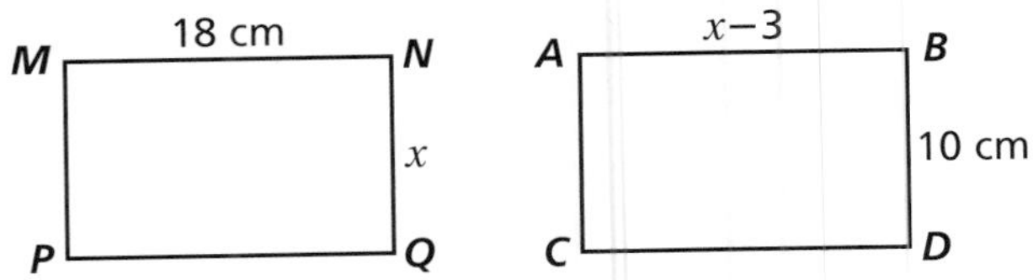

Ⓐ 44 cm^2 Ⓒ 120 cm^2
Ⓑ 66 cm^2 Ⓓ 270 cm^2

6. The simplest form of the product of the binomials $(2x - 6)$ and $(2x + 6)$ is which type of polynomial?

Ⓕ Zero Ⓗ Binomial
Ⓖ Monomial Ⓙ Trinomial

7. If the area of a circle is 49π and the circumference of the circle is 14π, what is the diameter of the circle?

Ⓐ 7 units Ⓒ 21 units
Ⓑ 14 units Ⓓ 49 units

8. Nationally, there were 217.8 million people age 18 and over and 53.3 million children ages 5 to 17 as of July 1, 2003, according to estimates released by the U.S. Census Bureau. How do you write the number of people age 5 and older in scientific notation?

Ⓕ 2.711×10^2 Ⓗ 2.711×10^7
Ⓖ 2.711×10^6 Ⓙ 2.711×10^8

9. What is the y-intercept of the line that passes through the points $(-3, 8)$ and $(2, -2)$?

(A) $(0, -2)$
(B) $(0, 0)$
(C) $(0, 2)$
(D) $(0, 6)$

HOT TIP! **If a problem involves decimals, you may be able to eliminate answer choices that do not have the correct number of places after the decimal point.**

Gridded Response

Use the following data for questions 10 and 11.

In 2003, the state of Virginia broke its record for the number of days in a row that it rained. The table shows the number of days in a row each rain station recorded rain.

Station	May 2003 Rain Days
Charlottesville	22
Bedford	20
Norfolk	17
Bremo Bluff	17
Brookneal	19
Lexington	19
Lynchburg	21
Meadows of Dan	18
Richmond	21
Somerset	20

10. Find the mean number of days in a row that it rained.

11. Find the median number of days in a row that it rained.

12. A fair number cube is rolled twice. What is the probability that the outcomes of the two rolls will have a sum of 4?

13. What is the length, in centimeters, of the diagonal of a square with side length 8 cm? Round your answer to the nearest hundredth.

14. If the rule for a geometric sequence is given by $a_n = 4\left(\frac{1}{2}\right)^{n-1}$, what is the 10th term of the sequence?

Short Response

15. A quilt is made by connecting squares like the one below.

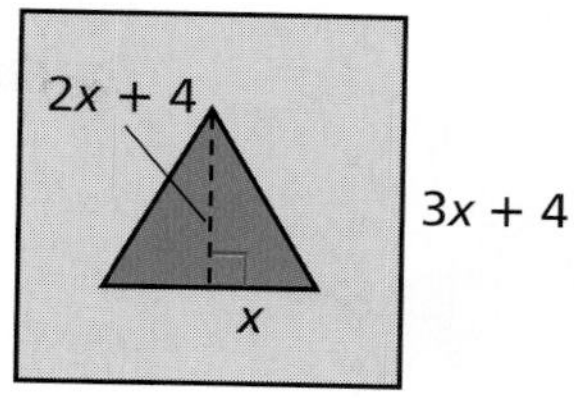

a. Write an expression for the area of the triangle and an expression for the area of the square.

b. Write an expression for the area of the blue region.

16. Draw a model for the product of the two binomials $(x + 3)$ and $(2x + 5)$ with the following tiles. Use the model to determine the product.

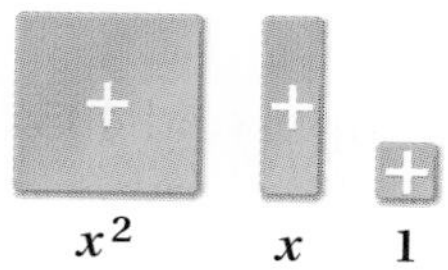

Extended Response

17. A cake pan is made by cutting four squares from a 18 cm by 24 cm piece of tin and folding the sides as shown.

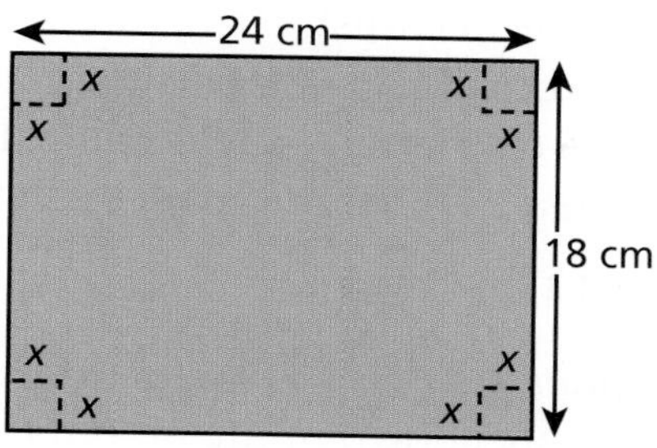

a. Write an expression for the length, width, and height of the cake pan in terms of x.

b. Multiply the expressions from part **a** to find a polynomial that gives the volume of the cake pan.

c. Evaluate the polynomial for $x = 1$, $x = 2$, $x = 3$, and $x = 4$. Which value of x gives the cake pan with the largest volume? Give the dimensions and the volume of the largest cake pan.

Problem Solving on Location

MISSISSIPPI

Catfish

Catfish is one of the five most popular seafoods in the United States. Mississippi produces about 75% of the nation's supply of catfish. Belzoni hosts the annual World Catfish Festival, an event that draws more than 20,000 catfish lovers each year.

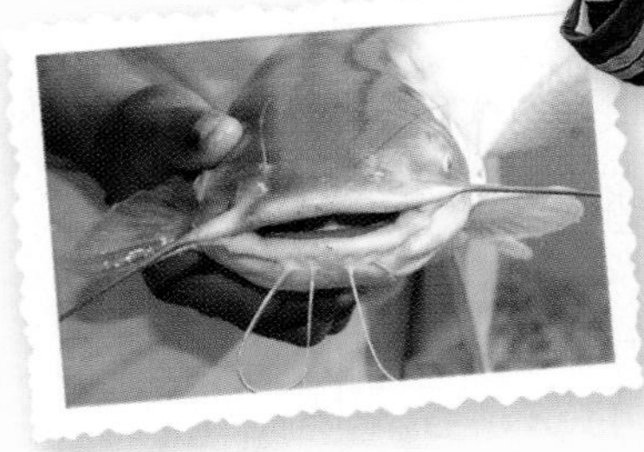

Choose one or more strategies to solve each problem.

1. In 2003, Mississippi had 405 catfish farms. In 2004, the number of farms in the state increased by 1.5%. If the number of catfish farms continues to increase by 1.5% each year, about how many catfish farms will the state have in 2011?

2. On a typical catfish farm, the pond is stocked with 6000 catfish per acre, the pond covers 17 acres, and the total weight of the fish in the pond is 153,000 pounds. On average, how much does each catfish weigh?

For 3 and 4, use the graph.

3. Assume that catfish production continues to increase at the rate shown in the graph. How many pounds of catfish will be produced in Mississippi in 2020?

4. In what year will catfish production in Mississippi hit 630 million pounds?

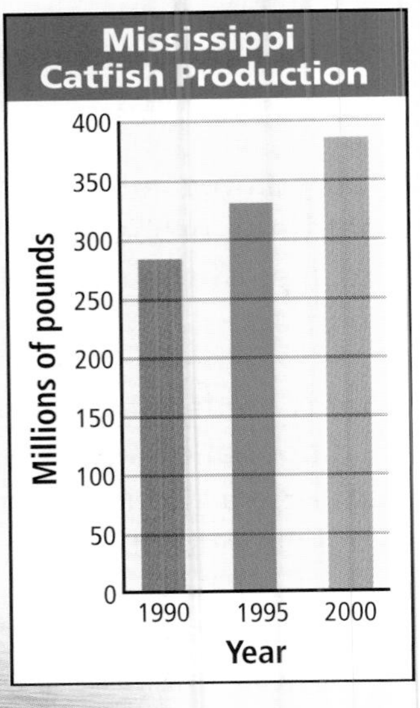

Problem Solving Strategies

Draw a Diagram
Make a Model
Guess and Test
Work Backward
Find a Pattern
Make a Table
Solve a Simpler Problem
Use Logical Reasoning
Act It Out
Make an Organized List

The Lauren Rogers Museum of Art

Since it opened in 1923, the Lauren Rogers Museum of Art had one of the finest—and most diverse—collections of art in the South. Nestled among the oaks of Laurel, Mississippi, the museum houses hundreds of Japanese prints, American and European paintings, and Native-American baskets.

Choose one or more strategies to solve each problem.

1. The museum's collection includes a painting called *Landscape with Windmill.* The length of the painting is 4 in. greater than its width. The perimeter of the painting is 52 in. What are the dimensions of the painting?

For 2 and 3, use the table.

2. The frame of *The Message* has an equal width on all sides of the painting. The perimeter of the frame is 132 inches. What is the width of the frame?
3. Only one painting in the table is by an English artist. The area of the painting is less than 800 in^2 and the perimeter of the painting is greater than 108 in. Which painting was painted by an English artist?

Paintings at the Lauren Rogers Museum of Art

Title	Dimensions
Knitting Reveries	55 in. by 37 in.
The Message	30 in. by 24 in.
Mythological Scene	38.5 in. by 51.6 in.
Miss Grace Hundley	30 in. by 25 in.
Young Girl Reading Beneath a Tree	32.9 in. by 27.2 in.

Knitting Reveries by Louis-Edouard Dubufe

Student Handbook

Extra Practice 782

Problem-Solving Handbook 810

Draw a Diagram 810
Make a Model 811
Guess and Test 812
Work Backward 813
Find a Pattern 814
Make a Table 815
Solve a Simpler Problem 816
Use Logical Reasoning 817
Act It Out 818
Make an Organized List 819

Skills Bank 820

Review Skills

Place Value to the Billions 820
Round Whole Numbers and Decimals 820
Long Division and Whole Numbers 821
Solve for a Variable 821
Factors and Multiples 822
Divisibility Rules 822
Prime and Composite Numbers 823
Percents Less Than 1% and Greater Than 100% 823
Greatest Common Factor (GCF) 824
Least Common Multiple (LCM) 824

Compatible Numbers 825
Mixed Numbers and Fractions 825
Multiply and Divide Decimal by Powers of 10 826
Multiply Decimals 826
Divide Decimals 827
Terminating and Repeating Decimals 827
Order of Operations 828
Properties 829
Cubes and Cube Roots 830
Skew Lines 830
Choose Appropriate Units of Measurements 831
Measure Angles 832
Informal Geometry Proofs 833
Iteration 834

Preview Skills

Relative, Cumulative, and Relative Cumulative Geometry 835
Frequency Polygons 836
Parallel Lines and Transversals 837
Circles 838
Matrices 839
Networks 840

Science

Compare and Order Measurements 841
Temperature Conversion 842
Customary and Metric Rulers 843
Precision and Significant Digits 844
Greatest Possible Error 845
pH 845
Richter Scale 846

Selected Answers 847

Glossary 859

Index 898

Table of Measures, Symbols, and Formulas .... inside back cover

Extra Practice ■ Chapter 1

LESSON 1-1

Evaluate each expression for the given value(s) of the variable(s).

1. $3 + x$ for $x = 5$
2. $6m - 2$ for $m = 3$
3. $2(p + 3)$ for $p = 8$
4. $4x + y$ for $x = 1, y = 3$
5. $2y - x$ for $x = 3, y = 6$
6. $5x + 1.5y$ for $x = 2, y = 4$

LESSON 1-2

Write an algebraic expression for each word phrase.

7. seven less than a number b
8. eight more than the product of 7 and a
9. a quotient of 8 and a number m
10. five times the sum of c and 18

Write a word phrase for each algebraic expression.

11. $9 + \frac{x}{3}$
12. $19x - 14$
13. $\frac{1}{3}(x + 1)$
14. $\frac{4}{x} - 100$
15. Write a word problem that can be evaluated by the algebraic expression $x - 122$, and then evaluate the expression for $x = 225$.

LESSON 1-3

16. In a miniature golf game the scores of four brothers relative to par are Jesse 3, Jack −2, James −5, and Jarod 1. Use <, >, or = to compare Jack's and Jarod's scores, and then list the brothers in order from the lowest score to the highest.

Write the integers in order from least to greatest.

17. −4, 6, −2
18. 1, −16, 9
19. −14, −2, −19

Find the additive inverse of each integer.

20. −10
21. 4
22. 1
23. −21

Evaluate each expression.

24. $|9| + |-4|$
25. $|-3| + |-19|$
26. $|52 - 12|$

LESSON 1-4

Add.

27. $-4 + 6$
28. $3 + (-8)$
29. $-6 + (-2)$
30. $7 + (-11)$

Evaluate each expression for the given value of the variable.

31. $x + 9$ for $x = -8$
32. $x + 3$ for $x = -3$
33. $x + 5$ for $x = -7$
34. The middle school registrar is checking her records. Use the information at right to find the net change in the number of students for this school for the week.

	Students Registering	Students Withdrawing
Monday	4	2
Tuesday	6	7
Wednesday	5	5
Thursday	1	4
Friday	4	0

Extra Practice ▪ Chapter 1

LESSON 1-5

Subtract.

35. $-6 - 4$ **36.** $8 - (-3)$ **37.** $-6 - (-3)$ **38.** $-5 - 8$

Evaluate each expression for the given value of the variable.

39. $7 - x$ for $x = -4$ **40.** $-8 - s$ for $s = -6$ **41.** $-8 - b$ for $b = 12$

42. An elevator rises 351 feet above ground level and then drops 415 feet to the basement. What is the position of the elevator relative to ground level?

LESSON 1-6

Multiply or divide.

43. $8(-6)$ **44.** $\frac{-63}{7}$ **45.** $-7(-3)$ **46.** $\frac{52}{-4}$

Simplify.

47. $8(4 - 5)$ **48.** $-5(9 - 11)$ **49.** $-4(-16 - 4)$ **50.** $3 + 7(10 - 14)$

51. A golfer plays 18 holes of golf. On 5 holes she is under par by 1. On 6 holes she is over par by 2. She is even on the remaining holes. What is her score?

LESSON 1-7

Solve.

52. $4 + x = 13$ **53.** $t - 3 = 8$ **54.** $17 = m + 11$ **55.** $5 + a = 7$

56. $p - 5 = 23$ **57.** $31 + y = 50$ **58.** $18 + k = 34$ **59.** $g - 16 = 23$

60. Richard biked 39 miles on Saturday. This is 13 more miles than Trevor biked. How many miles did Trevor bike on Saturday?

LESSON 1-8

Solve and check.

61. $\frac{a}{-4} = -2$ **62.** $-49 = 7d$ **63.** $\frac{c}{-2} = -8$ **64.** $-57 = 3p$

65. $-8b = 64$ **66.** $144 = -9y$ **67.** $\frac{x}{2} = -78$ **68.** $19c = 152$

69. Jessica hiked a total of 36 miles on her vacation. This is 4 times as far as she hikes on a typical weekend. How many miles does Jessica hike on a typical weekend?

LESSON 1-9

Compare. Write < or >.

70. $15 - 8$ ▢ 6 **71.** $3(7)$ ▢ 23 **72.** $51 - 18$ ▢ 34 **73.** $4(16)$ ▢ 62

Solve and graph each inequality.

74. $x - 3.5 \geq 7$ **75.** $5p < 40$ **76.** $2 \leq \frac{a}{3}$ **77.** $h - 5 \leq 13$

Extra Practice ■ Chapter 2

LESSON 2-1

Simplify.

1. $\frac{12}{96}$ 2. $\frac{6}{16}$ 3. $\frac{-10}{15}$ 4. $\frac{14}{42}$

Write each decimal as a fraction in simplest form.

5. 0.4 6. 0.05 7. 0.12 8. 0.625

Write each fraction as a decimal.

9. $\frac{3}{8}$ 10. $\frac{1}{4}$ 11. $\frac{9}{4}$ 12. $\frac{3}{5}$

LESSON 2-2

Compare. Write <, >, or =.

13. $\frac{6}{7}$ ■ $\frac{4}{5}$ 14. $\frac{11}{15}$ ■ $\frac{9}{10}$ 15. $\frac{1}{3}$ ■ $\frac{5}{6}$ 16. $-\frac{4}{5}$ ■ $\frac{1}{8}$

17. $1\frac{5}{8}$ ■ $1\frac{2}{3}$ 18. $-2\frac{1}{8}$ ■ $-2\frac{1}{5}$ 19. $\frac{12}{17}$ ■ 0.75 20. $5\frac{7}{8}$ ■ 5.9

LESSON 2-3

21. Hannah and Elizabeth drove to Niagara Falls for vacation. Hannah drove $98\frac{3}{4}$ miles and Elizabeth drove 106.44 miles. How far did they drive together?

Add or subtract. Write each answer in simplest form.

22. $\frac{3}{4} - \frac{7}{4}$ 23. $\frac{19}{8} + \frac{11}{8}$ 24. $\frac{5}{4} - \frac{15}{4}$ 25. $-\frac{7}{4} + \frac{11}{4}$

26. $\frac{9}{2} - \frac{15}{2}$ 27. $\frac{11}{2} + \frac{14}{2}$ 28. $\frac{9}{4} - \frac{22}{4}$ 29. $-\frac{21}{3} + \frac{16}{3}$

Evaluate each expression for the given value of the variable.

30. $32.9 + x$ for $x = -15.8$ 31. $21.3 + a$ for $a = -37.6$ 32. $-\frac{3}{5} + z$ for $z = 3\frac{1}{5}$

LESSON 2-4

Multiply. Write each answer in simplest form.

33. $-\frac{3}{4}\left(-\frac{5}{9}\right)$ 34. $\frac{7}{12}\left(-\frac{3}{5}\right)$ 35. $-\frac{4}{5}\left(-\frac{9}{10}\right)$ 36. $-\frac{3}{7}\left(\frac{13}{14}\right)$

37. $-4.7(-8)$ 38. $-4.1(8.6)$ 39. $-0.06(5.2)$ 40. $-0.003(-2.6)$

41. Rosie ate $2\frac{1}{2}$ bananas on Saturday. On Sunday she ate $\frac{1}{2}$ as many bananas as she ate on Saturday. How many bananas did Rosie eat over the weekend?

LESSON 2-5

Divide. Write each answer in simplest form.

42. $2\frac{3}{4} \div \frac{1}{3}$ 43. $5\frac{1}{5} \div \frac{7}{8}$ 44. $3\frac{5}{9} \div \frac{3}{4}$ 45. $3\frac{1}{8} \div \frac{2}{5}$

46. $5.68 \div 0.2$ 47. $7.65 \div 0.05$ 48. $1.76 \div 0.8$ 49. $0.744 \div 8$

Evaluate each expression for the given value of the variable.

50. $\frac{7.4}{x}$ for $x = 0.5$ **51.** $\frac{11.88}{x}$ for $x = 0.08$ **52.** $\frac{15.3}{x}$ for $x = -1.2$

53. Yolanda is making bows that take $21\frac{1}{2}$ inches of ribbon to make. She has 344 inches of ribbon. How many bows can she make?

LESSON 2-6

Add or Subtract.

54. $\frac{8}{9} + \frac{2}{7}$ **55.** $\frac{3}{8} - \frac{2}{3}$ **56.** $\frac{2}{3} + \frac{1}{7}$ **57.** $\frac{5}{6} - \frac{4}{9}$

58. $4\frac{1}{5} + \left(-2\frac{1}{7}\right)$ **59.** $3\frac{2}{3} + \left(-1\frac{7}{8}\right)$ **60.** $4\frac{1}{8} + \left(-1\frac{3}{5}\right)$ **61.** $8\frac{1}{7} + \left(-4\frac{1}{10}\right)$

Evaluate each expression for the given value of the variable.

62. $8\frac{1}{2} + x$ for $x = 4\frac{2}{9}$ **63.** $n - \frac{1}{9}$ for $n = -1\frac{7}{8}$ **64.** $1\frac{1}{8} + y$ for $y = -\frac{4}{7}$

65. A container has $10\frac{1}{2}$ gallons of milk. If the children at a preschool drink $7\frac{3}{4}$ gallons of milk, how many gallons of milk are left in the container?

LESSON 2-7

Solve.

66. $x - 3.2 = 5.1$ **67.** $-3.1p = 15.5$ **68.** $\frac{a}{-2.3} = 7.9$ **69.** $-4.3x = 34.4$

70. $m - \frac{1}{3} = \frac{5}{8}$ **71.** $x - \frac{3}{7} = \frac{1}{9}$ **72.** $\frac{4}{5}w = \frac{2}{3}$ **73.** $\frac{9}{10}z = \frac{5}{8}$

74. It is estimated that it will take Peter $9\frac{3}{4}$ hours to paint a room. If he gets two of his friends to help him and they work at the same rate as him, how long should it take them to paint the room?

LESSON 2-8

75. A bill from the plumber was $383. The plumber charged $175 for parts and $52 per hour for labor. How long did the plumber work at this job?

76. Alicia bought $116 worth of flowers and some bushes for around her house. The bushes cost $28 each, and the bill totaled $340. How many bushes did she buy?

Solve.

77. $\frac{a}{2} - 3 = 8$ **78.** $2.4 = -0.8x + 3.2$ **79.** $\frac{6 + z}{3} = 4$ **80.** $\frac{c}{6} + 2 = 5$

81. $0.9m - 1.6 = -5.2$ **82.** $\frac{x - 4}{3} = 7$ **83.** $\frac{b}{5} + 2 = -3$ **84.** $2.1d + 0.7 = 7$

85. $\frac{p + 5}{3} = 6$ **86.** $\frac{c}{6} - 8 = 3$ **87.** $\frac{r - 6}{9} = 5$ **88.** $-8.6 = 3.4k - 1.8$

Extra Practice ■ Chapter 3

LESSON 3-1

Determine whether each ordered pair is a solution of $2x + 3y = 16$.

1. (1, 5) **2.** (5, 2) **3.** (2, 4) **4.** (3, 3)

Use the given values to make a table of solutions.

5. $y = x - 3$ for $x = -2, -1, 0, 1, 2$

6. $y = 3x + 2$ for $x = -2, -1, 0, 1, 2$

7. The cost of mailing a letter is \$0.23 per ounce plus \$0.14. The equation that gives the total cost c of mailing a letter is $c = 0.23w + 0.14$, where w is the weight in ounces. What is the cost of mailing a 5-ounce letter?

LESSON 3-2

Graph each point on a coordinate plane.

8. (4, 3) **9.** (3, 0) **10.** (−1, 3)

11. (0, −5) **12.** (−2, −4) **13.** (4, −2)

Complete each table of ordered pairs. Graph each ordered pair on a coordinate plane.

14. $x + 3 = y$

x	$x + 3$	y	(x, y)
1			
2			
3			
4			

15. $3x = y$

x	$3x$	y	(x, y)
2			
4			
6			
8			

LESSON 3-3

Tell which graph corresponds to each situation described below.

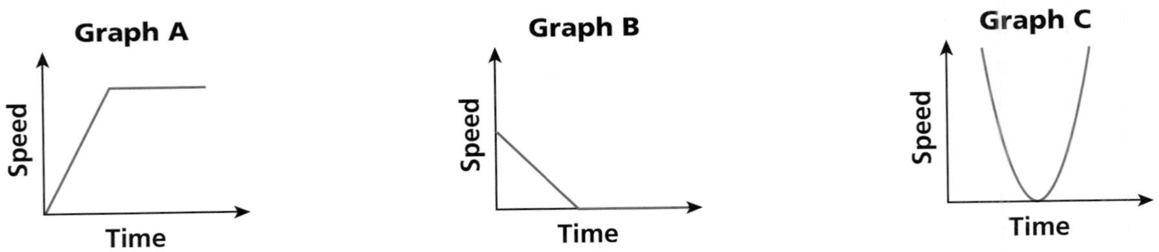

16. A person riding a bike increases speed and then maintains a high speed.

17. A person riding a bike goes up a hill and then accelerates going down the other side of the hill.

18. A person riding a race slows down after he reaches the finish line and then comes to a stop.

LESSON 3-4

Make a table and graph of each function.

19. $y = x + 1$ **20.** $y = -x - 2$ **21.** $y = 3x + 1$ **22.** $y = 4(x - 1)$

Determine if each relationship represents a function.

23.

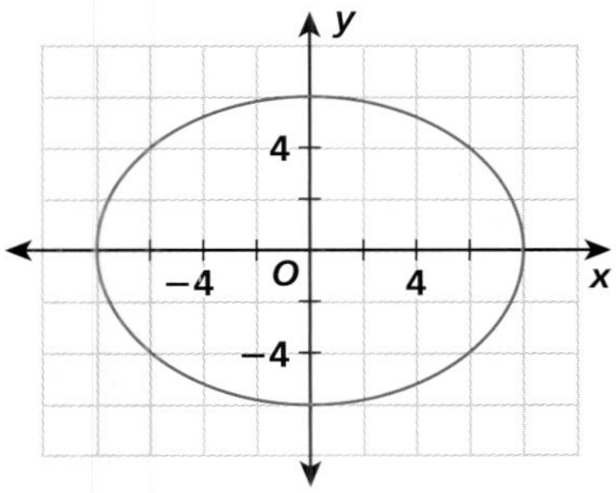

24.

x	y
−3	1
−1	−1
0	−2
2	0
4	2

25.

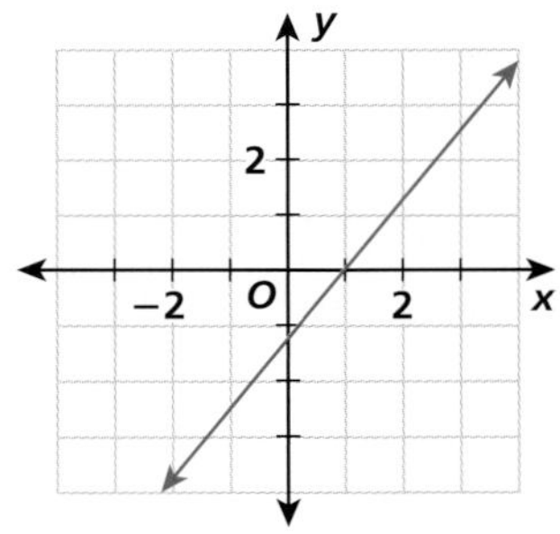

LESSON 3-5

26. The cost a caterer charges for a party is represented by the equation $c = \$13p$, where c is the amount paid to the caterer and p is the number of guests that will be attending the party. Make a table and sketch a graph of the equation.

27. Use the table to make a graph and write an equation.

x	0	3	6	9	12
y	2	4	6	8	10

28. Use the graph to make a table and write an equation for each line.

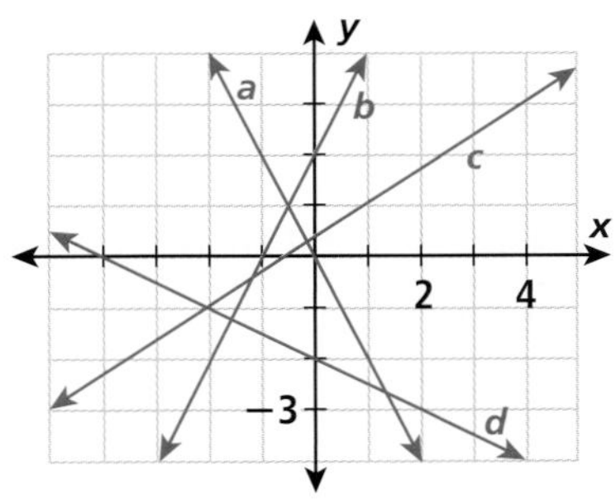

LESSON 3-6

Find the common difference and the next three terms in each arithmetic sequence.

29. 2, 7, 12, 17, . . . **30.** 16, 19, 22, 25, . . . **31.** 50, 44, 38, 32, . . .

32. −15, −6, 3, 12, . . . **33.** $\frac{1}{4}, \frac{3}{4}, 1\frac{1}{4}, 1\frac{3}{4}, \ldots$ **34.** −6, −10, −14, −18, . . .

Find a function that describes each arithmetic sequence. Use *y* to identify each term in the sequence and *n* to identify each term's position.

35. 1, 5, 9, 13, . . . **36.** 2, 11, 20, 29, . . . **37.** −2, −5, −8, −11, . . .

38. An air-conditioning repair company charges a \$54 service fee per visit, plus \$50 per hour for labor. Find a function that describes the arithmetic sequence. Then find the total charges for a service call that lasts $2\frac{1}{2}$ hours.

Extra Practice ■ Chapter 4

LESSON 4-1

Write in exponential form.

1. $3 \cdot 3 \cdot 3 \cdot 3$
2. $6a \cdot 6a \cdot 6a \cdot 6a \cdot 6a$
3. $(-9) \cdot (-9)$
4. b

Evaluate.

5. 2^5
6. 3^4
7. $(-6)^2$
8. $(-3)^5$
9. 5^3
10. 8^5
11. $(-2)^4$
12. $(-7)^3$

Evaluate each expression for the given values of the variables.

13. x^3 for $x = -3$
14. $k^2 + 3k$ for $k = -2$
15. $s^4 + y(s + 3)$ for $s = 1$ and $y = -2$
16. $10 + x^2 - \frac{x}{2}(y + 4)$ for $x = 3$ and $y = -2$
17. The formula for the area of a circle is $A = \pi r^2$. Use the formula to find the area of a circle with a radius of 7 cm.

LESSON 4-2

Evaluate the powers of 10.

18. 10^{-1}
19. 10^{-2}
20. 10^{-3}
21. 10^{-4}

Evaluate.

22. $(-4)^{-2}$
23. 3^{-3}
24. $(-5)^{-4}$
25. $\frac{3^2}{3^4} + (9 + 3)^0$
26. $13 - (-3) + 19(1 + 2)^2$
27. $4^5 \cdot 3^2 \cdot (-3)^{-3}$

LESSON 4-3

Multiply or divide. Write the product or the quotient as one power.

28. $2^4 \cdot 2^5$
29. $w^7 \cdot w^7$
30. $\frac{4^9}{4^9}$
31. $\frac{c^6}{c^2}$
32. $\frac{x^3}{y^3}$
33. $(3^0)^4$
34. $(3^{-2})^3$
35. $(-a^3)^4$

LESSON 4-4

Write each number in standard notation.

36. 2.4×10^3
37. 3.62×10^5
38. 5.036×10^{-4}
39. 8.93×10^{-2}

Write each number in scientific notation.

40. 0.00384
41. 1,450,000,000
42. 0.654
43. In the 2003 regular season, approximately 36,661,000 fans attended National League baseball games. The attendance for American League games was approximately 30,908,000 fans. Approximately how many more fans attended National League games than American League games? Write your answer in scientific notation.

LESSON 4-5

Find the two square roots of each number.

44. 25 **45.** 49 **46.** 289 **47.** 169

Evaluate each expression.

48. $2\sqrt{4}$ **49.** $3\sqrt{49}$ **50.** $\sqrt{99 + 45}$ **51.** $\sqrt{33 - 8}$

52. The area of a square garden is 1,681 square feet. What are the dimensions of the garden?

LESSON 4-6

Each square root is between two integers. Name the integers. Explain your answer.

53. $\sqrt{30}$ **54.** $\sqrt{61}$ **55.** $\sqrt{93}$ **56.** $-\sqrt{124}$

Use a calculator to find each value. Round to the nearest tenth.

57. $\sqrt{200}$ **58.** $\sqrt{185}$ **59.** $\sqrt{462}$ **60.** $\sqrt{219}$

61. Each tile on Michelle's patio is 18 square inches. If her patio is square shaped and consists of 81 tiles, about how big is her patio?

LESSON 4-7

Write all names that apply to each number.

62. $\sqrt{5}$ **63.** -61.2 **64.** $\frac{\sqrt{16}}{2}$ **65.** -6

State if the number is rational, irrational, or not a real number.

66. $\sqrt{\frac{4}{25}}$ **67.** $\sqrt{-9}$ **68.** $\sqrt{17}$ **69.** $\frac{13}{0}$

Find a real number between each pair of numbers.

70. $5\frac{1}{8}$ and $5\frac{2}{8}$ **71.** $4\frac{1}{3}$ and $4\frac{2}{3}$ **72.** $3\frac{5}{7}$ and $3\frac{6}{7}$

LESSON 4-8

Solve for the unknown side in each right triangle to the nearest tenth.

73.

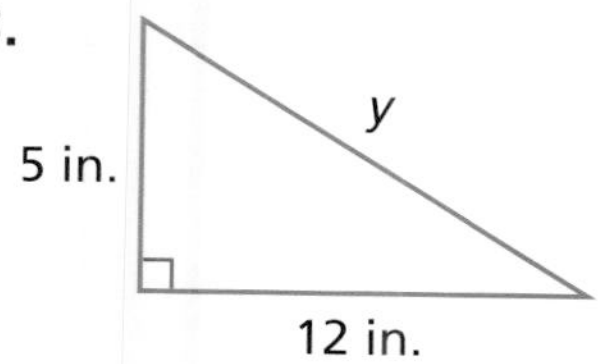

74.

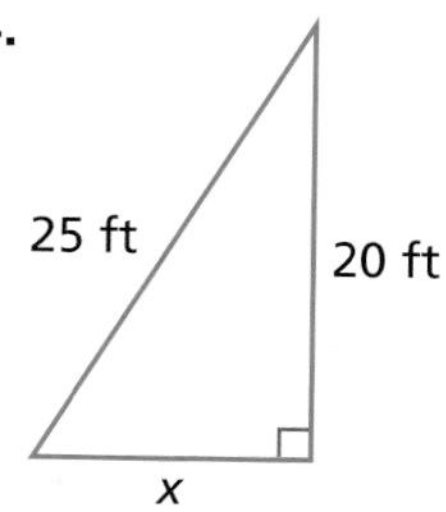

75.

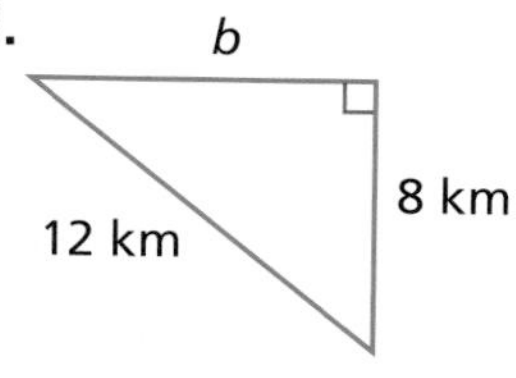

76.

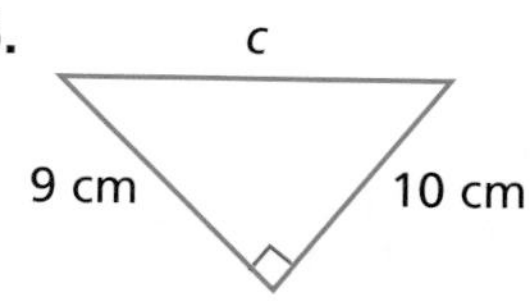

77. A professional tournament pool table typically measures 4.5 ft by 9 ft. How far is it from one corner pocket to the opposite corner pocket? Round to the nearest hundredth of a foot.

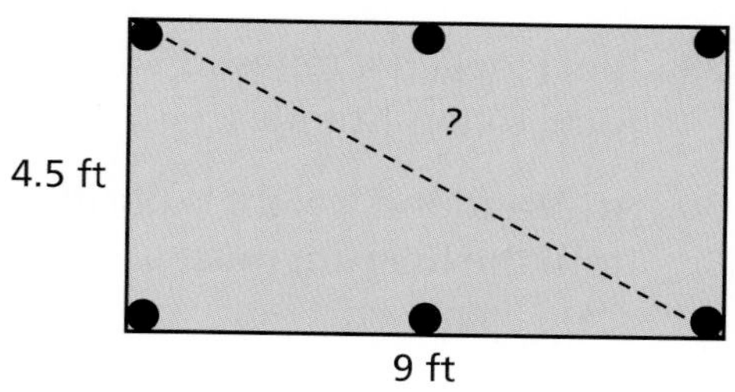

Extra Practice ■ Chapter 5

LESSON 5-1

Find two ratios that are equivalent to each given ratio.

1. $\frac{5}{10}$ **2.** $\frac{9}{12}$ **3.** $\frac{25}{35}$ **4.** $\frac{30}{35}$

Simplify to tell whether the ratios form a proportion.

5. $\frac{5}{30}$ and $\frac{3}{18}$ **6.** $\frac{12}{21}$ and $\frac{16}{28}$ **7.** $\frac{15}{21}$ and $\frac{10}{16}$ **8.** $\frac{52}{64}$ and $\frac{91}{112}$

LESSON 5-2

9. A penny has a mass of 2.5 g and a volume of approximately 0.442 cm^3. What is the approximate density of a penny?

10. Nikko jogs 3 miles in 30 minutes. How many miles does she jog per hour?

Estimate the unit rate.

11. 384 milligrams calcium for 8 oz of yogurt **12.** $57.50 for 5 hours

13. Find the unit rate for each brand of detergent, and determine which brand is the best buy.

Product	Size	Price
Pizzazz detergent	128 oz	$3.08
Spring Clean detergent	64 oz	$1.60
Bubbling detergent	196 oz	$4.51

LESSON 5-3

Find the appropriate factor for each conversion.

14. quart to gallon **15.** mile to foot

16. meter to centimeter **17.** milligram to gram

18. A three-toed sloth has a top speed of 0.22 feet per second. A giant tortoise has a top speed of 2.992 inches per second. Convert both speeds to miles per hour, and determine which animal is faster.

LESSON 5-4

Tell whether the ratios are proportional.

19. $\frac{7}{8}$ and $\frac{3}{4}$ **20.** $\frac{3}{4}$ and $\frac{24}{32}$ **21.** $\frac{32}{48}$ and $\frac{18}{27}$ **22.** $\frac{12}{20}$ and $\frac{6}{12}$

Solve each proportion.

23. $\frac{186 \text{ miles}}{3 \text{ hours}} = \frac{\blacksquare \text{ miles}}{5 \text{ hours}}$ **24.** $\frac{10 \text{ invitations}}{12 \text{ envelopes}} = \frac{15 \text{ invitations}}{\blacksquare \text{ envelopes}}$

25. $\frac{3}{8} = \frac{n}{12}$ **26.** $\frac{c}{15} = \frac{3}{45}$ **27.** $\frac{7}{18} = \frac{3}{m}$ **28.** $\frac{5}{f} = \frac{8}{12}$

29. Ricki jogged 4 miles in 36 minutes. At this rate, how long would it take Ricki to jog 12 miles?

30. An 18-pound weight is positioned 6 in. from a fulcrum. At what distance from the fulcrum must a 24-pound weight be positioned to keep the scale balanced?

LESSON 5-5

30. Khaled scans a photo that is 5 in. wide by 7 in. long into his computer. If he scales the length down to 3.5 in., how wide should the similar photo be?

31. Mutsuko drew an 8.5-inch-wide by 11-inch-tall picture that will be turned into a 34-inch-wide poster. How tall will the poster be?

32. A right triangle has legs that measure 3 cm and 4 cm. Another right triangle has legs that measure 5 cm and 12 cm. Are the triangles similar?

LESSON 5-6

Tell whether each transformation is a dilation.

33.

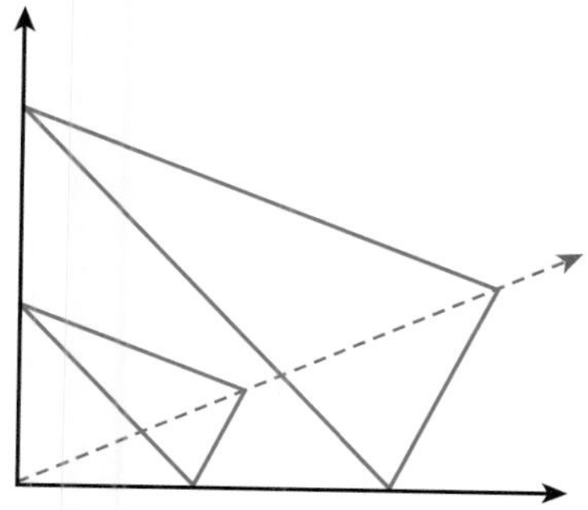

34.

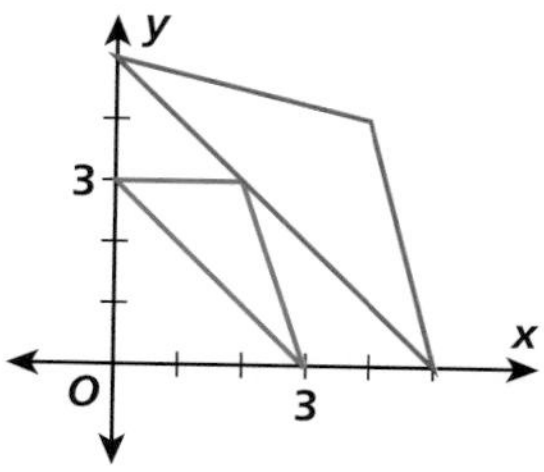

35.

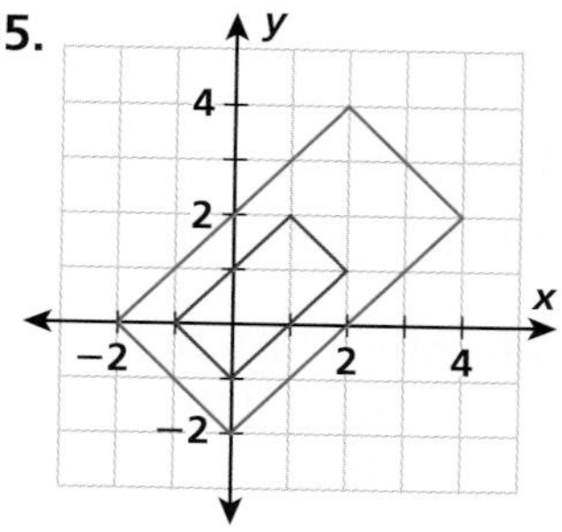

36. A figure has vertices at (2, 3), (3, 6), (6, 7), and (7, 2). The figure is dilated by a scale factor of 1.5 with the origin as the center of dilation. What are the vertices of the image?

LESSON 5-7

37. Brian casts a 9 ft shadow at the same time that Carrie casts an 8 ft shadow. If Brian is 6 ft tall, how tall is Carrie?

38. A telephone pole cast an 80 ft shadow, while a 3.5 ft tall child standing nearby casts a 6 ft shadow. How tall is the pole?

LESSON 5-8

39. What is the scale of a drawing where a 95 ft tall building is 6 in. tall?

40. On a scale drawing of a house plan, the master bathroom is $1\frac{1}{2}$ inches wide and $2\frac{5}{8}$ inches long. If the scale of the drawing is $\frac{3}{16}$ inches = 1 foot, what are the actual dimensions of the bathroom?

41. Julio uses a scale of $\frac{1}{8}$ inch = 1 foot when he paints landscapes. In one painting, a giant sequoia tree is 34.375 inches tall. How tall is the real tree?

42. A model of a skyscraper was made using a scale of 0.5 in:5 ft. If the actual skyscraper is 570 feet tall, how many feet tall is the model?

Extra Practice ■ Chapter 6

Extra Practice

LESSON 6-1

Compare. Write <, >, or =.

1. $\frac{3}{5}$ ■ 62% **2.** $\frac{2}{3}$ ■ $66\frac{2}{3}$% **3.** 24% ■ 0.25 **4.** 1% ■ 0.11

Order the numbers from least to greatest.

5. 0.11, 11.5%, 10%, $\frac{1}{8}$

6. $\frac{1}{5}$, 100%, $26\frac{2}{3}$%, 0.3

7. $\frac{7}{6}$, 115%, 83, 83.3%

8. 67.5%, $\frac{7}{3}$, 160%, 2.2

9. A molecule of ammonia is made up of 3 atoms of hydrogen and 1 atom of nitrogen. What percent of the atoms of an ammonia molecule are hydrogen?

LESSON 6-2

Estimate.

10. 51% of 1019 **11.** 33% of 60 **12.** 60% of 79 **13.** $66\frac{2}{3}$% of 211

14. Approximately 23% of each class walks to school. A student said that in a class of 20 students, approximately 2 students walk to school. Estimate to determine if the student's number is reasonable. Explain.

LESSON 6-3

15. What percent of 364 is 92?

16. What percent of 48 is 5?

17. What percent of 164 is 444?

18. 4 is what percent of 50?

19. Mt. McKinley in Alaska is 20,320 feet tall. The height of Mt. Everest is about 143% of the height of Mt. McKinley. Estimate the height of Mt. Everest. Round to the nearest thousand.

20. A restaurant bill for $64.45 was split among four people. Dona paid 25% of the bill. Sandy paid $\frac{1}{5}$ of the bill. Mara paid $14.25. Greta paid the remainder of the bill. Who paid the most money?

LESSON 6-4

21. 38 is 42% of what number?

22. 46 is 74% of what number?

23. 23 is 8% of what number?

24. 93 is 62% of what number?

25. 315 is 92% of what number?

26. 52 is 120% of what number?

27. A certain rock is a compound of several minerals. Tests show that the sample contains 17.3 grams of quartz. If 27.5% of the rock is quartz, find the mass in grams of the entire rock.

28. The Alabama River is 729 miles in length, or about 31% of the length of the Mississippi River. Estimate the length of the Mississippi River. Round to the nearest mile.

LESSON 6-5

Find each percent increase or decrease to the nearest percent.

29. from 10 to 17 **30.** from 38 to 65 **31.** from 91 to 44 **32.** from 3 to 25

33. from 86 to 27 **34.** from 38 to 46 **35.** from 19 to 60 **36.** from 88 to 23

37. A stereo that sells for $895 is on sale for 20% off the regular price. What is the sale price of the stereo?

38. Mr. Schultz owns a hardware store and typically marks up merchandise 28% over warehouse cost. How much would he charge for a wrench that costs him $12.45?

LESSON 6-6

39. An electronics salesperson sold $15,486 worth of computers last month. She makes 3% commission on all sales and earns a monthly salary of $1200. What was her total pay last month?

40. Jon bought a printer for $189 and a set of printer cartridges for $129. Sales tax on these items was 6.5%. What is Jon's total bill for these items?

41. Last year, Wendy earned $36,825. From this amount, $3830.50 was spent on food. What percent of her income went to food, to the nearest tenth of a percent?

42. In her shop, Stephanie earns 16% on all the clothes she sells. This month she earned $3920. What were her total sales of clothes?

43. Eli works in a clothes shop where he earns a commission of 8% and no weekly salary. What will Eli's weekly sales have to be for him to earn $425?

LESSON 6-7

44. Fatin borrowed $6500 to make home repairs and to put in a new skylight. The bank charges $7\frac{1}{2}$% simple interest over 5 years. What is the total Fatin will repay the bank?

45. Rebekah invested $15,000 in a mutual fund at a yearly rate of 8%. She earned $7200 in simple interest. How long was the money invested?

46. Shu earned $1000, which he used to buy a 10-year certificate of deposit (CD). The CD paid simple interest at 8%. What will the CD be worth at the end of 10 years?

47. Rich borrowed $16,000 for 12 years at simple interest to help pay for his schooling. If he repaid a total of $31,360, at what interest rate did he borrow the money?

Extra Practice ▪ Chapter 7

LESSON 7-1

Classify each angle as acute, obtuse, or right.

1.

2.
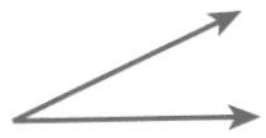

3.

In the figure, ∠1 and ∠3 are vertical angles, and ∠2 and ∠4 are vertical angles.

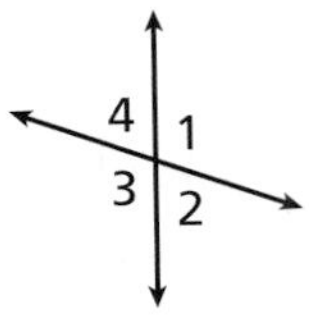

4. If m∠1 = 107°, find m∠3.

5. If m∠2 = 46°, find m∠4.

LESSON 7-2

In the figure, line $d \parallel$ line f. Find the measure of each angle.

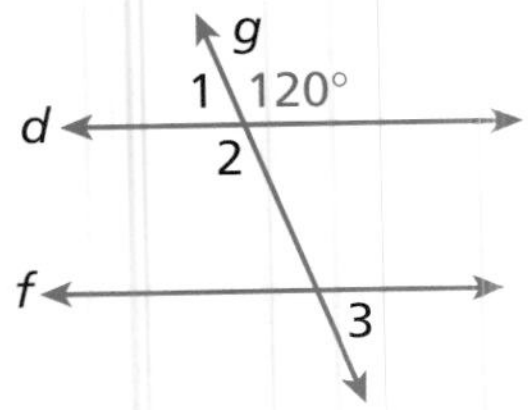

6. ∠1

7. ∠2

8. ∠3

LESSON 7-3

Find the missing angle measures in each triangle.

9.
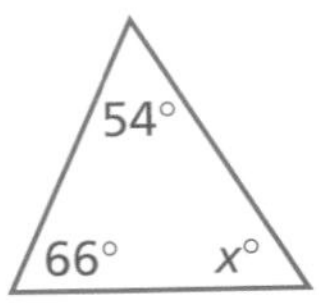

10.
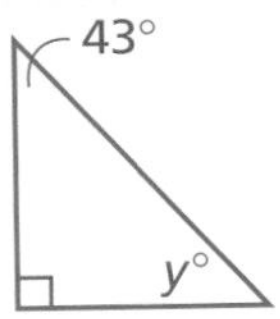

11.
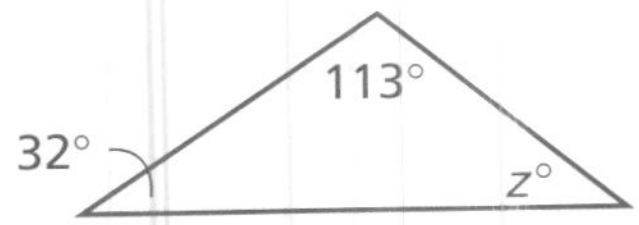

12. The first angle of a triangle is 3 times as large as the second angle. The third angle is twice as large as the second angle. Find the angle measures.

LESSON 7-4

Find the angle measures in each regular polygon.

13. pentagon (5 sides)

14. octagon (8 sides)

15. nonagon (9 sides)

Give all of the names that apply to each figure.

16.
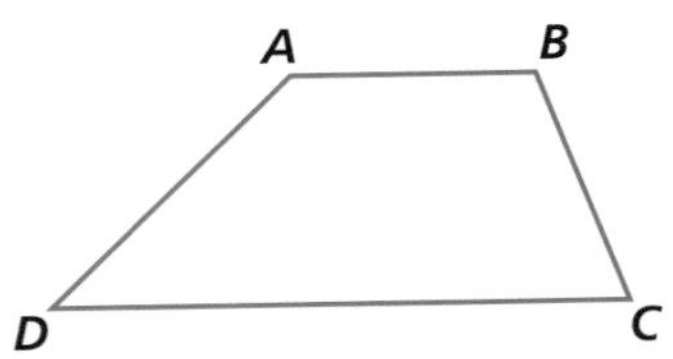

$\overline{AB} \parallel \overline{CD}$

17.
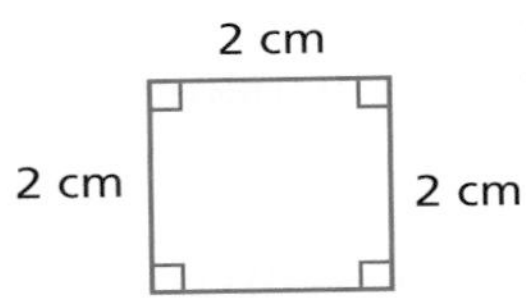

LESSON 7-5

Find the coordinates of the missing vertex.

18. rhombus $ABCD$ with $A(2, 3)$, $B(3, 0)$, and $D(1, 0)$

19. square $JKLM$ with $J(1, 1)$, $K(4, 1)$, and $L(4, -2)$

20. rectangle $ABCD$ with $A(-4, 3)$, $B(-1, 3)$, and $D(-4, -1)$

21. trapezoid $JKLM$ with $J(-2, 1)$, $K(2, 1)$, and $L(1, -1)$

Extra Practice · Chapter 7

LESSON 7-6

In the figure, quadrilateral $ABCD \cong$ quadrilateral $KLMN$.

22. Find x.

23. Find y.

24. Find z.

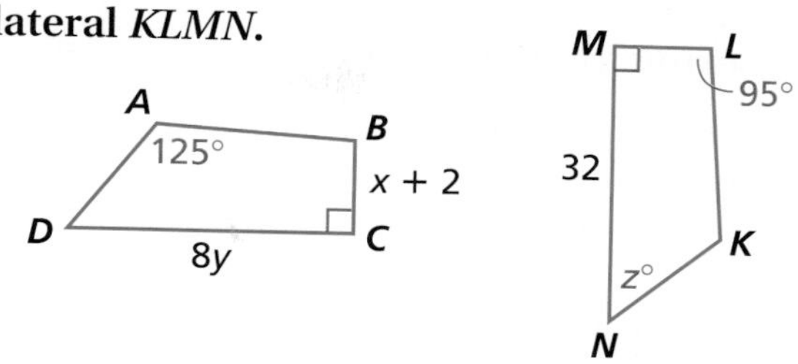

LESSON 7-7

Identify each as a translation, rotation, reflection, or none of these.

25.

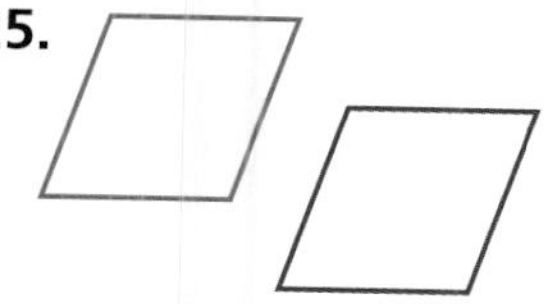

26.

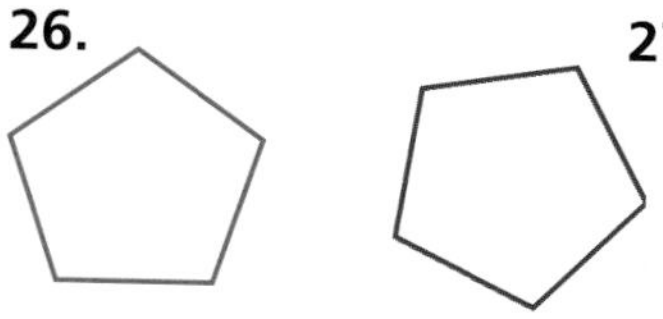

27.

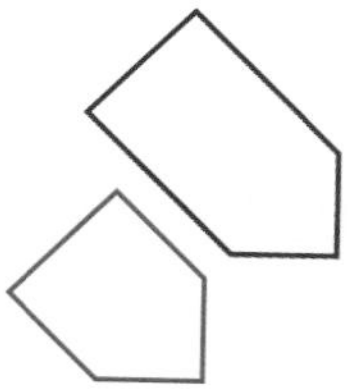

28.

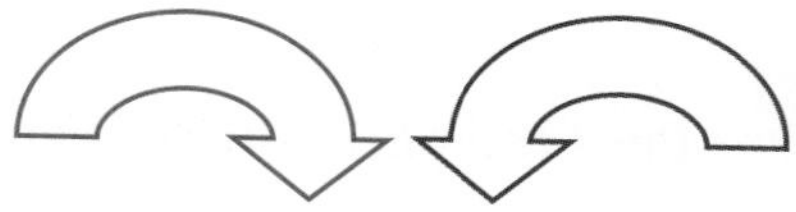

Draw the image of the triangle ABC with vertices (1, 1), (4, 2), and (4, 4) after each transformation.

29. reflection across the y-axis

30. translation 3 units down

31. rotation 180° around (0, 0)

32. translation 5 units left

33. translation 1 unit up

34. reflection across the x-axis

LESSON 7-8

Complete each figure. The dashed line is the line of symmetry.

35.

36.

37.

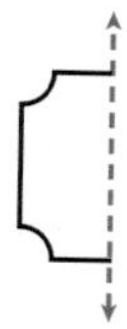

Complete each figure. The point is the center of rotation.

38. 4-fold

39. 6-fold

40. 2-fold

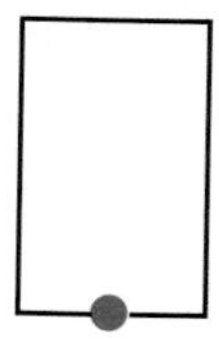

LESSON 7-9

Create a tessellation with each figure.

41.

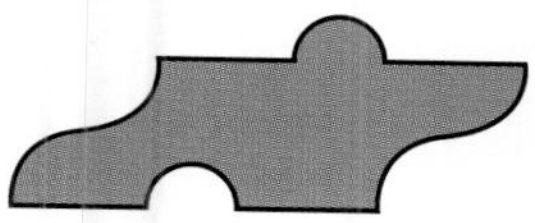

42.

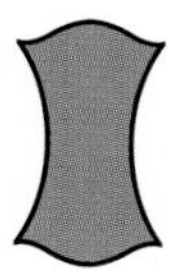

Extra Practice ■ Chapter 8

LESSON 8-1

Find the perimeter of each figure.

1.

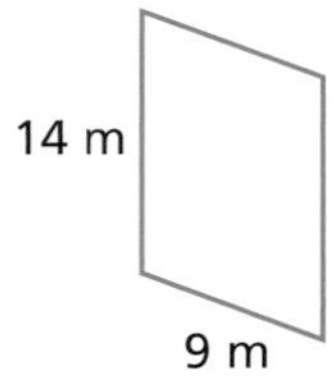

2.

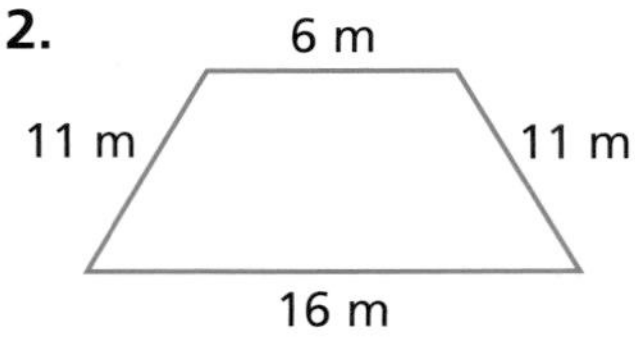

3.

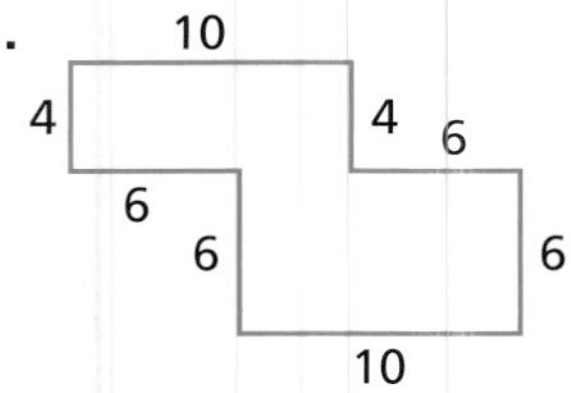

Graph and find the area of each figure with the given vertices.

4. $(-2, 1), (5, 1), (-2, 4), (5, 4)$

5. $(1, 2), (2, -1), (5, 2), (6, -1)$

LESSON 8-2

Find the perimeter of each figure.

6.

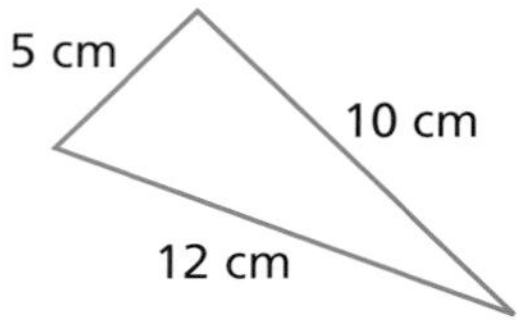

7.

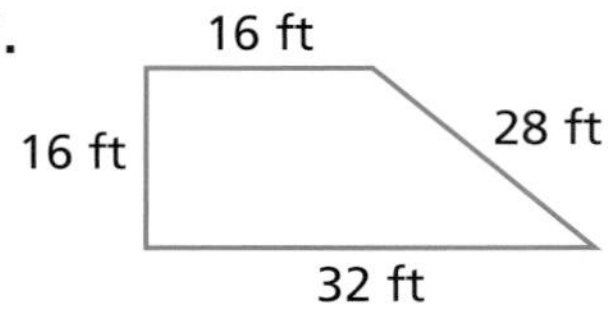

8.

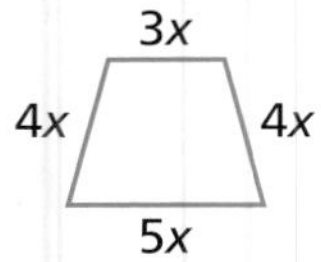

Graph and find the area of each figure with the given vertices.

9. $(-4, 3), (2, 3), (2, -1)$

10. $(2, -1), (5, 3), (0, -1), (-3, 3)$

LESSON 8-3

Find the circumference and area of each circle, both in terms of π and to the nearest tenth. Use 3.14 for π.

11.

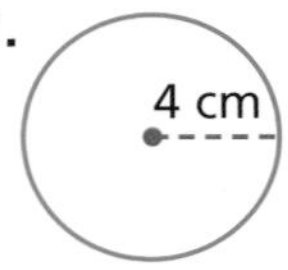

12.

13.

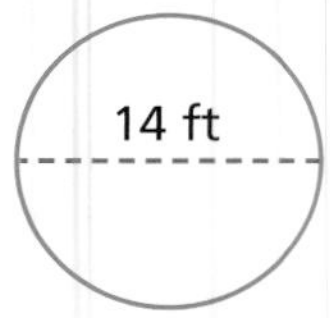

LESSON 8-4

Draw the front, top, and side views of each figure.

14.

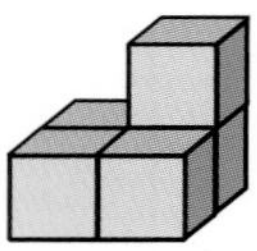

15.

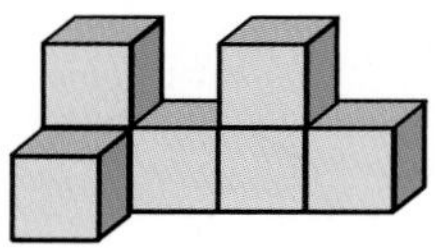

16.

LESSON 8-5

Find the volume of each figure to the nearest tenth. Use 3.14 for π.

17.

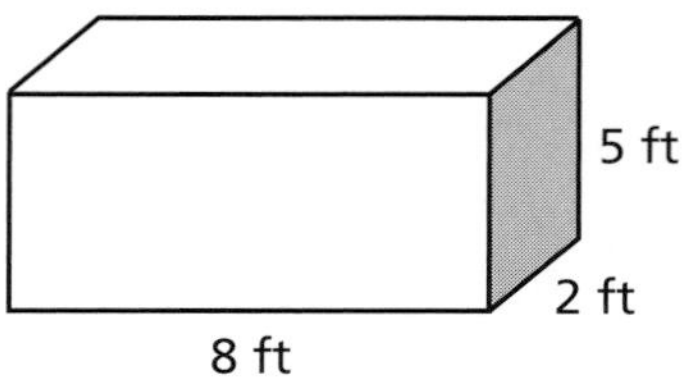

18.

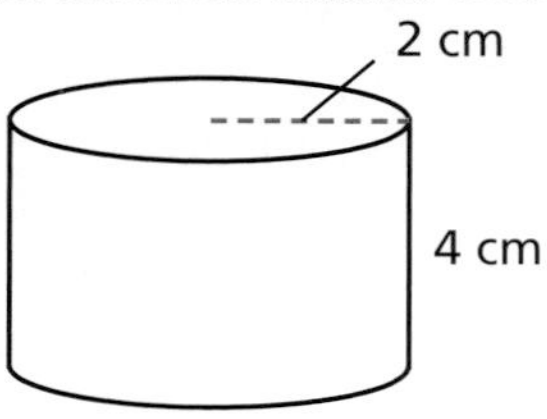

19.

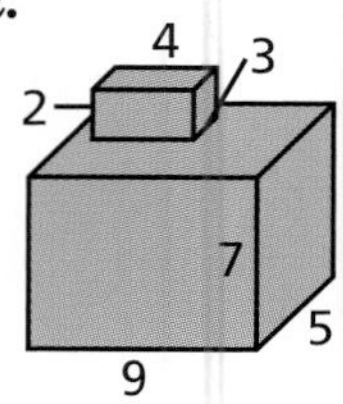

20. A can has a diameter of 3 in. and a height of 5 in. Explain whether doubling the height of the can would have the same effect on the volume as doubling the diameter.

21. A shoe box is 6.5 in. by 5.5 in. by 16 in. Estimate the volume of the shoe box.

LESSON 8-6

Find the volume of each figure to the nearest tenth. Use 3.14 for π.

22.

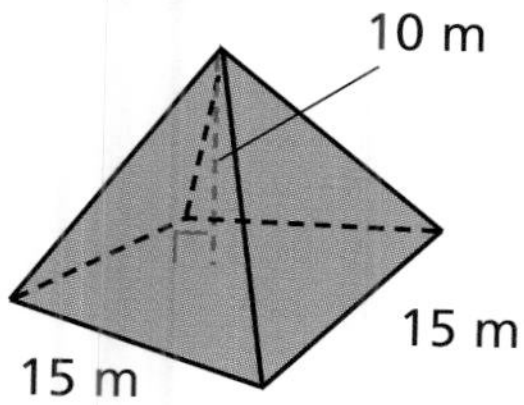

23.

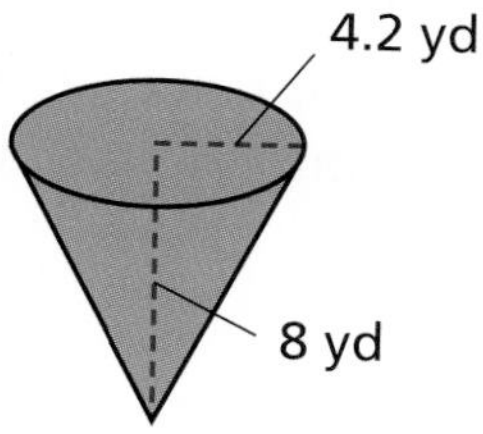

24.

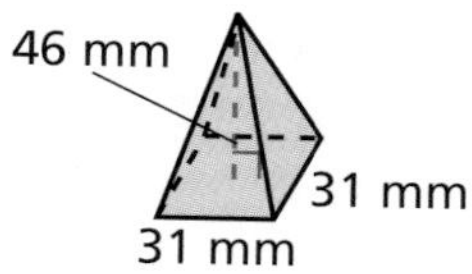

25. A rectangular pyramid has a height of 15 ft and a base that measures 5 ft by 7.5 ft. Explain whether doubling the height would double the volume of the pyramid.

LESSON 8-7

Find the surface area of each figure to the nearest tenth. Use 3.14 for π.

26. a cylinder with radius 10 cm and height 5 cm

27.

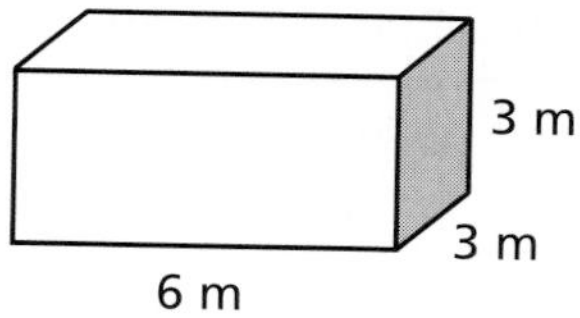

28.

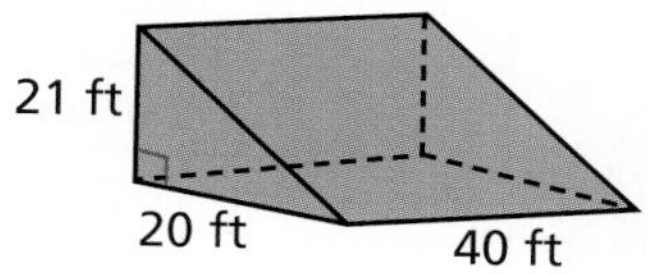

LESSON 8-8

Find the surface area of each figure to the nearest tenth. Use 3.14 for π.

29.

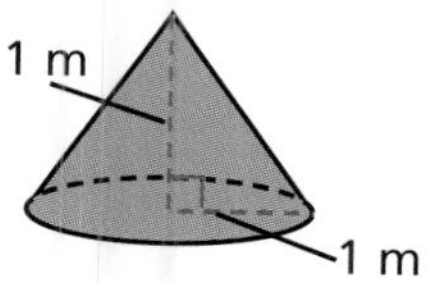

30. a square pyramid with an 8 in. by 8 in. base and a height of 3 in.

31. a pyramid with an equilateral triangle base with side length 12 units and all lateral faces equilateral triangles

LESSON 8-9

Find the volume and surface area of each sphere, both in terms of π and to the nearest tenth. Use 3.14 for π.

32. a sphere with radius 5 ft

33. a sphere with diameter 40 cm

LESSON 8-10

A 8 cm cube and a 5 cm cube are both part of a demonstration kit for architects. Compare the following values of the two cubes.

34. side length

35. surface area

36. volume

Extra Practice ■ Chapter 9

LESSON 9-1

Identify the sampling method used.

1. A questionnaire is distributed to every eighth diner entering a restaurant.
2. In a state survey, 10 cities are chosen at random, and 100 people are chosen from each city.

Identify the population and sample. Give a reason why the sample could be biased.

3. A company surveys 100 employees who belong to 5 different high tech companies about their opinion on company benefits.

LESSON 9-2

4. Use a line plot to organize the data of the number of miles biked by students over a weekend.

Number of Miles Biked by Students
12 21 12 8 10 15 15 18 12 11 9 10 9 6 0 5 12 5 14 14 10 8 12 10 9

5. **Use the given data to make a back-to-back stem-and-leaf plot.**

World Series Win/Loss Records of Selected Teams (through 2001)							
Team	Yankees	Pirates	Giants	Tigers	Cardinals	Dodgers	Orioles
Wins	26	5	5	4	9	6	3
Losses	12	2	11	5	6	12	4

LESSON 9-3

Determine and find the most appropriate measure of central tendency or range for each situation.

6. The number of animals seen each day of the week at a veterinarian's office was 22, 31, 20, 44, 39, 29. What number best describes the middle of this data?
7. Mr. Lucky sold five houses for the following prices: \$125,000; \$425,000; \$178,000; \$155,000; \$105,000. What measure of central tendency or range would make the house prices seem the highest?

LESSON 9-4

Find the first and third quartiles for each data set.

8. 27, 31, 26, 24, 33, 31, 24, 28, 31, 24, 22, 27, 31, 28, 26
9. 84, 79, 77, 72, 81, 82, 89, 94, 72, 80, 76, 80, 83, 86, 73

Use the given data to make a box-and-whisker plot.

10. 11, 4, 9, 17, 16, 12, 5, 16, 9, 11, 13
11. 57, 53, 52, 31, 48, 59, 64, 86, 56, 54, 55

LESSON 9-5

12. Organize the data into a frequency table and make a double-bar graph. The following are the ages of 24 men and women between the ages of 45 and 50 with high cholesterol.

Men: 48, 46, 50, 50, 45, 46, 45, 47, 49, 46, 45, 48

Women: 50, 47, 49, 49, 46, 48, 50, 49, 48, 49, 50, 45

LESSON 9-6

Explain why each graph or statistic is misleading.

13.

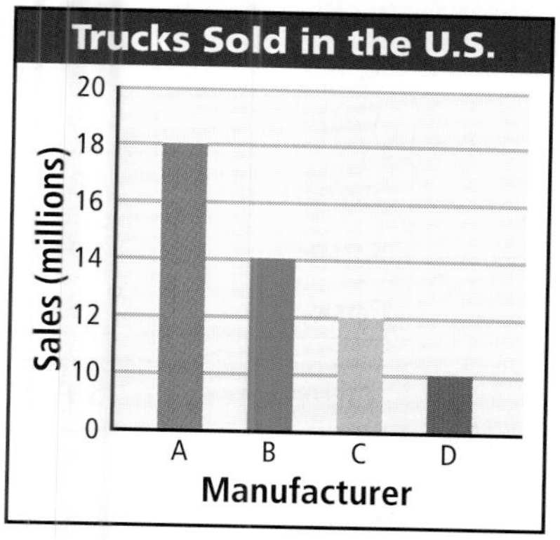

14. A market researcher randomly selected 12 shoppers to sample 4 brands of cereal labeled *A, B, C,* and *D.* Of the shoppers, 6 selected *C,* 2 selected *A,* 2 selected *B,* and 2 selected *D.* An ad for brand *C* is heard to say, "Preferred 3 to 1 over other brands."

15. A car lot has five cars for sale at the following prices: $14,000, $13,000, $15,000, $2,000, and $16,000. It has a banner boasting an average price of $12,000 per car.

LESSON 9-7

Use the given data to make a scatter plot.

16. The table shows the relationship between the number of years of post high school education and salary.

Number of Years of Post High School Education and Salary												
Years	1	1	3	4	4	4	5	5	6	6	8	8
Salary ($1,000's)	18	20.5	28	35	51	43	58	52	64	58	75	73.5

Do the data sets have a positive, a negative, or no correlation?

17. the number of sales and the amount of a salesperson's commission

18. the height of a dog and its life expectancy

LESSON 9-8

Choose the best data display for each situation. Explain your choice.

19. how Benetta spent her time one day

20. the price of Carlos' stock over one week

Extra Practice ■ Chapter 10

LESSON 10-1

Refer to the spinner at right. Give the probability for each outcome.

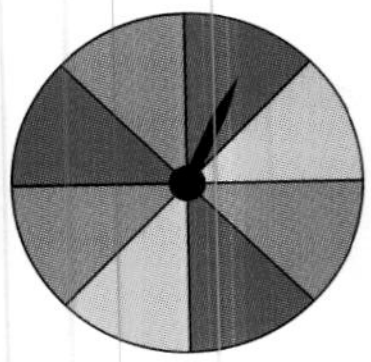

1. red
2. blue
3. yellow
4. not red
5. not blue
6. not yellow
7. The probability that Kim will win a game is $\frac{1}{4}$. Kelvin and Chelsea have half as much chance of winning as Kim does. Sasha is four times as likely to win the game as Kelvin is. Create a table of probabilities for the sample space.

LESSON 10-2

A utensil is drawn from a drawer and replaced. The table shows the results after 100 draws.

Outcomes	Draws
Spoon	33
Knife	36
Fork	31

8. Estimate the probability of drawing a spoon.
9. Estimate the probability of not drawing a spoon.

A sales assistant tracks the sales of a particular sweater. The table shows the data after 1000 sales.

Outcomes	Sales
White	361
Beige	207
Brown	189
Black	243

10. Estimate the probability that the next customer will buy a brown sweater.
11. Estimate the probability of the next sweater sold not being brown or beige.

LESSON 10-3

Use the table of random numbers to simulate each situation. Use at least 10 trials for each simulation.

53736 85815 87649 31119 16635 65161 27919 86585 32848 94425 61378 41256
11632 46278 38783 87649 13325 60848 74681 54238 94228 82794 23426 46498

12. A golfer has an 81% chance of making a putt on the first try. Estimate the probability that he will make the putt on the first try at least 9 of his next 10 times.
13. A field-goal kicker has a 74% chance of making successful field goals. Estimate the probability that he will make at least 8 of his next 10 field goal attempts.

LESSON 10-4

An experiment consists of rolling a fair number cube. There are 6 possible outcomes: 1, 2, 3, 4, 5, and 6. Find the probability of each event.

14. P(rolling an odd number)
15. P(rolling a 2)
16. P(rolling a number greater than 3)
17. P(rolling a 7)

An experiment consists of rolling two fair number cubes. Find each probability.

18. P(rolling a total of 4)

19. P(rolling a total less than 2)

20. P(rolling a total greater than 12)

21. P(rolling a total of 9)

LESSON 10-5

22. An experiment consists of rolling a fair number cube 3 times. For each toss, all outcomes are equally likely. What is the probability of rolling a 2 three times in a row?

23. A jar contains 3 blue marbles and 9 red marbles. What is the probability of drawing 2 red marbles at the same time?

LESSON 10-6

24. Kylie practiced barrel racing around a course 10 times. Her times, in seconds, were 13.849, 13.960, 14.133, 14.186, 13.946, 13.952, 14.054, 14.065, 14.296, and 14.383. If she practices 40 more times, what is the best prediction of the number of times that will be less than 14 seconds?

25. Toss four coins. Player A wins if exactly 3 heads land up. Otherwise Player B wins. Is this game fair?

LESSON 10-7

26. At a wrestling meet, 192 participants competed for 12 trophies. Estimate the odds of winning a trophy.

27. If the odds against winning a contest are 9999:1, what is the probability of winning the contest?

LESSON 10-8

A computer randomly generates a 4-character computer password of 3 digits followed by 1 letter.

28. Find the number of possible passwords.

29. Find the probability that an assigned password does not contain a *P*.

30. A dancer has a choice of 2 dresses, 4 scarves, and 4 pairs of shoes. Draw a tree diagram to show all the possible outcomes.

LESSON 10-9

Evaluate each expression.

31. $9!$

32. $\frac{6!}{3!}$

33. $\frac{5!}{11!}$

34. $\frac{7!}{(15-7)!}$

35. There are 10 college football teams in the conference. Find the number of orders in which all 10 teams can finish the season.

36. Find the number of ways the 10 teams can finish first, second, and third in the conference.

Extra Practice ▪ Chapter 11

LESSON 11-1

Combine like terms.

1. $5x + 4x + 7x$
2. $6x - 4x + 9 + 5x + 7$
3. $2x + 3 - 2x + 5$
4. $7a - 2b + 6 + 4b - 5a$
5. $4s + 9t - 9$
6. $6m + 4n - 6m + n$

Simplify.

7. $6(y + 4) - y$
8. $3(3b - 3) + 3b$
9. $4(x + 2) + 3x - 8$

Solve.

10. $4x + 7 = 87$
11. $2a - 3 = 41$
12. $9b + 4 = 67$
13. $6h - 12 = 78$
14. $5y + 3y = 24$
15. $8d - 3d = 40$
16. $2m + m = 42$
17. $9x - x = 48$
18. $a + 6a = 49$
19. $2p + 8p = 100$
20. $12y - 8y = 44$
21. $5f + 7f + 3f = 30$

LESSON 11-2

Solve.

22. $4a - 5 + 2a + 9 = 28$
23. $5 - 8b + 6 - 2b = 61$
24. $4x - 6 - 8x - 9 = 21$
25. $g - 9 + 4g + 6 = 12$
26. $2 - 3f - 5 + 5f = 6$
27. $4r - 8 + 7 - 6r = -9$
28. $\frac{4a}{5} - \frac{7}{5} = -\frac{3}{5}$
29. $\frac{1}{3} - \frac{2b}{3} = \frac{7}{3}$
30. $\frac{4z}{11} + \frac{3}{11} = -1$
31. $\frac{8}{9} - \frac{5m}{9} = \frac{23}{9}$
32. $\frac{9}{11} - \frac{3s}{11} = \frac{3}{11}$
33. $\frac{4p}{3} - \frac{2}{3} = 6$
34. $\frac{2f}{4} - 4 = -\frac{24}{12}$
35. $\frac{10c}{4} - \frac{16}{2} = \frac{56}{8}$
36. $\frac{9x}{3} - \frac{45}{9} + \frac{36x}{6} = \frac{-126}{9}$
37. $\frac{42y}{6} - \frac{9}{3} + \frac{16y}{8} = \frac{396}{12}$
38. $\frac{27a}{9} + \frac{15}{3} - \frac{8a}{2} = \frac{36}{6}$
39. $\frac{4b}{4} + \frac{b}{2} - \frac{6}{2} = \frac{12}{8}$
40. A round-trip car ride took 12 hours. The first half of the trip took 7 hours at a rate of 45 miles per hour. What was the average rate of speed on the return trip?

LESSON 11-3

Solve.

41. $5x - 6 = 2x$
42. $4w + 5 = 20 - w$
43. $3y + 12 = -3y$
44. $2b + 6 = -b + 3$
45. $4z - 2 = z + 1$
46. $-4a - 4 = a + 11$
47. $4p - 6 = 3 + 4p$
48. $6 + 5c = 3c - 4$
49. $7d - 3 + 2d = 5d - 8 + 1$
50. $3f - 4 - 5f = f + 4 + f$
51. $5k - 4 - k = 3k - 6 + 2k$
52. $\frac{w}{4} + \frac{5}{8} - \frac{2w}{2} = \frac{7}{8} - \frac{2w}{4}$
53. $\frac{a}{3} - \frac{1}{6} + \frac{5a}{6} = \frac{9}{6} + \frac{2a}{3} + \frac{a}{3}$
54. $\frac{2q}{3} + \frac{5}{9} - \frac{q}{6} = \frac{5q}{6} - \frac{2}{18}$
55. A cafeteria charges a fixed price per ounce for the salad bar. A sandwich costs \$3.10, and a large drink costs \$1.75. If a 7-ounce salad and a drink cost the same as a 4-ounce salad and a sandwich, how much does the salad cost per ounce?

LESSON 11-4

Solve and graph.

56. $3x > -36$

57. $5 \le \frac{v}{2}$

58. $\frac{2r}{3} < 8$

59. $6k > 24$

60. $-40 \ge 4q$

61. $\frac{3}{4}m > 18$

62. $-9x > 72$

63. $-2 \le -\frac{s}{3}$

64. $5 \ge -b$

65. $16 > -4c$

66. $\frac{p}{3} > -6$

67. $-3d < -12$

68. $3 > \frac{w}{-5}$

69. $-3h \ge -2$

70. $-f \le 4$

71. $-5y > -55$

72. Reese is running for student council president. In order for a student to be elected president, at least $\frac{1}{3}$ of the students must vote for him. If there are 432 students in a class, at least how many students must vote for Reese in order for him to be elected class president?

LESSON 11-5

Solve and graph.

73. $3a + 6 < 12$

74. $-5 \le 4x + 7$

75. $2b + 8 > 16$

76. $6c + 8 \ge -4$

77. $5 > 4d - 3$

78. $-8f + 6 \le 14$

79. $-3g + 2 \ge -4$

80. $-3 < 7h - 10$

81. $4z + 8 \le -4$

82. $7y + 1 > 8$

83. $9 < 3z - 9$

84. $a + \frac{3}{8} > \frac{1}{2}$

85. $\frac{x}{6} - \frac{1}{3} > -\frac{2}{3}$

86. $\frac{1}{2}k + 8 \ge 9$

87. $\frac{d}{2} + \frac{4}{5} < 2$

88. $\frac{2}{3} + \frac{p}{6} < \frac{7}{6}$

89. Nikko wants to make flyers promoting a library book sale. The printer charges \$40 plus \$0.03 per flyer. How many flyers can Nikko have made without spending more than the library's \$54 budget?

LESSON 11-6

Solve each system of equations.

90. $x - 2y = -10$
$5x + 2y = -2$

91. $y = 2x$
$y = x + 6$

92. $3x + 4y = 17$
$-2x + 4y = 2$

93. $y + 2x = 5$
$y = x - 4$

94. $y + 2x = -2$
$2y - 2x = 14$

95. $y = x + 4$
$y = 2x + 6$

96. $y = 3x - 1$
$y = 2x + 2$

97. $-y = x + 1$
$y = -2x - 4$

98. $2x + y = 0$
$2x + 3y = 8$

99. $x + y = -5$
$x - 2y = 7$

100. $y = x - 1$
$-3x + 3y = 4$

101. $-x - y = 0$
$y = x + 8$

102. $y = x - 5$
$x - y - 5 = 0$

103. $2y - x = 6$
$4y + 2x = -4$

104. $3y - 2x = -2$
$y + 2x = -6$

105. $y = -2x + 1$
$2x + y = 4$

106. $-3y - x = 2$
$2y + 2x = 4$

107. $y = 2x - 5$
$2x - y - 5 = 0$

108. $y = 3x$
$2y + 3x = -18$

109. $y = -x$
$4y + x = 21$

Extra Practice

Extra Practice ■ Chapter 12

LESSON 12-1

Graph each equation and tell whether it is linear.

1. $y = 4x - 2$
2. $y = -2x + 1$
3. $y = x^2 - 4$
4. $y = -x - 3$
5. A home improvement store charges a base fee of $150, plus $25 for each hour of machinery rental. The cost C for h hours is given by $C = 25h + 150$. Find the cost for 1, 2, 3, 4, and 5 hours. Is this a linear equation? Draw a graph that represents the relationship between the cost and the number of hours of rental.

LESSON 12-2

Find the slope of the line that passes through each pair of given points.

6. (3, 4) and (−2, 2)
7. (6, 2) and (−2, −6)
8. (3, 3) and (1, −4)
9. (−2, 4) and (1, 1)
10. The table shows how much money Andy and Margie made working at the concession stand at a baseball game one weekend. Use the data to make a graph. Find the slope of the line and explain what it shows.

Time (hr)	Money Earned
2	$15
4	$30
6	$45
8	$60

LESSON 12-3

Find the x-intercept and y-intercept of each line. Use the intercepts to graph the equation.

11. $5x - 3y = 8$
12. $3y - x = 9$
13. $7x + 1 = 4y$
14. $3y + x = 5$

Write each equation in slope-intercept form, and then find the slope and y-intercept.

15. $3x = y$
16. $3y = 5x$
17. $5x - y = 8$
18. $6y + 7 = 2x$

Write the equation of the line that passes through each pair of points in slope-intercept form.

19. (5, −1) and (−7, −4)
20. (5, 1) and (−1, −5)
21. (4, 9) and (−5, 3)

LESSON 12-4

Use the point-slope form of each equation to identify a point the line passes through and the slope of the line.

22. $y - 2 = \frac{1}{3}(x + 1)$
23. $y + 3 = -3(x - 2)$
24. $y - 4 = -\frac{1}{3}(x - 5)$
25. $y + 5 = 2(x - 1)$
26. $y - 2 = \frac{4}{7}(x + 5)$
27. $y = -\frac{3}{4}(x - 4)$

Write the point-slope form of the equation with the given slope that passes through the indicated point.

28. the line with slope 2 passing through (1, 4)
29. the line with slope $\frac{1}{4}$ passing through (−3, 2)

LESSON 12-5

Determine whether the data sets show direct variation.

30.

Weight of Patient	Medication Prescribed (mg)
100	50
120	60
140	70
160	80

31.

Cost of Item	Shipping and Handling
$10.80	$2
$27.82	$4
$43.20	$5
$55.00	$6

Find each equation of direct variation, given that y varies directly with x.

32. y is 24 when x is 8.
33. y is 18 when x is 12.
34. y is 96 when x is 3.
35. y is 8 when x is 4.
36. y is 102 when x is 17.
37. y is 17 when x is 6.

38. Instructions for a chemical concentrate swimming pool cleaner state that 2 ounces of concentrate should be added to every $1\frac{1}{2}$ gallons of water used. How many ounces of concentrate should be added to 18 gallons of water?

39. The distance d an object falls varies directly with the square of the time t of the fall. This is expressed by the formula $d = k \cdot t^2$. An object falls 90 feet in 3 seconds. How far will the object fall in 15 seconds?

LESSON 12-6

Graph each inequality.

40. $y \leq x - 3$
41. $y > x + 3$
42. $6x - 3y \geq 9$
43. $4y - 12 < 2x$
44. $3y - 9x < 15$
45. $3y + 9 > 5x$
46. $x - 5y < 2$
47. $-2y \geq x - 3$

48. A teacher needs to buy no more than 20 pens. Pens come in packages of 4 or 5. Write and graph an inequality showing the number of 4-pen and 5-pen packages the teacher can buy.

LESSON 12-7

Plot the data and find a line of best fit.

49.

x	6	4	8	5	1	7	2	3
y	5	3	6	2	2	5	1	4

50. Find a line of best fit for the men's Olympic winning times in the 50-meter freestyle. Use the equation of the line to predict what the winning time will be in 2068. Is it reasonable to make this prediction? Explain.

Year	1988	1992	1996	2000	2004
Winning Time (s)	22.14	21.94	22.13	21.98	21.93

Extra Practice ■ Chapter 13

LESSON 13-1

Determine if each sequence could be arithmetic. If so, give the common difference.

1. 213, 204, 195, 186, 177, 168, . . .
2. 13, 24, 36, 49, 63, 78, . . .
3. 16.5, 16.9, 17.3, 17.7, 18.1, . . .
4. 151, 156, 160, 165, 169, 174, . . .

Find the given term in each arithmetic sequence.

5. 15th term: 8, 16, 24, 32, . . .
6. 25th term: 100, 97, 94, 91, . . .
7. 17th term: 53, 44, 35, 26, . . .
8. 41st term: 841, 828, 815, 802, . . .
9. Meka received 2000 frequent flier miles when she applied for a credit card. For every $1000 she spends, she will receive 500 more miles. How much does she have to spend to have 5000 miles?

LESSON 13-2

Determine if each sequence could be geometric. If so, give the common ratio.

10. 8192, 4096, 2048, 1024, 512, 256, . . .
11. 1, 9, 81, 729, 6561, 59,049, . . .
12. 4, 8, 24, 120, 720, 5040, . . .
13. 13, 39, 117, 351, 1053, 3159, . . .

Find the given term in each geometric sequence.

14. 11th term: −5, 5 −5, 5, . . .
15. 44th term: 2, 4, 8, 16, . . .
16. 8th term: 236, 118, 59, 29.5, . . .
17. 20th term: 2, 6, 18, 54, . . .
18. The oil from a 12,000-gallon oil tank leaks at a rate of 6% per hour after being cracked in an accident. If the tank is not repaired, how many gallons of oil will be left after 6 hours?

LESSON 13-3

Use first and second differences to find the next three terms in each sequence.

19. 11, 18, 30, 47, 69, 96, . . .
20. 15, 22, 32, 45, 61, 80, . . .
21. 10.5, 15.25, 20.75, 27, 34, 41.75, . . .
22. 6, 11, 17, 25, 36, 51, . . .
23. 217, 231, 246, 262, 279, 297, . . .
24. 47, 52, 57.5, 64, 72, 82, . . .

Give the next three terms in each sequence using the simplest rule you can find.

25. 1, 3, 5, 7, 9, . . .
26. $1, \frac{1}{3}, \frac{1}{6}, \frac{1}{9}, \frac{1}{12}, \frac{1}{15}, \ldots$
27. 4, 7, 10, 13, 16, . . .

Find the first five terms of each sequence defined by the given rule.

28. $a_n = \frac{n}{n+1}$
29. $a_n = n(n + 2)$
30. $a_n = n(n - 1) + 3n$
31. $a_n = 3n\left(\frac{1}{n}\right)$
32. $a_n = 6n$
33. $a_n = \left(\frac{n}{n+2}\right)n$

LESSON 13-4

Determine whether each function is linear.

34. $f(x) = -\frac{1}{x} + 4$

35. $f(x) = 6^x + 2$

36. $f(x) = \frac{2}{3}x$

37. $f(x) = 3x^{-5}$

38. $f(x) = 0.5x + 8$

39. $f(x) = 9$

Write a rule for each linear function.

40.

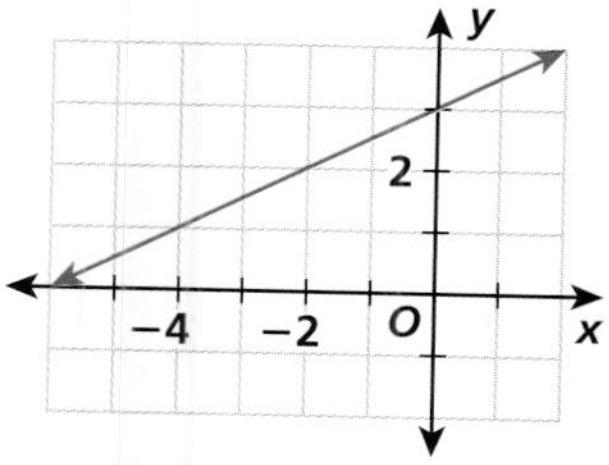

41.

x	y
−2	−5
−1	−3
0	−1
1	1
2	3

42.

x	y
−2	4
−1	3
0	2
1	1
2	0

43. Reo's cell phone company charges a monthly fee of \$12, plus \$0.10 each minute that he talks on the phone. Find a rule for the linear function that describes the monthly phone charges if Reo uses his phone x hours in a month, and use it to find how much he pays if he talks 72 minutes in a month.

LESSON 13-5

Create a table for each exponential function, and use it to graph the function.

44. $f(x) = 2 \cdot 3^x$

45. $f(x) = \frac{1}{4} \cdot 5^x$

46. $f(x) = 0.25 \cdot 3^x$

47. $f(x) = 3 \cdot 11^x$

48. The isotope cobalt-60, found in radioactive waste, has a half-life of 5 years. Predict how much of a 275 g sample of cobalt-60 would remain after 40 years.

LESSON 13-6

Create a table for each quadratic function, and use it graph the function.

49. $f(x) = x^2 - 2$

50. $f(x) = x^2 - x + 8$

51. $f(x) = (x - 2)(x + 3)$

52. The Taipei 101 skyscraper is 508 meters tall. The tallest occupied floor is 438 meters from the ground. The function $f(t) = -16t^2 + h$ gives the time t in seconds for an object to fall from height h. About how long would it take an object to fall from the tallest occupied floor in the Taipei 101 skyscraper?

LESSON 13-7

Determine whether the relationship is an inverse variation.

53. The table shows the number of trading cards a shop has listed at given prices.

Quantity of Trading Card	24,000	10,000	750	480	150
List Value (\$)	0.50	1.20	16.00	25.00	80.00

Create a table. Then graph each inverse variation function.

54. $f(x) = \frac{4}{x}$

55. $f(x) = \frac{-1.5}{x}$

56. $f(x) = \frac{5}{4x}$

57. $f(x) = \frac{1}{2}x$

Extra Practice ■ Chapter 14

LESSON 14-1

Determine whether each expression is a monomial.

1. $\frac{1}{4}r^2st^5$
2. $-6xy^3$
3. 2^yx^4
4. $\frac{3m^3}{n^5}$

Classify each expression as a monomial, a binomial, a trinomial, or not a polynomial.

5. $-4x^3 + x^2 + \frac{1}{4}$
6. $-9x^5y^2z^4$
7. $\frac{4}{5}m^4n^3 + m^3$
8. $h - 2h^{0.5} + 1$
9. $xw^7 - 7wz$
10. $-\frac{3}{z^4}$
11. $\frac{2}{3}a^4 + a^3 - 5$
12. $13st^6$

Find the degree of each polynomial.

13. $3x^3 + 4x^5 + 8$
14. $b^2 - 9b^3 - b^4 - 8$
15. $4 - t$
16. $z^2 + 5z^6 - 9z^3$

17. The trinomial $-16t^2 + vt + 12$ describes the height in feet of a baseball thrown straight up at a velocity of v ft/s from a 12-foot platform after t seconds. Find the height of the ball after 3 seconds if $v = 55$ ft/s.

18. The trinomial $-4x^2 + 270x - 2000$ gives the net profit, in dollars, that a custom bicycle manufacturer earns by selling x bikes in a given month. Find the net profit for a month if $x = 15$ bicycles.

LESSON 14-2

Identify the like terms in each polynomial.

19. $-s - 5r^2 + 7r - 9r^2 + 3s$
20. $4x^2 - 9 - 7x + x^5 + 10$
21. $5x^2y - 7x^2z + 7yz^2 - 3x^2y + xz^2$
22. $-3mn + 3p^2 + 3p - 5p^2 + 3mn$
23. $8s^2 + 6 - 7s + 6s^4 - 13$
24. $25 + 15xy - 10x^2 + 3xy - 5y^2 - 5$

Simplify.

25. $5z^2 + 2z - z^2 + 11z - 9$
26. $5 - 7(a^2 - 9) + 3a^2 - 7$
27. $-y^2z + 8xz - 6xy^2 + 10y^2z + xy^2$
28. $5c^2 + 11cd - d^2 - 5(c^2 - d^2) - 2c(c + d)$
29. $5(a^2b^2 + 3ab) + 3(ab^2 - 5ab)$
30. $2s^2t^2 + st^2 + 5s^2t^2 - 7s^2t - 3st^2 + s^2t$

31. A rectangle has a width of 12 cm and a length of $(2x^2 + 6)$ cm. The area is given by the expression $12(2x^2 + 6)$ cm^2. Use the Distributive Property to write an equivalent expression.

32. A parallelogram has a base of $(3x^2 - 4)$ in. and a height of 4 in. The area is given by the expression $4(3x^2 - 4)$ in^2. Use the Distributive Property to write an equivalent expression.

Extra Practice

Extra Practice ■ Chapter 14

LESSON 14-3

Add.

33. $(2x^2y^3 - 7x^3y^2 + xy) + (x^2y^3 + 2x^3y^2 + 3xy)$

34. $(3a^2 + 4ab^2) + (a^2b + 2b^2) + (-a^2b - 7ab^2)$

35. $(m^3 + 3m^2n^2 + 4) + (6m^2n^2 - 9)$

36. $(10r^3s^2 - 7r^2s + 4r) + (-4r^3s^2 + 3r)$

37. A rectangle has a width of $(x - 7)$ cm and a length of $(3x + 5)$ cm. An equilateral triangle has sides of length $x^2 - 2x + 3$. Write an expression for the sum of the perimeters of the rectangle and the triangle.

LESSON 14-4

Find the opposite of each polynomial.

38. $-6xy - 2y^3$

39. $4a^3b + 7ab - 8$

40. $-2x^6 - 3x + x^3$

41. $7g^5 + gh^4$

Subtract.

42. $(5x^2 + 2xy - 3y^2) - (3x^2 + 2y^2 - 8)$

43. $14a - (5a^3 - 3a + 6)$

44. $(5r^2s^2 + 9r^2s + rs) - (-3r^2s - 7rs + 2r^2)$

45. $(12y^3 - 6xy + 1) - (8xy - 2x + 1)$

46. The area of the larger rectangle is $10x^2 - 2x + 15$ cm^2. The area of the smaller rectangle is $5x^2 - 3x$ cm^2. What is the area of the shaded region?

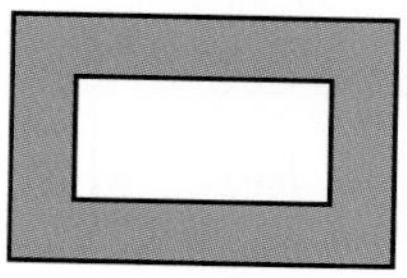

LESSON 14-5

Multiply.

47. $(5xy^2)(7x^3y^2)$

48. $(2a^2bc^2)(-5a^3b^2)$

49. $(6m^3n^4)(2mn)$

50. $6t(9s - 5t)$

51. $-p(2p^2 + pq - 5)$

52. $3xy^2(2x^3y^2 + 4x^2y - xy^6 - 11xy)$

53. A rectangle has a width of $3x^2y$ ft and a length of $2x^2 + 4xy + 7$ ft. Write and simplify an expression for the area of the rectangle. Then find the area of the rectangle if $x = 2$ and $y = 3$.

LESSON 14-6

Multiply.

54. $(y + 5)(y - 3)$

55. $(s + 3)(s - 5)$

56. $(3m + 2)(4m - 3)$

57. $(y + 1)^2$

58. $(d - 5)^2$

59. $(a + 9)(a - 9)$

Draw a Diagram

When problems involve objects, distances, or places, drawing a diagram can make the problem clearer. You can **draw a diagram** to help understand the problem and to solve the problem.

Problem Solving Strategies

Draw a Diagram	Make a Table
Make a Model	Solve a Simpler Problem
Guess and Test	Use Logical Reasoning
Work Backward	Use a Venn Diagram
Find a Pattern	Make an Organized List

June is moving her cat, dog, and goldfish to her new apartment. She can only take 1 pet with her on each trip. She cannot leave the cat and the dog or the cat and the goldfish alone together. How can she get all of her pets safely to her new apartment?

Understand the Problem The answer will be the description of the trips to her new apartment. At no time can the cat be alone with the dog or the goldfish.

Make a Plan **Draw a diagram** to represent each trip to and from the apartment.

Solve In the beginning, the cat, dog, and goldfish are all at her old apartment.

Old Apartment		New Apartment	
June, Cat, Dog, Fish	June, Cat →	June, Cat	*Trip 1: She takes the cat and returns alone.*
June, Dog, Fish	← June	Cat	
June, Dog, Fish	June, Dog →	June, Dog, Cat	*Trip 2: She takes the dog and returns with the cat.*
June, Cat, Fish	← June, Cat	Dog	
June, Cat, Fish	June, Fish →	June, Dog, Fish	*Trip 3: She takes the fish and returns alone.*
June, Cat	← June	Dog, Fish	
June, Cat	June, Cat →	June, Cat, Dog, Fish	*Trip 4: She takes the cat.*

Look Back Check to make sure that the cat is never alone with either the fish or the dog.

PRACTICE

1. There are 8 flags evenly spaced around a circular track. It takes Ling 15 s to run from the first flag to the third flag. At this pace, how long will it take her to run around the track twice?
2. A frog is climbing a 22-foot tree. Every 5 minutes, it climbs up 3 feet, but slips back down 1 foot. How long will it take it to climb the tree?

Make a Model

A problem that involves objects may be solved by making a model out of similar items. **Make a model** to help you understand the problem and find the solution.

Problem Solving Strategies

Draw a Diagram	Make a Table
Make a Model	Solve a Simpler Problem
Guess and Test	Use Logical Reasoning
Work Backward	Use a Venn Diagram
Find a Pattern	Make an Organized List

The volume of a rectangular prism can be found by using the formula $V = \ell wh$, where ℓ is the length, w is the width, and h is the height of the prism. Find all possible rectangular prisms with a volume of 16 cubic units and dimensions that are all whole numbers.

Understand the Problem You need to find the different possible prisms. The length, width, and height will be whole numbers whose product is 16.

Make a Plan You can use unit cubes to make a model of every possible rectangular prism. Work in a systematic way to find all possible answers.

Solve Begin with a $16 \times 1 \times 1$ prism.

$16 \times 1 \times 1$

Keeping the height of the prism the same, explore what happens to the length as you change the width. Then try a height of 2. Notice that an $8 \times 2 \times 1$ prism is the same as an $8 \times 1 \times 2$ prism turned on its side.

$8 \times 2 \times 1$

Not a rectangular prism

$4 \times 4 \times 1$

$4 \times 2 \times 2$

The possible dimensions are $16 \times 1 \times 1$, $8 \times 2 \times 1$, $4 \times 4 \times 1$, and $4 \times 2 \times 2$.

Look Back The product of the length, width, and height must be 16. Look at the prime factorization of the volume: $16 = 2 \cdot 2 \cdot 2 \cdot 2$. Possible dimensions:

$1 \cdot 1 \cdot (2 \cdot 2 \cdot 2 \cdot 2) = 1 \cdot 1 \cdot 16$

$1 \cdot 2 \cdot (2 \cdot 2 \cdot 2) = 1 \cdot 2 \cdot 8$

$1 \cdot (2 \cdot 2) \cdot (2 \cdot 2) = 1 \cdot 4 \cdot 4$

$2 \cdot 2 \cdot (2 \cdot 2) = 2 \cdot 2 \cdot 4$

PRACTICE

1. Four unit squares are arranged so that each square shares a side with another square. How many different arrangements are possible?

2. Four triangles are formed by cutting a rectangle along its diagonals. What possible shapes can be formed by arranging these triangles?

Guess and Test

When you think that guessing may help you solve a problem, you can use **guess and test.** Using clues to make guesses can narrow your choices for the solution. Test whether your guess solves the problem, and continue guessing until you find the solution.

Problem Solving Strategies

Draw a Diagram	Make a Table
Make a Model	Solve a Simpler Problem
Guess and Test	Use Logical Reasoning
Work Backward	Use a Venn Diagram
Find a Pattern	Make an Organized List

North Middle School is planning to raise $1200 by sponsoring a car wash. They are going to charge $4 for each car and $8 for each minivan. How many vehicles would have to be washed to raise $1200 if they plan to wash twice as many cars as minivans?

Understand the Problem

You must determine the number of cars and the number of minivans that need to be washed to make $1200. You know the charge for each vehicle.

Make a Plan

You can **guess and test** to find the number of cars and minivans. Guess the number of cars, and then divide it by 2 to find the number of minivans.

Solve

You can organize your guesses in a table.

	Cars	Minivans	Money Raised	
First guess	200	100	$4(200) + $8(100) = $1600	*Too high*
Second guess	100	50	$4(100) + $8(50) = $800	*Too low*
Third guess	150	75	$4(150) + $8(75) = $1200	

They should wash 150 cars and 75 minivans, or 225 vehicles.

Look Back

The total raised is $4(150) + $8(75) = $1200, and the number of cars is twice the number of minivans. The answer is reasonable.

PRACTICE

1. At a baseball game, adult tickets cost $15 and children's tickets cost $8. Twice as many children attended as adults, and the total ticket sales were $2480. How many people attended the game?

2. Angie is making friendship bracelets and pins. It takes her 6 minutes to make a bracelet and 4 minutes to make a pin. If she wants to make three times as many pins as bracelets, how many pins and bracelets can she make in 3 hours?

Work Backward

To solve a problem that asks for an initial value that follows a series of steps, you may want to work backward.

Problem Solving Strategies

Draw a Diagram	Make a Table
Make a Model	Solve a Simpler Problem
Guess and Test	Use Logical Reasoning
Work Backward	Use a Venn Diagram
Find a Pattern	Make an Organized List

Tyrone has two clocks and a watch. If the power goes off during the day, the following happens:

- **Clock A stops and then continues when the power comes back on.**
- **Clock B stops and then resets to 12:00 A.M. when the power comes back on.**

When Tyrone gets home, his watch reads 4:27 P.M., clock B reads 5:21 A.M., and clock A reads 3:39 P.M. What time did the power go off, and for how long was it off?

Understand the Problem You need to find the time that the power went off and how long it was off. You know how each clock works.

Make a Plan **Work backward** to the time that the power went off. Subtract from the correct time of 4:27, the time on Tyrone's watch.

Solve The difference between the correct time and the time on clock A is the length of time the power was off.

4:27 − 3:39 = 0:48 *The power was off for 48 minutes.*

Clock B reset to 12:00 when the power went on.

5:21 − 12:00 = 5:21 *The power came on 5 hours and 21 minutes ago.*

Subtract 5:21 from the correct time to find when the power came on.

4:27 − 5:21 = 11:06 *The power came on at 11:06 A.M.*

Subtract 48 minutes from 11:06 to find when the power went off.

11:06 − 0:48 = 10:18

The power went off at 10:18 A.M. and was off for 48 minutes.

Look Back If the power went off at about 10 A.M. for about an hour, it would come on at about 11 A.M., and each clock would run for about $5\frac{1}{2}$ hours.

PRACTICE

1. Jackie is 4 years younger than Roger. Roger is $2\frac{1}{2}$ years older than Jade. Jade is 14 years old. How old is Jackie?

2. Becca is directing a play that starts at 8:15 P.M. She wants the cast ready 10 minutes before the play starts. The cast needs 45 minutes to put on make-up, 15 minutes for a director's meeting, and then 35 minutes to get in costume. What time should the cast arrive?

Find a Pattern

If a problem involves numbers, shapes, or even codes, noticing a pattern can often help you solve it. To solve a problem that involves patterns, you need to use small steps that will help you **find a pattern**.

Problem Solving Strategies

Draw a Diagram	Make a Table
Make a Model	Solve a Simpler Problem
Guess and Test	Use Logical Reasoning
Work Backward	Use a Venn Diagram
Find a Pattern	Make an Organized List

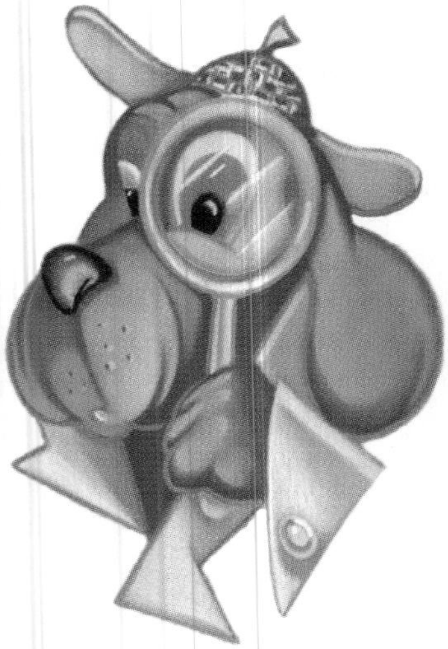

Gil is trying to decode the following sentence, which may have been encoded using a pattern. What does the coded sentence say?

QEB NRFZH YOLTK CLU GRJMP LSBO QEB IXWV ALD.

Understand the Problem You need to find whether there was a pattern used to encode the sentence and then extend the pattern to decode the sentence.

Make a Plan **Find a pattern.** Try to decode one of the words first. Notice that *QEB* appears twice in the sentence.

Solve Gil thinks that *QEB* is probably the word *THE*. If *QEB* stands for *THE*, a pattern emerges with respect to the letters and their position in the alphabet.

Q: 17th letter	*T*: 20th letter	*+ 3 letters*
E: 5th letter	*H*: 8th letter	*+ 3 letters*
B: 2nd letter	*E*: 5th letter	*+ 3 letters*

Continue the pattern. Although there is no 27th, 28th, or 29th letter of the alphabet, the remaining letters should be obvious ($27 = 1 = A$, $28 = 2 = B$, and $29 = 3 = C$).

```
QEB NRFZH YOLTK CLU GRJMP LSBO QEB IXWV ALD.
THE QUICK BROWN FOX JUMPS OVER THE LAZY DOG.
```

Look Back The sentence makes sense, so the pattern fits.

PRACTICE

Decode each sentence.

1. RFC DGTC ZMVGLE UGXYPBQ HSKN OSGAIJW.

(*RFC* = *THE*)

2. U PYLS VUX KOUWE GCABN DCHR TCJJS ZIQF.

(*U* = *A*)

Make a Table

To solve a problem that involves a relationship between two sets of numbers, you can **make a table.** A table can be used to organize data so that you can look at relationships and find the solution.

Problem Solving Strategies

Draw a Diagram	**Make a Table**
Make a Model	Solve a Simpler Problem
Guess and Test	Use Logical Reasoning
Work Backward	Use a Venn Diagram
Find a Pattern	Make an Organized List

Jill has 12 pieces of 2 ft long decorative edging. She wants to use the edging to enclose a garden with the greatest possible area against the back of her house. What is the largest garden she can make?

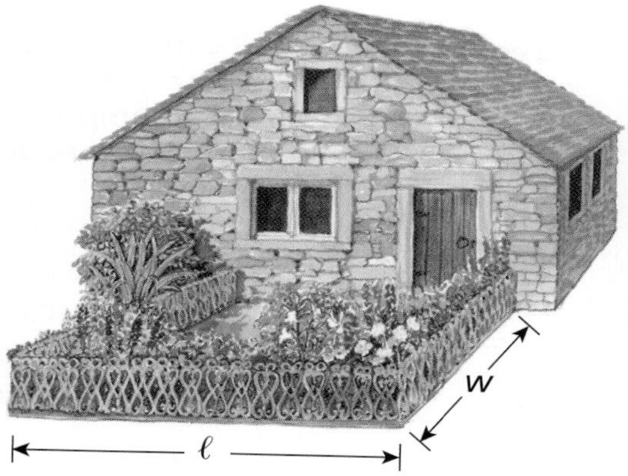

Understand the Problem

You must determine the length and width of the edging.

Make a Plan

Make a table of the possible widths and lengths. Begin with the least possible width and increase by multiples of 2 ft. Remember that the width is the same on two sides.

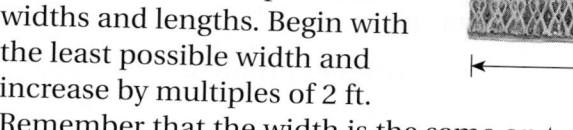

Solve

Use the table to solve.

Width (ft)	Length (ft)	Garden Area (ft^2)
2	20	40
4	16	64
6	12	72
8	8	64
10	4	40

The maximum area that the garden can be is 72 ft^2, with a width of 6 ft and a length of 12 ft.

Look Back

She can use 3 pieces of edging for the first side, 6 pieces for the second side, and another 3 pieces for the third side.

$3 + 6 + 3 = 12$ pieces
$6\text{ ft} + 12\text{ ft} + 6\text{ ft} = 24\text{ ft}$

PRACTICE

1. Suppose Jill decided not to use the house as one side of the garden. What is the greatest area that she could enclose?

2. A store sells batteries in packs of 3 for $3.99 and 2 for $2.99. Barry got 14 batteries total for $18.95. How many of each package did he buy?

Solve a Simpler Problem

If a problem contains large numbers or requires many steps, try to **solve a simpler problem** first. Look for similarities between the problems, and use them to solve the original problem.

Problem Solving Strategies

Draw a Diagram	Make a Table
Make a Model	**Solve a Simpler Problem**
Guess and Test	Use Logical Reasoning
Work Backward	Use a Venn Diagram
Find a Pattern	Make an Organized List

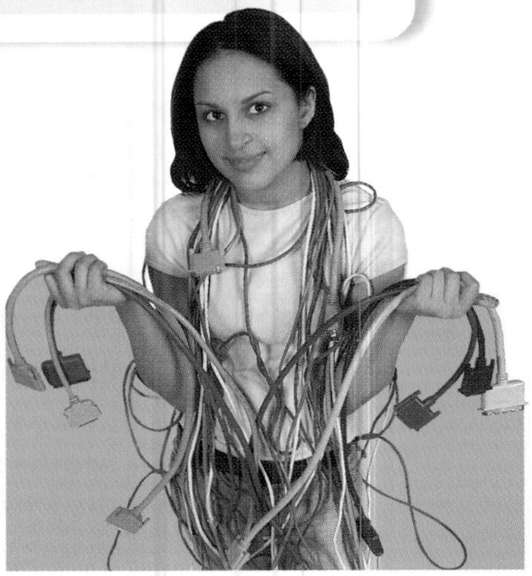

Noemi heard that 10 computers in her school would be connected to each other. She thought that there would be a cable connecting each computer to every other computer. How many cables would be needed if this were true?

Understand the Problem You know that there are 10 computers and that each computer would require a separate cable to connect to every other computer. You need to find the total number of cables.

Make a Plan Start by **solving a simpler problem** with fewer computers.

Solve The simplest problem starts with 2 computers.

2 computers
1 connection

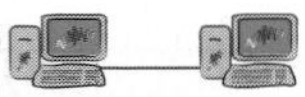

3 computers
3 connections

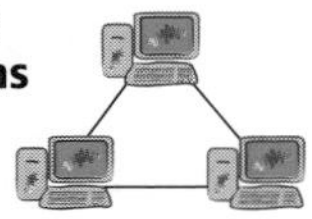

4 computers
6 connections

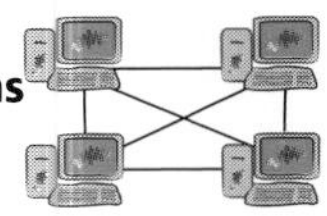

Organize the data in a table to help you find a pattern.

Number of Computers	Number of Connections
2	1
3	1 + 2 = 3
4	1 + 2 + 3 = 6
5	1 + 2 + 3 + 4 = 10
10	1 + 2 + 3 + 4 + 5 + 6 + 7 + 8 + 9 = 45

So if a separate cable were needed to connect each of 10 computers to every other one, 45 cables would be required.

Look Back Extend the number of computers to check that the pattern continues.

PRACTICE

1. A banquet table seats 2 people on each side and 1 at each end. If 6 tables are placed end to end, how many seats can there be?

2. How many diagonals are there in a dodecagon (a 12-sided polygon)?

Use Logical Reasoning

Sometimes a problem may provide clues and facts to help you find a solution. You can **use logical reasoning** to help solve this kind of problem.

Problem Solving Strategies

Draw a Diagram	Make a Table
Make a Model	Solve a Simpler Problem
Guess and Test	**Use Logical Reasoning**
Work Backward	Use a Venn Diagram
Find a Pattern	Make an Organized List

Kim, Lily, and Suki take ballet, tap, and jazz classes (but not in that order). Kim is the sister of the person who takes ballet. Lily takes tap.

Understand the Problem You want to determine which person is in which dance class. You know that there are three people and that each person takes only one dance class.

Make a Plan **Use logical reasoning** to make a table of the facts from the problem.

Solve List the types of dance and the people's names. Write *Yes* or *No* when you are sure of an answer. Lily takes tap.

	Ballet	Tap	Jazz
Kim		No	
Lily	No	**Yes**	No
Suki		No	

The person taking ballet is Kim's sister, so Kim does not take ballet. Suki must be the one taking ballet.

	Ballet	Tap	Jazz
Kim		No	
Lily	No	**Yes**	No
Suki	**Yes**	No	No

Kim must be the one taking jazz.

Kim takes jazz, Lily takes tap, and Suki takes ballet.

Look Back Make sure none of your conclusions conflict with the clues.

PRACTICE

1. Patrick, John, and Vanessa have a snake, a cat and a rabbit. Patrick's pet does not have fur. Vanessa does not have a cat. Match the owners with their pets.

2. Isabella, Keifer, Dylan, and Chrissy are in the sixth, seventh, eighth, and ninth grades. Isabella is not in seventh grade. The sixth-grader has band with Dylan and lunch with Isabella. Chrissy is in the ninth grade. Match the students with their grades.

Act It Out

Some problems involve actions or processes. To solve these problems, you can **act it out**. Actively modeling the problem can help you find the solution.

Problem Solving Strategies

Draw a Diagram	Make a Table
Make a Model	Solve a Simpler Problem
Guess and Test	Use Logical Reasoning
Work Backward	**Act It Out**
Find a Pattern	Make an Organized List

Kyle and Jared are playing Rock-Paper-Scissors. For each round, the players show either a fist (rock), an open hand (paper), or two fingers (scissors). The friends play many rounds. In what percentage of the rounds should they expect to show matching hands?

Understand the Problem

List the important information.

- The two players can each show one of three things: rock, paper, or scissors.

The answer will be the percentage of rounds in which the players can expect to match.

Make a Plan

Act it out to list all the possible outcomes of a round. Find the fraction of outcomes that involve matching hands and then write the fraction as a percent.

Solve

Work with a partner. Take the roles of the players and work together to show all the possible outcomes for one round. Circle the outcomes in which the players match.

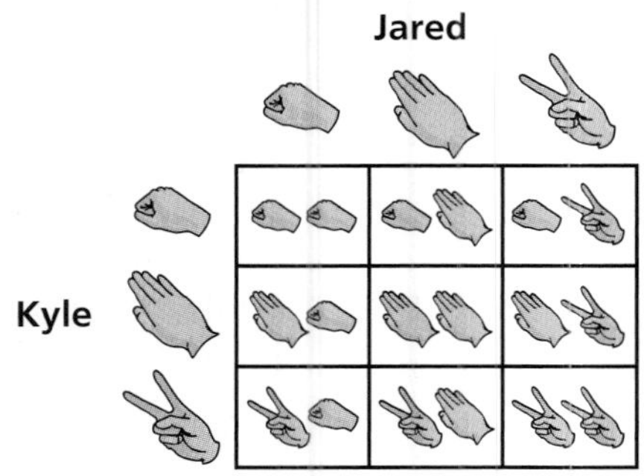

In each round, there are 9 possible outcomes. In 3 of these, the players show matching hands. The fraction of outcomes that involve matching items is $\frac{3}{9}$ or $\frac{1}{3}$. The players can expect to show matching hands in $\frac{1}{3}$ or $33\frac{1}{3}\%$ of the rounds.

Look Back

Double check to make sure you have all of the possible outcomes of the game. Also, check that your answer is in the form that the question requires.

PRACTICE

1. Mikiko flips a nickel and a dime together. She does this several times. What percentage of the time should she expect one coin to show heads and the other to show tails?

2. Leah rolls a blue number cube and a red number cube together. She does this several times. What fraction of the time should she expect to roll a sum of 6?

Make an Organized List

In some problems, you will need to find out exactly how many different ways an event can happen. When solving this kind of problem, it is often helpful to **make an organized list**. This will help you count all the possible outcomes.

Problem Solving Strategies

Draw a Diagram	Make a Table
Make a Model	Solve a Simpler Problem
Guess and Test	Use Logical Reasoning
Work Backward	Use a Venn Diagram
Find a Pattern	**Make an Organized List**

What is the greatest amount of money you can have in coins (quarters, dimes, nickels, and pennies) without being able to make change for a dollar?

Understand the Problem

You are looking for an amount of money. You cannot have any combinations of coins that make a dollar, such as 4 quarters or 3 quarters, 2 dimes, and a nickel.

Make a Plan

Make an organized list, starting with the maximum possible number of each type of coin. Consider all the ways you can add other types of coins without making exactly one dollar.

Solve

List the maximum number of each kind of coin you can have.

3 quarters = 75¢ 9 dimes = 90¢ 19 nickels = 95¢ 99 pennies = 99¢

Next, list all the possible combinations of two kinds of coins.

3 quarters and 4 dimes = 115¢
3 quarters and 4 nickels = 95¢
3 quarters and 24 pennies = 99¢

9 dimes and 1 quarter = 115¢
9 dimes and 1 nickel = 95¢
9 dimes and 9 pennies = 99¢

19 nickels and 4 pennies = 99¢

Look for any combinations from this list that you could add another kind of coin to without making exactly one dollar.

3 quarters, 4 dimes, and 4 pennies = 119¢
3 quarters, 4 nickels, and 4 pennies = 99¢
9 dimes, 1 quarter, and 4 pennies = 119¢
9 dimes, 1 nickel, and 4 pennies = 99¢

The largest amount you can have is 119¢, or $1.19.

Look Back

Try adding one of any type of coin to either combination that makes $1.19, and then see if you could make change for a dollar.

PRACTICE

1. How can you arrange the numbers 2, 6, 7, and 12 with the symbols +, ×, and ÷ to create the expression with the greatest value?

2. How many ways are there to arrange 24 desks in 3 or more equal rows if each row must have at least 2 desks?

Skills Bank Review Skills

Place Value to the Billions

A place-value chart can help you read and write numbers. The number 345,012,678,912.5784 (three hundred forty-five billion, twelve million, six hundred seventy-eight thousand, nine hundred twelve and five thousand seven hundred eighty-four ten-thousandths) is shown.

Billions	Millions	Thousands	Ones		Tenths	Hundredths	Thousandths	Ten-Thousandths
345,	012,	678,	912	.	5	7	8	4

EXAMPLE

Name the place value of the digit.

A the 7 in the thousands column
7 ⟶ *ten thousands place*

B the 0 in the millions column
0 ⟶ *hundred millions place*

C the 5 in the billions column
5 ⟶ *one billion, or billions, place*

D the 8 to the right of the decimal point
8 ⟶ *thousandths*

PRACTICE

Name the place value of the underlined digit.

1. 123,$\underline{4}$56,789,123.0594
2. 1$\underline{2}$3,456,789,123.0594
3. 123,456,789,123.05$\underline{9}$4
4. 123,456,789,12$\underline{3}$.0594
5. 123,456,789,123.$\underline{0}$594
6. 123,45$\underline{6}$,789,123.0594

Round Whole Numbers and Decimals

To round to a certain place, follow these steps.

1. Locate the digit in that place, and consider the next digit to the right.
2. If the digit to the right is 5 or greater, round up. Otherwise, round down.
3. Change each digit to the right of the rounding place to zero.

EXAMPLE

A **Round 125,439.378 to the nearest thousand.**
125,439.378 *Locate digit*
The digit to the right is less than 5, so round down.
125,000.000 = 125,000

B **Round 125,439.378 to the nearest tenth.**
125,439.378 *Locate digit.*
The digit to the right is greater than 5, so round up.
125,439.400 = 125,539.4

PRACTICE

Round 259,345.278 to the place indicated.

1. hundred thousand
2. ten thousand
3. thousand
4. hundred

Long Division with Whole Numbers

You can use long division to divide large numbers.

EXAMPLE

Divide 8208 by 72.

$$\begin{array}{r} 114 \\ 72\overline{)8208} \\ \underline{72} \\ 100 \\ \underline{72} \\ 288 \\ \underline{288} \\ 0 \end{array}$$

Place the first number under the long division symbol.
Subtract.
Bring down the next digit.
Subtract.
Bring down the next digit.
Subtract.

PRACTICE

Divide.

1. $125\overline{)4125}$
2. $158\overline{)20{,}698}$
3. $268\overline{)4556}$
4. $39\overline{)3471}$
5. $99\overline{)4653}$
6. $321\overline{)38{,}841}$
7. $120\overline{)5040}$
8. $108\overline{)10{,}476}$
9. $741\overline{)107{,}445}$

Solve for a Variable

In the equation $y = 2x + 3$, the variable y is isolated because it is alone on one side of the equation. You can use inverse operations to rearrange an equation and isolate any variable. This is called **solving for a variable**.

EXAMPLE

Solve $m - t = 6$ for m.

$$\begin{aligned} m - t &= 6 \\ \underline{+t} \quad &\quad \underline{+t} \\ m &= 6 + t \end{aligned}$$

Since t is subtracted from m, add t to both sides of the equation to undo the subtraction.

PRACTICE

1. Solve $r + s = 120$ for r.
2. Solve $\frac{x}{k} = 32$ for x.
3. Solve $y = x + 5$ for x.
4. Solve $3m = n + 1$ for m.
5. Solve $3s + 2 = t$ for s.
6. Solve $4p - 2r = 0$ for p.

Factors and Multiples

When two numbers are multiplied to form a third, the two numbers are said to be **factors** of the third number. **Multiples** of a number can be found by multiplying the number by 1, 2, 3, 4, and so on.

EXAMPLE

A **List all the factors of 48.**

$1 \cdot 48 = 48$, $2 \cdot 24 = 48$, $3 \cdot 16 = 48$, $4 \cdot 12 = 48$, and $6 \cdot 8 = 48$

So the factors of 48 are 1, 2, 3, 4, 6, 8, 12, 16, 24, and 48.

B **Find the first five multiples of 3.**

$3 \cdot 1 = 3$, $3 \cdot 2 = 6$, $3 \cdot 3 = 9$, $3 \cdot 4 = 12$, and $3 \cdot 5 = 15$

So the first five multiples of 3 are 3, 6, 9, 12, and 15.

PRACTICE

List all the factors of each number.

1. 8 **2.** 20 **3.** 9 **4.** 51 **5.** 16 **6.** 27

Write the first five multiples of each number.

7. 9 **8.** 10 **9.** 20 **10.** 15 **11.** 7 **12.** 18

Divisibility Rules

A number is divisible by another number if the division results in a remainder of 0. Some divisibility rules are shown below.

A number is divisible by . . .		Divisible	Not Divisible
2	if the last digit is an even number.	11,994	2,175
3	if the sum of the digits is divisible by 3.	216	79
4	if the last two digits form a number divisible by 4.	1,028	621
5	if the last digit is 0 or 5.	15,195	10,007
6	if the number is even and divisible by 3.	1,332	44
8	if the last three digits form a number divisible by 8.	25,016	14,100
9	if the sum of the digits is divisible by 9.	144	33
10	if the last digit is 0.	2,790	9,325

PRACTICE

Determine which of these numbers each number is divisible by: 2, 3, 4, 5, 6, 8, 9, 10

1. 56 **2.** 200 **3.** 75 **4.** 324 **5.** 42 **6.** 812

7. 784 **8.** 501 **9.** 2345 **10.** 555,555 **11.** 3009 **12.** 2001

Prime and Composite Numbers

A **prime number** has exactly two factors, 1 and the number itself.

2	Factors: 1 and 2; prime
11	Factors: 1 and 11; prime
47	Factors: 1 and 47; prime

A **composite number** has more than two factors.

4	Factors: 1, 2, and 4; composite
12	Factors: 1, 2, 3, 4, 6, and 12; composite
63	Factors: 1, 3, 7, 9, 21, and 63; composite

EXAMPLE

Determine whether each number is prime or composite.

A 17

Factors
1, 17 ⟶ prime

B 16

Factors
1, 2, 4, 8, 16 ⟶ composite

C 51

Factors
1, 3, 17, 51 ⟶ composite

PRACTICE

Determine whether each number is prime or composite.

1. 5 **2.** 14 **3.** 18 **4.** 2 **5.** 23 **6.** 27

7. 13 **8.** 39 **9.** 72 **10.** 49 **11.** 9 **12.** 89

Percents Less Than 1% and Greater Than 100%

You can convert a percent to a decimal by deleting the percent sign and moving the decimal point two places to the left. This can help you understand percents less than 1% and greater than 100%.

$$000.2\% = 0.002$$

$$135.\% = 1.35$$

EXAMPLE

Find the percent of each number.

A 0.5% of 280

0.5% of $280 = 0.005 \cdot 280$ *Write the percent as a decimal.*

$= 1.4$ *Multiply.*

B 140% of 60

140% of $60 = 1.4 \cdot 60$ *Write the percent as a decimal.*

$= 84$ *Multiply.*

PRACTICE

Find the percent of each number.

1. 0.8% of 90 **2.** 0.2% of 6 **3.** 150% of 88 **4.** 260% of 40

Greatest Common Factor (GCF)

The **greatest common factor (GCF)** of two whole numbers is the greatest factor the numbers have in common.

EXAMPLE

Find the GCF of 24 and 32.

Method 1: List all the factors of both numbers.

Find all the common factors.

24: 1, 2, 3, 4, 6, 8, 12, 24
32: 1, 2, 4, 8, 16, 32

The common factors are 1, 2, 4, and 8.
So the GCF is 8.

Method 2: Find the prime factorizations.

Then find the common prime factors.

24: $2 \cdot 2 \cdot 2 \cdot 3$
32: $2 \cdot 2 \cdot 2 \cdot 2 \cdot 2$

The common prime factors are 2, 2, and 2.
The product of these is the GCF.
So the GCF is $2 \cdot 2 \cdot 2 = 8$.

PRACTICE

Find the GCF of each pair of numbers by either method.

1. 9, 15 **2.** 25, 75 **3.** 18, 30 **4.** 4, 10 **5.** 12, 17 **6.** 30, 96
7. 54, 72 **8.** 15, 20 **9.** 40, 60 **10.** 40, 50 **11.** 14, 21 **12.** 14, 28

Least Common Multiple (LCM)

The **least common multiple (LCM)** of two numbers is the smallest common multiple the numbers share.

EXAMPLE

Find the least common multiple of 8 and 10.

Method 1: List multiples of both numbers.

8: 8, 16, 24, 32, 40, 48, 56, 64, 72, 80
10: 10, 20, 30, 40, 50, 60, 70, 80, 90

The smallest common multiple is 40.

So the LCM is 40.

Method 2: Find the prime factorizations. Then find the most occurrences of each factor.

8: $2 \cdot 2 \cdot 2$
10: $2 \cdot 5$

The LCM is the product of the factors.

$2 \cdot 2 \cdot 2 \cdot 5 = 40$ So the LCM is 40.

PRACTICE

Find the LCM of each pair of numbers by either method.

1. 2, 4 **2.** 3, 15 **3.** 10, 25 **4.** 10, 15 **5.** 3, 7 **6.** 18, 27
7. 12, 21 **8.** 9, 21 **9.** 24, 30 **10.** 9, 18 **11.** 16, 24 **12.** 8, 36

Compatible Numbers

Compatible numbers are close to the numbers in a problem and divide without a remainder. You can use compatible numbers to estimate quotients.

EXAMPLE

Use compatible numbers to estimate each quotient.

A $6134 \div 32$

$6134 \div 32$

$6000 \div 30 = 200$ ← *Estimate*

↑ ↑ *Compatible numbers*

B $647 \div 7$

$647 \div 7$

$630 \div 7 = 90$ ← *Estimate*

↑ ↑ *Compatible numbers*

PRACTICE

Estimate the quotient by using compatible numbers.

1. $345 \div 5$	**2.** $5474 \div 23$	**3.** $46{,}170 \div 18$	**4.** $749 \div 7$
5. $861 \div 41$	**6.** $1225 \div 2$	**7.** $968 \div 47$	**8.** $3456 \div 432$
9. $5765 \div 26$	**10.** $25{,}012 \div 64$	**11.** $99{,}170 \div 105$	**12.** $868 \div 8$

Mixed Numbers and Fractions

Mixed numbers can be written as fractions greater than 1, and fractions greater than 1 can be written as mixed numbers.

EXAMPLE

A **Write $\frac{23}{5}$ as a mixed number.**

$\frac{23}{5}$ *Divide the numerator by the denominator.*

$$5\overline{)23} = 4 \text{ R } 3 \quad (20,\ 3) \longrightarrow 4\tfrac{3}{5}$$

← *Write the remainder as the numerator of a fraction.*

B **Write $6\frac{2}{7}$ as a fraction.**

Multiply the denominator by the whole number. *Add the product to the numerator.*

$6\frac{2}{7} \longrightarrow 7 \cdot 6 = 42 \longrightarrow 42 + 2 = 44$

Write the sum over the denominator. → $\frac{44}{7}$

PRACTICE

Write each mixed number as a fraction. Write each fraction as a mixed number.

1. $\frac{22}{5}$	**2.** $9\frac{1}{7}$	**3.** $\frac{41}{8}$	**4.** $5\frac{7}{9}$
5. $\frac{7}{3}$	**6.** $4\frac{9}{11}$	**7.** $\frac{47}{16}$	**8.** $3\frac{3}{8}$
9. $\frac{31}{9}$	**10.** $8\frac{2}{3}$	**11.** $\frac{33}{5}$	**12.** $12\frac{1}{9}$

Multiply and Divide Decimals by Powers of 10

Notice the pattern below.

$0.24 \cdot 10 = 2.4$
$0.24 \cdot 100 = 24$
$0.24 \cdot 1000 = 240$
$0.24 \cdot 10{,}000 = 2400$

$10 = 10^1$
$100 = 10^2$
$1000 = 10^3$
$10{,}000 = 10^4$

*Think: When multiplying decimals by powers of 10, move the decimal point one place to the **right** for each power of 10, or for each zero.*

Notice the pattern below.

$0.24 \div 10 = 0.024$
$0.24 \div 100 = 0.0024$
$0.24 \div 1000 = 0.00024$
$0.24 \div 10{,}000 = 0.000024$

*Think: When dividing decimals by powers of 10, move the decimal point one place to the **left** for each power of 10, or for each zero.*

PRACTICE

Find each product or quotient.

1. $10 \cdot 9.26$ **2.** $0.642 \cdot 100$ **3.** $10^3 \cdot 84.2$ **4.** $0.44 \cdot 10^4$

5. $69.7 \cdot 1000$ **6.** $11.32 \div 10$ **7.** $678 \cdot 10^8$ **8.** $1.276 \div 1000$

9. $536.5 \div 10^2$ **10.** $5.92 \div 10^3$ **11.** $25 \div 10{,}000$ **12.** $6.519 \cdot 10^2$

Multiply Decimals

When multiplying decimals, multiply as you would with whole numbers. The sum of the number of decimal places in the factors equals the number of decimal places in the product.

EXAMPLE

Find each product.

A **81.2 · 6.547**

```
      6.547 ←— 3 decimal places
  ×    81.2 ←— 1 decimal place
     1 3094
     6 5470
   523 7600
   531.6164 ←— 4 decimal places
```

B **0.376 · 0.12**

```
      0.376 ←— 3 decimal places
  ×    0.12 ←— 2 decimal places
        752
       3760
    0.04512 ←— 5 decimal places
```

PRACTICE

Find each product.

1. $6.8 \cdot 3.4$ **2.** $2.56 \cdot 4.6$ **3.** $6.787 \cdot 7.6$ **4.** $0.98 \cdot 4.6$

5. $0.97 \cdot 0.76$ **6.** $0.5 \cdot 3.761$ **7.** $42 \cdot 17.654$ **8.** $7.005 \cdot 32.1$

9. $9.76 \cdot 16.254$ **10.** $296.5 \cdot 2.4$ **11.** $7.7 \cdot 6.5$ **12.** $8.92 \cdot 2.8$

13. $3.65 \cdot 4.2$ **14.** $0.002 \cdot 8.1$ **15.** $0.03 \cdot 0.204$ **16.** $98.6 \cdot 4.9$

Divide Decimals

When dividing with decimals, set up the division as you would with whole numbers. Pay attention to the decimal places, as shown below.

EXAMPLE

Find each quotient.

A **89.6 ÷ 16**

$$\begin{array}{r} 5.6 \\ 16\overline{)89.6} \\ \underline{80} \\ 96 \\ \underline{96} \\ 0 \end{array}$$

B **3.4 ÷ 4**

$$\begin{array}{r} 0.85 \\ 4\overline{)3.40} \\ \underline{3\,2} \\ 20 \\ \underline{20} \\ 0 \end{array}$$

Place decimal point.
Insert zeros if necessary.

PRACTICE

Find each quotient.

1. 242.76 ÷ 68 **2.** 40.5 ÷ 18 **3.** 121.03 ÷ 98 **4.** 3.6 ÷ 4

5. 1.58 ÷ 5 **6.** 0.2835 ÷ 2.7 **7.** 8.1 ÷ 0.09 **8.** 0.42 ÷ 0.28

9. 480.48 ÷ 7.7 **10.** 36.9 ÷ 0.003 **11.** 0.784 ÷ 0.04 **12.** 15.12 ÷ 0.063

Terminating and Repeating Decimals

You can change a fraction to a decimal by dividing. If the resulting decimal has a finite number of digits, it is **terminating**. Otherwise, it is **repeating**.

EXAMPLE

Write $\frac{4}{5}$ and $\frac{2}{3}$ as decimals. Are the decimals terminating or repeating?

$\frac{4}{5} = 4 \div 5$

$$\begin{array}{r} 0.8 \\ 5\overline{)4.0} \\ \underline{4\,0} \\ 0 \end{array} \longrightarrow \frac{4}{5} = 0.8$$

$\frac{2}{3} = 2 \div 3$

$$\begin{array}{r} 0.6666 \\ 3\overline{)2.0000} \\ \underline{1\,8} \\ 20 \end{array} \longrightarrow \frac{2}{3} = 0.6666...$$

$\longrightarrow$ *This pattern will repeat.*

The number 0.8 is a terminating decimal. The number 0.6666 . . . is a repeating decimal.

PRACTICE

Write as a decimal. Is the decimal terminating or repeating?

1. $\frac{1}{5}$ **2.** $\frac{1}{3}$ **3.** $\frac{3}{11}$ **4.** $\frac{3}{8}$ **5.** $\frac{7}{9}$ **6.** $\frac{7}{15}$

7. $\frac{3}{4}$ **8.** $\frac{5}{6}$ **9.** $\frac{4}{11}$ **10.** $\frac{5}{10}$ **11.** $\frac{1}{9}$ **12.** $\frac{11}{12}$

13. $\frac{5}{9}$ **14.** $\frac{8}{11}$ **15.** $\frac{7}{8}$ **16.** $\frac{23}{25}$ **17.** $\frac{3}{20}$ **18.** $\frac{5}{11}$

Order of Operations

When simplifying expressions, follow the order of operations.

1. Simplify within parentheses.
2. Evaluate exponents and roots.
3. Multiply and divide from left to right.
4. Add and subtract from left to right.

EXAMPLE

A **Simplify the expression $3^2 \times (11 - 4)$.**

$3^2 \times (11 - 4)$

$3^2 \times 7$ *Simplify within parentheses.*

9×7 *Evaluate the exponent.*

63 *Multiply.*

B **Use a calculator to simplify the expression $19 - 100 \div 5^2$.**

If your calculator follows the order of operations, enter the following keystrokes:

$19 - 100 \div 5$ [x^2] [ENTER] The result is 15.

If your calculator does not follow the order of operations, insert parentheses so that the expression is simplified correctly.

$19 - (100 \div 5$ [x^2] $)$ [ENTER] The result is 15.

PRACTICE

Simplify each expression.

1. $45 - 15 \div 3$

2. $51 + 48 \div 8$

3. $35 \div (15 - 8)$

4. $\sqrt{9} \times 5 - 15$

5. $24 \div 3 - 6 + 12$

6. $(6 \times 8) \div 2^2$

7. $20 - 3 \times 4 + 30 \div 6$

8. $3^2 - 10 \div 2 + 4 \times 2$

9. $27 \div (3 + 6) + 6^2$

10. $4 \div 2 + 8 \times 2^3 - 4$

11. $33 - \sqrt{64} \times 3 - 5$

12. $(8^2 \times 4) - 12 \times 13 + 5$

Use a calculator to simplify each expression.

13. $6 + 20 \div 4$

14. $37 - 21 \div 7$

15. $9^2 - 32 \div 8$

16. $10 \div 2 + 8 \times 2$

17. $\sqrt{25} + 4 \times 6$

18. $4 \times 12 - 4 + 8 \div 2$

19. $28 - 3^2 + 27 \div 3$

20. $9 + (50 - 16) \div 2$

21. $4^2 - (10 \times 8) \div 5$

22. $30 + 22 \div 11 - 7 - 3^2$

23. $3 + 7 \times 5 - 1$

24. $38 \div 2 + \sqrt{81} \times 4 - 31$

Properties

The following are basic properties of addition and multiplication when a, b, and c are real numbers.

Addition

Closure: $a + b$ is a real number.

Commutative: $a + b = b + a$

Associative: $(a + b) + c = a + (b + c)$

Identity Property of Zero: $a + 0 = a$ and $0 + a = a$

Multiplication

Closure: $a \cdot b$ is a real number.

Commutative: $a \cdot b = b \cdot a$

Associative: $(a \cdot b) \cdot c = a \cdot (b \cdot c)$

Identity Property of One: $a \cdot 1 = a$ and $1 \cdot a = a$

Multiplication Property of Zero: $a \cdot 0 = 0$ and $0 \cdot a = 0$

The following properties are true when a, b, and c are real numbers.

Distributive: $a \cdot (b + c) = a \cdot b + a \cdot c$

Transitive: If $a = b$ and $b = c$, then $a = c$.

EXAMPLE

Name the property shown.

A $4 \cdot (7 \cdot 2) = (4 \cdot 7) \cdot 2$
Associative Property of Multiplication

B $4 \cdot (7 + 2) = (4 \cdot 7) + (4 \cdot 2)$
Distributive Property

PRACTICE

Give an example of each of the following properties, using real numbers.

1. Associative Property of Addition
2. Commutative Property of Multiplication
3. Closure Property of Multiplication
4. Distributive Property
5. Multiplication Property of Zero
6. Identity Property of Addition
7. Transitive Property
8. Closure Property of Addition

Name the property shown.

9. $4 + 0 = 4$
10. $(6 + 3) + 1 = 6 + (3 + 1)$
11. $7 \cdot 51 = 51 \cdot 7$
12. $5 \cdot 456 = 456 \cdot 5$
13. $17 \cdot (1 + 3) = 17 \cdot 1 + 17 \cdot 3$
14. $1 \cdot 5 = 5$
15. $(8 \cdot 2) \cdot 5 = 8 \cdot (2 \cdot 5)$
16. $72 + 1234 = 1234 + 72$
17. $0 \cdot 12 = 0$
18. $15.7 \cdot 1.3 = 1.3 \cdot 15.7$
19. $8.2 + (9.3 + 7) = (8.2 + 9.3) + 7$
20. $85.98 \cdot 0 = 0$
21. If $x = 3.5$ and $3.5 = y$, then $x = y$.
22. $12a \cdot 15b = 15b \cdot 12a$
23. $(2x + 3y) + 8z = 2x + (3y + 8z)$
24. $0 \cdot 6m^2n = 0$
25. $8j + 32k = 32k + 8j$
26. If $3 + 8 = 11$ and $11 = x$, then $3 + 8 = x$.

Skills Bank

Cubes and Cube Roots

The volume of the cube at right is 5 · 5 · 5 or 125. Because 5 is a factor 3 times, you can use an exponent to write the expression as 5^3, which is read "5 cubed."

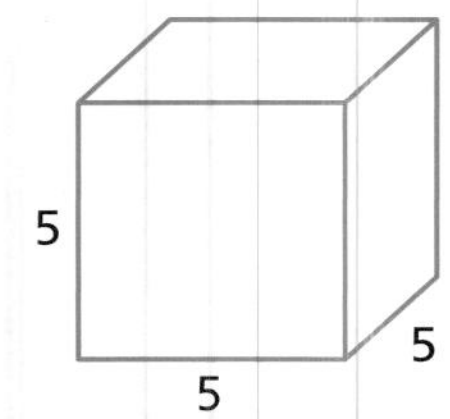

Finding **cube root** is the inverse of cubing a number. The symbol $\sqrt[3]{\ }$ means "cube root." For example, $\sqrt[3]{125} = 5$.

EXAMPLE

Evaluate each expression.

A 8^3

$8^3 = 8 \cdot 8 \cdot 8$ *Use 8 as a factor 3 times.*

$= 512$ *Multiply.*

B $\sqrt[3]{64}$

$\sqrt[3]{64} = 4$ *$4^3 = 4 \cdot 4 \cdot 4 = 64$, so $\sqrt[3]{64} = 4$.*

PRACTICE

Evaluate each expression.

1. 2^3
2. 1^3
3. 7^3
4. 10^3
5. $\sqrt[3]{8}$
6. $\sqrt[3]{27}$
7. $\sqrt[3]{1000}$
8. $\sqrt[3]{1}$

Skew Lines

Parallel lines are lines in the same plane that do not intersect. Skew lines also do not intersect. **Skew lines** are lines that are not parallel that lie in two different planes

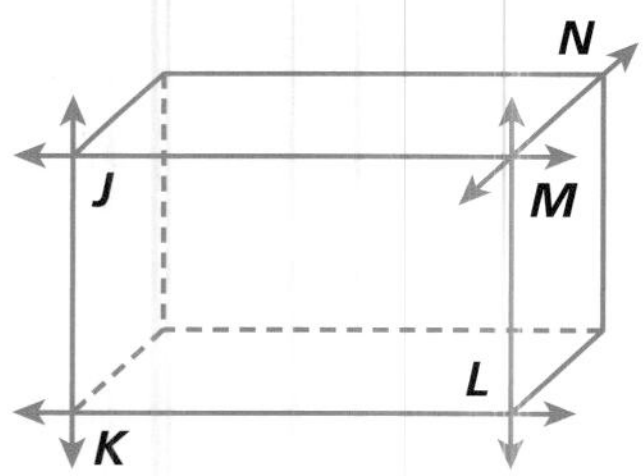

EXAMPLE

Tell whether the lines appear to be parallel, skew, or neither.

A $\overleftrightarrow{JK}$ and $\overleftrightarrow{MN}$

$\overleftrightarrow{JK}$ and $\overleftrightarrow{MN}$ are skew. *The lines are in different planes and are not parallel.*

B $\overleftrightarrow{JK}$ and $\overleftrightarrow{KL}$

$\overleftrightarrow{JK}$ and $\overleftrightarrow{KL}$ are neither parallel nor skew. *The lines intersect, so they are neither parallel nor skew*

PRACTICE

Tell whether the lines appear to be parallel, skew, or neither.

1. $\overleftrightarrow{AB}$ and $\overleftrightarrow{CD}$
2. $\overleftrightarrow{CD}$ and $\overleftrightarrow{DE}$
3. $\overleftrightarrow{BC}$ and $\overleftrightarrow{DE}$

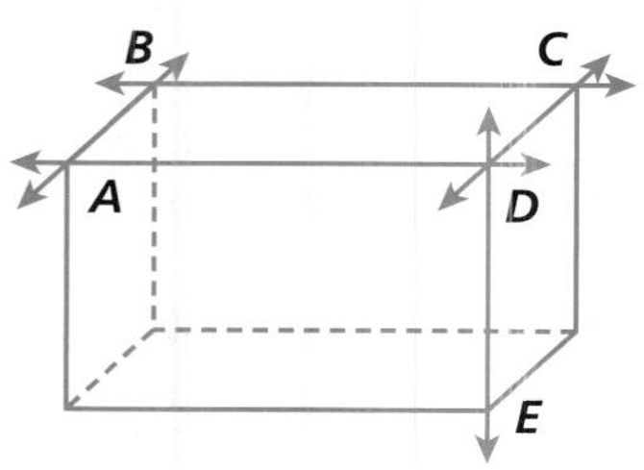

Choose Appropriate Units of Measurement

You can use the following benchmarks to help you choose appropriate units of measurement.

	Customary Unit	Benchmark
Length	Inch (in.)	Length of a small paper clip
	Foot (ft)	Length of a standard sheet of paper
	Mile (mi)	Length of about 18 football fields
Weight	Ounce (oz)	Weight of a slice of bread
	Pound (lb)	Weight of 3 apples
	Ton	Weight of a buffalo
Capacity	Fluid ounce (fl oz)	Amount of water in 2 tablespoons
	Cup (c)	Capacity of a standard measuring cup
	Gallon (gal)	Capacity of a large milk jug

	Metric Unit	Benchmark
Length	Millimeter (mm)	Thickness of a dime
	Centimeter (cm)	Width of your little finger
	Meter (m)	Width of a doorway
	Kilometer (km)	Length of 10 football fields
Mass	Milligram (mg)	Mass of a grain of sand
	Gram (g)	Mass of a small paper clip
	Kilogram (kg)	Mass of a textbook
Capacity	Milliliter (mL)	Amount of liquid in an eyedropper
	Liter (L)	Amount of water in a large water bottle
	Kiloliter (kL)	Capacity of 2 large refrigerators

EXAMPLE

A **Choose the most appropriate customary unit to measure the length of a sofa. Justify your answer.**
feet; the length of a sofa is similar to the length of several sheets of paper.

B **Choose the most appropriate metric unit to measure the capacity of a sink. Justify your answer.**
liters; the capacity of a sink is similar to the capacity of several large water bottles.

PRACTICE

Choose the most appropriate customary unit for each measurement. Justify your answer.

1. the weight of a laptop computer

2. the height of a sparrow

Choose the most appropriate metric unit for each measurement. Justify your answer.

3. the mass of a walnut

4. the thickness of a piece of cardboard

Measure Angles

You can use a protractor to measure angles. To measure an angle, place the base of the protractor on one of the rays of the angle and center the base on the vertex. Look at the protractor scale that has zero on the first ray. Read the scale where the second ray crosses it. Extend the rays, if necessary.

EXAMPLE

Use a protractor to measure the angles of quadrilateral *ABCD*.

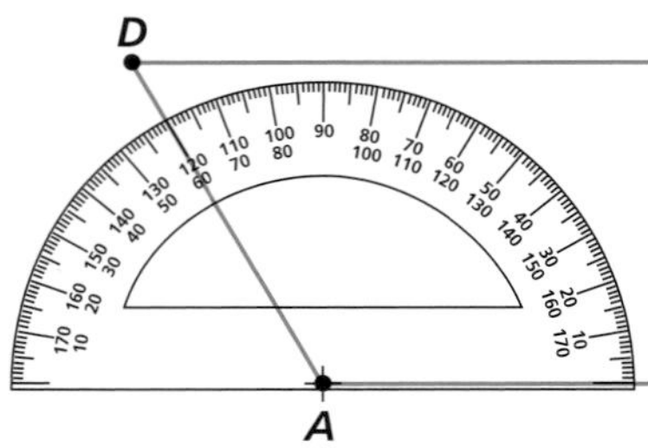

The measure of $\angle A$, or $m\angle A$, equals 120°.

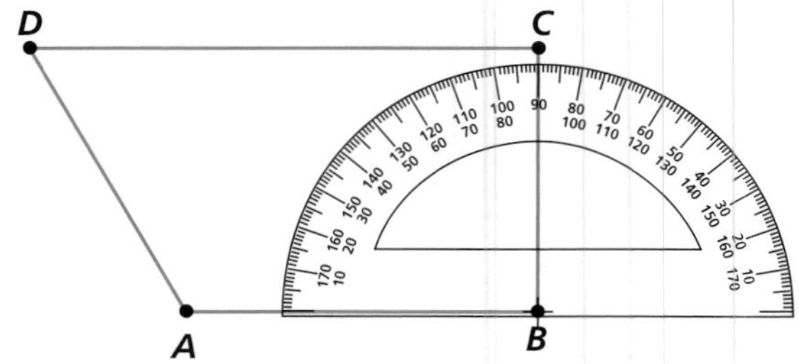

The measure of $\angle B$, or $m\angle B$, equals 90°.

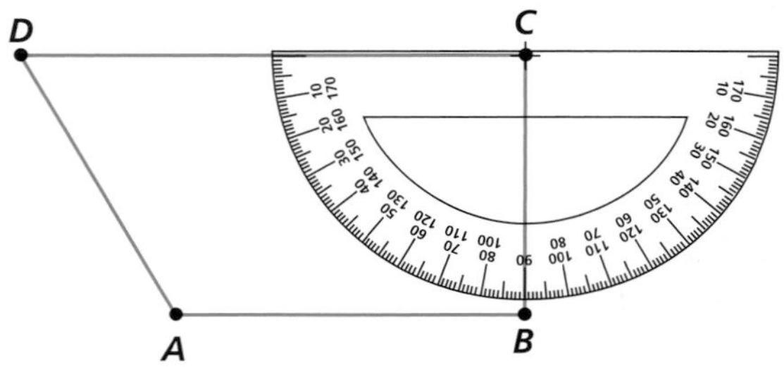

The measure of $\angle C$, or $m\angle C$, equals 90°.

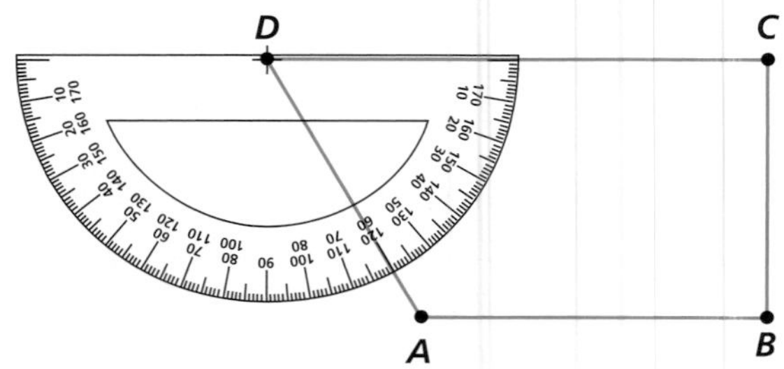

The measure of $\angle D$, or $m\angle D$, equals 60°.

PRACTICE

Use a protractor to measure the angles of each polygon.

1.
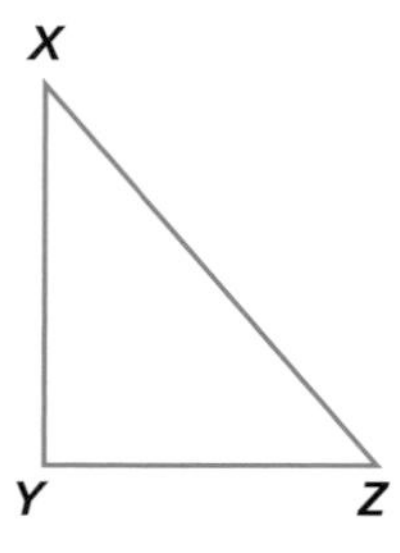

2.
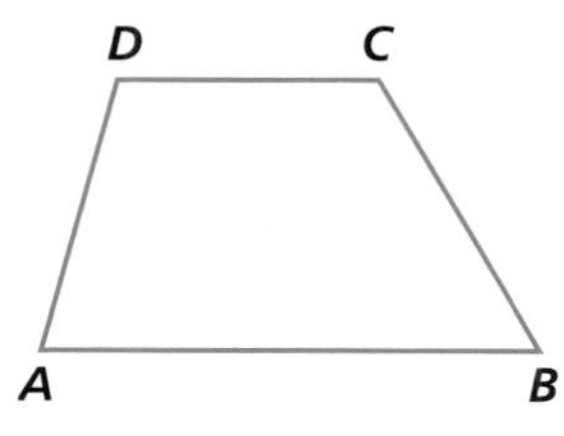

3.
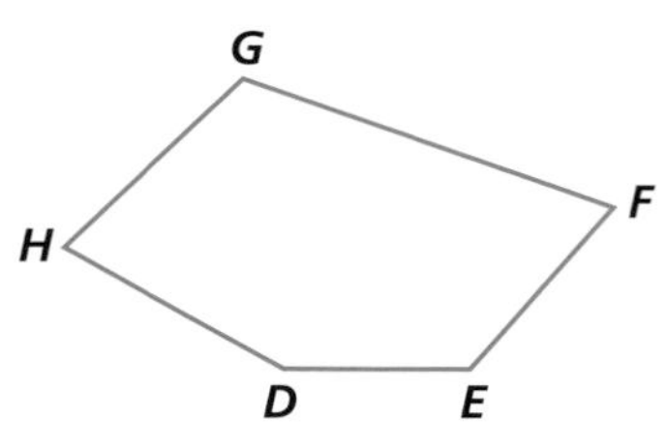

4.
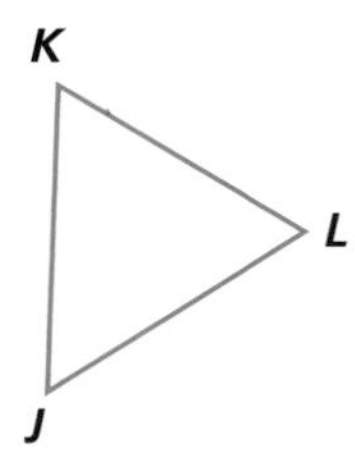

Informal Geometry Proofs

Inductive reasoning involves examining a set of data to determine a pattern and then making a conjecture about the data. In **deductive reasoning**, you reach a conclusion by using logical reasoning based on given statements or premises that you assume to be true.

EXAMPLE

A **Use inductive reasoning to determine the 30th number of the sequence.**

3, 5, 7, 9, 11, . . .

Examine the pattern to determine the relationship between each term in the sequence and its value.

Term	1st	2nd	3rd	4th	5th
Value	3	5	7	9	11

$1 \cdot 2 + 1 = 2 + 1 = 3$

$2 \cdot 2 + 1 = 4 + 1 = 5$

$3 \cdot 2 + 1 = 6 + 1 = 7$

$4 \cdot 2 + 1 = 8 + 1 = 9$

$5 \cdot 2 + 1 = 10 + 1 = 11$

To obtain each value, multiply the term by 2 and add 1. So the 30th term is $30 \cdot 2 + 1 = 60 + 1 = 61$.

B **Use deductive reasoning to make a conclusion from the given premises.**

Premise: Makayla needs at least an 89 on her exam to get a B for the quarter in math class.

Premise: Makayla got a B for the quarter in math class.

Conclusion: Makayla got at least an 89 on her exam.

PRACTICE

Use inductive reasoning to determine the 100th number in each pattern.

1. $\frac{1}{2}, 1, 1\frac{1}{2}, 2, 2\frac{1}{2}, \ldots$

2. 1, 4, 9, 16, 25, . . .

3. 4, 6, 8, 10, 12, . . .

4. 0, 3, 6, 9, 12, 15, . . .

Use deductive reasoning to make a conclusion from the given premises.

5. Premise: If it is raining, then there must be a cloud in the sky.

Premise: It is raining.

6. Premise: A quadrilateral with four congruent sides and four right angles is a square.

Premise: Quadrilateral *ABCD* has four right angles.

Premise: Quadrilateral *ABCD* has four congruent sides.

7. Premise: Darnell is 3 years younger than half his father's age.

Premise: Darnell's father is 40 years old.

Skills Bank

Iteration

An **iteration** is a step in the process of repeating something over and over again. You can show the steps of the process in an **iteration diagram**.

EXAMPLE

A **Use the iteration diagram below, and complete the process three times.**

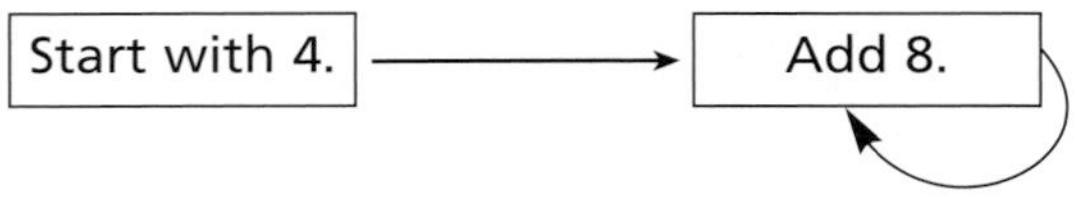

4	→	12	→	20	→	28
Start		Stage 1		Stage 2		Stage 3

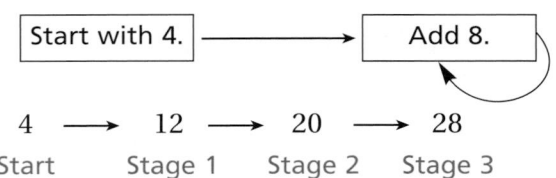

B **For the pattern below, state the iteration and give the next three numbers in the pattern.**

1, 5, 25, 125, . . .

To get from one stage to the next, the iteration is to multiply by 5.

$125 \cdot 5 = 625$ $\quad$ $625 \cdot 5 = 3125$ $\quad$ $3125 \cdot 5 = 15{,}625$

The next three numbers in the pattern are 625, 3125, and 15,625.

PRACTICE

Use the diagram at right. Write the results of the first three iterations.

1. Start with 1.
2. Start with 8.
3. Start with 2.
4. Start with 25.
5. Start with −3.
6. Start with −7.

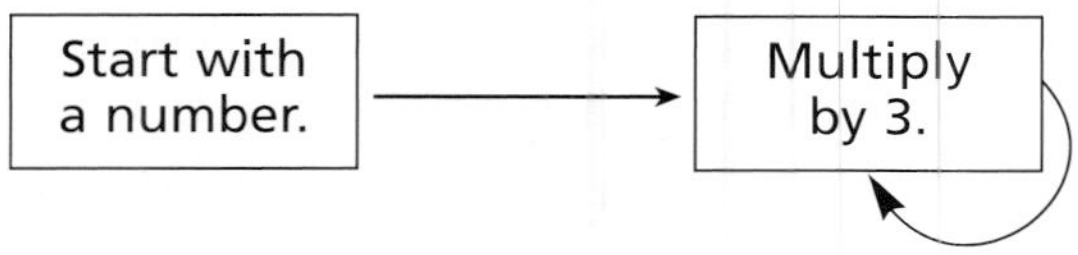

For each pattern, state the iteration and give the next three numbers in the pattern.

7. 11, 17, 23, 29, . . .
8. 5, 10, 20, 40, . . .
9. 345, 323, 301, 279, . . .
10. 30, 75, 120, 165, . . .
11. 15, 7, −1, −9, . . .
12. $1, 1\frac{2}{3}, 2\frac{1}{3}, 3, \ldots$

A **fractal** is a geometric pattern that is *self similar*, so each stage of the pattern is similar to a portion of another stage of the pattern. For example, the Koch snowflake is a fractal formed by beginning with a triangle and then adding an equilateral triangle to each segment of the triangle.

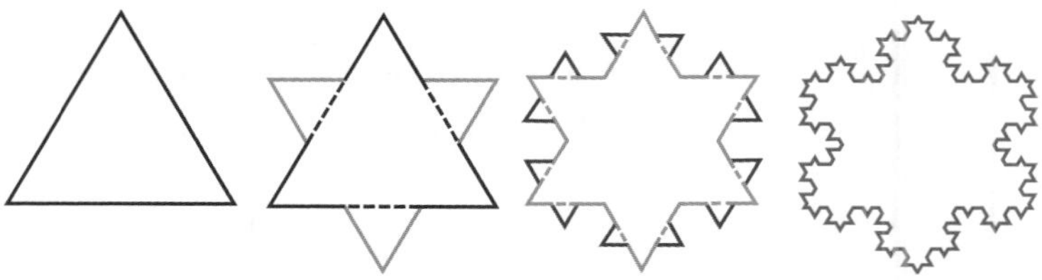

Draw the next two stages of each fractal.

13.

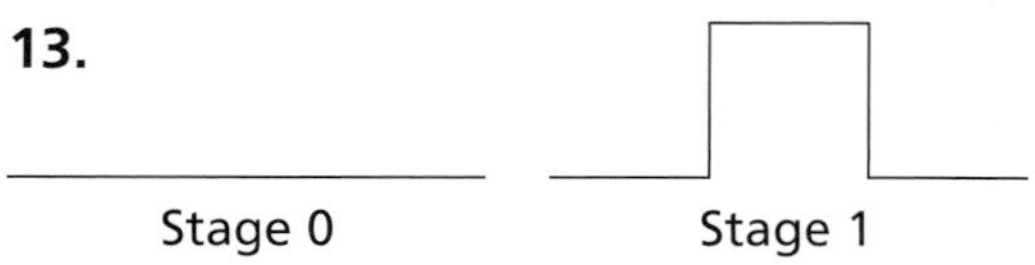

14.

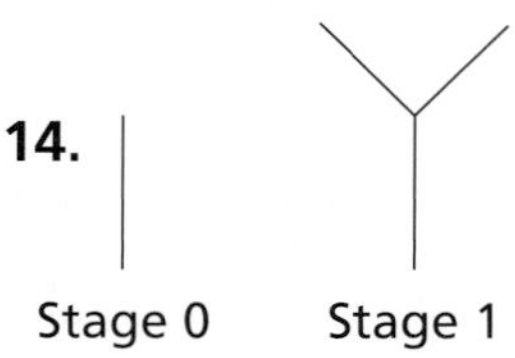

Preview Skills

Relative, Cumulative, and Relative Cumulative Frequency

A **frequency table** lists each value or range of values of the data set followed by its **frequency**, or number of times it occurs.

Relative frequency is the frequency of a value or range of values divided by the total number of data values.

Cumulative frequency is the frequency of all data values that are less than a given value.

Relative cumulative frequency is the cumulative frequency divided by the total number of values.

Test Score	Frequency
66–70	3
71–75	1
76–80	4
81–85	7
86–90	5
91–95	6
96–100	2

EXAMPLE

The frequency table above shows a range of test scores and the frequency, or the number of students who scored in that range.

A Find the relative frequency of test scores in the range 76–80.

$3 + 1 + 4 + 7 + 5 + 6 + 2 = 28$ *Find the total number of test scores.*

There are 4 test scores in the range 76–80. The relative frequency is $\frac{4}{28} \approx 0.14$.

B Find the cumulative frequency of test scores less than 86.

$7 + 4 + 1 + 3 = 15$ *Add the frequencies of all test scores less than 86.*

The cumulative frequency of test scores less than 86 is 15.

C Find the relative cumulative frequency of test scores less than 86.

$\frac{15}{28} \approx 0.54$ *Divide the cumulative frequency by the total number of values.*

The relative cumulative frequency of test scores less than 86 is 0.54.

PRACTICE

The frequency table shows the frequency of each range of heights among Mrs. Dawkin's students.

Height	Frequency
4 ft–4 ft 5 in.	2
4 ft 6 in–4 ft 11 in.	8
5 ft–5 ft 5 in.	10
5 ft 6 in–5 ft 11 in.	6
6 ft–6 ft 5 in.	1

1. What is the relative frequency of heights in the range 5 ft–5 ft 5 in.?
2. What is the relative frequency of heights in the range 4 ft–4 ft 5 in.?
3. What is the cumulative frequency of heights less than 6 ft?
4. What is the cumulative frequency of heights less than 5 ft?
5. What is the relative cumulative frequency of heights less than 5 ft 6 in.?
6. What is the relative cumulative frequency of heights less than 5 ft?

Frequency Polygons

A **histogram** is a common way to represent frequency tables. A histogram is a bar graph with no space between the bars. Each bar can represent a range of values of a data set.

A **frequency polygon** is made by connecting the midpoints of the tops of all of the bars of a histogram.

EXAMPLE

A **The frequency table shows the frequency of the number of push-ups done by the students in a gym class. Draw a histogram and frequency polygon of the data.**

Label the horizontal axis with the number of push-ups.
Label the vertical axis with the frequency.

Push-ups Done in 1 Minute	
Number of Push-ups	Frequency
0–9	3
10–19	6
20–29	11
30–39	10
40–49	4
50–59	2

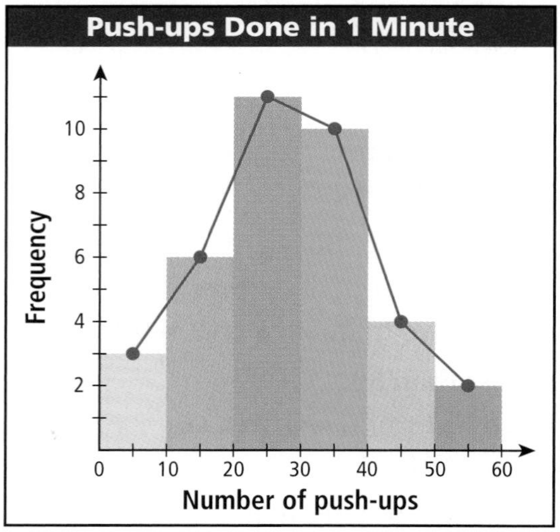

The frequency polygon is made up of the red points and red segments connecting the points.

PRACTICE

Use each frequency table to draw a histogram and frequency polygon of the data.

1.

Books Read over the Summer	
Number of Books	Frequency
0–2	5
3–5	8
6–8	12
9–11	6
12–14	4
15–17	2

2.

Miles Driven One Way to Work	
Number of Miles	Frequency
0–4	6
5–9	5
10–14	13
15–19	9
20–24	4
25–29	1

Parallel Lines and Transversals

Recall that a transversal is a line that intersects two or more other lines. When three parallel lines are intersected by two transversals, the parallel lines divide the transversals proportionally.

In the figure, lines ℓ, m, and n are parallel. Lines r and s are transversals. You can conclude that $\frac{AB}{BC} = \frac{DE}{EF}$.

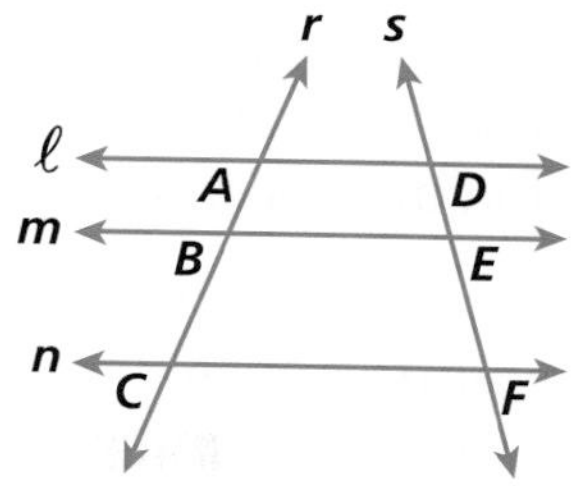

EXAMPLE

A Line $p \parallel$ line $q \parallel$ line r. **Write a proportion based on the figure.**

Lines j and k are transversals. The segments on the transversals are proportional.

$\frac{AC}{CE} = \frac{BD}{DF}$

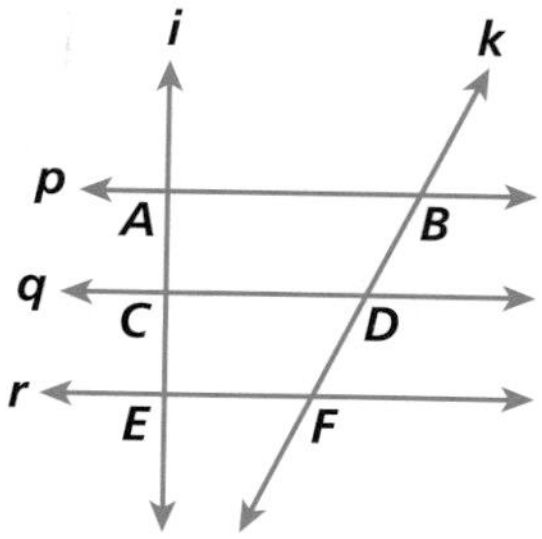

B Line $u \parallel$ line $v \parallel$ line w. **Find x.**

$\frac{DE}{EF} = \frac{GH}{HJ}$	*The segments on the transversals are proportional.*
$\frac{4}{6} = \frac{6}{x}$	*$DE = 4$, $EF = 6$, $GH = 6$, $HJ = x$*
$4x = 6 \cdot 6$	*Find cross products.*
$4x = 36$	*Multiply.*
$x = 9$	*Divide both sides by 4.*

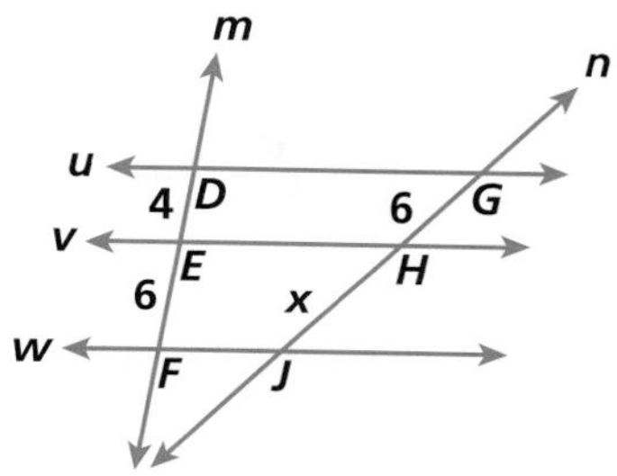

PRACTICE

Write a proportion based on each figure.

1. Line $u \parallel$ line $v \parallel$ line w

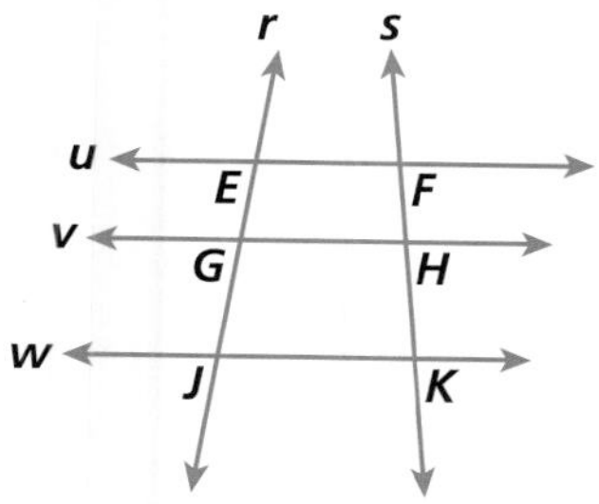

2. Line $\ell \parallel$ line $m \parallel$ line n

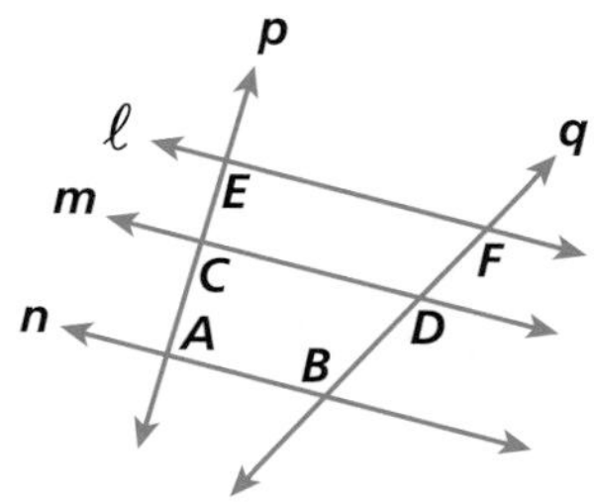

Find x.

3. Line $p \parallel$ line $q \parallel$ line r

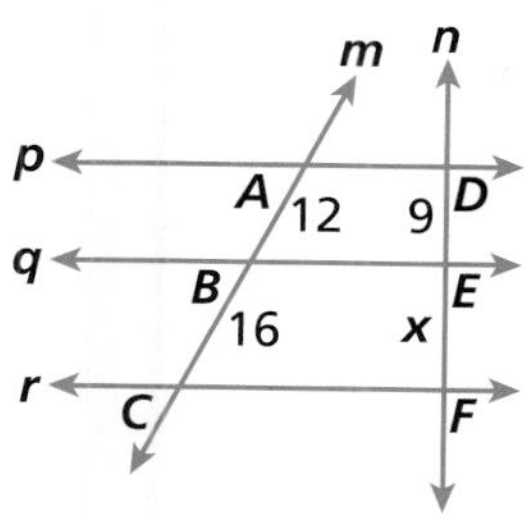

4. Line $u \parallel$ line $v \parallel$ line w

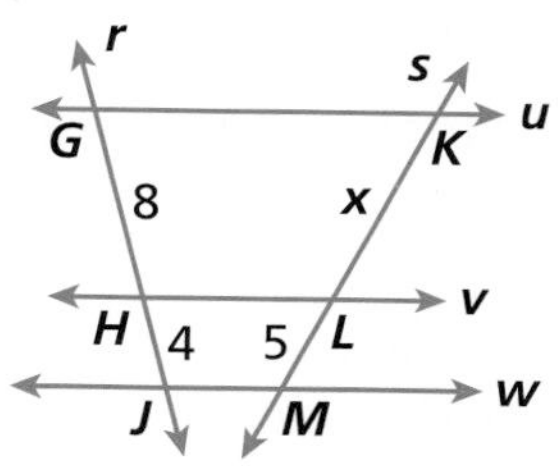

Skills Bank

Circles

A circle can be named by its center, using the ⊙ symbol. A circle with a center labeled C would be named $\odot C$. An unbroken part of a circle is called an **arc.** There are major arcs and minor arcs.

A **minor arc** of a circle is an arc that is shorter than half the circle and named by its endpoints. A **major arc** of a circle is an arc that is longer than half the circle and named by its endpoints and one other point on the arc.

$\widehat{AB}$ is a minor arc.

$\widehat{BAC}$ is a major arc.

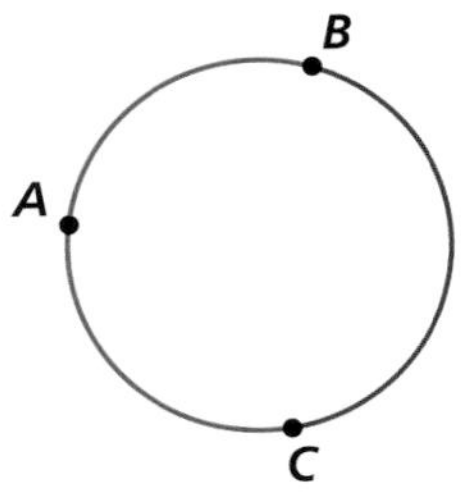

A **radius** connects the center with a point on a circle.

radius $\overline{CD}$

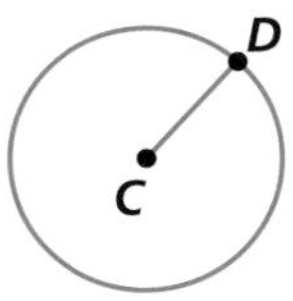

A **chord** connects two points point on a circle. A **diameter** is a chord that passes through the center of a circle. A **semicircle** is an arc whose endpoints lie on a diameter.

chord $\overline{AB}$
diameter $\overline{CD}$
semicircle $\widehat{CAD}$

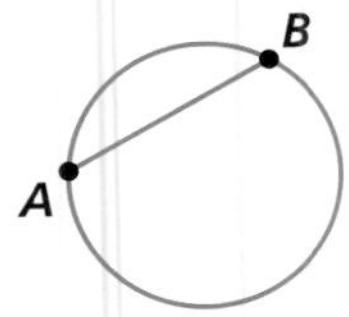

A **secant** is a line that intersects a circle at two points.

secant $\overleftrightarrow{EF}$

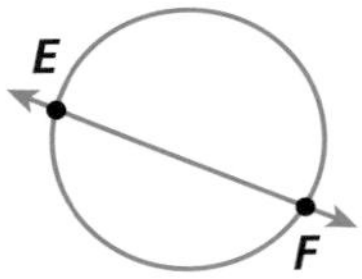

A **tangent** is a line that intersects a circle at one point.

tangent $\overleftrightarrow{GH}$

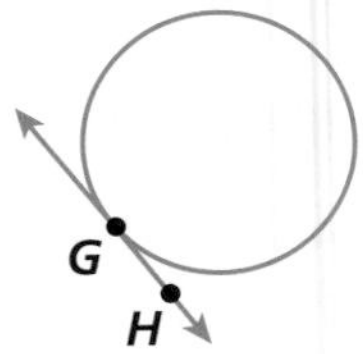

A **central angle** has its vertex at the center of the circle.

central angle
$\angle JKL$

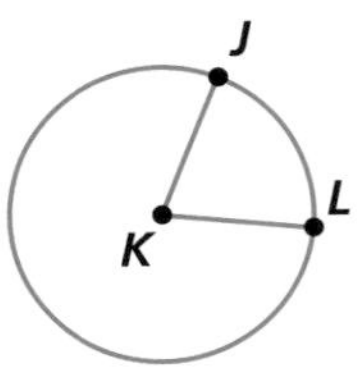

An **inscribed angle** has its vertex on the circle.

inscribed angle
$\angle MNP$

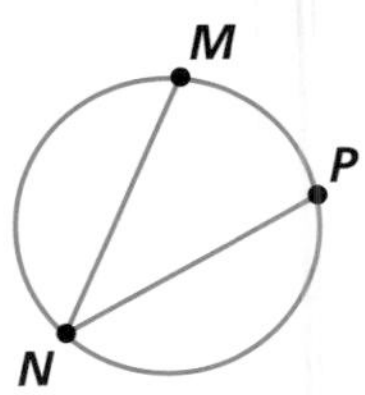

PRACTICE

Use the given diagram of $\odot A$ for exercises 1–6.

1. Name a radius.
2. What two chords make up the inscribed angle?
3. Name a secant.
4. Give the tangent line.
5. Name the central angle.
6. Name the inscribed angle.

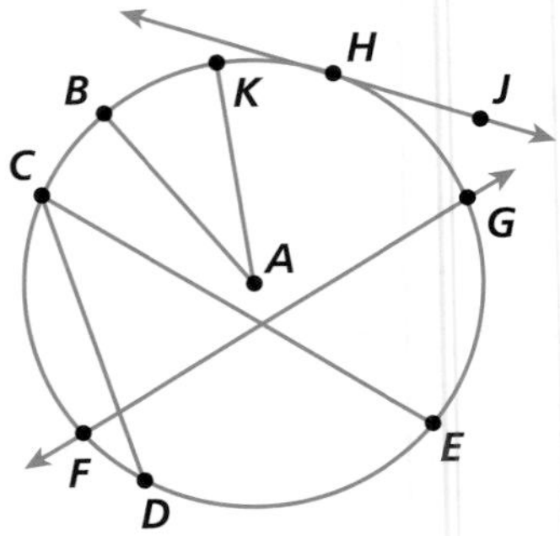

Matrices

A **matrix** is a rectangular arrangement of data enclosed in brackets. Matrices are used to list, organize, and sort data.

The **dimensions** of a matrix are given by the number of horizontal **rows** and vertical columns in the matrix. For example, Matrix A below is an example of a 3×2 ("3-by-2") matrix because it has 3 rows and 2 columns, for a total of 6 **elements**. The number of rows is always given first. So a 3×2 matrix is not the same as a 2×3 matrix.

$$A = \begin{bmatrix} 86 & 137 \\ 103 & 0 \\ 115 & 78 \end{bmatrix} \begin{matrix} \leftarrow \text{Row 1} \\ \leftarrow \text{Row 2} \\ \leftarrow \text{Row 3} \end{matrix}$$

↑ ↑

Column 1 Column 2

Each matrix element is identified by its row and column. The element in row 2 column 1 is 103. You can use the notation $a_{21} = 103$ to express this.

EXAMPLE

Use the data shown in the bar graph to create a matrix.

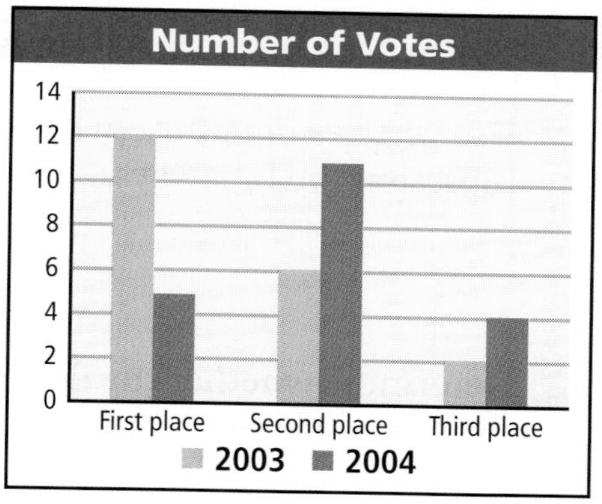

The matrix can be organized with the votes in each year as the columns:

$$\begin{bmatrix} 12 & 5 \\ 6 & 11 \\ 2 & 4 \end{bmatrix}$$

or with the votes in each year as the rows:

$$\begin{bmatrix} 12 & 6 & 2 \\ 5 & 11 & 4 \end{bmatrix}$$

PRACTICE

Use matrix B for Exercises 1–3.

$$B = \begin{bmatrix} 1 & 0 & 7 & 4 \\ 0 & 1 & 3 & 8 \\ 6 & 5 & 2 & 9 \end{bmatrix}$$

1. B is a ___ × ___ matrix.

2. Name the element with a value of 5.

3. What is the value of b_{13}?

4. A football team scored 24, 13, and 35 points in three playoff games. Use this data to write a 3×1 matrix.

5. The greatest length and average weight of some whale species are as follows: finback whale—50 ft, 82 tons; humpback whale—33 ft, 49 tons; bowhead whale—50 ft, 59 tons; blue whale—84 ft, 98 tons; right whale—50 ft, 56 tons. Organize this data in a matrix.

6. The second matrix in the example is called the *transpose* of the first matrix. Write the transpose of matrix B above. What are its dimensions?

Networks

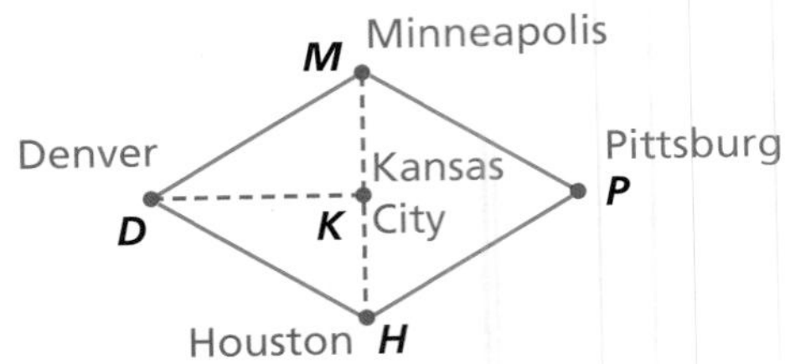

A **network** is a set of points and line segments or arcs that connect the points. Networks are useful in many real-world situations. The network at right at represents the flight routes of a small airline.

The points of a network are called **vertices**.
The line segments or arcs connecting the vertices are called **edges**.
The **degree** of a vertex is the number of edges touching the vertex. For example, vertex D has degree 3.

A **circuit** is a path along the edges that begins and ends at the same vertex and does not go through any edge more than once. An Euler circuit is a circuit that goes through every edge. An **Euler circuit** exists only when every vertex of a network has an even degree.

EXAMPLE

The map shows the highways that connect the cities on a florist's delivery route.

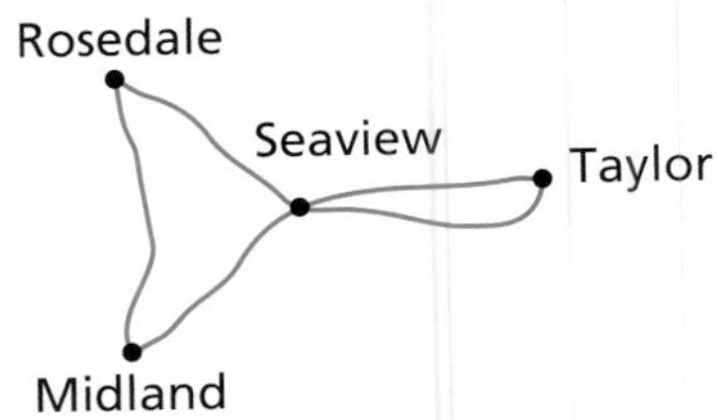

A Construct a network to represent the situation.

Use vertices to represent the cities and edges to represent the highways.

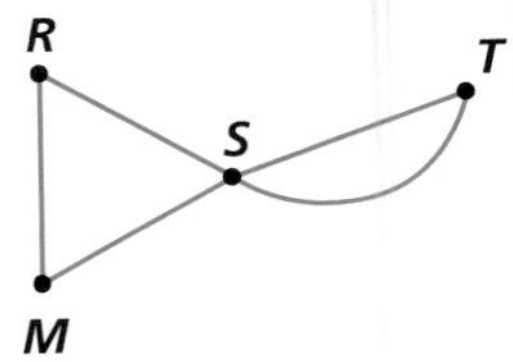

B Determine whether the network can be traveled through an Euler circuit. If so, show one possible Euler circuit. If not, explain why not.

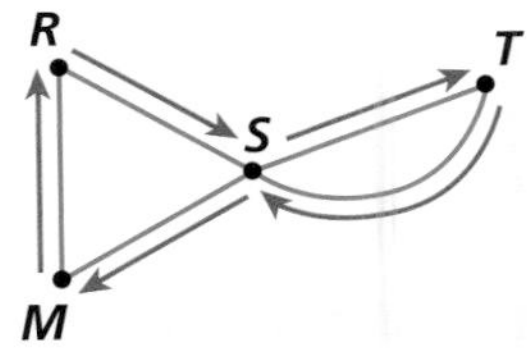

First find the degree of each vertex.

Vertex	M	R	S	T
Degree	2	2	4	2

Every vertex has an even degree, so the network can be traveled by an Euler circuit, as shown.

PRACTICE

The map shows the roads and the houses of five families on Jake's newspaper route.

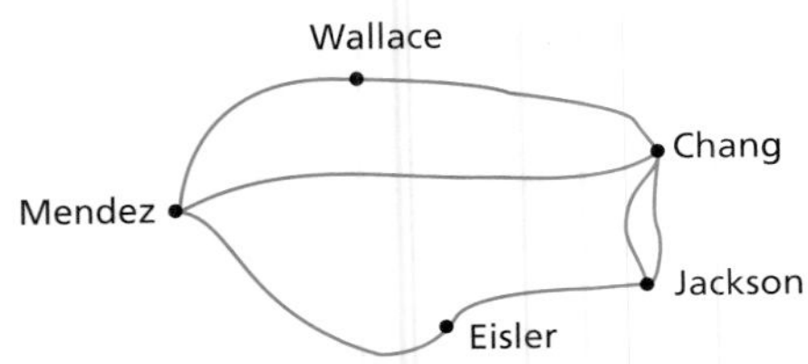

1. Construct a network to represent the situation.
2. Determine whether the network you drew in Exercise 1 can be traveled through an Euler circuit. If so, show one possible Euler circuit. If not, explain why not.

Science Skills

Compare and Order Measurements

You can use **conversion factors** to compare and order measurements.

Common Metric to Customary Conversions		
Length	**Mass**	**Capacity**
1 cm ≈ 0.394 in.	1 g ≈ 0.035 oz	1 mL ≈ 0.034 fl oz
1 m ≈ 3.281 ft	1 g ≈ 0.002 lb	1 L ≈ 33.814 fl oz
1 m ≈ 1.094 yd	1 kg ≈ 35.274 oz	1 L ≈ 1.057 qt
1 km ≈ 0.621 mi	1 kg ≈ 2.205 lb	1 L ≈ 0.264 gal

Common Customary to Metric Conversions		
Length	**Mass**	**Capacity**
1 in. ≈ 2.54 cm	1 oz ≈ 28.35 g	1 fl oz ≈ 29.574 mL
1 ft ≈ 0.305 m	1 oz ≈ 0.028 kg	1 fl oz ≈ 0.03 L
1 yd ≈ 0.914 m	1 lb ≈ 453.592 g	1 qt ≈ 0.946 L
1 mi ≈ 1.609 km	1 lb ≈ 0.454 kg	1 Gal ≈ 3.785 L

EXAMPLE

A **Compare 8 cm and 5 in. by writing < or >.**

1 cm ≈ 0.394 in. — *Find the conversion factor to convert centimeters to inches.*
8 cm ≈ 8(0.394) in. — *Convert 8 cm to inches.*
≈ 3.152 in. — *Multiply.*

Since 3.152 in. < 5 in., 8 cm < 5 in.

B **Write the measurements 700 g, 25 kg, and 50 lb in order from least to greatest.**

First convert the metric measurements to pounds.

700 g ≈ 700(0.002) lb — *Use the conversion factor 1g ≈ 0.002 lb.*
≈ 1.4 lb — *Multiply.*
25 kg ≈ 25(2.205) lb — *Use the conversion factor 1kg ≈ 2.205 lb.*
≈ 55.125 lb — *Multiply.*

Since 1.4 lb < 50 lb < 55.125 lb, the correct order is 700 g, 50 lb, 25 kg.

PRACTICE

Compare each set of measurements by writing < or >.

1. 3 gal and 12 L **2.** 6 km and 5 mi **3.** 20 kg and 40 lb

Write each set of measurements in order from least to greatest.

4. 60 ft, 4 yd, 12 m **5.** 23 oz, 2 lb, 0.5 kg **6.** 4 gal, 18.5 qt, 20 L

Temperature Conversion

In the United States, the Fahrenheit (°F) temperature scale is the common scale used. For example, weather reports and body temperatures are given in degrees Fahrenheit. The metric temperature scale is Celsius (°C) and is commonly used in science applications. Temperatures given in one scale can be converted to the other system using one of the formulas below.

Formulas

Fahrenheit to Celsius (°F to °C)	$\frac{5}{9}(F - 32) = C$
Celsius to Fahrenheit (°C to °F)	$\frac{9}{5}C + 32 = F$

EXAMPLES

A **Convert 77°F to degrees Celsius.**

$$\frac{5}{9}(F - 32) = C$$
$$\frac{5}{9}(77 - 32) = C$$
$$\frac{5}{9}(45) = C$$
$$25 = C$$

B **Convert 103°C to degrees Fahrenheit.**

$$\frac{9}{5}C + 32 = F$$
$$\frac{9}{5}(103) + 32 = F$$
$$185.4 + 32 = F$$
$$217.4 = F$$

PRACTICE

Convert each temperature to degrees Celsius. Give the temperature to the nearest tenth of a degree.

1. 7°F

2. 0°F

3. 12°F

4. 40°F

5. 100°F

6. 32°F

7. 25°F

8. 212°F

9. −50°F

10. −8°F

Convert each temperature to degrees Fahrenheit. Give the temperature to the nearest tenth of a degree.

11. 0°C

12. 10°C

13. 22°C

14. 55°C

15. 212°C

16. 1°C

17. 100°C

18. 80°C

19. 95°C

20. 32°C

21. 31°C

22. 42°C

23. −6°C

24. −40°C

Customary and Metric Rulers

A metric ruler is divided into centimeter units, and each centimeter is divided into 10 millimeter units. A metric ruler that is 1 meter long is a *meter stick*.

1 m = 100 cm
1 cm = 10 mm

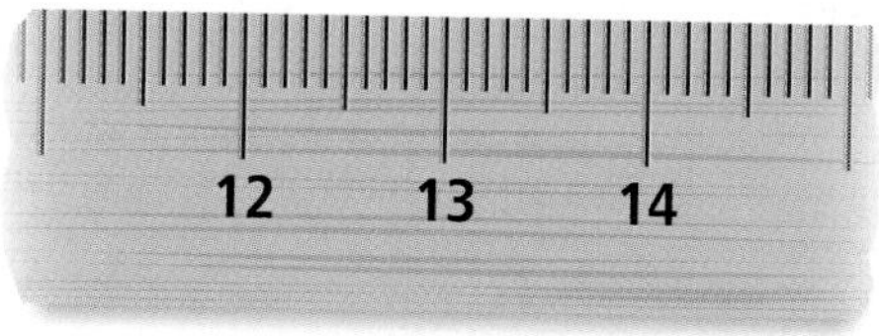

EXAMPLE

What is the length of the segment?

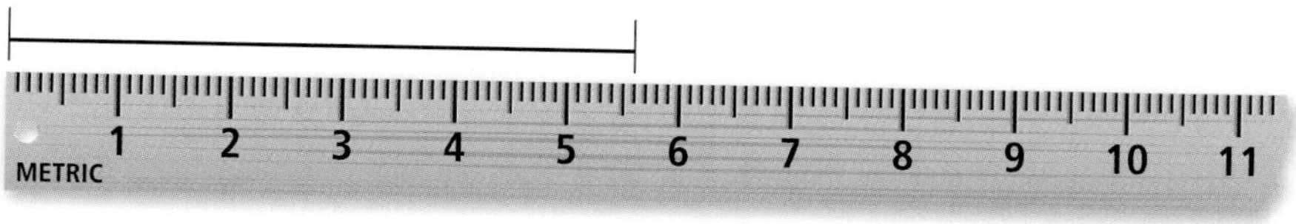

Since the segment is longer than 5 cm and shorter than 6 cm, its length is a decimal value between these measurements. The digit in the ones place is the number of centimeters and the digit in the tenths place is the number of millimeters. The length of the segment is 5.6 cm.

PRACTICE

Use a metric ruler to find the length of each segment.

1. |————| **2.** |————————|

A customary ruler is usually 12 inches long. The ruler is read in fractional units rather than in decimals. Each inch typically has a long mark at $\frac{1}{2}$ inch, shorter marks at $\frac{1}{4}$ and $\frac{3}{4}$ inch, even shorter marks at $\frac{1}{8}$, $\frac{3}{8}$, $\frac{5}{8}$, and $\frac{7}{8}$ inch, and the shortest marks at the remaining 16ths inches.

EXAMPLE

What is the length of the segment?

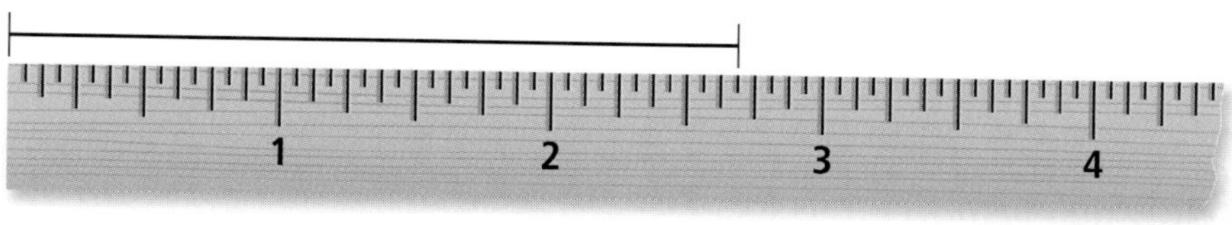

Since the segment is longer than 2 inches and shorter than 3 inches, its length is a mixed number with 2 as the whole number part. The fractional part is $\frac{11}{16}$. The length of the segment is $2\frac{11}{16}$ inches.

PRACTICE

Use a customary ruler to find the length of each segment.

3. |————————| **4.** |————|

Skills Bank

Precision and Significant Digits

In a measurement, all digits that are known with certainty are called **significant digits**. The more precise a measurement is, the more significant digits there are in the measurement. The table shows some rules for identifying significant digits.

Rule	Example	Number of Significant Digits
All nonzero digits	15.32	All 4
Zeros beween significant digits	43,001	All 5
Zeros after the last nonzero digit that are to the right of the decimal point	0.0070	2; 0.0070

Zeros at the end of a whole number are assumed to be nonsignificant. (Example: 500)

EXAMPLE

A **Which is a more precise measurement, 14 ft or 14.2 ft?**

Because 14.2 ft has three significant digits and 14 has only two, 14.2 ft is more precise. In the measurement 14.2 ft, each 0.1 ft is measured.

B **Determine the number of significant digits in 20.04 m, 200 m, and 200.0 m.**

20.04 All 4 digits are significant.
200 There is 1 significant digit.
200.0 All 4 digits are significant.

When calculating with measurements, the answer can only be as precise as the least precise measurement.

C **Multiply 16.3 m by 2.5 m. Use the correct number of significant digits in your answer.**

When muliplying or dividing, use the least number of significant digits of the numbers.

16.3 m · 2.5 m = 40.75

Round to 2 significant digits. ⟶ 41 m^2

D **Add 4500 in. and 70 in. Use the correct number of significant digits in your answer.**

When adding or subtracting, line up the numbers. Round the answer to the last significant digit that is farthest to the left.

4500 in. *5 is farthest left. Round to*
+ 70 in. *hundreds.*
4570 Round to the hundreds. ⟶ 4600 in.

PRACTICE

Tell which is more precise.

1. 31.8 g or 32 g **2.** 496.5 mi or 496.50 mi **3.** 3.0 ft or 3.001 ft

Determine the number of significant digits in each measurement.

4. 12 lb **5.** 14.00 mm **6.** 1.009 yd **7.** 20.87 s

Perform the indicated operation. Use the correct number of significant digits in your answer.

8. 210 m + 43 m **9.** 4.7 ft · 1.04 ft **10.** 6.7 s − 0.08 s

Greatest Possible Error

The smaller the units used to measure something, the greater the precision of the measurement. The **greatest possible error** of a measurement is half the smallest unit. This is written as ± 0.5 unit, which is read as "plus or minus 0.5 unit."

EXAMPLES

A Which is a more precise measurement, 292 cm or 3 m?

The more precise measurement is 292 cm because its unit of measurement, 1 cm, is smaller than 1 m.

B Find the greatest possible error for a measurement of 2.4 cm.

The smallest unit is 0.1 cm.

$0.5 \times 0.1 = 0.05$

The greatest possible error is ± 0.05 cm.

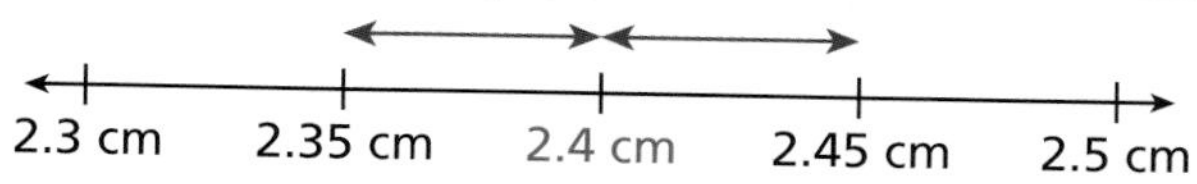

PRACTICE

Tell which is a more precise measurement.

1. 40 cm or 412 mm
2. 3.2 ft or 1 yd
3. 7 ft or 87 in.
4. 3116 m or 3 km
5. 1 mi or 5281 ft
6. 0.04 m or 4.2 cm

Find the greatest possible error of each measurement.

7. 5 ft
8. 22 mm
9. 12.5 mi
10. 60 km
11. 2.06 cm
12. 0.08 g

pH (Logarithmic Scale)

pH is a measure of the concentration of hydrogen ions in a solution. pH ranges from 0 to 14. An *acid* has a pH below 7 and a *base* has a pH above 7. A pH of 7 is *neutral* and a hydrogen ion concentration of 1×10^{-7} mol/L. The exponent is the opposite of the pH.

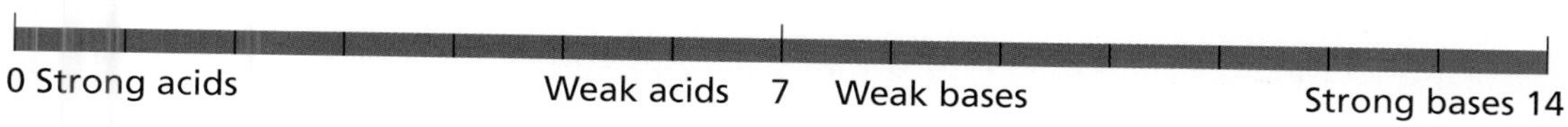

EXAMPLES

A Write the pH of the solution, given the hydrogen ion concentration.

coffee: 1×10^{-5} mol/L

The coffee is acidic, with a pH of 5.

B Write the hydrogen ion concentration of the solution in mol/L.

antacid solution: pH = 10.0

1×10^{-10} mol/L in the antacid solution

PRACTICE

Write the pH of each solution, given the hydrogen ion concentration.

1. seawater: 1×10^{-8} mol/L
2. lye: 1×10^{-13} mol/L
3. borax: 1×10^{-9} mol/L

Write the hydrogen ion concentration in mol/L.

4. drain cleaner: pH = 14.0
5. lemon juice: pH = 2.0
6. milk: pH = 7.0

Richter Scale

An earthquake is classified according to its magnitude. The Richter scale is a mathematical system that compares the sizes and magnitudes of earthquakes.

The magnitude is related to the height, or *amplitude,* of seismic waves as recorded by a seismograph during an earthquake. The higher the number is on the Richter scale, the greater the amplitude of the earthquake's waves.

Earthquakes per Year	Magnitude on the Richter Scale	Severity
1	8.0 and higher	Great
18	7.0–7.9	Major
120	6.0–6.9	Strong
800	5.0–5.9	Moderate
6200	4.0–4.9	Light
49,000	3.0–3.9	Minor
≈ 3,300,000	below 3.0	Very minor

The Richter scale is a *logarithmic scale,* which means that the numbers in the scale measure factors of 10. An earthquake that measures 6.0 on the Richter scale is 10 times as great as one that measures 5.0.

The largest earthquake ever measured registered 8.9 on the Richter scale.

Skills Bank

EXAMPLE

How many times greater is an earthquake that measures 5.0 on the Richter scale than one that measures 3.0?

You can divide powers of 10, with the magnitudes as the exponents.

$$\frac{10^5}{10^3} = 10^2$$

A 5.0 quake is 100 times greater than a 3.0 quake.

PRACTICE

Describe the severity of an earthquake with each given Richter scale reading.

1. 7.6 **2.** 4.2 **3.** 5.0

4. 2.0 **5.** 3.6 **6.** 8.4

Each pair of numbers repesents two earthquake magnitudes on the Richter scale. How many times greater is the first earthquake in each pair? (Use a calculator for 10–12.)

7. 6.0 and 4.0 **8.** 8.0 and 5.0 **9.** 7.0 and 3.0

10. 7.5 and 5.5 **11.** 5.7 and 5.3 **12.** 8.6 and 7.1

Selected Answers

Chapter 1

1-1 Exercises

1. 15 **3.** 3 **5.** 3 **7.** 2 c **9.** $2\frac{1}{2}$ c **11.** 37 **13.** 57 **15.** 13 pt **17.** 10 pt **19.** 13 **21.** 22 **23.** 20 **25.** 11 **27.** 10 **29.** 16 **31.** 51 **33.** 20.7 **35.** 18 **37.** 105 **39.** 14 **41.** 30.5 **43.** 21 **45.** 0 **47.** $110 **49b.** 165,600 frames **53.** D **55.** 23 **57.** 101, 411, 117, 121 **59.** All are odd. **61.** 100 **63.** 198 **65.** 1000 **67.** 199.8

1-2 Exercises

1. $3p - 5$ **3.** $16 + \frac{d}{7}$ **5.** 18 plus the product of 43 and s **7.** 10 plus the quotient of y and 31 **9.** $5n$; $75; $125; $175; $225 **11.** $1 + \frac{5}{n}$ **13.** $78j - 45$ **15.** $14 + 59q$ **17.** 12 more than the product of 16 and g **19.** 51 less than the quotient of w and 182 **23.** $\frac{1}{2}(m + 5)$ **25.** $\frac{1}{3 + g}$ **27.** $13y - 6$ **29.** $2\left(\frac{m}{35}\right)$ **31.** $8\left(\frac{2}{3} + x\right)$ **33.** 8 times the sum of m and 5 **35.** 17 times the quotient of 16 and w **37.** $\frac{1}{4}(x + 7)$ or $\frac{x + 7}{4}$ **41.** C **43.** $9n$; $9450 **45.** 24 **47.** 5; 7; 9; 11

1-3 Exercises

1. $-4 < -2$; Vijay Singh, Phil Mickelson, Tiger Woods, Justin Leonard **3.** −17, −8, 6 **5.** −7, 0, 3 **7.** −13 **9.** −25 **11.** 14 **13.** 15 **15.** −3°F < 2°F; Monday, Thursday, Tuesday, Wednesday **17.** −11, −5, 8 **19.** −2, −1, 4 **21.** 15 **23.** 31 **25.** 21 **27.** 10 **29.** < **31.** = **33.** > **35.** > **37.** −16, −12, 24 **39.** −45, −25, 35 **41.** 50 **43.** 1 **45.** 72 **47.** 6 **49.** 48 **51.** 2 **53.** Antarctica, Asia, North America, Europe, South America, Africa, Australia **57.** B **61.** 35 **63.** 57 **65.** $2p + 3$

1-4 Exercises

1. 6 **3.** 2 **5.** −7 **7.** 6 **9.** 11 **11.** −10 **13.** −2 **15.** −5 **17.** 22 **19.** −16 **21.** 7 **23.** −32 **25.** 23 **27.** 9 **29.** $-3 + (-4) = -7$ **31.** −12 **33.** −17 **35.** −22 **37.** 43 **39.** 8 **41.** −30 **43.** −15 **45a.** $1,146,137,000,000 **b.** −$1,763,863,000,000 **c.** about −$618,000,000,000 or −$618 billion **49.** C **51.** 4 **53.** 12 **55.** 13

1-5 Exercises

1. −14 **3.** 12 **5.** 17 **7.** −15 **9.** −10 **11.** 17 **13.** 17 **15.** −17 **17.** $-6 - (-4)$ **19.** 3 **21.** −56 **23.** −26 **25.** −20 **27.** −24 **29.** ≈ 190 ft above the starting point **31.** Great Pyramid to Cleopatra; about 500 years **33.** Cleopatra takes throne and Napoleon invades Egypt. **37.** 8 **39.** 3 **41.** −12

1-6 Exercises

1. −32 **3.** 28 **5.** 49 **7.** −24 **9.** gains $15 **11.** 21 **13.** −84 **15.** −60 **17.** −39 **19.** +100 **23.** −12 **25.** −4 **27.** 8 **29.** 36 **31.** 11 **33.** −8 **35.** −6 **41.** D **43.** $j - 18$ **45.** $y - 22$ **47.** 9 **49.** −254

1-7 Exercises

1. 12 **3.** −14 **5.** −23 **7.** 39 **9.** 15,635 ft **11.** 32 **13.** 44 **15.** −74 **17.** 35 **19.** 5 **21.** 24 **23.** 3 **25.** 949 **27.** 110 **29.** −17 **31.** −138 **33.** −1784 **35.** $t - 600 = -173$; 427°C **37.** 40 **39.** 1 **41.** −59 **47.** G **49.** −14 **51.** −13 **53.** −56 **55.** −2

1-8 Exercises

1. −7 **3.** 14 **5.** 2 **7.** 3 **9.** −60 **11.** −57 **13.** −207 **15.** −84 **17.** $\frac{1}{4}c = 60$; $c = \$240$ **19.** −40 **21.** 36 **23.** −15 **25.** 7 **27.** 2 **29.** −4 **31.** 54 **33.** 96 **35.** −161 **37.** −252 **39.** 2 **41.** −7 **43.** −7 **45.** 2 **47.** 56 **49.** −72 **51.** 17 **53.** −3 **55.** −48 **57.** 35 **61.** 48 hr **63.** 540 students and faculty **65.** $m + (505 + 262) = 1568$; $m = 801$ miles **69.** 9 **71.** 4 **73.** 20 **75.** $x = -5$ **77.** $x = 8$

1-9 Exercises

1. > **3.** > **5.** < **7.** $x < -7$ **9.** $m \leq 32$ **11.** $y \geq 17$ **13.** $z > 21$ **15.** < **17.** > **19.** > **21.** $b < 4$ **23.** $h \geq 5$ **25.** $a > 3$ **27.** $f \leq 11$ **29.** $x < 6$ **31.** $x > 4$ **33.** $x < 1$ **35.** $s \geq \$103,322$ **37.** $60 + 246 \overset{?}{\geq} 300$; $306 \overset{?}{\geq} 300$; no **39.** > **41.** < **43.** > **45.** $b \geq 34$ **47.** $q \geq -9$ **49.** $p \leq -16$ **51.** $y \geq -4$ **57.** D **59.** −2, 0, 1, 3 **61.** −23, −15, 0 **63.** $x = 67.2$ **65.** $y = -3$

Chapter 1 Study Guide: Review

1. equation **2.** opposite **3.** absolute value **4.** 147 **5.** 152 **6.** 278 **7.** $2(k + 4)$ **8.** $4t + 5$ **9.** 10 less than the product of 5 and b **10.** 32 more than the product of 23 and s **11.** 12 less than the quotient of 10 divided by r **12.** 16 more than the quotient of y divided by 8 **13.** 1 **14.** 15 **15.** 34 **16.** 21 **17.** 4 **18.** −1 **19.** −2 **20.** −12 **21.** −3 **22.** 1 **23.** −24 **24.** 8 **25.** −8 **26.** −16 **27.** 17 **28.** 3 **29.** 15 **30.** −22 **31.** −4 **32.** 16 **33.** −5 **34.** −35 **35.** −18 **36.** 52 **37.** 25 **38.** 120 **39.** 2 **40.** $z = 23$ **41.** $t = 8$ **42.** $k = 15$ **43.** $x = 11$ **44.** Let c = weight of sea cow; $c - 585 = 715$; $c = 1300$; a sea cow weighs 1300 lb. **45.** Let d = area of Death Valley;

$d + 11{,}700 = 15{,}000$; $d = 3300$; the area of Death Valley is 3300 mi^2. **46.** $g = -8$ **47.** $k = 9$ **48.** $p = -80$ **49.** $w = -48$ **50.** $y = -40$ **51.** $z = 192$ **52.** Let d = total distance; $\frac{1}{3}d = 235$; $d = 705$; the total distance was 705 mi. **53.** Let m = number of months; $390m = 9360$; $m = 24$; the loan is for 24 months. **54.** $h < 10$ **55.** $y > 7$ **56.** $x \geq 6$ **57.** $w \geq 2$ **58.** $x \leq 4$ **59.** $q \leq -3$ **60.** $p < -2$ **61.** $m \leq 48$ **62.** $y > 0$ **63.** $x > 3$ **64.** $y > 6$ **65.** $x \leq 4$

Chapter 2

2-1 Exercises

1. $\frac{1}{2}$ **3.** $-\frac{2}{3}$ **5.** $\frac{1}{3}$ **7.** $-\frac{3}{4}$ **9.** $\frac{7}{16}$ **11.** $\frac{3}{4}$ **13.** $\frac{2}{5}$ **15.** $22\frac{1}{5}$ **17.** $3\frac{21}{100}$ **19.** 0.625 **21.** 0.416 **23.** −0.1 **25.** 0.375 **27.** 1.25 **29.** $\frac{3}{4}$ **31.** $-\frac{1}{2}$ **33.** $\frac{5}{6}$ **35.** $\frac{22}{35}$ **37.** $-\frac{13}{21}$ **39.** $\frac{3}{5}$ **41.** $\frac{18}{25}$ **43.** $1\frac{377}{1000}$ **45.** $-1\frac{2}{5}$ **47.** −0.375 **49.** −1.8 **51.** 1.6 **53.** −4.6 **55.** $1.\overline{3}$ **59.** $3\frac{3}{8}$ **61a.** $\frac{4}{9}; \frac{1}{6}; \frac{1}{4}; \frac{7}{15}; \frac{9}{16}; \frac{12}{25}; \frac{5}{8}; \frac{3}{8}$ **63.** GCF = 2; $\frac{21}{34}$; No, the fraction cannot be further simplified because the numerator and denominator are relatively prime. **69.** F **71.** 11; 14 **73.** 6 **75.** −25 **77.** 156 **79.** −6

2-2 Exercises

1. < > **3.** = **5.** > **7.** > **9.** $7\frac{5}{16}$ in., 7.5 in., $8\frac{1}{8}$ in., 8.25 in. **11.** > **13.** = **15.** > **17.** < **19.** > **21.** < **23.** = **25.** = **27.** > **29.** < **37a.** apricot, sulphur, large orange sulphur, white-angled sulphur, great white **41.** $|0.62|$, $|-\frac{2}{3}|$, $|-0.75|$, $|\frac{5}{6}|$ **43.** J **45.** 10 **47.** −47 **49.** 0.75 **51.** 2.5 **53.** 0.95

2-3 Exercises

1. 0.56 s **3.** −3 **5.** $-2\frac{1}{2}$ **7.** $-1\frac{1}{5}$ **9.** $\frac{1}{5}$ **11.** $\frac{4}{9}$ **13.** 10.816 s **15.** $-1\frac{3}{4}$ **17.** $-\frac{1}{3}$ **19.** $-\frac{14}{17}$ **21.** $-\frac{8}{33}$ **23.** $\frac{1}{3}$ **25.** 7.9375 or $7\frac{15}{16}$ **27.** $4\frac{69}{200}$ or 4.345 **29.** $\frac{1}{3}$ **31.** $4\frac{1}{5}$ **33.** 1.9 **35.** −1.2 **37.** $\frac{3}{28}$ **39.** $1\frac{6}{41}$ **41.** $\frac{1}{4}$ in. **43.** 0.186 quadrillion Btu **47.** D **49.** $\frac{11}{15}$ **51.** $b = -7$ **53.** $a = -5$ **55.** < **57.** =

2-4 Exercises

1. $2\frac{1}{2}$ **3.** $1\frac{7}{8}$ **5.** $\frac{5}{32}$ **7.** $5\frac{5}{8}$ **9.** 14.7 **11.** 9.6 **13.** $\frac{1}{4}$ **15.** $-5\frac{1}{2}$ **17.** $-11\frac{2}{3}$ **19.** $-20\frac{1}{3}$ **21.** $-22\frac{2}{5}$ **23.** $-\frac{7}{36}$ **25.** $\frac{7}{24}$ **27.** $1\frac{1}{2}$ **29.** $\frac{21}{40}$ **31.** −0.235 **33.** −4.125 **35.** −0.496 **37.** −0.368 **39.** $\frac{3}{8}$ **41.** $-8\frac{7}{11}$ **43.** $15\frac{5}{9}$ **45.** 1.82 **47.** −0.558 **49.** $2\frac{53}{54}$ **51.** $-\frac{55}{192}$ **53a.** $1\frac{1}{4}$ tsp **b.** $1\frac{1}{2}$ tsp **c.** 2 tsp **57.** A **59.** C **61.** > **63.** > **65.** $-\frac{5}{6}$ **67.** $-\frac{2}{9}$

2-5 Exercises

1. $\frac{2}{3}$ **3.** $-\frac{2}{7}$ **5.** $1\frac{11}{80}$ **7.** $1\frac{2}{5}$ **9.** 12.4 **11.** 15.3 **13.** $4.2\overline{3}$ **15.** 490 **17.** −19.4 **19.** 45 **21.** −18 **23.** $\frac{1}{6}$ serving **25.** $1\frac{9}{35}$ **27.** $1\frac{3}{5}$ **29.** $-\frac{8}{21}$ **31.** $2\frac{1}{28}$ **33.** 83 **35.** 9.7 **37.** 40.55 **39.** 13.6 **41.** 12 **43.** −11 **45.** 370 **47.** 11 glasses **49.** $3\frac{31}{48}$ in. **55.** G **57.** 11 **59.** $\frac{13}{20}$ **61.** $\frac{723}{1000}$ **63.** $-\frac{4}{5}$

2-6 Exercises

1. $\frac{19}{21}$ **3.** $-\frac{3}{8}$ **5.** $-4\frac{3}{10}$ **7.** $\frac{47}{60}$ **9.** $1\frac{11}{72}$ **11.** $\frac{13}{14}$ **13.** $-\frac{41}{52}$ **15.** $6\frac{5}{8}$ yd **17.** $\frac{19}{21}$ **19.** $1\frac{1}{3}$ **21.** $-\frac{29}{126}$ **23.** $1\frac{4}{45}$ **25.** $\frac{1}{12}$ **27.** $\frac{19}{42}$ **29.** $\frac{7}{34}$ **31.** $72\frac{4}{5}$ in. **35.** $18\frac{21}{50}$ in. **37.** $47\frac{2}{25}$ meters **39.** C **41.** −4 **43.** −5 **45.** $\frac{1}{18}$ **47.** $4\frac{2}{7}$

2-7 Exercises

1. $y = -82.3$ **3.** $m = -19.2$ **5.** $s = 97.146$ **7.** $x = -\frac{5}{9}$ **9.** $w = -\frac{7}{15}$ **11.** $y = -8$ **13.** 18.7 days **15.** $m = -7$ **17.** $k = -3.6$ **19.** $c = 3.12$ **21.** $d = \frac{6}{25}$ **23.** $x = -\frac{1}{24}$ **25.** $r = -\frac{5}{7}$ **27.** $d = 1\frac{1}{21}$ **29.** 2.5 g **31.** $253\frac{4}{5}$ carats **33.** $z = \frac{1}{3}$ **35.** $j = -21.6$ **37.** $t = 7$ **39.** $d = -\frac{1}{2}$ **41.** $v = -30.25$ **43.** $y = -4.2$ **45.** $c = -\frac{1}{20}$ **47.** $y = 54.2$ **49.** $m = -1.4$ **55.** $3v = 6\frac{1}{4}$; $2\frac{1}{2}$ minutes **57.** $\frac{1}{2}(m + 19)$ **59.** $10\frac{5}{12}$ **61.** $2\frac{4}{45}$

2-8 Exercises

1. 7 hours **3.** 56 **5.** 114 **7.** 126 **9.** 125 **11.** −18 **13.** −90 **15.** 19 **17.** 94 **19.** 2.02 **21.** 15 **23.** $\frac{2}{30}$ **25.** 0.5 or $\frac{1}{2}$ **27.** 10 **29.** 21 **31.** 1.3 **33.** $-\frac{11}{5}$ **35.** $\frac{n-7}{5} = 13$; 72 **39.** 110,000 **41.** 25 in. **43.** B **45.** $x < 5$ **47.** $x \leq 2$ **49.** $y = -4.4$ **51.** $m = -25.6$

Chapter 2 Study Guide: Review

1. rational number **2.** relatively prime **3.** reciprocal **4.** $\frac{3}{5}$ **5.** $\frac{1}{4}$ **6.** $\frac{21}{40}$ **7.** 1.75 **8.** $0.2\overline{6}$ **9.** $0.\overline{7}$ **10.** $\frac{2}{3}$ **11.** $\frac{2}{3}$ **12.** $\frac{3}{4}$ **13.** < **14.** = **15.** $-0.9, -\frac{2}{3}, 0.25, \frac{1}{2}$ **16.** $-0.11, 0, 0.67, \frac{9}{10}$ **17.** $-\frac{6}{13}$ **18.** $\frac{7}{5}$ **19.** $\frac{5}{9}$ **20.** $\frac{1}{11}$ **21.** $\frac{1}{11}$ **22.** $\frac{12}{13}$ **23.** $-1\frac{1}{5}$ **24.** $7\frac{3}{5}$ **25.** $\frac{8}{15}$ **26.** −4 **27.** $2\frac{1}{4}$ **28.** $3\frac{1}{4}$ **29.** 13 **30.** $-\frac{7}{18}$ **31.** 6 **32.** $\frac{3}{8}$ **33.** $\frac{2}{9}$ **34.** −16 **35.** $\frac{5}{4}$ **36.** 2 **37.** $1\frac{1}{6}$ **38.** $\frac{5}{18}$ **39.** $11\frac{3}{10}$ **40.** $4\frac{7}{20}$ **41.** $3\frac{17}{60}$ **42.** $-9\frac{11}{36}$ **43.** −21.8 **44.** −18 **45.** $-\frac{5}{8}$ **46.** 2 **47.** $\frac{95}{99}$ **48.** −2 **49.** 44.6 **50.** −6 **51.** $126 **52.** $m = 10$ **53.** $y = -8$ **54.** $c = -16$ **55.** $r = -3$ **56.** $t = 16$ **57.** $w = 64$ **58.** $r = -42$ **59.** $h = -50$ **60.** $x = 52$ **61.** $d = -33$ **62.** $c = 90$ **63.** 11

Chapter 3

3-1 Exercises

1. yes **3.** yes **7.** \$2.95 **9.** no **11.** no **17.** yes **19.** yes **21.** no **23.** yes **25.** $c = 39.99 + 0.49m$; (29, 54.20) **31a.** (1980, 74) **b.** (2020, 81) **33.** $y = 5$ **37.** J **39.** 12.8 **41.** $\frac{3}{5}$ **43.** $\frac{1}{2}$

3-2 Exercises

1. (−2, 3); Quadrant II **3.** (2, −3); Quadrant IV **5.** (5, 5); Quadrant I **13.** (0, 3); no quadrant **15.** (2, −4); Quadrant IV **17.** (−2, 5); Quadrant II **19.** (2, −4); Quadrant IV **21.** (−2, 5); Quadrant II **27.** 7 studs **31.** C **33.** $y > -3$ **35.** $f \geq 5$ **37.** no **39.** yes

3-3 Exercises

1a. Rider 2 **b.** Rider 1 **c.** Rider 3 **5a.** Dog 2 **b.** Dog 3 **c.** Dog 1 **13.** Check students' graphs. **15.** $-1\frac{11}{36}$ **17.** $1\frac{5}{99}$

3-4 Exercises

5. The relationship is not a function. **7.** The relationship is a function. **13.** The relationship is not a function. **15.** D = 1, 4, 8, 14; **17.** D = 30, 40, 50, 60; **21a.** yes **b.** Domain: (0, 20, 40, 60, 80, 100); Range: (0, 150, 300, 450, 600, 750) **25.** D **27.** 23 **29.** −60 **31.** 104 **33.** −33.7 **35.** $\frac{1}{6}$

3-5 Exercises

3. $y = 3x$ **5.** $y = 12 - x$ **15.** −21 **17.** −4 **19.** 16

3-6 Exercises

1. 4 **3.** − 6 **5.** −3 **7.** 25, 30, 35 **9.** 12, 5, −2 **11.** −10, −12, −14 **13.** $y = 3n$ **15.** $y = 3n - 4$ **17.** 7 **19.** −6 **21.** −7 **23.** 45, 54, 63 **25.** −2, −11, −20 **27.** −15, −18, −21 **29.** $y = 4n$ **31.** $y = 7n - 4$ **33.** 65 **35.** 30 **37.** 44 **39.** 63 **41.** 77 **43.** 31 **47a.** no **b.** yes **c.** no **49.** 17 **51.** $\frac{1}{6}$

Chapter 3 Study Guide: Review

1. common difference **2.** function **3.** origin **4.** sequence; arithmetic sequence **5.** vertical line test **6.** x-axis; y-axis **7.** yes **8.** no **9.** yes **10.** no **23.** 5 **24.** 8 **25.** 20 **26.** 26 **27.** 10.1 **28.** $\frac{22}{3}$ **30.** Oven E **31.** Person B **36.** yes **37.** no **38.** $y = -2.3x$ **39.** $y = \frac{1}{2}x$ **40.** $y = x$ **41.** 29, 36, 43 **42.** 11.5, 14, 16.5 **43.** $3\frac{1}{3}$, 4, $4\frac{2}{3}$ **44.** 13, 15, 17 **45.** −15, −18, −21

Chapter 4

4-1 Exercises

1. 12^1 **3.** $(2b)^4$ **5.** 64 **7.** −125 **9.** 4096 **11.** −5 **13.** −710 **15.** 5^6 **17.** 3^3d^3 **19.** $(-4)^2c^3$ **21.** 256 **23.** 4096 **25.** 16 **27.** 173 **29.** 1 **31.** $(-3)^4$ **33.** 6^6 **35.** 125 **37.** −2744 **39.** −36 **41.** −1 **43.** −65 **45.** $2^{18} = 262{,}144$ bacteria **47.** approximately 1728 cm^3 **51.** B **53.** 125 **55.** −28 **57.** −47 **59.** $0.2\overline{6}$ **61.** $0.208\overline{3}$

4-2 Exercises

1. 0.01 **3.** 0.000001 **5.** $\frac{1}{64}$ **7.** $\frac{1}{27}$ **9.** $13\frac{1}{125}$ **11.** $\frac{1}{8}$ **13.** 0.1 **15.** 0.00000001 **17.** $-\frac{1}{4}$ **19.** $\frac{1}{10{,}000}$, or 0.0001 **21.** $-1\frac{3}{4}$ **23.** $11\frac{2}{81}$ **25.** $\frac{1}{128}$ **27.** $\frac{1}{729}$ **29.** $\frac{4}{9}$ **31.** 28 **33.** 13.02 **35.** $\frac{3}{4}$ **37.** $\frac{1}{11 \times 11 \times 11 \times 11} = \frac{1}{14{,}641}$ **39.** $-\frac{1}{6 \times 6 \times 6} = -\frac{1}{216}$ **45.** 38,340 lb **49.** C **51.** (2, 3); I **53.** (3, −1); IV **55.** 25 **57.** −729

4-3 Exercises

1. 5^{15} **3.** m^4 **5.** 6^2 **7.** $12^0 = 1$ **9.** 3^{20} **11.** 4^{-6} or $\frac{1}{4^6}$ **13.** 10^{17} **15.** r **17.** 5^4 **19.** t^{13} **21.** $5^0 = 1$ **23.** 3^{-4} **25.** 4^4 **27.** a^7 **29.** x^{10} **31.** 7^{12} **33.** cannot combine **35.** $y^0 = 1$ **37.** 26^2, or 676 **39.** 12^2, 12^1 **41.** 4 **43.** −6 **45a.** 10^{100} **b.** 10^{200} **49.** G **51.** 25 **53.** 22.8 **55.** $1\frac{1}{11}$ **57.** $\frac{1}{9}$ **59.** 1

4-4 Exercises

1. 4170 **3.** 62,000,000 **5.** 5.7×10^{-5} **7.** 6.98×10^6 **9.** 9.6×10^7 **11.** 9,200,000 **13.** 0.036 **15.** 7×10^{-5} **17.** 1×10^8 **19.** 9×10^9 kg **21.** 140,000 **23.** 78 **25.** 0.000000053 **27.** 559,000 **29.** 7,113,000 **31.** 0.00029 **33a.** 1.5×10^{-4} g **b.** 1.5×10^{26} g **35a.** $2(6.02 \times 10^{23}) = 1.505 \times 10^{24}$ atoms **b.** $10 \div 2.5 = 4$ g **c.** $4 \div (6.02 \times 10^{23}) \approx 6.64 \times 10^{-24}$ **37.** 8.56×10^{-3} **39.** 5.9×10^6 **41.** 7.6×10^{-3} **43.** 4.2×10^3 **45.** 4×10^2 **47.** 7×10^6 **49.** 5.85×10^{-3}, 1.5×10^{-2}, 2.3×10^{-2}, 1.2×10^6, 5.5×10^6 **55.** $y = 3x - 4$ **57.** 7^2 **59.** t^3

4-5 Exercises

1. ±2 **3.** ±8 **5.** ±1 **7.** ±3 **9.** 16 ft **11.** 3 **13.** −1 **15.** ±12 **17.** ±13 **19.** ±20 **21.** ±15 **23.** −1 **25.** −18 **27.** ±6 **29.** ±7 **31.** ±23 **33.** ±24 **37.** 26 ft **39.** $\pm\frac{1}{3}$ **41.** $\pm\frac{9}{4}$ **43.** ±2 **45.** $\pm\frac{1}{2}$ **47a.** 64 small squares; 1 small square left **b.** 16 small squares **51.** C **53.** $\frac{7}{20}$ **55.** $-7\frac{9}{50}$ **57.** 1.97×10^9 **59.** 3.14×10^{10}

4-6 Exercises

1. 6 and 7 **3.** 12 and 13 **5.** 15 and 16 **7.** 8.6 **9.** 60.0 **11.** 71.6 **13.** 1 and 215; −45 and −4417; ≈28.84 cm **19.** 9.6 **21.** 12.2 **23.** B **25.** E **27.** F **29.** 33.71 **31.** −14.66 **33.** −32.83 **35.** 40 ft **37a.** about 609.9 mi/h **b.** about 7.8 hours **39.** about 10,752.7 feet **41.** 62.83 **43.** 21 **45.** 18 **47.** ±8 **49.** ±36

4-7 Exercises

1. irrational, real **3.** rational, real **5.** rational **7.** irrational **9.** rational **11.** not real **15.** $\frac{3}{16}$ **17.** rational, real **19.** integer, rational, real **21.** rational **23.** irrational **25.** irrational **27.** no real **31.** whole, integer, rational, real **33.** irrational, real **35.** rational, real **37.** irrational, real **39.** rational, real **41.** rational, real **43.** $-\sqrt{16}$ is the negative of the square root of 1. $\sqrt{-16}$ is undefined and not real. **55.** $x \geq 0$ **57.** $x \geq 2$ **59.** $x \leq 5$ **63.** D **65.** C **67.** 17 **69.** 7 **71.** −27 **73.** 81

4-8 Exercises

1. 15 **3.** 8.5 **5.** 8 **7.** 16 **9.** 13 **11.** 11.7 **13.** 12.4 **15.** 17 mi **17.** $\sqrt{65} \approx 8.1$ **19.** 78 **21.** $\sqrt{1391} \approx 37.3$ **23.** no **25.** yes **27.** yes **29.** no **31.** 22.6 ft **37.** G **39.** 9 **41.** 51 **43.** 6.48 **45.** 8.19

Chapter 4 Study Guide: Review

1. base, exponent **2.** irrational number **3.** scientific notation **4.** Pythagorean theorem; legs; hypotenuse **5.** real numbers **6.** 7^3 **7.** $(-3)^2$ **8.** k^4 **9.** $(-9)^1$ **10.** $(-2)^2d^2$ **11.** $(3n)^3$ **12.** $6x^2$ **13.** 10^4 **14.** 625 **15.** −32 **16.** −1 **17.** 256 **18.** −3 **19.** 64 **20.** −27 **21.** 25 **22.** 15 **23.** 1296 **24.** 100,000 **25.** −128 **26.** $\frac{1}{125}$ **27.** $-\frac{1}{64}$ **28.** $\frac{1}{11}$ **29.** $\frac{1}{10{,}000}$ **30.** 1 **31.** $-\frac{1}{36}$ **32.** $-\frac{1}{81}$ **33.** $\frac{1}{100}$ **34.** $\frac{1}{8}$ **35.** $-\frac{1}{27}$ **36.** $\frac{1}{3}$ **37.** 1 **38.** $\frac{1}{2}$ **39.** $\frac{1}{72}$ **40.** 0 **41.** 4^7 **42.** 9^6 **43.** p^4 **44.** 15^3 **45.** cannot combine **46.** x^{10} **47.** 8^3 **48.** 9^2 **49.** m^5 **50.** 3^7 **51.** 4^0 or 1 **52.** y^9 **53.** 5^3 **54.** y^5 **55.** k^0, or 1 **56.** 1620 **57.** 0.00162 **58.** 910,000 **59.** 0.000091 **60.** 8×10^{-9} **61.** 7.3×10^7 **62.** 9.6×10^{-6} **63.** 5.64×10^{10} **64.** 4 and −4 **65.** 30 and −30 **66.** 26 and −26 **67.** 5 **68.** $\frac{1}{2}$ **69.** 9 **70.** 89.4 in. **71.** 167.1 cm **72.** 9 and 10 **73.** rational **74.** irrational **75.** not a real number **76.** irrational **77.** rational **78.** not a real number **80.** 10 **81.** 10 **82.** 14.1 inches

Chapter 5

5-1 Exercises

1. $\frac{3}{7}, \frac{12}{28}$ **3.** $\frac{3}{1}, \frac{42}{14}$ **5.** $\frac{24}{34}, \frac{60}{85}$ **7.** $\frac{2}{3} \neq \frac{5}{9}$; no **9.** $\frac{2}{3} = \frac{2}{3}$; yes **11.** $\frac{2}{14}, \frac{3}{21}$ **13.** $\frac{7}{6}, \frac{28}{24}$ **15.** $\frac{22}{100}, \frac{44}{200}$ **17.** $\frac{3}{5} = \frac{3}{5}$; yes **19.** $\frac{1}{3} \neq \frac{1}{4}$; no **21.** no; $\frac{1}{3}$ **23.** no; $\frac{8}{14}$ **25.** yes **27.** no; $\frac{3}{14}$ **29.** yes **31.** no **33.** $\frac{2}{4} = \frac{3}{6}$; $\frac{2}{5} = \frac{4}{10}$; $\frac{12}{3} = \frac{4}{1}$; $\frac{12}{8} = \frac{9}{6}$ **37.** C **39.** yes **41.** > **43.** > **45.** −5.44 **47.** 0.642

5-2 Exercises

1. $\approx 7.26\text{g/cm}^3$ **3.** about 40 students per bus **5.** about 500 Calories per serving **7.** 38 oz box **9.** $3.52\ \text{g/cm}^3$ **11.** about 30 chairs per row **13.** about \$12 per CD **15.** 1 yard of ribbon **17.** 50.25 mi/h **19.** \$2.35 per taco **21.** approximately \$5 per magazine **23.** approximately 50 words per minute **25.** \$0.16/fl oz; 90 fl oz **27.** 30.9 lb **29a.** Tom: $25\frac{3}{8}$ frames per hour; Cherise: 27 frames per hour; Tina: $28\frac{3}{8}$ frames per hour **b.** Tina **c.** $1\frac{5}{8}$ **d.** 24 **33.** F **35.** $p = 20$ **37.** $w = 15$ **39.** $\frac{6}{10}, \frac{9}{15}$ **41.** $\frac{8}{22}, \frac{12}{33}$

5-3 Exercises

1. $\frac{60\text{ s}}{1\text{ min}}$ **3.** $\frac{1\text{ kg}}{1000\text{ g}}$ **5.** 7.5 mi/h **7.** $\frac{1000\text{ mm}}{1\text{m}}$ **9.** $\frac{1\text{ hr}}{60\text{ min}}$ **11.** 1.8 km/h **13.** 480 cereal boxes **15.** 6 fish **17.** ≈ 5.8 mi **19.** ≈ 1.14 g **21.** 28.75 tons **23.** 10.3 m/s **25.** ≈ 2.85 gal **31.** B **32.** H **33.** 32 **35.** 4096 **37.** 0.00000001 **39.** 128 **41.** m^{13} **43.** ≈ \$0.175 per oz **45.** \$249 per monitor

5-4 Exercises

1. yes **3.** no **5.** no **7.** 330 mi **9.** \$9 **11.** 525 **13.** 10 **15.** $5\frac{1}{3}$ in. **17.** yes **19.** yes **21.** \$103.92 **23.** \$48 **25.** 9 **27.** 24 **29.** \$22.50 **31.** $\frac{8}{4}, \frac{24}{12}$ **33.** $\frac{81}{39}, \frac{27}{13}$ **35.** $\frac{0.5}{6}, \frac{1}{12}$ **37.** 14 molecules **41.** B **43.** 16 **45.** −33 **47.** $293\frac{1}{3}$ feet per second

5-5 Exercises

1. $\triangle ABC \sim \triangle FDE$ **3.** 16.5 cm **5.** ≈ 2.98 in. **7.** similar **9.** similar **13.** $x = 6$ ft **15.** 18 in. **17.** 8 cm **23.** 70 **25.** $y = x + 3$ **27.** $y = 5.4$ **29.** $k = 5$

5-6 Exercises

1. no **3.**

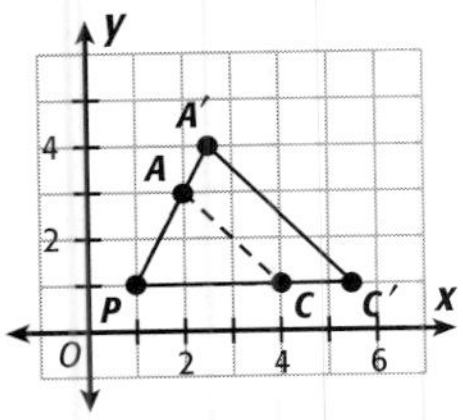

5. A′(2, −1); B′(1, −2); C′(4, −3); D′(3, −1) **7.** no **11.** A′(−9, 5); B′(15, 12); C′(−6, −9) **13.** A′(3, 6); B′(10.5, 6); C′(10.5, 0); D′(3,0) **19.** 19.2 ft; 76.8 ft; 368.64 ft² **21.** −15 **23.** 15 yd

5-7 Exercises

1. 128 yd **3.** 100 m **5.** 4 ft **7.** 7.2 m **9.** 85 ft **11.** 65 ft **15.** C **17.** $-\frac{1}{5}$ **19.** $\frac{1}{6}$ **21.** 3^4 **23.** $(-2)^3$

5-8 Exercises

1. 1 in.:1.25 ft **3.** 14 in. **5.** 1 cm = 1.5 m **7.** 7.5 ft **9.** enlarges **11.** reduces **13.** enlarges **15.** $\frac{12}{1}$ **17.** $\frac{1}{45}$ **19.** $\frac{1}{20}$ **21.** 630 ft **23.** 6.25 ft **25.** ≈18 in. **27.** ≈945 in.²; ≈6.6 ft² **29.** ≈298 ft² **31.** D **33.** rational **35.** irrational **37.** \$11.25 per hour **39.** 12 players per team

Chapter 5 Study Guide: Review

1. ratio; proportion **2.** rate; unit rate **3.** similar; scale factor
4. dilation; enlargement; reduction
5. Possible answers: $\frac{1}{2}, \frac{2}{4}$
6. Possible answers: $\frac{3}{6}, \frac{4}{8}$
7. Possible answers: $\frac{7}{12}, \frac{14}{24}$
8. yes **9.** no **10.** yes **11.** no
12. $0.30 per disk; $0.29 per disk; 75 disks **13.** $3.75 per box; $3.75 per box; unit prices are the same
14. $2.89 per divider; $4.00 per divider; 8-pack **15.** 90,000 m/h
16. 4500 ft/min **17.** $583\frac{1}{3}$ m/min
18. $x = 15$ **19.** $h = 6$ **20.** $w = 21$
21. $x = 29\frac{1}{3}$ **22.** 12.5 in.
23. 3.125 in.

24.

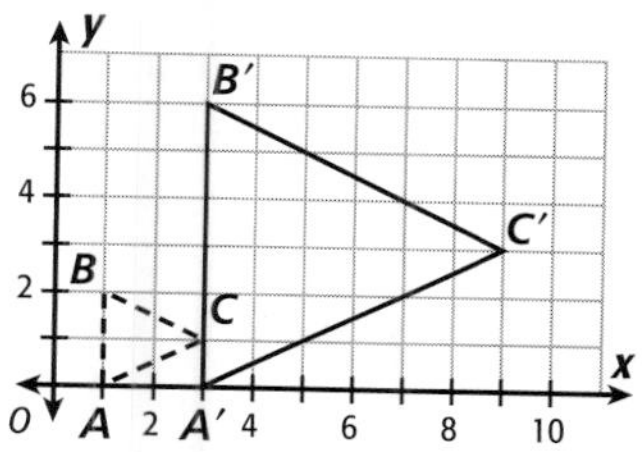

25.

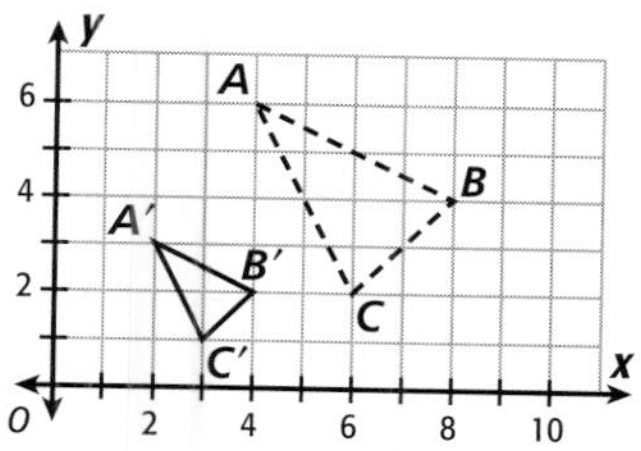

26.

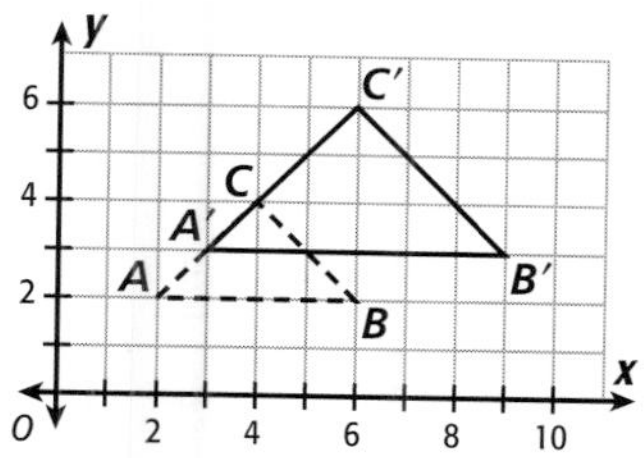

27. 18 ft **28.** 6.2 ft **29.** 64.8 m
30. 6.6 in. **31.** 1 in:16 ft **32.** 46 mi
33. 57.5 mi **34.** 153 mi **35.** 72.5 mi

Chapter 6

6-1 Exercises

1. $\frac{1}{4}$ **3.** 87.5% **5.** $<$ **7.** $=$
9. 0.3, $33\frac{1}{3}$%, 36%, $\frac{3}{8}$ **11.** $33\frac{1}{3}$%
13. $\frac{39}{100}$ **15.** 125% **17.** $<$ **19.** $=$
21. 0.04, $\frac{2}{5}$, 42%, 70%
23. 40%, 30%, 20%, 10%
25. 40%, 30%, 25%, 5% **33.** G
35. $<$ **37.** $=$ **39.** 4

6-2 Exercises

1. 50 **3.** 30 **5.** 13 **7.** 16 **11.** 100
13. 6 **15.** 32 **17.** 9 **21.** B **23.** B
25. C **27.** 150 **29.** 40 **31.** 800
33. 30 **35.** 100 **37.** ≈ 300 cars
39. ≈ 475,000 **41.** ≈ 12 hours
43a. No **b.** Yes **47.** B **49.** B
51. 9 **53.** −64 **55.** 125 **57.** 8
59. $\frac{23}{50}$ **61.** 0.5 **63.** 0.525

6-3 Exercises

1. 49.5% **3.** 17.8% **5.** 1.6 mi
7. 400% **9.** 1% **11.** 1.0% **13.** 604 ft
15. 10 **17.** 6.9 **19.** 498 **21a.** 32
b. 48 **c.** 160 **23a.** 150 **b.** 75
c. 37.5 **27.** ≈ 49 min **29.** Lena: $11.87, Ana: $12.36, Joseph: $12.50, George: $12.71 **33.** G **35.** $x = 2$
37. $b = 5$ **39.** 100 **41.** 40

6-4 Exercises

1. 60 **3.** 166 **5.** ≈ 2.4 oz **7.** 135
9. 1333.3 **11.** 400 cards **13a.** 250
b. 125 **c.** 62.5 **15a.** 30 **b.** 20
c. 15 **17.** 658,000 **19.** 6.7%
21. 98,000 **23.** C **25.** 5, 6 **27.** 7, 8
29. 11, 12 **31.** 2.12 **33.** $4.08\overline{3}$

6-5 Exercises

1. 48% increase **3.** 100% increase
5. $9773.60 **7.** 22% increase
9. ≈ 8.6% **11.** 33% decrease
13. 39% decrease **15.** 24% decrease **17.** $500 **19.** 120
21. 50 **23a.** $78 **b.** $117 **c.** $39
d. 80% **25.** 24,900% **31.** $7.49; $31.76 **33.** 50% **35.** 311.75

6-6 Exercises

1. $574 **3.** 11.6% **5.** $603.50
7. 3.1% **9.** $15.23 **11.** $38.07
13. $81,200 **17a.** $64,208
b. $12,717 **c.** ≈ 17.8% **d.** ≈ 19.8%
19. B **21.** yes **23.** yes
25. 50% decrease

6-7 Exercises

1. $2234.38; $9384.38 **3.** $1430.24
5. $23,032.50 **7.** $1473.60
9. $94.50, $409.50 **11.** $446.25, $4696.25 **13.** $9.26, $626.26
15. $195.75, $1,095.75 **17.** $340, $2040 **25.** G **27.** 1 gal/4 qt
29. 95

Chapter 6 Study Guide: Review

1. percent **2.** percent change
3. commission **4.** 0.4375
5. 43.75% **6.** $1\frac{1}{8}$ **7.** 112.5% **8.** $\frac{7}{10}$
9. 0.7 **10.** 30 **11.** 62 **12.** 3.3
13. 18 **14.** $7.50 **15.** $16.00
16. 33% **17.** 4200 ft **18.** 7930 mi
19. 5 lb 7 oz **20.** 16%
21. 472,750% **22.** 34.4%
23. $16,830 **24.** $3.55
25. $3171.88 **26.** $400 **27.** 7%
28. 0.5 yr **29.** $1000 at 3.75% for 3 years; $7.50

Chapter 7

7-1 Exercises

1. points X, Y, Z **3.** plane A or plane XYZ **5.** $\overrightarrow{XY}, \overrightarrow{YZ}, \overrightarrow{YX}$
7. $\angle BEC, \angle CED$ **9.** $\angle BEC$ and $\angle CED$ **11.** 105° **13.** points J, K, L, M **15.** plane N or plane JKL
17. $\overrightarrow{KJ}, \overrightarrow{KL}, \overrightarrow{KM}, \overrightarrow{LK}, \overrightarrow{MK}$
19. $\angle VWZ, \angle YWX$ **21.** $\angle VWZ$, $\angle YWX$ **23.** 126° **25.** False
27. False **29.** False **31.** False
33. False **35.** 30°, 60° **37.** 140°
41. 117° **43.** w^7 **45.** 11^{15}

7-2 Exercises

1. $\angle 1 \cong \angle 4 \cong \angle 5 \cong \angle 8 (45°)$; $\angle 2 \cong \angle 3 \cong \angle 6 \cong \angle 7 (135°)$ **3.** 62° **5.** 62° **7.** 70° **9.** 110° **11.** $\angle 4$, $\angle 5$, and $\angle 8$ **13.** Possible answers: $\angle 1$ and $\angle 2$, $\angle 1$ and $\angle 3$, $\angle 3$ and $\angle 4$ **15.** 129° **17.** 89° **27.** The measures of the remaining angles are 90°. The transversal is perpendicular to the parallel lines. **29.** 18,250 **31.** 25°

7-3 Exercises

1. 77° **3.** 120° **5.** 56° **7.** 60°, 30°, 90° **9.** 58° **11.** 60° **13.** $2g° = 20°$, $7g° = 70°$, $9g° = 90°$ **15.** 57° **17.** 30° **19.** 15° **27.** 52° **29.** 64° **31.** C **33.** $x° = 30°$, $y° = 100°$; $z° = 50°$ **35.** 105°, obtuse **37.** 8 and 9 **39.** 17 and 18 **41.** 55° **43.** 146°

7-4 Exercises

1. 360° **3.** 900° **5.** $v° \approx 128.6°$ **7.** quadrilateral, trapezoid **9.** quadrilateral, parallelogram, rectangle **11.** 1080° **13.** $m° = 135°$ **15.** $v° = 144°$ **17.** quadrilateral, parallelogram **19.** 3240°; 162° **21.** 10,440°; 174° **23.** 2520°; 157.5° **25.** $y° = 95°$ **27.** $z° = 97°$ **29.** $m° = 40°$ **31.** pentagon **33.** 11-gon **37.** not possible **43.** regular hexagon **45.** −50 **47.** −71

7-5 Exercises

1. 0 **3.** positive slope; 1 **5.** $\overleftrightarrow{AN} \parallel \overleftrightarrow{CD}$ **7.** parallelogram, rhombus, rectangle, square

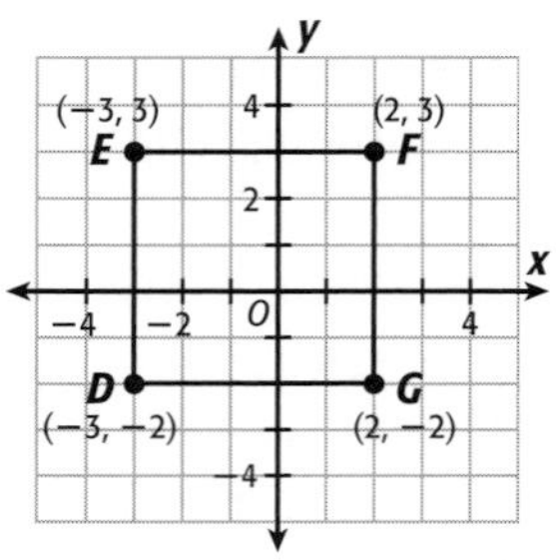

9. $C(2, -1)$ **11.** positive slope, 1 **13.** 0 **15.** $\overleftrightarrow{CD} \parallel \overleftrightarrow{AB}$

17.

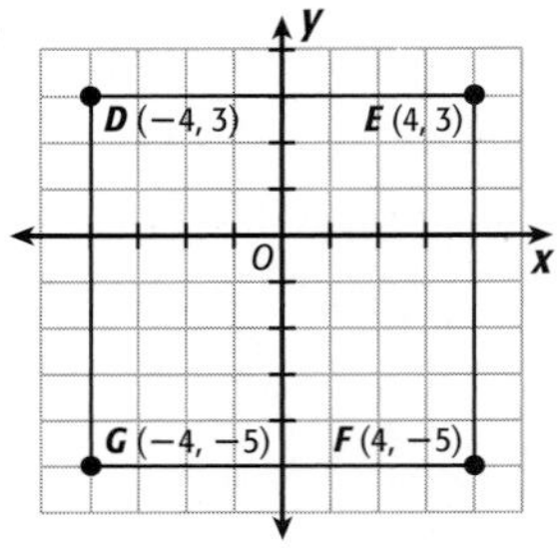

19. $C(4, -1)$ **21.** 3 **23.** 0 **25.** slope $\overleftrightarrow{PE} = 2$ **31.** true **33.** false **35.** true **37.** D; rectangle **39.** B; right triangle **45.** A **47.** 20 **49.** 1500 **51.** 2,340° **53.** $180°(n - 2)$

7-6 Exercises

1. triangle $ABC \cong$ triangle FED **3.** $q = 5$ **5.** $s = 7$ **7.** quadrilateral $PQRS \cong$ quadrilateral $ZYXW$ **9.** $n = 7$ **11.** $x = 19$, $y = 27$, $z = 18.1$ **13.** $r = 24$, $s = 120$, $t = 48$ **15.** 62° **19.** C **21.** 3 **23.** 2 **25.** 26 **27.** 90° **29.** 33

7-7 Exercises

1. reflection

3.

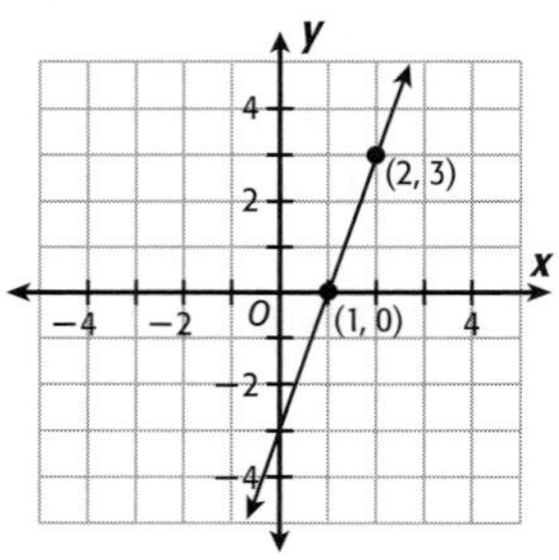

5.

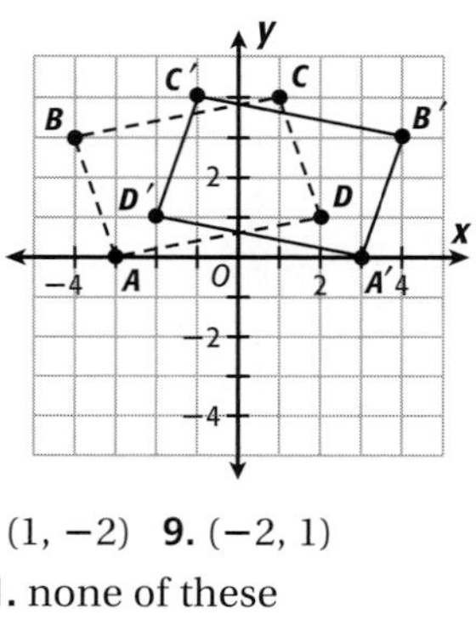

7. (1, −2) **9.** (−2, 1) **11.** none of these

13.

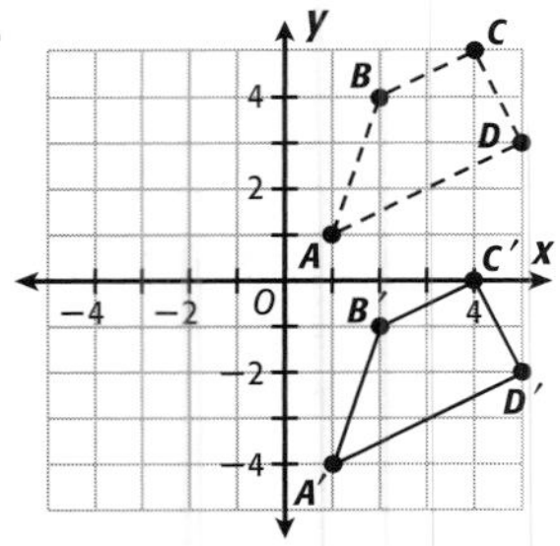

15.

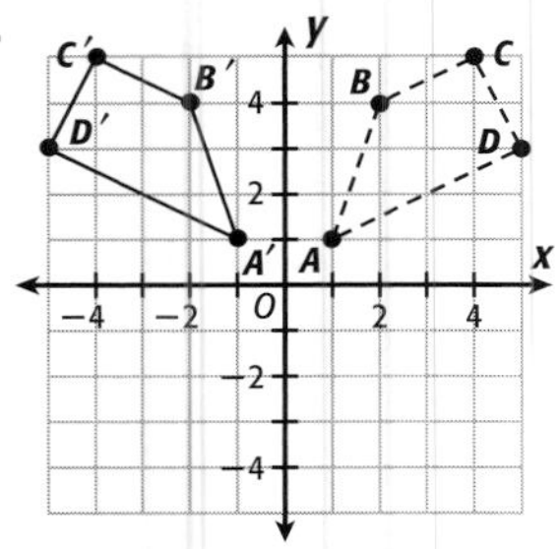

17. (−5, 2) **19.** (2, 2) **25.** (−3, −2) **27.** (−5, −2) **29.** $(-m, n)$ **31.** (4, −5) **37.** The vertices of the image are (1, 4), (5, 5), and (3, −1). **39.** 17% increase **41.** 0

7-8 Exercises

1.

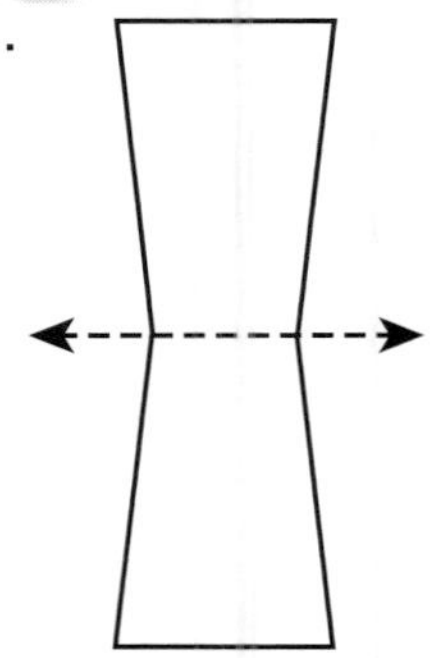

3.

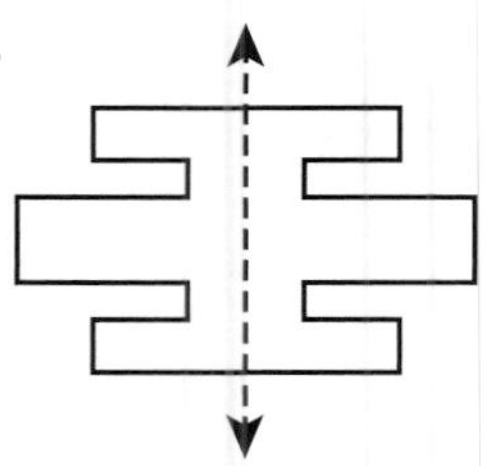

5.

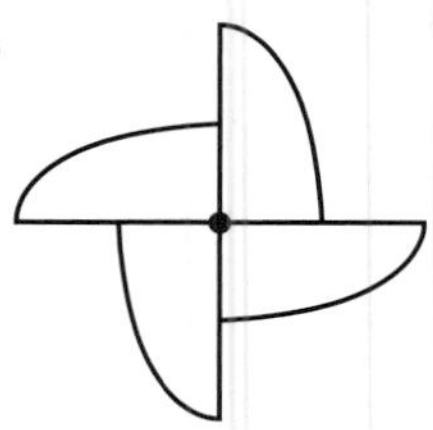

7.

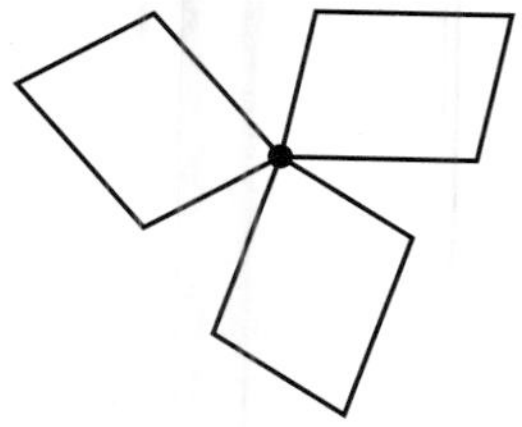

9.

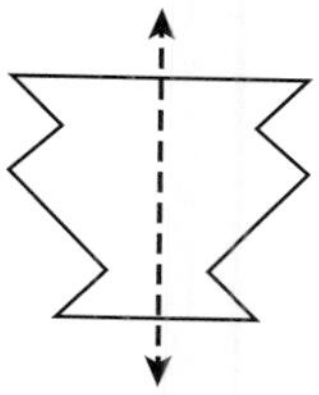

11.

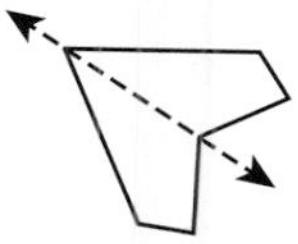

13.

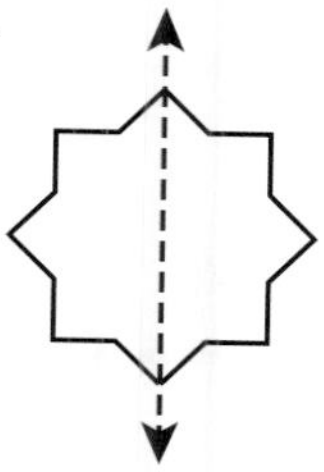

15.

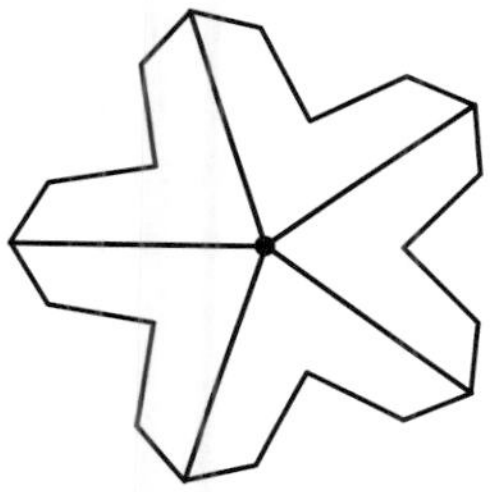

21. 2 lines **23.** 1 line **25.** 2 lines
31. G **33.** 31 mi/h **35.** $j = 5$
37. $m = 4$

7-9 Exercises

1.

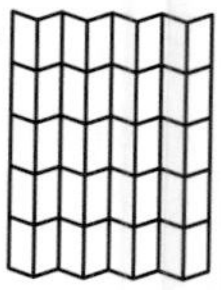

7.

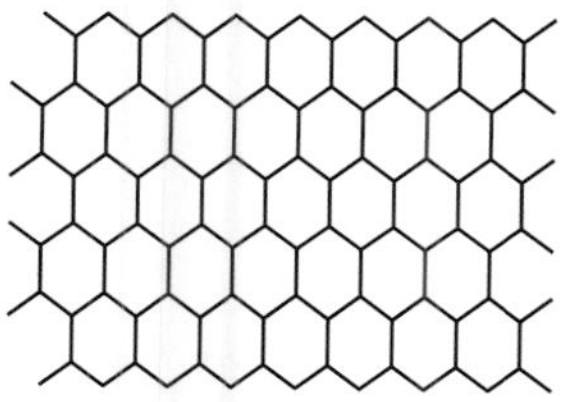

9.

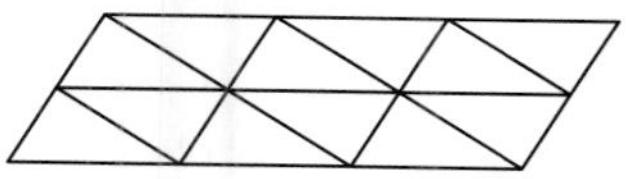

11. yes **15.** hexagon
21. 4.5×10^{-7} **23.** perpendicular

Chapter 7 Study Guide: Review

1. parallel lines; perpendicular lines **2.** rectangle; rhombus
3. 112° **4.** 68° **5.** 112° **6.** 66°
7. 114° **8.** 66° **9.** 66° **10.** 114°
11. $m^0 = 26°$ **12.** 135° **13.** 147.3°

14.

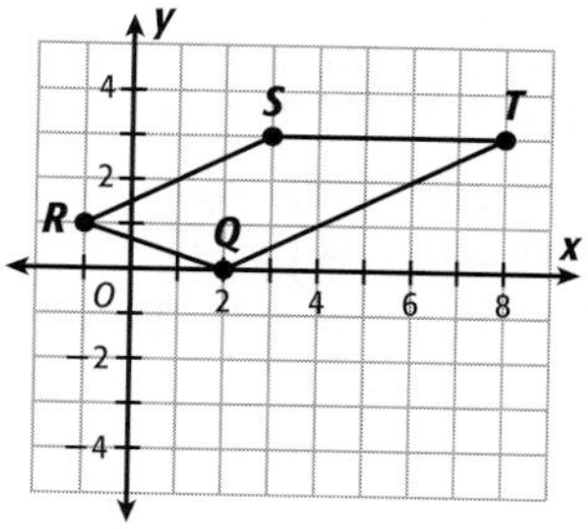

trapezoid

15.

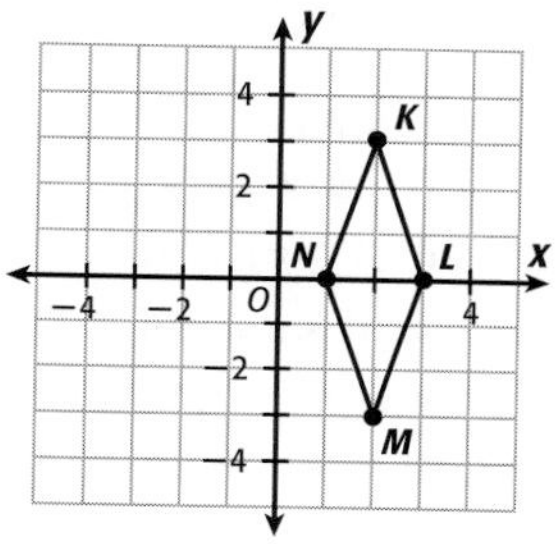

16.

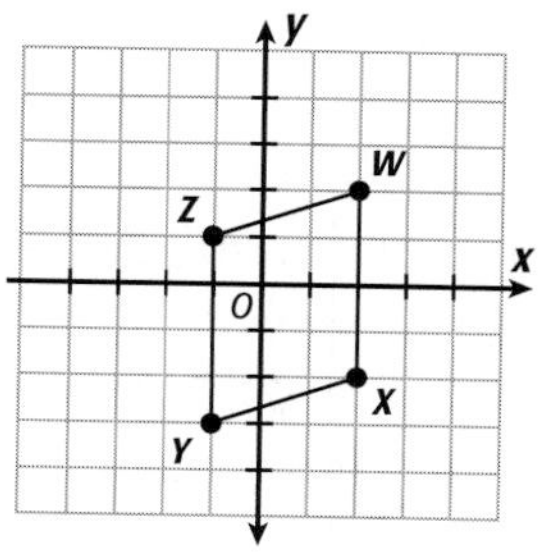

17. $x = 19$ **18.** $t = 2.4$
19. $q = 7$

20.

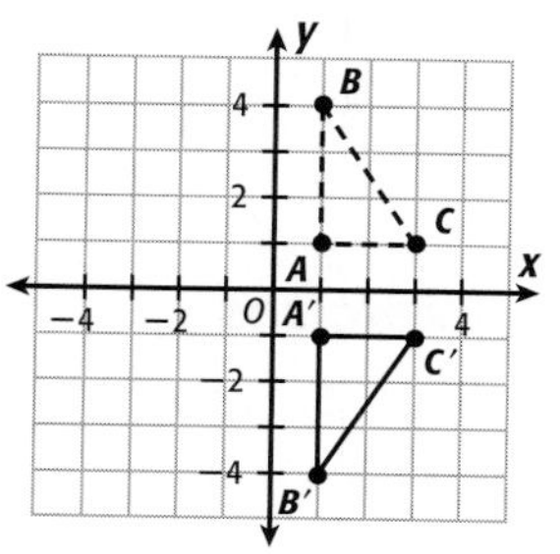

21.

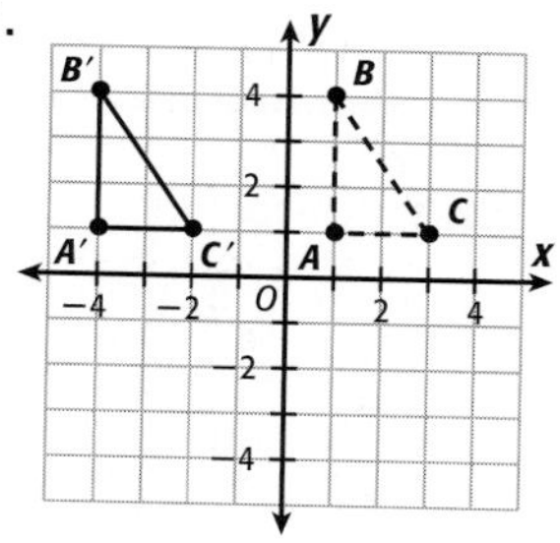

22.

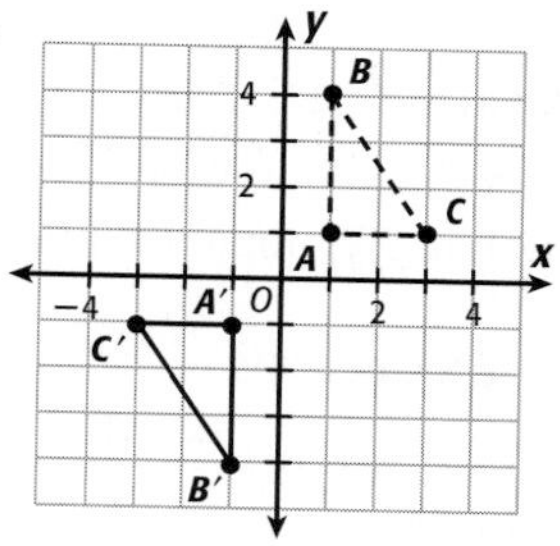

23.

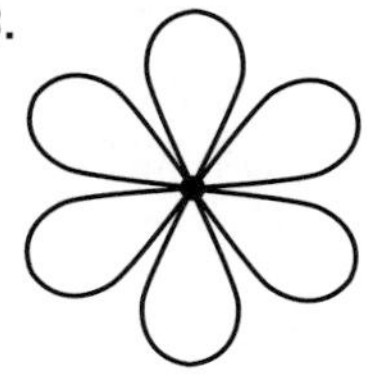

24.

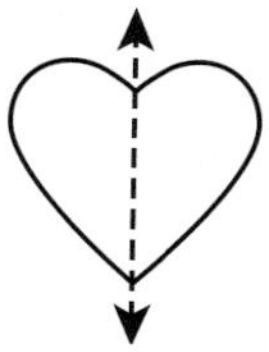

25.

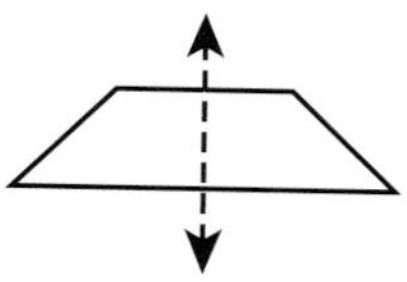

26. Possible answer:

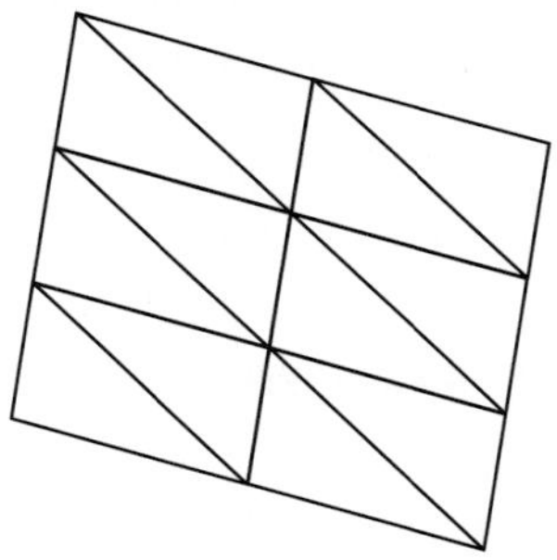

27. Possible answer:

Chapter 8

8-1 Exercises

1. 28 cm **3.** 12.2x ft **5.** 18 units^2 **7.** 14 units^2 **9.** 42 cm **11.** 26x units **13.** 24 units^2 **15.** 12 units^2 **17.** 64 units **19.** 18 ft; 10.5 ft^2 **21.** $3375 **23.** 42,000 mi^2 **27.** B **29.** $x = -4$ **31.** $a = -37$ **33.** rational **35.** rational **37.** not a real number

8-2 Exercises

1. 102 ft **3.** 30 units **5.** 19 **7.** 51.2 in. **9.** 42 units^2 **11.** 25 units^2 **13.** 70 ft **15.** 15 **17.** 21 **19.** 20 units^2 **21.** 12 units^2 **23.** 60 units^2 **25.** 25x units^2 **27.** 9.1 ft **29.** 1929.5 ft^2 **31.** 2747.9 ft^2 **33.** 273 ft^2 **37.** 7.1 **39.** $\frac{\text{1 quart}}{\text{2 pints}}$ **41.** 45 units^2

8-3 Exercises

1. 6π cm; 18.8 cm **3.** 16.8π ft^2; 52.8 ft^2 **5.** $A = 4\pi$ units^2; 12.6 units^2; $C = 4\pi$ units; 12.6 units **7.** 18π in.; 56.5 in. **9.** 256π cm^2 803.8 cm^2 **11.** $A = 16\pi$ units^2; 50.2 units^2; $C = 8\pi$ units; 25.1 units **13.** $C \approx 10.7$ m; $A \approx 9.1$ m^2 **15.** $C \approx 56.5$ in.; $A \approx 254.3$ in^2 **17.** 6.4 cm **19.** 6 cm **21.** 11.7 m **23.** 248.1 m^2 **25.** $C = 30\pi$ ft $\approx$ 94.2 ft; $A = 225\pi$ ft$^2 \approx 706.5$ ft^2 **31.** 785 **33.** 50° **35.** 65° **37.** 24 units^2

8-4 Exercises

1. vertices: J, K, L, M, N, P, Q, R edges: $\overline{JK}, \overline{KL}, \overline{LM}, \overline{MJ}$, etc.; faces: quadrilaterals $JKLM$, $PQRN$, etc. **17.** D **19.** $1.79 **21.** $128.58 **23.** 226.9 in.^{2}

8-5 Exercises

1. 463.1 cm^3 **3.** 1256 m^3 **5.** $\approx$ 1500 ft^3 **7.** 300 in^3 **9.** 351 m^3 **11.** $\approx$ 60 cm^3 **13a.** 800 in^3 **15a.** 46,200,000 in^3 **b.** about 18.8 ft **21.** J **23.** (5, −9) **25.** 4 in.

8-6 Exercises

1. 20 cm^3 **3.** 99.7 ft^3 **5.** 9.1 cm^3 **7.** Yes **9.** 160.29 in^3 **11.** 35.0 m^3 **13.** 66.2 ft^3 **15.** 5494.5 units^3 **17.** 13,083.33 m^3 **19.** 6 in. **21.** 11 ft **23.** 600 in^3 **25.** 301,056 ft^3 **29.** A **31.** 4 cm **33.** $t = 8$ **35.** $t = 0$

8-7 Exercises

1. 791.3 cm^2 **3.** 61.8 m^2 **7.** 1160 mm^2 **9.** no **11.** $1920\pi \approx$ 6028.8 mm^2 **13.** 4 m **15.** $34.56 **17.** at least 2 quarts **21.** J **23.** 0.3 **25.** −0.26 **27.** 12 units^2 **29.** 9 units^2

8-8 Exercises

1. 105 m^2 **3.** 144 m^2 **5.** $\approx$ 702.5 ft^2 **7.** 125.6 mm^2 **9.** no **11.** 0.18 km^2 **13.** $\approx$ 877,201,312 mi^2 **15a.** $\approx$ 481; $\approx$ 277 **b.** Menkaure; $\approx$ 191,684 ft^2 **c.** Khufu; 91,636,272 ft^3 **19.** B **21.** 8 **23.** 10 **25.** 120 ft^3

8-9 Exercises

1. 36π cm^3; 113.0 cm^3 **3.** 6.6π m^3; 207 m^3 **5.** 4π in^2; 12.6 in^2 **7.** 256π cm^2; 803.8 cm^2 **9.** The volume of the sphere and the cube are about equal **11.** 246.9π cm^3 **13.** 1.3π in^3 **15.** 207.4π m^2 **17.** 400π cm^2 **19.** 366.17π in^3 **21.** $V = 52.41\pi \approx 164.55$ yd^3; $S = 46.24\pi \approx 145.19$ yd^2 **23.** 30 km **25.** $\approx$ 5392 cm^3 **27.** $\approx$ 3.14 cm^2 **29.** J **31.** 12 **33.** 13 **35.** 1 **37.** 24,021 cm^2

8-10 Exercises

1. 4:1 **3.** 64:1 **5.** 112 min **7.** 4:1 **9.** 32 cm **11.** 1 cm **13.** 9 cm **15.** 7 cm **17.** 1,000,000 cm^3 **21a.** 2508.8 in^3; $\approx$ 10.9 gal **b.** about 2541 in^3 **25.** D **29.** $w = 2$ **31.** 1869.4 ft^2 **33.** 1256 cm^2

Chapter 8 Study Guide: Review

1. perimeter, area **2.** edge, vertex **3.** about 7.18 in^2, 12 in. **4.** 198 m^2, 80 m **5.** 9 cm^2 **6.** 16 in^2 **7.** 452.16 in^2 **8.** 55.3896 cm^2 **9.** 28.26 m^2 **10.** 1.1304 ft^2

11.
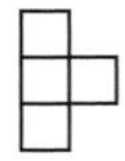

12.
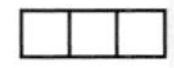

13.
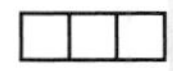

14. 339.12 cm^3 **15.** 1053 ft^3 **16.** 320 ft^3 **17.** 37.68 in^3 **18.** 680 mm^2 **19.** 132 cm^2 **20.** 439.6 in^2 **21.** 904.32 in^3 **22.** 24,416.64 m^3 **23.** 3 times as small **24.** 9 times as small **25.** 27 times as small

Chapter 9

9-1 Exercises

1. systematic **3.** Population: pet store customers **5.** voluntary response **7.** Population: people who attend the team's games **9.** convenience **11.** voluntary response **13.** stratified **15.** Population: city residents **21.** D **23.** 5 **25.** 6 **27.** 7^6 **29.** x^8

9-2 Exercises

1.
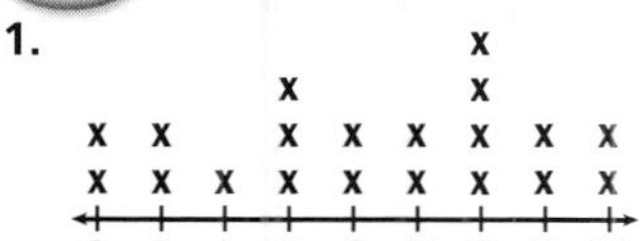

3. 63, 66, 68, 73, 73, 75, 77, 80, 81, 81, 90, 94, 95, 99 **7.** 50, 51, 54, 58, 62, 66, 67, 71, 74, 75, 76, 76, 82

9.

Coldest		Warmest
7 0	1	
7 5	2	
6 6 2	3	
8 6	4	0 3 4 7
	5	0 1 2 9
	6	2

Key: 7|1| means 17°
|4|0 means 40°

11. 13, 12, 11,14,10, 8, 9, 15 **13.** African Americans older than

40 years **15.** African Americans who are not married **17.** 27 **19.** 61 **25.** 3 **27.** 48 **29.** systematic

9-3 Exercises

1. ≈ 34, 43, 35, no mode **3.** 5 **5.** range **7.** mean **9.** 87.6 **11.** 5.85 **13.** median **15.** mean **17.** mode **19a.** 3,625,00,000 miles **b.** median **25.** 60.4 **27.** 564.7 **29.** Population: shoppers; sample: paid shoppers at a mall

9-4 Exercises

1. 52

3.

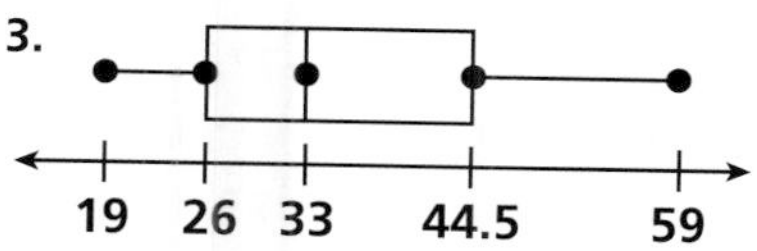

5. The medians are equal, but data set B has a much greater range.

7. 45.5

9.

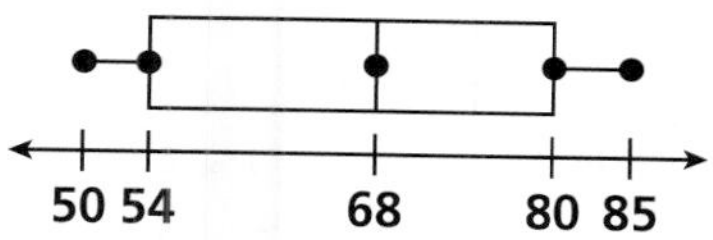

11. Data set X has a greater median. **13.** 68; 85 **15.** 35

17.

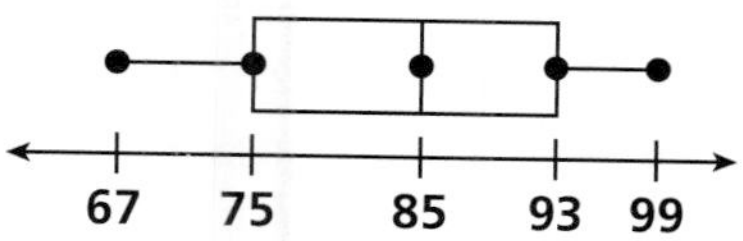

19.

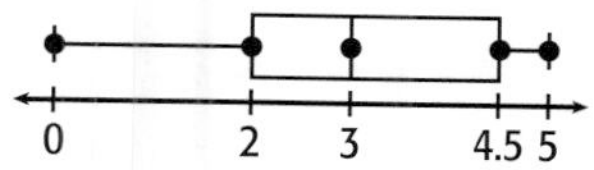

27. Range: 25 **29.** 9 and −9 **31.** 1 and −1 **33.** 15.5

9-5 Exercises

1.

Data	Frequency Data Set 1	Frequency Data Set 2
9	1	2
10	3	2
11	3	4
12	2	3
13	3	1

3. male: approximately 73.5 yr; female: approximately 79.5 yr

5.

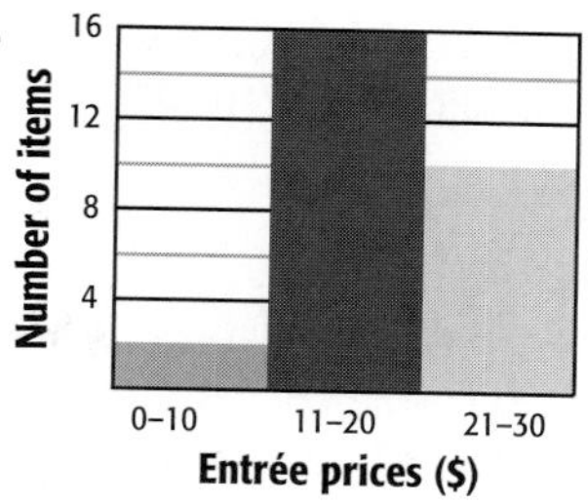

7.

Data	Frequency Data Set 1	Frequency Data Set 2
1	4	5
2	4	3
3	2	4
4	3	2
5	3	3
6	4	3

13. C **15.** 2,880 **17.** 900 **19.** 882

9-6 Exercises

1. Possible answer: The scale does not start at zero, so changes appear exaggerated. **3.** Possible answer: The fruits are all different sizes. **5.** Possible answer: The graph has no scale, so it's impossible to compare the money earned. **7.** Possible answer: The difference between the two groups' responses is only 2. **13.** B **15.** 32 units^2

9-7 Exercises

1.

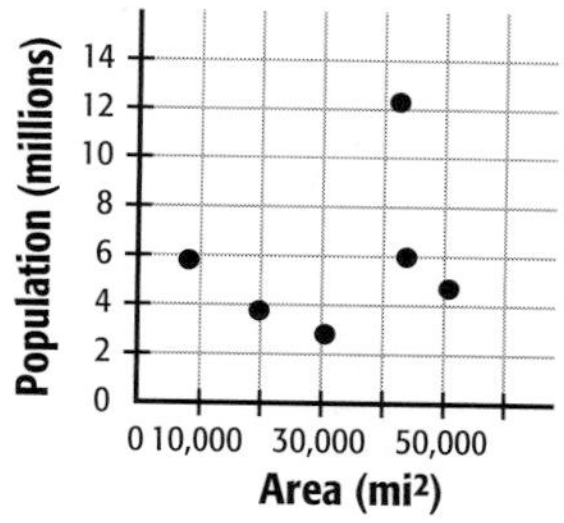

3. no correlation

5.

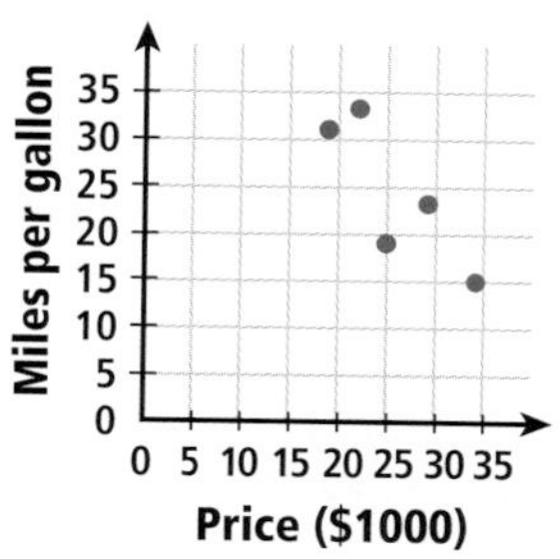

7. positive **9.** positive **11.** negative **15.** no correlation **17.** 3 **19.** The sample size is too small.

9-8 Exercises

1. bar graph **3.** circle graph **5.** line graph **7.** circle graph **15.** mode: 22 **17.** 84.9 yd^2

Chapter 9 Study Guide: Review

1. median **2.** variability **3.** line of best fit **4.** population: moviegoers **5.** sample: 100 people who own cell phones **6.** sample: 50 parents of middle-school-aged children

7.

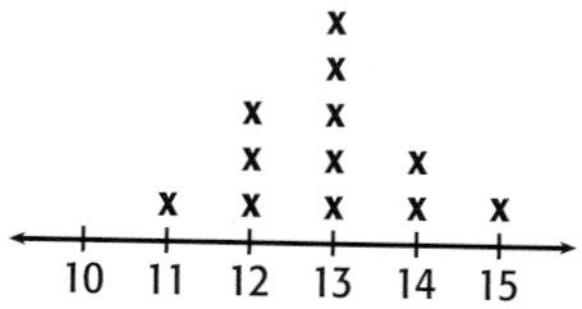

8. median

9.

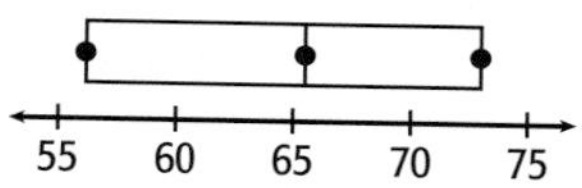

10.

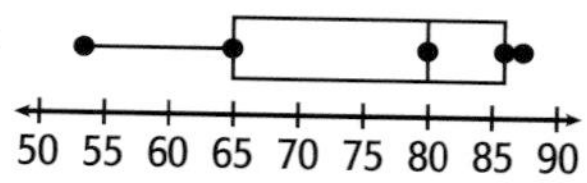

11.

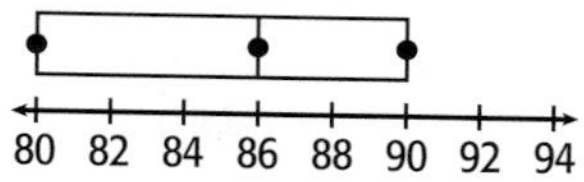

12.

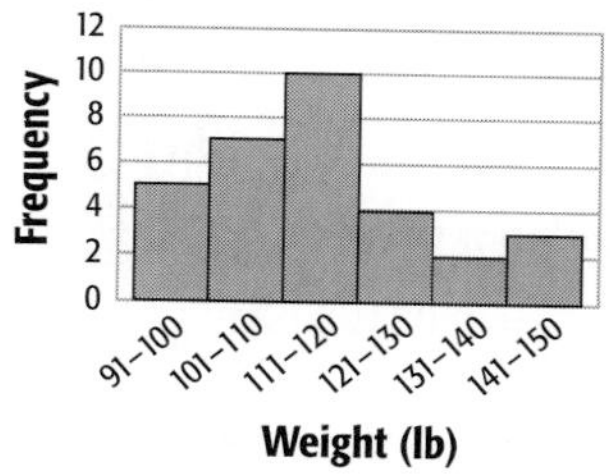

13.

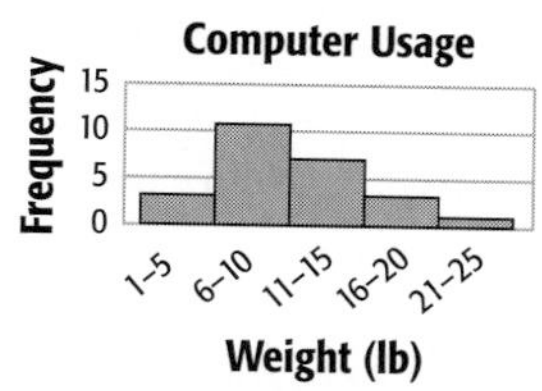

14. Different sized icons represent the same number of pizzas ordered. **15.** no correlation **16.** circle graph

Selected Answers

Chapter 10

10-1 Exercises

1. 0.6; 0.4 **3.** 0.709 **5.** $\frac{1}{3}$; $\frac{1}{3}$; $\frac{1}{6}$; $\frac{1}{6}$
7. 0.72 **9.** 0.885 **11.** 0.784
13. 0.545 **19.** A **21.** 0.0001
23. 0.00001 **25.** undefined
27. $-\frac{3}{2}$

10-2 Exercises

1. 0.34 **3.** more likely to walk
5. ≈ 0.319 **7.** more likely to have one sibling **9.** 0.25 **11.** 0.025
13. 0.35 **15.** 0.3 **19.** 51 **21.** −4.4
23. $\frac{3}{8}$ **25.** $\frac{1}{8}$

10-3 Exercises

13. B **15.** $\frac{2 \text{ pints}}{1 \text{ quart}}$ **17.** $\frac{1 \text{ m}}{1000 \text{ mm}}$
19. 0.16

10-4 Exercises

1. $\frac{1}{2}$ **3.** $\frac{1}{12}$ **5.** $\frac{1}{4}$ **7.** red **9.** 0 **11.** $\frac{5}{6}$
13. $\frac{1}{18}$ **15.** 1 **17.** 30 **19.** $\frac{1}{8}$ **21.** $\frac{1}{2}$
23. $\frac{1}{8}$ **25.** $\frac{1}{2}$ **29.** $\frac{5}{6}$ **31.** yes **33.** no

10-5 Exercises

1. dependent **3.** $\frac{1}{32}$ **5.** $\frac{10}{253}$
7. independent **9.** $\frac{1}{2}$ **11.** $\frac{5}{24}$ **13.** $\frac{4}{27}$
15. $\frac{1}{32} = 0.03125$ **21.** $\frac{1}{9}$ **23.** 52

10-6 Exercises

1. 525 **3.** 8 **5.** not fair **7.** 5
9. fair **11.** 25 **13.** 0 **17.** 54 **21.** A
23. 208 units^2 **25.** $40m$ units^2
27. The volume is 8 times as large.

10-7 Exercises

1. 1:135 **3.** $\frac{1}{142{,}000}$ **5.** 1:79
7. 1:2240 **9.** $\frac{1}{9000}$ **11.** 1:619
13. 1:35; 35:1 **15.** 1:11; 11:1
17. 1:1; 1:1 **19.** 1:1 **21.** 1:2 **27.** B
29. $30, $330 **31.** fair

10-8 Exercises

1. 676,000 **3.** 0.729 **5.** 8
7. ≈ 0.7865 **9.** 24 shirts **11.** 18
13. 9 **15.** 12 **17.** 2,176,782,336
19. 5400 **23.** G **25.** 16 **27.** $\frac{7}{4}$
29. 10%

10-9 Exercises

1. 720 **3.** 15,120 **5.** 39,916,800
7. 56 **9.** 24 **11.** 24 **13.** 5040
15. 10,518,300 **17.** 336
19. 3,628,800 **21.** 1 **23.** 132 **25.** 1
27. 1 **29.** 1 **31.** n **33.** 5040
35. 1320 **37.** 462 **41.** A **45.** 60

Chapter 10 Study Guide: Review

1. probability **2.** sample space
3. permutation **4.** 0.85, 0.15
5. 0.15 **7.** $\frac{4}{15}$ **8.** $\frac{1}{1296}$ **9.** $\frac{13}{51}$
10. 20 laps **11.** 3:10 **12.** 2,600,000
13. ≈ 0.59 **14.** 120 **15.** 210

Chapter 11

11-1 Exercises

1. $5x$ **3.** $12f + 8$ **5.** $6p - 9$
7. $5x + 8y$ **9.** $9x + y$
11. $7g + 5h - 12$ **13.** $r + 12$
15. $2t + 56$ **17.** $y = 15$ **19.** $13y$
21. $6a + 15$ **23.** $5x + 3$ **25.** $9p$
27. $13x + 5$ **29.** $6a + z$
31. $9x + 6q + 2$ **33.** $9a + 8c + 5$
35. $12y - 14$ **37.** $12y + 23$
39. $19x - 16$ **41.** $p = 6$ **43.** $y = 8$
45. $x = 12$ **47.** $12x$ **49.** $7d + 1$
51. $x = 3$ **53.** $49g + 53s + 44b$
59. D **63.** 28% increase
65. 57% increase

11-2 Exercises

1. $d = 3$ **3.** $e = 6$ **5.** $h = 7$
7. $x = -1$ **9.** $p = -1$ **11.** 6
13. $k = -10$ **15.** $w = 3$ **17.** $y = 5$
19. $h = 6$ **21.** $m = 2$ **23.** $x = -12$
25. $n = 2$ **27.** $b = -13$ **29.** $x = 17$
31. $y = -7$ **33.** $11.80 per hour
35. 31 and 32 **37.** 212°F **41.** C
43. 27 in^3 **45.** 15 **47.** $5a - b + 4$

11-3 Exercises

1. $x = 1$ **3.** $x = 2$ **5.** $x = -20$
7. $x = 1$ **9.** $d = 5$ **11.** 2.5 min
13. $n = 4$ **15.** $n = 1$ **17.** $x = 1$
19. $p = 2$ **21.** $n = 5$ **23.** 3 h
25. $y = 2$ **27.** $n = 5$ **29.** $x = 5$
31. 350 units **33.** 22, 23 **39.** J
41. 7.39×10^9 **43.** -4.1×10^6
45. $x = 0.5$

11-4 Exercises

1. $r > 18$ **3.** $120 \geq j$, or $j \leq 120$
5. $-40 \geq a$, or $a \leq -40$
7. $r > -63$ **9.** 104 sandwiches: $\frac{\$400}{\$3.85}$ **11.** $75 < x$, or $x > 75$
13. $-77 \geq p$, or $p \leq -77$
15. $h > 12$ **17.** $q \geq -4$ **19.** $6 > r$, or $r < 6$ **21.** $w \geq -3$ **23.** $t < 95$
25. $a < 120$ **27.** $x < 11$ **29.** $n \geq 9$
31. $x \geq -128$ **35.** C **39.** C
41. $\frac{3}{36}$, or $\frac{1}{12}$ **43.** $\frac{1}{36}$

11-5 Exercises

1. $k > 2$ **3.** $y < -8$ **5.** $y \geq 7$
7. $x < 3$ **9.** $h \leq 1$ **11.** $d < -1$
13. at least 21 caps **15.** $x > 4$
17. $q \leq 2$ **19.** $x \leq -7$ **21.** $a \geq -3$
23. $k \geq 3$ **25.** $r < 3$ **27.** $p \leq \frac{22}{3}$
29. $w > -1$ **31.** $a > \frac{1}{2}$ **33.** $q < 6$
35. $b < 2.7$ **37.** $f \leq -27$ **39.** 7
41. at least 31 beads **43a.** $158
b. 17 mo **47.** B **53.** $a = 4$

11-6 Exercises

1. (2, 3) **3.** (−4, 7) **5.** (0, 7)
7. (5, 3) **9.** (1, 10) **11.** (−9, 3)
13. (−1, 1) **15.** (2, 7) **17.** (2, 5)
19. (2, 3) **21.** (1, 3) **23.** (7, −3)
25. 4 bookmarks and 3 wall hangings **27.** (2, −17) **29.** (2, 1)
31. (−1.3, 5.8) **33.** no solution
35. 25 dimes and 10 quarters
37. $x = 11$ and $y = 6$ **41.** 6
43. $d = 21$ **45.** $w = 12$ **47.** $p = 3$

Chapter 11 Study Guide: Review

1. system of equations **2.** like terms **3.** solution of a system of equations **4.** terms **5.** $19m - 10$ **6.** $14w + 6$ **7.** $2x + 3y$ **8.** $2t^2 - 4t + 3t^3$ **9.** $y = 6$ **10.** $z = 7$ **11.** $y = 5$ **12.** $z = 8$ **13.** $y = -1$ **14.** $h = 2$ **15.** $t = -1$ **16.** $r = 3$ **17.** $z = 2$ **18.** $a = 12$ **19.** $s = 7$ **20.** $c = 24$ **21.** $x = \frac{1}{6}$ **22.** $y = \frac{2}{3}$ **23.** no solution **24.** $z = 5$ **25.** $m \geq 18$ **26.** $n \leq -3$ **27.** $t > -16$ **28.** $p < -3$ **29.** $b \geq -27$ **30.** $a > 8$ **31.** $z > 1$ **32.** $h \geq 6$ **33.** $a < 24$ **34.** $x \geq -1$ **35.** $k > 3$ **36.** $y > \frac{1}{8}$ **37.** $(-2, 1)$ **38.** $(2, 6)$ **39.** $(3, 5)$ **40.** $(3, -2)$ **41.** no solution **42.** infinite solutions **43a.** $x + y = 32$ **b.** $x = 8$

Chapter 12

12-1 Exercises

1. linear **3.** not linear **5.** linear **7.** not linear **9.** not linear **11.** linear **13.** 509.6 N **15.** $(-1, -2), (0, 0), (1, 2)$ **17.** $(-1, -6), (0, -1), (1, 4)$ **19.** $(-1, -5), (0, -3), (1, -1)$ **21.** $(-1, -6), (0, -4), (1, -2)$ **23.** $(-1, 1.5), (0, 3.5), (1, 5.5)$ **25.** $C = 2.25b + 3$ **29.** B **31.** $-8, -5, -2$ **33.** $\frac{1}{16}$ **35.** cannot combine

12-2 Exercises

1. 1 **3.** $\frac{1}{4}$ **5.** The graph shows a variable rate of change. **7.** The slope of the line is 5. **9.** $-\frac{1}{2}$ **11.** $-\frac{3}{4}$ **13.** $-\frac{6}{7}$ **15.** The graph shows a constant rate of change. **17.** The slope of the line is 4. **19.** Graph A **21.** Graph B **23.** $y = -\frac{4}{5}x + 350$ **25.** The roof is flat. **29.** H **31.** negative **33.** linear **35.** linear

12-3 Exercises

1. $(4, 0), (0, -4)$ **3.** $(-6, 0), (0, -4)$ **5.** $y = \frac{1}{3}x$ **7.** $y = \frac{1}{4}x - 4$ **9.** $m = 4.5$; $b = 25$ **11.** $y = -4x + 3$ **13.** $(2, 0), (0, 6)$ **15.** $(3, 0), (0, -12)$ **17.** $y = -3x$ **19.** $y = -2x - 2$ **21.** $m = 12$ **23.** $y = -x$ **31.** slope = 955 **33.** D **35.** \$6.35 per hour **37.** \$5.50 per burrito **39.** $\frac{5}{4}$ **41.** $\frac{1}{4}$

12-4 Exercises

7. $y - 6 = 5x$ **9.** $y - 840 = -10.5(x - 40)$ **17.** $y = 6(x + 3)$ **19.** $y - 3 = 4(x + 2)$ **21.** $y + 7 = -1(x + 5)$ **29.** G **31.** $7x - 5y + 18$ **33.** $-4x$ **35.** $y = x - 5$

12-5 Exercises

1. yes **3.** $y = 3x$ **5.** $y = \frac{1}{2}x$ **7.** $y = \frac{1}{9}x$ **9.** no **11.** $y = \frac{1}{3}x$ **13.** $y = \frac{2}{13}x$ **15.** $y = \frac{1}{10}x$ **17.** yes **19.** no **21.** No; **27.** 28 **29.** $m = 4$ **31.** $m = -0.25$

12-6 Exercises

7a. $18t + 15r \leq 450$ **b.** yes **17.** about \$70 **19.** no **21.** yes **23.** no **25.** B **29.** no **31.** $m = -6$ **33.** $y - 1 = 5(x - 4)$

12-7 Exercises

3. no **7.** positive **9.** negative **11a.** 7 **11b.** 14.6%, 22.8%, 36.6%, 51.0%, 56.4%; mean = 36.28% **15.** A **17.** $x > 4$ **19.** $x < -4$ **21.** $(16, 0), (0, -6)$ **23.** $(2, 0), (0, 13)$

Chapter 12 Study Guide: Review

1. x-intercept; y-intercept **2.** slope intercept form; point-slope form **3.** direct variation **4.** linear **5.** linear **6.** not linear **7.** not linear **8.** not linear **9.** linear **10.** not linear **11.** not linear **12.** $\frac{3}{4}$ **13.** -4 **14.** $\frac{6}{5}$ **15.** -1 **16.** -1 **17.** $\frac{3}{2}$ **18.** $-\frac{9}{4}$ **19.** $y = \frac{4}{3}x + 5$ **20.** $y = \frac{6}{5}x - 2$ **21.** $y = -\frac{2}{3}x + 4$ **22.** $y = \frac{7}{4}x + 3$ **23.** $y = 3x + 4$ **24.** $y = -3x + 2$ **25.** $y = -\frac{1}{3}x + 7$ **26.** $y = \frac{1}{2}x - \frac{5}{2}$ **27.** $y = 2x - 2$ **28.** $y = -4x - 5$ **29.** $y = -\frac{5}{6}x - 3$ **30.** $y = \frac{2}{7}x$ **31.** $y = 6x$ **32.** $y = 13x$ **33.** $y = \frac{1}{7}x$

Chapter 13

13-1 Exercises

1. yes **3.** yes **5.** no **7.** 37 **9.** -92 **11.** 6 oz **13.** yes **15.** yes **17.** yes **19.** 1.2 **21.** 1 **23.** 23, 26, 29 **25.** 51, 38, 25 **27.** 1, 3, 5, 7, 9 **29.** 0, 0.25, 0.5, 0.75, 1 **31.** 11:53, 11:46, 11:32 **33.** first: \$127.50, \$180, \$232.50, \$285 **37.** C **39.** $x = -1$ **41.** $k = -9.4$ **43.** sample: the cable companies customers whose last names begin with an "s."

13-2 Exercises

1. no **3.** yes **5.** yes **7.** 6144 **9.** $\frac{1}{9}$ **11.** \$7.18 **13.** no **15.** yes **17.** yes **19.** $952\frac{8}{49}$ **21.** 4374 **23.** 39.0625 **25.** 18, 6, 2 **27.** $-\frac{1}{27}$ **29.** 2 **31.** 30 **33.** 10 **35.** $\frac{1}{5}$ **37.** $\frac{2}{3}$ **39.** 27 **41.** 61,236 cells **43a.** yes; $\frac{3}{4}$ **b.** 26 ft **49.** yes **51.** $x = 16$ **53.** $-2p + 21$ **55.** $40 + 7y$

13-3 Exercises

1. 225 **3.** 178 **5.** $\frac{13}{15}$ **7.** 3 **9.** $\frac{2}{5}$ **11.** 2 **13.** 117 **15.** 106 **17.** 4 **19.** 2.00002 **21.** $-\frac{1}{3}$ **23.** $\frac{3}{2}$ **25.** 3rd, 6th, 9th, 12th terms **27.** 42 **29.** 880 Hz **33.** H **35.** 821,000 **37.** -1400 **39.** yes

13-4 Exercises

1. linear **3.** linear **5.** not linear **7.** $f(x) = 2x + 2$ **9.** $f(x) = 18x + 480$ **11.** linear **13.** not linear **15.** linear **17.** $f(x) = 6x - 5$ **19.** 16 lb **21a.** $f(x) = 5x + 1245$ **21b.** 2745 ft **27.** $f(t) = -50t + 1800$ **29.** $\frac{6}{19}$ **31.** $-\frac{21}{40}$ **33.** 6.7 **35.** 8.1

13-5 Exercises

7. 7.29×10^{-5} g **15.** $f(x) = 300 \cdot 3^x$ **17.** $\frac{1}{8}$, 1, 8 **19.** $\frac{1}{1000}$, 1, 1000 **21.** $f(x) = 3 \cdot 2^x$ **23.** $f(x) = 1 \cdot 4^x$ **25.** 3 hours **27.** 1.5625% **29.** It has no x-intercepts. **33.** C **35.** 1,257 mm^3 **37.** $\frac{1}{4}$

13-6 Exercises

5. 5.1 ft **11.** 15 **13.** 0 **15.** 37 **17.** $x = 4, x = -12$ **19.** $x = 1, x = -3$ **21.** 6 and 6 **27.** B **31.** 7 **33.** 7.5 ft **35.** 12.75 ft **37.** 45, 65

13-7 Exercises

1. no **7.** $y = \frac{12}{x}$ **9.** no **15.** $y = \frac{9}{x}$ **17.** $y = \frac{26}{x}$ **19.** 12 cm **21.** \$1600 **25.** D **27.** $x = 5$ **29.** $x = \frac{40}{3}$ **31.** $p < -1$

Chapter 13 Study Guide: Review

1. sequence **2.** arithmetic sequence; geometric sequence **3.** Fibonacci sequence **4.** 29 **5.** 0.85 **6.** $\frac{10}{3}$ **7.** -3072 **8.** $\frac{64}{625}$ **9.** -2 **10.** 7 **11.** 4 **12.** -3 **13.** 2 **14.** $f(x) = x - 1$ **15.** $f(x) = \frac{1}{2}x + 4$ **16.** $f(x) = -2$

Chapter 14

14-1 Exercises

1. yes **3.** no **5.** binomial **7.** not a polynomial **9.** 8 **11.** 0 **13.** yes **15.** no **17.** yes **19.** monomial **21.** trinomial **23.** not a polynomial **25.** 2 **27.** 4 **29.** 1 **31.** 8 in^3 **33.** monomial **35.** binomial **37.** trinomial **39.** not a polynomial **41.** trinomial **43.** not a polynomial **51.** 9 **53.** -3.5×10^{-5} **55.** $x = 13$ **57.** $m = 100$

14-2 Exercises

1. $-3b^2$ and $4b^2$ **3.** $7x^2 + 4x - 5$ **5.** $12x - 32$ **7.** $17a^2 - 21a$ **9.** $-t$ and $5t$ **11.** $9p^2 + 7p$ **13.** $9x^2 - 32x$ **15.** $6y^3 - 4$ **17.** $12s^2 + 2s - 3$ **19.** $2x^2 - 13x + 15$ **21.** $9m^2 - 20m$ **23.** $17mn$ **25.** $40 - 1000d^2$ **27.** $82xy + 82y$ in^2 **29.** C **31.** 51.2%

14-3 Exercises

1. $5x^3 + 3x + 6$ **3.** $11r^2s + 9rs$ **5.** $15ab^2 + 3ab - a^2b - 8$ **7.** $128 + 32w$ in. **9.** $7g^2 + g - 1$ **11.** $-3h^6 + 12h^4 - h$ **13.** $13t^2 - 4t + 12$ **15.** $-w^2 - 4w - 2$ **17.** $7w^2y + 2wy^24wy$ **19.** $\approx 6.19r^3 + 4r^2 + 5r + 2$ **27.** C **29.** 84 ft **31.** 42 ft **33.** $\frac{11}{10}$ **35.** $\frac{6}{25}$

14-4 Exercises

1. $-4x^2y$ **3.** $-3x^2 + 8x - 5$ **5.** $8x^3 - 5x + 6$ **7.** $-2b^3 + 5b^2 - b + 4$ **9.** $-4m^2n - 7mn + 3mn^2$ **11.** $-2x^2y - 5xy + 10x - 8$ **13.** $-4x^3 + 9x^2 - 12x + 21$ in^3 **15.** $-3v + 5v^2$ **17.** $-4xy^2 - 2xy$ **19.** $9b^2 + 2b + 9$ **21.** $5a - 8$ **23.** $x^2 - 3x + 4$ **25.** $-6p^3 - 5p^2 - 2p^2t^2 + 10pt^2$ **27.** $-2b + 2ab$ **29.** $6y^2 - 12x^2y + 5x^2$ **31.** $2x^2 - 6x - 1$ in^2 **33.** B **37.** $10x + 29$ **39.** ± 3 **41.** ± 13 **43.** $-zy^3 - 5zy$

14-5 Exercises

1. $-15s^3t^5$ **3.** $-35h^6j^{10}$ **5.** $35p^4r^5$ **7.** $6hm - 8h^2$ **9.** $-3x^3 + 15x^2 - 30x$ **11.** $A = \frac{1}{2}b_1h + \frac{1}{2}b_2h$ **13.** $2g^3h^8$ **15.** $-2s^5t^4$ **17.** $7.5h^3j^{10}$ **19.** $15z^3 - 12z^2$ **21.** $-6c^4d^3 + 12c^2d^3$ **23.** $-12s^4t^3 - 15s^3t^3 + 6s^4t^4$ **25.** $-24b^6$ **27.** $6a^3b^6$ **29.** $-3m^5 + 15m^3$ **31.** $x^5 - x^7y^5$ **33.** $3f^2g^2 + f^3g^2 - f^2g^5$ **35.** $20m^4p^8 - 12m^3p^7 + 24m^4p^5$ **37.** 63π **43.** $15c^3d^4 - 20c^2d^4$ **45.** 1,067.6 cm^2 **47.** $y = \frac{64}{x}$

14-6 Exercises

1. $xy + 4x - 5y - 20$ **3.** $12m^2 + 7m - 45$ **5.** $m^2 - 9m + 14$ **7.** $600 - 200x + 4x^2$ ft^2 **9.** $b^2 - 9$ **11.** $9x^2 + 30x + 25$ **13.** $v^2 + 4v - 5$ **15.** $3x^2 + 13x - 30$ **17.** $12b^2 + 11bc - 5c^2$ **19.** $12r^2 - 11rs - 5s^2$ **21.** $100 + 50x + 4x^2$ yd^2 **23.** $b^2 + 6b + 9$ **25.** $4x^2 - 9$ **27.** $a^2 + 14a + 49$ **29.** $b^2 + 7b + -60$ **31.** $t^2 - 13t + 36$ **33.** $3b^2 - 5b - 28$ **35.** $4m^2 + 11mn - 3n^2$ **37.** $r^2 - 25$ **39.** $15r^2 - 22rs + 8s^2$ **41.** $PV + bP + aV + ab = c$ **45.** B **47.** 1:5 **49.** 1:20 **51.** $-4m^2 + 12m - 24$ **53.** $-11x^2y + 4xy^2 + 16xy$

Chapter 14 Study Guide: Review

1. polynomial; degree of a polynomial **2.** FOIL; binomial **3.** binomial, trinomial **4.** trinomial **5.** not a polynomial **6.** not a polynomial **7.** monomial **8.** not a polynomial **9.** binomial **10.** 8 **11.** 4 **12.** 3 **13.** 5 **14.** 6 **15.** $7t^2 - 3t + 1$ **16.** $11gh - 9g^2h$ **17.** $20mn - 12m$ **18.** $8a^2 - 10b$ **19.** $36st^2 - 23st$ **20.** $6x^2 - 2x + 5$ **21.** $5x^4 + x^2 - x + 7$ **22.** $2h^2 + 8h + 7$ **23.** $2xy^2 - 2x^2y + 2xy$ **24.** $13n^2 + 12$ **25.** $6x^2 - 8$ **26.** $-w^2 - 12w + 14$ **27.** $-4x^2 - 16x - 14$ **28.** $4ab^2 - 11ab + 4a^2b$ **29.** $-p^3q^2 - 4p^2q^2 - 2pq^2$ **30.** $12s^2t^4 + 4s^2t^3 + 32st^3$ **31.** $12a^4b^3 + 30a^3b^3 - 36a^3b + 24a^2b^2$ **32.** $2m^3 - 16m^2 + 2m$ **33.** $10g^3h^3 - 15gh^5 + 20gh - 30h^2$ **34.** $2j^5k^3 - \frac{3}{2}j^4k^4 + j^6k^5$ **35.** $18x^7y^{14} - 15x^6y^{12} + 12x^3y^7 - 24x^3y^6$ **36.** $p^2 - 8p + 72$ **37.** $b^2 + 10b + 24$ **38.** $3r^2 + 11r - 4$ **39.** $3a^2 - 11ab - 20b$ **40.** $m^2 - 14m + 49$ **41.** $9t^2 - 36$ **42.** $6b^2 - 2bt - 28t^2$ **43.** $-3x^2 - 2x^2 + 40$ **44.** $y^2 - 22y + 121$

Glossary/Glosario

go.hrw.com
Multilingual Glossary Online
KEYWORD: MT7 Glossary

A

ENGLISH	SPANISH	EXAMPLES
absolute value The distance of a number from zero on a number line; shown by | |. (p. 15)	**valor absoluto** Distancia a la que está un número de 0 en una recta numérica. El símbolo del valor absoluto es | |.	$\|-5\| = 5$
accuracy The closeness of a given measurement or value to the actual measurement or value.	**exactitud** Cercanía de una medida o valor a la medida o valor real.	
acute angle An angle that measures less than 90°. (p. 325)	**ángulo agudo** Ángulo que mide menos de 90°.	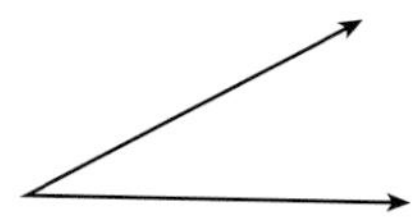
acute triangle A triangle with all angles measuring less than 90°. (p. 336)	**triángulo acutángulo** Triángulo en el que todos los ángulos miden menos de 90°.	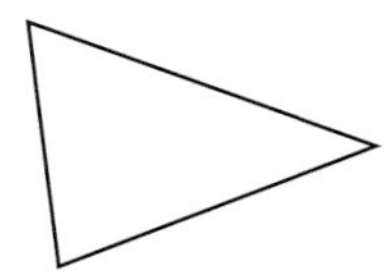
Addition Counting Principle If one group contains *m* objects and a second group contains *n* objects, and the groups have no objects in common, then there are $m + n$ total objects to choose from. (p. 559)	**Principio de conteo en suma** Si un grupo tiene *m* objetos, otro grupo tiene *n* objetos y los grupos no tienen objetos en común, entonces hay un total de $m + n$ objetos para elegir.	A restaurant offers 3 types of juice and 4 types of iced tea. There are $3 + 4 = 7$ total drinks to choose from.
Addition Property of Equality The property that states that if you add the same number to both sides of an equation, the new equation will have the same solution. (p. 34)	**Propiedad de igualdad de la suma** Propiedad que establece que puedes sumar el mismo número en ambos lados de una ecuación y la ecuación resultante tendrá la misma solución.	$\begin{array}{rcr} 14 - 6 & = & 8 \\ \underline{+6} & & \underline{+6} \\ 14 & = & 14 \end{array}$
Addition Property of Opposites The property that states that the sum of a number and its opposite equals zero.	**Propiedad de suma de los opuestos** Propiedad que establece que la suma de un número y su opuesto es cero.	$12 + (-12) = 0$
additive inverse The opposite of a number. (p. 14)	**inverso aditivo** El opuesto de un número.	The additive inverse of 5 is -5.
adjacent angles Angles in the same plane that have a common vertex and a common side.	**ángulos adyacentes** Ángulos en el mismo plano que están uno al lado del otro y comparten un vértice y un lado.	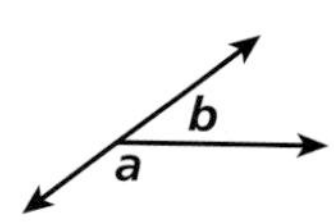

ENGLISH	SPANISH	EXAMPLES
algebraic expression An expression that contains at least one variable. (p. 6)	**expresión algebraica** Expresión que contiene una o más variables.	$x + 8$ $4(m - b)$
algebraic inequality An inequality that contains at least one variable. (p. 44)	**desigualdad algebraica** Desigualdad que contiene una o más variables.	$x + 3 > 10$ $5a > b + 3$
alternate exterior angles A pair of angles on the outer sides of two lines cut by a transversal that are on opposite sides of the transversal. (p. 331)	**ángulos alternos externos** Par de ángulos en los lados externos de dos líneas intersecadas por una transversal, que están en lados opuestos de la transversal.	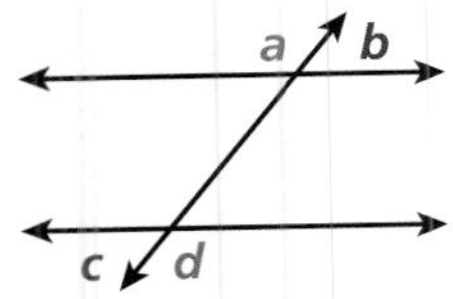 ∠a and ∠d are alternate exterior angles.
alternate interior angles A pair of angles on the inner sides of two lines cut by a transversal that are on opposite sides of the transversal. (p. 331)	**ángulos alternos internos** Par de ángulos en los lados internos de dos líneas intersecadas por una transversal, que están en lados opuestos de la transversal.	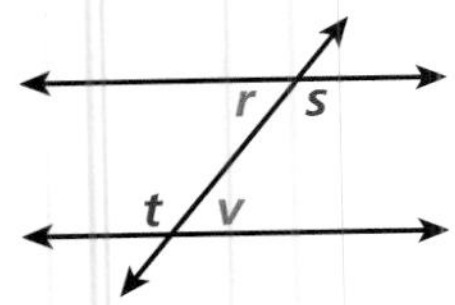 ∠r and ∠v are alternate interior angles.
angle A figure formed by two rays with a common endpoint called the vertex. (p. 325)	**ángulo** Figura formada por dos rayos con un extremo común llamado vértice.	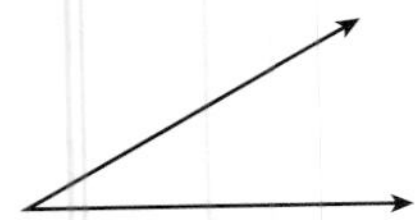
angle bisector A line, segment, or ray that divides an angle into two congruent angles. (p. 329)	**bisectriz de un ángulo** Línea, segmento o rayo que divide un ángulo en dos ángulos congruentes.	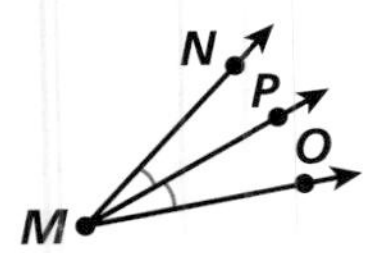
arc An unbroken part of a circle. (p. 838)	**arco** Parte continua de un círculo.	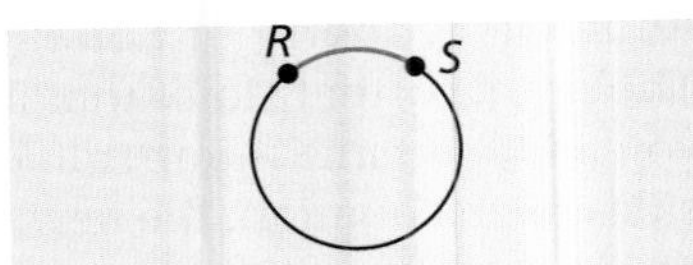
area The number of square units needed to cover a given surface. (p. 389)	**área** El número de unidades cuadradas que se necesitan para cubrir una superficie.	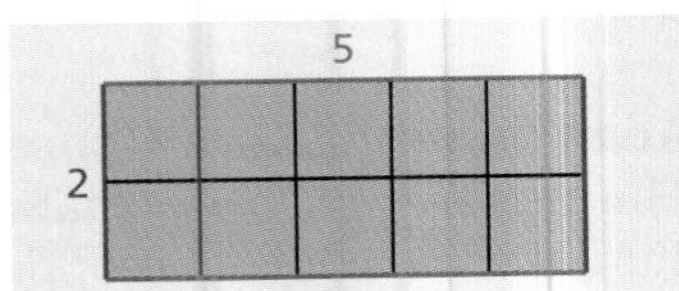 The area is 10 square units.
arithmetic sequence An ordered list of numbers in which the difference between consecutive terms is always the same. (p. 142)	**sucesión aritmética** Lista ordenada de números en la que la diferencia entre términos consecutivos siempre es la misma.	The sequence 2, 5, 8, 11, 14... is an arithmetic sequence.

ENGLISH	SPANISH	EXAMPLES
Associative Property of Addition The property that states that for all real numbers *a, b,* and *c,* the sum is always the same, regardless of their grouping. (p. 829)	**Propiedad asociativa de la suma** Propiedad que establece que para todos los números reales *a, b* y *c,* la suma siempre es la misma sin importar cómo se agrupen.	$a + b + c = (a + b) + c = a + (b + c)$
Associative Property of Multiplication: The property that states that for all real numbers *a, b,* and *c,* their product is always the same, regardless of their grouping. (p. 829)	**Propiedad asociativa de la multiplicación** Propiedad que establece que para todos los números reales *a, b* y *c,* el producto siempre es el mismo, sin importar cómo se agrupen.	$a \cdot b \cdot c = (a \cdot b) \cdot c = a \cdot (b \cdot c)$
average The sum of a set of data divided by the number of items in the data set; also called *mean.* (p. 472)	**media** La suma de todos los elementos, dividida entre el número total de elementos en el conjunto de datos. También se llama *promedio.*	Data set: 4, 6, 7, 8, 10 Average: $\frac{4+6+7+8+10}{5} = \frac{35}{5} = 7$

B

back-to-back stem-and-leaf plot A stem-and-leaf plot that compares two sets of data by displaying one set of data to the left of the stem and the other to the right. (p. 468)

diagrama doble de tallo y hojas Diagrama de tallo y hojas que compara dos conjuntos de datos presentando uno de ellos a la izquierda del tallo y el otro a la derecha.

Data set A: 9, 12, 14, 16, 23, 27
Data set B: 6, 8, 10, 13, 15, 16, 21

Set A		Set B
9	0	6 8
6 4 2	1	0 3 5 6
3 7	2	1

Key: |2| 1 means 21
7 |2| means 27

bar graph A graph that uses vertical or horizontal bars to display data. (p. 485)

gráfica de barras Gráfica en la que se usan barras verticales u horizontales para presentar datos.

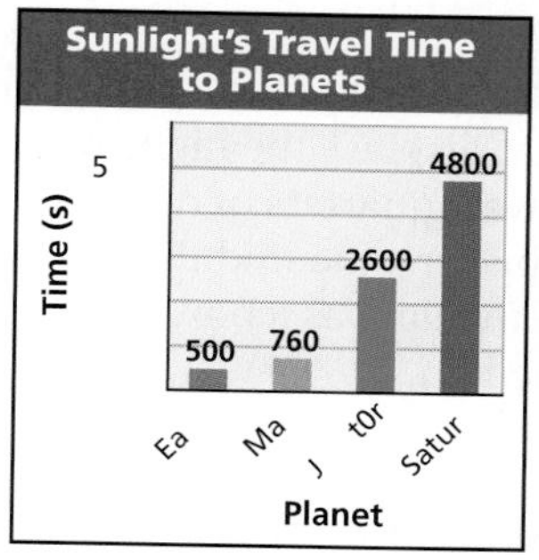

base When a number is raised to a power, the number that is used as a factor is the base. (p. 162)

base En un número elevado a una potencia, el número que se usa como factor es la base.

$3^5 = 3 \cdot 3 \cdot 3 \cdot 3 \cdot 3$; 3 is the base.

ENGLISH	SPANISH	EXAMPLES
base (of a polygon or three-dimensional figure) A side of a polygon; a face of a three-dimensional figure by which the figure is measured or classified. (p. 413)	**base (de un polígono o figura tridimensional)** Lado de un polígono; cara de una figura tridimensional según la cual se mide o se clasifica una figura.	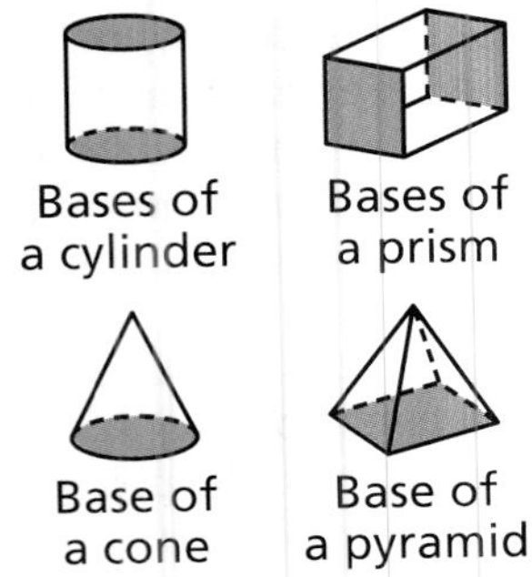
biased sample A sample that does not fairly represent the population. (p. 463)	**muestra no representativa** Muestra que no representa de forma justa la población.	
binomial A polynomial with two terms. (p. 734)	**binomio** Polinomio con dos términos.	$x + y$ $2a^2 - 3$ $4m^3n^2 + 6mn^4$
bisect To divide into two congruent parts. (p. 329)	**trazar una bisectriz** Dividir en dos partes congruentes.	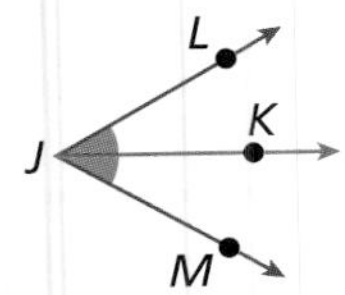 $\overrightarrow{JK}$ bisects $\angle LJM$
boundary line The set of points where the two sides of a two-variable linear inequality are equal. (p. 655)	**línea de límite** Conjunto de puntos donde los dos lados de una desigualdad lineal con dos variables son iguales.	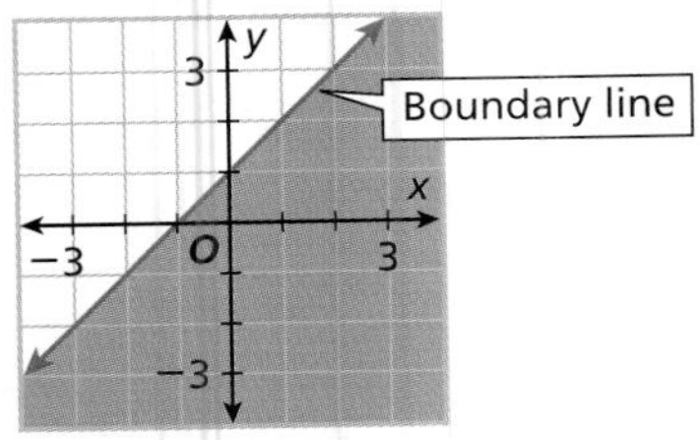
box-and-whisker plot A graph that displays the highest and lowest quarters of data as whiskers, the middle two quarters of the data as a box, and the median. (p. 477)	**gráfica de mediana y rango** También conocida como gráfica de "caja y bigotes" ya que muestra los cuartiles superior e inferior como "bigotes", los dos cuartiles intermedios como una "caja", así como la medana de los datos.	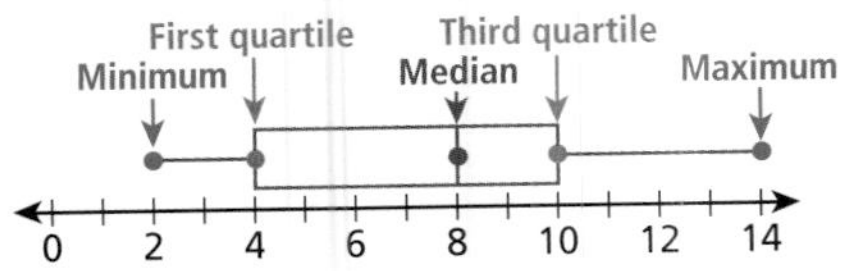
break (graph) A zigzag on a horizontal or vertical scale of a graph that indicates that some of the numbers on the scale have been omitted.	**discontinuidad (gráfica)** Zig-zag en la escala horizontal o vertical de una gráfica que indica la omisión de algunos números de la escala.	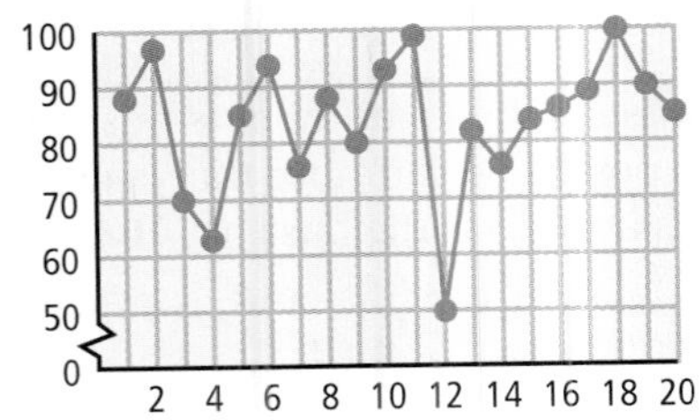

C

capacity The amount a container can hold when filled. (p. 440)	**capacidad** Cantidad que cabe en un recipiente cuando se llena.	A large milk container has a capacity of 1 gallon.

ENGLISH	SPANISH	EXAMPLES
Celsius A metric scale for measuring temperature in which 0°C is the freezing point of water and 100°C is the boiling point of water; also called *centigrade.*	**Celsius** Escala métrica para medir temperatura, en la que 0 °C es el punto de congelación del agua y 100 °C es el punto de ebullición. También se le llama *centígrada.*	
center (of a circle) The point inside a circle that is the same distance from all the points on the circle. (p. 294)	**centro (de un círculo)** Punto interior de un círculo que se encuentra a la misma distancia de todos los puntos de la circunferencia.	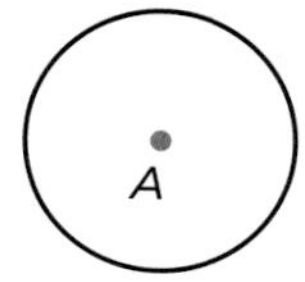
center of dilation The point of intersection of lines through each pair of corresponding vertices in a dilation. (p. 244)	**centro de una dilatación** Punto de intersección de las líneas que pasan a través de cada par de vértices correspondientes.	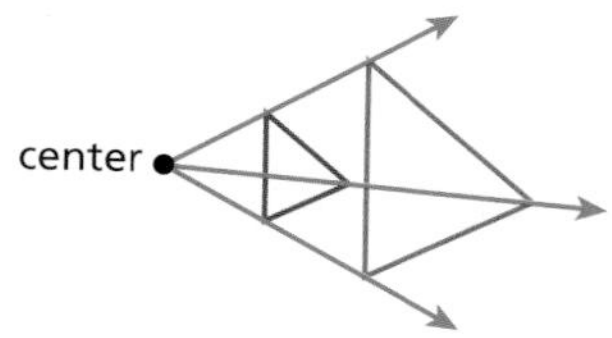
center of rotation The point about which a figure is rotated. (p. 358)	**centro de rotación** Punto alrededor del cual se hace girar una figura.	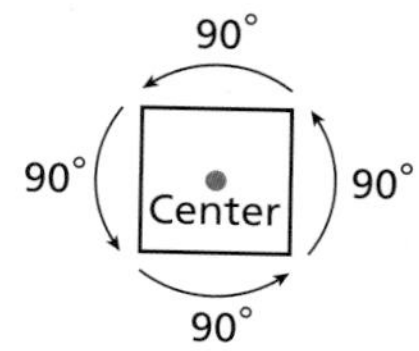
central angle An angle formed by two radii with its vertex at the center of a circle. (p. 838)	**ángulo central** Ángulo formado por dos radios y cuyo vértice se encuentra en el centro de un círculo.	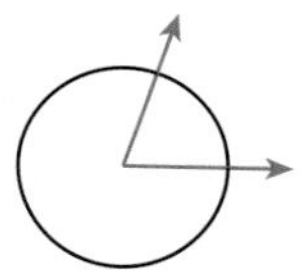
certain (probability) Sure to happen; an event that is certain has a probability of 1. (p. 522)	**seguro (probabilidad)** Que con seguridad sucederá. Representa una probabilidad de 1.	When rolling a number cube, it is certain that you will roll a number less than 7.
chord A segment with its endpoints on a circle. (p. 838)	**cuerda** Segmento de recta cuyos extremos forman parte de un círculo.	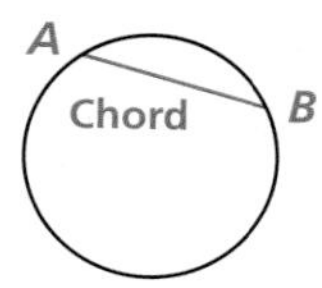
circle The set of all points in a plane that are the same distance from a given point called the center. (p. 400)	**círculo** Conjunto de puntos en un plano que se encuentran a la misma distancia de un punto llamado centro.	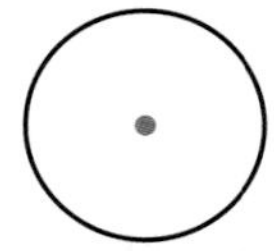
circle graph A graph that uses sectors of a circle to compare parts to the whole and parts to other parts. (p. 484)	**gráfica circular** Gráfica que usa secciones de un círculo para comparar partes con el todo y con otras partes.	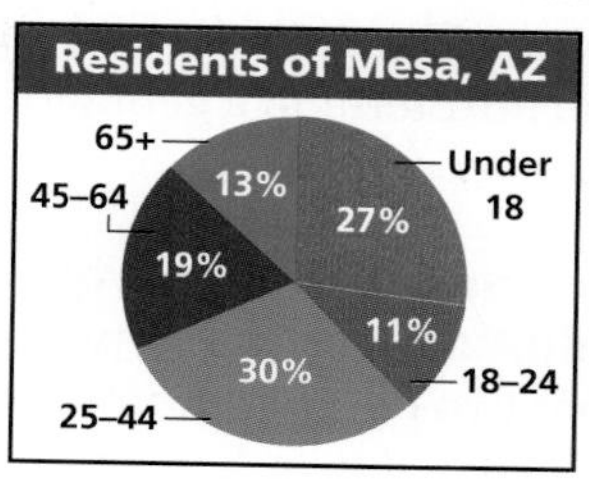
circuit A path in a graph that begins and ends at the same vertex. (p. 840)	**circuito** Una trayectoria en una gráfica que empieza y termina en el mismo vértice.	

ENGLISH	SPANISH	EXAMPLES
circumference The distance around a circle. (p. 400)	**circunferencia** Distancia alrededor de un círculo.	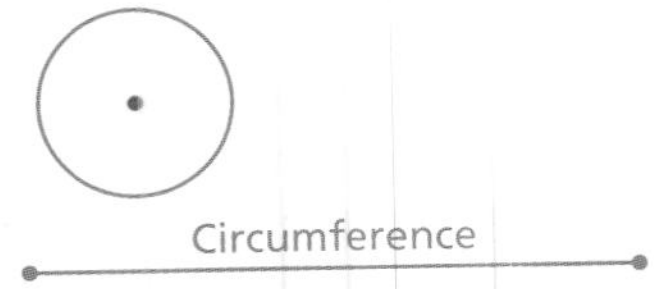
clockwise A circular movement to the right in the direction shown.	**en sentido de las manecillas del reloj** Movimiento circular hacia la derecha en la dirección que se indica.	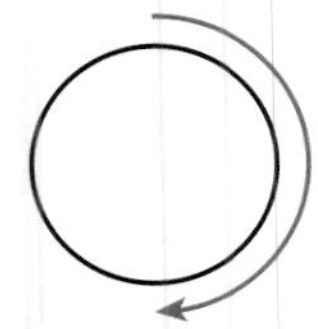
coefficient The number that is multiplied by the variable in an algebraic expression. (p. 6)	**coeficiente** Número que se multiplica por la variable en una expresión algebraica.	5 is the coefficient in $5b$.
combination An arrangement of items or events in which order does not matter. (p. 564)	**combinación** Agrupación de objetos o sucesos en la que el orden no es importante.	For objects *A, B, C,* and *D,* there are 6 different combinations of 2 objects: *AB, AC, AD, BC, BD, CD.*
commission A fee paid to a person for making a sale. (p. 298)	**comisión** Pago que recibe una persona por realizar una venta.	
commission rate The fee paid to a person who makes a sale expressed as a percent of the selling price. (p. 298)	**tasa de comisión** Pago que recibe una persona por hacer una venta, expresado como un porcentaje del precio de venta.	A commission rate of 5% and a sale of $10,000 results in a commission of $500.
common denominator A denominator that is the same in two or more fractions.	**común denominador** Denominador que es el mismo en dos o más fracciones.	The common denominator of $\frac{5}{8}$ and $\frac{2}{8}$ is 8.
common difference The difference between any two successive terms in an arithmetic sequence. (p. 142)	**diferencia común** Diferencia entre dos términos consecutivos de una sucesión aritmética.	In the arithmetic sequence 3, 5, 7, 9, 11, . . ., the common difference is 2.
common factor A number that is a factor of two or more numbers. (p. 824)	**factor común** Número que es factor de dos o más números.	8 is a common factor of 16 and 40.
common multiple A number that is a multiple of each of two or more numbers. (p. 824)	**común múltiplo** Número que es múltiplo de dos o más números.	15 is a common multiple of 3 and 5.
common ratio The ratio each term is multiplied by to produce the next term in a geometric sequence. (p. 687)	**razón común** Razón por la que se multiplica cada término para obtener el siguiente término de una sucesión geométrica.	In the geometric sequence 32, 16, 8, 4, 2, . . ., the common ratio is $\frac{1}{2}$.
Commutative Property of Addition The property that states that two or more numbers can be added in any order without changing the sum. (p. 828)	**Propiedad conmutativa de la suma** Propiedad que establece que dos o más números se pueden sumar en cualquier orden sin alterar la suma.	$8 + 20 = 20 + 8$; $a + b = b + a$

ENGLISH	SPANISH	EXAMPLES
Commutative Property of Multiplication The property that states that two or more numbers can be multiplied in any order without changing the product. (p. 828)	**Propiedad conmutativa de la multiplicación** Propiedad que establece que dos o más números se pueden multiplicar en cualquier orden sin alterar el producto.	$6 \cdot 12 = 12 \cdot 6$; $a \cdot b = b \cdot a$
compatible numbers Numbers that are close to the given numbers that make estimation or mental calculation easier. (p. 278)	**números compatibles** Números que pueden reemplazar a otros en un problema por ser más fáciles de usar en estimaciones o cálculos mentales.	To estimate 7,957 + 5,009, use the compatible numbers 8,000 and 5,000: 8,000 + 5,000 = 13,000.
complementary angles Two angles whose measures add to 90°. (p. 325)	**ángulos complementarios** Dos ángulos cuyas medidas suman 90°.	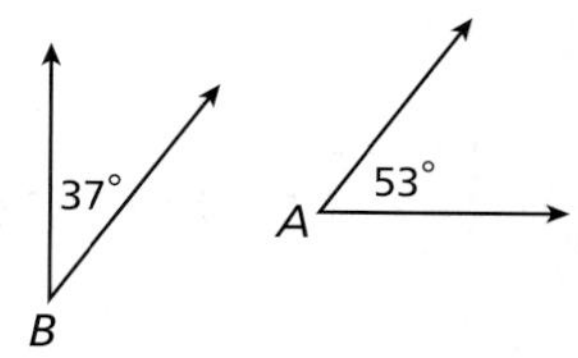 The complement of a 53°angle is a 37° angle.
composite number A number greater than 1 that has more than two whole-number factors. (p. 823)	**número compuesto** Número mayor que 1 que tiene más de dos factores que son números cabales.	4, 6, 8, and 9 are composite numbers.
compound event An event made up of two or more simple events.	**suceso compuesto** Suceso formado por dos o más sucesos simples.	Rolling a 3 on a number cube and spinning a 2 on a spinner is a compound event.
compound inequality A combination of more than one inequality.	**desigualdad compuesta** Combinación de dos o más desigualdades.	$x \geq -2$ or $x < 10$ $-2 \leq x < 10$
compound interest Interest earned or paid on principal and previously earned or paid interest. (p. 306)	**interés compuesto** Interés que se gana o se paga sobre el capital y los intereses previamente ganados o pagados.	If \$100 is put into an account with an interest rate of 5% compounded monthly, then after 2 years, the account will have $100\left(1 + \frac{0.05}{12}\right)^{12 \cdot 2} = \$110.49$
cone A three-dimensional figure with one vertex and one circular base. (p. 420)	**cono** Figura tridimensional con un vértice y una base circular.	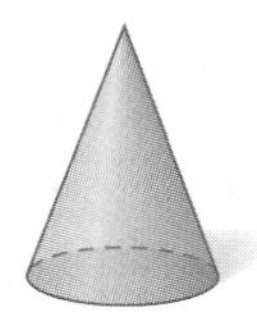
congruent Having the same size and shape. (p. 325)	**congruentes** Que tiene la misma forma y tamaño.	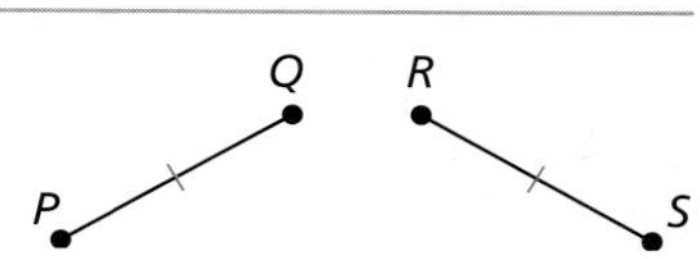 $\overline{PQ} \cong \overline{RS}$

ENGLISH	SPANISH	EXAMPLES
congruent angles Angles that have the same measure. (p. 238)	**ángulos congruentes** Ángulos que tienen la misma medida.	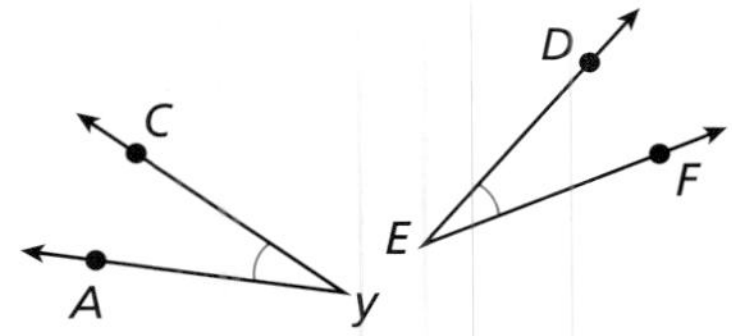 $\angle ABC = \angle DEF$
congruent segments Segments that have the same length. (p. 238)	**segmentos de recta congruentes** Segmentos que tienen la misma longitud.	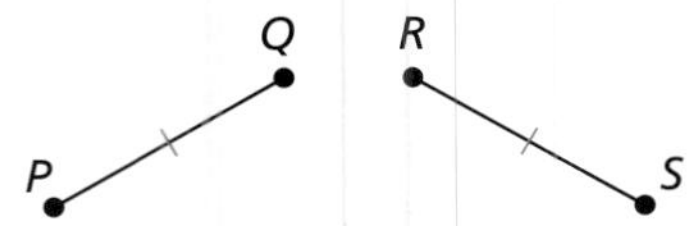 $\overline{PQ} \cong \overline{SR}$
constant A value that does not change. (p. 6)	**constante** Valor que no cambia.	3, 0, ?
constant of proportionality A constant ratio of two variables related proportionally. (p. 650)	**constante de proporcionalidad** Razón constante de dos variables que están relacionadas en forma proporcional. *Ejemplo:* $5 = k$, $10 = 2k$, y $15 = 3k$	In $y = 5x$, the constant of proportionality is 5.
convenience sample A sample based on members of the population that are readily available. (p. 462)	**muestra de conveniencia** Una muestra basada en miembros de la población que están fácilmente disponibles.	
conversion factor A fraction whose numerator and denominator represent the same quantity but use different units; the fraction is equal to 1 because the numerator and denominator are equal. (p. 224)	**factor de conversión** Fracción cuyo numerador y denominador representan la misma cantidad pero con unidades distintas; la fracción es igual a 1 porque el numerador y el denominador son iguales.	$\frac{24\text{ hours}}{1\text{ day}}$ and $\frac{1\text{ day}}{24\text{ hours}}$
coordinate One of the numbers of an ordered pair that locate a point on a coordinate graph. (p. 122)	**coordenada** Uno de los números de un par ordenado que localizan un punto en un plano cartesiano.	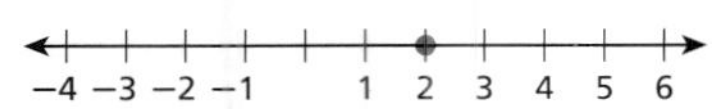 The coordinates of *A* is 2. 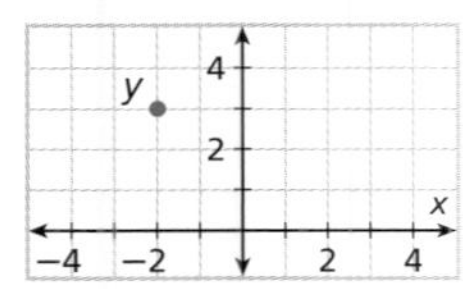 The coordinates of *B* are (−2, 3)
coordinate plane (coordinate grid) A plane formed by the intersection of a horizontal number line called the *x*-axis and a vertical number line called the *y*-axis. (p. 122)	**plano cartesiano (cuadrícula de coordenadas)** Plano formado por la intersección de una recta numérica horizontal llamada eje de las *x* y otra vertical llamada eje de las *y*.	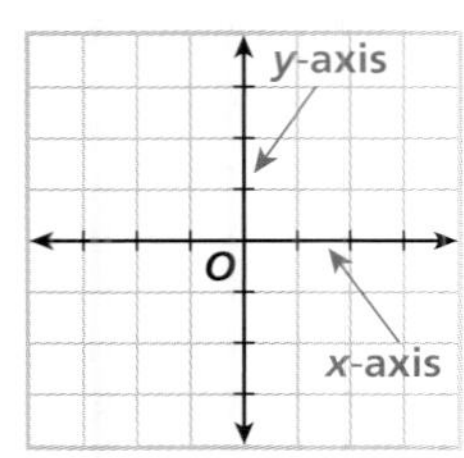

ENGLISH | SPANISH | EXAMPLES

correlation The description of the relationship between two data sets. (p. 494)

correlación Descripción de la relación entre dos conjuntos de datos.

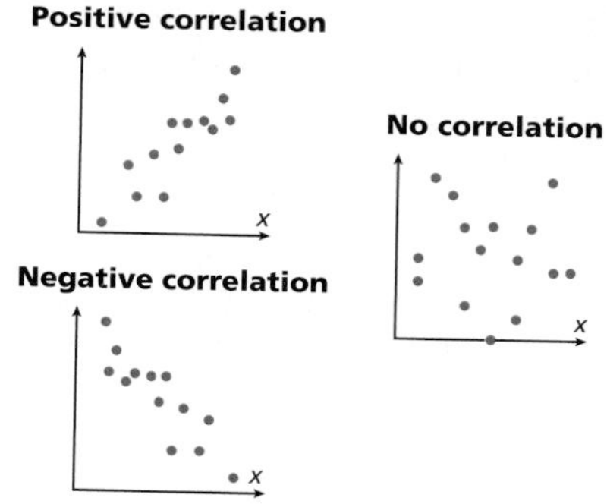

---

correspondence The relationship between two or more objects that are matched. (p. 354)

correspondencia La relación entre dos o más objetos que coinciden.

∠*A* and ∠*D* are corresponding angles.

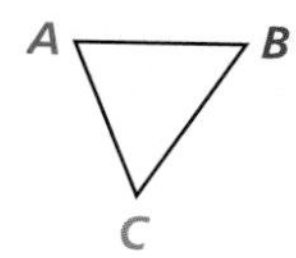

$\overline{AB}$ and $\overline{DE}$ are corresponding sides.

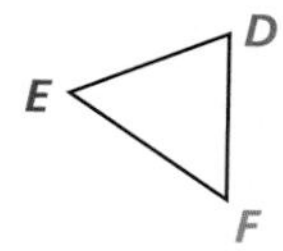

---

corresponding angles (for lines) Angles formed by a transversal cutting two or more lines and that are in the same relative position. (p. 331)

ángulos correspondientes (en líneas) Ángulos formados por una transversal que interseca dos o más líneas y que están en la misma posición relativa.

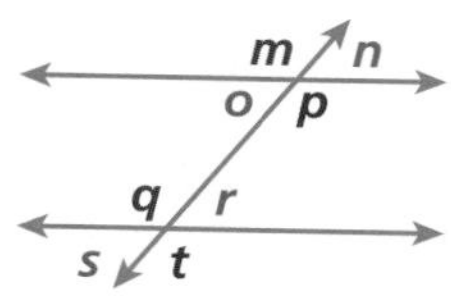

∠*m* and ∠*q* are corresponding angles.

---

corresponding angles (in polygons) Matching angles of two or more polygons. (p. 238)

ángulos correspondientes (en polígonos) Ángulos que están en la misma posición relativa en dos o más polígonos.

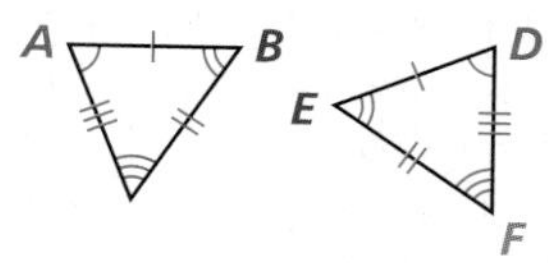

∠*A* and ∠*D* are corresponding angles.

---

corresponding sides Matching sides of two or more polygons. (p. 238)

lados correspondientes Lados que se localizan en la misma posición relativa en dos o más polígonos.

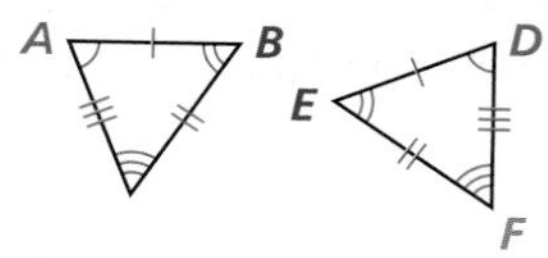

$\overline{AB}$ and $\overline{DE}$ are corresponding sides.

---

counterclockwise A circular movement to the left in the direction shown.

en sentido de las manecillas del reloj Movimiento circular hacia la derecha en la dirección que se indica.

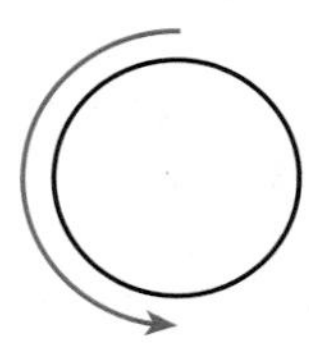

---

cross product The product of numbers on the diagonal when comparing two ratios. (p. 229)

producto cruzado Multiplicación cruzada de los numeradores y denominadores de dos razones.

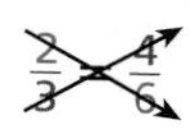

For the proportion $\frac{2}{3} = \frac{4}{6}$, the cross products are $2 \cdot 6 = 12$ and $3 \cdot 4 = 12$

ENGLISH	SPANISH	EXAMPLES
cube (geometric figure) A rectangular prism with six congruent square faces. (pp. 154, 300)	**cubo (figura geométrica)** Prisma rectangular con seis caras cuadradas congruentes.	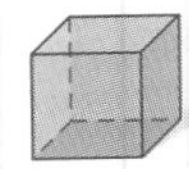
cube (in numeration) A number raised to the third power. (p. 830)	**cubo (en numeración)** Número elevado a la tercera potencia.	$2^3 = 2 \cdot 2 \cdot 2 = 8$ 8 is the cube of 2.
cumulative frequency The sum of successive data items. (p. 835)	**frecuencia acumulativa** Muestra el total acumulado de las frecuencias.	
customary system of measurement The measurement system often used in the United States.	**sistema métrico de medición** Sistema decimal de pesos y medidas empleado universalmente en las ciencias y de uso común en todo el mundo.	inches, feet, miles, ounces, pounds, tons, cups, quarts, gallons
cylinder A three-dimensional figure with two parallel, congruent circular bases connected by a curved lateral surface. (p. 413)	**cilindro** Figura tridimensional con dos bases circulares paralelas y congruentes, unidas por una superficie lateral curva.	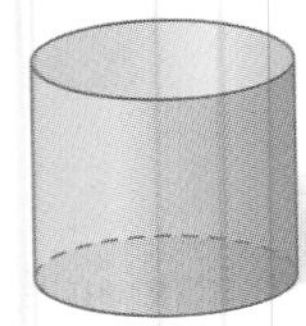

D

ENGLISH	SPANISH	EXAMPLES
decagon A polygon with ten sides.	**decágono** Polígono de diez lados.	
degree The unit of measure for angles or temperature. (p. 324)	**grado** Unidad de medida para ángulos y temperaturas.	
degree of a polynomial The highest power of the variable in a polynomial. (p. 735)	**grado de un polinomio** La potencia más alta de la variable en un polinomio.	The polynomial $4x^5 - 6x^2 + 7$ has degree 5
Density Property The property that states that between any two real numbers, there is always another real number. (p. 192)	**Propiedad de densidad** Propiedad según la cual entre dos números reales cualesquiera siempre hay otro número real.	
denominator The bottom number of a fraction that tells how many equal parts are in the whole. (p. 64)	**denominador** Número que está abajo en una fracción y que indica las partes en que se divide el entero.	In the fraction $\frac{2}{5}$, 5 is the denominator.
dependent events Events for which the outcome of one event affects the probability of the other. (p. 545)	**sucesos dependientes** Sucesos en los que el resultado del primero no afecta la probabilidad del segundo.	A bag contains 3 red marbles and 2 blue marbles. Drawing a red marble and then drawing a blue marble without replacing the first marble is an example of dependent events.

ENGLISH	SPANISH	EXAMPLES
diagonal A line segment that connect two non-adjacent vertices of a polygon.	**diagonal** Segmento de recta que une dos vértices no adyacentes de un polígono.	
diameter A line segment that passes through the center of a circle and has endpoints on the circle, or the length of that segment. (p. 400)	**diámetro** Segmento de recta que pasa por el centro de un círculo y tiene sus extremos en la circunferencia, o bien la longitud de ese segmento.	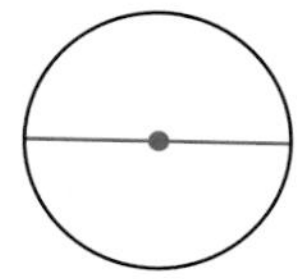
difference The result when one number is subtracted from another.	**diferencia** El resultado de restar un número de otro.	
dilation A transformation that enlarges or reduces a figure. (p. 244)	**dilatación** Transformación que agranda o reduce una figura.	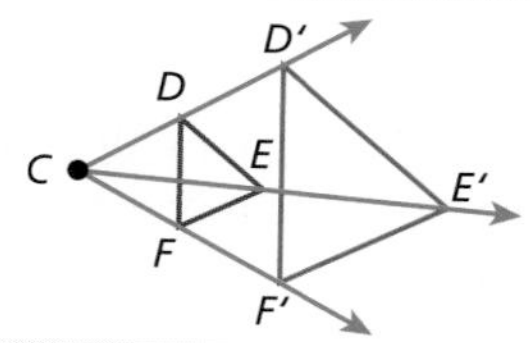
dimensions (geometry) The length, width, or height of a figure.	**dimensiones (geometría)** Longitud, anchura o altura de una figura.	
dimensions (of a matrix) The number of horizontal rows and vertical columns in a matrix. (p. 839)	**dimensiones (de una matriz)** Número de filas y columnas que hay en una matriz.	
direct variation A relationship between two variables in which the data increase or decrease together at a constant rate. (p. 650)	**variación directa** Relación entre dos variables en la que los datos aumentan o disminuyen juntos a una tasa constante.	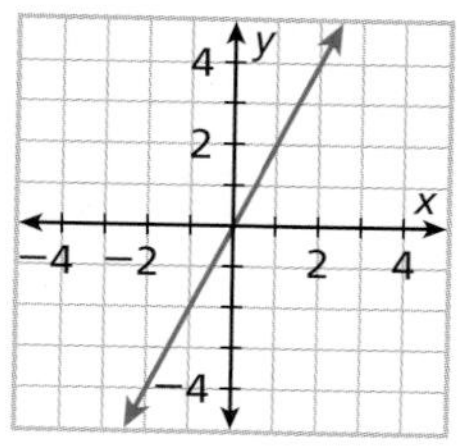 $y = 2x$
discount The amount by which the original price is reduced.	**descuento** Cantidad que se resta al precio original de un artículo.	
Distributive Property The property that states if you multiply a sum by a number, you will get the same result if you multiply each addend by that number and then add the products. (p. 829)	**Propiedad distributiva** Propiedad que establece que si multiplicas una suma por un número, obtienes el mismo resultado que si multiplicas cada sumando por ese número y luego sumas los productos.	$5 \cdot 21 = 5(20 + 1) =$ $(5 \cdot 20) + (5 \cdot 1)$
dividend The number to be divided in a division problem.	**dividendo** Número que se divide en un problema de división.	In $8 \div 4 = 2$, 8 is the dividend.
divisible Can be divided by a number without leaving a remainder. (p. 822)	**divisible** Que se puede dividir entre un número sin dejar residuo.	18 is divisible by 3.

ENGLISH	SPANISH	EXAMPLES
Division Property of Equality The property that states that if you divide both sides of an equation by the same nonzero number, the new equation will have the same solution. (p. 39)	**Propiedad de igualdad de la división** Propiedad que establece que puedes dividir ambos lados de una ecuación entre el mismo número distinto de cero, y la ecuación resultante tendrá la misma solución.	
divisor The number you are dividing by in a division problem.	**divisor** El número entre el que se divide en un problema de división.	In $8 \div 4 = 2$, 4 is the divisor.
dodecahedron A polyhedron with 12 faces.	**dodecaedro** Poliedro de 12 caras.	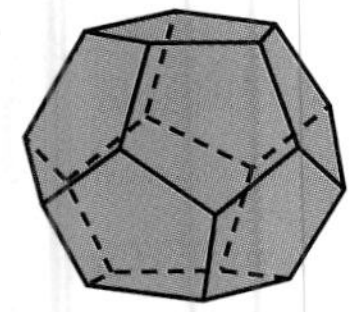
domain The set of all possible input values of a function. (p. 134)	**dominio** Conjunto de todos los posibles valores de entrada de una función.	The domain of the function $y = x^2 + 1$ is all real numbers.
double-bar graph A bar graph that compares two related sets of data. (p. 485)	**gráfica de doble barra** Gráfica de barras que compara dos conjuntos de datos relacionados.	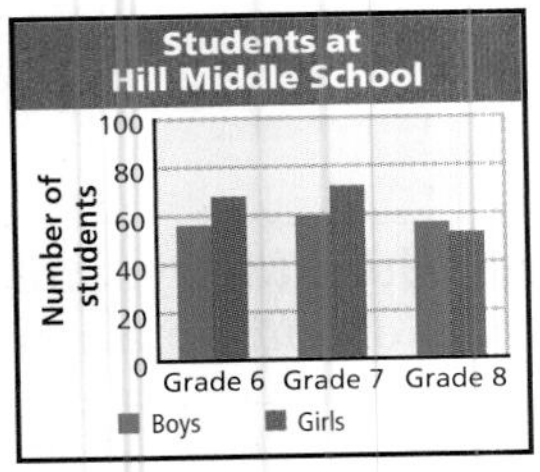
double-line graph A line graph that shows how two related sets of data change over time. (p. 486)	**gráfica de doble línea** Gráfica lineal que muestra cómo cambian con el tiempo dos conjuntos de datos relacionados.	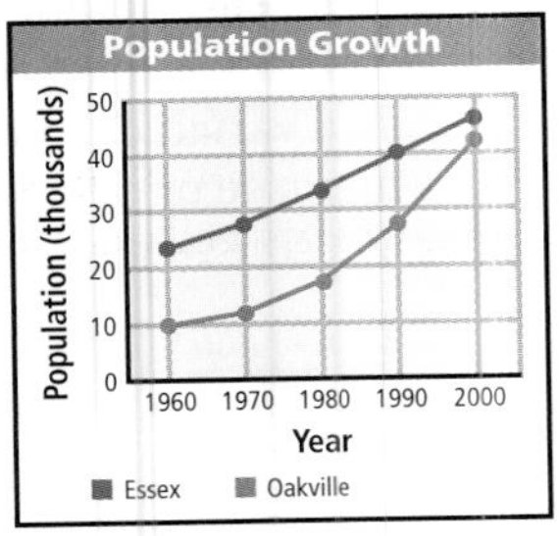

E

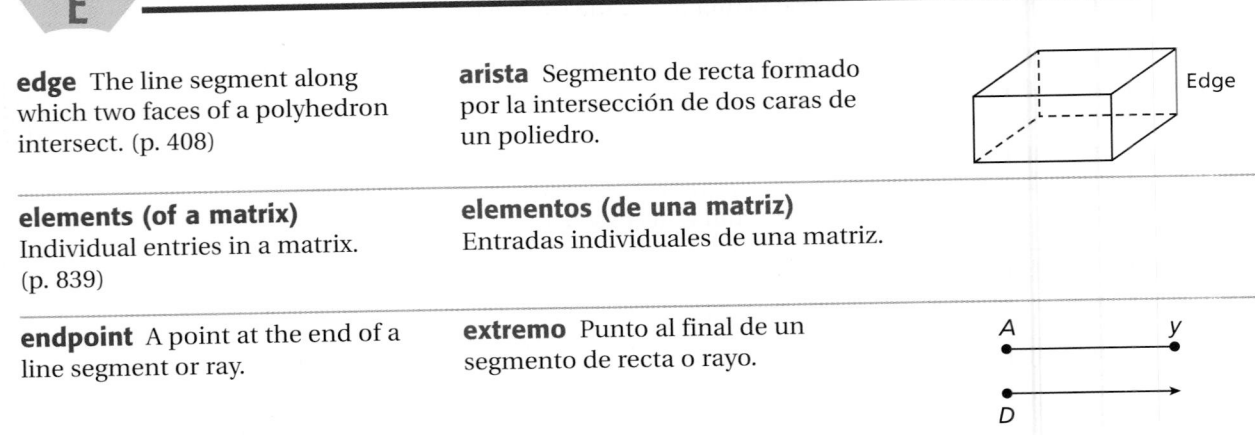

ENGLISH	SPANISH	EXAMPLES
edge The line segment along which two faces of a polyhedron intersect. (p. 408)	**arista** Segmento de recta formado por la intersección de dos caras de un poliedro.	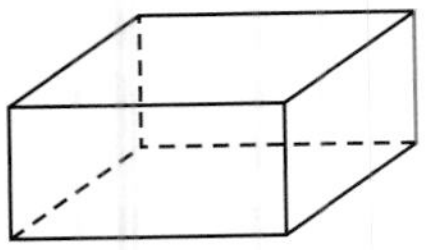
elements (of a matrix) Individual entries in a matrix. (p. 839)	**elementos (de una matriz)** Entradas individuales de una matriz.	
endpoint A point at the end of a line segment or ray.	**extremo** Punto al final de un segmento de recta o rayo.	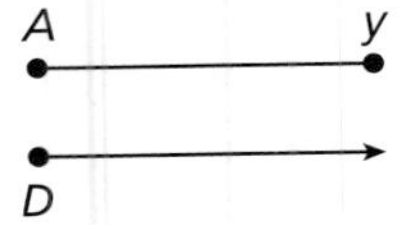

ENGLISH	SPANISH	EXAMPLES
enlargement An increase in size of all dimensions in the same proportions. (p. 253)	**agrandamiento** Aumento de tamaño de todas las dimensiones en las mismas proporciones.	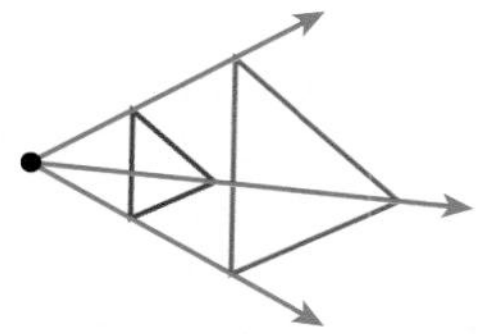
equally likely Outcomes that have the same probability. (p. 540)	**igualmente probables** Resultados que tienen la misma probabilidad.	When tossing a coin, the outcomes "heads" and "tails" are equally likely.
equation A mathematical sentence that shows that two expressions are equivalent. (p. 34)	**ecuación** Enunciado matemático que indica que dos expresiones son equivalentes.	$x + 4 = 7$ $6 + 1 = 10 - 3$
equilateral triangle A triangle with three congruent sides. (p. 337)	**triángulo equilátero** Triángulo con tres lados congruentes.	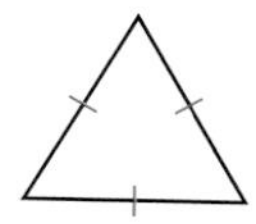
equivalent Having the same value. (p. 584)	**equivalentes** Que tienen el mismo valor. (pág. 28)	
equivalent expression Equivalent expressions have the same value for all values of the variables. (p. 584)	**expresión equivalente** Las expresiones equivalentes tienen el mismo valor para todos los valores de las variables.	$4x + 5x$ and $9x$ are equivalent expressions.
equivalent fractions Fractions that name the same amount or part.	**fracciones equivalentes** Fracciones que representan la misma cantidad o la misma parte de un todo.	$\frac{1}{2}$ and $\frac{2}{4}$ are equivalent fractions.
equivalent ratios Ratios that name the same comparison. (p. 216)	**razones equivalentes** Razones que representan la misma comparación.	$\frac{1}{2}$ and $\frac{2}{4}$ are equivalent ratios.
estimate (n) An answer that is close to the exact answer and is found by rounding or other methods. **(v)** To find such an answer. (p. 278)	**estimación (n)** Una solución aproximada a la respuesta exacta que se halla mediante el redondeo u otros métodos. **estimar (v)** Hallar una solución aproximada a la respuesta exacta.	500 is an estimate for the sum $98 + 287 + 104$.
evaluate To find the value of a numerical or algebraic expression. (p. 6)	**evaluar** Hallar el valor de una expresión numérica o algebraica.	Evaluate $2x + 7$ for $x = 3$ $2x + 7$ $2(3) + 7$ $6 + 7$ $13.$
even number A whole number that is divisible by two.	**número par** Número cabal divisible entre 2.	
event An outcome or set of outcomes of an experiment or situation. (p. 522)	**suceso** Resultado o conjunto de resultados posibles de un experimento o situación.	When rolling a number cube, the event "an odd number" consists of the outcomes 1, 3, and 5.

ENGLISH	SPANISH	EXAMPLES
expanded form A number written as the sum of the values of its digits.	**forma desarrollada** Número escrito como suma de los valores de sus dígitos.	236,536 written in expanded form is 200,000 + 30,000 + 6,000 + 500 + 30 + 6.
experiment (probability) In probability, any activity based on chance (such as tossing a coin). (p. 522)	**experimento (probabilidad)** En probabilidad, cualquier actividad basada en la posibilidad, como lanzar una moneda.	Tossing a coin 10 times and noting the number of "heads".
experimental probability The ratio of the number of times an event occurs to the total number of trials, or times that the activity is performed. (p. 527)	**probabilidad experimental** Razón del número de veces que ocurre un suceso al número total de pruebas o a las veces que se realiza el experimento.	Kendra attempted 27 free throws and made 16 of them. Her experimental probability of making a free throw is $\frac{\text{number made}}{\text{number attempted}} = \frac{16}{27} \approx 0.59$.
exponent The number that indicates how many times the base is used as a factor. (p. 162)	**exponente** Número que indica cuántas veces se usa la base como factor.	$2^3 = 2 \times 2 \times 2 = 8$; 3 is the exponent.
exponential form A number is in exponential form when it is written with a base and an exponent. (p. 162)	**forma exponencial** Un número está en forma exponencial cuando se escribe con una base y un exponente.	4^2 is the exponential form for $4 \cdot 4$.
exponential function A nonlinear function in which the variable is in the exponent. (p. 704)	**función exponencial** Función no lineal en la que la variable está en el exponente.	$f(x) = 4^x$
expression A mathematical phrase that contains operations, numbers, and/or variables. (p. 6)	**expresión** Enunciado matemático que contiene operaciones, números y(o) variables.	$6x + 1$

F

ENGLISH	SPANISH	EXAMPLES
face A flat surface of a polyhedron. (p. 408)	**cara** Superficie plana de un poliedro.	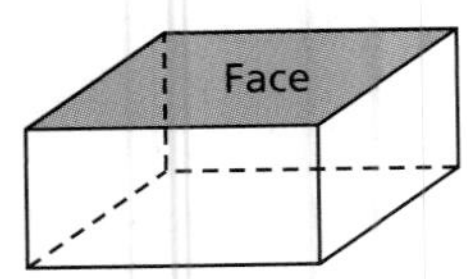
factor A number that is multiplied by another number to get a product. (p. 822)	**factor** Número que se multiplica por otro para hallar un producto.	7 is a factor of 21 since $7 \cdot 3 = 21$.
factorial The product of all whole numbers except zero that are less than or equal to a number. (p. 563)	**factorial** El producto de todos los números cabales menores o iguales a un número, excepto cero.	4 factorial $= 4! = 4 \cdot 3 \cdot 2 \cdot 1$

ENGLISH	SPANISH	EXAMPLES

Fahrenheit A temperature scale in which 32°F is the freezing point of water and 212°F is the boiling point of water.

Fahrenheit Escala de temperatura en la que 32° F es el punto de congelación del agua y 212° F es el punto de ebullición.

---

fair When all outcomes of an experiment are equally likely, the experiment is said to be fair. (p. 540)

justo Un experimento es justo si todos los resultados posibles son igualmente probables.

When tossing a coin, heads and tails are equally likely, so it is a fair experiment.

Fibonacci sequence The infinite sequence of numbers (1, 1, 2, 3, 5, 8, 13, ...); starting with the third term, each number is the sum of the two previous numbers; it is named after the thirteenth century mathematician Leonardo Fibonacci. (p. 695)

sucesión de Fibonacci La sucesión infinita de números (1, 1, 2, 3, 5, 8, 13...); a partir del tercer término, cada número es la suma de los dos anteriores. Esta sucesión lleva el nombre de Leonardo Fibonacci, un matemático del siglo XIII.

1, 1, 2, 3, 5, 8, 13, . . .

---

first differences A sequence formed by subtracting each term of a sequence from the next term. (p. 693)

primeras diferencias Sucesión que se forma al restar cada término de una sucesión del término siguiente.

For the sequence 4, 7, 10, 13, 16, . . . , the first differences are all 3.

---

first quartile The median of the lower half of a set of data; also called *lower quartile.* (p. 476)

primer cuartil La mediana de la mitad inferior de un conjunto de datos. También se llama *cuartil inferior.*

FOIL An acronym for the terms used when multiplying two binomials: the First, Inner, Outer, and Last terms. (p. 762)

FOIL Acrónimo en inglés de los términos que se usan al multiplicar dos binomios: Primeros (First), Internos (Inner), Externos (Outer), Últimos (Last).

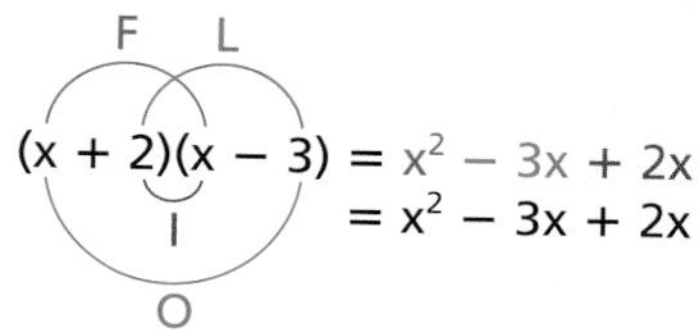

$$(x + 2)(x - 3) = x^2 - 3x + 2x$$
$$= x^2 - 3x + 2x$$

---

formula A rule showing relationships among quantities.

fórmula Regla que muestra relaciones entre cantidades.

$A = \ell w$ is the formula for the area of a rectangle.

---

fractal A structure with repeating patterns containing shapes that are like the whole but are of different sizes throughout. (p. 834)

fractal Estructura con patrones repetidos que contienen figuras similares al patrón general pero de diferente tamaño.

---

fraction A number in the form $\frac{a}{b}$, where $b \neq 0$.

fracción Número escrito en la forma $\frac{a}{b}$, donde $b \neq 0$.

$\frac{2}{3}$

---

frequency table A table that lists items together according to the number of times, or frequency, that the items occur. (p. 485)

tabla de frecuencia Tabla que organiza los datos de acuerdo al número de veces o frecuencia con que aparece cada valor.

Data set: 1, 1, 2, 2, 3, 4, 5, 5, 5, 6, 6
Frequency table:

Data	Frequency
1	2
2	2
3	1
4	1
5	3
6	2

ENGLISH	SPANISH	EXAMPLES

function An input-output relationship that has exactly one output for each input. (p. 134)

función Regla que relaciona dos cantidades de forma que a cada valor de entrada corresponde exactamente un valor de salida.

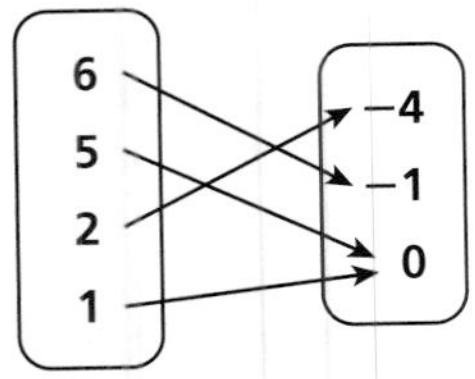

function notation The notation used to describe a function. (p. 700)

notación de funciones Notación que se usa para describir una función.

Equation: $y = 2x$
Function notation: $f(x) = 2x$

function table A table of ordered pairs that represent solutions of a function.

tabla de función Tabla de pares ordenados que representan soluciones de una función.

x	3	4	5	6
y	7	9	11	13

Fundamental Counting Principle If one event has m possible outcomes and a second event has n possible outcomes after the first event has occurred, then there are $m \cdot n$ total possible outcomes for the two events. (p. 558)

Principio fundamental de conteo Si un suceso tiene m resultados posibles y un segundo suceso tiene n resultados posibles, después de ocurrido el primer suceso, entonces hay $m \cdot n$ posibles resultados en total para los dos sucesos.

There are 4 colors of shirts and 3 colors of pants. There are $4 \cdot 3 = 12$ possible outcomes.

G

geometric sequence An ordered list of numbers that has a common ratio between consecutive terms. (p. 687)

sucesión geométrica Lista ordenada de números que tiene una razón común entre términos consecutivos.

The sequence 2, 4, 8, 16. . . is a geometric sequence.

graph A set of points and the line segments or arcs that connect the points. Also called a network. (p. 122)

gráfica Conjunto de puntos y los segmentos de recta o arcos que los conectan. También se le llama red.

graph of an equation A graph of the set of ordered pairs that are solutions of the equation. (p. 123)

gráfica de una ecuación Gráfica del conjunto de pares ordenados que son soluciones de la ecuación.

$y = x - 1$

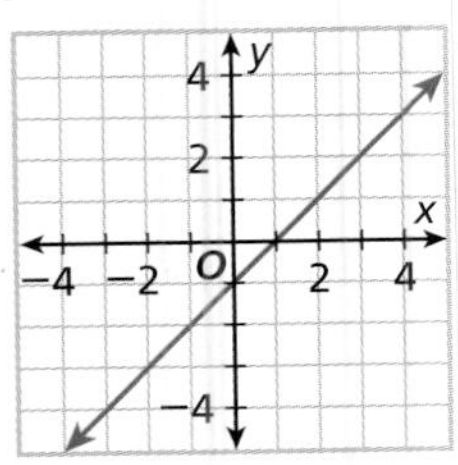

great circle A circle on a sphere such that the plane containing the circle passes through the center of the sphere. (p. 436)

círculo máximo Círculo de una esfera tal que el plano que contiene el círculo pasa por el centro de la esfera.

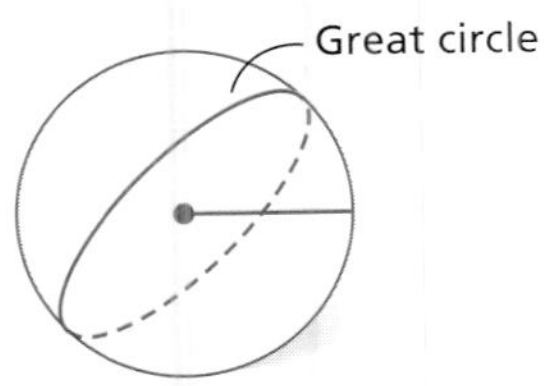

greatest common factor (GCF) The largest common factor of two or more given numbers. (p. 824)

máximo común divisor (MCD) El mayor de los factores comunes compartidos por dos o más números.

The GCF of 27 and 45 is 9.

ENGLISH	SPANISH	EXAMPLES

H

height In a pyramid or cone, the perpendicular distance from the base to the opposite vertex. (p. 420)

altura En una pirámide o cono, la distancia perpendicular que va de la base y al vértice opuesto.

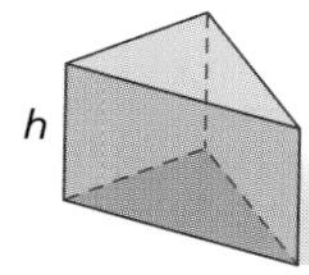

In a triangle or quadrilateral, the perpendicular distance from the base to the opposite vertex or side. (p. 395)

En un triángulo o cuadrilátero, la distancia perpendicular que va de la base de la figura al vértice o lado opuesto.

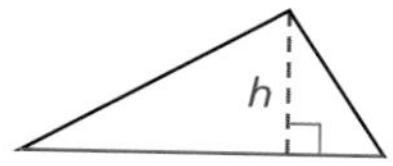

In a prism or cylinder, the perpendicular distance between the bases. (p. 413)

En un prisma o cilindro, la distancia perpendicular entre las bases.

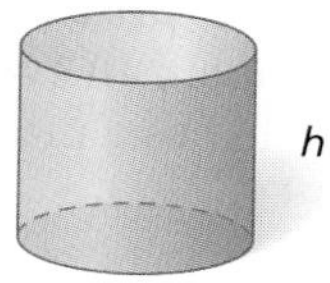

hemisphere A half of a sphere. (p. 436)

hemisferio La mitad de una esfera.

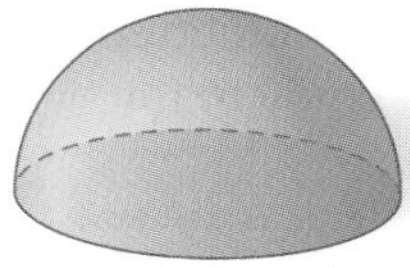

heptagon A seven-sided polygon. (p. 341)

heptágono Polígono de siete lados.

hexagon A six-sided polygon. (p. 341)

hexágono Polígono de seis lados.

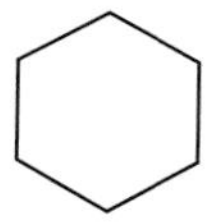

histogram A bar graph that shows the frequency of data within equal intervals. (p. 485)

histograma Gráfica de barras que muestra la frecuencia de los datos en intervalos iguales.

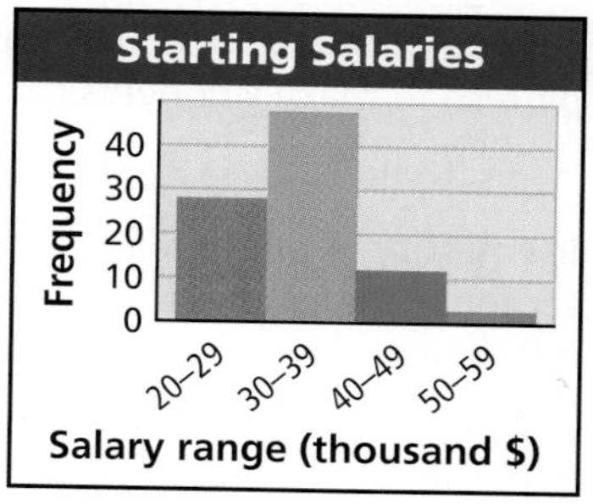

hypotenuse In a right triangle, the side opposite the right angle. (p. 196)

hipotenusa En un triángulo rectángulo, el lado opuesto al ángulo recto.

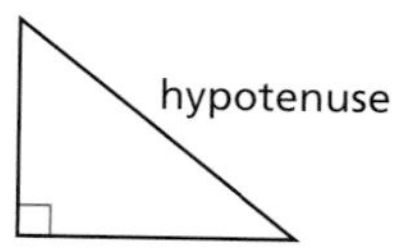

I

Identity Property of One The property that states that the product of 1 and any number is that number. (p. 829)

Propiedad de identidad del uno Propiedad que establece que el producto de 1 y cualquier número es ese número.

$4 \cdot 1 = 4$
$-3 \cdot 1 = -3$

ENGLISH	SPANISH	EXAMPLES
Identity Property of Zero The property that states the sum of zero and any number is that number. (p. 829)	**Propiedad de identidad del cero** Propiedad que establece que la suma de cero y cualquier número es ese número.	$4 + 0 = 4$ $-3 + 0 = -3$
image A figure resulting from a transformation. (p. 358)	**imagen** Figura que resulta de una transformación.	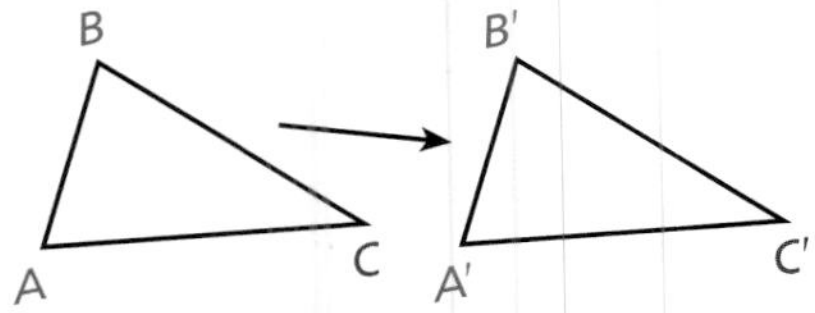
impossible (probability) Can never happen; an event that is impossible has a probability of 0. (p. 522)	**imposible (en probabilidad)** Que nunca puede ocurrir. Suceso cuya probabilidad de ocurrir es 0.	When rolling a standard number cube, rolling a 7 is an impossible event.
improper fraction A fraction in which the numerator is greater than or equal to the denominator. (p. 825)	**fracción impropia** Fracción cuyo numerador es mayor o igual que el denominador.	$\frac{17}{5}, \frac{3}{3}$
independent events Events for which the outcome of one event does not affect the probability of the other. (p. 545)	**sucesos independientes** Sucesos en los que el resultado del primero no afecta la probabilidad del segundo.	A bag contains 3 red marbles and 2 blue marbles. Drawing a red marble, replacing it, and then drawing a blue marble is an example of independent events.
indirect measurement The technique of using similar figures and proportions to find a measure. (p. 248)	**medición indirecta** La técnica de usar proporciones y figuras semejantes para hallar una medida.	
inductive reasoning Using a pattern to make a conclusion. (p. 833)	**razonamiento inductivo** Uso de un patrón para sacar una conclusión.	
inequality A mathematical sentence that shows the relationship between quantities that are not equivalent. (p. 44)	**desigualdad** Enunciado matemático que muestra una relación entre cantidades que no son equivalentes.	$5 < 8$ $5x + 2 \geq 12$
input The value substituted into an expression or function. (p. 134)	**valor de entrada** Valor que se usa para sustituir una variable en una expresión o función.	For the function $y = 6x$, the input 4 produces an output of 24.
inscribed angle An angle formed by two chords with its vertex on a circle. (p. 838)	**ángulo inscrito** Ángulo formado por dos cuerdas y cuyo vértice está en un círculo.	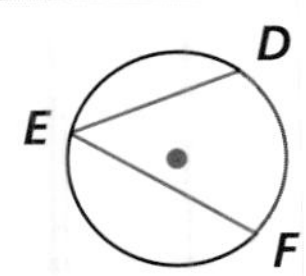
integers The set of whole numbers and their opposites. (p. 14)	**enteros** Conjunto de todos los números cabales y sus opuestos.	. . . −3, −2, (1, 0, 1, 2, 3, . . .

ENGLISH	SPANISH	EXAMPLES

interest The amount of money charged for borrowing or using money. (p. 302)

interés Cantidad de dinero que se cobra por el préstamo o uso del dinero, o la cantidad que se gana al ahorrar dinero.

---

interior angles Angles on the inner sides of two lines cut by a transversal.

ángulos internos Ángulos en los lados internos de dos líneas intersecadas por una transversal.

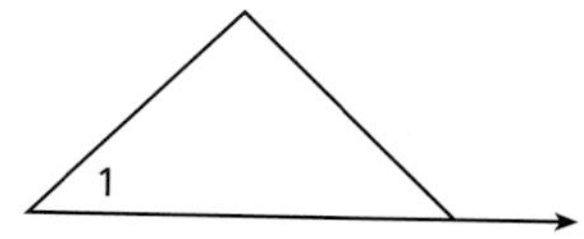

∠1 is an interior angle.

---

intersecting lines Lines that cross at exactly one point.

líneas secantes Líneas que se cruzan en un solo punto.

---

interval The space between marked values on a number line or the scale of a graph.

intervalo El espacio entre los valores marcados en una recta numérica o en la escala de una gráfica.

---

inverse operations Operations that undo each other: addition and subtraction, or multiplication and division. (p. 34)

operaciones inversas Operaciones que se anulan mutuamente: suma y resta, o multiplicación y división.

Addition and subtraction are inverse operations:
$5 + 3 + 8; 8 - 3 = 5$
Multiplication and division are inverse operations:
$2 \cdot 3 = 6; 6 \div 3 = 2$

---

inverse variation A relationship in which one variable quantity increases as another variable quantity decreases; the product of the variables is a constant. (p. 714)

variación inversa Relación en la que una cantidad variable aumenta a medida que otra cantidad variable disminuye; el producto de las variables es una constante.

$xy = 7, y = \frac{7}{x}$

---

irrational number A number that cannot be expressed as a ratio of two integers or as a repeating or terminating decimal. (p. 191)

número irracional Número que no se puede expresar como una razón de dos enteros ni como decimal periódico o cerrado.

$\sqrt{2}, \pi$

---

isolate the variable To get a variable alone on one side of an equation or inequality in order to solve the equation or inequality. (p. 34)

despejar la variable Dejar sola la variable en un lado de una ecuación o desigualdad para resolverla.

$$\begin{aligned} x + 7 &= 22 \\ \underline{\;-7} &\;\; \underline{-7} \\ x \quad &= 15 \end{aligned}$$

$$\frac{12}{3} = \frac{3x}{3}$$

$$4 = x$$

---

isometric drawing A representation of a three-dimensional figure that is drawn on a grid of equilateral triangles. (p. 302)

dibujo isométrico Representación de una figura tridimensional que se dibuja sobre una cuadrícula de triángulos equiláteros.

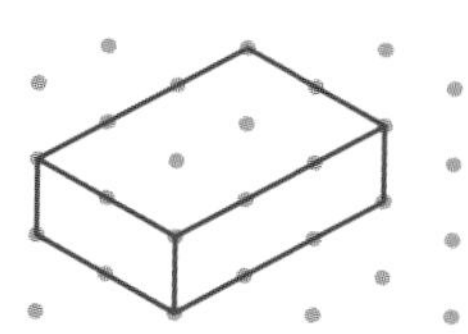

---

isosceles triangle A triangle with at least two congruent sides. (p. 337)

triángulo isósceles Triángulo que tiene al menos dos lados congruentes.

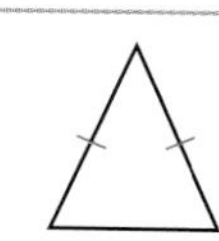

ENGLISH	SPANISH	EXAMPLES

L

lateral face In a prism or a pyramid, a face that is not a base. (p. 427)

cara lateral En un prisma o pirámide, una cara que no es la base.

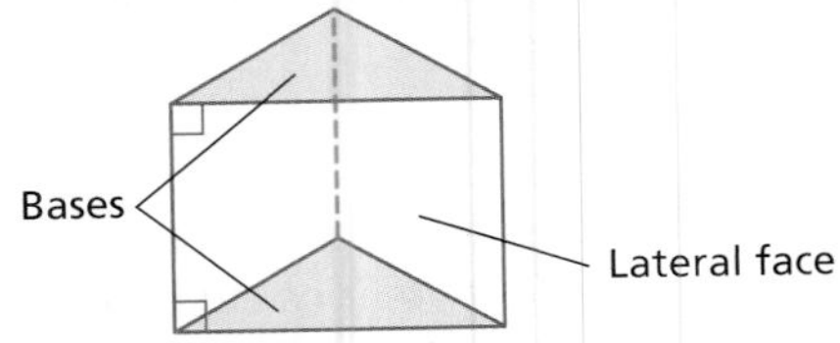

Right prism

lateral surface In a cylinder, the curved surface connecting the circular bases; in a cone, the curved surface that is not a base. (p. 427)

superficie lateral En un cilindro, superficie curva que une las bases circulares y forma los lados del cilindro; en un cono, la superficie curva que no es la base.

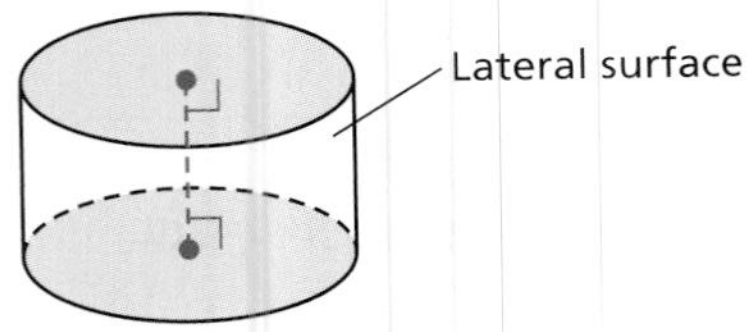

Right cylinder

least common denominator (LCD) The least common multiple of two or more denominators. (p. 68)

mínimo común denominador (mcd) El múltiplo común más pequeño de dos o más denominadores.

The LCD of $\frac{3}{4}$ and $\frac{5}{6}$ is 12.

least common multiple (LCM) The smallest whole number, other than zero, that is a multiple of two or more given numbers. (p. 824)

mínimo común múltiplo (mcm) El menor de los múltiplos de dos o más números que no sea cero.

The LCM of 6 and 10 is 30.

legs In a right triangle, the sides that include the right angle; in an isosceles triangle, the pair of congruent sides. (p. 196)

catetos En un triángulo rectángulo, los lados adyacentes al ángulo recto. En un triángulo isósceles, el par de lados congruentes.

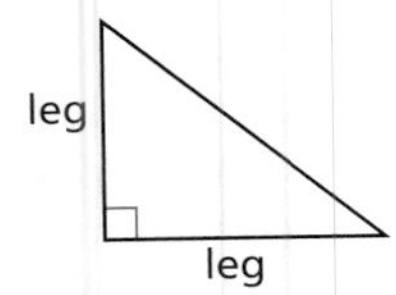

like fractions Fractions that have the same denominator.

fracciones semejantes Fracciones que tienen el mismo denominador.

$\frac{5}{12}$ and $\frac{7}{12}$ are like fractions.

like terms Two or more terms that have the same variable raised to the same power. (p. 584)

términos semejantes Términos que contienen la misma variable elevada a la misma potencia.

In the expression $3a + 5b + 12a$, $3a$ and $12a$ are like terms.

line A straight path that extends without end in opposite directions. (p. 324)

línea Trayectoria recta que se extiende de manera indefinida en direcciones opuestas.

line graph A graph that uses line segments to show how data changes. (p. 486)

gráfica lineal Gráfica que muestra cómo cambian los datos mediante segmentos de recta.

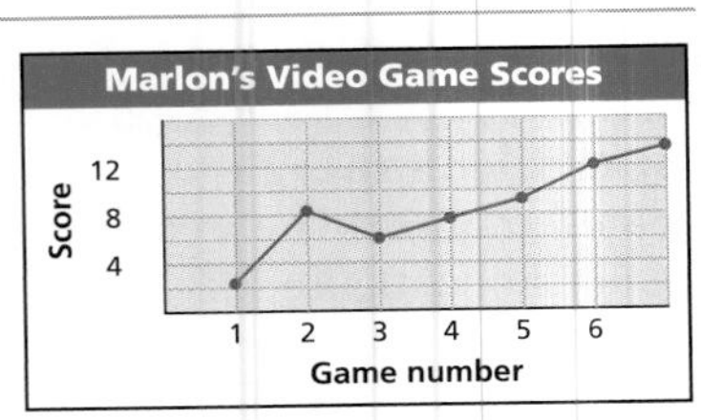

line of best fit A straight line that comes closest to the points on a scatter plot. (p. 494)

línea de mejor ajuste La línea recta que más se aproxima a los puntos de un diagrama de dispersión.

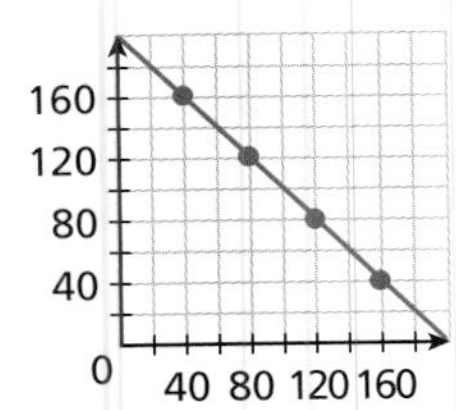

ENGLISH	SPANISH	EXAMPLES
line of reflection A line that a figure is flipped across to create a mirror image of the original figure. (p. 358)	**línea de reflexión** Línea sobre la cual se voltea una figura para crear una imagen idéntica de la figura original.	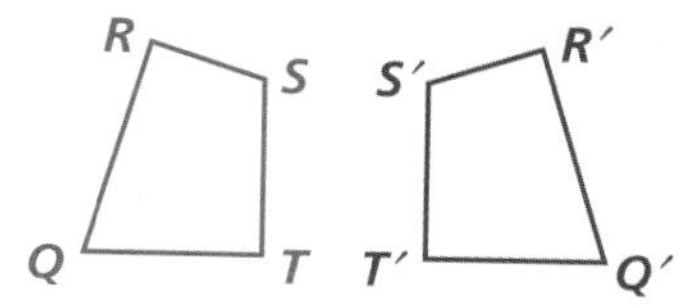
line of symmetry The imaginary "mirror" in line symmetry. (p. 364)	**eje de simetría** El "espejo" imaginario de una simetría axial.	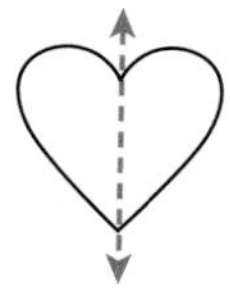
line plot A number line with marks or dots that show frequency. (p. 467)	**diagrama de acumulación** Una recta numérica con marcas o puntos que indican la frecuencia.	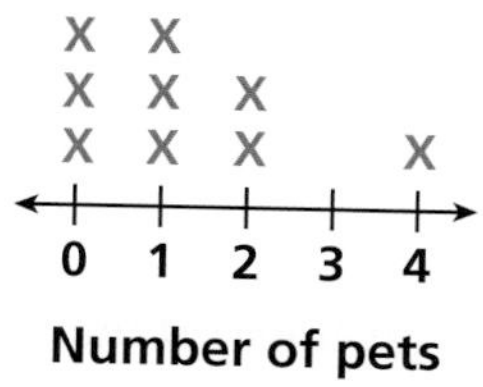
line segment A part of a line between two endpoints. (p. 324)	**segmento de recta** Parte de una línea entre dos extremos.	
line symmetry A figure has line symmetry if one half is a mirror-image of the other half. (p. 364)	**eje de simetría** El "espejo" imaginario en la simetría axial.	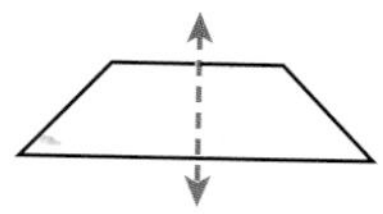
linear equation An equation whose solutions form a straight line on a coordinate plane. (p. 628)	**ecuación lineal** Ecuación cuyas soluciones forman una línea recta en un plano cartesiano.	$y = 2x + 1$
linear function A function whose graph is a straight line. (p. 700)	**función lineal** Función cuya gráfica es una línea recta.	$y = x - 1$ 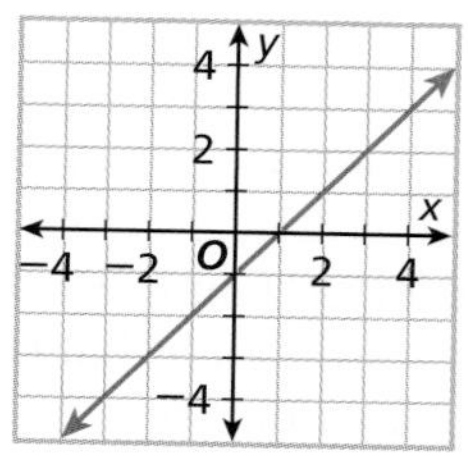
linear inequality A mathematical sentence using <, >, ≤, or ≥ whose graph is a region with a straight-line boundary. (p. 655)	**desigualdad lineal** Enunciado matemático que usa los símbolos <, >, ≤, o ≥ y cuya gráfica es una región con una línea de límite recta.	

M

major arc An arc that is more than half of a circle. (p. 838)	**arco mayor** Arco que es más de la mitad de un círculo.	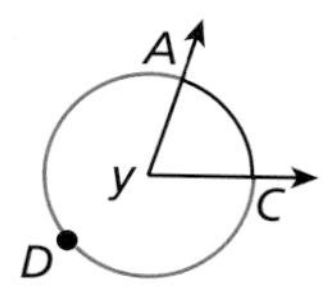 $\overparen{ADC}$ is a major arc of the circle.

ENGLISH	SPANISH	EXAMPLES
matrix A rectangular arrangement of data enclosed in brackets. (p. 839)	**matriz** Arreglo rectangular de datos encerrado entre corchetes.	$\begin{bmatrix} 1 & 0 & 3 \\ -2 & 2 & -5 \\ 7 & -6 & 3 \end{bmatrix}$
mean The sum of a set of data divided by the number of items in the data set; also called *average*. (p. 472)	**promedio** La suma de un conjunto de datos dividida entre el número de elementos en el conjunto. También se le llama *media*.	Data set: 4, 6, 7, 8, 10 Mean: $\frac{4+6+7+8+10}{5} = \frac{35}{5} = 7$
measure of central tendency A measure used to describe the middle of a data set; the mean, median, and mode are measures of central tendency. (p. 472)	**medida de tendencia dominante** Medida empleada para describir la parte media de un conjunto de datos; la media, la mediana y la moda son medidas de tendencia dominante.	
median The middle number, or the mean (average) of the two middle numbers, in an ordered set of data. (p. 472)	**mediana** El número intermedio, o la media (el promedio), de los dos números intermedios en un conjunto ordenado de datos.	Data set: 4, 6, 7, 8, 10 Median: 7
metric system of measurement A decimal system of weights and measures that is used universally in science and commonly throughout the world.	**sistema métrico de medición** Sistema decimal de pesos y medidas empleado universalmente en las ciencias y de uso común en todo el mundo.	centimeters, meters, kilometers, gram, kilograms, milliliters, liters
midpoint The point that divides a line segment into two congruent line segments.	**punto medio** El punto que divide un segmento de recta en dos segmentos de recta congruentes.	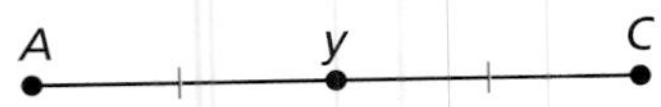 B is the midpoint of $\overline{AC}$.
minor arc An arc that is less than half of a circle. (p. 838)	**arco menor** Arco que es menor que la mitad de un círculo.	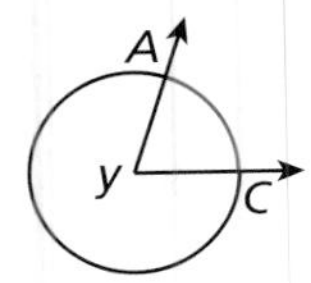 $\overset{\frown}{AC}$ is the minor arc of the circle.
mixed number A number made up of a whole number that is not zero and a fraction. (p. 825)	**número mixto** Número que contiene un número cabal mayor que cero y una fracción. (pág. 765)	$4\frac{1}{8}$
mode The number or numbers that occur most frequently in a set of data; when all numbers occur with the same frequency, we say there is no mode. (p. 472)	**moda** Valor o valores más frecuentes en un conjunto de datos; si todos los números aparecen con la misma frecuencia, no hay moda.	Data set: 3, 5, 8, 8, 10 Mode: 8
monomial A number or a product of numbers and variables with exponents that are whole numbers. (p. 734)	**monomio** Un número o un producto de números y variables con exponentes que son números cabales.	$3x^2y^4$

ENGLISH	SPANISH	EXAMPLES
Multiplication Property of Equality The property that states that if you multiply both sides of an equation by the same number, the new equation will have the same solution. (p. 40)	**Propiedad de igualdad de la multiplicación** Propiedad que establece que puedes multiplicar ambos lados de una ecuación por el mismo número y la ecuación resultante tendrá la misma solución.	$3 \cdot 4 = 12$ $3 \cdot 4 \cdot 2 = 12 \cdot 2$ $24 = 24$
Multiplication Property of Zero The property that states that for all real numbers a, $a \cdot 0 = 0$ and $0 \cdot a = 0$. (p. 829)	**Propiedad de multiplicación del cero** Propiedad que establece que para todos los números reales a, $a \cdot 0 = 0$ y $0 \cdot a = 0$.	
multiplicative inverse A number times its multiplicative inverse is equal to 1; also called *reciprocal.* (p. 80)	**inverso multiplicativo** Un número multiplicado por su inverso multiplicativo es igual a 1. También se le llama *recíproco.*	The multiplicative inverse of $\frac{4}{5}$ is $\frac{5}{4}$.
multiple The product of any number and a non-zero whole number is a multiple of that number. (p. 822)	**múltiplo** El producto de cualquier número y un número cabal es un múltiplo de ese número.	
mutually exclusive Two events are mutually exclusive if they cannot occur in the same trial of an experiment. (p. 542)	**mutuamente excluyentes** Dos sucesos son mutuamente excluyentes cuando no pueden ocurrir en la misma prueba de un experimento.	When rolling a number cube, rolling a 3 and rolling an even number are mutually exclusive events.

N

ENGLISH	SPANISH	EXAMPLES
negative correlation Two data sets have a negative correlation if one set of data values increases while the other decreases. (p. 495)	**correlación negativa** Caso en que los valores de un conjunto de datos aumentan mientras que los valores de otro conjunto de datos disminuyen.	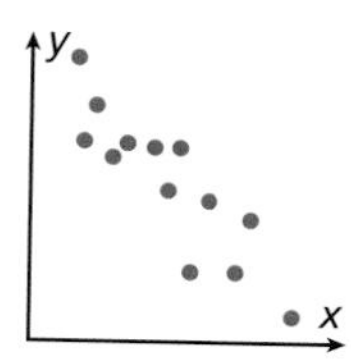
negative integer An integer less than zero. (p. 15)	**entero negativo** Entero menor que cero.	−2 is a negative integer. 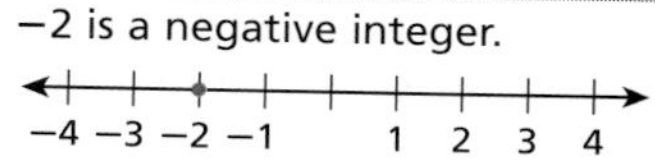
net An arrangement of two-dimensional figures that can be folded to form a polyhedron. (p. 406)	**plantilla** Un arreglo de figuras bidimensionales que se puede plegar o doblar para formar un poliedro.	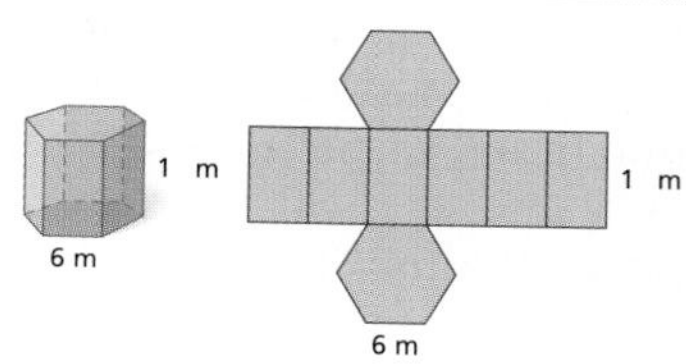
no correlation Two data sets have no correlation when there is no relationship between their data values. (p. 495)	**sin correlación** Caso en que los valores de los dos conjuntos no muestran ninguna relación.	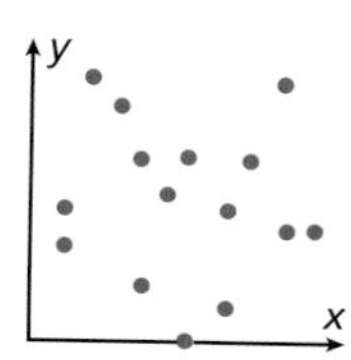

ENGLISH	SPANISH	EXAMPLES
nonlinear function A function whose graph is not a straight line.	**función no lineal** Función cuya gráfica no es una línea recta.	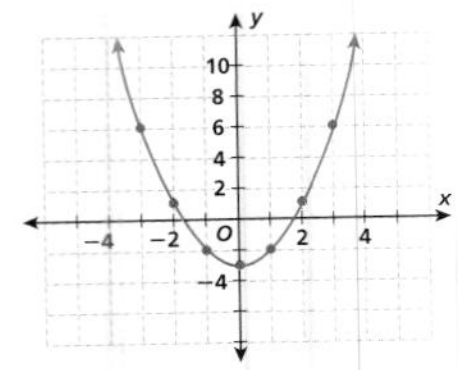 $y = x^2 - 3$
nonterminating decimal A decimal that never ends. (p. 191)	**decimal no cerrado** Decimal que nunca termina.	
numerator The top number of a fraction that tells how many parts of a whole are being considered. (p. 64)	**numerador** El número de arriba de una fracción; indica cuántas partes de un todo se están considerando.	$\frac{4}{5}$ ← numerator
numerical expression An expression that contains only numbers and operations.	**expresión numérica** Expresión matemática que incluye sólo números y operaciones matemáticas.	$(2 \cdot 3) + 1$

O

obtuse angle An angle whose measure is greater than 90° but less than 180°. (p. 325)	**ángulo obtuso** Ángulo cuya medida es mayor de 90° pero menor de 180°.	
obtuse triangle A triangle containing one obtuse angle. (p. 336)	**triángulo obtusángulo** Triángulo que tiene un ángulo obtuso.	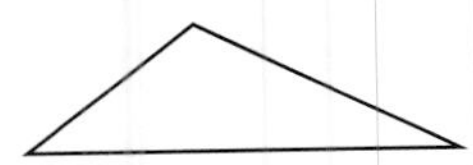
octagon An eight-sided polygon. (p. 239)	**octágono** Polígono de ocho lados.	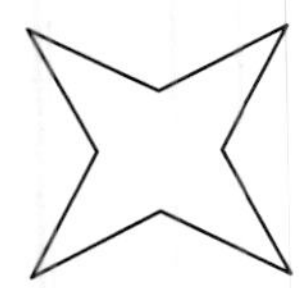
odd number A whole number that is not divisible by two.	**número impar** Número cabal que no es divisible entre 2.	
odds A comparison of favorable outcomes and unfavorable outcomes. (p. 554)	**posibilidades** Comparación de resultados favorables y no favorables.	
odds against The ratio of the number of unfavorable outcomes to the number of favorable outcomes. (p. 554)	**posibilidades en contra** Razón del número de resultados posibles no favorables con respecto al número de resultados posibles favorables.	The odds against rolling a 3 on a number cube are 5:1.
odds in favor The ratio of the number of favorable outcomes to the number of unfavorable outcomes. (p. 554)	**posibilidades a favor** Razón del número de resultados posibles favorables con respecto al número de resultados posibles desfavorables.	The odds in favor of rolling a 3 on a number cube are 1:5.

ENGLISH	SPANISH	EXAMPLES
opposites Two numbers that are an equal distance from zero on a number line; also called *additive inverse.* (p. 14)	**opuestos** Dos números que están a la misma distancia de cero en una recta numérica. También se llaman *inversos aditivos.*	5 and −5 are opposites. 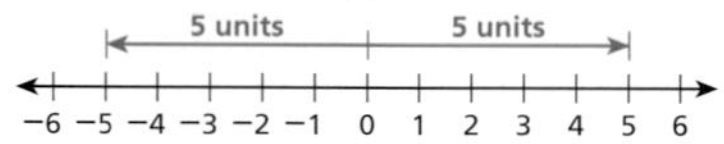
order of operations A rule for evaluating expressions: First perform the operations in parentheses, then compute powers and roots, then perform all multiplication and division from left to right, and then perform all addition and subtraction from left to right. (p. 828)	**orden de las operaciones** Regla para evaluar expresiones: primero se hacen las operaciones entre paréntesis, luego se hallan las potencias y raíces, después todas las multiplicaciones y divisiones de izquierda a derecha ,y por último todas las sumas y restas de izquierda a derecha.	$4^2 + 8 \div 2$ Evaluate the power. $16 + 8 \div 2$ Divide. $16 + 4$ Add. 20
ordered pair A pair of numbers that can be used to locate a point on a coordinate plane. (p. 118)	**par ordenado** Par de números que sirven para localizar un punto en un plano cartesiano.	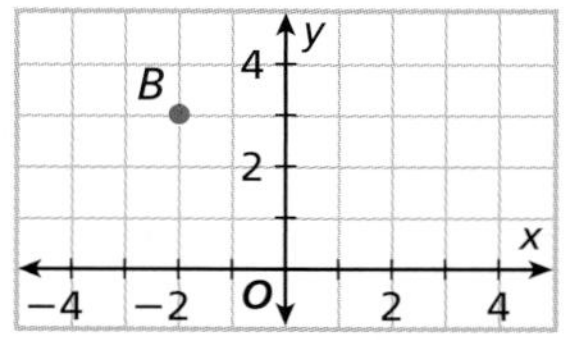 The coordinates of *B* are (−2, 3).
origin The point where the *x*-axis and *y*-axis intersect on the coordinate plane; (0, 0). (p. 122)	**origen** Punto de intersección entre el eje de las *x* y el eje de las *y* se cruzan en el plano cartesiano; (0, 0).	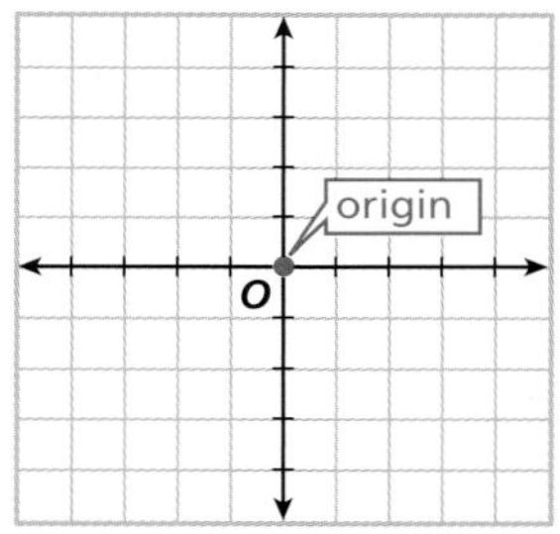
orthogonal views A drawing that shows the top, bottom, front, back, and side views of a three-dimensional object. (p. 408)	**vista ortogonal** Un dibujo que muestra la vista superior, inferior, frontal, posterior y lateral de un objecto de tres dimensiones.	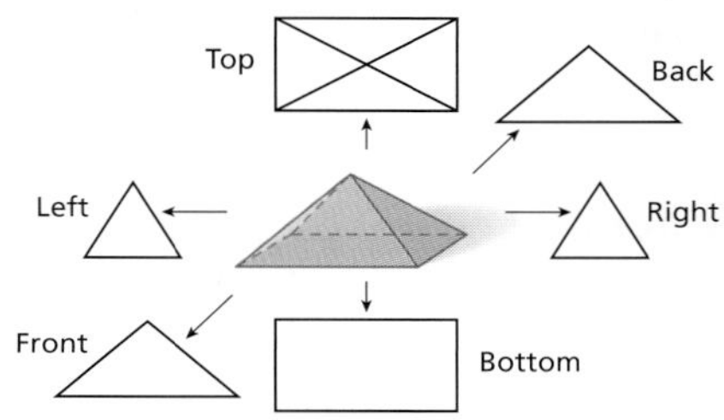
outcome (probability) A possible result of a probability experiment. (p. 522)	**resultado posible (en probabilidad)** Un posible resultado de un experimento de probabilidad.	When rolling a number cube, the possible outcomes are 1, 2, 3, 4, 5, and 6.
outlier A value much greater or much less than the others in a data set. (p. 472)	**valor extremo** Valor mucho mayor o mucho menor que los demás de un conjunto de datos.	
output The value that results from the substitution of a given input into an expression or function. (p. 134)	**valor de salida** Valor que resulta después de sustituir una variable con un valor de entrada en una función o expresión.	For the function $y = 6x$, the input 4 produces an output of 24.

ENGLISH	SPANISH	EXAMPLES

P

parabola The graph of a quadratic function. (p. 708)

parábola Gráfica de una función cuadrática.

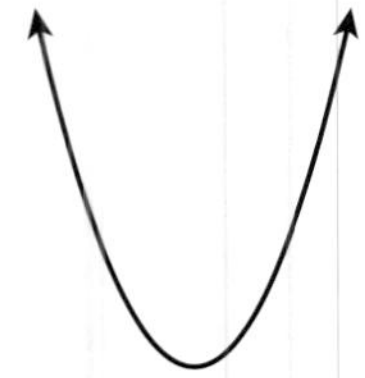

parallel lines Lines in a plane that do not intersect. (p. 330)

líneas paralelas Líneas que se encuentran en el mismo plano pero que nunca se intersecan.

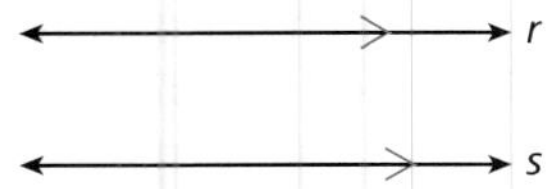

parallelogram A quadrilateral with two pairs of parallel sides. (p. 342)

paralelogramo Cuadrilátero con dos pares de lados paralelos.

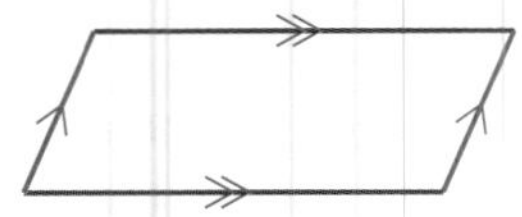

pentagon A five-sided polygon. (p. 341)

pentágono Polígono de cinco lados.

percent A ratio comparing a number to 100. (p. 274)

porcentaje Razón que compara un número con el número 100.

$45\% = \frac{45}{100}$

percent change The amount stated as a percent that a number increases or decreases. (p. 294)

porcentaje de cambio Cantidad expresada como un porcentaje en que un número aumenta o disminuye.

percent decrease A percent change describing a decrease in a quantity. (p. 294)

porcentaje de disminución Porcentaje en que una cifra disminuye.

An item that costs $8 is marked down to $6. The amount of the decrease is $2 and the percent of decrease is $\frac{2}{8} = 0.25 = 25\%$.

percent increase A percent change describing an increase in a quantity. (p. 294)

porcentaje de incremento Porcentaje en que una cifra aumenta.

The price of an item increases from $8 to $12. The amount of the increase is $4 and the percent of increase is $\frac{4}{8} = 0.5 = 50\%$

perfect square A square of a whole number. (p. 182)

cuadrado perfecto El cuadrado de un número cabal.

$5^2 = 25$, so 25 is a perfect square.

perimeter The distance around a polygon. (p. 388)

perímetro Distancia alrededor de un polígono.

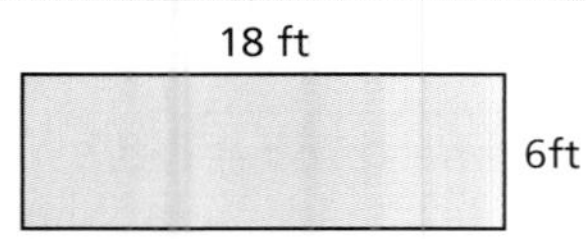

perimeter =
$18 + 6 + 18 + 6 = 48$ ft

permutation An arrangement of items or events in which order is important. (p. 563)

permutación Arreglo de objetos o sucesos en el que el orden es importante.

For objects *A, B,* and *C,* there are 6 different permutations: *ABC, ACB, BAC, BCA, CAB, CBA.*

perpendicular bisector A line that intersects a segment at its midpoint and is perpendicular to the segment. (p. 227)

mediatriz Línea que cruza un segmento en su punto medio y es perpendicular al segmento.

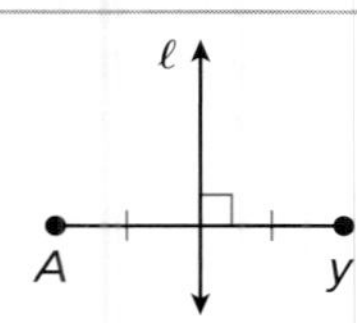

ENGLISH	SPANISH	EXAMPLES
perpendicular lines Lines that intersect to form right angles. (p. 330)	**líneas perpendiculares** Líneas que al intersecarse forman ángulos rectos.	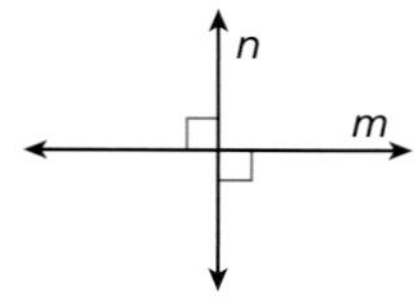
perspective A technique used to make three-dimensional objects appear to have depth and distance on a flat surface. (p. 408)	**perspectiva** Técnica que sirve para hacer que los objetos tridimensionales parezcan tener profundidad y distancia en una superficie plana.	
pi (π) The ratio of the circumference of a circle to the length of its diameter; $\pi \approx 3.14$ or $\frac{22}{7}$. (p. 400)	**pi (π)** Razón de la circunferencia de un círculo a la longitud de su diámetro; $\pi \approx 3.14$ ó $\frac{22}{7}$.	
plane A flat surface that extends forever. (p. 324)	**plano** Superficie plana que se extiende de manera indefinida en todas direcciones.	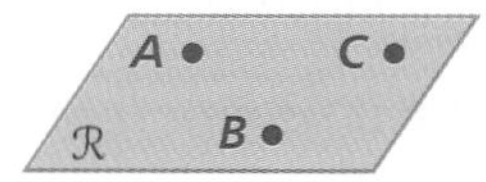
point An exact location in space. (p. 324)	**punto** Ubicación exacta en el espacio.	*P* •
point-slope form The equation of a line in the form of $y - y_1 = m(x - x_1)$, where m is the slope and (x_1, y_1) is a specific point on the line. (p. 644)	**forma de punto y pendiente** Ecuación lineal en la forma $y - y_1 = m(x - x_1)$, donde m es la pendiente y (x^1, y^1) es un punto específico de la línea.	$y - 3 = 2(x - 3)$
polygon A closed plane figure formed by three or more line segments that intersect only at their endpoints (vertices). (p. 341)	**polígono** Figura cerrada plana, formada por tres o más segmentos de recta que se intersecan sólo en sus extremos (vértices).	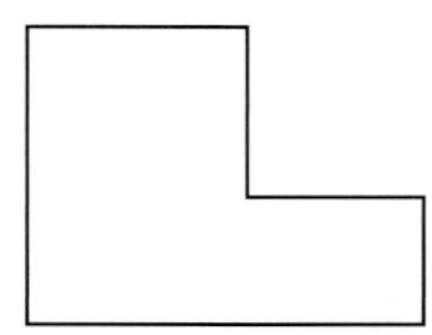
polyhedron A three-dimensional figure in which all the surfaces or faces are polygons.	**poliedro** Figura tridimensional cuyas superficies o caras tiene forma de polígonos.	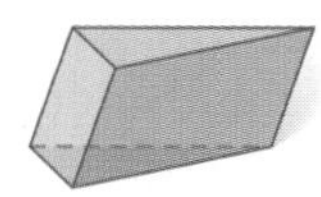
polynomial One monomial or the sum or difference of monomials. (p. 734)	**polinomio** Un monomio o la suma o resta de monomios.	$2x^2 + 3xy - 7y^2$
population The entire group of objects or individuals considered for a survey. (p. 462)	**población** Grupo completo de objetos o individuos que se desea estudiar.	In a survey about study habits of middle school students, the population is all middle school students.
positive correlation Two data sets have a positive correlation when their data values increase or decrease together.	**correlación positiva** Caso en el que los valores de ambos conjuntos de datos aumentan o disminuyen al mismo tiempo.	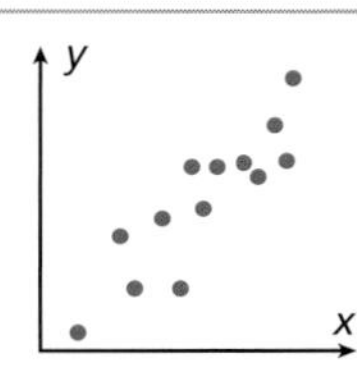

ENGLISH	SPANISH	EXAMPLES
positive integer An integer greater than zero. (p. 15)	**entero positivo** Entero mayor que cero.	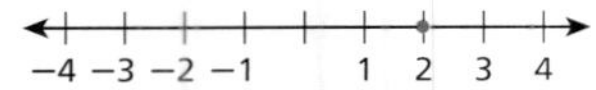 2 is a positive integer.
power A number produced by raising a base to an exponent. (p. 162)	**potencia** Número que resulta al elevar una base a un exponente.	$2^3 = 8$, so 2 to the 3rd power is 8.
prime factorization A number written as the product of its prime factors. (p. 823)	**factorización prima** Número que se escribe como el producto de sus factores primos.	$10 = 2 \cdot 5$, $24 = 2^3 \cdot 3$
prime number A whole number greater than 1 that has exactly two factors, itself and 1. (p. 823)	**número primo** Un número cabal mayor que 1 que tiene exactamente dos factores el l y sí mismo.	5 is prime because its only factors are 5 and 1.
principal The initial amount of money borrowed or saved. (p. 302)	**capital** Cantidad inicial de dinero depositada o recibida en préstamo.	
principal square root The nonnegative square root of a number. (p. 182)	**raíz cuadrada principal** Raíz cuadrada no negativa de un número.	$\sqrt{25} = 5$; the principal square root of 25 is 5.
prism A polyhedron that has two congruent, polygon-shaped bases and other faces that are all parallelograms. (p. 413)	**prisma** Poliedro con dos bases congruentes con forma de polígono y caras con forma de paralelogramos.	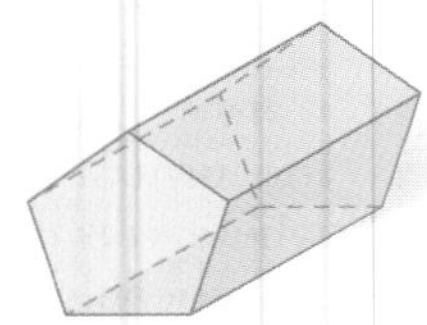
probability A number from 0 to 1 (or 0% to 100%) that describes how likely an event is to occur. (p. 522)	**probabilidad** Un número entre 0 y 1 (ó 0% y 100%) que describe la posibilidad de que un suceso ocurra.	A bag contains 3 red marbles and 4 blue marbles. The probability of randomly choosing a red marble is $\frac{3}{7}$.
product The result when two or more numbers are multiplied.	**producto** Resultado de multiplicar dos o más números.	The product of 4 and 8 is 32.
proper fraction A fraction in which the numerator is less than the denominator.	**fracción propia** Fracción en la que el numerador es menor que el denominador.	$\frac{3}{4}, \frac{1}{12}, \frac{7}{8}$
proportion An equation that states that two ratios are equivalent. (p. 216)	**proporción** Ecuación que establece que dos razones son equivalentes.	$\frac{2}{3} = \frac{4}{6}$
protractor A tool for measuring angles. (pp. 330, 832)	**transportador** Instrumento para medir ángulos.	
pyramid A polyhedron with a polygon base and triangular sides that all meet at a common vertex. (p. 420)	**pirámide** Poliedro cuya base es un polígono y tiene caras triangulares que terminan en un vértice común.	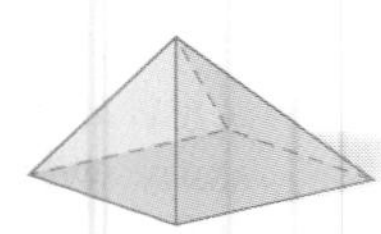

ENGLISH	SPANISH	EXAMPLES
Pythagorean Theorem In a right triangle, the square of the length of the hypotenuse is equal to the sum of the squares of the lengths of the legs. (p. 195)	**Teorema de Pitágoras** En un triángulo rectángulo, la suma de los cuadrados de los catetos es igual al cuadrado de la hipotenusa.	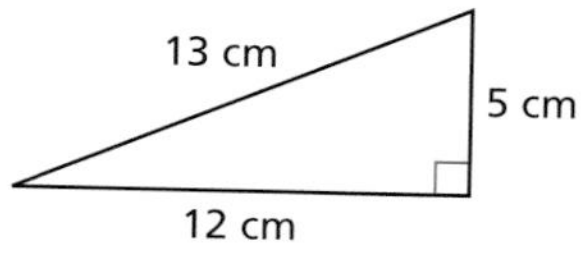 $5^2 + 12^2 = 13^2$ $25 + 144 = 169$

Q

quadrant The x- and y-axes divide the coordinate plane into four regions. Each region is called a quadrant. (p. 122)	**cuadrante** El eje de las x y el eje de las y dividen el plano cartesiano en cuatro regiones. Cada región recibe el nombre de cuadrante.	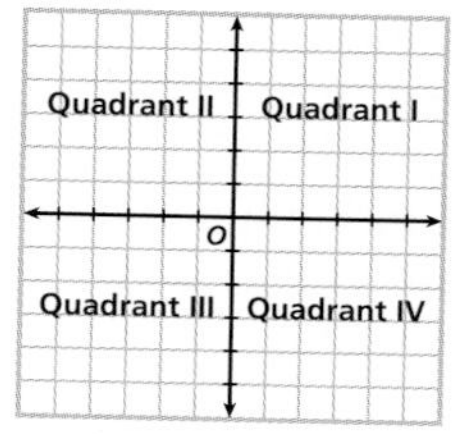
quadratic function A function of the form $y = ax^2 + bx + c$, where $a \neq 0$. (p. 708)	**función cuadrática** Función de la forma $y = ax^2 + bx + c$, donde $a \neq 0$.	$y = x^2 - 6x + 8$
quadrilateral A four-sided polygon. (p. 341)	**cuadrilátero** Polígono de cuatro lados.	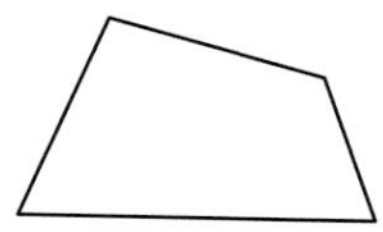
quarterly Four times a year. (p. 307)	**trimestral** Cuatro veces al año.	
quartile Three values, one of which is the median, that divide a data set into fourths. (p. 476)	**cuartil** Cada uno de tres valores, uno de los cuales es la mediana, que dividen en cuartos un conjunto de datos.	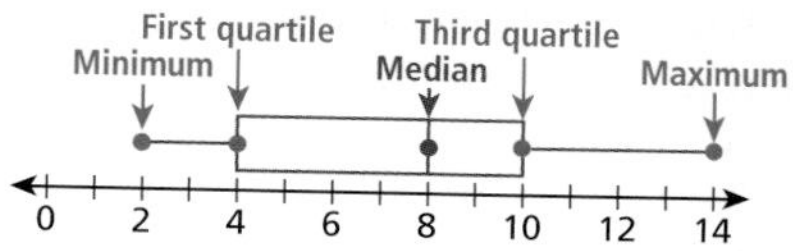
quotient The result when one number is divided by another.	**cociente** Resultado de dividir un número entre otro.	In $8 \div 4 = 2$, 2 is the quotient.

R

radical symbol The symbol $\sqrt{}$ used to represent the nonnegative square root of a number. (p. 146)	**símbolo de radical** El símbolo $\sqrt{}$ que se usa para representar la raíz cuadrada no negativa de un número.	
radius A line segment with one endpoint at the center of the circle and the other endpoint on the circle, or the length of that segment. (p. 400)	**radio** Segmento de recta con un extremo en el centro de un círculo y el otro en la circunferencia. También se llama radio a la longitud de ese segmento.	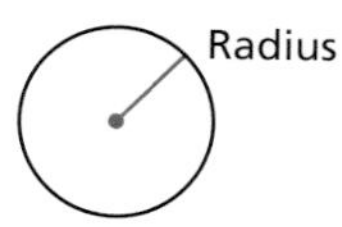
random numbers In a set of random numbers, each number has an equal chance of appearing. (p. 532)	**muestra aleatoria** Muestra que da a cada miembro de una población la misma posibilidad de ser elegido.	

ENGLISH	SPANISH	EXAMPLES
random sample A sample in which each individual or object in the entire population has an equal chance of being selected. (p. 462)	**números aleatorios** En un conjunto de números aleatorios, todos los números tienen la misma probabilidad de ser seleccionados.	
range (in statistics) The difference between the greatest and least values in a data set. (p. 472)	**rango (en estadística)** Diferencia entre los valores máximo y mínimo de un conjunto de datos.	Data set: 3, 5, 7, 7, 12 Range: $12 - 3 = 9$
range (of a function) The set of all possible output values of a function. (p. 134)	**rango (en una función)** El conjunto de todos los valores posibles de una función.	The range of $y = \|x\|$ is $y \geq 0$.
rate A ratio that compares two quantities measured in different units. (p. 220)	**relación** Comparación de dos cantidades expresadas con unidades diferentes.	The speed limit is 55 miles per hour or 55 mi/h.
rate of interest The percent charged or earned on an amount of money; see *simple interest.* (p. 302)	**tasa de interés** Porcentaje que se cobra por una cantidad de dinero prestada o que se gana por una cantidad de dinero ahorrada; ver *interés simple.*	
ratio A comparison of two quantities by division. (p. 216)	**razón** Comparación de dos cantidades mediante una división.	12 to 25, 12:25, $\frac{12}{25}$
rational number Any number that can be expressed as a ratio of two integers. (p. 64)	**número racional** Número que se puede escribir como una razón de dos enteros.	6 can be expressed as $\frac{6}{1}$. 0.5 can be expressed $\frac{1}{2}$.
ray A part of a line that starts at one endpoint and extends forever. (p. 324)	**rayo** Parte de una línea que inicia en un extremo y se extiende de manera indefinida.	
real number A rational or irrational number. (p. 191)	**número real** Número racional o irracional.	
reciprocal One of two numbers whose product is 1; also called *multiplicative inverse.* (p. 80)	**recíproco** Uno de dos números cuyo producto es igual a 1. También se llama *inverso multiplicativo.*	The reciprocal of $\frac{2}{3}$ is $\frac{3}{2}$.
rectangle A parallelogram with four right angles. (p. 342)	**rectángulo** Paralelogramo con cuatro ángulos rectos.	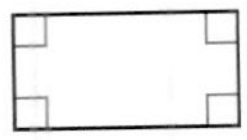
rectangular prism A polyhedron whose bases are rectangles and whose other faces are parallelograms. (p. 413)	**prisma rectangular** Poliedro cuyas bases son rectángulos y sus caras tienen forma de paralelogramos.	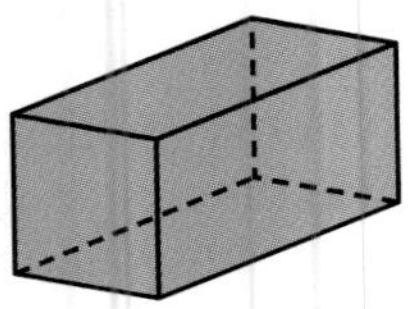
reduction A decrease in the size of all dimensions. (p. 253)	**reducción** Disminución de tamaño en todas las dimensiones de una figura.	

ENGLISH	SPANISH	EXAMPLES
reflection A transformation of a figure that flips the figure across a line. (p. 358)	**reflexión** Transformación que ocurre cuando se voltea una figura sobre la línea de reflexión.	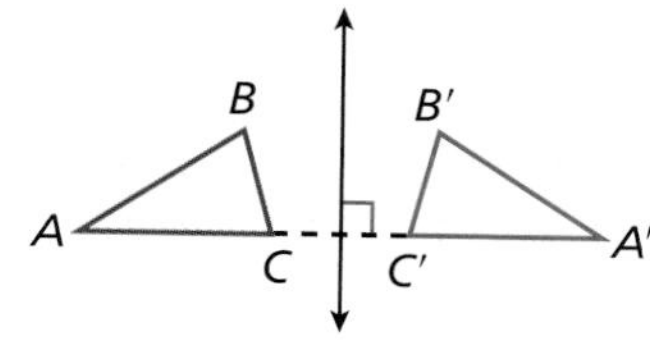
regular polygon A polygon with congruent sides and angles. (p. 342)	**polígono regular** Polígono con lados y ángulos congruentes.	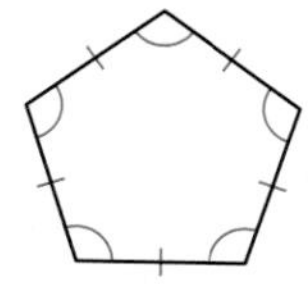
regular pyramid A pyramid whose base is a regular polygon and whose lateral faces are all congruent. (p. 432)	**pirámide regular** Pirámide que tiene un polígono regular como base y caras laterales congruentes.	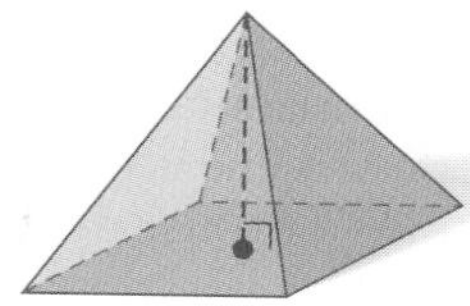
relatively prime Two numbers are relatively prime if their greatest common factor (GCF) is 1. (p. 64)	**primo relativo** Dos números son primos relativos si su máximo común divisor (MCD) es 1.	8 and 15 are relatively prime.
repeating decimal A decimal in which one or more digits repeat infinitely. (pp. 191, 827)	**decimal periódico** Decimal en el que uno o más dígitos se repiten de manera indefinida.	$0.757575\ldots = 0.\overline{75}$
rhombus A parallelogram with all sides congruent. (p. 342)	**rombo** Paralelogramo en el que todos los lados son congruentes.	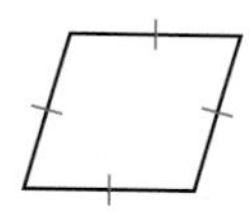
right angle An angle that measures 90°. (p. 325)	**ángulo recto** Ángulo que mide exactamente 90°.	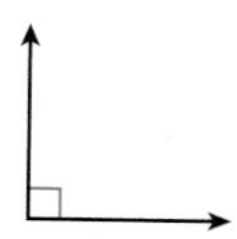
right cone A cone in which a perpendicular line drawn from the base to the tip (vertex) passes through the center of the base. (p. 432)	**cono regular** Cono en el que una línea perpendicular trazada de la base a la punta (vértice) pasa por el centro de la base.	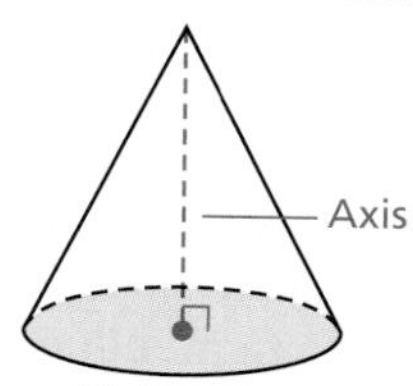 Right cone
right triangle A triangle containing a right angle. (p. 336)	**triángulo rectángulo** Triángulo que tiene un ángulo recto.	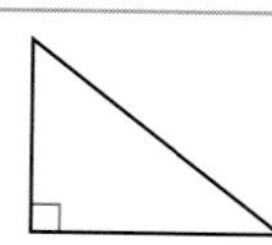
rise The vertical change when the slope of a line is expressed as the ratio $\frac{\text{rise}}{\text{run}}$, or "rise over run." (p. 347)	**distancia vertical** El cambio vertical cuando la pendiente de una línea se expresa como la razón $\frac{\text{razón distancia vertical}}{\text{distancia horizontal}}$, o "distancia vertical sobre distancia horizontal".	For the points (3, −1) and (6, 5) the rise is $5 - (-1) = 6$.

ENGLISH	SPANISH	EXAMPLES
rotation A transformation in which a figure is turned around a point. (p. 358)	**rotación** Transformación que ocurre cuando una figura gira alrededor de un punto.	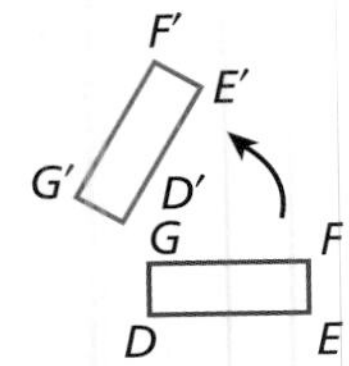
rotational symmetry A figure has rotational symmetry if it can be rotated less than 360° around a central point and coincide with the original figure. (p. 365)	**simetría de rotación** Ocurre cuando una figura gira menos de 360° alrededor de un punto sin dejar de ser congruente con la figura original.	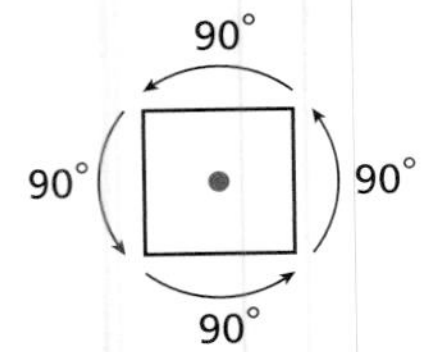
run The horizontal change when the slope of a line is expressed as the ratio $\frac{\text{rise}}{\text{run}}$, or "rise over run." (p. 347)	**distancia horizontal** El cambio horizontal cuando la pendiente de una línea se expresa como la $\frac{\text{razón distancia vertical}}{\text{distancia horizontal}}$, o "distancia vertical sobre distancia horizontal".	For the points (3, −1) and (6, 5) the run is 6 − 3 = 3.

S

ENGLISH	SPANISH	EXAMPLES
sales tax A percent of the cost of an item, which is charged by governments to raise money. (p. 298)	**impuesto sobre la venta** Porcentaje del costo de un artículo que los gobiernos cobran para recaudar fondos.	
sample A part of the population. (p. 462)	**muestra** Parte del grupo o población que se desea estudiar.	
sample space All possible outcomes of an experiment. (p. 522)	**espacio muestral** Todos los resultados posibles de un experimento.	When rolling a number cube, the sample space is 1, 2, 3, 4, 5, 6.
scale The ratio between two sets of measurements. (p. 252)	**escala** La razón entre dos conjuntos de medidas.	1 cm: 5 mi
scale drawing A drawing that uses a scale to make an object smaller than (a reduction) or larger than (an enlargement) the real object. (p. 252)	**dibujo a escala** Dibujo que usa una escala para que un objeto se vea proporcionalmente menor (reducción) o mayor (ampliación) que el objeto real al que representa.	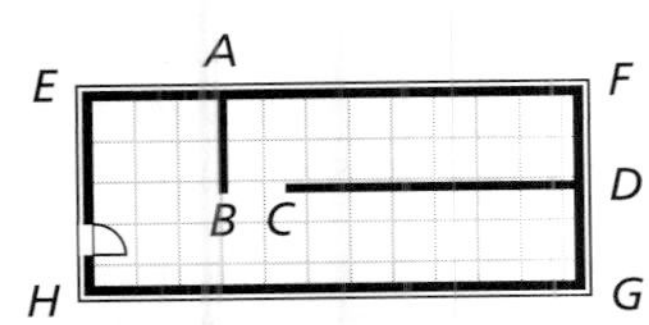 A blueprint is an example of a scale drawing.
scale factor The ratio used to enlarge or reduce similar figures. (p. 239)	**factor de escala** Razón empleada para agrandar o reducir figuras semejantes.	
scale model A proportional model of a three-dimensional object. (p. 253)	**modelo a escala** Modelo proporcional de un objeto tridimensional.	

ENGLISH | **SPANISH** | **EXAMPLES**

scalene triangle A triangle with no congruent sides. (p. 337)

triángulo escaleno Triángulo que no tiene lados congruentes.

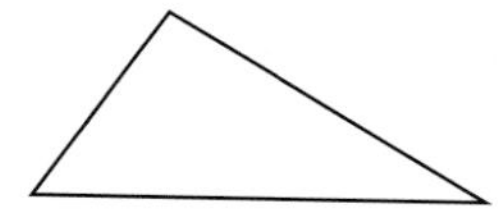

scatter plot A graph with points plotted to show a possible relationship between two sets of data. (p. 494)

diagrama de dispersión Gráfica de pares ordenados que se usa para mostrar una posible relación entre dos conjuntos de datos.

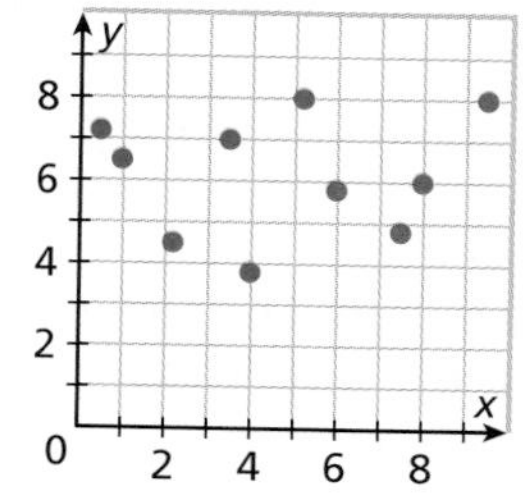

scientific notation A method of writing very large or very small numbers by using powers of 10. (p. 174)

notación científica Método abreviado que se usa para escribir números muy grandes o muy pequeños usando potencias de 10.

$12{,}560{,}000{,}000{,}000 =$
1.256×10^{13}

second differences A sequence formed from differences of differences between terms of a sequence. (p. 693)

segundas diferencias Sucesión formada a partir de las diferencias de diferencias entre términos de una sucesión.

For the sequence 1, 4, 9, 16, 25..., the first differences are 3, 5, 7, 9, ..., and the second differences are all 2.

second quartile The median of a set of data. (p. 476)

segundo cuartil La mediana de un conjunto de datos.

Data set: 4, 6, 7, 8, 10
Second quartile: 7

segment A part of a line between two endpoints. (p. 324)

segmento Parte de una línea entre dos extremos.

$\overline{GH}$

sequence An ordered list of numbers. (p. 142)

sucesión Lista ordenada de números.

2, 4, 6, 8, 10, . . .

side A line bounding a geometric figure; one of the faces forming the outside of an object. (p. 388)

lado Segmento de recta que delimita las figuras geométricas; una de las caras que forman la parte exterior de un objeto.

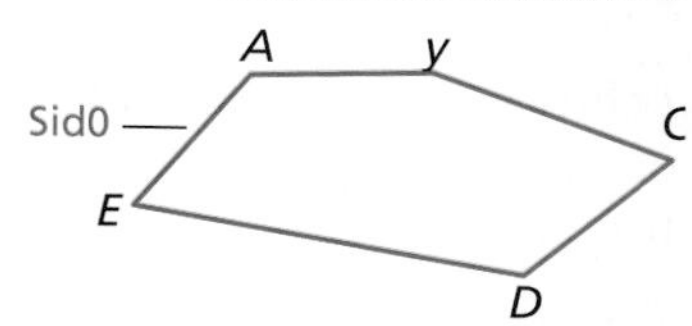

similar Figures with the same shape but not necessarily the same size are similar. (p. 238)

semejantes Figuras que tienen la misma forma, pero no necesariamente el mismo tamaño.

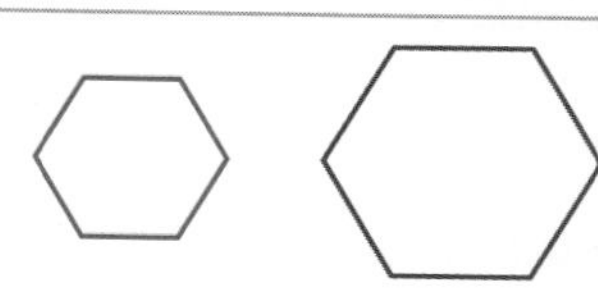

simple interest A fixed percent of the principal. It is found using the formula $I = Prt$, where P represents the principal, r the rate of interest, and t the time. (p. 302)

interés simple Un porcentaje fijo del capital. Se calcula con la fórmula $I = Crt$, donde C representa el capital, r, la tasa de interés, y t, el tiempo.

$100 is put into an account with a simple interest rate of 5%. After 2 years, the account will have earned $I = 100 \cdot 0.05 \cdot 2 = \$10$.

simplest form A fraction is in simplest form when the numerator and denominator have no common factors other than 1. (p. 64)

mínima expresión Una fracción está en su mínima expresión cuando el numerador y el denominador no tienen más factor común que 1.

Fraction: $\frac{8}{12}$
Simplest form: $\frac{2}{3}$

ENGLISH	SPANISH	EXAMPLES
simplify To write a fraction or expression in simplest form. (p. 585)	**simplificar** Escribir una fracción o expresión en su mínima expresión.	
simulation A model of an experiment, often one that would be too difficult or too time-consuming to actually perform. (p. 532)	**simulación** Representación de un experimento que en muchos casos sería demasiado difícil o tomaría demasiado tiempo realizarlo.	
slant height The distance from the base of a cone to its vertex, measured along the lateral surface. (p. 432)	**altura inclinada** Distancia de la base de un cono a su vértice, medida a lo largo de la superficie lateral.	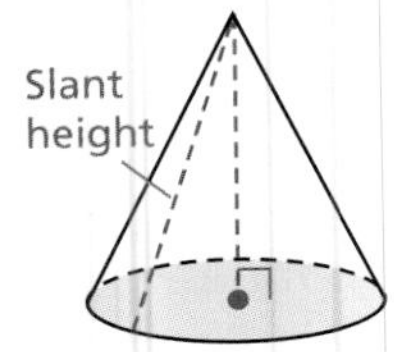
slope A measure of the steepness of a line on a graph; the rise divided by the run. (p. 347)	**pendiente** Medida de la inclinación de una línea en una gráfica. La distancia vertical dividida entre la distancia horizontal.	Slope = $\frac{\text{rise}}{\text{run}} = \frac{3}{4}$ 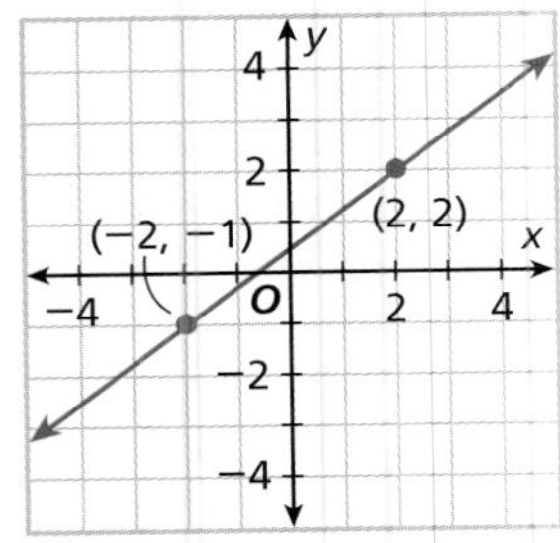
slope-intercept form A linear equation written in the form $y = mx + b$, where m represents slope and b represents the y-intercept. (p. 639)	**forma de pendiente-intersección** Ecuación lineal escrita en la forma $y = mx + b$, donde m es la pendiente y b es la intersección con el eje de las y.	$y = 6x - 3$
solution of an equation A value or values that make an equation true. (p. 34)	**solución de una ecuación** Valor o valores que hacen verdadera una ecuación.	Equation: $x + 2 = 6$ Solution: $x = 4$
solution of an inequality A value or values that make an inequality true. (p. 44)	**solución de una desigualdad** Valor o valores que hacen verdadera una desigualdad.	Inequality: $x + 3 \geq 10$ Solution: $x \geq 7$
solution of a system of equations A set of values that make all equations in a system true. (p. 608)	**solución de un sistema de ecuaciones** Conjunto de valores que hacen verdaderas todas las ecuaciones de un sistema.	System: $\begin{cases} x + y = -1 \\ -x + y = -3 \end{cases}$ Solution: (1, 2)
solution set The set of values that make a statement true. (p. 44)	**conjunto solución** Conjunto de valores que hacen verdadero un enunciado.	Inequality: $x + 3 \geq 5$ Solution set: $x \geq 2$ 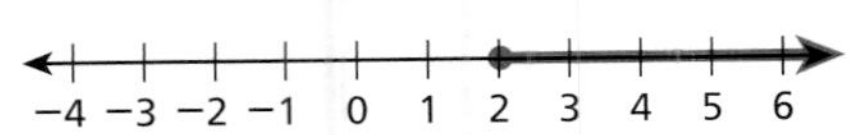
solve To find an answer or a solution. (p. 34)	**resolver** Hallar una respuesta o solución.	

ENGLISH	SPANISH	EXAMPLES

sphere A three-dimensional figure with all points the same distance from the center. (p. 436)

esfera Figura tridimensional en la que todos los puntos están a la misma distancia del centro.

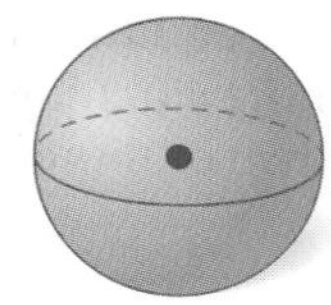

---

square A rectangle with four congruent sides. (p. 342)

cuadrado Rectángulo con cuatro lados congruentes.

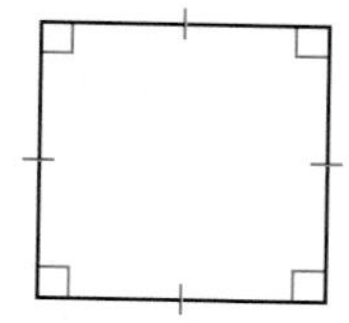

---

square (numeration) A number raised to the second power. (p. 182)

cuadrado (en numeración) Número elevado a la segunda potencia.

In 5^2, the number 5 is squared.

---

square root One of the two equal factors of a number. (p. 182)

raíz cuadrada Uno de los dos factores iguales de un número.

$16 = 4 \cdot 4$, or $16 = -4 \cdot -4$, so 4 and -4 are square roots of 16.

---

stem-and-leaf plot A graph used to organize and display data so that the frequencies can be compared. (p. 467)

diagrama doble de tallo y hojas Diagrama de tallo y hojas que compara dos conjuntos de datos presentando uno de ellos a la izquierda del tallo y el otro a la derecha.

Stem	Leaves
3	2 3 4 4 7 9
4	0 1 5 7 7 7 8
5	1 2 2 3

Key: 3|2 means 3.2

---

stratified sample A sample of a population that has been divided into subgroups. (p. 462)

muestra por estratos Muestra de una población que ha sido dividida en subgrupos.

In a nationwide survey, ten states are randomly chosen and 500 people are randomly chosen from each of these states.

---

substitute To replace a variable with a number or another expression in an algebraic expression. (p. 6)

sustituir Reemplazar una variable por un número u otra expresión en una expresión algebraica.

Substituting 3 for m in the expression $5m - 2$ gives $5(3) - 2 = 15 - 2 = 13$.

Subtraction Property of Equality The property that states that if you subtract the same number from both sides of an equation, the new equation will have the same solution. (p. 35)

Propiedad de igualdad de la resta Propiedad que establece que puedes restar el mismo número en ambos lados de una ecuación y la ecuación resultante tendrá la misma solución.

$$\begin{aligned} 14 - 6 &= 8 \\ \underline{\quad - 6} &= \underline{-6} \\ 14 - 12 &= 2 \end{aligned}$$

---

sum The result when two or more numbers are added.

suma Resultado de sumar dos o más números.

---

supplementary angles Two angles whose measures have a sum of 180°. (p. 325)

ángulos suplementarios Dos ángulos cuyas medidas suman 180°.

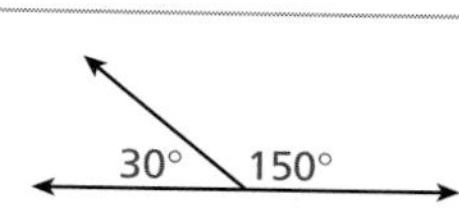

---

surface area The sum of the areas of the faces, or surfaces, of a three-dimensional figure. (p. 427)

área total Suma de las áreas de las caras, o superficies, de una figura tridimensional.

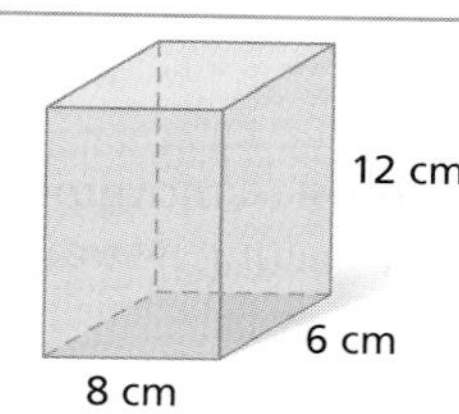

Surface area = $2(8)(12) + 2(8)(6) + 2(12)(6) = 432 \text{ cm}^2$

ENGLISH	SPANISH	EXAMPLES
system of equations A set of two or more equations that contain two or more variables. (p. 608)	**sistema de ecuaciones** Conjunto de dos o más ecuaciones que contienen dos o más variables.	$\begin{cases} x + y = -1 \\ -x + y = -3 \end{cases}$
systematic sample A sample of a population that has been selected using a pattern. (p. 462)	**muestra sistemática** Muestra de una población, la cual se elije mediante un patrón.	To conduct a phone survey, every tenth name is chosen from the phone book.

T

ENGLISH	SPANISH	EXAMPLES
term (in an expression) The parts of an expression that are added or subtracted. (p. 584)	**término (en una expresión)** Las partes de una expresión que se suman o se restan.	$3x^2 +$ $6x -$ 8 (↑ Term ↑ Term ↑ Term)
term (in a sequence) An element or number in a sequence. (p. 142)	**término (de una sucesión)** Elemento o número de una sucesión.	5 is the third term in the sequence 1, 3, 5, 7, 9, . . .
terminating decimal A decimal number that ends or terminates. (pp. 191, 827)	**decimal cerrado** Decimal que termina debido a que tiene un número determinado de posiciones decimales.	6.75
tessellation A repeating pattern of plane figures that completely cover a plane with no gaps or overlaps. (p. 368)	**teselado** Patrón repetido de figuras planas que cubren totalmente un plano sin traslaparse ni dejar huecos.	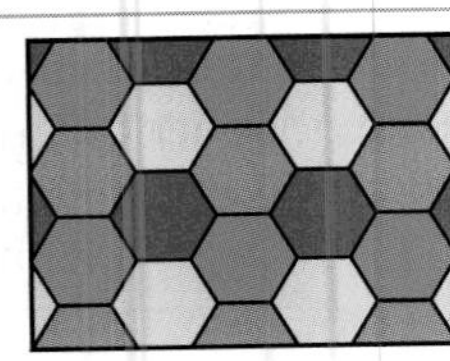
theoretical probability The ratio of the number of equally likely outcomes in an event to the total number of possible outcomes. (p. 540)	**probabilidad teórica** Razón del número de resultados igualmente probales al número de resultados posibles.	When rolling a number cube, the theoretical probability of rolling a 4 is $\frac{1}{6}$.
third quartile The median of the upper half of a set of data; also called *upper quartile.* (p. 476)	**tercer cuartil** La mediana de la mitad superior de un conjunto de datos. También se llama *cuartil superior.*	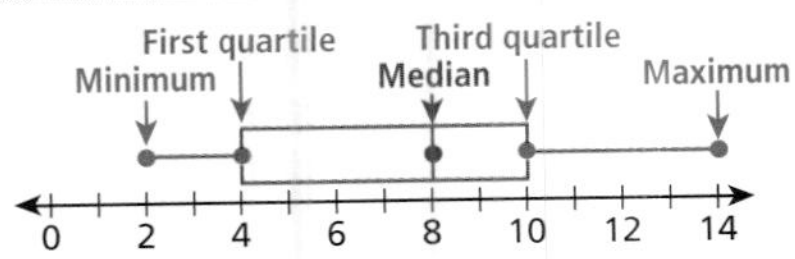
transformation A change in the size or position of a figure. (p. 358)	**transformación** Cambio en el tamaño o la posición de una figura.	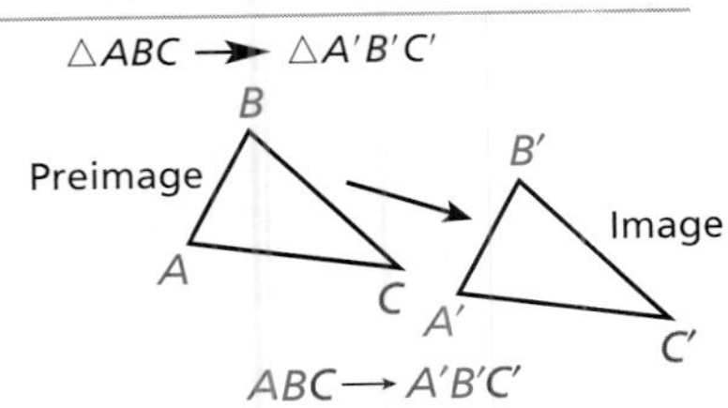
translation A movement (slide) of a figure along a straight line. (p. 358)	**traslación** Desplazamiento de una figura a lo largo de una línea recta.	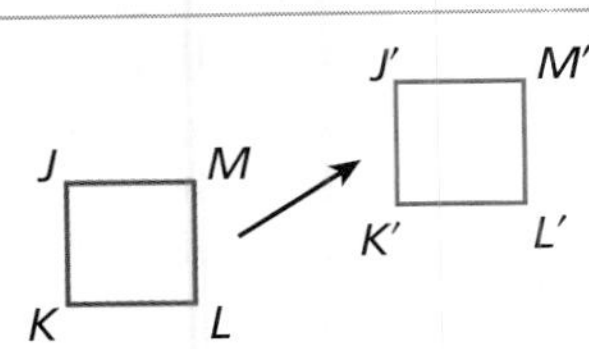

ENGLISH	SPANISH	EXAMPLES

transversal A line that intersects two or more lines. (p. 330)

transversal Línea que cruza dos o más líneas.

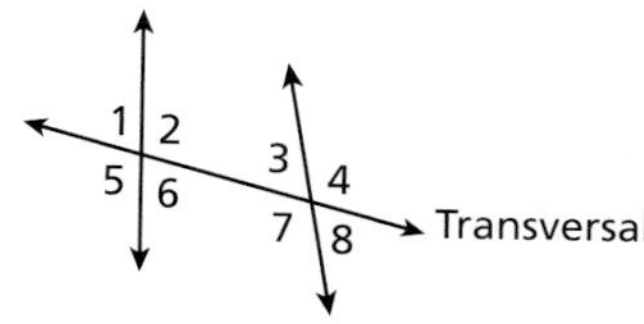

trapezoid A quadrilateral with exactly one pair of parallel sides. (p. 342)

trapecio Cuadrilátero que tiene exactamente un par de lados paralelos.

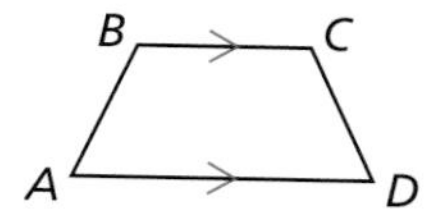

tree diagram A branching diagram that shows all possible combinations or outcomes of an event. (p. 559)

diagrama de árbol Diagrama ramificado que muestra todas las posibles combinaciones o resultados de un suceso.

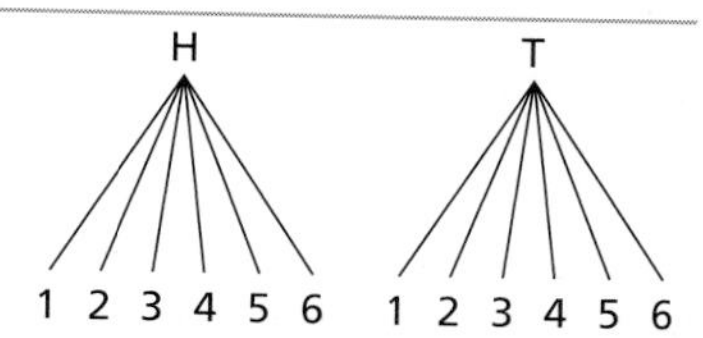

trial In probability, a single repetition or observation of an experiment. (p. 522)

prueba En probabilidad, una sola repetición u observación de un experimento.

When rolling a number cube, each roll is one trial.

triangle A three-sided polygon.

triángulo Polígono de tres lados.

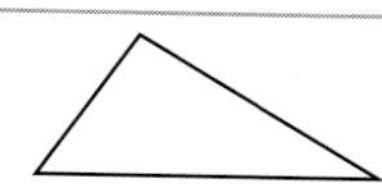

Triangle Sum Theorem The theorem that states that the measures of the angles in a triangle add up to 180°. (p. 336)

Teorema de la suma del triángulo Teorema que establece que las medidas de los ángulos de un triángulo suman 180°.

triangular prism A polyhedron whose bases are triangles and whose other faces are parallelograms. (p. 413)

prisma triangular Poliedro cuyas bases son triángulos y sus demás caras tienen forma de paralelogramos.

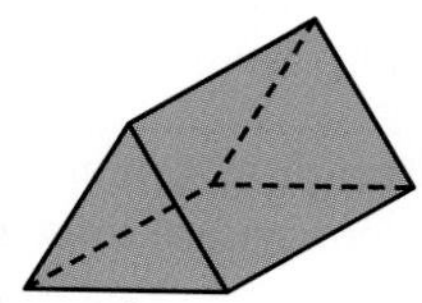

trinomial A polynomial with three terms. (p. 734)

trinomio Polinomio con tres términos.

$4x^2 + 3xy = 5y^2$

U

unbiased sample A sample is unbiased if every individual in the population has an equal chance of being selected. (p. 463)

muestra imparcial Una muestra es imparcial si cada individuo de la población tiene la misma posibilidad de ser seleccionado.

unit conversion The process of changing one unit of measure to another.

conversión de unidades Proceso que consiste en cambiar una unidad de medición en otra.

unit conversion factor A fraction used in unit conversion in which the numerator and denominator represent the same amount but are in different units. (p. 224)

factor de conversión de unidades Fracción que se usa para la conversión de unidades, donde el numerador y el denominador representan la misma cantidad pero con unidades distintas.

$\frac{60 \text{ min}}{1 \text{ h}}$ or $\frac{1 \text{ h}}{60 \text{ min}}$

ENGLISH	SPANISH	EXAMPLES
unit price A unit rate used to compare prices. (p. 221)	**precio unitario** Relación unitaria que sirve para comparar precios.	Cereal costs \$0.23 per ounce.
unit rate A rate in which the second quantity in the comparison is one unit. (p. 220)	**tasa unitaria** Una relación en donde la segunda cantidad de comparación es la unidad.	10 cm per minute

V

ENGLISH	SPANISH	EXAMPLES
variability The spread of values in a set of data. (p. 476)	**variabilidad** Medida en que se extienden los valores de un conjunto de datos.	The data set {1, 5, 7, 10, 25} has greater variability than the data set {8, 8, 9, 9, 9}.
variable A symbol used to represent a quantity that can change. (p. 6)	**variable** Letra o símbolo que representa una cantidad que puede cambiar.	In the expression $2x + 3$, x is the variable.
Venn diagram A diagram that is used to show relationships between sets. (p. 468)	**diagrama de Venn** Diagrama que sirve para mostrar las relaciones entre conjuntos.	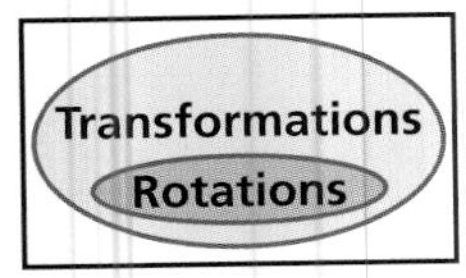
vertex On an angle or polygon, the point where two sides intersect; on a polyhedron, the intersection of three or more faces; on a cone or pyramid, the top point. (p. 408)	**vértice** En un ángulo o polígono, el punto de intersección de dos lados; en un poliedro, el punto de intersección de tres o más caras; en un cono o pirámide, la punta.	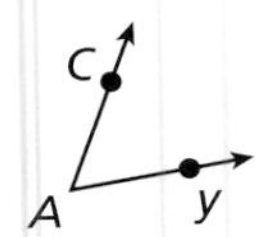 A is the vertex of $\angle CAB$.
vertical angles A pair of opposite congruent angles formed by intersecting lines. (p. 325)	**ángulos opuestos por el vértice** Par de ángulos congruentes y opuestos formados por líneas secantes. En el diagrama, $\angle a$ y $\angle c$ son opuestos por el vértice, lo mismo que $\angle b$ y $\angle d$.	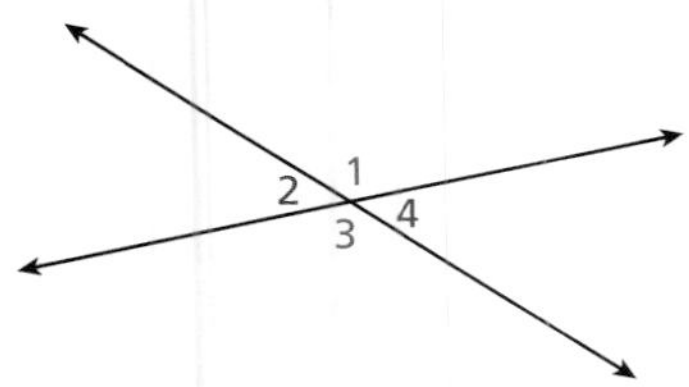 $\angle 1$ and $\angle 3$ are vertical angles.
volume The number of cubic units needed to fill a given space. (p. 413)	**volumen** Número de unidades cúbicas que se necesitan para llenar un espacio.	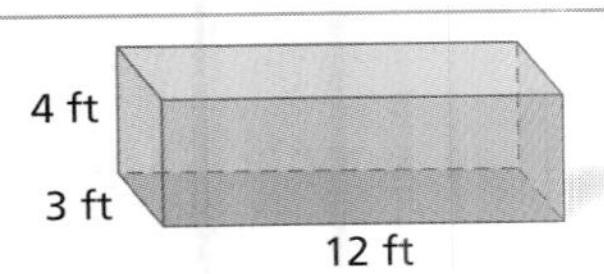 Volume $= 3 \cdot 4 \cdot 12 = 144$ ft^2
voluntary-response sample A sample in which members choose to be in the sample. (p. 462)	**muestra de respuesta voluntaria** Una muestra en la que los miembros eligen participar.	A store provides survey cards for customers who wish to fill them out.

ENGLISH	SPANISH	EXAMPLES

X

x-axis The horizontal axis on a coordinate plane. (p. 122)	**eje de las *x*** El eje horizontal del plano cartesiano.	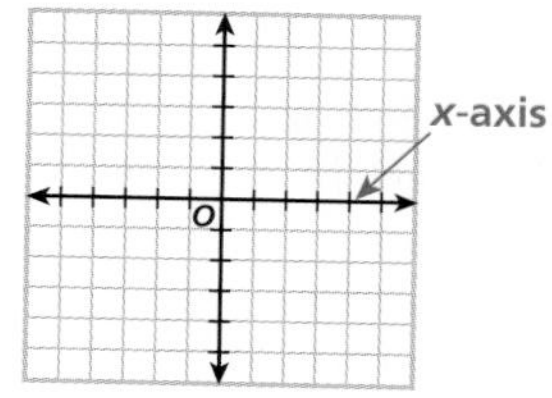
x-coordinate The first number in an ordered pair; it tells the distance to move right or left from the origin (0, 0). (p. 122)	**coordenada *x*** El primer número de un par ordenado; indica la distancia que debes moverte hacia la izquierda o la derecha desde el origen, (0, 0).	5 is the *x*-coordinate in (5, 3).
x-intercept The *x*-coordinate of the point where the graph of a line crosses the *x*-axis. (p. 638)	**intersección con el eje de las *x*** Coordenada *x* del punto donde la gráfica de una recta cruza el eje de las *x*.	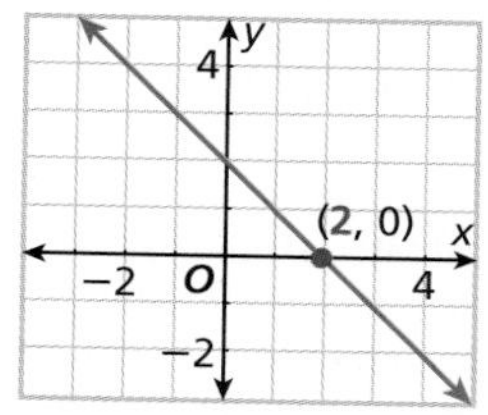 The *x*-intercept is 2.

Y

y-axis The vertical axis on a coordinate plane. (p. 122)	**eje de las *y*** El eje vertical del plano cartesiano.	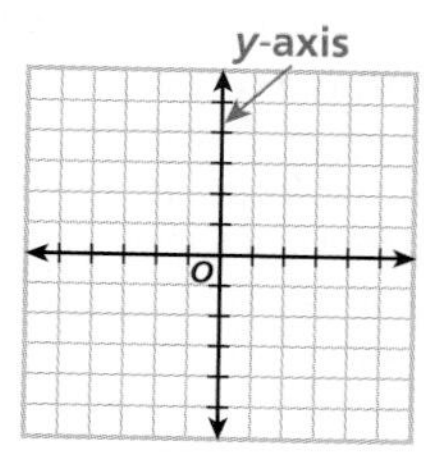
y-coordinate The second number in an ordered pair; it tells the distance to move up or down from the origin (0, 0). (p. 122)	**coordenada *y*** El segundo número de un par ordenado; indica la distancia que debes moverte hacia arriba o abajo desde el origen, (0, 0).	3 is the *y*-coordinate in (5, 3).
y-intercept The *y*-coordinate of the point where the graph of a line crosses the *y*-axis. (p. 638)	**intersección con el eje de las *y*** Coordenada *y* del punto donde la gráfica de una recta cruza el eje de las *y*.	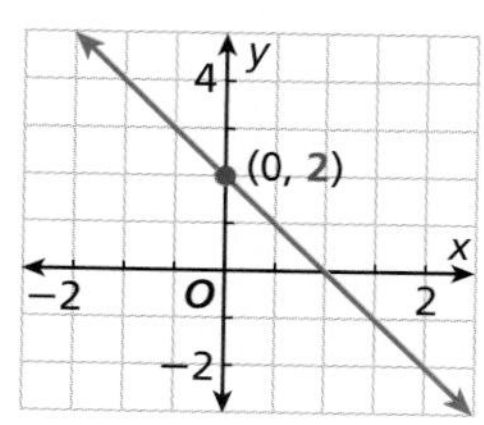 The *y*-intercept is 2.

Z

zero pair A number and its opposite, which add to 0.	**par nulo** Un número y su opuesto, cuya suma es 0.	18 and −18

Index

A

Absolute value, 15
Abstract art, 743
Acetaminophen, 707
Act It Out, 818
Acute angles, 325
Acute Mountain Sickness (AMS), 642
Acute triangles, 336
Addition
Associative Property of, 747
of fractions, 89
with unlike denominators, 85–86
of integers, 18–19
of polynomials, 747–748
modeling, 746
of rational numbers, 72–73
solving equations by, 34–36
Addition Counting Principle, 559–560
Addition Property of Equality, 34
Additive inverses, 14
AIDS Memorial Quilt, 388
Alaska, 282
Albers, Josef, 567
Algebra
The development of algebra skills and concepts is a central focus of this course and is found throughout this book.
absolute value, 15
arithmetic sequences and, 142–143
equations, 32–33, 34
addition, 34–35
checking solutions of, 34, 35, 39–40
decimal, solving, 92, 98
division, 39–40
linear, 628–630
multiplication, 39–40
multi-step, 588–589, 592, 593–595
solutions of, 32–33, 34
subtraction, 34–35
systems of, 608–609
two-step, 40, 96–97, 98–99
exponential functions, 704–705
expressions, 6–7, 10–11, 584–585
translating between tables and, 6, 11
variables and, 6–7
functions, 134–135
exponential, 704–705
graphing, 134–135, 138–139
linear, 700–701
tables and, 134–135, 138–139
quadratic, 708–709
inequalities, 44–45, 600–601, 604–605
proportions, 216–217
and indirect measurement, 248–249
in scale drawings, models, and maps, 252–253, 256–257
in similar figures, 236–237, 238–239
solving, 229–231
tiles, 32–33, 96–97, 592
Algebra tiles, 32–33, 96–97, 592
Algebraic expressions, 6, 10–11
simplifying, 584–585
Algebraic inequalities, 44
Allergies, 497
Alternate exterior angles, 331
Alternate interior angles, 331
American Samoa, 340
Amplitude, 846
AMS (Acute Mountain Sickness), 642
Amusement park rides, 358
Analysis
dimensional, 224–226
unit, 224
Analyzing, collecting, and displaying data, 458–517
Anamorphic images, 427
Anatomy, 176
Angles, 325
acute, 325
alternate exterior, 331
alternate interior, 331
bisector, 329
central, of a circle, 838
classifying, 325
complementary, 325
congruent, 238
corresponding, 331
exterior, of polygons, 346
measuring, 832
obtuse, 325
points and lines and planes and, 324–326
protractor, measuring with, 832
right, 325
supplementary, 325
in triangles, 336–338
vertical, 325
Animals, 79
Animals Link, 79
Answering context-based test items, 620–621
Ant lions, 433
Aperture, 247
Applications
Anatomy, 176
Animals, 79
Architecture, 254, 424, 637
Art, 241, 411, 428, 442, 567, 748
Astronomy, 37, 172, 475, 709
Business, 46, 136, 172, 218, 230, 281, 441, 465, 473, 557, 587, 595, 703, 711, 741, 750, 753, 755
Chemistry, 17, 220
Computer, 183
Conservation, 141
Construction, 125, 637, 764
Consumer application, 526, 640, 684
Consumer Economics, 78, 300
Consumer Math, 100, 119
Cooking, 567
Crafts, 610
Design, 74
Earth Science, 17, 23, 28, 29, 94, 297, 345, 435, 480, 557, 647, 659
Economics, 21, 607, 691, 703
Energy, 75
Entertainment, 9, 218, 223, 403, 535, 606, 611, 632
Environment, 217
Finance, 8, 281, 717
Fitness, 503, 686
Food, 227, 403, 658
Games, 185, 549
Geography, 248, 254, 277, 285, 480
Geometry, 120, 163, 586, 591, 611, 696, 750
Graphic Design, 9
Health, 19, 79, 759
History, 121
Hobbies, 185, 219, 586, 710
Home Economics, 137
Language Arts, 184, 287
Life Science, 71, 165, 177, 227, 228, 252, 253, 284, 288, 290, 294–295, 417, 433, 535, 567, 647, 654, 691, 742
Literature, 297
Measurement, 87
Medical, 645
Meteorology, 71
Money, 40, 175, 305, 689
Multi-Step, 395, 595, 763
Music, 125, 415, 715
Nutrition, 94
Patterns, 168, 277, 286
Photography, 247
Physical Science, 7, 38, 177, 226, 231, 232, 241, 275, 281, 288, 333, 401, 591, 597, 630, 631, 635, 652, 691, 701, 706, 711, 717
Physics, 735
Recreation, 42, 77, 86, 284, 443, 465, 686, 703
Safety, 528, 637
School, 475, 549, 553, 605
Social Studies, 37, 69, 84, 178, 282, 286, 340, 367, 392, 417, 421, 435, 602, 657
Sports, 14, 27, 47, 66, 70, 72, 74, 137, 145, 184, 227, 281, 403, 430, 503, 567, 587, 591, 607, 661, 690, 710
Technology, 562
Transportation, 227, 228, 632, 737
Travel, 140, 143, 589
Approximating pi by measuring, 399
Arc, of a circle, 838
Archerfish, 328
Architecture, 254, 424, 637
Architecture Link, 255
Are You Ready?, 3, 61, 115, 159, 213, 271, 321, 385, 459, 519, 581, 625, 679, 731
Area, 389
of circles, 401
of parallelograms, 388–390
perimeter and volume and, 384–457
of rectangles, 388–390
surface, 427

of cones, 432–433
of cylinders, 425–428
of prisms, 425–428
of pyramids, 431–433
of spheres, 437
of trapezoids, 394–396
of triangles, 394–396
Arguments, writing convincing, 215
Arithmetic sequences, 142–143
finding *n*th term of, 683–684
terms of, 682–684
Art, 241, 411, 428, 442, 567, 748
Art Link, 241, 371, 567, 743
Aspect ratio, 223
Assessment
Chapter Test, 55, 109, 153, 207, 265, 315, 379, 453, 513, 575, 673, 691, 725, 775
Cumulative Assessment, 58–59, 110–111, 156–157, 208–209, 268–269, 316–317, 382–383, 454–455, 516–517, 576–577, 622–623, 674–675, 728–729, 776–777
Ready to Go On?, 39, 48, 90, 102, 132, 146, 180, 200, 234, 258, 292, 308, 352, 372, 404, 444, 482, 506, 538, 568, 598, 612, 648, 664, 698, 718, 744, 766
Standardized Test Prep, 58–59, 110–111, 156–157, 208–209, 268–269, 316–317, 382–383, 454–455, 516–517, 576–577, 622–623, 674–675, 728–729, 776–777
Study Guide: Preview, 4, 62, 116, 160, 214, 272, 322, 386, 460, 520, 582, 626, 680, 732
Study Guide: Review, 52–54, 106–108, 150–152, 204–206, 262–264, 312–314, 376–378, 450–452, 510–512, 572–574, 616–618, 670–672, 722–724, 772–774
Test Tackler
All Types: Using a Graphic, 514–515
Extended Response: Write Extended Responses, 380–381
Gridded Response: Write Gridded Responses, 154–155
Multiple Choice
Answering Context-Based Test Items, 620–621
Eliminate Answer Choices, 56–57
Work Backward, 726–727
Short Response: Write Short Responses, 266–267
Associative Property, 747
of Addition, 829
of Multiplication, 829
Astronomy, 37, 172, 475, 709
Atlantic City boardwalk, 113
Atomic mass, 177
Atoms, 158
Axes, 122

B

Back-to-back stem-and-leaf plot, 467
Bacteria, 165, 201, 678
Balance of trade, 21
Baltimore Kinetic Sculpture Race, 677
Bar graphs, 500
histograms, 836
Bases, 162
Beavers, 719
Benchmarks, 278
Best fit, lines of, 494, 660–661
Best representations of data, choosing, 500–501
Biased samples, 463
Bilateral symmetry, 446
Binary codes, 518
Binary fission, 165
Binomials, 734
multiplication of, 760–761, 762–763
special products of, 763
Bisecting figures, 329
Blood pressure, 233
Board foot, 741
Boeing 747, 398
Bonds, Barry, 281
Bonsai, 212
Boundary line, 655
Box-and-whisker plots, 477, 500
creating, 481
Boyle's Law, 716
Brilliant cut, 345
British thermal units (Btu), 75
Business, 46, 136, 172, 218, 230, 281, 441, 465, 473, 557, 587, 595, 703, 711, 741, 750, 753, 755
Business Link, 465, 750
Butterflies, 71

C

Caffeine, 707
Calculator
graphing, *see* Graphing calculator
order of operations on a, 828
Calder, Alexander, 229
Camera lens, 247
Capacity, 440
Career
Bacteriologist, 678
Cryptographer, 518
Financial Analyst, 730
Firefighter, 2
Horticulturist, 212
Hydrologist, 580
Nuclear Physicist, 158
Nutritionist, 60
Pharmacist, 114
Playground Equipment Designer, 320
Quality Assurance Specialist, 458
Sports Statistician, 270
Surgeon, 384
Wildlife Ecologist, 624
Career Link, 424
Carlsbad Caverns, 22
Catfish, 778
Caution!, 45, 77, 163, 182, 191, 330, 388, 390, 421
CD-ROM, 562
Celsius temperature
converting between Fahrenheit and, 842
scale, 103
Center
of a circle, 400
of dilation, 242–243, 244
of rotation, 358
Central angle, 838
Central tendency, measures of, 472–473
Certain event, 522
Challenge
Challenge exercises are found in every lesson. Some examples: 9, 13, 17, 21, 25
Changing dimensions, exploring effects of, 393
Chapter Project Online, 2, 60, 114, 158, 212, 270, 320, 384, 458, 518, 580, 624, 678, 730
Chapter Test, 55, 109, 153, 207, 265, 315, 379, 453, 513, 575, 673, 691, 725, 775, *see also* Assessment
Chemistry, 17, 220
Chesapeake Bay Bridge, 676
Chess, 185
Chord, of a circle, 838
Choose a Strategy, 9, 29, 84, 165, 228, 247, 287, 297, 340, 430, 443, 562, 597, 659, 711, 750, 755
Choosing best representations of data, 500–501
Chord, 838
Cincinnati Zoo, 465
Circle(s), 400–401, 838
arcs of, 838
area of, 401
central angles of, 838
chords of, 838
circumference, 400
diameter, 400
great, 436
graphs, 484, 500
inscribed angles of, 838
radius, 400
secant of, 838
Circle graphs, 500
making, 484
Circuit, network, 840
Circumference, 400
Classifying
angles, 325
polygons, 341–343
real numbers, 191–192
three-dimensional figures, 413, 420
Clemson Tigers Football, 578

Closure Property
of Addition, 829
of Multiplication, 829
Coefficients, 6
Collecting, displaying, and analyzing data, 458–517
Combinations, 564–565
Combining like terms, 584–585
Combining transformations, 362–363
Commission, 298
Commission rate, 298
Common denominator, 68
Common difference, 142, 682
Common factor, 822
greatest (GCF), 824
Common multiple, 822
least (LCM), 824
Common ratio, 687
Communicating Math
apply, 415
choose, 221, 343
compare, 19, 27, 45, 163, 239, 245, 289, 295, 390, 422, 428, 433, 437, 478, 495, 528, 555, 605, 609, 630, 684, 689, 705, 709, 748, 753, 757
compare and contrast, 657
describe, 19, 23, 36, 69, 99, 119, 128, 135, 176, 183, 217, 231, 245, 253, 280, 359, 369, 396, 415, 422, 441, 463, 486, 501, 542, 585, 605, 609, 630, 640, 645, 652, 657, 661, 689, 701, 709, 715, 735, 748
decide, 183, 463
demonstrate, 285, 303
discuss, 187
determine, 176, 187, 221, 280
explain, 7, 15, 19, 23, 36, 41, 65, 69, 73, 86, 93, 99, 119, 143, 163, 171, 176, 183, 192, 197, 217, 226, 231, 249, 253, 275, 289, 295, 299, 303, 326, 331, 338, 343, 349, 355, 365, 369, 428, 433, 437, 441, 468, 473, 478, 491, 524, 533, 555, 565, 595, 601, 630, 635, 657, 684, 735, 753
express, 11, 167, 390
find, 695
give, 11, 41, 45, 65, 119, 123, 128, 217, 226, 409, 473, 501, 524, 528, 601
give an example, 7, 73, 77, 86, 217, 275, 415, 491, 495, 542, 547, 551, 565, 635, 640, 741, 763
identify, 135, 715
list, 27, 171, 589
model, 82
name, 77, 285, 303, 657
show, 163, 275, 285
suppose, 27, 560
tell, 7, 82, 86, 167, 192, 197, 231, 299, 303, 326, 331, 355, 359, 365, 533, 547, 585, 589, 645, 652, 661, 741
use, 192
Think and Discuss
Think and Discuss is found in every lesson. Some examples: 7, 11, 15, 19, 23
Write About It
Write About It exercises are found in every lesson. Some examples: 9, 13, 17, 21, 25
Commutative Property, 829
Comparing
customary units and metric units, 841
rational numbers, 68–69
Compass, 329, 334–335
Compatible numbers, 278, 825
Complementary angles, 325
Composite Figures
area of, 390
perimeter of, 390
volume of, 415
Composite Numbers, 823
Compound Events, 545–547
Compound interest, 306
computing, 306–307
Computer, 183
Computer graphics, 347
Computer ownership, 663
Computer viruses, 704
Computing compound interest, 306–307
Concept maps, 387
Conclusions, *see* Geometry proofs, informal
Concorde, 398
Cones, 420
right, 432
surface area of, 432–433
volume of, 420–422
exploring, 418–419
Congruence, 354–355
Congruent angles, 238
Congruent figures, 325
Congruent triangles, 354
Conjectures, *see* Geometry proofs, informal
Conservation, 141
Constant of proportionality, 650
Constants, 6
Constructing
graphs, using spreadsheets for, 504–505
nets, 406–407
Construction, 125, 637, 764
Constructions, 334–335
Consumer application, 526, 640, 684
Consumer Economics, 78, 300
Consumer Math, 100, 119
Context-based test items, answering, 620–621
Convenience samples, 462
Converse of the Pythagorean Theorem, 199
Conversion factors, 224, 841
units of measure, 224–226
Converting
customary units to metric units, 841
metric units to customary units, 841
odds to probabilities, 554–555
probabilities to odds, 555
Convincing arguments, writing, 215
Cooking, 567
Coordinate geometry, 347–349
Coordinate plane, 122
graphing on a, 122–123
Coordinates, 122–123
Cornell system of note taking, 161
Correlation, 494–495
Correspondence, 354
Corresponding angles, 331
Corresponding sides, 238, 354–355
Counting Principles, 558–560
Crafts, 610
Crazy Horse Memorial, 235
Creating
box-and-whisker plots, 481
histograms, 489
scatter plots, 498–499
Crelle's Journal, 184
Critical Thinking, 13, 17, 29, 42, 67, 70, 121, 145, 168, 199, 219, 227, 297, 305, 327, 333, 350, 351, 371, 480, 526, 557, 591, 606, 654, 686, 711, 737, 750
Cross products, 229
Cross section, 446
Crown of Great Britain, 345
Cube(s), 830
Cube roots, 830
Cubic functions, exploring, 712–713
Cubic units, 413
Cullinan diamond, 94
Cumulative Assessment, 58–59, 110–111, 156–157, 208–209, 268–269, 316–317, 382–383, 454–455, 516–517, 576–577, 622–623, 674–675, 728–729, 776–777, *see also* Assessment
Cumulative frequency, 835
relative, 835
Cumulative test, studying for a, 733
Customary system of measurement, 224–226, 837
converting between metric and, 841
measuring in, 843
Cylinders, 413
surface area of, 427–428
exploring, 425–426
volume of, 413–415
exploring, 412

D

da Vinci, Leonardo, 434
Dance rhythms, 125
Dase, Zacharias, 184

Index

Data, *see also* Displaying and organizing data
analyzing, collecting, and displaying, 458–517
choosing best representations of, 500–501
displaying, 485–486
organizing, 467–468
Decay, exponential, 705
Decimals
addition of, 72, 73, 92
comparing, 69
converting between percents and fractions and, 274–275
division, 81, 827
fractions and, 65
multiplication, 77, 92, 826
by powers of ten, 826
ordering, 69
repeating, 65, 827
rounding, 821
subtraction of, 72, 73, 92
terminating, 65, 827
writing as percents, 274–275
Decisions, making, 550–551
Deep Blue, 185
Degrees of polynomials, 735
Denominator(s), 64
like, adding and subtracting with, 73
unlike, adding and subtracting with, 85–86
Density, 220
Density Property of rational numbers, 192
Dependent events, 545–547
finding probability of, 546–547
Depreciation, linear, 703
Design, 74
Degree, of a network vertex, 840
Diagonals, 341
Diagram
iteration, 834
tree, 559
Diameter, 400
Diastolic blood pressure, 233
Difference, common, 142, 682
Differences, first, 693
Digits, significant, 844
Dilation, center of, 242–243, 244
Dilations, 244–245
exploring, 242–243
Dimensional analysis, 224–226
Dimensions
changing, exploring effects of, 393
matrix, 839
three, symmetry in, 446
Direct variation, 650–652
Discounts, 295
Disjoint events, 542
Displaying and organizing data, 485–486
bar graphs, 500
circle graphs, 484, 500
double-bar graphs, 485
double-line graphs, 486
frequency polygons, 836
frequency tables, 485, 835
histograms, 485, 489, 500, 836
line graphs, 500
misleading graphs, 490–491
stem-and-leaf plots
back-to-back, 467
Distracter, 56
Distributive Property, 741, 829
Divisibility rules, 822
Division
of decimals, 81, 827
by powers of ten, 826
of fractions, 80–81
of integers, 26–27
long, 821
of numbers in scientific notation, 179
of polynomials by monomials, 768–769
of powers, 170
of rational numbers, 80–82
solving equations by, 39–41
solving inequalities by, 600–601
Division Property of Equality, 39
DNA model, 253
Domain, 134
Double-bar graphs, 485
Double-line graphs, 486
Draw a diagram, 810
Drawing three-dimensional figures, 408–409
Drawings, scale, 252
Duckweed plants, 177

E

Earth, 436
Earth Science, 17, 23, 28, 29, 94, 297, 345, 435, 480, 557, 647, 659
Earth Science Link, 17, 29, 88, 131, 345, 530, 647, 659
Earthquakes, 530
Richter scale, 846
Economics, 21, 607, 691, 703
Economics Link, 21, 301, 663
Edge,
of a three-dimensional figure, 408
of a network, 840
Edison, Thomas, 137
Effective notes, taking, 161
Eggs, 439
Energy, 75
Entries, of a matrix, 838
Enlargement, 253
Entertainment, 9, 218, 223, 403, 535, 606, 611, 632
Entertainment Link, 403, 611
Environment, 217
Equality
Addition Property of, 34
Multiplication Property of, 40
Subtraction Property of, 35
Equally likely outcomes, 540
Equations, 34
graphs of, 123
linear, *see* Linear equations
multi-step, *see* Multi-step equations
in slope-intercept form, graphing, 643
solving, *see* Solving equations
Standard Form of, 638
systems of, *see* Systems of equations
tables and graphs and, 138–139
two-step, *see* Two-step equations
with variables on both sides, modeling, 592
Equilateral triangles, 337
Equivalent expressions, 584
Equivalent ratios, 216
Error, greatest possible, 845
Escher, M. C., 371
Estimate, 278
Estimating
with percents, 278–280
quotients, 825
square roots, 186–187
Estimation, 24, 84, 87, 165, 173, 184, 223, 281, 423, 480, 659, 703
Evaluating algebraic expressions, 6
powers and roots, 190
Events, 522
dependent, *see* Dependent events
disjoint, 542
independent, *see* Independent events
mutually exclusive, 542
Experiment, 522
Experimental probability, 527–528
Exploring
cubic functions, 712–713
dilations, 242–243
effects of changing dimensions, 393
right triangles, 195
sampling, 466
similarity, 236–237
Exponent(s), 162–163
integer, looking for patterns in, 166–167
negative, 166
properties of, 170–171
roots and, 158–211
Exponential decay, 705
Exponential form, 162
Exponential functions, 704–705
Exponential growth, 705
Expressions
algebraic, 6, 10–11
simplifying, 584–585
equivalent, 584
simplifying numerical, 828
variables and, 6–7
Extended Response, 88, 141, 169, 223, 297, 333, 380–381, 443, 480, 642, 703, 755
Write Extended Responses, 380–381

- **Extension**
  - Dividing Polynomials by Monomials, 768–769
  - Solving Systems of Equations by Graphing, 666–667
  - Symmetry in Three Dimensions, 446
- **Exterior angles of polygons,** 346
- **Extra Practice,** 782–809
- **Euler circuit,** 840
- **Eyes,** pupils of, 244

F

- **Faces,** 408
  - lateral, 427
- **Factorials,** 563
- **Factor(s),** 822
  - common, 822, 824
  - conversion, 224, 841
  - greatest common (GCF), 824
  - scale, 239
- **Fahrenheit temperature**
  - converting between Celsius and, 842
  - scale, 103
- **Fair objects,** 540
- **Family crests,** 367
- **Ferris wheel,** 403
- **Fibonacci sequence,** 692, 695
- **Fifth,** 697
- **Figures**
  - bisecting, 329
  - composite, 390, 415
  - congruent, 325
  - dilating, 244–245
  - similar, 238–239
  - three-dimensional, *see* Three-dimensional figures
- **Finance,** 8, 281, 717
- **Find a Pattern,** 814
- **Finding**
  - *n*th term of an arithmetic sequence, 683–684
  - *n*th term of a geometric sequence, 688
  - numbers when percents are known, 288–289
  - percents, 283–285
  - probability of dependent events, 546–547
  - probability of independent events, 545–546
  - surface area of prisms and cylinders, 425–426
  - surface area of pyramids, 431
  - volume of prisms and cylinders, 412
  - volume of pyramids and cones, 418–419
- **Fireworks,** 735
- **First differences,** 693
- **Fish weight,** 591
- **Fitness,** 503, 686
- **Flatiron Building,** 441
- **Flip,** *see* Reflection
- **Florida,** 121
- **Focus,** of a parabola, 708
- **Focus on Problem Solving**
  - Look Back, 91, 405, 745
  - Make a Plan, 133, 293, 483, 599
  - Solve, 31, 181, 235, 699
  - Understand the Problem, 353, 539, 649
- **FOIL mnemonic,** 762
- **Food,** 227, 403, 658
- **Foster, Don,** 471
- **Fountain of Youth,** 121
- **Formulas,** *see* inside back cover
- **Fractals,** 394, 834
- **Fraction(s)**
  - addition of, 72–73, 89
    - with unlike denominators, 85–86
  - relating, to decimals and percents, 274–275
  - subtraction of, 72–73, 89
    - with unlike denominators, 85–86
  - unit, 104
  - writing as mixed numbers, 825
  - writing as terminating and repeating decimals, 827
- **Fraction form, dividing rational numbers in,** 80
- **Frequency,** 835
  - cumulative, 835
  - polygons, 836
  - relative, 835
  - relative cumulative, 835
  - tables, 485, 835
- **Fulcrum,** 229
- **Fuller Building,** 441
- **Function notation,** 700
- **Functions,** 134–135
  - cubic, exploring, 712–713
  - exponential, 704–705
  - graphs and sequences and, 114–157
  - linear, 700–701
  - quadratic, 708–709
  - sequences and, 678–729
- **Fundamental Counting Principle,** 558–559

G

- **Game Time**
  - Coloring Tessellations, 374
  - Copy-Cat, 260
  - Crazy Cubes, 50
  - Distribution of Primes, 508
  - Egg Fractions, 104
  - Egyptian Fractions, 104
  - Equation Bingo, 202
  - Find the Phony!, 148
  - Graphing in Space, 668
  - Line Solitaire, 668
  - Magic Squares, 202
  - Math in the Middle, 508
  - Math Magic, 50
  - The Paper Chase, 570
  - Percent Puzzlers, 310
  - Percent Tiles, 310
  - Permutations, 570
  - Planes in Space, 448
  - Polygon Rummy, 374
  - Rolling for Tiles, 770
  - Short Cuts, 770
  - Sprouts, 148
  - Squared Away, 720
  - Tic-Frac-Toe, 260
  - Trans-Plants, 614
  - Triple Concentration, 448
  - 24 Points, 614
  - What's Your Function?, 720
- **Game Time Extra,** 50, 104, 148, 202, 260, 310, 374, 448, 508, 570, 614, 668, 720, 770
- **Games,** 185, 549
- **Games Link,** 185, 549
- **Garfield, James,** 196
- **Gas mileage,** 737
- **GCF (greatest common factor),** 824
- **Generating random numbers,** 531
- **Geography,** 248, 254, 277, 285, 480
- **Geometric sequences,** 687
  - finding *n*th term of, 688
  - terms of, 687–689
- **Geometry,** 320–383

  The development of geometry skills and concepts is a central focus of this course and is found throughout this book.
  - angles, 325–326, 330–331, 334–335, 336–338, 341–342, 346, 354–355
  - building blocks of, 324–326
  - circles, 400–401
    - area of, 401
    - exploring, 399
    - circumference of, 400
  - cylinders
    - volume of, 412, 413–415
    - surface area of, 425–426, 427–428
  - cones
    - volume of, 418–419, 420–422
    - surface area of, 432–433
  - coordinate, 347–349
  - lines, 324–326
    - parallel, 330–331
    - perpendicular, 330–331
    - of reflection, 358–359
    - skew, 830
    - of symmetry, 364–365
    - transversal, 330–331
  - measurement and, 832, 841, 843
    - parallel line relationships, 837
  - parallelograms, 342
    - area of, 389
    - perimeter of, 388
  - polygons, 341–343, 346, 355
    - diagonals in, 341
    - finding angle measures in, 341–342
    - regular, 342
  - prisms, 412, 413–415
    - volumes of, 412, 413–415
    - surface area of, 425–426, 427–428
  - proofs, informal, 833
  - pyramids, 418–419, 420–421
    - volume of, 418–419, 420–421
    - surface area of, 431, 432–433

rectangles, 388–390
area of, 389–390
exploring area and perimeter of, 393
perimeter of, 388–390
rhombuses, 342
software, 346
sphere, 436–437
three-dimensional figures, 406–407, 408–409, 440–441, 446
drawing views of, 406–407, 408–409
modeling, 256–257, 406–407, 408–409, 440–441,
trapezoids
area of, 395–396
perimeter of, 394
triangles, 195
area of, 395–396
perimeter of, 394
Geometry software, 346
Geysers, 131
Giant Ocean Tank, 417
Giant shark, 288, 289
Gigabyte, 173
Glenn Research Center, 211
go.hrw.com, *see* Online Resources
Global Challenge yacht race, 47
Global temperature, 71
Gold, 220
Gold bullion, 223
Googol, 173
Graphic Design, 9
Graph(s)
bar, 500
circle, *see* Circle graphs
constructing, using spreadsheets for, 504–505
double-bar, 485
double-line, 486
of equations, 123
equations and tables and, 138–139
functions and sequences and, 114–157
interpreting, 127–128
line, 500
misleading, 490–491
Graphics
interpreting, 461
using, 514–515
Graphing
on a coordinate plane, 122–123
equations in slope-intercept form, 643
inequalities, 45
in two variables, 655–657
linear equations, 628–630
lines, 624–677
points, 126
solving systems of equations by, 666–667
transformations, 359
Graphing calculator
adding and subtracting fractions, 89
computing compound interest, 306–307
creating box-and-whisker plots, 481
creating histograms, 489
creating a scatter plot, 498–499
evaluating powers and roots, 190
exploring cubic functions, 712–713
graphing equations in slope-intercept form, 643
graphing points, 126
multiplying and dividing numbers in scientific notation, 179
Great circle, 436, 838
Great Lakes, 31
Great Pyramid of Giza, 421
Greatest common factor (GCF), 824
Greatest possible error, 845
Gridded Response, 9, 21, 25, 38, 43, 67, 75, 84, 101, 137, 154–155, 165, 189, 199, 228, 233, 241, 287, 291, 301, 328, 351, 357, 398, 403, 424, 430, 435, 439, 475, 515, 526, 544, 549, 587, 591, 611, 637, 647, 654, 686, 707, 711, 717, 737, 750, 765
Write Gridded Responses, 154–155
Groundhogs, 318
Growth, exponential, 705
Guess and Test, 812
Gulliver's Travels, 239

H

Half-life, 707
Hands-On Lab
Approximate Pi by Measuring, 399
Bisect Figures, 329
Combine Transformations, 362–363
Construct Nets, 406–407
Constructions, 334–335
Explore Dilations, 242–243
Explore the Effects of Changing Dimensions, 393
Explore Right Triangles, 195
Explore Sampling, 466
Explore Similarity, 236–237
Fibonacci Sequence, 692
Find Surface Area of Pyramids, 431
Find Surface Areas of Prisms and Cylinders, 425–426
Find Volumes of Prisms and Cylinders, 412
Find Volumes of Pyramids and Cones, 418–419
Make a Circle Graph, 484
Make a Scale Model, 256–257
Model Equations with Variables on Both Sides, 592
Model Polynomial Addition, 746
Model Polynomial Subtraction, 751
Model Polynomials, 738–739
Model Solving Equations, 32–33
Model Two-Step Equations, 96–97
Multiply Binomials, 760–761
Use Different Models for Simulations, 536–537
Harmonics, 697
Hawaiian alphabet, 287
Health, 19, 79, 759
Health Link, 233, 707
Heart rate, target, 759
Height
of parallelograms, 388–390
slant, 432–433
using indirect measurement to find, 248–249
using scales and scale drawings to find, 440–441
Helpful Hint, 10, 11, 18, 34, 36, 76, 118, 119, 122, 138, 174, 175, 229, 239, 245, 253, 275, 285, 348, 354, 359, 364, 389, 413, 440, 486, 495, 533, 584, 594, 604, 608, 609, 638, 639, 640, 650, 655, 656, 657, 682, 714, 762
Hemispheres, 436
Henry, Jodie, 74
Heptagons, 341
Hertz (Hz), 697
Hexagons, 341
Hill, A. V., 765
Histograms, 485, 500, 836
creating, 489
History, 121
History Link, 121
Hobbies, 185, 219, 586, 710
Home Economics, 137
Home Economics Link, 137
Homework Help Online
Homework Help Online is available for every lesson. Refer to the go.hrw.com box at the beginning of each exercise set. Some examples: 8, 12, 16, 20, 24
Horned lizards, 191
Hot air balloons, 703
Hot Tip!, 57, 59, 111, 155, 157, 209, 267, 269, 317, 381, 383, 455, 515, 517, 577, 621, 623, 675, 727, 729, 777
Hurricanes, 480
Hypotenuse, 196
Hz (Hertz), 697

I

Ice Hotel, 17
Ice House, 112
Identity Property of One, 829
Identity Property of Zero, 829
Images, 358
anamorphic, 427
Impossible event, 522
Improper fractions, writing as mixed numbers, 825
Independent events, 545–547
finding probability of, 545–546
Indirect measurement, 248–249
Inductive reasoning, 833
Industrial supplies, 21

Inequalities, 44
algebraic, 44
graphing, 45
introduction to, 44–45
linear, 655
multi-step, 580–623
solving, 45
by multiplication or division, 600–601
two-step, solving, 604–605
in two variables, graphing, 655–657
Input, 134
Inscribed angle, of a circle, 838
Integer exponents, looking for patterns in, 166–167
Integers, 14
absolute value, 15
addition of, 18–19
division of, 26–27
multiplication of, 26–27
and order of operations, 27
ordering, 14–15
subtraction of, 22–23
Intercepts, using, 638–640
Interest, 302
compound, *see* Compound interest
rate of, 302
simple, 302–303
Interpreting
graphics, 461
graphs and tables, 127–128
Interstate highway system, 43
Inverse operations, 34, 80
Inverse variation, 714–715
Inverses, additive, 14
Investment time, 302
Ions, 38
Irrational numbers, 191
Isosceles triangles, 337
Iteration, 834
It's in the Bag
Canister Carry-All, 105
Clipboard Solutions for Graphs, Functions, and Sequences, 149
Data Pop-Ups, 509
Graphing Tri-Fold, 669
It's a Wrap, 203
Note-Taking Taking Shape, 51
Origami Percents, 311
Picture Envelopes, 615
Polynomial Petals, 771
Probability Post-Up, 571
Project CD Geometry, 375
Springboard to Sequences, 721
The Tube Journal, 449
A Worthwhile Wallet, 261

J

Journals, math, keeping, 323

K

Kasparov, Garry, 185
Keeping math journals, 323
Kente cloth, 373
Kilobyte, 173
Kites, 341
Koch snowflake, 394, 834
Krill, 169

L

Lab Resources Online, 32, 89, 96, 126, 179, 190, 195, 236, 242, 306, 329, 334, 346, 362, 393, 399, 406, 412, 418, 425, 431, 466, 471, 481, 484, 489, 498, 504, 531, 536, 592, 643, 692, 712, 738, 746, 751, 760
Language Arts, 184, 287
Language Arts Link, 471
Laser surgery, 384
Lateral faces, 427
Lateral surface, 427
Lauren Rogers Museum of Art, 779
LCD (least common denominator), 68
LCM (least common multiple), 68, 824
Learning math vocabulary, 521
Least common denominator (LCD), 68
Least common multiple (LCM), 68
Lee, Harper, 297
Legoland, 443
Legs, 196
Length
customary units of, 224–226, 837
metric units of, 837
Lessons, reading, for understanding, 117
LeWitt, Sol, 411
Life Science, 71, 165, 177, 227, 228, 252, 253, 284, 288, 290, 294–295, 417, 433, 535, 567, 647, 654, 691, 742
Life Science Link, 101, 165, 177, 417, 433, 439, 497, 535, 544, 642, 654, 765
Lift, 398
Light bulb filament, 137
Light sticks, 281
Like denominators, adding and subtracting with, 72–73
Like terms, 584, 740
Lilliputians, 239
Lincoln, Abraham, 86
Line(s), 324
of best fit, 494, 660–661
boundary, 655
graphing, 624–677
parallel, 330–331, 830, 837
perpendicular, 330–331
points and planes and angles and, 324–326
skew, 830
slope of a, 633–635
of symmetry, 364
symmetry, 364
transversals to, 331, 837
Line graphs, 500
Line plots, 467, 500
Line segments, 324
Line symmetry, 364–365
Linear depreciation, 703
Linear equations, 628
graphing, 628–630
Linear functions, 700–701
Linear inequalities, 655
Link
Animals, 79
Architecture, 255
Art, 241, 371, 567, 743
Business, 465, 750
Career, 424
Earth Science, 17, 29, 88, 131, 345, 530, 647, 659
Economics, 21, 301, 663
Entertainment, 403, 611
Games, 185, 549
Health, 233, 707
History, 121
Home Economics, 137
Language Arts, 471
Life Science, 101, 165, 177, 289, 417, 433, 439, 497, 535, 544, 642, 654, 765
Literature, 297
Meteorology, 71
Money, 305
Music, 125, 697
Photography, 247
Physical Science, 281, 328, 333, 398, 691, 705
Recreation, 86, 703
Science, 169, 189
Social Studies, 25, 43, 291, 367, 735
Sports, 47, 430, 503, 591
Technology, 562
Transportation, 632
Liquid mirror, 709
Literature, 297
Literature Link, 297
Logarithmic scale, 845–846
London Eye, 403
Long division, 821
Looking for patterns in integer exponents, 166–167
Loomis, E. S., 196
Louvre Pyramid, 239, 424
Luxor Hotel, 457, 637

M

Magic squares, 202
Make a Model, 811
Make an Organized List, 819
Make a Table, 815

Making
circle graphs, 484
decisions, 550–551
predictions, 550–551
scale models, 256–257
Maryland, 676–677
Math, translating between words and, 63
Math expressions
translating, into word phrases, 11
translating word phrases into, 10
Math journals, keeping, 323
Math vocabulary, learning, 521
Matrix (matrices), 839
Matrushka dolls, 84
Mean, 472
Measurement, 87
The development of measurement skills and concepts is a central focus of this course and is found throughout this book.
angle, 832
and approximating pi, 399
customary system of, 224–226, 837, 843
indirect, 248–249
metric system of, 831, 843
Measuring angles, 840
Measures of central tendency and range, 472–473
Median, 472
Medical, 645
Mercury (planet), 37
Metamorphoses, 371
Meteorology, 71
Meteorology Link, 71
Meter stick, 843
Metric system of measurement, 831
converting between customary and, 841
measuring in, 843
Metropolitan Opera House, 611
Midpoint, 329
Mirror, liquid, 709
Misleading graphs and statistics, 490–491
Mississippi, 778–779
Mixed numbers, 825
Mode, 472
Modeling
equations with variables on both sides, 592
polynomial addition, 746
polynomial subtraction, 751
polynomials, 738–739
solving equations, 32–33
two-step equations, 96–97
Models
scale, *see* Scale models
using different, for simulations, 536–537
Mole (mol), 177
Mona Lisa, 241
Money, 40, 175, 305, 689
Money Link, 305
Monomials, 734
division of polynomials by, 768–769
multiplication of polynomials by, 756–757
Monopoly, 540
Mount Etna, 647
Multi-Step, 42, 70, 87, 95, 120, 125, 188, 223, 287, 296, 392, 395, 430, 691
Multi-Step Application, 395, 595, 763
Multi-step equations
and inequalities, 580–623
solving, 588–589
Multi-Step Test Prep, 49, 103, 147, 201, 259, 309, 373, 445, 507, 569, 613, 665, 719, 767
Multiple, 822
least common (LCM), 824
Multiple Choice
Multiple Choice test items are found in every lesson. Some examples: 9, 13, 17, 21, 25
Answering Context-Based Test Items, 620–621
Eliminate Answer Choices, 56–57
Work Backward, 726–727
Multiple representations, using, 681
Multiplication
of binomials, 760–761, 762–763
of decimals, 77, 92, 826
by powers of ten, 826
of integers, 26–27
of numbers in scientific notation, 179
of polynomials, by monomials, 756–757
of powers, 170
of rational numbers, 76–77
solving equations by, 39–41
solving inequalities by, 600–601
Multiplication Property of Equality, 40
Multiplication Property of Zero, 829
Muscle contractions, 765
Music, 125, 415, 715
Music Link, 125, 697
Mutually exclusive events, 542

N

***n*-gons,** 341
Nanoguitar, 166
Negative correlation, 495
Negative exponents, 166
Negative slope, 633
Neptune, 177
Nets, 425–426
constructing, 406–407
Networks, 840
Neutrons, 177
Nevada, 456-457
Nevada State Capitol, 456
Newborns, 274
New Jersey, 112–113
Newtons (N), 36
Niagara Falls, 88
Nickels, 275
Nielsen Television Ratings, 283
No correlation, 495
Notation
function, 700
scientific, 174–176, 179
Note Taking Strategies, *see* Reading and Writing Math
Notes, taking effective, 161
***n*th term,** finding
of an arithmetic sequence, 683–684
of a geometric sequence, 688
Number line, 18
Numbers
compatible, 278, 825
composite, 823
division of, in scientific notation, 179
finding, when percents are known, 288–289
irrational, 191
mixed, 825
multiplication of, in scientific notation, 179
prime, 508, 823
random, 531–532
rational, *see* Rational numbers
real, 191–192
relatively prime, 64
triangular, 693
Numerator, 64
Nutrient requirements, 60
Nutrition, 94

O

Obtuse angles, 325
Obtuse triangles, 336
Ocean trenches, 29
Octagons, 341
Odds, 554–555
against, 554
converting, to probabilities, 554–555
converting probabilities to, 555
in favor, 554
Ohio, 210–211
Ohio & Erie Canal, 210
Ohm's Law, 716
Old Faithful, 131
Online Resources
Chapter Project Online, 2, 60, 114, 158, 212, 270, 320, 384, 458, 518, 580, 624, 678, 730
Game Time Extra, 50, 104, 148, 202, 260, 310, 374, 448, 508, 570, 614, 668, 720, 770
Homework Help Online
Homework Help Online is available for every lesson. Refer to the go.hrw.com box at the beginning of each exercise set. Some examples: 8, 12, 16, 20, 24
Lab Resources Online, 32, 89, 96, 126, 179, 190, 195, 236, 242, 306, 329,

334, 346, 362, 393, 399, 406, 412, 418, 425, 431, 466, 471, 481, 484, 489, 498, 504, 531, 536, 592, 643, 692, 712, 738, 746, 751, 760
Parent Resources Online
Parent Resources Online is available for every lesson. Refer to the go.hrw.com box at the beginning of each exercise set. Some examples: 8, 12, 16, 20, 24
State Test Practice Online, 58, 110, 156, 208, 268, 316, 382, 454, 516, 576, 622, 674, 728, 776
Web Extra!, 25, 101, 131, 185, 233, 255, 291, 333, 371, 398, 424, 497, 530, 611, 647, 663, 697, 703, 743, 750
Open circle, 45
Operations
inverse, 34, 80
order of, 6, 828
Opposites, 14
Order of operations, 6, 828
Ordered pairs, 118–119
Ordering
measurements, customary and metric, 224, 841
rational numbers, 68–69
Organizing data, 467–468
Origami, 311
Origin, 122
Orthogonal views, 408
Outcomes, 522
equally likely, 540
Outlier, 472
Output, 134

P

Pairs, ordered, 118–119
Pandas, 6
Parabola, 708
Parallel lines, 330–331, 837
properties of transversals to, 331, 837
and skew lines, 830
Parallelograms, 342
area of, 388–390
perimeter of, 388–390
Parent Resources Online
Parent Resources Online are available for every lesson. Refer to the go.hrw.com box at the beginning of each exercise set. Some examples: 8, 12, 16, 20, 24
Parentheses, 6, 828
Patterns, 168, 277, 286
in integer exponents, looking for, 166–167
and iterations, 834
Pediment, 405
Pei, I. M., 420, 424
PEMDAS mnemonic, 6
Pennsylvania, 318–319
Pentagons, 341
Percent(s), 270–319
applications of, 298–299
defined, 274
estimating with, 278–280
finding, 283–285
using an equation, 284
using a proportion, 283
greater than one hundred, 823
known, finding numbers for, 288–289
less than one, 823
relating, to decimals and fractions, 274–275
Percent change, 294
Percent decrease, 294–295
Percent increase, 294–295
Perfect squares, 182
Perimeter, 186, 388
area and volume and, 384–457
of parallelograms, 388–390
of rectangles, 388–390
of trapezoids, 394–396
of triangles, 394–396
Periscopes, 333
Permutations, 563–564
Perpendicular lines, 330–331
Perspective, 330–331
pH, 845
Philadelphia Mural Arts Program, 319
Phone numbers, 558
Photography, 247
Photography Link, 247
Physical Science, 7, 38, 177, 226, 231, 232, 241, 275, 281, 288, 333, 401, 591, 597, 630, 631, 635, 652, 691, 701, 706, 711, 717
Physical Science Link, 281, 328, 333, 398, 691, 705
Physics, 735
Pi (π), 194, 400
approximating, by measuring, 399
Piersol, Aaron, 72
Pitch, 697
Pixels, 183
Place value, 820
Planes, 324
points and lines and angles and, 324–326
Playground equipment, 320
Plimpton 322, 196
Pluto, 177
Point symmetry, *see* Rotational symmetry
Point-slope form, 644–645
Points, 324
graphing, 126
lines and planes and angles and, 324–326
Polygon(s), 341, 569
classifying, 341–343
exterior angles of, 346
frequency, 836
regular, 342
similar, 238
Polynomials, 730–779
addition of, 747–748
modeling, 746
defined, 734–735
degrees of, 735
division of, by monomials, 768–769
modeling, 738–739
multiplication of, by monomials, 756–757
simplifying, 740–741
subtraction of, 752–753
modeling, 751
Ponce de León, 121
Population, 462
Positive correlation, 495
Positive slope, 633
Power(s), 162
division of, 170
evaluating, 190
multiplication of, 170
raising powers to, 171
zero, 167
Precision, 844–845
Predictions, making, 550–551
Price, unit, 221
Prime factorization, 824
Prime numbers, 508, 823
Principal, 302
Principal square root, 182
Prisms, 413
lateral faces, 427
rectangular, 413
surface area of, 427–428
triangular, 413
finding, 425–426
volume of, 413–415
exploring, 412
Probability, 518–579
converting, to odds, 555
converting odds to, 554–555
defined, 522–524
of dependent events, finding, 546–547
experimental, 527–528
of independent events, finding, 545–546
theoretical, 540–542
Problem Solving
Problem solving is a central focus of this course and is found throughout this book.
Problem Solving Application, 36, 82, 98–99, 186–187, 225, 249, 279, 501, 524, 532–533, 601, 757
Problem Solving Handbook, 810–819, *see also* Problem Solving Strategies
Problem Solving on Location
Maryland, 676–677
Mississippi, 778–779
Nevada, 456–457
New Jersey, 112–113
Ohio, 210–211
Pennsylvania, 318–319

South Carolina, 578–579
Problem Solving Skill
analyze units, 224–226
estimate with compatible numbers, 278–280
look for patterns, 166–167
Problem Solving Strategies, 532–533
Act It Out, 818
Draw a Diagram, 810
Find a Pattern, 814
Guess and Test, 812
Make a Model, 811
Make an Organized List, 819
Make a Table, 815
Solve a Simpler Problem, 816
Use Logical Reasoning, 817
Work Backward, 813
Problems, reading, for understanding, 273
Production costs, 730
Projects, 2, 60, 114, 158, 212, 270, 320, 384, 458, 518, 580, 624, 678, 730
Proofs, informal geometry, 833
Properties
Associative, 747, 829
Closure, 829
Commutative, 829
Distributive, 829
Identity
of Zero, for addition, 829
of One, for multiplication, 829
Transitive, 829
Proportionality, constant of, 650
Proportions, 216
and indirect measurement, 248
and percent, 283
ratios and, 216–217
ratios and similarity and, 212–269
solving, 229–231
using, to find scales, 252
Protons, 177
Protractors, 330
Punnett squares, 544
Punxsutawney Phil, 318
Pupils of eyes, 244
Pyramid of the Sun, 424
Pyramids, 420
regular, 432
surface area of, 432–433
exploring, 431
volume of, 420–422
exploring, 418–419
Pythagoras, 196
Pythagorean Theorem, 195, 196–197
and area, 395
converse of the, 199
Pythagorean triples, 199, 448

Q

Quadrants, 122
Quadratic functions, 708–709
Quadrilaterals, 341
classifying, 348
Quartiles, 476
Quilts, 182
Quotients, estimating, 825

R

Radical symbol, 182
Radius, 400
Raising powers to powers, 171
Random numbers, 532
generating, 531
Random samples, 462
Range, 134, 472
measures of, 472–473
Rate of interest, 302
Rates, 220
commission, 298
ratios and unit rates and, 220–221
unit, *see* Unit rates
Rational numbers, 60–113, 191
addition of, 72–73
comparing, 68–69
defined, 64
Density Property of, 192
division of, 80–82
multiplication of, 76–77
ordering, 68–69
solving equations with, 92–93
subtraction of, 72–73
Ratios, 216
common, 687
equivalent, 216
proportions and, 216–217
proportions and similarity and, 212–269
rates and unit rates and, 220–221
Rays, 324
Reading and Writing Math, 5, 63, 117, 161, 215, 273, 323, 387, 461, 521, 583, 627, 681, 733
Reading Math, 162, 171, 216, 238, 252, 274, 325, 358, 395, 563, 628, 700
Reading problems for understanding, 273
Reading Strategies, *see also* Reading and Writing Math
Interpret Graphics, 461
Learn Math Vocabulary, 521
Read a Lesson for Understanding, 117
Read Problems for Understanding, 273
Use Your Book for Success, 5
Ready to Go On?, 39, 48, 90, 102, 132, 146, 180, 200, 234, 258, 292, 308, 352, 372, 404, 444, 482, 506, 538, 568, 598, 612, 648, 664, 698, 718, 744, 766
Real numbers, 191–192
properties of, 829
Reasoning, inductive and deductive, 833
Reciprocals, 80
Recreation, 42, 77, 86, 284, 443, 465, 686, 703
Recreation Link, 86, 703
Rectangles, 342
area of, 388–390
perimeter of, 388–390
Rectangular prism, 413
Rectangular pyramid, 420
Recycling, 217
Reduction, 253
Reflection symmetry, 446
Reflections, 358
Refraction, 328
Regular polygons, 342
Regular pyramids, 432
Regular tessellations, 368
Relating decimals, fractions, and percents, 274–275
Relative cumulative frequency, 835
Relative frequency, 835
Relatively prime numbers, 64
Remember!, 6, 14, 44, 64, 68, 73, 92, 167, 183, 224, 347, 349, 400, 585, 589, 600, 633, 660, 768
Repeating decimals, 65, 827
Representations of data, *see also* Displaying and organizing data
choosing best, 500–501
multiple, using, 681
Reptiles, **(M.C. Escher)** 371
Reptiles, 654
Reticulated python, 289
Rhode Island, 282
Rhombuses, 342
Richter scale, 846
Right angles, 325
Right cones, 432
Right triangles, 336
exploring, 195
finding angles in, 336
finding lengths of legs in, 195, 395
Rise, 347, 633
Rock and Roll Hall of Fame, 420
Roddick, Andy, 226
Roots
cube, 830
evaluating, 190
exponents and, 158–211
square, 182–187
Rotation, 358
center of, 358
Rotational symmetry, 365, 446
Rounding
decimals, 820
whole numbers, 820
Run, 347, 633

S

Safety, 528, 637
Sales tax, 298
Sample(s), 462
biased, 463
convenience, 462

random, 462
stratified, 462
surveys and, 462–463
systematic, 462
voluntary-response, 462
Sample space, 522
Sampling, exploring, 466
Scale, 252
logarithmic, 845
Scale drawings, 252
Scale factors, 239
Scale models, 253, 259
making, 256–257
Scalene triangles, 337
Scaling three-dimensional figures, 440–441
Scatter plots, 494–495, 500
creating, 498–499
School, 475, 549, 553, 605
Science Link, 169, 189
Scientific notation, 174–176
division of numbers in, 179
multiplication of numbers in, 179
Scrabble, 549
Secant, of a circle, 838
Second differences, 693
Sections, 445
Segments, line, 324
Selected Answers, 847–xxx
Self-similar patterns, 834,
Semiregular tessellations, 370
Sequences, 142
arithmetic, *see* Arithmetic sequences
Fibonacci, 692, 695
functions and, 678–729
geometric, *see* Geometric sequences
graphs and functions and, 114–157
other, 693–695
Shakespeare, William, 471
Short Response, 13, 29, 47, 95, 131, 145, 173, 178, 185, 219, 247, 251, 255, 266–267, 340, 345, 361, 371, 392, 411, 465, 471, 488, 493, 497, 503, 514, 515, 530, 553, 567, 607, 632, 659, 663, 691, 697, 743, 759
Write Short Responses, 266–267
Sieve of Eratosthenes, 508
Significant digits, 844
Silos, 416
Similar figures, 236–239
and dilations, 244–245
and indirect measurement, 248–249
and scale drawings and models, 252–253
Similar polygons, 238
Similarity
exploring, 236–237
ratios and proportions and, 212–269
Simple interest, 302–303
Simplify, 585
Simplifying
numerical expressions using a calculator, 828
algebraic expressions, 584–585
polynomials, 740–741
Simulations, 532
using, 532–533
using different models for, 536–537
Skew lines, 830
Slant height, 432
Slide, *see* Translation
Slope, 347, 633
of a line, 633–635
using, 638–640
Slope-intercept form, 639
graphing equations in, 643
Snakes, 101
Snowboard half-pipe, 430
Social Studies, 37, 69, 84, 178, 282, 286, 340, 367, 392, 417, 421, 435, 602, 657
Social Studies Link, 25, 43, 367, 735
Solid circle, 45
Solid figures, *see* Three-dimensional figures
Solution set, 44
Solutions of systems of equations, 608
Solve a Simpler Problem, 816
Solving
equations, *see* Solving equations
inequalities, *see* Solving inequalities
multi-step equations, 588–589
proportions, 229–231
systems of equations by graphing, 666–667
two-step equations, 98–99
two-step inequalities, 604–605
for a variable, 821
Solving equations
by addition, 34–36
using addition and subtraction properties, 34–36
with decimals, 92, 98
by division, 39–41
linear, 628–630
modeling, 32–33
multi-step, 588–589, 592–595
by multiplication, 39–41
with rational numbers, 92–93
by subtraction, 34–36
systems of, 608–609
two-step, 98–99
with variables on both sides, 593–595
Solving inequalities, 45, 600–601, 604–605
by multiplication or division, 600–601
South Carolina, 578–579
South Carolina Hall of Fame, 579
Special Olympics World Summer Games, 503
Special products, 763
Spheres, 436–437
surface area of, 437
volume of, 436
Spiral Review
Spiral Review questions are found in every lesson. Some examples: 9, 13, 17, 21, 25
Sports, 14, 27, 47, 66, 70, 72, 74, 137, 145, 184, 227, 281, 403, 430, 503, 567, 587, 591, 607, 661, 690, 710
Sports Link, 47, 430, 503, 591
Sports utility vehicles (SUV's), 527
Spreadsheets
generating random numbers, 531
using, to construct graphs, 504–505
Square(s), 342
magic, 202
perfect, 182
square roots and, 182–183
Square roots
estimating, 186–187
principal, 182
squares and, 182–183
Square units, 413
Standard Form of an Equation, 638
Standardized Test Prep, 58–59, 110–111, 156–157, 208–209, 268–269, 316–317, 382–383, 454–455, 516–517, 576–577, 622–623, 674–675, 728–729, 776–777, *see* also Assessment
Standardized Test Strategies, see Standardized Test Prep
State Test Practice Online, 58, 110, 156, 208, 268, 316, 382, 454, 516, 576, 622, 674, 728, 776
Statisticians, 270
Statistics, misleading, 490–491
Stem-and-leaf plot, 467
back-to-back, 468
Step Pyramid of King Zoser, 435
Stratified samples, 462
Strong correlation, 495
Study Guide: Preview, 4, 62, 116, 160, 214, 272, 322, 386, 460, 520, 582, 626, 680, 732, *see also* Assessment
Study Guide: Review, 52–54, 106–108, 150–152, 204–206, 262–264, 312–314, 376–378, 450–452, 510–512, 572–574, 616–618, 670–672, 722–724, 772–774, *see also* Assessment
Study Strategies, *see also* Reading and Writing Math
Concept Map, 387
Study for a Cumulative Test, 733
Take Effective Notes, 161
Use Multiple Representations, 681
Subscripts, 395
Substitute, 6
Subtraction
of fractions, 89
with unlike denominators, 85–86
of integers, 22–23
of polynomials, 752–753
modeling, 751
of rational numbers, 72–73
solving equations by, 34–36

Index

Subtraction Property of Equality, 35
Super Ball, 691
Supplementary angles, 325
Surface, lateral, 427
Surface area, 427
of cones, 432–433
of cylinders, 427–428
exploring, 425–426
of prisms, 427–428
exploring, 425–426
of pyramids, 432–433
exploring, 431
of spheres, 437
Surveys, samples and, 462–463
SUV's (sports utility vehicles), 527
Swift, Jonathan, 239
Symmetry, 364–365
bilateral, 446
line, 364
line of, 364
reflection, 446
rotational, 365, 446
in three dimensions, 446
Systematic samples, 462
Systems of equations, 608–609
solutions of, 608
solving, by graphing, 666–667
Systolic blood pressure, 233

T

Tables
equations and graphs and, 138–139
frequency, 485, 835
interpreting, 127–128
Taiwan, 178
Taking effective notes, 161
Target heart rate, 759
Tax, sales, 298
Tax brackets, 301
Technetium-99m, 705
Technology, 562
Technology Lab
Add and Subtract Fractions, 89
Compute Compound Interest, 306–307
Create Box-and-Whisker Plots, 481
Create Histograms, 489
Create a Scatter Plot, 498–499
Evaluate Powers and Roots, 190
Explore Cubic Functions, 712–713
Exterior Angles of a Polygon, 346
Generate Random Numbers, 531
Graph Equations in Slope-Intercept Form, 643
Graph Points, 126
Multiply and Divide Numbers in Scientific Notation, 179
Use a Spreadsheet to Construct Graphs, 504–505
Technology Link, 562
Television Ratings, Nielsen, 283
Temperature,
conversions, 842
global, 71
scales, 103
Terabyte, 173
Term number, 683
Terminating decimals, 65, 827
Terms, 142, 584
of arithmetic sequences, 682–684
finding nth, 683–684
of geometric sequences, 687–689
finding *n*th, 688
like, 584
Tessellations, 368–369
regular, 368
semiregular, 370
Test, cumulative, studying for a, 733
Test items, context-based, answering, 620–621
Test Prep
Test Prep questions are found in every lesson. Some examples: 9, 13, 17, 21, 25
Test Tackler, *see also* Assessment
All Types: Using a Graphic, 514–515
Extended Response: Write Extended Responses, 380–381
Gridded Response: Write Gridded Responses, 154–155
Multiple Choice
Answering Context-Based Test Items, 620–621
Eliminate Answer Choices, 56–57
Work Backward, 726–727
Short Response: Write Short Responses, 266–267
Test Taking Strategy, *see* Test Tackler
Test Taking Tips, *see* Hot Tip!
Tetris, 411
Think and Discuss
Think and Discuss is found in every lesson. Some examples: 7, 11, 15, 19, 23
Theoretical probability, 540–542
Three-dimensional figures
drawing, 408–409
scaling, 440–441
surface area of, 425, 431–433, 437
volume of, 412–415, 418–422, 436
Three dimensions, symmetry in, 446
Tides, 28
Time, investment, 302
Timeline, 25
Tips, 278
To Kill a Mockingbird, 297
Torus, 448
Toxic gases, 2
Toys, 750
Train à Grande Vitesse, 632
Transamerica Pyramid, 423, 447
Transformations, 358–359
combining, 362–363
graphing, 359
Translating
math expressions into word phrases, 11
word phrases into math expressions, 10
between words and math, 63
Translations, 358
Transpose, of a matrix, 839
Transportation, 227, 228, 632, 737
Transportation Link, 632
Transversals, 330
to parallel lines, properties of, 331
Trapezoids, 342
area of, 394–396
perimeter of, 394–396
Travel, 140, 143, 589
Tree diagrams, 559
Trenches, ocean, 29
Trial, 522
Triangle Sum Theorem, 336
Triangles, 341
acute, 336
angles in, 336–338
area of, 394–396
congruent, 354
equilateral, 337
isosceles, 337
obtuse, 336
perimeter of, 394–396
right, *see* Right triangles
scalene, 337
Triangular numbers, 693
Triangular prism, 413
Triangular pyramid, 420
Trinomials, 734
Trump Tower, 256
Tsunamis, 189
Turns, *see* Rotations
Twins, 354
Two-step equations
modeling, 96–97
solving, 98–99
Two-step inequalities, solving, 604–605

U

Umbra, 435
Unbiased sample, 463
Undefined slope, 633
Understanding
reading lessons for, 117
reading problems for, 273
Unit(s)
choosing appropriate, 831
conversion factors, 841
customary, 831
metric, 831
Unit analysis, 224
Unit fractions, 104
Unit price, 221

Unit rates, 220
ratios and rates and, 220–221
United States census, 291
Unlike denominators
addition of fractions with, 85–86
subtraction of fractions with, 85–86
Use Logical Reasoning, 817
Using
different models for simulations, 536–537
graphics, 514–515
intercepts, 638–640
multiple representations, 681
simulations, 532–533
slopes, 638–640
spreadsheets to construct graphs, 504–505
your book for success, 5
your own words, 627

V

Value, absolute, 15
Variability, 476–478
Variable(s)
on both sides
modeling equations with, 592
solving equations with, 593–595
expressions and, 6–7
solving for, 821
two, graphing inequalities in, 655–657
Variation
direct, 650–652
inverse, 714–715
Venn diagrams, 468
Vertex
of an angle, 325
of a three-dimensional figure, 408
of a network, 840
Vertical angles, 325
Vertical line test, 135
Views, orthogonal, 408
Viruses, computer, 704
Vocabulary, math, learning, 521
Vocabulary Connections, 4, 62, 116, 160, 214, 272, 322, 386, 460, 520, 582, 626, 680, 732
Volcanoes, 647
Volume
of cones, 420–422
exploring, 418–419
of cylinders, 413–415
exploring, 412
perimeter and area and, 384–457
of prisms, 413–415
exploring, 412
of pyramids, 420–422
exploring, 418–419
of spheres, 436
Voluntary-response samples, 462

W

Water discharge, 580
Weak correlation, 495
Weather balloons, 659
Web Extra!, 25, 101, 131, 185, 233, 255, 291, 333, 371, 398, 424, 497, 530, 611, 647, 663, 697, 703, 743, 750
Whales, 169
What's the Error?, 13, 21, 38, 67, 71, 79, 95, 121, 145, 173, 185, 189, 194, 219, 223, 228, 277, 333, 345, 350, 403, 417, 424, 480, 493, 526, 535, 553, 557, 587, 591, 603, 637, 691, 737
What's the Question?, 136, 305, 351, 392, 567, 632, 703, 759
Whole numbers
long division, 821
rounding, 821
Whooping cranes, 624
Word phrases
translating, into math expressions, 10
translating math expressions into, 11
Words
and math, translating between, 63
using your own, 627
Work Backward, 726–727, 813
Write About It
Write About It exercises are found in every lesson. Some examples: 9, 13, 17, 21, 25
Write a Problem, 47, 75, 125, 141, 178, 199, 241, 251, 282, 357, 361, 367, 435, 475, 488, 503, 549, 553, 607, 647, 654, 686, 717, 750
Writing
convincing arguments, 215
extended responses, 380–381
gridded responses, 154–155
to justify, 583
short responses, 266–267
Writing Math, 65, 331, 683
Writing Strategies, *see also* Reading and Writing Math
Keep a Math Journal, 323
Translate Between Words and Math, 63
Use Your Own Words, 627
Write a Convincing Argument, 215
Write to Justify, 583

X

***x*-axis,** 122
***x*-coordinate,** 122
***x*-intercept,** 638

Y

***y*-axis,** 122
***y*-coordinate,** 122
***y*-intercept,** 638
Yosemite National Park, 86

Z

Zero power, 167
Zero slope, 633

Credits

Staff Credits

Bruce Albrecht, Nancy Behrens, Justin Collins, Lorraine Cooper, Marc Cooper, Jennifer Craycraft, Martize Cross, Nina Degollado, Lydia Doty, Sam Dudgeon, Kelli R. Flanagan, Mary Fraser, Stephanie Friedman, Jeff Galvez, José Garza, Diannia Green, Jennifer Gribble, Liz Huckestein, Jevara Jackson, Kadonna Knape, Cathy Kuhles, Jill M. Lawson, Peter Leighton, Christine MacInnis, Rosalyn K. Mack, Jonathan Martindill, Virginia Messler, Susan Mussey, Kim Nguyen, Matthew Osment, Chris Rankin, Manda Reid, Patrick Ricci, Michael Rinella, Michelle Rumpf-Dike, Beth Sample, Annette Saunders, John Saxe, Kay Selke, Robyn Setzen, Patricia Sinnott, Victoria Smith, Jeannie Taylor, Ken Whiteside, Sherri Whitmarsh, Aimee F. Wiley, Alison Wohlman

Photo Credits

Student Handbook TOC: (standing boy), Sam Dudgeon/HRW; (sitting girl), John Langford.

Chapter 1: 2–3 (bkgd), Peter Skinner/Photo Researchers, Inc.; 2 (br), Tom Tracy/Getty Images/FPG International; 6 (tr), Keren Su/Animals Animals; 9 (tr), The Kobal Collection; 10 (t), Robert Landau/CORBIS; 14 (t), Don Couch/HRW; 17 (t), © Layne Kennedy/CORBIS; 18 (t), Victoria Smith/HRW; 21 (t), Peter Van Steen; 22 (t), Chad Ehlers/PictureQuest; 25 (coin), Araldo de Luca/CORBIS; 25 (pyramid), Steve Vidler/SuperStock; 25 (painting), The Art Archive/Napoleonic Museum Rome/Dagli Orti; 25 (Cleopatra), Bettmann/CORBIS; 26 (t), Dennis MacDonald/ PhotoEdit Inc.; 29 (tl), Peter David/Getty Images; 36 (tr), Sam Dudgeon/HRW; 39 (tr), Joseph de Sciose; 47 (l), Fotopress, Ross Setford/AP Photo; 49 (tl), iStock Photo; 49 (b), HRW; 50 (br), Randall Hyman; 51 (4), Sam Dudgeon/HRW. **Chapter 2:** 60-61 (bkgd), Kevin R. Morris/CORBIS; 60 (br), Sam Dudgeon/HRW; 60 (food pyramid), Courtesy Food & Drug Administration; 64, Ann Heisenfelt/AP Photo; 68 (t), Getty Images; 71 (tl), NASA; 72 (tr), © Lucy Nicholson/Reuters/CORBIS; 76 (t), Sam Dudgeon/ HRW; 79 (tl), John Giustina/Bruce Coleman, Inc.; 84 (tr), Mark Tomalty/Masterfile; 85 (tr), Jimmy Chin/National Geographic Image Collection; 86 (l), Library of Congress; 88 (tr), © Lester Lefkowitz/CORBIS; 088 (cr); 91 (b), Dean Conger/CORBIS; 98 (t), Eric Gaillard/Reuters/CORBIS; 101 (tr), AFP/CORBIS; 101 (cr), Karl H. Switak/Photo Researchers, Inc.; 103 (b), AP Photo; 104 (br), Jenny Thomas/HRW; 105 (br), Sam Dudgeon/HRW; 112 (hockey), Courtesy Ice House, Hackensack, NJ; 112 (br), Photodisc/Getty Images; 113 (all), Photos courtesy of the Atlantic City Convention & Visitors Authority. **Chapter 3:** 114–115 (bkgd), © Brooks/Brown/Photo Researchers, Inc.; 114 (b), © Jose Luis Pelaez, Inc./CORBIS; 118 (t), Sam Dudgeon/ HRW; 121 (tl), Bettmann/CORBIS; 125 (r), Laurence Fleury/Photo Researchers, Inc.; 127 (t), David Townsend Images; 131 (t), Alec Pytlowany/Masterfile; 133 (b), Sam Dudgeon/HRW; 137 (l), Schenectady Museum; Hall of Electrical History Foundation/CORBIS; 138 (t), U.S. Navy Photo; 147 (all), Sam Dudgeon/HRW; 148 (b), Victoria Smith/HRW; 149 (b), HRW. **Chapter 4:** 158–159 (bkgd), Science Photo Library/Photo Researchers, Inc.; 158 (b), Dean Conger/CORBIS; 165 (l), S. Lowry/Univ. Ulster/Getty Images/Stone; 166 (t), Lidija Sekaric/Harold G. Craighead, CCMR/CNF, Cornell University; 169 (t), Francois Gohier/Photo Researchers, Inc.; 169 (c), Flip Nicklin/Minden Pictures; 173 (c), PEANUTS © Universal Press Syndicate; 174 (t), Victoria Smith/HRW; 175, Peter Van Steen/HRW; 178 (bl), Joe McDonald/CORBIS; 182 (t), © Victoria & Albert Museum, London/Art Resource; 183 (t), © Roberto Rivera; 185 (l), Uimonen Ilkka/CORBIS/SYGMA; 185, Peter Van Steen/HRW; 186 (t), Sam Dudgeon/HRW; stained glass artist: Leanne Ohlenburg; 189 (t), Chris Butler/Photo Researchers, Inc.; 191 (tr), Joseph T. Collins/Photo Researchers, Inc.; 196 Loukas Hapsis/On Location; 201 (tl), Classic PIO Partners; 201 (b) SciMAT/Photo Researchers, Inc.; 202 (br), Randall Hyman; 203 (b) Sam Dudgeon/HRW; 210 (c), Photo by William C. Bennett, Collection of the Massillon Museum; 210 (b), Bruce S. Ford/City of Akron; 211 (all), NASA John H. Glenn Research Center at Lewis Field. **Chapter 5:** 212–213 (bkgd), Galen Rowell/ CORBIS; 212 (b), Michael S. Yamashita/CORBIS; 216 (tr), Dave Jacobs/Index Stock Imagery, Inc.; 219 Sam Dudgeon/HRW; 220 (tr), Courtesy Jens of Sweden; 224 (tr), Joe Skipper/Reuters/Corbis; 229 (tr), Art on File/CORBIS; 233 (tr), © 2004 EyeWire Collection; 233 (cr), © Andrew Syred/Microscopix Photolibrary; 233 (bc), Ed Reschke/Peter Arnold, Inc.; 235 (bl), Robb deWall/Crazy Horse Memorial; 238 (paper cube), HRW; 238 (tr), Rubberball/Alamy; 241 (tl), Layne Kennedy/CORBIS; 244 (eyes), Phil Jude/Science Photo Library/Photo Researchers, Inc.; 247 (cl), Peter Van Steen/HRW; 248 (tr), Courtesy Troop 32, Arlington Heights, IL; 252 (tr), "Iowa Countryside Outside of Cedar Rapids Iowa" by Stan Herd, photo © Jon Blumb; 253 (cl), Digital Art/CORBIS; 255 (tr), David Young-Wolff/PhotoEdit Inc.; 256 (c), Lee Snider/CORBIS; 257 (tc), Sam Dudgeon/HRW; 259 (br), Richard Meier & Partners Architects LLP; 259 (tl), Sam Dudgeon/HRW; 260 (t), Digital Image © 2004 PhotoDisc; 260 (br), Ken Karp/HRW; 261 (b), Sam Dudgeon/HRW.

Chapter 6: 270–271 (bkgd), Chuck Solomon/Sports Illustrated; 270 (b), Clive Mason/Allsport/Getty Images; 274 (tr), © Charles Gullung/Getty Images; 278 (tr), John Langford/HRW; 281 (bl), Peter Van Steen/HRW; 283 (c), PEANUTS © Universal Press Syndicate; 288 (tr), Jeff Rotman/Photo Researchers Inc.; 289 (tl), Hans Reinhard/Bruce Coleman, Inc.; 291 (tr), © Katy Winn/CORBIS; 293 (cricket, wasp, ladybugs), Digital Image © 2004 PhotoDisc; 293 (black & white beetles, European mantis), Stockbyte; 293 (ants, earwig, green beetle, mantis with extended wings), Brand X Pictures; 293 (harlequin beetle), Digital Image © 2004 Artville; 294 (tr), © *The New Yorker* Collection 1992 Danny Shanahan from cartoonbank.com. All Rights Reserved.; 297 (tr), Lyn Topinka/USGS/Cascades Volcano Observatory; 297 (tl), © Katy Winn/CORBIS; 299 (cr), Peter Van Steen/HRW; 301 (tr), Sam Dudgeon/HRW; 305 (tl), AFP/CORBIS; 309 (tl), Stephanie Friedman/HRW; 309 (b), Sam Dudgeon/HRW; 310 (br), Victoria Smith/HRW; 311 (b), Sam Dudgeon/HRW; 318 (c), Jacon Cohn/© Reuters/CORBIS; 319 (t), Bob Krist/CORBIS; 319 (br), © 2004 Conrad Gloos c/o MIRA. **Chapter 7:** 320–321 (bkgd), Richard T. Nowitz/CORBIS; 320 (br), Victoria Smith/HRW; 328 (tr), Stephen Dalton/Photo Researchers, Inc.; 330 (tr), Richard Meier & Partners Architects LLP; 333 (tl), Hulton-Deutsch Collection/CORBIS; 341 (tr), © Stockbyte; 345 (tl), Jonathan Blair/CORBIS; 347 (all), © Lucasfilm, Ltd.; 354 (tr), Seth Kushner/Getty Images/Stone; 354 (tl), Science Photo Library/Photo Researchers, Inc.; 358 (tr), © Carol Leigh/Grant Heilman Photography, Inc.; 364 (tc), Image © /Dmitriy Margolin; 364 (tr), PhotoDisc/Getty Images; 365 (tc), Garry Black/Masterfile; 367 (tl), Grant V. Faint/Getty Images/The Image Bank; 368 (tr), Harry Lentz/Art Resource, NY; 373 (bl), Bob Burch/Jenny Thomas/HRW; Index Stock; 373 (tl), Chris Barton/PhotographersDirect.com; 374 (br), 375 (b), Sam Dudgeon/HRW. **Chapter 8:** 384–385 (bkgd), UHB Trust/Getty Images/Stone; 384 (br), Rob Crandall/Alamy Photos; 388 (tr), Corbis/PictureQuest; 398 (tr), Benelux/ZEFA/H. Armstrong Roberts; 400 (tr), © 2005 David Farley; 403 (tl), © Robert Harding Picture Library Ltd/Alamy; 405 (b), Dave G. Houser/ Houserstock; 411 (cr), (photo) © 2006 Sol LeWitt//Artists Rights Society (ARS), New York. Photography by Mike Kilyon. 413 (tr), Kenneth Hamm/Photo Japan; 417 (tr), Dallas and John Heaton/CORBIS; 417 (tl), G. Leavens/Photo Researchers, Inc.; 420 (tr), Paul Spinelli/Getty Images Sport; 421 (br), Will & Deni McIntyre/Photo Researchers, Inc.; 424 (tl), Owen Franken/CORBIS; 424 (tr), Steve Vidler/SuperStock; 427 (tr), © 2004 Kelly Houle; 428 (c), Peter Van Steen/HRW; 430 (tl), © Todd Patrick; 433 (br), Robert & Linda Mitchell Photography; 434 (br), Baldwin H. Ward & Kathryn C. Ward/CORBIS; 436 (tr), Imtek Imagineering/Masterfile; 439 (tr), Darryl Torckler/Getty Images/Stone; 439 (turtle eggs), Dwight Kuhn Photography; 439 (fossil eggs), Sinclair Stammers/Science Photo Library/Photo Researchers, Inc.; 439 (br), Ron Austing; Frank Lane Picture Agency/CORBIS; 441 (tr), Gail Mooney/ CORBIS; 443 (tr), Chris Lisle/CORBIS; 445 (tl), PhotoDisc/Getty Images; 445 (b), © Grant Heilman/Grant Heilman Photography; 446 (tl), Sam Dudgeon/HRW; 446 (tc), Art Stein/Photo Researchers, Inc.; 446 (tr), Neil Rabinowitz/CORBIS; 447 (br), © John Elk III; 448 (br), HRW; 449 (br), HRW; 456 (cl), Library of Congress; 456 (bl), Joe Cavaretta/AP Photo; 456 (cr), Nevada State Museum; 457 (cr), © D. Hurst/ Alamy; 457 (tc), Bruce Cashin/Index Stock; 457 (bl), © D. Hurst/Alamy.

Chapter 9: 458–459 (bkgd), David Joel/Stone/Getty Images; 458 (br), Sam Dudgeon/HRW; 465 (tl), © Ron Austing; Frank Lane Picture Agency/CORBIS; 467 (tr), Digital Vision; 471 (tr), © Richard Schultz; 476 (tr), Peter Van Steen/HRW/Kittens courtesy of Austin Humane Society/SPCA; 483 (br), Richard Cummins/CORBIS; 485 (tr), Tracy Frankel/Getty Images; 494 (tr), Rudi Von Briel/PhotoEdit, Inc.; 497 (grass pollen), Dr. Jeremy Burgess/Science Photo Library/Photo Researchers, Inc.; 497 (weed pollen), Ralph C. Eagle, Jr. M.D./Photo Researchers, Inc.; 500 (tr), Michael Newman/PhotoEdit, Inc.; 507 (b), Design Pics; 507 (tl), PhotoDisc/Getty Images; 508 (b), HRW; 509 (b), Sam Dudgeon/HRW.

Chapter 10: 518–519 (bkgd), Erlendur Berg/SuperStock; 518 (br), Bettmann/ CORBIS; 522 (tr), © Royalty-free/Corbis; 522 (cr), Peter Van Steen/HRW; 527 (tr), AP Photo; 530 (tc), Reuters NewMedia Inc./CORBIS; 530 (tr), David Weintraub/Photo Researchers, Inc.; 532 (tr), Andy Hayt/Sports Illustrated; 535 (tl), Raymond Gehman/CORBIS; 539 (br), Simon Watson/FoodPix/Getty Images; 540 (tr), Sam Dudgeon/HRW; 542 (cr), Peter Van Steen/HRW; 544 (tr), Sam Dudgeon/HRW; 545 (tr), Digital Vision; 549 (tl), Corbis/Sygma; 550 (tr), HRW; 557 (tr), iStock Photo; 558 (tc), © Scott Adams, Inc. All rights reserved. Licensed by United Feature Syndicate; 562 (tl), Steve Kahn/Getty Images/FPG International; 563 (tr),

Rubberball/GettyImages; 567 (tl), The Newark Museum/Art Resource, NY; 570 (br), Jenny Thomas/HRW; 571 (b), Sam Dudgeon/HRW; 578 (cr), Craig Jones/Getty Images Sport; 578 (br), Doug Pensinger/Getty Images Sport; 578 (tr), Clemson University Athletics; 579 (tc), Courtesy Myrtle Beach Convention and Visitors Bureau; 579 (br), AP Photo; 579 (cr), The Granger Collection, New York; 579 (cr), Lucile Godbold Papers, J. Drake Edens Library Archives, Columbia College, Columbia, SC. **Chapter 11:** 580–581 (bkgd), Tom Bean/Getty Images/Stone; 580 (br), David Edwards Photography; 589 (cl), Stuart Dee/The Image Bank/Getty Images; 591 (tl), Buddy Mays/CORBIS; 591 (tr), Peter Van Steen/HRW; 593 (tr), © Margaret Bryant/Bryant Dog Photography; 597 (tl), Andrew Syred/Science Photo Library/Photo Researchers, Inc.; 599 (b), Sam Dudgeon/HRW; 600 (tr), Jeffrey Oh; 604 (tr), © Bill Bachman/Danita Delimont - Agent; 605 (c), Fotopic/Index Stock; 607 (t), Peter Van Steen/HRW; 608 (tr), Corbis; 611 (tl), Rafael Macia/Photo Researchers, Inc.; 613 (tl), © Comstock, Inc.; 613 (b), © Dean Fox/SuperStock; 614 (br), Jenny Thomas; 615 (b), Sam Dudgeon/HRW. **Chapter 12:** 624–625 (bkgd), Tom Stack/Painet; 624 (br), Gary Braasch; 628 (tr), Don Klumpp/Getty Images; 632 (tl), AP Photo; 633 (tr), Diaphor Agency/Index Stock; 642 (tr), Jeff Schultz/AlaskaStock Images; 644 (tr), John Greim/Science Photo Library/Photo Researchers, Inc.; 647 (tl), Art Wolfe/Getty Images/The Image Bank; 649 (b), Sam Dudgeon/HRW; 652 (tr), Patrick Gnan; 654 (tl), E.R. Degginger/Bruce Coleman, Inc.; 655 (tr), Chris Luneski/Alamy; 659 (tl), Nick Caloyianis/National Geographic Image Collection; 660 (tr), Duomo/CORBIS; 665 (tl), iStock Photo; 665 (b), © Michael Wong/Corbis; 668 (br), Jenny Thomas/HRW; 669 (b), Sam Dudgeon/HRW; 676 (cr), AP Photo; 676 (b), Kenneth Garrett/National Geographic Collection/Getty Images; 677 (tl), AP Photo; 677 (cr), Courtesy American Visionary Art Museum; 677 (tc), Courtesy American Visionary Art Museum. **Chapter 13:** 678–679 (bkgd), C.N.R.I./Phototake; 678 (br), Stevie Grand/Science Photo Library/Photo Researchers, Inc.; 682 (tr), Victoria Smith/HRW; 691 (tl), Courtesy Wham-O®; 699 (b), George McCarthy/CORBIS; 700 (tr), NASA; 703 (tl), Ron Johnson/Index Stock; 705 (bl), GJLP/Science Photo Library/Photo Researchers, Inc.; 707 (all), John Langford/HRW; 708 (tr), Chip Simons Photography; 711 (tr), Sam Dudgeon/HRW; 714 (tr), Louis Turner/Alamy; 719 (tr), Stephanie Friedman/HRW; 719 (cr), Harry Engels/Photo Researchers, Inc.; 719 (b), Alan and Sandy Carey/Photo Researchers, Inc.; 720 (br), Randall Hyman/HRW; 721 (b), Sam Dudgeon/HRW. **Chapter 14:** 730–731 (bkgd), © W. Cody/CORBIS; 730 (br), HRW; 734 (tr), iStock Photo; 735 (bl), © Dave G. Houser/CORBIS; 743 (cr), © Paul Eekhoff/Masterfile; 743 (tr), Private Collection/Bridgeman Art Library/ © 2002 Fletcher Benton/Artists Rights Society (ARS), New York; 745 (cr), Steve Gottlieb/Stock Connection/PictureQuest; 747 (tr), HRW; 748 (c), HRW; 750 (tl), Stephen Mallon/The Image Bank/Getty Images; 752 (tr), HRW; 753 (bl), HRW; 756 (tr), HRW; 757 (tr), Victoria Smith/HRW; 759 (tr), HRW; 762 (tr), Mark Gibson/Gibson Stock Photography; 769 (tl), iStock Photo; 769 (bl), © Jeff Greenberg/Photo Edit Inc.; 769 (br), Photodisc/Getty Images; 770 (br), Sam Dudgeon/HRW; 771 (b), Sam Dudgeon/HRW; 778 (all), Julian Toney/Belzoni Banner; 779 (all), Courtesy of the Lauren Rogers Museum of Art, Laurel, Mississippi.

Art Credits

Chapter 1: 5, Argosy; 12 (t), Jeffrey Oh; 25 (bkgd), Stephen Durke/Washington Artists; 27 (c), Argosy; 29 (cr), Argosy; 31 (bl), Argosy; 38 (tr), Argosy; 43 (tr), Mark Betcher; 44 (t), Nenad Jakesebic; 44 (c), Greg Geisler; 47 (r), Ortelius Design; 50 (tr), Ted Williams; 51 (all), Leslie Kell. **Chapter 2:** 63 (cards), Argosy; 67 (tr), Argosy; 79 (tr), Argosy; 82 (tr), Fian Arroyo; 92 (t), Cindy Jeftovic; 95 (r), Mark Heine; 103 (tl), Argosy; 104 (tr), Nenad Jakesevic; 105 (tr), Leslie Kell; 105 (cr), Leslie Kell; 112 (tr), Leslie Kell. **Chapter 3:** 122 (t), Mark Heine; 134 (tr), Jeffrey Oh; 134 (cl), Jeffrey Oh; 134 (cr), Jeffrey Oh; 145 (c), Tom Klare; 148 (t), Cindy Jeftovic; 149 (A–C), Leslie Kell; 149 (B), Leslie Kell; 149 (C), Leslie Kell. **Chapter 4:** 161 (c), Leslie Kell; 162 (tr), Greg Geisler; 174 (c), Leslie Kell; 177 (tr), Stephen Durke/Washington Artists; 178 (t), Argosy; 181 (b), Argosy; 189 (c), Argosy; 199 (t), Argosy; 202 (tr), Jeffrey Oh; 203 (all), Leslie Kell; 210 (tc), Leslie Kell.
Chapter 5: 215 (paper), Leslie Kell; 217 (cl), Leslie Kell; 218 (r), Argosy; 223 (tr), Argosy; 225 (tr), Argosy; 227 (br), Argosy; 248 (c), Karen Minot; 249 (c), Argosy; 250 (all), Argosy; 251 (c), Karen Minot; 255 (cr), © Jeremy Boon, Sam Dudgeon/HRW Photo; 257 (tr), Leslie Kell; 261 (A–C), Leslie Kell.
Chapter 6: 273 (tc), Leslie Kell; 277 (tr), Jane Sanders; 284 (br), Gary Otteson; 287 (tr), Doug Bowles; 301 (cr), Stephen Durke/Washington Artists; 305 (tr), Argosy; 309 (c), Argosy; 310 (tr), Gary Otteson; 311 (A–C) Leslie Kell; 318 (tc), Leslie Kell; 318 (b), Jeffrey Oh. **Chapter 7:** 323 (c), Leslie Kell; 328 (tr-inset), Argosy; 328 (cr), Argosy; 330 (c), Argosy; 333 (tr), Jeffrey Oh; 336 (tr), Argosy; 340 (tr), Argosy; 345 (cr), Argosy; 364 (cl), Argosy; 365 (tl), Argosy; 367 (a–c), Argosy; 367 (cr), Leslie Kell; 371 (cl), Argosy; 375 (A–C) Leslie Kell. **Chapter 8:** 387 (c), Leslie Kell; 389 (tc), Argosy; 392 (cr), Ortelius Design; 398 (c), Argosy; 400 (cl), Argosy; 400 (cr), Argosy; 403 (pancakes), Jeffrey Oh; 408 (tr), Dave Clegg; 411 (c), Argosy; 416 (tc), Mark Heine; 416 (bc), Karen Minot; 418 (all), Leslie Kell; 430 (cr), Argosy; 433 (br), Argosy; 435 (tr), Dan Stuckenschneider; 445 (cr), Argosy; 446 (cr), Argosy; 447 (1.), Argosy; 447 (2.), Argosy; 447 (3.), Argosy; 447 (7.), Argosy; 447 (8.), Argosy; 448 (cl), Argosy; 448 (c), Argosy; 448 (cr), Argosy; 449 (A–B), Leslie Kell; 456 (tc), Leslie Kell. **Chapter 9:** 461 (l), Leslie Kell; 462 (tr), Gary Otteson; 469 (c), Argosy; 469 (br), Ortelius Design; 475, Argosy; 479 (br), Argosy; 487 (b), Daniel James; 488 (t), Argosy; 490 (tr), Jeffrey Oh; 490 (c), Argosy; 491 (t), Argosy; 492 (tr), Argosy; 492 (br), Argosy; 493 (tl), Argosy; 496 (tr), Ortelius Design; 497 (cr), Argosy; 506 (food), Leslie Kell; 509 (A–C), Leslie Kell; 512 (food), Leslie Kell.
Chapter 10: 521 (cr), Argosy; 529 (br), Argosy; 546 (br), Jeffrey Oh; 554 (tr), Kevin Rechin; 554 (c), Greg Geisler; 559 (c), Argosy; 562 (tr), Jeffrey Oh; 569 (br), Dave Clegg; 569 (tl), Dave Clegg; 570 (tr), Gary Otteson; 571 (A–B), Leslie Kell; 578 (tc), Leslie Kell. **Chapter 11:** 584 (tc), Dave Clegg; 584 (c), Greg Geisler; 587 (t), Argosy; 593 (c), Leslie Kell; 613 (c), Leslie Kell; 614 (tr), John Etheridge; 615 (A–D), Leslie Kell. **Chapter 12:** 627 Leslie Kell; 633 (b), Greg Geisler; 638 (tr), Tom Klare; 639 (tc), Greg Geisler; 642 (cr), Nenad Jakesevic; 647 (all), Patrick Gnan; 650 (tr), Dave Clegg; 654 (tr), Christy Krames; 659 (r), HRW; 663 (tr), Gary Otteson; 668 (tc), Argosy; 668 (tr), Lance Lekander; 669 (A–D), Leslie Kell; 676 (tc), Leslie Kell.
Chapter 13: 686 (tr), Gary Otteson; 687 (tr), Fian Arroyo; 697 (t), Argosy; 704 (tr), Dave Clegg; 708 (c), Argosy; 720 (tr), Gary Otteson; 721 (A–C), Leslie Kell.
Chapter 14: 737 (tc), Argosy; 740 (tc), Greg Geisler; 762 (c), Greg Geisler; 763 (tr), Danial Stuckenschneider; 765 (tr), Gary Otteson; 770 (tr), Gary Otteson; 771 (A & B), Leslie Kell; 778 (tc), Leslie Kell.

Formulas

Perimeter

Square	$P = 4s$
Rectangle	$P = 2\ell + 2w$ or $P = 2(\ell + w)$
Polygon	$P =$ sum of the lengths of the sides

Circumference

Circle	$C = 2\pi r$ or $C = \pi d$

Volume

Prism	$V = Bh$
Rectangular prism	$V = \ell wh$
Cylinder	$V = \pi r^2 h$ or $V = Bh$
Pyramid	$V = \frac{1}{3}Bh$
Cone	$V = \frac{1}{3}\pi r^2 h$ or $V = \frac{1}{3}Bh$
Sphere	$V = \frac{4}{3}\pi r^3$

Area

Square	$A = s^2$
Rectangle	$A = \ell w$ or $A = bh$
Parallelogram	$A = bh$
Triangle	$A = \frac{1}{2}bh$ or $A = \frac{bh}{2}$
Trapezoid	$A = \frac{1}{2}(b_1 + b_2)h$ or $A = \frac{(b_1 + b_2)h}{2}$
Circle	$A = \pi r^2$

Surface Area

Prism	$S = 2B + Ph$
Cylinder	$S = 2\pi r^2 + 2\pi rh$
Regular Pyramid	$S = B + \frac{1}{2}P\ell$
Cone	$S = \pi r^2 + \pi r\ell$
Sphere	$S = 4\pi r^2$

Probability

Experimental	$\text{probability} \approx \dfrac{\text{number of times the event occurs}}{\text{total number of trials}}$
Theoretical	$\text{probability} = \dfrac{\text{number of outcomes in the event}}{\text{number of outcomes in the sample space}}$
Permutations	${}_nP_r = \dfrac{n!}{(n-r)!}$
Combinations	${}_nC_r = \dfrac{{}_nP_r}{r!} = \dfrac{n!}{r!(n-r)!}$
Dependent events	$P(A \text{ and } B) = P(A) \cdot P(B \text{ after } A)$
Independent events	$P(A \text{ and } B) = P(A) \cdot P(B)$